REVISED EDITION

Sociology of
DEVIANT BEHAVIOR

Marshall B. Clinard

University of Wisconsin

HOLT, RINEHART AND WINSTON, INC.

New York — Chicago — San Francisco
Toronto — London

To my children

from whom I have learned a great deal

MARSHA, STEPHEN, and LAWRENCE

Preface

Some five years have elapsed since this book first appeared. It has been gratifying to learn that it has been well received. In this revision I have followed essentially the approach of the original work: namely, the analysis of certain behavior in terms of deviations from norms. I have felt, however, that a text book not only should "grow" with the literature but also reflect changes in the author's thinking. Consequently, substantial revisions have been made in nearly all chapters. Four chapters have been almost completely rewritten. In each case I have included significant recent research and the latest statistical data, including 1960 United States Census figures. Two chapters have been added: Chapter 8, which emphasizes types of juvenile delinquents; and Chapter 21, which presents the sociological aspects of the prison and the mental hospital. More material has been included on juvenile delinquency.

Moreover, in this revision I have placed more emphasis on process in the analysis of deviant behavior and less on mere description or isolated facts. In line with more recent developments in sociology, I have added considerable comparative materials on deviant behavior from other societies. It is hoped that this material will place a number of issues presented here in a wider perspective.

This book is written as a text for courses designated as "social disorganization," "social problems," "social pathology," "deviant behavior," or some similar term. As its title suggests, I have tried to deal with certain deviations from social norms which encounter disapproval and to which theory and concepts derived from sociology and social psychology may be applied. Consequently, "problems" primarily of concern to economics, political science, or public health are not discussed.

The book has been organized in three parts: Social Deviation, Deviant Behavior, and Deviant Behavior and Social Control. Part I presents a general approach to social deviation, describing and defining various forms, introducing a number of sociological and sociopsychological concepts, and discussing the effects of contemporary urbanism. In addition, various theories of deviant behavior, such as those stressing poverty, cultural lag, and

vii

the psychiatric and psychoanalytic explanations of deviant behavior are presented in Part I rather than throughout the book, thus avoiding repetition. Part II presents a detailed analysis of a considerable number of forms of deviant behavior. In Part III, various types of proposed solutions are dealt with at one time rather than after the analysis of each form of deviant behavior, so that the similarity of various approaches may be seen. Chapter 22, for example, deals with various group approaches, such as group therapy, and their application to such fields as alcoholism, mental disorder, drug addiction, and criminal behavior.

In Chapters 1 and 2, I have explained, in terms of deviant behavior, various concepts which are applied throughout the book. They have included social norms and values, subcultural groups, social differentiation, social structure, societal reaction, socialization, social status, self-conception, social roles, and the definition of the situation. In particular, I have stressed role theory. The wide use of these concepts is based on the premise that deviant behavior is social behavior, to which the same concepts can be applied as to nondeviant behavior. It is hoped that the opening chapters will help those who have not previously had an introductory course in sociology; for those who have, it will serve as a transition and review. Except for the first chapter each one ends with a summary and all conclude with an annotated list of selected readings. Extensive case material and personal documents are included throughout.

I have appreciated the help and suggestions of several persons who have read parts of the original or revised text, particularly Frank E. Hartung, Kingsley Davis, Arnold W. Green, Lyle W. Shannon, Simon Dinitz, Michael Hakeem, David Mechanic, Thomas J. Scheff, Eugene A. Friedmann, Orville G. Brim, Jr., Ersel E. Le Masters, Alfred Kadushin, Leslie A. Osborn, Donald W. Olmstead, Andrew L. Wade, and Torgny Segerstedt. My research assistant on the revision, Virginia M. Lambert, has been particularly helpful to me. Several of my graduate teaching assistants have also furnished useful comments. I should like to acknowledge especially the help of my wife, Ruth, who has spent many long hours typing, retyping, and editing both editions of this book.

M. B. C.

Madison, Wisconsin
January, 1963

Contents

Tables

Figures

PART I

Social Deviation

Chapter

I

Social Deviation

Man's achievements in the area of social relationships have not equaled his achievements in physical science and technology. Within a few centuries man has solved many of the mysteries of the world around him. His endeavors have progressed from the realm of folklore and magic to that of science. His knowledge of the earth and all its resources, and even the vast areas of outer space, surpasses the wildest speculation of primitive man, medieval philosophers, or the early American colonists. The tremendous information he has amassed has enabled him to build great dams and irrigation projects to prevent catastrophic floods and droughts and open up marginal lands to cultivation. He has learned to control pestilence and many diseases so that his expected life span is greatly increased. In large parts of the Western world, at least, modern technical skills have provided food, clothing, and shelter for most of the population, and scientific research today increasingly deals with such intricate problems as nuclear fission, electronics, and changes in the human cell.

Unfortunately these technological advances have not brought with them a comparable degree of conquest over man's problems of relationships with other persons. His success in social relationships generally has not approached his progress in his physical environment. Although the physical scientists have fathomed the very structure of energy and have produced means of travel in outer space, man has been increasingly plagued with difficulties in his personal relationships.

Just as man has had to cope with mysticism and dogma in his understanding of the physical world, similar stumbling blocks have stood in his path as he has attempted to deal with problems in social relationships. Unscientific observations and theories of the behavior of man are as rampant today as they were concerning the physical world in the medieval ages. Many falsely consider the behavior of man, his achievements as well as his problems, as a product of individual strength or perversity. The behavior of persons who constitute problems to themselves and to others is falsely attributed to individual biological weaknesses in inheritance, to feeblemindedness, to body type, or even to racial origin, or is explained as the product of poverty or simply of the "moral" weakness of the individual.

Most people fail to realize that the scientific study of society, social behavior, and the social problems associated with them is fairly recent, though the basic discoveries which have culminated in the advances in the physical world go back many centuries. In fact, the basic knowledge for man's dramatic control of physical phenomena, resulting in the discovery of atomic energy, is the outcome of mathematical and other learning accumulated over at least two thousand years. Until fifty to a hundred years ago scientific methods were applied for the most part to the physical world only, whereas human personality and group behavior were left chiefly to philosophical and moral speculation. Scientific efforts in the latter areas have required the development of concepts and research tools for the study of human behavior. Some of the more important of these concepts will be discussed briefly in the following sections.

Society and Group Relationships

From birth man must depend upon other human beings. Physically and economically he is dependent upon others for his survival and, socially, he relies upon his fellow human beings for his personal development and his satisfactions. Man alone lives in true social groups. Like man, most animals form groups, and there may even be prolonged association, mutual dependence, and cooperation toward biologically common goals. The term *society or social group,* however, can be applied to no animal other than man, for the ties which bind a human group together are not merely biological needs but abstract social relationships. Shared sets of common meanings or symbols, feelings of unity, and systems of mutual obligation characterize man's social groups. Some may attempt to read human counterparts into the life of other animals, but man alone has such social institutions as a political state, an economic system, and religion. He alone has laws and moral judgments.

Social groups are more than simply a group or collection of persons. In a social group several persons are in interaction, there are social relationships among the persons, and, finally, there is a degree of consensus or concerted action. Social groups exist when there are *social relationships* among a number of persons. Social relationships, in turn, are a consequence of recurring or repeated *social interaction* between two or more persons. An individual, in his actions, takes into account what he considers to be the expectation of others, and his behavior, in turn, means that he expects others to act toward him in a certain way. These mutual expectations and a person's evaluation of them represent his *social role,* a term which will be more fully discussed in the following chapter.

Sociology is the study of groups. There are many kinds of groups, and one inclusive way of conceiving of them is in terms of concerted action. All joint enterprises involve some kind of social differentiation and an integration of the various contributions, and such coordination is facilitated when there is consensus. . . . From birth to death each human being is a participant in a variety of groups, and neither he nor anything he does or experiences can be understood when separated from the fact of such participation. As John Donne so eloquently expressed it, "No man is an island, entire of itself." Human conduct is continually subject to social control. What one does often depends more upon the demands he imputes to other people than it does upon his own preferences.[1]

As a result of his group experiences, a human being becomes dependent on others. The importance of this dependence on groups, and man's need for human group relationships, can be demonstrated in situations where group contacts are removed. For example, prison officials have learned that solitary confinement, with its almost complete isolation from human relationships, is one of the most severe forms of punishment for any human being. A few days of this type of treatment usually will render the most defiant prisoner tractable. Admiral Byrd voluntarily isolated himself for several months in the uninhabited polar regions of Antarctica more than a hundred miles from the nearest human being of his expedition. He described his experiences of being alone and vividly showed how dependent the individual is on social groups when he is removed from such contacts.

10 P.M. Solitude is an excellent laboratory in which to observe the extent to which manners and habits are conditioned by others. My table manners are atrocious—in this respect I've slipped back hundreds of years; in fact, I have no manners whatsoever. If I feel like it, I eat with my fingers, or out of a can, or standing up—in other words, whichever is easiest. What's left over, I just heave into the slop pail, close to my feet. Come to think of it, no reason why I shouldn't. It's rather a convenient way to eat; I seem to remember reading in Epicurus that a man living alone lives the life of a wolf.

A life alone makes the need for external demonstration almost disappear. Now I seldom cuss, although at first I was quick to open fire at everything that tried my patience. Attending to the electrical circuit on the anemometer pole is no less cold than it was in the beginning; but I work in soundless torment, knowing that the night is vast and profanity can shock no one but myself.

My sense of humor remains, but the only sources of it are my books and myself, and, after all, my time to read is limited. Earlier today, when I came into the hut with my water bucket in one hand and the lantern in the other, I put the lantern on the stove and hung up the bucket. I laughed at this; but, now when I laugh, I laugh inside; for I seem to have forgotten how to do it out loud. This leads me to think that audible laughter is principally a mechanism for sharing pleasure. . . . My hair hasn't been cut in months. I've let

---

[1] Tamotsu Shibutani, *Society and Personality: An Interaction Approach to Social Psychology*, p. 61. © 1961. Prentice-Hall, Inc., Englewood Cliffs, N.J.

it grow because it comes down around my neck and keeps it warm. I still shave once a week—and that only because I found that a beard is an infernal nuisance outside on account of its tendency to ice up from the breath and freeze the face. Looking in the mirror this morning, I decided that a man without women around him is a man without vanity; my cheeks are blistered and my nose is red and bulbous from a hundred frostbites. How I look is no longer of the least importance; all that matters is how I feel. However, I have kept clean, as clean as I would keep myself at home. But cleanliness has nothing to do with etiquette or coquetry. It is comfort. My senses enjoy the evening bath and are uncomfortable at the touch of underwear that is too dirty.[2]

In social groups, as well as in the larger society, there are social structures involving systems of relationships among the members. Members have definite reciprocal rights and duties which are the result of each person's *social status* or social position. An individual's definition of the world around him depends largely upon his social status, such as the class and subgroups to which he belongs. These interrelated status positions are based on such criteria as sex, age, race, family, and achievement. When status is based on one's position in the social structure at birth, regardless of personal attributes, it is referred to as *ascribed status*. When a person's social position is the product of achievement it is termed *achieved status*. In former times a person's status and role were clearly defined, and were largely fixed for life at the time of birth. In contemporary society it is possible that one's position at birth can be much altered through achievement. Changes in statuses and roles may give rise to conflicts within the person as well as among groups, a situation which we shall discuss frequently later.

Many people are as unaware of the great diversity and specialization among groups in modern society, and of the variations in their effects upon individual persons, as is a fish of the water around him. Groups, such as the neighborhood, village, or city, are based on physical proximity, and others, such as the family and larger groups of relatives, are based on kinship. Still others are based on congeniality, or on economic, technological, or other interests. The group nature of man is well indicated in Table 1.1, a list of groups based on interest.

Some social groups are informally organized and temporary, whereas others are highly formal and stable in their structure and in the specific duties and obligations of each member. The relatively permanent, stable, uniform, and formal manner in which social groups are interrelated produces what are termed *social institutions*. In addition, social institutions are generally distinguished by the fact that they encompass activities which are regarded as vital to certain ends, or as worthy in themselves by the

---

[2] Richard E. Byrd, *Alone* (New York: G. P. Putnam's Sons, 1938), pp. 139–140. Reprinted by permission of the publishers.

society in which they exist.[3] For example, government, which is a social institution, is regarded as vital for the maintenance of order or peaceable relations in society. Other institutions include the family, and the economic, religious, and educational institutions. The *social structure of an institution*

Table 1.1. Social Groups Which May Be Based on Interests

Interests	Groups
Congeniality	Friendship groups Social clubs Taverns Purely social groups, boys' gangs, etc.
Economic interests	Corporations, partnerships Professional societies Associations of commerce Labor unions
Technological interests	Crafts Some athletic associations and teams Police departments
Religious interests	Churches Sects and other organizations
Aesthetic interests	"Schools" of painting, sculpture, literature, etc. Bands, orchestras, choirs, etc.
Intellectual interests (science, philosophy, the intellectual aspects of the humanities, etc.	Research groups Learned societies
Educational interests	Schools Universities Study groups, etc.
Political interests	Political parties and machines Taypayers' associations, etc.
Recreational interests	Philatelists' societies Yacht clubs Bridge clubs Some sport teams and clubs, etc.
Ameliorative interests	Charitable societies Community welfare organizations Alcoholics Anonymous Minority group associations, etc.

SOURCE: Adapted from John L. and John P. Gillin, *Cultural Sociology* (New York: The Macmillan Company, 1948), pp. 291–292. These groups may arise through other factors than interests alone.

[3] See George C. Homans, *Social Behavior: Its Elementary Forms* (New York: Harcourt, Brace & World, Inc., 1961), p. 5.

or other stable group consists of shared understandings concerning the duties and obligations of participants, the ways in which activities are to be carried out, the proper order of activities, ideas about what is desirable and undesirable or good and bad, and evaluations of the relative importance of the contributions of given participants and of the deference to be accorded by one participant to another. In addition, there are usually prescribed methods for recruiting participants, for training or indoctrinating them, and for expelling them.

Stated most simply, the social structure of an institution is merely the form in which group activities are to be carried out. However, the form is not "visible" or "tangible," but consists of systems of shared understandings in the minds of human beings as to their obligations, as in the case of the family. The *function of a social institution,* on the other hand, is generally described as its central activity or purpose, as this is defined by the society in which the institution exists. Thus, the family may be viewed as primarily concerned with the rearing and care of children. In some societies the procreation of the family may be stressed as contributing to the strength of the state; whereas in others it may be stressed as an agency which contributes to the fulfillment of personal happiness. Changes in the specific functions and structures of institutions and in the relationship of one institution to another have an important bearing on social problems. The stability of any society depends greatly on the functioning of its institutions and on their ability, through formal and informal means, to maintain social control.

Culture and Social Norms

The concept of *culture* is closely related to the concept of social group, and others mentioned thus far, in that each of these concepts refers to phenomena which are constituted of the same basic social ingredients.[4] Culture may be distinguished from another concept, society, as involving primarily *normative standards* for conduct, rather than interaction and social relationships. Like society, culture arises out of the need of people to communicate about the meaning of things and to regulate social life. Culture is a system of symbols or meanings with three distinct properties. It is *transmittable, learned,* and *shared.* The fact that it is transmittable means that it is passed from one generation to another. The fact that it is learned means that it is not an innate or biological quality of persons, but that it is acquired and participated in by persons through association with others. The fact that it is shared means that there is a fair degree of consensus among a number of persons concerning what is proper and im-

---

⁴ See Talcott Parsons, *The Social System* (New York: The Free Press of Glencoe, 1951), especially Chaps. 1 and 12.

proper behavior, what meanings are to be attached to objects, situations, or events. It is only when such consensus exists that a group of persons can be said to be members of a "culture." Thus, it is evident that culture has existed before the individual's birth and will continue, though probably with modifications, beyond his lifetime. It is more than merely a description of ways of acting. It is a system of standards and evaluations of how to act. Culture is a "blueprint for behavior," telling what a person must do, ought to do, should do, may do, and must not do.[5]

Social relationships and behavior are regulated through *social norms*, often referred to as standardized ways of acting, or expectations governing limits of variation in behavior. Some social norms may be fairly widespread, whereas others are not. Some are temporary, and some are more permanent. Some may have considerable force to support compliance with them, whereas others have very little. Among the more universal and permanent social norms are many of those associated with institutions. Many *institutional norms*, but by no means all, are supported by a high degree of consensus and an intense reaction when violated.

Social values are simply those things to which a society or cultural group attaches value, worth, or significance.[6] Social values are described by some as the goals or objectives of a given society or culture. They are not only shared; they are regarded as matters of collective welfare to which is often attached a high degree of emotional belief that they are important. The distinction between social norms and social values can be illustrated by the criminal law. Although criminal laws are simply legal norms regulating various types of behavior and are enforced by the coercion of the state, certain values or basic goals are involved in some of them. Murder, manslaughter, bigamy, rape, theft, and burglary are violations of legal norms, but the social values involved include the protection of human life, the protection of sexual and family life, and the protection of property.[7] Among the value orientations which Williams feels are the objectives of such a complex society, as, for example, American society, are achievement and success, activity and work, efficiency and practicality, progress, material comfort, humanitarianism, equality, nationalism-patriotism, and democracy and individual personality.[8]

Rarely are individuals consciously aware of the often arbitrary nature of the social norms and social values of a culture or subculture, for they are introduced to them in the ongoing process of living. Social norms are transmitted from one generation to another through groups, and each

---

[5] Robin M. Williams, Jr., *American Society* (New York: Alfred A. Knopf, Inc., 1954), p. 23.

[6] Homans, *op. cit.*, Chap. 3.

[7] Hermann Mannheim, *Criminal Justice and Social Reconstruction* (New York: Oxford University Press, 1946). He also included the values of protection against property, protection of labor, and protection against labor.

[8] Williams, *op. cit.*, pp. 388–442.

individual largely incorporates into his life organization the beliefs, ideas, and language of the groups to which he belongs. Men thus come to see the world around them not with their eyes alone, for if they did they would see the same things, but rather through their cultural and other group experiences. Even the moral judgments of man are not generally his alone, but those of the group or groups to which he belongs.

In the following passage Ellsworth Faris has brilliantly pointed out the significance of seeing the world through group experiences:

> For we live in a world of "cultural reality," and the whole furniture of earth and choir of heaven are to be described and discussed as they are conceived by men. Caviar is not a delicacy to the general. Cows are not food to the Hindu. Mohammed is not the prophet of God to me. To an atheist God is not God at all. Objects are not passively received or automatically reacted to; rather is it true that objects are the result of a successful attempt to organize experience.[9]

The process by which persons learn and incorporate cultural meanings and values is called *socialization*. The process of socialization continues throughout life. Rarely are individuals consciously aware of the often arbitrary nature of the social norms and social values of a culture, for they are introduced to them in the ongoing process of living. Social norms are transmitted from one generation to another through groups, and each individual largely incorporates into his life organization the beliefs, ideas, and language of the groups to which he belongs. Man develops a set of social norms and values as he develops a social environment, which consists of people with whom he comes into contact first in the family, then in his neighborhood and school, and later in his economic, religious, or educational groups, and his social class.[10]

Social Differentiation and Subcultural Norms

Among more homogeneous peoples, such as primitive or folk societies, most norms and values are perceived in a somewhat similar, but by no means entirely so, way by various members of a society. Because of this fact members of the society come to share many common objectives and meanings. Modern societies are more complex and there is much *social differentiation*. In a highly differentiated society relatively distinct clusterings or groupings of persons will arise which have in common some socially assigned attribute or quality. Social clusterings arise around such attributes as race, occupation, ethnic background, religion, political party, residence,

---

[9] Ellsworth Faris, *The Nature of Human Nature* (New York: McGraw-Hill Book Company, Inc., 1937), pp. 150–151.

[10] Muzafer Sherif, *The Psychology of Social Norms* (New York: Harper & Row, Publishers, 1936), p. 46. For a general discussion of norms, also see Torgny T. Segerstedt, "The Uppsala School for Sociology," *Acta Sociologica* (Scandinavian Review of Sociology), 1:85–119, No. 2 (1955).

and many others. Modern societies are greatly differentiated by social class and into age or peer groups, into thousands of different occupational groups, often into a large number of religious groups, and even into rather distinct regional and neighborhood groups.

Sometimes social groupings which arise in the manner described may develop and share a set of values and meanings which are distinctive to some degree from the values and meanings shared by the society of which they are a part. When this occurs such a group may be called a *subculture*. A subculture is, simply speaking, a "culture within a culture." This implies that the subcultural group participates in and shares the "larger" culture of which it is a part, but also shares some meanings and values which are unique. A subculture is not necessarily in opposition to the larger culture, even though some conflict may arise between it and the larger culture.

Large modern societies consist of a variety of subcultures and social groups, each often with its own set of norms and values not only as to what constitutes proper conduct but also even as to the goals of life itself. Cohen has suggested that subcultures emerge in a highly differentiated society when, in effective interaction with one another, a number of persons have similar problems.[11] Sociological research has shown the existence of pronounced differences in normative structures of subcultures involving persons of different age groups, social classes, occupations, racial, religious, and ethnic groups, neighborhoods, and regions. In addition, there are some even more limited subcultures such as those among teen-age gangs, prostitutes, alcoholics, drug addicts, homosexuals, and professional and organized criminals. Even institutions for the treatment of deviants, such as prisons, actually develop subcultures with their own social systems.[12] In fact, so diverse are the subcultural norms of most large societies that there are probably only a few norms which are accepted as binding on *all* persons.

An American child raised as a member of another culture, whether Eskimo, Chinese, or Hottentot, would adopt the norms and values of that culture, just as the immigrants to America adopted the more general norms and values of American culture. Similarly, a person in modern society tends to acquire the norms of those subcultural groups of which he is a part. Although a modern society has certain common norms and values, there are many differences in norms and values.[13] As one writer has stated, "Within such complex aggregates as modern nations many norms are

---

[11] See, for example, Albert K. Cohen, *Delinquent Boys: The Culture of the Gang* (New York: The Free Press of Glencoe, 1955), p. 59.

[12] See Donald Clemmer, *The Prison Community* (rev. ed.; New York: Holt, Rinehart and Winston, Inc., 1958). Also see Donald R. Cressey ed., *The Prison: Studies in Institutional Organization and Change* (New York: Holt, Rinehart and Winston, Inc., 1961), and Richard A. Cloward, Donald R. Cressey, George H. Grosser, Richard McCleery, Lloyd E. Ohlin, Gresham M. Sykes, and Sheldon L. Messinger, "Theoretical Studies in Social Organization of the Prison" (Pamphlet 15; New York: Social Science Research Council, March, 1960).

[13] Frank E. Hartung, "Common and Discrete Values," *Journal of Social Psychology*, 38:3-22 (August, 1953).

effective only within limited subcultures, and there are wide differences in individual conformity and conceptions of normative structure." [14]

The norms and values of *peer groups*—persons of similar generations or ages—also may differ considerably. For example, a peer group, such as teen-agers in modern urban societies, often has standards of conduct and even goals which are quite different from those of other peer or age groups, and these may lead to misunderstandings and conflicts. The teen-age subculture is characterized by particular norms of dress, music, language, sexual activity, ways of regarding society and adults, and recreation.[15] Sometimes stealing, car theft, and vandalism become accepted norms among certain parts of the teen-age subculture.

Racial and religious discrimination may be greater in one part of a society than in another, depending on subcultural regional norms. Neighborhoods in the larger American cities often have distinct behavioral norms and values. The social norms and values in one neighborhood may contribute to the development of stealing by teen-age boys as a form of recreation and status, whereas in another the norms and values may encourage teen-age participation in scouting programs and similar forms of community-directed youth activities which lead toward nondelinquent behavior. Neighborhood norms may define policemen in one area as "enemies" and in the other as symbols of respect for law. Similarly, prostitutes, professional criminals, drug addicts, organized criminals, and similar groups may have a series of social norms and values distinct from those of the larger society. An understanding of this condition of highly differentiated and often conflicting norms as part of the way "modern" societies are organized is essential to a meaningful analysis of social deviation. A set of norms is not always supported in the same way by different subcultural groups.

There is a tendency for diversity of norms between groups to increase in a highly differentiated society. Often groups in such a society do not develop norms which are radically different from one another; the norms simply differ in emphasis. Nevertheless, if a person belongs to a number of groups in such a society, and if each group either holds different norms or emphasizes them differently, considerable personal conflict may ensue. The norms and social roles a person secures from the family group may not necessarily always agree with the norms and social roles of the play group, age or peer group, work group, or political group. Certain groups may become more important to an individual's life organization than

---

[14] Williams, *op. cit.*, p. 30.

[15] See, for example, "The Teen-Age Culture," *The Annals*, Vol. 338 (November, 1961), for a description of the characteristic norms of teen-agers in our culture as well as those of teen-agers in Europe. There is also a discussion of the Italian-American, Jewish, and Negro teen-age cultures. See also James S. Coleman, *The Adolescent Society* (New York: The Free Press of Glencoe, 1961).

others and, consequently, he may tend to conform to the norms of the groups with which he is more closely identified. The family, while important, is only one of many groups which may be related to a person's behavior, whether deviant or nondeviant. Among other important sources of norms and social relationships are social class, occupational, neighborhood, school, and religious groups, and the gang or clique.

All this means three things: (1) that within a modern society there may be almost as pronounced differences among various groups about the norms of accepted behavior as there are between large cultures; (2) that to explain logically how members of certain deviant subgroups in a society come to act the way they do can be explained in the same way, for example, that an Eskimo becomes culturally an Eskimo; and (3) that even when we speak of the norms of a given family we are likely to be referring actually to the social class, occupational, or some other subcultural group to which the family belongs.

Social Stratification and Deviant Behavior

Modern societies are socially differentiated in many ways: probably none is greater than the variations in behavior among the social classes in a society. Social class can be viewed as a hierarchical system by which large groups of families in society are ranked according to a social position of inferiority, equality, or superiority. Ranks may be based on six levels of stratification: prestige, occupation, possessions, interaction, class consciousness, and value orientations.[16] Studies of class structure have shown how value orientations, patterns of family life, and behavior in general not only represent but serve actually to integrate class ways of life.

So different are the social norms and other behavior of, for example, American social classes, that these differences are probably actually greater than those between members of the same social class but, say, from some other Western European or even Asiatic societies. The norms of longshoremen, for example, may differ markedly from those of doctors or professors. The norms and values of the middle class and lower class have been characterized in the studies by Miller and Cohen.

Kinsey and others, for example, have shown the existence of great class differences in sex behavior and even in the nature of the sex relation itself. Studies by Green,[17] Davis,[18] and others have shown that even family rearing patterns of the lower and middle classes are greatly different. The

---

[16] Joseph A. Kahl, *The American Class Structure* (New York: Holt, Rinehart and Winston, Inc., 1957), pp. 8–13.

[17] Arnold W. Green, "The Middle-Class Male Child and Neurosis," *American Sociological Review*, 11:31–41 (February, 1946).

[18] Kingsley Davis, "Mental Hygiene and the Social Structure," in Arnold Rose ed., *Mental Health and Mental Disorder* (New York: W. W. Norton & Company, Inc., 1955).

Lower Class (Miller) [a]	Middle Class (Cohen)
Concern with "trouble" involving official authorities or agencies of middle-class society	Cultivation of manners and courtesy
Toughness such as physical prowess, masculinity, fearlessness, bravery, daring	Control over physical aggression
Ability to outsmart others and to gain money by "wits"	Respect for property of others
Excitement of thrills, risk, and danger	Desire for wholesome recreation
Belief that people are favored by fate, fortune, and luck	Ambition; postponement of immediate goals for long-term objectives
Resentment of external controls of authority but at the same time dependence on them	Individual responsibility

[a] Although a useful characterization of general lower-class norms and values, particularly in larger cities, there are great variations within this broad category. The way of life of many lower-class families resembles, to some extent, middle-class norms and values.

SOURCES: Walter B. Miller, "Lower Class Culture as a Generating Milieu of Gang Delinquency," *Journal of Social Issues*, 14:5–19, No. 3 (1958); and Albert K. Cohen, *Delinquent Boys: The Culture of the Gang* (New York: The Free Press of Glencoe, 1955), pp. 88–91.

use of physical punishment, for example, is an acceptable form of disciplining children in lower-class families. The middle-class boy is more likely to be whipped if he fights; the lower-class boy if he does not, or if he loses. Studies have shown great differences in the norms, behavior, and family structure of teen-age youth by social class.[19]

Much of this research has directly or indirectly contributed to the understanding of deviant behavior. There are great differences in the incidence and nature of different types of deviant behavior by social class. Behavior may be approved in one class and disapproved in another. Class status may represent, for the individual, different neighborhood norms and different patterns of interpersonal relations, particularly between parents and children.[20] The greater incidence of juvenile delinquency among the lower class has been shown in many sociological studies.[21] Sociological investigations have suggested that auto theft is more likely to be a middle-

[19] August B. Hollingshead, *Elmtown's Youth* (New York: John Wiley & Sons, Inc., 1949). Also see Coleman, *op. cit.*

[20] The social behavior of particular adolescents was found to be largely a result of the social class they belonged to, according to one study in which adolescents were divided by class. Hollingshead, *op. cit.*

[21] See, for example, Terence Morris, *The Criminal Area: A Study in Social Ecology* (London: Routledge and Kegan Paul Ltd., 1957). Also see Albert J. Reiss, Jr. and Albert Lewis Rhodes, "Delinquency and Social Class Structure," *American Sociological Review*, 26:720–733 (October, 1961).

class juvenile offense.[22] The type and nature of sex offenses by juveniles appears to be related to social class.[23] The rates for adult crime in general are higher in lower-class areas. Nearly all crimes of violence, such as murder, are committed by lower-class adults, and the nature of lower-class sub-culture and family life seems to offer an explanation of the origin of most murders.[24] Prostitution appears to be consistently more prevalent among the lower classes. The more overt types of crime, such as burglary, are rare among members of the middle and upper classes, who become more often involved in types of crime to which the term "white-collar crime" has been applied. Sociological studies have shown the existence of wide-scale violations of law by persons in the upper and middle classes, politicians, government officials, businessmen, labor union leaders, doctors, and lawyers.[25]

Probably in no area has social class shown more pronounced differences than in the area of mental disorder. Faris and Dunham demonstrated years ago, in their Chicago study of the residences of public and private mental patients, that mental disorder was generally greater in the lower class.[26] More recently another study has revealed great differences in the relative incidence and nature of neuroses and psychoses by social class.[27] Schizophrenia, a common form of mental disorder, was nine times more prevalent among those of the lowest social class. There were even class differences in the type of the neuroses.

The incidence of suicide is related to occupation and social class. This has been established by many studies, including Sainsbury's study of London suicides.[28]

Merton has explained all deviant behavior in terms primarily of social structure, particularly social class. He suggests that all forms of deviant behavior result from differentials in the access to the success goals of a society by *legitimate* means.[29] Deviations are thus symptoms of dissociation

---

[22] William W. Wattenberg and James Balistrieri, "Automobile Theft: A 'Favored-Group' Delinquency," *American Journal of Sociology*, 57:575-579 (May, 1952).

[23] Albert J. Reiss, Jr., "Sex Offenses: The Marginal Status of the Adolescent," *Law and Contemporary Problems*, 25:309-334 (Spring, 1960).

[24] Henry Allen Bullock, "Urban Homicide in Theory and Fact," *Journal of Criminal Law, Criminology, and Police Science*, 45:565-575 (January-February, 1955); and Marvin E. Wolfgang, *Patterns in Criminal Homicide* (Philadelphia: University of Pennsylvania Press, 1958).

[25] Edwin H. Sutherland, *White Collar Crime* (New York: Holt, Rinehart and Winston, Inc., reissue 1960), and Marshall B. Clinard, *The Black Market: A Study of White Collar Crime* (New York: Holt, Rinehart and Winston, Inc., 1952).

[26] Robert E. L. Faris and H. Warren Dunham, *Mental Disorders in Urban Areas* (Chicago: The University of Chicago Press, 1939).

[27] August B. Hollingshead and Frederich Redlich, *Social Class and Mental Illness* (New York: John Wiley & Sons, Inc., 1958). Also see Jerome K. Myers and Bertram H. Roberts, *Family and Class Dynamics in Mental Illness* (New York: John Wiley & Sons, Inc., 1959).

[28] Peter Sainsbury, *Suicide in London* (London: Chapman & Hall, Ltd., 1955).

[29] Robert K. Merton, *Social Theory and Social Structure* (rev. ed.; New York: The Free Press of Glencoe, 1957), pp. 131-194.

between culturally prescribed aspirations and socially structured ways of realizing them, or a situation of *anomie,* meaning in general "normless-ness." [30] According to this theory, modern urban societies emphasize such status goals of competitive success as material gain and higher education, but provide limited means for everyone to achieve these goals legitimately because of the great differentials by age, sex, ethnic status, and particularly social class. "It is only when a system of cultural values extols, virtually above all else, certain *common* success-goals for the population at large while the social structure rigorously restricts or completely closes access to approved modes of reaching these goals *for a considerable part of the same population,* that deviant behavior ensues on a large scale." [31] Conse-quently, other means, some *illegitimate,* may be used to achieve, for ex-ample, the goal of material gain. Several categories or adaptations of be-havior may emerge to achieve such goals—conformity, innovation, ritual-ism, retreatism, and rebellion.[32] A particular adaptation is dependent on the individual's acceptance or rejection of cultural goals and on his ad-herence to, or violation of, accepted norms.

The greatest pressure for deviation arises among the lower socio-economic groups, where opportunities to acquire material goods are fewer and the level of education is lower. Innovation through ordinary stealing, vice, or organized crime may be ways of achieving goals of wealth and power. Retreat from the goal is still another possible reaction to a situation where a discrepancy exists between the goals and the means of achieving them. This may result in frustration and internal conflict and lead to the development of psychoses, neuroses, chronic alcoholism, or drug addic-tion.[33]

A reformulation of Merton's theory of anomie has been made by

---

[30] *Ibid.* Also Robert K. Merton, "Social Problems and Sociological Theory," in Robert K. Merton and Robert A. Nisbet, *Contemporary Social Problems* (New York: Harcourt, Brace & World, Inc., 1961), pp. 697–737. Also see Parsons, *op. cit.,* pp. 256–267. The con-cept of *anomie* was originally formulated by Émile Durkheim in *Suicide* (originally pub-lished 1896; tr. John A. Spaulding and George Simpson; New York: The Free Press of Glencoe, 1951).

[31] Merton, *Social Theory and Social Structure,* p. 146.

[32] Several other forms of adaptation have been added by Dubin. See Robert Dubin, "Deviant Behavior and Social Structure: Continuities in Social Theory," *American So-ciological Review,* 24:147–164 (April, 1959).

[33] Although the theoretical statement of the relation of anomie to deviant behavior has been widely quoted, little research has been done to establish its validity. Theoreti-cally it is a general explanation at the level of social structure rather than at the socio-psychological level of the individual. The success-goal aspirations of a society which are not achieved by the deviant are not clear or specific. Moreover, it does not adequately explain why, in American society, most lower-class males do not go beyond institutional goals to achieve them. Likewise, it does not explain deviant behavior in societies where "esteemed goals" are not thought of as available to everyone, i.e., where there is gen-erally ascribed rather than achieved status. Nor does the theory, based primarily on American goal orientation, explain, for example, why subcultural delinquency is be-coming a nearly world-wide phenomenon.

Cloward to include not only differentials in the availability of legitimate means, but variations in the access or opportunity for illegitimate means.[34] Within this context he has sought to explain delinquency, crime, alcoholism, drug addiction, mental illness, and suicide. In much the same way delinquency has been said to arise from the disparity between what lower-class youths are led to want and what is actually available to them. Desiring such conventional goals as economic and educational success, they are faced with limitations on legitimate avenues of success to these goals. Being unable to revise their goals downward, they experience frustration and turn to delinquency if the norms or opportunities are available to them.[35]

Cohen has stated a theory of gang delinquency which has a general approach similar to Merton's anomie but is considerably more specific.[36] Delinquent gangs, he suggests, arise as a consequence of the class structure of American society. Delinquent gang behavior is a product of group solutions to the status problems, needs, and frustrations of the American lower-class system in a world of predominantly middle-class values and virtues.

Social Deviation and Societal Reaction

Reactions to deviations from social norms can vary in the direction of approval, tolerance, or disapproval. Modern societies encourage a certain amount of nonconformity, provided it is in an approved direction. Deviations which society approves may be rewarded by admiration, prestige, money, or other symbols. Some deviations in the form of new mechanical inventions, new styles in architecture, painting, literature, music, and fashions may, on occasion, meet with general approval. Approved deviations may also include behavior which is more industrious, ambitious, pious, patriotic, brave, or honest than is called for by the norms of a particular situation. Everyone is supposed to be a careful driver, for example, but rewards are sometimes given for the driver who has never had an accident over a long period of years. A certain degree of heroism is expected of everyone, civilian or soldier alike, but medals or other forms of recognition are given to soldiers, and occasionally to civilians, who are particularly heroic and risk their own lives.

In general, however, a society is probably more concerned with punishing disapproved deviations from norms than with rewarding compliance with norms. Deviations may be reacted to with varying degrees of disapproval. What specific behavior is disapproved, and the point at which disapproval will be expressed, depends largely on the content of the norms

---

[34] Richard A. Cloward, "Illegitimate Means, Anomie, and Deviant Behavior," *American Sociological Review*, 24:164–176 (April, 1959).

[35] Richard A. Cloward and Lloyd E. Ohlin, *Delinquency and Opportunity: A Theory of Delinquent Gangs* (New York: The Free Press of Glencoe, 1960).

[36] Cohen, *op. cit.*

of the given society in question. Deviations which are disapproved may be reacted to with disgust, anger, hate, gossip, isolation, and ostracism, or even physical punishment. Deviations from orthodox political and religious thinking, approved sexual behavior, or certain legal codes may encounter strong disapproval.

Generally speaking, the norms of a given society or group may be known not only by observing what people do, but by observing when and how sanctions, both positive and negative, are applied. It is by observing what behavior is socially punished that we learn what behavior is disapproved and is therefore in violation of the norms. By observing what behavior is socially rewarded, or esteemed, we learn what behavior more nearly expresses the ideals embodied in the norms. Thus it is by observing the operation of sanctions, or in other words, *social control,* that we can infer the nature and the limits of acceptable and nonacceptable behavior implicit in given norms.

> In speaking of social control, then, reference is being made to the fact that men interact with one another in regularized ways as they cooperate to accomplish collective goals. In organized groups the activities of the participants are curtailed by the conventional roles that they play. But such control is not restricted to formalized settings. Participants in lynching mobs are not free to do as they wish; a man who is not in sympathy with the prevailing mood may be torn to pieces if he tries to assert his opposition. Even those who are physically alone often take into account what the reactions of other people are likely to be if they should find out about what he is doing. *Social control refers to the fact that human behavior is organized in response to expectations that are imputed to other people.* This does not necessarily involve coercion; various constraints are placed upon the things men do by virtue of their participation in groups.[37]

Behavior which is disapproved at one time may later become approved. This implies that ideas of what is proper or improper normative behavior may change. Over the years scientists who have challenged traditional beliefs have been scorned, ridiculed, ostracized, or even punished. Copernicus, Galileo, and many others who were regarded as deviants in their day would undoubtedly be regarded today with the same approval as was accorded Einstein. Within comparatively recent times there was strong disapproval of women's smoking, drinking alcoholic beverages, particularly in public, using make-up, wearing one-piece bathing suits, or engaging in political activity. Many religious offenses of various types, such as engaging in recreation on the Sabbath, were formerly considered crimes. Professional boxing matches or "prize fights" were generally a criminal offense during most of the nineteenth century in the United States. New York, for example, did not legalize prize fighting until 1896 and subse-

---

[37] Shibutani, *Society and Personality,* pp. 60–61. Italicized in the original.

quently changed the law several times so that present legalization of professional fighting actually dates from as late as 1920.

> It was a crime in Iceland in the Viking age for a person to write verses about another, even if the sentiment was complimentary, if the verses exceeded four strophes in length. A Prussian law of 1784 prohibited mothers and nurses from taking children under two years of age into their beds. The English villein in the fourteenth century was not allowed to send his son to school, and no one lower than a freeholder was permitted by law to keep a dog. The following have at different times been crimes: printing a book, professing the medical doctrine of circulation of the blood, driving with reins, sale of coins to foreigners, having gold in the house, buying goods on the way to market or in the market for the purpose of selling them at a higher price, writing a check for less than $1.00. On the other hand, many of our present laws were not known to earlier generations—quarantine laws, traffic laws, sanitation laws, factory laws.[38]

This means, of course, that the norms which define deviant behavior are not necessarily the same in various cultures, nor are they the same in a given culture over a period of time. Homosexual behavior, prostitution, or drunkenness does not constitute deviant behavior in some societies today. Some Scandinavian countries, for example, have such different interpretations of sexual norms that many delinquent and criminal acts in American society would not be regarded as such there. Changed attitudes in the United States over the past fifty years toward tobacco smoking by juveniles and young adults is an indication of how normative standards can be redefined in time. Formerly there was great preoccupation with smoking among younger groups, laws were passed forbidding it, and often were strictly enforced. Smoking was thought to be related to a variety of other social problems.

Deviations vary in the *intensity* of the reaction to the deviation, as well as in the *direction* of approval or disapproval. Some deviations from norms in a society are not only approved but encouraged. Likewise, disapproved deviations may encounter various degrees of sanction, varying all the way from a certain amount of tolerance to mild and even strong disapproval. Certain behavior of the "idle rich," of actors, musicians, and artists, or of extreme religious sects, although not approved, may be tolerated. Deviations from norms of politeness, dress, table manners, cleanliness, and the telling of risqué stories in public may encounter mild disapproval in the form of ridicule or scorn. Lying and malicious gossip may be more strongly disapproved, while certain behavior such as murder, burglary, and robbery may be punished by the political state through fine, imprisonment, or even death.

---

[38] Edwin H. Sutherland and Donald R. Cressey, *Principles of Criminology* (6th ed.; Philadelphia: J. B. Lippincott Company, 1960), p. 15.

Norms have varying degrees of strength, or "resistance potential," in the event of a disapproved deviation from them, "a power which may be measured in degrees of what the group regards as the severity of the sanction." [39] Each norm can be thought of as having a *tolerance limit,* that is, the ratio between violations of the norm and a society's willingness to tolerate it or suppress it.[40] Deviations from sexual norms, for example, have different tolerance limits, depending on the society. Over the centuries, prostitution has been approved, tolerated, or disapproved, depending on cultural norms. In certain Near Eastern countries and in ancient Greece prostitution was approved, and in Paris today it is not extensively suppressed. Some communities in the United States tolerate prostitution either by ignoring its presence and not enforcing the laws or by allowing a "red-light district" to exist. Other communities may take a strong position and attempt to wipe it out.

The concept of "tolerance limit" is in some respects, however, misleading, for it implies that there is a definite and absolute point at which norm violations will involve a reaction. Actually the relation between norm violation and the societal reaction is not as simple as this and may depend on the nature of the situation or on the social status of the deviant.

The Social Visibility of Deviant Behavior

Wide variations exist in the "social visibility" of negatively regarded deviations, that is, the extent to which behavior comes to the attention of people within a society and the acts are defined as "deviant." Certain crimes, such as kidnaping, violent sex offenses, murder, lynching, and armed robbery, for example, are highly visible and create much comment and action. Other offenses, such as white-collar crime, abortions, blackmail, rape, homosexuality, and petty theft, are not as socially visible; moreover, some of these are not even likely to be reported to the police.

Many reasons might be cited for this lower social visibility and the failure to report many of these crimes: (1) The offended person often fears unfavorable publicity and embarrassment if he is involved in blackmail, abortion, or sex offenses. (2) For other reasons he may not wish the offense to be discovered. In a case of theft he might not wish to have the police investigate because of his own illegal behavior or the nature of the stolen property. (3) The offense may be of a petty nature involving, for example, the theft of an article of little value and the victim may not take the time to report it. (4) Some offenses are known only to the offender and

---

[39] Thorsten Sellin, "Culture Conflict and Crime" (Bulletin 41; New York: Social Science Research Council, 1938), p. 34.

[40] Courtland C. Van Vechten, "The Tolerance Quotient as a Device for Defining Certain Social Concepts," *American Journal of Sociology,* 46:35–44 (July, 1940).

he would hardly report himself. These offenses would include vagrancy, disorderly conduct, or carrying concealed weapons. (5) Witnesses to a crime may not wish to report it because of fear, inconvenience, or embarrassment. (6) Friends and relatives may try to protect the offender or the victim and therefore do not report the offense.[41]

Symptoms of mental disorder are not always interpreted as such and so do not become visible to members of a society. In some instances the mentally ill person is considered simply as "eccentric," "odd," or "difficult." This is particularly true of many neurotic symptoms. In other cases interpretations may make the behavior less socially visible. Certain persons who are mentally ill may become members of a religious sect and claim to experience trances and visions without provoking much comment. In a society which emphasizes orderliness and cleanliness a neurotic with certain compulsive symptoms in this direction may not be conspicuous. Manic behavior is less visible in a dynamic society like America, whereas symptoms of mental depression or social withdrawal have a high degree of visibility. Mental illness is also less visible among some occupational groups than among others; manic behavior in certain salesmen is an example.

Generally, the physical symptoms of intoxication tend to be visible, as the intoxicated person usually displays such physical symptoms as thickened speech, flushed face, and unsteady gait, although certain physical illnesses may produce similar symptoms. It is the social behavior of the intoxicated person, however, which attracts the most attention from others and brings about the strongest reaction. Some persons can actually be quite intoxicated without exhibiting noticeable behavior patterns, but others may become quarrelsome, noisy, loquacious, silly, depressed, or otherwise annoying to other people so that the drunken behavior becomes even more conspicuous than the physical symptoms.

A person's status may largely determine whether or not deviant activity on his part is interpreted by others as deviant and, therefore, as disapproved behavior. In many instances deviant acts may be interpreted as attributes associated with the status the person occupies, and therefore not perceived as "deviant," with all that implies.[42]

The social visibility of many forms of deviant behavior varies by social class and by racial characteristics. Among the lower classes, or among a group of homeless transients, for example, drunkenness may

[41] Thorsten Sellin, "Research Memorandum on Crime and the Depression" (Bulletin 27; New York: Social Science Research Council, 1936), pp. 69–70.

[42] For further elaboration see Edwin M. Lemert, *Social Pathology* (New York: McGraw-Hill Book Company, Inc., 1951), Chaps. 2, 3, and 4. Also see Homans, *Social Behavior*, pp. 349–359 and S. Kirson Weinberg, *Social Problems in Our Time* (Englewood Cliffs, N.J.: Prentice-Hall, Inc., 1960).

provoke little comment, and an alcoholic may at times go largely unde-
tected. On the other hand, drunkenness or alcoholism in a middle-class
group may stand out like a fire on a hillside.

Deviant Behavior

Deviations from norms which are tolerated or which provoke only
mild disapproval are obviously of little concern to a society. Only those
situations in which behavior is in a disapproved direction, and of sufficient
degree to exceed the tolerance limit of the community, constitute *deviant
behavior* as it will be used here. This includes such deviations from norms
as delinquency and crime, drug addiction, alcoholism, mental disorders,
suicide, marital and family maladjustment, problems of old age, and
discrimination against minority groups. Obviously the extent and degree
of disapproval in a particular instance are dependent on the nature of the
situation and the community's degree of tolerance of the behavior involved.

Deviant behavior and *social problems* are not necessarily the same
thing. Not all social problems are instances of deviant behavior. For
example, soil erosion, flood damage, and forest destruction have for
decades been considered as social problems. Yet these problems can
hardly be considered as instances of deviant behavior. To be sure,
soil erosion may exemplify a variation from ideal standards of soil productivity, yet this variation is not a consequence of social behavior. The
same could be applied to social problems involving disease or physical
handicaps, such as cancer, heart disease, blindness, and crippling.[43]

Some writers refer to the existence of what has been described here
as deviant behavior as *social disorganization* and the society as being
"disorganized." A state of disorganization is often thought of as one in
which there is a "breakdown of social controls over the behavior of the
individual" and a decline in the unity of the group because former patterns of behavior and social control no longer are effective.[44] There are
a number of objections to this frame of reference. (1) Disorganization is
too subjective and vague a concept for analyzing a general society. Effective use of the concept, however, may be made in the study of specific
groups and institutions. (2) Social disorganization implies the disruption

---

[43] Such conditions, when dealt with in textbooks on "social problems," are completely
in order. It is only suggested here that they are not instances of deviant behavior within
the definition stated above.

[44] Contemporary use of the concept "social disorganization" comes largely from
W. I. Thomas and Florian Znaniecki, *The Polish Peasant in Europe and America* (New
York: Alfred A. Knopf, Inc., 1927). For criticisms of this concept see John F. Cuber,
Robert A. Harper, and William Kenkel, *Problems of American Society* (New York: Holt,
Rinehart and Winston, Inc., 1956), Chap. 22; Lemert, *op. cit.,* Chap. 1; and Hartung,
"Common and Discrete Values," *loc. cit.*

of a previously existing condition of organization, a situation which generally cannot be established. Social change is often confused with social disorganization without indicating why some social changes are disorganizing and others not. (3) Social disorganization is usually thought of as something "bad," and what is bad is often the value judgment of the observer and the members of his social class or other social groups. For example, the practice of gambling, the patronage of taverns, greater freedom in sex relations, and other behavior do not mean that these conditions are naturally "bad" or "disorganized." (4) The existence of forms of deviant behavior does not necessarily constitute a major threat to the central values of a society. The presence of suicide, crime, or alcoholism may not be serious if other values are being achieved. American society, for example, has a high degree of unity and integration despite high rates of deviant behavior if one considers such values as nationalism, highly developed industrial production, and goals of material comfort. (5) What seems like disorganization actually may often be highly organized systems of competing norms. Many subcultures of deviant behavior, such as delinquent gangs, organized crime, homosexuality, prostitution, and white-collar crime, including political corruption, may be highly organized. The slum sex code may be as highly organized and normative regarding premarital relations in one direction as the middle-class sex code is in the other.[45] The norms and values of the slums are highly organized, as Whyte has shown in his *Street Corner Society*.[46] (6) Finally, as several sociologists have suggested, it is possible that a variety of subcultures may contribute, through their diversity, to the unity or integration of a society rather than weaken it by constituting a situation of social disorganization.[47]

Types of Deviant Behavior

In the chapters which follow, a number of types of deviant behavior or, as they have been termed, "strongly disapproved deviations," are discussed. The following discussion presents a brief description of each of these types of deviant behavior, including the nature of the norms involved, the extent of the violation, and, in some cases, definitions of a few important concepts which are necessary to understand the deviation.

Most sociologists are skeptical of loose terms, such as "socially maladjusted," "antisocial," "emotionally disturbed," "abnormal," "mentally

---

[45] William F. Whyte, "A Slum Sex Code," *American Journal of Sociology*, 49:24–32 (July, 1943).

[46] William F. Whyte, *Street Corner Society* (Chicago: The University of Chicago Press, 1943).

[47] See Robin Williams, Jr., "Unity and Diversity in Modern America," *Social Forces*, 36:1–8 (October, 1957).

ill," "sexually deviant," and even an omnibus category, such as "delinquency," unless the norms are stated. The definition of excessive drinking and alcoholism, for example, involves norms, such as the amount of alcohol consumed, the purpose and meaning of the drinking, the social handicap to the individual, and the degree of inability to refrain from excessive drinking. Even the norms involved in mental disorder need to be so stated that we can determine with some precision who is mentally ill and who is not, whom we are to treat, and whom not to treat.

DELINQUENCY AND CRIME

Among the norms whose violation usually exceeds the tolerance limit of the community in even a highly differentiated society are the legal norms. To emphasize their importance and to force compliance with them, a series of penalties has been established by the political state. Enacted laws represent varying degrees of tolerance for the behavior outlawed. Some legal norms forbidding certain behavior are supported by nearly all segments of a society, the behavior in question being regarded as inimical to group welfare, whereas norms embodied in other laws have little support. Deviant behavior, such as murder, kidnaping, sexual abuse of young children, or incest, may be overwhelmingly and strongly disapproved. Other behavior, while disapproved legally, may have less public disapproval. Although persons differ about the validity of individual legal norms, there may be agreement that there is need for "obedience of the law" in general.

Most criminal behavior represents a conflict of the norms of particular groups or individuals against those norms which the law represents. Much juvenile delinquency, organized prostitution, gambling, traffic in narcotics, and homosexuality, for example, arise from the growth of subgroups which, although in physical contact with the rest of the society, may have different norms. Norms of subgroups which conflict with legal norms may be those of certain age groups, social classes, occupations, neighborhoods, or regions.

The exact amount of law violation in American society today is unknown, but the evidence points to its extensive nature. During 1960, 1.9 million serious crimes were reported to the police in the United States. Because some offenses, such as rape, are not frequently reported to the police, obviously more crimes were committed than these figures reveal. Reported to the police during 1960, according to the Federal Bureau of Investigation, were an estimated 432,906 cases of burglary, 88,970 robberies, usually with a gun, and 321,400 automobile thefts. There were 9140 murders and cases of nonnegligent manslaughter, 15,560 rape cases, and 130,230 cases of aggravated assault.

Property crimes, such as larceny, burglary, automobile theft, and robbery, constituted 91.7 percent of all crimes reported to the police in the United States in 1960. Murder and nonnegligent manslaughter, which are *personal crimes,* accounted for only 0.5 percent of the total. There is also a large group of *offenses against public order,* including vagrancy, disorderly conduct, prostitution, and gambling.

Certain types of offenses are often not included in the statistics for ordinary crimes. *White-collar crimes* are violations of laws by businessmen, professional men, and politicians in connection with their occupations. Their consequences are not usually tabulated as crimes, even though their effect on society as a whole may be far more serious than that of a typical burglary. These offenses include embezzlement and other trust violations, falsified income tax returns, political corruption, violations of food and drug laws, violations of banking and security laws, fee splitting by doctors, and violations of countless other regulations affecting persons of the white-collar class.

Antisocial acts committed by persons under a certain age, usually sixteen to eighteen, which are considered to be injurious to the person or society are classified as *juvenile delinquency.* Generally "delinquents" are not punished by the criminal law but are treated in other ways. Antisocial acts of juveniles include not only those which would be crimes if committed by adults but many other offenses which are peculiarly juvenile, such as truancy, incorrigibility, and vandalism. Although these latter acts are disturbing to community norms and are of increasing concern to American society, they are not generally included in national figures of "crimes" which have been committed.

In 1960 approximately 514,000 juvenile delinquency cases, involving about 443,000 children aged ten through seventeen, were handled by juvenile courts in the United States. These children represented about 1.8 percent of all children in this age group in the country, and represented a 6 percent increase over 1959 cases, in contrast to only a 2 percent increase in the child population. In addition, about 306,000 traffic cases were disposed of by juvenile courts in 1960, involving roughly 264,-000 different children, or about 1.0 percent of the child population.

DRUG ADDICTION

The use of such drugs as morphine, heroin, opium, cocaine, and marihuana, other than for medicinal purposes, is considered as a deviation from cultural or legal norms not only in the United States but also in many other Western societies. The use of drugs is disapproved because most of them are habit-forming. Their use tends either to decrease mental or physical activity or to overexcite and sustain such activity. Where a habit has been established, there may be excruciating physical and mental symptoms when the drugs are not used. Furthermore, drug addiction may become extremely expensive for a person who has been addicted for some time and has built up an increased tolerance for the drugs. Some addicts even commit thefts or engage in prostitution to finance their addiction.

ALCOHOLISM

The use of alcohol as a beverage is widespread in Western civilization and, by the majority of the population at least, its use in moderation is generally approved. Where alcohol is consumed mainly for purposes of conviviality or ceremony it is termed *social or controlled drinking*. The *social drinker* is able to control his drinking and rarely becomes intoxicated. Drinkers who deviate from the norms of the drinking patterns of a culture, and from such legal norms as those prohibiting drunkenness and driving while intoxicated, are referred to as *excessive drinkers*.

Excessive drinkers use alcohol for purposes of intoxication and some may even become completely dependent upon its effects. The *heavy drinker* uses alcohol more frequently than does the social drinker. He has occasional sprees of drunkenness, but in general his drinking does not seriously deviate from drinking norms. *Alcoholics* are those excessive drinkers who deviate markedly from drinking norms by the frequency and quantity of their consumption of alcohol and by the unconventional times and places selected for the drinking. Such excessive consumption of alcohol tends to disturb their interpersonal relationships in their family, occupational, and social groups. The alcoholic is unable to control consistently, or stop at will, either the start of drinking or its termination once started. Most deviant of all are those whose alcoholism has become chronic. *Chronic alcoholics* almost completely lose control over their drinking and become "compulsive" drinkers. They become so dependent upon alcohol that they live to drink and drink to live. Some of their characteristics are solitary drinking, morning drinking, and general physical deterioration.

In 1960 there were, in the United States, an estimated 4,470,000 alcoholics, which is equivalent to a rate of 4000 alcoholics per 100,000 adults aged twenty years and over. Of these alcoholics it was estimated that about a fourth were chronic alcoholics, or those alcoholics with complications.

MENTAL DISORDERS

When an individual's behavior patterns in interpersonal relationships persistently deviate from certain cultural norms to the extent that a society considers his conduct to be a nuisance, a danger, or a handicap to himself, the behavior is often regarded as deviant and the person as mentally disordered. Mentally ill persons have difficulty in relating to others and in sharing the norms and objectives of others in given situations. Every society tolerates a range of behavior and a certain amount of eccentricity, but mental disorders often exceed the "limits of eccentricity."

In its extreme form, behavior in mental disorders not only is disapproved but often is also unintelligible to others.[48] Violations of legal norms, on the other hand, are likewise disapproved, but criminal behavior is generally intelligible to others. Psychotic persons, for example, may exhibit hallucinations, delusions, losses of memory, peculiar construction in language, and inappropriate emotional responses. They may be unnecessarily seclusive, overexcited, extremely aggressive, or depressed. Psychotic individuals disturb other persons since it is difficult to interact with them, and the individual with a severe mental disorder may find it increasingly difficult to participate at all in a society.

Psychoses are of two types, organic and functional. *Organic psychoses* are presumed to have some connection with disturbances in the physical organism. They include the senile psychoses or mental disorders of old age; alcoholic psychoses, which are related to alcoholism; and paresis, which is caused by syphilis. The *functional psychoses* are those in which the mental disorder cannot be attributed to organic disturbances. The chief disorders of this type are schizophrenia, characterized by withdrawal from reality, hallucinations, and delusions; manic-depressive psychoses, with symptoms of extreme elation, deep depression, or both; and paranoia, characterized by illusions of grandeur and extreme beliefs of persecution. That these types are not disease entities in the sense of physical illness is shown by the fact that psychiatrists vary in their diagnoses of cases.

Traditionally psychiatrists have classified mental disorders into the neuroses and the psychoses. Neurotic conditions are not as noticeable to other persons generally as is psychotic behavior. In mild forms they may even be recognized as a problem only by the individual, his immediate family, or his friends. Consequently, deviations from cultural norms are less clear with neurotic than with psychotic behavior. Neurotic conditions include hypochondria, compulsions, phobias, and hysteria. Compulsive disorders comprise repetitive or ritualistic behavior, such as excessive hand washing or dressing in a precise manner. Phobias represent obsessive fears about something, such as high places, death, the loss of one's mind, or illness. If the individual is a hypochondriac he is unduly, and usually needlessly, concerned about the state of his health. Hysterical symptoms—which are without a physical basis—include fainting spells, tics or tremors, or the loss of sight or hearing or, for example, the ability to write.

It has been estimated that there are about 2 million psychotic persons

---

[48] Robert E. L. Faris, *Social Disorganization* (2d ed.; New York: The Ronald Press Company, 1955), p. 324.

in the United States and over 4 million so severely neurotic as to need psychiatric treatment. One study concluded that the probabilities are that about one person in twenty, by the age of forty-five, and one in ten, by the age of sixty-five, will develop a serious mental illness, either an episodic or a continuing one.[49] In 1959 there were 616,964 mental patients in long-term mental hospitals, about 88 percent of them in public mental hospitals, state, county, or city. Actually the total is much higher in view of the fact that the movements of patients in and out of these hospitals during a given year is extensive. From 1955 to 1960 there has been a slight decline in the resident population of these hospitals. In 1960, 235,-231 patients were admitted to state and local mental hospitals for the first time, and about 100,000 were admitted who had previously been in mental hospitals. In addition, many persons are treated outside a mental hospital by psychiatrists, clinical psychologists, social workers, counselors, and ministers.

The economic costs of mental disorders in terms of loss of earnings are extremely large. Losses in 1952, for all patients resident in mental institutions in the United States, were estimated at $700 million in one year.[50] The estimated losses during the first year for first admissions in 1954 were $160 million. Estimated present value of all future earnings of first admissions to public prolonged-care hospitals was $1.9 billion. First admissions (1954), based on probable discharge and death rates (but not including readmissions) will lose 556,000 labor-force years in their remaining years of life, or equal to a present value of $800 million.

SUICIDE

Many persons in Western civilization take their lives each year, but in no Western society is this action approved. There may be feelings of sympathy for the personal difficulties in certain cases of suicide, but this sympathy does not constitute approval. Norms opposed to suicide have a long historical background, including particularly strong attitudes against it in Christian theological doctrine. Also a factor is the general implication of cowardice in retreating from life through suicide and of disgrace to the family and even the associates of the suicide. Attempted suicide is even a crime in several countries and in a few states in the United States. This extreme and complete form of social withdrawal has long interested social scientists and others who consider suicide to be a reflection of difficulties in interpersonal relations.

During 1959 in the United States there were 18,330 deaths officially

[49] Herbert Goldhamer and Andrew W. Marshall, *Psychoses and Civilization* (New York: The Free Press of Glencoe, 1953), p. 11.
[50] See Rashi Fein, *The Economics of Mental Illness* (New York: Basic Books, Inc., 1958), p. 87

reported as suicides, or a rate of 10.4 per 100,000. Many more suicidal deaths undoubtedly occur but are not recorded as such because of the disgrace involved. The Metropolitan Life Insurance Company has estimated that more than 100,000 persons annually attempt suicide.

CONFLICTS IN MARITAL AND FAMILY ROLES

All societies recognize the importance of marriage and family relationships. Although great variations exist in marital and family systems, it is generally assumed in most Western European societies that marriage and family relationships have a high degree of permanence and are capable of satisfying the expectations of the marital partners. Marriage and family unity prevail where the roles and expectations of the members are satisfactorily achieved. If conflicts in marriage or family roles develop, the marital or family relationship is impaired.

Separation, desertion, and divorce, as they represent varying degrees of dissolution of the family, are generally strongly disapproved in Western societies. So also is wife beating or similar forms of physical violence. As scientific research and marriage counseling have advanced in recent years, the concept of marital maladjustment has been broadened. Increasingly it is being regarded as embracing those situations in which the marital partners display little marital affection, slight dependence on one another, and no sharing of satisfactions and decision making. Where these are present there may be indifference, dissatisfaction, and incompatibility between the marital partners and a situation deviating from the behavior expected by each partner in marriage.

Obviously the actual extent of the breakdown of interaction in the marital or family situation cannot be determined. Generally divorce statistics are cited as an objective, though limited, indication of the extent of role conflicts in marriages. The United States ratio is about one divorce to every four marriages; in 1959 about 1,500,000 marriages to about 400,000 divorces, affecting about 4 percent of all children under eighteen. In addition, many families are broken by legal separation or by desertion, either temporary or permanent, of one or the other marital partner, more frequently the husband. Even these figures on broken homes, however, do not indicate the full extent of marital and family role conflicts in the United States. Studies of married persons have revealed that a considerable proportion of marriages in certain samples are unhappy even though the marriage has not been physically or legally dissolved.[51]

---

[51] See Ernest W. Burgess and Paul Wallin, *Engagement and Marriage* (Philadelphia: J. B. Lippincott Company, 1953); Harvey Locke, *Predicting Adjustment in Marriage* (New York: Holt, Rinehart and Winston, Inc., 1951); and L. M. Terman, *Psychological Factors in Marital Happiness* (New York: McGraw-Hill Book Company, Inc., 1938).

ROLE AND STATUS CONFLICT IN OLD AGE

In growing older a person is faced with making adjustments so that his expectations and his evaluations of his social roles are in harmony with those of the persons with whom he interacts. The roles of the aged are not clearly defined in contemporary society, and often the aged person experiences conflicts where his expectations are based on roles which were formerly appropriate. To the extent that the aged person's behavior exhibits conflicting roles which are unsatisfactory to himself and to society it is deviant. This definition of certain behavior among the aged as social deviation is admittedly weak. A more precise statement is difficult until the status and roles of the aged in contemporary society are more clearly defined. Deviant behavior among older persons includes feelings of lowered social status, loneliness, unhappiness, or rejection.

As childhood and other diseases have been controlled and as man's life span has continued to increase, the proportion of older men and women in the United States has become significantly greater. At present in the United States 9.2 percent of the population is sixty-five or over. It might be supposed that technological developments and this increased life expectancy have added much to a fuller enjoyment of life by these older people. Unfortunately, many old people in the United States are unhappy in their daily living, feel frustrated in their relationships with other persons, and may even develop senile psychoses.

DISCRIMINATION AGAINST MINORITY GROUPS

Over the past few centuries a set of norms has evolved relating to certain rights for persons regardless of their race, creed, or ethnic derivation. These norms include political equality, due process of law and equal justice, freedom of opportunity to achieve economic and political success, and the right to express one's religious beliefs. A Universal Declaration of Human Rights embodying these norms was approved by the United Nations in 1948. A similar group of norms and values constitutes what is termed the American Creed.[52]

These norms and values in the United States developed out of the philosophy of the Enlightenment and the English, American, and French revolutions, with their emphasis on the importance of the individual; the traditional judicial procedures of English justice; Christianity, with its concept of universal brotherhood; capitalism, with its belief that individual success is based on individual initiative; and, finally, American na-

---

[52] Gunnar Myrdal, *An American Dilemma* (New York: Harper & Row, Publishers, 1944), Chap. 1.

tionalism itself, with its emphasis on the racial, religious, and ethnic diversity of America. These values are reflected in the Declaration of Independence, in the Constitution and its amendments, and in numerous decisions of the Supreme Court, particularly those in recent years dealing with the illegality of laws upholding segregation or denying equal citizenship rights to all persons.

When a group is placed in a lower status on the basis of race, religion, or ethnic background, the action is considered discrimination. It takes many forms and involves suffrage and public office, the administration of justice, employment and business opportunities, education, public accommodation and housing, and every form of social participation. Social norms and values sanctioning discrimination, such as beliefs about racial superiority and anti-Semitism, have a long history. Such discriminatory norms are derived from various subcultural groups and in some historic periods or in certain areas have even been enacted into law.

In the United States discrimination in varying degrees is directed at 18,000,000 or more Negroes, or approximately one in every ten Americans; at over 5,500,000 Jews; at over 3,500,000 Spanish-speaking people, primarily the Mexicans and Spanish-Americans of the Southwest and the Puerto Ricans of New York City; at over 500,000 Indians; and at over 700,000 of Japanese and Chinese origin.

The Scientific Study of Deviant Behavior

Many people believe that deviant behavior cannot be studied scientifically because scientific methods cannot be applied to them in the same manner as in the case of the physical sciences. Human behavior, they claim, is not the proper field for scientific research. This skepticism about the effectiveness of the social sciences is due, in large part, to the extreme complexity of the data which the research worker in these fields must use. In fact, the nature of human behavior is thought by some to be so different from other data that they would restrict the term "science" to the so-called exact or physical sciences such as biology, chemistry, and physics. They would even deny the use of the term "science" to such social or behavioral sciences as sociology, social psychology, anthropology, economics, and political science, upon which the solution of problems of deviant behavior ultimately depends. As Sellin has indicated, however, these, "are important considerations, but they do not permit us to assume that social facts cannot be studied scientifically and laws of social life gradually established. They merely recognize that the social scientist has great hazards to overcome." [53]

Part of this confusion is a result of failure to consider the nature of

[53] Sellin, "Culture Conflict and Crime," pp. 12–13.

scientific methods. The scientific study of human behavior assumes that the criteria of science can be applied to the data involved. This means that human behavior can be studied as a *natural process,* or as a sequence of events in which certain events follow from other events, in much the same way as the process through which a disease develops or a chemical process occurs. Whether events which follow are "caused" by preceding events cannot be determined by observing the order of occurrence of the events alone; they must be subjected to scientific investigation.

The scientific study of deviant behavior, like the scientific approach to any data, is an attempt to describe the *processes* associated with the behavior. Generalizations as to cause and effect relationships in such processes are the purpose of science. Such generalizations, if eventually achieved, are usually stated in terms of probabilities. A criminal career, for example, is generally found to have followed a long series of circumstances and incidents, usually beginning with juvenile delinquency and progressing to more serious acts. Likewise, the admission of a psychotic patient to a mental hospital is not the result of one experience but rather may be the culmination of many experiences. The series of steps which precede the chronic alcoholic's admission to the alcoholic ward may extend back for many years. A divorce is seldom the product of a single argument.

A science also tries to put some order into a series of heterogeneous data by reducing them to *types,* as, for example, when the zoologist or botanist classifies animals or plants into species. The scientific study of "criminals" has resulted in the discovery that not all criminals have the same characteristics, but instead that there are various types of criminal careers. Similarly, excessive drinkers are of various types. People suffering from mental disorders and suicides can also be subdivided into a number of types. Generally, such types or classifications are given names or terms in order to facilitate or simplify the manipulation of the mass of data involved in each type.

The social scientist, as contrasted with those who make unscientific claims about human behavior, is willing to do three things. First, he is willing to subject his hypotheses to tests. Second, he avoids making generalizations which are not based on empirical studies. Third, he will state his confidence in a proposition according to the degree to which it has been verified by a test using experimental or empirical data.

Scientific method is nothing more than a description or guide to the logic of scientific inquiry. It is generally stated as a series of steps, which in its simplest form involve:

1. the formulation of a hypothesis referring to the phenomenon to be studied;
2. the observation and collection of data which will test the hypothesis;
3. the classification and analysis of the data obtained; and
4. the arrival at conclusions as to whether, from the results of the analysis, the hypothesis is confirmed or not confirmed.

A *hypothesis* is a statement of a relationship that appears to exist, as, for example, "Delinquency is produced by crime stories on the radio and television." In this hypothesis the social scientist would define how he uses such terms as "delinquency," "crime stories," and other variables. In order to *test* such a hypothesis, however, it would have to be stated in a form which is testable, as "A significantly greater proportion of juveniles who listen to or watch crime stories on radio and television also have been legally classified as delinquent than have those who do not listen to or watch such crime stories." He then *observes* as much as he can of the relevant data, using the *research techniques* most appropriate to the data studied. It is usually not feasible for the social scientist to use mechanical instruments similar to those used in the physical science laboratories. Instead, he may rely on questionnaires and interviews, case histories, and personal documents, such as diaries. In other types of studies he may use ecological techniques, such as spot-mapping, community studies, and, finally, the comparative studies of people living in different cultures.

The social scientist in his research must see that the group he uses for study is representative of the phenomena he is studying. In most instances he also compares the group he is studying with a control group. For example, in testing the hypothesis about the relation of delinquency to crime stories on radio and television, the social scientist must select a *representative sample* of all juvenile delinquents. Since only relatively few juvenile delinquents are sent to correctional institutions, he might decide to select a random sample of those who had been arrested or had appeared before a juvenile court. It also would be necessary, as in most research studies on behavior problems, to compare the delinquents, or the *experimental group,* with a sample of nondelinquents, or a *control group,* in order to discover to what extent the latter also listen to or watch crime stories.

This hypothesis would be partially *verified* if the delinquents, or a statistically significant proportion of the experimental group, listened to or watched crime stories and the nondelinquents did not. The hypothesis would be rejected if no differences were found, or if the control group were discovered to have been listening to or watching crime stories as much as or more than the experimental group. Even after the conclusion of this study, a generalization could not be established until the study had been repeated on other samples of the delinquent and nondelinquent population.

Advances in any physical or social science are often made through efforts to predict or control real phenomena. Such efforts may reveal the inadequacies of scientific knowledge when applications fail to produce the expected results. Applications may also confirm and even extend scientific knowledge. In the physical world, for example, the application of astronomy to the problems of sea and air navigation resulted in improvements in both the theory of astronomy and the techniques of navigation. Efforts to control criminal behavior contribute not only to the field of criminology but also to the broader study of human behavior and society in general.

On the other hand, emphasis on the application, rather than the discovery, of basic scientific knowledge can be carried too far. Generally speaking, application of knowledge is not the *goal* of the science, but rather a by-product of or consequence of scientific discovery.[54] Preoccupation with social welfare and social legislation, where it has not been simultaneously concerned with scientific study of deviant behavior, has often hindered the development of basic knowledge in this area.[55] Unfortunately, attention has often been concentrated on the control of delinquency and crime, alcoholism, discrimination, mental illness, and marital difficulties without the accumulation and study of concepts, theories, and research upon which to base such a program of control.

The primary motivation of most scientists studying deviant behavior today, as of the physical scientist in his laboratory, is scientific curiosity. This does not mean that most social scientists who attempt to understand human behavior are uninterested in its practical application or that the two are necessarily opposed. Rather, students of society, as scientists, are interested chiefly in the discovery of knowledge.

Increasing recognition is being given to the importance of systematizing knowledge about deviant behavior, for without this systematization knowledge cannot be effectively utilized in social control. The mere description of the characteristics of deviants is of little use without some explanation of the development of their behavior. With the extension and systematic application of scientific knowledge, there appears to be no reason why many types of deviant behavior cannot be solved.

Selected Readings

The Annals. November, 1961, issue on "The Teen-age Culture." A series of articles dealing with the norms of a particular peer group subculture, namely, teen-agers. Includes a discussion of Italian-American, Jewish, and Negro subcultures in our society and also in several foreign countries.

GOODE, WILLIAM J., and PAUL K. HATT. *Methods in Social Research.* New York: McGraw-Hill Book Company, Inc., 1952. An excellent discussion of the scientific method in the study of human behavior. Discusses scientific design and the techniques used primarily in sociological research.

HOMANS, GEORGE C. *Social Behavior: Its Elementary Forms.* New York: Harcourt,

---

[54] In a similar way modern-day space explorations involve applications of previously discovered basic knowledge in sciences such as physics or astronomy, which, however, have been added to by testing this knowledge through space explorations.

[55] Edwin H. Sutherland, "Social Pathology," *American Journal of Sociology*, 50:429–436 (May, 1945).

Brace & World, Inc., 1961. An analysis of social behavior based on data obtained from observations of behavior in small groups in industry, in laboratory settings, and in communities. The social behavior of given group members is seen to depend upon a number of variables, such as their status, their role, the probability of rewards for given acts, and so forth.

JAHODA, MARIE, MORTON DEUTSCH, and STUART W. COOK. *Research Methods in Social Relations*. 2 vols. New York: Holt, Rinehart and Winston, Inc., 1952. An introductory statement of the basic processes and selected techniques in social research. Illustrative material primarily deals with the study of prejudice.

KAHL, JOSEPH A. *The American Class Structure*. New York: Holt, Rinehart and Winston, Inc., 1957. An analysis of the norms and behavior patterns of American social classes.

LEMERT, EDWIN M. *Social Pathology*. New York: McGraw-Hill Book Company, Inc., 1951, Chaps. 1–3. Discusses the nature of deviation and the societal reactions to deviations from norms. There is also an analysis of the concepts of social visibility as well as mention of the tolerance quotient.

MILLER, WALTER B. "Lower Class Culture as a Generating Milieu of Gang Delinquency," *Journal of Social Issues*, 14:5–19 (1958). A well-known description of some of the norms of the lower class in America.

SELLIN, THORSTEN. "Culture Conflict and Crime." New York: Social Science Research Council, Bulletin 41, 1938. Deals with the relation of science to criminology and presents a well-known discussion of the concept of "norms" in relation to crime and human behavior in general. Conduct norms have a varying degree of "resistance potential"; hence norms can be classified on this basis.

SUTHERLAND, EDWIN H. "Social Pathology," *American Journal of Sociology*, 50:429–436 (May, 1945). A theoretical survey of fifty years of research on deviant behavior.

Chapter

2

Deviant Behavior
as Social Behavior

Many people look upon such deviants as delinquents, criminals, mental patients, suicides, and alcoholics as strange varieties of human beings whose behavior arises in an entirely different way from that of the more balanced and respectable members of society. It is true that deviant behavior is one kind of human, or social, behavior, just as conforming behavior is another kind. However, the difference between conforming and deviant behavior does not mean that there are different physical or psychological qualities which the deviant, as compared with the conformist, possesses. This assertion is alien to the thinking of many persons. We often learn to look upon those who behave differently from the way "we" behave as possessing individual qualities unlike our own. We tend, furthermore, to believe that these "qualities" are the "causes" of the behavior involved. Thus, we say a person is an alcoholic, or "drinks" excessively because he is "weak," "has no character," "has no will power," or has "bad heredity." We tend, therefore, to believe that the excessive drinking of which we disapprove is due to some lack of "character" within the person. In the same way, we attribute excessive "sex drives" to the sex offender and prostitute, or we say that they are "emotionally insecure" and are attempting to find love and affection in sexual release. We describe delinquents as "having a need to rebel," or as "releasing aggressive drives which they have suppressed too long," or as "having hostile, aggressive, and rebellious personality traits." [1]

In various ways, therefore, our mode of perceiving and interpreting the world and the things about us is conditioned by meanings and categories with which our culture has provided us. As noted in the previous chapter, we see our world through a cultural mesh, and nowhere is this truer than in our perception of social deviants.

This attitude that deviants are inherently different is built upon a

---

[1] See Edwin H. Lemert, *Social Pathology* (New York: McGraw-Hill Book Company, Inc., 1951), Chaps. 3 and 4 for further elaboration on this problem.

series of false assumptions, for *all deviant behavior is human behavior*. By this is meant that the same fundamental processes which produce the "normal" person also produce the "abnormal," for both of them are human beings. If certain basic processes underlie the development of the normal person, the same processes and structures must be sought in the deviant. Common components of human nature are found in all types of normality and abnormality.

> One implication of the sociological approach to the study of human behavior is that men are always participants in joint enterprises of one sort or other and that all individualistic explanations of the things men do are necessarily incomplete. Men are rarely isolated and acting purely as independent agents. Respiration is essentially an involuntary organic process, but even that is subject to social control. Men deliberately check their panting if they do not wish to appear cowardly or weak, or they may sigh to indicate hopelessness. Even passive acquiescence and failure to act are social to the extent that such hesitation arises from the anticipated reactions of other people. Each person is involved in many transactions to which he may contribute and thereby modify but only in his capacity as a participant in them. This means that what a man does cannot be explained exclusively in terms of his personality traits, his attitudes, or his motives. People frequently do things they do not want to do. Human behavior is something that is constructed in the course of interaction with other people, and the direction it takes depends upon the inclinations of others as well as those of the actor.[2]

Differences in subprocesses exist; if they did not there would be no way to account scientifically for deviant behavior. The subprocesses affecting deviants, however, must operate within the general framework of a theory of human nature. The units of analysis, as well as the fundamental social processes in all human conduct, are the same whether the end products are inmates of correctional institutions or wardens, mental patients or psychiatrists, habitual criminals or ministers. Brown writes that abnormal behavior is not something outside nature: "It is a naturalistic phenomenon, socially defined as undesirable, but nevertheless a naturalistic phenomenon that developed as all other human nature developed."[3]

Moreover, there does not appear to be any general personality pattern of conformity or nonconformity with social norms or values.[4] Persons may

---

[2] Tamotsu Shibutani, *Society and Personality: An Interaction Approach to Social Psychology*, p. 60. © 1961. Prentice-Hall, Inc., Englewood Cliffs, N.J. By permission.

[3] Lawrence Guy Brown, *Social Pathology* (New York: Appleton-Century-Crofts, Inc., 1946), p. 62. This quotation has been used by permission of the publisher.

[4] Many psychiatrists and psychologists believe, however, that there is such a relationship. Talcott Parsons, a sociologist, has also suggested, without supporting evidence, that there is a relationship between a nonconformist personality pattern and deviant behavior. —*The Social System* (New York: The Free Press of Glencoe, 1951), Chaps. 7–9, and particularly pp. 256–267.

deviate from certain norms and comply with others.[5] Those who deviate from sex norms may not steal, for example, and many white-collar offenders may have a rigid sexual code. In most cases strongly disapproved deviations may be but a small proportion of a person's total life activities. Even where the deviations constitute a more organized subculture, as in certain types of crime, accepted conduct may coincide at many points with the norms and values of the larger community.[6] In the case of professional crime, for example, personal honor and "honesty among thieves" may be a reality because it would generally be inappropriate to depend on the police or other outside agencies for support.

Further confusion arises in the minds of some observers when they perceive that certain factors are associated with the occurrence of deviant behavior. They often jump to the conclusion that two phenomena are related when they may have no connection. When it is noted, for example, that delinquency and bad housing are often associated, a causal relationship may be presumed to exist. Others may perceive that delinquents read comic books, so they conclude that comic books cause delinquency. In both instances, the observer has failed to take into account how such situations may cause delinquency. Most important, however, they may have failed to observe that these same factors—bad housing and comic books—affect a large proportion of our population without necessarily producing deviant behavior. Although most delinquency occurs in so-called slum areas, where housing is poor, the relation has little direct connection with any theory of human behavior and must be discounted as an error in perception. Moreover, delinquency does occur in areas of good housing; hence, if the same logic is used, this situation might be attributed to the adequacy of the housing situation. In studying deviant behavior it is always necessary to consider whether similar influences are affecting non-deviants; therefore, some *theory of human behavior* must be devised which will account for the differential effects, if they exist.

With this statement of the thesis that, fundamentally, both deviant and nondeviant persons have essentially the same components, some further discussion of these components is necessary. Here the interest is not so much in society, culture, or the group as in the individual. The discussion will begin by analyzing what relation a person's biological structure has to his actions and what the differences are between the biological nature of man and that of other animals.

Biology and Social Behavior

Man has a biological nature and a social nature, but it is obvious that without a biological nature there could be no human nature. There is an

---

[5] Robert Harper, "Is Conformity a General or Specific Trait?" *American Sociological Review*, 12:81–86 (February, 1947).

[6] Lemert, *op. cit.*, p. 49.

interplay between the two rather than opposition. Man is an animal who must breathe, eat, rest, and eliminate. Like any other animal, he requires calories, salt and other chemicals, and a particular temperature range and oxygen balance. Man is an animal who is dependent upon his environment and limited by certain of his biological capacities. "Social influences profoundly affect the ways in which human bodies behave . . . but human bodies never cease to be animals." [7]

In the past it was customary for social scientists to engage in lengthy debates as to whether the social behavior of man was in any way biological. Modern social scientists are more likely to begin with the assertion that biology is of little relevance to social or symbolic behavior.[8] There are no physical functions or structures, no combination of genes, and no glandular secretions which contain within themselves the power to direct, guide, or determine the type, form, and course of the social behavior of human beings. Physical structures or properties set physical limits on the activities of persons, but whether such structures will set *social* limits depends on the way in which cultures or subcultures symbolize or interpret these physical properties.

INSTINCTS

Certain writers on deviant behavior, particularly psychoanalysts, have erroneously stressed the animal nature of man, especially with reference to the existence in man of an "unrepressed primitive" animal nature.[9] It is said that man has instincts and that many contemporary difficulties in social relations result from man's inability to overcome his real or original nature. Man has no primitive instinctive nature, however, for there are no universal or instinctive patterns of behavior common to all men and transmitted biologically from one generation to another. Man does not have instinctive patterns of behavior. Hunger can be satisfied with a variety of foods, many of which are injurious to men. Sex acts have no particular season, there is no inborn pattern of courtship, and no "natural" way of sexual intercourse. There is no instinct which makes man religious or irreligious, kind or cruel, a killer or a pacifist.

HEREDITY AND DEVIANT BEHAVIOR

If human behavior is to be inherited, it must have a direct connection with the biological structure, such as the tissue of the brain, the nervous

---

[7] Theodore M. Newcomb, *Social Psychology* (New York: Holt, Rinehart and Winston, Inc., 1950), p. 48. Copyright 1950 by Holt, Rinehart and Winston, Inc. The quotations from this book are reprinted by special permission.

[8] For further discussion see, for example, Alfred R. Lindesmith and Anselm L. Strauss, *Social Psychology* (rev. ed.: New York: Holt, Rinehart and Winston, Inc., 1955), Chaps. 1 and 2.

[9] See the discussion of psychoanalysis, pp. 126–139.

system, the glands, or the blood. Moreover, the specific factor or factors must be present when the ovum is fertilized by the spermatozoon. An inherited quality must be reasonably specific, and must be stable enough that it might be able to affect all members of the species. Regardless of these prerequisites, some biologists still believe that crime, alcoholism, certain types of mental illness, and certain sexual deviations can be carried as specific unit factors in biological inheritance. According to this biological theory, certain specific deviant behavior can be inherited in much the same manner as eye or hair color, through the genes and the chromosomes, at the time of the fertilization of the ovum. Persons with this scientific orientation speak of "born criminals," "born alcoholics," or "inherited insanity."

The evidence today is overwhelmingly against such a view. For example, the following conclusion about criminal behavior has been reached.

> It is obviously impossible for criminality to be inherited as such, for crime is defined by acts of legislatures and these vary independently of the biological inheritance of the violators of the laws. If persons with certain inherited traits are more likely to commit crimes than persons with other inherited traits, these traits have not been identified and their connection with criminal behavior has not been demonstrated. Anyone who speaks of the direct or indirect inheritance of criminality except in the senses stated in the first two propositions in this paragraph is speaking from his preconceptions and assumptions and not from factual evidence.[10]

Although the evidence is incomplete and contradictory, the numerically important types of mental disorder do not appear to be biologically inherited.[11] The evidence on the inheritance of alcoholism was surveyed by Jellinek, a biologist, who combined fifteen studies of heredity made of 4372 clinical alcoholics, of whom, 2799, or 52 percent, were found to have had at least one inebriate parent. He found that the estimates of the several investigators as to the percentage of alcoholics who had a possible history of hereditary factors varied from a high of 83 percent to a low of 23 percent. In his conclusions Jellinek, having left out some of the studies which dealt exclusively with persons suffering from alcoholic psychoses in which other factors besides alcoholism might be present, stated that the studies surveyed showed that "the incidence of hereditary taint in the total group of alcoholics probably does not exceed 35 percent. This leaves us with a large alcoholic population in which inebriety has developed independently of any hereditary liability." [12] This is far too cautious a state-

---

[10] Edwin H. Sutherland and Donald R. Cressey, *Principles of Criminology* (6th ed.; Philadelphia: J. B. Lippincott Company, 1960), p. 90.

[11] This will be discussed in Chapter 13, "The Functional Mental Disorders."

[12] E. M. Jellinek, "Heredity of the Alcoholic," in *Alcohol, Science, and Society* (New Brunswick, N.J.: Quarterly Journal of Studies on Alcohol, 1945), p. 109.

ment, for the presence of an alcoholic parent by no means represents necessarily a biological rather than a social influence.

In order to prove that crime or other deviant behavior is inherited, the nature of the inheritance must be stated in such precise terms as to suggest what part of the physical organism is affected or how the organism as a whole is affected. This has not been done. Since attitudes derived from the norms of the culture cannot be inherited, deviant attitudes derived from other sources cannot be inherited. Likewise, deviant behavior cannot be hereditary because such a theory assumes that what constitutes disapproved behavior is the same in all societies, which is not necessarily the case.

What many persons confuse as inheritance in behavior is the social transmission of somewhat similar ways of behaving from one generation to another in a culture, or from one family to another. Actually none of this is hereditary, for there is no way in which so-called family traits or culture can be inherited through the genes. The inheritance of eye color is one thing; the inheritance of thousands of social norms and values is another. Anthropologists have demonstrated conclusively that there is no connection between the biological features of race and culture. A typical American Negro, for example, would have little in common culturally with an African Negro. The American Negro has no appreciable vestige of his African culture left today. The social organization, the language, the African gods, the witchcraft, the food habits have all been supplanted by a Western European culture. The complexity of gene structure which would be required to transmit a culture as part of the biological heritage would be inconceivable.

One of the reasons for the belief in constitutional differences was the error in perceiving the reasons for resemblances and differences in the trait structures of father and son, mother and daughter, and brothers and sisters. The experiences of no two children are exactly the same even for an hour or a day, let alone a month, a year, or more. The child learns to adapt to the world around him and to the people in the world. Thus it can be understood that the experiences of two brothers, particularly if there is a considerable age disparity, may be even more distinct than the experiences of friends of either one. Among these differences in experiences are obviously the addition of siblings to the family, playmates, school classes, and teachers. If the family has moved during the childhood of two brothers, as many families do, the neighbors and the general environment may be quite different. What is probably most important is the change in attitudes of the father and mother with additional children, and changes in social status and possibly in occupation. The method of treating an older and a younger child may be quite different because of changes in the parents' social situation.

The relevance of all this discussion to deviant behavior should be clear.

If one can inherit only something which is carried physiologically, and none of the social norms or values of one's culture or subculture are thus transmitted, much of what are termed "family traits" are eliminated. It is obvious, however, that behavioral traits can be passed on from grandfather to father and son through sharing common experiences and attitudes without recourse to inheritance. Likewise, there is no way in which such deviant attitudes as disrespect for laws, sexual licentiousness, or, in mental illness, for example, difficulties in interpersonal relations such as fear of other people, can be inherited. It is intriguing to consider what might happen in each instance if it were possible to cross such traits. Such possibilities include crossing a shoplifter's genes with a forger's genes, the genes of a person who likes people with those of one who does not, or those of a teetotaler with those of an alcoholic.

Neither moral behavior nor immoral behavior is biologically inherited. This would be impossible, for, as we have said above, the definitions of what constitutes such behavior vary not only among societies, but, as Kinsey showed about sex behavior, primarily by social class within a society. Morality also varies by generation, as illustrated by the changes in norms designated in the criminal code each year. Thus the gene structure would have to be extremely variable to keep up with these changes in moral definitions. Moreover, as indicated before, any propositions about the inheritance of deviant behavior would have to apply as well to the nondeviant.

GLANDS

Some writers have sought a more specific explanation of certain forms of deviant behavior in the malfunctioning of certain glands of the human body, particularly the endocrine glands. Berman suggested that persons who are criminal, irresponsible, and unable to adjust to society have disturbances in the thymus gland.[13] Schlapp and Smith explained criminal behavior as being due to malfunctioning of the glands,[14] a theme which has become a particular favorite of many European, particularly Italian, criminologists. Efforts have also been made to trace some forms of mental disorders and alcoholism to the improper functioning of certain glands, particularly the thyroid and adrenal glands.[15] Others have suggested that malfunctioning of the gonads and abnormal secretion of the sex hormones

---

[13] Louis Berman, *The Glands Regulating Personality* (New York: The Macmillan Company, 1922).

[14] Max Schlapp and E. H. Smith, *The New Criminology* (New York: Liveright Publishing Corporation, 1929).

[15] J. M. Nielsen and George N. Thompson, *The Engrammes of Psychiatry* (Springfield, Ill.: Charles C. Thomas, Publisher, 1947), pp. 357–362.

produce not only the effeminate homosexual and the oversexed personality types but the prostitute.[16]

In spite of these claims, research on glandular structure has as yet produced no conclusive explanations in any area of deviant behavior, with the possible exception of certain unique cases. Part of this inability to prove a relationship can be attributed to the fact that little is known about the relationship of endocrine glands to disorders in behavior.[17] In fact, very little is known about the functioning of glands among nondeviant persons. Ashley-Montagu states unequivocally that "not one of the reports on the alleged relationship between glandular dysfunctions and criminality [has] been carried out in a scientific manner, and that all such reports are glaring examples of the fallacy of false cause." [18] Somewhat similar statements have been made about efforts to relate schizophrenia or the manic-depressive psychoses to endocrine disturbances.[19]

Even if there were evidence that disturbances in the endocrine glands were related to certain forms of deviant behavior, it would be difficult to establish the fact that the glandular disturbances preceded the deviant behavior. Incarceration in a prison or a long period of mental illness might upset the glandular functioning of an individual. The association of glandular deficiencies with the development of alcoholism is even more difficult, for alcoholics may consume large quantities of alcohol over long periods during which their diet is anything but balanced. It is likely that glandular secretions occasionally may affect a personality, but there seems to be no general correlation between certain behavioral characteristics and endocrine disturbance. Further research using control groups is imperative in order to pass beyond speculation to facts in this area.

PHYSICAL CHARACTERISTICS AND DEFECTS

Some persons claim that certain antisocial behavior is often produced by poor health or disease. In particular, there has been an interest in the relation of deviant behavior to brain pathology, infectious diseases, heart lesions, and such foci of infection as tonsils or teeth.[20] Crossed eyes, facial

[16] See, for example, A. Myerson and R. Neustadt, "Bisexuality and Male Homosexuality," Clinics, 1:956 (December, 1943).

[17] R. G. Hoskins, Endocrinology: The Glands and Their Functions (New York: W. W. Norton & Company, Inc., 1941).

[18] Montague Francis Ashley-Montagu, "The Biologist Looks at Crime," in J. P. Shalloo ed., "Crime in the United States," The Annals, 217:55 (September, 1941).

[19] See Roy M. Dorcus and G. Wilson Shaffer, Textbook of Abnormal Psychology (3d ed.; Baltimore: The Williams & Wilkins Company, 1945), p. 307. Also see Kimball Young, Personality and Problems of Adjustment (New York: Appleton-Century-Crofts, Inc., 1947), p. 743.

[20] H. Cotton, The Defective, Delinquent and Insane: The Relation of Focal Infections to Their Causation, Treatment, and Prevention (Princeton, N.J.: Princeton Uni-

deformities such as large nose or acne, and other physical defects, such as clubfeet, have also been said to have an important relationship to delinquency and crime.[21] There is, however, no one-to-one relationship between physical defects and social maladjustment. There are undoubtedly criminals, for example, who are physically weak, have infected tonsils, or are cross-eyed, but there are many persons with these characteristics who are not criminals, and the incidence of these conditions may be even greater among the noncriminal population.

Some biological or physical characteristics, while not having a direct effect on social behavior, may have some indirect effect. "It has been said that if Cleopatra's nose had been a half inch longer, she would have had a different kind of influence on history. Certainly physique, including health, appearance, physical strength and coordination, skin pigmentation, growth rate, height, weight, etc., are important factors in developing the kind of attitudes that a person has about himself." [22] What is important is the individual's conception of people's attitudes toward his appearance. A physical handicap, such as crossed eyes, may cause a person *indirectly* to seek certain antisocial contacts and participate in criminal activity. The expected social roles of women are different, however, and the chance of their participation in serious crime for this reason may be limited. The fact that a male has what appear to be feminine characteristics may make his indulgence in homosexual practices more likely, even though homosexual behavior does not appear to be inherited. Finally, a person who has a dark skin or other Negroid features is forced to assume a series of subservient roles in a culture and often must live in city slums where criminal norms are more prevalent, and where there is greater temptation to adopt delinquent and criminal patterns of behavior.

INTELLIGENCE

Although the limits of intelligence are probably set at birth, the development of intelligence is greatly dependent on such variables as social experience, language, and education. Intelligence tests measure only intelligence as liberated through specific environmental forces. They do not measure innate intelligence, for such a form exists only in the abstract. Intelligence existing in any individual (which present intelligence tests attempt to measure) is a product of both environment and potentialities.

versity Press, 1921); and W. Hunter, "Chronic Sepsis as a Cause of Mental Disorder," *Journal of Mental Science,* 73:549–563 (October, 1927). Formerly case histories of deviants often included a question about whether there had been a difficult pregnancy or a traumatic birth.

[21] See, for example, Ralph S. Banay, "Physical Disfigurement as a Factor in Delinquency and Crime," *Federal Probation,* 7:20–24 (January–March, 1943).

[22] Richard Dewey and W. J. Humber, *Development of Human Behavior* (New York: The Macmillan Company, 1951), p. 87.

A succeeding chapter will present a discussion of intelligence and deviant behavior with largely negative conclusions.[23]

Social Nature of Man

Despite the fact that man is an animal, little that has a meaningful relationship to the essential qualities of human behavior can be derived from the study of lower forms of animal life. No matter how anthropomorphic we are in seeing human qualities in ants, bees, mice, dogs, and horses, there are extremely important differences that cannot be bridged. The behavior of lower forms of animal life is largely controlled by a series of innate reflexes and instincts, whereas man's behavior patterns are transmitted by culture from one generation to another. Man alone among the animals possesses language with which to convey abstract meanings. He alone has the language and intelligence needed to convey highly technical ideas, such as mathematical concepts. Man alone has a self, plays a variety of social roles, and makes moral distinctions. Lower animals are not nearly as dependent on others of their kind as is man. The limitations on the possibility that animals can approach human beings in their behavior far outweigh the few similarities. Even some comparative psychologists have pointed out the fallacy of trying to derive valid knowledge about human beings from experiments on animals. Hilgard, a well-known psychologist, has summed it up as "the price paid for overmuch experimentation with animals is to neglect the fact that human subjects are brighter, are able to use language—and probably learn differently because of these advances over lower animals. . . . Only if a process demonstrable in human learning can also be demonstrated in lower animals is the comparative method useful in studying it." [24]

LANGUAGE

Without language there can be no abstract reasoning, no social interaction, no self or conception of self; without language the human animal cannot play social roles. The possession of language is the most important distinguishing characteristic separating man from other animals. No matter how many experiments reveal subhuman or pseudohuman qualities in the learning process of rats and apes, the dividing line between the two groups is impossible to bridge without language. Language enables the human being to deal with norms and values. Scientific, moral, and religious ideas are carried and expressed through language. "The absence of morality, religion, conscience, etc., among both adult apes and human infants is

---

[23] See Chapter 5.
[24] Ernest R. Hilgard, *Theories of Learning* (New York: Appleton-Century-Crofts, Inc., 1948), p. 329.

based upon the same inability to represent to oneself in terms of a human language, one's own goals, purposes, or principles." [25] Even terms like "criminal," "drunk," "mental patient," "Negro," or "Jew" take on abstract or stereotyped meanings in common language.

A child acquires the language of his parents; he also acquires cultural meanings or evaluations which are communicated principally through language.[26] Conceptual categories are merely our general modes of viewing or relating to things, but our more specific modes of perceiving and feeling are closely aligned with the linguistic categories we have acquired. For example, the white child who learns that "dirty Negro" refers to dark-skinned persons will probably perceive or see a dark-skinned person as "dirty" whether he actually is dirty or not. In addition, the child may thus learn to have a feeling of revulsion or disgust when he sees a Negro.

The human infant, whether he turns into a criminal or a noncriminal, is born into this world the most plastic of all animals. A few reflexes, some drives, such as hunger and sex, and a potentiality for human behavior are about all he has. In turn, a human being requires a longer time to mature than any other animal. The child becomes socialized through the use of language. In communication through language with others over a long infancy, childhood, and young adulthood the human being interacts with others and both his and other personalities become modified. One social psychologist has defined *social interaction* as the "process by which an individual notices and responds to others who are noticing and responding to him." [27] This reciprocal process of interaction with other persons and through them with culture and subculture enables the child or adult to develop a unique personality, whether deviant or not.

CONCEPTION OF SELF

Man is the only animal who has a "self" in the sense that he conceives of himself as a separate being, has an understanding of who and what he is, and is even able to talk to evaluate himself in ways which are sometimes laudatory and at other times reproving. The human being is not born with a self; he acquires one through social interaction.[28] Like other, but mature, animals, a young infant cannot distinguish between himself

---

[25] Lindesmith and Strauss, *op. cit.*, p. 25.

[26] Should the student doubt this he might ask himself how often he has heard the following phrases: "She's a nice prostitute," "He's a kind murderer," or "He's a very sincere thief." Such phrases have a peculiar sound—the adjectives "kind," "nice," and so on, are incongruent with the invidious images portrayed by the nouns "prostitute," "murderer," or "thief."

[27] Newcomb, *op. cit.*, p. 21.

[28] Perhaps some persons would rush to defend a pet dog and say that he not only conceives of himself as a separate being, but when punished he has been observed to sulk. We would be the last to disturb such a pleasant fantasy, but it might be well to

and others. He and everything else in the world are part of a confusing hodgepodge with little meaning except in the immediate present. As speech develops, he realizes that he has a self separate from others. He acts out roles or parts, such as a cowboy, a fireman, an Indian chief, a policeman, his father or his mother. In this role playing it is not someone else who does the things that the child does, but he himself. This constitutes the "play stage" of personality growth where dolls, toys, and other similar objects become an indispensable part of this acting process. Later the child develops a further conception of self through playing games of various types where there must be an ability to shift roles by playing the parts of the other players. The growing child learns to internalize the roles of others and in so doing to distinguish his own role from that of others. When the internalization of these roles has been sufficiently developed to give the child a conception of a generalized "other" person to whom he can respond, he has also achieved what might be referred to as a generalized self. As George H. Mead has written: "No hard-and-fast line can be drawn between our own selves and the selves of others, since our own selves exist . . . only insofar as the selves of others exist." [29]

As the child learns that he is a separate person, that is, as he learns to think of himself as "Johnny" and not as Billy, Fred, or Daddy, he also learns that "Johnny" has certain attributes. He learns this not from himself alone, but from the reactions of others toward him, and eventually from these actions plus his interpretations of them. In effect, Johnny learns to apply to himself both the words and the attitudes of others. He may become unhappy because the words "bad boy" conjures up a thought image of something he has learned to dislike and fear, and the idea of "Johnny, you are bad" which occurs in the momentary reflection of himself as others see him arouses a feeling of fear, shame, and dislike all at once. This is what we mean when we say that the child's self-concept develops as he, by means of language, takes the attitude of others toward himself and then calls out in himself (in his symbolic response) the attitude of others. This process is instantaneous and is not at all prolonged, as our description might suggest.

The three steps involved in each phase of this process, from the standpoint of the individual, are

> *Perception:* Attending to the other's action
> *Interpretation:* Attribution of meaning to the other's action
> *Response:* Acting or feeling on the basis of the meaning attributed [30]

---

suggest the absence of two elements that make this improbable, namely, that a dog has no way to refer himself to himself and, second, he possesses no words with which to talk to himself about the errors of his ways.

[29] George H. Mead, *Mind, Self, and Society* (Chicago: The University of Chicago Press, 1934), p. 164.

[30] *Ibid.*, Chaps. 1 and 2. Actually, the three steps above characterize all social behavior, in the sense that all action (or response) which is social is preceded by perception and interpretation (or definition).

The normal person is able to call out the same responses in himself that he calls out in others. An organized and integrated self permits him to put himself in the place of another, while still maintaining his own identity. This growth of self-realization can be illustrated by the development of children's moral ideas. In a study of lower-class children in Switzerland, Piaget showed that a child's ideas of fair play move from self-centered judgments to seeing them through the eyes of others.[31] Until about the age of five a child has an absolute idea of right and wrong, and from then until about the age of ten the child comes to realize that moral ideas are not real in themselves but are related to numerous group ideas. Finally, the child learns that the group can make exceptions to rules and that new ones can be made by the group. In this way the child learns to acquire abstract, generalized ideals. He is not born with "natural" moral judgments; instead, children in the early grades have "abstract conceptions of justice and 'fairness' [which] are not yet very clear." [32]

The self-concept is not static, but is subject to change and modification throughout a person's life. It changes as the others with whom one identifies change, or as the expectations of these others alter. The concept of self which one has as a child will be decidedly different from one's concept of self as an aged person.[33]

> In recent years more and more students of human behavior have come to recognize the importance of personal identity, for what a man does or does not do depends in large measure upon his conception of himself. Each individual is tied to a pattern of communal life by the manner in which he is identified. By virtue of being who he is, he assumes status in a group. He can locate himself and is recognized by others, and his relationship to each of the others is thereby defined. Far from being creatures of impulse, men generally inhibit their organic dispositions in order to live up to the standards of conduct that they set for themselves. They are constantly responding to what they believe themselves to be. . . . Many of the distinctive features of human behavior arise from the fact that men orient themselves within a symbolic environment and strive to come to terms with what they believe themselves to be. Men give their lives willingly for a variety of worthy causes; they deny themselves many joys in order to build gigantic political or industrial empires; they build up social barriers to protect their progeny against miscegenation; they plot vengeance for a wrong suffered long ago by their ancestors; they create monuments in their own honor; they push their children to "make a name" for themselves; lovers commit suicide when they are denied the right to marry; artists paint happily for "posterity," serenely indifferent to the fact that their contemporaries regard them as mad. Al-

---

[31] Piaget, *Moral Judgment of the Child* (London: Routledge and Kegan Paul Ltd., 1932).
[32] Gardner and Lois Murphy and Theodore Newcomb, *Experimental Social Psychology* (New York: Harper & Row, Publishers, 1937), p. 650.
[33] See, for example, Zena S. Blau, "Changes in Status and Age Identification," *American Sociological Review*, 21:198–203 (1956).

though men take these activities for granted as a part of human life, no other animal is known to engage in such conduct. It is unlikely that any creature without self-conceptions would do any of these things. Human behavior consists of a succession of adjustments to life conditions, but each man must come to terms with himself as well as with other features of his world. To understand what men do we must know something about what each person means to himself.[34]

The self-conception, therefore, is an important aspect of the person, and whether one is dealing with deviant or nondeviant behavior it is necessary to recognize this. It is the image in our minds of the "self" (ourselves) that we try to enhance and defend whether we are a judge or a criminal. When this self-image gets out of line with the conception which others have of a person, the result may even be the "great inventor" or similar figures found in mental hospitals. As a person's conception of himself changes, so may a large part of his personality, as is indicated in what is termed the "successful treatment" of mental patients, alcoholics, and delinquents. What, in part, happens is that the deviant comes to view himself differently, placing new expectations on his conduct, as well as new demands.

Social Roles

Up to now the discussion has been about the fact that all social behavior is human behavior and that people have language and a conception of self that other animals do not have. This leads us to a further discussion of why people act the way they do. Social behavior has to be acquired. It is not there at birth but develops through experiences. Behavior becomes modified in response to the demands and expectations of others. Personality, or a person's general *pattern* of behavior, is produced by social interaction in the sense that practically all behavior is only in relation to other people. Terms like "honesty," "friendliness," "shyness" have meaning only in relation to other people. Even expressions of emotionality, such as anger or depression, although they have physiological concomitants, are mostly the expressions of social reactions. They can be expressed, controlled, or accentuated according to a variety of social and cultural definitions.

The process described in the development of the self is also descriptive of the process involved in the development of other social behavior. Social behavior develops not only as we respond in relation to other people, but also as we anticipate the responses of other people to us and incorporate them into our conduct. When two people converse, both are more or less aware of the fact that each is evaluating the other's behavior. In

---

[34] Shibutani, *op. cit.*, pp. 247–248.

this process each person evaluates his own behavior as well as the behavior of other persons. The person's behavior, based on his estimate of how he should act, is called *role playing,* and his idea of the other person's behavior is called *role taking.* A *social role* more specifically involves four parts: (1) the person's identification or conception of himself; (2) the appropriate behavior he displays according to his conception of the situation; (3) the roles which are acted out by other persons in response to his role; and (4) the evaluation by the individual of these roles.[35] The activities of a human being in the course of a day can be regarded as the performance of a series of roles which he has learned and which others expect him to fulfill. The most important part of this process is role taking. Through role taking, or assuming the attitudes of others toward ourselves, we not only gain an idea of what kinds of persons we are, but also of what other persons expect of us. When we direct our actions according to these expectations we are, in effect, engaging in *self-control. Social control,* on the other hand, becomes possible through the fact that persons acquire the ability to behave in a manner consistent with the expectations of others.[36]

Like the actor who plays many stage parts, even though they are exaggerated, all persons fill numerous roles. A person's social roles are linked with his position in society. There are age roles, sex roles, social class roles, occupation roles, and family roles. Such roles are, for example, those of an old or a young person, a man or a woman, a husband or a wife, a parent or a child, a doctor, a lawyer, or a salesman. The student and the professor play a series of roles in the lecture room, in the office discussing a subject or bargaining for a grade, and often in their greeting and demeanor toward one another on the campus. Negroes, in their relations with whites, often act out roles, and the problems arising from these interacting roles are an important aspect of what are called race relations. For example, in the South, there is often a "continued flow of agreement by the Negro while a white man is talking, such as 'Yes, boss,' 'Sho nuff,' 'Well, I declare' and the like." [37]

It is through the expectations of others that persons are assigned roles and statuses and are expected to engage in the behavior prescribed for these roles and statuses. The status and role (or roles) which a person is assigned cannot be easily changed by his own desires: whether a person plays the role which society has assigned to him or not, his behavior is still interpreted by society as consistent with this role and its corresponding status. For example, the behavior of the ex-inmate of a prison in his home

---

[35] Lindesmith and Strauss, *op. cit.,* p. 166.

[36] Shibutani, *op. cit.,* pp. 118–121, 197. Self-control is, in essence, social control, for persons see themselves from the standpoint of the group and thus they try to maintain self-respect through achieving social respect by meeting the group's expectations. Also see S. F. Nadel, "Social Control and Self-Regulation," *Social Forces,* 31:265–273 (1953).

[37] John Dollard, *Caste and Class in a Southern Town* (New Haven, Conn.: Yale University Press, 1937), p. 180.

community may be interpreted in a manner consistent with real or imagined criminal "tendencies," even if he is making a determined effort to "go straight." The power of community interpretations in perpetuating a person's occupancy of a criminal status and role may have several consequences. Sometimes such persons will "give in" to the societal definition and actively play the role which has been expected of them. In other cases, such persons may move to different communities where presumably their past experiences are unknown, and where their noncriminal behavior may provide the basis for assignment of a conventional and "respectable" status and role.[38]

On the basis of social roles, deviants can be distinguished as to whether they represent primary or secondary deviation.[39] Persons may engage in deviant behavior but continue to occupy a conventional status and role. Such deviant behavior constitutes *primary deviation* when it is rationalized and considered as a function of a socially acceptable role. On the other hand, deviant actions may be reacted to by arrest, imprisonment, or other sanctions; the deviant then becomes officially labeled as such and may even be socially isolated as a deviant. Consequently the deviant has less opportunity to play conventional roles and comes to incorporate a societal image of himself as a deviant. When this occurs there is *secondary deviation.* "When a person begins to employ his deviant behavior or a role based upon it as a means of defense, attack, or adjustment to the overt and covert problems created by the consequent societal reaction to him, his deviation is secondary." [40]

Thus persons may commit delinquencies and crimes without becoming secondary deviants and without being regarded as "delinquents" and "criminals." Women may engage in sex acts under conditions similar to that of the "prostitute" but do not consider themselves as one. There are persons who engage in homosexual acts but are not "homosexuals" in the sense of secondary deviation. A person may be a heavy drinker and not be designated a "drunk." But once the label of "deviant" has been given a person it may have important consequences for further deviant behavior.

Human behavior fundamentally represents a series of social roles which may be deviant or nondeviant. Professional thieves, for example, play a variety of roles. Punctuality in keeping appointments with partners and the code of not "squealing" on another thief are of particular importance in their profession. Social status or position among thieves is based on their technical skill, connections, financial standing, influence, dress, manners, and wide knowledge. Their status is also reflected in the attitudes which ordinary criminals have toward them as well as the attitudes of lawyers, the police, court officials, and newspaper reporters. The profes-

---

[38] See Shibutani, *op. cit.*, and Lemert, *op. cit.*
[40] *Ibid.*, p. 76.

[39] Lemert, *op. cit.*, pp. 75-76.

sional criminal may likewise play different roles toward victim, friend, wife, children, father, mother, grocer, or minister.

Most of the "script" for these deviant roles, as for nondeviant ones, is derived from group experience and cultural or subcultural situations. On occasions, however, where appropriate roles are not provided they may be unique to the individual's own life experience. The diversity of social roles in modern urban society, as will be indicated later, is an important factor in the extent of social deviation of modern society. Because of this diversity and lack of coordination of social roles, the actual behavioral responses of persons to certain situations fail to conform to what would ordinarily be expected. A person's own evaluation of his role is often not the same as that of others.

THE DEFINITION OF THE SITUATION

A *definition of a situation* is merely an anticipation of action in a given situation.[41] In defining a situation one assumes the standpoint of real or imagined others and imaginatively rehearses the action expected by these others of oneself. Role taking, or assuming the attitude of others, is the elementary process involved in defining a situation.

> In the drama of life, as in the theater, everyone performs for some kind of audience. In a small community the observers are easy enough to find; but in our complex, pluralistic society the people in whose eyes a person seeks to preserve and enhance his status are not so apparent. Much depends upon the communication channels in which he regularly participates. . . . The comprehension of what a man does requires a record of (1) his definition of the situation, (2) the kind of creature he believes himself to be, and (3) the audience before which he tries to maintain his self-respect.[42]

The definition of the situation is essentially a means by which an individual organizes his behavior. In order imaginatively to rehearse his own action, he takes into account the anticipated responses of others and organizes them into his own behavior.[43] In defining situations with which we are unfamiliar, we often look for "cues" which allow us to assess the present circumstances in terms of contexts with which we are more familiar. For example, in meeting a stranger, as on a train, we usually inquire as to his destination, where he is from, and what he does for a living. With such questions, we are actually trying to determine the stranger's social status. We do this because if we know what his status is, we can anticipate much of his behavior, and much about his life circumstances as well. If the stranger is an unemployed, poorly dressed man of middle age, we make

---

[41] William I. Thomas and Florian Znaniecki, *The Polish Peasant in Europe and America* (New York: Alfred A. Knopf, Inc., 1927), II, 1846–1849.
[42] Shibutani, *op. cit.*, p. 279.   [43] *Ibid.*, pp. 118–119.

certain assumptions about him, and base our own responses to him on these assumptions. We may define him as "not in our class," and thus treat him in a way such as to keep interaction at a minimum. Or we might make an entirely different definition.[44]

The particular definition a given individual makes will be influenced by all that he has known and experienced until that time. The latter would include the set of attitudes, norms, and values which the person has acquired or known, the particular set of statuses and roles he has occupied, or is familiar with, and the particular cumulation of experiences and situations he has known of or participated in. For example, if a teen-ager perceives a set of keys left in a car he may interpret the situation as an opportunity to steal it; another may pay no attention to the same situation. A difficult situation may be perceived one way by a person contemplating suicide, and a completely different way by someone else.

ATTITUDES

Certain definitions of situations are relatively conventional or stabilized. These will be referred to as *attitudes*.[45] Every individual has literally thousands of such attitudes which provide the basis for his actions in many situations. On the basis of acquired attitudes a flavored solution of a chemical called alcohol may be regarded as a delectable beverage by a habitual drinker, whereas that same chemical may not only taste highly disagreeable to a teetotaler but be regarded as poisonous and sinful to drink. A Negro may be thought of as quite similar in his personality to most white men or he may be thought of as shiftless, immoral, oversexed, and naturally superstitious, thus causing behavior with reference to the Negro to vary correspondingly. Objects or social norms in our culture are defined by a person's experiences, as the following case illustrates.

A novel example is furnished by Fung Kwok Keung, born Joseph Rinehart of American parents living in Long Island, New York. At the age of three, his parents deserted him, and he was adopted by Chinese, taken to China and reared there for nineteen years. Recently he returned to the United States. He is Chinese in manner, speech, habit, outlook—in all ways but appearance.[46]

---

[44] See Erving Goffman, *The Presentation of Self in Everyday Life* (New York: Doubleday Anchor Books, 1959), Chap. 1.

[45] "Attitudes denote these [states of readiness] which are learned [formed] in relation to definite stimuli [objects, persons, situations, values, or norms] and which are more or less lasting."—Muzafer Sherif, *An Outline of Social Psychology* (New York: Harper & Row, Publishers, 1948), p. 207.

[46] Quoted in William F. Ogburn and Meyer F. Nimkoff, *Sociology* (Boston: Houghton Mifflin Company, 1946), p. 8. As the groups to which a person belongs differ, then so do his attitudes.

Most attitudes are developed through group associations rather than as a result of individual experience. Inasmuch as people are all, in one way or another, members of groups, attitudes generally represent shared meanings. Hence most attitudes are derived from cultural norms. Groups, then, to which the individual may belong serve as a frame of reference and undoubtedly influence his attitudes. A group in terms of whose norms a person orients his behavior is a *reference group*. Such groups are not necessarily the same as *membership groups* to which a person is recognized as belonging.[47] A delinquent gang may be the reference group of a delinquent rather than such membership groups as family, church, and similar groups.

Although cultural experiences are often superficially similar, they are not the same in detail, nor are they experienced in the same way by two individuals. As mentioned above, attitudes are derived from social experiences, and thus may differ according to such variables as the country or part of the country in which we live, the part of the city or town in which we have been raised, the social class and occupation to which we belong, and the amount of our education. These differences in attitudes have been reflected in numerous surveys of public opinion. People have been shown to differ a great deal in their attitudes toward things simply on the basis of their religious training. The attitudes of a slum neighborhood toward crime, delinquency, the police, gambling, premarital sex relations, and prostitution are often much different from those held in middle-class residential areas. To the average white man in Iowa a Negro is not quite the same person that he is to the average white man in Mississippi.

Of fundamental importance in the development of attitudes are those groups which are described as "primary." Primary groups include the family, the neighborhood, and various friendship groups such as high school cliques and boys' gangs—all groups from which basic attitudes are acquired, particularly those attitudes involving social values. These *primary groups* are extremely important because social interaction tends to be intimate and "face to face," which makes a greater impression on the person than the less intimate type of group. These primary groups affect the individual early in life, presenting the child with the first ways of acting, and with the only possible "right" conception of a situation. Early attitudes become important whether they are about foods, manners, and religion or about Negroes, Jews, and honesty. These attitudes are called primary not only because they develop first but because they have attached to them strong personal ties which are more difficult to modify later in life. Among deviants, for example, the corner gang may supply the child with a view of the world in general, including conceptions of such broad

---

[47] Newcomb, *op. cit.*, p. 225.

categories as the police and schoolteachers, or stealing and truancy in particular. Likewise, another boy may secure many different definitions of behavior from his family, the YMCA, and his Cub Scout den.

As distinguished from "primary group attitudes," there is another source, called *secondary groups*. These are somewhat later associations based on common interests, abilities, roles, and status position and include occupational groups, labor union or professional groups, church, tavern, club, or lodge. Members of these groups are not emotionally tied together, and the members might not even know each other well. The norms which are present usually refer to a specific area of life and may not be those of all the members. It is in this sense that it is often possible to speak of a person as belonging to such a secondary group without really becoming a part of it. Although a person undoubtedly acquires many attitudes from secondary groups, they are not likely to be the first presented to him on such important questions of behavior as racial or sexual attitudes. Oftentimes primary groups, such as the family, tend to channel persons, particularly when young, into secondary groups with similar norms, and in such circumstances what may appear to be a continuous hold of the family on the individual turns out to be a partial illusion.

Although people secure most of their attitudes from the general culture and from subcultural situations that differ according to region, neighborhood, class, occupation, religion, and education, some attitudes are the result of unique personal experiences. An example is the favorable change in attitudes toward Negroes that sometimes occurs among soldiers under battle conditions. This method of acquiring attitudes through unique experiences is not common, but probably everyone has had such experiences. Most attitudes involving disrespect for law are acquired through group experiences but some persons who have had particularly brutal experiences in a correctional institution or in a so-called reformatory may have attitudes of disrespect turn into hatred for law and law officers, as happened to John Dillinger.

A differential process of acquiring attitudes has been suggested by Sutherland, particularly in connection with his fourfold theory of criminal behavior.[48] The theory can be applied in general, however, to the acquisition of many other forms of deviant behavior involving cultural norms. He has suggested that variables such as the following would account both for the difference in the development and for the continuance of delinquent and criminal deviant attitudes: (1) How early in life did the association with a certain deviant norm begin? (2) How many and how extensive were the facets of the person's life associated with the deviant behavior? Did the definition of a social situation include only one social role or all the per-

---

[48] Sutherland and Cressey, *op. cit.*, Chap. 4.

son's activities? (3) How continuous was the contact with the deviations? Did the association continue over a period of years, or was it limited to only a brief period? (4) How important was the association with the person who furnished a deviant model? In this connection, how much did the person identify himself with the deviant model, whether it was a companion, a member of the family, a play group, or other models? [49]

Research on attitudes has brought out the fact that, while they may be relatively stabilized definitions of situations, they can and do change. Among the more important variables which change attitudes appear to be such factors as the following: first, the strength of a particular attitude in the presence of external influences; second, increased familiarity due to firsthand experience; and third, the prestige of the model presenting a given attitude. These three ideas can be illustrated by the resistance to the influence of crime stories on the part of a middle-class boy who has attended a high school where there is little deviant behavior, who has been an active Boy Scout, and who has conceived of himself as a "model boy." Suppose that a boy who has long been a delinquent moves into his neighborhood. Under the personal influence of this boy the first youngster may tend to alter his attitudes. If the new boy is someone with considerable prestige and one whom he admires, there is an increased possibility that he himself may engage in delinquent behavior. If the prestige model in this example were reversed the delinquent boy might well become nondelinquent.

In summary, then, the definition of a situation which a person makes is, in part, dependent upon his past experiences and learning. It is also dependent on the responses of others in the immediate situation, for it is these responses which the individual takes into account in defining the situation and organizes into his own behavior. Consequently, no two individuals, not even identical twins, could be expected to perceive and define all situations in precisely the same way. The assumption that, if persons have been reared in the same home and have had the same general experiences, their definitions should be uniform in all situations is naïve. Of course, however, greater similarity would be expected among such persons than among those having had dissimilar general experiences.

Some tend to attribute socialization primarily to early childhood, and particularly to experiences in the family. It is argued that, since the first experiences of the child with others are within the family group, trait structures arising there form the basis for the entire structure of personality. The evidence about this stability or the all-important emphasis on the family is not conclusive. Much of the research on personality to date

---

[49] For an application of these ideas as applied to delinquent and criminal behavior, see pp. 184–186.

has been concerned primarily with the family and has not taken sufficiently into account the play group and other influences which the child encounters in early life, particularly in street play in urban areas and in preschool and kindergarten activities.[50]

Even so-called *motives* are acquired as the result of social experience. They are socially molded, usually in accord with the prevailing norms of particular groups to which the individual belongs. For example, the possession of an automobile and the status it would give might be so important a goal to a delinquent boy that he would steal one. If his goals were directed toward a status based on higher grades in school or on some conventional hobby the end results would be different. Reference groups to which an individual belongs or from which he wishes to gain acceptance have an important bearing on the attitudes of a person. If the group is important to him he will often do everything demanded of him to secure or maintain acceptance. If a delinquent gang is important to him, a boy will do all he can to conform to the gang, whereas a boy in a Scout troop may have entirely different demands placed upon him. The negative attitudes of a group of teetotalers toward liquor may be as strong as the positive attitudes of a group of regular tavern patrons. Thus people tend to respond to the attitudes of the group to which they belong.

Persons appear to vary in their emphasis on given motives, depending on cultural and subcultural norms, the definition of the situation, and the life organization of the individual. In the process of reaching goals, deviants and nondeviants may adopt what might appear to be different patterns of behavior, but in reality they may be achieving similar goals in their own way. Some boys may have fun playing baseball or indulging in other sports, whereas others may find even more fun in stealing automobiles, slashing tires, wrecking a school, or beating up a stranger. Some may find companionship in a delinquent gang rather than in a Boy Scout troop; some people may prefer the fellowship of drinking companions in a tavern to the fellowship offered by a church. A young "punk" in a city slum may seek to gain a status of a far different kind from that sought by a college student. Some men would probably prefer to have the prestige and acclaim accorded them in an organized criminal syndicate or in professional crime than be president of a university. Businessmen and politicians have engaged in illegal behavior in order to secure funds with which to buy material goods which, in turn, bring them greater recognition in society.

---

[50] Likewise, research has not stressed experiences in later life as factors in personality orientation. Most studies of personality traits have been based on evidence derived from memories in which childhood experiences, particularly in the family, are likely to be recalled without their necessarily having much bearing on why a person acts as he does later in life.

LIFE ORGANIZATION

Social roles weld themselves into a continuous pattern of behavior, referred to as *life organization*. Thus it is possible to speak of the life organization of a college professor, an alcoholic, a suicide, a professional criminal, or any person, whether he is deviant or nondeviant. This life organization is unique to each individual, although much may be derived from the general culture, subculture, and unique experiences. The life organization of some persons results in a well-integrated personality, whereas in that of others there may be conflicting elements. The life organization of some types of deviants is often well integrated, as is true of organized and professional criminals. Conflicts within the life organization, on the other hand, play an important part in the development of mental illness, alcoholism, or suicide. Such difficulties in life organization may develop when there are marked discrepancies between the person's appraisal of various situations and the interpretation by other persons of his behavior. This conflict may be seen in an individual who becomes mentally ill when faced with a variety of conflicting roles involving his parents, wife, wife's family, employer, and his own friends. Conflicts between role expectations and evaluation are also important in marital maladjustment.

Summary

The same fundamental processes are involved in deviant and nondeviant behavior. Differences in subprocesses exist; if they did not, there would be no way to account for deviant behavior. The biological structure of man is of little importance in accounting for deviant or nondeviant behavior. He does not have instincts which could account for such behavior. Deviant behavior cannot be inherited, and there is no evidence that glandular malfunctioning is involved in the great majority of cases. Physical defects do not distinguish the deviant from the nondeviant. Physical characteristics are not directly important, although they may have an indirect influence in some cases of deviant behavior.

It is the social rather than the physical nature of man which is important in studying deviant and nondeviant behavior. This includes attitudes, social roles, and life organization. The fact that man has language and a conception of self makes him different from other animals. Attitudes are important components of personality or behavior and are acquired primarily through relations with others. Attitudes are secured from primary and secondary groups and from unique experiences.

All persons play a variety of social roles which involve the way a person conceives of himself, the behavior he displays according to this conception, the roles acted out by others in response to his behavior, and his evaluation of his role. Deviants as well as nondeviants play social roles, and this fact must be understood in analyzing such behavior. The organization of social roles is called a person's life organization. A well-integrated life organization may characterize some deviants, whereas others may be the product of conflicting roles. Persons tend to define a given social situation in terms of past experiences.

Selected Readings

CAMERON, NORMAN. *The Psychology of Behavior Disorders.* Boston: Houghton Mifflin Company, 1947. An analysis of mental disorder primarily in terms of difficulties in role playing and self-conception.

CLINARD, MARSHALL B. "Criminal Behavior Is Human Behavior," *Federal Probation,* 13:21–26 (March, 1949). A discussion of the importance of considering criminal and noncriminal behavior within the same frame of reference and with the same concepts.

CRESSEY, DONALD R. *Other People's Money.* New York: The Free Press of Glencoe, 1953. This study is a sociopsychological analysis of embezzlement emphasizing particularly self-conception.

GOFFMAN, ERVING. *The Presentation of Self in Everyday Life.* New York: Doubleday Anchor Books, 1959. A discussion of the self and its importance in social interaction with others.

LEMERT, EDWIN H. *Social Pathology.* New York: McGraw-Hill Book Company, Inc., 1951, Chap. 4, "Sociopathic Individuation." This is an excellent application of the concept of social role to the study of deviant behavior.

LINDESMITH, ALFRED R. *Opiate Addiction.* Bloomington: University of Indiana Press, 1947. A sociopsychological interpretation of opiate addiction using many of the concepts presented here.

LINDESMITH, ALFRED R. and ANSELM L. STRAUSS. *Social Psychology.* Rev. ed. New York: Holt, Rinehart and Winston, Inc., 1955. Discusses human nature, language, the self, and social roles. Chapter 13, "Deviant Behavior," is a sociopsychological discussion of a number of areas.

SHIBUTANI, TOMATSU. *Society and Personality.* Englewood Cliffs, N.J.: Prentice-Hall, Inc., 1961. Discusses the fundamental processes and concepts involved in socialization. An unusually clear and interesting discussion of social behavior.

Chapter

3

Urbanization, Urbanism,
and Deviant Behavior

City living has characterized some areas for centuries, but has spread with such acceleration over the past century as to encompass hundreds of millions of people throughout the entire world. This process of urban life has produced what some have called the "Mass Society." Urban life has greatly increased social differentiation, the clash of norms and social roles, and the breakdown in interpersonal relations among persons. Modern urban life has presented opportunities for the development of such a "way of life" on a tremendous scale.[1]

The Growth of World Urbanization

Cities first appeared in the Near East, in Mesopotamia, in the region between the Tigris and Euphrates rivers, about 3500 B.C.[2] A few centuries later they also appeared in the Nile Valley of Egypt and the valley of the Indus River, in what is now West Pakistan. The emergence of the earliest cities, according to Sjoberg, required (1) that the surrounding region have a climate and soil sufficiently favorable to support a large population, (2) relatively speaking, an advanced technology in both agricultural and non-agricultural spheres, and (3) a complex social organization, particularly in political and economic spheres.[3]

Thus cities have existed for thousands of years. Some cities, such as those of the Orient, were of considerable size. In general, however, only a small proportion of the people lived in them, as compared with urban populations today, and few cities had over 100,000 persons. Athens, at its

---

[1] Rose Hum Lee, *The City: Urbanism and Urbanization in Major World Regions* (Philadelphia: J. B. Lippincott Company, 1955). Also see special issue, "World Urbanism," *American Journal of Sociology*, Vol. 60 (March, 1955), and Nels Anderson, *The Urban Community* (New York: Holt, Rinehart and Winston, Inc., 1959).

[2] Gideon Sjoberg, *The Preindustrial City: Past and Present* (New York: The Free Press of Glencoe, 1960), pp. 25–51. Also see Kingsley Davis, "The Origin and Growth of Urbanization in the World," *American Journal of Sociology*, 40:429–437 (March, 1955).

[3] Sjoberg, *op. cit.*, p. 27.

peak in the fifth century B.C., was estimated to have had between 120,000 and 180,000 persons; Rome had several hundred thousand; Florence in 1338, 90,000; and London in 1377, 30,000.[4]

Life in the large cities of several hundred years ago, both in Europe and in the Orient, was quite different from life in the same cities today. There were no forms of rapid or extensive communication and transportation, nor were there the means of distribution and preservation of food which modern inventions have made possible. Consequently, cities, even though large, tended to be actually clusters of villages. Urban populations were much more permanent and settled than they are today, there was less migration into the cities from rural areas, and because of this and because of the absence of media of mass communication as we have them today, people were able to know one another much better than they do now.

In 1800 only about 3 percent of the world's estimated population of 906 million lived in places of more than 5000 persons. By 1950 this percentage had increased to about 30 percent. Whereas the world population had increased by nearly 165 percent during these one hundred and fifty years, the urban population of the world had risen by 2535 percent to what has been termed not merely a population explosion but a world "urban explosion." In 1800 the proportion of the world's population living in cities of 20,000 or more was 2.4; in 1950 it was 20.9 percent.[5] Cities of 100,000 or more were 1.7 percent of the total world population in 1800; in 1950 they were 13.1. In 1800 there were fewer than 50 cities in the entire world with 100,000 or more inhabitants and none with a million persons, a figure which is smaller than the number of cities in the million class today.

The increase in the proportion of urban population in the underdeveloped areas of the world, such as those in South America, Africa, and Asia, has been particularly great. In India, for example, which is thought of as a rural nation, 8.2 percent of the population in 1941 lived in cities of 20,000 or more, whereas in 1961, 17.8 percent lived in cities of that size. This amounts to over 75,000,000 urban persons in India in 1961, or a number larger than the population of most countries of the world. Only 2 Indian cities had over a million population in 1941; by 1961 there were 6, and Davis estimates that by 1970 there will be 10.[6] In 1951 there were 77 cities with 100,000 or more persons; in 1961 there were 121.

Australia leads the world in the proportion of its population living in cities of 100,000 or more. (See Table 3.1.) The United Kingdom with 51.0, Japan with 41.2, and Argentina with 39.5 percent follow in that

---

[4] Davis, "Origin and Growth of Urbanization," *loc. cit.*   [5] *Ibid.*
[6] Kingsley Davis, "Urbanization in India: Past and Future," in Roy Turner ed., *India's Urban Future* (Berkeley: University of California Press, 1962), p. 25.

order. The United States has 28.4 percent of its population living in cities of this size.

Table 3.1. Estimated Proportion of Population Living in Cities
of 100,000 or More

Country	Percent
Australia (1959)	57.4
United Kingdom (1958)	51.0
Japan (1959)	41.2
Argentina (1958)	39.5
Israel (1959)	34.3
Denmark (1958)	34.2
West Germany (1959)	30.7
United States (1960)	28.4
Union of South Africa (1960)	25.4
Sweden (1959)	24.7
Italy (1959)	23.9
USSR (1959)	23.5
United Arab Republic (1958)	22.2
Brazil (1959)	17.6
France (1954)	16.8
Indonesia (1959)	9.4
Ghana (1960)	7.3
India (1951)	6.6
Congo (1959)	5.9
Burma (1958)	5.3

SOURCE: Prepared from *United Nations Demographic Yearbook, 1960* (New York: 1960).

The number of large cities in the major regions of the world is shown in Table 3.2. In 1950, there were over nine hundred cities of 100,000 or more persons and over forty-nine cities with more than a million inhabitants. Twenty percent of the world's population lived in cities of 20,000 or more, and 13 percent in cities of 100,000 or over. Asia has the largest number of cities with a population of 1 million and over. According to 1960 estimates, Tokyo is the largest city in the world, with nearly 10 million persons, or one in ten persons in Japan.

Behind this growth of modern urbanization, particularly in the Western European world, have been many forces which can only be listed here: the breakdown of the feudal system with its loss of prescribed duties and obligations and integrated way of village life; the Commercial and later the Industrial Revolution, which produced a wide dispersion of the population, particularly to cities; the development of the factory system of production, and extensive occupational differences; the development of science, which brought a secular way of life by destroying many age-old traditions of thought, also produced new forms of transportation as well as improvements in agriculture so that millions of people were freed from immediate dependence on the land, and enabled to work and live in cities. The virtual disappearance of the large family and with it the loss of many family functions and responsibilities further weakened the ties of family members to the land. All these forces produced drastic changes in the interpersonal relations of those who moved to cities.

Table 3.2. Cities over 100,000 Population in Major Regions of the World, 1950

Area	1,000,000 and over	500,000 to 1,000,000	250,000 to 500,000	100,000 to 250,000	Total cities over 100,000
Africa	1	3	6	27	37
Asia (excludes USSR) (includes Near East)	20	22	43	178	263
Europe	14	28	46	187	364
USSR (1939 figures)	2	9	20	58	89
North America	7	15	27	91	140
Oceania	2		3	5	10
South America	3	4	11	26	44
Total	49	81	156	572	947

SOURCE: Rose Hum Lee, *The City: Urbanism and Urbanization in Major World Regions* (Philadelphia: J. B. Lippincott Company, 1955), p. 55. Data secured by Lee from *United Nations Demographic Yearbook, 1952*, Table 8, pp. 202–214.

Also essential for this growth of modern cities are more specific conditions. The level of agricultural production must be sufficiently high to provide a surplus which will allow people to concentrate in areas for non-agricultural production. Sources of power, such as coal, electricity, or oil, are also necessary to provide large concentrations of persons with the means of industrial production. Electricity, for example, has become essential not only in such production but as part of mass communication through the telephone, radio, and television.

Urbanization in the United States

The United States, following the Civil War, changed from a society of rural communities to one of the most urbanized in the world. So rapid and extensive has been this urbanization that it is now possible to refer to America as an "urban society." As Table 3.4 shows, in 1790 only 5.1 percent of the population lived in cities. By 1880 this proportion had increased to 28.2 and in 1920 approximately half the people were urban. Using a slightly different definition, in 1950 the urban population of the United States was 64 percent of the total, and in 1960, 69.9. In 1960 this amounted to 125,268,750 persons. In nine states the percentage of urban population exceeds 75: in order they are New Jersey, Rhode Island, New York, Massachusetts, Illinois, Connecticut, Hawaii, and Texas.

Perhaps even more drastic has been the increase in the United States in the number of places with 2500 population or over—from 236 in 1850 to 2262 in 1910. By 1940 this figure had increased to 3464, and by 1950 to 4284, although the latter figure represented, in part, a change in the definition of an urban place. The number of cities, however, gives no idea of the increasing concentration of population in and around a small number of places. The 132 cities of 100,000 persons and over contained more than one fourth (28.4 percent) of the total population of the United States in 1960. One out of ten Americans lives in a city of one millon or more. A measure of urbanization, namely "urbanized areas," which includes cities with a population of 50,000 or more and those persons residing in certain contiguous areas which are not part of the city, is now used. The fourteen largest urbanized areas in the United States in 1960 are shown in Table 3.3.

Table 3.3. The Fourteen Largest Urbanized Areas in the United States

Area	Population in millions
New York—northeastern New Jersey	14.1
Los Angeles—Long Beach area	6.5
Chicago—northwestern Indiana	6.0
Philadelphia—New Jersey area	3.6
Detroit	3.5
San Francisco—Oakland area	2.4
Boston	2.4
Washington–Md.–Va.	1.8
Pittsburgh	1.8
Cleveland	1.8
St. Louis, Mo.–Ill.	1.7
Baltimore	1.4
Minneapolis—St. Paul	1.4
Milwaukee	1.1

SOURCE: *United States Census of Population, 1960. Summary of Number of Inhabitants* (Washington, D.C.: Bureau of the Census, 1961), pp. 1–50.

Slightly more than one half of the total, and more than three fourths of the urban, population of the United States in 1960 was living in 213 urbanized areas. Of the 95.8 million persons living in urbanized areas, 58.0 million lived in the 254 central cities and 37.8 million lived in the urban-fringe area outside the city. The 16 urbanized areas with more than 1 million inhabitants had a combined population of 51.7 million, or more than half of the 213 urbanized areas.

*Table 3.4. Growth of the Urban Population in the United States,
1790–1960*

Year	Percent urban	Percent rural
1790	5.1	94.9
1800	6.1	93.9
1810	7.3	92.7
1820	7.2	92.8
1830	8.8	91.2
1840	10.8	89.2
1850	15.3	84.7
1860	19.8	80.2
1870	25.7	74.3
1880	28.2	71.8
1890	35.1	64.9
1900	39.7	60.3
1910	45.7	54.3
1920	51.2	48.8
1930	56.2	43.8
1940	56.5	43.5
1950	64.0	36.0
1960	69.9	30.1

SOURCE: *United States Census of Population, 1960. Summary of Number of Inhabitants* (Washington: Bureau of the Census, 1961), pp. 1–4. The definition of "urban" changed in 1950, so that the comparable figure for that year was 59.6, and in 1960, 63.1.

Urbanism as a Way of Life

The growth of modern cities has meant the development of a way of life much different from that of the rural world. Urbanism as a way of life is often characterized by extensive conflicts of norms and values, by rapid social change, by increased mobility of the population, by emphasis on material goods and individualism, and by a marked decline in intimate communication.[7] The relation of these factors to the size, density, and heterogeneity of an urban area can be seen in the schematic presentation in Table 3.5.

[7] See Louis Wirth, "Urbanism as a Way of Life," *American Journal of Sociology,* 44:1–24 (July, 1938). Wirth's statement was based in part on Georg Simmel, "The Metropolis and Mental Life," in Paul K. Hatt and Albert J. Reiss, Jr. eds., *Reader in Urban Sociology* (New York: The Free Press of Glencoe, 1951), pp. 563–574; Robert E. Park, *The City* (Chicago: The University of Chicago Press, 1925); Anderson, *op. cit.;* and Kingsley Davis, H. C. Bredemeier, and Marion J. Levy, Jr. eds., *Modern American Society* (New York: Holt, Rinehart and Winston, Inc., 1949). Other terms, such as "mass society" or "secular," have been used which in general reflect the same process. For a discussion of secular societies, see Howard Becker, *Man in Reciprocity* (New York: Frederick A. Praeger, Inc., 1956), pp. 169–197.

Table 3.5 Schematic Version of Urbanism as a Way of Life

	Greater the number of people interacting, greater the potential differentiation (mobility).
	Dependence upon a greater number of people, lesser dependence on particular persons.
Size An increase in the number of inhabitants of a settlement beyond a certain limit brings about changes in the relations of people and changes in the character of the community	Association with more people, knowledge of a smaller proportion, and of these, less intimate knowledge.
	More secondary rather than primary contacts—increase in contacts which are face to face, yet impersonal, superficial, transitory, and segmental.
	More freedom from personal and emotional control of intimate groups.
	Association in a large number of groups, no individual allegiance to a single group.
Density Reinforces the effect of size in diversifying men and their activities, and in increasing the structural complexity of the society.	Tendency to differentiation and specialization.
	Separation of residence from work place.
	Functional specialization of areas—segregation of functions.
	Segregation of people: city becomes a mosaic social world.
Heterogeneity Cities products of migration of peoples of diverse origin. Heterogeneity of origin matched by heterogeneity of occupants. Differentiation and specialization reinforces heterogeneity	Without common background and common activities premium is placed on visual recognition: the uniform becomes symbolic of the role.
	No common set of norms and values, no common ethical system to sustain them; money tends to become measure of all things for which there are no common standards.
	Formal controls as opposed to informal controls. Necessity for adhering to predictable routines. Clock and the traffic signal symbolic of the basis of the social order.
	Economic basis: mass production of goods, possible only with the standardization of processes and product.
	Standardization of goods and facilities in terms of the average. Adjustment of educational, recreational, and cultural services to mass requirements.
	In politics, success of mass appeals—growth of mass movements.

SOURCE: Schematic version by E. Shevky and W. Bell, *Social Area Analysis* (Stanford, Calif.: Stanford University Press, 1955), pp. 7–8, derived from Louis Wirth, "Urbanism as a Way of Life," *American Journal of Sociology*, 44:1–24 (July, 1938). Copyright 1938 by The University of Chicago.

Cities vary in the extent or degree to which they are characterized by urban qualities. Some cities have much less norm conflict, social change, mobility, individualism, and impersonality than others. Likewise, great variations in such characteristics often exist among local areas of a given city. Moreover, certain cultural values in a society may increase the effects of urbanization. If a culture emphasizes material possessions as a central value, the impersonality of urban life will tend to increase that emphasis. Furthermore, in a culture where people are formal in their behavior and where the people are, as a cultural pattern, more self-contained, the impact of urban life may further intensify impersonality in relationships.

All too frequently the shortcomings of urban life are emphasized. Cities have several advantages over rural areas. Certainly they have been the centers of industrial production and distribution and as such have contributed much to higher standards of living. Cities, to a greater degree than rural areas, have been centers for inventions and the modification of cultural patterns. This is partly due to the anonymity of the city and its diversity of cultural patterns which provide more freedom for creative thought than do rural areas. As a result, artistic and intellectual centers have developed in many larger cities. Cities have also been the centers of great public health advances, particularly in sanitation and the prevention of disease. In fact, without good sanitation it would be difficult for many cities to exist. City living, as a way of life, is associated with many aspects of "civilization."

> What we call civilization as distinguished from culture has been cradled in the city; the city is the center from which the influences of modern civilized life radiate to the ends of the earth and the point from which they are controlled; the persistent problems of contemporary society take their most acute form in the city. The problems of modern civilization are typically urban problems.[8]

City living does not, of course, directly result in deviant behavior, but many of the conditions associated with city life are, to a preponderant degree, conducive to deviation.[9] It should be kept in mind, however, that the set of variables associated with the concept of urbanism may be found independent of city environments. In other words, "urbanism" is not synonymous with "city." Whereas "city" refers to an area distinguished principally by population size, density, and heterogeneity, "urbanism" refers to a complex of social relationships. Although urbanism may more fre-

---

[8] Louis Wirth, "The Urban Society and Civilization," *American Journal of Sociology,* 45:744 (March, 1940).

[9] For a discussion of rural and urban ways of life and the manner in which they may lead toward or away from various forms of deviation, see Eleanor Leacock, "Three Social Variables and Mental Illness," in Alexander H. Leighton, John A. Clausen, and Robert N. Wilson eds., *Explorations in Social Psychiatry* (New York: Basic Books, Inc., 1957), pp. 308–338.

quently arise within city environments, this does not mean that it is limited to them. Rural areas are also becoming "urbanized" as their way of life is experiencing such changes. Some of these changes represent the spread of behavior patterns emanating from cities, but much of the change in rural areas has come about as the result of new relations among people who live in these areas. Some of the conditions of an urban way of life will be discussed in the following sections.[10]

NORM AND SOCIAL ROLE CONFLICTS

A major characteristic of urbanism is the diversity of interests and backgrounds of persons who at the same time live in close contact with one another. People living in urban communities vary in age, race, ethnic background, occupation, interests, attitudes, and values. Moreover, urban life is characterized by contrasts in wealth, abilities, and class structure. "Cities generally, and American cities in particular, comprise a motley of peoples and cultures, of highly differentiated modes of life between which there is often only the faintest communication, the greatest indifference and the broadest tolerance, occasionally bitter strife, but always the sharpest contrast." [11] Large cities, in particular, have generally been cities within cities in the form of areas with subcultures, religious affiliations, or racial characteristics. These are often groups with different customs as well as separate languages. Although in the United States there is the idea that eventually these will disappear as separate areas, in cities in other parts of the world the existence of such diverse areas has been, and is often expected to continue as, a "natural" part of city existence.

Urban life attracts people with varying values and ideologies, and it also fosters the growth of differences. Because of the greater density of the population and increased mobility, individuals under urban conditions are exposed to a great variety of social contacts. Media of mass communication, such as the newspaper, radio, and television, constantly bring individuals in an urban world into contact with divergent ideologies. Furthermore, the relative impersonality of city life permits the development of special-interest groups, whether a racketeering political machine or a Society for the Prevention of Cruelty to Animals.

The heterogeneity of the population, the complex division of labor, and the class structure existing in the larger communities generally result in divergent group norms and values and conflicting social roles. In

---

[10] See Charles T. Stewart, Jr., "The Urban and Rural Dichotomy: Concepts and Uses," *American Journal of Sociology*, 64:152–158 (September, 1958) and Richard Dewey, "The Rural–Urban Continuum: Real but Relatively Unimportant," *American Journal of Sociology*, 66:60–66 (July, 1960). Also see Paul Hatt and Albert J. Reiss, Jr. eds., *Cities and Society* (New York: The Free Press of Glencoe, Inc., 1957), especially pages 35–45, and Anderson, *op. cit.*

[11] Wirth, "Urbanism as a Way of Life," *loc. cit.*, p. 20.

modern urban societies, so differentiated and so conflicting have become the ends sought by different groups that individuals are often in the position of not knowing in many areas of life exactly what are the conventional ways of behaving and the proper social roles. Persons who are conventional in their sexual behavior live alongside those who are sexually promiscuous. The city harbors those who respect the law and are honest in most of their social relationships as well as those who have little respect for laws, officials, or property. Variations exist in religious beliefs, family systems, and the means of achieving satisfying human relationships.

At the same time the impersonality of urban life tends to foster increased individual freedom. This freedom in a mass society, as Rose has pointed out, means that "there are fewer standards to which the individual must conform and the concepts of 'right' and 'good' are relative. To an individual without the training to make up his mind on such ethical matters, or the strength of character to conform to standards which he thinks proper, freedom may be demoralizing." [12]

Norm and role conflicts, or diversities of norms and behavioral standards, create a situation where no single standard is likely to be upheld and where deviation from it is not met with penalizing sanctions. Individuals who have been taught to accept the supremacy of a single rule may become skeptical of its validity when they discover, under urban conditions, that breaking the rule does not bring about social ostracism or censure as supposed.

RAPID CULTURAL CHANGE

Rapid social and cultural change, disregard for the importance of stability of generations, and untempered loyalties also generally characterize urban life. New ideas are generally welcome, inventions of mechanical gadgets are encouraged, and new styles in such arts as painting, literature, and music are often approved. Becker has characterized urban society as a secular one or "one in which resistance to change is at a minimum or, to say the very least, where change in many aspects of life is quite welcome." [13] Consequently, elements which are traditional, or "sacred," dwindle in importance and "cynicism with reference to the alleged values of contending groups and skepticism with reference to the alleged truths have become marks characteristic of the modern [urban] sophisticated man." [14]

Urban life itself also tends to facilitate changes in norms and ideol-

---

[12] Arnold Rose, "The Problem of a Mass Society," in Arnold Rose, *Theory and Methods in the Social Sciences* (Minneapolis: University of Minnesota Press, 1954), p. 37.

[13] Howard Becker, *Through Values to Social Interpretation* (Durham, N.C.: Duke University Press, 1950), p. 67.

[14] Louis Wirth, "Ideological Aspects of Social Disorganization," *American Sociological Review*, 5:482 (August, 1940).

ogies, as well as systems of behavior, which may greatly alter the nature of the social structure and the relationships of people to one another. Sometimes these changes appear to result partly from the practical exigencies of urban life; at other times they seem to be outgrowths of the failure of informal controls to uphold and maintain the older values and ideologies. Urban living has brought such great changes in the modern family, for example, that it has come to be called the urban family. The reduced size of the modern family has been both a characteristic and a result of urban life. Urban life has developed the concept of the equality of the sexes in marriage, a concept which has caused considerable conflict with rural definitions of family roles. The structuring of urban society into often fairly distinct peer groups has resulted in the magnification of age differences and the widening of the gap between teen-age persons and older generations. Likewise, the emphasis on youthful values in urban life has meant that as people grow older they are faced with new definitions of roles which may necessitate considerable readjustment.

MOBILITY

An urban population exhibits considerable horizontal and vertical mobility. Horizontal mobility involves physical movement in connection with occupation and other activities, or it may mean change of residence within a community or to another. Vertical mobility involves changes in occupational and social status.

Modern transportation, particularly in urban areas, enables persons to move about rapidly and to come into frequent contact with many different people. It has been said that less than a century ago a man might live a lifetime without ever going far from his home, and without seeing more than a handful of strangers.

One writer has stated that speed is the most common characteristic of urban life.[15] Time has become an extremely important factor, and it is seldom possible for urbanites to relax. Transportation, job, meetings, recreation, home—all move in response to the clock. Even children learn to hurry at an early age. They must get to school on time, be dismissed on the minute, and head toward home on some sort of transportation which often leaves "on the dot." When they arrive home they rush out to play and then run home to dinner. "In spite of many time-saving gadgets and devices invented to leave more and more minutes free from some drudgery or operation, the urban day is still too short." [16]

Figures of the United States Census Bureau reveal how frequently families move in contemporary society. Less than 2 percent of the adult population in 1952 could be called "old-timers" in their communities in

---

[15] Lee, *op. cit.*, p. 459.   [16] *Ibid.*

that they had always lived in their present homes. The number of persons who move each year is approximately one in five. Each year about 30 million persons move (see Table 3.6), and of this number about 5

Table 3.6. Internal Migration in the United States

| Year | Total number of persons | Persons moving their home | |
		Within same state	From one state to another
1948–49	27,127,000	22,783,000	4,344,000
1949–50	27,526,000	23,637,000	3,889,000
1950–51	31,158,000	25,970,000	5,188,000
1951–52	29,840,000	24,728,000	5,112,000
1952–53	30,786,000	25,264,000	5,522,000
1953–54	29,027,000	23,993,000	5,034,000
1954–55	31,492,000	26,597,000	4,895,000
1955–56	33,098,000	28,045,000	5,053,000
1956–57	31,834,000	26,758,000	5,076,000
1957–58	33,263,000	27,679,000	5,584,000

SOURCE: U.S. Bureau of the Census, *Current Population Reports; Population Characteristics.* October 13, 1958, Series P-20, No. 85, pp. 8–9.

million cross county lines. Another 5,000,000 move across state lines. Two out of five move across regional lines as well, many of them one or two thousand miles. Younger persons are more mobile than older persons; yet a large number of persons age sixty-five and over also move. During the years 1951–1952, 38 percent of those between twenty and twenty-four changed their places of residence, and the proportion was almost as great for those between twenty-five and twenty-nine. Nearly 9 percent of those sixty-five and over changed their residence during this period.

Although urban societies generally tend to regard mobility favorably, such frequent moves may have unsatisfactory effects. They tend to weaken attachments to the local community, particularly among primary or face-to-face contacts, to make persons less interested in maintaining certain community standards, and to increase contact with secondary groups of diverse patterns, "thus weakening the bonds which provide the basis for social control among members of local groups." [17] As a person becomes more mobile he comes into contact with many different norms and comes to understand that other codes of behavior are different from his own. Mobility often means the loss of personal relationships, such as kinship ties, neighbors, and close friendships. For child and adult alike, it may be

[17] Paul H. Landis, *Rural Life in Process* (New York: McGraw-Hill Book Company, Inc., 1940), p. 320.

necessary to acquire new friends and new norms, to change social roles, and to reconcile old norms and roles with new ones.

As close relations with neighbors and relatives are severed, there is less control over the mobile person's behavior and a decline in the importance to him of having a "good reputation" in the eyes of these persons. Too, the standards by which reputation is judged may become more diverse and may depend less upon the specific ethical and moral qualities of the person than upon the "general impression" of him as a person. Children may have increasingly fewer contacts with their grandparents and other relatives. Largely because of this mobility it is likely that a large proportion of young people today, living under urban conditions in America, cannot give the names of great-grandparents on either side of the family. The identification of third cousins usually becomes impossible.

As an illustration of the role mobility may play in some types of criminal behavior, in a study of farm, village, and city offenders in Iowa and in a replication of this study in Iowa and one in Sweden, mobility was found to play an important part in the development of criminal behavior.[18] Those from rural areas were found to have had extensive contacts with persons outside their home communities. This mobility, as measured by changes in residence and the frequency of outside contacts, was greater than that of a group of nonoffenders from the same area. It was also greater than that of their parents.

MATERIALISM

External appearances and material possessions become of primary importance in an urban society, where people are more often known for their gadgets than for themselves. People increasingly come to judge others by how well they display their wealth, a display which Veblen has called "conspicuous consumption." Under urban conditions the type of clothes a man wears or the automobile he drives, the costliness of his home and its furnishings, the exclusiveness of the club or association to which he belongs, and the knowledge of his salary or the amount of his financial assets are often the sole means others have of judging him or his success in life. It is on the basis of readily "visible" criteria such as these that status is assigned. Some persons emphasize the importance of "status symbols" in urban society.[19]

---

[18] Marshall B. Clinard, "The Process of Urbanization and Criminal Behavior," *American Journal of Sociology*, 48:202–213 (September, 1942). Also see his "Rural Criminal Offenders," *American Journal of Sociology*, 50:38–45 (July, 1944) and his "A Cross-Cultural Replication of the Relation of Urbanism to Criminal Behavior," *American Sociological Review*, 25:253–257 (April, 1960). Also see Harold D. Eastman, "The Process of Urbanization and Criminal Behavior: A Restudy of Culture Conflict." Unpublished doctoral thesis, University of Iowa, Iowa City, 1954.

[19] See Erving Goffman, *The Presentation of Self in Everyday Life* (Edinburgh: University of Edinburgh Social Science Research Center, 1956), especially Chap. 1. Also see Vance Packard, *The Hidden Persuaders* (New York: Pocket Books, Inc., 1958).

INDIVIDUALISM

In modern urban societies two almost contradictory trends are taking place which affect the position of the individual. On the one hand, the focus is on the individual, as urban persons have more and more come to regard their own interests as paramount in their social relationships.[20] Thus "I" feelings come to replace much of the cooperation characteristic of rural life. People feel that they must look after their own interests and increase their status through their own efforts. The urban person's strong belief in hedonism or personal happiness as the goal of life is increasingly reflected, for example, in modern marriage, the function of which is thought to be primarily personal happiness, all other functions being regarded as subordinate.

As individualism in urban society has increased, competition has also been intensified. Each individual may feel that he is in ceaseless competition with the remainder of society, or at least with that part of the society in which he operates. The intensity with which the goals are striven for is, generally, in proportion to the values attached to them and the extent to which they can satisfy socially induced needs of the individual.

The role of this individual competition in modern urban societies is difficult to evaluate. Ordinary competition has many favorable aspects. Where it is fair it minimizes such factors as favoritism, prejudice, or other bias in the struggle for status in social life. Competition can also serve as an important dynamic force for production, as laboratory experiments have shown. Competition can also, on the other hand, make the desire to achieve social status through the acquisition of wealth and other means assume an importance out of all relation to other factors. It often condemns the loser to a feeling of failure and frustration or it may force him to resort to unconventional methods of achieving status. One psychiatrist has pointed out the effect of competition in the development of mental illness: "Some of our mental breakdowns are caused by the kind of society in which we live—a highly competitive society in which there are few winners and many losers. Everyone is in competition with everyone else—not only for economic gain, but for esteem, love, respect, and recognition." [21]

On the other hand, there is a contrary stress in the modern urban world away from this type of individualism and aptly referred to by

---

[20] There is much emphasis on individualism within contemporary economic, political, religious, and philosophical thinking. This individualism is also related to the Protestant Reformation, the seventeenth- and eighteenth-century political revolutions of England, America, and France, and the development of the American frontier. For some examples see Abbott P. Herman, "Our Values of Individualism," in *An Approach to Social Problems* (Boston: Ginn and Company, 1949), Chap. 8.

[21] George Thorman, "Toward Mental Health" (No. 120; New York: Public Affairs Pamphlets 1946), pp. 19–20.

Riesman as "The Lonely Crowd." [22] According to him, there are three types of personalities in modern societies, each one "directed" in a different way. The "tradition-directed" type almost unthinkingly conforms to the norms of his culture. "Inner-directed" persons have some degree of independence in their actions. Regardless of conflicts with society, such individuals do not necessarily follow what others do but try to ignore the environment or shape it to fit their needs. The third type is what might be thought of as the modern urban type of personality, who loses his individuality and constantly follows the dictates of others. He wishes to conform and to be like others, and consequently becomes what Riesman has termed an "other-directed" person, his actions being directed not by himself but by others.

Decline in Intimate Communication and Modification of Mechanisms of Informal Social Control

Central to the problem of urbanization is the decline in intimate communication among the members of society. Urbanized areas, particularly those where the population is dense and mobile, tend to create an extensive area of impersonality for their residents. Associations among people are not so much on the basis of knowing each other's total personality as acquaintance with particular social roles. Human beings tend to be regarded categorically much as other physical objects, often to be "manipulated" without much feeling and, primarily, for personal satisfaction. Most urban associations with people are brief and fragmentary, and tend to be stereotyped because of the impossibility of dealing with each association individually. Max Weber suggested that density and the presence of large numbers of persons decrease the possibility of mutual acquaintanceships between individuals.[23]

Although a person meets many people face to face in his daily contacts, these contacts in the city are, nevertheless, often "impersonal, superficial, transitory, and segmental." [24] The urban world is one of anonymity where there are few ties or interests to bind a person to others. Urban conditions generally do not provide means for getting psychologically "close" to other persons, and the so-called blasé, sophisticated attitude of many big-city dwellers represents in part a way of protecting their privacy from the intrusions of others. When they encounter difficulties in their inter-

---

[22] David Riesman, *The Lonely Crowd: A Study of Changing American Character* (New Haven, Conn.: Yale University Press, 1950).

[23] Max Weber, *Wirtschaft und Gesellschaft* (Tübingen, Germany: Mohr, 1925), Pt. II, p. 514.

[24] Wirth, "Urbanism as a Way of Life," *loc. cit.,* p. 12. There is often a tendency to overlook the fact that intimate contacts may exist in a city. See, for example, William F. Whyte, *Street Corner Society* (Chicago: The University of Chicago Press, 1943).

personal relations they consequently must often turn to professional counselors or psychiatrists. In many of the transitory relationships encountered, the only things of interest are those directly pertaining to the situation; for example, whether a man will "stand" for a round of drinks, is a "good talker," or has a new car or some new and expensive gadget. This has helped to produce the loneliness of the urban world so well described by Auden:

> . . . This stupid world where
> Gadgets are gods and we go on talking,
> Many about much, but remain alone,
> Alive but alone, belonging—where?—
> Unattached as tumbleweed.[25]

This decline in close personal relations is reflected in contemporary American films about urban life where the hero and heroine are usually not identified with strong family ties and often are even without any strong attachments.[26] This is in marked contrast to the close personal contacts of the less urbanized small town where the townspeople may know large numbers of people by name or sight and know many of them even intimately.[27] Generally speaking, under the urban conditions of a larger city a person may be "acquainted" with many more people than he would under rural conditions, but a rural person may "know" more people intimately than does an urban individual.

Whereas "anonymity" is virtually impossible in a rural society, it is the "norm" in a predominantly urban society. This is why, in the absence of intimate personal acquaintances, a person's status and character are judged by others from his "self-presentation," or the external indices of that self. Thus symbols of wealth, sophistication, or other forms of influence are of special significance to urban society.[28]

Many of those who migrate to our larger cities pride themselves on the fact that "Now, thank God, I don't *have* to know my neighbors, go to Rotary, belong to a church, or participate in an annual Community Chest drive!" And the big city does little to disabuse them of this attitude. Individuals can and do live comfortably in our large cities with no formal ties between themselves and the structures of the culture save the money tie between them and their

---

[25] W. H. Auden, *The Age of Anxiety* (New York: Random House, 1946), p. 44. Reprinted by permission of the publisher.

[26] Martha Wolfenstein and Nathan Leites, *Movies: A Psychological Study* (New York: The Free Press of Glencoe, 1950).

[27] Albert Blumenthal, *Small-Town Stuff* (Chicago: The University of Chicago Press, 1932). For example, in Mineville the average person knew nine tenths of the townspeople by sight or name and a large number intimately.

[28] See Goffman, *op. cit.* for a discussion of the way in which personal impressions are formed in a mass society. See also C. Wright Mills, *The Power Elite* (New York: Oxford University Press, 1956), especially pp. 71–93, for a discussion of "elites" (high-status persons) in modern society.

jobs. One may or may not elect to exercise one's political right to vote; one may or may not own property, marry, or belong with anybody else to anything; but one must tie into the structure to the extent of getting money regularly. . . .

Urban folk delay marriage and in some cases elect not to marry; and kinship ties are narrowing and attenuating. Citizenship ties are weakening in our urban world to the point that they are largely neglected by large masses of people. Neighborhood and community ties are not only optional but generally growing less strong; and along with them is disappearing the important network of intimate, informal social controls traditionally associated with living closely with others.[29]

Generally speaking, where intimate group participation languishes, the incidence of social deviation is high.[30] Others have suggested that the breakdown of intimate communication in an urban society lies at the center of social problems in that the individual finds that he cannot easily communicate with his fellows and thus cannot orient his own values or put himself into harmony with the group.[31]

It has been said that as urbanism has increased, as man's behavior has become more individual, competitive, and materialistic, and as his conformity to social norms has become less affected by informal group controls, greater opportunities and inducements appear to develop for behavior which deviates from accepted norms.

Urban Characteristics a Matter of Degree

The description of the characteristics of the urban way of life which has been presented here should be considered only as an abstract ideal type which can be compared with the characteristics of rural society. It does not mean that the life of all persons in a city is so characterized. One may have considerable personal relationships, for example, with others in a city. Limited studies have shown that primary group life survives in urban areas and is effective over considerable segments. For example, a Detroit study of family patterns found that neighborliness was widespread, with about 75 percent reporting that they got together with neighbors as well as with relatives; 55 percent got together with "other friends" once or twice a week or a few times each month.[32] In addition, only 11 percent had no relatives at all in the Detroit area, and 54 percent

[29] Robert S. Lynd, *Knowledge for What?* (rev. ed.; Princeton, N.J.: Princeton University Press, 1946), p. 83.

[30] Stuart A. Queen and Jeannette Gruener, *Social Pathology: Obstacles to Social Participation* (rev. ed.; New York: Thomas Y. Crowell Company, 1948).

[31] Rose, *op. cit.*, p. 25.

[32] Cited in Harold L. Wilensky and Charles N. Lebeaux, *Industrial Society and Social Welfare* (New York: Russell Sage Foundation, 1958), p. 122. Also see Whyte, *op. cit.* Sjoberg has stated that preindustrial cities of underdeveloped countries do not have as much of the characteristics of urbanism. While there is a difference in degree,

saw one or more related units of the family once or twice a week. Other studies in Chicago have shown that customer-clerk relations in smaller city stores can be quite intimate.[33]

As one study has suggested, the role of mobility and impersonality in urban life should not be overstated either in the local community or in the factory and other work situations.

> Whatever the mobility of the population, intimate contacts with relatives, neighbors, and friends are a universal feature of urban life at home and in the local community (as indeed they were in an earlier day among the Little Polands and Little Sicilies of the slum). Such contacts are also a universal feature of life at work. Even in the huge workplace where many thousands mass for the daily routine, the informal workgroup seems destined to go on performing its usual functions of controlling the workpace, initiating new members, deciding how far to go along with the boss, and making work a bit more like play. There is no evidence that human relations are any more atomized at work than in the local community and neighborhood, though the liveliness of informal groups may, of course, vary from place to place.[34]

Although the life of suburbia has been described among the young upwardly mobile middle class as often a transient superficial life,[35] others have pointed out that areas with single-family dwellings, particularly those with more factory workers, have considerable stability in their family life and local community relations.[36] Even where people move within the city some retain active friendships over the city in neighborhoods where they once lived. "Spatial mobility makes for city-wide ties; stability makes for local area ties; and most urban residents have both." [37]

Certainly a degree of intimate life does exist in any city, in both the local community and the work place, but it is not anywhere near the same as it is in the villages or rural areas. Moreover, in the city a person experiences almost daily large areas of impersonal relations where his personal identity is not recognized. To admit the need for exercising caution in order to avoid overstating the universal presence of urban characteristics does not minimize, however, their importance as a framework for understanding much of contemporary life and deviant behavior.

---

the characteristics of an urban way of life can be found in cities like those of India. See Marshall B. Clinard and B. Chatterjee, "Urban Community Development in India: the Delhi Pilot Project" in Turner, *India's Urban Future*, pp. 71–93.

[33] Gregory P. Stone, "City Shoppers and Urban Identification: Observations on the Social Psychology of City Life," *American Journal of Sociology*, 60:36–45 (July, 1954).

[34] Wilensky and Lebeaux, *op. cit.*, p. 124.

[35] See William F. Whyte, Jr., *The Organization Man* (New York: Simon and Schuster, Inc., 1956).

[36] Flint City—Fringe Survey. Social Science Research Project, University of Michigan, Ann Arbor, 1955, as cited in Wilensky and Lebeaux, *op. cit.*, pp. 126–127.

[37] Joel Smith, William H. Form, and Gregory P. Stone, "Local Intimacy in a Middle-Sized City," *American Journal of Sociology*, 60:284 (November, 1954). See also Peter H. Rossi, *Why Families Move: A Study in the Social Psychology of Urban Residential Mobility* (New York: The Free Press of Glencoe, 1956).

The discussion to this point has been in terms of the world-wide growth of urbanization and the development of urbanism as a way of life. If it can be demonstrated that this frame of reference is useful in explaining the incidence of deviant behavior, it will furnish overwhelming evidence against the contention that deviant behavior is the product of biological or individual psychological forces. It will also help to explain the rising problems of deviant behavior, such as crime and delinquency, in underdeveloped countries undergoing rapid industrialization and urbanization.[38] The following section will compare the incidence and prevalence of certain forms of deviant behavior in rural and urban areas, between cities of various sizes, and within areas of a city. Such material should furnish some evidence for the contention that urbanization and urbanism are related to the extent and increase of deviant behavior in modern societies.

Comparisons of Certain Forms of Deviant Behavior in Rural and Urban Areas

For centuries writers have been concerned about the debauchery and moral conditions of the cities and have generally praised rural life. Hesiod, for example, wrote about the corrupt justice of the cities.[39] The Greeks and Romans compared the city with agricultural areas, noting the greater evils and sources of criminality in the cities. One of the first systematic comparisons of rural and urban peoples was made by Ibn Khaldun in the fourteenth century. This famed Arab historian compared life in the city with that among the nomadic tribes. He found that the nomads had good behavior, whereas evil and corruption were abundant in the city; that honesty and courage were characteristic of the nomads, whereas lying and cowardice were prevalent in the city; and that the city caused decay, stultified initiative, and made men depraved and wicked. In general, rural life has been, and still largely is, a world of close personal relationships which Burgess has thus described:

> But the main characteristics of small-town life stand out in clear per-
> spective: close acquaintanceship of everyone with everyone else, the dominance
> of personal relations, and the subjection of the individual to continuous ob-
> servation and control by the community. . . . This fund of concrete knowl-
> edge which everyone has of everyone else in the small town naturally em-

---

[38] See J. J. Panakal and A. M. Khalifa, *Prevention of Types of Criminality Resulting from Social Changes and Accompanying Economic Development in Less Developed Countries*, Reports on the Second United Nations Congress on the Prevention of Crime and the Treatment of Offenders, London, August, 1960 (New York: United Nations Department of Economic and Social Affairs, 1960).

[39] See Pitirim Sorokin, Carle Zimmerman, and Charles Galpin, *A Systematic Sourcebook in Rural Sociology* (Minneapolis: University of Minnesota Press, 1930), pp. 27-52, 54-68.

phasizes and accentuates the role of the personal in all relationships and activities of community life. Approval and disapproval of conduct, likes and dislikes of persons, play correspondingly a tremendous part in social life, in business, in politics, and in the administration of justice.[40]

DELINQUENCY AND CRIME

The types, incidence, and reactions to rural crime, as with urban crime, are a function of the type of life and the various norms and values of the communities. Delinquency and crime rates today are generally much lower in rural areas than in urban. In general, the differences between rural and urban property crimes are greater than the differences in crimes against the person.

Some delinquent and criminal acts committed in rural areas are dealt with informally and not officially reported, and there are undoubtedly more opportunities to commit offenses in urban as compared with rural areas. The differences between rural and urban rates, however, are so great that differential reporting or opportunity could, at most, account for only a small part. Also, there is little evidence to support the theory held by some that the city attracts deviants from rural areas.[41]

As Table 3.7 shows, burglary rates in the United States, as a whole,

Table 3.7. *Rates per 100,000 Population for Crimes Known to the Police in Rural and Urban Areas, United States, 1960*

Offense	Rate	
	Urban	Rural
Murder and nonnegligent manslaughter	4.9	6.4
Forcible rape	10.3	6.8
Robbery	70.7	11.9
Aggravated assault	88.7	42.2
Burglary—breaking or entering	568.9	210.9
Larceny—theft ($50 and over)	340.8	102.8
Automobile theft	243.7	42.1

SOURCE: Derived from Federal Bureau of Investigation, *Uniform Crime Reports* (Annual Bulletin, 1960; Washington, D.C.: Government Printing Office, 1960), p. 33. The population figures used were based on the 1960 census. Rates for the above are based on 1960 census data. "Urban areas" include Standard Metropolitan Statistical Areas.

are generally almost three times as great in urban areas as in rural, larceny is over three times as great, and robbery over six times.[42] The rates for burglaries known to the police per 100,000 population in 1960

[40] Ernest W. Burgess, in Blumenthal, *op. cit.*, pp. xii–xiii.   [41] See page 95.
[42] In such countries as France, Belgium, Switzerland, Holland, Germany, Sweden, Finland, Denmark, and Italy the incidence of urban offenses, crimes known, and con-

were, for example, 568.9 in urban areas and 210.9 in rural areas. Crimes such as murder, which are relatively infrequent as compared with property crimes, are about the same, with a somewhat higher rate in rural areas, where the rate is 6.4 as compared with 4.9 in urban. Rape rates are much higher in urban areas, 10.3 in urban as contrasted with 6.8 in rural.

Specific studies, rather than statistical comparisons, also seem to support the thesis that the urbanization of rural areas and an increase in crime go hand in hand. A study of the southern mountain villages showed that as the hill country was opened to outside contacts criminal activities increased.[43] The most important factor associated with this increase was the growing lack of community identification on the part of individuals as the villages became more urbanized. A study of rural inmates in an Iowa reformatory revealed that characteristics associated with an urban way of life played a significant role in their criminal behavior.[44]

MENTAL DISORDERS

Most contemporary data on mental disorders, but not all, show that the rates are generally higher in urban than in rural areas. As with crime, many writers feel that the expansion of urbanism is significant in the production of mental illness in our society.[45] One writer has stated that "the data also show that insanity is much more prevalent in urban than in rural areas, a fact of no little significance for the student of rural sociology. . . . there seems to be no doubt of the association between urbanity and insanity." [46] After a study of the prevalence of mental disorder among the urban and rural populations of New York State, Malzberg concluded that

victions per population have been reported as generally higher than among rural areas. In Finland, for example, during the years 1930–1933 there were approximately seven times as many property crimes known to the police in urban areas as in rural.—Hans H. Burchardt, "Kriminalität in Stadt und Land," *Abhandlungen des Kriminalistischen Instituts an der Universität Berlin* (4. Folge, 4 Bd., 1. Heft [1936]). Louis Wirth and Marshall B. Clinard, "Public Safety," in *Urban Government*, Supplementary Report of the Urbanism Committee to the National Resources Committee (Washington, D.C.: Government Printing Office, 1939), I, 247–303. Also see Sorokin, Zimmerman, and Galpin, *op. cit.*, II, 266–302, 315–329.

[43] M. Taylor Mathews, *Experience Worlds of the Mountain Peoples* (New York: Columbia University Press, 1937).

[44] Clinard, "Rural Criminal Offenders," *American Journal of Sociology*, 50:38–45 (July, 1944). A replica of Clinard's study made several years later found that these characteristics also played a role in the lives of offenders.—Eastman, "The Process of Urbanization and Criminal Behavior: A Restudy of Culture Conflict," cited above.

[45] For an over-all picture of the general distribution of mental disorder, see Stuart A. Queen, "The Ecological Study of Mental Disorder," *American Sociological Review*, 5:201–209 (April, 1940); Robert E. L. Faris, "Ecological Factors in Human Behavior," in James McV. Hunt ed., *Personality and the Behavior Disorders* (New York: The Ronald Press Company, 1944), pp. 736–757; C. W. Schroeder, "Mental Disorders in Cities," *American Journal of Sociology*, 47:40–47 (July, 1942); and Abraham Myerson, "Review of Mental Disorders in Urban Areas," *American Journal of Psychiatry*, 96:995–999 (January, 1940).

[46] T. Lynn Smith, *The Sociology of Rural Life* (New York: Harper & Row, Publishers, 1940), p. 125.

the rural regions of the state had less mental disorder than the urban.[47]

In another study, Texas rates for all persons who became psychotic for the first time were found to be two and a half times greater in urban areas than in rural, a difference which was statistically significant.[48] The same differential held for the sexes with an average annual rate per 100,000 for males in urban areas of 76 in contrast with 44 in rural areas; for females an even greater difference—99 as compared with 36. Even the age-specific psychoses rates were consistently higher in urban areas than for the same rural age group. The disparity between rates for rural and urban areas increased with advancing age. Jaco has summarized the results of the Texas study as follows: "In examining the overall results concerning the incidence rates of mental disorders in the rural and urban areas, no significant evidence was found to support the notion that the large rate differentials between urban and rural areas were due to differences in accessibility to psychiatric treatment facilities or to the type of psychiatric facilities available in the two areas." [49]

Not all the evidence supports the conclusion that the incidence of mental illness is much less in rural areas. The differences may actually be smaller than they now appear to be because of the likelihood that rural families may keep mentally disturbed members at home rather than hospitalize them. A study made in Tennessee concluded that mental health in rural areas is not necessarily as good as the smaller number of commitments to mental institutions might indicate, for almost half the psychotic individuals in rural areas were found to be cared for by their families.[50] For this reason it is possible that mental deviants in urban society may be somewhat more socially visible, and that both unofficial and official tolerance of the deviation will be less.

ALCOHOLISM

The chances that rural persons will become chronic alcoholics are less than half as great as those for urban dwellers, according to estimates made by Yale University's Section on Alcohol Studies. In 1940 the rate per 100,000 adult population in areas of less than 2500 population was 474 as compared with 972 in cities of 100,000 population or over. There were 821 male alcoholics for every 100,000 rural males, as compared with 1894 in large cities; the difference between rural and urban women, com-

[47] Benjamin Malzberg, "The Prevalence of Mental Disease among the Urban and Rural Populations of New York State." *Psychiatric Quarterly* 9:55–88 (January, 1935).

[48] E. Gartly Jaco, *The Social Epidemiology of Mental Diseases* (New York: Russell Sage Foundation, 1960). Also see Leacock, "Three Social Variables and Mental Illness," *loc. cit.*, p. 314.

[49] Jaco, *op. cit.*

[50] William F. Roth, Jr., and Frank H. Luton, "The Mental Health Program in Tennessee," *American Journal of Psychiatry*, 99:662–676 (January, 1943). A study of the Eastern Health District of Baltimore found that one fourth of the rural psychotics were not hospitalized.

puted on a standardized population, is somewhat less. The rates of reported deaths from alcoholism per 100,000 adults in 1940 was nearly twice as great in cities of over 100,000 as in rural areas.[51] Urban commitments for alcoholic psychoses are reported to be three and a half times the rate for rural areas.[52]

The principal reasons for this lower rate of alcoholism in rural areas are the social norms and the amount of social control at the personal level over drinking or excessive drinking. Farm people in the United States are much less likely to drink alcoholic beverages than are city dwellers. One half of the rural people are abstainers, but this proportion decreases as the size of the city increases, until in cities with a population of over 500,000 only one fourth do not drink. Both farm rearing and farm residence are associated with lower proportions of heavy drinkers. A recent Iowa study showed that 58 percent of drinkers in the city were either moderate or heavy drinkers as compared with 43 percent of the farm drinkers.[53] Moreover, the extent of drinking increased among the farm-reared who had migrated to the city but this increase was in moderate rather than heavy drinking.

SUICIDE

On the whole, persons living on farms and villages either in Europe or in America are much less likely to take their lives than persons living in cities. In London the standardized rate, expressed as a percentage of that for the whole of England and Wales, is 115, for the county boroughs 106, for other urban districts 97, and for rural districts 88.[54] In Sweden, Denmark, and Finland wide differences exist between farm and city in the suicide rates, in Finland the urban rate being over twice as high.[55] A detailed study of suicide in France showed that the chances that farm people and persons living in places of less than 2000 population would take their lives were considerably less than for city people.[56] Only in the Irish Free State and the Netherlands have suicides been reported to be greater in rural than in urban areas.[57] This has been partially explained as being due to the large number of old persons in rural areas who, feeling useless from an economic point of view, commit suicide.

[51] E. M. Jellinek, "Recent Trends in Alcoholism and Alcohol Consumption," *Quarterly Journal of Studies on Alcohol,* 8:23 (June, 1947).

[52] Landis and Page, *op. cit.*

[53] Harold A. Mulford and Donald E. Miller, "Drinking in Iowa. II. The Extent of Drinking and Selected Socio-cultural Categories," *Quarterly Journal of Studies on Alcohol,* 21:34–35 (March, 1960).

[54] Figures cited in Peter Sainsbury, *Suicide in London: An Ecological Study* (New York: Basic Books, Inc., 1956).

[55] Louis I. Dublin and Bessie Bunzel, *To Be or Not to Be* (New York: Harrison Smith and Robert Haas, 1933), p. 82.

[56] Maurice Halbwachs, *Les Causes du Suicide* (Paris: Librairie Félix Alcan, 1930).

[57] Dublin and Bunzel, *op. cit.*, pp. 82–83.

The suicide rate in cities of the United States of a population of over 10,000 has generally been almost twice as great as that in smaller cities and rural areas. A student from a small western Kansas town has written of suicides in his community over the past twenty years.

> I know of only four suicides in the last twenty years in the town and its agricultural hinterland. Two of these are dramatic memories of my childhood and occurred in 1932. Both suicides were men (one the president of the Citizens State Bank and the other the county treasurer) who had become involved in dishonest financial affairs. The other two suicides were individuals past middle age and without kinship or community ties. One, a man, whose wife had died several years previously and who was without children, had spent his savings in an attempted rejuvenation. The other suicide, a woman, was separated from her husband and son and was shunned by the women of the community because she talked incessantly. One of the local ministers created a sensation in connection with this woman's funeral sermon—he accused the women of the town of murdering the woman who had committed suicide by refusing to associate with her. To my knowledge, no farmers have committed suicide in this area in the last twenty years.[58]

The differential in rural and urban suicide rates appears to be declining because of the tendency for an urban way of life to characterize rural areas. An analysis of 3081 cases of suicide in Michigan between 1945 and 1949 revealed that rural males exhibited higher suicide rates than urban males.[59] Although "farmers and farm managers" had a high suicide rate in Michigan, the majority of "rural" males who committed suicide were engaged in urban occupations and resided in urbanized fringe areas. It is possible that the high rural rate in this sample was due to two factors: as urban values become more widely disseminated in rural areas they create an intense personal conflict because of the disparity between urban and rural values as they affect behavioral alternatives; and the occupations of rural males who committed suicide are characteristic occupations of urban groups, thus suggesting exposure to conflicting values and norms. Although they lived in the country, these people were oriented to an urban way of life.

Social Deviation and City Size

The higher incidence of certain forms of deviant behavior in urban communities has been, in general, demonstrated by a comparison of urban with rural rates, but several questions remain to be answered: (1) If urban rates for certain forms of deviation are, in turn, analyzed by the size of the community, is there a proportional increase as one proceeds from the small city to the great metropolis? (2) Do deviation rates vary according to

---

[58] From an unpublished personal document.
[59] W. Widick Schroeder and Allan J. Beegle, "Suicide: An Instance of High Rural Rates," *Rural Sociology*, 18:45–52 (March, 1953).

the distance from a large community? (3) Within any city are there variations in the rates of deviation according to the degree of urbanism of the area?

CRIME RATES BY CITY SIZE

Comparisons in the United States of crime rates by city size show some startling differences and, in most crimes even a continuous progression in rates as the size of the city increases.[60] (See Table 3.8.) In 1960

Table 3.8. Rates per 100,000 for Crimes Known to the Police
by City Size, United States, 1960

	Population	Murder—Nonnegligent manslaughter	Manslaughter by negligence	Forcible rape	Robbery
I	Over 250,000	6.8	4.4	15.2	117.6
II	100,000–250,000	5.6	4.1	7.6	57.5
III	50,000–100,000	3.3	2.9	5.5	36.6
IV	25,000– 50,000	2.9	2.3	4.7	22.6
V	10,000– 25,000	2.4	1.5	4.0	15.7
VI	Under 10,000	2.7	1.3	3.3	12.8

	Population	Aggravated assault	Burglary—Breaking or entering	Larceny $50 and over	Larceny Under $50	Auto theft
I	Over 250,000	154.1	742.1	477.5	1,070.8	368.8
II	100,000–250,000	83.3	668.3	371.2	1,322.6	288.2
III	50,000–100,000	58.9	512.8	343.1	1,107.9	199.0
IV	25,000– 50,000	39.9	433.0	282.9	1,057.7	154.1
V	10,000– 25,000	35.2	347.9	200.1	923.3	112.8
VI	Under 10,000	28.9	288.9	140.8	650.0	82.1

SOURCE: Federal Bureau of Investigation, *Uniform Crime Reports* (Annual Bulletin, 1960; Washington, D.C.: Government Printing Office, 1961), pp. 81–82. Included in this report were 49 cities over 250,000 population; 80 cities from 100,000 to 250,000; 189 cities from 50,000 to 100,000; 379 cities from 25,000 to 50,000; 880 cities from 10,000 to 25,000; and 1789 cities under 10,000. Population figures on which these rates are based are those included in the 1960 census reports.

[60] Durkheim in France, some fifty years ago, maintained that crime increases directly with the volume and density of the population. A later study by Burchardt concluded that crime rates in European cities generally increase directly with the size of the city. The only exceptions which he found were in the Netherlands and Austria, where the largest cities have the least crime, a situation which he explained as due to unique factors. A comprehensive study of crime in France and Belgium has shown major differences in rates of urban and rural areas, and in those of cities of different sizes. The study found, however, that such rates are affected by the extent of industry and other social factors. See Denis Szabo, *Crimes et Villes* (Louvain: Catholic University of Louvain, 1960).

the rate per 100,000 population for burglaries reported to the police, for example, which is probably the best comparable index of crime, rose steadily from cities of less than 10,000, with a rate of 288.9, to cities over 250,000 population, with a rate of 742.1, or over twice as great.[61] Robbery rates were nine times as great in the larger cities as compared with the smaller ones.

It is interesting to note that rates by city size are often affected, however, by the cultural factors in the area in which the cities are located.[62] In fact, the regional location of a city seems often to be more related to the crime rate than is the extent of urbanization in the state. Some states, such as California, with a large proportion of urban population, also have high crime rates, whereas Massachusetts, which is also heavily urbanized, has a comparatively low rate. It is likely that the urban "way of life" in a more recently developed area like California is characterized by norm conflicts, rapid change, and other unsettling conditions, whereas in older areas, such as New England, these aspects of urbanism may be somewhat attenuated.

ALCOHOLISM

Although cities with a population over 100,000 have estimated rates for chronic alcoholism which are considerably higher than the rates for cities up to 10,000 population, as shown in Table 3.9, the progression

Table 3.9. Estimated Rates of Chronic Alcoholism in the
Adult Population by Sex and Population Size
Groups, United States, 1940

Population size group	Males per 100,000 adult males	Females per 100,000 adult females	Both sexes per 100,000 adult population
Places of 100,000 and over	1,894	294	972
Places of 10,000 to 100,000	1,422	190	727
Places of 2,500 to 10,000	1,428	217	743
Rural (less than 2,500)	821	154	474

SOURCE: E. M. Jellinek, "Recent Trends in Alcoholism and Alcohol Consumption," Quarterly Journal of Studies on Alcohol, 8:23 (June, 1947). Reprinted by permission of the Journal.

[61] Federal Bureau of Investigation, Uniform Crime Reports (Annual Bulletin, 1960; Washington, D.C.: Government Printing Office, 1961), pp. 81–82. The rates for reported burglaries appear to decline in cities of 500,000 or more population, which may be due to a saturation point in urbanization above which size burglary rates do not materially increase.—Wirth and Clinard, "Public Safety," loc. cit., p. 265.

[62] Wirth and Clinard, "Public Safety," loc. cit., p. 265. Also see Lyle Shannon, "The Spatial Distribution of Criminal Offenses by States," Journal of Criminal Law, Criminology and Police Science, 45:264–274 (September–October, 1954).

by city size is not continuous. A suggested explanation is that cities of from 10,000 to 100,000 contain many suburban areas where the rate of alcoholism may be high. This irregular progression in rates for alcoholism is in contrast to the continuous increase in the percentage of drinkers as the size of the city increases.[63]

SUICIDE

Suicide rates appear to increase with the size of the community, until cities of 500,000 and over are reached. The suicide rate per 100,000 population during 1927–1933 ranged from 15.9 in cities of 10,000 to 25,000 population to 19.9 in the 250,000 to 500,000 group, with the rates in cities of over half a million population declining slightly.[64] It has been noted that fast-growing cities tend to have a higher suicide rate.[65]

RACIAL DISCRIMINATION

In larger urban communities, where contacts between racial groups become more impersonal and segmental, there is often a decline in discrimination in some areas and an increase in others. Compared with smaller communities there is likely to be less emphasis on patterns of subservience or etiquette and less segregation of facilities such as parks, libraries, and the like, which serve to symbolize status differences. Often the enforced segregation in social contacts of a small community are replaced by "voluntary" segregation or social separation of the races. After examining the correlation of various indices of urbanization with discrimination it was found that while the relative gain from urbanization for nonwhites may be substantial, because of a low starting point, the absolute differences may be maintained so that urbanization does not mean the lessening of all types of discrimination.[66]

On the other hand, urban racial social violence has occurred in every geographic region in the United States, including such cities as Chicago, Detroit, Tulsa, New York, Washington, East St. Louis, and Atlanta. There are four patterns of urban racial violence: [67]

1. Spontaneous brawls over an immediate disturbance, among bystanders.
2. The "mass, uncoordinated battle" occurring when groups of one race

---

[63] American Institute of Public Opinion Survey, December, 1947.

[64] Wirth and Clinard, "Public Safety," loc. cit., p. 271.

[65] Henry Wechsler, "Community Growth, Depressive Disorders, and Suicide," American Journal of Sociology, 67:9–17 (July, 1961).

[66] H. M. Blalock, Jr., "Urbanization and Discrimination in the South," Social Problems, 7:146–152 (Fall, 1959).

[67] See Allen D. Grimshaw, "Urban Racial Violence in the United States: Changing Ecological Considerations," American Journal of Sociology, 66:110 (September, 1960).

attack usually isolated members of the other. Mobs of one race seldom engage mobs of the other race in open battle.

3. The "urban pogrom," which is the full-scale assault of one group, almost always white, upon Negroes, and which has occurred particularly where whites have assumed the tacit approval of local government. These "pogroms" have resulted in the flight of large numbers of the minority community.

4. Stray assaults and stabbings on the part of individuals or small groups of one race upon individuals of the other.

Distribution of Deviant Behavior within a City

According to the most generally accepted theory, the characteristic spatial pattern of cities is a series of concentric circles, with each circle having certain distinctive characteristics moving out from the central business district into increasingly better areas of housing.[68] The ecological pattern of the city in terms of concentric zones leading out from the first circle are Zone I, the central business district; Zone II, an area known variously by a number of names such as the slums, zone in transition, or interstitial area; Zone III, an area of two- and three-family flats or dwellings; Zone IV, an area of single-family dwellings; and Zone V, the suburban or commutation area. These circles can be thought of as undergoing constant movement in the form of expansion outward, much like the movement taking place on the surface of water when a pebble is dropped into it. The central business district is constantly expanding into the slum much as many persons living in each successive zone may eventually move outward to another area.

Although this theory implies equal expansion in all directions, few cities ever completely approximate a series of concentric circles. Rivers, mountains—or a lake, as in the case of Chicago—interfere with this natural growth. Even so, there are some cities, such as Rochester, New York, which closely resemble this pattern.[69] This abstraction of concentric circles is no different from the law of falling bodies wherein the principle of an equal rate of fall between an iron ball and a feather is valid only if both are in a vacuum.

---

[68] Ernest W. Burgess, "The Growth of the City," in Robert E. Park and Ernest W. Burgess, *The City* (Chicago: The University of Chicago Press, 1925). Later theory based on city growth is that cities have a pattern of sectors like pieces of a pie. According to this theory, industrial areas follow river valleys, water courses, and railroad lines out from the city and become surrounded by workingmen's housing, with factories tending to locate even along the outer fringe of the city. According to the sector view, the best housing then does not fringe the entire city but only parts of it. The main industrial areas of the future may well be located on the outskirts of cities in new industrial towns and suburbs as is now taking place.—Homer Hoyt, *The Structure and Growth of Residential Neighborhoods in American Cities* (Washington, D.C.: Federal Housing Administration, 1939), pp. 75–77, and his "The Structure of American Cities in the Post-War Era," *American Journal of Sociology*, 48:475–481 (January, 1943).

[69] William Ogburn and Meyer Nimkoff, *Sociology* (Boston: Houghton Mifflin Company, 1946), pp. 414–416.

The slum is an area of particular interest to sociologists. It is an area of high land values but cheap rents. This curious contradiction is the result of such land being held "in pawn," so to speak, on the assumption that the central business district will expand into the area and will bring its business firms, manufacturing establishments, and high-priced rental units such as hotels and apartment hotels. The landowners, who seldom live in the area, do not wish to improve slum housing since it will eventually be torn

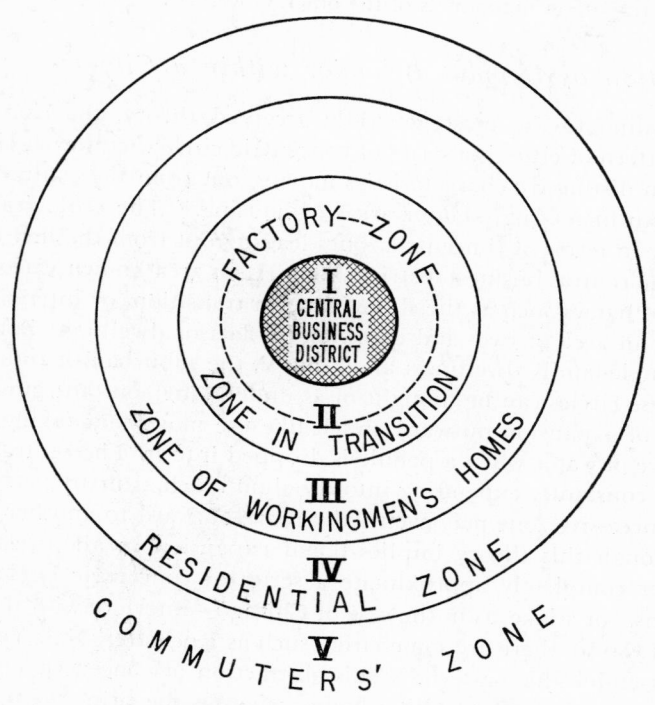

FIGURE 1.—The Growth of a City

SOURCE: Adapted from Burgess, "The Growth of a City," in Park and Burgess, *The City.*

down. This fact and the rather undesirable location make for cheap rentals. Yet the land remains so high-priced that when an occasional apartment hotel is erected in the area, as in the case of Chicago's Gold Coast, it must be of skyscraper proportions to be profitable. Zorbaugh has described the slum of Chicago in this way:

> One alien group after another has claimed this slum area. The Irish, the Germans, the Swedish, the Sicilians have occupied it in turn. Now it is being invaded by a migration of the Negro from the South. It has been known successively as Kilgubbin, Little Hell, and, as industry has come in, as Smoky

Hollow. The remnants of these various successions have left a sediment that at once characterizes and confuses the life of this district. . . .

It is an area in which encroaching business lends a speculative value to the land. But rents are low; for while little business has actually come into the area, it is no longer desirable for residential purposes. It is an area of dilapidated dwellings, many of which the owners, waiting to sell the land for commercial purposes, allow to deteriorate, asking just enough in rent to carry the taxes. . . .

The city, as it grows, creates about its central business district a belt of bleak, barren, soot-begrimed, physically deteriorated neighborhoods. And in these neighborhoods the undesirable, and those of low economic status, are segregated by the unremitting competition of the economic process in which land values, rentals, and wages are fixed.[70]

In each section of the city there are wide variations in age, sex, nationality and racial origins, occupation, social class, homeownership, condition of housing, literacy, and education. Differences in social class are one of the most important characteristics of various areas of a city. The shifting of persons under *ecological* pressures brings about an association of like with like and a tendency for population specialization in certain areas.[71]

The central business district and the "zone in transition" have accentuated urban characteristics. The population of these areas is heterogeneous. The residents are chiefly unskilled workers and their families, and include migrants from rural and other areas, and various nationality and racial groups. People tend to move in and out of the areas with great frequency. For a long period of time prostitutes, vagrants, homeless men, delinquents, and criminals have often been concentrated in these areas. The norms and values of these areas, consequently, do not always agree with those of the more stable areas of the city. The residents of these areas are often more likely than those of other areas to regard delinquency and crime without as much disfavor as other areas of the city and to have different norms about sexual behavior,[72] political honesty, or similar behavior. Considerable differences also exist in other social norms and values of various individuals and groups who live there. Patterns of parent-child relation-

---

[70] Harvey Zorbaugh, *The Gold Coast and the Slum* (Chicago: The University of Chicago Press, 1929), pp. 127–129.

[71] For many years botanists and geologists have been interested in studying the pattern of distribution and movement in space of plant and animal life, which they call plant and animal ecology. Following this, interest grew in human ecology, or the study of the distribution of man and his institutions in space, which includes the study of rural-urban differences as well as differences in city size and within cities. The study of the ecology or distribution of deviant behavior has largely developed in the past forty years.

[72] The sex code of these areas, while often different from that of the middle-class regarding, for example, premarital sex relations, is just as highly organized.—William F. Whyte, "A Slum Sex Code," *American Journal of Sociology*, 49:24–32 (July, 1943).

ships of persons residing there and in Zone III may be considerably different from those in the middle-class areas of Zones IV and V.[73]

This does not mean that the slum is "disorganized," for about some
norms and values there may be considerable agreement among all groups;
moreover, each group may have a high degree of organization of its own.
Whyte, in a study of an Italian slum of a large American city, found that
both formal and informal groups among the Italians generally had a complex and well-established organization.[74] Nationality and racial groups,
however, tend to live in close association with one another even though
there may be considerable social isolation from a different group living
geographically close. This means in general that few close interpersonal
relationships are developed among the diverse groups constituting the
population of these areas.

Zone III has a more stable population, more skilled workers, and fewer
foreign-born or racial groups. Second-generation immigrant groups moving
out of the slum generally move here first. Zones IV and V largely consist of
apartment houses, single-family dwellings, and commuters' houses, which
means that they are chiefly upper-middle and upper class.

Over a century ago a few studies were made of the distribution of
deviant behavior within a city,[75] but most of this type of research began
with the stimulation of sociological studies by Park, Burgess, and their
students of the Chicago community in the 1920's. The spot-mapping of
deviants by place of residence has revealed that, on the whole, certain types
of social deviation tend to be concentrated in specific areas. For example,
conventional crime, delinquency, mental illness in general and schizophrenia in particular, suicide, prostitution, vagrancy, dependency, illegitimacy, infant mortality, as well as associated problems such as high death
and disease rates, have been found to vary with the areas of the city. The
highest rates are in Zones I and II, and become successively lower out
from this area. The evidence on alcoholism and the manic-depressive psychoses does not show quite this pronounced pattern for, although there are
probably higher rates in Zones I and II, the differences are not as marked
from one part of the city to another. White-collar crime, on the other hand,
is greater in Zones IV and V of the city. Gambling and prostitution are
prevalent not only in Zone II but sometimes beyond the suburban fringe
of the city.[76]

---

[73] Arnold W. Green, "The Middle-Class Male Child and Neurosis," *American Sociological Review*, 11:31–41 (February, 1946).

[74] Whyte, *Street Corner Society*.

[75] Yale Levin and Alfred Lindesmith, "English Ecology and Criminology of the
Past Century," *Journal of Criminal Law and Criminology*, 27:801–816 (March–April,
1937), and Alfred Lindesmith and Yale Levin, "The Lombrosian Myth in Criminology,"
American Journal of Sociology, 42:653–679 (March, 1937).

[76] Walter C. Reckless, *Vice in Chicago* (Chicago: The University of Chicago Press,
1933).

Delinquent gangs were found by Thrasher to be largely concentrated in the zone of transition.[77] The spot-mapping of some 60,000 cases of delinquency, truancy, and crime by Shaw and McKay showed a close correlation among the rates of all three groups, with wide variation in their distribution among the local communities of the city.[78] The slum area near the centers of commerce and industry had the highest rates, whereas those in outlying residential communities of higher economic status were uniformly low. In a later study of some 25,000 juvenile court delinquents, distributed over thirty-three years, Shaw and McKay reported additional evidence of the consistency of high rates of delinquency in Zone II.[79]

Findings similar to those in Chicago have been reported for eight other large metropolitan cities and eleven other cities, all widely separated geographically, including Boston, Philadelphia, Cleveland, Richmond, Birmingham, Omaha, and Seattle.[80] Higher rates of delinquency were found in the inner zones and lower rates in the outer zones, and in all nineteen cities, except for Boston, Birmingham, and Omaha, the rates also declined regularly from innermost to outermost zones. Even in these cities where rates in the outermost zones were somewhat higher than in the intermediate, as in Boston, the explanation may possibly be the fact that the industrial areas are near the periphery as well as the differences in the policies of the courts in the various areas. A study of Croydon, a large English city near London, revealed that the highest rates for delinquency were concentrated in areas of the city populated by unskilled and semiskilled workers' families.[81]

The correlation of delinquency rates with economic factors should not be interpreted as indicating any direct relation to poverty or bad housing, as Shaw and McKay have indicated. They point out that in rural areas there may be poverty but little delinquency. Poverty, moreover, does not produce a tradition of delinquency because of a lack of money in itself; rather, it may interfere with the realization of status or prestige. The explanation of delinquency, they believe, is to be found in the general social situations in delinquency areas.

The rate of arrests of adults per 10,000 population seventeen years of age and over was more than ten times as great in the central areas of Chi-

---

[77] Frederic M. Thrasher, *The Gang* (Chicago: The University of Chicago Press, 1927).

[78] Clifford R. Shaw and Henry D. McKay, *Delinquent Areas* (Chicago: The University of Chicago Press, 1929). Jonassen has criticized the limitations of data, the methodology, and the internal consistencies of the data.—Christen T. Jonassen, "A Re-evaluation and Critique of the Logic and Some Methods of Shaw and McKay," *American Sociological Review*, 14:608–614 (October, 1949).

[79] Clifford R. Shaw, Henry D. McKay, *et al.*, *Juvenile Delinquency and Urban Areas* (Chicago: The University of Chicago Press, 1942).

[80] *Ibid.* Automobile theft may often be somewhat of an exception to the generalization that delinquency tends to be concentrated in areas such as these.

[81] Terence Morris, *The Criminal Area: A Study in Social Ecology* (London: Routledge and Kegan Paul Ltd., 1958).

cago as in the outlying areas of the city.[82] The rates for nearly all 29 types of crimes known to the police in Seattle, and arrests for these crimes during the period 1949–1951 showed a decline as one moved out in six one-mile concentric zones from the highest land value in the central business district.[83] There was a tendency for 23 out of the 29 types of crime known to the police to decrease more or less in direct proportion from the center of the city, in particular shoplifting, theft, arson, rape, sodomy, and burglary. Bicycle theft was the only crime known to the police which had a higher rate in Zone VI (149.5) than in Zone I (65.3). The differentials between inner and outer zones were relatively small for Peeping Toms, obscene telephone calls, indecent liberties, and carnal knowledge. Not a single category in the arrest series showed a higher rate in the peripheral zones. Arrest rates for fraud, rape, prostitution, lewdness, robbery, gambling, and common drunkenness showed the greatest difference, while auto theft and indecent exposure showed the least.

White-collar crime, as one might expect, follows a reverse pattern, with concentration in Zones IV and V of the city. In a study of wartime black-market offenders in the wholesale meat industry in Detroit, Hartung found that more than 80 percent of them lived in the most desirable areas of the city. (See Table 3.10.) Of the ten who lived in the least desirable areas (4 and 5), three lived in good downtown hotels.

Table 3.10. Distribution of Meat Black-Market Offenders
According to Desirability of Residence

Residentially de-sirable quintile	Number of personal defendants	Percentage of total
1	62	48.4
2	41	32.0
3	15	11.7
4	4	3.1
5	6	4.7

SOURCE: Frank E. Hartung, "A Study in Law and Social Differentiation: As Exemplified in Violations of the Emergency Price Control Act of 1942 and the Second War Powers Act, in the Detroit Meat Industry." Unpublished doctoral dissertation, University of Michigan, Ann Arbor, 1949, p. 221. Index of residence desirability constructed by Detroit Bureau of Governmental Research on the basis of twenty criteria.

[82] Ernest R. Mowrer, *Disorganization, Personal and Social* (Philadelphia: J. B. Lippincott Company, 1942), p. 143.

[83] Calvin F. Schmid, "Urban Crime Areas: Part II," *American Sociological Review;* 25:655–678 (October, 1960). There also appears to be a remarkable constancy and uniformity in the spatial patterning of crime by gradients. A comparison of two series of offenses known to the police in Seattle, 1939–41 and 1949–51, shows a close correspondence with high correlations for burglary and robbery.—*Ibid.,* p. 669.

MENTAL DISORDERS

Over fifty years ago British writers raised the question as to why, if there was a specific diathesis (condition in the body) governing insanity, there should be such vast differences in its geographical distribution.[84] Recent ecological research in urban areas has similarly raised some important questions concerning the connection between social relationships in local urban communities and mental disorders. Such ecological research on the distribution of mental illness dates from the 1939 study of Faris and Dunham in Chicago and Providence, in which the residences of 34,864 cases admitted to state and private mental hospitals during a thirteen-year period were spot-mapped.[85] Subsequent research in seven other cities has largely substantiated their findings.

At the present time the evidence derived from these studies indicates that mental illness within a city increases, in general, with the degree of urbanization of the area.[86] There are three major conclusions. (1) All types of mental disorders show a marked concentration in Zones I and II, and the rates successively decline in all directions as one goes out from the center of the city. Faris and Dunham have reported that the highest average annual rate per 100,000 population in Chicago was 499, occurring in the central business district, which includes the hotel and homeless-men area. The next highest rate of 480 was found in other vagrant and rooming-house areas. Lowest in the incidence of mental disorder was the outlying residential district, with a rate of 48, or only one tenth that of the highest areas. (2) The rates of schizophrenia follow the same pattern of distribution as for all psychoses. The highest rates are found in the rooming-house areas, where impersonality and social isolation are most pronounced. In the Chicago study the differences between the rates for schizophrenia in the rooming-house areas and those in the better residential area ranged from fivefold to ninefold. (3) As opposed to the pattern of schizophrenia, the manic-depressive rates show a much wider distribution within the city and do not follow the concentric pattern closely.

Interpretations of the significance of these distributions, particularly with reference to the difference in the distribution of schizophrenia and manic-depressive psychoses, have suggested the hypothesis that the former is a product of residence in areas of extensive social isolation, whereas the latter is related to too intense social contacts in a society. Evidence of this

---

[84] W. R. MacDermott, "The Topographical Distribution of Insanity," *British Medical Journal*, September 26, 1908, p. 95.

[85] Robert E. L. Faris and H. Warren Dunham, *Mental Disorders in Urban Areas* (Chicago: The University of Chicago Press, 1939).

[86] H. Warren Dunham, "Current Status of Ecological Research in Mental Disorders," *Social Forces*, 25:321–327 (March, 1947).

relationship to schizophrenia is suggested by the fact that persons—Negroes are an example—residing in areas not primarily populated by those with similar ethnic or racial backgrounds, show a higher incidence of such a disorder than those who live in areas in which they are more integrated. The variations in rates among the Negroes of Chicago, according to the type of area in which they lived, were greater than the differences, however, between all Negroes and all whites.

Explanation of Distributions of Deviant Behavior within Cities

Some have suggested that the explanation of variations in deviant behavior within cities is differential reporting in various areas to authorities. Actually, however, the official rate differences between various areas of a city are so marked, often being, two, five, and even ten times as great, that even if reporting errors were overcome the rates probably would be little changed. As Schmid has written after studying the spatial distribution of crime in Seattle, "In spite of crime statistics and distortion in the derivation of rates resulting from differentials in population mobility and composition, there is still a very considerable portion of the high incidence of crime in the central segment of the city that must be explained on grounds other than these circumstances." [87]

There have been various explanations of these variations in the distribution of deviant behavior within a city. Some authorities explain the variations as the result of the greater number of urban characteristics in the areas closest to the center of the city.[88] Different areas certainly exhibit considerable variations in such factors as ethnic and racial diversity, differential norms, social cohesion, family life, socioeconomic status, physical deterioration of the area, and population mobility.

The differences in social class subcultures in each of the areas may account in large part for the variations in the incidence of deviant behavior. The subculture of lower-class urban areas is characterized by norms conducive to high delinquency, crime, prostitution, drug addiction, and other deviant behavior. Thus Miller explains the high concentration of delinquency and crime in certain areas as a product of lower-class culture which contrasts sharply with middle-class legal values, characterized particularly by values of toughness, "smartness"—mainly to outsmart or dupe someone—and excitement.[89] If this type of explanation is general, it would mean that the different systems of norms, values, and social relation-

[87] Schmid, "Urban Crime Areas: Part II," *American Sociological Review*, 25:675 (October, 1960).

[88] Some have referred rather to the "social disorganization" in each area with much the same meaning.

[89] Walter B. Miller in W. C. Kvaraceus and W. B. Miller, *Delinquent Behavior: Culture and the Individual* (Washington, D.C.: National Education Association, 1959), pp. 8–13.

ships which are associated with the different social classes may directly influence the degree of deviant behavior. Or it could mean that whatever the differences in the values and norms of the different classes, the deviant actions of persons in certain social classes, particularly the lower classes, are more likely to be noticed and to be dealt with officially.

It has also been suggested that certain areas of the city attract rather than produce deviants, and that those who are economically poor, or who are physically or socially deficient, tend to go from rural areas to the more urbanized area of the city.[90] If one considers the "skid row" concentration of alcoholics, criminals, prostitutes, and drug addicts there may be some justification for the view, since the way of life in these areas tends to enhance such concentration. As one writer has stated: "No doubt, the clustering of arrestees charged with drunkenness, vagrancy, prostitution, lewdness, disorderly conduct, and similar crimes in Seattle's Skid Road can be explained in part by the drift hypothesis." [91] This "drift" hypothesis is supported by little evidence as far as other areas of the city are concerned. People may migrate because of differences in economic or educational status or because their friends migrated and told them about a new place to live, but there is little evidence to indicate that persons migrate because they are deviant. For example, there is no indication of selective migration of deviants to Harlem in New York City, which has a high delinquency and crime rate. Furthermore, there are indications that deviant behavior is as common among those who were reared, for example, within certain areas of a city as among those who were migrants to them. Faris has this to say about the theory that persons with mental illness in a large city have migrated there:

> It has been contended that persons who are mentally abnormal tend to fail in their economic activities and as a consequence drift into the slum areas, from which they are eventually committed to a hospital. The concentration of rates, therefore, would represent not the areas in which mental illness develops, but areas to which persons drift after they became abnormal. An unpublished study of the Chicago cases of catatonic schizophrenia, however —a group sharply concentrated in the foreign-born and Negro slum areas— found that most of the patients were born and brought up in the areas from which they were committed and had not drifted into these areas. Rate computations were also made separately for younger (twenty-nine years and less) and older (thirty and over) schizophrenics of both the paranoid and the catatonic types, and of first commitments and recommitments. If drift were important, there should be a sharper concentration of older cases and of recommitted cases, for these would have had more time to fail and to drift to the slums. The findings, however, were that the amount of concentration was

---

[90] See, for example, Donald R. Taft, *Criminology* (New York: The Macmillan Company, 1950).

[91] Schmid, "Urban Crime Areas: Part II," *loc. cit.*, p. 676.

approximately the same, except for some indications of a drift of some of the catatonic schizophrenics from one low-income area to another, that is, from foreign-born slum areas to hobo areas. Their highest rates, nevertheless, were in the foreign-born areas. . . .

Once more it may be pointed out that the contrast between distributions of different mental disorders is inconsistent with the hypothesis that a drift to the slums as a result of economic failure is the principal cause, for there is no reason to assume that the drift would follow such precise patterns.[92]

It seems more likely that the distribution of deviant behavior, with high and low rates in certain areas, has suggested possible factors for such distribution since it furnishes us with leads as to the social factors which may produce given forms of deviant behavior. Consequently, treatment and prevention might be concentrated in certain local areas where the rates are highest in much the same way as public health officers concentrate their work in certain areas of the city. The latter often use spot maps of the city showing typhoid, scarlet fever, poliomyelitis, and similar contagious diseases and, with this information, concentrate on measures like vaccination, quarantine, and control of carriers, the elimination of outside toilets, and the institution of better hygienic practices. A similar approach to deviant behavior would not eliminate the problem but would tend to lower the overall urban rate.[93]

Present-day trends in city growth emphasize suburbanization and decentralization, particularly in the location of plants outside the city. The factors contributing to this growth have been stated by Harris as (1) the greater mobility made possible by automobiles, (2) lower taxes on the periphery, and (3) a greater number of small dwelling units due to the decrease in the size of the family.[94] These general changes in city patterns are bound to influence current theories on the concentration of deviant behavior. Through decentralization, contacts with deviant forms of behavior may become less intensive, and clusters of deviation may come to assume different patterns.

Summary

Urbanism, with its mobility, impersonality, individualism, materialism, norm and role conflicts, and rapid social change, appears to be associated with higher incidence of deviant behavior. Some evidence has been presented here about the comparative incidence of crime, mental illness, alcoholism, and suicide in rural and urban areas, in cities of different size, and within cities.

---

[92] Robert E. L. Faris, *Social Disorganization*, 2d ed., pp. 337, 339. Copyright 1955, The Ronald Press Company.

[93] John B. Martin, "New Attack on Delinquency," *Harper's Magazine* 189:97–109 (July, 1944).

[94] Chauncy D. Harris, "Suburbs," *American Journal of Sociology*, 49:1–13 (July, 1943).

Delinquency and crime rates, as computed from official statistics, are almost universally lower in rural as compared with urban areas. Other forms of deviant behavior also tend, in general, to be statistically more frequent in urban areas. There are also regional and area variations in rates. Although considerable variation in urban characteristics exists from one area of a city to another, further research may possibly indicate that some of the variation may arise from differences in the way of life of social classes residing in each area.

Some persons have attempted to explain these differences in the extent of deviant behavior as being almost entirely due to differences in reporting or opportunity. Others have suggested that the inner zones of the city attract deviants from the other zones or from rural areas, but little evidence exists for either of these contentions. Obviously, these great differences are not due to variations in the biological constitution of individuals. Consequently, the variations among the zones can be thought of as important in suggesting social and cultural explanations for deviant behavior as well as indicating what areas should receive the greatest attention in any effort to reduce it.

Selected Readings

ANDERSON, NELS. *The Urban Community: A World Perspective.* New York: Holt, Rinehart and Winston, Inc., 1959. A view of the impact of urbanism in a world-wide perspective, including a discussion of the characteristics of urbanism, its effect on the family and other groups, and a discussion of social change and conformity under urbanism.

BURGESS, ERNEST W. "The Growth of the City," in Logan Wilson and William Kolb, *Sociological Analysis.* New York: Harcourt, Brace & World, Inc., 1949, pp. 407–414. This is a reprint of the original article, which described the concentric patterns of the city using data from Chicago.

CLINARD, MARSHALL B. "The Process of Urbanization and Criminal Behavior," *American Journal of Sociology,* 48:202–213 (September, 1942). A study of the incidence of the urban characteristics of mobility, impersonality, and contacts with differential norms among farm, village, and city criminal offenders.

CLINARD, MARSHALL B. "Urbanization, Urbanism, and Criminal Behavior," in Ernest W. Burgess and Donald Bogue eds., *Research Contributions to Urbanism.* Chicago: The University of Chicago Press, 1962.

DUNHAM, H. WARREN. "Current Status of Ecological Research in Mental Disorders," *Social Forces,* 25:321–327 (March, 1947). A survey of all ecological studies of mental illness up to that time and an evaluation of the ecological research technique in this area.

MALZBERG, BENJAMIN, and EVERETT S. LEE. *Migration and Mental Disease.* New York: Social Science Research Council, 1956. A study of the extent of migration among all admissions to hospitals for mental disorder in New York during a three-year period. Includes an excellent introduction by Dorothy I. Thomas, summarizing and evaluating other similar research, including ecological studies and other studies of mental illness among migrants and nonmigrants.

MORRIS, TERENCE. *The Criminal Area: A Study in Social Ecology.* London: Routledge & Kegan Paul Ltd., 1957. An ecological study of crime and delinquency in an English city. Has an excellent survey and critique of nearly all studies of the ecology of delinquency both in America and in foreign countries.

RIESMAN, DAVID. *The Lonely Crowd: A Study of Changing American Character.* New Haven, Conn.: Yale University Press, 1950. An important discussion of "tradition-directed," "inner-directed," and "other-directed" personality patterns. He states that the modern urban person is losing his individuality and tends to conform to the dictates of others.

ROSE, ARNOLD. *Theory and Methods in the Social Sciences.* Minneapolis: University of Minnesota Press, 1954, "The Problem of the Mass Society," pp. 25–49. This is a discussion of the relation of social problems to the rise of urban or the "mass society" of today. There are also some suggestions for the solution of some of the difficulties presented by a "mass society."

SCHMID, CALVIN F. "Urban Crime Areas: Parts I and II." *American Sociological Review,* 25:527–542 and 655–678 (August and October, 1960). A detailed ecological study of urban crime areas in Seattle involving 20 crime variables and 18 social, economic, and demographic indices for 93 census tracts. Contains several maps showing distribution of crimes.

SHAW, CLIFFORD, HENRY D. MCKAY, *et al. Juvenile Delinquency and Urban Areas.* Chicago: The University of Chicago Press, 1942. A series of studies of the ecological distribution of juvenile delinquency in twenty large American cities.

SJOBERG, GIDEON. *The Pre-Industrial City.* New York: The Free Press of Glencoe, 1960. A discussion of the historical development of the city and the differences between preindustrial cities of the past as well as those of underdeveloped areas today and the industrial city.

WILENSKY, HAROLD L., and CHARLES N. LEBEAUX. *Industrial Society and Social Welfare.* New York: Russell Sage Foundation, 1958. Contains an excellent statement of the nature of urban-industrial society and its effects, particularly on juvenile delinquency.

WIRTH, LOUIS. "Urbanism as a Way of Life," *American Journal of Sociology,* 44:1–24 (July, 1938). Probably the best statement of the characteristics of the urban way of life.

Chapter

4

Economic and Technological
Factors in Social Deviation

Economic distress has long been considered as the basic cause of society's ills. Economists and others, including some sociologists, have contributed many studies attempting to show that the underlying basic factors in social deviation originate in economic forces. Among the approaches which might be termed economic are those relating social problems to the lag of nonmaterial parts of culture behind technological development, to the depressed phase of the business cycle, to the economic strength of a given area, and to poverty and substandard housing. Many of these writers have recognized the fact that economic factors are extremely important in social life and that most modern societies are built around an essentially economic ideology. They believe that the explanation of deviant behavior lies in the malfunctioning of the technological and economic system, the failure to control the machine age and to provide adequate goods and services for everyone in a society. Thus it has seemed reasonable to them to correlate the incidence of social deviation with various economic indices.

There have been exclusively economic explanations of delinquency and crime, alcoholism, prostitution, mental illness, race prejudice, and other social problems. Implicit in all these studies is the assumption that if "poverty" could be abolished, the business cycle eliminated, technological developments properly controlled, and "adequate" housing provided for everyone, we would then enter a social millennium largely devoid of social deviation.

Poverty and Deviant Behavior

Since the great economic writings of Adam Smith economic explanations of deviant behavior have been advanced by many students of social problems. Such spokesmen of the classical economic theory as Smith, Ricardo, and others discussed the degrading role of poverty. Alfred Marshall, in the introduction to his now historic work in the field of capitalist economic theory (1891), wrote:

And very often the influence exerted on a person's character by the amount of his income is hardly less, if it is less, than that exerted by the way in which it is earned. . . . It is true that in religion, in the family affections and in friendship, even the poor may find scope for many of those faculties which are the source of the highest happiness. But the conditions which surround extreme poverty, especially in densely crowded places, tend to deaden the higher faculties. Those who have been called the Residuum of our large towns have little opportunity for friendship. . . . No doubt their physical, mental, and moral ill-health is partly due to other causes than poverty, but this is the chief cause.

. . . Although then some of the evils which commonly go with poverty are not its necessary consequences; yet, broadly speaking, "the destruction of the poor is their poverty," and the study of the causes of poverty is the study of the causes of the degradation of a large part of mankind.[1]

Writers who mentioned social problems in the nineteenth and early twentieth centuries often stressed the need for socioeconomic surveys, settlement houses, philanthropy, and other economic uplift procedures, as well as socialism or even communism, to deal with the moral decay of society. Writers such as Henry George, Karl Marx, Charles Booth, Jacob Riis, Jane Addams, and William Bonger felt that we should concentrate our efforts on correcting the maldistribution of income and overcoming economic fluctuations, not only because they were bad in themselves but because they produced most of the vices and evils besetting the world.[2]

Marx felt that crime, prostitution, vice, and moral evils were primarily due to the poverty produced by the capitalistic system, with its ownership of the means of production by a few, the general maldistribution of wealth, and an inevitable class struggle. The solution to these problems would eventually come in the establishment, first, of a dictatorship of the proletariat (i.e., world-wide communism), and, later, of a classless society in which each person would contribute according to his ability and receive according to his needs.[3] Many writers of Marx's day were socialists and were thus strongly influenced by the classic statement of Marx. Today, this general position has swelled into a dynamic communistic doctrine carrying an economic explanation of the world's difficulties into the farthest corners of the globe.

Every person who subscribes to the paramount importance of economic factors in societal development is by no means a communist. In fact, ardent believers in capitalism imply another materialistic emphasis by insisting

---

[1] Alfred Marshall, *Principles of Economics* (8th ed.; London: Macmillan & Co., Ltd., 1936), pp. 1–3.

[2] See Charles Booth, *Life and Labour of the People in London* (London: Macmillan & Co., Ltd., 1892).

[3] Karl Marx, *Das Kapital* (S. Moore and E. Aveling, trans.; F. Engels, ed.; Hamburg, Germany: Otto Meisner, 1890). See also Karl Marx and Friedrich Engels, *The Communist Manifesto* (F. Engels, ed.; London: 1848).

that a higher standard of living will lead to the elimination of most social difficulties. The same line of reasoning prompts philanthropists to assume that merely by distributing some of their wealth among the poor they will eliminate much deviant behavior.

Many studies have tried to show that poverty is the basic cause of social deviation. Probably the most widely known of all exponents of the view was William Bonger, a Dutch social economist who used European data to ascribe practically every social problem to poverty.[4] He attempted to develop the thesis that the mental state of criminals is an outgrowth of economic degradation on the one hand and class cleavage on the other. One of his most common devices was to compare fluctuations in the price of grain with fluctuations in the amount of crime. Other later investigations have attempted to show that most delinquents or criminals and other deviants come from the unskilled, poor population.

EVALUATION OF POVERTY AND DEVIANT BEHAVIOR

Without question poverty has serious consequences for health, the cultural quality of family life, and educational opportunity. Above all, it limits social participation, particularly in the political, social, and economic sphere. There are a number of objections, however, to poverty as a basic explanation of deviant behavior: the meaning of the concept of poverty itself is relative; studies of poverty have been derived from biased samples; noneconomic factors are often of primary importance in deviation; and, finally, deviation may be reduced without a great deal of change in economic conditions.

1. The entire emphasis on "poverty," "lower economic group," or "minimum standard of living" can be challenged by questioning the meaning of these expressions. They cannot be regarded as absolute and timeless designations in terms of either money or material goods. If poverty is regarded as a relative term, both from the standpoint of other cultures and in time, it has little utility as a universal explanation of deviant behavior. A poor person in America may have infinitely more material goods than a poor person in India or China; a relatively poor family today may have technological possessions and education superior even to those of the upper classes of the American Revolutionary period. Poverty must be defined in terms of the aspirations and expectations of a culture and its capacity to produce these goods. Thus radio, television, electricity, inside plumbing, central heating, an old car or a washing machine, canned foods, and so on, are material possessions which the poor generally have in this country today but which would have been considered luxuries years ago. In fact, it is of

---

[4] William A. Bonger, *Criminality and Economic Conditions* (Henry P. Horton, trans.; Boston: Little, Brown & Company, 1916).

interest that even though there has been a constant increase in the living standards of Western European countries over the past century, there is no indication that deviant behavior has decreased.

Many studies of the economic background of deviants represent biased samples. Most economic studies, for example, have neglected to indicate that a considerable proportion of our nondeviant population also has a low income and also is poorly housed. A considerable number of American families in recent years have had an income below the minimum standards recommended for health and welfare by the Bureau of Labor Statistics.

It is likely that the proportion of deviants from lower socioeconomic groups would generally be much smaller if the samples were more representative. Probably a greater proportion of deviants among the lower socioeconomic group comes to the attention of authorities, both in detection and in commitment, than the proportion of deviants from the wealthier classes. Delinquents among the higher economic groups, for example, are often dealt with by informal means. Crime of the white-collar type among the upper classes is seldom prosecuted, and few persons of this group are imprisoned for it. After surveying the extent of crime among business and professional men, Sutherland has written:

> The theories of criminologists that crime is due to conditions statistically associated with poverty are invalid because, first, they are derived from samples which are grossly biased with respect to socio-economic status; second, they do not apply to the white collar criminals; and third, they do not even explain the criminality of the lower class, since the factors are not related to a general process characteristic of all criminality.[5]

Alcoholics and mental patients from the upper socioeconomic groups are less likely to be included in many studies of alcoholics who come to the attention of public agencies, for they are often treated privately either by psychiatrists or in private clinics or hospitals. A study of 2023 male patients from the Connecticut outpatient alcoholism clinics which were created in recent years tends to contradict previous impressions of the alcoholic population.[6] According to this study, rather than being "alcoholic bums" and derelicts, "nearly two-thirds of the men were gainfully employed when they first came to the clinic; 56 per cent were known to have held steady employment on one job for at least 3 years; 25 per cent for at least 10 years. At least seven out of ten have held jobs involving special skills or responsibility." Sex deviants such as prostitutes likewise appear to exist among all classes; yet those arrested for sexual promiscuity are more likely to be from the poorer classes.

2. Several investigations have indicated that poverty is by no means

---

[5] Edwin H. Sutherland, "White-Collar Criminality," *American Sociological Review* 5:1–12 (February, 1940).

[6] Robert Straus and Selden D. Bacon, "Alcoholism and Social Stability," *Quarterly Journal of Studies on Alcohol*, 12:231–260 (June, 1951). Quotation from page 259.

the only factor accounting for the deviant behavior. Poverty alone does not explain the hobo and the migratory worker, the shelter-house man, and even the beggar. Anderson has presented several other factors of importance, including personality defects.[7] Certain crises, such as family conflict, feelings of failure, disgrace, or embarrassment, and fear of punishment might cause a man to desert his home or community. In some cases racial or national discrimination has resulted in a man's becoming a tramp (one who won't work) or a hobo (one who works only occasionally). In still other situations the longing for new experiences has led a man to develop wanderlust and join the ranks of the homeless man.

After studying 20,000 occupants of shelter houses, Sutherland and Locke also indicated that economic destitution is not the only factor.[8] Many others besides strictly economic considerations were found to be significant in the development of a homeless man. Most of these men had never been really part of any community. More than half of them had been primarily engaged in transient or seasonal labor during most of their lives. Others had moved, before the depression, from one job to another. Few of them had had close relations with their families even when they were young men. Only one third had ever married, and nearly all of these were either divorced, separated, or widowed. Rarely had any of them been connected with a church, and in general they had few personal friends. Thus the road to dependency generally involved not only such factors as prolonged marginal dependency or a long period of economic deterioration, but marital and sexual problems, excessive drinking, cultural conflicts, detachment from family and personal friends, and personal crises.

On the whole, the helpless, ragged shelter-house man has become so demoralized that he is not generally what would be termed a beggar. The latter capitalizes on the contrast between his appearance and that of others, appeals to pity, and generally exploits his lowered economic status. In fact, it is questionable whether an economic factor such as poverty alone explains the beggar seen on the streets of many cities. In a detailed study of beggars, Gilmore found that begging is generally a highly organized activity with general acceptance of a role of begging rather than working. Professional beggars know what types of begging are most productive, such as exhibiting deformities or "hitting" for a handout young people on dates, and where to beg, as in crowds of persons in the theater district or going to or from church. Careful attention is paid to styles of dirty dress and the use of certain words and signs. Some of this knowledge is transmitted from

---

[7] Nels Anderson, *The Hobo* (Chicago: The University of Chicago Press, 1923; reissued by Phoenix, 1961); pp. 72–86.

[8] Edwin H. Sutherland and Harvey J. Locke, *Twenty Thousand Homeless Men* (Philadelphia: J. B. Lippincott Company, 1936). Also see H. Warren Dunham, *Homeless Men and Their Habitats: A Research Planning Report* (Detroit: Department of Sociology and Anthropology, Wayne University, 1953).

generation to generation in begging families; where begging is organized in teams, as in the following case, it distinguishes the professional from the amateur:

> An organization of beggars formerly had their headquarters in the rear of a saloon run by Joe Thomas on a side street just off the central business section. In this back room the beggars kept a supply of old clothes, crutches, false legs, collodion to put in the eyes to make "blind men," acid to make "jiggers" on the arms, and other articles needed in their make-up. They would come here in the morning dressed in their regular street clothes and would change to their "begging" togs. At the end of the day, they would return to head-quarters and change back to their street clothes. There were usually about 70 members of this gang, including ten or twelve women. They were in charge of a precinct captain for an alderman who was a political friend of a state senator. For protection each paid $1.50 to $4.00 per day depending on his "stand." This protection consisted of security from police interference and assurance that other beggars would not be allowed in the loop area.[9]

In the cities of India a common feature in many bazaar areas, as well as in the central shopping areas, temples, and railway stations, is the inevitable beggar who makes his rounds daily. Although a certain type of mendicancy, such as religious begging, has long been common in India, professional begging has become an urban phenomenon for the simple reason that it is a lucrative "trade." [10] One survey reported that in the city of Bombay alone there are about 10,000 beggars, some 47 percent of whom are able-bodied. The total beggar population of Delhi has been estimated at about 3000, 44.5 percent of whom are able-bodied. Many beggars "earn" more than the daily wage of nonbeggars.

3. There are indications, moreover, that the social integration of an area can be improved without major material changes. For example, the Chicago Area Projects, where neighborhood councils in the slums have dealt with problems of delinquency, appear to have made a reduction in these rates without changing either economic or housing conditions.[11] Treatment in general and group methods in the treatment, in particular, of mental disorder, crime, and alcoholism, for example, through Alcoholics

---

[9] Harlan W. Gilmore, *The Beggar* (Chapel Hill: University of North Carolina Press, 1940), p. 117.

[10] M. V. Moorthy ed., *Beggar Problem in Greater Bombay* (A Research Study; Bombay: Indian Conference of Social Work, 1959), p. 14, and *The Beggar Problem in Metropolitan Delhi* (Delhi: Delhi School of Social Work, 1959).

[11] H. L. Witmer and E. Tufts, *The Effectiveness of Delinquency Prevention Programs*, Children's Bureau, United States Department of Health, Education, and Welfare, Publication 350 (Washington, D.C.: Government Printing Office, 1954), p. 15. Also see Solomon Kobrin, "The Chicago Area Project: A 25 Year Assessment," *The Annals*, 322:19–29 (March, 1959), and Anthony Sorrentino, "The Chicago Area Project After 25 Years," *Federal Probation*, 23:40–45 (June, 1959).

Anonymous, do not necessarily require marked changes in the economic status of the individual.[12]

Fluctuations in the Business Cycle and Deviation

Modern society has been characterized by recurrent fluctuations in economic conditions, fluctuations commonly referred to as prosperity, recessions, and depressions. During periods of recession or depression there is an increase in unemployment and poverty, along with a general decline in morale. It is believed by some people that these conditions are associated with increased juvenile delinquency, crime, prostitution, mental disorder, marital maladjustment, suicide, and racial tensions. On the other hand, many believe that prosperity is accompanied by "high" living and increased alcohol consumption. In the scientific study of these relationships, different rates of deviant behavior have been compared with various economic indices, generally utilizing measures of statistical correlation.

From the evidence available it can be concluded that the business cycle has little or no direct relation to most forms of social deviation with the exception of suicide. The processes of urbanism and norm conflicts must be regarded as the more basic factors in producing social deviation. Whereas deficiencies in given economic processes may intensify urbanism, they certainly are not the prime causes of our contemporary difficulties. It is likely that a balanced economic system would still have most of our contemporary problems since most of them involve conflicts in norms and difficulties in interpersonal relations rather than technological or strictly economic issues.

Technological Development and the Cultural Lag

The machine age and all of its complexity have been blamed by a number of scientists, including sociologists, for the confusion and deviation of the world in which we live. Their ideas have been reflected in the beliefs of many laymen that if we could only master the machine we would be able to build a world free of crime and other social problems. This theory, with different solutions proposed for the problems, has wide acceptance both in the West and in the communist countries. The idea has been illustrated in countless cartoons, such as those showing a complex machine and a socially incompetent modern "caveman."

In fact, no explanation of social deviation has enjoyed a popularity equal to that of the scientific theory based upon the "cultural lag," a con-

---

[12] Marshall B. Clinard, "The Group Approach to Social Reintegration," *American Sociological Review*, 14:257–262 (April, 1949).

cept first suggested by Ogburn in 1922.[13] All social problems, according to him, resulted basically from social change, which creates maladjustments among various parts of a culture. Today, the term is part of everyday speech, and many editorials and cartoons dwell on the theme. A survey of the literature of social science indicates that practically every conceivable problem at one time or another has been considered to be a cultural lag. "At the basis of all social problems are culture lags. . . . The maladjustments create confusion and inject uncertainties in the relations of individual to individual, individual to group, and group to group." [14] A text on social problems stated that the cultural lag concept is as basic to sociology as the theory of gravitation is to physics:

> Although mankind has become adapted to the new tempo of living and has accepted and exploited scientific and technological achievements, it has failed to adjust the social structure—economic, political, and social ideas and institutions—to the new pattern of material culture. Indeed, men are trying to manage the new world of machines with the ideas and institutions of horse-and-buggy days and, in some cases, of the Stone Age. This failure to modernize social ideas and institutions has produced the serious "cultural lag" that confronts our society and causes most of our social problems.[15]

Such unrelated social problems as unemployment and labor conflicts, congestion and insufficient housing construction, inadequate medical care, educational problems, traffic casualties, juvenile delinquency, crime, mental illness, moral conflicts, the costs and destruction of war, and adolescent instability have been attributed to technological maladjustments. Other studies have ascribed the decline of family ethics to a lag behind technological advance. Some would explain increased crime as partly due to the lag in the number of police behind the more rapid growth in population, as well as to the failure of modern mechanical devices for dealing with criminals to keep pace with the growth of crime.[16] One writer has well summarized the impact of this materialistic interpretation of human history:

---

[13] William F. Ogburn, *Social Change* (New York: The Viking Press, Inc., 1922). For further elaboration of his theory, see William F. Ogburn ed., *Recent Social Trends in the United States* (New York: McGraw-Hill Book Company, Inc., 1933); National Resources Committee, *Technological Trends and National Policy* (Washington, D.C.: Government Printing Office, 1937); William F. Ogburn, *The Social Effects of Aviation* (Boston: Houghton Mifflin Company, 1946); and William F. Ogburn and Meyer Nimkoff, *Sociology* (Boston: Houghton Mifflin Company, 1940). An earlier writing by the sociologist Charles Cooley stated the somewhat similar view that social problems grew out of the "formalism" of certain social institutions which became ossified or fixed, while others undergo transformations.—Charles Cooley, *Social Organization: A Study of the Larger Mind* (New York: Charles Scribner's Sons, 1919).

[14] Elio Monachesi, "Sociology and Culture," in Emerson P. Schmidt ed., *Man and Society* (Englewood Cliffs, N.J.: Prentice-Hall, Inc., 1938), p. 46.

[15] Harry Elmer Barnes and Oreen M. Ruedi, *The American Way of Life* (2d ed.; Englewood Cliffs, N.J.: Prentice-Hall, Inc., 1950), pp. 2–3.

[16] Ogburn and Nimkoff, *op. cit.*, pp. 886–887.

Anyone who fondly retains his foreign language, who doesn't believe in divorce, who bakes his own bread, or who is slow to accept the technological improvements of his business competitor, these are all "in lag." Circumstances such as the congested condition of the streets, the regular delay in the appearance of subject matter in secondary texts after its general acceptance, and scores of other cases, are also "evidence of lag" and have been uncritically classified under that omnibus rubric.[17]

According to the cultural lag thesis, various parts of modern culture are not changing at the same rate. Some parts, the technological, are changing more rapidly than the nontechnological aspects of society, such as the family, religion, and the political system. Since there are a correlation and an interdependence of parts among all social institutions, a rapid change in one part of a culture requires readjustments through changes in the various other correlated parts. Technological changes eventually cause alterations in other parts of the culture, but corresponding changes in the nonmaterial culture do not occur simultaneously with the changes in the material sphere.[18] This differential time sequence results in the cultural lag.

The nonmaterial aspects of culture change much more slowly than the material for several reasons: (1) there is more emotional opposition to change in the former; (2) improvements resulting from changes in the material culture are more readily received since they are more observable; (3) a materialistic emphasis is itself a supreme value in our society; and (4) habit, vested interests, and ignorance all combine to favor the maintenance of the *status quo* in the nonmaterial sphere. "Social problems arise, and existing problems are aggravated, when a society creates or accepts instruments of change, yet fails to understand, anticipate, or deal with the consequences of such action." [19]

Most so-called "lags" are thought to indicate that certain technological revolutions have far outsped economic and other social changes, thus creating maladjustments. Not only are adherents of this approach certain that a lag can be shown to exist in social areas but also that the extent of the lag and the severity of the maladjustment can be measured. With the present-day emphasis on machines and the rapidity with which these ma-

---

[17] John H. Mueller, "Present Status of the Cultural Lag Hypothesis," *American Sociological Review*, 3:320 (June, 1938).

[18] Ogburn, as well as others, in more recent writings has tried to place less stress on technological changes and has implied that lags could take place between any two parts of the culture even if both were adaptive: "The strain that exists between two correlated parts of culture that change at unequal rates of speed may be interpreted as a lag in the part that is changing at the slowest rate, for the one lags behind the other." In another connection Ogburn has written that "the lag of social changes behind technological progress is simply a special case of the general phenomenon of unequal rates of change of the correlated parts of culture."—Ogburn and Nimkoff, *op. cit.*, pp. 886, 893.

[19] Abbott Herman, *An Approach to Social Problems* (Boston: Ginn and Company, 1949), p. 51.

terial aspects are changing, the lag between the technological and the adaptive culture has become increasingly great. Steam power replaced hand power; electrical power and electronics, together with the gasoline engine, have made great inroads into the use of steam power; and now nuclear fission has become a source of power.

AN EVALUATION OF THE CULTURAL LAG THEORY
OF DEVIANT BEHAVIOR

Regardless of whether cultural lag is restricted to the material-nonmaterial definition or is described as a lack of synchronization in social institutions in the general culture, those who hold this theory believe that social problems can be explained by cultural lags, that they have been constantly increasing rather than decreasing, and that the most important factors are technological and economic. The proposed solution to the problem of cultural lag obviously lies in social planning in order to restore balance within the culture. Such planning would include a study of past changes in the material culture and a prediction of future changes and of the resistances in a society which prevent adjustment to technological change.

The cultural lag explanation impresses many students of social problems, for it focuses attention on culture as a unified whole and stresses the interdependence of institutions in a society. In fact, properly employed, the cultural lag concept is extremely useful as a theoretical instrument to explain some disunities in a culture that are primarily economic. The cultural lag hypothesis may even have some predictive value, primarily in economic areas. For example, Ogburn has demonstrated how future consequences of technological devices can be predicted, making it possible for society to avoid many of the dislocations of the past.[20]

Despite the wide following that the cultural lag theory has had among social scientists interested in problems of deviant behavior, however, there are a number of serious objections to it. These include the fact that norms and values, other than technological and materialistic ones, are often involved in deviant behavior; moreover, consideration of the individual is omitted, and the term "cultural lag" is loosely used.

1. The problems of modern society involve, fundamentally, conflicts of norms and values which are many and of diverse origins. The cultural lag theory, even though there have been recent attempts at modification, is essentially an overstatement of the role that technological and economic

---

[20] Ogburn, *The Social Effects of Aviation.* See also "National Policy and Technology," in *Technological Trends and National Policy,* Pt. I, sec. 1; and William F. Ogburn ed., *Technology and International Relations* (Chicago: The University of Chicago Press, 1949). Also see Charles R. Walker ed., *Modern Technology and Civilization* (New York: McGraw-Hill Book Company, Inc., 1962).

forces play in conflicts in a society. It assumes that the norm conflicts disturbing a society are largely derived from these sources. Undoubtedly some social change does originate in technological factors, but much social change has been brought about by ideas not connected with material culture. They include Christianity and other great religious doctrines, the growth of secularism, democracy, the humanistic philosophy, communism, individualism, equal rights for women, and the English concept of justice in law. Questions involving the use of alcoholic beverages and conflicts stemming from racial and religious discrimination disturb modern societies a great deal, but only by the widest stretch of the imagination can they be brought within the lag concept. Actually most social change is a product of inextricably connected forces, both material and nonmaterial. Wallis puts it thus: "It seems to us unwarranted and also historically inaccurate to say that society must always hop when technology swings the rope." [21]

2. Attitudes, motivations, and social roles of the individual person are of little consequence because impersonal forces far more basic are said to be in operation. The cultural lag theory falsely implies that the person is an automaton, controlled almost entirely by impersonal forces, largely technological and economic.

3. "Cultural lag" is used so loosely that it often has little meaning. Instead of a single concept to be applied indiscriminately to all types of change, Mueller, for example, has suggested two types of lags: those that are really delayed responses and those that are spurious, that is, are actually not lags at all.[22] Most of the applications of the social lag concept turn out on close analysis to be spurious lags. Examples of true lags are seen in the workmen's compensation laws, which followed considerably behind the development of machine technology, and the development of other measures to deal with unemployment arising from new inventions. In cases of this type the relation between the variables, between one cultural element and another, can be established. Many supposed lags are not lags at all because the variables assumed to be closely related are actually not. It would be impossible to relate, for example, divorce rates as measures of marital difficulties and industrial production or other similar economic indices unless one had a rather unusual concept of what basically were the causes of such marital maladjustment.

Actually, the existence of a lag and its direction rest inevitably on a question of values. What is a lag to one scientist may not be to another.[23] A large percentage of women working in industry may suggest that the family system is lagging behind the industrial system and that later adjust-

---

[21] Wilson D. Wallis, in Letters to the Editor, *American Journal of Sociology,* 43:807 (March, 1938).

[22] Mueller, "Present Status of the Cultural Lag Hypothesis," *loc. cit.,* p. 320.

[23] *Ibid.*

ments will take women out of the economic system and back into the home. On the other hand, the same facts might as plausibly suggest that more industrial work should be provided for women because of equalitarian treatment of women, because of the decline of various functions of the family, and because some psychiatrists might believe it good mental hygiene to provide useful tasks for women who have little to do in modern urban society. Similarly, how can we be assured, as some have suggested, that contemporary marriage ethics and sexual morals are lagging behind industrial development, and if they are, is it known how much they lag? Persons with opposite value systems might reach opposite conclusions. Mumford, too, has pointed out that the idea implies that man must always make an adjustment to the machine, whereas on occasions what may be required is adjustment away from the machine: "In truth, interactions between organisms and their environments take place in both directions, and it is just as correct to regard the machinery of warfare as retarded in relation to the morality of Confucius as to take the opposite position." [24]

Substandard Housing and Deviant Behavior

Probably few people believe that inadequate housing, by itself, is a cause of deviant behavior, but many consider it to be one of the major causes. Considerable evidence has been submitted to indicate that substandard housing plays a major role in deviant behavior.[25] In Detroit fifteen times as many criminals per unit of population came from a blighted area as from a normal residential area. In Cleveland 21 percent of the murders and 26 percent of the vice centers were in a deteriorated housing area representing only 1 percent of the land area and 2.5 percent of the population. A study of Jacksonville, Florida, showed that the cost of police protection in blighted areas was twelve times more per unit of area than in the remainder of the city. An Indianapolis study of census tracts (enumerative areas in a population census) near the center of the city, where the housing had deteriorated, showed that whereas only 10.4 percent of the city population lived there, these people utilized some 30 percent of the city hospital service and made up 24 percent of the cases in the venereal disease clinics and 19 percent of the patients in mental hospitals. Almost 25 percent of the cost to the city of arresting, trying, and imprisoning misdemeanants and 36 percent of the cost of felony cases involved residents of this area. In addition, this district accounted for 16.7 percent of the city's fire cost.[26]

---

[24] Lewis Mumford, *Technics and Civilization* (New York: Harcourt, Brace & World, Inc., 1934), p. 317.

[25] S. E. Sanders and A. J. Rabuck, *New City Patterns* (New York: Reinhold Publishing Corporation, 1946), p. 12.

[26] R. Clyde White, "The Relation of Felonies to Environmental Factors in Indianapolis," *Social Forces*, 10:498–509 (May, 1932).

A study by a federal housing agency indicated that poor housing is an important element in nearly all phases of social deviation, particularly juenvile delinquency. The relation of housing to delinquency was indicated as follows: (1) Physically deteriorated areas in which there is much congestion, together with many pool halls, beer taverns, and houses of ill repute, have larger proportions of delinquency. (2) Because of overcrowding at home, young boys and girls have to share rooms with adults, not always members of their own families, adolescents of different sexes have to share rooms, and there may be three or more individuals sleeping in the same room. (3) Those places in the city characterized by land crowding, inadequate recreation areas, and buildings so crowded that there is inadequate light and ventilation often have more than their share of delinquents. (4) Homes from which come delinquent children are usually found to be substandard from the standpoint of physical conditions and modern facilities.[27]

Research in the fields of racial, ethnic, and religious prejudice has consistently indicated three major effects of segregated housing in deteriorated areas: (1) It represents symbolically in an observable form the subordination of certain peoples to those with more adequate housing. (2) It perpetuates intergroup tensions, prejudice, and stereotypes by largely eliminating the opportunity for personal contacts among members of different groups. When certain minority groups attempt to move into areas populated by a dominant group the resistance of the latter may increase tension and prejudice and even result in vandalism or race riots. (3) It makes for serious health problems, and some claim it directly or indirectly affects other problems of a more social nature, such as juvenile delinquency.

The exceptionally bad housing among Negroes may have an effect on their family system. Because of the Negroes' economic situation, two or more families may occupy the same set of rooms without any semblance of privacy. When the family lives separately, it may take in lodgers, a practice that is more frequent when the household is headed by a woman. These living arrangements may seriously affect family morale and sex patterns. Bad housing "probably explains why so many Negroes congregate on the streets of Negro neighborhoods. So far as the children are concerned, the house becomes a veritable prison for them. There is no way of knowing how many of the conflicts in Negro families are set off by the irritations caused by overcrowding people, who come home after a day of frustration and fatigue, to dingy and unhealthy living quarters." [28]

Conclusions about Housing and Deviant Behavior. A more careful

---

[27] Federal Emergency Administration of Public Works Housing Division, "The Relation between Housing and Delinquency" (Research Bulletin 11; Washington, D.C.: Government Printing Office, 1936), p. 40.

[28] E. Franklin Frazier, *The Negro in the United States* (rev. ed.; New York: The Macmillan Company, 1957), p. 636.

analysis of the high deviation rates of the slums does not indicate that either low economic status or bad housing is the explanation. Rather, low economic status or racial prejudice forces persons to reside in low-rent areas which are characterized by the presence of accentuated urban characteristics and norm conflicts. Although it is true that sociological studies of the ecological distribution of delinquency and of mental illness within cities have indicated that such deviation and poor housing are correlated, this fact in itself is not the important variable. Rather, the explanation of the deviation appears to be a product primarily of the social conditions and the extensive urbanism of the area. One comprehensive report on housing lists as a popular fallacy "that substandard housing is the direct cause of delinquency and crime and that its elimination would result in a crimeless world." [29]

Part of the difficulty in attempting to show such relationships has been the research techniques employed. Such studies are based merely on large statistical comparisons, disregarding for the most part individual case studies where the meaning of the economic factors could be better understood. Summarizing available evidence and suggestions, Chapin has concluded that adequate housing can neither produce new and desirable personality traits nor cure mental disorders. [30]

What sometimes appears to be significant is often a crude relationship at best. Some studies have attempted to prove that when housing is improved, general social conditions, including the incidence of delinquency, also improve. It has been claimed, for example, that the juvenile delinquency rates in one particular housing development dropped from 3.18 per 100 children to 1.64 [31] as a result of changes in housing facilities. A study of 171 relocated families in Minneapolis revealed that families which moved to less crowded quarters gained in five out of eight indices of social conditions. [32] As compared with the children of a control group, there was a decline in juvenile delinquency among the children of a group of Negro families in Newark who were rehoused during World War II. [33] There is some question, however, as to whether in such situations housing accounted for the decline or whether it was due to changes in social conditions. A New York study compared the housing facilities of 277 delinquency cases from 196 city blocks in East Harlem with the homes of more than 31,000

---

[29] Quoted in Edith Elmer Wood, *Introduction to Housing: Facts and Principles* (Washington, D.C.: U.S. Housing Authority, Federal Works Administration, 1939), p. 55.

[30] F. Stuart Chapin, "Some Housing Factors Related to Mental Hygiene," in "Social Policy and Social Research in Housing," *Journal of Social Issues*, Nos. 1 and 2 (1951).

[31] Naomi Barer, "Delinquency before, after Admission to New Haven Housing Development," *Journal of Housing* 3:27 (December, 1945–January, 1946).

[32] F. Stuart Chapin, "The Effects of Slum Clearance and Rehousing on Family and Community Relationships in Minneapolis," *American Journal of Sociology*, 43:744 (March, 1938).

[33] Housing Authority of the City of Newark, *The Social Effects of Housing* (Newark, N.J.: 1944).

nondelinquent children of the same age in the area.[34] The study found no relationship between the physical aspects of bad housing and juvenile delinquency as revealed by court records, although the social relationships connected with housing were found to be important. Finally, it has not always been demonstrated that the families which moved into a housing project had previously lived in the area. After studying an English city Morris concluded that physical characteristics of an area are of little relevance to crime and delinquency, except as an indirect determinant of the social status of the area. Even after the construction of new government housing projects the high rates of delinquency remained.[35]

Summary

In the light of all this evidence it appears that it is not poverty, the amount of income, or economic factors generally which are crucial for understanding the dynamics of social and personal deviation. The relation of economic factors to deviant attitudes, social roles, and life organization must be demonstrated before much reliance can be placed on explanations based on economic factors. Although no one would imply that economic factors are not significant, they must have a demonstrated meaningful relationship to human behavior if they are to be considered as basic.

What is important is the urbanized setting in which economic factors function, and the interpretation given by the person and the group to the economic situation in which they find themselves. Poverty and deprivation, prosperity and depressions are important only in terms of the aspirations, needs, socially defined status, and cultural conditionings of the person. A sudden improvement in earning power may have as much of a disorganizing influence on a person as a decrease, but a different kind of deviant behavior will result.

Countries with much material welfare, such as the United States, have some of the highest deviation rates in the world, and these rates are extremely high during times of great economic prosperity. Comparisons of rural and urban deviation rates in most societies, including America, indicate much lower rural rates even though tenant farmers and farm laborers often may be generally poorer and live under housing conditions almost as unsatisfactory as those in large urban centers.

There is some indication that juvenile delinquency, rather than being a product of poverty, may, if anything, be related to "the affluent society." Certainly there is some evidence for this in the increasing delinquency of Western society and, in particular, in such countries as the United States

---

[34] Wood, op. cit., p. 56.
[35] Terence Morris, The Criminal Area: A Study in Social Ecology (London: Routledge & Kegan Paul Ltd., 1957).

and Sweden. Writing of the relation of juvenile delinquency to American prosperity of recent years, Galbraith has stated:

> Thus an aspect of increasing private production is the appearance of an extraordinary number of things which lay claim to the interest of the young. Motion pictures, television, automobiles, and the vast opportunities which go with the mobility, together with such less enchanting merchandise as narcotics, comic books, and pornographia, are all included in an advancing gross national product. The child of a less opulent as well as a technologically more primitive age had far fewer such diversions.[36]

Speaking of communities where private consumer goods are far more developed than public services, such as the school, Galbraith says:

> Here, in an atmosphere of private opulence and public squalor, the private goods have full sway. Schools do not compete with television and the movies. The dubious heroes of the latter, not Miss Jones, become the idols of the young. The hot rod and the wild ride take the place of more sedentary sports for which there are inadequate facilities or provision. Comic books, alcohol, narcotics, and switchblade knives are, as noted, part of the increased flow of goods, and there is nothing to dispute their enjoyment. There is an ample supply of private wealth to be appropriated and not much to be feared from the police. An austere community is free from temptation. It can be austere in its public services. Not so a rich one.[37]

Actually the basic process through which social deviation increases appears to lie in the urban way of life which is found today in all communities, regardless of the economic system. Urbanism is present whether a society is capitalist, democratic socialist, communist, or fascist. Forces tending to emphasize urban ways of life are present in all systems, and their influences range from New York City and Chicago to Moscow, Madrid, Stockholm, and the islands of Indonesia. This emphasis on urbanism rather than the economic system as the basic problem for society does not imply that a given economic system may have no relation to the characteristics of urbanism which we have described. All society is an interrelated whole, and each institution, whether it be the economic, religious, or family system, may affect the central ideologies of a society. Consequently, one economic system may accentuate urban ways of life while another may help to minimize them. An economic system which does not protect the individual from depressions, unemployment, and lack of social security in childhood and old age, or which stresses individual materialistic success at the expense of others will accentuate urban characteristics of individualism, materialism, and the role of competition. An economic system which so regulates all phases of the individual's life that he becomes dependent upon, and subservient to, the central political organization will result in great empha-

[36] John Kenneth Galbraith, *The Affluent Society* (Boston: Houghton Mifflin Company, 1958), pp. 256–257. Used by permission of the publishers.
[37] *Ibid.*, pp. 257–258.

sis on impersonality in social relations and upon the importance of technology and the state rather than human welfare. Such an economic system will emphasize not only materialism and striving for individual advantage through special rewards and favors but also self-interest through the growth of the fear and helplessness of the individual in the face of impersonal and bureaucratic forces.

Selected Readings

ANGELL, ROBERT C. *The Family Encounters the Depression.* New York: Charles Scribner's Sons, 1936. The effect of the depression on the family was not primarily one of economic insecurity.

CAVAN, RUTH S., and KATHERINE H. RANCK. *The Family and the Depression.* Chicago: The University of Chicago Press, 1938. A study of the effect of the depression on a group of families.

GALBRAITH, JOHN K. *The Affluent Society.* Boston: Houghton Mifflin Company, 1958. A somewhat different view of the role of economic factors and social problems, namely, that affluence, rather than poverty, is important.

GILMORE, HARLAN W. *The Beggar.* Chapel Hill: University of North Carolina Press, 1940. A study of begging as a highly organized activity and not one primarily arising from economic need.

MORRIS, TERENCE. *The Criminal Area: A Study in Social Ecology.* London: Routledge & Kegan Paul Ltd., 1957. An analysis of crime and delinquency areas in an English city, with one conclusion being that physical deterioration or new housing has, on the whole, little direct relation to crime.

MUELLER, JOHN H. "Present Status of the Cultural Lag Hypothesis," *American Sociological Review,* 3:320–327 (June, 1938). An excellent criticism of the cultural lag theory in which he distinguishes particularly between "spurious" and true lags.

OGBURN, WILLIAM F. *Social Change.* New York: The Viking Press, Inc., 1950. This book is the classic statement of the cultural lag theory. Originally published in 1922, it was reprinted again in 1950 with a supplementary chapter.

STRAUS, ROBERT, and SELDEN D. BACON. "Alcoholism and Social Stability," *Quarterly Journal of Studies on Alcohol,* 12:231–260 (June, 1951). This study of 2023 male alcoholics who visited outpatient clinics for treatment, indicated that many alcoholics come from the middle class.

SUTHERLAND, EDWIN H. "White-Collar Criminality," *American Sociological Review,* 5:1–12 (February, 1940). In this well-known presidential address to the American Sociological Society, Sutherland stated that crime cannot be explained by poverty, for it occurs among the middle and upper socioeconomic groups as well. Criminological research should be conducted on broader samples of criminal offenders.

WALKER, CHARLES R. ed. *Modern Technology and Civilization.* New York: McGraw-Hill Book Company, Inc., 1962. This book of readings explores the relationship between man and the machine, and assumes that the future of all civilizations is closely linked to the manner in which man may either use or misuse modern technology. It also explores the human problems and promises of the machine age in which man now lives.

Controversial Theories
of Deviant Behavior

Approaching the problem of deviant behavior—either the general problem or specific types of behavior—with a background of particularistic knowledge derived from their own specialties, some scientists have on occasion shown little or no grasp of the principles of human behavior. In this chapter the following theories will be discussed: that deviants are feeble-minded, have certain body types, or can be explained entirely by psychiatric or psychoanalytic principles.

Deviant Behavior and Feeble-Mindedness

In the past, and to some extent today, constitutional inferiority in the form of subnormal intelligence has been frequently advanced as one of the principal causes of certain forms of deviant behavior. Hundreds of studies of intelligence have been made of juveniles and criminals, prostitutes, alcoholics, and hoboes. The assumption has been made that either low intelligence and deviant behavior are directly associated, or that low intelligence is likely to lead a person into patterns of such behavior.[1]

The theory that there is a relationship between intelligence and deviant behavior is now on its way out of accepted literature. The reasons for this are based on actual intelligence scores of deviants, on the fact that certain data are largely derived from biased samples, and on the fact that a direct relationship between intelligence and deviant behavior is simply an assumption.

More careful study of the empirical evidence has not substantiated earlier beliefs about subnormal intelligence. Not only are there wide variations in the intelligence scores of deviants, but in general their scores do not appear to differ too much from those of the general population. Sutherland examined 350 studies of the intelligence of some 175,000 criminals

---

[1] Goddard was one of the earliest writers to advocate this theory. See Henry H. Goddard, *Human Efficiency and Levels of Intelligence* (Princeton, N.J.: Princeton University Press, 1922), pp. 72–73.

and delinquents and found such great variations in the percentage of offenders diagnosed as feeble-minded that any relationship had little meaning. In the period 1910–1914 the feeble-minded so diagnosed averaged 50 percent; between 1925 and 1928 they were 20 percent.[2] He also found that if allowances were made for selective factors in conviction and imprisonment the scores did not differ materially from those of the general population. Zeleny, too, found that a comparison of scores of inmates of correctional institutions with those of the general population showed little difference, the ratio being only 1.2 to 1.0.[3] Another study covering some 10,000 Illinois prisoners found that their intelligence scores differed little from those of the normal population.[4]

Several wartime studies of prostitutes for the United States Public Health Service have failed to confirm the belief that girls from such groups are necessarily feeble-minded.[5] The Kinsey report, as well as other similar studies which have indicated widespread sexual deviation on the part of the general population, would serve to confirm the idea that sexual promiscuity certainly cannot be directly associated with intelligence scores.[6]

Now that more extensive studies have been made of alcoholism and mental disorder in all social groups, the intelligence quotient is no longer considered to be significant in their etiology. One test group of 47 compulsive drinkers had a mean I.Q. of 114.9, which is somewhat above the average, their standard deviation was 14.3 and their range was 73–139 on the Wechsler-Bellevue Adult Intelligence Test. Halpern, who made the study, said: "In general, then, this group of alcoholic subjects showed no characteristic organization of mental abilities which would serve to distinguish them either from normal subjects or from other clinical groups. For this group there was no evidence of mental impairment or deterioration."[7] Bühler subsequently corroborated these findings in her study of 100 alcoholics. They had an average I.Q. score of 103.2, or well within the normal range.[8]

---

[2] Edwin H. Sutherland, "Mental Deficiency and Crime," in Kimball Young ed., *Social Attitudes* (New York: Holt, Rinehart and Winston, Inc., 1931), pp. 357–375.

[3] Leslie D. Zeleny, "Feeble-Mindedness and Criminal Conduct," *American Journal of Sociology*, 38:564–578 (January, 1933).

[4] Simon H. Tulchin, *Intelligence and Crime* (Chicago: The University of Chicago Press, 1939).

[5] H. L. Rachlin, "A Sociological Analysis of 304 Female Patients Admitted to the Midwestern Medical Center, St. Louis, Mo.," *Venereal Disease Information,* U.S. Public Health Service, 25:267 (September, 1944).

[6] Alfred C. Kinsey, Wardell B. Pomeroy, and Clyde E. Martin, *Sexual Behavior in the Human Male* (Philadelphia: W. B. Saunders Company, 1948).

[7] Florence Halpern, "Psychological Test Results," in Jane F. Cushman and Carney Landis, *Studies of Compulsive Drinkers* (New Haven, Conn.: Quarterly Journal of Studies on Alcohol, 1946), p. 83.

[8] Charlotte Bühler and D. Welty Lefever, "A Rorschach Study of the Psychological Characteristics of Alcoholics," *Quarterly Journal of Studies on Alcohol,* 8:197–260 (September, 1947).

EVALUATION OF DEVIANT BEHAVIOR AND FEEBLE-MINDEDNESS

Most of the studies of the intelligence of deviants have been based on institutional populations or detected deviants, and the fact that the studies sometimes indicate that deviants may have a low intelligence may simply mean that the samples are biased. Various investigators agree that there are fewer mental defectives among randomly chosen school children than among the delinquents who get caught, and that institutionalized delinquents have an average I.Q. below that of school children.[9] If professional and white-collar criminals, persons who are seldom detected or go to prison, were added to the sample of persons in penal institutions, the intelligence scores would undoubtedly increase. There may be, however, a relation between intelligence and certain types of offenses, with the habitual petty offender generally having a lower intelligence than the white-collar or professional criminal. If alcoholics from the more educated groups were added to drunks tested in Skid Rows, the I.Q. distribution would be skewed upward.

No one knows the actual components of innate intelligence because the effect of social experience on the latter is such that it appears to be impossible to measure.[10] It is now generally agreed that the so-called intelligence test measures only "test intelligence" and not innate intelligence. Moreover, there is increasing evidence that the I.Q. can be somewhat modified by social experience.[11] On logical grounds, moreover, there is nothing in the nature of subnormal intelligence that implies a relationship with either social attitudes or social roles. The idea that persons with low intelligence are likely to engage in deviant behavior must be regarded simply as an assumption, since one might also argue that low intelligence could lead to rigid compliance with traditional ways of acting and higher intelligence could be associated with deviant behavior when traditional values are violated. Although studies have not been made, the great proportion of persons with low intelligence scores undoubtedly are nondeviants, whereas there are large numbers of persons with above normal intelligence who are.

A feeble-minded boy may associate with a delinquent group and engage in delinquencies much as would a boy of normal intelligence. It is conceivable that where the deviant actions require skill and initiative the feeble-minded person might, however, be excluded. On the other hand,

---

[9] Maud A. Merrill, *Problems of Child Delinquency* (Boston: Houghton Mifflin Company, 1947), p. 162.

[10] See George L. Stoddard, *The Meaning of Intelligence* (New York: The Macmillan Company, 1943).

[11] *Ibid.*

without the acquisition of deviant attitudes and certain social roles the feeble-minded boy might never become a deviant. In terms of human behavior the concept of feeble-mindedness has little significance. After surveying various delinquency studies Merrill has stated: "As measured in terms of I.Q., intelligence has little relation to the choice or persistence of a criminal career. Of young people who break the law, we have more opportunities to observe the behavior of the less intelligent than of the more intelligent." [12] In the total pattern of personality, intelligence may in a given case have some relation to delinquent behavior but the degree of intelligence alone does not account for the delinquency.

Deviant Behavior and Body Type

In the past the writings of Lombroso on crime and Kretschmer on mental illness—and in more recent years of Hooton on crime and of Sheldon on mental illness, crime, and alcoholism—have tried to correlate deviant behavior with certain body types. These studies have aroused great controversy among those interested in deviation and have captured the imagination of many laymen. The public has been quick to accept these ideas, for carried in the folklore of our culture is a common belief in the direct relationship between physiognomy and personality. Crippled hunchbacks appear in literature as stereotypes of evil or as court jesters, fat persons are presumed to be jolly, thin persons are sad and melancholy, and the red-haired are hot-tempered. Commonly cartoons and literature picture the criminal, for example, as of middle age, hard in appearance and often with a malformation in the ear and in general facial structure. The myth of racial superiority and inferiority has served to perpetuate in the popular mind these ideas about differences in the physical appearance of deviants.

Lombroso, in the latter part of the nineteenth century, made studies to show that most criminals were characterized by certain physical characteristics.[13] On the basis of his studies in Germany in the 1920's, Kretschmer believed that he could classify human beings into three rather distinct physical types which were differently associated with certain forms of mental illness.[14] The asthenic type, who had a thin, narrow build, particularly in the shoulders and chest, long thin arms and delicately shaped hands, was associated with schizophrenia, as was the athletic type. The

---

[12] Merrill, *op. cit.*, p. 180.   [13] See Chapter 6.

[14] E. Kretschmer, *Physique and Character* (London: Routledge & Kegan Paul Ltd., 1925). Although Mohr and Gundlach, attempting to test Kretschmer's body types, found some agreement in their study of Illinois prisoners, they found the same distribution of physical traits among the noncriminal population.—George J. Mohr and Ralph H. Gundlach, "The Relation between Physique and Performance," *Journal of Experimental Psychology,* 10:117–157 (February, 1927).

latter, as the name indicates, was a strong, muscular, well-developed physical type with broad shoulders and a thick chest. The pyknic type, on the other hand, was round and fat in appearance and was associated with the manic-depressive psychoses.

Somewhat later, Hooton, a physical anthropologist, made an elaborate study in which he compared several thousand prisoners with a control group.[15] He attempted to revive in many respects the Lombrosian theory—which started the science of criminology—that most criminals are some sort of atavistic, "primitive" men with observable physical features. Hooton reported that criminals are more likely to have long thin necks and sloping shoulders, low and sloping foreheads, thinner beard and body hair, more red-brown hair, thin lips, compressed jaw angles, and a small, extremely protruding ear. He stated, in addition, that certain body types are connected with certain types of crime, tall, thin men tending to murder and rob; tall, heavy men to kill and commit forgery and fraud; undersized men to steal and to commit burglary; and short, heavy persons to assault, rape, and commit other sex crimes.

Von Hentig went even further and suggested, on the basis of a study of Western outlaws, that criminals who committed frontier depredations were primarily red-haired and that red-haired persons are physiologically more active, impulsive, and with "accelerated motor innervation." Hence he concluded "that the number of red-headed men among the noted outlaws surpassed their rate in the normal population." [16] Another writer has presented contrary evidence, indicating that of fifty-eight frontier bad men only two were red-haired.[17]

The general thesis of Lombroso, Kretschmer, and Hooton has been elaborated since 1940 by Sheldon into a much more complex theory. Sheldon is a medically trained psychologist who for several years has been Director of the Constitution Laboratory and Professor of Medicine at Columbia University. His studies have been widely publicized and have come to the attention of millions of persons both here and abroad.[18] His thesis that a human being's behavior and personality are closely related to the structure of his body has been set forth in three volumes.[19] Sheldon has

[15] E. A. Hooton, *Crime and the Man* (Cambridge, Mass.: Harvard University Press, 1939), and *The American Criminal: An Anthropological Study* (Cambridge, Mass.: Harvard University Press, 1939).

[16] Hans von Hentig, "Redhead and Outlaw," *Journal of Criminal Law and Criminology*, 38:6 (May–June, 1947).

[17] Philip J. Rasch, "Red Hair and Outlawing," *Journal of Criminal Law and Criminology*, 38:352–356 (November–December, 1947).

[18] See, for example, Robert Coughlan, "What Manner of Morph Are You?" *Life*, 30:65–66 (June 25, 1951).

[19] William H. Sheldon, S. S. Stevens, and W. B. Tucker, *The Varieties of Human Physique* (New York: Harper & Row, Publishers, 1940); William H. Sheldon and S. S. Stevens, *The Varieties of Temperament* (New York: Harper & Row, Publishers, 1942); and William H. Sheldon, *Varieties of Delinquent Youth* (New York: Harper & Row, Publishers, 1949).

offered, in terms of his system, an explanation of mental illness, crime, delinquency, and, indirectly, homosexuality.

Sheldon has attempted to isolate three poles of physique, through the use of numerous anthropometric measurements and profile photographs delineated as the somatotypes or body types of the endomorph, mesomorph, and ectomorph, which correspond roughly to the pyknic, athletic, and asthenic types of Kretschmer.[20] These types—which may be thought of as the round, soft, and fat type, the muscular and big-boned type, and the thin, small, bony type—are by no means the distinct entities that they were to some of his predecessors. Rather, persons possess all three components, which are indicated by a subjective rating scale of 1 to 7. Thus the endomorph might be a 5–3–1 with 5 parts of endomorph, 3 of mesomorph, and 1 of ectomorph. Sheldon, moreover, goes far beyond either Kretschmer or Hooton in attempting to correlate psychological or temperamental factors with each body type. A body type of endomorphy is correlated with what he calls a psychological temperamental type of viscerotonia, mesomorphy with somatotonia, and ectomorphy with cerebrotonia. The somatotype, psychological characteristics, and the culture interact to produce deviant behavior (see Figure 2).

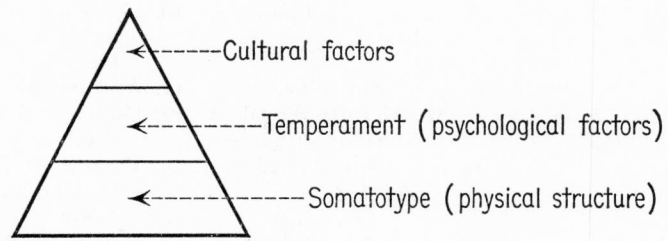

FIGURE 2.—Interaction of Factors That Produce Deviant Behavior

The characteristics of each type of temperament are indicated in the scale in Table 5.1. Round types, for example, tend to like people, muscular types to be aggressive, and thin types to avoid people.

Generally, the mesomorphs with psychological characteristics of somatotonia do not fare well. Sheldon's more recent work has dealt with a study of 200 delinquent boys in the Hayden Goodwill Inn, a Boston social agency. According to his findings, delinquents and criminals are heavy, insensitive, aggressive mesomorphs.[21] In a study of 312 psychotic cases Sheldon found that endomorphy and mesomorphy are correlated with manic-depressive behavior reactions, that mesomorphy was also associated with paranoid reactions, and that ectomorphy was related to certain schizo-

---

[20] He also refers to a T component of thoroughbreddedness or "fine breeding."
[21] Sheldon, *Varieties of Delinquent Youth.*

Table 5.1. The Scale for Temperament

I *Viscerotonia*	II *Somatotonia*	III *Cerebrotonia*
1. Relaxation in Posture and Movement	1. Assertiveness in Posture and Movement	1. Restraint in Posture and Movement, Tightness
2. Love of Physical Comfort	2. Love of Physical Adventure	2. Physiological Overresponse
3. Slow Reaction	3. The Energetic Characteristic	3. Overly Fast Reactions
4. Love of Eating	4. Need and Enjoyment of Exercise	4. Love of Privacy
5. Socialization of Eating	5. Love of Dominating, Lust for Power	5. Mental Overintensity, Hyperintentionality, Apprehensiveness
6. Pleasure in Digestion	6. Love of Risk and Chance	6. Secretiveness of Feeling, Emotional Restraints
7. Love of Polite Ceremony	7. Bold Directness of Manner	7. Self-Conscious Motility of the Eyes and Face
8. Sociophilia	8. Physical Courage for Combat	8. Sociophobia
9. Indiscriminate Amiability	9. Competitive Aggressiveness	9. Inhibited Social Address
10. Greed for Affection and Approval	10. Psychological Callousness	10. Resistance to Habit, and Poor Routinizing
11. Orientation to People	11. Claustrophobia	11. Agoraphobia
12. Evenness of Emotional Flow	12. Ruthlessness, Freedom from Squeamishness	12. Unpredictability of Attitude
13. Tolerance	13. The Unrestrained Voice	13. Vocal Restraint, and General Restraint of Noise
14. Complacency	14. Spartan Indifference to Pain	14. Hypersensitivity to Pain
15. Deep Sleep	15. General Noisiness	15. Poor Sleep Habits, Chronic Fatigue
16. The Untempered Characteristic	16. Overmaturity of Appearance	16. Youthful Intentness of Manner and Appearance
17. Smooth, Easy Communication of Feeling, Extraversion of Viscerotonia	17. Horizontal Mental Cleavage, Extraversion of Somatotonia	17. Vertical Mental Cleavage, Introversion
18. Relaxation and Sociophilia under Alcohol	18. Assertiveness and Aggression under Alcohol	18. Resistance to Alcohol, and to Other Depressant Drugs
19. Need of People When Troubled	19. Need of Action when Troubled	19. Need of Solitude When Troubled
20. Orientation toward Childhood and Family Relationships	20. Orientation toward Goals and Activities of Youth	20. Orientation toward the Later Periods of Life

SOURCE: William H. Sheldon, *Varieties of Delinquent Youth* (New York: Harper & Row, Publishers, 1949), pp. 26–27. Reprinted by permission of the publishers.

phrenic responses.[22] Neurosis was explained by Sheldon as a conflict arising primarily from a person's attempting to be different from what is expected "normally" from his somatotype and temperament.

He has also associated physique with certain degrees of alcoholism. According to Sheldon, alcohol agrees with fat, soft persons and they seldom become addicted to it. Even a moderate quantity of alcohol serves, however, to accentuate the personality traits of persons who are of a hard, athletic body build. In conjunction with other situational components, individuals with such a body type become chronic alcoholics. Finally, those persons who are primarily thin and who have flat chests and a generally weak physical constitution find alcohol unpleasant, for it increases strain and brings on fatigue and dizziness. Consequently, they generally dislike alcohol and avoid its use.

The Gluecks employed the logic of Sheldon and Lombroso in their study of physical types and delinquency in 1956.[23] In their study approximately 60 percent of a group of 500 delinquent boys in a correctional training school were classified mesomorphs, and with traits of temperament and character associated with this body type, as compared with 30 percent of 500 boys in a control group. They thus suggested that "some body types have a greater delinquency potential than do others," implying that a mesomorphic body build may have etiological significance in the commission of delinquent behavior. This study seems to indicate little more than that these boys, most of whom belonged to delinquent groups and who were in correctional institutions, tended to be more muscular than other boys, which is what one might expect and proves nothing more than that about the relation of delinquency and body type. From these figures it is somewhat difficult, however, to explain any actual connection because of the overlap in body types, including mesomorphs, between the two groups.[24]

EVALUATION OF DEVIANT BEHAVIOR AND BODY TYPE

These studies of the relation of physique to deviant behavior have been attacked on numerous grounds:

[22] Phyllis Wittman, William H. Sheldon, and Charles J. Katz, "A Study of the Relationship between Constitutional Variations and Fundamental Psychotic Behavior Reactions," *Journal of Nervous and Mental Diseases,* 108:470–476 (December, 1948).

[23] See Sheldon and Eleanor Glueck, *Physique and Delinquency* (New York: Harper & Row, Publishers, 1956).

[24] See also Eleanor Glueck, "Body Build in the Prediction of Delinquency," *Journal of Criminal Law, Criminology and Police Science,* 48:577–579 (March–April, 1958). For a more recent study of the relation of appearance and criminal behavior, see Raymond J. Corsini, "Appearance and Criminality," *American Journal of Sociology,* 65:49–51 (July, 1959). Corsini found that the most physically attractive sex offenders tended to be those whose crimes had involved having sexual relations with adults (rape), while the least attractive sex offenders tended to be those who had victimized children (pedophilia).

1. They have not actually demonstrated the relation between physique and behavior. Hooton and Sheldon both tried to suggest that criminal types are the result of the selection of organically inferior types by the environment. Inferiority is judged by the presence of deviant behavior. Even if an association were proved statistically between constitutional features and behavior, before the theory could be accepted, there would still be need for an adequate general theory of human nature which would incorporate such findings.[25] The jump from body type to temperament is similarly assumed rather than explained. Even if high statistical correlations were to be found, and they were not, the correlations in themselves would not prove the meaningful association of such variables.

2. Most of the argument involves, in general, jumping from certain anatomical characteristics to deviant behavior. In nearly all such studies cultural factors either are not considered at all or occupy a position subordinate to physical factors. All these three studies deal with undefined, unstable, and relative terms, such as "crime" and "delinquency," which involve value judgments, and attempt to relate them to a more stable factor, such as physique. Although Sheldon considers the family, he leaves out for the most part such factors as the neighborhood and the community.

3. The contention that certain physical characteristics are by their very nature inferior is simply an assumption and nothing more. The physical appearance of the organism is naturally neither "good" nor "bad." It is significant that Hooton and Sheldon reach opposite conclusions as to what is "inferior." According to the former the criminal is an inadequately developed, runty physical type, whereas Sheldon finds the criminal and alcoholic inferior because they are a husky, athletic type.

4. None of these studies have used adequate control groups. Sheldon, for example, used no control group in his study of 200 delinquents, and Hooton compared 4200 native white prisoners with 300 noncriminals—150 Nashville firemen and 150 others, including outpatients of a Boston clinic, militiamen, and patrons of a bathhouse. Neither firemen nor militiamen belong in a control group because they are selected on the basis of a physical examination. Nevertheless, the statistical differences between Hooton's criminal and control groups were insignificant; moreover, comparisons of the Nashville and Boston control groups showed greater differences than those between the criminal and control groups. In Hooton's study the physical differences among these various types of offenders, such as robbers and burglars, were almost infinitesimal and generally statistically insignificant.

5. These studies have been largely conducted on institutionalized populations, or very select groups, such as Sheldon's, which probably do

[25] Edwin H. Sutherland, "A Critique of Sheldon's *Varieties of Delinquent Youth*," *American Sociological Review*, 16:10–13 (February, 1951).

not represent a normal sample of the total population. This is particularly true of persons who are imprisoned, for they are not representative of all criminals.

The Psychiatric Theory of Deviant Behavior

In recent years the theory that deviant conduct is a result of childhood experiences in the family has gained great popularity. This theory is shared by representatives of many academic disciplines and laymen. It is the view of causation which is most frequently displayed in popular magazines, the press, and other mass media of communication, and propounded by most social welfare workers and psychiatrists and many psychologists.

To a great extent this theory owes its ascendancy to the dissemination of psychiatric and psychoanalytic thought over the past several decades.[26] Yet it could be said that both this idea and, indeed, psychiatric thought itself derive from more fundamental values which are rooted in the traditions of our culture. Prominent among these values are the beliefs in the responsibility of parents for the training and preparation of children for adult life, and the relation between early training and adulthood.

Undoubtedly there is much solid common sense in the idea that childhood experiences may influence later behavior—*if* childhood is regarded as the primary arena in which culture is acquired. Robert Merton has suggested that whatever prominence childhood and family experience may be assigned is due to the fact that the family is the principal transmitting agency of culture to the child.[27]

While many would agree with Merton, there are others who imply that *certain childhood experiences have effects which transcend all other social and cultural experiences.* These proponents suggest that certain childhood incidents or family relationships lead to the formation of certain types of personalities which contain within themselves seeds of deviant or conforming behavior, irrespective of culture. Thus childhood is the arena in which personality traits toward or away from deviance are developed, and a person's behavior after the childhood years is fundamentally the acting out of tendencies formed therein. Thus essentially these proponents offer the following formula.

---

[26] Psychiatrists are medical doctors who have had specialized training beyond their M.D. degree in a medical school, generally from other psychiatrists. Psychoanalysts are nearly always medically trained persons who have received special training, usually in a psychoanalytic institute. The differences in psychiatric thinking are great and the discussion here does not deal with those psychiatrists who take a nearly biochemical or organic approach to human behavior.

[27] See Robert K. Merton, "Social Structure and Anomie: Revisions and Extensions," in Ruth N. Anshen, *The Family: Its Function and Destiny* (rev. ed.; New York: Harper & Row, Publishers, 1959), p. 275.

1. All deviant behavior is a product of something in the individual, such as personal disorganization or "maladjusted" personality. Deviants are individuals who are psychologically "sick" persons. Culture is seen not as a determinant of deviant and conforming behavior but rather as the context within which these tendencies are expressed.

2. All persons at birth have certain inherent basic needs, in particular the need for emotional security.

3. Deprivation of those universal needs in men during the early years of childhood leads to the formation of given personality types of structure. The degree of conflict, disorder, retardation, or injury to the personality will vary directly with the degree of deprivation.

4. Childhood experiences, such as emotional conflicts, will determine personality structure and thus the pattern of behavior in later life.

5. Family experiences of the child almost exclusively determine the pattern of behavior in later life, whether deviant or nondeviant, by affecting the personality structure of the child. The need for the mother to provide maternal affection is particularly stressed.

6. A high degree of certain so-called general personality traits, such as emotional insecurity, immaturity, feelings of inadequacy, inability to display affection, and aggression characterize the deviant but not the nondeviant. Such traits are the product of early childhood experience in the family. It is argued that, since the first experiences of the child with others are within the family group, traits arising there form the basis for the entire structure of personality. Deviant behavior is often a way of dealing successfully with such personality traits, for example, "immature" persons may commit crimes or "emotionally insecure" persons may drink excessively and become alcoholics.

This, then, is the theoretical framework with which psychiatry largely explains deviant behavior. Each year are published many books and articles written by psychiatrists who attempt to explain such diverse problems as stealing, murder, sex offenses, delinquency, alcoholism, narcotic addiction, marital difficulties, and the psychoses and the neuroses, as well as racial and religious prejudice.

The Psychoanalytic Explanation of Deviant Behavior

One part of the general field of psychiatry is called psychoanalysis, which has in addition to the psychiatric frame of reference its own particular system of explaining deviant behavior. This, as we shall shortly point out, involves what psychiatrists call conflicts between the id and the superego; the masculinity-femininity conflict, infantile regression, and parent fixation. We shall discuss this approach in detail because its followers publish widely on deviant behavior and their approach has greatly affected not only American psychiatry in general but many social workers and others who deal with deviants.

Because of their emphasis on sex and symbolism, psychoanalytic works in particular make fascinating reading for both professional people and laymen, with the result that probably no approach to deviant behavior has a wider audience. Sigmund Freud, the Viennese psychiatrist who died about twenty years ago, founded psychoanalysis, which has become an important part of the contemporary vocabulary and thinking of Western Europeans.

According to psychoanalytic writers, the chief explanation of behavior disorders must be sought in an analysis of the *unconscious mind,* which consists of a world of inner feelings that are unlikely to be the obvious reasons for behavior or to be subject to recall at will. Antisocial conduct is a result of the dynamics of the unconscious rather than of the conscious activities of mental life. Much of the adult's behavior, whether deviant or nondeviant, owes its form and intensity to certain instinctive drives and to early reactions to parents and siblings. A leading analyst once stated this in emphatic terms: "One thesis is that the child's relation to his family remains throughout life the prototype of its relation to its fellows in general, that this exercises the profoundest influence on its character and conduct." [28]

METHOD

Psychoanalysts generally rely on the use of lengthy free association and the analysis of dreams to infer unconscious experience and motivations. The analyst listens, often taking notes, while the patient, usually in a reclining position, rambles on, presumably verbalizing all his thoughts. Through this "free association" the patient is thought to be able to reveal words, phrases, and ideas ordinarily excluded from consciousness. The same principle holds in hypnosis, which is sometimes used, but the latter technique has many physical disadvantages over free association.

Dreams are supposed to have an obvious meaning as well as a hidden one. That part of the dream which one can recall is its obvious content, whereas the unconscious processes which give rise to the dream are its hidden meanings. Since the latter are generally not acceptable to the dreamer, they must be transformed in some symbolic way to be made acceptable. The "censor," a mechanism of importance in this scheme, decides what may come to the dreamer's conscious mind and what may not. It also transforms, condenses, elaborates, and dramatizes the hidden content, through symbols, into the obvious content. These symbols often have sexual connotations. In dreams the father may be said to be symbolized as

[28] E. Jones, "Relationship of Psychoanalysis to Sociology," in E. Jones ed., *Social Aspects of Psychoanalysis* (London: Williams & Norgate, Ltd., 1924), p. 37.

a king and/or various animals, the mother thought of as nature, and pro-creation by sowing or tilling.

CONFLICTS OF THE ID AND THE SUPEREGO

In the psychoanalyst's scheme, personality is thought of as composed of three parts: the primitive animal *id,* the *ego,* and the *superego.* Psycho-analysis assumes that the conscious self is built over a great reservoir of biological drives. Although biology, in the form of basic animal drives, plays an important part in psychoanalytic theory, these drives are present in everyone and do not necessarily represent individual biological differ-ences.

1. The *id* is the buried reservoir of unconscious instinctual animal tendency or drive. From the Freudian standpoint these instincts are of two major types: the *libido,* including chiefly sexual drives, but not exclusively limited to this drive, and the love or life-trend instincts; and the sadistic or destructive instincts. These instincts operate in every activity.

2. The *ego* is elaborated from the large tract of instinctual tendencies as a result of the contact of the individual with the outer social world. Freud postulated here a dualistic conception of mind: the "id" or internal unconscious world of native or biological impulses and repressed ideas, and the "ego," the self, operating on the level of consciousness. These two may sometimes be compatible but more often are incompatible, unless adjusted through some psychological mechanism. There may be constant conflict between the "ego," the conscious part of the mind representing the civilized aspect of man, and the "id," the unconscious or "primitive" in man.

3. The *superego,* on the other hand, is partly conscious, partly un-conscious, and it is the conscious part which corresponds to the conscience. It is man's social self, derived from cultural definitions of conduct, the mores.

Some writers on psychoanalysis have made almost synonymous with criminal behavior the unresolved conflicts between the primitive id and its instinctive drives and the requirement of society. According to this view, crime arises out of inadequate social restrictions which society has placed on what psychoanalysts assume to be the original instinctive, unadjusted nature of man, which is savage, sensual, and destructive. Criminal behavior is thought of as an almost necessary outcome or expression of the personal-ity, and hence does not always necessitate contacts with a "criminal" cul-ture. According to Karpman, all persons are born criminals in the sense that they come into the world unconditioned and unrepressed. Society, therefore, is the mechanism through which we are conditioned so as to re-press our criminal tendencies: "To put it in other words, we are born selfish, hateful, spiteful, mean; and it is the culture that makes us devoted, loving, kind and sympathetic. . . . criminality . . . [is viewed] as being expressive of the anti-social feelings that each of us carries within him. And it is out of this criminal basis our normal citizenry carried that our criminal population is evolved." [29] Zilboorg writes that crime results from the temporary overcoming of the resistance of the superego and then the ego by instinctive drives from the id.[30] After the discharge of such impulses and the consequent silencing of id drives, the superego reasserts itself and a sense of guilt is felt. According to Abrahamsen, murder arises from the expression of the individual's natural aggressions: "Murder has psychological root in the person's aggressions related to attack and defense. These are expressions of his fight for survival or may be due to an erotic drive, no matter how distorted or concealed it may be." [31]

Psychoanalytic writers dealing with the problems of suicide have stressed the polarity principle of the life (love) and death (hate) instincts of the id.[32] According to this view, there is a strong desire in the id for self-destruction, such as mutilation or suicide, and at the same time a desire for self-preservation. The superego, in turn, contains various social and moral restrictions on personal violence or self-destruction. The forces pulling toward self-destruction and self-preservation are in constant interaction, and when the former overcomes the latter, self-inflicted death ensues. In the course of normal mental development toward maturity, the destructive drives are directed outward in the form of aggression or are sublimated. Failure to direct these tendencies outward results in the individual's fighting or destroying himself.

Psychoanalysts often find hidden motives behind suicides as, for example, self-mutilation or self-destruction in place of injury to another person. Menninger has described three varieties of suicide: the wish to kill; the wish to be killed, which may take the form of hypochondria or alcoholism, or exposure of oneself to diseases; and the wish to die. According to him, the death wish, which is part of the id, may occur in alcoholics where chronic drunkenness is in a sense a slower method of self-annihilation than some of the others customarily employed. Alcoholism may also be a means of self-punishment, the desire for which stems from guilt feelings created by incessant war between the id and the superego.

Some psychoanalysts have suggested that the conflicts between the id

---

[29] Ben Karpman, *The Individual Criminal: Studies in the Psychogenetics of Crime* (Washington, D.C.: Nervous and Mental Diseases Publishing Co., 1935), p. ix.

[30] Gregory Zilboorg, *Mind, Medicine and Man* (New York: Harcourt, Brace & World, Inc., 1943).

[31] David Abrahamsen, *Crime and the Human Mind* (New York: Columbia University Press, 1944), p. 148. Also see Karl Menninger, "Verdict Guilty—Now What?" *Harper's Magazine* 210:60–64 (August, 1959).

[32] Karl Menninger, *Man against Himself* (New York: Harcourt, Brace & World, Inc., 1938).

and the superego explain prejudice. In our modern complex society the natural drives and personal wishes of the id meet all varieties of blocks in the path of achievement. More and more frustrations being forced upon individuals result in greater inner tensions and anxieties. Yet there are no standard cultural means of relieving this pressure. Tensions must somehow be relieved, either directly or through "free-floating aggression" against persons and groups. Just as the mother or other disciplinarian becomes the object of conscious or unconscious hatred and hostility of the child, so "out-groups" and other people with assumed or real divergences in physical or other characteristics become objects of hate through the displacement mechanism, i.e., hatred is shifted from the persons and groups who stand in the way of one's fulfillment of goals to a more convenient object.

As a consequence of these frustrations of the id the hostility toward the Jew in the world today may emanate from a transference of the hatred of Christians for Christ and Christianity itself. According to this explanation, Christ, a Jew, gave the world a morality which curbed the id impulses of Western mankind. But since men do not relish these restrictions on their material desires, they unconsciously fear and hate not only Christ but his doctrines as well. On the one hand they overcompensate these feelings by strict adherence to the church, and on the other by sympathizing unconsciously with all those persons who do not uphold this morality. The Jews serve as the objects of hate because it was they who produced a religious leader who introduced this hard morality. The Jews, in other words, are hated because they gave the world a Christ. This theory of prejudice is called Christophobia, meaning an irrational fear of Christ.[33]

Prejudice against the Negro has been explained as resulting from the white man's desire for sexual relations with Negroes or from his envy of their so-called hypersexuality. According to this explanation, white people believe that Negroes are less inhibited and more passionate sexually, that colored males have larger sexual organs than do white males, and that colored females can experience more orgasms than can white women. White persons who do not have sexual relations with Negroes feel that they must repress their desires, whereas those who do have relations with Negroes experience marked guilt feelings.[34] McLean believes that southern whites think themselves somewhat lacking in sexual expression, while the Negro has a superabundance of such feelings. Their jealousy of the Negroes and the need to repress the id desires toward them result in prejudice. She says that as whites are "devoid of the capacity for the expression of genuine warmth unconsciously they feel that the Negro has what they lack. They anxiously search for something which will give meaning to their lives

---

[33] For a description of this explanation of anti-Semitism see Maurice Samuel, *The Great Hatred* (New York: Alfred A. Knopf, Inc., 1940), pp. 105–115.

[34] See discussion of this theory in Arnold and Caroline Rose, *America Divided* (New York: Alfred A. Knopf, Inc., 1948), p. 290.

through their contacts with the Negro. These contacts, however, are fraught with the terror of the forbidden. Their inflexible consciences, in seeking a victim to punish for all manner of forbidden impulses, must keep in subservience those who represent the temptation." [35]

MASCULINITY-FEMININITY CONFLICT

Every person, psychoanalytically, has both masculine and feminine tendencies or, to put it another way, is naturally bisexual with homosexual and heterosexual components. Within each individual this fact results in a certain amount of conflict. Many psychoanalytic writers have emphasized the conflict of the masculine and feminine components which are a part of everyone's original make-up, the one being aggressive and the other passive. The rapist, for example, has a feeling of inferiority and fear of sexual inadequacy which prevents normal permanent sexual alliances. Murder may even be a defense against "feminine" traits which are abhorred by the murderer.

Some psychoanalytic writers believe that alcoholism in the male represents the direct expression of his homosexual drives. Drinking often enables him to be in male company exclusively, particularly in bars and taverns, and it also enables him to overcome his feeling of sexual impotency. Eventually the inebriate substitutes the consumption of alcohol for heterosexual contacts. After analyzing the hangovers of seven men and seven women alcoholics, Karpman has concluded that they reflect guilt over homosexual feelings. [36]

INFANTILE REGRESSION

Psychoanalysts think of a normal personality as having developed through a series of four stages. The development of personality involves shifting interests and changes in the nature of sexual pleasure from the oral and the anal preoccupation of infant life, to love of self, love of a parent of the opposite sex, and, finally, love of a person of the opposite sex and other than one's parent. Some of these stages overlap and may go on simultaneously. Some persons do not progress through all these stages, have conflicts, and develop personality difficulties.

According to psychoanalysts, the newborn individual operates on a pain-pleasure principle, and the environment is viewed merely as consisting of desirable objects which serve to bring about bodily comfort and satisfaction, such as oral gratification through nursing and preoccupation with

[35] Helen V. McLean, "Psychodynamic Factors in Racial Relations," *The Annals*, 244:164 (March, 1946).

[36] Ben Karpman, *The Hangover* (Springfield, Ill.: Charles C Thomas, Publisher, 1957).

activities of elimination. This stage, from the point of view of the affectional or libidinal development, is one of preoccupation with one's own body. From the start, however, this interest becomes increasingly blocked by cultural controls and restrictions. The adult world insists on adjustment to social patterns and an increasingly greater restriction on freely expressed biological drives and fantasies.

Many psychoanalysts stress the fact that deviants are immature persons who have not developed into fully socialized adults. The activities of deviants unconsciously represent unresolved infantile desires to which they have returned. Others believe that the type of crime, the type of objects involved in the crime, and the person from whom something was stolen often indicate infantile regression. Stealing from superiors, for example, may be symbolic of original childhood envy of adult sexual organs. Burglary has been traced by one psychoanalyst to fixation in the oral stage of development, and arson has been explained as a regression to an infantile stage of development.[37] Foxe has even classified various types of crime in terms of trauma and fixation in childhood. Automobile theft is due to regression to the early oral stage; burglary, forgery, and embezzlement are due to regression to the late oral stage; and armed robbery and swindling are due to regression to the late anal.[38]

> Earliest training leaves its impress upon one's constitution and character and so it is not surprising that so many individuals in whom the training deviated considerably from average showed strong marks of primitive infantile patterns [anal-oral stage]. . . . That even crime should show such impression —the tooth-like dagger of the assaulter and the tooth-like sadistic pen of the forger, the anal explosiveness of the gun-holding robber—is not at all remarkable.[39]

Many psychoanalysts have concluded that the etiology of schizophrenia lies in the regression of the total personality to the stage in life in which the ego is not completely molded. It is, therefore, a retreat to a form of infantilism. The alcoholic has often been characterized by psychoanalysts as a passive, insecure, dependent, "oral" personality of an infantile type, with his latent hostility being thereby obscured.

PARENT FIXATION AND CONFLICTS

Generally psychoanalysts regard patterns of behavior as having been formed in the early years, in many before five years, in nearly all before

---

[37] Otto Fenichel, *The Psychoanalytic Theory of Neurosis* (New York: W. W. Norton & Company, Inc., 1945).

[38] Arthur N. Foxe, "Classification of the Criminotic Individual," in Robert M. Lindner and Robert V. Seliger eds., *Handbook of Correctional Psychology* (New York: Philosophical Library, Inc., 1947).

[39] Arthur N. Foxe, "Criminoses," in V. C. Branham and S. B. Kutash eds., *Encyclopedia of Criminology* (New York: Philosophical Library, Inc., 1949), p. 117.

adolescence. Normal psychic development involves not only the question of normal affectional development but also a gradual emergence from a condition of dependence on parental authority and care to one in which the individual achieves a greater degree of independence. Failure to do so results in a socially inadequate adult personality.

In infancy the mother becomes definitely an object of the child's libido. She is the first object to whom love impulses are directed, but since she is the first person who restricts pleasure she is also one to whom hate is first directed. Based on this early attachment to the mother, there arises an *Oedipus phase* in libidinal development in which the male child unconsciously becomes a rival of his father for the mother's sexual affections and, therefore, comes to hate his father. In the case of girls, the conflict with the mother over the father is called the *Electra complex*.[40] Psychoanalytic writers have tried to show that many social phenomena can be understood only when viewed in the light of the Oedipus complex, which produces significant manifestations in almost every sphere of human activity.

An outstanding example of this approach is the view held by many, but not all, psychoanalysts, that the Oedipus complex is universal in all cultures.[41] Sexual adjustments become heterosexual, with the love object outside the family. With the deviant, however, this conflict is not solved; there are guilt feelings over the incestuous desires for the parent of the opposite sex, and an unsatisfactory shift to other heterosexual persons. These guilt feelings are relieved by deviant behavior or by the punishment that arises from antisocial behavior.

Criminals and neurotics have much in common, for example, for both feel that they need punishment to relieve guilt feelings arising from an Oedipus situation. The individual may feel a need for punishment because of the hostility he has harbored against a member of his family. He may commit a crime and seek punishment by society, whereas another may seek self-punishment through a neurosis. Self-destructive tendencies may result in a murder's being committed in order to receive punishment.

Many psychoanalysts believe that the behavior difficulties associated with alcoholism lie in various Oedipus or Electra conflicts. Alcoholism is interpreted as an escape valve from these intolerable inner battles.

Homosexuality in a man has been explained as a result of overattachment for the mother in an unresolved Oedipus complex which results in his rejecting sex relations with other women. Psychoanalytic theories of prostitution often explain it as caused by the individual's failure

---

[40] Another conflict may result from overattachment to the mother, which turns to violent dislike and is called the *Orestes complex*. All these terms have their origin in the characters and plots of the classic Greek plays.

[41] Many psychoanalysts use the Oedipus complex symbolically but do not regard it as universal.

to reach sexual maturity. Some psychoanalysts characterize the prostitute as a person who has been denied sufficient parental love, affection, and security in childhood and who therefore establishes liaisons because she wants to feel that she is wanted and needed. She also suffers from, or has never outgrown, her Electra complex for her father, and is often incapable of receiving real sexual gratification.

SOME SPECIFIC CRITICISMS OF PSYCHOANALYTIC THEORY

1. *Contrary to psychoanalysis, evidence suggests that human behavior is a product of social experience and that it is not determined by an innate reservoir of animal impulses termed the id.* Depending upon his social and cultural experiences, a man can be either cruel or gentle, aggressive or pacifist, sadistic or loving. He can be either a savage Nazi Jew-baiter or a compassionate and tender human being like Albert Schweitzer or Mohandas Gandhi. No detailed refutation is necessary, therefore, to disprove a psychoanalytic theory that some forms of criminality, for example, should be envisaged as outbursts of unsocialized original animal impulses. What constitutes criminal behavior is a matter of social determination, and impulses secure their social meaning only through the medium of social interaction. There is no savage man lurking under a veneer of socialization. This belief in something resembling human instincts, which was common until the 1920's, has been completely refuted by a large number of studies by social psychologists, psychologists, and anthropologists. It is no longer even a debatable subject.

2. *There is no evidence to support the theory that sex represents an all-inclusive factor which explains a host of mental conflicts.* The psychoanalytic emphasis on sexual eroticism is a great overstatement of an important aspect of human behavior. As Horney has indicated, conflicts can arise in many areas of human experience, particularly through excessive competition.[42] Likewise, religion, the achievement of status, and various conflicts in social roles—all constitute wide areas of possible mental conflict.

3. *The entire psychoanalytic scheme is bodily conscious rather than primarily socially conscious for the child's development is greatly influenced by social relationships which have little or no connection with bodily functions.* The evidence does not support the view that these rather presocial experiences involving oral and anal stimulation affect the entire course of human life. The idea that frustrations of the libidinal infantile drives universal in all human beings will necessarily affect personality has been rejected by Orlansky after an extensive survey of anthropological literature. In a study of various societies he considered the effects on personality of different methods of nursing, mothering, bowel training, and

---

[42] Karen Horney, *New Ways in Psychoanalysis* (New York: W. W. Norton & Company, Inc., 1939).

restraint of motion, and reached negative conclusions about their "specific invariant psychological effect upon children." [43] He concludes that parental attitudes which are derived from the culture are the chief variables. Sewell, likewise, has concluded from a study of 162 farm children that different methods of infant breast feeding, weaning, and bowel training have practically no subsequent effect on personality.[44]

4. *Psychoanalytic theory has assumed certain universal uniformities in human behavior as arising from the assumed uniformities in human biological drives, irrespective of cultural influences, or historical eras, or of variations in social structure.* Actually "drives," if they exist, have no inherent direction or aim; but the complex behaviors necessary to relieve the physical tensions, which we term "drives," are learned through social experiences. For example, the stomach contractions which we refer to as "hunger" do not in themselves explain why Americans eat hamburgers, Koreans prefer rice, and Eskimos prefer seal blubber. The kinds of food eaten and the methods of obtaining and preparing them are culturally learned.

An outstanding example of this approach is the view that the Oedipus complex is universal in all cultures. One survey of Freudian concepts has stated that "Freud assumed the Oedipus relationship to exist universally, and while other investigations have found instances of it, no indications of a universal cross-sex parental preference have been discovered in either children or adults." [45] It appears that Freud overrated the uniformity of family patterns and failed to perceive that sexual definitions are products of the child's social relationships. Even in our culture families do not exhibit a similar culture pattern, and there is considerable variability in the specific behaviors expected of persons in their family roles. In turn, if various family patterns throughout the world are examined, these patterns and roles become even more variable.

> It is a truism today that adult behavior is a function of the culture in which it was learned. Psychiatric thought had not gone so far at the beginning of the century, however, and Freud's notion of the universal Oedipus complex stands as a sharply etched grotesquerie against his otherwise informative description of sexual development. From the analysis of data relating to object choice, it is apparent that in this matter perhaps more than in any other the nature of the chosen object and the reactions to other similar or dissimilar objects are dependent on the early home environment of the child. So far we are in agreement with Freud. But, beyond this, Freud seeks a common or typical pattern of development. If such existed, it should come only from a

---

[43] Harold Orlansky, "Infant Care and Personality," *Psychological Bulletin*, 46:1–48 (January, 1949).

[44] William H. Sewell, "Infant Training and the Personality of the Child," *American Journal of Sociology*, 58:150–159 (September, 1952).

[45] Robert R. Sears, "Survey of Objective Studies of Psychoanalytic Concepts" (Bulletin 51; New York: Social Science Research Council, 1943), pp. 134–135.

common culture pattern, i.e., from a constant situation in which learning could take place in a uniform way.[46]

General Evaluation of the Psychiatric and Psychoanalytic Explanations

Psychiatry and psychoanalysis have a large following in present-day society and their literature is extensive. Psychoanalysis has emphasized the meaningfulness of subjective experience and as a theory it has contributed to the understanding of various psychological processes through which the mind avoids certain painful experiences. The emphasis on the unconscious, on symbolic expressions, and on mental conflict has been noteworthy, even if overstressed in the explanation. Some have increasingly recognized the importance of the larger world of cultural definitions and interpersonal relationships in the development of deviant behavior. Moreover, the remarks presented here are focused on the *theoretical explanation, and not on therapy.* Certainly some favorable therapeutic results are achieved by psychiatrists and psychoanalysts working with deviants. Therapy, however, does not necessarily always follow the theory but may be improvised to fit an individual case. Moreover, the results achieved by therapy may be due to other factors, such as the intimate social relationship between practitioner and patient.

1. *Psychoanalytic as well as psychiatric theory has all too frequently assumed that adult behavior and personality are almost wholly determined by childhood experiences, most of them in the family, whereas the overwhelming bulk of evidence suggests that behavior varies according to situations and social roles and that personality continues to develop throughout life.* Such early family influences have probably been greatly overemphasized, sometimes to the virtual exclusion of the effect on personality of other groups such as the peer group, occupation, neighborhood, marriage, and other later social situations. Even in early life the socialization of the child is greatly influenced by the play group, by street play in urban areas, by preschool and kindergarten activities, and by neighbors and others, such as relatives. Largely on the basis of current anthropological studies, Orlansky has concluded that "the rigidity of character structure during the first year or two of life has been exaggerated by many authorities and that the events of childhood and later years are of great importance in reinforcing or changing the character structure tentatively found during infancy."[47] This seems plausible, for life must be regarded as a continuous experience of social interaction which cannot be arbitrarily divided between infancy, childhood, and adult experience. To psychiatrists and

---

[46] *Ibid.,* p. 136.   [47] Orlansky, "Infant Care and Personality," *loc. cit.*

psychoanalysts, events occurring at forty years of age, for example, may be explained by some occurrence at age four. The theory of predetermination of adult behavior on the basis of heredity has largely disappeared; in its place is predetermination based on early family interaction. For the most part, the sociological approach to deviant behavior, while certainly recognizing the importance of the family, does not agree with this theory in even paramount or exclusive emphasis on the family or on parental models as necessarily the determinants of either deviant or nondeviant behavior.

2. *Despite their claims, the explanations of psychiatrists and psychoanalysts and their proponents concerning deviant behavior have not, for the most part, been scientifically verified.* Psychiatrists and psychoanalysts have generally failed, and even have often refused, to use experimental or more verifiable situations, or other more rigorous and controlled techniques, to test their hypotheses.[48] For evidence, there is reliance on verbal recall of childhood experiences, which are interpreted by the psychiatrist or psychoanalyst. Much of that evidence is derived from memories in which childhood experiences, particularly in the family, are likely to be recalled without their necessarily having much bearing on why a person acts as he does in later life. Much of this type of activity has been criticized for using imagination and guesswork too freely. Another person going over the same material might find some other equally valid and significant explanation which did not employ the theory, for example, of psychoanalysis.[49] Most psychiatric and psychoanalytic studies have been concerned only with deviant persons, and only a few studies have employed control groups of nondeviant persons. This is understandable if one considers that they specialize in treatment, but they frequently generalize without utilizing accepted scientific procedures, such as samples of sufficient size or representativeness. One important psychoanalytic volume, for example, covered only six cases and yet was called *Roots of Crime*.[50]

3. *Psychiatric and psychoanalytic explanations of deviant behavior exemplify a blurring of the line between "sickness" and simply deviations from norms.* According to these explanations the presence of mental aberra-

---

[48] See, for example, Lyle W. Shannon, "The Problem of Competence to Help," *Federal Probation*, 25:32–39 (March, 1961). He suggests a number of positive criteria in evaluating a professional person's ability to deal effectively with deviant behavior: (1) the ability to predict human behavior, (2) the ability to control or modify human behavior, and (3) the existence of a body of scientific research which tends to support the explanation of the professional group in question and with which the therapy in question appears to be consistent.

[49] Sears, "Survey of Objective Studies of Psychoanalytic Concepts," p. 133. Some psychoanalysts maintain that successes in therapy are proof of the validity of their theoretical systems. This is no more proof than the "cures" of patent medicine. Other factors, such as the subject's belief and acceptance of the interpretation, as well as his personal relations with the analyst, also enter into the so-called successful treatment.

[50] Franz Alexander and William Healy, *Roots of Crime* (New York: Alfred A. Knopf, Inc. 1935).

tions explains the occurrence of certain antisocial actions, such as crime. Thus, criminal or socially deviant behavior is itself made the criterion for the diagnosis of mental abnormality. In this sense deviations from norms of "sinful behavior," such as delinquency and crime, are used as the basis for inferring the presence of "sickness" or mental aberration. This tendency is similar to older attempts to link behavioral deviations with "possession by devils." [51]

4. *Some writers, after extensive investigations, have concluded that psychiatric and psychoanalytic diagnoses are unreliable, and that there is absence of agreement among psychiatrists themselves concerning what objective criteria are to be employed in assessing degrees of mental well-being or mental aberration.*[52] To a great extent it is the very absence of objective criteria of either mental illness or mental health which is responsible for the psychiatrists' and psychoanalysts' tendencies to equate "sickness" and, for example, delinquency and crime. This is because, lacking such criteria, there is no way of distinguishing between those whose criminal acts are excusable on the basis of mental disorder from those who, though committing criminal acts, are not mentally disordered. Finding themselves unable thus to distinguish "mentally healthy" criminals from "mentally unhealthy" ones, criminal behavior itself is used as a criterion of mental disorder, or of other abnormalities within the person. This dilemma, in essence, underlies the psychiatric explanation of deviant behavior and the psychiatric view concerning the treatment of deviants.[53]

5. *No evidence has been produced, despite these claims, that so-called personality traits are associated with deviations from disapproved norms.* Comparisons with control groups have revealed that no series of traits can distinguish deviants from nondeviants in general.[54] Some de-

---

[51] Barbara Wootton, *Social Science and Social Pathology* (New York: The Macmillan Company, 1957), p. 207.

[52] See Wootton, *op. cit.*, especially Chap. 7; Michael Hakeem, "A Critique of the Psychiatric Approach to Crime and Corrections," *Law and Contemporary Problems*. 22:681–682 (Autumn, 1958); Michael Hakeem, "A Critique of the Psychiatric Approach," in Joseph Roucek ed., *Juvenile Delinquency* (New York: Philosophical Library, Inc., 1958), pp. 79–112; Arthur P. Miles, *American Social Work Theory* (New York: Harper & Row, Publishers, 1954), pp. 122–130; Percival Bailey, "The Great Psychiatric Revolution," *American Journal of Psychiatry*, 113:387–406 (November, 1956); Marshall B. Clinard, "Contributions of Sociology to Understanding Deviant Behavior," *British Journal of Criminology*, in press; Thomas S. Szasz, "Malingering: Diagnosis or Social Condemnation?" *American Medical Association Archives of Neurology and Psychiatry*, 76:432–438 (1956); and Thomas S. Szasz, *The Myth of Mental Illness* (New York: Paul B. Hoeber, Inc., 1961).

[53] See Wootton, *op. cit.*, and Hakeem, "A Critique of the Psychiatric Approach to Crime and Corrections," *loc. cit.*, for further elaboration of this problem.

[54] See, for example, Karl F. Schuessler and Donald R. Cressey, "Personality Characteristics of Criminals," *American Journal of Sociology*, 55:476–484 (March, 1950), and Edwin H. Sutherland, H. C. Schroeder, and C. L. Tordella, "Personality Traits and the Alcoholic: A Critique of Existing Studies," *Quarterly Journal of Studies on Alcohol*, 11:547–561 (December, 1950). Also see Leonard Symes, "Personality Characteristics and

viants are "emotionally insecure," but some nondeviants are also "emotionally insecure." On the other hand, some deviants are "emotionally secure." One is never sure whether given personality traits were present before the deviant behavior developed or whether experiences encountered as a result of the deviation produced the traits. Thus the fact that a boy or a girl in a correctional institution is "emotionally insecure" is no proof that he or she was so prior to commitment to the institution or prior to the first delinquency. The alcoholic who is "emotionally insecure" may have developed this trait as a result of reactions of others during a long period of alcoholism. Moreover, a personality trait does not indicate how a person will act in a given situation or explain how specific definitions of situations, such as techniques of stealing, are acquired. Part of the difficulty has arisen from the fact that psychiatrists, being practitioners, see deviants almost entirely and obviously do not have an opportunity to study many nondeviants. They erroneously assume, therefore, that such traits as they find characterize only deviants.

Summary

In this chapter three theories of the cause of deviant behavior—feeble-mindedness, body type, and childhood experiences (the psychiatric and psychoanalytic explanations)—have been discussed. Although these theories have much support, for a number of reasons they do not offer a valid explanation of deviant behavior. Much of the inadequacies in their explanations can be attributed to the training and background of the investigators. Since deviant behavior is seen and experienced from this frame of reference, more often than not the facts are manipulated to fit the theory, rather than altering the theory to fit the facts. This is particularly true of psychoanalysis.

On the whole, these theories tend to be explanations of the social behavior of human beings without full consideration of the social nature of man. That consideration is necessary if one is to attempt to explain behavior as it actually occurs within society, instead of in what Planck has called the "picture world," or the world of "other things being equal."

Satisfactory control groups of nondeviants have not been utilized in most of the studies. Explanations have been largely based on the analysis of deviants only, such as delinquents, criminals, or alcoholics, without reference to other persons who do not exhibit this behavior.

Many of the concepts of psychiatry and psychoanalysis have been valuable contributions to a science of human behavior. Despite the vociferous claims of the psychiatrists and the psychoanalysts, however, that their *general theory* offers a solution to deviant behavior, they are more a system

---

the Alcoholic: A Critique of Current Studies," *Quarterly Journal of Studies on Alcohol,* 18;288–302 (June, 1957).

of beliefs than scientifically verified bodies of knowledge. Until psychiatry and psychoanalysis are supported by extensive research using accepted scientific methods they will continue to remain largely a body of intriguing speculation.

Superficially, these three theories seem to be simple ways of dealing with deviant behavior. It is fortunate that there is so little validity in the theories, however, for they would mean that it would be virtually impossible ever to control deviant behavior effectively. If feeble-mindedness or body type were associated with certain deviations, control would have to be through selective eugenic breeding and sterilization. Both methods may be applicable to other animals, but for man it would be virtually impossible because of the extensive nature of deviations, the possibility of biological inheritance through recessive characteristics, the relatively free marriage selection system in modern society, and the democratic rights of each individual. The application of psychiatric and psychoanalytic principles on a large scale and the use of psychiatry and psychoanalysis as treatment devices for millions of deviants would be an extremely complex solution.

Selected Readings

BAILEY, PERCIVAL. "The Great Psychiatric Revolution," *American Journal of Psychiatry*, 113:387–406 (November, 1956). The many conflicting approaches to treatment of specific forms of deviant behavior by psychiatrists are a cause of concern, according to this well-documented article.

GLUECK, SHELDON, and ELEANOR GLUECK. *Physique and Delinquency*. New York: Harper & Row, Publishers, 1956. A study of the physique of 500 delinquent boys in a correctional training school, as compared with a control group of boys.

HAKEEM, MICHAEL. "A Critique of the Psychiatric Approach," in Joseph Roucek ed., *Juvenile Delinquency*. New York: Philosophical Library, Inc., 1958, pp. 79–112. A critical appraisal of the methods and evidence on which psychiatric theory is based.

MONROE, RUTH L. *Schools of Psychoanalytic Thought*. New York: Holt, Rinehart and Winston, Inc., 1955, Chaps. 2, 3, 5, and 7. A comprehensive description of the concepts and methods of psychoanalysis with critical comments. Chapter 7 deals with the theoretical explanations of certain deviant behavior and the use of psychoanalysis in treatment.

ORLANSKY, HAROLD. "Infant Care and Personality," *Psychological Bulletin*, 46:1–48 (January, 1949). A study of whether any universal findings could be established when psychoanalytic theory was applied to a large number of primitive societies.

SCHUESSLER, KARL F., and DONALD R. CRESSEY, "Personality Characteristics of Criminals," *American Journal of Sociology*, 55:476–484 (March, 1950). A survey of all studies which sought to differentiate the personality traits of delinquents and criminals, with a control group. The survey concluded that such differences have not been established.

SEARS, ROBERT R. "Survey of Objective Studies of Psychoanalytic Concepts." New York: Social Science Research Council, Bulletin 51, 1943. This well-known critique of psychoanalysis criticizes writers in this field for not generally employing scientific methods of proof.

SEWELL, WILLIAM H. "Infant Training and the Personality of the Child," *American Journal of Sociology*, 58:150–159 (September, 1952). An attempt to test empirically the effect of certain child-rearing practices on personality emphasized by the Freudians. The conclusions were negative.

SHANNON, LYLE. "The Problem of Competence to Help," *Federal Probation*, 25: 32–39 (March, 1961). A discussion of the positive and negative criteria which should be used in evaluating a professional person, such as a psychiatrist, on his competence to help a deviant.

SUTHERLAND, EDWIN H. "A Critique of Sheldon's *Varieties of Delinquent Youth*," *American Sociological Review*, 16:10–13 (February, 1951). An excellent criticism of one of the leading books dealing with the relation of body type and deviant behavior.

SZASZ, THOMAS S. *The Myth of Mental Illness*. New York: Paul B. Hoeber, Inc., 1961. A psychoanalyst states the view that what is considered to be mental illness has come to be defined as whatever psychiatrists say it is, and that psychiatry has, with increasing and misplaced zeal, called more and more kinds of behavior "illness."

WOOTTON, BARBARA. *Social Science and Social Pathology*. New York: The Macmillan Company, 1959. Includes an appraisal of current psychiatric beliefs and concludes that there is little evidence that antisocial attitudes are due to lack of maternal affection in infancy. She particularly condemns the blurring of the line between "sickness and sin" for which she holds contemporary psychiatry responsible.

PART
II

Deviant Behavior

The Nature of Delinquency
and Crimes

In the previous discussions, which have covered many forms of deviant behavior, the air has been cleared of some fundamental misconceptions about deviant behavior in general; urbanization has been found to be a profitable over-all frame of reference for the analysis of deviant behavior; and, finally, several key concepts of considerable utility have been presented. They include the society, culture, groups, social norms, values, attitudes, conception of self, and social roles. Beginning with crime and criminal behavior, these concepts will be applied more specifically to a number of important forms of deviant behavior.

For many hundreds of years men have been intrigued with crime and criminals, if numerous songs, poems, and stories in the literature of many cultures are any indication of this interest. Ballads dealing with thieves and highwaymen, gaols and sheriffs, have been passed down from generation to generation. Today this interest in criminal offenders has come into even greater prominence as evidenced in the subject matter of many contemporary novels, newspapers, magazines, radio and television plays, and motion pictures. In fact, so large is the proportion of popular mass communication devoted to criminal behavior that one is tempted to speculate about the content of fictional literature in that millennium of a crimeless society.[1]

The Scientific Study of Criminal Behavior

Despite these centuries of interest in crime, it is only within the past seventy-five years that men have sought to study scientifically the factors underlying criminal behavior. Previously there had been considerable writing and speculation about the nature of crime, but little interest in the criminal. Near the end of the eighteenth century, several writers, notably Cesare Beccaria in Italy and Jeremy Bentham in England, suggested that

---

[1] So much space is devoted to the reporting of various crimes in the daily press of Western society that the difference between most papers and one like the *Christian Science Monitor,* which seldom prints crime news, is striking.

a crime was simply an act wherein the pleasure derived from illegal behavior exceeded the possible pain that might consequently be imposed as
punishment. This conception of crime was based on the principles of he-
donistic psychology, which assumed that the behavior of all persons was
completely a matter of individual responsibility and that their misbehavior
was motivated by pain and punishment.

Basing his ideas on this belief, but with no actual studies of criminals
and noncriminals to prove it, Beccaria expressed his views in a famous
essay on crime and punishment. He suggested that there should be uniform
penalties for given crimes but that they should vary according to the
severity of the crime.[2] Crimes were punished differently by various judges,
with little or no punishment for a nobleman and great severity for a serf;
hence Beccaria's idea was revolutionary at that time. His conception of
punishment, with so many years for burglary and so many more for robbery,
still underlies the criminal law of nearly all countries today.

It was not until 1876, however, that there was any really scientific
study of criminals. It was begun by Cesare Lombroso, an Italian army
doctor. The abstract methods of studying crime did not appeal to him;
instead, he began the study of the anatomy of various criminals. Lombroso
was influenced by some work he had done in taking various physical measurements of patients in mental hospitals and by the still controversial
Darwinian theory of evolution, and its corollary, that contemporary man
had antecedents in various forms of primitive man.[3] While he was dissect-
ing the famous brigand Vilella, Lombroso discovered a distinct depression
in the back part of the skull similar to one he had found in lower animals.
Becoming convinced that some criminals were characterized by certain
physical features, he later classified criminals into two additional categories,
insane and criminaloids, persons who were not born with physical stigmata
but who actually had innate tendencies toward crime. Lombroso vividly
describes his findings:

> This was not merely an idea, but a revelation. At the sight of that skull I
> seemed to see all of a sudden, lighted up as a vast plain under a flaming sky,
> the problem of the nature of the criminal—an atavistic being who reproduces
> in his person the ferocious instincts of primitive humanity and the inferior
> animals. Thus were explained anatomically the enormous jaws, high cheek-
> bones, prominent superciliary arches, solitary lines in the palms, extreme size
> of the orbits, handle-shaped or sessile ears found in criminals, savages, and
> apes, insensibility to pain, extremely acute sight, tattooing, excessive idleness,
> love of orgies, and the irresistible craving for evil for its own sake, the desire

[2] Cesare Beccaria, *An Essay on Crimes and Punishments* (New York: Stephen Gould, 1809).
[3] Cesare Lombroso, *L'uomo delinquente* (Turin: Bocca, 1896–1897). Also see Gina Lombroso Ferrero, *Lombroso's Criminal Man* (New York: G. P. Putnam's Sons, 1911); and Cesare Lombroso, *Crime, Its Causes and Remedies* (H. P. Horton, trans.; Boston: Little, Brown & Company, 1912).

not only to extinguish life in the victim, but to mutilate the corpse, tear its flesh, and drink its blood.

I was further encouraged in this bold hypothesis by the results of my studies on Verzeni, a criminal convicted of sadism and rape, who showed the cannibalistic instincts of primitive anthropophagists and the ferocity of beasts of prey.

The various parts of the extremely complex problem of criminality were, however, not all solved hereby. The final key was given by another case, that of Misdea, a young soldier of about twenty-one, unintelligent but not vicious. Although subject to epileptic fits, he had served for some years in the army when suddenly, for some trivial cause, he attacked and killed eight of his superior officers and comrades. His horrible work accomplished, he fell into a deep slumber which lasted twelve hours and on awaking appeared to have no recollection of what had happened. Misdea, while representing the most ferocious type of animal, manifested in addition, all the phenomena of epilepsy, which appeared to be hereditary in all the members of his family. It flashed across my mind that many criminal characteristics not attributable to atavism, such as facial asymmetry, cerebral sclerosis, impulsiveness, instantaneousness, the periodicity of criminal acts, the desire of evil for evil's sake, were morbid characteristics common to epilepsy, mingled with others due to atavism.[4]

In developing their theories, Lombroso and his followers, Garofalo and Ferri, who modified his theory, measured thousands of offenders. The work of the Italian school of criminology aroused world-wide interest in the study of criminals. Although some accepted the idea that a criminal was characterized by innate stigmata and did further research and writing along these lines, others were convinced that the idea was sheer nonsense. Goring in England led the main attack with a study which found no appreciable physical difference, except in weight, between a large group of university students and inmates of English prisons.[5]

In the early part of this century, the two main developments in criminology were Gabriel Tarde's theory of imitation and crime and the theories based on the mentality of criminals. Tarde, a French judge and later a professor, had worked out a theory which, being sociopsychological rather than biological, was the complete opposite of Lombroso's. He believed that crime resulted from the imitation of antisocial behavior in others.[6] This idea came to him when, as a French judge, he sentenced fathers, then sons, and sometimes even an older brother, and later a younger brother. His general ideas of social factors in crime were in advance of his time, although they were not valid with respect to his theory of imitation.

---

[4] Gina Lombroso Ferrero, *Lombroso's Criminal Man* (New York: G. P. Putnam's Sons, 1911), pp. xiv–xvi. Reprinted by permission of the publisher.

[5] Charles Goring, *The English Convict* (London: His Majesty's Stationery Office, 1913). He offered an explanation that offenders inherited an inadequate personality.

[6] Gabriel Tarde, *Penal Philosophy*, tr. by Rapelje Howell (Boston: Little, Brown & Company, 1912).

Americans have played an important role in the development of criminology. Goddard and others stressed mental deficiency as the explanation of crime. In 1915, William Healy, a psychiatrist, published his famous volume, *The Individual Delinquent,* which, in addition to presenting material on delinquents, for the first time offered detailed case studies of individuals with an emphasis on their personality traits. Sutherland, beginning in 1924, eventually developed the important sociological theory that differential association with criminal norms is the cause of criminal behavior.[7] Criminological theory in America and Europe has increasingly emphasized social and group factors in the explanation of delinquency and crime.[8] European criminologists in general, however, consider biological factors as much more important than do American writers.[9]

Crime and Social Control

All societies and groups develop ways of dealing with behaviors which fall outside the range of tolerance of given societal or group norms. These methods are ordinarily called "negative sanctions" because they impose penalties on those whose behavior has transcended the range of tolerance of the norms. "Positive sanctions," on the other hand, consist of special rewards, such as praise, recognition, or prestige which are bestowed on persons whose behavior has conformed, or has exceeded conformance, to prescribed norms.

Both negative and positive sanctions are categories of social control. Social control may, in turn, be classified as either "formal" or "informal." In general, formal controls are the *official* actions of a group or society in response to the behavior of group members, whereas informal controls such as gossip or ostracism consist of *unofficial* group actions. Official actions or formal controls, such as the criminal law, derive from the official group machinery set up to carry out the functions of the group or agency. These controls are, in effect, imbedded in the formal structure of the group. However, these formal controls are generally backed by certain beliefs, ideals, customs, convictions, attitudes and opinions which in

---

[7] Edwin H. Sutherland, *Principles of Criminology* (Philadelphia: J. B. Lippincott Company, 1924, and subsequent revisions of 1934, 1939, 1947, 1955, and 1960). Also see Marshall B. Clinard, "Sociologists and American Criminology," *Journal of Criminal Law and Criminology,* 41:549–577 (January–February, 1951).

[8] See Albert Geis, "Sociology and Crime," in Joseph S. Roucek ed., *Sociology of Crime* (New York: Philosophical Library, Inc., 1961), pp. 7–33, and Clinard, "Sociologists and American Criminology," *loc. cit.*

[9] See, for example, Stephan Hurwitz, *Criminology* (Elsie Giering, trans.; London: George Allen & Unwin Ltd., 1952), and Olof Kinberg, *Basic Problems of Criminology* (Copenhagen: Levin and Munksgaard, 1935). Not all European criminologists take this position. See Hermann Mannheim, *Group Problems in Crime and Punishment* (London: Routledge & Kegan Paul Ltd., 1955). Also see Wolf Middendorff, *Soziologie des Verbrechens (Sociology of Crime)* (Dusseldorf: Eugen Diederichs Verlag, 1959).

themselves are actually informal controls. Thus, in this sense, informal and formal controls cannot be considered as completely discreet categories.[10]

The use of penalties through the criminal law is, therefore, but one of the formal methods of control, and it is a small part of the total system of social controls which operate to create and maintain order in society. Likewise, crime, which is behavior that is defined by law or legal norms, is nevertheless relative to the legal norms of a given area, community, state, or nation.

> What is crime to one city, county, or nation may not be to another. What was crime yesterday may not be today, and what people consider crime today may not be tomorrow. . . . Moreover, laws are but one facet of the regulations we impose on individuals which may vary all the way from ordinary customs, social conventions such as good manners, rules and regulations of a church or lodge, the mores, to other rules such as those called public regulations and laws. All of them represent simply variations in norms and are all part of a continuum. Sometimes, in fact, we may punish some acts which are not crimes more severely than if they were. Examples of such are public reactions to some unconventional manners, the punishment of illegitimacy, or the religious penalty of excommunication.[11]

No effort is required on the part of the group to secure compliance with most of our group norms, for they are the spontaneous and unconscious ways of acting which characterize the bulk of the customs of any culture. Generally speaking, mechanisms of control, such as customs, mores, traditions, beliefs, attitudes, and ideals, are taught through prolonged interaction between persons. Likewise, *informal control* of behavior may be observed in specific behaviors, such as gossip, ridicule, reprimands, praise, criticism, gestural cues, glances of approval or disapproval, emotional expressions, denial or bestowal of affection, ostracism, verbal rationalizations, verbal expressions of opinion, and many other methods. These specific modes of responding to the behavior of group members are generally learned without conscious awareness through group participation. Moreover, because they have been incorporated into their behavior systems and outlooks they are used in a way which seems "natural" or "spontaneous" to the persons involved. Unlike formal controls, informal controls are not exercised through official group mechanisms. Gossip, as an example of an informal social control, is undoubtedly one of the most effective instruments yet devised for disciplining people. These controls are extremely important in any society, for they bulwark the more formal

---

[10] See Paul H. Landis, *Social Control* (rev. ed.; Philadelphia: J. B. Lippincott Company, 1956).

[11] Marshall B. Clinard, "Criminal Behavior Is Human Behavior," *Federal Probation,* 13:24 (March, 1949).

controls of law. They are extremely effective in a folk society and in rural neighborhood situations of primary personal relationships.

To summarize, the difference between formal and informal controls does not depend on the specific behavior necessary for their operation, but depends instead on the source of origin of societal reaction to such behavior, whethey they derive from formal machinery and relationships or from informal personal relationships.[12]

FORMAL CONTROLS

Formal controls involve organized systems of specialized agencies and standard techniques. There are two main types: those instituted by agencies other than the state, and those imposed by the political state. Rules of a more abstract nature are formulated and authority is given such agents as the clergy or police for their interpretation and application.

A series of specific actions is established to punish the transgressor and to reward those whose compliance with the norms is regular or beyond the expectation of the group. Curiously, nonpolitical agencies, such as business concerns and professional, religious, or social groups, probably use rewards more than penalties, which is just the reverse of formal governmental controls. Through promotions, bonuses, or some token of merit, business organizations frequently reward those who have made an outstanding contribution to the firm, who have never been absent, or who have an unusual safety record. Professional groups often reward outstanding service with election to office or some citation. Religious groups reward faithful adherents by promises of a future state of euphoria, by positions of leadership, and by pins or scrolls given for faithful attendance at Sunday school or similar activities. Clubs, lodges, fraternities, and sororities likewise offer a large number of prestige symbols for those who walk the path from neophyte to full-fledged member without reflecting dishonor on the group. Recognition of a type similar to military rewards is given to a small number of civilians each year in the United States through the Carnegie awards for outstanding heroism.

Nonpolitical groups also impose penalties, some of which may be more severe than punishments imposed for crimes. A business concern may fire a man from his job, and a professional group or a union may suspend a member or even expel him from the group, which may mean a loss of livelihood. Baseball players who do not obey the rules of the league or the ball club are usually fined $50 or $100 for an infraction and they may be suspended. Religious organizations may demand penance or withhold

---

[12] See Landis, *op. cit.*, and Robert Bierstedt, *The Social Order* (New York: McGraw-Hill Book Company, Inc., 1957), pp. 188–189.

certain religious services such as the wedding privilege or religious service at death. They may even use what is, to members of a particular faith, the most drastic punishment of all—excommunication from the church. Clubs and similar groups generally utilize a scale of fines, withdrawal of membership privileges, or even expulsion as formal means of controlling their members.

The other type of formal control is exercised by the state through its political and legal institutions. Unfortunately, this control is seldom exerted through positive sanctions or rewards. Some cities occasionally give publicity to safe and courteous drivers, but the reward is seldom more than a pleasant notoriety. The Mr. Milquetoast who goes through life obeying nearly all the requirements imposed upon him by law seldom receives any rewards. Of course, a man's good reputation may be of benefit to him in connection with certain occupational or community responsibilities, and if he should be apprehended for violation of law his past conduct may mitigate the punishment. An important exception to this failure of the state to use rewards as a means of control is the practice in our armed services of giving good-conduct ribbons, medals, or special leaves for faithful adherence to duty or for outstanding bravery, even though every soldier is supposed to do his duty.

Social control of civilians is characterized by a variety of punishments which may be imposed by the state. If a person is below the legal adult age, he comes under the jurisdiction of the courts as a "delinquent." If the offender has reached the legal age of adulthood he is subject to punishment under the criminal law. He can be put on probation, fined, imprisoned, or even condemned to death. The state of Delaware still flogs persons for certain offenses, and in the past various other cruel and inhumane methods of punishing criminals have been authorized by governments.

The measures at the disposal of the state for the control of violations by its members are not confined to the penalties available through the criminal law. The state has many ways of compelling individuals, business concerns, and labor unions to obey the law. It may withdraw a doctor's, lawyer's, or druggist's right to practice, and it may suspend a tavernkeeper or a restaurateur from doing business for a few days, a year, or even permanently. If an individual or a company makes a product illegally, such as alcohol, or if a concern manufactures foods in violation of pure-food laws, the products may be seized and destroyed by the government without compensation. In settling claims for back payment of taxes or fraudulent returns on taxes, the government may require an additional payment which may be quite a severe penalty. If a business concern or a union is defying a law, the government may institute an injunction "to cease and desist" from further violations, and if further violations occur, contempt of court proceedings may be instituted. Many other examples of government penalties could be cited to indicate that the criminal law is not the only sanction used by political institutions to secure compliance with conduct norms.

What Is a Crime?

The nature of a criminal act may be considered from two points of view, either as a violation of the criminal law or as a violation of any law punished by the state, depending upon the particular assumption with which illegal behavior is approached.

A CRIME AS A VIOLATION OF THE CRIMINAL LAW

First, from a strictly legal position, an act is a crime only when the statutes so specify. These statutes, and the subsequent interpretations of them by the court, constitute the criminal law. Most of the conventional crimes, such as burglary and robbery, were crimes under the common law long before the enactment of any legislation.

At one time or other beliefs of all kinds have been punished by the state under the criminal law, which has developed as a result of legislative and court action. Violations of the criminal law have included such behavior as engaging in recreational activities on the Sabbath, practicing witchcraft, smoking, failing to show proper respect to a noble, wearing one-piece bathing suits, listening to illegal radio programs, and selling alcoholic beverages. Slavery was at one time supported in the United States by laws which severely punished any person opposing slavery or aiding slaves to escape. In 1931 a study of the inmates of the prisons of the federal government showed that, primarily because of the Prohibition laws, 76 percent of them had been convicted of crimes which were not crimes sixteen years earlier.[13]

On the other hand, many parts of the criminal law today, such as the laws against armed robbery, have a long history of being regarded under the common law as antisocial. When written criminal codes came into being, sanctions against these acts were included, since many of them had their origin in institutional norms and values. Even though at one time they were primarily settled through fights or duels, murder, libel, and assault, for example, became crimes largely because private settlements of such disputes tended to disorganize the stability of social relationships. Occasionally one sees the continuation of this process when a relative of a victim takes the law into his own hand. Violations of these laws, which have their origin and partial support in the mores and are offenses bad in themselves, are referred to by lawyers as *mala in se*.

---

[13] George W. Kirchwey, "The Prison's Place in the Penal Systems," *The Annals*, 157:13–22 (September, 1931).

Certain types of behavior which constitute a considerable portion of the criminal law have no such basis in the mores or common law. Lawyers refer to this general group of criminal offenses as *mala prohibita,* or bad simply because they have been prohibited. Most of these offenses have grown out of more recent technological and cultural changes in society. Many are associated with the automobile, with building codes, with hygiene, and with foods and drugs. Other acts have become crimes because of the activities of some pressure group. Types of behavior which have been so outlawed through this means include the sale of alcoholic beverages, unfair trade practices, cruelty to animals, and the teaching of evolution. Other behavior which has become criminal under changing social conditions includes misuse of trademarks, false advertising, the manufacture of impure foods and drugs, acts in restraint of trade, fraudulent or negligent acts of bank officials resulting in insolvency of banks, sale of fraudulent securities, and improper conduct of labor relations.

In order to deal with crime effectively it is necessary not only to get people to modify their ideas about the extreme seriousness of certain crimes but more frequently to get society to take a stronger view toward certain acts which are not regarded as serious even though they are prohibited. Sutherland summarized the problem in this manner: "Laws have accumulated because the mores have been weak and inconsistent; and because the laws have not had the support of the mores they have been relatively ineffective as a means of control. When the mores are adequate, laws are unnecessary; when the mores are inadequate, the laws are ineffective." [14]

The Criminal Law in Practice. A number of misapprehensions about the nature of the criminal law should be removed before criminals are discussed. Since people are often confused by what they hear about criminal behavior, a few general principles or observations about the criminal law are presented below.

1. The first common misapprehension involves the distinction between two commonly used terms, *felonies* and *misdemeanors.* In general, felonies are offenses which are punished by a sentence of one year or more to a state prison or reformatory. Misdemeanors, on the other hand, are generally dealt with under municipal or county ordinances and involve sentences of less than a year in local institutions. Actually there are few clear-cut distinctions between the two in relation to the acts involved. Often the decision is quite arbitrary, so that a theft of an article worth over $50 is a felony, whereas a theft of one of less value is a misdemeanor. Many offenses, such as burglary and assault, involve various degrees of seriousness, some of which arbitrarily constitute felonies and others misdemeanors. In fact, studies have shown that a felony in one state is often considered a mis-

---

[14] Edwin H. Sutherland and Donald R. Cressey, *Principles of Criminology* (6th ed.; Philadelphia: J. B. Lippincott Company, 1960), p. 11.

demeanor in another, and vice versa. At the discretion of the prosecuting attorney misdemeanant categories, such as "disorderly conduct," can be used to cover a variety of offenses which would otherwise be felonies. This is particularly true of many sex and assault cases.

2. Many people assume that a crime always involves a question of *intent*. Although this is generally the case, there are many exceptions. Statutes are increasingly being enacted which do not incorporate this element. In many states today the criminal law provides that persons may be convicted for crimes, such as adultery, bigamy, selling mortgaged property illegally, and passing bad checks, without criminal intent being established. People have also been convicted of injuring someone because of negligence or because of driving in an intoxicated condition; yet in none of these cases did the person have intent, unless one were to assume that he intended to be negligent or to get drunk in order to harm someone.

3. Only a person who is *competent* can commit a crime. In most states he cannot be adjudged a criminal if he is suffering from a psychosis. Also, the individual must be of legal age. This age is usually eighteen, although in the case of certain felonies there may be concurrent jurisdiction at sixteen, and in the case of murder the act may constitute a crime from the age of twelve. Although a person below the age of eighteen is generally regarded as a delinquent rather than a criminal, it would be an error to assume that all or even a large part of delinquency is comparable to adult criminality, or that boys and girls who are picked up for delinquency or are sent to our state training schools are always "junior criminals."

Actually the behavior covered by the term "delinquency" goes beyond any definition of crime; many acts, if committed by adults, would not even appear before the courts. The delinquent child is not technically prosecuted, nor is there a formal trial with a prosecutor and a defense attorney, or a list of witnesses testifying either against or for someone. There are no specific penalties for delinquent acts, and the judge is permitted great latitude in his judgment, although this latitude is not permitted beyond the delinquent's twenty-first birthday. In Wisconsin, for example, a delinquent child is "any child under the age of eighteen years who has violated any law of the state or any county, city, town or village ordinance, who by reason of being wayward or habitually disobedient, is uncontrolled by his parent . . . who is habitually truant from home or school, who habitually so deports himself as to injure or endanger the morals or health of himself." [15] The following are some of the offenses for which juveniles are apprehended, a list which should certainly remove the erroneous impres-

[15] *Wisconsin Laws Relating to Juvenile Delinquency* (Madison: State Department of Public Welfare, Division for Children and Youth, March, 1952). For a discussion of the legal aspects of juvenile delinquency, see Donald J. Newman, "Legal Aspects of Juvenile Delinquency," in Joseph S. Roucek ed., *Juvenile Delinquency* (New York: Philosophical Library, Inc., 1958), pp. 29–56.

sion that boys and girls picked up for delinquency or committed to training schools are all "junior criminals."

1. Violates any law or ordinance
2. Engages in immoral or indecent conduct
3. Knowingly associates with vicious or immoral persons
4. Knowingly enters or visits house of ill repute
5. Patronizes gambling establishments
6. Patronizes a tavern where intoxicating liquor is sold
7. Uses intoxicating liquors
8. Patronizes a public poolroom
9. Smokes cigarettes around public places
10. Is habitually truant from school
11. Is incorrigible and will not obey parents
12. Absents self from home without consent
13. Wanders in streets at night, not on lawful business (curfew)
14. Habitually wanders about railroad yards or tracks
15. Begs or receives alms
16. Engages in an illegal occupation
17. Is in occupation or situation dangerous to self or others
18. Deports self so as to injure self or others
19. Habitually uses vile, obscene, or vulgar language in public places
20. Jumps train or enters car or engine without authority

4. An *attempt* to commit a crime is also punishable under many circumstances, although usually in a lesser degree, on the theory that the act was intended even though it did not occur. This includes, for example, attempted murder or rape, or the carrying of a concealed weapon, which has been changed from a misdemeanor to a felony on the assumption that the possession of a concealed weapon implies an intent to commit a crime.

5. Under most criminal laws an *accomplice* is considered equally guilty in the commission of an offense. If a group of persons robs a filling station and the operator is shot and killed in the process, not only is the person who held the gun liable for prosecution for murder but all the others, including the lookout, are liable. In a recent English case a man was executed for the killing of a police officer even though at the time of the murder he was being physically held by the arresting officers while his accomplice did the shooting.

6. The criminal law contains no implication that differentials exist in the treatment of crime on the basis of social class, race, and sex. Actually the differences are so great that one criminologist has even questioned the possibility of determining the causes and processes of crime.[16] There are certainly marked differences in the arrests of lower- and upper-class persons

---

[16] Walter C. Reckless, *The Crime Problem* (3d ed.; New York: Appleton-Century-Crofts, Inc., 1961), Chap. 3. He would substitute for causes "categoric risks" of getting arrested and involved in the administrative process.

for the crimes they commit, a fact which will be discussed in more detail later. Likewise, Negroes are more likely to be arrested, convicted, and sentenced to prison than will a comparable group of white offenders. Although the ratio of crimes committed is lower for women than for men, a large proportion of crime committed by women is not reported or prosecuted. This is particularly true of women shoplifters, who are often not reported. When women are involved in offenses with men, as they often are, they are seldom prosecuted and even if convicted are rarely sent to prison. A woman committing murder is seldom given the death penalty.

Trends in the Criminal Law. There are a number of significant trends in the development of the criminal law. Some of them represent improvements; others do not.

1. There has been a trend toward the wider use of probation, the suspended sentence, and the indeterminate sentence, rather than imprisonment. The former method of a flat sentence of so many years for certain crimes is being replaced by the use of indeterminate sentences of, for example, from one to ten years, one to twenty years, or one to life, depending upon the offense. Most criminologists believe that an indeterminate sentence makes it possible for an administrative board, rather than the judge, to study the offender and determine how long an offender should stay in prison, how best to rehabilitate him and at the same time protect society.

2. There has been a marked increase in the use of compulsory psychiatric examinations of offenders for purposes of informing the court in certain sex or personal offenses, or in cases of previous felony conviction. A somewhat similar trend has been the widespread enactment of sex-deviate laws which require the psychiatric examination of certain types of offenders and their indefinite detention for treatment.

3. Physical punishment for crimes has been decreasing. A study of history will reveal that there are probably few methods of physical punishment which have not been used to enforce the criminal law. Men have been tortured and maimed in a variety of ingenious ways; they have been forced to man galleys or transported overseas to penal colonies; they have been executed by various devices. Beginning with the end of the eighteenth century, offenders were more likely to be imprisoned, fined, or placed on probation. These forms of punishment are now almost the only methods that our society uses to punish criminal offenders.

Physical punishment has constituted such a large part of the criminal law in the past that we should examine the philosophies which have been advanced to support it. According to one view, physical punishment exacts retribution; here we have *lex talionis* and vengeance, or an "eye for an eye and a tooth for a tooth." The offender should pay his debt to society. Another view, similar to Beccaria's idea of long ago, is that the punishment of an offender deters others from similar acts. Then there is the concept that punishment restores the social equilibrium, which has been upset by certain crimes. In such cases the offender might be considered to expiate his offense through suffering. Finally, in addition to these theories of punishment, some people have felt that punishment reforms, something it obviously cannot do. On the contrary, physical punishment, whether by imprisonment or otherwise, appears to produce a number of harmful effects.[17]

1. It tends to isolate the individual. Some have remarked that what society holds against a man is not the crime he committed but the fact that he has been physically punished, as by imprisonment.

2. Punishment may simply develop cautious actions in the individual so that instead of changing his attitudes he may simply try harder not to be apprehended again.

3. It frequently creates new and undesirable attitudes in the individual, such as fear, and lack of self-confidence.

4. Punishment may even give the offender status. Delinquents and adults who have been punished often occupy a higher position in the eyes of other deviants and sometimes even in the eyes of the general public simply because of this fact.

5. Any attempt to reform an individual must be a constructive process, but physical punishment is the opposite of this. In fact, in many instances the application of force may stop any efforts on the part of the individual to change his personal behavior voluntarily.

The death penalty has been rapidly declining as a form of punishment. At the end of the eighteenth century it could be employed in at least 240 crimes in England, and there were almost as many capital crimes in the United States. With the development of the idea of prisons, the wider extension of equality before the law affecting noble and serfs alike, and the greater respect for human life, there has been a gradual trend toward the abolition of capital punishment.[18]

Many countries have abolished the death penalty during peacetime: Belgium, Denmark, Holland, Iceland, Italy, New Zealand, Norway, Portugal, Sweden, Switzerland, Argentina, Brazil, Colombia, Peru, Uruguay, Venezuela, and Costa Rica. Although in the Soviet Union the death penalty had been reserved for cases of high treason, espionage, sabotage, terrorist acts, banditry and premeditated murder under certain aggravated circumstances, it was announced in May, 1961, that the death penalty might be applied to large-scale embezzlers of state property and to counterfeiters. The death penalty, all executions being by a firing squad, was also sanc-

---

[17] Sutherland and Cressey, *op. cit.*
[18] See George Rusche and Otto Kirchheimer, *Punishment and Social Structure* (New York: Columbia University Press, 1939).

tioned for especially dangerous habitual offenders and for prisoners who committed violence in their place of confinement.[19] In 1962 the death penalty was further extended to certain public officials who receive bribes, to those who make attempts "under aggravating circumstances" on the life of a policeman or a citizen-volunteer charged with maintaining public order, and to those who commit some types of forcible rape.[20]

After discussions going back over many years, the English Parliament passed the Homicide Act of 1957 which restricted the number of cases in which the death penalty could be imposed.[21] At the time of the passage of this act it was anticipated that the number of executions would be reduced about five sixths, and so far this estimate has been proved to be substantially accurate.

In the United States persons can still be executed for such crimes as murder, kidnaping, treason, rape, and for armed robbery in many southern states. Of the 42 states with capital punishment in 1960, 24 of them use electrocution, 11 lethal gas, 6 hanging, and in 1 state, Utah, the prisoner has the choice of shooting or hanging. During the twenty-four-year period, 1930 through 1953, a total of 3281 persons were executed by civil authorities, 87.0 percent of them for murder and 11.4 percent for rape. There has been a marked decline in the use of capital punishment in the United States, from an annual average of 167 between 1930 and 1939 to 80 per year for the period 1950–1953. In the calendar year 1960, 57 prisoners were executed in this country, somewhat above the figure of 49 for each of the years 1958 and 1959, which was a record low. Twenty states with capital punishment conducted one or more executions in 1960, five of them accounting for 37 executions: California with 9, Arkansas and Texas 8 each, and Georgia and New York 6 each. Of all the executions, 45 were for murder, 8 were for rape, 2 were for kidnaping, 1 was for robbery, and 1 was for aggravated assault by a life prisoner.

A number of arguments can be advanced against capital punishment: (1) There appears to be little evidence that capital punishment has a deterrent effect. Homicide rates in the United States are generally much lower in the states which have abolished capital punishment than in those which have not. This may simply mean that the presence or absence of capital punishment has no relationship to the homicide rate and that the entire question probably rests on more basic factors in the social environment. Vermont, for example, has a mandatory death penalty; yet it has one of the lowest homicide rates in the country. There are such marked differ-

---

[19] As reported in *The New York Times,* May 7, 1961, p. 28.

[20] As reported in *The New York Times,* February 28, 1962, pp. 1, 5.

[21] For example, treason, piracy, killing of a law officer, and murder connected with the commission of another crime such as robbery would be subject to the death penalty. For a complete discussion of the history of capital punishment in Great Britain and this new law, see Gerald Gardiner, "Criminal Law: Capital Punishment in Britain," *American Bar Association Journal,* 45:259–261 (March, 1959).

ences in the homicide rates within a state that the deterrent effect of the death penalty is doubtful. (2) The abolition of the death penalty has resulted in no consistent reaction. Sometimes there has been an increase in murder and sometimes not. (3) Moreover, evidence indicates that juries are less willing to convict a person when the penalty is death. (4) Another argument against capital punishment is that if an injustice has been done it can never be remedied. (5) A disproportionate number of persons executed are Negroes, young people, and the poor. Of those persons executed for rape from 1930 to 1960, for example, 89.9 percent were Negroes. Over 60 percent of all those executed during 1960 were Negroes, and of these over three fourths were under thirty-five. (6) Finally, there is the debasing effect of executions on societies where the taking of human life is contrary to most religious and social beliefs. It is not in line with contemporary scientific thinking, which emphasizes the treatment and rehabilitation of criminals.

Although there has been a trend away from the use of physical punishments, greater severity in the use of imprisonment has developed in two directions. In response to public hysteria, particularly in the case of certain crimes of violence and sex offenses, penalties of imprisonment up to 199 years have been provided by some states. This sentence is more severe than even a so-called life sentence, since a person becomes eligible for release from prison after serving about one third of his sentence. In the case of life imprisonment this period is from eleven to fifteen years, a figure based on approximately a forty-five-year life expectancy beyond the average age at commission of the crime. The second direction has been the passage of habitual-criminal laws (sometimes called Baumes Laws, after the first one passed in New York), which often require incarceration for life, with no parole, after four felony convictions.[22] On the whole, criminologists look with disfavor on both these trends because they emphasize the crime and not the possible rehabilitation of the offender, and because they often remove all hope from him. Thus not only is further rehabilitation almost impossible: the individual becomes a difficult custodial problem in a correctional institution.

An interesting and significant trend has been the expansion of federal criminal law, which has resulted in making many crimes national crimes. Some of these laws which have developed during the past half century follow:

1910 The White Slave Act (Mann Act)
1925 National Motor Vehicle Theft Act (Dyer Act)
1932 Extortion Act (prohibition of the sending of such notes through the
       mails)

---

[22] Great Britain uses preventive detention of from five to fourteen years for habitual criminals. Norval Morris, *The Habitual Criminal* (Cambridge, Mass.: Harvard University Press, 1951).

1934   Kidnaping Act (Lindbergh Act)

1934   National Firearms Act (registration and taxation of machine guns and similar weapons)

1934   National Bank Robbery Act (robbery of banks connected with the Federal Reserve System or insured by the federal government)

1934   National Stolen Property Act (transportation in interstate commerce of stolen articles worth more than $5000)

1934   Anti-Racketeering Statute (prohibition of racketeering in interstate commerce)

1951   Slot machines and other gambling devices (machines cannot be moved in interstate commerce)

1951   Occupational tax on gamblers ($50 tax on bookies)

Federal laws of this type have been enacted primarily because of the difficulty in dealing with crime on a restricted political basis when criminals, like other persons, move freely and rapidly across state lines. Without the authority provided by a federal law, officers must depend upon the cooperation of officials in other states. Moreover, the cost of extraditing an offender from one state to another has discouraged the prosecution of many crimes. The Bank Robbery Act was enacted in 1934 when the Federal Deposit Insurance Corporation began to insure deposits in most banks, many of which are also members of the Federal Reserve System. Robberies of these banks actually constitute robbery of the federal government.

Although there will probably be further federal expansion of such specific laws in the future, most of them will be restricted to interstate commerce. Other expansion of the enforcement of federal laws has come from more general federal laws, such as postal regulations and tax laws of the Internal Revenue Service.

WHITE-COLLAR CRIME

The definition of a crime solely in terms of the criminal law seems to be too restrictive, however, for the adequate explanation of criminal behavior. Many students of the problem, particularly scientists with a broad point of view, feel that a crime should be defined not only in terms of the criminal law but in broader terms as any act punishable by the state, regardless of whether the penalty is a criminal one or is administrative or civil in nature. They believe that the strict legal definition of a crime is too limited and biased and does not include what has been termed "white-collar crime."

Lawbreaking is often divided into two neat categories: the conventional crimes, such as larceny, burglary, and robbery, which are usually punished under the criminal law; and those violations of law which have come to be known as "white-collar crimes" and which are seldom punished in this way. They include violations of law by businessmen, politicians and government employees, labor union leaders, doctors, and lawyers.[23]

Many investigations by governmental committees, both state and federal, have revealed that white-collar crime among business concerns is extensive. These investigations have covered banking operations, the oil industry, stock exchanges, public utilities, munitions, real estate, insurance, and railways. Violations of law by businessmen include the illegal activities of reorganization committees in receiverships and in bankruptcies; restraint of trade such a monopoly, illegal rebates, infringements of patents, trademarks, and copyrights; misrepresentation in advertising; unfair labor practices; financial manipulations; and wartime crimes, such as black marketeering.[24]

Employers seem to have extensively violated federal laws regulating wages, hours, and public contracts, as well as labor relations and trade practices.[25] A study covering seventy large corporations which, with two exceptions, are included among the two hundred largest nonfinancial institutions in the United States, found that they had had 980 decisions rendered against them for violations of government regulations, an average of 14 per corporation.[26] Sixty corporations had had decisions against them for restraint of trade, 53 for infringement of patents, 44 for unfair labor practices, 28 for misrepresentation in advertising, 26 for rebates, and 43 for miscellaneous offenses. Sixty percent of these adverse decisions were rendered during the ten-year period 1935–1944, during which time there was increased government enforcement of business regulations. After a careful analysis Sutherland concluded that although 158 cases were dealt with by the criminal courts, in actuality crimes were committed in 779 out of the 980 cases, 583 being decisions by civil courts. Even if the analysis were restricted to the criminal courts, it would show that almost two thirds of the corporations had been convicted at one time or another and had an average of 4 convictions each.

Various offenses of a white-collar nature are committed by politicians and government employees. They include direct misappropriation of public funds or the illegal acquirement of these funds through padded payrolls, through relatives illegally on the government payroll, or through

---

[23] One might ask about college professors. There is the possibility of accepting bribes for higher grades, but this has never been a part of the pattern of college teaching. If it was, the results would be as chaotic as politics are.

[24] See Frank Gibney, *The Operators* (New York: Harper & Row, Publishers, 1960) for an account, with many case histories, of unethical and illegal practices in business and politics.

[25] Robert A. Lane, "Why Business Men Violate the Law," *Journal of Criminal Law, Criminology, and Police Science,* 44:151–165 (July–August, 1953).

[26] Edwin H. Sutherland, *White Collar Crime* (New York: Holt, Rinehart and Winston, Inc., 1949, reissued 1960), p. 20.

monetary "kickbacks" from appointees. Usually, however, the illegal activities are more subtle. Politicians and government employees may gain financially by furnishing some favor to business firms or to criminal syndicates. Favors for which politicians may be rewarded by certain businessmen include illegal commissions on public contracts, issuance of licenses or certificates of building or fire inspections, and tax exemptions or lowered tax valuations. Criminal syndicates may share the proceeds of gambling or other profits with public officials who give protection from arrest.

Labor union officials may engage in a variety of criminal activities, such as the misappropriation or misapplication of union funds, defiance of the government by failure to enforce laws affecting their labor unions, collusion with employers to the disadvantage of their own union members, and the use of fraudulent means to maintain their control over the union.[27]

Certain activities in the medical profession are not only unethical but illegal. They include giving illegal prescriptions for narcotics, performing illegal abortions, making fraudulent reports and giving false testimony in accident cases, and fee splitting. Fee splitting, in which a doctor splits the fee he charges with the doctor who referred the case to him, is against the law in many states because of the danger that such referrals will be based on the size of the fee rather than on the proficiency of the practitioner. This practice actually involves the very life of the patient if a doctor refers him to an inferior surgeon in order to secure a part of the surgeon's fee. One study reported that two thirds of the surgeons in New York City split fees.[28] Dr. Paul R. Hawley, Director of the American College of Surgeons, declared that the American people would be shocked at the extent of this practice as well as at the amount of unnecessary surgery performed on patients throughout the country.[29]

Lawyers engage in such illegalities as misappropriating funds in receiverships, securing perjured testimony from witnesses, and "ambulance chasing" in various forms, usually to collect fraudulent damage claims arising from an accident. When cases of these types are discovered the offender is more apt to be disbarred from practice than prosecuted.

The consideration of only conventional crimes gives an erroneous impression of the extent and effects of crimes on society as well as of the nature of criminals.[30] Persons sentenced to prison are usually rather poor

---

[27] Malcolm Johnson, *Crime on the Labor Front* (New York: McGraw-Hill Book Company, Inc., 1950). See also Robert Kennedy, *The Enemy Within* (New York: Harper & Row, Publishers, 1960).

[28] Cited in Sutherland, *White Collar Crime*, p. 12.

[29] "Too Much Unnecessary Surgery," *United States News & World Report*, 34:47-55 (February, 1953). Also see H. Whitman, "Why Some Doctors Should Be in Jail," *Collier's*, 132:23-27 (October, 1953).

[30] Frank E. Hartung, "White Collar Crime: Its Significance for Theory and Practice," *Federal Probation*, 17:31-36 (June, 1953). See also Donald J. Newman, "White-Collar Crime," in *Law and Contemporary Problems*, 23:735-753 (Autumn, 1958).

and relatively uneducated, whereas white-collar criminals are usually in the higher income brackets and are better educated. There is considerable difference in the effect on society of ordinary crimes as compared with white-collar offenses. Sutherland has made these comparisons:

> The financial loss to society from white-collar crimes is probably greater than the financial loss from burglaries, robberies, and larcenies committed by persons of the lower socio-economic class. The average loss per burglary is less than one hundred dollars, a burglary which yields as much as fifty thousand dollars is exceedingly rare, and a million-dollar burglary is practically unknown. On the other hand, there may be several million-dollar embezzlements reported in one year. Embezzlements, however, are peccadilloes compared with the large-scale crimes committed by corporations, investment trusts, and public utility holding companies; reports of fifty-million-dollar losses from such criminal behavior are by no means uncommon.[31]

Many people believe, however, that white-collar crimes are not crimes, and that "crime" and "criminal" should be arbitrarily restricted to the more overt acts of ordinary criminals which fit the common stereotype and which they themselves would never do. This arbitrary distinction is made not on the basis of illegal behavior but on the basis of how the judicial process—namely, the criminal law—reacts to it. Sociologically a crime is any act which is considered socially injurious and which is punished by the state, regardless of the type of punishment. The difficulty in limiting the definition of a crime in terms of the criminal law becomes evident when one compares the punishment of a fine, jail sentence, or probation given an apprehended burglar or bank robber with the different kind of punishment often given a person of white-collar status who violates the law. A doctor who violates the law might be punished by having his license revoked, a lawyer by being disbarred, or a businessman by being enjoined by the government, being required to pay civil damages, having his license to do business suspended, or, in some cases, having his product seized and destroyed. Several factors may enter into the decisions on the dispositions of tax violations which are ordinarily settled by an additional payment of money rather than by criminal prosecution. Tax cases involving large sums of money and flagrant law violations may sometimes be handled administratively, such as being "settled," or by criminal prosecution.

The reports of the Federal Food and Drug Administration carry evidence of widespread violations of laws whose purpose is to safeguard the nation's health and welfare. Such cases include selling various types of food contaminated by filth, hair, and rodents; misrepresenting products, such as selling horse meat as beef, mixing mineral oil with salad oil, or

---

[31] Edwin H. Sutherland, "Crime and Business," *The Annals*, 217:113 (September, 1941). Also see Marshall B. Clinard, "Corruption Runs Far Deeper Than Politics," *The New York Times Magazine*, August, 1952, p. 21.

mixing ground chick-peas or cereal with coffee; short-weighting or using deceptive containers; and, occasionally, selling products which contain physically harmful ingredients. These violations may result in a variety of possible actions: issuance of a civil court injunction to cease further viola- tions; seizure and destruction of the product; and, in the case of the federal law, a fine of up to $5000 and imprisonment of up to five years. It seems logical to regard these violations as crimes, whether or not those responsible for them appeared in the criminal courts. All these sanctions imply that this behavior is socially injurious, that punishment is involved, and that the offender is being stigmatized by society.

Sutherland has shown that unless a more inclusive concept of what constitutes "crime" is used, it is impossible to deal analytically with the different illegal activities which are punished according to occupation and social class.[32]

> White-collar crime is real crime. It is not ordinarily called crime, and calling it by this name does not make it worse, just as refraining from calling it crime does not make it better than it otherwise would be. It is called crime here in order to bring it within the scope of criminology, which is justified because it is in violation of the criminal law. The crucial question in this analysis is the criterion of violation of the criminal law. Conviction in the criminal court, which is sometimes suggested as the criterion, is not adequate because a large proportion of those who commit crimes are not convicted in criminal courts. This criterion, therefore, needs to be supplemented. When it is supplemented, the criterion of the crimes of one class must be kept con- sistent in general terms with the criterion of the crimes of the other class. The definition should not be the spirit of the law for white-collar crime and the letter of the law for other crimes, or in other respects be more liberal for one class than for the other.[33]

Why White-Collar Crime Is Punished Differently. Punishments for white-collar crimes vary considerably, and are in a striking contrast to the punishment for ordinary crimes. There are several reasons for this differ- ence. First of all, many acts of businessmen which are socially harmful were not made illegal until rather recent times. Embezzlement and some forms of fraud, for example, were not designated as crimes until late in the eight- eenth century, and it was not until after the beginning of the nineteenth century that the following acts were outlawed in this country: restraint of trade, false advertising, insolvency of banks due to fraud or negligence of officials, sale of fraudulent securities, and misuse of trade-marks. This slow development was partly due to the fact that the philosophy of laissez faire

---

[32] This sociological conception of crime does not include as crime behavior which is solely antisocial, injurious to society, unfair, greedy, but not necessarily illegal.

[33] Edwin H. Sutherland, "White Collar Criminality," *American Sociological Review* 5:5 (February, 1940), and Hartung, "White Collar Crime," *loc. cit.* Also see Marshall B. Clinard, *The Black Market: A Study of White Collar Crime* (New York: Holt, Rinehart and Winston, Inc., 1952), pp. 226–262.

and *caveat emptor* ("let the buyer beware"), which characterized our general social, political, and economic thinking, prohibited the development of certain needed legal prohibitions regardless of occupation or social class.

Second, there has been little organized public resentment against many socially injurious white-collar crimes, and without great public pressures it has been difficult to get criminal laws passed against this behavior. As one writer has pointed out, white-collar crime differs from other crime, not only in the methods of dealing with it but in the status of the offender, the toleration of the public, and the support which offenders may receive from other groups in the society.[34] This confusion over white-collar crime is a reflection of the diversity of status systems in present-day society. White-collar crimes are usually more complex and are often diffused over a longer period of time than are simple and overt crimes, such as burglary, a fact which tends to obscure the essential criminality of the acts.[35] Furthermore, white-collar crimes are publicized differently from ordinary crimes; consequently, they usually arouse less public resentment.

Summary

A crime may be defined broadly as any act punishable by the state or, in a restricted fashion, as any act punishable by the criminal law. The former definition would include as white-collar crime a host of offenses against the law which are socially injurious but not often punished with a criminal penalty. In either case the use of formal punishment by the state is only one way in which society seeks to secure support for its social norms. What situation is defined as a crime may be relative to both place and time. The criminal law has been characterized by a number of trends, including the wider use of probation, compulsory psychiatric examinations for certain offenses, the decreasing use of the death penalty, and, unfortunately, a trend toward severe penalties for particular types of offenses and for repeaters. Society should more properly consider the offender and not merely the criminal act.

Selected Readings

CLINARD, MARSHALL B. *The Black Market.* New York: Holt, Rinehart and Winston, Inc., 1952, Chaps. 1, 2, and 9. An analysis of price and rationing violations during World War II. Chapter 9 discusses white-collar crime and, in particular, whether black-market activities were crimes.

FULLER, RICHARD C. "Morals and the Criminal Law," *Journal of Criminal Law and Criminology,* 32:624-630 (March–April, 1942). A discussion of the relation of social norms and values to ordinary crimes and to white-collar crimes.

---

[34] Vilhelm Aubert, "White Collar Crime and Social Structure," *American Journal of Sociology,* 58:263-271 (November, 1952).

[35] See Sutherland, *White Collar Crime,* pp. 50-51.

HARTUNG, FRANK E. "White Collar Crime: Its Significance for Theory and Practice," *Federal Probation*, 17:31–36 (June, 1953). This article surveys the research on white-collar crime and suggests its theoretical and practical implications.

NEWMAN, DONALD J. "Legal Aspects of Juvenile Delinquency," in Joseph S. Roucek ed., *Juvenile Delinquency*. New York: Philosophical Library, Inc., 1958, pp. 29–56. A discussion of the difference between delinquency and crime and of some of the important issues in dealing with juveniles as delinquents and not criminals.

NEWMAN, DONALD J. "White-Collar Crime," *Law and Contemporary Problems*, 23:735–753 (Autumn, 1958). A survey of the literature and discussion of the definition and legal basis of white-collar crime and the positive and negative view of whether white-collar violations are crime and white-collar violators criminals.

SUTHERLAND, EDWIN H. *White Collar Crime*. New York: Holt, Rinehart and Winston, Inc., 1949, reissued 1961, Chaps. 1–3. The first comprehensive work dealing with white-collar crime. Chapter 3 is a discussion of the problem of whether such crime is actually crime.

SUTHERLAND, EDWIN H., and DONALD R. CRESSEY. *Principles of Criminology*. 6th ed. Philadelphia: J. B. Lippincott Company, 1960, Chap. 1. This chapter presents some of the essential aspects of the criminal law which are necessary for the study of criminology.

TAPPAN, PAUL W. "Who Is the Criminal?" *American Sociological Review*, 12:96–103 (February, 1947). The position of this article is that the definition of crime in criminology should be restricted to the criminal law and that to include white-collar crime is confusing.

Sources of Delinquent and
Criminal Attitudes

Thus far this discussion of crime has attempted to clarify the nature of delinquent and criminal acts. It has shown that behavior becomes criminal because it is socially harmful and subject to punishment by the state. This chapter will focus attention on the sources of various conflicting norms which either are in opposition to laws forbidding certain behavior or fail to support them.

Criminals and delinquents develop attitudes and definitions of situations through group association in the same fashion as do noncriminals and nondelinquents. This group experience involves not only the family about which we now hear so much, but also the play group, the school, the neighborhood, clubs, church, marriage, occupation—in fact, all life in its interaction with culture and subculture. Both criminality and noncriminality are "natural" in the sense that they are the outgrowths of processes of social definitions.

First of all, in a consideration of these group experiences, some of the factors in the general culture should be examined, including cultural ideologies which might enhance criminal behavior, the effect of law-enforcement agencies on criminal behavior, and the effects of such secondary influences as motion pictures, radio, television, newspapers, and comic books. The role of the neighborhood or occupational group, the subculture of delinquent companions and gangs, and the role of the family will also be discussed. All these areas, it is contended, are potential sources of criminal attitudes and thus should be considered in developing any program to control delinquency or crime.

Although there is evidence which seems to indicate that certain types of neighborhoods are one of the most important bases for an attack on delinquency, efforts at control should go beyond the neighborhood. The larger society, as it impinges on the community as well as on the adult and the juvenile, must be dealt with in any realistic analysis of delinquency and criminal behavior. Moreover, the attempt to draw a line between the world of the juveniles and young adults and the larger world of the adult is theoretically indefensible, for both groups secure deviant and non-deviant norms within the social framework of our general culture.[1]

The General Culture

Great Britain, New Zealand, and the Scandinavian countries appear to have much lower crime rates than does the United States. This fact is significant, for even a superficial comparison with these countries reveals some striking differences. Several characteristics of American culture un-doubtedly account for its high rate of crime. Taft has suggested the following as characteristic aspects of American culture and significantly related to its high crime rate.

1. American culture is dynamic.
2. American culture is complex.
3. American culture is materialistic.
4. American culture is individualistic.
5. American social relations are increasingly impersonal.
6. American culture fosters restricted group loyalties.
7. American culture encourages survival of frontier values.
8. American culture lacks the viewpoint of social science.
9. American culture has faith in law without expecting or even approving obedience to all laws.[2]

Although several of these characteristics have already been discussed in the analysis of the role of urbanism in producing deviant behavior, some need further elaboration in the sections which follow. They will include the general disobedience to law, the selective obedience to law, the illegal behavior of law-enforcement officers, and the relation to delinquency and crime of such secondary media of communication as the press and its treatment of crime and motion pictures, television, radio, and comic books and their treatment of crime.

GENERAL DISOBEDIENCE TO LAW

Although American culture professes obedience to law, there is ex-tensive flaunting of these taboos on the part of the general adult popula-tion. There are indications that disobedience to law is far more widespread than reports of crimes committed show; indeed, Reckless has asserted that many violations of the criminal code are not officially known.[3]

Several studies have been made of the extent of unreported delin-

---

[1] Marshall B. Clinard, "Secondary Community Influences and Juvenile Delinquency," *The Annals*, 261:42–43 (January, 1949).

[2] Adapted from Donald R. Taft, *Criminology* (3d ed.; New York: The Macmillan Company, 1956), pp. 38–43. Item 4 has been added by the author.

[3] Walter C. Reckless, *The Crime Problem* (3d ed.; New York: Appleton-Century-Crofts, Inc., 1961), pp. 23–25.

quency and crime. A comparison of a group of 337 Texas college students
with a group of 2049 delinquents who came to the attention of the Fort
Worth juvenile court revealed that the delinquent acts of these college
students had been as serious, although probably not as frequent, as those
of the delinquents.[4] Although the college students had rarely appeared in
court except for traffic offenses, everyone had committed other offenses for
which he could have been charged. For example, on the average every 100
male students committed 116 precollege thefts and 36 thefts during college.
Of 49 criminology students at a midwestern university, 86 percent had
committed thefts, and about 50 percent had committed acts of vandalism.[5]

An interesting study was made of criminal behavior among the general
adult population in metropolitan New York City.[6] Of 1698 persons who
answered a questionnaire anonymously, 91 percent stated that they had
committed one or more crimes after they were sixteen years of age. (See
Table 7.1.) Sixty-four percent of the men and 29 percent of the women

*Table 7.1. Percentage of 1698 Persons Who Had
Committed Offenses*

Offense	Men	Women
Malicious mischief	84%	81%
Disorderly conduct	85	76
Assault	49	5
Auto misdemeanors	61	39
Indecency	77	74
Gambling	74	54
Larceny	89	83
Grand larceny (except auto)	13	11
Auto theft	26	8
Burglary	17	4
Robbery	11	1
Concealed weapons	35	3
Perjury	23	17
Falsification and fraud	46	34
Election frauds	7	4
Tax evasion	57	40
Coercion	16	6
Conspiracy	23	7
Criminal libel	36	29

SOURCE: James S. Wallerstein and Clement J. Wyle, "Our Law-Abiding Law-Breakers,"
Probation, 25:112 (April, 1947).

[4] Austin L. Porterfield, *Youth in Trouble* (Fort Worth, Tex.: Leo Potishman Foundation, 1946), pp. 32–35.
[5] Unpublished material collected by the author.
[6] James S. Wallerstein and Clement J. Wyle, "Our Law-Abiding Law-Breakers," *Probation,* 25:107–112 (April, 1947). The immediately following statistics are from this study.

could have been convicted of felonies. The mean number of offenses committed by the men in adult life (over sixteen years of age) was eighteen and
ranged from 8 percent for ministers to 20 percent for laborers. Between
eight and nine in every ten men and women had stolen things; one in four
of the men admitted stealing an automobile; and one in ten of this group
had robbed someone. From this study it was concluded that "the number
of acts legally constituting crimes are far in excess of those officially reported. Unlawful behavior, far from being an abnormal social or psychological manifestation, is in truth a very common phenomenon."

The types of violation varied greatly according to occupation: "Businessmen and lawyers were highest in perjury, falsification, fraud and tax
evasion; teachers and social workers in malicious mischief; writers and
artists in indecency, criminal libel and gambling; military and government
employees in simple larceny; mechanics and technicians in disorderly conduct; farmers in illegal possession of weapons; laborers in grand larceny,
burglary and robbery; students in auto misdemeanors."

Many different reasons were given for the violations of law. A doctor,
for example, admitted taking a car without permission, explaining it as an
"emergency." A laborer who had broken in and taken property said that
he "put it back later."

> Several persons stated that they had had to falsify their religion to get a
> certain job, others reporting violation of birth control or gambling laws re
> garded the laws themselves as stupid and therefore they saw nothing wrong in
> violating them. Larceny of objects under $100 in value covered such items as
> towels, a bathmat, a spoon and stamps. One man asserted that his high bill
> gave him at least a moral right to steal from the hotel where he was staying.
> Another excused himself for stealing from his employer by observing, "My boss
> is a jerk." A mechanic who falsified to get someone to sign a document ex
> plained that the paper in question was his marriage license. Another man
> learned that crime did not pay when he used a falsehood in the matter of
> signing a document. He added to his admission, "My uncle's will, but got
> nothing, anyway." A farmer faced with the issue of whether or not he had been
> guilty of assault without provocation wrote "no" in the designated space, but
> added the comment, "Thrashed a lot of men in my time but they all jolly well
> deserved it." A woman artist decided to call herself guilty of assault but with
> the qualifying phrase "Threw ash tray at an unbearable cad." A self-styled
> criminologist over sixty gave up after reading the questionnaire and returned
> it with the sweeping comment, "Too much trouble, I've done them all."

The Kinsey report on sexual conduct in American society—although
the sample used is only partially representative—revealed the startling
presence of serious violations of criminal law of which the public had not
been aware.[7] The study revealed that nearly all men with less than an

---

[7] A. C. Kinsey, W. B. Pomeroy, and C. E. Martin, *Sexual Behavior in the Human Male*
(Philadelphia: W. B. Saunders Company, 1948). This study has been criticized for the lack

eighth-grade education and about three fourths of those with a college training had had premarital intercourse, an offense which is punishable in every state as fornication, about one third of the sample had had homosexual experiences, and nearly three fourths had had relations with prostitutes. There were extramarital relationships in a third of the marriages, a violation of our laws relating to adultery. Kinsey concluded that "the persons involved in these activities, taken as a whole, constitute more than 95 per cent of the total male population. Only a relatively small proportion of the males who are sent to penal institutions for sex offenses have been involved in behavior which is materially different from that of most of the males in the population." [8]

Few evidences of our lawless behavior would be more startling to people of another culture than the widespread indirect association of the American people with organized crime through their participation in organized gambling. In 1951 the Kefauver Committee found that widespread illegal gambling was being practiced in nearly every city of any size in the United States. People illegally bet billions of dollars through organized racketeers on policy and numbers rackets as well as on the outcome and point range of many amateur and professional athletic contests. Within recent years some athletes have become involved with the law either because they did not report an offer of a bribe or because they accepted one. From 1956 through 1961 twenty college basketball players were paid $44,500 in bribe money to fix forty-four games, according to statements and indictments by prosecutors in New York and North Carolina. Another six players were charged with accepting money in "softening-up" cash, as potential or actual contact men.[9]

This public lawlessness undoubtedly has its effects on other criminals as well. Ten years ago Senator Paul Douglas made some significant remarks on the effects of this and other types of illegal behavior upon American society.

> Other events during the year [1951] have also shown that the evils which have been revealed are far more pervasive than we should like to believe. They go deep into our social life and are not confined to politics. Thus, large numbers of players on leading college basketball teams have confessed to accepting money from gamblers in order to "fix" the point score in games. Further inquiry has developed that the colleges themselves were not guiltless, since they have allowed both the sport and the players to be professionalized. It has also been revealed that the major portion of the football team at the United States Military Academy—an institution which has prided itself upon its honor—

---

of representativeness of the sample and for the inaccuracy of some of the data furnished by some of the subjects as well as for other flaws. See Paul Wallin, "An Appraisal of Some Methodological Aspects of the Kinsey Report," *American Sociological Review*, 14:197–211 (April, 1949).

[8] Kinsey, *et al.*, *op. cit.*, p. 392.

[9] See Tim Cohane, "Behind the Basketball Scandal," *Look*, 26:85 (February 12, 1962).

systematically cheated in their examinations in order to maintain their eligibility. Informal polls of the student bodies of a number of colleges have indicated that cheating is apparently a widespread practice while the professionalization of college football has become more and more evident. In one FBI district alone, the number of cases of embezzlement from banks by trusted officials has reached a startling figure. These and other developments are symptoms of ethical weaknesses which permeate wide sections of our society from which we had expected higher standards. They have brought a feeling of disgust to most Americans and have made them skeptical about the existence either of integrity in active life or of any real professional virtue.[10]

In 1959 the shock of television scandals on several nationally televised "quiz shows" swept through the American public, an estimated fifty million of whom, in 1958, had been watching the three leading quiz programs. A number of programs were found to have been rigged by feeding the contestants answers in advance. On this basis one contestant, whose father and uncle each had won a Pulitzer Prize in literature, defeated thirteen opponents and therefore won $129,000. Others confessed to winning large amounts fraudulently, as much as $237,500 in one case and $98,500 in another. Altogether, ten contestants were brought before the courts on charges of perjury since they had denied the charges under oath before a grand jury. They were given suspended sentences, but were allowed to keep their "earnings."

SELECTIVE OBEDIENCE TO LAW

Much more common than general disobedience to law is the tendency in American culture for persons to obey laws on a selective basis. Instead of obeying all laws one disregards those types of law which directly affect his own occupation and social class. Sutherland, as well as others, emphasized this public attitude that one can use his own discretion as to which laws he must obey. Some laws are obeyed, others are not, according to a person's own beliefs rather than the general welfare.[11]

Many businessmen believe that such laws as those regulating securities and banking procedures, tax collections, restraint of trade, labor relations, wartime price control and rationing, and others of a similar nature, are not as binding on the individual as are our burglary and robbery laws. Some labor leaders see no reason for obeying laws prohibiting labor "racketeering" or laws affecting the conduct of labor relations and strikes if it is to their advantage to break them. Farmers have been known, too, to disobey the law selectively; examples include their failure to pay proper income

---

[10] Paul H. Douglas, *Ethics in Government* (Cambridge, Mass.: Harvard University Press, 1952), pp. 9–10. Also see "Ethical Standards in Public Life," *The Annals*, Vol. 280 (March, 1952).

[11] Edwin H. Sutherland and Donald R. Cressey, *Principles of Criminology* (6th ed.: Philadelphia: J. B. Lippincott Company, 1960), p. 86.

taxes, their intimidation of farm auctioneers, and their dumping of milk trucks to keep up the price of milk in the depression of the thirties.[12] Government officials operate in a situation where bribes and favors are on occasion offered by businessmen and where politicians, including congressmen, may exert influence in behalf of special interests. A political scientist has this to say about political corruption:

> The record indicates that the political morality reflects, rather than shapes, the society in which it operates and that, more pertinently, it is naïve in the extreme to expect from politicians a far different ethical standard from that which prevails throughout the country. Indeed, were today's politicians to adopt such a standard they would almost certainly be rejected by the voters as idealists, dreamers, crackpots, or visionaries.[13]

The implications of selective obedience to law can be seen more clearly if ordinary crimes are considered. Many persons who engage in such crimes as robbery and burglary consider some of our laws unjust and too severe, and they often have a number of rationalizations for these attitudes. They point to the general dishonesty of the public, the brutality of the police, and the corruption of public officials, including those in the courts. A professional confidence man who is smart enough to outtrick a "sucker" may contend that the law should not punish him, or in any event not as severely as it does. A man with a prison record who has a dependent family, whose wages are too low, and whose record interferes with employment possibilities may advance such arguments as rationalizations for thefts or burglaries. Certainly ordinary criminals are acquainted with the effects of this selective obedience to law, and this attitude presents a major problem in the rehabilitation work of our correctional institutions. As the warden of one of our prisons said in 1946, "What am I supposed to do, retrain people to be honest in a dishonest world of black markets and frauds?" Perhaps Willy Sutton, a well-known professional bank robber, put it best when he told a group of New York reporters some years ago: "Others accused of defrauding the government of hundreds of thousands of dollars merely get a letter from a committee in Washington asking them to come in and talk it over. Maybe it's justice but it's puzzling to a guy like me."

Great inconsistency exists in modern urban society between the behavior required of a child and that of an adult, and these differences are not clearly defined as a correlate of age. In fact, adults are permitted increasing transgressions of the conduct norms, whereas juveniles are expected to conform to ideals. In many simpler societies the situation is reversed. It is the juveniles who have considerable freedom, whereas the behavior of

---

[12] James O. Babcock, "The Revolt in Iowa," *Social Forces*, 12:369–373 (March, 1934).
[13] H. H. Wilson, *Congress: Corruption and Compromise* (New York: Holt, Rinehart and Winston, Inc., 1951), p. 234.

adults is one of rigid conformity.[14] The inconsistent value patterns of the adult world constitute one of the chief moral hazards to the juvenile in the modern world. The relation between the differing degrees of latitude allowed in the behavior norms of the adult and the juvenile worlds can best be illustrated by the fact that if we were to insist on the same, or comparable, behavior standards among our adults as among our juveniles, our police, jails, or courts could not possibly deal with the consequent avalanche of cases. There are few adults, particularly in large urbanized areas, whose conduct would approach the standards set by that ideal for juveniles, the Boy Scout Code.

THE BEHAVIOR OF LAW-ENFORCEMENT OFFICERS AND AGENCIES

The general attitude of the American public toward law-enforcement officers is certainly not conducive to obedience. The American people generally do not have the same degree of respect that the English have for their "bobbies," barristers, and judges. In general, legislative bodies, considered as corporate bodies and not as individuals, are regarded with suspicion and distrust, and the police are looked upon as harsh, corrupt, and inefficient. There is a more favorable public attitude toward the courts, but the higher courts are often ridiculed because of their corporate inefficiency; the lower courts, for their inefficiency and dishonesty.

Although there is much evidence of this disrespect for law-enforcement agencies, it is possible that it may represent simply a vicious circle in that what the American people expect their law-enforcement officers to be is actually what they often are. Certainly, numerous studies have indicated that the police and other law-enforcement agencies, instead of preventing the development of criminal attitudes and acts, actually constitute one of the chief sources of indoctrination in attitudes of disrespect for law.[15] The all too common practice of employing police personnel and electing judges who in no way exemplify the type of conduct required of those charged with enforcing the law adds both directly and indirectly to the production of delinquency and crime. Far too many police officers, both urban and rural, are simply political appointees. Many are intellectually unfit, inefficient, brutal in making arrests and securing evidence through the third degree, and frequently willing to accept bribes even from juveniles. In

---

[14] For example, see Margaret Mead, *Coming of Age in Samoa* (New York: William Morrow & Company, Inc., 1928), and the works of Bronislaw Malinowski on the Trobriand Islanders.

[15] William Westley, "Violence and the Police," *American Journal of Sociology*, 59:34–41 (July, 1953). Also Ernest J. Hopkins, *Our Lawless Police* (New York: The Viking Press, Inc., 1931).

some instances police officers may even go further than this, as in the case of several Chicago policemen who in 1961 were convicted of collaborating with criminals in a number of burglaries.[16] Such behavior does not encourage respect for law nor aid in the prevention of delinquency or the rehabilitation of offenders.

Many judges also do not merit the respect of juveniles, for their attitudes on the bench and the general atmosphere of their courtrooms often seem to indicate a lack of understanding. This situation is understandable when one realizes that most law schools and the legal system itself do not provide adequate, or indeed, any training for lawyers or judges in juvenile or adult rehabilitation work. Very few jurists apply scientific knowledge in the treatment of crime in the courts. Cases of political influence, bribery, and outright violations of law by jurists occur in American society in sufficient numbers partially to endanger the concept of "justice" which has come over to us from English law. In 1949, a police judge in Newark pleaded guilty to stealing over $630,000 through a rigged-up series of fictitious mortgages. He had used the money to cover his losses in horse racing bets. The serious injuries in such cases lie not only in the crime but in its effects on other offenders.

The Kefauver Committee found that organized crime in American cities could not exist or flourish without extensive bribery of politicians, public officials, sheriffs, police officers, and others. As Tannenbaum has stated, "He who would ask the question 'Why have we as much crime as we do have and why do we have this kind of crime?' must first be asked to answer the larger question, 'Why do we have the kind of political life that we do have in our larger cities?'"[17] A Scandinavian criminologist once wrote the author that bribery of police and judicial officials is almost non-existent in Sweden. Yet in the United States the "fix" is so common that Sutherland's comment about it is no different from that of others who have studied the relation between crime and law enforcement in this country:

---

[16] See Virgil W. Peterson, "The Chicago Police Scandals," *The Atlantic*, 206:58 ff. (October, 1960). See also Barron Beshoar and George Harris, "How Denver's Cops Turned Burglar," *Life*, 51:18 ff. (November 3, 1961).

[17] Frank Tannenbaum, *Crime and the Community* (Boston: Ginn and Company, 1938), pp. 150–151. Reprinted by permission of the publishers. "The evidence . . . is perhaps sufficient to indicate that a considerable portion of crime in our larger cities, and also its character, are reflections of, and are intimately bound up with, the kind and character of the political organizations that exist in these cities. The political machine, the gamblers and the gangsters, the police and the local ward heelers, the city magistrates and the court clerks, the lawyers who practice in the courts, the bondsmen, the local attendants, the 'fixers,' the hangers-on, the good fellows about the political clubs, the dispensers of favors and the securers of jobs, the people willing to 'go to the front' for the less fortunate who have been arrested, the givers of political jobs to honest political workers, are all intertwined into a system, or still better, a way of life, for that part of our community which occupies itself with the business of governing under the conditions that make this kind of governing both possible and necessary."—*Ibid.*

When one is caught the problem is to "fix" things. This occurs very commonly in the so-called law-abiding groups in relation to traffic violations, gambling, smuggling liquor, and certain other crimes. In other circles it occurs in relation to shoplifting, picking pockets, robbery, burglary, and murder. There is a prevalent belief among prisoners that their own cases could have been "fixed" if they had had sufficient money. According to that belief the only reason for being arrested or convicted is poverty. It is probable that no part of the population is better acquainted with the corruption and graft in the legislative, judicial, and police systems, so far as they exist, than are the professional criminals.[18]

The methods of dealing with crime often constitute little subcultures for the transmission of criminal norms.[19] According to reports of state and federal inspectors, many American jails fail to meet standards of health and welfare. Conditions in many of our boys' training schools, our reformatories, and our prisons are not much better. The large number of criticisms of such institutions can be summarized by stating that most of them, as now constituted, probably produce more crime in a society than they eliminate.[20] Although there are small islands of exceptions in the correctional systems, scientific studies, reports of inmates and wardens, the high percentage of repeaters, and the frequent prison riots by outraged inmates —all justify this conclusion.

The prisoners' idle hours are primarily devoted to conversations about crime and sex. The more sophisticated offenders provide tutelage for the naïve in both the techniques and the philosophy of crime. Fellow inmates of detention houses and cell mates tutor others in how to "strip" a car properly, how to "blow" a safe or successfully counterfeit money; moreover, there is frequently indoctrination in homosexual practices. Most prisons are far too large to deal with human beings on a personal basis, the strict discipline antagonizes men, the one-sex community stimulates unhealthy sex attitudes, the supervisory personnel is often inferior, and there is all too frequently little that is rehabilitative. Since the bulk of the several hundred thousand persons in our jails and prisons annually receives these experiences, they represent a contribution of the general culture to the American crime problem.

Fortunately, there is evidence that this situation is changing. More often than in the past policemen are being selected on a merit basis and given training in proper police conduct. Some judges receive training at professional institutes which deal with delinquency and crime. Jail and prison conditions are slowly being improved, although most of them still have a long way to go to achieve recommended standards.

---

[18] Sutherland and Cressey, op. cit., p. 198.
[19] Donald Clemmer, "Observation on Imprisonment as a Source of Criminality," Journal of Criminal Law and Criminology, 41:318 (September–October, 1950).
[20] For a complete discussion of prisons see Chapter 21.

THE NEWSPAPER AND CRIME

The press has been charged with generally promoting and glorifying crime because of the volume of its news items and its continual elevation of so-called public enemies by building them up as success stories: "When a newspaper carries the story that a certain criminal is the worst, or the best, or the most dangerous, or some other superlative appellation, it is one of the few consolations this criminal will have, in case of conviction, while he is in prison." [21]

Unusual events are newsworthy and gain ready access to the printed page, for the urban American reader is little concerned with the ordinary happenings in everyday life. Only the unusual, the different, and the new attract his attention. He dotes on war, rape, murder, and crime. The breaking of the law is an event that captures reader interest. The amount and prominence of space devoted to crime in the newspapers and the amount of conversation based on these stories present a bewildering picture of immortality in our society. By continually playing up crime, it is likely that newspapers are important in making us a crime-centered culture. As a result, crime often seems more frequent than it really is. Perhaps to some, crime stories resemble the folk tales of frontier bad men. They provide vicarious emotional thrills which are seldom derived from conventional institutions. The newspapers also provide information about the techniques of committing crime, although this is probably not too important in individual cases.

There is a difference between reporting a crime in simple, verifiable factual statements, as is often done in many countries, and loading a long, detailed crime story with emotionally charged words. Crime receives particular prominence in American newspapers because of the amount of space given to crime stories and because of their position on the front page. The proportion of crimes stories to the rest of the news is not an adequate basis for comparison, for the front page sells the paper. Even a reader on his way to the comic section cannot help noticing front-page crime stories and pictures. If he misses it there he is sure to hear it included in the dinner-table conversation. Under the guise of supplying what the reader demands, crime is not merely made prominent: it is supplied to the reader in colorful exposition and frequently with "on the scene" lurid photographs. A person is not merely murdered or slain; he is brutally slain with a blunt instrument. The suspect does not merely attempt to escape capture; the desperate killer, his cunning increased by his emotional stimulation, gives the inept police a terrific run for their money.

There is general indifference on the part of the newspapers to the

[21] Sutherland and Cressey, op. cit., p. 211.

serious moral implications of this almost universal practice. Admittedly such a statement raises the problem of the function of the newspapers. On the one hand, the concept of free enterprise condones the collection of sordid tales as a valuable vehicle for selling advertisements; on the other, the concept of social responsibility suggests that some newspapers might re-evaluate their role in a society.

Television, Motion Pictures, Radio, and Comic Books

The great interest of juveniles and adults in television, motion pictures, the radio, and comic books has caused some people to overestimate their importance, whereas others tend to discount them in their explanations of delinquency and crime. It is conceivable, however, that even if all these media were to disappear from our culture we probably would still have almost as much delinquency and crime as we now have. Certainly we had delinquency and crime before any of them were considered of consequence.

A recent survey of television, covering such questions as types of programs, time spent watching television, and the like, was conducted by a research team at the Stanford University Institute for Communication Research.[22] The findings of this survey were based on responses from 6000 children, 2000 parents, and 300 teachers. It was found that from the age of three to sixteen the average child devotes about a sixth of his waking hours to watching television, and more than half the children studied watched "adult" programs, such as crime plays, westerns, and shows featuring emotional problems. The investigators analyzed 100 hours of programs in the so-called children's hours, the period from 4:00 to 9:00 P.M. In those 100 hours they counted twelve murders, sixteen major gun fights, twenty-one persons shot, twenty-one other violent incidents in which one person slugged another, an attempted murder with a pitchfork, two stranglings, one stabbing in the back with a butcher knife, three successful suicides (and one unsuccessful suicide), four people pushed over a cliff, two attempts made to run over persons with automobiles, a raving psychotic loose in an airliner, two mob scenes (in one the wrong man was hanged), a horse grinding a man under his hoofs, two robberies, a woman killed by falling from a train, a tidal wave, an earthquake, a hired killer stalking his victim, and, finally, one guillotining. Although admitting the disturbing effects of such violence on children, they concluded that almost invariably delinquent children who blamed television for their crimes had something seriously wrong with their lives quite apart from watching television and that with few exceptions these problem children had problems before they learned anything about crime from television.

[22] Wilbur Schramm, Jack Lyle, and Edwin B. Parker, *Television in the Lives of Our Children* (Stanford, Calif.: Stanford University Press, 1961).

There has also been much public indignation against the misnamed "comic" books, particularly their vicious crime content. It is reported that over fifty cities have taken steps to ban objectional ones. After studying some delinquents and the contents of comic books, a psychiatrist concluded that comic books produce a great deal of serious delinquency.[23] In his opinion, comic books suggest delinquent ideas to children, stimulate unwholesome fantasies, suggest sexually abnormal behavior, emphasize deceit and cruelty, and supply techniques for committing delinquencies. Most of the material he presents is based on a few cases, little of it is of a scientific, factual nature, and he does not make any study of the effect of comic books on nondelinquents.

It is doubtful if many cases can be found where, even though there was no evidence of prior deviant behavior, such behavior could be attributed only to reading comic books. Much of the material represents fantasy and makes no attempt at reality. To those already delinquent, comic books may furnish techniques and even additional reasons for committing an offense.[24] One psychiatrist, in suggesting a cautious approach to the problem of comic books, has summarized what appears to be a realistic view:

a. No one has conclusively demonstrated that the comic books are detrimental in any way.
b. Campaigns to eliminate them are useless and serve only to release the aggressive feeling of the crusaders.
c. No normal child under the age of 12 is likely to be harmed by them. Neurotic children need treatment and would be equally affected by the movies or the radio.
d. Normal adolescents may be harmed by certain types of comics, especially the "jungle adventure" type.
e. Parents are the best judges of what their children should read. If parents supervise their children's reading of comics the undesirable ones would soon disappear.
f. The argument that children waste time on the comics, which could be better spent, needs further study.
g. More study should be devoted to eliciting the facts about the comics.[25]

Research indicates that although both delinquents and nondelinquents attend motion pictures, the delinquents attend more often and exhibit greater interest in them. In some studies marked differences were noted between delinquents and their control groups in this regard. Although this

[23] Frederic Wertham, *Seduction of the Innocent* (New York: Holt, Rinehart and Winston, Inc., 1953).

[24] In his study of 1313 delinquent gangs in Chicago, Thrasher found that comic strips in the newspapers did influence these groups and their activities. Not only did many of the gangs obtain their names from the comic strips but suggestions for vandalism and other destructive activities were directly traceable to this source.—Frederic M. Thrasher, *The Gang* (rev. ed.; Chicago: The University of Chicago Press, 1936), p. 113.

[25] John R. Cavanagh, "The Comics War," *Journal of Criminal Law and Criminology*, 40:34–35 (May–June, 1949).

fact may have significant implications, careful additional study would be required to ascertain them.[26] There is no question that the motion picture often presents a version of our culture emphasizing wealth, materialism, and immoral conduct, both criminal and sexual, which, as far as juveniles are considered, furnishes them approved models conducive to delinquency. Approximately half of the motion pictures produced during 1948 dealt with murder or the activities of criminals.[27]

A realistic appraisal of these forms of entertainment indicates, therefore, that on the whole their direct influence on the juvenile only serves to aggravate whatever existent deviant attitudes and personality traits there may be. Schramm has stated that children both learn and are influenced by the various media of mass communication, but that what they receive from the mass media is first passed through another set of influences, such as family, school, and church, before it becomes a very important guide to actions. "We might say that what television does to children is less significant than what children do with television; and what children do with television . . . depend[s] on their homes, their schools, their peer group relations, and many other factors quite outside the mass media." [28]

This does not mean, however, that such media have no effect. In 1961 a Senate committee looked into the problem of the large proportion of television programs dealing with crime and violence. In general, the conclusion was reached that this material might have an indirect effect on many youths by presenting a distorted picture of approved American values. The vivid pictures of juvenile delinquents and criminal offenders presented on television serves to perpetuate a stereotyped picture, in the minds of the public, of *all* delinquents and criminals as tough and vicious. Consequently, this makes it difficult to bring about changes in the punitive aspects of the criminal law and correctional programs and to utilize measures to bring about reformation. From such a view, television programs may be thought of more directly as increasing, in the long run, the seriousness of delinquency and crime.

It is unfortunate that few actual scientific investigations have been made of the influence of these various forms of entertainment on delinquency and crime. Certainly there has been only limited investigation of

---

[26] See Maud A. Merrill, *Problems of Child Delinquency* (Boston: Houghton Mifflin Company, 1947), p. 91. Also see William Healy and Augusta F. Bronner, *New Light on Delinquency and Its Treatment* (New Haven, Conn.: Yale University Press, 1936), p. 72. In a study made almost thirty years ago Blumer and Hauser found that motion pictures represented important factors in only about one in ten of the delinquent boys and one in four of the delinquent girls. See Herbert Blumer and Philip M. Hauser, *Movies, Delinquency and Crime* (New York: The Macmillan Company, 1933), p. 198.

[27] For this reason, in Sweden, children under fourteen are not permitted to see most motion pictures, which are primarily American; moreover, certain crime films are censored for adults.

[28] Wilbur L. Schramm ed., *Mass Communications* (Urbana: University of Illinois Press, 1960), p. 466.

the millions of nondelinquent juveniles who avidly attend crime movies, nightly watch several television programs dealing with crime and violence, or read comic books regularly. In most cases the result of the preoccupation of the public with the effect on juvenile delinquency of television, motion pictures, radio, and comic books is merely to release the feeling that something should be done. The deeper question of why juveniles are interested in this entertainment raises issues which adults often do not wish to face because of their own interests in similar material. Likewise, this problem is evidence of a reluctance on the part of the adult world to deal effectively with factors basic to it—general disobedience to law, the presence of disorganizing influences in local neighborhoods, political corruption, and certain emphases in our culture, such as materialism and extreme individuality. The existence of gangs of delinquent boys is a more important and more difficult immediate problem than television, motion pictures, radio, or comic books, but few communities have the necessary vision to attack it. In dealing with social difficulties the public tends to take the easiest course.

Neighborhoods and Occupations

So far these comments about the inconsistency of cultural norms have referred to the social heritage as a whole. This section will describe the role of neighborhoods and occupations in transmitting criminal norms. The neighborhood or local community is one primarily of personal relationships, where people live and where their local institutions are located. It is an area of more personal social participation in which the activities of child and adult tend to be organized around agencies, such as the local stores, the school, the church, playgrounds, and sometimes even a motion-picture theater. This local world may include taverns, lodges, gangs, athletic teams, and sports organizations. The members of the neighborhood tend sometimes to share in other activities, such as weddings and funerals, picnics and carnivals. It is a world of meaningful experiences to the individual. At the same time, the neighborhood reflects some of the norms and evaluations of the outside world. A child who lives "back of the yards" or "across the tracks" develops a conception of himself as being different from children in other neighborhoods. As a recent major work on delinquency concluded, "the major effort of those who wish to eliminate delinquency should be directed to the reorganization of slum communities." [29]

Neighborhoods often differ as to social class, in the variety of the

---

[29] Richard A. Cloward and Lloyd E. Ohlin, *Delinquency and Opportunity: A Theory of Delinquent Gangs* (New York: The Free Press of Glencoe, 1960), p. 211. They point out that whereas slum areas used to be organized, they are now becoming "disorganized" because of such factors as the decline of the local political power structure and new housing developments.

composition of racial, ethnic, and religious groups, and in the stability of the population. Even more important, there may be pronounced differences in the social norms of the local community. There are local areas which are organized principally around conventional norms, and there are other areas in which unconventional standards predominate. In either instance no local community has norms exclusively of one type or another; rather, conflicting standards are present in varying proportions. A person in a delinquent area may have close associations with persons who engage in, or encourage him to engage in, delinquency and at the same time have similar contacts with law-abiding persons.

Some local communities maintain the middle-class virtues of pride in family status, of obedience to the sexual mores, of respect for the police and law, at least insofar as the more overt crimes are concerned. These local communities have considerable stability and relatively little racial and ethnic diversity. These areas do not tolerate such establishments as taverns, houses of prostitution, gambling, and "fences" for the disposal of stolen goods. Most of the boys and girls belong to such traditional groups as the Scouts, and the adults are actively organized in conventional groups like the parent-teacher association. Other groups are patterned along conventional ways, engaging in woodcraft, hikes, and games. Occasionally there is some vandalism but there is little theft. The social norms of the community are largely conventional, and conventional institutions exist to support these norms. The moral responsibilities of the outside world and general culture are continually brought into the lives of juvenile and adult alike.

Many local communities have norms so different from those of middle-class neighborhoods that they might be a part of a separate culture. A considerable proportion of our population lives in these areas. They are represented by Zone I and mainly by Zone II of our large cities, and by an area "back of the tracks" in our smaller cities and towns.[30] The moral values in these areas are reflected in the types of recreational facilities, consisting of places of prostitution, strip-tease joints, burlesque shows, public drinking places, and taxi dance halls. Many of the taverns permit gambling and sell liquor to minors and drunks. There are secondhand stores which often dispose of shady merchandise, and "fences" and junkmen who foster

---

[30] See pages 87–90. In some places our farming areas are characterized by these pockets of moral deterioration, as has been satirized in *Tobacco Road*, and suggested by differentials in the moral standards of owners and some farm labor. Farming districts and small towns probably do not have nearly as distinct local areas as do the large urban communities, because of personal relationships which transcend the immediate neighborhood. A study of one small city showed that although counterparts to delinquency areas in large cities produced crime, localizations of deviant values were not entirely confined to a neighborhood but rather were associated with membership in certain families and small groups with deviant attitudes.—Donald R. Taft, "Testing the Selective Influence of Areas of Delinquency," *American Journal of Sociology*, 38:699–712 (March, 1933).

delinquencies and crimes because of their willingness to purchase stolen goods. Premarital and extramarital relations are common, many girls are expected to engage in such relations or in sexual promiscuity, and many girls and boys believe that such conduct is proper.

The norms of conventional society are not nonexistent in these areas, however, and they include some traditional organizations such as youth groups, lodges, and churches. There are families who have traditional virtues, and there are persons who live in the area but whose standards are not part of it. On the whole, however, these conventional organizations are not too effective. These neighborhoods are often insulated from much of conventional society and its norms.[31]

Far too often the "big shots" of these areas are successful young "punks," criminals, shady politicians, or owners of vice resorts. Their position of high social status is a demonstration that participation in the activities of conventional society is not the only way to achieve success. This world with prestige values different from other neighborhoods has been described by two delinquents.

> Every boy has some ideal he looks up to and admires. His ideal may be Babe Ruth, Jack Dempsey, Al Capone, or some other crook. His ideal is what he wants to be like when he grows up and becomes a man. When I was twelve years old we moved into a neighborhood where there lived a mob of gangsters and big crooks. They were all swell dressers and had big cars and carried "gats." Us kids saw those swell guys and mingled with them in the cigar store on the corner. Jack Gurney was the one in the mob that I had a fancy for. He used to take my sis out and that was how I saw him often. He was in the stick-up racket before he was in the beer racket and was a swell dresser and had lots of dough. He was a nervy guy and went in for big stuff. He was a mysterious fellow and would disappear sometimes for several days but always came back. He was looked up to as the leader of his mob and anybody would gladly be in his place.

> Naw, I don't wanna be a big lawyer or business man, I wanna amount to something. I wanna be a big shot, like "P.J." [well-known beer baron]. Have all the guys look up to me, and have a couple of Lincolns, lots of molls, and all the coppers lickin' my shoes.[32]

Similar to the impact of neighborhood norms on the individual are those of certain occupations. In some, norms may be law-abiding, whereas in others they may not be. This will be discussed in detail in a more extensive presentation of white-collar crime in a later chapter.

---

[31] Sutherland and Cressey, *op. cit.*, pp. 160–161.
[32] Chicago Area Project, "Juvenile Delinquency," A Monograph Prepared by the Institute for Juvenile Research and the Chicago Area Project (rev. ed.; Chicago: 1953), pp. 8–9.

Associates

The role of cultural, neighborhood, and occupational norms and values in the development of criminal attitudes has been discussed, but the method of transmittal to the individual delinquent or criminal has not been indicated. These attitudes are primarily acquired through companions and by participation in small intimate groups in much the same manner as law-abiding norms are transmitted. Companions who play a major part in the acquisition of these norms include the play group or gang, siblings in the family, associates in one's occupation, and other persons. Popular thinking about delinquency and crime is, for once, quite correct in its emphasis on the role of "evil companions" in this behavior.

Most delinquents are arrested in company with others, and it can be safely assumed that those who had no companions at the time of their arrest had had at least one in the beginning of their delinquency.[33] In one study of 5480 Chicago delinquents Shaw found that 81.8 percent of those brought into juvenile court had one or more companions.[34] Considering those with one or more companions, he found that 30.3 percent had one companion, 27.7 percent had two, 10.8 had three, 7.1 had four, and 5.9 percent had five or more.

In one of their studies Healy and Bronner found that two thirds of a group of 3000 Chicago and Boston delinquents had had bad companions. In another of their studies 70 percent of the delinquents were found to have had delinquent companions.[35] After comparing 500 delinquents with an equal number of nondelinquents, the Gluecks reported that "delinquents almost without exception chummed largely with other delinquents while the nondelinquents, despite the fact that they too lived in the slums, had few intimates among delinquents."[36] Although 98.4 percent of the delinquents associated with other delinquents, only 7.4 percent of the nondelinquent group had done so. Two previous studies of the Gluecks had revealed a similar picture, with 70 percent of a group of 1000 Boston delinquents and 60 percent of a group of Massachusetts reformatory men having committed their offenses with companions.[37]

---

[33] For a current survey of various findings, see Thomas G. Eynon and Walter C. Reckless, "Companionship at Delinquency Onset," *British Journal of Criminology*, 2:162–170 (October, 1961).

[34] Clifford R. Shaw and Henry D. McKay, "Social Factors in Juvenile Delinquency," National Commission on Law Observance and Enforcement, *Report on the Causes of Crime* (Washington, D.C.: Government Printing Office, 1931), II, 195–196.

[35] Healy and Bronner, *op. cit.*, p. 52.

[36] Sheldon and Eleanor T. Glueck, *Delinquents in the Making* (New York: Harper & Row, Publishers, 1952), p. 89. Also see their original study, *Unraveling Juvenile Delinquency* (Cambridge, Mass.: Harvard University Press, 1950).

[37] Sheldon and Eleanor T. Glueck, *One Thousand Juvenile Delinquents* (Cambridge, Mass.: Harvard University Press, 1934), p. 100, and their *Five Hundred Criminal Careers* (New York: Alfred A. Knopf, Inc., 1930), p. 152.

Some persons are critical of the emphasis on neighborhood and associational factors on the ground that generally only about one fourth of the boys even in the worst delinquency areas have appeared before the juvenile courts. One writer has attempted to answer this by pointing out that official delinquency, as measured by juvenile court statistics, represents only a small proportion of actual offenders.[38] If police records in Chicago are used, this figure increases to nearly two thirds. Boys in areas of high delinquency simultaneously exhibit socially approved and disapproved behavior; hence the term "nondelinquent" becomes a rather meaningless one and represents middle-class standards of behavior. A substantial number of boys who engage in juvenile delinquency, however, presumably grow up to be law-abiding persons.

This view that most crime and delinquency arise from the adoption of deviant norms, particularly through the tutelage of others, has been supported by other studies of petty thievery, of highly organized thievery, of organized crime, and of white-collar crime.[39]

NONGANG COMPANIONS

Most persons who consider the role of companions in crime have in mind only juvenile gangs or the more organized criminal syndicate. A great deal of this type of juvenile association, however, is not with organized groups but instead with one or two companions. In a large study of 4663 Chicago delinquents who had been brought before the juvenile court for committing thefts, 33 percent had only one companion and 31 percent had two companions.[40] Although seven in every ten of a group of 1000 Boston delinquents had committed offenses with companions, less than one in ten (7.3 percent) belonged to a gang.[41] Another study found that approximately only half of the delinquents who had delinquent companions belonged to gangs.[42]

It is possible, of course, that some nongang offenders at one time had an association with a gang; yet many of the nongang associates are undoubtedly those who have acquired deviant attitudes through other sources, particularly through contact with someone who has been in a correctional institution. Differential association with criminals or delinquents by means

---

[38] Solomon Kobrin, "The Conflict of Values in Delinquency Areas," *American Sociological Review*, 16:653–661 (October, 1951).

[39] Clifford R. Shaw and Henry McKay, *Juvenile Delinquency and Urban Areas* (Chicago: The University of Chicago Press, 1942); Edwin H. Sutherland, *The Professional Thief* (Chicago: The University of Chicago Press, 1937); Edwin H. Sutherland, *White Collar Crime* (New York: Holt, Rinehart and Winston, Inc., 1949, reissued 1961), and Clinard, *The Black Market*.

[40] Shaw and McKay, "Social Factors in Juvenile Delinquency," *loc. cit.,* p. 196.

[41] Glueck and Glueck, *One Thousand Juvenile Delinquents*, p. 94.

[42] Glueck and Glueck, *Unraveling Juvenile Delinquency*, pp. 163–164.

of contacts with one or two persons appears to be more characteristic of rural and village areas than of urban ones. In urban areas larger group patterns of delinquency are the more typical method of association. In rural areas these companions are more often chance acquaintances. A study of rural offenders found that almost two thirds of them had not been associated with groups of boys who stole, and if this category is restricted to those who committed serious thefts, 87 percent had never had such previous association.[43] This apparent difference in the pattern of associates is due to the existence of a predominant measure of personal relations and informal social control in farm and village areas.

Delinquent Gangs or Subcultures

Many studies have shown the high incidence of gang membership among youthful offenders. Approximately two thirds, for instance, of a sample of Iowan and Swedish criminal offenders had belonged to a group of boys who stole.[44] During later childhood and early adolescence nearly all normal children associate in groups for play, religious activities, or other special interests. Some of these groups develop into conflict groups or gangs in the sense that they are in conflict with some other groups in society. Some of these gangs turn from mere conflict with other gangs, the family, or the school to conflict with the police, property owners, and certain moral standards of a society. Our interest here is not in the gang but in the delinquent gang. Thrasher has described the emergence of such a gang:

> Natural leaders emerge, a relative standing is assigned to various members and traditions develop. It does not become a gang, however, until it begins to excite disapproval and opposition, and thus acquires a more definite group-consciousness. It discovers a rival or an enemy in the gang in the next block; its baseball or football team is pitted against some other team; parents or neighbors look upon it with suspicion or hostility; "the old man around the corner," the storekeepers, or the "cops" begin to give it "shags" (chase it); or some representative of the community steps in and tries to break it up. This is the real beginning of the gang, for now it starts to draw itself more closely together. It becomes a conflict group.[45]

Gangs grow out of the play activities and come to acquire a definite organization. They tend to reflect neighborhood values. If located in cer-

---

[43] Marshall B. Clinard, "Rural Criminal Offenders," *American Journal of Sociology*, 50:38–45 (July, 1944).

[44] Marshall B. Clinard, "A Cross Cultural Replication of the Relation of the Process of Urbanism to Criminal Behavior," *American Sociological Review*, 25:253–257 (April, 1960). Also see Marshall B. Clinard, "The Relation of Urbanization and Urbanism to Criminal Behavior," in Ernest W. Burgess and Donald J. Bogue eds., *Research Contributions to Urban Sociology* (Chicago: The University of Chicago Press, 1962).

[45] Thrasher, *op. cit.*, p. 30.

tain areas, primarily middle-class, the members of the play groups may engage in harmless club activities. In other areas, on the other hand, gangs may bring the delinquent norms of these areas into intimate contact with the individual. Such gang delinquency, in the form of stealing and vandalism, may be regarded as a natural adjustment not only to the social roles, behavior patterns, and norms of the group but to those of the neighborhood of which the group is a part.

Many delinquent groups in the more urban areas in America have a past history; some have been in existence for many years, long enough so that their members may have older brothers or even fathers who were once members. Gangs which have directed their activities toward crime and delinquency for some time have an opportunity to furnish excellent training in criminal techniques. They teach new members how to empty slot machines, shoplift, obtain junk illegally, open freight cars, snatch purses, "roll" drunks, secure skeleton keys, purchase guns, steal automobiles, engineer holdups, sell stolen goods to "fences," and, finally, bribe a policeman or otherwise "fix" a case. New members may progress from truancy and stealing petty objects and junk to the more serious activities of breaking into freight cars, purse snatching, jack-rolling drunks, burglaries, automobile thefts, and even armed robbery.

When the gang develops considerable skill and the individual stays with it for a long enough period of time, he may acquire a considerable knowledge of crime, moving from the more simple offenses to the serious rackets. Many gangs furnish the training in techniques, the rationalizations, and the social status that accrue to those who have developed skill in crime. The following account of the "copper-wire" gang is typical of a large city gang.

> Police held 10 Milwaukee boys Sunday night on suspicion of stealing 42 cars and forging near-perfect street car passes in water colors. The "copper-wire gang," so-called because it used copper wires to "jump" cars' ignitions, was taken into custody when a 16-year-old member was picked up in a stolen car, police said. Authorities said they would be charged with stealing 42 cars over a two months' period. Two 18-year-olds were being held by police and the eight younger members were at the detention home. The 16-year-old who was arrested Friday had two guns in the car with him, police said. They believed they were to be used in holdups. They said the 16-year-old had perfected the copper-wire technique and taught it to the others. Donald H_____, 18, was accused of counterfeiting street car passes in water color so well they could hardly be distinguished from the originals. He allegedly produced as many as 40 a week and sold them for a quarter apiece.[46]

The effectiveness of delinquent gangs in disseminating knowledge of crime lies in the fact that through mutual excitation the gang makes illegal

---

[46] *Milwaukee Journal*, March 27, 1950.

acts attractive to the individual. In this sense gangs represent the spontaneous development of a form of group life to satisfy needs for new experiences, response, security, and recognition which are not met by conventional institutions, such as religious organizations, youth activities, and
clubs. Members enjoy the thrill of common intimate participation in interests involving conflict.

> When we were shoplifting we always made a game of it. For example, we
> might gamble on who could steal the most caps in a day or who could steal in
> the presence of a detective and then get away. We were always daring each
> other that way and thinking up new schemes. This was the best part of the
> game. I would go into a store to steal a cap, by trying on one and when the
> clerk was not watching walk out of the store, leaving the old cap. With the
> new cap on my head I would go into another store, do the same thing as in
> the other store, getting a new hat and leave the one I had taken from the
> other place. I might do this all day and have one hat at night. It was fun I
> wanted, not the hat. I kept this up for months and then began to sell the
> things to a man on the west side. It was at this time that I began to steal for
> gain.[47]

Each gang is a social system. Many common symbols and activities
hold it together, and each of its members is assigned a social status or
position. Common symbols include gang names such as the Dirty Dozen,
the Purple Gang, So So's, the Onions, the Torpedoes, the Wolves, White
Rocks, the Murderers, Bat-Eyes, Dukies, and the Hawthorne Toughs. They
have their own universe of discourse and argot, as well as songs and
stories which have become traditional with them. Common activities of
various types hold them together: gang fighting, raiding, robbing, defending
a hang-out, getting "shagged" (group sexual activities), holding smut sessions, drinking, playing games and pranks, maintaining clubrooms, gambling, and committing acts of vandalism.[48] These common activities give a
gang unity in its endeavors, and *esprit de corps*. Part of its integration
comes from warfare with other groups which have different names and
territories, or which are organized along different racial, religious, or ethnic
lines. Gangs develop common traditions not only through conflict with
other gangs but through warring with the police, who represent more conventional norms. Many juvenile gangs in New York City have terms for
various forms of gang fighting:

Sounding: A dirty or questioning look.
Roughing: A jostling of one member of a gang by a rival gang member.
Fair one: A fist fight between two boys.
Rumble: A gang fight of the less serious kind, sometimes produced by a
    "sounding."

---

[47] Chicago Area Project, *op. cit.*, p. 5.   [48] Thrasher, *op. cit.*, p. 277.

Stomping: A gang fight in which the enemy is knocked to the ground and kicked while down.

Burn, waste, or go down: To hold a gang fight in which "blades" [knives] and "pieces" [guns] are used.

Call it on: To hold a prearranged grudge fight in which anything goes.[49]

The position or social status of gang members is measured in ways entirely different from those used by such conventional groups as the YMCA or the Boy Scouts. A gang member achieves high status by displaying courage and skill in the commission of a crime, by having a long record of delinquencies, and, better still, by having been incarcerated in a correctional institution. Each boy comes to be designated by a nickname which is somewhat indicative of his social status in the gang.

When I was 8 years old I did my first job in the racket. This job was the biggest thrill I ever got in my life. . . . When it got too dark to play ball we all went into the alley to have a smoke and tell stories. The big guys got talking about stealing, and my brother said he had a good place spotted where we could get some easy "dough." The place was a butcher shop on Thirty-first Street. The big guys planned everything, and I only listened. These guys were seven or eight years older than me and had pulled off a lot of big jobs before. They would never let me go with them on big jobs; this night I went along and they didn't say a word. . . .

Everything was locked tight. The owner lived over the butcher shop, so we couldn't make much noise by breaking the glass or jimmying the door. We all went up to the back door, and then my brother got a box and stood on it and tried the transom—and it opened. It was too little for my brother or the other guys to get through. Then I was thrilled when they said I'd have to crawl through the transom. That was the kick of my whole life. I was only 8 and always very little so I could get through the transom easy. I was scared but made up my mind to go through anyway. I was too thrilled to say no.

My brother lifted me up on his shoulders and I crawled through the transom. I hung down on the inside and stood on an ice-box and then crawled down on the floor. The door was locked with a padlock and chain, but I was able to unlock the window and let the big guys in that way. The big guys looked for money first and found $22. Then we all got everything we wanted to eat and several cartons of cigarettes and ditched the place. When we got out, my brother divvied up everything and I got $4 and a lot of cigarettes. I felt like a "big-shot" after that night because the big guys said I could go with them every time they went robbin', and many times I had to crawl through transoms and one time through an ice-box hole. That's why the big guys called me the "baby bandit." [50]

As a result of participation in gang behavior its members develop fairly uniform attitudes toward "opposition to authority, contempt for the

---

[49] *The New York Times,* May 15, 1955, sec. 4.

[50] Chicago Area Project, *op. cit.,* pp. 7–8.

traitor, recognition and prestige through delinquency, hero-worship, stigma of petty stealing, and control of the gang over its members." [51] Nowhere are these values of the gang better seen than in the gang leader who comes to exemplify them. His control over the gang depends on such qualities. It is he who helps to invoke the code of the gang and to punish and ridicule those who do not live up to the standards of conduct the gang demands. One leader of a delinquent gang has written:

> The boys I ran around with were just like me, steal anything they get their hands on. One boy would make plans for stealing money, and we would give him jiggers and help him out if he needed help, and the other boys would do the same. We would meet every Saturday night in the pool room and set down in the pool room and plan our schemes out for the following week. The leader of each group was supposed to be tough. He would take most of the money and split the rest of it with the rest of the boys. I was leader, and never did cheat the other fellows out of a dime, and they had me for their leader until I was sent to Eldora Training School. The gang then got them a different leader, and they continued to take part where I left off. Then in Eldora they came and seen me and told me I could be their leader when I was released, but I said I wasn't going to be another leader, and they called me names such as coward. Well, I couldn't very well take those names, so I was their leader again when I was released, but I wished I wouldn't of for it got me only in trouble again, while the other boys was released on probation. It didn't offer me nothing but bad luck.[52]

Some boys' gangs disappear after a while, and others continue for many years. Although there is no hard-and-fast line of demarcation between a gang of younger offenders and one of older offenders, the latter tend to drift into more serious crimes. The membership of older criminal gangs appears to be drawn chiefly from those juveniles who have had a record of incarceration in correctional institutions. Criminal gangs become tied up with politics and organized criminal rackets. They develop connections as part of criminal syndicates, work with political machines, and specialize in types of rackets.

TYPES OF DELINQUENT SUBCULTURES

Five types of delinquent subcultures have been distinguished by Cohen and Short: the parent male subculture, the conflict-oriented subculture, the drug-addict subculture, the semiprofessional theft subculture and the middle-class delinquent subculture.[53] (1) The parent male subculture is the more common, involving a small gang whose behavior is nonutilitarian, malicious, negativistic, versatile and characterized by short-

---

[51] *Ibid.*, p. 5.   [52] From a personal document.
[53] Albert K. Cohen and James F. Short, Jr., "Research in Delinquent Subcultures," *Journal of Social Issues*, 14:20–37, No. 3 (1958).

run hedonism and group automony. These characteristics form the common core from which the other types develop, hence the idea of "parent." (2) The conflict-oriented gang may be a much larger group with a high degree of organization and a definite territory, and in readiness to engage in physical conflict and "rumbles" with other gangs. (3) The drug-addict subculture centers around the use of narcotic drugs and a distinct way of dress; its members are often referred to as the "cats." (4) Semiprofessional theft has a utilitarian, systematic, and pecuniary character using strong-arm methods and is characterized by the sale of stolen articles. (5) The middle-class delinquent fosters "the deliberate courting of danger (suggested by the epithet 'chicken') and a sophisticated, irresponsible 'playboy' approach to activities symbolic, in our culture, of adult roles and centering largely around sex, liquor, and automobiles." [54] A more limited typology of delinquent subcultures has been made by Cloward and Ohlin: the criminal, the conflict, and the retreatist or drug-culture gang.[55] They will be discussed shortly.

THEORIES OF GANG DELINQUENCY

Although the delinquent subculture of the gang has generally been explained as a product of neighborhood values of certain areas and the process of gang behavior itself, several recent theories have been advanced to explain gang delinquency in a larger context. The theories are that gang delinquency arises from (1) the characteristics of lower-class culture, (2) hostility and rejection of middle-class values, (3) anomie and differential opportunity, or (4) conflict in the transition from adolescence to adult status.

1. Gang delinquency, according to Miller, is concentrated in the male lower class and is a product of lower-class culture.[56] The chief concerns of lower-class culture are trouble, toughness, smartness, excitement, fate, and autonomy. "Getting into trouble" and "staying out of trouble" are chief concerns of lower-class individuals. "Toughness" is highly valued in the form of "masculinity," physical prowess, strength, and athletics. The gangster, the boxer, the tough guy, or the "hard" teacher become models. "Smartness" is represented by duping and outsmarting the other guy. Such models are seldom the teacher but the "con" man or the "fast-man-with-a-buck." "Excitement" relieves the dullness of hanging around drab areas. Taking a risk appeals a great deal and is evident in goading teachers and policemen, picking up girls, destroying public property, participating

---

[54] *Ibid.*   [55] Cloward and Ohlin, *op. cit.*

[56] Walter B. Miller, "Lower Class Culture as a Generating Milieu of Gang Delinquency," *Journal of Social Issues*, 14:9, No. 3 (1958). Also see Miller's remarks in W. C. Kvaraceus and W. B. Miller, *Delinquent Behavior: Culture and the Individual* (Washington, D.C.: National Education Association, 1959).

in a rumble, stealing a car, and joy-riding. "Fate" is represented by the idea of being caught because of bad luck. "Autonomy" is the desire to be bossed around by others even when the members say they want to be their own bosses. There is a testing of authority to see if it is strict enough.

The lower-class boy, therefore, wishing to belong and to achieve status, often participates in delinquent groups which express these values. Delinquent acts not only provide status but are means for satisfying those factors which dominate the way of life of the lower class.

Although the values of the lower class, such as toughness, have meaning and significance for the lower-class teen-agers, this behavior among the middle class assumes the characteristics of an adolescent fad, although it may have repercussions in real delinquent behavior.

> In the United States every generation of youngsters espouses a current fad which will distinguish it from the adult population. One function of such fads is to provide a vehicle of rebellion against parents; the fad is effective to the degree that it succeeds in shocking and dismaying the older generation. Today's middle-class youngster finds that he cannot get much of a rise out of his parents by "free" sexual references; Freud is too well known and accepted. Nor can he shock them by political radicalism; this is currently too dangerous. But he has discovered that one *really* effective way to appall his parents is to assume behavior patterns characteristic of lower-class culture. The black leather jacket, tight dungarees, a D.A. haircut, a Marlon Brando intonation pattern, or a James Dean stance—as concrete symbols of lower-class culture—or truanting, failing grades, threatening to quit school, or belittling the worth of college—as indications of a general lower-class set—are sure-fire methods for producing maximum parental agitation.[57]

2. Another explanation has suggested that the behavior of such delinquent gangs is a consequence of hostility toward middle-class values.[58] Such pertinent middle-class values include ambition, self-reliance, the postponement of immediate satisfactions, good manners and courtesy, wholesome recreation, opposition to physical violence, and respect for property. Lower-class boys, according to this theory, resent such dominant values because they have not been part of their world. Consequently, they also resent middle-class people, such as their schoolteachers, who consider them to have low status because they do not exhibit middle-class values. Lower-class delinquent gangs are a natural consequence of certain boys of this class coming together because of common hostilities. The subculture which they form is the opposite of middle-class values and is characterized by malice toward things that are virtuous, a versatility in types of delin-

---

[57] Kvaraceus and Miller, *op. cit.*, p. 82.
[58] Albert K. Cohen, *Delinquent Boys: The Culture of the Gang* (New York: The Free Press of Glencoe, 1955). This provocative approach to delinquent gang behavior will have to be affirmed or rejected by subsequent research, as Cohen does little more than suggest it as a hypothesis.

quent behavior, short-run hedonism involving nonutilitarian types of "fun" rather than long-range goals, and, finally, group automony or opposition to social control other than control by the group itself.

3. Somewhat related is the theory of anomie and differential opportunity of Cloward and Ohlin, who believe that delinquent subcultures arise where legitimate means to the attainment of the success goals of the dominant society, such as economic and higher educational opportunities, are blocked.[59] "The disparity between what lower-class youth are led to want and what is actually available to them is the source of a major problem of adjustment. Adolescents who form delinquent subcultures, we suggest, have internalized an emphasis upon conventional goals. Faced with limitations on legitimate avenues of access to these goals, and unable to revise their aspirations downward, they experience intense frustrations; the exploration of non-conformist alternatives may be the result." [60] Whether this deprivation will result in delinquency as well as the three types of gang delinquency which may arise depends, however, on the opportunity or availability of illegitimate means to obtain their goals and consequent status. In integrated slum areas where adult criminal patterns serve as models and opportunity structures are available, the subcultures will be *criminal* gangs engaged in thefts, extortion, and similar activities to achieve an illegal income and status. In unintegrated areas, characterized by mobility, transiency, and instability, such as new urban housing developments, where criminal patterns and opportunity structures are unavailable, models for delinquent behavior to achieve status come from other adolescents and tend to take the form of a *conflict* gang engaging in violence and vandalism. Another type, the "retreatist" gang or subculture, although its members live in the slum, use drugs and engage in other sensual experiences because its members find both legitimate and other illegitimate means to success closed to them and refuse to accept the moral validity of illegitimate means to status and success exemplified by stealing and vandalism.

4. Finally, a fourth explanation by Bloch and Niederhoffer is that gangs arise out of the conflict arising from the transition from adolescence to adult status.[61] In urban society there is no equivalent of the ceremonies

---

[59] Cloward and Ohlin, *op. cit.* According to their definition of delinquent subcultures, certain forms of delinquent activity are essential requirements for the performance of dominant social roles provided and supported by the subcultures. Such delinquent subcultures are characterized by a great frequency of criminal acts, stability, and resistance to change, and the recognition by members of a system of rules as binding upon their behavior. Legitimacy has been withdrawn from certain norms of law whose violations are regarded as illegitimate by official agency representatives. To these authors the acts of delinquent subcultures are much more deliberate and rational than Cohen, for example, has contended.

[60] *Ibid.*, p. 86.

[61] Herbert Bloch and Arthur Niederhoffer, *The Gang: A Study in Adolescent Behavior* (New York: Philosophical Library, Inc., 1958).

and other "rites of passage," such as puberty ceremonies, found among preliterate societies which symbolized transition to adult status. Despite his aspirations and his physical readiness for adult status the adolescent is kept in a condition of social and economic and legal dependency by the withholding of adult symbols, such as money, personal automony, and sexual relations, thus creating pressure to engage in deviant behavior to secure what adolescents regard as symbols of this adult status. One method is to form gangs whereby the adolescent may gain among his peers the equivalent of adult status through demonstrating that he is independent, tough, and capable of flaunting adult authority. In delinquent gangs this is expressed to the full. As an illustration, possession of an automobile becomes among adolescents a symbol of adulthood, and may often be used for sexual experiences as well. Some may steal automobiles for this purpose and to demonstrate their toughness.

The aspirations satisfied by the gang are supported more by the lower-class culture, but it is difficult to distinguish lower- from middle-class delinquency on this basis alone. In this connection some have suggested that one solution to gang delinquency might be to find some really constructive work for adolescents to perform for themselves and for the community, so that they would be able more adequately and quickly to achieve adult status.[62]

EVALUATION

These four theories of gang behavior have all attempted to provide a central framework for explaining delinquency in terms of basic concepts such as class, role, and status aspirations. But they are recent, and thus far little research has been done to prove or disprove them. Each seems to make a contribution, but each, as an all-inclusive explanation, is deficient. Most of them are actually attempts to explain the reasons for gang delinquency in lower-class areas in large urban communities of the United States. Whether such explanations would apply to middle-class or rural areas in the United States, or to the delinquency of other countries with different values and class structures, is open to some question. Certainly delinquency, primarily gang delinquency, is a world-wide phenomenon today and not confined to the United States. "The most important new type of juvenile delinquency found in nearly all parts of the world is the formation of juvenile gangs which commit delinquent acts." [63]

[62] Erik Erikson, *Childhood and Society* (New York: W. W. Norton & Company, Inc., 1950).

[63] *New Forms of Juvenile Delinquency: Their Origin, Prevention and Treatment*, General Report by Wolf Middendorff, Judge, Federal Republic of Germany, Second United Nations Congress on the Prevention of Crime and the Treatment of Offenders, London, August 8–20, 1960 (New York: United Nations Department of Economic and

They are reported to be extensive in places far apart, for example, England, South Africa, Sweden, Australia, the Federal Republic of Germany, France, Japan, and the Philippines. Group delinquency of a non-gang type, largely involving mass rioting and other forms of antisocial behavior, is widespread in many countries where they are known as "halb-starke" (the half-matured) in Germany, "blousons noir" in France, "teddy boys" in England, "vitelloni" in Italy, "hooligans" in Poland and Russia, "bodgies" and "widgies" (girls) in Australia and New Zealand, "tsotsio" in South Africa, and "mambo" boys and girls in Japan.[64] The problems of youth gangs are not confined to the Western world, but have been reported in the Soviet Union and its satellite countries. "East Germany's Communist rulers acknowledged today their deep concern over widespread juvenile delinquency and 'hooliganism' in the country. . . . Gangs of youthful trouble-makers have been arrested in recent months in Leipzig, Dresden and other East German industrial centers. In some cases the youths, armed with clubs, knives or pistols, battled the police, attacked passers-by or committed robberies." [65]

Subcultural gang delinquency may be more accurately explained by the lack of communication among age peer groups which has arisen with pronounced urbanism and by the lack of well-defined national goals than as being a product of class deprivation. This explanation probably accounts, in part, for the increasing juvenile delinquency among the middle class.

A number of specific criticisms have been raised about each theory of delinquency.[66] Sykes and Matza, for example, question whether a gang member actually rejects middle-class standards as Cohen claims, but, instead, rationalizes his deviant behavior by five techniques of neutralization or rationalization.[67] These are "denial of responsibility" by blaming parents, and so on; "denial of injury," by claiming, for example, that the act was a prank or the stolen car was "borrowed"; "denial of the victim," namely, that the delinquency was justified under the circumstances; "condemnation of the condemners," such as cruel police methods; and, finally, the "appeal to higher loyalties," association in gangs being more important than the larger society. In Cloward and Ohlin's theory the success-goal

---

Social Affairs, 1960), p. 43. See, for example, a study of French gangs in Philippe Parrot and Monique Gueneau, *Les Gangs d' Adolescents* (Paris: Presses Universitaires de France, 1959). A study has also been made of adolescent delinquents in Sweden. See Dick Blomberg, *Den Svenska Ungdomsbrottsligheten* (Stockholm: Falu Nya Boktryckeri AB, 1960).

[64] *New Forms of Juvenile Delinquency*, pp. 35–36.

[65] *The New York Times*, February 12, 1961.

[66] For a detailed criticism of the theories of Miller, Cohen, and Bloch and Niederhoffer, see Cloward and Ohlin, *op. cit.*, pp. 47–76. For a specific critique of Cohen's theory, see J. I. Kitsuse and D. C. Dietrick, "Delinquent Boys: A Critique," *American Sociological Review*, 24:211–212 (April, 1959).

[67] Gresham M. Sykes and David Matza, "Techniques of Neutralization," *American Sociological Review*, 22:664–670 (December, 1957).

aspirations of slum boys are not clearly stated, except the economic and educational goals, and they assume that these goals are more uniformly appreciated by subcultures in a society than is warranted. Bloch and Niederhoffer fail to show how the status deprivation of adolescence leads some but not others to delinquency.

After studying street corner gangs in Chicago, Short has proposed that gang delinquency is not so much a failure to achieve membership in the middle class, or because certain adult goals in society are denied them, as it is a failure to achieve status within the context of adult, middle-class-dominated institutions such as the school, the church, and economic and political institutions.[68] The formation of the delinquent subculture involves the establishment of new groups with new rules by which they may compete successfully to obtain status. "Participants in delinquent subcultures appear to be oriented primarily toward members of their own gangs and/or toward other individuals and gangs who share their respective subcultures rather than toward adults as status reference objects." [69] The solutions for lower-class boys provided by delinquent subcultures are primarily status-rewarding rather than economically rewarding, as suggested by Ohlin and Cloward. Money acquired by gang boys tends to be spent for status rewards within the group (e.g., $20 hats) and for "kicks" (alcoholic beverages and drugs).

The Family

Some people believe that the chief source of delinquent behavior lies in unhealthy family influences. This idea has become so strong that judges in several cities have been punishing the parents of delinquents, although they seldom specifically indicate the nature of the family influences that might be related to illegal behavior other than sometimes "lack of parental supervision." It is difficult for a number of reasons to indicate specifically what influence the family may have on delinquency and crime.

In the first place, families are not all the same; among some there are strong personal ties, but others are hardly integrated. Second, the family is an institution which has been undergoing great social change, as will be indicated later. The result of this change has been a decline in the importance of the family's role in general social life. Because many of the traditional functions of the family have declined, the socialization of young children is increasingly being done by other groups, such as the school and the street gang. As the strength of kinship ties becomes weaker and as the mother is increasingly employed outside the home, the urban child may

---

[68] James F. Short, Jr., "Street Corner Groups and Patterns of Delinquency," A Progress Report from the National Institute of Mental Health Research Grant M-3301 (Mimeographed; March 1, 1961).

[69] *Ibid.*, p. 13.

spend less time with members of his immediate family. Among large sections of the urban population today the family no longer plays the dominant idealized role that certainly is in the minds of those who think of it as the primary factor in encouraging or preventing delinquency and crime.

There are, however, a number of specific family influences which may possibly be related to delinquent and criminal behavior. These influences are the family as a source of delinquent patterns, the broken-home situation, and emotional insecurity within the family.

THE FAMILY AS A SOURCE OF DELINQUENT PATTERNS

There is the possibility that delinquent patterns of behavior may be derived directly from the family. Although there may be some direct tutelage in criminal acts by father, mother, or brother, current evidence indicates that this is of minor importance. The influence of siblings on one another is not common, however, for in many families only one or two children may be delinquent. One study, in fact, has compared a delinquent group with their nondelinquent siblings on this basis.[70]

It is more likely that the family may furnish other influences, such as sexual immorality, drunkenness, and other socially unacceptable patterns of behavior which may or may not be conducive to specific acts of delinquency or crime. Certainly studies have revealed some families with different standards in regard to stealing, gambling, or sex relations, particularly a mother-daughter situation where the former is sexually promiscuous.

Nevertheless, it is probably the contemporaries of persons who engage in crime and delinquency who are the important influences. Even a higher incidence of delinquent patterns in a home does not mean that deviant standards could not have been acquired from the outside. The family can enhance the effect of deviant patterns or it can help to inhibit them, but those who regard the family as the exclusive source of social norms and therefore put the blame on the family fail to see that the family is simply a part of the larger culture and tends to reflect the norms of its neighborhood. The difficulty which any family encounters in trying to keep a child away from delinquent influences in a neighborhood well illustrates this point.

It has also been said that families of delinquents have been either too lax or too strict in their punishment. In two studies the Gluecks discovered that discipline was either insufficient or too severe for seven in ten male prisoners and for nearly two in three women prisoners.[71]

Parental discipline is, of course, not the only factor in the dynamics

---

[70] Healy and Bronner, *op. cit.*

[71] Glueck and Glueck, *Five Hundred Criminal Careers*, and their *500 Delinquent Women*.

of family interaction. Nye has attempted to study this and other factors, such as value agreement, mutual recreation, parental interaction, and rejection by parents in the lives of a group of delinquents and non-delinquents.[72] The study was not conclusive but direct control techniques were found to have a greater influence for girls than for boys, and the father's behavior was more significantly related to delinquent behavior than was that of the mother.

THE BROKEN HOME

Persistent efforts have been made to link delinquency to homes broken by separation, desertion, divorce, or death, on the assumption that such a break in the family ties would lead the child to commit delinquent acts. The United States Children's Bureau, in a report covering cases for 1936, for example, found that about one third of the delinquent boys and one half of the delinquent girls came from broken homes.[73] The Gluecks, in a study of 1000 Boston delinquents, found that 48 percent came from broken homes, and in another study of 500 inmates of the Massachusetts Reformatory found that about 60 percent came from broken homes.[74] It is quite likely, however, that there would be a higher incidence in correctional institutions of those from broken homes than in the general population because offenders with this type of background might more frequently be sent there.

A few studies have been made comparing a group of delinquents with a control group of nondelinquents. In a Chicago study the home status of 1675 delinquents was compared with that of 7278 schoolboys from the same type of residential area and of the same age and nationality background.[75] It was found that among the delinquents 42.5 percent came from broken homes, as compared with 36.1 percent of the nondelinquents. This study has been criticized because no effort was made to ascertain whether the control group actually contained no delinquents. In a later study, 300 consecutive court arraignments were matched with a control group for age, sex, and nationality, with the result that about 50 percent of the former group were found to come from broken homes as compared with one fourth of the control group.[76] Another study by Jackson Toby has shown that if the variables of sex, age, and race are considered, which was

---

[72] F. Ivan Nye, *Family Relationships and Delinquent Behavior* (New York: John Wiley & Sons, Inc., 1958).

[73] U.S. Department of Labor, Children's Bureau, *Juvenile Court Statistics* (Publication 245; Washington, D.C.: 1939), p. 49.

[74] Glueck and Glueck, *One Thousand Juvenile Delinquents*, p. 75, and *500 Criminal Careers*, p. 117.

[75] Shaw and McKay, "Social Factors in Juvenile Delinquency," *loc. cit.*, pp. 262–285.

[76] Merrill, *op. cit.*, p. 77.

not done in the Shaw and McKay study, a relationship can be shown between family control over young children and girls.[77]

The effort to link delinquency with broken homes is probably a blind
alley, since the concept of a broken home is by no means a constant factor,
and the relationship of broken homes to delinquency has never been conclusively demonstrated: "It is, however, clear that the broken home does
not always cause delinquency. It makes a great difference how and when
the home was broken and what was the effect upon family relationships
and the attitudes of the children." [78] There are certainly millions of
families which are broken in one form or another but whose members
are not delinquent. No one knows what this exact proportion is, but some
idea can be gained by the fact that there are annually about 400,000
divorces. Some homes where there is friction between the parents may, as
will be indicated later, be improved by separation. How closely identified
a child is with a particular parent is another question, for the effect of a
broken home on one child may be quite different from its effect on another.

EMOTIONAL SECURITY AND THE FAMILY

Several studies have suggested that the family's failure to provide
the child with a proper degree of security and affection produces delinquency and crime. Healy and Bronner compared 105 delinquents with
105 nondelinquent siblings from the same families,[79] and concluded that
the major differences accounting for delinquency were the delinquents'
experiences and attitudes. These differences were attributed to the differential treatment of the children by their parents. This study has also been
criticized in a number of ways, particularly for its relative disregard of influences outside the home. The fact that 70 percent of the delinquents had
delinquent companions is mentioned, for example, but not amplified.

A more recent and comprehensive study with similar conclusions about
the importance of satisfactory family relationships has been made by the
Gluecks.[80] They selected two groups, one of 500 Boston delinquents in a
boys' training school and 500 Boston nondelinquents whom they matched
with the delinquents according to the areas of the city, age, ethnic or racial
derivation, and general intelligence. They then compared the differences
between the two groups in family and personal background, body types,
health, intelligence, temperament, and character.

As a result of this study the Gluecks recommended a prognostic in-

[77] Jackson Toby, "The Differential Impact of Family Disorganization," *American Sociological Review*, 22:505–512 (October, 1957).

[78] Taft, *Criminology*, p. 192.

[79] Healy and Bronner, *New Light on Delinquency and Its Treatment*.

[80] Glueck and Glueck, *Unraveling Juvenile Delinquency;* also the abridged version of this study, *Delinquents in the Making*.

strument to predict delinquency at about six years of age. It emphasized the role of the family and consisted of prediction tables which involved the following as the more important items: adequacy of discipline of boy by father, supervision of boy by mother, affection of father and mother for boy, and family cohesiveness. To this they added five personality traits from the Rorschach tests and five from psychiatric interviews. It seems unlikely that delinquency, which involves social definitions, could be predicted at an age when the child has not participated much in the wider community. This study can be criticized for its lack of an integrated theory of human behavior, its disregard of cultural factors, and the overemphasis on family and personality factors.

Such studies as those by the Gluecks, which emphasize the family, assume that a neighborhood is necessarily experienced socially in the same way by all boys simply because they live in it. This is a false idea of the impact of attitudes, motivations, and social contacts on personality. Four fifths of the delinquents had moved five times or more, as compared with two fifths for the nondelinquents, and their mobility may well have exposed them to more deviant patterns. Other equally startling differences between the groups were sneaking into motion-picture theaters (62%: 4%), running away from home (59%:1%), gambling (53%:9%), hanging around street corners (95%:58%), truancy (95%:11%). Whereas 42 percent of the delinquents spent some of their leisure time at home and 29 percent on playgrounds, the corresponding figures for the nondelinquents were 93 percent and 61 percent. Although the authors state that these "were maladjusted and delinquent children long before they were gang members," [81] no convincing evidence was given for this statement. Half of the five hundred delinquents belonged to gangs, as compared with only three of the nondelinquents. Delinquents likewise tended to be attracted to older boys and to have had more heterosexual experiences. In the light of this one wonders whether the emotional setting of the family was really of such great importance.

Alcohol and Delinquency or Crime

Some people believe that most delinquency or crime is committed under the influence of alcohol. On numerous occasions offenders have even excused their behavior as due to "one or two beers" or "drinking."

There is evidence that large numbers of arrests are for common drunkenness. Such drunkenness does have an important relation to misdemeanors and the police problem. When all offenses are examined, it is found that of all arrests, including misdemeanors as well as crimes, some one half to two thirds are for drunkenness, or for some related offense, such as

[81] Glueck and Glueck, *Delinquents in the Making*, pp. 88–89.

disorderly conduct or vagrancy. An alcoholic may be arrested and imprisoned as many as twenty to thirty times a year.

In some serious crimes of murder, aggravated assault, and forcible rape, drunkenness is undoubtedly of some significance.[82] After studying 588 criminal homicides in Philadelphia, Wolfgang concluded that there is a significant association between violent homicide and the presence of alcohol in the offender of either sex. "Approximately 60 per cent of all offenders who committed homicide violently had been drinking prior to the crime, while 40 per cent had not been drinking. On the other hand, among those who killed nonviolently, half had been drinking and half had not been drinking before the crime." [83]

Likewise, drunken driving is particularly serious as far as criminality is concerned. In 1959, in cities in the United States of over 2500 population, there were slightly over 104,000 arrests for drunken driving. Some of these cases involved the injury or possible injury to persons, and, where death resulted, the drivers could be charged with negligent homicide.

The very volume of drinking by offenders and nonoffenders in the United States would suggest that there are other variables involved in the problems of crime and delinquency besides alcohol. There are about 200,000 taverns in the country, and about one in five adults drinks regularly, more than one in two drinks occasionally.

It is probable that in most cases where alcohol was associated with criminal behavior, it acted as a depressant and made the person temporarily less cognizant of the probable consequences of deviant behavior, or else less able to respond in terms of his ordinary system of values and norms. In a sense it simply "released" behavior patterns already there instead of "causing" them. Although alcohol may "release" an individual's criminal attitudes, such criminal activities, involving either property or personal crimes, might have taken place sooner or later irrespective of his alcohol intake. When murders and assaults are committed under the influence of alcohol, they usually represent long-standing quarrels or difficulties in relationships with others which may culminate in violence depending upon the definition of the situation and the response of the persons involved. Forcible rape may represent the enactment of definitions of sexual behavior already present.

Summary

The chief sources of delinquent and criminal behavior appear to be the general culture, the neighborhood, and associates. Of particular im-

---

[82] See, for example, Julian Roebuck and Ronald Johnson, "The Negro Drinker and Assaulter as a Criminal Type," *Crime and Delinquency*, 3:21–33 (January, 1962).

[83] Marvin E. Wolfgang, *Patterns in Criminal Homicide* (Philadelphia: University of Pennsylvania Press, 1958), p. 166.

portance in the culture as a whole are the general and selective disobedience to law and the behavior of law-enforcement officers and agencies.
Newspapers may also contribute toward the increase of criminal behavior
in a society, and motion pictures, radio, television, and comic books play
similar roles. It is unlikely, however, that any person, without previous
deviant patterns, would engage in delinquency or crime only because of
crime stories and influences arising from these sources. Delinquents who
have already had association with deviant norms through other influences
may be further stimulated by certain types of motion pictures, radio and
television programs, or comic books.

Present evidence seems to indicate that social norms, both deviant and
conventional, are primarily acquired through personal experiences of a
face-to-face nature. Neighborhood influences and certain occupational
situations may furnish a setting favorable to the development of delinquent and criminal behavior.

Delinquent companions are extremely important, as are delinquent
gangs. Such gangs disseminate techniques of committing offenses, help the
individual delinquent to progress in crime, encourage mutual excitation
and common activities in connection with delinquency and crime, give
social status to the delinquent, and develop in him opposition to authority.

The role of the family in delinquency and crime does not appear to
be as important as many think. There is considerable variation in family
integration, and there are now other institutions and influences which are
also sources of deviant norms. There is little evidence to indicate that the
family is the source of delinquent patterns, or that broken homes are significantly related to delinquency. Similarly, there is no conclusive evidence
that the lack of emotional security in family relationships leads to delinquency and crime. There is little evidence, furthermore, to indicate that
the use of alcohol plays an important part in delinquent or criminal behavior.

Selected Readings

BLOCH, HERBERT A., and ARTHUR NIEDERHOFFER. *The Gang: A Study in Adolescent Behavior.* New York: Philosophical Library, Inc., 1958. An analysis of the behavior of adolescents in a variety of cultures. Gang delinquency in American
society, they maintain, results from the difficulty of adolescents in achieving
adult status.

CLINARD, MARSHALL B. "Secondary Community Influences and Juvenile Delinquency," *The Annals,* 261:42–55 (January, 1949). Other influences in the general culture besides the family and neighborhood must be considered in explaining juvenile delinquency.

CLOWARD, RICHARD A., and LLOYD E. OHLIN. *Delinquency and Opportunity: A Theory
of Delinquent Gangs.* New York: The Free Press of Glencoe, 1960. An explanation of how delinquent gangs arise, recruit their members, develop law-

violating ways of life, and persist or change. Basically the explanation follows anomie with the addition of the concept of differential opportunity.

COHEN, ALBERT K. *Delinquent Boys: The Culture of the Gang.* New York: The Free Press of Glencoe, Inc., 1955. An analysis of delinquent gangs in terms of social class differences.

DOUGLAS, PAUL H. *Ethics in Government.* Cambridge, Mass.: Harvard University Press, 1952. Lectures given at Harvard University by a leading economist and United States senator who headed a series of investigations of unethical practices in government. He makes several proposals to improve ethics in government.

GLUECK, SHELDON and ELEANOR. *Unraveling Juvenile Delinquency.* Cambridge, Mass.: Harvard University Press, 1950. A comparison of 500 delinquents and nondelinquents on a large number of factors. Probably the best-known study of delinquency chiefly in terms of the family and certain personality traits.

KOBRIN, SOLOMON. "The Conflict of Values in Delinquency Areas," *American Sociological Review,* 16:653–661 (October, 1951). A discussion of the social norms and values of areas of high delinquency.

MILLER, WALTER B. "Lower Class Culture as a Generating Milieu of Gang Delinquency," *Journal of Social Issues,* 14:5–19, No. 3 (1958). Juvenile delinquency is explained as a product of the way of life of lower-class subculture.

ROBISON, SOPHIA M. *Juvenile Delinquency: Its Nature and Control.* New York: Holt, Rinehart and Winston, Inc., 1960. An analysis of theories seeking to explain juvenile delinquency and the research data used to support them. Includes a discussion of social class, family, the gang, the school, and mass media in relation to juvenile delinquency.

SCHRAMM, WILBUR, JACK LYLE, and EDWIN B. PARKER. *Television in the Lives of Our Children.* Stanford, Calif.: Stanford University Press, 1961. An analysis of the effects of television in the lives of over 6000 children.

SUTHERLAND, EDWIN H. *White Collar Crime.* New York: Holt, Rinehart and Winston, Inc., 1949, reissued 1961. This study of the illegal behavior of seventy large American corporations indicates that there is extensive disobedience to law among the upper classes in our society.

THRASHER, FREDERIC M. *The Gang.* Chicago: The University of Chicago Press, 1936. This study of 1313 gangs in Chicago is one of the most widely known books on criminology.

Chapter

8

Types of Delinquent and
Criminal Offenders

The terms "delinquent" and "criminal" do not refer to a homogeneous group and have little meaning except as they refer to lawbreakers. There are various types and kinds of delinquent and criminal offenders, depending upon whether the offenders are classified by types of crime committed, by characteristics such as sex and age, or in terms of behavior systems. Classification by offense is useful in studying the legal definitions of offenses. Sex, age, and other characteristics of offenders are necessary in enumerations for statistical purposes. From a scientific or sociological point of view, however, offenders are best grouped according to their behavior patterns and the processes through which they develop. An adequate explanation of delinquent and criminal behavior should show how it applies to all delinquent and criminal behavior, and how it should be modified to explain various types.

> For the purposes of understanding and controlling criminal behavior, definitive generalizations are needed regarding criminal behavior as a whole, with specifications of the general theory applied to particular criminal behaviors. The relation between the general theory and the particular criminal behaviors is analogous to the relation between a germ theory of disease and the particular germs which cause particular diseases. . . . Continued efforts should be made to state valid generalizations regarding criminal behavior as a whole, and continued efforts should be made to explain particular criminal behaviors. . . . Just as the germ theory of disease does not explain all diseases, so it is possible that no one theory of criminal behavior will explain all criminal behavior. In that case, it will be desirable to define the areas to which any theory applies, so that the several theories are co-ordinate and, when taken together, explain all criminal behavior.[1]

Type of Crime

As noted above, criminal offenders are often classified, from a legal point of view, by the type of crime, such as murder, burglary, and arson.

---

[1] Edwin H. Sutherland and Donald R. Cressey, *Principles of Criminology* (6th ed.; New York: J. B. Lippincott Company, 1960), p. 71.

Such a classification enables us, presumably, to group offenders neatly according to what they did, and to show something of these tolerance limits of crimes as reflected in the different penalties of the criminal law. This classification may be quite misleading, inasmuch as persons of extremely diverse types may commit the same crime; moreover, the seriousness of a criminal act is not always correlated with criminal behavior patterns in offenders. And, as has been indicated in a previous chapter, distinctions based on misdemeanants and felons are also unsatisfactory.

There are three main categories of crimes: crimes against the person, crimes against property, and crimes against public order. Crimes against persons involve such acts as murder, manslaughter, assault, and rape. Property crimes include burglary, larceny, forgery, automobile theft, and robbery. Crimes against public order consist of such behavior as prostitution, gambling, the use of narcotics, and drunkenness.

Of the three groups, crimes against the person receive the most publicity in newspapers, on radio and television programs, and in motion pictures. It is not surprising that most people believe, therefore, that the greatest amount of crime, as well as our most serious offenses, involve personal crimes. When murder and rape cases increase or are widely publicized in the newspapers and it is intimated that crime has materially increased, the public erroneously concludes that a "crime wave" is occurring. A single case involving the killing of one juvenile by another, or a particularly vicious sex killing of a child by an adult, immediately becomes news from coast to coast in the United States among 180 million people.

Personal crimes actually constitute a small proportion of all reported crime, less than 5 percent in 1960, with murders and nonnegligent manslaughter but a tiny fraction of all crime. During 1960 an estimated 1,767,389 major property crimes were reported to the police, but only some 82,909 personal crimes. (See Table 8.1). There were 1,104,048 reported larcenies and 432,906 burglaries, as compared with 3371 murders and cases of nonnegligent manslaughter. The distribution of types of crimes varies somewhat between different countries and between developed and underdevelopd countries.[2]

If one were trying to gauge the increase or decrease of crime it would be incorrect to cite personal crimes. Some states, for example, have so few murders that an increase of only two or three may change the proportion profoundly. Wisconsin, for example, had 45 homicides (murder and nonnegligent manslaughter) in the year 1959–1960, with a population of

[2] *Prevention of Types of Criminality Resulting from Social Changes and Accompanying Economic Development in Less Developed Countries,* General Reports to the Second United Nations Congress on the Prevention of Crime and the Treatment of Offenders (London, 8–20 August, 1960) by J. J. Panakal and A. M. Khalifa (New York: United Nations Department of Economic and Social Affairs, 1960).

*Table 8.1. Major Crimes Reported to the Police
in the United States During 1960*

Crime index classification	Estimated number of offenses [a]	Percentage of total
Murder and nonnegligent manslaughter	9,140	0.5
Forcible rape	15,560	0.8
Robbery	88,970	4.7
Aggravated assault	130,230	7.0
Burglary	821,100	44.0
Larceny $50 and over	474,900	26.0
Auto theft	321,400	17.0
Total	1,861,300	100.0

[a] Based on reports to law enforcement agencies in 1960.
SOURCE: Federal Bureau of Investigation, *Uniform Crime Reports* (Annual Bulletin, 1960; Washington, D.C.: Government Printing Office, 1961), p. 2.

almost 4 million. Thus a difference of a few cases would alter the percentage either way.

Sex of Offenders

Delinquents and criminals may be classified according to sex. This distinction had more significance when nearly all offenses committed by women were prostitution and drunkenness, but women now engage in as wide a variety of offenses as do men, although not as frequently. Women are increasingly becoming involved in cases of embezzlement and forgery. They are also involved as associates of men in many cases of property crime, although they are rarely charged. During 1952 women committed about 9 percent of a selected group of major offenses in cities with 25,000 population and over. (See Table 8.2.) In cases of embezzlement and fraud, larceny and theft, and homicide their proportion was considerably greater. The ratio of arrests for embezzlement and fraud, larceny and theft, and murder is approximately 7 men to every 1 woman; assault, 10 to 1; robbery, 25 to 1; and burglary, 40 to 1.

Although it is increasingly difficult to distinguish clearly among offenses in terms of the sex of the offender, the apparently low ratio of crimes committed by women raises a number of questions. Some people have attributed this low ratio to factors other than the low criminality rate of women.[3] Some have suggested that women offenders often play a part in crimes committed by men offenders but that they are not as easily detected

[3] See, for example, Otto Pollak, *The Criminality of Women* (Philadelphia: University of Pennsylvania Press, 1950).

*Table 8.2. Number and Percentage of Crimes for Which Women Were
Arrested in Cities with 25,000 Population and Over, 1952*

	Number	Percent of all arrests
Embezzlement and fraud	951	14.6
Larceny and theft	5,541	14.0
Criminal homicide	297	13.2
Assault	6,050	10.5
Driving while intoxicated	1,724	4.2
Robbery	277	4.2
Burglary—breaking and entering	548	2.4

SOURCE: Federal Bureau of Investigation, *Uniform Crime Reports* (Annual Bulletin, 1952; Washington, D.C.: Government Printing Office, 1953), Vol. 23, No. 2, p. 116.

in crime as men. Others have suggested that since women can engage in prostitution they need not turn to burglary or larceny.

Criminologists, on the other hand, have felt that, even with these allowances, the low incidence of crime among women is indicative of the importance of social rather than personality factors in crime. Certainly there must be the same range of personality traits among women as among men and the former now participate sufficiently in the general society to be able to steal a car or burglarize a home. More significant is the fact that women do not as frequently belong to gangs and are more isolated from criminal norms. And it has been suggested that women more often develop a conception of themselves in terms of future parental responsibilities, making their participation in serious crimes less likely.

Age of Offenders

Another distinction often made is the classification of offenders by age, with younger and older offenders supposedly denoting different degrees of criminal development. Cartoons usually picture the confirmed criminal as a man in his late thirties or forties, heavy set with jutting jaw and large ears, and in general a rather hardened, forbidding creature. The question is how close this stereotype of age and criminal hardness fits reality. Offenders committing serious crimes are most frequently under twenty-five years of age, and a considerable proportion are under twenty-one, according to nation-wide arrest figures collected by the FBI.

Although all types of crimes are committed by persons of all ages, there is a much greater probability of young persons being arrested for the most serious felonies. (See Table 8.3.) During 1960, in cities over 2500 population, approximately one in every two burglars and thieves ar-

*Table 8.3. Number and Percentage of Arrests of Persons under 18,
under 21, and under 25 Years of Age, 1960, in 2460 Cities
over 2500 in Population*

Offense charged	Number of persons arrested				Percentage		
	Total	Under 18	Under 21	Under 25	Under 18	Under 21	Under 25
Criminal homicide:							
a. Murder and nonnegligent manslaughter	4,507	346	827	1,393	7.7	18.3	30.9
b. Manslaughter by negligence	1,766	131	336	618	7.4	19.0	35.0
Robbery	29,326	8,154	13,892	19,333	27.8	47.4	65.9
Aggravated assault	52,277	6,074	10,715	17,463	11.6	20.5	33.4
Burglary—breaking and entering	110,047	56,221	72,867	85,554	51.1	66.2	77.7
Larceny—theft	207,548	102,093	127,284	145,334	49.2	61.3	70.0
Auto theft	54,024	33,558	42,472	47,082	62.1	78.6	87.2
Forcible rape	6,068	1,242	2,556	3,684	20.5	42.1	60.7
Prostitution and commercialized vice	25,851	424	2,523	8,447	1.6	9.8	32.7
Narcotic drug laws	23,430	956	3,965	9,190	4.1	16.9	39.2
Weapons: carrying, possessing, etc.	34,520	6,567	11,146	16,419	19.0	32.3	47.6
Driving while intoxicated	146,381	1,128	6,852	21,985	0.8	4.7	15.0

SOURCE: *Uniform Crime Reports,* Annual Bulletin, 1960, p. 93. Total population 81,660,735, based on 1960 U.S. decennial census.

rested was under eighteen. Two thirds of all those arrested for auto theft were under eighteen, and one fourth of all those arrested for robbery. Almost half of the persons arrested in 1960 for robbery and two thirds of those arrested for larceny were under twenty-one, as well as approximately four fifths of the automobile thieves and two thirds of the burglars. If the age is moved up to those under twenty-five years of age, two out of every three persons arrested for robbery and two in three arrested for larceny are included, as well as about three in four burglars, and nearly nine tenths of the automobile thieves. Younger offenders do not constitute as large a percentage of arrests for criminal homicide and aggravated assault, but one fifth of all forcible rapes are committed by those under eighteen and nearly one half by those under twenty-one.

In all probability the age at which ordinary crimes are committed is even lower than has been indicated. In the first place, many of those in the age group from fourteen through sixteen are not included, for the figures cited above are computed from fingerprint cards, and often either juvenile offenders are not fingerprinted or their fingerprints are not always reported to the FBI. In the second place, arrests tabulated in a given year do not indicate the age at first arrest. If it were possible to know when offenses first started, a greater frequency might be found even below fourteen years of age. For example, one research study of five brothers who had a long career in crime revealed that all had started their delinquency before the age of ten.[4]

In this connection, however, a somewhat different picture is revealed for other offenses, particularly those involving alcohol and gambling violations, murder, and white-collar and professional crime. About 90 percent of all persons arrested for drunkenness or for gambling are twenty-five years of age or older. Nearly two thirds of the persons arrested in 1960 for murder or for nonnegligent manslaughter, in cities over 2500 population, were twenty-five or over. Nine in ten white-collar offenders are over thirty, and one fourth over fifty, as indicated by a study of World War II black-market offenses involving price violations.[5] Four fifths of those arrested for embezzlement and fraud during 1960 were twenty-five years of age or over. About two thirds of all arrests for forgery and counterfeiting were in the older age categories. Most professional criminals are well over twenty-five.

Classification of offenders by age has little merit, for the "hardness" of an offender has little relation to his age. An offender is "hardened" if he has definite antisocial attitudes toward laws, property, and the police, professional knowledge of techniques to commit crimes and avoid prosecution, and a framework of rationalizations to support his conduct. These attitudes may be well developed in a boy of seventeen and yet be absent in a "criminal" of forty. For example, 65.9 percent of all robberies are committed by persons under twenty-five, an offense which is almost always preceded by other crimes, involves the use of a gun, and indicates definite antisocial attitudes.

There are several reasons for the decline of felonies with age. The Gluecks have referred to this as "maturation," and although they have stressed the possibility of biological factors, it seems possible to find in the social frame of reference an explanation for the differences in offenses of the various age groups.[6] Younger men are more daring and possess more physical ability, two qualities necessary for burglary and robbery. Probably the chief reason for the age differential is that the group association of those with deviant norms is greatest among younger people. Except for certain types of crime, as a person grows older he tends to lose touch with deviant associates because of marriage and family responsibilities, and there is a change in his conception of himself.

[4] Clifford R. Shaw, *Brothers in Crime* (Chicago: The University of Chicago Press, 1938).
[5] Marshall B. Clinard, *The Black Market* (New York: Holt, Rinehart and Winston, Inc., 1952), p. 287.
[6] Sheldon and Eleanor T. Glueck, *500 Criminal Careers* (New York: Alfred A. Knopf, Inc., 1930).

Delinquent and Criminal Behavior Systems

A more useful method of distinguishing the various types of delinquent and criminal offenders is based on social processes and behavior systems: how delinquent and criminal norms were incorporated in the individual to produce the delinquent or criminal act and what this criminal behavior means to him. The distinguishing characteristics of types of delinquent and criminal offenders are the degree of development of criminal social roles and life organization, identification with others, and progression in crime.

Noncareer offenders are, for example, represented by occasional offenders, such as most of those who commit assault or murder, statutory rape, and a rare theft, embezzlement, or forgery. Likewise, many sex offenses, such as exhibitionism, fall into this type. The most highly developed career criminals are professional and organized criminals.

A criminal career as distinguished from a noncriminal career involves a life organization of roles built about criminal activities, such as identification with crime, a conception of self as a criminal, extensive association with criminal activities, including other criminals, and, finally, progression in crime. Progression in crime means the acquisition of more complex techniques, more frequent offenses, and, ultimately, dependence on crime as a frequent or sole means of livelihood. Among career offenders group and subcultural factors are extremely important.

Career criminals make crime a definite part of their life organization. They maintain association not only with other criminals but with those persons, such as shady politicians, who may be helpful in the continuation of their way of life. They develop techniques, "a level of operation," and a philosophy of life to go with it. Frequently it is a full-time occupation and their sole means of livelihood. These offenders often concentrate in certain fields of crime. In fact, the police often proceed on this assumption and develop a *modus operandi* file which frequently enables them to pick up burglars, forgers, counterfeiters, safe-crackers, or armed robbers. Professional criminal careers are developed almost entirely within the field of property crimes.[7] For example, in American society, murderers do not ordinarily make a career out of killing, although this practice exists in the Middle East, where one may hire a professional killer for a price. Likewise, rape and aggravated assault are seldom thought of as career crimes. Even persons who participate in a long series of criminal activities may not have a real criminal career.

---

[7] Walter C. Reckless, *The Crime Problem* (3d ed.; New York: Appleton-Century-Crofts, Inc., 1961), p. 153.

Offenders can thus be classified according to the degree to which they make a long-term career out of crime, with the criminally insane at one end and the professional criminal at the other. (See Figure 3.) In between may be ranged extreme sex deviates, occasional offenders, homosexuals and prostitutes, habitual petty criminals, white-collar criminals, those with ordinary criminal careers, and organized criminals.[8]

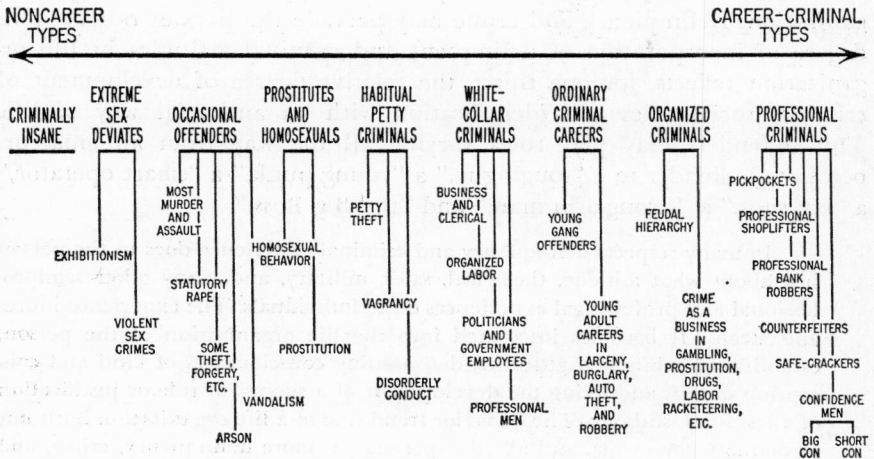

FIGURE 3.—Selected Types of Delinquent and Criminal Behavior

Most personal offenders are of the noncareer type, whereas property offenders are more likely to be of the career type.[9] Some personal offenses are the result of gang or organized groups and are of a career type. Although murder is generally regarded as an individual noncareer type of offense, it may grow out of a career situation. In fact, in New York City there was an unusual organized group, called Murder, Inc., which hired out men to kill other persons for a fee. They approached murder as though it were any property offense, and it has been claimed that during the 1930's this group committed some 1000 murders from coast to coast.[10]

[8] Other types have been devised for classification of prison inmates. Hayner, for example, divides them into types such as the "con forger," "the alcoholic forger," "the rapo," the "heavy," and the "graduate."—Norman S. Hayner, "Characteristics of Five Offender Types," *American Sociological Review*, 26:96–102 (February, 1961). Also see Don C. Gibbons and Donald L. Garrity, "Some Suggestions for the Development of Etiological and Treatment Theory in Criminology," *Social Forces*, 38:51–58 (October, 1959).

[9] See, for example, Alfred R. Lindesmith and H. Warren Dunham, "Some Principles of Criminal Typology," *Social Forces*, 19:307–314 (March, 1941). They use the terms "individual" and "social," which are somewhat misleading.

[10] Burton B. Turkus and Sid Feder, *Murder, Inc.* (New York: Farrar, Straus and Cudahy, Inc., 1952).

SOCIAL ROLES

Although individuals may commit offenses which are legally similar, this behavior actually has a different significance for each. In some individuals their delinquent and criminal activity may represent only a minor and relatively unimportant part of their social roles and life organization. Delinquency and crime may pervade the lives of others. This degree of incorporation of delinquent and criminal attitudes in life organization reflects, for one thing, the relative degree of development of criminal social roles and identification with an antisocial way of life. Thus offenders may play roles varying all the way from an amateur, occasional offender to a "tough guy," a "young punk," a "smart operator," a "big shot," a "strong-arm man," and "the Big Boss."

> In many respects delinquency and criminal experience does to the person just about what athletic, theatrical, sales, military, and many other semiprofessional and professional experiences do to individuals. The experience inures and steeps. It becomes integrated into the life organization of the person, establishing habits and attitudes, determining consciousness of kind and conception of self, and fixing the development of a successful role or justification of a less successful one. The behavior trend line of a life organization built out of delinquency, crime, and allied experience is more delinquency, crime, and allied behavior. The problem is for the person to revise his scheme of life and reorganize himself on a different basis. This would be true if the person took a desk job in an office and left the road as a salesman or if a newspaper reporter became an undertaker or a university professor became a barker in a circus.[11]

Similarly the social role of a "delinquent" is often different from the legal category in which he is placed by the courts. The labeling of delinquent may bring with it the playing of a definite social role, as Cohen and Short have indicated.

> But the category "delinquent" as a social "role" of everyday life is not identical with "delinquent" as a legal category. That is, the criteria by which the man in the street defines somebody as delinquent and the images, feelings and dispositions that the word arouses are not identical with the criteria and consequences in the world of the courts. The social role of delinquent entails consequences over and above those provided by law. If a boy is defined as delinquent in the world of everyday life, his whole social world may be transformed: the ways in which other people see him, how they feel toward him, their willingness to associate with him, the activities and opportunities that are open to him. In consequence of these changes, the way in which the boy sees, labels and evaluates himself, his estimate of his chances and prospects

---

[11] Walter C. Reckless, *The Crime Problem* (New York: Appleton-Century-Crofts, Inc., 1950), p. 35.

in the world of nondelinquent and conventional people, his notion of whether trying to avoid delinquency is worth the trouble, may be profoundly affected. It is quite possible, indeed, that being invested with the social role may so narrow a person's opportunities for the rewards and gratifications of nondelinquent society that it may strengthen his tendency to behavior that is delinquent in the legal sense.[12]

IDENTIFICATION WITH CRIME

The individual may gain considerable satisfaction from the acceptance of group norms and orient his life around them. Thus if a boy identifies himself with the activities of a group of "young punks," this relationship may become as satisfying as if he identified his activities with a group of Boy Scouts. Yet mere membership in a group or contact with deviant norms does not tell us what such behavior means to the individual. Criminality is the result of a person's identification with others from whose perspective his criminal behavior seems acceptable.[13] For example, for rural offenders their lack of identification with delinquent groups is almost as important in explaining their behavior as their membership in such a group.[14] The sophisticated criminal, likewise, may secure a certain status from his identification with other offenders. His knowledge of criminal techniques becomes part of his life organization and as a result he wishes constantly to add to it.

CONCEPTION OF SELF

Closely associated with identification with delinquency or crime is the conception of himself and of his social role which a delinquent or criminal offender develops. He may feel that he is essentially a "good boy" who has really done nothing more than make a technical mistake from the legal point of view, or he may regard his activities as isolated transgressions. On the other hand, he may regard himself as tough, antisocial, or even criminal. In one study farm boys were found to have conceptions of themselves as "wild" and "reckless," whereas city offenders with more pronounced activities in crime spoke of themselves as "hard," "tough," "criminal," "mean," or "no good." [15]

---

[12] Albert K. Cohen and James F. Short, Jr., "Juvenile Delinquency," in Robert K. Merton and Robert A. Nisbet eds., *Contemporary Social Problems* (New York: Harcourt, Brace & World, Inc., 1961), pp. 80–81.

[13] Daniel Glaser, "Criminality Theories and Behavioral Images," *American Journal of Sociology*, 61:433–445 (March, 1956).

[14] Marshall B. Clinard, "Rural Criminal Offenders," *American Journal of Sociology*, 50:38–45 (July, 1944).

[15] Marshall B. Clinard, "The Process of Urbanization and Criminal Behavior," *American Journal of Sociology*, 48:202–213 (September, 1942). Also see Walter C. Reckless, Simon Dinitz, and Ellen Murray, "Self Concept as an Insulator against Delinquency," *American Sociological Review*, 21:744–746 (December, 1956).

A conception of oneself as a delinquent or a criminal may become so well developed that the individual believes he is at war with society and that he is constantly being mistreated and persecuted by the police. In fact, the relation of law-enforcement agencies to the acquisition of one's conception of self often makes the first arrest or incarceration of prime importance in an offender's life organization. Tarde, the early French sociologist and judge, was one of the first to state that a criminal is created, first, by the offense and, second, by the way society treats the act. About delinquency a recent article has stated:

> Although being a "delinquent child" and having the social role of delinquent are not the same thing, if one has been legally declared a "delinquent child" and the fact is known, he is likely to be invested with the social role. Indeed, if he has merely been processed by the courts without having been found delinquent, this may suffice to endow him with the social role. This by-product of legal processing may have more far-reaching consequences in the life of the child than what happens to him in court. For this reason, it is not possible to appraise the law and the judicial institutions without considering the extrajudicial social role of delinquency and its meaning for the child.[16]

Once an offender has developed the conception of himself as a delinquent, prostitute, confidence man, robber, or forger, it is often hard to change it. The following comments show how a group of reformatory inmates looked upon themselves.

> The gang I went with was some older boys than me and some were younger than I was, and all of us thought we were very tough.

> I had the reputation of being a tough guy. I am afraid that if there was anybody that had anything that I wanted I would find some way to get it if I had to steal it.

> I got in so many fights that some people started calling me a roughneck.

> My two brothers next to my age are staying to home and taking care of the folks. They both are older than twenty-one but do not seem to care for women or dances or care for liquor. I am the only one that seems to be getting into trouble. . . . I guess it is that I am carefree and seem to try anything that comes along. I like to go out on parties. I seem to be like a clown, I guess, when I am on parties, and it seems that I have the gang in an uproar most of the time. . . . I seem to have quite a few friends. Some, of course, think that if I would leave the liquor alone and quit my stealing I would be a good boy. Some think that I just ain't no good and never will be any good.[17]

Recent sociological studies have suggested differences in self-conception as the reason that certain children residing in a delinquency area

---

[16] Cohen and Short, "Juvenile Delinquency," *loc. cit.*, p. 81.
[17] From personal documents.

do not become delinquents.[18] In a study of 125 "good boys" and 108 potential delinquents in this area, the authors concluded: "Conception of self and others is the differential response component that helps to explain why some succumb and others do not, why some gravitate toward socially unacceptable patterns of behavior and others veer away from them." [19] Additional research in this direction may furnish valuable insights into why so many middle- and upper-class boys do not engage in delinquency and may help to explain the differential response patterns of adults, including white-collar workers, to criminal norms.

DIFFERENTIAL ASSOCIATION

In addition to identification and conception of self as an important part of an offender's social role is the extent to which a lawbreaker acquires the techniques and philosophy of a criminal type. There is differential association with the pushes and pulls of conventional and criminal norms. Some tend to push the individual away from criminal behavior while others pull him toward it.

Intimate and personal associations undoubtedly have the greatest influence in the acquisition of delinquent and criminal norms. Although one may not entirely agree with Sutherland's arbitrary statement that a person who becomes delinquent does so because of an excess of definitions favorable to violations of law over definitions unfavorable to violation of law, much of crime is a product of differential association with criminal norms.[20] The effect of such association depends on the frequency, duration, priority, and intensity of exposure to conventional and criminal norms. The frequency of such association and the length of their duration have much to do with the development of a delinquent or criminal career. The priority of such association with criminal norms means that the exposure to delinquent norms early in life may have a profound subsequent effect in determining the development of a criminal career. The intensity of such association is related to the prestige of persons with criminal norms with whom an individual associates and with his reactions to such persons.

PROGRESSION IN CRIME

The history of a criminal career type is a progressive series of steps in the acquisition of criminal techniques and knowledge. This progression

[18] Reckless, Dinitz, and Murray, "Self Concept . . . ," loc. cit.; Walter C. Reckless, Simon Dinitz, and Ellen Murray, "The 'Good Boy' in a High Delinquency Area," Journal of Criminal Law, Criminology, and Police Science, 48:18–25 (1957); and Walter C. Reckless, Simon Dinitz, and Barbara Kay, "Self-Component in Potential Delinquency and Non-Delinquency," American Sociological Review, 22:566–570 (1957).

[19] Reckless, Dinitz, and Kay, "Self-component . . . ," loc. cit., p. 570.

[20] Edwin H. Sutherland and Donald R. Cressey, Principles of Criminology (6th ed.; Philadelphia: J. B. Lippincott Company, 1960), pp. 74–81.

varies with different types of crimes. Burglars and robbers, for example, show a progression from petty theft to more serious larcenies, to crimes such as ordinary burglary or automobile theft, and then on to highly skilled burglary or armed robbery. Criminality may proceed from trivial to more serious crimes, from being a sport to being a business, and from occasional crime to more frequent crime. Along with progression in crime the offender develops a philosophy of life which justifies his criminal actions.

Personality Traits and Criminal Behavior

Many psychologists and psychiatrists have sought to explain nearly all forms of delinquent and criminal behavior as due primarily to abnormalities in the psychological structure of the individual. They believe that inadequacies in the individual's personality traits interfere with his adjustment to the demands of society. The assumption of this approach to criminal behavior is that if it were possible to ascertain the nature of trait structures which are related to criminal behavior, and if formation of these structures could be prevented or if they could be treated successfully, most crime could be eliminated. To them, delinquent or criminal behavior, even of a group nature, consists mainly of the actions of separate individuals.

There are several major difficulties in distinguishing between the personality traits of offenders and those of nonoffenders. Samples of institutionalized offenders are customarily used, which are probably unrepresentative; moreover, the test performances may be unreliable. It is also possible that experiences, such as arrests, court appearances, or imprisonment, may so affect the personality traits of offenders that it is impossible to determine what they were like prior to such experiences. Comparisons of delinquents, who are of a certain age and often of a particular cultural background, with a general test norm may be misleading. Finally, very few studies of personality traits have distinguished among types of offenders.

Some evidence that there is no necessary relationship, however, between personality traits and criminal behavior has been shown in a survey by Schuessler and Cressey. They took all 113 known studies (up to 1950) which had compared the personality characteristics of delinquents and nondelinquents, criminals and noncriminals. Although 42 percent of the studies showed differences in favor of the nondelinquents and noncriminals, in 58 percent of the studies the results, for various reasons, were indefinite: "The doubtful validity of many of the obtained differences, as well as the lack of consistency in the combined results, makes it impossible to conclude from these data that criminality and personality elements are associated." [21]

---

[21] Karl F. Schuessler and Donald R. Cressey, "Personality Characteristics of Criminals," *American Journal of Sociology*, 55:476 (March, 1950). For attempts to show the relationship of personality traits to delinquency, see Starke Hathaway and Elio D. Monachesi, *Analyzing and Predicting Juvenile Delinquency with the MMPI* (Minneapolis: University

One theory of the relation of personality traits and certain criminal behavior needs more detailed analysis. The literature of many phases of deviant behavior has had references to the existence of a deviant personality type termed a "criminal psychopath" or "psychopathic personality," a habitual antisocial deviant.[22] It has been suggested that nearly all sexual offenders are psychopaths, or that the prison population is composed partly of psychopaths. Numerous popular articles have contained such statements as "Most of the sex killers are psychopathic personalities. No one knows or can even closely estimate how many such creatures there are, but at least tens of thousands of them are loose in the country today." [23]

Since 1937, at least twenty states, acting in response to a rather hysterical belief in the wholesale existence of dangerous "psychopaths," have passed specific laws dealing with the treatment of sexual psychopaths. Although there are some variations, for the most part they provide for the indefinite incarceration of such diagnosed persons in state mental hospitals. As Sutherland has pointed out, most of these laws have had their origin in emotional and nonrational processes.[24] Generally they have been enacted after a state of fear has been aroused in a community from a small number of sex crimes occurring over a short period of time.

Although there has been considerable dispute over the meaning of the term "psychopath," some of the characteristics of a so-called psychopath are said to be that he is free from the signs or symptoms generally associated with psychoses, neuroses, or mental deficiency, and that he demonstrates poor judgment and an inability to learn by experience, which is seen in "pathological lying," repeated crime, delinquencies, and other antisocial acts.[25] "Patients repeat apparently purposeless thefts, forgeries, bigamies, swindlings, distasteful or indecent acts in public, scores of times." [26]

---

of Minnesota Press, 1953); Elio D. Monachesi, "Personality Characteristics and Socio-Economic Status of Delinquents and Non-Delinquents," *Journal of Criminal Law and Criminology*, 40:570–583 (January–February, 1950); Elio D. Monachesi, "Personality Characteristics of Institutionalized and Non-Institutionalized Male Delinquents," *Journal of Criminal Law and Criminology*, 41:167–179 (July–August, 1950).

[22] Harrison Gough, "A Sociological Theory of Psychopathy," *American Journal of Sociology*, 53:365 (March, 1948). There are few more unprecise psychiatric terms, or with a longer history, than the term "psychopath." Originally the terms "moral insanity" and "moral imbecility" were used. In the trial of Charles Guiteau in 1881 for the assassination of President Garfield, the issue of "moral" insanity was raised by the defense. Koch is credited with originating the term "psychopathic personality" in 1888 when he referred to a group of patients having no proper class of mental disorder but who could not be considered as entirely sane.

[23] David G. Wittels, "What Can We Do about Sex Crime?" *Saturday Evening Post*, 221:31 (December 11, 1948).

[24] Edwin H. Sutherland, "The Sexual Psychopath Laws," *Journal of Criminal Law and Criminology*, 40:543–554 (January–February, 1950).

[25] Hervey Cleckley, *The Mask of Sanity* (St. Louis: C. V. Mosby Co., 1950), and "The Psychopath, a Problem for Society," *Federal Probation*, 12:3–8 (June, 1948). Also see his "Psychopathic Personality," in the *Encyclopedia of Criminology* (W. C. Branham and E. B. Kutash, eds.; New York: Philosophical Library, Inc., 1949), pp. 413–416.

[26] Cleckley, "Psychopathic Personality," *loc. cit.*, p. 415.

Although many believe that the concept of a psychopath is real and that such a personality type sufficiently explains numerous antisocial acts, the term is used so imprecisely and with such a variety of meanings by people who are not clear as to the developmental processes of a psychopath that its entire usefulness can be seriously questioned. In fact, the authors of one study have reported that they found some 202 different terms applied in one form or another to the psychopath.[27] After a study of several years the Committee on Forensic Psychiatry of the Group for the Advancement of Psychiatry issued a warning against the use of a term in statutes with such a wide variety of meanings as the word "psychopath." [28]

The lack of precision in describing psychopathic traits has been shown by the wide differences in the diagnoses of "psychopathic" criminal offenders in various institutions and by research on the traits. Cason and Pescor isolated fifty-four traits commonly held to be characteristic of psychopaths. They selected 101 persons diagnosed as psychopathic by the Psychopathic Unit of the Federal Medical Unit at Springfield, Missouri, and from them took two groups, the 23 least psychopathic and the 29 most psychopathic.[29] This distinction was made on the basis of the number of characteristics described as psychopathic. Their findings were that forty-six of the fifty-four traits were not statistically significant in distinguishing between those least and those most psychopathic. Of the remaining eight traits, six were only slightly significant, and the two significant characteristics were being intolerant and making threats.

The view that a person is a psychopath merely because he is a repeater or is persistent in his behavior is circular reasoning.[30] Writing on the characteristic of persistent antisocial behavior as a criterion of a psychopath, Sutherland stated: "This identification of an habitual sexual offender as a sexual psychopath has no more justification than the identification of any other habitual offender as a psychopath, such as one who repeatedly steals, violates the antitrust law, or lies about his golf scores." [31]

---

[27] Halsey Cason and M. J. Pescor, "A Statistical Study of 500 Psychopathic Prisoners," *Public Health Reports*, 61:557–574 (April 19, 1946). Also see their "A Comparative Study of Recidivists and Non-Recidivists among Psychopathic Federal Offenders," *Journal of Criminal Law and Criminology*, 36:236–238 (September, 1946).

[28] Group for the Advancement of Psychiatry, Report No. 9. Also see *The Habitual Sex Offender*, Report and Recommendations of the Commission on the Habitual Sex Offender as formulated by Paul W. Tappan, Technical Consultant (Trenton: State of New Jersey, 1950), p. 38.

[29] Cason and Pescor, "A Statistical Study of 500 Psychopathic Prisoners," *loc. cit.*

[30] The question of the point at which persistent lying and evasiveness become psychopathic was an important issue in the Alger Hiss case when his defense attorneys sought to prove, by testimony of a psychiatrist, that the chief prosecution witness, Whittaker Chambers, was a psychopath. In relentless cross-examination, which at times became humorous, the prosecutor showed conclusively that the term "psychopath" lacked preciseness.—James Bell, "Your Witness, Mr. Murphy," *Life*, 28:41–42 (January 23, 1950). Also see Alistair Cooke, *A Generation on Trial* (New York: Alfred A. Knopf, Inc., 1952).

[31] Sutherland, "The Sexual Psychopath Laws," *loc. cit.*, p. 549.

Types of Delinquents

Among the many problems confronting the student of juvenile delinquency there is probably none more perplexing or elusive than the designation "juvenile delinquency." The many definitions of this term as found in recent textbooks and monographs attest to the lack of agreement as to what juvenile delinquency is. Not only has the concept been subject to a variety of definitions; it has also been utilized as an omnibus designation. Thus, as currently employed, the term "juvenile delinquency" has the doubtful function of being an inclusive category, applied without too much foresight to much juvenile behavior in general.[32]

A typological approach to delinquency permits concentration upon problems of limited scope and enables one to deal with manageable groups characterized by relatively homogeneous behavior.[33] Some of the difficulties in the prediction and control of delinquency are probably due to limited typological research on juveniles.[34] To understand delinquency more fully the various career patterns and types of offenses of delinquents must be studied. A fundamental question still to be answered is why a given delinquent engages in a particular act, such as vandalism or sex offenses, rather than in some other form of delinquency, although, to be sure, some delinquents are involved in several forms of delinquent behavior.[35] Two types of delinquency will be discussed here, vandalism and auto theft.[36]

Vandalism

Vandalism is an example of the typological approach to juvenile delinquency.[37] By vandalism is meant the deliberate defacement, mutilation,

---

[32] This confusing situation has affected the type of research done in this area, especially the prevailing emphasis on the early discovery and prediction of the potential delinquent. The usual procedure is to take a random and representative sample of delinquents, match it with an equally random and representative sample of nondelinquents, subject the samples to a variety of diagnostic tests, and thus arrive at a "scientific" formula which supposedly aids the investigator to predict with some degree of accuracy the potential delinquent, regardless of type.

[33] Marshall B. Clinard and Andrew L. Wade, "Toward the Delineation of Vandalism as a Sub-Type in Juvenile Delinquency," *Journal of Criminal Law, Criminology, and Police Science,* 48:493–499 (January–February, 1958).

[34] Steps in the right direction are the following: William W. Wattenberg and James Balistrieri, "Automobile Theft: A 'Favored-Group' Delinquency," *American Journal of Sociology,* 57:575–579 (May, 1952), and William W. Wattenberg and John B. Moir, "A Study of Teen-Agers Arrested for Drunkenness," *Quarterly Journal of Studies on Alcohol,* 17:426–436 (September, 1956).

[35] See William W. Wattenberg and David Faigenbaum, "Patterns in Delinquency," *Journal of Clinical Psychology,* 9:78–81 (January, 1953).

[36] For a discussion of types of delinquency, such as auto theft, traffic violations, vandalism, sex delinquency, drunkenness, and drug addiction in various countries, see *New Forms of Juvenile Delinquency: Their Origin, Prevention and Treatment,* General Report by Wolf Middendorff, Judge, Federal Republic of Germany (New York: United Nations Department of Economic and Social Affairs, 1960).

[37] Much of the material in this section is derived from Clinard and Wade, "Toward

or destruction of private or public property by a juvenile or group of juveniles not having immediate or direct ownership of the property so abused. Although a common type of property offense among adolescent boys, the term itself is a relatively recent one, having come into official use as applied to delinquency only since the late thirties. What is here defined as vandalism is often included in such designations of delinquent activity as "malicious mischief," "acts of carelessness or mischief," "willful and wanton misconduct," "destructiveness," "disorderly conduct," "incorrigibility," or even "assault."

Vandalism includes many acts of destruction which have been described as follows:

> Studies of the complaints made by citizens and public officials reveal that hardly any property is safe from this form of aggression. Schools are often the object of attack by vandals. Windows are broken; records, books, desks, typewriters, supplies, and other equipment are stolen or destroyed. Public property of all types appears to offer peculiar allurement to children bent on destruction. Parks, playgrounds, highway signs, and markers are frequently defaced or destroyed. Trees, shrubs, flowers, benches, and other equipment suffer in like manner. Autoists are constantly reporting the slashing or releasing of air from tires, broken windows, stolen accessories. Golf clubs complain that benches, markers, flags, even expensive and difficult-to-replace putting greens are defaced, broken or uprooted. Libraries report the theft and destruction of books and other equipment. Railroads complain of and demand protection from the destruction of freight car seals, theft of property, wilful and deliberate throwing of stones at passenger car windows, tampering with rails and switches. Vacant houses are always the particular delight of children seeking outlets for destructive instincts; windows are broken, plumbing and hardware stolen, destroyed, or rendered unusable. Gasoline operators report pumps and other service equipment stolen, broken, or destroyed. Theater managers, frequently in the "better" neighborhoods, complain of the slashing of seats, wilful damaging of toilet facilities, even the burning of rugs, carpets, etc.[38]

The available statistics on juvenile court referrals reported annually to the United States Children's Bureau indicate that property destruction is a common offense among adolescent boys. The cost to the American public of this deliberate damage is probably greater than the combined costs of other forms of juvenile property offenses. Vandalism is not confined to the United States; in Sweden, for example, the increases in willful damage committed by those aged fifteen to seventeen increased nearly 200 percent between 1950 and 1953.

The cost of an offense is not the only way to measure seriousness. Re-

---

the Delineation of Vandalism . . . ," *loc. cit.* By special permission of the *Journal of Law, Criminology and Police Science* (Northwestern University School of Law).

[38] J. P. Murphy, "The Answer to Vandalism May Be Found At Home," *Federal Pro-*

search has shown that attitudes toward respect for property are not always the same and that any concept of property rights is to a considerable extent fluid and conditional.[39] Actually a violation of property rights is not, of itself, necessarily serious. Its seriousness is dependent on such factors as the relationship of the owner to the offender, the danger of punishment for the offender, the likelihood of real injury to the owner, the kind of property involved, and the value of the property. Studies attempting to measure the relative seriousness of this offense have shown that vandalism ranks low in order of seriousness when compared with other typical juvenile offenses and that within the general designation of "vandalism" there are different types of property destruction, each with its relative degree of seriousness.[40]

Comparing a group of vandals in the Bronx of New York City with other delinquents reported during 1955, Martin found that while both vandals and other delinquents live largely in deteriorated neighborhoods there were differences. The vandal is more likely to be a male, is younger than most delinquents, more likely to be white, from less mobile families, and more likely to commit vandalism in company with others.[41]

SEX AND AGE

Statistics from the Children's Bureau, over the years it has published such figures, show that, as might be expected, far more boys than girls are involved in vandalism. Studies in such diverse localities as Denver, Detroit, Connecticut, and Great Britain also bear out this relationship.[42] There is, on the other hand, considerable disagreement as to whether the typical age group involved in this offense is preadolescent or adolescent.[43] Some of this disagreement may be due to the type of vandalism engaged in by juveniles. Some kinds of destruction of property are probably associated with certain age groups since these acts may call for the ingenuity which comes with

bation, 18:8–10 (March, 1954). This issue of Federal Probation contains a symposium on vandalism.

[39] See John C. Eberhart, "Attitudes toward Property: A Genetic Study by the Paired-Comparisons Rating of Offenses," Journal of Genetic Psychology, 60:3–25 (March, 1942).

[40] See Mervin A. Durea, "An Experimental Study of Attitudes toward Juvenile Delinquency," Journal of Applied Psychology, 17:522–534 (1933), and Edwin Powers and Helen Witmer, An Experiment in the Prevention of Delinquency (New York: Columbia University Press, 1951), pp. 329–332.

[41] John M. Martin, Juvenile Vandalism (Springfield, Ill.: Charles C Thomas, Publishers, 1961).

[42] A Study of Vandalism (Denver: Denver Area Welfare Council, Inc., April, 1954), p. 5; William W. Wattenberg and Frank Saunders, "Sex Differences among Juvenile Offenders," Sociology and Social Research, 39:26 (September–October, 1954); Needs of Neglected and Delinquent Children (Hartford, Conn.: Public Welfare Council, 1946), p. 14; and Hermann Mannheim, "The Problem of Vandalism in Great Britain," Federal Probation, 18:14 (March, 1954).

[43] See Ben Solomon, "Vandalism," Youth Leaders Digest, 17:162 (February, 1955);

more age and experience. There is some evidence that vandalism among children diminishes during the summer months. Most vandalism seems to occur when juveniles are en route to school or have just left school.[44]

SOCIAL CLASS

Evidence concerning the relationship of vandalism to social class position is conflicting and fragmentary. Shulman has speculated that while offenses among lower-class boys consist largely of various types of theft, malicious mischief occurring under group stimulus is more characteristic of middle-class juveniles.[45] The evidence is contradictory, however. Gingery's survey of vandalism in twenty-five cities revealed that this offense is just as high in the poorer sections as in the higher socioeconomic districts of the city.[46] On the other hand, a recent Denver study of vandalism showed that the majority of offenders lived in low-income sections, whereas Mannheim's study of juvenile delinquency in Kansas City disclosed that the highest incidence was among youth from areas composed of middle-class families.[47] A few studies have indicated that acts committed by vandals tend to be nearer the homes of their perpetrators than are any other offenses typical of juveniles.[48]

Cohen suggests that vandalism, for the middle-class boy, constitutes a protest against identification with his mother. Because of the small family, the boy's isolation from socially significant adults other than his parents, and the curtailment of his movement outside the neighborhood, the boy's mother becomes the principal agent of socialization and indoctrination of "good" behavior. Thus goodness comes to symbolize femininity for the middle-class boy. Feeling this a threat to his status as a male, he reacts negatively to those social conduct norms associated with "mother" by engaging in behavior which functions as a denial of his femininity and an assertion of his masculinity. Because property has great symbolic value for the middle-class adult as an attribute of status, a destructive attack on this

---

and Henry S. Dewhurst, *The Railroad Police* (Springfield, Ill.: Charles C Thomas, Publisher, 1955), p. 114.

[44] William W. Wattenberg, "Delinquency During Summer Months," *Journal of Educational Research*, 42:262 (December, 1948). Burt has concluded that acts of property destruction showed irregular fluctuations, revealing small correlation with the weather. See Cyril Burt, *The Young Delinquent* (New York: Appleton-Century-Crofts, Inc., 1925), p. 162.

[45] Harry M. Shulman, "The Family and Juvenile Delinquency," *The Annals*, 261: 30 (January, 1949).

[46] S. L. Gingery, "Vandalism in Schools," *School Business Affairs*, 12:5 (September, 1946).

[47] *A Study of Vandalism*, p. 7, and Ernest Mannheim, *Youth in Trouble* (Kansas City, Mo.: The Community Service Division, Department of Welfare, 1945).

[48] *A Study of Vandalism*, p. 7, and Mannheim, *Youth in Trouble*, pp. 88 f.

symbol becomes especially meaningful to the middle-class boy who has been reared to believe that property should be treated carefully, not carelessly abused or destroyed.[49]

Vandalism for the lower-class boy, on the other hand, has the same protest function but a different basis. Whereas the adult world defines the middle-class boy as a "good" boy, the definition of the lower-class boy indicates suspicion, contempt, and hostility. This negative definition is transmitted to him through the attitudes of middle-class adults with whom he has categoric contacts. His participation in property destruction constitutes an attack on the symbols of middle-class respectability and serves as a protest of this imputation of inferiority and devaluation of personal worth by the middle-class group. Destructive behavior emphasizes the difference between himself and middle-class conventionality and demonstrates a contempt for its way of life.[50]

RELATION OF VANDALISM TO OTHER DELINQUENCY

One study found that 61.8 percent of the delinquent boys and only 3.8 percent of the nondelinquent controls had previously indulged in various acts of destructiveness.[51] On this evidence the statement was made that destructive mischief is one of the first clear signs of the delinquent's social maladaptation.[52] However, this idea of vandalism as a first or eventual step in a career of crime is yet to be empirically confirmed by others. Furthermore, little is known about the amount and kind of recidivism in vandalism. Merrill's delinquency study found that only 4 percent of the delinquents had "malicious mischief" as a first offense, whereas theft was the first offense in 57 percent of the cases studied.[53]

GROUP NATURE OF VANDALISM

Studies have shown that in nearly all cases of destruction the acts are performed with companions.[54] In certain communities an additional ele-

---

[49] Albert K. Cohen, *Delinquent Boys* (New York: The Free Press of Glencoe, 1955), pp. 91 ff. and 164 f.

[50] Solomon Kobrin, "The Conflict of Values in Delinquency Areas," *American Sociological Review*, 16:656 and 659 f. (October, 1951).

[51] Sheldon and Eleanor Glueck, *Unraveling Juvenile Delinquency* (New York: The Commonwealth Fund, 1950), p. 162.

[52] *Ibid.*, p. 28.

[53] Maud A. Merrill, *Problems of Child Delinquency* (Boston: Houghton Mifflin Company, 1947), Appendix B, Table 2, p. 346.

[54] Walter Houston Clark, "Sex Differences and Motivation in the Urge to Destroy," *Journal of Social Psychology*, 36:170 (November, 1952). Also see Clifford R. Shaw and Henry D. McKay, *Social Factors in Juvenile Delinquency*, Report on the Causes of Crime, National Commission on Law Observance and Enforcement, No. 13; (Washington D.C.: Government Printing Office, 1931). II, 122 f.

ment of gang rivalry is apparent: sometimes rival gangs will compete in destructive acts.[55] There is also some evidence that such vandalism is related to racial, ethnic, or religious prejudice.[56] It is unlikely, however, that such behavior is more typical of certain racial or ethnic groups than of others. Data from the Children's Bureau indicate that there is little difference between Negro and white groups in the amount of vandalism committed.

DIMENSIONS IN A TYPOLOGY OF VANDALISM

Provided there is not serious injury to property, the American public tends to view pranks with a kind of careless tolerance, probably because most American males were once participants in this kind of activity. However, certain implied limits exist to juvenile vandalism growing out of ambiguous definitions of the roles and status of children in contemporary society. The destructiveness of very young children is often excused with the rationalization that they have not yet matured to a responsible understanding of property rights and values. Much of the damage by this group is probably accidental, hence more readily excusable. Furthermore, most of this vandalism seems to grow out of random play-group activity. In its beginning stages this activity is inherently neither recreational nor delinquent. Later it may be defined as one or the other, depending upon whether the culmination of the activity is acceptable or unacceptable to the community. With younger children vandalism is not, therefore, necessarily malicious; rather, it is more often destructive play motivated largely by curiosity.[57]

The adolescent, on the other hand, is generally held morally culpable for his destructiveness. More often than not, his vandalism is considered deliberate and malicious even by the juvenile, as a fourteen-year-old boy has stated:

> Well, my parents came over to Gene's. I told my father we'd go over to the [drugstore] . . . . Went over to the apartment house where cars were parked . . . wanted to "split tires" and did . . . meanness, I guess,—get an urge to do it—start with one and keep on doing it. . . . Well, it didn't matter, any car would do. . . . Teen-agers are different from adults, feel urge to do something ornery. . . . I didn't know the people, of course, just something mean to do . . . everybody does something mean.[58]

---

[55] Lloyd T. Delaney, "Establishing Relations with Anti-Social Groups and an Analysis of Their Structure," *British Journal of Delinquency*, 5:43 (July, 1954) and Barbara Bellow *et al.*, "Prejudice in 'Seaside,' " *Human Relations*, 1:112 (June, 1947).

[56] Raymond Gordon, "Vandalism," *Federal Probation*, 18:50 (September, 1954). See also Shaw and McKay, *op. cit.*, p. 117.

[57] A. H. Maslow, "A Comparative Approach to the Problem of Destructiveness," *Psychiatry*, 5:520 (November, 1942).

[58] This and subsequent undesignated interviews are from a study in Kansas City of teen-age vandalism, financed by Community Studies, Inc., Kansas City, Mo., and also from Clinard and Wade, "Toward the Delineation of Vandalism . . . ," *loc. cit.*

How severely the teen-ager is censured is often dependent on the nature of the damage and the property vandalized. Community tolerance limits of various types of property destruction also appear to be affected by whether it occurs in a rural or an urban area. As Ellingston has suggested, to overturn a truck in the urban community is labeled destruction of property.[59]

These normative aspects are important in the assessment of the meaning of vandalism to the community. It is commonplace for the community to overlook certain forms of vandalism on Halloween. But even within this institutionalized setting the norms are undergoing change and less destructive behavior is approved than formerly.[60] The social situation in which the offense takes place is another important dimension. Although the society may not have a well-structured and consistent set of norms relative to property destruction, within the society certain groups, or members of particular social classes, may be accorded a well-defined field in which to indulge in vandalism. One British writer has stated:

> . . . the party of public schoolboys who damage property during the course of a "rag" are behaving very differently from the street corner gang who smash street lamps or shop windows "just for the fun of it," or to work off their aggression. The mores of the Public School community allow and even encourage such explosively expressive behaviour and the scholars' participation in rowdyism has the sanction of authority in its restricted setting, whereas the casual destructiveness of promiscuous gangs has no such social approval to sustain it.[61]

Often there is a certain flavor of spontaneity present indicating the type of criminal behavior characterized by Reckless as "a striking back against authority figures" in response to certain situations.[62] Much teen-age vandalism appears to be of this kind; it is extemporaneous behavior, adventitious and fortuitous in character, an outgrowth of the restless and exuberant nature of the adolescent boy.

> In the evening, between five or six, we was out to _____ Center (this center had been burned) messin' around. We was gonna play some ball. It was gettin' too dark for that, so one of us suggested to go in; so we went in. . . . Climbed up on the rest room roof. See, it used to be a school, that's where the exits outside from the rest rooms were. We climbed up on there and went in through the window. . . . Well, first we went up and we thought

---

[59] John Ellingston, *Protecting Our Children from Criminal Careers* (Englewood Cliffs, N.J.: Prentice-Hall, Inc., 1948), pp. 197 f.

[60] See Ralph and Adelin Linton, *Halloween: Through Twenty Centuries* (New York: Abelard-Schuman, Ltd., 1950). In Great Britain, the Guy Fawkes Day Celebration (November 5) is an institutionalized occasion for college-boy pranks; students let off "steam" mainly by setting bonfires.

[61] John Barron Mays, *Growing Up in the City* (Liverpool: University of Liverpool Press, 1954), pp. 18–19.

[62] Reckless, *op. cit.*, 3d ed., p. 5.

we'd see what the Teen Town room looked like. Went up there, it wasn't bothered or burnt too much—floor was a little weak, dirty. Then we come back downstairs—we was gonna go in the art room but we couldn't get in there, the floor, it was burnt through. There was, oh, about an eighth of an inch of wood left. So we couldn't get in there. Uh—we just went messin' around. Started throwin' rocks. . . . From what we heard they was gonna tear the building down, build one the full length of the lot down there. . . . In there about an hour; just went around—throw one or two (rocks) . . . pretty soon we were going like mad. . . . While we were doing it we didn't think nothing about doing it because, like I said, what we heard they was going to tear the whole building down and I didn't think they would save them (windows)—big percentage of them were cracked and discolored, anyway. . . . What we was doing there would be about three of us outside and three of us inside and we would have wars, throwing rocks back and forth at each other. . . . I guess anybody likes to get in trouble once in a while . . . not actually go out to look for trouble, but I mean at the time we thought it was fun until the police came; that was all.

On the other hand, the differential social expectations as to the roles of boys and girls are important in the inhibition of destructive behavior by girls. Since American culture does not place the same inhibitions on the boy's outward expression of his feelings, positive or negative, as it does on that of girls, the male youth, as one author has suggested, often appears to feel it essential to be self-directive in order to be considered masculine and acceptable to his peers.[63] Participation in vandalism is one way of meeting these needs for autonomy and peer-group acceptance.

Fundamentally related is the frustration felt by the adolescent in a culture in which his role and status lack a well-defined normative structure. Moreover, there is little consensus on values and no consistency in adult behavior which might serve as guideposts. This absence of dominant and clearly defined norms, coupled with the factor of peer-group loyalty, with its attendant norms and values, results in conflict between the adolescent and authority figures, usually his parents and teachers. The consequence is behavior often termed delinquent by the adult world, while the adolescent defines it in terms of conformity to peer-group expectations.[64]

This difference in the definition of behavior is true of vandalism. Whereas the adult world thinks of the teen-age vandal as a delinquent, the vandal may often have an entirely different self-conception. His self-image is frequently that of a prankster:

We did all kinds of dirty tricks for fun. We'd see a sign, "Please keep the street clean," but we'd tear it down and say, "We don't feel like keeping

---

[63] See Aileen Schoeppe, "Sex Differences in Adolescent Socialization," *Journal of Social Psychology*, 38:175–185 (November, 1953).

[64] For a criticism of the view that adolescent culture is in conflict with its adult counterpart, see Frederick Elkin and William A. Westley, "The Myth of Adolescent Culture," *American Sociological Review*, 20:680–684 (December, 1955).

it clean." One day we put a can of glue in the engine of a man's car. We would always tear things down. That would make us laugh and feel good, to have so many jokes.[65]

One time . . . four or five of us boys went to an apartment just being built, took a whole wall of cement down. We took a chisel and knocked down hundreds of cinder blocks, just mischievous. We went to old houses, broke windows. . . . In one house we found a big Victrola. We threw it down the stairs, we pushed down the bannister, we broke the chandelier. We didn't steal anything, just broke things. . . . I had to do it so they wouldn't call me chicken.[66]

The fact that often nothing is stolen during such acts of vandalism tends to reinforce the vandal's conception of himself as merely a prankster and not a delinquent. Some writers have pointed this out as a distinguishing characteristic of the vandal when compared with other property offenders, assuming that since nothing is taken vandalism has a nonutilitarian function. However, these acts often do have a real meaning and utility for the participants, even though the reasons for participation are not expressed. Property destruction appears to function for the adolescent as a protest against his ill-defined role and ambiguous status in the social structure. Although role frustration is basic to this protest, the nature of the frustration differs as to the position of the vandal in the social structure, as implied in this statement by a sixteen-year-old delinquent.

Well, he accused us of stealing some stuff out of his joint. He didn't come right out and say it was us, but the way he talked he made it sound like it—particularly us. . . . Yeah, we was kidding him about an old rifle he had in there, about ninety years old, and he wanted fifteen dollars for it and the stock on it was all cracked up and everything. And we kept kidding his mother—she's in there (the store) with him—and we kept kidding her, and old Gay (the store owner), himself, come over there and started raising the devil, blowing off steam and everything. We didn't like it too well. We left and came back later. . . . I told him (his companion) let's go down and break those windows. He said OK and we went down there and picked up some rocks along the way. We got down there and stood in front of the place till there weren't any cars very close to it and we threw the rocks and ran. . . . I guess you gotta get into something once in a while or you don't live right out there. It didn't seem like then that it would amount to this much.

SUBTYPES OF VANDALISM

Acts of vandalism may be divided into three types: predatory, vindictive, and wanton vandalism.[67] The first type involves acts which, although

[65] Frederick M. Thrasher, *The Gang* (2d ed.; Chicago: The University of Chicago Press, 1936), pp. 94 f.

[66] Benjamin Fine, *1,000,000 Delinquents* (Cleveland: World Publishing Company, 1955), pp. 36–37.

[67] Martin, *op. cit.*, pp. 72–103.

destructive, end in some financial reward to the vandals. For example, metal pipes may be ripped out of a building and later sold. In vindictive vandalism the chief motivation is antagonism and hatred for individuals or groups. A Negro's home may be stoned or a Jewish synagogue desecrated with a swastika. School property may be destroyed by a boy who hates his teacher or the school in general. In the third type—wanton vandalism— we have "at one extreme, destruction of this type [occurring] as simply part of the play activity of children, particularly relatively young children. At the other it appears to be a spontaneous and wild destruction by individuals who are 'mad at the world' or by groups of marauding youths who are in open conflict with the community." [68]

A special study of vandalism in all the junior and senior high schools of Syracuse found important differences between those schools with a high rating of damage and those with a low rating:

> Low socio-economic status and high instability or transiency in the community in which the school was located, and change and instability in the school situation were found related to the . . . amount of school damage. A low level of personal identification with the school and its goals among students, teachers, and parents was found positively associated with a high rate of vandalic behavior among students. High-damage schools, also, were found characterized by inadequate administration and leadership, with poor communication among the various members of the school. In such schools, furthermore, relatively poor interpersonal relations were found between principal and teacher, teacher and teacher, student and teacher, parent and teacher, and custodian and student. The feeling that the school administration was not sufficiently concerned with the welfare of staff and students was found associated with a low level of school morale.[69]

Automobile Theft by Juveniles

In many parts of the world there has been an increase in auto thefts and in the proportion of those committed by juveniles. Such a situation has been observed in Great Britain, France, West Germany, and Sweden. The larceny of motor vehicles has been steadily increasing in metropolitan London, where 20,557 motor vehicles were stolen or driven away during 1958. Two thirds (62.6 percent) of those arrested for the larceny of motor vehicles were under twenty-one, and one in five (21.7 percent) was under seventeen.[70] The percentage of offenders arrested in West Germany for car theft who were under twenty-one increased from 46.2 in 1954 to 61.8

---

[68] *Ibid.*, p. 90.

[69] Nathan Goldman, "A Socio-Psychological Study of School Vandalism," Final report on Office of Education Contract No. SAE 181 (8453) (Mimeographed; Syracuse: University Research Institute, 1959), p. 109.

[70] In *New Forms of Juvenile Delinquency: Their Origin, Prevention and Treatment*, p. 6.

in 1958. Juveniles arrested in Sweden for the unauthorized borrowing and theft of motor vehicles (including autos, motorcycles, and power bicycles) increased from 7065 per month to 32,902, or 463.4 percent, from 1950 to 1957. About the Swedish situation Torsten Eriksson has written: "In comparison with what we know about other countries, the most striking development in Sweden is the emphasis on crimes involving automotive vehicles. Car thefts (unlawfully stolen and borrowed cars) are the main cause for concern in the case of youthful offenders. They have increased enormously and, compared with the pre–World War II era, they represent a new form of criminality." [71]

In 1960 nearly two thirds of all persons arrested for automobile theft in 2460 cities in the United States were under eighteen. Even the number of arrests for automobile theft by those under sixteen is large. In New York City in 1959 there were 1011 such arrests, or 17.3 percent of all arrests of persons under sixteen.

Two samples of eighty-one New York boys between twelve and seventeen who stole cars and a similar number who did not, have shown some statistically significant differences.[72] Boys who stole cars were more often white rather than Negro or Puerto Rican, their homes were in better economic circumstances, and fewer came from broken homes. Their delinquency generally started at an earlier age, and they were more intelligent.

Almost all the boys in the New York study stole cars more frequently from areas with a homogeneous population, lived in single-family dwellings, and had only one parent employed. Similar findings were reported in a Detroit study.[73] Such boys are well socialized as far as primary group relations are concerned, commit their offenses with companions, and are not isolated, peculiar individuals. The Detroit study reported that such boys, however, easily accept the values of companions but respond weakly to the prohibitions of the larger society. "Thus, if a boy's friends got pleasure from riding in automobiles, he would oblige in carefree fashion by borrowing a car." [74]

Summary

The term "criminal" has little real meaning, for actually there are many types of criminals. Classifications of criminals based on the type of crime, age, or sex of the offender are useful for legal or statistical purposes. From a scientific approach, behavior systems represent a more satisfactory classification, for offenders may be grouped along a continuum of noncareer and career types, with the criminally insane at one end and the professional

---

[71] *Ibid.*, p. 26.
[72] Erwin Schepses, "Boys Who Steal Cars," *Federal Probation*, 25:56–62 (March, 1961).
[73] Wattenberg and Balistrieri, "Automobile Theft . . . ," *loc. cit.*
[74] *Ibid.*, p. 578.

criminal at the other. Career types of offenders largely represent deviant attitudes which are the result of group association. Noncareer offenders generally commit personal offenses; career types, property offenses.

A behavior system considers social roles, identification with crime, conception of self, pattern of differential association with others, progression in crime, and the degree to which criminal behavior has become a part of the life organization. Persons have associations which are criminal and noncriminal, and the effect of these seems to depend in part on the frequency, duration, priority, and intensity of these associations. It has not been possible to demonstrate that certain personality traits are related to all delinquent and criminal behavior. The concept of "psychopath" or "sexual psychopath" does not appear to be a useful one in the study of criminal careers.

Delinquency should be analyzed by types rather than considered as an entity. Two types of delinquencies are vandalism and auto theft.

Selected Readings

CLINARD, MARSHALL B. and ANDREW L. WADE, "Toward the Delineation of Vandalism as a Sub-Type in Juvenile Delinquency," *Journal of Criminal Law, Criminology, and Police Science,* 48:493–499 (January–February, 1948). A discussion of the need for typological studies of delinquency as a detailed illustration of a type.

GIBBONS, DON C. and DONALD L. GARRITY, "Some Suggestions for the Development of Etiological and Treatment Theory in Criminology," *Social Forces,* 38:51–58 (October, 1959). Types of criminal behavior and the need for relating treatment programs to types rather than general programs for treating criminal offenders.

LINDESMITH, ALFRED R., and H. WARREN DUNHAM. "Some Principles of Criminal Typology," *Social Forces,* 19:307–314 (March, 1941). In this article a distinction is made between individual and social types of offenders. Psychiatrists who study primarily the individual type of offender tend to generalize about all offenders, and sociologists who study primarily social types do the same.

MARTIN, JOHN M. *Juvenile Vandalism.* Springfield, Ill.: Charles C Thomas, Publisher, 1961. One of the few studies of vandalism. Discusses the extent of vandalism. Several case histories are included.

RECKLESS, WALTER C. *The Crime Problem.* 3d ed. New York: Appleton-Century-Crofts, Inc., 1961. The concept of a criminal career is discussed, and in particular, ordinary types of criminal careers.

SUTHERLAND, EDWARD H., and DONALD R. CRESSEY. *Principles of Criminology.* 6th ed. Philadelphia: J. B. Lippincott Company, 1960, Chap. 13. A discussion of behavior systems in crime from a somewhat different viewpoint.

Chapter

9

Types of Offenders: Murderers
and Sex Offenders

In the following discussion two types of offenders will be analyzed—murderers and sex offenders. Very few persons have ever made a career out of murder or become what might be called career sex offenders. Although this is less true of prostitution, many prostitutes are so engaged only temporarily and do not make a career out of such sex activities. All murder and sex offenses, however, must be viewed in the perspective of social behavior and social norms. In the case of murder we shall refer to it as arising within the general framework of a "subculture of violence." Most homosexuality and prostitution will be seen in a group and subcultural context.

Murderers

The type of criminal homicide which we shall discuss here as murder consists of both murder and nonnegligent manslaughter, but does not include justifiable homicide or attempts or assaults to kill, or accidental deaths. Another type of criminal homicide also not included is negligent manslaughter, in which a death is attributable to the negligence of some other person than the victim. Technically "murder" is determined by the police and the court through a legal process.

Criminal homicide, or what is generally referred to as murder or nonnegligent manslaughter, is one of the most socially visible crimes; yet it comprises a small proportion of the total crime. The general trend in urban murder rates in the United States has been downward. The rate in 1933 per 100,000 population was 7.1. This rate continued to move downward, with slight upward changes in 1945 and 1946, until 1954, when it was 4.8.[1] The 1960 rate was 5.1. A Philadelphia study has indicated that the decline in criminal homicide may be misleading.[2] Since rates for aggravated

---

[1] *Uniform Crime Reports,* Annual Bulletins of the Federal Bureau of Investigation, Washington, D.C.

[2] Marvin E. Wolfgang, *Patterns in Criminal Homicide* (Philadelphia: University of Pennsylvania Press, 1958), pp. 332–333.

assault and assault with intent to kill have increased, the decline in criminal homicide appears to be the result of better communication with the police to prevent homicides, more rapid transportation to a hospital, and advances in medical technology.

Popular interest has always centered on murder. In spite of this widespread public interest, however, scientific knowledge about murder and murderers is limited. It is known that murderers only occasionally have criminal careers, and that they are seldom repeaters. Most studies show that they are one of the best risks for successes on parole. It is commonly said that wardens frequently use murderers as chauffeurs and as household servants on the assumption that they are the least criminal. Warden Lawes of Sing Sing used to remark that the barber who shaved him for years had been convicted of a particularly brutal murder. Further evidence of this fact is that about half (46.7 percent) of ninety-six Wisconsin prisoners serving time for murder had never been arrested before, whereas only one in three of the sex offenders and only one in eleven of the property offenders could make this claim.[3]

TYPES OF MURDER

Murders can be classified on the basis of the situation in which they occurred. There are murders which result from a long period of hostility, those which occur in sudden anger, and, finally, those committed in connection with another crime.[4]

Prolonged Personal Disputes. The first type generally takes place after a long period of interpersonal difficulties for which murder represented a possible solution. Most murders of this cumulative type arise out of these long-standing personal frictions. They may involve disputes between neighbors and work associates, between husbands and wives or other close relatives, or between former lovers. In the case of the following murder, the difficulties extended over a long period of years and involved increasing hostility.

> The inner conflict engendered by his childhood and adolescent upbringing was not mitigated by his marriage. He and his wife had had sexual relations before their marriage, and F claims that this was part of a plot to force him to marry her. However that may be, their first child was born two months after their marriage. Shortly thereafter a friend of his wife's teasingly asked F how he could be sure that the child was his own, unnerving him so much that he fled to another room and wept. His wife induced her friend to tell him that she was merely joking, but the suspicion thus implanted continued to linger and impair the conjugal relationship.

[3] John L. Gillin, *The Wisconsin Prisoner* (Madison: The University of Wisconsin Press, 1946).

[4] Ralph S. Banay, "Study in Murder," *The Annals*, 284:26–35 (November, 1952).

After three years of married life F was in a very disturbed emotional state. He was afflicted with dizziness, which sometimes caused him to topple over, and with impairment of memory. Obviously he was suffering from a typical neurosis, an escape from thoughts about the unpleasant situation at home. His wife was totally lacking in sympathy; she mocked, tantalized, and ridiculed him for innocence and lack of virility. She neglected her home to visit at her mother's or sister's, where she sought the companionship of a male boarder. When F learned of this situation, he warned her to stay away, and she promised to do so. One day shortly thereafter, however, finding his wife absent when he returned home early, he found her again in her mother's house, joking and fooling with the man she had promised to avoid. She introduced F to him as "nothing but a fool of mine." She tortured her husband by telling him that she was trying to drive him insane, by comparing his sexual potency with that of other men she had known, and by reminding him that there was nothing to prevent her from entertaining other men without his knowledge. The check he gave her each week she turned over to her sister and sister-in-law, stoutly denying that she did so. He not only decided that his wife was an inveterate liar but became convinced, after learning that her mother had once been hospitalized for insanity, that she was also insane. He says she made grimaces at him and called him names, neglected the child and the house, and was disgustingly dirty in her personal habits. He was told by a number of persons that she was unfaithful to him.

All these disturbing factors—his wife's general attitude toward him, her nagging and mocking, her criticism of his sexual weakness, the evidence that she cared nothing for him, the current gossip about her, and his long-standing feeling of inferiority, which her superior air intensified—led to terrific emotional upheavals, heavy drinking, neglect of his work, and frequent changes of occupation. Eventually the situation reached such a pass that he no longer could face it, and he shot and killed his wife.[5]

Hostility in these cases has often accumulated over a long period of time. In one case Banay has traced this long developmental process in the life history of a murderer, a war veteran in this case. The history included frustrations in preschool and school life, the first marriage, army life, a second marriage, and, finally the climax, a mass murder which occurred after the second wife left him with the children.

Suddenly on this day, as he paced the floor or sat brooding on his bed, an upsurge of hostility and frustration told him to take matters into his own hands. If he could not see his children he would at least frighten his in-laws. He put three revolvers in his pockets, threw an army carbine into his car, and drove to the house where his family lived. There was a short conversation with his father-in-law. "No," he could not see the children. "Throw him out," urged the mother-in-law. Then his wife appeared and he pleaded "Do you love me?" "You are crazy," she answered. That was the fatal moment. He pulled his guns and shot several people in the house; chased his mother-in-law

_____

[5] From John L. Gillin, *The Wisconsin Prisoner* (Madison: The University of Wisconsin Press, 1946), pp. 40–42.

to another house, shooting at anyone who came between them, and shot her. Then he drove to other relatives of his wife and shot them.[6]

Crisis Situation. In the second type of murder there has not been any building up of hostility; rather, it results from a crisis which demands an immediate solution, but for which the only immediate solution is seen as some form of violent action. Berg and Fox concluded that a violent argument plays an important role in the perpetration of certain types of homicide.[7] In such arguments verbalization tends to decline and emotionality to increase until, finally, a sudden assault with fist or weapons results in the death of the victim. Banay cites the case of a fifty-three-year-old president of a large industrial firm who shot his long-time friend and partner during an argument over the way in which the partner had represented the company at a hearing on a compensation award for an employee.

> Shortly after the death of his wife, on whom he had been very dependent, the commitment of his son to a state hospital further shook his confidence and outlook. His sexual life had been at a standstill for a number of years, and he began to feel a physical decline. His generous and open-hearted attitude began to change to a more scrupulous one, and he became overconcerned with finances. His shrinking income symbolized the waning of his power, influence, and potency. He began to transfer his dependence from his wife to his friend and partner. The feeling of impoverishment and infidelity, which so often is part of the involutional state, began to be projected on his partner. Therefore a relatively small incident acted as a fuse for the underground explosion.[8]

In Connection with a Crime. Some murders are committed in connection with a robbery or burglary, or in some sex offense, such as rape. In these cases the murder is usually an indirect result of resistance on the part of the victim or in order to forestall detection of the crime. Actually such murders are a minor part of the total crime picture. Gang murders of various types, although rare, represent efforts to remove certain opposition or hostile witnesses.

MURDER AS A BEHAVIOR SYSTEM

In the etiology of murder, the general cultural pattern seems to determine its frequency. The acceptance of murder as a method of solving interpersonal conflicts varies a great deal from country to country, region to region, and state to state. Finland, for example, has one of the highest

---

[6] Banay, "Study in Murder," *loc. cit.,* pp. 31–32.
[7] Irvin A. Berg and Vernon Fox, "Factors in Homicides Committed by 200 Males," *Journal of Social Psychology,* 26:109–119 (August, 1947).
[8] Banay, "Study in Murder," *loc. cit.,* p. 33.

homicide rates in the world, whereas the rate is quite low in Great Britain and Canada.[9] Ceylon also has a high rate in Asia.[10] A study of personal offenses in Puerto Rico indicated that the high rates of these crimes in such Latin cultures are related to personal insult or honor. In situations of personal vilification or marital triangles the culture may require the individual to attack the offender.[11] Two thirds of the offenders were found to have had some personal association with persons who had also resorted to violence under somewhat similar circumstances.

Most African homicides among tribal peoples today occur within an institutional setting which defines the social relationship between killer and victim.[12] These relationships tend to be different from Western societies, such as a woman killing her children rather than her husband in a domestic quarrel. Likewise altercations over money are rare, but fear of witches or land disputes may be more common reasons for the homicide.

Brearley's study of *Homicide in the United States* revealed that cultural definitions play an important role in murder.[13] In fact, the regional differences in the United States are so wide that "a general murder rate for the United States as a whole has no very close relation to the actual rate of any specific area or section." [14] The homicide rates of the South are considerably higher than those in other regions, and Brearley suggests that this difference is due to the fact that cultural definitions call for personal violence in certain situations and that weapons are carried more frequently in some areas than in others. The 1959 rate for murder and nonnegligent manslaughter for the New England area was 1.3; for the East North Central states 3.6; on the other hand, the South Atlantic area rate was 9.2, and the East South Central area, 9.0, or about twice the national average. In 1959, Vermont had a murder and nonnegligent manslaughter rate of 0.3 and Minnesota 1.0, in contrast with Georgia's rate of 13.4 and Alabama's 12.9.

Murder rates vary a great deal according to ethnic, racial, and class lines: "Murder would seem culturally to be somewhat more acceptable as a

[9] Veli Verkko, *Homicides and Suicides in Finland and Their Dependence on National Character* (Copenhagen: G. E. C. Gads Forlag, 1951).

[10] See Jacqueline and Murray Straus, "Suicide, Homicide, and Social Structure in Ceylon," *American Journal of Sociology*, 58:461–469 (March, 1953), and Arthur Wood, "Murder, Suicide, and Economic Crime in Ceylon," *American Sociological Review*, 26:744–753 (October, 1961).

[11] Jaime Toro-Calder, "Personal Crimes in Puerto Rico." Unpublished master's thesis, University of Wisconsin, Madison, 1950.

[12] Paul Bohannan, *African Homicide and Suicide* (Princeton, N.J.: Princeton University Press, 1960).

[13] H. C. Brearley, *Homicide in the United States* (Chapel Hill: University of North Carolina Press, 1932).

[14] George B. Vold, "Extent and Trend of Capital Crimes in the United States," *The Annals*, 284:3 (November, 1952).

way of expressing resentment directly among certain social classes than others." [15] Although the high rate of the southern regions reflects in part the high proportion of Negro population among which homicide is quite prevalent, the 1951 rates for southern whites is from three to seven times as great as for New England whites. Taking the years 1920 and 1925 together, Brearley found that the homicide rate for Negroes in Florida was 62.9 as compared with 12.8 for Massachusetts Negroes.[16]

Some indication of subcultural components in criminal homicide is the fact that of 489 cases in Houston, Texas, over 87 percent occurred in four areas, not far apart, located near the center of the city.[17] For the most part, outlying areas within the city had no homicides at all. Nearly all the homicides occurred in areas populated chiefly by Negroes and Spanish-Americans. In more than 70 percent of the cases victim and murderer lived less than two miles apart, and in 32.8 percent lived in the same house or the same block. The conflicts which gave rise to the disputes were chiefly between members of the same social group and in 87 percent of the cases the murderer and his victim had known each other before. The conflict patterns grew out of arguments, love triangles, and marital discord. The arguments arose from gambling disputes or in private parties in which there were drinking and boisterous conduct, all made more violent by the social concepts and the relaxed social control of the areas.

In a tabulation of the murders of 324 females, Sutherland found that nearly 60 percent were committed by relatives or other close associates. He reported that 102 of the murders were committed by husbands, 37 by fathers or other relatives closely associated with the victim, and 49 by lovers or suitors.[18]

A study of Wisconsin prisoners charged with murder disclosed in many cases a previous history of difficulties with the victim. Some were farmers who committed murder after a dispute with a neighbor over a cow or some similar matter. Two thirds of the Wisconsin murders grew out of a long-standing or an immediate quarrel, the remainder being connected with some crime. Many murders involved situations in which the marital situation was primarily important.[19]

Wolfgang's study of 588 victims and 621 slayers in Philadelphia, between 1948 and 1952, has given us many insights into what he terms the "subculture of violence." [20] Murder was found to be highest among Ne-

---

[15] Austin L. Porterfield and Robert H. Talbert, *Crime, Suicide and Social Well Being* (Fort Worth, Tex.: Leo Potishman Foundation, 1948), pp. 102–103.

[16] Brearley, *op. cit.*

[17] Henry Allen Bullock, "Urban Homicide in Theory and Fact," *Journal of Criminal Law, Criminology, and Police Science*, 45:565–575 (January–February, 1955).

[18] Edwin H. Sutherland, "The Sexual Psychopath Laws," *Journal of Criminal Law and Criminology*, 40:543–554 (January–February, 1950).

[19] Gillin, *op. cit.*, p. 60.

[20] Wolfgang, *op. cit.* Also see, for a summary, "A Sociological Analysis of Criminal Homicide," *Federal Probation*, 25:48–55 (March, 1961).

groes, males, those in the age group 20–24 and 30–34, from the lower social classes, and related to certain occupations. The rate among Negroes was four times that of whites, indicating the role of subculture and the isolating effects of segregation from the general norms of society. In fact, the rate was greatest among recent Negro migrants. The role of subcultural factors is that

> the significance of a jostle, a slightly derogatory remark, or the appearance of a weapon in the hands of an adversary are stimuli differentially perceived and interpreted by Negroes and whites, males and females. Social expectations of response in particular types of social interaction result in differential "definitions of the situation." A male is usually expected to defend the name and honor of his mother, the virtue of womanhood (even though his female companion for the evening may be an entirely new acquaintance and/or a prostitute), and to accept no derogation about his race (even from a member of his own race), his age, or his masculinity. Quick resort to physical combat as a measure of daring, courage, or defense of status appears to be a cultural expectation, especially for lower socio-economic class males of both races. When such a culture norm response is elicited from an individual engaged in social interplay with others who harbor the same response mechanism, physical assaults, altercations, and violent domestic quarrels that result in homicide are likely to be relatively common. The upper-middle and upper social class value system defines and codifies behavioral norms into legal rules that often transcend sub-cultural mores, and considers many of the social and personal stimuli that evoke a combative reaction in the lower classes as "trivial." Thus, there exists a cultural antipathy between many folk rationalizations of the lower class, and of males of both races, on the one hand, and the middle-class legal norms under which they live, on the other. The fate of 206 victims and the 227 offenders responsible for their death, whose motive has been classified as "altercation," can be partially interpreted in terms of the foregoing remarks.[21]

Nine out of ten murderers were in lower-class occupations, laborers, for example, committing more homicides than did clerks. Nearly one half of the offenders who had a previous arrest record of some type had been arrested for some form of assault more characteristic of lower-class behavior, such as wife beating and fighting.[22] Some indication of the relation of homicide to the pattern of life in certain areas of the city is suggested by the fact that 65 percent of all homicides occur during week ends, particularly on Saturday night.

---

[21] Marvin E. Wolfgang, *Patterns in Criminal Homicide* (Philadelphia: University of Pennsylvania Press, 1958), pp. 188–189. Reprinted by permission of the publishers.
[22] Wolfgang, *op. cit.*, p. 178. His study of urban offenders, largely Negro, indicated a large previous arrest record: 68 percent of the males and 48 percent of the females. Of them, 66 percent had been arrested for offenses against the person (48 percent for aggravated assault which is also included in this figure) and 34 percent for property and other offenses.

THE MURDERER AND HIS VICTIM

In a tabulation of the murders of 324 females, Sutherland found that nearly 60 percent were committed by relatives or other close associates.

A study of 713 New Jersey murderers classified according to victims and the situations in which the murders took place found that less than one fourth committed murder in connection with another crime. The largest group, about two thirds, of the murders grew out of some altercation with male acquaintances, relatives, mistresses, or sex rivals (see Table 9.1). Ap-

Table 9.1. Motivation of Murderers [a]

	Numbers	Totals	Percent
Premeditated murder	79	79	11.1
Of relatives		37	5.2
Wives	24		
In-laws	4		
Immediate blood-relatives	4		
Distant blood-relatives	5		
Of non-relatives		42	5.9
Mistresses	15		
Sex rivals	4		
Male acquaintances	23		
In connection with other crimes		134	18.8
During robbery, burglary, etc.	129		
During rape	2		
During kidnaping	3		
Resisting arrest		22	3.1
Resisting police officer	20		
Resisting jail keeper	2		
Result of altercation		478	67.0
With relatives		110	15.4
Wives	78		
In-laws	19		
Immediate blood-relatives	8		
Distant blood-relatives	5		
With non-relatives		368	51.6
Mistresses	45		
Sex-rivals	25		
Male acquaintances	298		

a New Jersey State Prison; total murders, 713.
SOURCE: E. Frankel, "One Thousand Murderers," *Journal of Criminal Law and Criminology,* 29:687–688 (1938–1939). Reprinted by special permission of the *Journal of Criminal Law and Criminology* (Northwestern University School of Law), Vol. 29, No. 5 (1939).

proximately one third (35 percent) of 588 male and female criminal homicides in Philadelphia were the result of general altercations, family and domestic quarrels accounted for 14 percent, jealousy 12 percent, altercation over money 11 percent, and, contrary to popular impression, robbery only 7 percent.[23] Close friends and relatives accounted for over half (59 percent) of all the homicides and four fifths of the women. In 28 percent of the cases the victim was a close friend of the murderer, in 25 percent a family relative, in 14 percent an acquaintance. In only one out of eight murders was the victim a stranger. Women, as contrasted with men, generally kill someone in their own family or one in two of those murders committed by women in Philadelphia as compared with one in six committed by men. In all, one in five homicides represented husband or wife killings. Since the number of wives killed by their husbands constituted 41 percent of all women killed, and husbands only 11 percent of the men killed, it can be concluded that "when a woman committed homicide she was more likely to kill her mate; and when a man was killed by a woman he was most likely to be killed by his wife." [24]

Personal contacts have been found to play a significant role in murders in Denmark and India.[25] In a Danish study it was found that the murderer's victim was a relative or an acquaintance in nine out of ten cases. Strangers were seldom the victims. Most murders in India occur within the same caste and also frequently involve husband and wife.

Where there are racial aspects in homicide, as shown in a study of 500 Alabama homicides, the circumstances of the murder differ according to whether a Negro male killed a Negro male, a Negro male killed a Negro female, a Negro female killed a Negro male, a Negro female killed another Negro female, a white man killed another white man, and a white man killed a white female.[26] In the Philadelphia study reported above, 94 percent of all homicides were within the same race.

In one study over one in four criminal homicides were precipitated by the victim in that the victim was the first to show or use a deadly weapon, or to strike a blow in an altercation.[27] Victim-precipitated homicides were found to be significantly associated with Negroes, victim offender relationships involving male victims of female offenders, mate slayings, alcohol in the homicide situation, or in the victim, and victims with a previous record of assault or arrest. Other homicides, not included in this figure, involved the infidelity of a mate or a lover, failure of the victim to pay a debt, use

[23] Wolfgang, op. cit., p. 191.   [24] Ibid., p. 325.

[25] Kaare Svalastoga, "Homicide and Social Contact in Denmark," American Journal of Sociology, 62:37–41 (July, 1956), and Edwin D. Driver, "Interaction and Criminal Homicide in India," Social Forces, 40:153–158 (December, 1961).

[26] Howard Harlan, "Five Hundred Homicides," Journal of Criminal Law and Criminology, 40:736–752 (March–April, 1950).

[27] Wolfgang, op. cit., p. 252. Also see Hans von Hentig, The Criminal and His Victim (New Haven, Conn.: Yale University Press, 1948).

of vile names by the victim in such a way that the victim had a great deal to do with the homicide. Even in robbery the behavior of the victim may incite the robber to kill.

Sex Offenders

Many people today believe that all sex offenders are "beasts" and should be put away for life either in a prison or in a mental hospital. Such a belief is based on many misconceptions about sex offenders, the principal one being a rather general confusion in definition of the term "sex offender." Some people have the erroneous idea that all sex offenders are sexual degenerates who have, or try to have, sex relations with young children or who engage in sexual delinquencies accompanied by acts of violence.

Actually, sex crimes involve many different acts, most of which are unaccompanied by violence. Sex offenses which are considered deviations and punishable by law consist, mainly, of rape, homosexual behavior (sodomy), adultery, fornication, indecent exposure, incest (intercourse with a relative, as prohibited by law), and prostitution. The following is a classification of sex offenses by the nature of the deviant behavior.[28]

Sexual assault
  Mild sexual assault
  Serious sexual assault
Forcible rape
Statutory rape
Incestuous relations
Noncoital sex relations with a minor
Exhibitory acts
Disseminating "obscene" material
Homosexual relations
  Homosexual relations with adults
  Homosexual relations with minors
Bestiality

Forcible rape should be distinguished from statutory rape—sexual intercourse, with or without force, with a female below the age of consent, which is usually set at sixteen or eighteen years of age. Although we do not know what percentage of all rapes are statutory, it appears likely that they are in the majority. Only about one in six convictions for rapes in New York City during 1930–1939 involved force, and these cases represented only 12 percent of all serious sex offenses.[29] In a group of Wisconsin sex offenders in the state prison, only 14 had been convicted of forcible rape,

[28] Albert Ellis and Ralph Brancale, *The Psychology of Sex Offenders* (Springfield, Ill.: Charles C Thomas, Publisher, 1956), p. 31.
[29] Sutherland, "The Sexual Psychopath Laws," *loc. cit.*, p. 545.

as compared with 89 who had been convicted of statutory rape.[30] Many statutory, as well as some forcible rapes, are legally so called, but they may have been committed with passive consent, or they may have involved blackmail or prostitution on the part of the woman.

What is sexually normal or deviant behavior can be looked at from a number of ways, all involving cultural norms. One is a statistical definition of normality which might, for example, follow the most prevalent sex practices disclosed by the Kinsey report. Still another would be whether the sex practices lead to procreation, thus excluding acts of homosexuality and exhibitionism. Finally, the most likely definition would be acts which are prescribed by law. While there are variations in different cultures, most sex laws in American society govern four relationships: the degree of consent, such as forcible rape; the nature of the object, restricting legitimate sex objects to human beings of the opposite sex, of a certain age, of a defined distance in kinship, and to the spouse; the nature of the sexual act to certain behavior in heterosexual intercourse; and, finally, the setting in which the sex act occurs.[31]

Some persons who have studied the operation of sex laws have maintained that the regulations of law are too wide and that those sex acts which should be punishable are those which involve (1) the use of force or duress, (2) adults who take advantage of a minor, and (3) public sex acts which are distasteful to the majority of those in whose presence they are committed.[32] They maintain that it is questionable whether sex acts, other than those in which adults engage publicly, should be punished. Such a view would affect the legality of many present-day sex acts, including much of unmarried adult heterosexual relations and adult homosexuality, as is the case in many European countries such as Sweden and Denmark.[33] It has also been suggested that the age of statutory rape, or age of consent, be lowered from eighteen to fifteen, as is generally the case in Europe. Originally, in common law, the age of consent was under ten, but this age has been moved upward to what one leading legal writer claims is entirely unrealistic because of the voluntary nature of much of such sex relations in middle and late adolescence and the knowledge of sex relationships on the part of the girl. In the United States "each such sexual contact may

---

[30] Gillin, op. cit., p. 120.

[31] Stanton Wheeler, "Sex Offenses: A Sociological Critique," in Law and Contemporary Problems, 25:258–259 (Spring, 1960). Also see Morris Ploscowe, "Sex Offenses: The American Legal Context," in the same issue, which is a symposium on sex offenses, pp. 217–225, and Morris Ploscowe, Sex and the Law (Englewood Cliffs, N.J.: Prentice-Hall, Inc., 1951).

[32] Ellis and Brancale, op. cit., pp. 88–89.

[33] Even in Britain the well-known Wolfenden Parliamentary Committee on Homosexual Offenses and Prostitution of 1957 recommended the legalizing of homosexual acts between consenting adults in private. For a discussion see J. E. Hall Williams, "Sex Offenses: The British Experience," Law and Contemporary Problems, 25:334–360 (Spring, 1960).

technically be rape under some law and may subject the male to ferocious penalties." [34]

MISCONCEPTIONS ABOUT SEX OFFENDERS

In many ways the term "sex offender" is misleading. Sex is but one, and often a minor, aspect of a person's total life; it is not independent, but rather is often an expression of other aspects of personality, so that to speak of a person as a "rapist" or a "homosexual," or to use the general term "sex offender," tends to make an aspect of a person's life cover his entire personality. The same comment might also be made of many other types of criminal offenders, including particularly the murderer and the occasional property offender. One writer has objected to the title of sex offender being applied to juveniles.

> One technically violates the sexual conduct norm through behavior and thereby commits a *delinquent* offense. The term sex offender should perhaps signify no more nor less than this. Certainly, it should not imply that this is the only major kind of delinquent activity the person has committed. To classify a person as a sex offender may only serve to develop self and public definitions of the person as a sex offender.[35]

Many other misconceptions exist about sex offenders. Contrary to popular belief, a study of the first 300 sex offenders committed to a state diagnostic center revealed that the majority of sex offenders were rather harmless "minor" deviates rather than dangerous "sex fiends." [36] Of the sex offenders, 58 percent had committed relatively minor sex offenses. Only 10 in the entire group of 300 were considered to be dangerous in the sense that they had used force or duress. Moreover, aside from those convicted of statutory rape and incestuous relations, most sex offenders tend to be "sexually inhibited" rather than oversexed persons.

Another report on sex offenders has summarized a number of facts about them.

1. There are not tens of thousands of homicidal sex fiends abroad in the land.
2. Sex offenders are usually not recidivists (repeaters), at least in police and other official records.
3. Sex offenders do not progress to more serious types of sex crimes.
4. It is impossible at the present time to predict the danger of serious crimes being committed by sex deviates.

---

[34] Ploscowe, "Sex Offenses: The American Legal Context," *loc. cit.*, p. 222. The age of consent is generally sixteen in England and Norway, fifteen in Sweden, Denmark, and France, and fourteen in Belgium and Germany.

[35] Albert J. Reiss, Jr., "Sex Offenses: The Marginal Status of the Adolescent," *Law and Contemporary Problems*, 25:311 (Spring, 1960).

[36] Ellis and Brancale, *op. cit.*, p. 32.

5. "Sex psychopathy" is not a clinical entity.

6. Sex offenders are not oversexed.[37]

After the elimination of statutory rape, incest, and the majority of homosexual cases, which as a general rule do not constitute a serious menace to females, there remains a relatively small number of violent sex cases in most countries. Sutherland estimated that in the United States there are annually about 5.7 sex killings of women and 4 of children.[38] He suggested that if these figures seem to be too low they could be multiplied fivefold or twentyfold and still not be large. He made a tabulation of all murders of women and of children as reported in *The New York Times* during the years 1930, 1935, and 1940, on the assumption that it would carry nearly all offenses of this type reported in the United States. He found that of the 324 murders of women reported, only 17 involved rape or suspicion of rape. Since the latter type of case would be more completely reported nationally, the ratio of such cases may be actually smaller. During these three years only 39 murders of children were reported and only 12 were indicated to be rape-murders.

There is considerable doubt about sex offenders being psychopathic, not only because this term is vague but because the percentage of them diagnosed as such varies tremendously. The Psychiatric Clinic of the Court of General Sessions in New York City diagnosed 15.8 percent of its sex offenders as psychopathic, but the psychiatrists in Bellevue Hospital in the same city diagnosed 52.9 percent as psychopathic.[39] A more recent study has shown that the term "sexual psychopath" is applicable to only a small minority (about 3 percent) of convicted sex offenders.[40] Sutherland has concluded that "the concept 'sexual psychopath' is too vague for judicial or administrative use either as to commitment to institutions or as to release as 'completely or permanently cured.' " [41] He states, moreover, that there is no indication that such laws are extensively used or that their enactment in such states as California, Illinois, Michigan, and Minnesota has resulted in any different trend in rape rates of adjoining states which do not have the law. Morris Ploscowe, a well-known legal authority has written:

---

[37] Derived from *The Habitual Sex Offender,* Report and Recommendations of the Commission on the Habitual Sex Offender as formulated by Paul W. Tappan, Technical Consultant (Trenton: State of New Jersey, 1950), pp. 13–16.

[38] Sutherland, "The Sexual Psychopath Laws," *loc. cit.,* pp. 545–546.

[39] Jack Frosch and Walter Bromberg, "The Sex Offender—A Psychiatric Study," *American Journal of Orthopsychiatry,* 9:761–776 (October, 1939); and Benjamin Apfelberg, Carl Sugar, and Arnold Z. Pfeffer, "A Psychiatric Study of 250 Sex Offenders," *American Journal of Psychiatry,* 100:762–770 (May, 1944).

[40] Ellis and Brancale, *op. cit.,* p. 37.

[41] Sutherland, "The Sexual Psychopath Laws," *loc. cit.,* p. 551.

Any revision of sex offender laws must also repeal much of the sexual psychopath legislation that is presently in force. These laws were passed to provide a means for dealing with dangerous, repetitive, mentally abnormal sex offenders. Unfortunately, the vagueness of the definition of sexual psychopaths contained in these statutes has obscured this basic underlying purpose. There are large numbers of sex offenders who engage in compulsive, repetitive sexual acts, which may be crimes, who may be mentally abnormal, but who are not dangerous. The transvestite, the exhibitionist, the frotteur, the homosexual who masturbates another either in the privacy of his bedroom or in a public toilet, the "peeping tom"—are typical of large numbers of sex offenders who are threatened with long-term incarceration by present sexual psychopath legislation. And what is even worse is that such legislation has not usually been implemented by facilities for treatment. The result is that many nuisance-type, nondangerous sex offenders have been imprisoned for long periods of time, without treatment, in those jurisdictions where such laws have been enforced. This is not to say that the compulsive nondangerous types of sex offenders should be immune from prosecution and punishment; but short sentences or probation are more than adequate to deal with these derelictions, unless better treatment facilities are provided.[42]

Evidence indicates that sex offenders, contrary to common beliefs, have a low rate of recidivism in comparison with other types of offenders. Out of a total of twenty-five kinds of crime reported in the FBI's *Uniform Crime Reports* for 1937, rapists ranked nineteenth as repeaters and the category "Other sex offenses" was seventeenth. Only 1 in 20 of 1447 males arrested in 1937 for rape had previously been convicted of rape. A special study of New York City juvenile delinquents revealed that only 3 boys in 108 brought in for sex delinquencies had subsequent appearances, none of which were sex offenses.[43] Between two thirds and three fourths of the sex offenders referred to the New Jersey Diagnostic Center were first offenders.[44] Of 1985 convicted English sex offenders over four out of five (83 percent) had no previous conviction for a sex offense.[45]

A California study covering sex offenders committed to correctional institutions during the five years 1945–1949 reported that one half of all sex offenders had a prior commitment record and one fifth a previous record. Recidivism was greater among the homosexuals than among any other group. On the other hand, sex offenders who had been committed to prison were found to be fairly good risks on parole. Only 31.8 percent of 568 California sex offenders committed another offense while on parole, as

[42] Reprinted from a symposium, *Sex Offenses*, by permission from *Law and Contemporary Problems*. Vol. 25, No. 2, Spring 1960. Published by the Duke University School of Law, Durham, North Carolina. Copyright, 1960, by Duke University.

[43] Lewis I. Doshay, *The Boy Sex Offender and His Later Career* (New York: Grune & Stratton, Inc., 1943).

[44] *The Habitual Sex Offender*, p. 24.

[45] Leon Radzinowicz ed., *Sexual Offenses: A Report of the Cambridge Department of Criminal Science* (London: Macmillan & Co., Ltd., 1957), p. 137.

compared with 50.3 percent of all offenders.[46] Of these violators, less than 10 percent committed a serious offense.

Of 206 patients committed under the New Jersey sex offender law between June, 1949, and April, 1953, 57 were released on parole or discharged by this latter date, but no offender had violated his parole even though half had been out more than six months.[47] In Illinois, sex offenders have the lowest parole violation rate of any group of offenders, being about one third that of those committed for property offenses.[48] In England, of a group of 1985 convicted sex offenders who had been released for four years, 85 percent had no subsequent convictions.[49]

SUBCULTURAL FACTORS AND SEX OFFENDERS

The most feasible distinction which can be made of sex offenders is between aggressive and passive offenders. The aggressive are those who attempt rapes and sexual assaults on persons of the opposite sex beyond the age of puberty. Passive offenses include exhibitionism and noncoital sex play with children. Offenders of the aggressive type, in comparison with the passive type, appear to exhibit less clear-cut psychological symptoms and have more in common with nonsexual offenders. They are more likely to be judged normal on psychiatric diagnosis and to be regarded as less inhibited sexually, and to have fewer symptoms of emotional disturbances. Their prior arrest records show fewer sex and more nonsexual offenses. Finally, they show the attitudes that one finds among those from delinquent subcultures. Frequently their offenses are committed in gangs. Consequently, instead of thinking of their behavior as sexually motivated in nature or that they are "sick offenders," it would be better to view their "offenses as part of a broader system in which force may be used to attain their goals. It is the use of force, rather than any specifically deviant sexual motivation that distinguishes these offenders from those who fall within the law." [50] The victim may also play a part in an act of rape where the offense may be a product of an evening of drinking or sexual arousal. "Consideration of the victim's role means that the offense can be viewed as a product of a social situation; its explanation cannot easily be reduced

[46] *California Sexual Deviation Research,* January, 1953 (Sacramento: State Printing Office, 1953), pp. 21–22.

[47] *A Follow-Up Study of 206 Sex Offenders Committed to State Mental Hospitals in New Jersey* (Trenton: New Jersey Department of Institutions and Agencies, June, 1953), pp. 1–2.

[48] *Report of the Illinois Commission on Sex Offenders,* To the 68th General Assembly of the State of Illinois (Springfield: State Printing Office, March 15, 1953), p. 25.

[49] Radzinowicz, *op. cit.,* p. 268.

[50] Wheeler, "Sex Offenses . . . ," *loc. cit.,* p. 277. Also see Eugene J. Kanin, "Male Aggression in Dating-Courtship Relations," *American Journal of Sociology,* 63:197 (September, 1957).

to a search for the childhood emotional disorders of the party who becomes labeled the offender." [51]

Some striking variations exist in the norms of sex conduct, reported by Kinsey and various public opinion surveys, according to education, social class, race, religion, and region.[52] Sexual offenses may be the result of the influence of different subcultural definitions of sexual behavior. Commenting on sexual offenses in Michigan, one report stated that when some southern rural families move north into more urban, middle-class areas, certain types of sexual behavior which previously received little attention in the old permissive environment are looked upon as sex offenses.[53]

The Illinois report likewise referred to cultural factors in sex offenses. This report further indicated that the stability of sexual patterns is related to the stability of the social structure. "For example, the sex conduct of soldiers exposed to disorganized social conditions overseas varied widely from their sex conduct at home. Modern, industrialized, mobile, impersonal living has also affected traditional standards of sex behavior." [54] Sutherland has referred to cultural influences in the etiology of sex offenses:

> The absurdity of this theory [sexual psychopathy] should be evident to anyone who has an acquaintance with the variations in sexual behavior and sexual codes throughout the history of mankind; practically all of the present sex crimes have been approved behavior for adults in some society or other. Similarly within our society deviant cultures with references to sex behavior prevail in sub-groups. The manner in which juveniles are inducted into the cultures of these sub-groups in the toilets of schools, playgrounds, and dormitories, as well as in other places, has been shown in many research reports on juvenile sex behavior.[55]

Sex violations, both heterosexual and homosexual, occurring among juveniles appear largely to take place with other juveniles rather than with adults and are the result of definitions of sexual behavior by the peer group.[56] The sexual behavior of adolescents is primarily peer-organized and peer-controlled.

> Adolescents themselves set standards for what is a violation of their sexual codes. The standards in these adolescent codes vary considerably according to the social status position of the adolescent and his family in the larger society. A comparison of the prescribed heterosexual coition patterns

[51] Wheeler, "Sex offenses . . . ," loc. cit., p. 278. Also see von Hentig, op. cit.

[52] Alfred C. Kinsey, Wardell B. Pomeroy, Clyde E. Martin, and Paul H. Gebhard, Sexual Behavior in the Human Female (Philadelphia: W. B. Saunders Company, 1953) and Alfred C. Kinsey, Wardell B. Pomeroy, and Clyde E. Martin, Sexual Behavior in the Human Male (Philadelphia: W. B. Saunders Company, 1948).

[53] Report of the Governor's Study Commission on the Deviated Criminal Sex Offender (Lansing: State of Michigan Printing Office, 1951), p. 31.

[54] Report of the Illinois Commission on Sex Offenders, p. 10.

[55] Sutherland, "The Sexual Psychopath Laws," loc. cit., p. 549.

[56] Reiss, "Sex Offenses . . . ," loc. cit.

of middle- and lower-status boys and girls may illustrate this variability. Among the lower-status white adolescent boys in our society, premarital heterosexual intercourse is prescribed to secure status within the group, while it is not necessary to secure status within most middle-peer status groups, even though it does confer some status.[57]

HOMOSEXUALITY

There is ample evidence that cultural attitudes toward homosexual or one-sex behavior have differed from one period in history to another. In Greek and Roman times this behavior was prevalent, and in some societies homosexual practices were related to certain religious rites. Ford and Beach studied 76 folk societies and found that among 49 of them, or 64 percent, "homosexual activities of one sort or another are considered normal and socially acceptable for certain members of the community." [58] Some of the attitude in parts of Western society that homosexuality is deviant behavior can be explained by certain aspects of the Christian tradition.[59]

There are indications that overt homosexuality, that is, sex relations with one's own sex, is much more prevalent now than many assume. A great deal of this behavior is unknown to the public and to the law authorities. Kinsey reports that about 37 percent of the white male population has had some homosexual experience and to the point of orgasm somewhere between adolescence and old age. Only half as many females as males have had homosexual experiences, and males have more frequent relations, continue their activities for more years, and are more promiscuous.[60] There is ample evidence that homosexual relationships exist to a considerable extent in our prisons and other one-sex communities. Most homosexual relationships are of a transitory nature, occurring perhaps only once or twice over a number of years, or as a result of a unique social situation. Kinsey reports that 4 percent of his sample of males were career homosexuals.

Some studies have shown that homosexuals are generally above average in intelligence and education and that, except for their sex behavior, they are generally law-abiding and hard working.[61] Most of them are unmar-

---

[57] *Ibid.*, p. 312.

[58] Clellan S. Ford and Frank A. Beach, *Patterns of Sexual Behavior* (New York: Harper & Row, Publishers, 1951), p. 130. Also see Ruth Benedict, *Patterns of Culture* (Boston: Houghton Mifflin Company, 1934).

[59] David S. Bailey, *Homosexuality and the Western Christian Tradition* (New York: David McKay Company, Inc., 1955).

[60] Kinsey *et al.*, *Sexual Behavior in the Human Female*, and Kinsey, *et al.*, *Sexual Behavior in the Human Male*.

[61] L. H. Loeser, "Sexual Psychopaths in the Military Service," *American Journal of Psychiatry*, 102:92–101 (July, 1945). Also see Kinsey *et al.*, *Sexual Behavior in the Human Male*.

ried, separated, or divorced, and they come primarily from cities rather than from the country.

Homosexual behavior appears to be a product of the adoption of certain homosexual cultural norms and a conception of self. The channeling of sexual expressions into homosexual patterns must come through some cultural or subcultural definitions, just as do heterosexual relations. The very first homosexual experience among 127 homosexuals studied in Great Britain was usually with a school boy of the same age and generally constituted sex play, often in a school situation.[62] These experiences, however, did not necessarily lead to homosexuality as a pattern of sex behavior. The first "significant homosexual experience" can be defined as one carried out with an adult or repeated acts carried out with the same boy over a year or so. Over two thirds of such experiences were with another boy. Only 18 percent were first introduced to homosexuality as boys by adults and a further 11 percent had no experience of any sort until they were adults, and in all such cases their partner was an adult. Contrary to the popular view, seduction is not a very important factor. With most homosexuals there was a long period during which they fought against their homosexual activity before recognizing it as permanent behavior and assuming a conception of themselves as homosexuals.

Although our culture as a whole does not approve of this type of sex behavior, there exists a subcultural world of homosexuals who indoctrinate new individuals into it. This subcultural world consists of a special language which serves to keep its members secret from the out-group. There are special words for this sex behavior, such as "gay," "straight," and "queen," which are "similar in some respects to that of the underworld; in others to that of the theater." [63] Recognition by other homosexuals appears to involve particularly gestures, walk, clothes, and a special vocabulary.[64] There are subculturally defined ways in which homosexual relations are established. Many communities have special meeting places where homosexuals gather, usually at certain street corners, parks, taverns, clubs, or lavatories.[65] After an intensive study of 60 homosexuals in a large Canadian city the following conclusions were reached about the homosexual community.

The homosexual community thus consists of a large number of distinctive groups within which friendship binds the members together in a strong and

---

[62] Gordon Westwood, *A Minority: A Report on the Life of the Male Homosexual in Great Britain* (London: Longmans, Green & Co., Ltd., 1960), pp. 24–39.

[63] Donald W. Cory, *The Homosexual in America* (New York: Greenberg: Publisher, Inc., 1951), p. 90. Also see J. D. Mercer, *They Walk in the Shadow* (New York: Comet Press, 1959).

[64] Westwood, *op. cit.*, pp. 83–86.

[65] For discussion see Gordon Westwood, *Society and the Homosexual* (New York: E. P. Dutton & Co., Inc., 1953), Chaps. 19–21, and Cory, *op. cit.* Also see Westood, *A Minority*, pp. 68–77.

relatively enduring bond and between which the members are linked by tenuous but repeated sexual contacts. The result is that homosexuals within the city tend to know or know of each other, to recognize a number of common interests and common moral norms. . . . This community is in turn linked with other homosexual communities in Canada and the United States chiefly through the geographic mobility of its members.[66]

PROSTITUTION

While the extent of prostitution and the reaction of society to it has fluctuated over many years, the definition has remained the same. Prostitution is sexual intercourse on a promiscuous and mercenary basis, with emotional indifference.[67] The patron pays for this intimacy, but the method of payment often serves to cloud the definition of a true prostitute. For example, when a customer "dates" a shopgirl for an evening dinner and show and later has sex relations with her, the relationship is often on a mercenary, emotionally indifferent basis; yet the girl may not be considered, or consider herself, a real prostitute. Such a girl has a job, may have a family and other group attachments, and may not make a practice of exchanging sexual favors for an evening's entertainment.

Many women are promiscuous but are not prostitutes, for their sex relations have an element of affection, even if transitory. The prostitute "sells" her sex relations with an element of indifference. While some prostitutes may be selective of their customers on the basis of race, age, economic status, or physical attractiveness, generally an act of intercourse may be carried out with almost anyone. So indifferent are most prostitutes to the emotional aspect of sex relations that they rarely experience an orgasm with a customer, although they frequently do with their "pimp" or male consort.

Extent. The true prostitute might be considered as one who primarily makes her living from selling, for money, her sexual favors, but there is no way of ascertaining the number of these women.[68] Some of them have part- or full-time legitimate jobs which serve to cover up their real occupation. Usually statistical reports of prostitution are gathered from arrest figures, which themselves are not always reliable. Estimates have ranged from around 100,000 for the United States to as high as Reitman's estimate of 100,000 in 1931 for the city of Chicago alone.[69] It is likely that a much

[66] Maurice Leznoff and William A. Westley, "The Homosexual Community," *Social Problems*, 3:263 (Spring, 1956).

[67] In some countries, as well as in many of our states, it is not prostitution which is legally a criminal offense; rather, soliciting is the offense for which the prostitute is punished. See Williams, "Sex Offenses: The British Experience," *loc. cit.*

[68] There are also male prostitutes in homosexuality, and Kinsey estimates their number to be as high in large cities as the number of female prostitutes.

[69] Ben L. Reitman, *The Second Oldest Profession: A Study of the Prostitutes' "Business Manager"* (New York: Vanguard Press, Inc., 1931).

more conservative estimate than Reitman's figure is more nearly correct—possibly 275,000 live, in America, by prostitution alone.[70] About 69 percent of the total male population has some experience with prostitutes, but a large part have had only one or two experiences and some 15 to 20 percent have relations more than a few times a year.[71] Prostitution accounts for less than 10 percent of the total nonmarital sexual outlet for males. Not more than 1 percent of extramarital sexual intercourse is with prostitutes.

There appears to have been a steady decline in prostitution throughout the past two decades, except for periodic increases in wartime. During World War II it was estimated that in America there were about 600,000 regular prostitutes and about an equal number who were engaged in prostitution but had other means of livelihood.[72] Kinsey states that the frequency with which American males go to prostitutes has been reduced by about one half of what it was prior to World War I.[73] Kingsley Davis has explained the decrease in prostitution as a result of increased sexual freedom for women. As young women have less restraint in their sexual relations, it is easier for men to have sex relations without recourse to prostitutes.[74] Even if prostitution continues to decrease there will probably always be a certain amount of it, because there will continue to be a group of men who are able to secure sexual satisfactions only through payment for such services.

Patrons. Kinsey has indicated a number of reasons for the existence of prostitution, which has often been referred to as the oldest profession.[75] Men go to prostitutes because they do not have sufficient other sexual outlets. It is simpler and often cheaper to secure extramarital intercourse through a prostitute than by dating. Likewise, there are no responsibilities for a resulting pregnancy. Married men also go to prostitutes for the sake of variety in sexual intercourse, a variety often not otherwise available even to married persons. Others go if they are ineffective in securing sexual relations with women because they are timid, deformed, deaf, blind, or otherwise physically handicapped. Kingsley Davis has summarized the appeals of prostitution.

> In short, the attempt of society to control sexual expression, to tie it to social requirements, especially the attempt to tie it to the durable relation of marriage and the rearing of children, or to attach men to a celibate order, or to base sexual expression on love, creates the opportunity for prostitution.

[70] Edwin M. Lemert, *Social Pathology* (New York: McGraw-Hill Book Company, Inc., 1951), p. 231.

[71] Kinsey *et al.*, *Sexual Behavior in the Human Male*, p. 597.

[72] "Regulations of Vice," *Encyclopedia Americana* (1945 ed.; New York: Encyclopedia Americana), XXVIII, 58.

[73] Kinsey *et al.*, *Sexual Behavior in the Human Female*, p. 300.

[74] Kingsley Davis, "The Sociology of Prostitution," *American Sociological Review*, 2:744–755 (October, 1937).

[75] Kinsey *et al.*, *Sexual Behavior in the Human Male*, pp. 606–609.

It is analogous to the black market, which is the illegal but inevitable response to an attempt fully to control the economy. The craving for sexual variety, for perverse gratification, for novel and provocative surroundings, for ready and cheap release, for intercourse free from entangling cares and civilized pretense—all can be demanded from the woman whose interest lies solely in the price. The sole limitation on the man's satisfactions is in this instance not morality or convention, but his ability to pay.[76]

Societal Reactions. Attitudes toward prostitution have varied historically, and today vary in different countries. The attitude toward, and the social status of, the prostitute, as Davis has suggested, vary according to three conditions: (1) if the prostitute practices a certain discrimination in her customers, (2) if the earnings are used for some socially desirable goal, and (3) if the prostitute combines with her sexual role others which are more acceptable.[77] In ancient Greece, for example, brothel prostitutes were given a different status from the hetaerae who, educated in the arts, often were wealthy, powerful personages who had great influence on many important leaders. Although prostitutes, they generally were highly respected. The devadasis, or dancing girls, were connected with the temples of India for centuries and, besides singing and dancing, they engaged in temple prostitution. In general, these girls were the only Indian women who learned to read. Because the devadasi was one of a social group of religious prostitutes attached to the temple, the money was given to the temple and the act of intercourse was, to some extent, a religious ritual. Finally, the famous Japanese geishas can be cited as another example of women who could often engage in prostitution but still have high status in their society. They were trained in the arts, such as music, in conversation, and in social entertaining.

In France prostitution is illegal but condoned, and in many other parts of the world, particularly in Latin American, it is countenanced. Prostitution, particularly soliciting, is strongly disapproved under Anglo-American law, but there are persons who would tolerate it as necessary and even have certain areas of a city set aside for prostitutes who could, they naïvely believe, be regularly inspected for venereal disease. Prostitution is opposed on many grounds: (1) the degradation of the women who engage in it; (2) the threat to public health because of the transmission of venereal disease; (3) the effect on general law enforcement through police protection; (4) the effect on marital relations where recourse is had to prostitutes; and (5) the patronage of prostitutes by young persons, soldiers in particular, and its effect on national values.

Types of Prostitutes. Prostitutes can generally be classified according

---

[76] Kingsley Davis, "Prostitution," in Robert K. Merton and Robert A. Nisbet, eds., *Contemporary Social Problems* (New York: Harcourt, Brace & World, Inc., 1961), pp. 275–276.

[77] *Ibid.,* p. 267.

to their methods of operation. There are individual common prostitutes, organized houses of prostitution, call-girl and similar arrangements, and the high-class independent prostitute.[78] The individual common prostitute operates alone, procuring her trade as she can, on the streets or in such places as bars and hotel lobbies. She takes her customers to a prearranged cheap rooming house or hotel. Generally she has no connection with organized crime, but often she must pay for her own protection.

Similar to this kind of prostitute is the girl who works in an organized house or brothel. Such houses, which flourished in the red-light districts, were probably more predominant a few decades ago than they are today. They vary a great deal as to size, type of customers, and degree of respectability. New girls are "broken in" to the rules and regulations of the house, and each new prostitute soon learns various sex techniques. She learns how to handle a large number of customers without running the risk of losing them as patrons, how to deal with rough and uncouth men, and how to protect herself against venereal disease. These girls are often exploited by the madame or the manager of the house, for they have small chance to protect themselves, and a high percentage of their earnings, from 50 to 60 percent, is deducted for the "house," for linens, medical examinations, police protection, and the like. Usually these houses are operated in conjunction with some type of organized crime, through which police "protection" is usually secured. They are also usually associated with panderers who solicit for the girls, taxicab drivers who receive commissions, and pimps who live off the girls' earnings.

Another type of organized prostitution has become more and more prominent as police and health authorities have become more effective in doing away with street soliciting and red-light houses. This is the so-called call girl, who depends upon some organization for recruiting her patrons, although she may operate independently and have her own list of patrons who call upon her services. More frequently these patrons are secured through the intermediary services of a bellhop, a hotel desk clerk, a taxi driver or other type of agent who, for a fee, will give her telephone number to the patron or arrange for a room in a hotel where the girl is known. Usually call girls work in lower-class hotels, but even some of the best-known expensive hotels allow this type of prostitute to operate on their premises. During the past few years the call girl has become widely known, and her methods of operating have been thoroughly publicized. In some New York City cases patrons are reported to have paid large sums of money, reputedly as high as $500, for an evening's entertainment. Since this type of prostitution is less visible than the "parlor house" type, it gives more concealment to the prostitute and more anonymity to the patron.

---

[78] For a discussion of prostitutes see Walter C. Reckless, *Vice in Chicago* (Chicago: The University of Chicago Press, 1933). Also see Sheldon and Eleanor T. Glueck, *500 Delinquent Women* (New York: Alfred A. Knopf, Inc., 1934).

Some prostitution is not strictly organized as such, but is knowingly permitted and often even encouraged, through legitimate, but often shady, businesses, especially those in the commercial recreation industry, such as burlesque shows, night clubs, amusement parks, and the like. Taxi-dance halls particularly afford opportunities for the dancers to make engagements with their patrons, either in a room hired for the occasion or in the dancer's own room or apartment.[79] Through a variety of techniques performers in cabarets or burlesque shows recruit patrons for later dates.

There is, finally, the independent professional prostitute who lives in her own apartment house or flat, often in a more expensive part of town, and encourages middle- and upper-class patrons. Most of her clientele is secured on an individual basis through referrals from taxicab drivers or other persons.

Backgrounds of Prostitutes. Inasmuch as physical attractiveness and youth are a necessity for the prostitute, she is usually between seventeen and twenty-four years old, the peak ages being twenty and twenty-one years. Some prostitutes are older, but most of these have taken up the profession for special reasons, such as drug addiction, where their need for a continued supply of drugs has brought about increased financial demands. Single girls constitute the largest proportion of prostitutes, although many prostitutes are divorced or separated. Many of those who give their marital status as married are either living with or are married to pimps. On the whole, the professional common prostitute has less opportunity for marriage than the "high-class" type of prostitute.

Prostitutes are highly mobile persons, being often recruited from those classes and groups in society which are the most mobile. In the past the most recent migrant groups have swelled the ranks of prostitution, and at one time there was probably a disproportionate number of prostitutes from various foreign-born groups. Contemporary studies, however, seem to refute the idea the foreign-born are overrepresented among prostitutes, although there is a disproportionate percentage of racial minorities.[80] The high mobility among Negroes, together with their lower socioeconomic conditions and their cultural standards of less rigid sex mores, has no doubt accounted for the higher proportion of Negro prostitutes. Other than the fact that prostitutes may primarily come from the lower socioeconomic groups, from which many women come, there is no evidence that they enter this profession because of poverty even though they may desire to better their economic status.

Although the modern prostitute differs a great deal from her flamboyantly dressed and heavily made-up predecessor, they still have characteristics in common. They have often been indoctrinated into the profession

---

[79] Paul Cressey, *Taxi-Dance Hall* (Chicago: The University of Chicago Press, 1932).
[80] Lemert, *op. cit.*, pp. 240–241.

by those who have been closely associated with prostitution, they have usually been poorly integrated into socially acceptable groups, and they seldom develop a high degree of organization within their profession. The very nature of the profession is competitive, each prostitute attempting to build up and keep her own clientele; hence there is little group solidarity except for cases where they must band together for protection from the police or from others who threaten their profession. Prostitutes have a limited argot or special language of their own, which is a mark of a degree of association and group cohesiveness.[81]

The Process of Prostitution. At one time it was rather widely believed that the prostitute was often the victim of a "white slaver" who had induced a sexually unexperienced girl to go into prostitution. The White-Slave-Traffic Act (the Mann Act) was aimed at eliminating what was called white slavery. Movies and sermons were used to portray graphically the evils which might befall an unsuspecting young girl, and it was believed that once a girl had thus been seduced her only alternative was to continue a life of prostitution. Another theory with very little substance to it is that women enter prostitution because of economic necessity. Actually, the earnings of most prostitutes, even allowing for deductions in payments to a madame, to a pimp, or for "protection" from the police, are higher than the earnings of most working women. The prostitute is paid for her loss of esteem through the societal reaction. In fact, Davis concludes that "since the occupation is lucrative, the interesting question is not why so many women become prostitutes, but why so few of them do." [82]

Present-day studies of girls who make their living in this way indicate that the process of becoming a prostitute is quite different. Generally there is agreement that most girls of this type have lived in local communities where the moral standards about sex have not been high. Although most have had considerable sexual experience, either with or without marriage, this fact in itself does not account for the prostitution. Generally the important other factor is association with persons on the fringe of prostitution:

> In the United States, these contacts with persons in or on the fringe of prostitution are largely with women, practitioners of prostitution themselves. Although some prostitutes are exploited by pimps, this parasitism is not usually the mode. One should expect that those girls who acquire pimps do so after they have entered the trade. It is very rare to find a case in American prostitution in which a girl who has never been a prostitute was persuaded or forced into the business by a pimp.[83]

---

[81] David Maurer, "Prostitutes and Criminal Argots," *American Journal of Sociology,* 44:546–550 (January, 1939).

[82] Davis, "Prostitution," *loc. cit.*, p. 277.

[83] Walter C. Reckless, *The Crime Problem* (2d ed.; New York: Appleton-Century-Crofts, Inc., 1955), p. 275. Reprinted by permission of the publisher.

Mere sexual experiences do not make the prostitute, for prostitution is largely a product of playing a social role.[84] Quasi-prostituting experiences, such as those of a waitress who after hours accepts favors from customers in return for sexual intercourse, may lead to prostitution. Arrest or treatment for venereal disease may strengthen this concept of self, as will the attitude of other prostitutes and persons associated with them.

After going into prostitution the girls tend to develop attitudes and behavior patterns which are a part of the social role they play. In this connection they develop an argot or special language for their work, special acts and services, patterns of bartering with their customers and an impersonal relationship with them, as well as a large number of rationalizations for their activities.[85]

Many prostitutes are able to leave this occupation for marriage or for employment as waitresses, domestic servants, or salesgirls. A few others are able to achieve a high standard of living and maintain it. But for many of them, eventually ravaged by venereal disease, alcoholism, and drug addiction, the end result is a derelict life, punctuated more or less regularly by arrests and jail sentences. From there it is an easy step to petty stealing and shoplifting.

Summary

Murderers and sex offenders generally are not of the career type. They should be looked at, however, from the perspective of social behavior and social norms. Murder can be thought of as arising primarily from a subculture of violence. Most homosexuality and prostitution can also be explained within a group and subcultural context.

Selected Readings

DAVIS, KINGSLEY. "Prostitution," in Robert K. Merton and Robert A. Nisbet eds., *Contemporary Social Problems*. New York: Harcourt, Brace & World, Inc., 1961. A sociological explanation of prostitution in terms of its relation to the general society.

LEMERT, EDWIN M. *Social Pathology*. New York: McGraw-Hill Book Company, Inc., 1951, Chap. 8. A comprehensive discussion of prostitution, including an analysis of the social visibility, societal reaction, and tolerance of prostitution.

RECKLESS, WALTER C. *Vice in Chicago*. Chicago: The University of Chicago Press, 1933. Although an older study, this is one of the best on prostitution. Includes case material.

"Sex Offenses." Volume 25 (Spring, 1960) of *Law and Contemporary Problems*. A symposium on the legal, anthropological, ethical, sociological, clinical, and

---

[84] Lemert, *op. cit.*, p. 270.   [85] Reckless, *The Crime Problem*, 2d ed., pp. 276–277.

medical-legal aspects of sex offenses. Includes also a study of British and Scandinavian experiences with sex offenders.

SUTHERLAND, EDWIN H. "The Sexual Psychopath Laws," *Journal of Criminal Law and Criminology*, 40:543–554 (January–February, 1950). A criticism of the concept of a psychopath and of the sexual psychopath laws.

WESTWOOD, GORDON. *A Minority: A Report on the Life of the Male Homosexual in Great Britain*. London: Longmans, Green & Co., Ltd., 1960. A study of 127 homosexuals primarily from a sociological approach.

WOLFGANG, MARVIN E. *Patterns in Criminal Homicide*. Philadelphia: University of Pennsylvania Press, 1958. Surveys the literature on homicide and studies nearly 600 cases of criminal homicide in Philadelphia, including both the offender and the victim. Presents the legal aspects of homicide, an analysis of race, sex, and age differences; methods and weapons used to inflict death; spatial patterns; relation to the use of alcohol; the degree of violence in homicide; and victim-precipitated homicide.

Career Criminals

The characteristics of a fully developed criminal career have been previously indicated. This is a life organization built about criminal activities which include identification with crime, a conception of the self as a criminal, extensive association with criminal activities including other criminals, and, finally, progression in crime. The last represents progression toward more complex techniques and more frequent offenses, and, ultimately, making crime a frequent or a sole means of livelihood.

Obviously, persons who commit personal offenses such as murder and sex offenses can rarely be thought of as having criminal careers. It is true that professional murderers can be hired in other parts of the world, but seldom in the Western world. Those who have criminal careers generally commit theft or a crime involving some other form of gain. In this chapter three main types of criminal careers will be discussed, the ordinary criminal career, the organized criminal, and the most highly developed of all criminal careers, the professional. To serve as a contrast to them, three types of offenders who generally do not represent fully developed careers in crime will first be discussed—the occasional property offender, the habitual petty offender, and the white-collar offender.

Occasional Property Offenders

There are many offenders whose entire criminal records rarely consist of more than an occasional theft of some kind. Such offenses are incidental to their way of life and are so rare that these offenders in no way make a living from crime and they do not play a criminal role. This type of criminal behavior is often of a fortuitous nature, embarked upon at a particular moment, perhaps for a thrill or for suddenly needed funds. Often the offense is committed alone, and without prior criminal contacts; at other times there may be one companion, or at most two.

The occasional offender does not conceive of himself as a criminal. His offenses show little sophistication in the techniques of crime; he has small knowledge about crime and no vocabulary of criminal argot. To him stealing an automobile is more like "borrowing" the car and does not involve any of the techniques commonly associated with career types of offenders—selecting a special type of car, knowing how to open car locks, strip cars, find "fences," and so on. The occasional criminal makes no effort to progress to types of crimes requiring greater knowledge and skill.

It has been estimated that some 75 percent of all check forgeries are committed by persons who have no previous pattern of such behavior. Analyzing a small sample of twenty-nine cases, Lemert concluded that such persons generally do not come from a delinquency area, have no previous criminal record, or have had no previous contact with delinquents and criminals. He suggests that the novice check forger, who generally comes from the higher socioeconomic groups, is a product of certain difficult social situations in which he finds himself, a certain degree of social isolation, and a process of "closure" or "constriction of behavior alternatives subjectively held as available to the forger." [1]

Rural persons who commit theft usually have these characteristics of an occasional property offender. Many white-collar offenders also have them but these will be discussed in a separate section. A rural offender has described his offense in this way:

> The crime I done was a few miles from home. Perhaps I would of done it anywhere, as I had to be at a certain place at a certain time. I wanted to go to a dance, and my folks would not give me any money, so I really didn't care what I done. I had a car, but it was getting fixed and I didn't have the money to pay for it, so I stole my neighbor's car, just to show my folks I was not scared. I told them I was going to do it, but they didn't think I would. I have never thought about any crime as far as that goes. Like breaking into a place is way out of my line. I always was honest. My father is one of the best citizens. I consider him one of the best in that county. The boys I went with never stole anything. I never had any experience stealing cars. Guess it don't take any practice. When a boy I would use dad's car without asking him, but he didn't care. Sometimes he didn't like it very well, but he always got over it somehow.[2]

The Habitual Petty Offender

Habitual petty offenders [3] are one of the largest criminal groups. They constitute a large proportion of arrests, but since they do not often commit serious felonies they are commonly confined in city and county jails. Generally they begin their criminal activities while young, and they continue in petty crime, vagrancy, and disorderly conduct for a long period of time. These offenders have long criminal records, maintain extensive connections with a criminal underworld, and conceive of themselves as criminals. Habitual petty offenders do not, however, possess much sophistication about

---

[1] Edwin M. Lemert, "An Isolation Closure Theory of Naïve Check Forgery," *Journal of Criminal Law and Criminology*, 44:298 (September–October, 1953).

[2] From Marshall B. Clinard, "Rural Criminal Offenders," *American Journal of Sociology*, 50:44 (July, 1944).

[3] Here this term is being used to describe a behavior system and is not the legal term discussed on page 159.

crime, do not employ elaborate techniques, and are not particularly effective at "fixing" their cases in court.

The criminal pattern of habitual offenders is complicated by their conception of themselves as failures in social adjustment. This self-conception has considerable basis in fact in their tendency to be lazy, shiftless, and irresponsible; moreover, they are likely to have been arrested not only for petty stealing but also for alcoholism, for the sale of or addiction to drugs, for vagrancy, or for other similar offenses: "Consequently they are easily caught, and, since they have no means of protection such as the professional criminal has established, are easily convicted. They do not steal consistently at first, but as their reputation becomes known they find it more and more difficult to find employment and live without criminal activity." [4] The following is a good example of a habitual criminal career.

Doe was born in S. County, Washington, June 10, 1908, the second child in a family of 3 girls and 2 boys. Father was a blacksmith in a rural community, who provided very poorly for family. Mother divorced him when subject was 15 years old. Since 1928, defendant has traveled about the country, supporting himself chiefly by gambling. He has a delinquency record going back to the age of 15. He was married in 1931, separated six years later, divorced in 1941. No children. Wife had 8th grade education and a good reputation. Father was a heavy drinker, a cruel personality, and a poor provider for the family. The mother had an 8th grade education. Married again. Stepfather was a naturalized Austrian, mill worker and logger, 3 years of schooling, has police record for drunkenness in A. Was once on relief and certified for W.P.A. Has had no effective ties with defendant and no interest in him. Records on sisters and brothers are clear.

The defendant lived mainly in cheap hotels, although he considers his mother's address as his permanent address. Mother says John "just comes and goes, where, we don't know." Doe completed the 8th grade. According to mother he made a good record in school, leaving school when he was 13. As a child he attended the Church of God but does not now attend any church. He was never a member of any character building organization. He bowls and "does some drinking." He admitted that he often associated with prostitutes, gamblers, and "because of the need for narcotics," with addicts and peddlers. His mother said he "chased around with just no good people."

He weighs 185 pounds and is 5′ 11″ in height. His health history discloses the usual childhood diseases. He denied he was a narcotic addict. He admitted he had syphilis, and also "social drinking of whiskey." At the Veterans' Hospital he was given malarial fever treatment for tertiary syphilis. He was also diagnosed here as "psychopathic personality with asocial trends." His employment history is as follows, verified only in case of the shipyard job and Army service: 6–9–43 to 9–29–43, U.S. Army, private, discharged because of syphilis, 3–3–42 to 12–10–42 the Q.R. Shipyard, S. as shipfitter's helper, 95 cents per hour, left to enter army; 1937 to 1942, "several" employers as a gambler; 1928, salesman for used cars. The subject has also worked as a cigar salesman, traveled about the country as a gambler and salesman of electric razors. Refer-

[4] Ruth S. Cavan, *Criminology* (New York: Thomas Y. Crowell Company, 1948), p. 218.

ences consulted expressed the opinion that many of the defendant's activities were illegal "rackets," and that he had the reputation of being connected with prostitution as a pimp.[5]

The following is the report of [his] FBI fingerprint clearance, with explanatory comments given by the defendant.

Date	Place	Charge	Disposition	Defendant's Comment
4-26-26	PD A., Wn.	Dis. Con.	Dismissed	None
1-16-29	SO M., Wn.	Assault & Bat.	30 days: $22.80	"Drunk, hotel fight."
12-27-34	PD P. A., Wn.	Opera. auto with revoked driver's lic.	$75 fine and costs	"Served 5 days, paid fine."
12-20-34	PD S., Wn.	Manslaughter, reduced to accessory after fact	6 months jail, 5 months suspended	"Loaned friend car, who killed person getting off bus."
7- 5-38	PD B., Ida.	Investigation	None	"Gambling, picked up, told to get out of town."
7-31-39	SO L., Ida.	Susp. Vag.	None	"Just gambling, released."
7- 1-40	PD M., Wis.	Inv. Vag.	Susp. Sent. on vag. charge	"Served 10 days, released."
12-19-40	SO S., Calif.	Vio. Sec. 502 CVC	None	"Lost license, paid $75 fine, got 60 days on drunken driving."
4- 8-41	PD L., Neb.	Susp. white slavery	Released	"Roe and I were arrested, just asked taxi driver to get us a girl."
11-13-41	PD W.W., Wn.	Drunk	None	"Got $10 fine."
2- 4-42	SO T., Wn.	Burglary 2nd degree	0-15 yrs., deferred on condition join Army	"Could not get into Army, reported to parole officer until case dismissed 5-19-43" (verified)
6- 6-42	USM S., Wn.	O.P.A. (gas without coupons)	65 days jail	None
2-22-44	Bur. Narc., Wash.	Conceal. transp. poss. of opium	Current case	
2-22-44	PD S., Ore.	Burglary	Pending, warrant with USM	"Not guilty of charge"

---

[5] Walter C. Reckless, *The Crime Problem* (New York: Appleton-Century-Crofts, Inc., 1950), p. 104. Reprinted by permission of the publisher.

The following additional information, which does not duplicate the above, was obtained from the records of the sheriff's office in A., H., and M., Washington. (Offenses were committed in A.)

Date	Charge	Disposition	Explanation
9–11–23	Vagrancy	Dismissed	Police dismissed, subject only 15 yrs old
11–29–25	Drunk	Forfeited $25	Subject then only 17
7–18–27	Vagrancy	No disposition	Defendant not consulted for comment
6– 2–27	No driver's license	$5 fine	Defendant not consulted for comment
4–16–29	Vagrancy	None	Defendant not consulted for comment
1– 1–34	Drunken driving	$50 fine, license suspended	Defendant not consulted for comment
10–10–40	Drunk	$10 fine	Defendant not consulted for comment

SOURCE: Walter C. Reckless, *The Crime Problem* (New York: Appleton-Century-Crofts, Inc., 1950), pp. 103–104. Reprinted by permission of the publisher.

White-Collar Offenders

White-collar crime is committed by persons of high occupational status in connection with their occupations: it includes crimes by businessmen, politicians, doctors, and lawyers. Offenses by labor union officials are also included, since these leaders increasingly enjoy reasonably high status and are in important positions of trust where both power and influence can be exercised. White-collar crime does not include such crimes as murder or robbery, which could be committed by persons of any occupation. As has been pointed out in the discussions of crime, no act committed by white-collar groups, however unethical, should be considered as crime unless it is punishable by the state in some way. For example, the deliberate sale of a pair of odd-lot shoes which are too small for a customer is unethical but it is not a crime. This is also true of advertising which is unethical but not necessarily illegal.

One of the most significant recent cases of white-collar crime involved conspiracy in price-fixing and price-rigging violations of the federal antitrust laws by many of the leading electrical concerns of the United States. Twenty-nine leading electrical companies, including General Electric and Westinghouse and forty-five executives of the companies involved, were convicted in 1960 of illegalities in sales of heavy electrical equipment amounting to $1,750,000,000 a year. Such violations meant that government and private purchasers of equipment had been deceived about the open competitive nature of bids and had to pay sums far in excess of a regular bid. In the end, such illegal behavior, when perpetrated against a government agency, costs the taxpayers. Consequently, the convictions were later followed by civil suits amounting to millions of dollars filed by various federal, state, and local agencies to recover damages from the illegal price fixing and price rigging.

Fines amounting to $1,924,000 were imposed by the federal court, including a fine of $437,000 against General Electric and $372,000 against Westinghouse. Seven executives who were high enough in their companies to make policy were sentenced to thirty days in jail and twenty-four other executives received suspended jail sentences. Those sentenced to jail included three officials from General Electric and two from Westinghouse. Among the seven receiving sentences of thirty days in prison was a vice-president of General Electric, who also received a $12,500 fine, and a vice-president of Westinghouse, who was fined $2000. General Electric was fined $437,000, and Westinghouse $372,500. The salaries of the convicted executives ranged from $25,000 to $135,000 a year.

The jail sentences imposed on these business executives of this high status, and the severity of the fines, were unique punishments for white-collar crime. In pronouncing sentence, Judge Ganey said: "This is a shocking indictment of a vast section of our economy, for what is really at stake here is the survival of a kind of economy under which this country has grown great, the free enterprise system." The judge then noted that the court did not yet have enough evidence to convict the highest echelons in the electrical firms, but he went on to state the following: "One would be most naïve . . . to believe . . . these violations . . . so long persisted in and affecting so large a segment of the industry and involving so many millions upon millions of dollars were facts unknown to those responsible for the corporation and its conduct." [6]

Secret meetings had been arranged by representatives of the companies in hotel rooms. Participants were cautioned to conceal their bids in expense-account reports. At the secret meetings pricing schedules were arranged and arrangements were made for each company to submit the lowest bid for each of various contracts.

As an example of how the conspiracies worked, one of the most involved conspiracies, and also of longest duration, was in the switchgear division, which handles the sale of electric circuit breakers and the like.[7] This conspiracy operated for a number of years and was well organized. Conspirators had their own lingo and operating procedures. Attendance lists at secret meetings of the companies were called "Christmas card

[6] Quoted in Richard A. Smith, "The Incredible Electrical Conspiracy: I," *Fortune*, April, 1961, p. 133. Also see John Herling, *The Great Price Conspiracy: The Story of the Antitrust Violations in the Electrical Industry* (Washington: Robert B. Luce, Inc., 1962.)

[7] Herling, *op. cit.*, pp. 106–114.

lists"; meetings were known as "choir practices." The companies involved in this conspiracy—General Electric, Westinghouse, Allis-Chalmers, Federal Pacific, and I.T.E.—were given a code number which was used in the book price listings, and in communications between executives. The job of initiating memos on the subjects of jobs coming up, and on book price listings by each company, was rotated among executives, each performing this task for thirty days. Several times over a period of about eight years the conspiracy was given up because participants from the different firms tended to cheat on the "rules" of the conspiracy itself and attempted to "chisel" one another. However, slumps in profits and sales, combined with productive overcapacity, would generally force the executives to do something to remedy this situation. Since price fixing had succeeded before in solving the low-profit versus overcapacity dilemma, it was easily resorted to again. During slumps in profits and sales the division executives would be pressured from the central echelons to "do something" to raise profits and sales. This appeared to contribute to the decisions of lower-echelon executives to resume conspiracies. Through searching investigations during which extensive records, including minutes, of the conspiracy meetings were obtained, the government was able to secure sufficient evidence to indict the forty-five executives. Also, executives of one company decided to go along with the government and submitted documents and other supporting evidence to the investigators.

One writer has suggested that in these cases a factor of major importance was the separation of business and personal ethics.[8] In the minds of the executives there was a cleavage between ordinary morals and business morals; what applied in one area did not in another. Following these cases Henry Ford II, President of the Ford Motor Company, delivered a major address calling for strong condemnation by businessmen of violations of law.

CONCEPTION OF SELF

The major difference between white-collar crime and other forms of crime lies in the offender's conception of himself.[9] A white-collar offender does not play as consistent a criminal role as do many other types of offenders. He may play a variety of other roles, such as that of a respected citizen; hence the degree of recognition of the conflict between this role and that of a criminal offender may vary with different individuals. Since he is likely to regard himself as a respectable citizen, at most he regards himself as a "lawbreaker" and not as a "criminal." In this sense he has the attitude

---

[8] Smith, "The Incredible Electrical Conspiracy: II," *Fortune*, May, 1961, pp. 161–164 and 210–224.

[9] Edwin H. Sutherland, *White Collar Crime* (New York: Holt, Rinehart and Winston, Inc., 1949, reissued 1960), pp. 223–224.

of some offenders convicted of such crimes as statutory rape, nonsupport, or drunken driving.

Most career offenders, such as the ordinary, professional, or organized, think of themselves primarily as "criminals," and do not ordinarily put white-collar offenders in the same category with themselves. The higher social status of white-collar criminals makes it difficult for the general public, while not condoning their activities, to conceive of them as being associated with real criminal behavior, which is largely stereotyped as the more overt offenses. This attitude is, in turn, reflected in the conception that white-collar offenders have of themselves.[10]

DIFFERENTIAL ASSOCIATION

A new man in some white-collar occupations may learn the techniques by which the law can be violated, and he may build up a series of rationalizations such as "Business is business," or "One cannot conduct a profitable business or profession in any other way." This diffusion of illegal practices is spread from a person already in the occupation to new persons entering it, and from one business establishment, political machine, or other white-collar group to another. Sometimes the diffusion may be the result of an effort to meet illegal competitive activities of another business or political machine. How this diffusion of unethical and illegal behavior works is described by a person in the used-car business.

When I graduated from college I had plenty of ideals of honesty, fair play, and cooperation which I had acquired at home, in school, and from literature. My first job after graduation was selling typewriters. During the first day I learned that these machines were not sold at a uniform price but that a person who haggled and waited could get a machine at about half the list price. I felt that this was unfair to the customer who paid the list price. The other salesmen laughed at me and could not understand my silly attitude.

---

[10] Some people would, therefore, define behavior as really "criminal" only when it is considered so by general public opinion. According to such a definition neither violations of Prohibition laws, many types of gambling, nor similar kinds of illegal behavior should be considered as crimes. The same reasoning would be offered by those who feel that a crime has been committed only when an individual conceives of his offense as being criminal. According to this position, if persons do not think of their acts as violations of law either because of personal, situational, or occupational reasons, their acts would not be crimes no matter what the law or public opinion felt. Thus a person who refuses to register for the draft because of religious reasons, as did thousands of Jehovah's Witnesses during World War II, would not be considered a criminal even though many were sentenced to prison. Nor would a person necessarily be a criminal if he held certain political beliefs that were opposed by the majority. Many feel that statutory rape is often not criminal, since these cases, which involve sexual intercourse with girls under the age of eighteen, usually are with consent and seldom are the result of coercion. The same argument might apply to persons sentenced to prison for nonsupport of their families or for injuring someone through their negligent or drunken driving.

They told me to forget the things I had learned in school, and that you couldn't earn a pile of money by being strictly honest. When I replied that money wasn't everything they mocked at me: "Oh, no? Well, it helps." I had ideals and I resigned.

My next job was selling sewing machines. I was informed that one machine, which cost the company $18, was to be sold for $40 and another machine, which cost the company $19, was to be sold for $70, and that I was to sell the de luxe model whenever possible in preference to the cheaper model, and was given a list of the reasons why it was a better buy. When I told the sales manager that the business was dishonest and that I was quitting right then, he looked at me as if he thought I was crazy and said angrily: "There's not a cleaner business in the country."

It was quite a time before I could find another job. During this time I occasionally met some of my classmates and they related experiences similar to mine. They said they would starve if they were rigidly honest. All of them had girls and were looking forward to marriage and a comfortable standard of living, and they said they did not see how they could afford to be rigidly honest. My own feelings became less determined than they had been when I quit my first job.

Then I got an opportunity in the used-car business. I learned that this business had more tricks for fleecing customers than either of those I had tried previously. Cars with cracked cylinders, with half the teeth missing from the fly wheel, with everything wrong, were sold as "guaranteed." When the customer returned and demanded his guarantee, he had to sue to get it and very few went to that trouble and expense: the boss said you could depend on human nature. If hot cars could be taken in and sold safely, the boss did not hesitate. When I learned these things I did not quit as I had previously. I sometimes felt disgusted and wanted to quit, but I argued that I did not have much chance to find a legitimate firm. I knew that the game was rotten but it had to be played—the law of the jungle and that sort of thing. I knew that I was dishonest and to that extent felt that I was more honest than my fellows. The thing that struck me as strange was that all these people were proud of their ability to fleece customers. They boasted of their crookedness and were admired by their friends and enemies in proportion to their ability to get away with a crooked deal: it was called shrewdness. Another thing was that these people were unanimous in their denunciation of gangsters, robbers, burglars, and petty thieves. They never regarded themselves as in the same class and were bitterly indignant if accused of dishonesty; it was just good business.

Once in a while, as the years have passed, I have thought of myself as I was in college—idealistic, honest, and thoughtful of others—and have been momentarily ashamed of myself. Before long such memories became less and less frequent and it became difficult to distinguish me from my fellows. If you had accused me of dishonesty I would have denied the charge, but with slightly less vehemence than my fellow businessmen, for after all I had learned a different code of behavior.[11]

---

[11] Personal document in Sutherland, *White Collar Crime*, pp. 235–236. Copyright 1949 by Holt, Rinehart and Winston, Inc. Reissued 1961. Reprinted by special permission.

Most World War II black-market violations, involving violations of price and rationing regulations, appear to have had their origin in behavior learned in association with others.[12] Unethical and illegal practices were circulated in the trade as part of a definition of the situation, and rationalizations to support these violations of law were transmitted by this differential association. Many types of violations were picked up from conversations with businessmen and from descriptions of violations in trade newspapers and the general press. The following case illustrates, at least in part, the explanation of the violations through differential association:

> During 1942 two eastern tire salesmen were instrumental in organizing a state-wide ring which purchased, received, and transferred new rubber tires and tubes without exchanging rationing certificates. In this case the two principal defendants arranged a meeting with retail tire dealers, who later became involved also, and explained the method that they were using to transfer tires without surrendering rationing or replenishment certificates and advised them that they could get any tires they needed. The plan was to have signed blank billheads on printed stationary to be used as "sign-offs," giving the impression that the principals were bona fide agents when acquiring tires in large metropolitan centers. The tires were then sold to the retailers at a cash profit and then resold to the latter mostly in bulk sales. No certificates were to be used in transferring these tires, and no accurate records were to be kept of the transactions, since it was suggested that the retailers bill these tires to "phony" individuals or to defunct garages which had been out of business for many years. The eventual tire ring involved a large number of dealers in scattered cities and towns who disposed of thousands of tires through this illegal device.[13]

When one considers that the social background of persons engaging in white-collar crime is different from that of such types as the ordinary, habitual, or organized criminal, one might ask why such exposure to illegal norms has any effect. Sutherland has listed a number of factors which tend to isolate businessmen from unfavorable definitions of illegal activity.[14] Agencies of mass communication play up conventional crime as abhorrent but treat white-collar crime much more leniently. Also, businessmen are often shielded from severe criticism by government officials, many of whom either were formerly in business or accepted contributions from business sources. Finally, businessmen chiefly associate with other businessmen, both at work and in their social life, so that the implications of white-collar crime are shielded from objective scrutiny.

---

[12] Marshall B. Clinard, *The Black Market* (New York: Holt, Rinehart and Winston, Inc., 1952), pp. 298–313.

[13] *Ibid.*, pp. 301–302.   [14] Sutherland, *op. cit.*, pp. 247–253.

ORGANIZATION AND WHITE-COLLAR CRIME

In many areas of white-collar crime there is often considerable organization. In fee splitting, for example, there must be a reciprocal relationship between the doctors. In political corruption there is an organized tie-up with businessmen or criminal syndicates. After studying the criminal behavior of seventy large corporations, Sutherland has pointed out a number of ways in which crimes among this type of business are organized: [15]

1. The criminality of corporations is persistent. In fact, in his study he found that 97.1 percent of the corporations were repeaters.[16]

2. The illegal behavior is far more extensive than the prosecutions would indicate; in many violations they are industry-wide. The fact that there are few prosecutions is due to the differential implementation of the criminal law.

3. There is generally no loss of status by an offender among his business associates.[17] In fact, while some members of his group may look down upon his behavior, others may even admire him for it. The shrewdness of the illegal transacation in which he was involved may give him added status.

4. In those areas which immediately affect white-collar offenders there is apt to be fairly general contempt for the law, the government as a whole, and for the personnel who administer the law.

5. Most white-collar business crimes are organized in the sense that the violation is a corporation affair or may extend to several corporations or subsidiaries. The organization may be more informal, as in false advertising. The organization of white-collar crime is indicated by the selection of certain types of illegal behavior. The selection of a particular form of illegal behavior, as Sutherland points out, may be either on the basis of the smallest danger of detection and difficulty in obtaining proof, or on the basis of the firm's capacity to "fix" the case, have the law not properly enforced, or change the law itself.[18]

ROLE ORIENTATIONS

Although many cases of white-collar crime can be satisfactorily explained by a theory of differential association, particularly if there had been

---

[15] *Ibid.*, pp. 217–220.

[16] Lane, in another study of business violations, did not reach such a conclusion and states that "unlike the crime records, the records of business violation show that recidivism is infrequent."—Robert E. Lane, "Why Business Men Violate the Law," *Journal of Criminal Law and Criminology*, 44:162 (July–August, 1953).

[17] In 1961 several high executives of the leading American electric companies referred to above were sentenced to jail for serious violations of law and some also received large fines. A number who resigned from their companies within a short time were appointed to positions of nearly equal executive responsibility in other companies—*The New York Times*, June 23, 1961, p. 37.

[18] Sutherland, *op. cit.*, pp. 230–233.

continuous and intimate association with unethical and illegal differential norms and at the same time some isolation from other norms, such a general theory as an explanation for *all* cases has several limitations. Some individuals do not engage in such practices, even though they are familiar with the techniques and the rationalizations of violations and frequently associate with persons similarly familiar. It is doubtful if any businessman could be in a given line of business for any length of time, either in peacetime or in wartime, without acquiring a rather complete knowledge of the illegalities practiced in it.

Persons tend, in part, to accept or reject opportunities for white-collar crime according to their orientations toward their roles and their attitudes toward general social values. Some of these factors are negative attitudes toward other persons in general, the relative importance attached to status symbols of money as compared with law obedience, and the relative importance attached to personal, family, or business reputation.[19]

EMBEZZLEMENT AND OTHER VIOLATIONS OF TRUST

Embezzlement, a form of white-collar crime, is more common than most people assume. During 1951, for example, there were 608 reports of defalcations among banks insured by the Federal Deposit Insurance Corporation. These defalcations involved 759 persons, including 217 bank officials, 412 employees, and 130 other persons. An analysis of the irregularities showed currency manipulation, deposit manipulation, and loan manipulation as the chief violations. Some examples of such violations included mislabeling money bags of $50 in pennies as $500 in dimes, withholding deposits or making unauthorized charges to deposit accounts, extending credit to certain customers by means of unauthorized and unrecorded overdrafts, withholding interest or principal payments, forging or fabricating notes, and diverting income from service charges.[20]

Contrary to popular views and some scientific writers, white-collar crimes involving violations of trust, such as embezzlement, cannot be ex-

---

[19] Clinard, *The Black Market*. See also Lane, "Why Business Men Violate the Law," *loc. cit.*, pp. 161–163. Sutherland has stated, however, that he believes the variation in crimes of a group of corporations which he studied was not the result of personality factors.—Sutherland, *op. cit.*, p. 265. For example, corporations which have violated the antitrust laws have been doing so for over forty years. The presence of philanthropists and public-spirited citizens on boards of directors at various times has made little difference in the extent of violations. Moreover, the composition of boards of directors may vary from one concern to another and yet there are similar violations, indicating that personalities have little bearing on violation. These conclusions, however, have been reached with only preliminary research and, while true in some cases, cannot be taken as evidence that individuals have little to do with the violations.

[20] For a general account of the extent of embezzlement as well as many case histories, see Norman Jaspan with Hillel Black, *The Thief in White Collar* (Philadelphia: J. B. Lippincott Company, 1960).

plained simply by gambling, extravagant living standards, unusual family expenses, undesirable associates, inadequate income, or personality.[21] There have been a number of different classifications of embezzlers. Redden, after studying 7629 cases of embezzlement,[22] classified them into the more or less self-explanatory types of the little-fellow embezzler, the grab-and-run embezzler, the little-fellow-who-becomes-a-big-fellow embezzler, the one-hundred-thousand-dollar embezzler, the clever-account embezzler, the un-trained bookkeeper embezzler who pockets errors he makes, the prevari-cator embezzler who denies he receives goods or reports them as lost, dam-aged, or the like. Probably a more meaningful type was developed by Cressey, who used 65 cases and divided them on the basis of the systems of trust violation and on the basis of their rationalizations.[23] Thus he di-vided embezzlers into "independent businessmen," violators who were in business for themselves and who converted "deposits" which were entrusted to them for a specific purpose while at the same time maintaining their regular business. The second group was composed of the "long-term" violators or those individuals who as employed persons converted their employers' funds, or funds belonging to their employers' clients, by taking relatively small amounts over a period of time. "Absconders" were those who converted funds or property at hand and absconded with it, regardless of whether or not they were employed by the person or institution in whose trust the funds or property had been placed.

After studying 133 persons imprisoned for violations of trust as well as cases collected by others, Cressey has developed what he claims to be a universal explanation of trust violation. According to him, there are three elements which are necessary in a trust violation and all must be present: (1) opportunity and a nonsharable financial problem, (2) knowledge of how to violate, and (3) rationalizations about the violations.

First are the opportunity to commit a trust violation and the presence of what Cressey terms a nonsharable problem which, if revealed, would have lost the individual group approval: "Trusted persons become trust violators when they conceive of themselves as having a financial problem which is nonsharable." [24] These difficulties include important obligations where the status of the individual might be interfered with, a feeling of per-sonal responsibility, or a business reversal. Others involve situations where the individual is isolated from others who might help him in his financial

[21] For some beliefs along this line see Virgil W. Peterson, *Why Honest People Steal* (Chicago: Chicago Crime Commission, 1947), p. 4, and *1000 Embezzlers* (Baltimore: United States Fidelity and Guaranty Co., 1937).

[22] Elizabeth Redden, "Embezzlement: A Study of One Kind of Criminal Behavior, with Prediction Tables Based on Fidelity Insurance Records." Unpublished doctoral dissertation, University of Chicago, 1939.

[23] Donald R. Cressey, *Other People's Money* (New York: The Free Press of Glencoe, 1953).

[24] *Ibid.*, p. 30.

difficulties, situations where the person's general behavior is not approved by others, and problems arising from employer-employee relations where the individual feels underpaid or overworked, or has a "grudge."

The second aspect of a violation is the knowledge of how to violate. Trust violators are aware "that this problem can be secretly resolved by a violation of the position of financial trust." Finally, the third necessary part of a violation is the presence of acceptable explanations "which enable them to adjust their conception of themselves as users of the entrusted funds or property." The potential trust violator defines the situation through rationalizations in terms which enable him to look upon his criminality as essentially noncriminal, such as merely "borrowing," as justified, as part of the "general irresponsibility" for which he is not completely accountable, or as due to unusual circumstances which are different in his case. Both the rationalizations and the techniques for violating are acquired through differential association. Indirectly the acceptance of a position of trust carries with it some idea of possible violation through the mere fact of being bonded; moreover, there are conversations with others about violations of trust, and observance of others who are dishonest.

Unfortunately, Cressey's study describes only the process of violation and not the characteristics of a person who violates a trust obligation. Moreover, it does not tell us what specific situations are likely to be more productive of violations. Perhaps future studies will enable us to predict with some accuracy who will violate, and what situations are more likely than others to lead to violations of trust.[25]

Ordinary Criminal Careers

A criminal career more typical than any previously described is the one which moves from juvenile gang associations to adult criminal behavior of a more serious type, primarily in burglary, automobile theft, or robbery. Such a career involves early group experience with delinquent behavior patterns. These experiences are intense in the sense that effective delinquent models have been furnished to the individual. There is a continuous acquisition of techniques and rationalizations about crime, and the delinquent acts move from petty to more serious offenses. During this progression there are usually a considerable number of experiences with official agencies including the police courts, juvenile authorities, juvenile institutions, reformatories and, finally, prison. Institutional experience adds to the offender's status and sophistication and helps mold his conception of himself as a criminal. The degree of development and sophistication

---

[25] Some suggestions for the prevention of embezzlement have been given by Cressey. *ibid.*, pp. 153–157, and by Jaspan and Black, *op. cit.*, pp. 233–254.

in crime of an ordinary career, however, is much less than among professional criminals. It is for these reasons that they are termed "ordinary" criminal careers.[26] These careers, as noted in an earlier chapter, usually terminate somewhere between the early twenties and the late twenties or early thirties. This type has been referred to by Cohen and Short as those gang subcultures which carry out semiprofessional theft with a utilitarian emphasis and represent the later stages of a long history of frequent stealing which began at an early age.[27] It is likely that boys going in for these activities represent small cliques in larger gangs who are "serious minded" about their delinquency rather than being nonutilitarian and malicious. They are characterized by

   a. the use of strong-arm methods (robbery) of obtaining money.
   b. the sale of stolen articles, versus using for oneself, giving or throwing away, or returning stolen articles.
   c. stating, as a reason for continued stealing, "want things" or "need money" versus stealing for excitement, because others do it, because they like to, or for spite.[28]

A comparison of 32 Negro armed robbers with 368 other Negro offenders revealed a pattern which can be designated as an ordinary criminal career.[29] Their arrest histories showed a mean of 18.2 arrests.

> An early patterning of stealing from their parents, from school, and on the street; truancy, and suspension or expulsion from school; street fighting, association with older delinquents, and juvenile delinquent gang memberships, all were usually evident in their social backgrounds. When compared with the men in the other criminal categories it was found that there was more destruction of property in their delinquent activities, and there were more frequent fights with schoolmates, male teachers, and delinquent companions. There was a higher incidence of "mugging" and purse snatching. They had more often been the leaders of delinquent gangs, and, they claimed they were leaders because of their superior size and physical strength. . . . Criminal progression appeared to occur at a more rapid rate with an early trend toward crimes of violence—from petty thefts and playground fights, to the rolling of drunks and homosexuals, and on to holdups with such weapons as pistols and knives.[30]

As juvenile delinquents they frequently carried and used weapons of violence.

---

[26] Much the same distinction is made by Walter C. Reckless. See his chapter, "Ordinary and Professional Criminal Careers," in *The Crime Problem* (3d ed.; New York: Appleton-Century-Crofts, Inc., 1961), Chap. 9.

[27] Albert K. Cohen and James F. Short, Jr., "Research in Delinquent Subcultures," *Journal of Social Issues*, 14:20–37, No. 3 (1958).

[28] *Ibid.*, p. 13.

[29] Julian B. Roebuck and Mervyn L. Cadwallader, "The Negro Armed Robber as a Criminal Type: The Construction and Application of a Typology," *Pacific Sociological Review*, 4:21–26 (Spring, 1961).

[30] *Ibid.*, p. 24.

"Sometimes you gotta carry some heat to put the pressure on. Some people won't get up off that money less they see you are ready. The studs I ran with, Jack, had to have some kind of heat . . . knife, gun, blackjack or something." [31]

One study has described five brothers whose criminal careers cost the state of Illinois $25,000 for board alone during the total of fifty-five years they spent in institutions.[32] All five brothers started begging at around five years of age. John and Elwood, the oldest brothers, began their delinquency in company with a gang of twelve boys ranging in age from five to twelve. "Their playgrounds were the alleys, streets, and railroad yards; their activities were largely spontaneous, random, and unsupervised; simple forms of stealing were interspersed with nondelinquent activities with little realization of their moral implications." They stole all varieties of objects, most of them for fun. The more experienced and older delinquents furnished the models and encouraged the younger and less experienced to engage in more serious thefts.

The three younger brothers became involved in this network chiefly through the indoctrination of their older brothers and other boys. All moved from begging to truancy and petty stealing, then to stealing more valuable objects. All of them were arrested by the police many times from the age of five on, for wandering the streets late at night, begging and stealing. They all appeared frequently in courts on dependency and delinquency complaints and all served at least ten periods of confinement in correctional and penal institutions besides being placed on probation and parole several times.

The delinquent and criminal acts of the five brothers were not isolated acts but were rather part of the organized life of the community. Their contacts with conventional society were limited. They had intimate association with at least 250 known delinquents and criminals. "They lived in a social world in which delinquency served a dual purpose—on the one hand, it was a means by which they secured the friendly regard, approval, and approbation of their fellows, while on the other hand, it served as a source of economic gain." Their associations gave them the moral sanction to commit crime and sell their stolen articles. Edward was arrested at twenty-one for stealing a car and at twenty-four for carrying a concealed weapon, James at seventeen was arrested four times for attempted or actual theft of autos; Michael at fifteen for robbery with a gun, burglary and larceny of cars, and Carl at thirteen for the theft of two cars. Nearly all their crimes were committed in company with either a brother or a brother and other persons. All except one had terminated their criminal careers by the time they were twenty-five years of age.

---

[31] *Ibid.*

[32] Clifford R. Shaw, Henry D. McKay, and James F. McDonald, *Brothers in Crime* (Chicago: The University of Chicago Press, 1938). Quotations are from pages 109 and 119.

Organized Crime

Organized crime is represented by criminal syndicates or rings which engage in criminal activities as a career. The public bestows the epithet "mobster" or "gangster" upon those active in organized crime, even though these terms technically should be reserved for those few individuals of this group who use force and violence. Criminal syndicates are usually well organized, with a boss, lieutenants, and subaffiliates, and their operations often are of an intracity, intercity, or interstate character. The characteristic features of organized crime are these:

1. Hierarchy involving a system of specifically defined relationships with mutual obligations and privileges.
2. Not confined by political or geographic boundaries. Intracity or intercity; intra- or interstate.
3. Dependence upon
   a. the use of force and violence to maintain internal discipline and restrain competition;
   b. the securing and maintaining of permanent immunity from interference from law enforcement and other agencies of government.
4. Criminals operating for large financial gains and specializing in one or more combinations of enterprises which fall in the area of moral problems where public opinion is divided.
5. Striving for either monopolistic control or establishment of spheres of influence between or among different organizations.

FEUDAL STRUCTURE

The most important characteristic of organized crime is its feudal pattern. All-powerful "lords of the underworld" or leaders of particular syndicates have the allegiance of several underlords who, in turn, have coteries of henchmen varying from lieutenants to what might be termed "serfs." Burgess has stated that an organized crime syndicate is "held together by powerful leaders, by intense personal loyalties, by the gangsters' code of morals, by alliances and agreements with rival gangster chiefs, and by their common warfare against the forces of organized society." [33]

There are interlocking relations between one syndicate and another and between one individual leader and another so that a given syndicate or leader may be engaged in several areas of crime. These syndicates may use strong-arm techniques to enforce their rules among their own members, to eliminate other syndicates when peaceful methods have failed, and to secure the cooperation of intended victims among the general public. Al-

---

[33] Ernest W. Burgess, "Summary and Recommendations," *Illinois Crime Survey* (Chicago: Illinois Association for Criminal Justice, 1929), Pt. 3, p. 1092.

though this use of force is becoming much less a feature of organized crime than it was in the Capone era of Prohibition days, it still is a characteristic of organized as compared with professional crime.

WIDESPREAD OPERATIONS

Organized criminal operations involve branches of the syndicate as well as tie-ups with legitimate enterprises which give them public respectability and power in the community. The Senate Special Committee to Investigate Organized Crime found that organized criminals were engaged in about fifty areas of legitimate business enterprises, in particular the liquor industry, automobile and trucking business, steel, oil, banking and finance, the garment industry, juke boxes, cigarette-vending and slot machines, real estate, hotels, restaurants, night clubs, food products, and unions.[34]

In 1951 the two major crime syndicates in this country were the Accardo-Guzik-Fischetti syndicate, whose headquarters were in Chicago but whose influence was felt in Kansas City, Dallas, Miami, Las Vegas, and the West Coast, and the Costello-Adonis-Lansky syndicate, emanating from New York City, with operations in Saratoga, New Jersey, New Orleans, Miami, Las Vegas, and the West Coast.[35] Both groups had close relationships, and their leaders appeared to know one another personally.

ORGANIZED CRIME AND POLITICS

Organized crime is more than a feudal hierarchy built to carry on particular criminal activities; it is also organized to keep its members out of legal entanglements. Connections with political machines or with branches of the legal system, such as the police or courts, bring almost permanent immunity from arrest or, if there should be an arrest, enable the "fix" to be applied.

The Kefauver Committee reported in 1951 that in New York City the Gross bookmaking empire had paid over $1,000,000 a year for police protection; in Philadelphia approximately $152,000 was paid each month in thirty-eight police districts.[36] The fix is not worked out individually by each criminal when a need arises; instead, organized criminal syndicates maintain such close political connections that local immunity for their members is almost assured, especially for the top men in the syndicate.

---

[34] Third Interim Report of the Special Committee to Investigate Organized Crime in Interstate Commerce, United States Senate, 82d Cong., 1st Sess., S.R. 307 (Washington, D.C.: 1951), pp. 171–181. Also see Estes Kefauver, *Crime in America* (New York: Doubleday & Company, Inc., 1951).

[35] Third Interim Report of the Special Committee to Investigate Organized Crime in Interstate Commerce, pp. 1–2.

[36] *Ibid.*, p. 184.

The same pattern of organized crime found in large metropolitan areas exists in the medium-sized cities with similar evidence of official sanction or protection. In some cases the protection is obtained by the payment of bribes to public officials, often on a regular basis pursuant to a carefully conceived system. In other cases, the racketeering elements make substantial contributions to political campaigns of officials who can be relied upon to tolerate their activities. Sometimes these contributions will support a whole slate of officers in more than one political party, giving the racketeers virtual control of the governing body.[37]

Organized criminal syndicates maintain their close association with political machines either through direct payoffs or through delivery of votes, honest or fraudulent. The payoffs are used by politicians, police commissioners, or police captains or lieutenants either as personal assets or as contributions for the political machine. Both the contributions and the aid in delivering votes, which usually requires only the endorsement of the party by the syndicate leader in local community areas, bring immunity, either direct or indirect. Immunity also comes through the appointment of councilmen, police officers, prosecutors, judges, and other government officials who will cooperate with the leaders of organized crime and who will pass the word along that the syndicate is to be let alone. The head of the Department of Justice's Special Group on Organized Crime declared in 1960: "The underworld gets about $9 billion of the estimated $47 billion spent annually on illegal gambling. . . . Fully half of the syndicates' income from gambling is earmarked for protection money paid to police and politicians." [38]

The relation of political machines to organized crime has been repeatedly demonstrated in the past by the close relationship of Chicago Democratic and Republican organizations to various gang leaders such as Al Capone.[39] The bosses of the Chicago underworld were, first, Big Jim Colosimo, then John Torrio, Mont Tennes, Scarface Al Capone, and a host of others. Even the funerals of underworld leaders have revealed the closeness of the relation between politicians and organized criminals. In the 1920's two congressmen and seven aldermen were honorary pallbearers at Big Jim Colosimo's funeral; at Anthony D'Andrea's funeral twenty-one judges were honorary pallbearers.[40]

The Seabury investigation in New York City in 1930 and 1931 showed

---

[37] Final Report of the Special Committee to Investigate Organized Crime in Interstate Commerce, United States Senate, 82d Cong., 1st Sess., S.R. 725 (Washington, D.C.: 1951), p. 5.

[38] Quoted in Daniel P. Moynihan, "The Private Government of Crime," *The Reporter*, July 6, 1961, p. 14.

[39] Virgil W. Peterson, *Barbarians in Our Midst* (Boston: Little, Brown & Company, 1952).

[40] John Landesco, "Organized Crime," *Illinois Crime Survey*, Pt. 3, pp. 1033–1034.

that Tammany Hall controlled the judges and at the same time performed services for organized crime. James J. Hines, leader of Tammany Hall in New York City in the 1930's, had close relations with New York underworld leaders, for which he finally was sent to Sing Sing. Frank Costello, leader of an organized criminal syndicate who was later sent to prison, was found in 1950 to have been friendly with many of the district leaders of the Democratic party and with many judges in New York City. Some political appointments were Costello's friends. Asked about them, Costello replied, "I know them, know them well and maybe they got a little confidence in me." [41]

AREAS OF ORGANIZED CRIME

Organized crime largely operates in those areas which are "moral problems," areas where public sentiment is divided over the actual immorality of such behavior.[42] As a result, organized crime finds less coordinated opposition from the general public and law-enforcement agencies in these areas. Furthermore, since so many people want some of these services, the illegal revenues from them are large. It is thus possible for organized racketeers to make a substantial income and at the same time pay off properly those political officials without whose connivance no organized criminal activity could operate. Some of the more important areas in which organized crime has operated include the following: liquor, prostitution, narcotics, gambling, union shakedowns, and industrial and business shakedowns.

During Prohibition organized crime operated most extensively in prostitution and in alcohol, which largely went out with the repeal of the Prohibition Amendment, except for running liquor into some dry states. Prostitution is still a large area for racketeering but not as large or as profitable as it was formerly. It now usually involves a syndicate of many prostitutes who are chiefly "call girls" and for whom the organized syndicate helps arrange the necessary "fix" or other over-all business arrangements. Another area of organized crime has been, and still is, the drug traffic.

GAMBLING

Organized crime today finds that gambling and various forms of labor and industry racketeering bring the highest returns; hence it dominates these activities. To wager money or other objects upon an outcome which

---

[41] Third Interim Report of the Special Committee to Investigate Organized Crime in Interstate Commerce, p. 121.

[42] Richard Fuller and Richard R. Myers, "Some Aspects of a Theory of Social Problems," *American Sociological Review*, 6:24–32 (February, 1941).

largely depends on chance is gambling.[43] Gambling is illegal in nearly all parts of the United States, although most forms of gambling are legal in Nevada.

There are wide variations in the attitudes of people toward private and public gambling. Gambling among friends for small stakes in such card games as poker, blackjack, and bridge is generally not regarded as gambling which is essentially bad. When gambling becomes public and commercialized so that its operation requires bets from a great many persons in an impersonal urban situation over which the individual has practically no control, public attitudes are divided over its social usefulness; moreover, it is an inviting situation for organized racketeers.

Generally, wherever opportunities are presented for gambling, large numbers of persons are interested in participating, even though they may be publicly against it. There appear to be a number of reasons for this.[44] Gambling appeals because of the chance factor for success, regardless of the type of skill involved in it. In some societies, generally those where social status is achieved by, and depends upon, successful competition for money and material goods, the chance element is more important than in others. In Western European society it is very difficult to distinguish between situations in which there is a chance element called gambling and those situations like stock market or commodity speculations or, indeed, many other financial transactions which also contain a chance element and yet are not officially classified as forms of gambling.

Gambling also represents relief from the routine and boredom of contemporary urban life. Betting on something is often fascinating both to the participant and to the spectator. Whether one wins or not, for a while there is excitement over the possible result. The appeal of different forms of gambling varies according to social class, sex, and other differences.

In some parts of Western society opposition to commercialized gambling seems to be based on the fact that gambling does not perform any socially productive economic functions, for in a sense it is securing money without earning it through work. Moreover, the fact that some people have lost all their money through excessive gambling has stirred up much opposition to it. The odds in some forms of gambling, particularly organized gambling, are so great that the chances of winning are actually very small. Finally, because commercialized gambling must bribe law-enforcement officers and other public officials in order to secure the necessary "protection," it is opposed by many because of the effect of its methods.

---

[43] For a full discussion, see the series of articles on "Gambling," *The Annals*, Vol. 269 (May, 1950). This issue dealt with the legal status, various forms of gambling, the gambler, and gambling in foreign countries.

[44] Herbert A. Bloch, "The Sociology of Gambling," *American Journal of Sociology*, 57:215–221 (November, 1951), and David D. Allen, *The Nature of Gambling* (New York: Coward-McCann, Inc., 1952).

Commercialized gambling is of two types. In one, the person gambles in an establishment with such devices as roulette wheels, dice, or slot machines. In the other, bets are placed on larger events, such as illegal lotteries and "policy," the "numbers racket," horse or dog races, or various sports events. Policy is a variation of the lottery in that bets are placed on the drawing of numbers. The numbers racket involves a bet placed on the three digits of certain events such as, for example, the daily United States Treasury balance of clearinghouse totals or racing pari-mutuels. In both policy and the numbers racket the amount of the wager, as well as the chance of winning, is small, but the odds paid are large.

The lucrative returns from gambling enterprises make them most attractive to organized crime. A considerable organization is required to distribute forms and collect bets. In the Detroit numbers racket, which has been studied by Carlson, there were some thirty-five separate organizations, some of which were grouped into syndicates. These organizations had "cover banks" which underwrote the bets placed by the local gambling place as a protection against a run on a particular number. For efficient operation the gambling syndicate employed writers or runners, pick-up men or collectors of bets, cashiers, clerks, checkers, and operators. Tickets with winning numbers were redeemed by cashiers on the spot; if the holders were not present, the money was delivered by a runner.[45] There is also the "fix," as one New York bookmaker has stated:

> "The whole business is pretty damn complicated, let me tell you. I gotta worry about my runners so I gotta pay off beat cops, squad cars, detectives, everybody. In the last ten years I paid off $1 million to cops. It cuts into the profits, but, what the hell, a business is a business." [46]

The present-day bookmaker with whom the public deals is often nothing more than a runner or contact man who tells his customers what unlisted telephone number to use to place their bets. He gives the bettor a code, such as the cryptic words: "This is Doc for Hollywood." The bettor then simply phones his bets directly to headquarters, and the runner later settles with the bettor for his wins or losses.

Gambling interests are protected through collusion between politicians and organized criminal syndicates. In 1951 the Special Senate Committee to Investigate Organized Crime reported that the most shocking thing about organized criminal activities in gambling was "the extent of official corruption and connivance in facilitating and promoting organized crime." Top mobsters were found to be immune from prosecution, policemen and

---

[45] Gustav G. Carlson, "Number Gambling: A Study of a Culture Complex." Unpublished doctoral dissertation, University of Michigan, Ann Arbor, 1940.

[46] Roger Kahn and Richard Schaap "The Mania to Bet on Sports," *Newsweek*, June 6, 1960, p. 41. Reprinted by permission.

sheriffs were bribed, and political leaders were bought off. The committee gathered evidence of corruption of law-enforcement officers in practically all the numerous cities in which it held hearings. In New York City a threat of testimony by a bookmaker brought about the resignation of many police officials. The sheriff of the county in which Miami is located was reported to have had $2500 in assets when elected, and six years later $75,000; one deputy testified that another deputy had delivered a $36,000 pay-off from gamblers to the sheriff's wife.

Betting on horse races began as a personal type of gambling, later shifted to clubs and county fairs, and now operates almost exclusively in a complex urban environment, largely indulged in by millions of urban persons who seldom see horses, let alone horse races. Although several states permit pari-mutuel betting at race tracks, almost every state prohibits absentee betting through bookmakers. In many states, regardless of whether pari-mutuel betting is legal or not, absentee betting through organized criminal syndicates constitutes a large-scale violation of law.

In many large cities, as well as elsewhere, some bookmakers specialize in bets on other events—professional boxing matches, baseball, hockey, and professional or amateur football and basketball games. Formerly the betting was concentrated on professional events, but college football and basketball games have drawn more and more of it. In fact, one reason given for canceling the Army–Notre Dame football game series in 1948 was the extremely heavy betting, one estimate on the gamblers' pay-off wires being as high as $15,000,000 to $20,000,000. Investigations have also revealed extensive syndicated betting on college basketball games in Madison Square Garden in New York. In 1951 a series of gambling cases involved a large number of star basketball players of four New York colleges, a midwestern, and a southern university, who were bribed either to throw important games or to keep the point score within a range designated by gambling syndicates. The usual price received by these college athletes was $500 to $1500 a game. A similar series of cases occurred in 1961. (See page 171.)

In 1951 the Special Senate Committee to Investigate Crime found that organized criminals derive enormous profits from gambling. The "take" on a slot machine is about $50 a week; thus a mere two hundred machines would bring in $10,000 weekly. A single one of the eight large policy wheels in Chicago made an annual net profit of over $1,000,000. One New Jersey gambling casino made over $250,000 a year; another, in Florida, $205,000; and a Kansas City newsstand handbook, $100,000. According to a 1960 survey, week-end bets alone on football, baseball, basketball, horse racing, and boxing were as follows:

Football: On a typical fall week end, with 30 to 35 college and professional football games on the bookmakers' boards, the illegal betting (the "handle") fluctuates between $50 million and $60 million.

Baseball: Throughout the summer, with sixteen or more major-league games scheduled each week end, the handle runs between $40 million and $50 million.

Basketball: On a Friday–Saturday week end, with a full schedule of 40 college and professional games, the basketball handle approaches $15 million, but is gradually slipping. The reason: suspected fixes.

Horse Racing: Except for special races (off-track betting on the Kentucky Derby may exceed $30 million), the racing handle is roughly $25 million on any week end. As a twelve-month, daily enterprise, racing has the largest illegal handle of any sport.

Boxing: Except for a heavyweight championship fight, two-day action rarely exceeds $2 million. Boxing has lost much of its betting appeal in the sport's general decline.[47]

Some people believe that the solution to illegal gambling in the United States is to legalize it as it is in Nevada. Most countries have state lotteries, sweepstakes, or other forms of betting which bring in much revenue for the state after the winners are paid off. Sweden, for example, legalized betting on sports pools in 1934, the betting being supervised by a corporation consisting of members of several sports organizations. Some of the revenue is used for such organizations and for expenses, but the largest share goes to the government.

There is some question as to whether commercialized gambling could be legalized throughout the United States. Most but not all students of the problem believe that legalization is not the solution.[48] They argue that it would be too large an enterprise for the government and, in the long run, would add nothing to the economy even if it did produce revenue. In other countries gambling has not been associated with organized crime; in fact, most European countries do not have this type of crime. Legalized gambling in the United States might tend to become infiltrated by the same criminal elements that now control illegal gambling, as has happened to a considerable extent in Nevada.[49] Moreover, politicians and public officials would be even more vulnerable to corruption. Finally, the American people, on the whole, do not participate in commercialized forms of gambling, according to a Gallup poll taken in 1951.[50] Should gambling be legalized they might engage in it more extensively than they do now, or than is done in countries where gambling is legal.

Probably the most effective way to deal with gambling in the United States is to develop in the public a realization not only of the effects of

---

[47] Kahn and Schaap, *loc. cit.*, p. 39.

[48] See, for example, Virgil W. Peterson, "Gambling: Should It Be Legalized?" *Journal of Criminal Law and Criminology,* 40:259–329 (September, 1949), and Allen, *op. cit.*

[49] See Kefauver, *op. cit.*, pp. 229–237.

[50] Public Opinion News Service, June 11, 1951, American Institute of Public Opinion, Princeton, N.J. Cited in Herbert L. Marx ed., *Gambling in America* (New York: The H. W. Wilson Company, 1952), p. 26.

commercialized gambling on law-enforcement personnel and other public officials but of the need for stronger enforcement of the laws against gambling. The states will need help from the federal government, which can give it because commercialized gambling is interstate. Since 1951, for example, there has been a federal tax on bookmakers amounting to 10 percent of the gross bets each month and a $50 tax on those who accept bets. Finally, federal lotteries might succeed in diverting some illegal betting, but their use would present many difficulties. In 1961 three new federal laws were passed making it a federal crime to

1. cross state lines or use the mails to distribute the proceeds of gambling, prostitution, narcotics, or illegal liquor sales. The law was aimed at "absentee" organized criminals who operate outside the jurisdiction of state officials. Violators face a maximum sentence of five years in jail and a $10,000 fine.
2. carry or send across state lines records, ticket slips or other data used in bookmaking, the numbers racket, or sports wagering pools. Exempted were betting slips sent to Nevada, a state where gambling is legal, and pari-mutuel tickets used at tracks where betting is legal.
3. use such communication facilities as cables, telephones, or the telegraph to transmit across state lines any information useful to gamblers. Common carriers under the jurisdiction of the Federal Communications Commission must withdraw service from subscribers known to be using the facility for gambling.

RACKETEERING IN LABOR UNIONS AND BUSINESS

Second only to gambling in its attractiveness to organized crime is racketeering in labor unions and business. The term "racketeering" is often loosely used to refer to almost any criminal activity. In a strict sense, however, it refers to the use of organized force to maintain control over some organization, to extort money from it, or to force some services upon it. Racketeering has been used to maintain control of the members of a union or to defeat another union which is competing with it for members. In business racketeering, efforts are made to force concerns to pay tribute to "protect" themselves from violence, such as damaging clothes in a cleaning and dyeing establishment, or to maintain price fixing. Tribute may also be demanded to avoid a wildcat strike. Although racketeering activities have affected many industries, they have been particularly prevalent in the movies, building trades, liquor, laundry and cleaning establishments, and the waterfront, trucking, and loading businesses.[51] Senate investigations of the relation of certain union officials with organized criminals have in recent years brought this area of organized crime particularly to the

[51] Malcolm Johnson, *Crime on the Labor Front* (New York: McGraw-Hill Book Company, Inc., 1950).

public's attention.[52] The New York water front, for example, has a long history of domination by labor racketeers, and repeated attempts on the part of local and state officials to control this situation in the past have proved unsuccessful. Investigations in 1953 indicated that the average pier boss is largely "responsible for the crime and corruption on the water-front." [53] The pier boss usually operates from his position within the union, and his "ultimate power rests in his control of some number of the locals that supply the dock-wallopers to the stevedoring concerns." He has close connections with the underworld, and "in some instances his rise to power has been sponsored by unscrupulous management officials. Connivance with such individuals has also been necessary, at times, to insure the retention of his position. More than one industry spokesman has openly boasted that such men are good for the waterfront because they 'keep the dock-walloper in his place and maintain order.' "

Racketeers in unions and businesses may use overt force in the form of property damage or physical violence to intimidate; or they may be more subtle and simply threaten a strike. Hostetter has distinguished two types of rackets, the simon-pure collusive and the collusive agreement.[54] The former is usually a one-man operation in which an individual coerces a business firm into cooperating. For example, the notorious racketeer Bioff, a high official of a motion-picture union, shook down certain Hollywood producers on threat of a strike. The collusive agreement is a much more complex operation and generally involves a criminal syndicate. Here a hierarchy of henchmen may maintain a certain leadership in control of a union, or may force certain retail outlets to pay a money tribute or to purchase a designated commodity, on the threat of destroying their merchandise or equipment. In return for acquiescence in its demands the syndicate may offer to "protect" members of a given trade association not only from outside forces but even from unfair competition in their own field, thus providing something in return for its exactions.

There are two types of rackets in business, monopoly and association.[55] The monopoly, with the aid of politicians, coerces businessmen to buy through an unnecessary middleman. An association type of racketeering denotes just that, businessmen being forced to join an association and pay dues to it in order to be protected from violence. In its more extreme form "the association" may also control and fix prices in order to avoid price cutting. The Special Senate Committee to Investigate Organized

---

[52] See Robert Kennedy, *The Enemy Within* (New York: Harper & Row, Publishers, 1960).

[53] George C. Wright, "The Boss on the Pier: Waterfront Portraits," *The New York Times*, January 25, 1953, sec. 4.

[54] Gordon L. Hostetter and Thomas Q. Beesley, *It's a Racket!* (Chicago: Les Quin Books. Inc., 1929), p. 4.

[55] Murray L. Gurfein, "Racketeering," *Encyclopedia of the Social Sciences* (New York: The Macmillan Company, 1934), VII, 45–46.

Crime reported that in "some instances legitimate businessmen had aided the interests of the underworld by awarding lucrative contracts to gangsters and mobsters in return for help in handling employees, defeating attempts at organization, and in breaking strikes. And the committee has had testimony showing that unions are used in the aid of racketeers and gangsters, particularly on the New York water front." [56]

It is extremely difficult for law-enforcement officers to control such activities. Seldom has prosecution been as successful as that of District Attorney Thomas E. Dewey in the convictions of many racketeers in New York City in the 1930's. Intimidation through fear of violence, the tie-ups among politicians, police, and organized criminals, the "fix," the difficulty of securing legal evidence, and inadequate laws interfere with the successful prosecution of racketeering. Occasionally businessmen have banded together to form a crime commission, as in the case of Chicago, and to resist racketeering pressure more effectively through the threat of publicity.

ORGANIZED CRIME AS A CAREER

The feudal organization of a crime syndicate makes generalization about the backgrounds of its members difficult. Many have histories similar to the ordinary criminal career, in which there is progression in a long series of delinquencies and crime and of association with a tough gang of young offenders. Instead of ending their careers in their twenties, however, they have continued their criminal activities in association with some syndicate. One significant factor in this continuance is their habituation to crime, which means that they may attach themselves to criminal groups as conditions seem suitable. "Organized crime, manifesting itself in gangs and in the larger structures within which gangs function, may be regarded as the result of a process of sifting and selection whose final product is a criminal residue." [57]

The delinquent gang of the slum produces the adult "gangster" who uses strong-arm methods and is employed for this very purpose by the organized criminal groups. Gangsters usually come from our large cities, frequently have long criminal records of armed robberies, and have a conception of themselves as "tough." Those who are successful in the syndicate sometimes take it over.

In many instances organized criminal machines have called upon the services of gangsters for protective or offensive operations only to have the

---

[56] Third Interim Report of the Special Committee to Investigate Organized Crime in Interstate Commerce, p. 5. Also see Wright, "The Boss on the Pier," *loc. cit.*

[57] Alfred R. Lindesmith, "Organized Crime," *The Annals*, 217:123 (September, 1941). Also see life history of a gangster in John Landesco's "The Gangster's Apologia Pro Vita Sua," in *Illinois Crime Survey*, Pt. 3, pp. 1043–1057.

gangsters take over the operations themselves. In other instances gangsters have been content to be on the payroll of a prosperous organization and to get a considerable cut of the profits without assuming full control. Gangsters are usually recruited from the slums of American cities. They have come up through the sand lots of crime and have made crime their career. Most of them have been members of small boys' gangs and have graduated to larger boys' gangs and later to affiliation with organized crime and political machines. They have made themselves useful to both political machines and organized crime. The gangster is the toughest of American criminals and invariably his is a blatant career of criminal activity.[58]

The Professional Offender

Of all criminal offenders the "professionals" have the most highly developed criminal career, social status, and skill. The use of the respected term "professional" to apply to criminal activities requires some explanation. The characteristics of any professional man, whether a doctor, an accountant, a lawyer, a professor, or a professional criminal, involve differential association, technical skill, consensus, organization, and status.[59] Since the professional criminal has all these attributes, the designation "professional" can be challenged only on the basis that a term carrying with it such high status is applied to an activity whose ends are hardly legitimate.

Professional criminals as a group engage in a variety of highly specialized crimes. They develop a great deal of skill in a particular type of offense. Their activities include pickpocketing (cannon), shoplifting (the boost), sneak-thieving from stores, banks, and offices (the heel), stealing from jewelry stores by substituting inferior jewelry for valuable ones (penny-weighting), stealing from hotel rooms (hotel prowling), and a variety of miscellaneous rackets such as passing illegal checks (hanging paper), and extorting money from others engaged in illegal activities (the shake). These professional criminals seldom use force in connection with their activities, as is done in the "heavy rackets," although occasionally certain of them, particularly bank robbers and safe-crackers, are professionals.

Confidence games are divided into the "short con" and the "big con." In the former, money is secured illegally from an individual directly and in a brief time, through the sale, for example, of false jewelry. The "big con" usually requires a longer period of time and involves a larger sum of money, which is secured, for example, through the operation of a

---

[58] Reckless, *op. cit.*, 3d ed., p. 203. Reprinted by permission of Appleton-Century-Crofts, Inc.

[59] Edwin H. Sutherland, *The Professional Thief* (Chicago: The University of Chicago Press, 1937), p. 197. Written by a professional thief and annotated and interpreted by Sutherland.

"money-making machine" or the sale of fraudulent securities. These professionals, particularly those operating in the "big con," must be highly intelligent, well organized, and able to "fix" law-enforcement agencies. These abilities account, in part, for the fact that few confidence men ever go to prison or are even brought to trial. A great asset of the "con" man is the fact that his victim is often also out to violate the law, either in accepting the illegal proposition of the confidence man or engaging in illegal activity to raise money for the confidence game. Probably 90 percent of the victims, therefore, never complain to the police.

One of the most famous of all confidence men was "Yellow Kid" Weil, who is estimated to have made some $8,000,000 in a variety of swindles over a lifetime.[60] Weil, who was always well dressed, wore yellow gloves. He specialized in the sale of stolen and fraudulent securities, as well as in "money-making" machines and other devices. Because of his ability to fix his cases, the "Yellow Kid" was rarely arrested and served only one prison term, five years in Leavenworth, in a lifetime of criminal activities. Maurer has sketched the steps in rackets such as the "Yellow Kid" used:

1. Locating and investigating a well-to-do-victim. (Putting the mark up.)
2. Gaining the victim's confidence. (Playing the con for him.)
3. Steering him to meet the inside man. (Roping the mark.)
4. Permitting the inside man to show him how he can make a large amount of money dishonestly. (Telling him the tale.)
5. Allowing the victim to make a substantial profit. (Giving him the convincer.)
6. Determining exactly how much he will invest. (Giving him the breakdown.)
7. Sending him home for this amount of money. (Putting him on the send.)
8. Playing him against a "big store" (a false permanent setup with props and assistants, often in a store, to convince the victim) and fleecing him. (Taking off the touch.)
9. Getting him out of the way as quietly as possible. (Blowing him off.)
10. Forestalling action by the law. (Putting in the fix.) [61]

SOCIAL ROLE

Highly skilled criminal activities, however, do not alone make a criminal a professional, for even more important are other characteristics of his social role. In terms of social role, according to Sutherland, "a person who is received in the group and recognized as a professional thief is a professional thief." This role is the result of extensive contacts with others. Professional thieves have in common "acquaintances, congeniality, sym-

---

[60] Joseph R. Weil, "Yellow Kid" Weil (as told to W. T. Brannon; New York: A. S. Barnes and Company, 1948).
[61] David W. Maurer, The Big Con (New York: Pocket Books, Inc., 1949), pp. 3-4.

pathy, understandings, agreements, rules, codes of behavior, and language." [62]

In comparison with other offenders, an extremely high degree of consensus exists among professional criminals. Professional criminals develop common attitudes toward themselves, toward their crimes, and toward their common enemy, the police. These common attitudes include the support of other thieves in order to overcome the ostracism of conventional society. Other thieves help the individual to find solace and rationalizations for his behavior. The group gives him a cultural situation in which to carry on his social existence and a group of values held in common by all thieves. More specifically, the relationships among professional criminals are characterized by a "code of honor." In a sense this corresponds to the code of ethics and standards governing conduct in the more respectable professions. A professional thief, for example, is always punctual about his obligations and appointments. He must never "squeal" on another member of the profession. In fact, a professional thief will endure severe punishment rather than inform on another. There is considerable agreement on this rule, for it is supported by loyalty and identification with other thieves. It is also supported by certain motives of self-interest, including loss of prestige, danger of reprisal, and the difficulty of finding other thieves with whom to work if one fails to live up to the code of honor among them.

Probably the best example of consensus in any profession, including professional crime, is the special language or argot by which members communicate with one another in a separate set of symbols. Various academic departments—sociology is one example—have separate symbols for conversation, as do the medical and legal professions.

This language is not employed to hide anything, for its use in public would attract considerable attention among laymen. It is handed down from one generation to another; hence many of the terms used by professional criminals, like the terms used by doctors, can be traced back several hundred years.[63] Hundreds of terms are used and understood by professional criminals, but rarely by other criminals. Their argot refers to other criminals, the rackets, the public, law-enforcement officers, and many other aspects of their lives.

Bandhouse (n): House of correction or workhouse.
Big-time (adj): Theft in which preparations are elaborate and prospective gains large.
Boost (n): The racket of shoplifting.
Cannon (n): The pickpocket racket; a member of a mob engaged in the racket of picking pockets.
Clip (v): Steal from, beat.

---

[62] Sutherland, *op. cit.*, pp. 207, 4.
[63] Sutherland, *op. cit.* Also see Eric Partridge, *A Dictionary of Slang and Unconventional English* (New York: The Macmillan Company, 1950).

Fix (v): Arrange immunity for a thief on a criminal charge.

Fix (n): The act of arranging immunity; one who arranges immunity.

Hang paper (v): Write fradulent checks.

Hook (n): A member of a pickpocket mob who extracts the pocketbook from the pocket of the victim.

Inside man (n): A member of a confidence mob to whom a victim is brought.

Moll-buzzer (n): One who steals from pockets of women.

Poke (n): Pocketbook.

Push grift (n): Theft in a crowd by pickpockets.

Score (n): Successful theft, referring to the value of the stolen property.

Slave (n): A workingman, wage earner.

Sucker (n): Victim; anyone who is not a thief.[64]

ROLE SKILLS OF A PROFESSIONAL CRIMINAL

In addition to tutelage, however, the new recruit for professional crime must develop certain abilities. He must demonstrate such role attributes as "front," wits, talking ability, honesty, nerves, determination, and reliability, for without these qualities he could never be a successful thief. Sutherland writes the following about a professional thief:

> Chic Conwell was an attractive person. A friend made the comment: "Chic was a confidence man and a good one. A good confidence man must have something lovable about him." He could have passed readily as a lawyer, a banker, or a merchant so far as personal appearance and casual conversation were concerned. He had the initiative, ingenuity, and abilities that are characteristic of leaders. He was near the top of his profession.[65]

Without association and tutelage with other professional thieves, the mere possession of certain abilities would be insufficient, for specific knowledge of professional crime must be transmitted to the individual. As in all professions, a certain amount of withdrawal from association with others occurs, as well as a maximum of participation with those of one's own group.

HIGH STATUS OF PROFESSIONAL CRIME

The high status of professional criminals is reflected by the attitudes of other criminals and by the special treatment usually accorded them by the police, court officials, and others. This social status of the professional criminal is the result of several factors including "technical skill, financial standing, connections, power, dress, manners, and wide knowledge acquired in his migratory life." [66] Offenders of lower status groups tend to

---

[64] Edwin H. Sutherland, *The Professional Thief* (Chicago: The University of Chicago Press, 1937), pp. 235–243. Copyright 1937 by the University of Chicago.

[65] *Ibid.*, p. ix.   [66] *Ibid.*, p. 200.

look up to the professional, whereas professional thieves are contemptuous of amateurs and have many epithets for them, such as "snatch-and-grab thief," "boot-and-shoe thief," and "best-hold cannon." A professional thief has nothing in common with those who commit sexual or other emotional crimes, and he would not even be courteous to them if he chanced to meet them in jail. He also has little in common with an occasional or ordinary offender, other than sympathy for a fellow lawbreaker, for they would seldom have common acquaintances or similar techniques of stealing.

Evidence of social gradations within the profession appears to be contradictory. Some professional thieves state that there are no gradations, but others make a division within professional theft into "big-time" and "small-time" thieves, according to the size of the theft involved, the complexity of the preparations, and the status of the connections. One professional criminal has written:

> While he is undoubtedly a professional thief, I should a few years ago (before he was committed to prison) have been ashamed to be seen on the street with him. I say this not out of a spirit of snobbishness but simply because for business reasons I feel that my reputation would have suffered in the eyes of my friends to be seen in the company of a booster (shoplifter).[67]

A COMPLEX OF TECHNIQUES

The professional's time is spent in planning and carrying out crimes, disposing of stolen goods, "fixing" cases in the event of arrest, and, finally, developing other useful skills and techniques to add to those he possesses. He has been highly trained by other professionals and frequently the techniques he uses have a long history.[68]

The newcomer in the profession is first given preliminary instruction about the crime. His first efforts are made in a minor capacity, and he is given the kind of assistance he would later resent. If he does these minor assignments well, he is promoted to more important ones. During this probationary period he is taught the morality and etiquette of his profession. He acquires "larceny sense," learns how to dispose of stolen goods, and how to "fix" cases. He builds up associations with other criminals and the appropriate public officials. If successful, he is admitted to full status with other thieves.

How to arrange the "fix" is one of the more skilled techniques which the professional criminal learns: how to keep out of prison by knowing

---

[67] *Ibid.*, p. 201.
[68] Arthur V. Judges, *The Elizabethan Underworld* (London: Routledge & Kegan Paul, Ltd., 1930).

how to have the case dismissed or have no disposition entered; how to secure the unwilling assistance of the victim, witnesses, police, court clerks,
jury, prosecutor, judge, and others in order to escape a conviction. Some
work through a "fixer" with connections, whereas others use direct bribery,
restore the stolen property, jump a small bail bond, or buy off the victim.
Often subtle legal procedures are resorted to, such as the use of a writ
of habeas corpus.

ORGANIZATION OF PROFESSIONAL CRIME

Although professional crime is not characterized by the same degree of
formal organization as is organized crime, there is a system of extensive
informal unity and reciprocal relations among thieves. In fact, the system
consists of the whole complex of techniques, status, consensus, and differential association among thieves. Each professional thief, because of his extensive mobility, is known personally by a large number of professional
thieves. He not only knows thieves in other cities but usually knows them
by a nickname—Yellow Kid, Curly, or Chic. Information regarding methods and situations becomes known and shared by all professionals, as is
illustrated by phrases such as "Toledo is a good town," "The lunch hour
is the best time to work that spot," "Look out for the red-haired saleslady
—she's double smart," and "See Skid if you should get a tumble in Chicago." Likewise, any thief will assist another if he is in difficulty. A professional thief may warn another, or he may take up a collection to help
a thief who is in jail or to assist the man's family. Although these services
may be reciprocal, they are not performed with this purpose in mind.

Summary

Career criminals identify themselves with crime, have a conception of
themselves as criminals, have extensive association with criminal activities,
and have progressed in criminal techniques and in the frequency of offenses.
Crime is a chief source of income. Career criminals, who are largely of the
group type of offender, are the ordinary, the organized, and the professional.

Habitual petty offenders have had long criminal careers, but their
criminal pattern is complicated by certain life organizations and conceptions of themselves. White-collar offenders are largely products of differential association, but in some instances it is important to take into account
their role organization. There is considerable organization in white-collar
crime. A white-collar offender does not generally conceive of himself as a
criminal. Violations of trust appear to be products of opportunity and the
existence of a nonsharable problem, along with the knowledge of how to
violate and rationalizations about the violation.

In ordinary criminal careers the offender moves from juvenile gang associations to adult criminal behavior of a more serious type. There is a continuous acquisition of techniques and rationalizations about crime.

Organized crime is a feudal structure involving widespread criminal operations, often of an interstate nature. There is a close relation between organized crime and political corruption. Areas of organized crime are largely those in which public sentiments are divided over the actual immorality of the behavior. Gambling today is one of the chief areas of organized crime. Professional criminals are characterized by a high degree of differential association, technical skill, consensus, organization, and status.

Selected Readings

BLOCH, HERBERT A. "The Sociology of Gambling," *American Journal of Sociology*, 57:215–221 (November, 1951). An analysis of the function of gambling in a society and the reasons for opposition to gambling in Western European society.

CLINARD, MARSHALL B. *The Black Market*. New York: Holt, Rinehart and Winston, Inc., 1952. A study of price and rationing violations during World War II and an explanation of this white-collar crime.

CLINARD, MARSHALL B. "Rural Criminal Offenders," *American Journal of Sociology*, 50:38–45 (July, 1944). One of the few studies made of rural property offenders. They were found to be chiefly occasional offenders.

CRESSEY, DONALD R. *Other People's Money*. New York: The Free Press of Glencoe, 1953. A study of 133 violators of trust, primarily embezzlers, in which a universal explanation was suggested for this kind of criminal behavior.

GIBNEY, FRANK. *The Operators*. New York: Harper & Row, Publishers, 1960. A highly readable account of white-collar crime which originally appeared as a series in *Life* magazine.

HERLING, JOHN. *The Great Price Conspiracy: The Story of the Antitrust Violations in the Electrical Industry*. Washington: Robert B. Luce, Inc., 1962. A detailed and comprehensive analysis of probably the most important case of white collar crime. In this study of antitrust violations in the electrical industry use was made of Senate committee investigations, court records, and interviews.

KEFAUVER, ESTES. *Crime in America*. New York: Doubleday & Company, Inc., 1951. A nation-wide investigation of organized crime was conducted by a United States Senate committee during 1951, many of the hearings being televised. Senator Kefauver, who was chairman of the committee, writes of the findings of this investigation.

KENNEDY, ROBERT. *The Enemy Within*. New York: Harper & Row, Publishers, 1960. Describes the findings of the Senate investigations of the connections of certain labor unions with organized criminals.

MAURER, DAVID W. *The Big Con*. New York: Pocket Books, Inc., 1949. Originally published in 1940 by Bobbs-Merrill Company. An excellent description of the activities of confidence men by a professor of English who had a particular interest in their special vocabulary.

PETERSON, VIRGIL W. *Barbarians in Our Midst.* Boston: Little, Brown & Company, 1952. An account by the Operating Director, Chicago Crime Commission, of organized crime in Chicago and its relation to politics.

RECKLESS, WALTER C. *The Crime Problem.* 3d ed. New York: Appleton-Century-Crofts, Inc., 1961. See Chaps. 10 and 11 for a comprehensive discussion of white-collar, organized, and professional crime. In the chapter dealing with white-collar crime the author discusses the issue of considering white-collar violations as crimes.

SHAW, CLIFFORD R. *The Jack Roller.* Chicago: The University of Chicago Press, 1930. A life history and analysis of a delinquent.

SHAW, CLIFFORD R. *The Natural History of a Delinquent Career.* Chicago: The University of Chicago Press, 1931. A life history and analysis of a delinquent career.

SHAW, CLIFFORD R., HENRY D. MC KAY, and JAMES F. MC DONALD. *Brothers in Crime.* Chicago: The University of Chicago Press, 1938. In these well-known life histories the process of development of the ordinary criminal career is outlined. Each life history is analyzed.

SUTHERLAND, EDWIN H. *The Professional Thief.* Chicago: The University of Chicago Press, 1937. This account of stealing as a profession was written by a professional thief and analyzed by Sutherland.

SUTHERLAND, EDWIN H. *White Collar Crime.* New York: Holt, Rinehart and Winston, Inc., 1949, reissued 1960. Chapters 13 and 14 deal with white-collar crime as organized crime and present a general theory of white-collar crime.

Drug Addiction

Men have used drugs for centuries. Opium, which is easily grown from a poppy, was and is, in its various forms, the most widely used drug, not only in Europe and America but particularly in the Orient.[1] Its early use in medical treatment helped to spread it. Two important drugs were derived from opium: morphine, a potent drug, in 1804; and heroin, about three times as powerful as morphine, in 1898. These drugs, as well as opium, which could be smoked or drunk, became widely used in America in the nineteenth century, when many of them could be easily purchased.

According to Lindesmith, the public's attitude toward drug users was different then from that of today.[2] Although the use of drugs was not approved, there was considerable tolerance about it, drug addiction was regarded as a personal problem, and in general drug addicts were pitied. It was later that they came to be regarded as derelict characters, most people associating addiction with criminal behavior. This change in the public attitude was partly due to the prevalence of opium smoking among the criminal underworld in the nineteenth century.

The Harrison Act, passed in 1914, strictly regulated opiates and cocaine. This legislation, and subsequent statutes, made the sale and use of such drugs and marihuana illegal without a doctor's prescription.[3] Actually, it made drug users "criminals," and drugs something mysterious and evil, further influencing public attitudes against their use and making it difficult for persons to secure or use them without associating with other drug users. Within recent years the use of drugs by juveniles has created even greater public concern. In fact, the Federal Narcotics Control Act of 1956 imposes a severe penalty for selling, bartering, or transferring any

---

[1] According to a British government report in 1960, Hong Kong had an estimated 250,000 drug addicts, or one in every twelve of that British colony's population. A bill has been introduced into the Legislative Council to establish treatment centers where an addict would be able voluntarily to obtain treatment. Under present legislation an addict would have to commit a crime and be arrested before being sent to a hospital.

[2] Alfred R. Lindesmith, *Opiate Addiction* (Bloomington: University of Indiana Press, 1947), p. 183.

[3] See Donald J. Cantor, "The Criminal Law and the Narcotics Problem," *Journal of Criminal Law, Criminology and Police Science,* 51:512–527 (January–February, 1961).

narcotic drug or marihuana to a person under eighteen. If the offender is himself over eighteen a sentence of from ten to forty years' imprisonment is mandatory in addition to a possible fine of $20,000.

The Effect of Drugs

According to the federal statutes, a drug addict is any person who "habitually uses any habit-forming narcotic drug as defined . . . so as to endanger the public morals, health, safety, or welfare, or who is or has been so far addicted to the use of such habit-forming narcotic drugs as to have lost the power of self-control with reference to his addiction." [4]

Although habit-forming narcotic drugs include many compounds, addiction is generally from morphine and heroin, which are derived from opium, and cocaine and marihuana.[5] From the standpoint of physiological effect, these drugs fall roughly into two categories, the depressants and the stimulants. As their names imply, depressants decrease mental and physical activity in varying degrees, depending upon the dosage, whereas the stimulants excite and sustain activity and diminish symptoms of fatigue.

The most important depressant drugs are marihuana, morphine, and heroin. Marihuana (or marijuana), which is derived from the hemp plant and often known as "Indian hemp," is usually inhaled by smoking specially prepared cigarettes called "reefers." Although there is some controversy about the effects of marihuana, it is not usually considered by investigators in this country as a real form of narcotic addiction. The usual effect is giggling and laughter, accompanied by a distorted sense of time and space, but there are no unpleasant aftereffects and little physical dependence upon the drug. It has been said that it is easier to quit smoking marihuana than to quit smoking cigarettes. Although the prolonged use of marihuana in this country is an exception rather than the rule, it often serves as a preliminary to heroin or morphine addiction, particularly for juveniles.

The other depressant drugs most commonly used—morphine and heroin—account for the greatest proportion of drug addiction in the United States. A study of 1036 addicts, patients at the United States Public Health Service Hospital at Lexington, Kentucky, showed that morphine was the drug most often used first, most preferred, and also the last used. Other drugs used are also listed in Table 11.1.

Morphine, a white powder derived from opium, ranks highest in usage, and heroin is next. They are most frequently taken by injections either subcutaneously or directly into the vein. Almost immediately after the injection of either drug the person becomes flushed and he experiences a mild itching and tingling. Gradually he becomes drowsy and relaxed and

[4] *Code of Laws of the United States of America*, sec. 221, Title 21.
[5] See Nathan B. Eddy, "The History of the Development of Narcotics," *Law and Contemporary Problems*, 22:3–9 (Winter, 1957).

enters a state of reverie. Soon this state of euphoria is reached only with larger injections of the drug. Thus the addict builds up his tolerance for the drug as well as his dependence upon it. As this tolerance builds up, the addict becomes comparatively immune to the toxic manifestations of the drug. With morphine, for example, the tolerance may be as high as seventy-eight grains in sixteen hours, a dosage strong enough to kill twelve or more unaddicted persons. The safe therapeutic dosage of morphine given in hospitals is usually considered to be about one grain in the same period of time.

Table 11.1. Drugs Used First and Last, and Drug Preferred
by 1036 Patients at the United States Public Health
Service Hospital at Lexington

Drugs	First used	Preferred	Last used
Morphine	63.1%	67.3%	50.7%
Opium smoking	14.7	6.9	3.0
Heroin	12.3	23.2	43.3
Cocaine	4.8	0.7	0.2
Opium, orally	2.5	0.5	1.3
Others	2.0	0.7	0.8
No record, or no drug used	0.6	0.7	0.7
Total	100.0%	100.0%	100.0%

SOURCE: Michael J. Pescor, "A Statistical Analysis of the Clinical Records of Hospitalized Drug Addicts," *Public Health Reports,* Supplement 143 (1938), Appendix, p. 24.

The heroin or morphine addict becomes dependent upon his injections over a varying length of time, usually quite short, the addiction increasing slowly in intensity thereafter. Authorities are generally agreed that this dependence is favored more by the regularity of administration than by the amount of the drug or the method of administration. The addict becomes as dependent on drugs as he is on food, and if he is receiving his usual daily supply he is not readily recognized as an addict. Even intimate friends and family may not know of the addiction. If the individual does not receive this daily supply, however, clearly characteristic symptoms, referred to as withdrawal distress or the abstinence syndrome, will appear within approximately ten to twelve hours. He may become nervous and restless, he may develop acute stomach cramps, and his eyes may water and his nose run. Later he stops eating and he may vomit frequently, develop diarrhea, lose weight, and suffer muscular pains in the back and legs. During this period the "shakes" may develop, and if the addict cannot get relief by obtaining drugs he is in for harrowing mental and physical tortures. Consequently, an addict will go to almost any lengths to obtain a supply of drugs to relieve the suffering of withdrawal distress. Once the drugs are obtained, he appears normal again within about thirty minutes.

Cocaine is the best-known stimulant drug, but it is not as popular now as it once was. Taken intravenously, this drug produces pleasurable sensations, described by addicts as similar to sexual orgasm. The pleasurable sensations, however, are so fleeting that repeated doses must be taken to recapture them. These cumulative dosages often result in such disagreeable symptoms as heavy perspiration, trembling hands, and even, occasionally, convulsions. Hallucinations may occur, and those who become addicted to this drug may develop delusions of persecution; hence the cocaine addict is potentially dangerous.

This physiological and psychological dependence on drugs, with the stage being set for the withdrawal syndrome, makes the drug addict a serious problem, both for himself and for society. As tolerance for the drug is developed and more and more must be taken to relieve the physiological and psychological symptoms of withdrawal distress, the habit is well established. It is difficult, if not impossible, to break the habit. A Bureau of Naroctics agent once said, "When you're hooked your chances are 10,000 to 1 of ever snapping out of it." It is generally said that only a negligible number of addicts have been known to break their habit "cold," "riding out" the tortures of the withdrawal syndrome.

Extent of Addiction

It is impossible to know how many drug addicts there are in the United States today. Since the taking of drugs for nonmedical purposes is illegal, in all probability many of them are neither reported officially as such nor arrested. Most users carefully protect those who supply them so that to detect both users and suppliers requires great skill. Therefore the number of persons arrested for narcotic violation is probably representative of only a small proportion of actual violators.

According to estimates of the Federal Bureau of Narcotics, there were, on January 1, 1960, in the United States, 45,391 active drug addicts, which is 5000 to 15,000 less than were reported in 1951. Some estimates are much higher than this. Using the number of arrests of narcotic peddlers by the New York City Police Department, one study estimated that there were 90,000 addicts in that city alone.[6]

According to reports of various governmental committees investigating the problem, drug addiction has been increasing among younger persons, although arrests for the use of drugs constitute but a small proportion of all arrests for persons in this age group. It has been estimated that about

---

[6] New York City Mayor's Committee on Drug Addiction, *Report of Study of Drug Addiction among Teen-Agers* (New York: 1951).

60 percent of these young addicts use marihuana and the rest use heroin. According to FBI records of arrests for violation of the narcotic drug laws, there has been an increase in the percentage of those under twenty-five years of age, 31.4 percent being under twenty-five in the period January–June, 1941, as contrasted with 48.8 percent in the same period in 1951. Most of those arrested for federal narcotic law violations during 1955 were thirty years of age or under. Those under twenty-one constituted 9 percent, and those between twenty-one and thirty made up 54.2 percent of the total.[7] It has been estimated that of the reported 7500 addicts in the city of Chicago in 1952 approximately 60 percent were in the age group seventeen to twenty-five.[8] The changing pattern of rates of drug addiction arrests in Chicago between 1934–1938 and 1951 is shown in Table 11.2. By 1951 the rates for younger age groups had become much higher.

Table 11.2. Rates of Arrest for Narcotic Drug Law Violations (Chicago) per 10,000 Population for Different Age Groups

Age group	1934–1938	1951
16–20	0.43	13.64
21–30	2.10	10.08
31 and over	1.09	1.48

SOURCE: Table from Harold Finestone, "Narcotics and Criminality," *Law and Contemporary Problems,* 22:70 (Winter, 1957).

Approximately the same sex ratio, nine men to every one woman, exists for arrested addicts as for general crimes. Whereas about a fourth of those arrested for crimes in general are Negroes, this ratio is even higher for drug violations. According to the Federal Bureau of Narcotics in 1960 over half (57.6 percent) of the active addicts in the United States were Negroes. This greater ratio does not necessarily mean, however, that Negroes actually constitute this proportion of drug addicts, for it is known that they are less likely than others to be protected for this specific crime and more likely to be arrested.[9]

Drug addiction in the United States appears to be much more prevalent in large urban centers, particularly New York, Philadelphia, Washing-

[7] Report of the United States Treasury Department, Bureau of Narcotics, *Traffic in Opium and Other Dangerous Drugs* (Washington, D.C.: Government Printing Office, 1956).

[8] "Children and Drugs" (Madison, Wisc.: State Department of Public Welfare, Division for Children and Youth, March, 1952). Also see *Drug Addiction among Young Persons in Chicago* (Chicago: The Illinois Institute for Juvenile Research and The Chicago Area Project, October, 1953).

[9] The Narcotics Bureau figures of 1960 also reveal that 9 percent of the active addicts are Puerto Ricans and 6 percent are Mexicans.

ton, Baltimore, Chicago, Cleveland, Detroit, and Los Angeles.[10] In these cities drug addicts seem to come largely from the transitional areas, although addiction is by no means restricted to the lower socioeconomic classes. Faris and Dunham report the highest rates of addiction in the hobo and rooming-house districts, although some high rates appeared in the apartment and apartment-hotel districts. They concluded that drug addicts tend to select areas of the city where they can associate with other addicts and be more easily supplied by peddlers, and where, because of the mobility of the areas, their habits and activities are much less likely to be carefully scrutinized.[11]

Age and Length of Addiction

The United States Public Health Service maintains hospitals for the treatment of committed and voluntary narcotic drug addicts at Lexington, Kentucky, and Fort Worth, Texas. The age at addiction of 1036 of the patients at the Lexington hospital indicated that two thirds of those persons who became addicted did so before they were thirty. (See Table 11.3.) About two fifths were below the age of twenty-five. According to the Federal Narcotics Bureau, in 1960 over half the addicts in this country were between the ages of twenty-one and thirty.

Table 11.3. Age at Beginning of Addiction of 1036 Patients at the United States Public Health Service Hospital at Lexington

Age at onset of addiction	Percent
19 or less	16.5
20–24	28.1
25–29	25.1
30–34	14.2
35–39	6.9
40–44	5.4
45–49	1.7
50–54	0.8
55–59	0.5
60 or over	0.5
No record	0.3
Total	100.0

SOURCE: Michael J. Pescor, "A Statistical Analysis of the Clinical Records of Hospitalized Drug Addicts," *Public Health Reports*, Supplement 143 (1938), Appendix, p. 24.

---

[10] H. J. Anslinger and William F. Tompkins, *The Traffic in Narcotics* (New York: Funk & Wagnalls Company, 1953), p. 281.

[11] Robert E. L. Faris and H. Warren Dunham, *Mental Disorders in Urban Areas* (Chicago: The University of Chicago Press, 1939).

According to a study of these same 1036 patients, the length of addiction had generally been considerably more than five years; in fact, over 10 percent had been addicted more than twenty-five years. (See Table 11.4.)

Table 11.4. Length of Addiction among 1036 Patients at the United States Public Health Service Hospital at Lexington

Duration of addiction	Percent
1 year or less	4.1
Over 1 year, under 2	4.5
Over 2 years, under 3	6.4
Over 3 years, under 4	5.3
Over 4 years, under 5	5.3
Over 5 years, under 10	24.7
Over 10 years, under 15	15.3 (Average: 12.5 yrs)
Over 15 years, under 20	13.7
Over 20 years, under 25	9.9
Over 25 years	10.4
No record or no drugs used	0.4
Total	100.0

SOURCE: Michael J. Pescor, "A Statistical Analysis of the Clinical Records of Hospitalized Drug Addicts," *Public Health Reports,* Supplement 143 (1938), Appendix, p. 24.

These patients, of course, were more likely to be adults, and the length of addiction should be somewhat less for adolescents.

A New York City study of 115 adolescent users reported that 61 had used narcotics less than six months, and 24 had used them more than a year.[12] In another study the range was from one to eighteen months, with an average of five to six months.[13]

Education and Occupation of Drug Addicts

About one third of the drug addicts who undergo treatment at the United States Public Health Service Hospital at Lexington have high school educations or more. The distribution for educational attainment was comparable to that of the general population. One can assume that most patients in private hospitals have an even higher average level of education.

Although there is a wide divergence in the occupations of narcotic addicts, certain occupations are known to offer more hazards. The medical

[12] Welfare Council of New York City, *The Menace of Narcotics to the Children of New York: A Plan to Eradicate the Evil* (New York: The Council, 1951).

[13] Paul Zimmering, James Toolan, Ranate Safrin, and S. P. Wortis, "Heroin Addiction in Adolescent Boys," *Journal of Nervous and Mental Diseases,* 114:19–34 (July, 1951).

profession, for example, has an excessive share of addicts.[14] The United States Commissioner of Narcotics has estimated the incidence of opiate addiction among physicians as being about 1 addict among every 100 physicians, as contrasted to a rate of about 1 in 3000 in the general population.[15] The Federal Bureau of Narcotics reported that 1012 physicians were addicts, while 659 were found guilty of illegal narcotics sales or prescription activities from 1942 through 1956. Other countries have reported a substantial incidence of addiction among physicians. In England physicians are reported as being the occupational group most heavily represented among addicts, accounting for 17 percent of the addicts there. One report, summarizing United Nations data on the subject, has stated that 1 physician in every 550 in England, and 1 in every 95 in Germany, was an addict.[16] A study of 457 consecutive admissions to the United States Public Health Service Hospital at Lexington, for meperidine ("Demerol," an opiate derivative) addiction, revealed that 32.7 percent of the cases of primary addiction were physicians and osteopaths.[17] Doctors can obtain drugs easily and rather inexpensively. Moreover, physicians have knowledge of what drugs can do for someone who is tense or tired, which is an important factor in their becoming addicted. Many of these physicians do not come to the attention of authorities because they can often maintain their addiction without detection.

In a study of 98 physicians who either were or had been opiate addicts, pronounced differences were found between them and the typical addict who buys drugs from a "pusher."

> The most obvious difference is that the age at which the physicians began to use drugs is just about the age that the typical addict stops using drugs, whether by "maturing out" or for other reasons. The "street" addict typically begins drug use in adolescence, while the physician begins when he is an established community and professional figure. The "street" addict takes heroin, while the typical physician addict took meperidine. The physician can get a pure quality of his drug, although it is not as strong as heroin. The "street" addict gets a diluted drug. He often starts with marijuana, although none of the physicians ever smoked marijuana.
>
> The physician is usually discovered by the indirect evidence of a check of prescription records, while the "street" addict is usually arrested either because he has narcotics in his possession or has been observed making an illegal purchase. The physician is usually not arrested, while the typical "street" addict is arrested. Money to obtain drugs was not a problem for the

---

[14] Charles Winick, "Physician Narcotic Addicts," *Social Problems*, 9:174–186 (Fall, 1961).

[15] "Interview with Hon. Harry J. Anslinger," *Modern Medicine*, 25:170–191 (October 15, 1957).

[16] Lawrence Kolb, "The Drug Addiction Muddle," *Police*, 1:57–62 (January–February, 1957).

[17] Robert W. Rasor and H. James Crecraft, "Addiction to Meperidine," *Journal of the American Medical Association*, 157:654–657 (February 19, 1955).

physicians, as it usually is for the typical addict who must steal in order to obtain money to buy drugs illegally. The physicians could use their professional access to narcotics to obtain drugs without much money. Even if they paid, the legal prices of narcotic drugs are very low.

Most non-physician addicts associate with other addicts. In contrast, the physicians interviewed almost never associated with other physician addicts, or did not do so knowingly. They did not have any occasion for doing so, either for the purpose of getting drugs or for passing time, or for emotional support. They were solitary about their addiction. The "street" addict usually talks in a special jargon and often has a kind of wry insight into drug use, which stems from his extended discussions with his peers. The physicians did not talk in jargon and manifested very little insight into their drug use.[18]

Performers in the entertainment world, such as jazz musicians, sometimes become marihuana users, largely because such deviant behavior appears to be much less disapproved by their associates. The use of drugs has been studied among 357 jazz band musicians in New York City, 73 percent of whom were white. It was reported that 82 percent had tried marihuana at least once, 54 percent were occasional users, and one in four, or 23 percent, were regular users.[19] Heroin was used less than marihuana, but still by a large proportion: 53 percent at least once, 24 percent occasionally, and by one in six, or 16 percent, regularly. Only 3 percent expressed any moral objections to the use of either marihuana or heroin by their musical colleagues, and while two thirds of the nonusers felt sorry for the drug users, the common reaction was, "It's their business if they want to do it."

Over a third of the sample believed that most jazz musicians think they play better when using marihuana, even if they actually are playing worse. Nearly one in five believed that it actually helps a musician to play better, and 31 percent felt that the musicians played worse. More specifically, marihuana seems to establish "contact high," a special kind of emotional group contagion, among those taking marihuana, resulting in "musical whimsy or humor," and can permit the musician to perceive new space-time relationships by altering his perception of time. In general the comments were much more negative in relation to heroin. No significant relation, however, could be found between the use of heroin or marihuana and the degree of professional success attributed to the musician by his peers.

A number of group factors are related to the musician's drug use. One was the extent of use by the band itself. About half (53 percent) felt that the use of drugs was related to upward or downward mobility. For ex-

---

[18] Winick, "Physician Narcotic Addicts," *loc. cit.*, pp. 178–179.

[19] Charles Winick, "The Use of Drugs by Jazz Musicians," *Social Problems,* 7:240–254 (Winter, 1959–1960).

ample, a young musician may take a drug to accelerate his progress to the top. Drugs may be used to help tide a musician over when he is out of work. About one in five, especially those over thirty, felt that drug usage was related to "one nighters" as this type of traveling is tiring for musicians. As one heroin user described it:

> "I was traveling on the road in 1952. We had terrible travel arrangements and traveled by special bus. We were so tried and beat that we didn't even have time to brush our teeth when we arrived in a town. We'd get up on the bandstand looking awful. The audience would say, 'why don't they smile? They look like they can't smile.' I found I could pep myself up more quickly with heroin than with liquor. If you drank feeling that tired, you'd fall on your face." [20]

The Process of Opiate Addiction

To be an addict, a person must use the drug consciously. He must be aware of the drug, know how to administer it, and recognize its effects.

> Beyond this, one must have some motivation for trying the drug—whether to relieve pain, to produce euphoria, to please a loved person, to achieve acceptance in a group, or to achieve some other goal. The goal need have little to do with the specific effects of the narcotic. Moreover, the motivation or goal of initial drug use must be sharply distinguished from the motivation to maintain a drug habit. The latter is a product of learning which seems to depend on the interaction between drug effects, especially in the first experience of withdrawal, and the self-conception of the drug user.[21]

Generally addicts have personality disturbances, but it is not sound reasoning to assume that such personality traits necessarily existed before addiction.[22] In only a few cases are comparisons made with the traits of the population as a whole, and there is some doubt as to whether the addicts studied are always representative of the entire population.

The most significant sociological work in this field has challenged the general view that differences in personality traits or need for an escape mechanism accounts for addiction to opiates. Lindesmith explains addiction on the basis of the addict's association of the drug with the distress which accompanies the sudden cessation of its use. "If he fails to realize the connection between the distress and the opiate he escapes addiction, whereas if he attributes it to the opiate and thereafter uses the opiate to

---

[20] *Ibid.*, p. 246.

[21] John A. Clausen, "Social and Psychological Factors in Narcotics Addiction," *Law and Contemporary Problems*, 22:38–39 (Winter, 1957).

[22] Donald Gerard and Conan Kornetsky, "Adolescent Opiate Addiction: A Study of Control and Addict Subjects," *Psychiatric Quarterly*, 29:457–487 (1955).

alleviate it he invariably becomes addicted. Addiction is generated in the process of using the drug consciously to alleviate withdrawal distress." [23]

Addiction is impossible without recognizing the withdrawal distress which may come several hours after a "shot" and in some cases may be difficult to detect. In support of his argument Lindesmith claims that there are no persons who have not become addicts after experimenting with withdrawal symptoms. Doctors may successfully prevent addiction by keeping patients unaware of the effects of the drug upon them. Patients who have experienced withdrawal distress without understanding the connection between it and the drug have therefore escaped addiction.

Lindesmith cites several crucial cases of persons who were receiving drugs without becoming addicted, but when they later took drugs and began to associate the taking of drugs with the fear of withdrawal symptoms they became addicted. This interpretation is supported by the fact that an addict seldom experiences the uplift or buoyancy attributed to the drugs unless he has been "taught" to expect it. Even the argot of addicts themselves in the word "hooked" indicates the process of addiction. The following case shows how a person begins to realize that he is addicted.

> Mr. G. was severely lacerated and internally injured in an accident. He spent thirteen weeks in a hospital, in the course of which he received opiates frequently both by mouth and hypodermically. He was unconscious part of the time and suffered considerable pain during convalescence despite the intake of opiates. He did not know what he was getting and noticed no effects except that his pain was relieved by the shots. He was discharged from the hospital but in several hours he began to feel restless and uncomfortable, without recognizing his condition. That night he became nauseated and vomited blood. Fearing that he was going to die, he summoned his family doctor. The physician did not realize what was the matter and administered a mild sedative. During the next day Mr. G.'s condition became steadily worse, and by the second night he was in such misery that, as he said, he began to wish that he would die. He again summoned his family doctor. This time the doctor began to suspect that Mr. G. was suffering from opiate withdrawal and prepared an injection of morphine. Mr. G. remembers nothing after the injection except that the doctor sat down by his bed and asked him how he felt. He replied that he noticed no effect, but the doctor said, "You will in a few minutes." Soon the patient fell asleep and continued in perfect comfort for many hours. When he awoke, he was informed of the true nature of the relieving dose by his wife and by the physician's comment: "Now we're going to have a hell of a time getting you off." The patient remained free of the drug for a few days and then purchased a syringe and began to use it himself.[24]

---

[23] Alfred R. Lindesmith, "A Sociological Theory of Drug Addiction," *American Journal of Sociology*, 43:599 (January, 1938).

[24] Alfred R. Lindesmith, *Opiate Addiction* (Bloomington: University of Indiana Press, 1947), p. 72. This extract and others reprinted from this work are used with the permission of the author and the publisher.

In becoming an opiate addict the individual changes his conception of himself and of the behavior he must play as a "drug addict." These new conceptions have both social psychological and sociological implications. The more he associates with others who are "hooked" and finds that he cannot free himself from dependence on drugs, the more he comes to play the new role of the addict.

> It is evident that the drug addict assumes the group's viewpoint with respect to his experience of withdrawal distress by virtue of the fact that, prior to addiction, he has been a non-addict and a participating member of society. In view of the very use of language symbols, in terms of which the processes of re-evaluation which constitute addiction proceed, the addict necessarily shares the traditional heritage which includes knowledge of, and attitudes toward, the drug habit. Prior to addiction addicts acquire the attitudes of non-addicts, and when they become addicted they must adjust themselves to these attitudes. In other words, as our theory emphasizes, addiction pre-supposes life in organized society. Children and animals can not become addicts because they lack the ability to use and respond to the complex linguistic structures which have grown up in human society.[25]

Drug addiction is learned just as other behavior is learned, primarily from association with others who are addicts. The usual pattern is that of association for other means, rather than the person seeking another simply because the other person is a drug addict. Dai found that some were introduced to drugs at "pleasure parties," through co-workers, at dance halls and pool rooms, by prostitutes or in homosexual experiences, and, in some cases, by peddlers.[26] Similarly, younger persons learn addiction from the group, as has been previously discussed. Dai has thus summarized the role of association in drug addiction:

> The process in which this pattern of opium addiction is taken over by an individual is not very much different from that in which other cultural patterns are transmitted. In a number of cases we found that the drug habit was started less for the effect of the drug than as a sign of identification with the group they happened to be in. . . . This process of identification is found to take place when a young person associates with an older one who uses drugs and who, because of the habit or otherwise, commands the former's admiration and respect, or when two persons are in some form of love relationship . . . when one of them is a drug user.[27]

The Process of Using Marihuana

There are two objections to the claim that the use of marihuana, which actually does not cause addiction, is associated with personality

---

[25] *Ibid.*, p. 168.
[26] Bingham Dai, *Opium Addiction in Chicago* (Shanghai: The Commercial Press, 1937).
[27] *Ibid.*, p. 173.

traits.[28] First, marihuana users do not exhibit any uniform personality traits; second, there is great variation in the use of the drug by a given person. At one time the individual may be unable to use the drug for pleasure, on a later occasion he may use it, and still later not do so.

To use marihuana for pleasure a person must learn to conceive of the drug as something which can produce pleasurable sensations.[29] The user of marihuana drugs must learn three things: (1) to smoke the drug in a way which will produce certain effects; (2) to learn to recognize the effects and connect the drug with them; and (3) finally, to enjoy the sensations he feels. These three steps occurred in the case of fifty marihuana users whom Becker studied. He claims that when a person first uses the drug he does not ordinarily "get high" because he does not know the proper technique of drawing on the cigarette and holding the smoke. Even after learning the technique he does not form a conception of the smoking as being related to pleasure. Even though there are pleasurable sensations, the new marihuana user may not feel that they are enough, or he may not be sufficiently aware of their specific nature to become a regular user. He learns to feel the sensations of "being high" as defined by others. With greater use he learns to appreciate more of the sensations of the drug.

Finally, one more step is necessary to continue the use of marihuana. The person must learn to enjoy the sensations he has experienced. Feeling dizzy, being thirsty, misjudging distances, or a tingling scalp may not of themselves be pleasurable experiences. He must learn to define them in this way. Association with other marihuana users helps to define sensations that were frightening into something pleasurable and to be looked forward to. An experienced marihuana user has described how newcomers are helped to define the use of the drugs as giving pleasurable sensations:

> "Well, they get pretty high sometimes. The average person isn't ready for that, and it is a little frightening to them sometimes. I mean, they've been high on lush (alcohol), and they get higher that way than they've ever been before, and they don't know what's happening to them. Because they think they're going to keep going up, up, up till they lose their minds or begin doing weird things or something. You have to like reassure them, explain to them that they're not really flipping or anything, that they're gonna be all right. You have to just talk them out of being afraid. Keep talking to them, reassuring, telling them it's all right. And come on with your own story, you know: 'The same thing happened to me. You'll get to like that after awhile.' Keep coming on like that; pretty soon you talk them out of being scared. And besides they see you doing it and nothing horrible is happening to you, so that gives them more confidence." [30]

---

[28] Howard S. Becker, "Becoming a Marihuana User," *American Journal of Sociology*, 59:235–243 (November, 1953).

[29] *Ibid.*, pp. 235–242.   [30] *Ibid.*, p. 240.

The Culture of Drug Addiction

Much of drug addiction involves an elaborate subculture. The drugs must be imported illegally into the country and then distributed through suppliers or peddlers. There are "pushers" who help to indoctrinate new persons into addiction. Those who use the drugs are, to a large extent, also part of this subculture, since drug addicts must generally associate with peddlers and other addicts in order to secure their supply.

To understand why this illegal trade in narcotics flourishes and why it is so difficult to wipe out, one must realize the potential large profit in the handling of illegal drugs. The price for a shot of heroin varies considerably, and is often what the traffic will bear. Although police often have little difficulty in apprehending the common addict who is searching restlessly for his next shot, it is much more difficult to track down the supplier or successive line of suppliers to the source. Many addicts would rather sweat out the "shakes" than disclose the name of their supplier, and often there is a high degree of organization among those who manage to get supplies of drugs illegally into the country.

The extremely high profits involved in the sale of illegal drugs can be seen from the return which is likely on one kilogram (approximately thirty-five ounces) of heroin. This amount of 86 percent pure heroin in Italy costs about $1000, and it might cost as much as $5000 more to smuggle it into the United States. However, this kilogram of heroin, which will be diluted as much as 90 percent with milk sugar, will eventually be made into about 20,000 capsules (at $437\frac{1}{2}$ grains to an ounce and $1\frac{1}{2}$ grains to a capsule of the cut product) which will sell for about $2 to $3 apiece. Thus the return on the original investment is up to $40,000 to $60,000. Where profits as high as this exist it is inevitable that well-organized techniques will be developed to protect them. It is also inevitable that such an enterprise should become a fertile field for organized crime.

Most drug addicts are introduced to the habit knowingly. Only rarely does the use of drugs during illness lead to addiction; probably not more than 5 percent of the cases have this origin. As for the large numbers who take them because of curiosity, there has usually been some association with addicts. There is a desire to "try something once," especially if it happens to be something as frowned upon by society in general as is drug addiction. The chain-reaction process of addiction has often been called a "sordid and tragic pyramid game" in which the average addict can be counted on to lure several friends into the habit, often as a means of solving his own supply problem. Persons are often initiated at parties where the first several marihuana cigarettes or "shots" are "on the house" in order to initiate the beginner.

Teen-age addiction is more group in nature. In their attempts to acquire status, adolescents in certain areas often appear to be willing to explore socially unacceptable areas of behavior. Drug use among juveniles, consisting primarily of heroin and marihuana, flourishes in the interstitial areas of cities. In New York, for example, almost 90 percent of the cases are concentrated in only 13 percent of the census tracts.[31] In fact, in some of the tracts as many as 10 percent of the young men, aged sixteen to twenty, were known, during a three-year period, to be involved with drugs. In such areas the desire to enjoy life by having new experiences and taking chances means that there is a readiness to try the drug, as it, they are told, will give them an immediate "kick" or a "high" feeling. In some groups, namely delinquent gangs, this idea is even more widespread than among others. Great determination is required to escape the pull or, rather, push of delinquent subcultures which are associated with the use of drugs. "The pressure to fall in with the fast, noisy, aggressive 'cats' is great. The derisive taunts of 'chicken,' 'yellow,' 'punk,' and 'square' are powerful weapons to use against an adolescent boy."[32]

In spreading to young persons, as it did, narcotics use made its inroads within a distinctive and uniquely vulnerable social milieu, the world of the adolescent in the most disadvantaged areas of the city. Like their age-mates everywhere, these adolescents spontaneously form peer groups, which exert a significant influence upon their conduct. In other types of communities, however, particularly those of higher socioeconomic status, the control over behavior exerted by the peer group is subject to restraint by the obligations and loyalties binding the individual adolescent members to other conventional groups, such as the family and the school. By way of contrast, such competing obligations and loyalties fail to exert their limiting and moderating influences in the most disadvantaged areas, and the peer group assumes a virtually sovereign control over the behavior of the individual adolescent. Under such conditions, the introduction of a novel practice may lead to its rapid diffusion, and, because it is unchecked by pressures counter to those exerted by the peer group itself, go to extremes that are not possible among adolescents elsewhere. In this milieu, narcotics use could spread more selectively and with somewhat greater difficulty, perhaps, but in a manner analogous to a new fashion in language, dress, or music. . . .

It is evident from this description that there are significant influences originating in street-corner society itself that would be hospitable to experimentation with narcotics. An orientation to life which gives zestful sanction to many forms of unconventional activity appears to have spread the welcome mat for narcotics use. Much of the behavior reported by these young addicts clearly indicates that they had actively sought out narcotics—and not only heroin, but every other substance of which they had heard which yielded a "kick" such as marijuana, cocaine, benzedrine, and the barbiturates. The

---

[31] Isidor Chein and Eva Rosenfeld, "Juvenile Narcotics Use," *Law and Contemporary Problems*, 22:52–69 (Winter, 1957).

[32] *Ibid.*, p. 56.

activity centering around these narcotics had many of the characteristics of a fad—that is, the restless searching, the uncertainty and excitement and exclusive preoccupation with a novel experience, the pressures to "go along," and the final capitulation on the part of many, despite the existence of strong initial doubts and inhibitions.[33]

Teen-agers in high delinquency areas, which are also high drug use areas, can be divided into four groups: (1) delinquents who also use drugs, (2) delinquents who do not use drugs, (3) drug users who were not drug users prior to involvement with heroin, and, finally (4) nondelinquent nondrug users. Not all delinquent groups engage in the use of drugs, a fact which appears to be related to the area where they are located. Finestone has suggested that the use of narcotics spreads to adolescents in those communities deficient in two essential types of social control: "first, controls originating in conventional institutions which define the limits of permissible behavior for adolescents; and secondly, the controls by means of which the community is enabled to resist encroachments by those espousing values to which it is strongly antagonistic." [34] In regard to lack of the first type of social control he writes:

> In the localities frequented by adult criminals, the notoriety, glamour, and symbols of material success that are sometimes associated with them enhance their attractiveness as role-models to members of street-corner society, who, as adolescents, may find it easier to identify with them than with conventional role-models. In a similar vein, interviews with young narcotic addicts in 1952 suggested the observation that in at least certain social circles where these youngsters sought status and recognition, adult addicts or "junkies" enjoyed a certain prestige. Many of these young addicts reported that they and others had tried to simulate the mannerisms and philosophy of life of addicts before they themselves had become addicted.[35]

Most juvenile gangs that use drugs, however, often try to set the limits of drug usage by their members. In a study of eighteen gangs by Chein and Rosenfeld it was found that 65 percent of the members were opposed to the use of heroin, or felt ambivalent about it, but very few gang members had strong feeling about the use of marihuana.[36] Any leader who became a drug addict was demoted. Delinquent gangs are more tolerant of occasional use, but resist immoderate usage, on the grounds that it interferes with their stealing or that it will get the gang into trouble. Some writers, such as Ohlin and Cloward, have referred to a type of delinquent gang which, in its inability to achieve the conventional goals of society,

---

[33] Harold Finestone, "Narcotics and Criminality," *Law and Contemporary Problems,* 22:73–74 (Winter, 1957).

[34] *Ibid.,* p. 74.

[35] *Ibid.,* p. 75. For discussion of some group factors in younger drug addicts also see Alexander H. Leighton, John A. Clausen, and Robert N. Wilson, *Explorations in Social Psychiatry* (New York: Basic Books, Inc., 1957), pp. 230–277.

[36] Chein and Rosenfeld, "Juvenile Narcotics Use," *loc. cit.*

becomes preoccupied with the use of drugs rather than stealing except to get money for drugs.[37]

There is a widespread assumption that juvenile addicts are introduced to the drug habit by drug peddlers. One study has shown that the first shot of heroin came through some adult in only 10 percent of the cases.[38] Nearly all were introduced to the drug in the company of a boy their own age or in a group of boys. The first trial use of drugs was free to most. Only 10 percent had to pay for the first "shot" or "snort." The first dose was often taken in the home of one of the boys, although a large number tried it on the street, in a cellar, or even on a roof top. Frequently, it was taken before a party as a bracer to give poise and courage. Clausen reports: "There is general agreement that the great majority of these [marihuana and heroin] users were not tricked into addiction by drug peddlers." [39]

Once the adolescent becomes involved in a group which is using drugs and becomes addicted, it is difficult for him to withdraw from the group. Later his whole life may revolve around maintaining a regular supply of "shots," and there is consequently less and less opportunity for him to have any contacts with acceptable groups. In these groups of youthful addicts loyalties become intensified because of the constant fear of being arrested and cut off from sources of supply. And the constant search for sources of supply compels them to seek the company of known adult addicts.

Suppliers and most addicts live in a world that often has its own meeting places and its own argot. Possibly nothing more clearly demonstrates the fact that addiction has cultural components than the argot which is used. It includes special names for the drugs, for those who supply the drugs, and for addiction. It also includes special descriptive terms for those who use drugs.

Selected Glossary of Terms Used by Addicts
Bang: The thrill in drug taking.
Being on the nod: Peculiar semisomnolent condition after taking injection.
Belong: After habit is formed, individual "belongs" to pusher.

---

[37] Richard A. Cloward and Lloyd E. Ohlin, *Delinquency and Opportunity* (New York: The Free Press of Glencoe, 1960). Also see Harold Finestone, "Cats, Kicks, and Color," *Social Problems,* 5:3–13 (July, 1957). In this study some fifty Negro male users of heroin in their late teens and early twenties were selected from areas of highest incidence of drug usage in Chicago. Through intensive interviews between 1951 and 1953, these drug users served as subjects to elicit expression of many common values, schemes of behavior and general social orientation, suggesting the existence of a social type, "the cat." It was concluded that "the cat" is a product of social change, representing a reaction to a feeling of exclusion from adequate access to the goals of our society. Therefore, measures, such as improved educational opportunities which put these means within his grasp, will hasten the extinction of this type.
[38] Chein and Rosenfeld, "Juvenile Narcotics Use," *loc. cit.,* p. 58.
[39] Clausen, "Social and Psychological Factors in Narcotics Addiction," *loc. cit.,* p. 40.

Boy: Another name for heroin.

Burned out: A vein no longer useful for injection because of numerous puncture wounds.

Chicken: One who declines to take drugs because he is fearful.

Cold turkey: Complete and sudden withdrawal from drugs in jail.

Den: Place where several gather to use narcotics.

Drive: Addict's description of feeling good.

Fad party: Group of cats gathered.

Good ball: A pill or capsule of barbiturate used by addicts when they cannot get their supply of narcotics.

Girl: Slang for cocaine.

Hard stuff: Heroin, when compared to marihuana.

High: When an individual is under the effect of marihuana or other drugs.

Hooked: One who no longer can resist taking drugs.

Hophead: One who has become addicted to use of drugs.

Horse: Another name for heroin.

Hot shot: An overdose of drugs, sometimes fatal.

Joy popper: One who takes drugs only occasionally.

Junk: Any illegal drug.

Junkie: A drug addict.

Kick: Feeling of satisfaction after taking drugs (also lift).

Kicking the habit: Constant twitching of arms, legs and feet, some twenty-four hours after last dose of morphine, during withdrawal.

Main-liner: Any addict who uses intravenous injections.

Muggles: Marihuana cigarettes.

Pusher: Makes first contact for recruits. May give first few samples free.

Reefer: Marihuana cigarette.

Shakes: Uncontrolled physical tremors of addict when withdrawn from drugs.

Skin-popping: Injection of drugs, but not intravenous.

Sniffer: Inhalation of cocaine from thumbnail or match cover.

Snorting: Inhaling cocaine.

Snow: Slang for cocaine.

Speedball artist: One who mixes cocaine and heroin.

Stick: A marihuana cigarette.

Stuff: Any drug used illegally.

Wigged: An addict who can no longer think clearly.

Yen sleep: Restless, tossing sleep, eight to fourteen hours after last dose of morphine, during withdrawal.[40]

The argot of professional musicians makes use of many expressions which are widely used by addicts. They use terms and phrases to describe the music they like, such as "frantic," "it kills me," "wild," "crazy," "the end," "hip."[41]

---

[40] Derived from Lindesmith, *Opiate Addiction*, pp. 211–221; Anslinger and Tompkins, *op. cit.*, pp. 305–316; and "Children and Drugs," pp. 23–25. Also see J. E. Schmidt, *Narcotics Lingo and Lore* (Springfield, Ill.: Charles C Thomas, Publisher, 1959).

[41] Winick, "The Use of Drugs by Jazz Musicians," *loc. cit.*, pp. 249–250. "Drug users probably developed most of the key phrases in this jargon as outgrowths of various aspects

Since the 1920's, one popular procedure for combining musical expression with interest in drugs was to make records or perform pieces with thinly veiled references to narcotics in their titles: Hophead, Muggles, Reefer Song, Viper's Drag, Sweet Marijuana Brown, Weed Smoker's Dream, Chant of the Weed, Pipe Dream Blues, Kicking the Gong Around, You're a Viper, Reefer Man, Doctor Freeze, and Vonce, are among many such titles, some of which achieved considerable success. The lyrics as well as the title of many jazz pieces have dealt with narcotics, at least up to fairly recently.[42]

Delinquency, Crime, and Drug Addiction

Two factors are involved in the relationship between delinquency, crime, and drug addiction. First of all, the use of narcotics is so expensive that an addict must often engage in various illegal activities to maintain his supply. Second, the influence of drugs upon human behavior varies, and it is difficult to determine how much effect narcotics have on criminal behavior generally.

Once an individual becomes addicted to a narcotic drug, such as morphine or heroin, his dependence upon a continuous supply usually becomes the most important single aspect of his daily life. Although they took the drug earlier for pleasure or for an effect, most addicts soon take it to ward off withdrawal symptoms. The addict knows that conventional society is extremely hostile to his use of drugs, so he resorts to devious ways in his attempt to secure them. As his tolerance is built up and he requires more and larger dosages, it may cost as much as from fifteen to forty dollars a day to support the habit. This daily expenditure is generally much more than the addict earns, and thus he or she is literally compelled to engage in theft or prostitution in order to maintain an adequate supply.

Most crimes associated with drug addiction involve direct or indirect violations of narcotic laws. Drug addicts may engage in petty stealing, and occasionally robbery, to get enough money to buy their drugs, break into hospitals and doctors' offices to steal drugs, turn to prostitution, or sell drugs and become drug peddlers or "pushers." Drug addicts may also purchase a small supply of a drug from a peddler and then "water" down the powder with the addition of milk sugar before selling it to the next in line. By the time the last packet is bought by an addict it is mostly milk sugar. Doctors sometimes illegally prescribe drugs for an extra fee; indeed, some addicts have paid thousands of dollars to doctors for illegal prescriptions. One writer has thus described the young addict or "junky" and the need to commit crimes in order to secure drugs.

---

of drug-taking activity. For example, the key concept of being 'hip' (a member of the in-group) derives from the slight atrophy of the hip which resulted from lying on one preferred hip and balancing opium on the other hip. A 'hip' person was thus originally an opium smoker."—*Ibid.*, p. 250.

[42] *Ibid.*, p. 251.

At the time when many of these young addicts were interviewed in 1952, most were still in the early stages of their addiction. They were "snatch-and-grab" junkies, supporting their habits through petty thievery, breaking into cars, shoplifting, and a variety of "scheming," such as "laying a story" on "a sucker" in the hope of gaining sympathy and some cash. Some enterprising ones actually had girls out "hustling" for them through "boosting" (shoplifting) and "turning tricks" (prostitution). Despite the ragged state of their clothing and the harried nature of their existence, they regarded themselves as the members of an elite, the true "down cats" on the best "kick" of them all, "Horse" (heroin). Many of them were still living at home, although they had long since exhausted the last reserves of patience of their families and "fenced" much of their movable property. Few, if any, of them had finished high school, and, on the average, they had little or no employment experience. Their attitudes towards work and the daily routine that steady employment presupposed were entirely negative. Their number-one hazard was the "man" (the police). Once they became "known junkies"—that is, known to the police—they were frequently picked up and sometimes sentenced—mostly for misdemeanors and, consequently, for short sentences. . . . The impression gained from interviewing them was that these addicts were petty thieves and petty "operators" who, status-wise, were at the bottom of the criminal population or underworld. It is difficult to see how they could be otherwise. The typical young junkie spent so much of his time in a harried quest for narcotics, dodging the police, and in lockups, that he was hardly in a position to plan major crimes.[43]

The second factor is the relationship of drug addiction to crime in general and to crimes of violence in particular. In a study of the criminal records of 1036 patients at the United States Public Health Service Hospital in Lexington it was found that 75.3 percent had no official record of delinquency prior to addiction.[44] Generally they were not involved in offenses other than drug violations and where they were involved the offenses were not serious. Most younger drug users appear to have engaged in prolonged delinquent activities either prior to their first arrest or prior to their first regular use of drugs. A report of a Chicago study states:

With few exceptions known drug users engage in delinquency in more or less systematic form. Contrary to the widely held view that the delinquency of the young addict is a consequence principally of addiction, it was found that delinquency both preceded and followed addiction to heroin. Persons who became heroin users were found to have engaged in delinquency in a group-supported and habitual form either prior to their use of drugs or simultaneously with their developing interest in drugs. There was little evidence of a consistent sequence from drug use without delinquency to drug

[43] Finestone, "Narcotics and Criminality," loc. cit., pp. 76–77.
[44] Michael J. Pescor, "A Statistical Analysis of Clinical Records of Drug Addicts," Public Health Reports, Supplement 143 (1938), p. 26.

use with delinquency. Three observations may be made about the effect of
addiction upon the delinquent behavior of the person: (1) The pressure of
need for money to support his addiction impels the user to commit violations
with greater frequency and with less caution than formerly. (2) Delinquents
after becoming addicted to heroin do not engage in types of delinquency in
which they are not already skilled. The post-addict delinquent, in other words,
does not generally engage in more serious crimes than those he committed
prior to his addiction. (3) Delinquents who as pre-addicts tended to engage
in riotous behavior such as street fighting and gang attacks tend after addiction to abandon this kind of activity. Three elements are probably responsible for the change: (a) the sedative effect of the opiate; (b) the desire
to avoid attracting the attention of public and police; and (c) the tendency
for adolescents to become quieter in their conduct as they approach maturity.[45]

According to 1951 Chicago data, arrests for nonviolent property offenses is proportionately higher among addicts, whereas arrests of addicts
for violent offenses against the person, such as rape and aggravated assault, are only a fraction of the proportion among the population at large.
(See Table 11.5.) A group of young addicts was found seldom to have

*Table 11.5 The Percentage Distribution of Arrests for the Most
Serious Types of Offenses in the Narcotic Bureau and the
Chicago Police Department, 1951*

	Narcotic Bureau	Chicago Police Department
Larceny—theft (except automobile theft)	58.8	31.0
Robbery	16.2	7.3
Burglary—breaking and entering	9.9	9.4
Stolen property: buying, receiving, possessing	5.1	3.2
Forgery and counterfeiting: embezzlement and fraud	4.2	4.9
Sex offenses: Rape	1.6	11.0
Automobile theft	1.5	9.1
Weapons: carrying, possessing, etc.	1.4	4.4
Aggravated assault: other assault	1.3	19.7
	100.0	100.0

SOURCE: Chicago Police Department, Annual Report (1951), p. 13.

committed serious offenses against either persons or property, and those
who did generally had committed similar offenses before becoming ad-

[45] The Illinois Institute for Juvenile Research and Chicago Area Project, "Drug Addiction among Young Persons in Chicago," Summary Report of a Study Made by the Staff
of the Chicago Area Project for the National Institute of Mental Health (Mimeographed;
October, 1953).

dicted, so that violence was only a part of the total picture. The conclusion was: "Addiction, thus, appears to reduce both the inclination to violent crime and the capacity to engage in sophisticated types of crime requiring much planning." [46] Reckless concludes that there is little evidence to support the idea that addicts commit violent crimes: "One notices that sex crimes and crimes against the person are not the sorts of crime committed by the drug addict, in spite of the marihuana mythology. The most commonly used drugs, morphine and its derivatives, decrease an individual's aggressive tendencies." [47]

Treatment

All studies of the results of treatment indicate that drug addiction is one of the most difficult forms of deviant behavior to treat effectively. The rate of relapse is high. A follow-up study of 4776 addicts was made six months after their discharge from the United States Public Health Service Hospital at Lexington. Although the status of 39.6 percent of the patients could not be ascertained, it was revealed that 39.9 percent had relapsed, 7.0 percent had died after release, and only 13.5 percent were abstinent.[48]

Lindesmith attributes the high recidivism rate of the opiate addict to social psychological, rather than merely physiological, reasons. Recidivism in drug addiction is the result of long experience with the drugs and a conception of oneself as an addict, association with other addicts, and recognition of the importance of the drug in relation to withdrawal symptoms. It is often difficult to quit the use of drugs, or to abstain from beginning to use them again, because many friends and acquaintances are addicts. This feeling of boredom at being a nonaddict is also a factor in relapse. After the addict has been taken off drugs the old attitudes persist.

> The former user still believes in the efficacy of the drug. He still interprets the vicissitudes of life to some degree in terms of opiates and never again exhibits a feeling of disgust or moral indignation toward drug usage such as he may have had before addiction. These changes are produced by the influence of withdrawal distress, as has been demonstrated, but once formed, they are independent of the withdrawal symptoms.[49]

Addicts generally cannot be treated properly in their own homes or in general hospitals, for it is essential that they be under constant specialized observation.[50] Most treatment of this type is given in only a few private

---

[46] Finestone, "Narcotics and Criminality," *loc. cit.,* p. 77.

[47] Walter C. Reckless, *The Crime Problem* (2d ed.; New York: Appleton-Century-Crofts, Inc., 1950), p. 356.

[48] Michael J. Pescor, "Follow-Up Study of Treated Narcotic Addicts," *Public Health Reports,* Supplement 170 (1943), pp. 1–18.

[49] Lindesmith, *Opiate Addiction,* p. 139.

[50] For a description of specific methods of treatment, see Marie Nyswander, *The Drug Addict as a Patient* (New York: Grune & Stratton, Inc., 1956).

sanatoria, to a limited extent in some state hospitals, and in two federal hospitals, at Lexington, Kentucky, and at Fort Worth, Texas. The latter two institutions were established by Congressional action in 1929 for the confinement and treatment of narcotic addicts. They are now under the Mental Hygiene Division of the Public Health Service under the Department of Health, Education, and Welfare. Voluntary commitments are accepted at these institutions, but the majority of patients are those who have failed on probation and have been committed by federal courts.

The optimum treatment period is from four to six months. The longer a patient stays at a hospital the less likely he is to return, for there is little opportunity for him to continue treatment outside. A newly admitted drug addict is, first of all, given a thoroughgoing medical examination and treatment, which includes building up his general physical condition along with removal of drugs. The use of drugs is reduced gradually to minimize the severity of the symptoms. Currently the most frequently used drug is methadon, for it has much milder abstinence symptoms than either heroin or morphine. The next step—removal of the patient's psychological dependence on drugs—is a much more difficult process. It usually involves psychiatric treatment, recreational and occupational therapy, and vocational training. It is also important that the addict receives follow-up supervision, as most relapses among addicts occur within the first two years after their release from the hospital. If cure is to be permanent, any problems in the home which have directly or indirectly led to the addiction must be corrected. Through an organization called Narcotics Anonymous some use has been made of group therapy after release. See pages 653–655 for a description.

The Control of Drug Addiction

The best approach to the entire difficult problem of drug addiction is, of course, prevention. This means efforts to prevent the individual from coming into illegitimate contact with the drug. Prevention is largely a function for law-enforcement agencies through international agreements, federal agencies, and local authorities. Two United Nations groups, the Permanent Central Opium Board and the Narcotic Drugs Supervisory Body, control the lawful traffic in drugs.[51] In 1961, thirty-eight members of the United Nations agreed to a new, more rigid international regulation and control of drugs, subject to ratification by their home countries. A third group, the United States Commission on Narcotic Drugs, watches over lawful opium traffic in the United States, and suggests measures for controlling all illegal trade. The task of preventing unlawful trade in nar-

---

[51] See Bertil A. Renborg, "International Control of Narcotics," in *Law and Contemporary Problems*, 22:86–112 (Winter, 1957).

cotics within the United States is assigned to the Bureau of Narcotics, a branch of the Treasury Department, which administers the Harrison Narcotic Act. This act requires the registration and payment of a graduated occupational tax by all persons who import, manufacture, produce, compound, sell, deal in, dispense, or give away narcotic drugs. In addition, it provides for a commodity tax imposed on the drug. The Bureau of Narcotics also administers the Marihuana Tax Act, which has regulatory features similar to those used in the control of narcotics. There are about two hundred federal Bureau of Narcotics agents for the entire country, but they are aided by state and local enforcement officers.

Uniform state laws are now in operation in forty-two states, and there is increased cooperation among various enforcement agencies. Although greater penalties are being demanded for violators of narcotic laws and for some drug users, it is being urged that the penalties imposed on young novices be less severe than those given the organized dope peddler. One reason advanced is that long sentences for peddlers keep them out of circulation and thus make it harder for them to re-establish connections later.

In the United Kingdom, where a much different procedure from that used in the United States is in effect, there were only 335 heroin and morphine addicts known to the authorities in 1955, as compared with the estimated minimum of about 60,000 in the United States, a country three and a half times larger. Even if the official figure is inaccurate, the actual number is said to be probably not large.[52] The black market in drugs there is not great, nor are there many addicts who are "pushers" (peddlers of drugs). There drug addiction is considered as a medical problem, a matter to be treated by the physician with prescription of drugs at low cost, often not as high as the price of cigarettes.[53] Doctors are supposed to prescribe a minimum dosage and to make prolonged attempts to cure the addict. British officials, as well as the public, do not regard the addict as a criminal. The addict does not have to steal, become a prostitute, or peddle drugs in order to secure drugs, and addicts are therefore relatively noncriminal. The system does not appear to have brought about an increase in drug addiction. Lindesmith states that since the present British system seems to work, in that the problem is small and is not growing larger, there is an understandable reluctance to change it in any important way.[54]

Based on British and other experience, a different approach to this

[52] Alfred R. Lindesmith, "The British System of Narcotics Control," *Law and Contemporary Problems*, 22:141–142 (Winter, 1957).

[53] Marihuana is not prescribed, as it is regarded as an illicit drug and is dealt with by the police. It does not appear to lead often to heroin addiction, as it appears to do in the United States.

[54] Lindesmith, "The British System of Narcotics Control," *loc. cit.*, p. 147.

problem in the United States has been suggested by several authorities.[55] They believe that suppression has actually increased the difficulties of controlling the drug traffic because it has made necessary the development of an elaborate organization for illicit supply which seeks to extend itself by inducing nonaddicts to become users of narcotics. They also believe that crime has been increased because of addicts' efforts to obtain enough money to buy illicitly the high-priced drugs which could be obtained legally for a fraction of the cost charged by peddlers. After a two-year study Schur suggested that the British policy might well be applied to the American drug situation, even allowing for differences in the public image of the addict and in the detection and prevention of drug smuggling.[56] He feels that drug addiction should not be treated as a crime: "One also becomes aware that current American policies cannot help but fail. The policy of withholding legal satisfaction of the demand for narcotics inevitably leads to a profit-motivated and socially-dangerous illicit market in drugs." [57] Finally, the Joint Committee on Narcotic Drugs (of the American Bar Association and the American Medical Association) has recommended that drug addiction be viewed as a disease rather than a police problem. They have recommended a review of laws to abolish prison terms for addicts, to allow qualified doctors to dispense narcotics, and to establish an experimental outpatient clinic for the care of addicts.

Summary

At one time drug users were tolerated, even in the United States, but later the use of drugs was made illegal. Men use drugs much more than do women, and the use of drugs appears to be increasing among younger persons.

In order to become an addict a person must be aware of the drug, know how to administer it, and recognize its effects. Drug addiction has a culture associated with it. This includes a system of sale and distribution of the drugs and the indoctrination of many persons into the use of drugs by others who are already addicted. Drug addicts have an elaborate argot.

The use of drugs does not appear to be an important factor in crime.

---

[55] Lindesmith, *Opiate Addiction*, pp. 204–210, and August Vollmer, *The Police and Modern Society* (Berkeley: University of California Press, 1936), pp. 117–118. Also see *Drug Addiction: Crime or Disease*, Interim and Final Reports of the Joint Committee of the American Bar Association and the American Medical Association on Narcotic Drugs (Bloomington: Indiana University Press, 1960), and Edwin M. Schur, "British Narcotics Policies," *Journal of Criminal Law, Criminology and Police Science*, 51:619–630 (March–April, 1961). Also see Edwin M. Schur, "Drug Addiction under British Policy," *Social Problems*, 9:156–157 (Fall, 1961).

[56] Schur, "British Narcotics Policies," *loc. cit.*   [57] *Ibid.*, pp. 628–629.

Most criminals do not appear to use drugs. Addicts, however, may commit offenses in order to secure drugs or the money with which to purchase them.

There are two different approaches to the control of drug addiction. Some believe in rigid suppression, whereas others feel that this procedure has increased the deviant behavior by causing the development of an organization for illicit supply. They feel that drugs should be supplied to addicts through governmental and medical agencies.

Selected Readings

ANSLINGER, H. J., and WILLIAM F. TOMPKINS. *The Traffic in Narcotics.* New York: Funk & Wagnalls Company, 1953. A general description of drugs, the methods of their use, and the laws controlling them. Anslinger, for many years United States Commissioner of Narcotics, resigned in 1962.

BECKER, HOWARD S. "Becoming a Marihuana User," *American Journal of Sociology,* 59:235–243 (November, 1953). This study of a group of marihuana users describes the process of becoming a user. A good deal of case material is included.

Drug Addiction: Crime or Disease? Interim and Final Reports of the Joint Committee of the American Bar Association and the American Medical Association on Narcotic Drugs. Bloomington: Indiana University Press, 1960. Contains a comprehensive analysis of the drug problem in the United States by Morris Ploscowe, as well as a survey of drug control programs in Britain and other European countries. The reports reveal widespread dissatisfaction with existing legislation and law enforcement among medical and legal authorities in this country.

Law and Contemporary Problems. "Narcotics" Vol. 22, No. 1 (Winter, 1957). Contains a series of articles on many phases of drug addiction including the history of the development of narcotics, addiction and its treatment, social and psychological factors in narcotics addiction, juvenile narcotics use, narcotics and criminality, international control of narcotics, narcotic drug laws and enforcement policies, alternative solution to the problem, and the British system of narcotics control.

LINDESMITH, ALFRED R. *Opiate Addiction.* Bloomington: University of Indiana Press, 1947. A social psychological study of the process of opiate addiction containing many cases.

SCHUR, EDWIN M., "British Narcotics Policies," *Journal of Criminal Law, Criminology and Police Science,* 51:619–630 (March–April, 1961).

Chapter

12

Alcohol Drinking
and Alcoholism

Problems related to the consumption of alcohol, the role of the tavern in a society, and the alcoholic are far from being unique to any culture or age. Researches on the contents of the tombs of ancient Egypt and in the buried cities of Babylon reveal that as early in history as three thousand years ago the use of wine and beer was a subject of moral concern.

Socrates, Aristotle, Plato, Cicero, and others inveighed against intoxication as debasing the dignity of man. The Spartans and Carthaginians limited drinking among soldiers on active duty for reasons of efficiency. The Ethiopians, who were water drinkers, boasted of their long life and vigor in contrast to the shorter life span of their wine-using neighbors, the Persians.

The barbarian Gauls invading Roman territories reacted violently when they discovered the effects of wine. This was noticed by Roman leaders and by the Greeks, who avoided giving battle until the invaders were stuporous from drinking, then slaughtered them easily. But it should be noted that although Egyptian civilization attained a remarkably high level, both men and women gorged themselves with wine to the point of deep intoxication. The Spanish and Portuguese people, on the other hand, appear to have been remarkably abstemious.

Various attempts at regulatory controls of drinking appear in the ancient literature. In China during the Chou Dynasty (1134–256 B.C.) and the reign of the fourth emperor of the Yuan Dynasty, about 1312 A.D., laws against the manufacture, sale, and consumption of wine were established and repealed no less than forty-one times. Penalties for violation of the decrees were extremely severe.[1]

Today the use of alcohol represents a conflict of values, while excessive drinking and alcoholism may be considered as deviant behavior. The value conflicts over the use of alcohol actually represent a struggle between a Calvinistic tradition that it is the community's responsibility to

---

[1] Raymond G. McCarthy ed., *Drinking and Intoxication* (New York: The Free Press of Glencoe, 1959), pp. 39–40.

supervise the individual's drinking and an individualistic tradition that regards drinking as a matter of free choice.

In 1959, 85.3 percent of the population of the United States resided in areas where alcoholic beverages were sold.[2] Local option is provided in many states so that the percentage of population living in "wet" areas was less than two thirds in many states: in Tennessee, 33.1; Georgia, 38.1; Kentucky, 42.5; Alabama, 51.1; Texas, 54.1; Kansas, 50.1; Arkansas, 57.0; and North Carolina, 57.1. Mississippi is the only completely dry state, Oklahoma having repealed its dry law in 1959. Moreover, some counties in many states do not permit alcoholic beverages to be drunk where it is sold; that is, liquor is sold only in the bottle in privately or publicly owned liquor stores. In nineteen states, in 1960, the sale of distilled spirits by the bottle was controlled by a state board selling through state stores.

As a result of their continually conflicting claims and propaganda, temperance organizations and concerns manufacturing and distributing alcoholic beverages have done much to crystallize value judgments surrounding the use and misuse of alcoholic beverages. Frederick Lewis Allen in *Only Yesterday* wrote about the conflict during the Prohibition era:

> Whatever the contributions of the Prohibition regime to temperance, at least it produced intemperate propaganda and counter-propaganda. Almost any dry could tell you that Prohibition was the basis of American prosperity as attested by the mounting volume of savings-bank deposits . . . or that Prohibition had reduced the deaths from alcoholism, emptied the jails, diverted the workman's dollars to the purchase of automobiles, radios, and homes. Almost any wet could tell you that Prohibition had nothing to do with prosperity but it caused the crime wave, the increase of immorality and of the divorce rate, and a disrespect for all law which imperiled the very foundations of free government. The wets said the drys fostered Bolshevism by their fanatical zeal for laws which were inevitably flouted; the drys said the wets fostered Bolshevism by their cynical lawbreaking. Even in matters of supposed fact, you could find, if you only read and listened, any sort of ammunition that you wanted. One never saw drunkards on the streets any more; one saw more drunkards than ever. Drinking in the colleges was hardly a problem now; drinking in the colleges was at its worst. There was a still in every other home in the mining districts of Pennsylvania; drinking in the mining districts of Pennsylvania was a thing of the past. Cases of poverty as a result of drunkenness were only a fraction of what they used to be; the menace of drinking in the slums was three times as great as in Pre-Volstead days.[3]

---

[2] The Joint Committee of the States to Study Alcoholic Beverage Laws, *Alcoholic Beverage Control* (Washington, D.C.: 1960). The data for the states presented here were furnished to the Joint Committee by the Distilled Spirits Institute.

[3] Frederick Lewis Allen, *Only Yesterday* (New York: Harper & Row, Publishers, 1931), pp. 254–255. For a discussion of the issues and organizations involved in Repeal, see Raymond G. McCarthy and Edgar M. Douglass, *Alcohol and Social Responsibility* (New York: Thomas Y. Crowell Company and the Yale Plan Clinic, 1949), pp. 25–41, also reprinted in McCarthy, *Drinking and Intoxication*, pp. 368–435. Sweden has tried

The Drys have concentrated their attack by upholding the home, family, children, religion, and morality, which they claim are endangered by the use of alcohol and the existence of taverns. Newspaper headlines assist them in their attempts to show the deleterious consequences of the use of alcohol: "Stampede for Holiday Liquor"; "Drink Turns Patrolman into Murderer"; "Paralytic Struck by Drunk Driver"; "Liquor and Bad Company Lead to Jail"; "Drunken Boys Led to Jail"; "Man Killed in Tavern Brawl"; "Drunken Father Beats Family"; "Drunken Driver Kills Three." A speaker at a convention of the National Temperance Movement stated:

> At the close of the first ten years of repeal a committee of fifty, after extensive research, reported that the use of liquor is responsible for 20 per cent of divorces, 20 per cent of fatal accidents, 25 per cent of insanity, 37 per cent of poverty, 50 per cent of crime, 75 to 90 per cent of venereal infection. My guess is that every one of these percentages is now greater after five additional years of repeal—with the possible exception of the one of poverty.[4]

Although many of these claims cannot be supported, there is no question that the excessive use of alcoholic beverages is costing industry huge sums of money in the form of absenteeism, inefficiency on the job, and accidents. Landis, in 1945, for example, estimated the total monetary cost of excessive drinking as nearly $800 million; it is, of course, impossible to estimate the indirect social cost.[5]

A comparison between a group of industrial workers who were problem drinkers and two control groups revealed that the problem drinkers had 2.9 times as many days absent and 2.5 times as many cases of illness or injury-caused absences of eight days or more as the control groups.[6] The cost of sickness payments was 3.3 times as great and, in the case of women problem drinkers, twice as great.

There are conflicts not only about the use of alcohol but also about the tavern as a public institution. An investigation in Wisconsin revealed that both patrons and nonpatrons of taverns differ within each group in their attitudes toward the tavern and drinking in general.[7] Some non-

---

modified prohibition, and Finland, prohibition, but both countries have changed their laws. For a discussion of some of the results see McCarthy, *op. cit.*, pp. 347–367.

[4] Paul S. Rees, "Forward to Victory," a synopsis of his closing address at the Biennial Convention of the Convention of the National Temperance Movement in *The National Temperance Digest*, 3:5 (February, 1949).

[5] Benson Y. Landis, "Some Economic Aspects of Alcohol Problems," *Memoirs of the Section on Alcohol Studies* (No. 4; New Haven, Conn.: Quarterly Journal of Studies on Alcohol, 1945), pp. 28–29.

[6] Observer (a pseud.) and Milton A. Maxwell, "A Study of Absenteeism, Accidents and Sickness Payments in Problem Drinkers in One Industry," *Quarterly Journal of Studies on Alcohol*, 20:302–312 (June, 1959). Also see Harrison M. Trice, "Work Accidents and the Problem Drinker: A Case Study," *ILR Research*, 3:2–6, No. 2 (1957).

[7] Boyd E. Macrory, "The Tavern and the Community," *Quarterly Journal of Studies on Alcohol*, 13:609–637 (December, 1952).

patrons, for example, believe that the contemporary tavern is a lesser evil than the speakeasy of bootleg days and that there is no harm in an occasional drink with friends in a tavern; other nonpatrons think of the tavern as a place to relax and meet friends; but other nonpatrons view the tavern as an unmitigated evil related to drunkenness, unhappy home life, marital difficulties, and neglect of children. Regular tavern patrons were similarly divided in their opinions. Some believed that the tavern is useful because it provides a place for relaxation, a meeting place, and an orderly place for drinking as opposed to Prohibition days. Other regular patrons, however, believed that the tavern contributed to various types of crime, loss of jobs, domestic difficulties, highway accidents, and alcoholism.

The attitudes of certain groups in the population toward drinking and public drinking houses are also reflected in the rigid regulation of alcohol distribution through taverns.[8] These regulations imply that the tavern is the source of immorality, delinquency, and drunkenness and that a man of high moral character must be in charge if the community is to be protected. Regulations generally limit the number of taverns to a certain ratio of the population and specify high license fees, generally between $200 and $900 a year, regardless of the size of the establishment. Some states closely scrutinize prospective tavernkeepers' past histories for records of criminal or other immoral behavior. In some communities, the license of a tavern owner who knowingly employs a bartender with a criminal background is subject to revocation. Taverns must observe strict closing hours, they must generally remain closed on election days, on Christmas Eve, and on certain other holidays. They must not permit minors on the premises, are not allowed to obscure a full view of the interior from the outside, may not give "credit," and may not serve visibly intoxicated persons. Women, except relatives, are generally prohibited from working in taverns, although the employment of women is customary in Great Britain. In several states so-called dram acts make the tavern owner responsible for injuries incurred by a patron after leaving the tavern.

Physiological Effects of Alcohol

Alcohol is a chemical substance which is derived through a process of fermentation or by distillation. Although the process of distillation of alcoholic beverages from barley, corn, wheat, and other grains is fairly recent in human history, nearly all societies have made fermented beverages, such as wine, beer, and similar products, for thousands of years.[9]

[8] See Marshall B. Clinard, "The Public Drinking House and Society," in David J. Pittman and Charles R. Snyder eds., *Alcohol, Culture and Drinking Patterns* (New York: John Wiley & Sons, Inc., 1962), pp. 270–292.

[9] Clarence H. Patrick, *Alcohol, Culture and Society* (Durham, N.C.: Duke University Press, 1952), pp. 12–39.

Following the intake of alcoholic beverages, a certain amount of alcohol is absorbed into the blood stream from the stomach, but most of it is absorbed in the small intestine. It is carried in the blood to the liver and then disseminated in diluted form to every part of the body. Because there can never be more than 1 percent of alcohol in the blood stream, it cannot directly cause organic brain damage, neither "corroding," "dissolving," nor in any way directly harming the brain cells.[10] In fact, all substances classed as volatile anesthetics, such as ether, can produce precisely the same reactions upon the brain.[11] Alcohol is not physiologically habit-forming in the sense that certain narcotics are. One does not become a chronic drinker as the result of the first, twentieth, or even one hundredth drink. Moreover, it has never been demonstrated that the craving for alcohol is inherited.[12]

Actually the effect of alcohol is determined by the rate at which it is absorbed into the body, which depends upon the kind of alcoholic beverage consumed, the proportion of alcohol it contains, the speed with which it is drunk, and the amount and type of food in the stomach, as well as on certain minor physiological differences among individuals.[13] In moderate quantities alcohol has relatively little effect on a person, but large quantities disturb the activity in the organs controlled by the brain and cause the phenomenon known as "drunkenness." The effect on behavior of different kinds and quantities of alcoholic beverages on the human system of a 150-pound person is shown in Table 12.1.

As alcohol is consumed, it acts increasingly as a depressant and as an anesthetic.

> The prime action of alcohol in the body is its depressant action on the function of the central nervous system, the brain. This is an anesthetic action no different from that of ether or chloroform. The part of the brain affected and the degree of impairment depend on the concentration of alcohol in the blood and therefore acting on the brain. Although this action is entirely on the brain, disturbance in behavior is manifested in the organs controlled by the particular brain areas affected. Speech is thick, hands clumsy, knees sag, the person appears drunk—not because of the presence of alcohol in his tongue, hands or knees, but because it has depressed those parts of his brain controlling these organs.
>
> In a person of average size, 2 or 3 ounces of whisky present in the body will produce 0.05 per cent of alcohol in the blood. With this amount the uppermost levels of brain functioning are depressed, diminishing inhibi-

---

[10] McCarthy and Douglass, *op. cit.*, pp. 89–93.

[11] See Howard W. Haggard, "The Physiological Effects of Large and Small Amounts of Alcohol," in *Alcohol, Science and Society* (New Brunswick, N.J.: Quarterly Journal of Studies on Alcohol, 1945), pp. 59–72.

[12] Anne Roe, "Children of Alcoholic Parents Raised in Foster Homes," in *Alcohol, Science and Society*, p. 124.

[13] McCarthy and Douglass, *op. cit.*, p. 89.

Table 12.1. The Effect of Alcoholic Beverages

Amount of beverage consumed	Concentration of alcohol attained in blood	Effect		Time required for all alcohol to leave the body
1 highball (1½ oz. whisky) or 1 cocktail (1½ oz. whisky) or 3½ oz. fortified wine or 5½ oz. ordinary wine or 2 bottles beer (24 oz.)	0.03%	No noticeable effects on behavior		2 hrs.
2 highballs or 2 cocktails or 7 oz. fortified wine or 11 oz. ordinary wine or 4 bottles beer	0.06%	Increasing effects with variation among individuals and in the same individuals at different times	Feeling of warmth—mental relaxation—slight decrease of fine skills—less concern with minor irritations and restraints	4 hrs.
3 highballs or 3 cocktails or 10½ oz. fortified wine or 16½ oz. (1 pt.) ordinary wine or 6 bottles beer	0.09%		Buoyancy—exaggerated emotion and behavior—talkative, noisy, or morose	6 hrs.
4 highballs or 4 cocktails or 14 oz. fortified wine or 22 oz. ordinary wine or 8 bottles (3 qts.) beer	0.12%		Impairment of fine coordination—clumsiness—slight to moderate unsteadiness in standing or walking	8 hrs.
5 highballs or 5 cocktails or (½ pt. whisky)	0.15%	Intoxication—unmistakable abnormality of gross bodily functions and mental faculties		10 hrs.

For those weighing considerably more or less than 150 pounds the amounts of beverage indicated above will be correspondingly greater or less. The effects indicated at each stage will diminish as the concentration of alcohol in the blood diminishes.

SOURCE: Leon A. Greenberg, "Intoxication and Alcoholism: Physiological Factors," *The Annals*, 315:28 (January, 1958). Reprinted by permission of the American Academy of Political and Social Science.

tion, restraint, and judgment. The drinker feels that he is "sitting on top of the world," many of his normal inhibitions have vanished; he takes many personal and social liberties as the impulse prompts; he is long-winded and has an obvious blunting of self-criticism. At a concentration of 0.10 per cent of alcohol in the blood, resulting from 5 or 6 ounces of whisky in the body, function of the lower motor area of the brain is dulled. The person sways perceptibly; he has difficulty putting on his coat; he fumbles with the key at the door; words stumble over a clumsy tongue.

The states so far described are popularly designated as mild intoxication or "feeling high." The significant feature of these states is depression and dulling of sensory and motor function and, contrary to popular belief, not stimulation. The illusion of stimulation is given by the increased tempo and altered quality of behavior occurring when the normally prevailing inhibitions and restraints are removed by alcohol. The effect may be compared to releasing the brakes rather than stepping on the accelerator. Notwithstanding this illusion there is actually measurable reduction in sensitivity, impaired discrimination, and diminished speed of motor responses. The drinker, however, often denies that this occurs; often asserts, on the contrary, that after a few drinks his reactions, perception, and discrimination are better. This is an important effect of alcohol; his judgment about himself and his own activities is blunted, allowing for an inflated feeling of competence and self-confidence.

With increasing concentrations of alcohol in the blood there is a corresponding progression of impairment of functions. At 0.20 per cent, resulting from about 10 ounces of whisky, the entire motor area of the brain is profoundly affected. The individual tends to assume a horizontal position; he needs help to walk or undress. At 0.30 per cent, from the presence of a pint of whisky in the body, sensory perception is so dulled that the drinker has little comprehension of what he sees, hears, or feels; he is stuporous. At 0.40 per cent, perception is obliterated; the person is in coma, he is anesthetized. At 0.60 or 0.70 per cent, the lowest, most primitive levels of the brain controlling breathing and heartbeat cease to function and death ensues. Throughout this entire progression the concentrations of alcohol in the body are far too low to cause any direct organic damage to the tissues. The disturbance is entirely one of nerve function and is reversible; short of death, when the alcohol disappears the effect goes with it.[14]

If taken in moderate amounts, alcohol can lessen tensions and worry, and in general it may ease the fatigue associated with anxiety.[15] It presents an illusion of being a stimulant because it reduces or alters the cortical control over action. Under the influence of alcohol a person may become active, boisterous, aggressive, silent, or even fall into a stupor, all as a result of this reduction in cortical control and not from stimulation.

Much has been made of the so-called alcoholic diseases, such as beriberi, pellagra, and cirrhosis of the liver. Although these diseases are found among nonalcoholics as well as among alcoholics, the continuous drinking of alcohol brings about an almost complete loss of appetite, and, if this drinking is not curbed, disease may follow, not from the alcohol consumed but rather because of the nutritional deficiencies resulting from prolonged drinking. These deficiencies may produce an organic ailment called polyneuritis, or, less technically, beriberi, caused by a lack

---

[14] Leon A. Greenberg, "Intoxication and Alcoholism: Physiological Factors," *The Annals*, 315:26–27 (January, 1958). Reprinted by permission of the American Academy of Political and Social Science.

[15] Haggard, "The Physiological Effects . . . of Alcohol," *loc. cit.*, p. 63.

of vitamin B_1; or pellagra, caused by a deficiency of niacin. The fact that these deficiencies are present has caused some researchers to believe that alcoholism can be prevented or controlled by proper nutrition.[16] The disease which the man in the street most often associates with chronic alcoholism is cirrhosis of the liver. Although this disease occurs proportionately more often among inebriates than among nondrinkers, medical men state that it is not caused directly by alcohol but instead is due to some nutritional deficiency which has not as yet been conclusively demonstrated.[17]

Drinking as a Social Phenomenon

Alcoholic beverages of one type or another have been widely used for centuries by most ancient and modern peoples.[18] The people of Western Europe, and those who first colonized America, were no exception.

> In New England and the Middle and Southern colonies along the eastern seaboard, beer and ale were part of the daily diet and believed necessary to maintain health. However, from the earliest days, drunkenness was frowned upon and punishments were imposed on those who consumed more than was considered seemly. During the late eighteenth century, rum, which has a far higher alcohol content than ale or beer, became an integral part of the economic and social life of the colonies. Numerous distilleries were established in all the population centers.[19]

Drinking patterns today appear to vary in terms of the beverage used, the circumstances under which drinking takes place, the time, the amount, and the individual's own attitude and that of others toward his drinking. All drinking patterns are learned, just as other behavior is learned. As one writer on alcohol has stated, there are no universal drinking patterns for John, the average citizen: "In any event, John will not drink like a Zulu or an Austrian or a Japanese; in fact, he will not drink like a New Yorker or a Californian or a ditch digger or a Yale man or a Kentucky mountaineer, unless he is or has been in socially significant contact with such a group." [20] Patterns of drinking come down to us from

[16] Roger J. Williams, *Alcoholism: The Nutritional Approach* (Austin: University of Texas Press, 1959).

[17] Norman Jolliffe, "Alcohol and Nutrition: The Diseases of Chronic Alcoholism," in *Alcohol, Science and Society*, pp. 76–77.

[18] For a discussion of drinking practices of ancient Greece and Rome, the Far East, Central and South America, as well as France, England, Canada, and Russia, see McCarthy, *op. cit.*, pp. 39–179.

[19] Raymond G. McCarthy, "Alcoholism: Attitudes and Attacks, 1775–1935," *The Annals*, 315:13 (January, 1958).

[20] Selden D. Bacon, "Sociology and the Problems of Alcohol," *Memoirs of the Section of Studies on Alcohol* (No. 1; New Brunswick, N.J.: Quarterly Journal of Studies on Alcohol, 1946), pp. 17–18.

a long past in which alcohol has been used. The knowledge, ideas, norms, and values involved in the use of alcoholic beverages which have passed from generation to generation have thus maintained the continuity of an alcohol culture.

Drinking plays a significant role in everyday interpersonal affairs. Alcohol is used by many people to celebrate national holidays, such as Christmas and New Year's, and to rejoice in victories, whether those of war, the football field, or the ballot box. The bride and groom are often toasted, and the father may celebrate the birth of a child with a drink "all around." Promotions, anniversaries, and important special events of achievement by the family and close friends often call for a drink. Businessmen may negotiate contracts over a few glasses, and meeting an old friend is often the occasion for a drink. In some homes guests are welcomed with a drink or cocktails before dinner to help get the guests acquainted.

Even some church ceremonials and, on occasion, the bereavement of death are accompanied by alcoholic beverages. On a more inclusive level, it has been said: "The custom of drinking together to symbolize common feeling and unity is almost universal in present-day culture. . . . Thus imbedded in the culture pattern is the notion that in alcohol is magic which, in sorrow and in joy, in elation and in depression, in rebellion against the misery of travail and the restraints which hem one in, frees the human spirit and permits it to soar into the heavens unhampered by the ills of the flesh." [21]

Drinking by teen-agers is almost entirely a group activity and represents culturally patterned and socially controlled behavior. The drinking of teen-agers is almost entirely "partying action." [22] Drinking, for at least some teen-agers, is related to the passage from youth into young male adult roles in our society. Teen-age groups are important reference groups to the members.

There are also drinking patterns among college students. Dating often includes having a drink before or after a dance, show, or party. In some places college men have a tradition of drinking to celebrate the conclusion of examinations. "Bull sessions" often involve beer drinking, and some fraternities and other social organizations have drinking traditions. In European universities there were, and still are, "drinking fraternities" for which members qualified by their ability to consume a large quantity of wine, beer, ale, or other liquor. College drinking songs, expressing friendship and other deep feelings, have at times attained great popularity. A detailed study of college drinking habits found that motivations for

[21] Ernest R. Mowrer, *Disorganization: Personal and Social* (Phildelphia: J. B. Lippincott Company, 1942), pp. 263–264. Reprinted by permission of the publisher.
[22] Christopher Sower, "Teen-Age Drinking as Group Behavior," *Quarterly Journal of Studies on Alcohol*, 20:656 (September, 1959).

drinking, as given by men and women who drink, were approximately the same.[23] However, women more frequently felt that they drank in order to get along better on dates and they drank more often than men did to relieve illness and physical discomfort.

Despite the widespread use of alcohol in connection with many social functions, one writer has contrasted the value systems implicit in American drinking patterns with those on the Continent.

> Traditionally, in European cultures, aside from past dietetic necessity, drinking has been a phase of a deeply rooted, stable and integrated social and recreational pattern. Among Europeans, drinking may remain a satisfying social practice rather than a vice or social problem, largely because it remains an element within otherwise integrated and participating recreational practices. . . . With Europeans, for example, drinking has traditionally been a phase of the occasion of the group's coming together; with Americans, conversely, coming together has all too frequently provided the occasion for drinking. In this distinction, and its historical evolution, appears to lie one of the salient factors in the more disturbing features of our drinking habits.[24]

Public Drinking Houses and Society

A large proportion of drinking is done in groups, much of it in public drinking houses, which are found in most of the world today under a variety of names: American taverns and bars, British pubs, French bistros, German beer halls, Italian wine houses, and Japanese bars. In the United States alone there are over 200,000 bars and taverns.

A tavern, as we shall refer to a public drinking house, is more than a place where alcoholic beverages are sold for consumption on the premises. There are several important characteristics of a contemporary tavern: (1) A tavern involves group drinking. (2) This drinking is commercial in the sense that the ability to buy a drink is available to all as opposed to the bars of private clubs. (3) A tavern serves alcohol, however, and can thus be distinguished from the modern soda fountains, the coffeehouses of the Middle East, or the teahouses of the Orient. (4) It has a tavernkeeper or bartender who serves as a functionary of the institution and around whom, in part, the drinking gravitates. (5) There are many customs connected with a tavern, including the physical surroundings, types of drinks, and hours of sale.[25]

---

[23] Robert Straus and Selden D. Bacon, *Drinking in College* (New Haven, Conn.: Yale University Press, 1953), p. 71. Also see C. A. Hecht, R. J. Grine, and S. E. Rothrock, "Drinking and Dating among College Women," *Quarterly Journal of Studies on Alcohol*, 9:252–259 (September, 1948); and F. C. Berezin and N. R. Roth, "Drinking Practices of College Women," *Quarterly Journal of Studies on Alcohol*, 11:212–221 (June, 1950).

[24] Herbert A. Bloch, "Alcohol and American Recreational Life," *American Scholar*, 18:56–57 (January, 1949).

[25] Clinard, "The Public Drinking House and Society," *loc. cit.*

Taverns can be traced to Babylon, where the Code of Hammurabi provided for their regulation. In ancient Greece there were many taverns, although they had quite an unsavory reputation.[26] In Roman times there was a great variety of public drinking houses, ten different types being distinguished according to location, type of patron, and type of tavern operator. Some Roman taverns were regarded unfavorably and some were well accepted. One writer has flatly stated that more harm to Roman society would have resulted from their abolition than actually resulted from their continued existence.[27]

The inns of seventeenth- and eighteenth-century England, however, are more generally regarded as the forerunners of the modern tavern. In the earliest of these inns alcoholic beverages were served in the kitchen to travelers and persons of the local community. Eventually a special room was set apart for serving alcoholic beverages to persons who were of the upper classes and who did not care to associate with others in the kitchen. There were two classes of public houses in England, the ale and the wine taverns. The latter were considered more "respectable than the ale taverns and catered to a wealthier clientele." [28] Although some people regarded taverns as dens of iniquity, others considered them as necessary public institutions. One writer has stated that many of the public drinking houses in London were the meeting places of politicians and traders and were "the only places of convenient sojourn and pleasant sociality." [29]

Taverns played a significant role not only in England, where they came from, but in colonial America. In part because they believed that drinking not done in public was likely to be excessive and that the sale of liquor in a tavern could be regulated, the Puritan authorities in Massachusetts in 1656 even enacted a law making towns liable to a fine for not maintaining an ordinary (tavern).[30] During Puritan times tavernkeepers enjoyed a rather high status, and attempts were made to attract the right kind of person into this occupation. Tavernkeepers were granted land or pasturage and were often exempted from school taxes and church rates.[31]

In colonial America taverns served as coach stations or wayside stops and as places of lodging for strangers in the community. They were used as schools, courthouses, public meeting houses, post offices, job markets, and

---

[26] W. C. Firebaugh, *Inns of Greece and Rome* (Chicago: F. M. Morris, 1928).

[27] *Ibid.*, p. 65.

[28] J. D. Rolleston, "Alcoholism in Medieval England," *British Journal of Inebriety*, 31:46 (October, 1933).

[29] Frederick W. Hackwood, *Inns, Ales and Drinking Customs of Old England* (New York: Sturgis and Walton Co., 1911), p. 172.

[30] Eugene Field, *The Colonial Tavern* (Providence: Preston and Rounds, 1897), pp. 11–12.

[31] Herbert Asbury, *The Great Illusion* (New York: Doubleday & Company, Inc., 1950), p. 8.

as places for celebrations of weddings and national holidays.[32] One writer asserts that in colonial America the people found that "the tavern was their club, their board of trade, their 'exchanges,' and indeed, to most of the colonists it served as their newspapers." [33]

In both England and the United States the coming of the railroads gradually eliminated the necessity for taverns as coach stations, and their number declined. The Industrial Revolution, in turn, brought thousands of migrants, particularly single men, to work in the factories. A new type of public drinking house, the saloon, replaced the wayside taverns. The saloon became the urban standard characterized by strictly male patronage, drinking at an elaborate bar with free meals, and a special "family entrance." The overelaborate *décor* was in dramatic contrast to the squalid everyday environment of the workingman.[34] Most saloons performed an important function by helping to relieve the poverty, loneliness, and monotony of city life, although some were centers of deviant behavior such as drunkenness, gambling, and prostitution. A sociological study of saloons in the nineteenth ward of Chicago between 1896 and 1897 found that most saloons in this area were not centers of intemperance or vice.[35] In fact, the saloon was found to have many other functions:

> It [the saloon] is the workingman's club. Many of his leisure hours are spent here. In it he finds more of the things which approximate to luxury than he finds at home, almost more than he finds in any other public place in the ward. . . . But his demand for even these things is not fundamental, they are but the means to his social expression. It is the society of his fellows that he seeks and must have.[36]

After enactment of the Eighteenth Amendment in this country the saloon as a type became legally extinct. It was replaced by the illicit "speakeasy" with its select clientele, often adulterated alcoholic beverages, and an urban sophisticated setting. After the repeal of Prohibition the modern tavern made its appearance; more correctly, at least five different varieties of public places emerged, these types being largely associated with certain areas of the city. They were different from the saloon in that women in general were permitted, the surroundings were more attractive, and patrons more frequently drank while seated at tables rather than while standing at a bar. Contemporary taverns may be classified as Skid Row, the downtown

---

[32] Simon Dinitz, "The Relation of the Tavern to the Drinking Phases of Alcoholics." Unpublished doctoral dissertation, University of Wisconsin, Madison, 1951.

[33] Field, *op. cit.*, pp. 232–233.

[34] Maurice Gorham and M. McDunnett, *Inside the Pub* (London: The Architectural Press, 1950), p. 68.

[35] Ernest C. Moore, "The Social Value of the Saloon," *American Journal of Sociology*, 3:1–12 (July, 1897). Also see Raymond Calkins, *Substitutes for the Saloon: An Investigation Made for the Committee of Fifty* (Boston: Houghton Mifflin Company, 1901).

[36] Moore, *loc. cit.*, pp. 4–5.

bar, the dine and dance establishment, the night club, and the neighborhood tavern, which is divided primarily by location, and secondarily by patronage, into four subtypes: the rural, village, suburban, and city neighborhood types.

1. The Skid Row tavern is located close to the business district of urban centers. It offers little more than drinking and the blaring juke box. The bulk of its patrons are drifters, transients, and alcoholics. Drunkenness, prostitution, gambling, and violations of other state laws and ordinances are frequent.

2. The downtown bar is located in the business district, has long bars, few tables, and a predominantly male patronage. There are few recreational facilities but much drinking over business agreements or prior to going home from work.

3. The drink and dine establishment is located in the business district or close to the city limits, where it competes with night clubs which not only often serve fine food but afford an opportunity to dance as well. It has well-kept and often spacious dining rooms where fine food is served; yet much of its income and most of its profit are derived from the sale of alcoholic beverages.

4. The night club is usually located near the city limits along main highways. This type of tavern offers drink, food, and dancing, and the seating arrangement usually centers about the stage and dance floor. A larger proportion of women patronize both this type of tavern and the drink and dine establishment than the downtown bar. It is patronized by the business and professional classes, as well as by draftsmen and laborers.

5. The neighborhood tavern is the most numerous, constituting probably three fourths of all taverns. Most drinking is done seated around tables. It is patronized by people, largely couples, in the neighborhood. There are several subtypes, the city, suburban, village, and rural. It has many functions as a meeting place for regular patrons, offering them amusement, recreation, a chance to talk and to enjoy music, and general relaxation.[37]

Public drinking houses, as well as package liquor stores, are disproportionately concentrated in lower-class areas and constitute a highly visible symbol of the lower-class way of life.[38] There tends to be little distance between the place of residence and public facilities for alcohol consumption. This suggests that "people in the upper reaches of the social hierarchy might do most of their drinking at home or in downtown lounges and hotels, public places for imbibing being separated by some distance from place of residence."[39]

[37] Condensed from Macrory, "The Tavern and the Community," loc. cit.

[38] Harold W. Pfautz and Robert W. Hyde, "The Ecology of Alcohol in the Local Community," Quarterly Journal of Studies on Alcohol, 21:447–456 (September, 1960).

[39] Ibid., p. 455.

It appears that the functions of a tavern reflect the type of tavern and the conditions of its neighborhood. Examples are the Skid Row taverns, where drunkenness and other deviant behavior may flourish, and respectable neighborhood taverns, each of which reflects the norms of the local community. Drinking does not appear to be the actual reason for patronizing most neighborhood taverns.[40] Rather, such taverns function primarily as a place for people to meet for the sake of establishing and maintaining social relationships.[41] People also go to taverns to avoid loneliness and to relax from the cares and problems of the home and the factory, office, or farm. The neighborhood tavern also serves as a place for recreation, which includes such entertainments as card games, shuffleboard, pinball machines, juke boxes, or television. Finally, sympathetic tavern-keepers, bartenders, and others give the patron an opportunity to talk over his personal problems. Much the same reasons appear to account for the extensive participation in British pubs (public drinking houses) and French bistros.[42] According to one study, British pubs are patronized not only for the sake of drinking but for the opportunities for sociability and recreation they provide.[43]

> No pub can simply be regarded as a drinking shop. It may be lacking in facilities for games and music, present no organized forms of social activity and its actual accommodation be of the crudest, but none the less the activities of the drinkers are not confined to drinking. . . . The pub is a centre of social activities—for the ordinary pub goer the main scene of social life. Worktown working people rarely meet in each other's homes for social activities in the way middle classes do. For some there is the social activity of politics, football, or cricket clubs. But participators in these activities are a small minority. The place where most Worktowners meet their friends and acquaintances is the pub. Men can meet and talk [out] of the way of their womenfolk.[44]

Finally, the neighborhood tavern exercises a degree of control over the drinking behavior of those who patronize it. As one writer who studied

---

[40] Clinard, "The Public Drinking House and Society," *loc. cit.* and Margaret K. Chandler, "The Social Organization of Workers in a Rooming House Area." Unpublished doctoral dissertation, University of Chicago, 1948.

[41] Macrory, "The Tavern and the Community," *loc. cit.*, pp. 630–636.

[42] Joseph Wechsberg, "They Debate L'Alcoolisme—Over Their Drinks," *The New York Times Magazine*, March 26, 1961. Wechsberg remarks that the French bistros are the hub of French democracy and where the average Frenchman spends most of his leisure time. Also see Gabriel Mouchot, "France: Drinking and Its Control," in McCarthy, *Drinking and Intoxication*, pp. 149–158.

[43] Mass-Observation, *The Pub and the People* (London: Victor Gollancz, Ltd., 1943), pp. 82–83. Authorities on British labor history, such as the Webbs, have shown that a significant portion of the old union budgets went to supply the members with ale and other drinks at meetings and social gatherings. Also see B. Seebohm Rowntree and G. R. Lavers, *English Life and Leisure* (New York: David McKay Company, Inc., 1951), pp. 159–198.

[44] Mass-Observation, *The Pub and the People*, p. 311.

a number of them stated, "Each tavern seems to set its own norms as to what degree of inebriation it will tolerate. The old timers are allowed a certain freedom. In others, drunkenness and boisterousness are generally not acceptable. . . . The sense of participation is rewarding; loss of it hurts him." [45]

Attitudes toward the tavern are influenced by a person's position in the social structure as well as by his tavern patronage.[46] While a large proportion of the general population in all social strata drink alcoholic beverages, not all go to taverns. Many consumers of alcohol, particularly those of the middle and upper classes, drink at home, at cocktail parties, or at the bars of private clubs, such as golf clubs. While they may go to cocktail lounges or night clubs, they seldom visit neighborhood taverns. Taverns are often not even located in the immediate vicinity of their homes.

Extent of Drinking in the United States

In the United States the drinking of alcohol, in order of amount consumed and cost, consists chiefly of beer, followed by distilled spirits, and wine fermented from grapes. Over the past eighty years there has been a downward trend in the drinking of distilled spirits and an increase in the consumption of beer. From the period 1860–1870 to 1960 the consumption of distilled spirits declined well over a third, while the consumption of beer almost doubled. (See Table 12.2.) In the year 1850 almost 90 percent of the absolute alcohol consumed, that is, the alcohol content of a beverage, in the United States was in the form of distilled spirits, and nearly 7 percent was beer. A century later only 38 percent was in the form of spirits; 51 percent was beer. In 1948, $8.8 billion were spent on alcoholic beverages of all types, and in 1959, $9.6 billion. In the fiscal year 1960 the United States Treasury Department reported excise tax collections of $3,193,714,000 on alcoholic beverages, or one fourth of all excise taxes, and exceeding by far those collected on tobacco, automobiles, or gasoline.[47]

Approximately two thirds of the adult population over twenty-one years of age drink some type of alcoholic beverage during the year. (See Table 12.3). A larger proportion of men drink than women, three in four men as compared with one in two women. There is considerable evidence, however, that with the increasing trend toward equality in the behavior of the sexes drinking patterns may eventually become nearly the same.[48]

[45] David Gottlieb, "The Neighborhood Tavern and the Cocktail Lounge: A Study of Class Differences," *American Journal of Sociology*, 62:561 (May, 1957).

[46] Clinard, "The Public Drinking House and Society," *loc. cit.*

[47] The federal excise tax rate on distilled spirits is $10.50 per proof gallon.

[48] John W. Riley and Charles F. Marden, "The Social Pattern of Alcoholic Drinking," *Quarterly Journal of Studies on Alcohol*, 8:265–273 (September, 1947).

Table 12.2. Apparent Consumption of Alcoholic Beverages, per Capita (Aged 15 and Over), United States, 1850–1960, in United States Gallons

Year	Spirits Beverage	Spirits Absolute alcohol	Wine Beverage	Wine Absolute alcohol	Beer Beverage	Beer Absolute alcohol	Total absolute alcohol
1850	4.17	1.88	0.46	0.08	2.70	0.14	2.10
1860	4.79	2.16	0.57	0.10	5.39	0.27	2.53
1870	3.40	1.53	0.53	0.10	8.73	0.44	2.07
1881–90	2.12	0.95	0.76	0.14	17.94	0.90	1.99
1906–10	2.14	0.96	0.92	0.17	29.27	1.47	2.60
1916–19	1.68	0.76	0.69	0.12	21.63	1.08	1.96
1940	1.48	0.67	0.91	0.16	16.29	0.73	1.56
1950	1.72	0.77	1.27	0.23	23.21	1.04	2.04
1960	1.90	0.86	1.32	0.22	21.95	0.99	2.07

SOURCE: Mark Keller and Vera Efron, *Selected Statistical Tables on Alcoholic Beverages, 1850–1960, and on Alcoholism, 1930–1960* (New Brunswick, N.J.: Quarterly Journal of Studies on Alcohol, Inc., 1961), p. 3. Used by permission of the publisher.

The number of taverns in the United States gives an additional indication of the extent of drinking, even though only about one third of all liquor sales are made in taverns. In spite of the enormous value conflicts raging over the tavern, there are over 200,000 in the United States. Chicago has more than 9000; New York City alone has 12,000. Wisconsin has 14,000 taverns which sell beer, four in every five of them also serving

Table 12.3. Proportion of United States Population Twenty-one Years and Over Who Drink Alcoholic Beverages

Study	Total population %	Men %	Women %
Ley (1940)	57	60	34
Riley and Marden (1946)	65	75	56
Gallup (1947)	63	72	54
Maxwell (1951)	63	76	51
Mulford and Miller (1960)	60	69	51

SOURCES: H. A. Ley, "Incidence of Smoking and Drinking Among 10,000 Examinees," *Proceedings of the Life Extension Examiners*, 2:57–63 (May–June, 1940); John W. Riley and Charles F. Marden, "The Social Patterns of Alcoholic Drinking," *Quarterly Journal of Studies on Alcohol*, 8:265–273 (September, 1947); News Release, American Institute of Public Opinion (Princeton, N.J.: December 18, 1948); Milton A. Maxwell, "Drinking Behavior in the State of Washington," *Quarterly Journal of Studies on Alcohol*, 13:221 (June, 1952); Harold A. Mulford and Donald E. Miller, "Drinking in Iowa: II. The Extent of Drinking and Selected Socio-cultural Categories," *Quarterly Journal of Studies on Alcohol*, 21:28 (March, 1960).

distilled spirits. A Chicago study found that the tavern has more buildings, accommodates more people, and takes more of the money and time of people in that city than do all the motion-picture houses, sporting events, and other forms of commercial recreation put together.[49]

FREQUENCY OF DRINKING

Statements about the proportion of the general population that drinks are often misleading, however, because they give no indication of the frequency of drinking. In one national survey some 17 percent of the total group (27 percent of the men and 8 percent of the women) were regular drinkers defined as those who drank three or more times a week.[50] In a sample of the state of Washington only one in ten persons was found to drink this frequently, one in five men and only three in a hundred women. (See Table 12.4.)

Table 12.4. Drinking Frequency by Percentage of Drinkers, Washington, 1951

	Total	Men	Women
Each day	3.6	7.5	0.0
4–6 times a week	2.5	4.0	1.2
3 times a week	4.9	7.9	2.0
1–2 times a week	8.0	10.1	6.1
2–3 times a month	14.2	15.9	12.7
Once a month	11.9	14.5	9.4
1–5 times a year	18.2	16.3	20.0
Total drinkers	63.3	76.2	51.4

SOURCE: Milton A. Maxwell, "Drinking Behavior in the State of Washington," *Quarterly Journal of Studies on Alcohol*, 13:221 (June, 1952). Reprinted by permission of the Journal.

Using both an index of drinking frequency and the amount of alcohol consumed, a more recent Iowa study found that 40 percent of the population are abstainers, 22 percent drink infrequently (not more than once a month) and consume small amounts of alcohol at a single sitting (not more than 1.6 ounces of absolute alcohol). Using three various similar indices, the same study classified 27 percent as light drinkers, 20 percent as moderate drinkers, and, at the extreme, the 9 percent who drank more than

---

[49] Walter O. Cromwell, "The Tavern in Community Life" (Chicago: Juvenile Protective Association, 1940), p. 11. Similar statements have been made about the English pub, to which it is estimated about one in twelve adults go on a Saturday night.— *The Pub and the People*.

[50] Riley and Marden, "The Social Pattern of Alcoholic Drinking," *loc. cit.*

once a week and consumed medium (1.6 to 2.88 ounces) or large (more than 2.88 ounces) at one sitting.[51]

There is little information on the proportion of drinking done in taverns. The Washington survey found that most drinking is done either at home or in the homes of friends.[52] About 70 percent of the men and 83 percent of the women did their drinking at home, which meant that a relatively small proportion drank in taverns, cocktail lounges, clubs, or other places. Only 2.4 percent of the women patronized taverns as compared with 14.1 percent of the men.[53] In a sample of Wisconsin replies from 872 men and 569 women, it was found that three fourths of the men patronized taverns, about half of them regularly, that is, once a month or more, whereas only about two fifths of the women went to taverns, only one in seven women being a regular patron.[54]

A larger proportion of the population drink in New England, the Middle Atlantic states, and the Pacific Coast than in the Middle West or the South.

DRINKING AND AGE

One of the most striking differences in drinking is that between various age groups. A large proportion of the younger age groups drink. A survey of high school drinking studies has concluded: "A considerable proportion of young people 14–18 years of age have had some experience with drinking. This has frequently been done with parental consent. However, drinking practices of young people can only be understood in terms of their social class, economic status, religious affiliation and drinking customs of their parents." [55]

In a study of a highly urbanized and industrialized county in Wisconsin, two in three high school students reported that they used alcoholic drinks, almost entirely beer, on social and other nonreligious occasions.[56] There was a steady increase in age until the proportion who drank at the age of eighteen was four in five. Girls drank slightly less in most age

---

[51] Harold A. Mulford and Donald E. Miller, "Drinking in Iowa. II. The Extent of Drinking and Selected Socio-cultural Categories," *Quarterly Journal of Studies on Alcohol*, 21:26–39 (March, 1960).

[52] Milton A. Maxwell, "Drinking Behavior in the State of Washington," *Quarterly Journal of Studies on Alcohol*, 13:224 (June, 1952).

[53] This figure should be slightly larger because the study combined drinking in "clubs or cocktail lounges," which accounted for 7.9 percent of the women and 9.1 percent of the men.

[54] Macrory, "The Tavern and the Community," *loc. cit.*, pp. 611–612.

[55] Raymond G. McCarthy, "High School Drinking Studies," in McCarthy, *Drinking and Intoxication*, p. 205.

[56] John L. Miller and J. Richard Wahl, *Attitudes of High School Students toward Alcoholic Beverages* (New York: The Mrs. John S. Sheppard Foundation, 1956). This was a study of Racine County, Wisconsin.

groups, but there was little difference by the age of seventeen or eighteen. Some 17 percent of the Kansas high school students in the urban Wichita area had one or more drinks of alcoholic beverages, generally beer or wine, in the week before a survey was made, compared with 11 percent in Kansas rural counties.[57] The amount of drinking was small, 9 percent of the urban students and less than half of that number in the rural areas having had four or more drinks during the previous week. Although drinking among teen-agers was positively associated with the frequency of drinking by the parents and with the fact that alcoholic beverages were kept in the home, the drinking patterns generally followed were those considered appropriate to the member of the group. A Michigan study of 2000 persons, junior and senior students in six high schools, showed even more drinking. One in every ten students considered himself a person who drinks and about one third drank with some regularity.[58]

In a national sample, approximately three fourths of those between twenty-one and twenty-nine years of age drink, two thirds between thirty and forty-nine, and only one half of those fifty years and older.[59] Those adults with a higher education drink more than those with less education. In a Washington study, similar age differences in drinking were found.[60] One survey revealed that 70 percent of those with more than a high school education drank as compared with 62 percent of the less educated group.[61] The proportion among city residents of light drinkers declines and that of heavy drinkers increases as education increases, but among farm and town dwellers the reverse is true.[62]

A large proportion of college students, some 74 percent, drink alcoholic beverages, according to Straus and Bacon's survey of 15,747 students in twenty-seven American colleges.[63] Of the total group, 80 percent of the men and 61 percent of the women belong in this category. Actually these figures are misleading, for the drinking of college students varies a great deal by the type of institution, income, family drinking, religion, and ethnic background.[64] In addition, the extent of drinking increases with each year in college. More students drink at private, nonsectarian colleges attended only by men or by women than at any other type. The least amount of drinking is done at private, coeducational, "dry" colleges. (See Table 12.5.)

The frequency of drinking among college students who drink, how-

---

[57] E. Jackson Baur and Marston M. McCluggage, "Drinking Patterns of Kansas High School Students," *Social Problems*, 5:317–326 (Spring, 1958).

[58] Christopher Sower, "Teen-Age Drinking as Group Behavior," *Quarterly Journal of Studies on Alcohol*, 20:655—668 (September, 1959).

[59] Riley and Marden, "The Social Pattern of Alcoholic Drinking," *loc. cit.*

[60] Maxwell, "Drinking Behavior in the State of Washington," *loc. cit.*, p. 229.

[61] News Release, Institute of Public Opinion (Princeton, N.J.: December 18, 1948).

[62] Mulford and Miller, "Drinking in Iowa," *loc. cit.*, p. 33.

[63] Straus and Bacon, *op. cit.*, p. 46.   [64] *Ibid.*

Table *12.5. Incidence of Drinking, by Type of College*

| | Users of Alcoholic Beverages | |
	Men (%)	Women (%)
Private, men or women only, nonsectarian	92	89
Private, coeducational, nonsectarian	92	84
Private, coeducational, "dry"	65	39
Public, coeducational, general	83	74
Public, coeducational, teachers	79	44
Public, coeducational, southern Negro	81	40

SOURCE: Robert Straus and Selden D. Bacon, *Drinking in College* (New Haven, Conn.: Yale University Press, 1953), p. 47. Reprinted by permission of the publisher.

ever, is not great. Only 21 percent of the men and 10 percent of the women are reported to drink more than once a week, and two fifths of the men and more than half of the women drink no more than once a month. (See Table 12.6.)

Table *12.6. Frequency of Drinking During Past Year*

| | Users of Alcoholic Beverages | |
Frequency	Men	Women
1 to 5 times	19%	26%
6 to 12 times	24	27
Twice a month to once a week	36	37
2 or 3 days a week	18	9
4 or more days a week	3	1
Total	100%	100%

SOURCE: Robert Straus and Selden D. Bacon, *Drinking in College* (New Haven, Conn.: Yale University Press, 1953), p. 101. Reprinted by permission of Yale University Press.

Types of Drinkers

Drinkers can be classified in terms of the deviation from norms of drinking behavior within a culture and dependence on alcohol in the life organization of the individual. Persons learn in interaction with others to think and converse about alcohol in terms of what should be done with alcohol and what it will do to and for them. This includes the amount of alcohol consumed, the purpose and meaning of drinking as an aspect of role playing, the degree to which such drinking handicaps the individual in his interpersonal relations, and his ability to refrain from taking a drink. More specifically, the classification of types of drinkers involves

the analysis of behavioral phenomena involving (1) the amount of consumption of beverage alcohol (2) in an excessive manner indicating preoccupation with alcohol which (3) interferes with the drinker's interpersonal
relations.[65] One study has devised a scale to measure preoccupation with
drinking so that the differences between types of responses to the use
of alcohol may be measured with Group I, representing the most highly
preoccupied, and with IV, the least preoccupied, with alcohol. (See Table
12.7.)

There are several types of drinkers: the social or controlled drinkers,
the heavy drinkers, the alcoholics, and the chronic alcoholics.

A *social or controlled drinker* drinks for reasons of sociability, conviviality, and conventionality. He may or may not like the taste and
effects produced by alcohol. Above all else, he is able to desist from the
use of intoxicating beverages when he chooses to do so. He drinks in a
take-it-or-leave-it manner. There are two types of social drinkers, the occasional and the regular drinker. The former drinks sporadically and
may have only a few drinks a year, whereas the regular social drinker
may drink three or more times a week.

Not only does the *heavy drinker* make more frequent use of alcohol
than the regular social drinker; in addition and occasionally, he may
consume such quantities that intoxication results. Some studies have defined a heavy drinker as one who takes three or more drinks of liquor at
a "sitting" more than once a week. He is sometimes, but not always, given
to week-end binges or, at a party, may be drinking too heavily or just
having a few more than anyone else in the place. Whatever else may
be said about the excessive drinker, this type, in common with social
drinkers, but with greater difficulty, may be able to curtail or completely
cease drinking on his own volition. Depending upon circumstances, he
may continue drinking in this manner for the rest of his life, he may
later reduce the frequency and quantity of his alcohol consumption, or
he may become an alcoholic.

Alcoholics are those whose frequent and repeated drinking of alcoholic beverages is in excess of the dietary and social usages of the community and is to such an extent that it interferes with health or social
or economic functioning. The alcoholic is unable to control consistently,
or to stop at will, either the start of drinking or its termination once
started.[66] Some of the elements in this definition are (1) reliance on al-

---

[65] Harold A. Mulford and Donald E. Miller, "Drinking in Iowa. IV. Preoccupation
with Alcohol and Definitions of Alcohol, Heavy Drinking and Trouble Due to Drinking," *Quarterly Journal of Studies on Alcohol*, 21:279–291 (June, 1960).

[66] See Mark Keller, "Alcoholism: Nature and Extent of the Problem," *The Annals*,
315:1–11 (January, 1958) and Mark Keller, "Definition of Alcoholism," *Quarterly
Journal of Studies on Alcohol*, 21:125–134 (March, 1960). Some authorities feel that
such definitions make it difficult for scientists to replicate research. Consequently, an
operational definition of alcoholism in terms of community standards and societal re-

coholic beverages, (2) repetitiveness or chronicity of the drinking in the sense that the drinking does not take place on rare occasions, (3) ill effects which derive from the drinking and not from other causes. The drinking must affect the drinker's life and not just society. These ill effects may be either definite ill-health, social or interpersonal ill effects, such as disruption of the family or ostracism which would not occur if the drinking were stopped, or economic effects, such as inability to keep a job, work efficiently, or take care of one's property as well as one could without the drinking.

Alcoholism is drinking behavior which is conceived of by others as an extreme deviation. While the drinking of alcoholic beverages and heavy drinking are the necessary prerequisites, it should be regarded as behavioral phenomena and not as a biological or psychological entity. On a scale of preoccupation with alcohol it would probably fit in as responses to Groups I and II. (See Table 12.7.)

Chronic alcoholics characteristically have a "compulsion" to drink continually. Of particular importance are such other characteristics as solitary drinking, morning drinking, and general physical deterioration.

In the United States an estimated 3,760,000 men and 710,000 women, or a total of 4,470,000 were alcoholics in 1960.[67] This is equivalent to a rate of 4000 alcoholics per 100,000 adults aged twenty years and over.[68] Chronic alcoholics (alcoholics with complications) were estimated to be 1,147,000 in 1953, or one fourth of the alcoholics. Of this total, 971,000 were men and 176,000 were women. California and New Jersey had the highest rates, and South Carolina and Wyoming the lowest.

Although it is difficult to compare the alcoholism rates of various countries, the most accurate figures indicate that in terms of total population the United States has the highest rate, or 4390, followed by France and Sweden. (See Table 12.8.) Rates for chronic alcoholism are highest in Switzerland, with the United States being fourth.

During the past several decades there has been a great increase in the number of American women who drink, and while the rate of alcoholism has tended to increase there are indications that this increase has

---

action has been used involving frequent arrests for drunkenness, contact with social agencies, clinics, mental hospitals, or Alcoholics Anonymous. See William and Joan McCord, *Origins of Alcoholism* (Stanford, Calif.: Stanford University Press, 1960), pp. 10–11.

[67] Mark Keller, "The Definition of Alcoholism and the Estimation of Its Prevalence," in *Society, Culture and Drinking Patterns.* Estimates of the number of alcoholics with complications (chronic alcoholism) are derived by multiplying the reported number of deaths from cirrhosis of the liver by a certain ratio, usually by three in the United States. To arrive at the estimated number of alcholics in the United States, this figure is then usually multiplied by four.

[68] Mark Keller and Vera Efron, *Selected Statistical Tables on Alcoholic Beverages, 1859–1960, and on Alcoholism 1930–1960* (New Brunswick, N.J.: Quarterly Journal of Studies on Alcohol, 1961).

Table 12.7. The Iowa Scale of Preoccupation with Alcohol

Item	Content of Statement	Method of scoring
I	I stay intoxicated for several days at a time. I worry about not being able to get a drink when I need one. I sneak drinks when no one is looking.	Agree on any two.
II	Once I start drinking it is difficult for me to stop before I become completely intoxicated. I get intoxicated on work days. I take a drink the first thing when I get up in the morning.	Agree on any two.
III	I awaken next day not being able to remember some of the things I had done while I was was drinking. I take a few quick ones before going to a party to make sure I have enough. I neglect my regular meals when I am drinking.	Agree on any two.
IV	I don't nurse my drinks; I toss them down pretty fast. I drink for the effect of alcohol with little attention to type of beverage or brand name. Liquor has less effect on me than it used to.	Agree on any two.

SOURCE: Adapted from Harold A. Mulford and Donald E. Miller, "Drinking in Iowa. IV. Preoccupation with Alcohol and Definitions of Alcohol, Heavy Drinking and Trouble Due to Drinking," *Quarterly Journal of Studies on Alcohol*, 21:281 (June, 1960). The scale is cumulative in that with few exceptions respondents beginning with the bottom item agree to each item up to a point and then reject the remaining items.

been small.[69] Several reasons appear to account for the differences between the rates of alcoholism among men and women. First, proportionately fewer women than men drink. Second, greater social stigma is attached to excessive drinking by women than by men. Third, a housewife does not face the same occupational drinking hazards that men face. Fourth, women are generally not as directly involved in the competitive economic struggle, and, since they have the responsibility for the care and upbringing of the children, are not as "free" to drink regularly as are men, especially in the lower classes. Fifth, a woman's self-image is not as seriously threatened. Because her role is more restricted, primarily to that of a wife and mother, failure in this role is less likely to be known to outsiders. "A man, on the other hand, can fail not only in his familial

[69] Edith S. Lisansky, "The Woman Alcoholic," *The Annals*, 315:73–82 (January, 1958).

Table 12.8. Estimated Rates of Alcoholism in Various Countries

Country	Year	With complications (chronic alcoholism)	With and without complica- tions (alcoholism)
Switzerland	1947	1590	2385
Chile	1946	1497	1500
France	1945	1420	2850
United States	1953	1098	4390
Australia	1947	671	1340
Sweden	1946	646	2580
Denmark	1948	487	1950
Italy	1942	476	500
Canada	1952	407	1630
Norway	1947	389	1560
Finland	1947	357	1430
England and Wales	1948	278	1100

SOURCE: Mark Keller and Vera Efron, "The Prevalence of Alcoholism," *Quarterly Journal of Studies on Alcohol*, 16:634 (December, 1955). Reprinted by permission of the Journal.

but also in his occupational role; the possibility that a man's self-image will be *publicly* deflated is greater." [70]

The Alcoholic Process

Shifts from the excessive drinking to the alcoholic stage with its social and often physical deterioration, and to the chronic alcoholic state are imperceptible transitions. One is never a full-blown alcoholic after a few experiences with the effects of liquor, for alcoholism means more than sporadic intoxication. It implies changes in the nature of interpersonal relations with others, in attitudes toward drinking, in social roles, and in conceptions of the self, including increasing dependence on drinking, attitudes which are at variance with those held by others and which were developed through a marginal social existence, numerous rebuffs, social isolation, and physical deterioration.

The alcoholic process usually extends over a period of ten to twenty years of drinking, and can be sketched by the drinking symptoms of alcoholism in a group of 252 alcoholics.[71] These alcoholics became in-

[70] McCord and McCord, *op. cit.*, p. 163.

[71] Harrison M. Trice and J. Richard Wahl, "A Rank Order Analysis of the Symptoms of Alcoholism," *Quarterly Journal of Studies on Alcohol*, 19:636–648 (December, 1958). Also see E. M. Jellinek, "Phases in the Drinking History of Alcoholics," *Memoirs of the Section of Studies on Alcohol* (No. 5; New Brunswick, N.J.: Quarterly Journal of Studies on Alcohol, 1946).

toxicated for the first time at a mean age of 18.3 years, and within 11 years, or at age 29.5 they had already experienced "blackouts," or amnesia during intoxication. By 35.6 years they were engaging in morning drink ing, and at 36.1 they began to drink alone on a regular basis. At 37.8 they were first protecting their supply of alcohol, and by 38.6 years were first experiencing tremors. (See Table 12.9.)

Table 12.9. Symptoms and Mean Onset Ages (Years) of 13 Selected Symptoms in a Wisconsin Study Group of 252 Alcoholics, 1955

Symptoms	Mean age
First drink for self	17.6
First intoxication	18.3
First blackout	29.5
First frequent blackouts	33.6
First morning drinking	35.6
First "benders"	36.0
First daytime bouts	35.7
First loss of control	36.0
First drinking alone	36.1
First convulsions	37.6
First protecting of supply	37.8
First tremors	38.6
First drunk on less liquor	38.4

SOURCE: Derived from Harrison M. Trice and J. Richard Wahl, "A Rank Order Analysis of the Symptoms of Alcoholism," *Quarterly Journal of Studies on Alcohol*, 19:637 (December, 1958).

Alcoholics, on the average, reach their lowest point and conceive of themselves as having reached this lowest point in their late thirties, and after one or two decades of drinking. In the interim they have tried to change their drinking patterns; have "gone on the water wagon"; have experienced daytime drunks, "benders," or prolonged drinking sprees; have begun taking drinks in the morning; have sought to escape their environment; and have begun losing working time, jobs, and friends. They also have irrational fears, resentments, and "remorse," the latter being particularly characteristic. Alcoholics then often drink alone, "protect their supply," and experience tremors.

A more detailed description of the alcoholic process can be sketched in terms of early, middle, and late stages of alcoholism.[72] Many persons, of

[72] Derived from Jellinek, "Phases in The Drinking History of Alcoholics," *loc. cit.*; Marty Mann, *A Primer on Alcoholism* (New York: Holt, Rinehart and Winston, Inc., 1950), pp. 18–57; and Simon Dinitz, "The Relation of the Tavern to the Drinking Phases of Alcoholics," cited above.

course, do not inevitably go on to the next stage. Each stage can be divided into physical symptoms and drinking roles.

EXCESSIVE DRINKING STAGE

In the excessive drinking stage the drinker begins to lose control over his drinking, finding it difficult to stop at one or two drinks or from going on occasional week-end drunks. Blackouts frequently begin at this stage, although generally not until the end of a hard-drinking evening. He begins to gulp drinks, and he may take a drink *before* going to a party where there undoubtedly will be drinking, or *before* an appointment at which drinking would be quite in order. He feels the necessity of having drinks at certain regular times and the need for a certain amount of time spent in drinking before dinner, regardless of the inconvenience to others. He also needs to drink before special events, and he must have a drink for "that tired feeling," or for his "nerves," or to forget his worries or troubles for a while, or to avoid depression.

MIDDLE OR ALCOHOLIC DRINKING STAGE

The prealcoholic at this stage begins to have ugly hangovers, which include physical near collapse, mental remorse and self-disgust, and a terrifying self-doubt because his schemes for control of his drinking no longer work. Nausea is still rare during drinking, but it now has become a frequent morning-after experience. Blackouts are increasing, and the time of their onset grows steadily earlier. He now passes out frequently, sometimes early in the course of an event to which he had genuinely looked forward.

His growing dependence on alcohol is indicated by the fact that he no longer seems able to function well without drinks, and apparently makes little effort to do so. He is less willing to talk about drinking especially his own. The increasing use of alcohol often masks his real feelings toward himself and his role aspirations, as it also does toward increasing feelings of isolation and of "not belonging."

At this middle stage the alcoholic promises over and over again to stop drinking, but his drinking by now is so obviously different from other people's drinking that he lies about it to prevent discovery of this difference. He gulps drinks, makes sure of having enough "under his belt" before going anywhere, even to a scheduled drinking party, and to avoid any risks he carries his own supply. At this stage the alcoholic prefers to spend the allotted span of drinking time before meals at a tavern rather than at home, and he often arrives home late. He must be "well away" for any special event, he is always "dog-tired and cannot go on without something to drink." He is generally "nervous," plagued with worries and troubles, and life seems unbearable without drinks. His almost constant depression, often about his drinking, cannot be dealt with except by drinking.

The alcoholic at this stage now adds to the accepted drinking time, he may no longer care whether friends go with him, and he may prefer to sneak off-hour drinks. He keeps a bottle in his desk or hidden at home for purely private consumption, and signs of his drinking, even actual intoxication, begin to show up at the wrong time, such as at work or at gatherings where everyone else is sober. He no longer admits to having been drunk; he says he "wasn't up to par," "had eaten something," or was "under the weather." He does not usually admit having hangovers, an admission which might lead to inquiries about how much he has been drinking, a fact which he wishes to conceal carefully.

Episodes of drunkenness occur more and more often during this middle phase of alcoholism. Week ends are often real drinking bouts, with Sundays still reserved for "straightening out," but often matching Saturday in drinking intensity. Extravagance in buying drinks and other things for people and excessive tipping are characteristic of his drinking behavior. Some persons also commit various antisocial acts, such as fighting with others, vandalism in the form of malicious destruction, and practical jokes. Then the morning drink to "get going" increases rapidly in frequency as its efficacy becomes appreciated. As drinking behavior changes and the drinker's situation becomes more difficult, he starts "going on the wagon," something he is able to do at this stage for extended periods of time. He has a false sense of power over his alcoholism during these periods of nondrinking, but he is noticeably irritable, his family, friends, and business colleagues label him as a "difficult" person.

LATER OR CHRONIC ALCOHOLIC STAGE

At the chronic alcoholic stage it is no longer a question of merely gulping drinks, either publicly or privately; there is now a pressing physical need to get and keep a certain amount of alcohol in the system at all times. Although hangovers are not now the usual morning-after discomfort known to social drinkers, they do make themselves felt in the peculiarly horrible form known to the chronic alcoholic. If at all possible they are immediately wiped out by drinks. An added problem, however, is nausea, and the morning drinks often do not stay down. Blackouts set in, and disappear, at any time, leaving unaccountable memory blanks possibly lasting for several days. Passing out also occurs at any time, and much of the alcoholic's sleep is actually no more than this.

The major psychological symptom is now an overwhelming compulsion to drink, and the greatest difficulty of all is the inability to control drinking. Drinking is apparently completely accepted as natural and inevitable. When sober, he does not admit or discuss his drinking, drunkenness, or behavior, although there are rare outbursts, usually when half-drunk, of horror and self-disgust, as well as the expression of a tragically real desire to "be like other people." His ordinary morning hang-over is not allowed to occur, for round-the-clock drinking generally prevents it. A feeling of inferiority because of his drinking now frequently appears in an extreme form, contrasting sharply with equally extreme swings toward grandiosity.

The alcoholic now drinks to live and lives to drink. The full-fledged alcoholic's eating behavior is phenomenal: he seems to many people not to eat at all, a fact which is often quite true. He now maintains an adequate supply of liquor at all times in order to be able to "sneak drinks" because of the psychological need and desire for liquor during various parts of the day and night. It is almost impossible to describe adequately the terror that getting "caught short" holds for the addict, and the lengths to which he will go to prevent what to him would be a catastrophe of the most major proportions. Ingenious methods of safeguarding an ever-present supply indicate more clearly than almost anything else the compulsive need to drink experienced by the chronic alcoholic.[73]

Drunken behavior now usually, almost inevitably, takes place at the wrong time, drinking bouts occur regardless of the time of week, month, or year, their duration depending upon the financial and physical condition of the alcoholic, from a day or so to a week or longer. Even at this late stage, however, there may be times when the alcoholic manages his drinking well. Morning drinks and solitary drinking are indices of the chronic inebriate. He needs a few sips on awakening because he feels unsteady, has a headache, or has the "shakes" or tremors. This morning drink makes him "normal," if only psychologically so, and he feels he can meet his obligations for the day. In one novel the alcoholic is described as waiting for the corner tavern to open so that he can get his morning "shot." [74] This effect, unfortunately for the alcoholic, may wear off, and he is forced to resort to his hidden stock repeatedly during the day. "He may start utilizing techniques for the ingestion of alcohol which are beyond the pale of any conceivable development in the drinking usages of his

---

[73] To keep a supply of alcohol available alcoholics devise many original schemes for hiding their bottles from the family. Some hang bottles just outside the window below the ledge on strings, others under their pillows, under porches, in stockings, and in every other conceivable place. One informant stated that he would return in the evening with a large supply of alcohol and since his wife anticipated this, he would hide one or two bottles in a conspicuous place so that his wife would find them. The remainder he hid more securely. When his wife located the decoys she would feel relieved and he would put on a most pitiable mien. Of course, what she did not know was that several times during the course of a night, when alcoholic tremors would awaken him, he would repair to his supply and after a few drinks would be quieted down enough to go back to sleep.

[74] Charles Jackson, *The Lost Weekend* (New York: Holt, Rinehart and Winston, Inc., 1948).

group: starting off the day with 7 or 8 ounces of gin or whiskey; spending 4 or 5 days of the ordinary work-a-day week doing nothing but ingesting alcohol; taking alcohol in such forms as mouth-wash, canned heat preparations, vanilla extract, and so on; in addition, he may omit such practices (if they were the norm in his group) as using ice, glasses, chasers, mixes." [75]

Periods of being "on the wagon" still occur, although less often unless the patient is under treatment. Complete drunkenness is his condition most of the time, although this is not always evident, and he has great difficulty on the job. This produces another unpleasant situation, the necessity for getting money to pay for drinks; this is often difficult, and ordinary borrowing soon deteriorates into the "touch." He often watches his family sink into destitution, or leave him, without showing any feeling about it. His behavior at this time shows an almost complete loss of time sense.

In areas other than drinking there develop socially unacceptable changes in his relations with others. Their strong societal reaction to him in turn causes further drinking. "Dishonesty, excessive rationalization, avoidance, and the other deviations, once perhaps even rare in his behavior, then noticeable where alcohol was concerned, now begin to appear in the family situation or perhaps in friendship groups or on the job. Accidents, job losses, family quarrels, broken friendship, even trouble with the law may take place, not just when he is under the influence of alcohol, but even when he is not. And such occasions quite usually set off further drinking." [76]

Personality Traits and Excessive Drinking

Why some social drinkers become excessive drinkers and some excessive drinkers develop into alcoholics is not entirely clear at the present time. Most psychiatrists believe that alcoholism is a consequence of personality maladjustment. According to this view, certain childhood experiences produce feelings of insecurity which, together with difficulties in interpersonal relationships of adult life, produce tensions and anxieties. Because the use of alcohol reduces anxiety some persons may come to depend upon it. Over a period of years this dependence on alcohol as a way of escaping hidden or obvious difficulties with which the individual cannot deal increases.

The psychiatric explanation, although widely held, has several limitations. In the first place, such a theory is largely dependent for evidence on the personality traits of alcoholics and the differences between them and

---

[75] Selden D. Bacon, "Alcoholics Do Not Drink," *The Annals*, 315:62 (January, 1958).
[76] *Ibid.*, p. 63.

nonalcoholics. The personality traits of an alcoholic are measured after some ten to fifteen years of drinking in which the individual has usually had many problems due to his drinking, problems not only with his family but with his employer and others, and experiences which the nonalcoholic has probably not had.

Although efforts have been made to sketch an "alcoholic personality," presumably applicable to all alcoholics, more recent surveys have concluded that scientific reports to date do not permit us to define such an alcoholic personality, or even to come to any substantial agreement as to what it might be like. For example, two reviews of all personality studies of alcoholics and nonalcoholics up to 1956, using projective and nonprojective tests, found that there was no reason for concluding that persons of one type are more likely to become alcoholics than persons of another type.[77] Moreover, it cannot be assumed that the personality traits displayed by the alcoholic were there *before* excessive drinking began. It is possible that a number of types, such as the person who takes pride in his ability to consume large quantities of alcohol without becoming drunk, have a susceptibility for alcoholism, but more research is needed before any definite conclusions of this type can be reached.

Group and Subcultural Factors in Alcoholism

Rather than seek any universal explanation of alcoholism, either in the biological constitution or the personality trait structures, one should look for a variety of social and group situations under which alcoholism develops. Excessive drinking, for example, does not itself make the alcoholic. If it is continued over a long enough time he may increasingly become involved in difficulties which arise from the drinking itself. He may lose his job, his friends, and his wife because of his drinking, and he may even be arrested and placed in jail. Drinking may become a way of getting away from problems caused by drinking. He "is involved in a circular process whereby his excessive drinking creates additional problems for him which he can only face with the aid of further excessive drinking. The condition of true alcoholism has been established." [78] The Protestant ethic appears to play a role in this, since drunkenness is regarded as a lack of moral strength, will power, and devotion to the goals of personal discipline and work. The societal reaction to excessive drunk-

---

[77] Edwin H. Sutherland, H. C. Schroeder, and C. L. Tordella, "Personality Traits and the Alcoholic: A Critique of Existing Studies," *Quarterly Journal of Studies on Alcohol,* 11:547–561 (December, 1950) and Leonard Symes, "Personality Characteristics and the Alcoholic: A Critique of Current Studies," *Quarterly Journal of Studies on Alcohol,* 18:288–302 (June, 1957).

[78] Expert Committee on Mental Health, "Second Report of the Alcoholism Subcommittee" (Technical Report No. 48; Geneva, Switzerland: World Health Organization, 1952).

enness may be expressed through the husband or wife, employer, work associates, parents, in-laws, neighbors, church members, and the police representing the larger community. The comparatively low rate of alcoholism in Japan may be due, in part, to the fact that drunkenness does not seem to provoke quite the same reaction. It is largely regarded as a personal matter, often with good humor by other members of society.

Group associations and cultural factors, therefore, play an important part in determining who becomes an excessive drinker and who does not. There are differences not only in the drinking customs of societies but in those of subgroups within a modern society. Subgroups differ in the way in which alcohol is used, the extent of drinking, and attitudes toward drunkenness. The correlation of diverse drinking patterns with alcoholism can help us to test a number of hypotheses. Some believe that frequent drinking will lead to alcoholism; yet those groups with relatively high frequency of drinking, such as the American Jews, particularly the Orthodox, and the Italian-Americans, have low rates of alcoholism.[79] Still others say that frequency of drunkenness leads to alcoholism, and yet the Aleuts, the Andean Indians, and those of the northwest coast of America, among whom drunkenness is common, appear to have little alcoholism.[80] In an isolated Peruvian mestizo community drinking and drunkenness among adult males over fifteen years of age is virtually universal.[81] The few who abstain plead health reasons, but since liquor is regarded as "healthful," their lot is hard. Alcoholism is rare, however.

Ullman has stressed the role of the integration of drinking behavior patterns in low rates of alcoholism.[82] If conformity to drinking standards is supported by the entire culture or subculture, there will be low rates. If the individual drinker does not know what is expected or if the expected situation varies, he is in a position of ambivalence. Therefore, "in any group or society in which the drinking customs, values and sanctions —together with the attitudes of all segments of the group or society—

---

[79] See Charles R. Snyder, *Alcohol and the Jews* (New York: The Free Press of Glencoe, 1958) and Giorgio Lolli, Emilio Serianni, Grace M. Golder, and Pierpaolo Luzzatto-Fegis, *Alcohol in Italian Culture* (New York: The Free Press of Glencoe, 1958).

[80] See Gerald D. Berreman, "Drinking Patterns of the Aleuts," *Quarterly Journal of Studies on Alcohol*, 17:503–514 (September, 1956), William Mangin, "Drinking among Andean Indians," *Quarterly Journal of Studies on Alcohol*, 18:55–66 (March, 1957), and Edwin M. Lemert, *Alcohol and the Northwest Coast Indians* (University of California Publications in Culture and Society, Vol. 2, No. 6; Berkeley: University of California Press, 1954).

[81] Ozzie G. Simmons, "Drinking Patterns and Interpersonal Performance in a Peruvian Mestizo Community," *Quarterly Journal of Studies on Alcohol*, 20:103–111 (March, 1959).

[82] Albert D. Ullman, "Sociocultural Backgrounds of Alcoholism," *The Annals*, 315: 48–55 (January, 1958).

are well established, known to and agreed upon by all, and are consistent with the rest of the culture, the rate of alcoholism will be low." [83]

COMPANIONS AND EXCESSIVE DRINKING

In modern society, group patterns of excessive drinking, of companions, of social class, and of religious and ethnic groups are important.

There seems to be a good deal of evidence to the effect that many problem drinkers are "processed" into it, that is, they are encouraged by informal drinking groups to use alcohol as a way to adjust to anxiety and difficulty. Having once been conditioned by such experiences to use alcohol as a way to manage the ever-present problems of living, it is a simple step to increase its use when these problems become larger, as they do at one time or another for all of us. To this group encouragement there is frequently added the reward of group recognition. Often the early symptoms of problem drinking are given prestige in such groups. For example, the ability to "drink 'em under the table" may provide the person so characterized with the esteem of a drinking group. At the same time, it may well signal a dangerous increase in the tolerance to alcohol. Furthermore, drinking groups have a subtle "limit" beyond which they believe a drinker gets "sloppy" and disgusting. At this point the rewards and recognition previously accorded tend to become rejection. This constitutes a further anxiety that must be met by a technique already well known: more alcohol. . . .[84]

Drinking generally takes place in small groups, and within these groups drinking norms tend to develop. More than two thirds of the drinking occasions among men, for example, in rural Finland involve groups of two to four persons.[85] Moreover, while conformity between drinking habits and drinking norms is the rule in small groups, identification with a group is a variable on the basis of which it is possible to explain an individual's norms and his behavior.[86]

---

[83] *Ibid.*, p. 50. Also see Harrison M. Trice and David J. Pittman, "Social Organization and Alcoholism: A Review of Significant Research Since 1940," *Social Problems*, 5:294–308 (Spring, 1958). Among folk societies prior to contact with Western Europeans, alcoholism appears to have been infrequent. The ceremonial use of alcohol to produce mass intoxication among male adults was permitted in many folk societies but drinking for individualistic reasons was rare and alcoholism virtually unknown.—Donald Horton, "The Functions of Alcohol in Primitive Societies," in *Alcohol, Science and Society*, p. 157. For a general discussion of group association and cultural factors, also see Edwin M. Lemert, "Alcoholism and the Sociocultural Situation," *Quarterly Journal of Studies on Alcohol*, 17:306–317 (June, 1956).

[84] Harrison M. Trice, "The Problem Drinker in Industry," *ILR Research* (Ithaca: New York State School of Industrial and Labor Relations, Cornell University, June, 1956), II, 11. Reprinted by permission of the New York State School of Industrial and Labor Relations.

[85] P. Kuusi, *Alcohol Sales Experiment in Rural Finland* (Helsinki: Finnish Foundation for Alcohol Studies, 1957).

[86] Eric Allardt, "Drinking Norms and Drinking Habits," in *Drinking and Drinkers* (Helsinki: Finnish Foundation for Alcohol Studies, 1957).

The drinking norms of an individual appear to conform closely to those of age contemporaries, and particularly of friends or the marital partner.[87] These individuals appear to be more influential than the drinking partners of the parental generation in determining how people drink. In fact, wives of alcoholics have been found to have encouraged their husbands' alcoholism.[88] Another study has reported a close relation between the development of alcoholism and the type of companion with whom the individual associates and drinks.[89] Of twenty-eight excessive drinkers under thirty-five, nearly all belonged to social groups in which regular drinking and drunkenness were accepted and approved. Becoming drunk became a pattern of behavior from about nineteen years. Before they began drinking about half felt that they had been isolated and ridiculed for not drinking. It has been suggested, in one study, that the first drinking experience of potential alcoholics may have a particular meaning.[90] Excessive drinkers, as compared with nonexcessive drinkers, had their first drink in a place other than a private home or tavern but with friends or older persons who were not members of the family. Moreover, the prealcoholic more often became intoxicated in his first drinking and was ridiculed by his drinking companions. Later he seemed to take pride in having learned how to "drink like a man."

Studying the work experiences in industry of problem drinkers, Trice found that their drinking was influenced by the fellow employees with whom they drank after work. In fact, fellow workers were first to notice the problem drinker's developing loss of control. With their drinking problem becoming greater they tended to stop drinking with their work companions and to look for those whose drinking norms were more in line with their own.[91]

After studying two hundred homeless men, Straus found that only seven abstained entirely, and seventeen were moderate drinkers.[92] Suther-

[87] John L. Haer, "Drinking Patterns and the Influence of Friends and Family," *Quarterly Journal of Studies on Alcohol*, 16:178–185 (March, 1955).

[88] Samuel Futterman, "Personality Trends in Wives of Alcoholics," *Journal of Psychiatric Social Work*, 23:37–41 (October, 1953); Thelma Whalen, "Wives of Alcoholics: Four Types Observed in a Family Service Agency," *Quarterly Journal of Studies on Alcohol*, 14:632–641 (December, 1953); and G. M. Price, "A Study of the Wives of 70 Alcoholics," *Quarterly Journal of Studies on Alcohol*, 5:620–627 (March, 1945).

[89] Marvin Wellman, "Towards an Etiology of Alcoholism: Why Young Men Drink Too Much," *Canadian Medical Association Journal*, 73:717–719 (November 1, 1955).

[90] Albert D. Ullman, "The First Drinking Experience of Addictive and 'Normal' Drinkers," *Quarterly Journal of Studies on Alcohol*, 14:181–191 (June, 1953). Unfortunately, the addictive drinkers were prison inmates and the normal drinkers college students; thus they may represent samples which are not completely comparable.

[91] Harrison M. Trice, "Identifying the Problem Drinker on the Job," *Personnel Magazine*, 33:527–533 (May, 1957).

[92] Robert Straus, "Alcohol and the Homeless Man," *Quarterly Journal of Studies on Alcohol*, 7:360–404 (December, 1946). See also Robert Straus, "Some Sociological Concomitants of Excessive Drinking in the Life History of the Itinerant Inebriate," *Quarterly Journal of Studies on Alcohol*, 9:1–52 (June, 1948).

land and Locke, who studied several thousand shelter-house men in Chicago, wrote of them:

> Drinking is one of the most pervasive elements of shelter life. The men fall into four classes with reference to drinking. There is a comparatively small number of teetotalers. The majority partake of intoxicating drinks occasionally but rarely become drunk. A number go on periodic sprees and become completely drunk. Possibly 10 per cent of the men are chronic alcoholics. The chronic alcoholics are called "booze hounds" and are divided into yaki dockers, or those who make every effort to secure palatable liquor, and derailers, or those who drink denatured alcohol, sterno or anything "that will give them a bang." [93]

Many homeless persons become excessive drinkers but by no means all become alcoholics. In a study of 444 homeless men, 10.6 percent were found to be nondrinkers, 16.9 percent moderate drinkers, 28.0 percent "heavy controlled" drinkers, 43.2 percent heavy "uncontrolled" drinkers or alcoholics, while 1.3 percent were not classified.[94]

Skid Row excessive drinkers can be classified into six types: "older alcoholics," "bums," "characters," "winos," "ruby-dubs," and "lushes," the last referring to the prestige group of alcoholics.[95] Among those alcoholics with the most prestige on Skid Row, few are solitary drinkers. There are group definitions of behavior in the sharing of alcohol and, when drunk, in protecting each other from the police. Such alcoholics share in the financing of a bottle, and in drinking from a bottle to which an alcoholic has contributed: "he should drink in turn, his turn being dictated by the size of his donation, and he should take only one gulp with each round." [96] So great are the group influences on Skid Row that if an individual is to deal effectively with his alcoholism he must leave.

Group life and cultural factors play a role among "winos" studied in Seattle's Skid Row (or Road). Winos are those who habitually get drunk on wine, with a consequent unpleasant characteristic odor, and who exhibit an extremely rundown appearance. They drink wine not only because it is the cheapest but because the subculture believes it to have the longest and the most deadening effect, to kill the appetite, and to be the easiest drink to keep down. The wino has association with small groups of men with whom he does almost all of his drinking. Among the most imperative mores is the obligation to share: "Winos are not

[93] Edwin H. Sutherland and Harvey Locke, *Twenty Thousand Homeless Men* (Philadelphia: J. B. Lippincott Company, 1936), p. 113.

[94] Robert Straus and Raymond G. McCarthy, "Nonaddictive Pathological Drinking Patterns of Homeless Men," *Quarterly Journal of Studies on Alcohol*, 12:601–611 (December, 1951).

[95] W. Jack Peterson and Milton A. Maxwell, "The Skid Road 'Wino,'" *Social Problems*, 5:308–316 (Spring, 1958).

[96] Joan K. Jackson and Ralph Connor, "The Skid Road Alcoholic," *Quarterly Journal of Studies on Alcohol*, 14:475 (September, 1953).

isolates. Instead, they are found to live as social beings within a society of their fellows. It is a society which prescribes and provides mutual aid in meeting the problems of survival: food, drink, shelter, illness and protection. But more than that it is a society which also provides the emotional support found in the acceptance by, and the companionship of, fellow human beings." [97]

A study of a random sample of 187 chronic police case inebriates, most of them from a predominantly lower-class background, showed that their drinking occurred in small intimate groups, less than 8 percent being usually solitary drinkers.[98] "The major function of these drinking groups . . . is in providing the context, social and psychological, for drinking behavior. In reality we have subcommunities of inebriates organized around one cardinal principle: drinking. The fantasies concerning the rewards of the drinking experiences are reinforced in the interaction of the members, who mutually support each other in obtaining alcohol and mutually share it." [99]

CLASS DIFFERENCES IN EXCESSIVE DRINKING

Drinking customs and attitudes toward drinking vary in terms of the class structure. Dollard has shown, for example, that in the upper classes both sexes drink a good deal, and their drinking generally does not involve a moral issue, provided it is done "properly." "One is condemned in the Upper classes, not for drinking, nor for drunkenness, but for anti-social acts while drunk. Fighting is taboo; aggressive behavior is heavily penalized even when expressed only in verbal assaults." [100]

The lower-upper class is said to be distinguished from the other members of the upper class by the "cocktail set." In this particular group there is more alcoholic drinking in general and some excessive drinking which may result from the fact that the persons in the lower-upper class, in striving to reach the top of the social ladder, feel more insecure. The role of the host varies with the structure of the cocktail party, the composition of the guests, and the objectives of the party.[101] Cocktail parties

---

[97] Peterson and Maxwell, "The Skid Road 'Wino,'" loc. cit., p. 316. "For a wino to survive as a wino he needs someone to get him something to drink when he is sick and broke. Where it would be difficult for an individual to keep enough money for liquor coming in, two or three men bumming together can usually manage to keep enough money coming in for wine."—Ibid., p. 312.

[98] David J. Pittman and C. Wayne Gordon, Revolving Door (New York: The Free Press of Glencoe, 1958). Also see Earl Rubington, "Relapse and the Chronic Drunkenness Offender," Connecticut Review on Alcoholism, 12:9–12 (November, 1960).

[99] Pittman and Gordon, op. cit., p. 71.

[100] John Dollard, "Drinking Mores of the Social Classes," in Alcoholic, Science and Society, p. 99.

[101] David Riesman, Robert J. Potter, and Jeanne Watson, "The Vanishing Host," Human Organization, 19:17–28 (Spring, 1960).

vary in the degree to which persons "responsible" for them can influence course. At the large urban cocktail party, for example, the host tends to be relatively powerless, for such parties most often lack formal structure. The array of guests is heterogeneous, consisting of a wide cross section of persons of varying social statuses. Lack of space forces persons into little clusters where they may offer bits of polite small talk. Other persons, whose isolation is concealed by the unstructured nature of the group, may find solace in the food and drink. Such parties as these cannot be described as purely "sociable" occasions; rather, they are often "coming-out" parties for men, products, or ideas. Thus, the socially mobile couple who would not ordinarily give such a party, because of their lack of money and experience, may find themselves in a position which demands that they preside over such an affair.

On the upper-middle rungs of the success ladder, men drink at social gatherings and for business reasons. Women generally refrain from much drinking, however, and on the whole there seems to be a neutral attitude toward the consumption of liquor. Drinking parties seem to be increasing among middle-class groups who find escape, relaxation, and release through alcohol. A study of drinkng parties, as compared with nondrinking parties, revealed that they were attended by white-collar groups who, among the men, found increasing tensions in the insecurity of their status in an era of high-speed industrial and commercial activity and high-pressure salesmanship.[102] Members of the lower-middle class, striving desperately for recognition and status, and, in fact, for anything which would widen the gap between them and those whom they consider lower than themselves, have strong taboos against drinking, particularly among the women, because excessive drinking is associated in their minds with the behavior of the lower classes.

According to Dollard, the lower classes, in contrast to the lower-middle class, often do not exert restraints on drinking.[103] Both men and women may consume alcoholic beverages, and many, including primarily workers for whom drinking is in the norms, come, with few exceptions, to think of the tavern as the "poor man's club." The rates for military rejections during World War II for alcoholism were greater in the lower social strata of the population.[104] A study of a working class area in Santiago, Chile, found that 30 percent of the adult males have an episode of drunkenness every week end, twice a month, or once a month.[105]

[102] Duane Robinson, "Social Disorganization Reflected in Middle-Class Drinking and Dancing Recreational Patterns," *Social Forces*, 20:455–459 (May, 1942).

[103] Dollard, *loc. cit.*, pp. 99–101.

[104] R. W. Hyde and L. V. Kingsley, "Studies in Medical Sociology: The Relation of Mental Disorders to the Community Socioeconomic Level," *New England Journal of Medicine*, 231:543–548 (October, 1944).

[105] McCarthy, *Drinking and Intoxication*, pp. 99–105.

OCCUPATION AND EXCESSIVE DRINKING

Social patterns call for more immoderate drinking in certain occupational categories than in others. This view has been supported by the finding that a heavy disproportion of alcoholic psychoses are found in jobs with relatively low income and prestige, a result of the acceptance of heavy drinking as a norm in certain lower-class occupational groups.[106] On the other hand, McCord and McCord, after studying a group of 254 persons, found that middle-class Americans were significantly more prone to alcoholism than were members of the lower-lower class.[107]

Business is an occupation with which is often associated frequent and heavy drinking. Salesmen away from home for varying lengths of time stop overnight in towns where they have few acquaintances. They find people in taverns to talk to and with a few drinks the long hours pass quickly. Drinking is also a common practice among salesmen who travel in groups, drinking parties in hotel rooms being a particularly relaxing way to break monotony. Taking prospective customers out to dinner and having a few cocktails before the meal is often regarded as a traditional way of doing business and is provided for in the expense account.

A business executive in New York City has described how his daily luncheons are usually preceded by Martinis, followed by the leisurely drinking of highballs after the luncheon. In addition, important negotiations are often conducted over a drink in a bar. The executives who commute generally leave the office early enough to have two or three "for the road" before boarding the train. When they arrive home they usually find that their wives have cocktails ready, or that they have been invited out for cocktails at the home of some acquaintance. One alcoholic, in giving the reasons which led to his heavy drinking, has written:

> After finishing college and at the age of 27 I married and also picked up a job as an insurance salesman. Both my social life and my business life called for a good bit of social drinking and this was particularly true for the latter. To make a long story short, my drinking became progressively worse for fifteen years and it wasn't long before I was drinking almost daily.[108]

Seamen are an excellent illustration of occupational heavy drinkers. Life at sea for many becomes monotonous, frustrating, and socially isolating. Seamen have limited social outlets aboard ship, and often gain the satisfactions they need by looking forward to docking at the various ports of call in order to "have a good time." Enjoying oneself in port involves a

---

[106] Robert E. Clark, "The Relationship of Alcoholic Psychoses Commitment Rates to Occupational Income and Occupational Prestige," *American Sociological Review*, 14:539–543 (August, 1949).

[107] McCord and McCord, *op. cit.*, p. 41.   [108] From a personal document.

good many things, and almost invariably excessive drinking. It is no wonder, then, that the percentage of seamen who eventually become alcoholics is high. In the traditions of the trade, some form "bottle gangs," and tend to lose their individuality in these gangs. Often men in these gangs know little about each other, sometimes nothing more than their nicknames; yet in reference to norms such as excessive drinking and sexual promiscuity they may act as one.[109] Sailors often share their pay, for example, in order to continue drinking. During World War II an Alcoholic Seaman's Club was set up along the pattern of Alcoholics Anonymous. Treatment was directed toward breaking down the social isolation of the men and redirecting their desire for importance and recognition by letting them participate in more conventional social groups.[110]

It is not surprising that drinking is almost universal among migratory workers, "hoboes," and "tramps," and that drunkenness is frequent. In his classic study of this group Anderson stated:

> The only sober moments for many hobos and tramps are when they are without funds. The majority, however, are periodic drinkers who have sober periods of a week, a month or two, or even a year. These are the men who often work all summer with the avowed purpose of going to some lodging-house and living quietly during the winter, but usually they find themselves in the midst of a drunken debauch before they have been in town more than a day or two. Rarely does one meet a man among migratory workers who does not indulge in an occasional "spree"; the teetotalers are few indeed.[111]

A large percentage of chronic police-case inebriates studied by Pittman and Gordon had experience with all-male institutional living, and this experience appears to have affected their heavy drinking patterns.

> The Army, the Navy, the work camp, the railroad gang, and the lake steamer, all are rich in drinking culture. In these groups the harsh, the monotonous and the protective but controlled routines are broken by the nights, weekends and lay-offs which offer opportunities to drink. Drinking is a preoccupation and conversations at work are filled with talk of drink. The imagery and love of drinking are built up through these talks and stories. Fantasy around future drinking episodes serves the function of reducing the impact of heavy jobs in heat and cold, and of alleviating dull routines, sexual deprivation, and the loneliness of the all-male group. Drinking becomes a symbol of manliness and group integration.[112]

On the other hand, drinking does not appear to constitute a major problem among domestic servants. The close supervision exercised in this

---

[109] Anonymous, "Alcoholism—An Occupational Disease of Seamen," *Quarterly Journal of Studies on Alcohol*, 8:498–505 (December, 1947).

[110] R. G. Heath, "Group Psychotherapy of Alcohol Addiction," *Quarterly Journal of Studies on Alcohol*, 5:555–562 (March, 1945).

[111] Nels Anderson, *The Hobo: The Sociology of the Homeless Man* (Chicago: The University of Chicago Press, 1923, reissued by Phoenix, 1961), pp. 134–135.

[112] Pittman and Gordon, *op. cit.*, p. 67.

occupation means that a developing alcoholic is quickly noticed and dismissed from his position as a domestic servant.[113]

RELIGIOUS DIFFERENCES IN EXCESSIVE DRINKING

Differences in drinking patterns also exist among religious groups. One study, for example, revealed that 41 percent of the Protestants, 21 percent of the Catholics, and only 13 percent of the Jews abstained from drinking.[114] Studies have indicated that in spite of the fact that drinking is quite pervasive among the Jewish people, their rates for alcoholism fall far below what one would expect.[115] Only 4 percent of Jewish students in one study experienced social complications on account of their drinking; Episcopalians, 39 percent; Methodists, 50 percent; and nonaffiliates, 57 percent.[116]

In a comparative study Orthodox Jews have been found to have less drunkenness than more secular Jews, and, in general, to use alcohol differently.[117] A number of subcultural factors seem to explain the low alcoholism rates among Orthodox Jews. Among Orthodox Jews wine drinking is almost universal, since nearly all occasions, such as births, deaths, confirmations, and religious holidays, require it both by prescription and by tradition. Thus the Orthodox Jew becomes used to alcohol in moderation. He starts to use alcohol in childhood, later drinks with great frequency, but largely in a ritualistic context. Early socialization in the use of alcohol and ceremonial drinking is not as common among non-Orthodox Jews, and therefore they use alcohol in less moderation. Patterns of Orthodox drinking and their ritualistic associations are further supported by a normative structure of ideas of drunkenness as a gentile vice. The strength of the taboo among Orthodox Jews against conspicuous or excessive drinking can be seen from an old folk saying sometimes heard: "Drunk he is, drink he must, because he is a gentile."

Through the internalization of ideas and sentiments associated with Jewishness and the Jewish situation, and ideas of sobriety as a Jewish virtue,

---

[113] Robert Straus and Miriam Winterbottom, "Drinking Patterns of an Occupational Group: Domestic Servants," *Quarterly Journal of Studies on Alcohol,* 10:441–460 (December, 1949).

[114] Riley and Marden, *loc. cit.*

[115] Charles R. Snyder, *Alcohol and the Jews* (New York: The Free Press of Glencoe, 1958) and Robert F. Bales, "Cultural Differences in Rates of Alcoholism," *Quarterly Journal of Studies on Alcohol,* 6:480–500 (March, 1946).

[116] Jerome H. Skolnick, "Religious Affiliation and Drinking Behavior," *Quarterly Journal of Studies on Alcohol,* 19:452–470 (September, 1958). "The interpretation given to this finding is that abstinence teachings, by associating drinking with intemperance, inadvertently encourage intemperance in those students of abstinence background who disregard the injunction not to drink. However, frequent religious participation, even among students who drink, seems to diminish social complications."—*Ibid.,* p. 470.

[117] Snyder, *Alcohol and the Jews,* Chap. 6.

drunkenness as a Gentile vice, Jews bring to the drinking situation powerful moral sentiments and anxieties counter to intoxication. That these factors do not derive from the specific experience of drinking does not preclude their being a part of the normative orientation toward the act of drinking itself. We might say, then, that through the ceremonial use of beverage alcohol religious Jews learn how to drink in a controlled manner; but through constant reference to the hedonism of outsiders, in association with a broader pattern of religious and ethnocentric ideas and sentiments, Jews also learn how not to drink.[118]

The implications of these findings are great, as Snyder has suggested.

More generally, the findings of this study indicate that the problems of alcohol which beset American society cannot be understood apart from a consideration of the broader sociocultural matrix in which drinking occurs. Drinking itself is obviously not the exclusive cause of these problems since Orthodox Jews clearly demonstrate that virtually every member of a group can be exposed to drinking alcoholic beverages with negligible departure from a norm of sobriety and without the emergence of drinking pathologies such as alcoholism. Still more important, these findings suggest that the emergence of drinking pathologies where drinking is prevalent cannot be explained by exclusive reference to individual psychology or to a mysterious "craving" for alcohol presumed to be physiologically determined. The possible role of psychophysical processes is not denied but social and cultural phenomena, especially those related to normative or cultural traditions regarding drinking, appear to be essential for the emergence of these pathologies. Where drinking is an integral part of the socialization process, where it is interrelated with the central moral symbolism and is repeatedly practiced in the rites of a group, the phenomenon of alcoholism is conspicuous by its absence. Norms of sobriety can be effectively sustained under these circumstances even though the drinking is extensive. Where institutional conflicts disrupt traditional patterns in which drinking is integrated, where drinking is dissociated from the normal process of socialization, where drinking is relegated to social contexts which are disconnected from or in opposition to the core moral values and where it is used for individual purposes, pathologies such as alcoholism may be expected to increase.[119]

ETHNIC DIFFERENCES IN EXCESSIVE DRINKING

The extent and differences in drinking patterns of various ethnic groups are so pronounced that some people believe they have a biological rather than a cultural origin. The Irish, for example, have long been associated with traditions of excessive drinking. Studies indicate that their rates of chronic inebriety probably exceed those of any other single ethnic

---

[118] *Ibid.*, p. 182.   [119] *Ibid.*, p. 202. Reprinted by permission.

group.[120] It appears that the prevalence of the drinking habits in this group cannot be attributed, however, to any biological basis. Irish men drink because their culture permits drinking, particularly whiskey, probably more than many other ethnic groups permit it, although alcohol is not used in this group extensively for ceremonial purposes. After an examination of differences in Irish and Jewish rates of public drinking, one writer has suggested this as one of the chief reasons for the differences in the two groups.[121]

Bales has suggested that the explanation for the high rate of alcoholism among the Irish can be traced to a number of other factors.[122] In the 1840's the Irish farmer lived a marginal existence, the sexes were strictly separated, and at the same time there was difficulty in getting married because of economic conditions. The "older" young men were expected to spend their spare time with others drinking in the tavern. When relatives met in the tavern it was a matter of obligation to "stand" a drink for the others, who then had to reciprocate. The teetotaler was a suspicious character because he was not one of the "boys" in his drinking. Some of these drinking patterns have been carried on by immigrants who have left Ireland.

Italians in Italy have always had a tradition of using wine with the meals. Despite their extensive use of alcohol, the Italians have a low incidence of alcoholism. In fact, the United States rate is eight times as great. While the rate of alcoholism is also low among Italian-Americans, it appears to be higher than in Italy, even though the consumption of total alcoholic beverages was higher among the Italians. This was the problem of a unique joint research project on the use of alcohol in Italian culture among Italians and first-, second-, and third-generation Italian-Americans, conducted by the University of Rome and Yale University. In Italy milk is regarded primarily as a drink for children, whereas wine is for adults. Italians regard wine as healthful and a part of their tradition. Of 1459 adults interviewed in Italy, 79 percent said it was healthful to drink wine with the meals, 1 percent claimed it was not, and only one person expressed the fear that wine would lead to alcoholism.[123] Such an attitude appears, in part, to prevent alcoholic excesses and addiction. Most Italians first drink wine early in life, both men and women drink wine, and there

[120] William and Joan McCord, with Jon Gudeman, "Some Current Theories of Alcoholism: A Longitudinal Evaluation," *Quarterly Journal of Studies on Alcohol*, 20:746 (December, 1959).

[121] D. D. Glad, "Attitudes and Experiences of American-Jewish and American-Irish Male Youth as Related to Differences in Adult Rates of Inebriety," *Quarterly Journal of Studies on Alcohol*, 8:452 (December, 1947).

[122] Robert F. Bales, "Cultural Differences in Rates of Alcoholism," *Quarterly Journal of Studies on Alcohol*, 6:480–500 (March, 1946).

[123] Lolli *et al.*, *Alcohol in Italian Culture*. Also see Pierpaolo Luzzatto-Fegis and Giorgio Lolli, "The Use of Milk and Wine in Italy," *Quarterly Journal of Studies on Alcohol*, 18:355–381 (September, 1957).

is little opposition to the drinking of wine by young persons. Drinking is generally done in connection with meals. An interesting fact is that single persons appear to drink less wine, and "it would appear, therefore, that the use of wine—linked as it is with food events—loses much of its appeal for the unattached individual in the Italian culture, where alcoholic beverages are seldom used for 'escape' purposes." [124]

These drinking patterns were, in general, found to be present among Italian-Americans, although they are undergoing change. For example, 70 percent of Italian men, and 94 percent of the women, did all of their drinking at mealtimes, in comparison with 7 percent of the first-generation Italian-American men and 16 percent of the women, and 4 percent of the men and 11 percent of the women in the second generation. All of these factors, particularly drinking with the meals, tend to "inoculate" the Italian and Italian-Americans from alcoholism, and as they decline in importance alcoholism increases. Neither the cocktail hour, nor drinking after meals is a feature of Italian drinking; moreover, drinking with meals constitutes a safety factor for intoxication, as pointed out by Lolli:

> The relationship between the beverage used and the frequency of episodes of intoxication is outstanding. The occurrence of such episodes is lowest among the Italians, who drink almost exclusively table wine. The frequency increases among the first-generation Italian-Americans, who begin to drink more of other beverages. It is highest in the succeeding generations, who move still further away from the ancestral drinking customs and, presumably, the associated behaviors, attitudes and controls.[125]

Alcoholic beverages are widely used among the Chinese of New York City, but the incidence of excessive drinking or alcoholism is low.[126] The social control exercised by the Cantonese or Chinese subcultural pattern is such that alcohol is largely consumed as a part of social functions, public drunkenness is disapproved, and children are educated to observe these patterns. Unlike the Jews, frequent mild intoxication may occur, but statistics show low prevalence of alcoholism among Chinese-Americans.

Summary

The problems related to the consumption of alcohol, the role of the tavern, and the alcoholic in modern society are far from unique to any culture and age. Today there are extensive value conflicts over the use of alcohol as well as over taverns.

---

[124] Lolli *et al., op. cit.*, p. 79.   [125] *Ibid.*, p. 85.
[126] Milton L. Barnett, "Alcoholism in the Cantonese of New York City: An Anthropological Study," in Oskar Diethelm ed., *Etiology of Chronic Alcoholism* (Springfield, Ill.; Charles C Thomas, Publisher, 1955), pp. 179–227. Also see Merrill Moore, "Chinese Wine: Some Notes on Its Social Use," *Quarterly Journal of Studies on Alcohol,* 9:270–279 (September, 1948).

Alcohol acts physiologically as a depressant. The effect of alcohol depends on the rate at which it is absorbed, the kind of beverage consumed and the proportion of alcohol it contains, the amount and type of food eaten, and certain individual physiological differences. In moderate quantities alcohol does not appear to be harmful, but larger quantities can produce drunkenness.

Drinking is a social phenomenon. Group associations determine the kind of beverage and the amount used, the circumstances under which drinking takes place, the time of drinking, and the individual's, as well as others', attitudes toward drinking. Most taverns are of the neighborhood type, and their chief functions appear to be to provide social relationships, recreation, and a place to talk over common problems.

Approximately two thirds of the adult population of the United States drink alcoholic beverages. The proportion who drink varies by sex, religion, age, and education.

Those who drink can be classified in terms of deviations from norms of drinking behavior within a culture or subculture, and their dependence on alcohol in their life organization. This dependence includes the purpose and meaning of drinking, the degree to which such drinking handicaps the individual in his interpersonal relations, and his ability to refrain from taking a drink. On this basis drinkers can be classified as social or controlled drinkers, heavy drinkers, alcoholics, and chronic alcoholics.

The excessive use of alcohol seems to be learned from others. Group associations and cultural factors are important in determining who will become excessive drinkers and who will not. The drinking norms of the individual appear to be associated with those of his associates. They learn to drink excessively because of the type of drinking behavior of their companions, social class, occupation, or ethnic status. Involvement in difficulties because of their excessive drinking leads some into a circular process of further excessive drinking.

Selected Readings

Alcohol, Science and Society. New Brunswick, N.J.: Quarterly Journal of Studies on Alcohol, 1945. The first comprehensive discussion of alcoholism, and still one of the best. Many topics are discussed by different writers.

CLINARD, MARSHALL B. "The Public Drinking House and Society," in David J. Pittman and Charles R. Snyder eds., *Alcohol, Culture and Drinking Patterns*. New York: John Wiley & Sons, Inc., 1962. A comprehensive discussion of the tavern or public drinking house from the standpoint of the value conflicts involved, types of taverns, functions of taverns, and the relation of the tavern to alcoholism and delinquency.

JELLINEK, E. M. "Phases in the Drinking History of Alcoholics," *Memoirs of the Section of Studies on Alcohol*. No. 5. New Brunswick, N.J.: Quarterly Journal of Studies on Alcohol, 1946. An analysis of the symptoms of the various stages in the development of alcoholism, with a number of cases.

LOLLI, GIORGIO, EMILIO SERIANNI, GRACE M. GOLDER, and PIERPAOLO LUZZATTO-FEGIS, *Alcohol in Italian Culture*. New York: The Free Press of Glencoe, 1958. A comparative study of drinking patterns and attitudes of Italians in Italy and Americans of Italian extraction, based on interviews and dietary diaries. An analysis of the place of alcoholic beverages in the total pattern of eating and drinking behavior in Italian culture.

MC CARTHY, RAYMOND G. ed. *Drinking and Intoxication*. New York: The Free Press of Glencoe, 1959. A comprehensive selection of materials on historical and contemporary drinking customs, attitudes toward drinking, and methods of control of drunkenness from earliest times to the present.

MC CARTHY, RAYMOND G., and EDGAR M. DOUGLASS. *Alcohol and Social Responsibility*. New York: Thomas Y. Crowell Company, 1949. A general survey of the literature dealing with the use of alcohol in our society. Various issues are discussed, in particular education about the use of alcohol.

PATRICK, CLARENCE H. *Alcohol, Culture and Society*. Durham, N.C.: Duke University Press, 1952. A study of alcohol in a cultural context, including the influence of society on the use of alcohol and its effects on society.

PITTMAN, DAVID J., and C. WAYNE GORDON. *Revolving Door*. New York: The Free Press of Glencoe, 1958. An intensive, systematic study of the men who are repeatedly jailed for drunkenness. Analyzes and interprets the family backgrounds, childhood and adolescent experiences, and criminal careers of men caught up in the circular process of arrest, imprisonment and rearrest on charges related to public intoxication. Illustrated with cases.

PITTMAN, DAVID J. and CHARLES R. SNYDER eds. *Alcohol, Culture and Drinking Patterns*. New York: John Wiley & Sons, Inc., 1962. A collection of articles, many of them original, by sociologists on various aspects of the use of alcohol, including drinking patterns and the public drinking house and society.

SNYDER, CHARLES R. *Alcohol and the Jews*. New York: The Free Press of Glencoe, 1958. A study of the influence of cultural norms on patterns of drinking behavior. Based on interviews with a random sample of adult Jewish men and on the results of a questionnaire study of the drinking practices of college students of various religious denominations.

SYMES, LEONARD. "Personality Characteristics and the Alcoholic: A Critique of Current Studies," *Quarterly Journal of Studies on Alcohol*, 18:288–302 (June, 1957). A follow-up of an earlier survey by Sutherland and Tordella covering all studies from 1949 to 1956 which tried to differentiate the personality traits of alcoholics from nonalcoholics. Reaches a largely negative conclusion about the relationship.

"Understanding Alcoholism." *The Annals*, Vol. 315 (January, 1958). Contains chapters by specialists on every phase of the problem of alcoholism: the alcoholic personality, sociocultural backgrounds, the chronic drunken offender, the woman alcoholic, the family, psychiatric treatment, Alcoholics Anonymous, physiological factors, role of the physician, social work, nature and extent of the problem of alcoholism, current therapy, education, and research.

The Functional Mental Disorders

Mental disorders have long constituted a vast, mysterious, and challenging frontier in contemporary society. The basis of mental illness and the appropriate methods of preventing it are still frequently elusive. Only within recent times has society come to regard the mentally disturbed person as a "sick person." Yet this recognition has not completely eliminated the societal attitude of rejection of the mentally ill. Indeed, rejection is manifested in many ways, including often the disposal of society's "insane" to the "human dumping grounds" found in many state mental hospitals.[1] That state mental hospitals should function as dumping grounds was not, of course, the manifest intent of their founders. This situation has arisen largely from the divergent attitudes which society holds toward physical as opposed to mental disorder. Toward the physically disordered there is generally a societal attitude of sympathy, perhaps because of the fact that the features of physical disorders can be seen, felt, and objectively observed. On the other hand, mental disorders, which involve intangibles, such as feelings and ideas which are often incomprehensible to other persons, are ordinarily reacted to with fear, revulsion, and ridicule. Despite this societal pattern of rejection toward the mentally ill, frank recognition of the problem of mental illness constitutes the first step in its control.[2]

There are increasing scientific interest and research on mental disorders on the part of sociologists and anthropologists as well as psychiatrists and psychologists. The role which social and cultural factors play in the development of such disorders is of particular interest. Of concern also have been the effects on society of mental disorder, including the concepts of mental disorder held by society, the status and role of the mentally ill, and the changing nature of treatment.

---

[1] *Action for Mental Health*, The Final Report of the Joint Commission on Mental Illness and Health (New York: Basic Books, Inc., 1961), pp. 56-63.

[2] *Ibid.* Also see Ernest M. Gruenberg and Seymour S. Bellin, "The Impact of Mental Disease on Society," in Alexander H. Leighton, John A. Clausen, and Robert N. Wilson eds., *Explorations in Social Psychiatry* (New York: Basic Books, Inc., 1957), pp. 341-364.

Problems of Definition

It is difficult to define adequately such terms as "mental health" and, consequently, to define "mental illness" or "mental disorder." It is not easy to say who is mentally ill and who is not.[3] Mental health or mental disorder can be defined in several ways—statistically, clinically, operationally, and in terms of value judgments and middle-class standards.

Mental health is not the same as the statistically normal in terms of averages. According to this view, the mental health of the person in the "middle" would represent what might be termed "normality." It is difficult to measure the mental health of the average citizen either in terms of averages, such as the mean, median, or mode, because there is no satisfactory frequency curve of mental health as in the case of intelligence curves. A norm of this type would also mean one which changed with the state of mental health of a given population.

In clinical medicine the terms "normal" and "health" are used in the same sense. The problem of definition of normality in organic medicine, while difficult enough, cannot quite compare with the complexities in behavioral disorders. From a clinical point of view, mental disorder is often regarded as behavior which does not "function according to design." [4] Thus a catatonic stupor would be clinically regarded as maladjusted behavior. It is difficult for the clinician to measure the signs of the beginning of mental disorder as distinguished from mental health. Hallucinations, for example, which are often considered to be signs of mental disorder, may be found in normal people. Catatonic stupor may be thought to be maladjustive in our society, but in Asia it might be associated with religious mysticism. As Redlich has written, there are three ideas which must be met before behavior can be labeled clinically as normal or abnormal.[5] (1) The motivation of the behavior must be taken into account, such as "normal" washing of the hands and a neurotic washing compulsion. (2) The context or situation in which the behavior occurs must also be considered. Wearing swimming trunks on a New England street in winter is one thing; on a summer bathing beach, another. (3) By whom is the judgment made that the behavior is clinically abnormal—the experts, such as the psychiatrist, or the general public? "As we do not possess a universal, rigorous science of man, many propositions on normality of behavior have a palpably low degree of validity and reliability and are apt to be chal-

[3] See Thomas S. Szasz, *The Myth of Mental Illness* (New York: Paul B. Hoeber, Inc., 1961).

[4] Psychoanalysts would regard mental health as freedom from anxiety and where the rational replaces the irrational.

[5] Frederick C. Redlich, "The Concept of Health in Psychiatry," in *Explorations in Social Psychiatry*, pp. 145–146.

lenged by a startled public, especially if scientific evidence for them is not particularly strong or runs counter to prevalent public opinion." [6]

The clinical definition of mental health gets us into the area of value judgments. Mental health is thus defined by listing certain traits, capacities and relationships which are considered to be "normal." All kinds of criteria exist. Among the definitions which have been used by leading psychiatric writers are strivings for happiness and effectiveness and sensitive social relationships, freedom from symptoms, being unhampered by conflict and having the capacity to love other than himself; successful integration of personality and the balance of instinctual and ego force. Karl Menninger, in a widely quoted definition, has stated: "Let us define mental health as the adjustment of human beings to the world and to each other with a maximum of effectiveness and happiness. Not just efficiency, or just contentment, or the grace of obeying the rules of the game cheerfully. It is all of these together. It is the ability to maintain an even temper, an alert intelligence, socially considerate behavior, and a happy disposition. This, I think, is a healthy mind." [7]

With such criteria it is often difficult to see how anyone could be regarded as normal. A state of emotional health is thus regarded as par (to use the golf term) for the upper levels of health attainment.[8] They are ideals and are often contradictory. Actually behavior contrary to such ideal values may often be considered normal in another society. Hysterical reactions, for example, are common and normal in many societies.

So-called mental disorders have been studied in a number of preliterate societies, and the findings have a bearing on our understanding of the definition of mental disorders in more complex urban societies. The Berens River Ojibwa in northern Canada, for example, have various fears about encounters with animals, as well as phobias about snakes and huge imaginary animals, such as toads.[9] The belief also exists that personal transgressions are related to disease. Finally, their most pronounced fear concerns beliefs about Windigo, or cannibals. Human beings can be transformed into cannibals, and this fact may be perceived by certain phenomena exhibited by individuals. To an outsider these fears appear to be

---

[6] *Ibid.*, p. 146. Also see Jurgen Ruesch and Gregory Bateson, *Communication: The Social Matrix of Psychiatry* (New York: W. W. Norton & Company, Inc., 1951). See also H. Warren Dunham, *Sociological Theory and Mental Disorder* (Detroit: Wayne State University Press, 1959); Joseph W. Eaton, "The Assessment of Mental Health," *American Journal of Psychiatry*, 108:81–89 (August, 1951); and Marie Jahoda, *Current Concepts of Positive Mental Health* (New York: Basic Books, Inc., 1958).

[7] Karl Menninger, *The Human Mind* (New York: Alfred A. Knopf, Inc., 1946), p. 1.

[8] Leslie A. Osborn, *Psychiatry and Medicine* (New York: McGraw-Hill Book Company, Inc., 1952), p. 211. See Jahoda, *op. cit.*, for a critique of ideal definitions of mental health, pp. 5–9 and 65–80.

[9] A. Irving Hallowell, "Fear and Anxiety as Cultural and Individual Variables in a Primitive Society: Ojibwa," in Marvin K. Opler ed., *Culture and Mental Health* (New York: The Macmillan Company, 1959), pp. 41–62.

"neurotic" in the sense that there is no real danger and they arise from fantasies. Hallowell believes we should distinguish between individual fears and such culturally induced fears. This is a prevalent problem in the diagnosis of mental disorder in more complex societies with various subcultures and social classes.

> In the first place, the Berens River Indian *is* responding to a *real* danger when he flees from a cannibal monster or murders a human being who is turning into a *windigo,* or when he becomes apprehensive in a certain disease situation. To act or feel otherwise would stamp an individual either as a fool or as a phenomenal example of intellectual emancipation. For, psychologically, the actual order of reality in which human beings live is constituted in a large measure by the traditional concepts and beliefs that are held. Furthermore, the Indians themselves are able to point out plenty of tangible empirical evidence that supports the interpretation of the realities that their culture imposes upon their minds. They are naïve empiricists but not naïvely irrational.[10]

Value judgments about mental health, moreover, often merely represent certain middle-class criteria, thus implying lower-class behavior to be the reverse. Frequently mental health is defined in middle-class terms, and an attempt is made to associate the definition with the Protestant ethic.[11] An analysis of the content of pamphlets attempting to improve the mental health of the general population has revealed these middle-class themes in the definition of the mentally healthy person: [12] adjustment to group and prevailing norms by getting along with others, facing up to problems and then doing something about them, the value of work through enjoying it and getting satisfaction out of one's job, control of emotions, planning ahead without fear of the future, striving to achieve goals and community participation.

An operational definition of mental normality has been proposed by Redlich as "normal for what" and "normal for whom." [13] This definition seems to be helpful for our purposes. The extent to which mental problems, for example, can be tolerated by others may be different for a business executive or a person employed in a minor capacity in an industrial plant, both in terms of what is presumed to be "normal" and what is the societal reaction of others. "The self-perception of the person with the problem and the role assignment of all actors involved will determine subsequent labeling (normal or abnormal with reference to certain tasks) and subsequent action." [14]

---

[10] *Ibid.,* p. 53.

[11] Kingsley Davis, "Mental Hygiene and the Class Structure," *Psychiatry,* 1:55–64 (February, 1938).

[12] Orville R. Gursslin, Raymond G. Hunt, and Jack L. Roach, "Social Class and the Mental Health Movement," *Social Problems,* 7:210–218 (Winter, 1959–1960).

[13] Redlich, "The Concept of Health in Psychiatry," *loc. cit.*   [14] *ibid.,* p. 155.

Operationally it is difficult, therefore, to draw a sharp line between mental health and mental disorder. What we really have is the problem of the social limits of "eccentricity," as an English writer has concluded: "It appears in fact that there is *no* clear-cut criterion of what constitutes a psychiatric case. Whether a person is regarded as in need of medical treatment is always a function of his behavior *and* the attitude of his fellows in society." [15] The person may be slightly, moderately, or severely impaired, depending upon the way his behavior is evaluated by others.[16] An operational definition depends also upon the societal reaction, including urgency of treatment as this is defined by society, and disorders may be divided into two groups.[17] One category is the severely mentally ill or psychotic, those cases in which the societal reaction to the behavior is strong and treatment is often urgent. Their behavior is regarded as social or antisocial in terms of the prevailing cultural norms and their level of social performance is not in conformity with norms current for persons of their particular age and status.[18] Such deviations are more easily recognized by the expert and the lay public with whom the persons are in contact, and they may even be treated without the consent of the patient. The second category represents those mild and transitory mental disturbances where there is little urgency and the problem is felt more by the individual than by others. The more moderately disturbed group includes those persons whose behavior deviates less markedly from the norms (of perception, belief, and feeling) and who may or may not be reacted to by most lay persons as "odd" or "peculiar." Professional persons would probably describe these persons with technical terms, such as the neuroses.[19]

In evaluating the criteria by which visible symptoms might be judged, one practical basis is the extent to which the person failed to fulfill adequately expectations in performing his primary social roles (especially his familial and occupational roles), and the extent to which he violated legal and moral norms and highly important values of the group. Whether a definition of deviancy is made and acted upon will depend, largely, on how serious the consequences of this deviation are for the social group. Some deviant behaviors are rewarded and tolerated, others have some idiosyncratic function for the group as is often the case with the "comic," or the deviant may be thought of as "eccentric," "queer," or "strange" but not sufficiently so to merit a definition of illness. On the other hand, should the deviancy begin to

---

[15] G. M. Carstairs, "The Social Limits of Eccentricity: An English Study," in Opler, *op. cit.*, p. 377.
[16] See A. Hollingshead and F. Redlich, *Social Class and Mental Illness* (New York: John Wiley & Sons, Inc., 1958), Chaps. 1, 2, 6.
[17] Redlich, "The Concept of Health in Psychiatry," *loc. cit.*, pp. 154–158.
[18] Norman Cameron, *The Psychology of Behavior Disorders* (Boston: Houghton Mifflin Company, 1947), p. 8.
[19] See Hollingshead and Redlich, *op. cit.*, Chap. 6, and *Action for Mental Health*, Chap. 3.

have serious consequences, either in that it is damaging or harmful to the individual, a group, or both, or becomes so visible to external groups that the family suffers status loss, it might be redefined as "mental illness" and the person sent for treatment. In some groups, of course, the stigma attached to a definition of mental illness is sufficiently great to bring about group resistance to such a definition.[20]

Traditionally, mental ill-health has been classified as the neuroses and the psychoses. Neuroses are the mildest and the most common type. Among psychotics, thoughts, feelings, expressions, beliefs, and acting deviate more markedly from approved norms. Psychotic behavior, as contrasted with neurotic, is often characterized by a loss of contact with reality. Furthermore, the psychotic's ability to communicate intelligently with others may be partially or completely interrupted, a factor which is not generally characteristic of the neurotic. The essential feature of the neuroses is that they involve behaviors which deviate less markedly from societal norms than is true of the psychoses. They are therefore regarded as "less serious," and generally there is greater societal tolerance for them.[21]

Actually, it is much easier to recognize the behavior which is labeled psychotic because the deviation from norms is often more pronounced and visible. The so-called neuroses are much harder to designate and label. Role distortions or role inadequacies are not generally apparent. Consequently, among psychiatrists and others there is little agreement on the definition of a neurosis. This fact is shown by estimates of the neurotics in the general population. Some estimate as high as 40 percent, others about 5 percent. Some have gone so far as to suggest that nearly everyone in a modern urban society is neurotic. Obviously, the concept becomes almost meaningless when used in this way.

Extent of Mental Disorders in the United States

It is impossible to know the extent of mental illness in the United States today. Even if one knew how many are so incapacitated mentally that they require hospitalization, are being treated by psychiatrists, or are being counseled by their clergymen or by others, this total might well exclude many others who are mentally ill. The sources of knowledge about the extent of mental illness have been chiefly from (1) data on patients in mental hospitals, (2) data from Selective Service examinations and the records of the armed forces, and (3) community surveys of the prevalence of mental disorders.[22]

---

[20] David Mechanic, "Some Factors in Identifying and Defining Mental Illness," *Mental Hygiene*, 46:66–74 (January, 1962).

[21] *Action for Mental Health*, Chap. 3.

[22] These data have several limitations. They have largely not been made on random samples of the population, and they have not used "standardized methods of case finding,

In 1959 there were 616,964 mental patients in long-term mental hospitals, about 88 percent of them in public mental hospitals—state, county, or city. The movement of patients in and out of these hospitals during a given year is so extensive that the total is actually much higher, and on any one day of the year, patients in mental hospitals make up almost half of all the patients in all the hospitals of the United States. From 1955 to 1960 there had been a slight decline in the resident population of mental hospitals, which has been thought to be due to the increased use of tranquilizers as well as to a spreading conviction that patients should, if possible, be treated without hospitalization.[23]

These figures are not an actual index of mental disorder because the proportion with mental disorders not hospitalized is not known. Also, there are considerable variations throughout the country: "Hospitalization rates are a resultant not only of the true incidence of mental disorder but of a number of factors such as availability of mental hospital beds, public attitudes toward hospitalization, and availability and use of other community resources for diagnosis and treatment."[24] These other resources include such facilities as general hospitals with psychiatric treatment services, psychiatric clinics, and private psychiatrists.

More Selective Service registrants were rejected during World War II for personality defects other than mental deficiency than for any other cause. Up to August 1, 1945, 900,000 men between the ages of eighteen and thirty-seven were rejected for military service and classed as neuropsychiatric casualties, a figure which represented 18 percent of all men rejected in the armed forces.[25] In a study of the prevalence of defects among those between the ages of eighteen and forty-four who were examined during the period 1940–1943, mental illness ranked sixth in prevalence, with a rate of 55.8 per 1000 men. During World War II the armed services gave a medical discharge to about 460,000 men for neuropsychiatric reasons, or about 36 percent of all medical discharges. Such figures, high as they are, should not be taken as representative of the general male population of military age. Persons were deferred for a large number of reasons, others volunteered, and some of those with certain physical defects or low educational standards were not examined at all. Furthermore, the standards for military acceptance changed, and draft boards did not use

---

diagnosis, and classification, as well as comparable definitions of case and prevalence."— R. H. Felix and Morton Kramer, "Extent of the Problem of Mental Disorders," *The Annals*, 286:13 (March, 1953).

[23] For a discussion of mental hospital populations see Chapter 21.

[24] Felix and Kramer, "Extent of the Problem of Mental Disorders," *loc. cit.*, p. 12.

[25] United States Selective Service System, *Physical Examination of Selective Service Registrants* (Special Monograph No. 15; Washington, D.C.: Government Printing Office, 1948). This figure did not include those rejected because they were mentally deficient (feeble-minded) or those who were in mental hospitals.

identical methods in screening.[26] Moreover, the figures should be regarded with extreme caution because of inefficiencies in the general screening process for military service.

Estimates of the incidence of mental disorder in the general population have been made, but it is difficult to know the true rate. Most of the estimates appear to be highly exaggerated. To give some estimate they will be presented with this reservation. A community survey was made in the Eastern Health District, Baltimore, Maryland, in 1936, and another in Williamson County, Tennessee, in 1938.[27] The Baltimore study found 3337 "active" cases of mental illness during the year in a population of 55,129, or 60.5 per 1000 population. The Williamson County survey found that there were 1721 cases of mental illness in a population of 24,804. The two studies cannot be compared, however, because of demographic differences and the methods they used.[28]

One of the most intensive metropolitan surveys ever made in the field of mental health involved a cross-section of a heterogeneous midtown Manhattan residential population of 110,000 persons.[29] From interviews with 1660 residents the conclusion was reached that only 18.5 percent were free enough of emotional symptoms to be considered "well." A total of 58.1 percent were found to have mild to moderate symptoms, such as tensions, nervousness, and other indications of emotional disturbances, although not to the extent of impairing life functioning. Marked, severe, and incapacitating symptoms were found in 23.4 percent of the cases.

---

[26] William A. Hunt and Cecil L. Wittson, "Some Sources of Error in the Neuropsychiatric Statistics of World War II," *Journal of Clinical Psychology*, 5:350–358 (October, 1949). Also see Eleanor Leacock, "Three Social Variables and the Occurrence of Mental Disorder," in Leighton, Clausen, and Wilson, *op. cit.*, pp. 308–340. Leacock points out that a good proportion of those rejected as "neuropsychiatric casualties" were actually mentally deficient and/or illiterate.

[27] Paul Lemkau, Christopher Tietze, and Marcia Cooper, "Mental Hygiene Problems in an Urban District," *Mental Hygiene*, 25:624–646 (October, 1941), 26:100–119, 257–288 (January, 1942), and 27:279–295 (April, 1943). Also see William F. Roth and Frank Luton, "The Mental Health Program in Tennessee, I: Description of the Original Study Program; II: Statistical Report of a Psychiatric Survey in a Rural County," *American Journal of Psychiatry*, 99:662–675 (January, 1943). It is unfortunate that the studies were not confined to mental illness, for the Baltimore study also included about 6.8 percent cases of mental deficiency, and the Tennessee study 8.2 percent. Feeble-mindedness, which represents a lack of intellectual development for organic or other reasons, is not considered here as a mental disorder. The distinction is often made between *amentia,* or the absence of mental faculties, and *dementia,* which is the disorder of such faculties. Occasionally feeble-minded persons develop disorders, but these generally have no connection with the feeble-mindedness. Feeble-minded persons probably have no more, and possibly even less, personality disorders than those with higher intelligence.

[28] In the former study, for example, "active" meant being a client of certain social agencies, whereas in the other "active" meant cases presenting both serious and mild personal problems.

[29] Leo Srole *et al., Mental Health in the Metropolis: The Midtown Manhattan Study,* (New York: McGraw-Hill Book Company, Inc., 1962). The validity of this study depends, of course, upon the criteria used to determine degrees of mental health.

A study of Texas has used a different measure, namely, of incidence of first cases of psychoses who came under diagnosis and treatment during the two-year period 1951 through 1952, whether private or public and whether in or outside a hospital, rather than merely hospitalization.[30] Jaco found the average number of Texans considered to be psychotic for the first time in their lives was 5649, or a crude annual incidence rate of 73.3 per 100,000. The age-adjusted rate was 68 for males and a higher rate of 78 for females. The median age was 44 for males and 40 for females. The incidence increased with each advancing age-group category in the total group and among males, although there were some slight exceptions among the female groups. As other studies have shown, highest standardized rates for psychoses were found among the divorced, followed in order by those who were single, separated, widowed, or married.

Trends in Mental Illness

There is some question as to whether there has been a real increase in the rate of resident patients in mental hospitals in the United States. Actually, the rate has about doubled, from nearly 200 per 100,000 population in 1903 to nearly 400 in 1950.[31] It may actually represent a real increase in mental disorders, or it may reflect an increase in the age of the general population, a greater awareness of mental illness on the part of laymen and professional men, more hospital space, or increased difficulties encountered by mentally ill persons who remain outside hospitals in urban areas where living conditions are crowded. One study suggests that the apparently greater flow to mental hospitals may be also a function of our highly complex, industrial society.[32] Thus some elderly persons who have simply outlived their function and who have difficulties in interpersonal relations may be placed in mental hospitals because there is no place for them outside.

A study of first-admission rates to Massachusetts and New York institutions for the mentally ill for the periods 1840–1885 and 1917–1940, a detailed comparison of 1885 and 1939–1941 being made, concluded that "there has been no long-term increase during the last century in the incidence of the psychoses of early and middle life." [33] More specifically, it was claimed that when comparisons are made which take into account the class of patients received, and the conditions affecting hospitalization, that the

[30] E. Gartly Jaco, *The Social Epidemiology of Mental Disorders* (New York: Russell Sage Foundation, 1960).

[31] Felix and Kramer, "Extent of the Problem of Mental Disorders," *loc. cit.*, p. 9.

[32] *Action for Mental Health*, Chap. 3.

[33] Herbert Goldhamer and Andrew W. Marshall, *Psychoses and Civilization* (New York: The Free Press of Glencoe, 1953), p. 92.

rates by age for first admissions under fifty "are revealed to be just as high during the last half of the 19th century as they are today." [34] A marked increase in the older groups was attributed to the increased tendency today to hospitalize older persons suffering from mental disorders.

A number of major objections to this study can be raised, however, some of which the authors recognize. First of all, Massachusetts has been highly urban for a long time: 75 percent in 1880 as compared with 90 percent in 1940; therefore conclusions drawn from this sample do not measure the possible increase in mental disorders in larger areas of the country where urbanization has been more recent and more rapid. There has been a decline in the relative incidence of organic psychoses, such as paresis, which is caused by syphilis, a disease more common a century ago. Moreover, the study did not include most neurotic cases, since they are only infrequently hospitalized; but, as will be indicated, these cases constitute a large proportion of contemporary mental illness. In addition, there are today a large number of persons with mental illness who are treated by outpatient clinics and private practitioners who could not have been so treated to any large extent a hundred years ago because there were few such facilities.

Organic Mental Disorders

According to conventional classification, there are two types of mental illness: those having an organic basis, and those having a nonorganic, or functional, basis. Organic types of mental disorders are usually linked to some germ, to a brain injury, or to other physiological disorder, and, in certain rare types of mental disorders, possibly to some hereditary factors. The three most important organic mental disorders are the arteriosclerotic senile psychoses, paresis, and the alcoholic psychoses, none of which is really hereditary.

The senile or old-age psychoses, which are generally classified as organic on the assumption that they are produced by certain physiological processes of aging, accounted for about a fourth of all admissions to state hospitals in 1957. Some of these cases are arteriosclerotic and result from changes in the circulatory system, but others are not. Senile psychoses are characterized by a loss of memory, particularly for recent events, inability to concentrate, or certain delusional thoughts. There is increasing evidence that many of the psychoses due to aging are the product of nonorganic conditions arising from interpersonal relations, such as social isolation and loss of status.[35]

Paresis, or dementia paralytica, is caused by syphilis, and accounts for

---

[34] *Ibid.*, p. 91.   [35] See Chapter 16.

about 4 percent of all state hospital admissions. This illness begins at least ten years after the initial syphilitic infection, and there is often progressive degeneration in the brain of untreated patients. Although the symptoms of a paretic may not be different from those of many functional psychoses, the paretic may be relatively easy to diagnose through positive Wassermann and Kahn reactions. There may also be tremors, convulsive seizures, and a lack of coordination in bodily movements. The mental symptoms are often a complete alteration in the personality traits: "The neat well-dressed individual becomes careless and slovenly; the efficient businessman shows poor judgment in the office; the moral, upright man suddenly becomes degraded." [36] Eventually memory about time and places may become defective and in some cases there is depression. As a rule, paretics do not live long. The elimination of syphilis would end paresis, and great advances have been made toward this goal. Today a number of factors have reduced not only the incidence of syphilis but, particularly, that of paresis. Widespread public health methods, including education, have reduced the incidence of syphilis; and drugs, including formerly arsenic and now the more effective antibiotics, which work on the nervous system, have helped to cure syphilis and thus prevent paresis. Some evidence exists, moreover, that present-day syphilis is of a milder form than that of a half century or so ago.

The psychoses resulting from alcoholism are not as definitely organic as paresis, although they are usually classified as the same type. Only relatively few alcoholics develop psychoses. In 1949 there were only 5381 new admissions to state mental hospitals for this illness as a result of alcoholism, or 5.2 percent of all admissions. In 1957 17,286 persons were admitted to public, prolonged-care hospitals, with mental disorders associated with alcoholic intoxication or alcohol addiction. Of this total, 10,527 were classified under "personality disorders" with "alcoholism addiction." There is some doubt as to how much mental illness is organically produced by the alcohol and what proportion is the result of certain socio-psychological conditions.[37] The prolonged existence of chronic alcoholism, with its vitamin and nutritional deficiencies, may in some cases produce such deterioration in physical and psychological behavior that alcoholic psychoses may result. Some patients become rigid and develop terrifying hallucinations, others have tremors which are often referred to as delirium tremens or "D.T.'s," and still others show general progressive deterioration. Not all cases of D.T.'s indicate a psychosis, however, for many of these symptoms may be short-lived and without marked personality changes.

[36] Roy M. Dorcus and G. W. Shaffer, *Textbook of Abnormal Psychology* (3d ed.; Baltimore: Williams & Wilkins Company, 1945), p. 278.
[37] See Chapter 12.

Functional or Nonorganic Mental Disorders

Previously we have indicated that mental disorder should be regarded as a deviation from norms and can be understood only in terms of the societal reaction to certain behavior. What may be regarded as mental disorder—that is, beyond the tolerance limit of eccentricity—is therefore not necessarily the same from one culture to another.

Such a view conflicts with the general psychiatric tendency which regards such behavior as clinical entities, as constituting a type of "sickness" which would, presumably, be the same in all cultures. Because of their medical training, psychiatrists obviously look for disease entities and think in terms of a medical diagnosis.[38] In the case of mental disorder these diagnoses have come to be known as neuroses and psychoses, and the latter in turn have been divided into schizophrenia, manic-depressive disorders, paranoia, and other entities. They have come to be regarded as real disease entities which are important to the psychiatrist who, being a physician, assumes that this enables him to deal with the "causes" and therefore to suggest treatment of the mental disorders. Rather than being disease entities they are actually *descriptions* of certain behavior.

The diagnostic categories themselves, and the adequacy of the diagnosis by psychiatrists, have been severely criticized by many writers. As Hollingshead has written: "Currently, psychiatry does not have a standard test which researchers may use to diagnose any of the functional mental illnesses. A standardized, valid, diagnostic test would enable a researcher to determine the presence or absence of functional mental illness in individuals. Until this problem is solved, research into mental illness will continue to be hampered." [39]

The lack of reliability and validity of psychiatric diagnosis has been shown in several studies. For example, it was recently reported by Hoch that the ratio of first admissions, with a diagnosis of manic depressive in comparison with schizophrenia, reversed itself over a five-year period in one state hospital system. He attributed this reversal to a change in personnel and policy in the hospital system, not to a shift in the distribution of disease in the population of the state.[40] This report was supplemented by Pasamanick, with findings from another hospital where from one ward to another significant differences were found in the diagnostic classifications

---

[38] For a critical discussion of the implications of medical training for psychiatric treatment, see Erving Goffman, *Asylums* (New York: Doubleday Anchor Books, 1961), pp. 320–386.

[39] August B. Hollingshead, "The Epidemiology of Schizophrenia," *American Sociological Review*, 26:10 (February, 1961).

[40] Paul H. Hoch, in "Work Conference in the Mental Disorders" (Mimeographed; New York: February 15–19, 1959), pp. 145–146.

of patients with functional psychoses.[41] For example, on one ward the diagnosis changed with the change in the ward administrator. The diagnoses had been made by residents, as well as by the ward administrator, who was a trained psychiatrist. Whereas these data were based on reports of hospitalized patients, Leighton did research in which he attempted to assess the mental status of a nonpatient group. In his study six psychiatrists were asked to read the field protocols on fifty adult white males, and were instructed to assess whether each man was mentally "ill" or "well." Fifteen were placed in an equivocal category, and five were thought to be "well," although these five men diagnosed as "well" differed for each of the six psychiatrists. In fact, one psychiatrist's five "wells" had been placed in another's "sickest" group.[42]

Having stated such criticisms, one might well question the relevance of including in the following section a description of various types of mental disorder. In the first place, they are terms widely used by psychiatrists, who are the persons mainly responsible for the treatment of mental disorders. Second, they are terms used by laymen. It is therefore necessary to become familiar with such terms and their use. Again, however, it should be understood that actually these are not clear-cut entities in the sense, for example, of tuberculosis. In fact, many persons exhibit the behavior described in each type, although in all probability to a lesser degree and in a manner which does not provoke much societal reaction. Probably all persons have, to some degree, exhibited such behavior as hallucinations, phobias, persecution complexes, and emotional extremes of elation and depression. For example, everyone will remember how many times during his lifetime he has had irrational fears, daydreams, flights of idea, and disorders of memory:

> . . . sense of inferiority, sublimation, imperception, illusion, hallucinations, delusions, disorders of judgment, disturbance of the train of thought, flight of ideas, nonessential ideas and thoughts, incoherence, retardation or inhibition of thought, disorders of orientation, disturbance of consciousness, clouding of consciousness, confusion, dream states, negativism, inaccessibility, obsession, fears, phobias, disorders of attention, disorders of memory, conflict, complexes, compensation, symbolization, etc.—all of these are found operating in varying degrees in minds that are considered normal, as well as in minds that are disordered to such an extent that the case is diagnosed as insanity.[43]

According to many psychiatrists, the functional or nonorganic mental disorders "function" to adjust the individual to his particular difficulties;

---

[41] Benjamin Pasamanick, in "Work Conference in the Mental Disorders," pp. 143–145.
[42] Alexander H. Leighton, in "Work Conference in the Mental Disorders," pp. 147–148.
[43] Lawrence Guy Brown, *Social Pathology* (New York: Appleton-Century-Crofts, Inc., 1946), p. 62. This quotation and others from this work have been used by permission of the publisher.

hence the term "functional." The idea that such mental disorders are necessarily an adaptation to stress is difficult to prove, although in many cases this adaptation may play an important part. As yet no one has been able to demonstrate conclusively that functional disorders result from heredity, physiological disorders, or other organic deficiency. Although there have been reports of organic deficiencies in some cases, most leading authorities in psychiatry today agree that nothing of a universal nature has so far been established. The neuroses and the psychoses are the two types of these disorders.

THE NEUROSES

Some neurotic symptoms can be classified as dissociated behavior and others as compulsive disorders. In all of them the societal reaction to the behavior is not as great as with the psychoses. Hysteria, amnesia, and disturbances of speech, hearing, and sight are examples of dissociated behavior. It was once thought that hysteria, which was quite common, was a peculiarly feminine disease, since women were frequently given to "swooning." In addition to hysterical fainting, there may often be facial tics or uncontrolled movements. Ingenious tests have been devised, for example, to separate the person who is hysterically blind in one eye from the truly blind.[44]

Compulsive behavior is a form of neurosis where there are "irrepressible tendencies to do, say or think something in a particular way which persist in spite of strong contrary tendencies. In this situation anxiety reactions develop and their periodically rising intensity leads to indulgence, followed by temporary relief."[45] This behavior includes stepping on cracks in the sidewalk, excessive washing of the hands or bathing, counting telephone poles, dressing in a certain set manner, and requiring everything to be in a certain meticulous order, such as all drawers carefully closed or shoes or other objects lined up in order.

Often the compulsive behavior is not physical in nature but consists of obsessions or persistent ideas, emotional fears of objects, acts, or a situation. Some obsessions may be a more or less constant fear of death, of losing one's mind, or of losing one's friends, prestige, or job. A fairly common neurotic fear is anxiety about one's health, hypochondria, which may involve fears about the general state of health or about nonexistent heart conditions, cancer or tuberculosis. Sometimes neurotic obsessions are di-

---

[44] Red and green letters are put on a card so that the letters are alternately colored. On one there may be the red letters JHSOKN and the green letters ONHPIS. The subject is given glasses, through one lens of which he can see only the red letters, the other only green. If he reads "Johns Hopkins" it is apparent that he is using both eyes even if he reports he has vision in only one eye.

[45] Cameron, *op. cit.*, p. 12.

rected at destructive notions of injuring someone. Neurotic phobias are often of a general nature such as fear of confinement (claustrophobia) or its opposite, fear of open places, and fear of high places. Persons suffering from these fears are generally not only ashamed of this behavior but become perplexed and resentful of it as absurd and burdensome.[46]

Studies have shown that members of the upper class are more likely to be given the polite label of "neurotic," whereas those in the lower class are labeled as psychotic or, more specifically, schizophrenic.[47] In this connection Clausen has stated:

> Every community has some members who are regarded by their fellow citizens as "queer," "mean," "shy," "offensive," and the like. Many of these persons would be diagnosed by a psychiatrist as neurotic and some as psychotic, even though other community members may not regard them as mentally ill. It is not unlikely that many persons whose social background is grossly divergent from that of the psychiatrist (e.g., lower-class persons) will be seen as sicker than those whose attitudes and behaviors are closer to the psychiatrist's own outlook.[48]

THE FUNCTIONAL PSYCHOSES

The functional psychoses are generally divided into three main types: schizophrenia, the manic-depressive psychoses, and paranoia. In all of these the societal reaction tends to be greater than it is toward the neuroses. About 21 percent of all new admissions to state mental hospitals each year are diagnosed as schizophrenic. This illness is sometimes referred to as dementia praecox, because it develops primarily between the ages of fifteen and thirty. Few persons develop schizophrenia after the age of fifty. The manic-depressive psychotics constitute about 15 percent of all institutionalized patients, women making up roughly three quarters of all these cases. Only about 1 percent of all new admissions to state mental hospitals each year have a diagnosis of true paranoia.

Schizophrenic Behavior. The most characteristic symptom of a schizophrenic is his withdrawal from contact with the world around him and his inability to play the roles expected of him. Even before institutionalization becomes necessary, the schizophrenic may show a great deal of emotional indifference and inattention. He does not share the expectations and interest of the group, and there is a great indifference to things previously considered important. In addition, the emotional tone is passive, often even negative, so that the patient has little interest in activities.

---

[46] *Ibid.*, p. 281.   [47] See, for example, Hollingshead and Redlich, *op. cit.*
[48] John A. Clausen, "The Sociology of Mental Illness," in Robert K. Merton, Leonard Broom, Leonard S. Cottrell, Jr., *Sociology Today* (New York: Basic Books, Inc., 1959), p. 494.

Finally, his thought processes are so disturbed that he builds a world of his own imagination, including false perceptions and hallucinations of various kinds, such as ideas, voices, and forces which enter his daily living and which he cannot control. Schizophrenics have undergone a collapse in their personalities which involves a detachment of their emotional selves from their intellectual selves. It is for this reason that the term "schizophrenia," or "split personality," as it is often called, is used to refer to this illness.

Several subtypes of schizophrenia have been identified. A conventional distinction has been a fourfold classification of simple, hebephrenic, paranoiac, and catatonic schizophrenia. The symptoms of severe hebephrenics and catatonics are not seen as frequently today in institutions because of the use of tranquilizers. In simple schizophrenia patients begin from early life to show increasing tendencies to withdraw, to daydream, and to be unable to concentrate. They become exceedingly careless of their personal appearance, manners, and speech, are listless and apathetic, and lose their interests and ambitions. There is little loss of memory and no serious mental deterioration, if any. Many of these cases are never institutionalized because they are not harmful to themselves or to others and because they may make some sort of adjustment to the world, inadequate as that adjustment may be.

Hebephrenic symptoms include a pronounced silliness of behavior with a great deal of situationally unwarranted smiling, giggling, odd mannerisms, gesturing, and incoherent speech and thought. There is pronounced mental deterioration with bizarre delusions and auditory and visual hallucinations.

Unlike those of the true paranoid, to be discussed shortly, the delusions of persecution of the schizophrenic paranoid are transitory and are based on his own social reality. Moreover, the schizophrenic with a paranoid reaction hears and sees varying images and noises and exhibits the characteristic emotional indifference of the schizophrenic. The following case illustrates a typical paranoid schizophrenic patient.

A 46-year-old laborer admitted to the state hospital with complaint of feeling weak, mixed up, unable to work. Following admission to hospital he appeared shy, mixed poorly, and complained that someone was following him and wanted to get rid of him. He improved spontaneously, was discharged to his family, then readmitted seven years later. On readmission he had a crutch and cane, claimed he had not been working for several years because of a spinal injury. He offered various ideas of persecution and strange expressions, i.e., that he was surrounded by detectives who were trying to "run a secret world." He was being bothered by "radio tones." After a course of 23 electric shock treatments he discarded his cane and crutch and gave up his ideas about not being able to walk. He has remained chronic with persistent delusions, some persecutory and others grandiose, e.g., identifying himself with Roosevelt and Truman, thinks he has done important "government work" in the past and that he is entitled to a large pension. He was well adjusted in the hospital.[49]

Catatonic schizophrenics have episodes of excitement and stupor. Since they live in a private world of their own, their behavior is characterized by apathy and impulsiveness. They display the most complete withdrawal from the social world of any mental patients. Many catatonics' withdrawal may be so complete that the muscular or waxy rigidity of the limbs and the stuporous appearance of the catatonic reminds an observer of a dummy. Such catatonics may sit for hours and days in the same position without movement or speech, and some have to be fed. One is able to lift the arm of many catatonics in such a stupor or place them in an uncomfortable position and for an indefinite time they will make no effort to alter their position. They seem to take no interest in things going on around them; yet they are often conscious of the most minute details in their surroundings. The catatonic syndrome also includes a manic state, with increased speech, muscular movements, and action. Gesturing and frenzy are also common. Probably most catatonics, but not all, alternate between these periods of severe depression, frenzied excitation, and stupor.

Some have suggested that some of the more bizarre reactions of hospitalized patients may, in fact, be reactions to their institutionalization and complete deprivation of civil rights. This might apply not only to the catatonic but to other types of patients as well.[50]

Manic-Depressive Behavior. As the name implies, manic-depressive behavior may be extremely elated, in the manic stage, or depressed, although manic-depressives do not necessarily pass through cyclical stages of mania and depression.[51] In the manic stage the patient is agitated and excited, elated and aggressive. He rapidly shifts from one topic, object, or activity, and there is a constant flow of manic talk, which, although continuous, is socially understandable. This method of talking is often filled with quips, rhymes, poems, and other witticisms, much with a personal reference. The manic patient sings or whistles, shouts, dances, walks, teases or clowns. He may dress himself lavishly or prefer to go unclothed. Since he often disregards such bodily needs as food, rest, and elimination, he may be in need of immediate physical attention.[52]

---

[49] From a case record collected by the author.

[50] *Action for Mental Health.* See also M. Greenblatt, D. Levinson, and R. Williams, *The Patient and the Mental Hospital* (New York: The Free Press of Glencoe, 1957), pp. 438–471, 517–526.

[51] Thomas Rennie, "Prognosis in Manic-Depressive Psychoses," *American Journal of Psychiatry*, 98:801–814 (May, 1942). In this study of 208 manic-depressive cases Rennie found that about one fourth had both manic and depressive attacks, although not as often in cycles.

[52] Cameron, *op. cit.*, p. 513.

In the depressed phase there is much brooding and unpleasantness, but little serious mental deterioration. Agitated depression involves restless overactivity and despair, whereas activity is minimized and stupor is not uncommon in retarded depression. This disturbance is generally characterized by feelings of dejection, sadness, and self-deprecation. The patient seems to have lost friends, home, family, and all purpose in life. He feels guilty about acts committed or omitted, and he believes he has grievously wronged and been wronged. Contact with reality is nonetheless maintained, as are memory and place-time orientation.

Not all depressed behavior is symptomatic of a manic-depressive psychosis. Neurotics may display secondary depression. Involutional melancholia is another fairly common mental disorder characterized largely by depression. This condition may occur among women during the menopause period and among men at a slightly older age. For example, it is difficult to distinguish schizophrenia from the extreme or manic phases of the manic-depressive disorders. In fact, today schizophrenia is apt to be a more popular diagnosis than formerly, and the manic-depressives are likely to be largely the depressive cases.

Paranoia and Paranoid Behavior. At one time a large proportion of mentally ill persons were diagnosed as suffering from paranoia, but today paranoia is not widely used as a diagnostic category. Most of those suffering from paranoid disorders are now considered to exhibit a form of schizophrenic behavior. Paranoids are thought to be extremely suspicious and have ideas of persecution with an intellectual defense which often appears to have plausible reasons for it. Their delusions are usually limited to a few areas and may even be centered on a single person. The behavior of most people who are paranoid, however, does not seriously interfere with most of their life activities; their personalities do not deteriorate nor do they have hallucinations.

Mental Disorder as a Process

Although a description of the symptoms of neurotic and psychotic behavior has been presented, it gives little insight into the developmental process in mental disorders. The mere description of mental disorders has, in fact, become an increasingly sterile approach in their understanding, prevention, or treatment. Although there are various biological, psychoanalytic, sociocultural and other explanations of mental disorder, none as yet offer an adequate explanation of mental disorder. We shall emphasize the sociocultural explanation, with the full realization that it is recent and requires much more research before it can be fully accepted. As explained in a sociocultural framework, the functional mental disorders are primarily the product of a breakdown of effective communication between persons and defective role playing.[53] Although the psychoses may sometimes be more severe disorders than the neuroses, both arise from, and are perpetuated by, the use of the same unskilled and inappropriate adjustive techniques in dealing with other persons and social situations in general.[54] Not everyone, of course, who has difficulties in dealing with other people has a mental disorder, for many people, regardless of occasional erratic behavior, are progressively effectual as social persons.

Mental disorders appear to be continuous, dynamic processes, and not a series of separate stages. There are periods of childhood, adolescent, and adult influences, but actually all the experiences which affect the person have a profound effect on his relationships with others and his self-reactions. A mother, for example, may be overprotective and thus produce in a child techniques of dealing with people or situations which may continue throughout life. If the child is pampered and spoiled he may develop and use techniques of getting his own way through bullying, fighting, and temper tantrums. On the other hand, the child who is dominated by his mother may become withdrawn, timid, and submissive. The child who does not know how to deal effectively with other people may become shy, and this shyness, in turn, may make him excessively obedient and submissive. It is out of such childhood training and later influences that the "shut-in," seclusive characteristics of many mental disorders develop, including the neurotically withdrawn person and the schizophrenic. The relation of family dynamics to schizophrenia has been described thus:

> The mothers of schizophrenics have been characterized as cold, perfectionistic, anxious, over-controlling, and unable to give spontaneous love and acceptance to the child. They often seem unwilling to accord the child any privacy, attempting to intrude even into its thoughts. . . . The family network appears to be characterized by great stress and conflict, though often this is covered over by a desire to conceal the existence of differences. The net effect of most of the patterns noted is that they would make it difficult for a child to achieve an identity of his own, to be able to confront life situations with self-reliance and confidence.[55]

---

[53] A well-known psychiatrist stated that the objectives of psychiatry should be the study of processes that involve or go on between people: "The field of psychiatry is the field of interpersonal relations, under any and all circumstances in which these relations exist."—Harry Stack Sullivan, "Conceptions of Modern Psychiatry—The First William Alanson White Memorial Lectures," *Psychiatry*, 3:5 (February, 1940). Also see Osborn, *Psychiatry and Medicine.*

[54] Cameron, *op. cit.*, p. 11.

[55] John A. Clausen, "Mental Disorders," in Robert K. Merton and Robert A. Nisbet eds., *Contemporary Social Problems* (New York: Harcourt, Brace & World, Inc., 1961), p. 164. Also see J. A. Clausen and M. L. Kohn, "Social Relations and Schizophrenia," in Don Jackson ed., *Etiology of Schizophrenia* (New York: Basic Books, Inc., 1960), pp. 295–320.

Such patterns may be carried over into social situations outside the home where such techniques, not being replaced by new ones, are used on others. As a result, these children may not be accepted into normal play groups and the development of more adequate role taking on their part is hindered. They are often ostracized by their peers or tend to avoid playing with those of a similar age. Not every child who is overprotected or reared in an unhappy family situation, however, will necessarily develop a pronounced mental illness. Childhood patterns can be altered at any time if the strategy of dealing with people can be reversed. Other influences may help this change: the social relations of the wider community, the reaction of the child himself, and adjustments to other children in the family. In fact, efforts to predict the personalities of children from early rearing experiences have not been successful.[56]

The patterns of childhood strategy in dealing with others may be carried on indefinitely and, by recurring at each successive phase of growth, may result in a feeling of successful interpersonal relations or one of personal failure. In fact, the difficulties in adolescence, when serious, are often simply a reflection of past situations. The child who reaches this stage, not liking people and having personal difficulties, will probably continue to have these difficulties. Adjustment difficulties become important when there are excessive conflicts in social roles, habitual anxieties over other persons' attitudes, or little real satisfactions in other aspects of life organization.[57]

Mental disorders thus generally have a long history and are cumulative rather than products of a single circumstance or a few situations. Childhood experiences and those of early and later adult life have their influence. Difficulties in interpersonal relations and social roles, as well as faulty conception of self, may continue for years before there is the full-fledged development of a mental disorder. The more a person becomes mentally ill the more sensitive he becomes to events that probably would not affect him at all if he were well. A depressed person, for example, may increasingly find more and more types of situations to depress him. This cumulative nature of mental illness often makes its treatment a long and laborious process.

One study of schizophrenia, for example, has emphasized the distinctive effects of social relationships in many areas of life.[58] The reactions of the schizophrenic, his withdrawal, his attitudes of low self-worth, his anx-

---

[56] William H. Sewell, "Infant Training and the Personality of the Child," *American Journal of Sociology*, 58:150–159 (September, 1952).

[57] Cameron, *op. cit.*, pp. 48, 52, and 499.

[58] S. Kirson Weinberg, "Social Psychological Aspects of Schizophrenia," in Lawrence Appleby, Jordan M. Scher, and John Cumming, *Chronic Schizophrenia* (New York: The Free Press of Glencoe, 1960).

iety concerning further social rejection, and his distorted meanings of reality all emerge from a series of social relationships. The weakening of the self-system is a product of social isolation and difficulties in interpersonal relations in the family, in peer relations, and with the opposite sex, as well as in work associations. In the following case the patient was unable to deal with a series of frustrations and conflicts in interpersonal relations and finally developed schizophrenia.

The subject, when last seen, was 28 years old and married. She had been committed in the hospital as schizophrenia undetermined, remained four months and then was discharged outright. After her discharge her general personality condition was perhaps better than it was before the schizophrenic onset.

The youngest of three siblings, she was always an obedient and "model" child. Though she claims never to have wanted for affection from her parents, she felt certain subtle attitudes of rejection because the parents had hoped for a boy and were disappointed with a girl. Though the center of attention, and considered the baby of the family, she felt lonely because of the age discrepancy between herself and her sisters. As a child she often played alone but made friendships which were cut short by the family movements. Her predominant feeling, even as a child, was that of being "different" and "inferior" because her playmates dressed better than she did; she felt that she was poorer than other girls, notions which her parents laughingly dispelled. During early adolescence the initial rejection which she formerly felt in a vague way became more manifest. This feeling was aggravated because she could not compete successfully with her older sisters. In addition, her parents set such high standards for the children that she often felt that she was a "failure" in anything she attempted. Because the father was so intent upon his daughters getting married, she made every effort to know boys. With this outlook she was seduced when she was 16 by a man 25, who promised to marry her.

At 17 she left home to attend college; had a difficult time in her studies and was unable to foster friendships with other students. After one year she transferred to another college. Apart from her studies her main preoccupation was in getting dates. Since this was during the war years, male students were fewer and dates harder to get. In a trial and error process she finally met, became enamored of and engaged to a soldier. Having been sexually intimate with him, she became struck with periodic guilt, but became very dependent upon him because, as she stated, he proved she "was worthy enough to be loved." She made friends at her dormitory, was pledged to a sorority and became an accepted member of the group. After getting to know them well she quarrelled with these dormitory friends. By siding with one group who promised to get her into a sorority she so antagonized her other friends that they would not speak to her. Very lonely and dejected, she felt that her chief self-support and fulfillment of her father's desire were concentrated in sustaining her engagement and the hope of eventually getting married. When her fiancé broke the engagement because he preferred another girl, she became despondent and confused, had a spree of crying, feared she would never get married, and considered herself a failure. But she had no one to whom to turn for consolation or advice. She dared not tell her parents, whom she felt were nicer to her during her engagement. She could not go to her friends who were not on speaking terms with her. Perplexed, distracted and depressed, she was unable to study, would stare about her until finally a glass caught her eye. She kept thinking "how easy it would be" to eat some glass and get out of her misery. The next day, while attempting to study, she abruptly got up, broke the glass, ate some splinters, became frightened at what she had done, ran to the psychiatrist who also became upset, but who said she could not stay in school and advised her to become a volunteer patient at a mental hospital.

When she entered the hospital she was uncommunicative, disoriented and intermittently agitated. She received seven shock treatments and improved continually until her release.[59]

Notwithstanding the cumulative nature of mental disorders, immediate situations occasionally do have a bearing. They act as precipitants and bring the process to a climax. The effect of an immediate situation is particularly important in the manic-depressive disorders, where the anxiety builds up and tends to be set off by it. Although the underlying process would still be there, more study of precipitating situations might reduce the incidence or at least the recurrence of these disorders. A study of a group of manic-depressive cases, for example, revealed that nearly four fifths of them were precipitated by some particularly disturbing life situation, a marital disagreement, the death of someone, a crisis situation in a career, or a feeling of personal failure induced by harsh criticism.[60] These conditions cause particularly severe anxiety and tension. In most cases there had been a period of from one to six months in which anxiety and conflict had been built up.

STRESS AND MENTAL DISORDER

In social living all persons frequently encounter circumstances in which their personal desires are not achieved. These conflicts bring about a situation of stress. An interference of one kind or another may prevent the adequate development or achievement of a person's desires. In fact, one theory of schizophrenia is that it arises from a situation called the "double bind," a situation in which no matter what a person does he cannot win.[61] Davis has classified the conflicts which may be involved in mental disorder thus: (1) ends may be incompatible because they are opposite in character, (2) different ends many compete for scarce means, and

---

[59] S. Kirson Weinberg, "Sociological Analysis of a Schizophrenic Type," *American Sociological Review,* 15:605–606 (October, 1950).

[60] Rennie, "Prognosis in Manic-Depressive Psychoses," *loc. cit.*

[61] Gregory Bateson, Don D. Jackson, Jay Haley, and John Weakland, "Toward a Theory of Schizophrenia," *Behavioral Science,* 1:251–264 (October, 1956).

(3) conflict may arise from too great a disparity between ends and means.[62]

A certain amount of conflict is a part of the normal process of social living. Life is not all clear and precise; there is always an unknown quantity. The individual is faced throughout life with conflicts, hazards, and overwhelming demands and perplexities. These tend to produce a certain amount of anxiety which many claim plays an important part in mental illness. In many ways anxiety resembles fear. Like fear, it is an emotional reaction produced by stimulation with which one is unable to deal, leaving the person with a feeling of possible loss of security and support. Unlike fear reactions, however, which call forth avoidance and even flight from a real danger when this is possible, in anxiety the emotional reaction does not go on to completion. Fear is overt but anxiety is covert, and leaves the person in an undefined emotional state with which he would like to cope but cannot. He is afraid, but since he is unable to identify what he fears he cannot eliminate it. As contrasted with overt fear reactions which can be identified, anxiety reactions are less visible and are often inaccessible both to the individual and to others.

With most people conflicts tend to solve themselves or become reformulated. Many people find that other activities and interests help the tensions of anxiety to disappear or to be absorbed. And there are some people who, through adequate role playing in their interpersonal relations and an adequate estimate of themselves, are able to continue to have anxieties, even of a cumulative nature, for a long period of time without developing a mental disorder.

In a nation-wide survey, anxiety, expressed through physical symptoms, has been found to be more prevalent in the lower-income groups where "low income" suggests current unhappiness and worries, no confidence in the future, and anxiety expressed through physical symptoms. On the other hand, psychological anxiety is more common at both extremes, the high and low income, with middle-income groups expressing the least.

It may be that psychological anxiety symptoms reflect blocking and consequent indirect expression of energy. In both high- and low-income groups, this blocking of energy and inability to find direct outlets may derive from an inability to give it direct expression in one's interaction with the world, specifically, in this instance, in efforts directed toward bringing about concrete environmental changes that have visible effects on one's status. For the economically deprived groups, this inability would spring from overwhelming environmental blocks; for the economically privileged group it would spring from the fact that many concrete aspirations were already

---

[62] Kingsley Davis, *Human Society* (New York: The Macmillan Company, 1949), pp. 260–262.

fulfilled. Thus, under highly dissimilar conditions, these two groups may experience similar problems.[63]

Some persons cannot endure the tensions of anxiety. This difference in the tolerance for anxiety and in the extent of its stress may explain why some persons develop mental disorders while others do not. The inability to deal with frustrations and conflicts producing anxiety appears to be the result of previous inadequate interpersonal relations over perhaps many years which have left the individual without the adequate supports with which to face anxiety-producing situations. If the anxiety-producing situation is one of difficult interpersonal relations, as it frequently is, anxiety reactions may be even further increased because the individual can neither deal with the situation nor face the fact that he cannot meet it.

If the tensions develop beyond the limits of the individual, there may be chronic anxiety reactions and even acute anxiety attacks. Not only do the symptoms of anxiety continue for a long time; a person may be subject to very pronounced anxiety attacks and even panic reactions. With mounting anxiety the individual may reach the end of his tolerance limit and be subject to great fright. Such persons may become agitated, there may be nausea and salivation, dizziness, weakness in the knees, and hot flushes. He may feel that impending disaster is at hand—that he is going insane, is about to die, is on the verge of a heart attack, and so on. One patient described her anxiety attack after a hot, tiring day in which she had to deal with a domineering superior: "My heart suddenly stopped. Then it came up in my throat and turned over and quivered so fast you couldn't count it. I had a pain in my chest and down my arm. I was like in a tight vice, I couldn't breathe. It seemed like I was going to die." [64]

Likewise, neurotic compulsive behavior, such as orderliness and obsessional ideas, helps to relieve the anxiety. The acts, words, and thoughts involved in the relief of the anxiety may include tapping, counting, saying a set word, recalling or imagining a certain scene, and even snapping the fingers. In hypochondria, for example, the individual's constant preoccupation with his health simply constitutes solutions in which this preoccupation diverts and releases anxiety. In fact, "the fruit of resistance to the compulsion is mounting anxiety, while the reward of indulgence is a temporary respite." [65] Although tendencies to compulsive neurotic behavior are an irritation and are opposed, the momentary feelings of anxiety lead to the behavior and the subsequent relief. The relief is always temporary, for eventually the anxiety begins to mount again and the pa-

---

[63] Gerald Gurin, Joseph Veroff, Sheila Feld, *Americans View Their Mental Health*, Joint Commission on Mental Illness and Health (Monograph Series No. 4; New York: Basic Books, Inc., 1960), p. 218.

[64] Cameron, *op. cit.*, p. 255.   [65] *Ibid.*, p. 277.

tient has to give in to the compulsive behavior in order to reduce it. Moreover, the societal reaction of others to the bizarre behavior, whether neurotic or psychotic, may tend to increase anxiety.

In the schizophrenic disorders and depression, the individual may withdraw and find anxiety fended off as he retreats from threat and conflict to what Cameron calls a "protective shell of incapacity." The paranoid may relieve the prolonged excessive anxiety by focusing it on some individual or situation to which he can attribute his uncomfortable feelings. Manic behavior may constitute "an escape from insupportable anxiety into overt action," or, as often stated, constitute "an escape into reality." [66] Like depressions, this excitement begins after prolonged stress. There is a period of greatly increased anxiety of from a few hours to several weeks. In his excited behavior, shifting as he does from one thing to another, the patient is able to find some avoidance of his anxiety feelings. There is an increase in initiative and through what appears to be boundless energy he seeks to avoid his anxiety and, therefore, his problems.

SELF-REACTIONS AND COMMUNICATION

All persons have a self-reaction to their appearance, status, and conduct. They come to conceive of themselves not only as physical objects but as social objects as well. Likewise, human beings learn to express approval of themselves and they are able to reproach themselves. This capacity of self-conception which all persons have plays an important part in mental illness.[67]

Mentally disordered persons develop distorted self-conceptions or self-images which are reflections of difficulties in interpersonal relations and continuing anxiety. Other persons may come to think of them as "odd," "crazy," or "difficult." Some may become less confident and more preoccupied with themselves. Without logical reasons they may adopt egocentric ideas of being either a great success or a great failure. Where interpersonal relations have been difficult, the mentally ill person may learn to use his self-reactions in fantasy. He may dream of himself as someone he is not in order to overcome conflicts. A seventeen-year-old dishwasher who became mentally disordered built up a strongly organized role of fantasy so that she considered herself a "beautiful duchess, walked on her tiptoes, her mien proud and sweet, her gestures graceful and commanding" [68]

---

[66] *Ibid.*, p. 276.
[67] See, for example, William R. Rosengren, "The Self in the Emotionally Disturbed," *American Journal of Sociology*, 66:454–463 (March, 1961).
[68] Cameron, *op. cit.*, p. 101.

The schizophrenic has a self-feeling of social isolation and does not strive for social relationships any more, as Weinberg has indicated:

> The process of schizophrenic breakdown involves the recasting of selfhood on several levels. . . . First, when the schizophrenic feels that he is losing hold of himself or even anticipates a disordered reaction in a projected intolerable situation, he frequently reaches for some means to regain control of his capacities, or at least to regain his self-esteem on an acceptable level. This bid for regaining an acceptable self-esteem, without having the defensive techniques for doing so, intensifies his panic reactions. The intensity of this bid for regaining self-acceptance is measured by the degree of explosiveness and conflict during the breakdown. With a gradual, insidious lapse into a disorder, the conflict to regain a former self-esteem is minimal. On the other hand, the schizophrenic with few settled defenses, in a state of panic, may resort to random aggression and abusive declamation as a futile means of self-reclamation.
>
> Second, the normal individual's range of identity is circumscribed subjectively by reactions which he can consciously control or intentionally will. The schizophrenic, however, is beset by uncontrollable impulses, somatic reactions, and inner experiences which challenge the range of his identity. Since he cannot control his inner experiences, he attributes them to forces or agents external to his identity and disrupts his ability to differentiate the self from the outer environs.[69]

Third, as Weinberg has indicated, the schizophrenic's continued preoccupation with self and his lessened ability to share his experiences with others intensifies self-centeredness. His self-centered reactions obstruct his capacity to relate, and this consequently magnifies his own concern about his symptoms and his conflicts, so that he is less able to act with emotional feeling. The reactions and interpretations of a schizophrenic to his hallucinatory behavior are illustrated by the following statement of a patient.

> When I first commenced hearing these voices I am hearing and having them unusual feelings in the arms I could tell by them feelings that I was having was caused by electric flashing and drawing through my body and head and them voices I was hearing about everything that I thought and I knew at the time that it was someone communicating with me in the way of having a short wave connected to me; and I knew that the short wave was working on my heart for every time I heard a voice my heart fluttered and pounded; and at night when I went to bed in the army barracks that electric would make me shake all over and I knew it was someone broadcasting to me in the way of having a short wave connected to me, but I could not figure out what they could have to do me them ways or who they was and when they first commenced talking to me.[70]

---

[69] S. Kirson Weinberg, "Social Psychological Aspects of Schizophrenia," *loc. cit.*, pp. 81–82.

[70] As quoted in Weinberg, *ibid.*, p. 82.

The paranoid self-reaction is one of conceit and suspicion which affects his relations with others. The overprotected child may develop an idea of his abilities which is entirely divergent from the opinions of those outside his closed family circle. The self-delusions of grandeur that develop out of this glorified self-conception are seen in extreme form in the paranoids who claim that they "own the entire world."

What a person does can result in self-approval or self-reproach. He can praise himself for what he has said or done, or he may be disturbed by what he has done and rebuke himself, producing frustration and conflict. For adults with a depressive psychosis, this self-punishment, representing an internalization of difficulties with their outside social situations, can become a "tragic melodrama, where the depressed self-accused lashes himself so mercilessly in talk and fantasy that death seems the one promise of penance and relief." [71] If the depressed person feels guilty, self-hostility may result in such a loss of self-respect and so much self-reproach that suicide may even result. In such mental disorders the self may become so detached from the individual that it becomes not a social object but a physical object to be mutilated and punished for sin.

In certain forms of neurotic behavior involving dissociation the person may even be able to forget his own identity. In some cases of hysteria and amnesia the person may even identify with a past role or with another self. In these cases there is an attempt to get away from one's conflicts by changing oneself. The new selves may be alternating or coexisting and one self may not be aware of the other.

Disturbances in language, which are often a part of the symptoms in mental illness, indicate rather clearly its connection with interpersonal relations.[72] Although verbal imagination is perfectly normal, for without it books, poems, or great music could not be written, a person with a mental disorder, being socially isolated, verbalizes his thoughts and then becomes afraid of what he has created. The mentally disordered person is able to invent a world of his own through his thought processes. With language the neurotic is able to conjure up all types of evil thoughts of which he is afraid. The depressed person is able to talk himself into self-depreciation; the manic, into a frenzy. The schizophrenic is able to invent a world of private fantasy which lifts him in his own estimation. This expansion of fantasy, growing out of inadequate responses to shared social situations, continues until it no longer responds to the role taking of others in the culture. The disorders in thought processes are eventually expressed through his language and are a result of retreat from reality.

---

[71] Cameron, op. cit., p. 101.

[72] A recent study has indicated that part of what is called disturbances in language or meaningful conversation of the mentally ill is actually a reflection of social class. See Lloyd H. Rogler and August B. Hollingshead, "Class and Disordered Speech in the Mentally Ill," Journal of Health and Human Behavior, 2:178–185 (Fall, 1961).

The fact that the schizophrenic lives in a world of his own making, through verbal imagery, not only reflects and influences his thought processes but distorts his verbal reactions until they swing completely away from socially adequate responses. Language becomes private and not social; whether the other person understands it is immaterial.

The schizophrenic patient, living in his private world, invents his own common words and links them in such a fashion as to make his speech seem incoherent to others. In response to the question, "Why are you in the hospital?" one patient replied:

> I'm a cut donator, donated by double sacrifice. I get two days for every one. That's known as double sacrifice; in other words, standard cut donator. You know, we considered it. He couldn't have anything for the cut, or for these patients. All of them are double sacrifice because it's unlawful for it to be donated any more. (Well, what do you do here?) I do what is known as the double criminal treatment.
>
> Something that he badly wanted, he gets that, and seven days criminal protection. That's all he gets, and the rest I do for my friend. (Who is the other person who gets all this?) That's the way the asylum cut is donated. (But who is the other person?) He's a criminal. He gets so much. He gets twenty years' criminal treatment, would make forty years; and he gets seven days' criminal protection and that makes fourteen days. That's all he gets.[73]

MENTAL DISORDER AND INAPPROPRIATE ROLE PLAYING

As has been indicated, we do not yet have, despite many claims, any final, definitive answers as to the causes of mental disorders. Role-playing difficulties seem to offer, however, a profitable clue. More specifically, difficulties in interpersonal relations found among persons with functional mental disorders appear to arise from inappropriate role playing. As has been indicated, social roles are organizations of attitudes and responses to certain social situations. Roles must be played so that the points of view and expectations of others in society are shared. In mental disorder the individual in varying degrees either never acquired this ability, or, having acquired it, later lost it. The social roles of a person with a mental disorder, for example, may appear rigid and unalterable, or they may be unstable and confused. His responses to social stimuli may be extremely inappropriate, contradictory, exaggerated, ineffectual, or apathetic.

Paranoid behavior, according to Cameron,[74] appears to be a product of inappropriate role playing and role taking. There is an inflexible way of looking at things, they cannot shift roles or see alternative explanations for the behavior of others. Gradually a private world is built up in which the

---

[73] Cameron, op. cit., pp. 466–467.

[74] Norman Cameron, "The Paranoid Pseudo-Community," *American Journal of Sociology*, 49:32–38 (July, 1943.)

self as a social object becomes central and in which slights and discriminations, some real and some imagined, from the outside world are interpreted to fit their preconceptions. The paranoid develops a "pseudo community" which is a product of his unique interpretation of "persecucution" in the ordinary behavior of others toward him. He is unable to interpret adequately the roles of others and is therefore not socially competent to interpret their motives and intentions. His systematized paranoid or paranoiac delusions of discrimination and persecution develop out of his attempt to account for situations and happenings which are the products of his own lack of socialization and his fantasies. "His socially inaadequate interchange of attitudes and interpretations with others not only throws him upon his own limited resources for explanations and hypotheses but allows these also to be elaborated without the checks and modifications that the contrary opinions of others, if entertained seriously, would inevitably induce. Such preoccupation, with its collection and noting of incidents, becomes more and more engrossing; it narrows down the interests and activities of the person and further isolates him from the affairs of others." [75]

The pseudo community in which the paranoid lives is a private world which is real but not shared with others. Often his public world in the earlier stages of paranoid behavior gives little overt indication of his thoughts. He may be quite adequate in his manners, in courtesy, in impersonal conversation, and in community activities. As his delusions grow in intensity the paranoid becomes, however, more and more suspicious. On those rare occasions when he comes later to share his suspicions with others their ridicule makes him even more convinced that he is right. As a result he may suddenly decide that an extensive plot is being directed against him. The reactions of the real community in the form of restraint or retaliation to any of his vengeful or defensive overt behaviors make him convinced that the interpretations of his paranoid pseudo community are correct.

Recently, Lemert, a sociologist, has challenged this interpretation of a "pseudocommunity." He maintains, after studying a number of cases of paranoia, that the community to which the paranoid reacts is real and not a pseudo or symbolic fabrication.[76] Lemert states that "while the paranoid person reacts differentially to his social environment, it is also true that 'others' react differentially to him and this reaction commonly if not typically involves covertly organized action and conspiratorial behavior in a very real sense." Moreover, the reaction of the future paranoid with others is reciprocal and results in exclusion. The delusions and associated

---

[75] *Ibid.*, p. 35.
[76] Edwin M. Lemert, "Paranoia and the Dynamics of Exclusion," *Sociometry*, 25:2–20 (March, 1962). Quotations are from pages 2 and 7.

behavior which develop must be understood in the context of a process of exclusion which disrupts his social communication with others.

> The paranoid process begins with persistent interpersonal difficulties between the individual and his family, or his work associates and superiors, or neighbors, or other persons in the community. These frequently or even typically arise out of bonafide or recognizable issues centering upon some actual or threatened loss of status for the individual. This is related to such things as the death of relatives, loss of position, loss of professional certification, failure to be promoted, age and physiological life cycle changes, mutilations, and changes in family and marital relationships. The status changes are distinguished by the fact that they leave no alternative acceptable to the individual, from whence comes their "intolerable" or "unendurable" quality.

Inappropriate role playing takes several forms: (1) Some persons are unable to play certain roles. (2) There may be contradictions in role playing to which persons cannot adjust. (3) Some individuals are unable to make the necessary shifts from one role to another as required in normal social relationships.

Incapacity for Certain Roles. Some neurotic difficulties appear to develop when a person who is much more suited to one role tries to play another that is beyond his capabilities, leaving him in a state of chronic anxiety. This results partly from the contradictions between sheltered successful role playing in the family and the often brutal competitive adjustments required in the outside world. These contradictions are largely a product of segmentalized urban living: "Thus, the individual who emerges from the family as a dependent person may acquire the hard-driving, indirectly aggressive way of life from his secondary groups. The contradiction between these two sets of relationships is perhaps the basis of many of our disorders." [77]

Many neurotic persons have tried to achieve success beyond their ability. Because of their conception of themselves or the driving impetus of their parents, wives, or friends, they cannot retreat to a lesser goal. Ambitious parents or ambitious wives undoubtedly have much to do with the formation of a neurosis.

Contradictory Roles. The necessity for persons to play many and contradictory roles is perfectly normal. With normal activity an individual can meet this contradiction in roles. A woman, for example, can give solicitous affection to all members of her immediate family and at the same time be an aggressive leader in her relations outside it. A person may have to play one role with the marital partner and another with his parents. Individuals who cannot adjust to these changes often develop anxiety and mental disorder.

---

[77] Weinberg, *Society and Personality Disorders*, p. 156.

It has been suggested that the causal agent in the manic-depressive psychoses may be such intense group relationships and so many conflicting and contradictory roles that the resulting strain is enough to cause a breakdown. The individual who is all things to all people in his desire to please and to gain attention and prestige and who is continually participating in group activities may lose his basic and characteristic orientation. The demands and values of too many groups and too fervent participation leave him in a position in which he is unable to incorporate them coherently into his life organization.

The hypothesis has been advanced by some writers that the intense striving for material goods and the enormous competitive emphasis lead many persons to irreconcilable conflicts. The sacrifice of mental health to the ever-continuing struggle for goods, possessions, power, and status appears to be more characteristic of men than of women and of urbanites than of rural persons. Group contacts are maintained not for the social and personal gratifications to be derived from them, but because they might serve as steppingstones to getting ahead. Should prestige, status, class position, or material goods be threatened, the individual's world may collapse, leaving him with no supports. Economic competition, for example, operated in five hundred psychiatric cases as a factor in their mental illness.[78] The struggle for achievement liberated in some patients feelings of hostility. In other cases the culturally prescribed standards of success and prestige presented goals impossible of achievement, which augmented already existing conflicts. In still others, economic life offered a new arena for the enactment of competitive struggles which had been going on in one guise or another since early childhood.

Inability to Shift Roles. The main characteristic of many persons who develop mental illness is their inability to shift from one social role to another. They have not had the kind of social experiences to develop such skill. As has been indicated, everyone normally plays many roles, even in a single day, depending upon the situation and the expectations of others. An inflexible personality that cannot adapt to social situations will develop anxiety. Muncie has referred to the "rigid personality" pattern of an individual who develops a psychosis.[79] He is unable to abandon one role in a situation that calls for different behavior; his activity seems incongruous. Likewise, such a person cannot satisfactorily predict the behavior of others.

An individual's inability to shift roles means that when "insurmountable personal difficulties arise [he] cannot abandon the non-adaptive

[78] Stanley A. Leavy and Lawrence Z. Freedman, "Psychoneurosis and Economic Life," *Social Problems*, 4:55–67 (July, 1956). Also see Karen Horney, *The Neurotic Personality of Our Time* (New York: W. W. Norton & Company, Inc., 1937).

[79] Wendell Muncie, "The Rigid Personality as a Factor in Psychoses," *Archives of Neurology and Psychiatry*, 26:359–370 (August, 1931).

perspective by shifting through roles to one that might offer a different solution. This fixity of perspective, so characteristic of nearly all delusions, is what psychiatrists mean when they say that a patient lacks insight. He sees things only from a single standpoint for which he seems unable to substitute any other, even for the purposes of the moment." [80]

The schizophrenic person, for example, often does not play the roles expected of him in normal social relations. He has never developed the necessary skill, when under stress, to be able to change his role in social situations. He is so closely identified with his parents and an older generation that he does not know how to work and play with others of his own age. This social incompetence means that situations which require social adjustment, and are easily handled by the average person, take on enormous proportions for the preschizophrenic. Shy and retiring as a child, he may not only be misunderstood by his more active playmates but be the subject of their abuse as well. The so-called period of strain and stress of adolescence, during which time schizophrenic disorders begin to make their appearance, carries some of the elements of isolation. In a detailed study of forty-two catatonic schizophrenics in Chicago, Dunham has shown that their solitary social roles prior to the onset of the illness was different from those of other boys in the community. These future patients could not establish intimate and informal relationships with others their age and as a result were unable to gain an adequate social conception of themselves.[81] In a study of fifty-three transitory schizophrenics, Weinberg found that their isolation resulted from the fact that they were unable to communicate their conflicts to others and assumed their characteristic role taking as a matter of self-protection. By withdrawing they avoided the evaluation of others, building, in turn, a world which they did not share. After a study of schizophrenics from upper and lower social classes, the patterns of withdrawal were described as follows:

> Briefly, schizophrenics in both classes displayed patterns of submissive and withdrawn behavior. They complied with parental and community authority and were inhibited socially and sexually. At the same time, certain pressures bore more heavily upon the schizophrenics than upon the neurotics in both classes. Specifically, most schizophrenic patients had few positive or rewarding contacts with family members. The home was disorganized and full of tension and antagonism. . . . Their mothers showed little genuine interest or affection for the schizophrenic patients. Their fathers were inadequate both at home and in the community, so that their mothers had to assume responsibility for family affairs.
>
> Whatever the factors responsible for the schizophrenics' shy personalities, be they constitutional, social, interpersonal, or other, it was clear that the

---

[80] Cameron, *op. cit.*, p. 94.

[81] H. Warren Dunham, "The Social Personality of the Catatonic-Schizophrenic," *American Journal of Sociology*, 49:508–518 (May, 1944).

above presses supported the further development of their deviant adjustments. Feeling neglected and overwhelmed by the chaos of the home, it was easy for the schizophrenics to avoid unpleasantness and seek the affection and guidance they lacked in autistic withdrawal. It was also clear that these presses gave rise to certain common stresses among schizophrenics. They felt isolated from warm intrafamilial relationships and neglected and rejected by their parents.[82]

In fact, Robert Faris has concluded that there is limited evidence to support the hypothesis that "in primitive culture the nature of social life is such that a 'shut-in' personality type, and consequently [the psychotic state] schizophrenia, could not occur." [83] Deveraux contends that this relative lack of schizophrenia among folk cultures is due to their "one-answer" universe, that is, the consistent set of norms and values in their societies.[84] Others, however, have reported evidence of schizophrenia among folk societies.[85] Some believe that much of the research on this problem to date has been unscientific and not based on a really intensive survey, so that no worthwhile conclusions can be drawn.[86]

Cultural Factors in Mental Disorders

Sociocultural factors have been shown in a variety of studies to play a significant role in the development of the functional mental disorders. These have included studies of mental disorders in comparative cultures and subcultures, social stratification and occupation, and ecological studies of distributions within cities.[87] Finally, another aspect has been the effects of mental hospital environment on the treatment of mental disorders.

---

[82] Reprinted with permission from Jerome K. Myers and Bertram H. Roberts, *Family and Class Dynamics in Mental Illness,* copyright 1959, John Wiley & Sons, Inc. Contrary to most previous findings, one study of schizophrenic children found that only one third had been isolated from their peers prior to the development of the disorder.—M. L. Kohn and J. A. Clausen, "Social Isolation and Schizophrenia," *American Sociological Review,* 20:265–273 (June, 1955).

[83] Robert E. L. Faris, "Some Observations on the Incidence of Schizophrenia in Primitive Societies," *Journal of Abnormal and Social Psychology,* 29:30 (April–June, 1934).

[84] George Deveraux, "A Sociological Theory of Schizophrenia," *Psychoanalytic Review,* 26:315–342 (June, 1939).

[85] Berend J. F. Laubscher, *Sex, Custom and Psychopathology* (London: Routledge & Kegan Paul, Ltd., 1938). James C. Carrothers, "A Study of the Mental Derangement in Africans and an Attempt to Explain Its Peculiarities More Especially in Relation to the African Attitude to Life," *Psychiatry,* 1:47–86 (February, 1948). Margaret Mead found schizoid personalities among the wives of the Manus who live in the Admiralty Islands in the South Pacific. See Margaret Mead, "Adolescence in Primitive and Modern Society," in V. F. Calverton and S. D. Schmalhausen eds., *The New Generation* (New York: The Citadel Press, 1930). Also see Opler, *Culture and Mental Health.*

[86] N. J. Demareth, "Schizophrenia among Primitives," *American Journal of Psychiatry,* 98:703–707 (March, 1942); and John Gillin, "Personality in Preliterate Societies," *American Sociological Review,* 4:681–702 (October, 1939).

[87] For a discussion of the ecological aspects of mental disorders, see Chapter 3.

(See Chapter 21.) Our knowledge is, as yet, only suggestive as to clues to the origins of the functional mental disorders. Most studies are recent, and much more research needs to be done.

Cultural factors play an important role in mental disorders. The incidence of mental illness, for example, varies widely in different cultures. Eaton and Weil's comparison of ten intensive studies of the incidence of mental disorder in different societies has shown considerable variation in the total incidence of the psychoses.[88] These authors suggest that this variation is a product of the amount of stability and integrated cultural traits, consistent role expectation, and close interpersonal, family, and community ties. Hindus, Chinese, and Malayans in Singapore, for example, have differing amounts and types of disorders depending upon their cultural experiences.[89] In our own society differences in the nature of schizophrenic symptoms have been found between persons from Irish and Italian subcultures, the former favoring fantasy and withdrawal to the extent of paranoid reactions, while the Italian patients suffered from poor emotional and impulse control.[90] Jaco has found pronounced differences in the extent and nature of mental disorders among Spanish-Americans and Anglo-Americans in Texas.[91]

The relation of community social structure and culture has been studied among the Hutterites, members of a religious sect of European origin who have lived in South Dakota, North Dakota, Montana, Manitoba, and Alberta for over sixty years.[92] This group of 8542 persons was studied for any incidence of mental illness, since commitment to a mental hospital had been reported as rare among the group. When studied, their incidence of diagnosed mental disorder was not too different from that of other populations, but they tended to deal with it by unofficial means. Moreover, there were few cases of schizophrenia and little free-floating anxiety or physical aggression. Diagnosed manic-depressive behavior, nearly all of it depressive, was much more common than schizophrenia, or the reverse of data in most urban studies. Very few persons diagnosed as mentally disordered had ever been admitted to mental hospitals for treatment. In fact, only five persons had been admitted, and these five for a short time, ranging from a day to several months. The recovery rate among the Hutterites was also found to be very high—far in excess of that found for the general United States population of mentally ill. The

[88] Joseph W. Eaton and Robert J. Weil, *Culture and Mental Disorders* (New York: The Free Press of Glencoe, 1955).

[89] H. B. M. Murphy, "Culture and Mental Disorder in Singapore," in Opler, *op. cit.*, pp. 291–316.

[90] Marvin K. Opler, "Cultural Differences in Mental Disorders: An Italian and Irish Contrast in the Schizophrenias—U.S.A.," in Opler, *op. cit.*, pp. 425–442.

[91] E. Gartly Jaco, "Mental Health of the Spanish-American in Texas," in Opler, *op. cit.*, pp. 467–489.

[92] Eaton and Weil, *op. cit.*

explanation of the low incidence of hospitalized mental illness, both the neuroses and the psychoses, may be in the homogeneous and highly integrated social system of the Hutterites. Instead of rejecting and segregating their mentally ill by having them committed to public hospitals, the Hutterites attempt to keep these persons within their own group. Arrangements are made for necessary care, and the mentally ill person is given affection and understanding and offered a situation which is favorable to recovery.

Other cultural situations furnish illustrations of conflict. Many Andean Indians who migrate to coastal urban centers of Peru have pronounced psychiatric problems, in part because of the migrations but also because of "the extreme differences between the cultures of the Sierran Indians and the coastal urban populations which magnify the dimensions of change required of the Indian." [93] Mental disorders were increased among the Ifaluk of Micronesia as a result of culture conflict arising from the Japanese occupation during World War II.[94]

Social Stratification and Mental Disorders

There is evidence that diagnosed mental disorders are related to differences in occupation and social class. Mental illness is not distributed either as a whole or by type randomly in the population. Schizophrenic behavior appears to be most common among unskilled laborers, farmers, urban residents in rooming-house areas, as well as others who are isolated.[95] On the other hand, manic-depressive behavior seems to be more prevalent among professional and socially prominent persons. Most studies have found a higher incidence rate of first admissions to mental hospitals of those from the lower occupational categories.[96]

In a Texas study adjusted incidence rates for persons who became psychotic for the first time showed the highest rates among the unemployed,[97] which might, in fact, reflect the fact that psychotic persons are often less likely to be employed. Among those who were employed at the time of the psychosis, the highest standardized rates of diagnosed illness were found among the professionals and semiprofessionals, followed by

[93] Jacob Fried, "Acculturation and Mental Health Among Indian Migrants in Peru," in Opler, op. cit., p. 136.

[94] Melford E. Spiro, "Cultural Heritage, Personal Tensions, and Mental Illness in a South Sea Culture," in Opler, op. cit., pp. 141–171.

[95] See Johns Hopkins University research referred to by Eaton and Weil in Arnold M. Rose ed., Mental Health and Mental Disorder (New York: W. W. Norton & Company, Inc., 1955), p. 233.

[96] See, for example, Robert E. Clark, "Psychoses, Income and Occupational Prestige," American Journal of Sociology, 54:433–440 (March, 1949) and "The Relationship of Schizophrenia to Occupational Income and Occupational Prestige," American Sociological Review, 13:325–330 (June, 1948).

[97] Jaco, The Social Epidemiology of Mental Disorders, pp. 125–148.

managerial, official, and proprietary occupations, clerical and sales workers, service workers, agricultural workers, and manual workers of all levels of skill. Jaco included public and private cases but maintains that this occupational difference does not reflect any bias in ability to pay.

A study of all persons in New Haven, Connecticut, who were patients of a psychiatrist or a psychiatric clinic, or were in psychiatric institutions on December 1, 1950, revealed rather decided class differences.[98] The total group of 1891 patients was compared with a 5 percent random sample of the normal population, or 11,522. When both groups were divided into five classes and compared, with Class I at the top and Class V at the bottom, it was found that the lower the socioeconomic class the more prevalent the diagnosis of disorder. Class I contained 3.1 percent of the population and only 1.0 percent of the mental patients, whereas the lowest group, with 17.8 percent of the population, had almost twice as many mental patients. When sex, age, race, religion, and marital status were analyzed, social class was still found to be the important factor.

The diagnosis of neuroses was found to be more prevalent at the upper-class levels, whereas the psychoses were more frequent in the lower groups. Neurotics constituted nearly two thirds of all patients in the two upper-class levels, but among the lowest level, neurotics were less than 10 percent of the patients. A further analysis of the 847 diagnosed schizophrenic cases showed that in comparison with the normal population, the diagnosis of this disorder is disproportionately high among the lower classes. In Class I this disorder was found to be only one fifth as great as it would be if proportionately distributed, whereas among those in Class V it was two and a half times as great.

Some comparison of the dynamic factors in the relation of social class and family dynamics to mental disorders has been made of a small sample of schizophrenics and psychoneurotics in Class III and Class V.[99] Those in Class III were believed to supervise their families more closely, but threats to economic, social and physical security were judged stronger in Class V than in Class III. The schizophrenic patients, who were largely concentrated in Class V, were found to be withdrawn and submissive personalities, to have unstable parental relationships and home situations, and to lack parental interest and affection. On the other hand, the neurotics, mainly from Class II, were thought to have more stable home environments, to have the presence of more affection and positive emotional attachment between parents and the family members, and to be characterized by greater rebellion than were the schizophrenics.

Two values appeared to permeate all aspects of Class III—respectability and success; throughout life they reported being taught to focus

[98] Hollingshead and Redlich, *Social Class and Mental Illness.* Some of this difference was undoubtedly due to differential diagnosis on the part of the psychiatrist.

[99] Myers and Roberts, *op. cit.*

their energies on social acceptance and upward mobility. Both of these objectives were difficult for many Class III persons who later developed mental disorders. First, they had difficulty in enjoying the more sensual aspects of life. Second, they expressed frustration in living up to respectability and success values, and "when their behavior did not measure up to these standards they were likely to develop serious inner conflicts, manifested in feelings of shame and guilt." [100] Third, they appeared to be under constant tension because of pressures toward upward social mobility. As they moved upward in social status, they felt a need to modify continually their behavior to conform to new roles, and were under constant tension. Furthermore, in upward mobility they tended to alienate their families and former friends and were never fully accepted by the new groups. Fourth, they apparently were taught to curb aggressive behavior. Fifth, their relations to their mothers were described as very close and the patients had difficulty in emancipating themselves. Warner and Green have tried to show that class structure affects the production of mental disorders. [101]

Heredity and Schizophrenia

Geneticists have attempted to demonstrate that heredity plays a leading part in schizophrenic disorders. For example, in Sweden there have been a number of studies which have indicated the possibility of genetic family patterns. While the incidence of the disorder may be 1 percent in the general population, the incidence in those persons with schizophrenic parents is 10 to 12 percent. In the case of brothers and sisters it was found to be 10 to 15 percent. [102] This finding obviously does not refute the fact that social situations in a schizophrenic family may be the cause rather than heredity.

Kallman has been a leading proponent of the theory that the functional mental disorders are inherited. He studied 1087 Berlin schizophrenic cases selected from 15,000 cases between the years 1893 and 1902; later, in New York, he made a study of pairs of twins of which one or both were diagnosed as schizophrenic. [103] He diagnosed the Berlin cases

[100] *Ibid.*, p. 251. Reprinted with permission of the publisher.

[101] W. Lloyd Warner, "American Caste and Class," *American Journal of Sociology*, 42:234–237 (September, 1936), and "The Society, the Individual, and His Mental Disorders," *American Journal of Psychiatry*, 94:275–284 (September, 1937); and A. W. Green, "The Middle-Class Male Child and Neurosis," *American Sociological Review*, 11:31–41 (February, 1946).

[102] J. A. Böök, "A Genetic and Neuropsychiatric Investigation of a North Swedish Population," *Acta Genetica et Statistica Medica*, 4:1–100, 133–139, 345–414 (1953).

[103] Franz J. Kallman, *The Genetics of Schizophrenia* (Locust Valley, N.Y.: J. J. Augustin, Inc., 1938). Also Franz J. Kallman, "The Genetic Theory of Schizophrenia," *American Journal of Psychiatry*, 103:309–322 (November, 1946); reprinted in Clyde Kluckhohn, Henry A. Murray, and David M. Schneider, *Personality in Nature, Society, and Culture* (rev. ed.; New York: Alfred A. Knopf, Inc., 1959), pp. 80–100.

from information which he secured and then compared them with the case histories of relatives. He found that 68.1 percent of the children whose parents were both schizophrenic developed the disease. Where there was one schizophrenic parent the chances were about one in six; with brothers and sisters, one in ten; nephews and nieces, one in twenty-five; and grand-children, one in twenty. In the later study Kallman used 794 twin index cases, obtained over a nine-year period from New York mental hospitals, and compared them with the case histories of relatives. He also concluded that the more distant the relationship the less likelihood of schizophrenia. Among his findings were the following:

(1) The morbidity rate [of schizophrenics] obtained with the "Abridged Weinberg Method" are in line with the genetic theory of schizophrenia. They amount to 1.8 per cent for the step-siblings; 2.1 per cent for the marriage partners; 7.0 per cent for the half-siblings; 9.2 per cent for the parents; 14.3 per cent for the full-siblings; 14.7 per cent for the dizygotic cotwins; and 85.8 per cent for the monozygotic cotwins. This morbidity distribution indicates that the chance of developing schizophrenia in comparable environments increases in proportion to the degree of blood relationship to a schizophrenic index case.

(2) The differences in morbidity among the various sibship groups of the index families cannot be explained by a simple correlation between closeness of blood relationship and increasing similarity in environment. The morbidity rates for opposite-sexed and same-sexed two-egg twin partners vary only from 10.3 to 17.6 per cent, and those for non-separated and separated one-egg twin partners from 77.6 to 91.5 per cent. The difference in morbidity between dizygotic and monozygotic cotwins approximates the ratio of 1:6. An analysis of common environmental factors before and after birth excludes the possibility of explaining this difference on non-genetic grounds.

(3) The difference between dizygotic and monozygotic cotwins increases to a ratio of 1:55, if the similarities in the course and outcome of schizophrenia are taken as additional criteria of comparison. This finding indicates that constitutional inability to resist the progression of a schizophrenic psychosis is determined by a genetic mechanism which seems to be non-specific and multifactorial.

(4) The predisposition to schizophrenia—that is, the ability to respond to certain stimuli with a schizophrenic type of reaction—depends on the presence of a specific genetic factor which is probably recessive and autosomal.[104]

Although Kallman's is the leading study, others have tried to show that schizophrenia is hereditary. All of these efforts have been subject to severe criticism.[105]

---

[104] Franz J. Kallman, "The Genetic Theory of Schizophrenia," *American Journal of Psychiatry*, 103:321 (November, 1946). By permission of the author and the Journal.

[105] Don D. Jackson, "A Critique of the Literature on the Genetics of Schizophrenia," in Jackson, *The Etiology of Schizophrenia*, pp. 37–87.

1. Kallman's study has been accepted by many writers as demonstrating the link between schizophrenia and heredity. Today his work is the single major source referred to by most authors writing on schizophrenia. In spite of this, Jackson made an exhaustive search of American and European literature of the past forty years and uncovered only two cases of twins who developed schizophrenia after having been allegedly reared apart. These two cases of twins who developed schizophrenia could have occurred on a chance basis, considering the incidence of schizophrenia. "Evidently the rumor that there are many such cases stems from . . . the fact that Kallman in his 1946 paper designated a category among identical twins of 'separated' and 'nonseparated.' However, his terms refer only to *separation five years prior to the psychosis*." [106] The average age of Kallman's twins was 33; thus they had, in most instances, remained together well into adult life.

2. A Yale sociologist and psychiatrist who made a comprehensive study of schizophrenic cases in the Greater New Haven area failed to show a significant number of relatives with schizophrenia.[107] Their cases consisted of all private and public mental hospital cases, as well as cases treated privately outside the hospital by psychiatrists. Of the 847 schizophrenic cases studied, only 25 percent of the cases studied had schizophrenic relatives.[108]

3. A truly Mendelian approach to the inheritance of schizophrenia cannot be carried out with human beings in the same manner as with plants and animals because human environments do not remain constant as is required in Mendelian studies.[109]

4. The problem of diagnosis is the greatest obstacle in the genetic study of schizophrenia. Often the diagnosis of schizophrenia is made on the basis of family history, a person being diagnosed as schizophrenic if someone in his family has been so diagnosed. There is a tendency even among clinicians to see twins as similar, whether they actually are or not.

5. Diseases may run in families, even physical ones, without having a genetic basis. For example, beriberi does so, but "what is 'inherited' is the pattern of preference for vitamin-poor foods which children pick up from their parents." [110] The fact that mental disorder may appear in a family line does not prove that it is inherited. These studies need to take into account the effects on children of being reared in a family where one or both parents are mentally disturbed and the effect of the total environment.

6. Jackson notes that the genetic mode of transmission has not been determined, and until this is done the genetic nature of schizophrenia will remain questionable. Also there has been no relationship established

---

[106] *Ibid.*, p. 40.   [107] Hollingshead and Redlich, *op. cit.*
[108] From a private communication from A. B. Hollingshead.
[109] Jackson, *op. cit.*   [110] Jackson, *op. cit.*, p. 44.

between hereditary taint, type of schizophrenia, age of onset, and outcome. Such studies do not tell us how the symptoms of mental disorder are related to hereditary transmission. In schizophrenia, for example, the person does not share reality with others, he has blunted emotional behavior, and he has disrupted role playing. Just how social behavior of this type is carried in the genes is not only not clarified; this crucial question is rarely raised. As Hollingshead has concluded about the inheritance of schizophrenia, "This theoretical approach has not been explored adequately; its validity remains in doubt." [111]

Summary

Mental disorders involve behavior which deviates from approved norms of perceiving, feeling, and interpreting. The psychoses encounter stronger societal reaction than do the neuroses. Regardless of type, the so-called functional mental disorders appear to arise from fundamentally the same processes, namely, difficulties in interpersonal relations expressed through inappropriate role playing. Inappropriate role playing includes the incapacity for certain roles, contradictions in role playing, and an inability to shift from one role to another.

Selected Readings

CAMERON, NORMAN. *The Psychology of Behavior Disorders.* Boston: Houghton Mifflin Company, 1947, Chap. 4. One of the best discussions of role playing, language, and self-conception in relation to personality disorders. The author is both a psychiatrist and a psychologist.

CLAUSEN, JOHN A. "Mental Disorders," in Robert K. Merton and Robert A. Nisbet eds., *Contemporary Social Problems.* New York: Harcourt, Brace & World, Inc., 1961. A critical discussion of the sociological aspects of mental disorder.

DUNHAM, H. WARREN. *Sociological Theory and Mental Disorder.* Detroit: Wayne State University Press, 1958. A collection of both new and previously published papers on mental disorder. The author adds a new section on epidemiology and details the underlying assumptions of two current alternative conceptions of mental illness and health.

EATON, JOSEPH W., and ROBERT J. WEIL. *Culture and Mental Disorders.* New York: The Free Press of Glencoe, 1955. This is primarily a study of the limited extent of mental disorders among a religious sect, the Hutterites. In this joint study by a sociologist and a psychiatrist there is also a detailed comparison of ten other studies of mental disorder in various cultures.

HOLLINGSHEAD, AUGUST B., and FREDERICK C. REDLICH. *Social Class and Mental Illness.* New York: John Wiley & Sons, Inc., 1958. An analysis of the incidence and types of mental disorders in terms of social class.

HORNEY, KAREN. *Our Inner Conflicts.* New York: W. W. Norton & Company, Inc.,

---

[111] Hollingshead, "Epidemiology of Schizophrenia," *loc. cit.*

1945. A study of neuroses primarily in terms of reactions of going away from, against, and toward other people.

JAHODA, MARIE. *Current Concepts of Positive Mental Health.* New York: Basic Books, Inc., 1958. Monograph Series: Joint Commission on Mental Illness and Health. A discussion of the problems involved in attempting to define mental illness. The author does not resolve any of the issues which her discussion raises, but she specifies the necessary considerations involved.

LEIGHTON, ALEXANDER H., JOHN A. CLAUSEN, and ROBERT N. WILSON. *Explorations in Social Psychiatry.* New York: Basic Books, Inc., 1957. A collection of papers by representatives of several disciplines dealing with the issues, approach, and specific problems studied in social psychiatry.

ROSE, ARNOLD ed. *Mental Health and Mental Disorder.* New York: W. W. Norton & Company, Inc., 1955. This is a collection of articles having a sociological approach to mental disorder. Nearly all important articles written by sociologists about mental disorders to this date are in this book.

WEINBERG, S. KIRSON. *Society and Personality Disorders.* Englewood Cliffs, N.J.: Prentice-Hall, Inc., 1952. A study of mental disorder by a sociologist in which there is a more complete discussion of several topics presented here.

Chapter

I4

Suicide

Generally, suicide refers to the destruction of one's self, self-killing, or, in a legalistic sense, self-murder. In one widely quoted definition, suicide is either "the intentional taking of one's life or the failure when possible to save one's self when death threatens." [1] Durkheim, the leading authority on suicide, defined it in a way as to include such acts of altruism as religious martyrs, "all cases of death resulting directly or indirectly from a positive or negative act of the victim himself, which he knows will produce the result." [2]

Two main forms of suicide may be distinguished.[3] One form is the definite desire on the part of a person to take his own life largely for this reason only. In the second form there is the additional desire to attract attention, to secure sympathy, or to revenge oneself on someone. Sometimes the same objective is then accomplished by a mere attempt at suicide.

Many persons commit suicide each year, although in comparison with such forms of deviant behavior as crime or mental disorders the number is small. During 1949 in the United States, 18,330 persons took their lives, a rate of 10.4 per 100,000 population. Probably at least another 100,000 made unsuccessful attempts to kill themselves.[4] Since 1950 the suicide rate in this country, per 100,000 population, has fluctuated from a high in 1950, of 11.4, to a low of 10.0 in 1952, (See Table 14.1.) Over a long period of time the fluctuation in suicide rates is more marked. The rate in 1900 in the United States was 10.2, 15.3 in 1910, 10.2 in 1920, and 15.6 in 1930. As has been previously indicated, suicide rates are responsive to

---

[1] Ruth S. Cavan, *Suicide* (Chicago: The University of Chicago Press, 1928), p. 3.

[2] Emile Durkheim, *Suicide*, tr. by John A. Spaulding and George Simpson (New York: The Free Press of Glencoe, 1951), p. 44.

[3] Ernest R. Mowrer, *Disorganization, Personal and Social* (Philadelphia: J. B. Lippincott Company, 1942), p. 332.

[4] Harry Alpert, "Suicides and Homicides," *American Sociological Review*, 15:673 (October, 1950). The statistical department of the Metropolitan Life Insurance Company estimates that the number of attempted suicides is six to seven for each actual suicide. Quoted in G. L. Williams, *The Sanctity of Life and the Criminal Law* (New York: Alfred A. Knopf, Inc., 1957), p. 272. For an interesting, semipopular analysis of the problem of suicide, see Edward R. Ellis and George N. Allen, *Traitor Within: Our Suicide Problem* (New York: Doubleday & Company, Inc., 1961).

Table 14.1. Number and Rate of Suicides per 100,000 Population,
United States, 1950–1960

Year	Number	Rate per 100,000
1950	17,145	11.4
1951	15,909	10.4
1952	15,567	10.0
1953	15,947	10.1
1959	18,633	10.6
1960	19,450	10.8

SOURCES: *Statistical Abstracts of the United States, 1950–1961.* Rate of 1953 computed from data in *Vital Statistics of the United States, 1953* (National Office of Vital Statistics, Public Health Service, U.S. Department of Health, Education, and Welfare; Washington, D.C.: Government Printing Office, 1955). Population estimates July 1 each year. Data for 1959, 1960 obtained from *Monthly Vital Statistics Report,* Provisional Statistics, Annual Summary for 1960, Part II, U.S. Department of Health, Education and Welfare, Vol. 9, No. 13 (July 28, 1961). Data for 1959 includes Alaska; data for 1960 includes both Alaska and Hawaii.

marked economic changes, being generally higher during periods of depression and lower during periods of prosperity.[5] Wars are usually characterized by a marked decline in suicide rates.[6]

Suicide and Cultural Norms

So strongly is suicide condemned by Western European peoples that one might assume this attitude to be universal. Both today and in the past, however, attitudes toward self-destruction have varied widely. Mohammedan countries strongly condemn suicide, and in actuality it rarely occurs there. The people of the Orient, however, do not disapprove of suicide. In fact, suttee, or the suicide of a widow on her husband's death, was common in India until well into the last century. Priests taught that such a voluntary death would be a passport to heaven, atone for the sins of the husband, and give social distinction to the relatives and children. Other aspects of the Hindu religious philosophy encouraged suicide, particularly the tendency to disregard the physical body. Suicide has been regarded as acceptable in China; when committed for revenge it was considered a particularly useful device against an enemy because it not only embarrassed him but enabled the dead man to haunt him from the spirit world. Voluntary death has been given an honorable place in Buddhist countries, but for devout Buddhists there is neither birth nor death, the individual being

[5] See pp. 427–428.   [6] See p. 586.

expected to prepare himself to meet all types of fate with stoical indifference.

For many centuries suicide has been favorably regarded in Japan. Among all classes, but particularly among the nobility and the military, it was traditionally taught that one must surrender to the demands of duty and honor. Hara-kiri, originally a ceremonial form of suicide to avoid capture after military defeat and later to avoid disgrace or other punishment, was practiced even during and after World War II. The suicide compact of lovers who wish to terminate their existence in this world and to go to another is not unusual in Japan, nor is suicide for revenge or as a protest against the actions of an enemy.

The attitude of contemporary Western European peoples toward suicide originated mainly in the philosophies of the Jewish and later the Christian religions. The Talmudic law of the Jewish religion takes a strong position against suicide: respect should not be paid the memory of the suicide although comfort should be given to his family. Suicide and infanticide had been prevalent in ancient Rome, but with the spread and acceptance of Christianity came a change in the attitude toward human life. Basic to the Christian condemnation of suicide were the concepts that human life is sacred, that the individual is subordinate to God, and that death should be considered an entrance to a new life to which one's behavior in the old is important. Moreover, death was followed by Purgatory, in which an individual suffered in order to expiate some types of sins, but those who had committed sins such as suicide were banished eternally to the torments of Hell. Death, to the Christians, unlike the pagans of Rome, was not something to look forward to without some misgivings. This concept of life after death strengthened the position of the Church.[7] In addition, Christian doctrine looked upon life as an opportunity for moral discipline and resignation in the presence of pain and suffering endured in the hope of another and happier world.

Although at first Christians sanctioned suicide connected with martyrdom or the protection of virginity, eventually they disapproved of it for any reason and it became not only a sin in Christian countries but a crime against the state. The property of a suicide might, for example, be confiscated and the corpse subjected to various mutilations. The laws of some European countries provided that the body of a suicide could be removed from a house only through a special hole in the wall, should be dragged through the streets, might be hung on the gallows, thrown into a sewer, burned, or even transfixed by a stake on a public highway as a sign of disrespect.

In the medieval ages church leaders denounced suicide, particularly Augustine, who stated, in the *City of God*, that suicide is never justifiable.

---

[7] William E. H. Lecky, *A History of European Morals* (3d ed.; New York: Appleton-Century-Crofts, Inc., 1906), pp. 209–211.

He maintained that suicide precludes the possibility of repentance, that it is a form of murder prohibited by the Sixth Commandment, and that a person who kills himself has done nothing worthy of death. Similarly, Thomas Aquinas opposed it on the grounds that it was unnatural and an offense against the community. Above all, he considered it a usurpation of God's power to grant life and death. Generally, in both England and Scotland, as well as on the Continent, laws provided for special treatment of the bodies of suicides, often outside regular graveyards. Throughout the medieval ages and well into modern times the strong religious opposition, the force of condemnatory public opinion, and the severe legal penalties were so effective that few had the temerity to take their lives, despite infrequent sporadic outbreaks of mass suicide on certain occasions such as epidemics, religious fanaticism to gain martyrdom, or crises.[8]

These views did not go unopposed by later philosophers, particularly those of the Age of Enlightenment, who challenged many existing institutions and discussed the importance of individual choice, even of life and death. David Hume, in his *Essay on Suicide,* argued that man has the right to dispose of his life without its being sinful. Other writers, such as Montesquieu, Voltaire, and Rousseau in France, challenged the laws on suicide and the denial of individual choice about life and death. In Germany, however, Kant opposed such views and said that suicide was contrary to reason. Today both Catholics and Protestants are opposed to suicide, although the Catholic position is a stronger one and the rates in such Catholic countries as Italy, Spain, and Ireland are generally lower. (See Table 14.2.)

Variations by Country

In 1958 Japan had the highest suicide rate in the world, followed by Hungary and Austria (see Table 14.2). The United States ranked fifteenth. Comparisons of the suicide rates of different countries indicate such great variations, however, that it is difficult to establish many uniformities. For example, among the Scandinavian countries Denmark, Finland and Sweden were high, but Norway was quite low. While the six highest countries are industrialized and urbanized, the United States, England and Wales, and Canada were not as high as some countries which are less developed in this respect. Predominantly Catholic countries were generally lower in the scale, but Austria, also a Catholic country, had the third highest rate. Asiatic countries had the lowest rates generally. Next to Japan, Ceylon had the highest rate of suicide in Asia, but it ranks nineteenth in the world.

---

[8] Louis I. Dublin and Bessie Bunzel, *To Be or Not to Be: A Study of Suicide* (New York: Harrison Smith and Robert Haas, 1933), p. 210.

Table 14.2. Suicide Rates for Selected Countries, 1958

Country	Rate per 100,000 population	Country	Rate per 100,000 population
Japan	25.9	Portugal	8.8
Hungary	23.5	Scotland	8.5
Austria	23.3	Ceylon	8.3
Finland	21.3	Canada	7.5
Denmark	21.2	Norway	7.3
Switzerland [a]	20.9	Israel	7.0
West Germany	18.9	Netherlands	6.8
Sweden	17.3	Italy	6.3
France	16.6	Poland	6.1
Belgium	14.9	Venezuela	6.0
Union of South		Spain [a]	5.8
Africa		Mauritius	5.5
white	12.4	Iceland	5.4
colored	3.1	Trinidad and Tobago	3.7
Asiatic	8.5	Greece	3.2
Australia	12.3	Guatemala	3.2
England and Wales	11.5	Ireland	2.7
El Salvador	11.5	Costa Rica	2.7
United States	10.7	Dominican Republic	2.1
New Zealand	9.9		

[a] Rates are for 1957.

SOURCE: World Health Organization, *Epidemiological and Vital Statistics Report,* Vol. 13, No. 10 (1960), p. 466. The accuracy of official reports has been questioned because of the possibility of relatives and others concealing the actual facts in some cases. It is generally concluded that, while the figures are not accurate, the amount of error may not be great. See Jack P. Gibbs, "Suicide," in Robert K. Merton and Robert A. Nisbet eds., *Contemporary Social Problems* (New York: Harcourt, Brace & World, Inc., 1961), pp. 227–229.

Suicide and the Law

Suicide was punished as a felony or crime in England for centuries, and the suicide's property was forfeited to the Crown. In fact, these provisions were not abolished until 1870, although they had been largely in disuse since the eighteenth century. In his famous *Commentaries* on the law Blackstone had given these reasons for forfeiture: "The suicide is guilty of a double offense: one spiritual, in evading the prerogative of the Almighty and rushing into his immediate presence uncalled for; the temporal, against the King, who hath an interest in the preservation of all his subjects." [9] To a certain extent, this concept, but without the law of

[9] William Blackstone, *Commentaries on the Laws of England* (1765–1769), IV, 188.

forfeiture, was carried to America. In 1660 the Massachusetts law forbade burial of a suicide in the common burying place of Christians. Instead, burial was in some common highway, with a cartload of stones laid upon the grave, as a brand of infamy, and as a warning to others to beware of similar "damnable practices." This law was repealed in 1823, but it helped shape the attitude toward attempted suicide in America.

In England, in some states in the United States, and in a number of other countries it is against the law to attempt suicide. It is not against the law in any other European country, including the Soviet Union, nor is it against the law in Scotland. This is a fairly recent development, having been applied in England in 1854.

Prior to World War II in England, most attempted suicides were punished by a short period of imprisonment and for a second attempt up to six months. Since then it has largely been used only in those cases where there have been repeated attempts, where the would-be suicide threatens to try it again, refuses treatment, or becomes an unnecessary nuisance.[10] Actually, in 1955, out of 5220 attempted suicides (a large number are not reported), only 535, or about 1 in 10, were brought before the courts. Of these cases, only 43 were sentenced to prison. Nearly all, however, are found guilty, and, as a result, have a criminal record.[11]

Attempted suicide is also a crime in New Jersey and in North and South Dakota. As in England, there is a general rule in the United States, under common law, that in the case of a suicide the life insurance policy is not recoverable. Several states, however, have statutes providing that a suicide does not affect the policy if it occurs after a certain period of time, unless it can be proved that the insured intended to take his life when he took out the policy.

Attempted suicides raise an interesting legal problem, since by definition "a suicidal act is not punishable as an attempt unless it was intended to result in suicide." [12] Some cases are genuine attempts; others are suicidal demonstrations where what is done is not really a serious attempt; and, finally, there are probably cases which fall in between. Many attempts, whether real or not, may endanger the lives of other persons or rescuers, as do those who resort to carbon monoxide gas in rooms or garages, who try to drown themselves, or who use firearms.

Suicide and the Type of Society

Self-destruction is reported as not occurring among some folk societies. One observer who asked Australian natives about suicide stated that whenever he interrogated them on this point they invariably laughed at him

[10] Williams, *op. cit.*, p. 280.

[11] Kenneth Robinson, "Suicide and the Law," *The Spectator*, March 14, 1958, p. 317.

[12] Williams, *op. cit.*, p. 283.

and treated the question as a joke.[13] A similar response was reported from natives of the Caroline Islands. A survey of some twenty sources dealing with the Bushmen and Hottentots of South Africa revealed no references to suicide among these people.[14] The Andaman Islanders in the Indian Ocean appear to have had no knowledge of suicide prior to their association with people from India and Europe. Nor has suicide been reported among such folk societies as the Indians of Tierra del Fuego and the Zuñi of southwestern United States.

It would be simple to analyze the problem of suicide in folk societies if other data were as consistent as those just cited. Suicide occurs among some folk societies, however, some having a much higher rate than others. Suicides have been reported among the natives of Borneo, the Eskimos, and many African tribes. It is also said to have been fairly common among the Dakota, Creek, Cherokee, Mohave, Ojibwa, and Kwakiutl Indians, and the Fiji Islanders, the Chuckchee, and the Dobu Islanders.

Since folk societies are generally well integrated, the problem of any suicide among them particularly interested the French sociologist Durkheim. As a result of his studies he classified suicides by type, and examined the different motives underlying suicide.[15] On the whole, according to Durkheim, suicide occurring among a folk people is considerably different from that in modern society. To him suicide was a measure of the degree of social integration in a society. Suicide occurring in Western European countries is generally either *egoistic* or *anomic,* whereas nearly all suicide among folk peoples is of an *altruistic* nature.

Among folk societies suicides tend to be altruistic in that a person takes his life with the idea that by doing so he will benefit others. The individual in such societies thinks primarily of the group welfare. When his actions or his continued living hurts the group he may turn to suicide so that the group will have one less mouth to feed or so that he may protect it from the gods. Suicides among folk peoples which may be classified as altruistic are those arising from physical infirmities, or connected with religious rites or with warfare, or in expiation for the violation of certain mores, such as tabus. Under such conditions suicide does not constitute a deviation; in fact, it would be considered a transgression to refrain from the act.

1. Suicides occur in certain primitive societies where limited food supplies make an old or infirm person a burden to the tribe. Among the

[13] Edward Westermarck, *Origin and Development of the Moral Ideas* (London: Macmillan & Co., Ltd., 1908), II, 220.

[14] Robert E. L. Faris, *Social Disorganization* (New York: The Ronald Press Company, 1948), p. 198.

[15] Durkheim, *op. cit.* Gibbs feels that while Durkheim's theory is important, he did not really test his data in terms of a set of rigorous criteria of social integration. See Gibbs, "Suicide," in Robert K. Merton and Robert A. Nisbet eds. *Contemporary Social Problems* (New York: Harcourt, Brace & World, Inc., 1961), pp. 255–256.

Eskimos and the Chuckchee, for example, old people who can no longer hunt or work kill themselves so that they will not consume food needed by other adults in the community who produce it.

2. On the death of certain persons in some folk societies it is customary to commit suicide as part of a religious observance. Women, for example, commit suicide on the death of their husbands, and relatives may kill themselves in order to propitiate the souls of the dead. In some societies when a chieftain dies his retainers kill themselves. At one time it was the custom among certain Indian tribes of the Pacific Northwest for slaves to commit suicide on the death of their masters. It has been reported that some Central American Indian tribes required the wives, servants, and friends to kill themselves following a chieftain's death. Certain warriors among some Brazilian tribes commit suicide on the death of the tribal leader.

3. Some suicide occurs in warfare when persons kill themselves to avoid capture and slavery or because of the disgrace of their failure as warriors.

4. Probably the most common form of altruistic suicides among folk societies is the suicide committed as expiation for a violation of the mores, such as a tabu. In these cases the society itself feels that since it has been made unclean, the only recourse for the offender is death by execution or by his own hand to avoid public disgrace. This type of suicide may occur, as among the Dobu, in connection with marital infidelity. Unmarried pregnant girls may kill themselves, as happens occasionally among the Kwakiutl Indians. Among the Indians of British Columbia a forbidden marriage between two persons closely related is reported to have ended in a double suicide as a result of public ostracism. Individuals who fail to commit suicide in atonement for these wrongs risk the imposition of other sanctions, such as perpetual public disgrace. Malinowski thus describes the motives of Trobriand Islanders, who generally commit suicide by climbing a palm tree, from which they give a speech before jumping to their deaths:

> Two motives must be registered in the psychology of suicide: first, there is always some sin, crime or passionate outburst to expiate, whether a breach of exogamous rules, or adultery, or an unjust injury done, or an attempt to escape one's obligations; secondly, there is a protest against those who have brought this trespass to light, insulted the culprit in public, forced him into an unbearable situation. One of these two motives may be at times more prominent than the other, but as a rule there is a mixture of both in equal proportions. The person publicly accused admits his or her guilt, takes all the consequences, carries out the punishment upon his own person, but at the same time declares that he has been badly treated, appeals to the sentiment of those who have driven him to the extreme if they are his friends or rela-

tions, or if they are his enemies appeals to the solidarity of his kinsmen, asking them to carry on a vendetta (lugwa).[16]

The types of suicide found in modern Western European society, egoistic and anomic, must be clearly distinguished from the group-oriented, altruistic type which is common among folk societies. Egoistic suicides are not the products of a tightly integrated society but of one in which interpersonal relations are neither close nor group-oriented. These suicides, which are the most common in modern societies, are a measure of a lack of close personal identity with others. In such societies, individualistic motives for suicide are not unusual and are associated with such personal problems as financial difficulties, loss of a desired goal, or ill-health.

The anomic type of suicide occurs when the individual "feels lost" in the face of situations where the values of a society or group are confused or break down. In such instances the equilibrium of society has been severely disturbed. There exists a social void in which the social order cannot adequately satisfy the desires of the person, and he does not know which way to turn. Commonly such anomic suicides occur in modern society as an aftermath of severe economic "crashes" or depressions, such as the stock market crash of 1929, which was followed by a large number of suicides. A similar situation has confronted persons after a severe political crisis or a defeat in war. In Hong Kong the suicide rate for post–World War II immigrants, who were mainly refugees, was five times greater than the combined rate for prewar immigrants and those born in Hong Kong.[17]

It would be a mistake to assume that all suicides among folk societies are altruistic. For example, although a recent study of suicide found little or no egoistic suicide among African tribes, they did find a moderate amount of anomic suicide: suicides committed by Africans who are not integrated satisfactorily into operating institutions.[18] Conversely, in modern societies, occasionally in peacetime but more frequently during war, individuals may give their lives in order to accomplish some goal involving group values. Sometimes this behavior is approved as being heroic. These suicides in modern society resemble the altruistic type found among folk people. In peacetime people will give their lives to save others. Soldiers volunteer for dangerous missions knowing that there is no chance of returning alive. The Japanese on many occasions during World War II engaged in what was termed suicidal behavior. Faced with certain

---

[16] Bronislaw Malinowski, *Crime and Custom in Savage Society* (London: Routledge and Kegan Paul, Ltd., 1926), p. 97.

[17] P. M. Yap, *Suicide in Hong Kong* (Hong Kong: Cathay Press, 1958), p. 76.

[18] Paul Bohannan, "Patterns of Murder and Suicide," in Paul Bohannan ed., *African Homicide and Suicide* (Princeton, N.J.: Princeton University Press, 1960), pp. 262–264.

death, large numbers of Japanese troops died to a man in suicidal banzai charges. In the latter days of that war the Kamikaze pilots became legendary for their disregard for their own lives. Loading their planes with explosives, they dived into Allied warships in order to make sure of destroying them completely.

Because of the peculiar settings in which the altruistic type of suicide takes place in modern society, however, much of it cannot be classed with typical altruistic suicides in folk societies. Group attitudes and pressures in a military unit under battle conditions and the emotional nature of a peacetime crisis situation involving the saving of a human life are not found in most ordinary modern situations giving rise to suicide. Elderly or incurably sick persons may sometimes end their lives so as not to become a burden on others, but this type of altruistic suicide is generally not approved.

Social Differentials in Suicide

Few forms of deviant behavior exhibit such pronounced differences in rates among various segments of the population as does suicide. Great differences can be found by sex, race, age, marital status, and religion. These differences in social factors have, in general, been found not only in Western societies but in most societies, as has been shown in studies of suicide in the Philippines, Ceylon, Singapore, and Hong Kong.[19] Many of these factors operated in the same fashion in these cultures.

Sex. Suicide is much more common among men than among women in Western European civilization, generally three to four times higher. In Norway, South Africa, Finland, and Ireland four times as many men as women commit suicide. (See Table 14.3.) In France, for example, three times as many men as women commit suicide.[20] In 1958 in the United States nearly four times as many men as women committed suicide. In the older age group the ratio of male to female suicides is even greater. In one American study of insurance policyholders the rate rose steadily with each age group: twice as many men as women committed suicide between twenty to twenty-four years of age; three and a half as many between thirty-five to forty-four; five and a half as many between fifty-five and sixty-four; and seven times as many in the age group over seventy-five.[21] On the other hand, the difference in adolescence is generally not nearly as great. One study found the rate for boys and girls to be the same among those fifteen to nineteen years of age.[22]

---

[19] See references in Yap, *op. cit.*

[20] Jean Daric, *L'Évolution de la Mortalité par Suicide en France et à l'Étranger* (Trends in Deaths from Suicide in France and Abroad), *Population*, II, No. 4, 673–700, October–December, 1956.

[21] Dublin and Bunzel, *op. cit.*, pp. 44–45.   [22] *Ibid.*, p. 43.

Table 14.3. Suicides by Sex by Country, 1958, 1959

Country	Male		Female	
	Number	Rate per 100,000 population, male	Number	Rate per 100,000 population, female
Norway (1959)	208	11.7	71	4.0
Union of South Africa (1958)	283	18.9	91	6.0
Finland (1959)	677	31.9	204	9.0
Ireland (1959)	55	3.8	17	1.2
United States (1959)	14,250	16.4	4,080	4.6
France (1959)	5,496	25.1	2,075	8.9
Canada (1959)	1,017	11.5	270	3.1
Spain (1958)	1,077	7.5	417	2.7
Sweden (1959)	1,012	27.2	338	9.0
New Zealand (1959)	154	14.1	48	4.4
Portugal (1959)	659	15.1	170	3.6
Belgium (1959)	843	18.8	351	7.5
Switzerland (1958)	794	31.6	299	11.2
Australia (1959)	827	16.3	288	5.8
Hungary	1,808	37.6	572	14.6
Italy (1958)	2,151	8.8	928	3.6
Austria (1959)	1,176	35.8	573	15.2
Denmark (1959)	647	28.7	309	13.5
West Germany (1959)	6,377	25.7	3,514	12.6
Ceylon (1958)	580	11.7	197	4.4
Netherlands (1959)	488	8.6	306	5.4
England and Wales (1959)	3,116	14.2	2,091	8.9
Japan (1958)	13,895	30.7	9,746	20.8

SOURCE: World Health Organization, *Epidemiological and Vital Statistics Report*, Vol. 14, No. 5 (1961), pp. 144–151.

With few exceptions, the same ratio of suicides seems to apply regardless of the type of situation.[23] Whether it be a love affair, an economic situation, or an illness, for example, approximately three to four men kill themselves to every woman. One cannot be sure if this is the result of men's being involved in more critical situations, or if they are less able to adjust to them. In Asia, however, women commit suicide much more frequently than they do in Western Europe and America. Hence, there the difference in the ratios is much less. In Japan the rate for males in 1958 was 30.7 and for females 20.8.

In some areas of India the suicide rate for women is greater than

[23] Cavan, *op. cit.*, pp. 309–310.

that for men, as shown in a study of 1129 cases of suicide between 1952 and 1955 in Sarashtra, in the state of Gujarat, where the rate was twice as great.[24] The reasons appear to lie in the conflicting roles and subordinate status of women in the Indian family. The realization of their often difficult family role has become greater with increasing freedom for women. Some of the factors given for the high suicide rate among Indian women follow.

1. Inferior social status of the women, discrimination shown against girls since birth and childhood.
2. Desire on the part of parents to marry off the daughter as soon as she reaches puberty.
3. Caste system and endogamy which restrict a wide choice for the bridegroom.
4. Child marriages, marriages against the will of the boy or the girl, and incompatibility in marriage.
5. Dowry and related customs. Girls from poor homes have to suffer taunts, humiliation, and persecution for not bringing a handsome dowry.
6. Oppression of the daughter-in-law in the joint family at the hands of the in-laws.
7. Unhelpful attitude of the parents of the woman. Even when they come to know that the daughter is unhappy in her family they are hesitant to give her shelter for long for the sake of social prestige.
8. Dual standard of morality for man and woman. While all actions of men are condoned, young widows or unmarried mothers are ostracized for any moral lapse.
9. Lack of education, confidence, and courage among women. Lack of knowledge regarding alternative arrangements should she decide to leave home.
10. Economic dependence of women, inability to stand on their own and make a living, due to lack of educational and vocational opportunities.

From American studies more women *attempt* suicide than do men. Many of these attempts by women, however, do not appear to be entirely sincere, for the suicidal arrangements are too often such that rescue is not only a possibility but even a probability.[25] In a study of 1000 attempted suicides in Detroit, the rate per 100,000 population was nearly twice as great for females as that for males: 35.5 as compared with 18.4.[26] This fact invited at least two interpretations: women were less successful in committing suicide, or, more likely, women more frequently use the

---

[24] Jyatsna H. Shah, "Causes and Prevention of Suicides." Paper read at the Indian Conference of Social Work, Hyderabad, India, December 29, 1959.

[25] Dublin and Bunzel, *op. cit.*, p. 55.

[26] F. C. Lendrum, "A Thousand Cases of Attempted Suicide," *American Journal of Psychiatry*, 13:479–500 (November, 1933). Also see Calvin F. Schmid and Maurice D. Van Arsdol, Jr., "Correlated and Attempted Suicides: A Comparative Analysis," *American Sociological Review*, 20:273–283 (June, 1955).

threat of suicide to accomplish a certain goal.[27] Threats or attempts at suicide must, however, be taken seriously, at least among men. Three fourths of a group of Los Angeles County male suicides had previously threatened or attempted to take their own lives.[28]

Race. White persons in the United States generally have a much higher suicide rate than do nonwhite persons. In 1953, 15,307 white persons committed suicide, a rate of 10.7 per 100,000 population, or approximately three times as great as the nonwhite rate of 3.8, or 640 nonwhite suicides in the entire country. In 1959, of the total of 18,633 suicides in the United States, 17,719 were committed by white persons and 914 by nonwhites. This ratio increases in the older age groups. In a Chicago study Negroes had a rate of 7.7 as contrasted with 28.8 for native whites.[29] The rate for white females was 4.6 with only 1.3 for nonwhite females. There is some evidence, however, that suicide attempts are approximately twice as great among Negroes as among whites.[30]

The probable explanation for the differences between white and Negro suicide rates is the more rural background of the Negroes, even where they have moved to a city. This factor tends to inhibit suicide. Furthermore, Negroes, because of racial discrimination, are more accustomed to restrictions on their participation in the general society, so that crises are less likely to produce disastrous results. Higher status opportunities for Negroes have developed only recently; as a consequence there have been, in the past, few competitive status pressures at a high level. That the Negro rate may be expected to increase as Negroes experience greater equality and urbanization is indicated by the fact that the northern Negro suicide rate is much higher than that of the southern Negro.

Age. The older a person is, in the United States and generally in Western European countries, the more likely he is to take his own life. This likelihood progresses steadily with each age category. (See Table 14.4.) The rates in 1959 for those between forty-five and sixty-four were nearly three times as great as for those between fifteen and forty-four. The rates for those over sixty-five in the United States was approximately twice as high as for those between thirty-five and forty-four. Suicide is largely a product of the weariness and disillusionment of the older years. Youthful optimism offers some protection against the temptation to commit suicide. Conversely, in Japan in 1956 the age group with the highest suicide was fifteen through forty-four, with a rate of 34.6, as compared with a rate of 31.0 for those forty-five through sixty-four.

---

[27] Mowrer, *op. cit.,* p. 339.

[28] Edwin S. Schneidman and Norman L. Farberow, "Clues to Suicide," in Edwin S. Schneidman and Norman L. Farberow, eds. *Clues to Suicide* (New York: McGraw-Hill Book Company, Inc., 1957), p. 9.

[29] Cavan, *op. cit.,* p. 78.

[30] Lendrum, "A Thousand Cases of Attempted Suicide," *loc. cit.*

Other variations can be seen in suicides by age and sex when one compares the rate in the United States with that of Japan, which has the highest suicide rate in the world. The rates for both sexes in the United States show a steady rise, although much less for females. The suicide rate for Japanese males rises sharply through adolescence up to twenty-four, when it reached 60 per 100,000 in 1952–1954. It then fell to a rate of about 25 between thirty to fifty, and then rose steadily until at seventy it was 95. The rate for females follows a similar but lower pattern.

Table 14.4. Suicide Rates in the United States, by Age, 1959

Age	Number	Rate
Below 1 year	—	0
1–14	70	0.1
15–24	1,230	5.2
25–34	2,250	9.9
35–44	3,240	13.7
45–54	4,060	19.8
55–64	3,640	23.7
65–74	2,460	24.5
75–84	1,160	25.8
85 and over	20	23.3

SOURCE: *Monthly Vital Statistics Report,* Annual Summary for 1959, Part II; U.S. Department of Health, Education, and Welfare.

Adolescent suicides receive so much publicity that their number has been exaggerated in the popular mind. Actually, the rate for those fifteen to twenty is exceedingly low, being less than a fifth the rate for all age groups and amounted, as reported in one study, to about 3 percent of all suicides.[31] In 1959 there were 1230 suicides, or a rate of 5.2, for the ages fifteen through twenty-four. The rate for those aged twenty-five through thirty-four was twice as great, and for every age group thereafter the rate increased, as shown in Table 14.4.

Children under ten practically never commit suicide, and only occasionally are there suicides between the ages of ten and fifteen. No suicides were reported, for example, of children under ten years of age during 1953. During this same year only 58 children, aged ten to fourteen, in the entire United States, committed suicide. In 1959 there were only 70 suicides, or a rate of 0.1, among those aged one through fourteen. These figures do not mean that many children, as they grow up, do not on occasion, when encountering frustrating situations, "wish they were dead," as studies have shown. This is particularly the case following certain

[31] Dublin and Bunzel, *op. cit.,* p. 39.

punishment situations. That these do not end in suicide seems partly the result of an incomplete formation of a definite conception of self, status, and social roles which are endangered by certain situations. Also, childhood crises are usually temporary, and there is seldom the long-term "brooding" which often occurs among adults.

Marital Status. In general, marriage, with its personal relationships, seems to be one of the best guarantees against the desire to commit suicide, although some situations produced by an unsatisfactory or a broken marriage may be conducive to it. The rate for married persons is considerably lower than that for widowed or divorced persons. In 1940 the rate per 100,000 married persons was 18.0, as compared with rates of 30.9 for the widowed and 64.3 for divorced persons.[32] Regardless of the age grouping over twenty years of age, the pattern is the same, although there is a much greater difference in the older age categories. Single persons had a lower rate in 1940 than married, or 6.8. The probable explanation is that single persons are largely in the younger age groups and younger persons generally have a lower suicide rate. Further evidence for this is the fact that in each age grouping over age twenty the suicide rate is lower for married persons than for single persons of the same age group. On this basis it would be correct to say that married persons have a lower rate than the single, the divorced, or the widowed. Yet these comparisons should not minimize the fact that many married persons take their lives. About half (50.3 percent) of the 50,047 suicides in the United States from 1949 to 1951 were married persons, between fifteen and sixty-four years of age.[33]

Another indication that the family has an important relationship to suicide is the fact that suicide appears to be greater among couples without children than among couples with children, who naturally have greater personal ties and feelings of responsibility that act as inhibiting factors.

Religion. Suicide rates among the main religious groups in Western European civilization vary greatly. In general, both in Europe and in America, Catholic rates are much lower than Protestant. Formerly the Jewish rate appears to have been lower than the Catholic, except that, on occasions when persecution made their situation particularly difficult or hopeless, waves of suicides occurred. Within recent years the Jewish suicide rate has risen considerably, perhaps reflecting changes in religious influence and greater participation in the general society. Both Catholic and Protestant rates have increased during the past century.

Religious differences in suicide rates have been interpreted as meaning in part the degree of integration of the various religious groups. Protestant religious groups tend to be more individualistic than Catholic.

---

[32] Andrew F. Henry and James F. Short, Jr., *Suicide and Homicide* (New York: The Free Press of Glencoe, 1954), p. 73.

[33] National Office of Vital Statistics, *Vital Statistics—Special Reports, Selected Studies,* 39:370 (May, 1956).

The Catholic position on suicide is more specific than that of most Protestant groups, at least in regard to the effect of suicide on the individual's afterlife and on the right to burial in consecrated ground.

Analysis of data from countries with large Catholic and Protestant populations, such as Germany and Switzerland, shows that even when all other factors are similar, fewer Catholics commit suicide. Catholic countries, such as Spain and Portugal, Ireland, and Italy, have low suicide rates, and predominantly Protestant countries, such as Denmark and Sweden, have high rates. (See Table 14.2.) Even this general rule does not explain the relatively low rate of Norway and Scotland.

It is difficult, however, to place too much emphasis on the factor of religious affiliation alone. The rate of Italian suicides for the period 1947–1951 in northern Italy is almost exactly twice as great as in the south, where economic conditions are poorer, there is less education, and adherence to Catholicism seems greater.[34] Most of the conclusions about the relation of religion, moreover, are based on large statistical categories and not on the effect of Catholicism at the individual level. Ferracuti has emphasized the possible role which the Catholic confession may play in furnishing a mechanism which might reduce the number of suicides.[35]

Occupation. In his classic study of suicide, Durkheim found that occupational status is linked to suicide, occurring more frequently in the upper ranks of various occupations as well as in positions of higher status. Suicides, for example, were found to be more frequent among army officers in proportion to population than among enlisted men, a fact which he attributed to the officers' feeling of status responsibility.[36] In later studies in America it has been found that United States Army officers are more likely to kill themselves than do enlisted men of the same race.[37] In a study of 955 persons who committed suicide in New Zealand between 1946 and 1951 the suicide rates were significantly greater among persons of high prestige, upper-class fathers producing more than their proportion of suicidal sons.[38] Moreover, suicide occurred more often when there was pronounced climbing and descending on the prestige scale. In Hong Kong attempted and actual suicide rates are highest at the two ends of the economic scale—businessmen and the unemployed—with high rates also among entertainers and prostitutes. Lowest rates were among the police, farmers, and fishermen. The explanation given was that rates tend to be higher among groups subject to great economic insecurity and uncer-

---

[34] Franco Ferracuti, "Suicide in a Catholic Country," in Schneidman and Farberow, *op. cit.,* p. 74.

[35] *Ibid.,* pp. 76–77.   [36] Durkheim, *op. cit.*

[37] Dublin and Bunzel, *op. cit.,* pp. 112–113.

[38] Austin L. Porterfield and Jack P. Gibbs, "Occupational Prestige and Social Mobility of Suicides in New Zealand," *American Journal of Sociology,* 66:147–153 (September, 1960).

tainty, and lower among those groups with security of employment or from well-integrated groups.[39]

In America suicide is more common among those with high social status. Although suicides occur disproportionately among those at both extremes of socioeconomic status, they are higher among those who are more wealthy.[40] Studies have shown that Londoners from the higher occupational status groups are more given to suicide, a fact attributed by those making the study that such groups are more subject to changes and social isolation.[41] Gibbs has summarized the relation of occupation, social status, and suicide as follows:

> Extremely high suicide rates generally prevail in occupations at the extremes: those with either very high income and prestige or very low income and prestige. For example, high rates are often found in both the professional-managerial category and the category of unskilled laborers, with occupations ranking midway between these two in status having lower rates. The high rate that typically prevails among the unemployed and retired appears to fit the low income-low prestige pattern.[42]

The Suicide Process

Although only a relatively few persons commit suicide, one writer claims that over half the people of the United States have contemplated it.[43] Death wishes are expressed in a variety of ways. One is the vague wish "never to have been born." Others occur in daydreams of death in which the person is likely to imagine himself dead and to speculate on the reaction of others to his death. By doing so the person lives out an experience which he desires but which he probably wishes will not occur. Similar death wishes are felt by those who wish for it but have no particular suicidal plans. Some persons may express a contingent wish for suicide about which they feel fairly safe, such as "If this thing happens, I will kill myself." Still others may make specific threats of suicide. In such cases if the threat is not effective, or the crisis is of long duration, suicide may result.

Suicides may be definitely planned without being carried to completion. Some persons may even have planned to kill themselves on a number of occasions, the final act being prevented by the removal of the original cause, an alternative solution, or the reinforcement of some attitude, particularly a strong religious one, opposed to self-destruction. A clinical investigation of material, obtained from the psychiatric inter-

---

[39] Yap, op. cit., pp. 33–36.   [40] Dublin and Bunzel, op. cit.
[41] Peter Sainsbury, Suicide in London: An Ecological Study (London: Chapman & Hall, Ltd., 1955), p. 91.
[42] Gibbs, "Suicide," in Merton and Nisbet, op. cit., p. 244.
[43] Cavan, op. cit., p. 178.

views of 100 attempted suicides, confirmed the social isolation hypothesis in that it was found that suicides have had some difficulty in forming friendships. In addition, the study found that "the human being . . . wants to exist for somebody and for something . . . [he] wants his achievements to be accepted and acknowledged. . . . he wants his place to be defined clearly by love and work." [44] The individual wants an accepted, useful role in a community which provides him with the means of satisfying his needs and desires. When such things are lacking he becomes demoralized and confused, life loses its meaning, and he resorts to suicide.

Various types and stages of the suicidal process have been identified. A distinction can be made between those suicides which are situational in pattern and those which represent an escape.[45] Situational suicides may range from those in which the act is impulsive and unpremeditated to those in which the individual deliberately plans to end his life. The former may be illustrated by adolescent suicides, which are usually impulsive actions after a broken infatuation, the denial of some privilege, or a severe rebuke. These situations may be of minor importance to an adult, but to the adolescent, suicide seems the only solution. Such adolescent suicides may be inspired by revenge or the desire for attention. Conversely, some persons, such as old people, may shrewdly calculate the balance between the difficulties of continued living and death. Situations such as ill-health and the loss of loved ones and friends may lead to suicide. Between the extremes of impulsive and planned suicides are others in which each of these patterns may play an important or a minor part. Most suicides among Africans, for example, appear to take place around domestic situations involving the husband and wife, or in status-linked situations.

> These additional, non-domestic situations in which men commit suicide in Africa are for the most part seen by Africans in terms of over-all status or rank in the society. The high suicide rates for Gisu, for example, come at an age when a man's total status is in some doubt—in the years immediately following initiation, and in the years when a man should be settling down to assume the status of elder. The Luo, to take another example, phrase their loss or uncertainty of total social status in terms of shame. The loss of status or "face" may occur in institutional contexts of the traditional tribal system or of the modern system of Kenya, but can nonetheless be recognized as status problems.[46]

Other suicides represent escape patterns from the responsibilities of continued life. The individual does not wish to face reality and instead seeks a way out of a dilemma which may seem impossible of fulfillment or

---

[44] Margarethe von Andics, *Suicide and the Meaning of Life* (London: William Hodge & Co., Ltd., 1947), p. 173.

[45] Mowrer, *op. cit.*, pp. 357–365.

[46] Bohannan, *op. cit.*, p. 262.

change. Such suicides may have a long history of continuous struggle against various circumstances.

Another type of escape pattern is exemplified by those suicides who take a calculated risk to achieve a goal. For example, after killing another person some commit suicide. In a Philadelphia study about 4 percent of those who committed homicide took their own lives. Other studies in America have shown an incidence of from 2 to 9 percent in such suicides.[47] In England and Wales the proportion is much larger; in 1950, for example, it was 35 percent [48] and between 1900 and 1949, 31 percent in cases of the murder of a person one year or older.[49] Likewise, when a law violator escapes the consequences of his acts by committing suicide when caught, he does so in the same calculated manner in which he planned his illegal activities. Many swindlers, such as Ivar Kreuger, the Swedish match king, or embezzlers may take this way out of their predicaments.

Suicides have also been classified into other types: those which result from an unidentified craving for a goal, from a recognized wish, from a specific wish, from mental conflicts, or from a broken life organization.[50] These types of suicidal processes represent interruptions or blocked desires which occur at different stages in some ongoing enterprise. Such suicidal processes are somewhat similar to any other behavior involving a social act which is blocked.

One type of suicidal process may simply be a general dissatisfaction with life or some unsatisfied need, or what might be termed an undefined craving. The idea of suicide is often vague and there is a high degree of restlessness, although the nature of this dissatisfaction is often not specified. The person feels "disgusted with life," or "useless." Emotional tone is low, but there is "no sharp crisis, no mourning for something lost, no resentment toward anyone, no impassioned emotions, no self-judgment, but a strong desire to stop living, since life is flavorless." [51] A divorced man of fifty left this suicide note.

To the Police—
    This is a very simple case of suicide. I owe nothing to anyone, including the World; and I ask nothing from anyone. I'm fifty years old, have lived violently but never committed a crime.
    I've just had enough. Since no one depends upon me, I don't see why I shouldn't do as I please. I've done my duty to my Country in both World

---

[47] Marvin E. Wolfgang, *Patterns in Criminal Homicide* (Philadelphia: University of Pennsylvania Press, 1958), p. 274.
[48] *Criminal Statistics for England and Wales, 1950* (London: 1951, p. xxiv) as cited by Max Grünhut, "Murder and the Death Penalty in England," *The Annals*, 284:158 (November, 1952).
[49] Based on *Royal Commission on Capital Punishment, 1949-53 Report*, Appendix 3, Table 1, pp. 298-301.
[50] Cavan, *op. cit.*, pp. 148-177.   [51] *Ibid.*, p. 149.

Wars, and also I've served well in industry. My papers are in the brown leather wallet in my gray bag.

If you would be so good as to send these papers to my brother, his address is: John Smith, 100 Main Street.

I enclose five dollars to cover cost of mailing. Perhaps some of you who belong to the American Legion will honor my request.

I haven't a thing against anybody. But, I've been in three major wars and another little insurrection, and I'm pretty tired.

This note is in the same large envelope with several other letters—all stamped. Will you please mail them for me? There are no secrets in them. However, if you open them, please seal them up again and send them on. They are to the people I love and who love me. Thanks.

George Smith [52]

Another case of this type was a wealthy, middle-aged businessman who had devoted his life to building up his company to achieve something he had always wanted, namely, a merger with a larger company. In this merger he retained the presidency of his own concern and became the vice-president of the larger company. After the agreement was concluded he immediately went into a depression. As the coroner commented, "The action was the reaction of a man who had built his business, makes the deal he wanted to make and then realizes he is no longer the direct owner of the business he spent his life building." He had no financial troubles, health problems, or marital difficulties to cause suicidal despondency.

Like the person with the unidentified craving, the individual with the specific need has not focused on a particular object or person. He is aware of how he feels and what he wants, but he is unaware of how this general need can be satisfied. The feeling may be one of loneliness, a wish for a better job, or something equally vague. Various situations are available for the potential suicide. A married woman, aged twenty-four, left this note.

I've proved to be a miserable wife, mother and homemaker—not even a decent companion. Johnny and Jane deserve much more than I can ever offer. I can't take it any longer. . . . This is a terrible thing for me to do, but perhaps in the end it will be all for the best. I hope so.

Mary [53]

The specific wish is at a more advanced level of needs, namely, a specific object or person. A person who is lonely may find other ways of overcoming his loneliness besides suicide. If he centers his interests on a specific goal or a love object which cannot be achieved, the situation be-

---

[52] From *Clues to Suicide,* Farberow and Schneidman eds., p. 44. Copyright, 1957. McGraw-Hill Book Co., Inc. Used by permission.
[53] *Ibid.,* pp. 43–44.

comes less one to which alternative solutions besides suicide can be applied. As attention is centered in a certain definite direction for a particular girl, man, or job, frustrated emotion tends to build up, until the suicidal process has moved decidedly from a condition of general dissatisfaction to a recognized wish. Any thwarted wish may take on the character of a "fixed idea" and become a predominant part of the person's life organization. Sometimes such suicides take the form of hate for the person who had been desired; suicide then becomes a form of revenge. In one case a husband wrote his reactions while taking gas because his wife had fallen in love with his brother.

A young clerk twenty-two years old killed himself because his bride of four months was not in love with him but with his elder brother and wanted a divorce so that she could marry the brother. The letters he left showed plainly the suicide's desire to bring unpleasant notoriety upon his brother and his wife, and to attract attention to himself. In them he described his shattered romance and advised reporters to see a friend to whom he had forwarded diaries for further details. The first sentence in a special message to his wife read: "I used to love you; but I die hating you and my brother, too." This was written in a firm hand; but as his suicide diary progressed, the handwriting became erratic and then almost unintelligible as he lapsed into unconsciousness. Some time after turning on the gas he wrote: "Took my 'panacea' for all human ills. It won't be long now. I'll bet Florence and Ed are having uneasy dreams now." An hour later he continues: "Still the same, hope I pass out by 2 A.M. Gee, I love you so much, Florence. I feel very tired and a bit dizzy. My brain is very clear. I can see that my hand is shaking—it is hard to die when one is young. Now I wish oblivion would hurry"—the note ended there.

Another note regretted the inconvenience to the landlady for using her premises as a death-house. Still another read: "To whom it may interest: The cause of it all: I loved and trusted my wife and trusted my brother. Now I hate my wife, despise my brother and sentence myself to die for having been fool enough to have ever loved any one as contemptible as my wife has proven to be. Both she and her lover (my brother) knew this afternoon that I intended to die tonight. They were quite pleased at the prospect and did not trouble to conceal their elation. They had good reason to know that I was not jesting."

The brother who is twenty-three years old spoke frankly to the police about his friendship with his brother's wife. Though separated in childhood when the parents had drifted apart, the two brothers had later on become inseparable companions until shortly before the tragedy, when both fell in love with the same girl. The younger man attempted suicide when his love was not returned and upon his recovery, the girl agreed to marry him out of pity—but later on she found she could not live up to her bargain. After a few weeks of married life, the husband discovered the relationship existing between his wife and his brother. He became much depressed and threatened suicide. The day before his death, there was a scene and when assured that the two were really deeply in love with each other, the clerk retorted: "All right, I can do you more harm dead than alive." [54]

Instead of a specific wish involving a person or object, another type represents a conflict between two social roles which the individual holds and which he cannot reconcile. On the one hand, he may wish to be married, for example, but at the same time he has responsibilities to his family which make it necessary to postpone marriage. Conflicts growing out of participation in two different sets of cultural groups or sets of ethical norms are also examples of a situation which has potentialities for suicide.

Suicides as the result of a broken life organization represent those cases where individuals, whose lives had previously been satisfactory, encounter some crisis. If this crisis is associated with great emotional disturbance and no alternative action seems available they may feel they can no longer continue to face life. This type of suicide, in a broad way, resembles the anomic type of Durkheim, and includes crises like blindness, incurable illness, arrests, breaking up of a home, death of a marital partner, or sudden loss of a business. The individual is unable to reconcile his previous conception of himself with the change required by a new situation. The individual's life organization has collapsed through no fault of his own. In the following case the crisis situation in the death of the wife led to the suicide.

> The entire life-organization of Dr. A. B. was centered about his one object of interest and affection. The death of Mrs. A. B. was a vital turning-point in his personality, for it necessitated either a thoroughgoing reorganization of his fundamental interests and attitudes, or else an indefinite period of unadjustment and later personal demoralization. What actually happened is well attested to by the ensuing events. In order to regain a state of healthy equilibrium, it would have been necessary for Dr. A. B. to find an interest, or interests, . . . as absorbing as the one he lost, something that he could reaccommodate himself to and continue his role in society. However, this tremendous disturbance to his personality resulted in a feeling of loneliness, hopelessness, futility, and inadequacy. He was unable to cope with such a radically new situation born of this change; nothing could satisfy this one dominant interest. He just literally "went to pieces." [55]

Prolonged frustrations and crises by no means always result in suicide, and it is not clear as yet just why some do. People face innumerable unpleasant crises in different ways. Some people may become drunk, others may seek religion, some will make light of the situation, and others will evade the issue or even consciously try to avoid it. The person who commits suicide is unable to find a satisfactory alternative solution.

---

[54] Dublin and Bunzel, op. cit., pp. 294–295.
[55] Calvin F. Schmid, "Suicides in Seattle, 1914 to 1925: An Ecological and Behavioristic Study," University of Washington Publications in the Social Sciences, 5:71 (October, 1928).

Several factors probably play a significant role in a suicide. First, the desired goal may become so *dominant* that in many cases it becomes almost an obsession. A girl, for example, whose engagement has been broken may feel that nothing else—parents, career, or other interests—is of any consequence. Second, there is a *fixity* in the interest so that nothing else can satisfy it: "In the suicide, this non-adaptability seems unusually prominent. If he has determined upon a certain way to satisfy it he can consider no alternative way. If a system of relationships once found satisfactory is for any reason broken, he can conceive of no system doing the work of the old." [56] Third, a particular *lack of objectivity* on the part of those who commit suicide makes them see the difficulty only from their own point of view. A fourth factor is the *interpretation of the difficulty* by the person. Circumstances such as economic losses or other difficulties which may seriously disturb one person may have little effect on another. The need for the object desired or his loss of status may be interpreted by a suicide as destroying all future hope. A prosperous businessman who has lost his fortune and commits suicide may have felt that because of the loss of money his previous social status is irrevocably ended. Satisfaction and material comforts, the future of his family, and the plans for his old age have all come tumbling down at once and he has no desire to try to rebuild his life. Sometimes persons commit suicide for some provocation which might seem unimportant or even trivial to others but which to the suicide has assumed tremendous proportions. The situation is defined as irremediable, intolerable, or even hopeless:

> The man who kills himself is through with life; he has literally died psychologically before he kills his body. Over and over again in the notes left by suicides appears the phrase, "I can't stand it any longer." It is a crisis which cannot be adjusted to—which ends in defeat. Externally, there may be little or even no evidence of the difficulty, but in his subjective life the person is enduring doubts, unsatisfied longings and finally hopelessness and inability to struggle longer.[57]

Suicide and Mental Disorder

Persons who commit suicide are not generally "mentally deranged," or suffering from "temporary insanity." Such an idea has developed from the assumption that "no one in his right mind" would take his own life. To be considered a suicide resulting from a psychosis the patient generally must have been under treatment or there must exist some other demonstrable evidence of psychosis. Hearsay evidence from relatives cannot be accepted. Reliable studies indicate that only approximately 15 to 30 percent of suicides are suffering from a psychosis. In a study of 291 Chicago

---

[56] Cavan, *op. cit.*, p. 173.   [57] *Ibid.*, p. 177.

suicides, only 58 were presumed to have had a psychosis.[58] Approximately 20 percent of 22,000 suicides among industrial policyholders of a large life insurance company were found to have had a recognized mental illness.[59]

From a study of suicides in New York mental hospitals, severe depression, either involutional melancholia or manic-depressive psychosis, seems to be the most common form of psychosis associated with suicide, although paranoia, senile dementia, and dementia praecox are also found.[60] The percentage of psychotic disturbances, although not large, is great enough to account for concern, in most cases of attempted suicide, lest there be present some severe mental disorder which will lead to a repetition of the attempt unless the disturbance is discovered and treated. Likewise, psychiatrists must be on guard for such possibilities in patients suffering from severe depression.[61]

On the other hand, a much larger percentage of suicides, at the time of the suicide, are in some way emotionally disturbed, although not to the point where their disturbance explains their action. In many instances they may have been agitated over a period of several days prior to the suicide. Some of these undoubtedly have acted "strange" or "queer." This is a different conception from that of suicide being basically a result of prolonged mental disturbance. Actually many suicides are rationally planned and carried out with no more evidence of mental disorder than would be found in the so-called normal person. The goals sought by most suicides, no matter how exaggerated, generally are real goals, the personal losses suffered are real losses, and are usually not the product of psychotic hallucinations or delusions having little or no basis in reality.

Suicide and Status

An explanation of suicide and homicide within the framework of different adjustments to status frustrations which produce aggression has been offered by two sociologists, Henry and Short.[62] Suicide and homicide, they claim, can be differentiated in terms of the target of the aggression; in suicide the aggression is directed at the self, whereas in homicide it is directed at others.

> The sociological evidence suggests that suicide is a form of aggression against the self aroused by some frustration, the cause of which is perceived by the person as lying within the self. Failure to maintain a constant or ris-

[58] *Ibid.*, p. 569.   [59] Dublin and Bunzel, *op. cit.*, p. 300.

[60] Study by H. M. Pollock of 200 suicides among patients with mental illness in New York mental hospitals, 1919–1929, quoted in Dublin and Bunzel, *op. cit.*, p. 11.

[61] Dublin and Bunzel, *op. cit.*

[62] Henry and Short, *op. cit.* Suicide and homicide are related in that both respond to the business cycle and are, they claim, therefore simply common responses to frustration.

ing position in the status hierarchy relative to others in the same status reference system is one—but by no means the only—important frustration arousing aggression. When this frustration is perceived as being the fault of the self, the aroused aggression may flow against the self. This is most likely when the person is relatively freed from the requirement that his behavior conform to the demands and expectations of others. Persons of high status and those isolated from meaningful relationships are most likely to blame themselves and commit suicide when frustration occurs, since their behavior is relatively independent of the demands and expectations of others.[63]

Suicide is related to three things: (1) the strength of the relational systems of a given population, (2) this strength of relational system varies with the external restraints on the behavior of the population, and, finally, (3) the external restraints placed on the behavior of the members of a population varies inversely with their status position.

As evidence of this relation they explain the lower suicide rate of married persons as compared with those who are single, divorced, or widowed as due to the fact that married persons are involved in a stronger relational system in which they must conform more to the demands and expectations of others. The degree of involvement with other persons also explains the lower rates of rural areas, the high rates in the central parts of the city, and the general tendency for suicide rates to increase as the person grows older and has fewer close relations with others.

For some time it has been well established that suicide rates fluctuate with the business cycle. Henry and Short offer the explanation that status frustrations caused by the business cycle, such as depressions, result in different degrees of aggressive behavior in the form of suicide according to the status position of persons. Groups in higher status positions react more violently to fluctuations in the business cycle, they claim, than do those in lower status positions. The rate of male suicides reacts more to economic fluctuations than that of women. Similarly, white suicide rates change more than Negro, and those in higher-income groups more than those in lower-income groups. The likelihood of suicide is thus related not only to the degree of interpersonal relations but also to position in the status hierarchy. Here external restraint, demands, and expectations by those in higher status categories operate to control the behavior of those in lower status and prevent suicide. Thus the lower suicide rate of the Negro and those in lower status occupational categories, such as an employee, can be partly explained in this way. The higher the status category the less restraint imposed on a person if he desires to commit suicide. This general explanation of suicide in terms of status frustration is intriguing

---

[63] Andrew F. Henry and James F. Short, Jr., "The Sociology of Suicide," in *Clues to Suicide,* p. 68.

but does not seem to be proved by the evidence presented and is largely a theory read into certain broad statistical findings.

Another recent sociological theory has attempted to link suicide to a particular pattern of status occupancy or the degree of status integration in a society.[64] There is less suicide in populations where one status position is closely associated with other status positions and, consequently, the members are likely to experience less role conflict, are more capable of conforming to the demands and expectations of others, and are more capable of maintaining stable and durable social relationships. As an illustration, of the males in 1950 from sixty to sixty-four, 79.3 percent were married, 9.6 widowed, 8.6 single, and 2.5 percent divorced. The corresponding suicide rates for each of the four marital status groups was 36.2, 64.7, 76.4, and, finally, for the divorced, 111.1. This presumably indicates that, although an older age group, the infrequently occupied status clusters, e.g., the divorced, are assumed to be characterized by role conflict and consequently weak social relationships.

Summary

Suicide is strongly condemned among Western European peoples and in Mohammedan countries. The negative attitude in Western European civilization can be traced primarily to the attitude of the Christian and Jewish religious teachings toward self-destruction.

Suicides appear to differ in their nature according to the type of society. Among folk societies most suicides are altruistic, whereas in modern societies they tend to be predominantly egoistic or anomic.

Rates of suicide fluctuate with the business cycle, being higher during periods of depression and lower at times of prosperity. Suicide rates for males are much higher than those for females. White persons in the United States have a higher rate than nonwhites.

The likelihood of suicide increases with age. In general, married persons have a lower suicide rate than do single, divorced, or widowed persons. Rates for Catholics are, in general, lower than those for Protestants.

Suicides can be distinguished according to whether they are situational or escape patterns. They can be classified into those arising from an unidentified craving for a goal, a recognized wish, a specific wish, mental conflicts, and a broken life organization. Whether a person commits suicide appears to be dependent upon the dominance of the goal, the fixity, the lack of objectivity, and the interpretation of the difficulty. Various theories have attempted to associate social status with suicide.

---

[64] See Jack P. Gibbs and Walter T. Martin, "A Theory of Status Integration and Its Relationship to Suicide," *American Sociological Review*, 23:140–147 (April, 1958). Also see Gibbs, "Suicide," in Merton and Nisbet, *op. cit.*, pp. 257–259.

Selected Readings

BOHANNAN, PAUL, ed. *African Homicide and Suicide.* Princeton, N.J.: Princeton University Press, 1960. A study of homicide and suicide among seven African tribes. Contains case materials and statistical comparisons with Western society.

CAVAN, RUTH S. *Suicide.* Chicago: The University of Chicago Press, 1928. This is one of the leading reference materials on suicide. Has considerable case material and statistical data from Chicago.

DUBLIN, LOUIS I., and BESSIE BUNZEL. *To Be or Not to Be: A Study of Suicide.* New York: Harrison Smith and Robert Haas, 1933. A comprehensive study of suicide, using in particular Metropolitan Life Insurance Company data on suicides.

DURKHEIM, ÉMILE. *Suicide.* John A. Spaulding and George Simpson, trans. New York: The Free Press of Glencoe, 1951. This is one of the most important books by the famous French sociologist. Originally published in 1897, it has been translated into English for the first time. Contains a detailed discussion of egoistic, altruistic, and anomic types of suicide.

HENRY, ANDREW F., and JAMES F. SHORT, JR. *Suicide and Homicide.* New York: The Free Press of Glencoe, 1954. An explanation of suicide and homicide primarily in terms of a theory of frustration and aggression. Contains considerable recent statistical data on suicides analyzed by race, sex, age, and income.

SAINSBURY, PETER, *Suicide in London: An Ecological Study.* London: Chapman & Hall, Ltd., 1955. An ecological study of 409 suicides occurring in North London analyzed according to residence, occupation, and other factors.

Chapter

15

Conflicts in Marital
and Family Roles

At present one divorce is granted in the United States for every four marriages performed. Although this represents a marked decline from the immediate postwar peak, when the ratio was one to two and a half, there has been in general an increase over the past sixty years in the proportion of divorces to marriages. These statistics, however, do not give the full account of contemporary marital unhappiness. Many more applications for divorce are filed than are finally granted, and none of these figures includes separations and desertions.

Various studies have shown that a legally intact marriage is not necessarily a "happy" one, indicating that marital unhappiness is far more pervasive than divorce statistics alone show. In general, marital unhappiness is taken as evidence of marital and family conflict. Conflict specifically refers to a situation where there is a discrepancy between the role expectations and role behaviors of family members in relation to one another. A conflict may thus be temporary or permanent. In its temporary aspects, it may hasten or assist the ability of marital partners to develop role skills or to deal with problems which arise.

Concept of Marital and Family Conflict

A marriage or family operates as a group in much the same manner as other social groups. Certain characteristics of such groups, however, make for a greater degree of interdependence, and hence interaction, than is true of most groups. The interlocking of the roles comprising the family group means that many of the actions of a family member deeply affects the other members. There are parallel intimate relations between many members, such as the parents' relations between themselves and with their children. Each of these conditions interacts with others and tends to intensify them.[1]

---

[1] Kurt Lewin, *Resolving Social Conflicts* (New York: Harpers & Row, Publishers, 1948). See also Talcott Parsons, "The Social Structure of the Family," in Ruth Nanda Anshen ed. *The Family: Its Function and Destiny* (rev. ed.; New York: Harper & Row, Publishers, 1959), p. 241.

When the beliefs and expectancies about the bonds in a family remain fairly constant over a period of time and from situation to situation, the family is able to perform its functions, the individuals within the marital group are comparatively free of tension, and the interacting individuals form a "unity." [2] Thus when all these conditions exist, the family is organized; that is, there is cooperation in the "process of building up organized attitudes in which all concur." [3] This set of mutually shared attitudes or expectations comprises what we call the organization or structure of the family, or the network of statuses and roles, common aims, and values, which make up the system of relationships. When family members share the same expectations and aims, and are able to act in accordance with them, the day-to-day needs of family members are generally met. Sometimes, however, obstructions to understanding or to role enactment may arise—either from within the family group or outside it. When this occurs, there may be a temporary conflict between the expectations of different family members. This conflict may, if it is permanent, affect the family unit as a whole.[4] In the same manner, social changes occurring in the society of which the family is a part can impinge upon the family structure. For example, an economic depression may leave a father unemployed. Not only will this alter the father's breadwinning role; it will affect the attitudes and expectations of family members in relation to one another, and so affect, in varying degrees, the total network of relationships.[5]

Interpersonal relations in marriage and family relations have many facets. Some involve intimacy of association, others influence the development of such an association, and still others affect the ability to meet these demands after association is developed.[6] The intimate relations of companionship can give great strength to the marriage relationship. Some of these intimate relationships involve the development and expression of sentiment, such as love and affection, physical contact, such as sexual relations, and sharing of valued experiences and hopes.[7] Generally, it is supposed that marital happiness and stability are greater in marriage relationships characterized by affection, mutual dependence and compati-

[2] Ernest W. Burgess, "The Family as a Unity of Interacting Personalities," *Family*, 7:3–9 (March, 1926). Some writers have suggested that the family, rather than a "unity" is more of an "arena" of interacting personalities.—Willard Waller, *The Family* (revised by Reuben Hill; New York: Holt, Rinehart and Winston, Inc., 1951), pp. 25–37.

[3] Annabelle Bender Motz, "Conceptions of Marital Roles by Status Groups," *Marriage and Family Living*, 12:136 (Winter, 1950).

[4] Elizabeth Bott, *Family and Social Network* (London: Tavistock Publications Ltd., 1957), p. 59.

[5] J. Cohen, R. Robson, A. Bates, *Parental Authority: The Community and the Law* (New Brunswick, N.J.: Rutgers University Press, 1958), p. 197.

[6] Ernest W. Burgess and Paul Wallin, *Engagement and Marriage* (Philadelphia: J. B. Lippincott Company, 1953), p. 418.

[7] Parsons "The Social Structure of the Family," in Anshen, *op. cit.*

bility, and shared satisfactions. On the other hand, it is believed that marital unhappiness and instability are more common where there is indifference, hostility, dissatisfaction, mutual independence, and incompatibility. Marital role relationships may be predominantly "joint": that is, they may involve many shared or similar activities carried out by husband and wife together. Or they may be "segregated": that is, they may involve many independent activities carried out by husband and wife separately. But marital stability and happiness seem to occur with about equal frequency among "joint" and "segregated" marital role relationships. Happiness and stability appear to be influenced more by the total social system of which the husband-wife relationship is a part, than by the marital relationship alone.[8]

In the marriage situation a number of factors may operate to produce marital stability or success. In each instance, however, they may operate in reverse and contribute, instead, to lack of success or instability in marriage. The similarities or differences in cultural backgrounds which each partner contributes to the marriage can make for harmony or for conflict. The development of interests and values likewise can strengthen the association through mutual stimulation and complementary interests or it can take a course which may produce boredom and conflict. Domestic activities, including household tasks, the rearing of children, family activities, illness, friends, may be mutually shared or, as in some marriages, one partner may escape to activities outside the family circle. One study has even shown the importance of social approval from others in the adjustment of a married couple, particularly to new situations.[9]

The dynamics of a marriage are more, however, than the development of intimacy and association. Marriage also means decision making and adaptability. In such activities the marriage means not individuals making separate decisions but a couple deciding together. If mutual decisions are made about such things as expenditures and the children, they serve to integrate the marriage; if they are made in an authoritarian way or unilaterally they weaken it.

If the partners in a marriage adapt to one another, a marriage can be greatly strengthened. Adaptability represents a process of change. "In marriage, adaptability enables husband and wife to adjust successfully despite the conflicting facets of their personalities which reveal themselves in the exigencies of marriage, and to cope with changes in the social situation which impinge upon and affect their roles as husband and wife." [10] Although there are other facets, one of the most important is the determination that the marriage will succeed.

---

[8] Bott, *op. cit.*, pp. 53-58, p. 219; and Carle C. Zimmerman and Lucius F. Cervantes, *Successful American Families* (New York: Pageant Books, Inc., 1960), pp. 35-55.

[9] Motz, "Conceptions of Marital Roles by Status Groups," *loc. cit.*

[10] Ernest W. Burgess and Paul Wallin, *Engagement and Marriage* (Philadelphia: J. B. Lippincott Company, 1953), p. 623. Excerpts from this work are used with the permission of the publisher.

Burgess and Wallin have constructed an index of marital adjustment which stresses the need for consensus or common agreement, common interests and activities, demonstration of affection, satisfaction with marriage, and absence of feelings of unhappiness and loneliness. Their list of the developmental and integrative, as opposed to the frustrative and disruptive, forces in interpersonal relations in marriage appears in Table 15.1.

Table 15.1. Interpersonal Relations in Modern Marriage

	Developmental and integrative	Frustrative and disruptive
I. Intimacy of Association:		
Love and affection	Mutual love, affection	Indifference, hostility
Sexual relations	Enjoyment and satisfaction	Dissatisfaction
Emotional interdependence	Mutual dependence	Emotional independence
Temperamental interaction	Compatibility	Incompatibility
II. Development of the Association:		
Cultural interaction	Assimilation and creativity	Accommodation and conflict
Interests and values	Stimulation and complementation	Boredom and conflict
Domesticity	Mutual enjoyment of home activities	Escape into outside activities
III. The Association in Operation:		
Decision making	Interdependent	Authoritarian and unilateral
Adaptability	Mutual adaptability	Unadaptability of one or both

SOURCE: Ernest W. Burgess and Paul Wallin, *Engagement and Marriage* (Philadelphia: J. B. Lippincott Company, 1953), pp. 418–419. They also include a factor "Expectations of Continuity," which is not discussed in this section.

The Process of Family Disintegration

Every family has its breaking point, and it is possible to sketch the process through which marital and family conflicts may pass to their culmination in crisis. After the first aura of passion and erotic newness of marriage has worn off, a monotonous pattern of day-to-day living may begin. Many withstand ripples of discontent and difficulties, finding more in the marital relationship than any contemplated escape from it would provide. For others, however, small difficulties mount in frequency and intensity until one of the partners feels that there are more satisfactions to be gained outside marriage than within it. The series of steps in this process as it leads finally to divorce have been listed by Locke as follows:

1. Developing tensions and difficulties between family members
2. Debating the issues of the conflict within oneself
3. Overtly expressing the conflicts
4. Intermittently attempting to solve marital difficulties
5. Sleeping in different beds or in different rooms
6. Mentioning divorce as a possibility to the mate
7. Separating into different domiciles
8. Making a temporary reconciliation
9. Making application for a divorce
10. Getting the application discussed
11. Reapplying for a divorce
12. Getting the application dismissed
13. Reapplying for a divorce
14. Securing the divorce
15. Trying to achieve emancipation from the mate
16. Adjusting to the crisis of the divorce.[11]

In the following case is a sequence of some of these steps. The woman, who was quite dominant, had worked in her husband's business and after it failed he was no longer important to her. There was a separation after which she applied for a divorce, only to have it dismissed.

> We were happy as could be for the first twenty years of our marriage. Then two things occurred which changed our marriage into unhappiness. I lost most of my business; second, my wife had the change of life. I would come home and would be worried about my business, and then she would argue and fuss and make me nervous, and I would have indigestion. So I got to staying down town and eating out.
>
> Then she became cold. We were very active sexually in our earlier life. Now she wouldn't have anything to do with me. I moved into another bed and then into another room. I told her that I would give her time to adjust to her change—four or five years. At the end of that time things were no better, so I packed up and left.
>
> Since I went away, I have been back occasionally. But when I go back for Christmas or Thanksgiving, she does not pay any attention to me. She talks and laughs with the others, but not with me. I may go out to the kitchen and try to wipe the dishes like I used to, but she says that she can get along all right by herself.
>
> A few weeks ago she suggested that I come back; we would live as man

---

[11] Derived from Harvey Locke, *Predicting Adjustment in Marriage* (New York: Holt, Rinehart and Winston, Inc., 1951), p. 71.

and wife; and I went over and talked with her. I found that the old trouble would still be there.[12]

Marital unhappiness may find a number of outlets short of annulment, separation, desertion, or divorce. Some persons resort to a world of fantasy and daydreams to escape a difficult marital situation. Through their emphasis on romantic love, motion pictures, romantic stories, and particularly the soap operas of radio and television furnish escapes. Chronic "illness" may also provide escape from an unpleasant marital situation. If either person feels neglected, dissatisfied, or unloved, he may resort to "illness" to obtain care and attention or to inflict discomfort on the other. Being constantly "tired" without a physical basis may be indicative of dissatisfaction with marriage. Studies have also shown that alcohol and other substitute satisfactions offer escapes from unsatisfactory marital situations. Some may take a more conventional outlet for such frustrations by minimizing interaction in the family and instead devote all their spare time to housework, their hobbies, their jobs, or to golf, music, art, or club activities. Finally, many parents who are not happy in their marital situation may project their frustrations through displaying excessive affection for their children and excessive interest in their children's goals.

Desertion

Some couples separate without a divorce, maintaining the fiction of marriage but with two households. Some separations are temporary, but others may be permanent. The law may even recognize this fact by providing for a "legal separation." Separations may meet religious objections to divorce or one partner's refusal to grant a divorce. Some partners simply desert by leaving home without making provisions for financial or other responsibilities. It is usually the husband who deserts. This does not always mean that he is the more dissatisfied partner; rather, he is more mobile.

The number of separations and desertions can be but an estimate. However, some idea of the total may be obtained from the number of divorces granted for desertion, from the census enumeration which shows the number of husbands or wives absent from the household, and from child-support cases. The number of divorces granted for desertion in the United States has increased during the past several decades. A peak of 112,000 was reached in 1946. By 1950 there was a decline to 68,000 divorces granted for desertion. Estimates of the extent of separation and desertion may be found in census data which show that, in 1957, 791,000 men and 1,146,000 women were listed as "separated." These figures include

---

[12] Locke, *op. cit.*, pp. 72–73. Reprinted by permission of Holt, Rinehart and Winston, Inc., publishers.

only those legally separated, those expecting to obtain a divorce, and those temporarily or permanently estranged. These data showed 1.9 percent of all married women to be separated from their husbands. Of nonwhite women only, chiefly Negro, 8 percent were separated from their husbands.[13] Desertions accounted for 33 percent, and divorce 5 percent, of all cases of children receiving aid in Philadelphia.[14] Over the past thirty years new desertion and nonsupport cases in Philadelphia were twice the number of divorce cases. In 1955, of the 2,600,000 children receiving aid-to-dependent children grants in the United States, the fathers of 1,400,000 were separated from their families.[15]

Desertion appears to be more frequent among groups where social controls are weaker, and where family groups may be presented with conflicting norms. Thus, it is observed that desertion occurs more frequently in "newer cities" which are presumably undergoing more rapid change, and in which associations may occur more frequently among heterogeneous groups.[16] Desertion is also more frequent among those religious groups for whom divorce is not acceptable. Among Catholics, for example, desertion is much more common than among Protestants. According to estimates, the desertion rate for Catholics in the United States exceeds that for the general population by about 40 percent.[17]

Divorce

Although many persons regard divorce as the only index of family disintegration, it is but one of many signs. Since it represents the legal dissolution of the marriage, it certainly is the final one. Two major types of legal divorce can be distinguished: absolute divorce, which restores marital partners to the status of single persons, completely absolving marital rights; and partial divorce, or legal separation, which gives legal status to separate maintenance without dissolving marital rights.[18]

EXTENT OF DIVORCE

About 400,000 divorces and annulments are granted annually in the United States. The ratio of divorces to marriages is about one in four,

---

[13] Bureau of the Census, *Population Characteristics, Marital Status, Economic Status, and Family Status:* March, 1957, *Current Population Reports*, Series P-20, No. 81 (March 19, 1958), Table 1.

[14] William M. Kephart and Thomas P. Monahan, "Desertion and Divorce in Philadelphia," *American Sociological Review*, 17:719 (December, 1952).

[15] Jessie Bernard, *Social Problems at Midcentury* (New York: Holt, Rinehart and Winston, Inc., 1957), p. 383, from a report from the Commissioner of Social Security.

[16] Zimmerman and Cervantes, *op. cit.*, pp. 51–55.

[17] Thomas P. Monahan and William M. Kephart, "Divorce and Desertion by Religious and Mixed Religious Groups," *American Journal of Sociology*, 59:454–465 (March, 1954).

[18] Mabel Elliott and Francis E. Merrill, *Social Disorganization* (New York: Harper & Row, Publishers, 1961), p. 390; and Paul H. Jacobson, *American Marriage and Divorce* (New York: Holt, Rinehart and Winston, Inc., 1959).

and about 4 percent of the children in the population who are under eighteen have been affected by divorce. In 1956 there were 2,418,000 divorced persons, 60 percent of whom were women. These figures do not include all persons who had been divorced, for about two thirds of divorced women and three fourths of divorced men eventually remarry.[19]

Divorce rates per 1000 marriages have increased in general since 1890, in the United States and in some Western European countries and Australia.[20] "It is therefore not merely an 'American' phenomenon, but is somehow related to the evolution of the family in Western society in general." [21]

The number of divorces increased during and after World War II. In the United States an all-time high of approximately 610,000 divorces were granted in 1946. (See Table 15.2.) The annual number of divorces

Table 15.2. Divorces and Divorce Rates in Relation to Population, United States, 1890–1957 (Rates per 1000 of mid-year Population)

Year	Population in millions	Divorces Number	Rate
1890	63.1	33,461	0.5
1900	76.1	55,751	0.7
1910	92.4	83,045	0.9
1920	106.4	170,505	1.6
1930	123.1	195,961	1.6
1940	131.97	264,000	2.0
1946 [a]	141.2	610,000	4.3
1950	150.7	385,144	2.6
1956	167.2	382,000	2.3
1957	170.3	381,000	2.2

[a] Peak year.

SOURCE: Table, "Marriages and Divorces, United States and Each State and Alaska, Hawaii, Puerto Rico and the Virgin Islands," 1957, *Vital Statistics: Special Reports*, Vol. 50, No. 7 (June, 1959), p. 187; and Table IX, "Provisional Marriage and Divorce Statistics," United States, 1948, *Vital Statistics: Special Reports*, Vol. 31, No. 16 (November 4, 1949), p. 229; and Paul H. Jacobson, *American Marriage and Divorce* (New York: Holt, Rinehart and Winston, Inc., 1959), p. 90.

has gradually decreased. In 1957 there were approximately 381,000 divorces, a fact which suggests that the increase in divorces during and after World War II may have been due, in part, to the increase in marriages.[22]

[19] Elliott and Merrill, *op. cit.*, p. 391.
[20] William J. Goode, "Family Disorganization," in Robert K. Merton and Robert R. Nisbet eds., *Contemporary Social Problems* (New York: Harcourt, Brace & World, Inc., 1961), Table 3, p. 406.
[21] Kingsley Davis, "Statistical Perspective on Marriage and Divorce," *The Annals*, 272:17 (November, 1950).
[22] Goode, "Family Disorganization," in Merton and Nisbet, *op. cit.*, p. 411.

Although the total number of divorces in the United States, as well as the rate of divorce in relation to the population and divorces per 1000 married females fifteen years and over, has decreased in the past few years, the number of divorces relative to the number of 1000 yearly marriages has, in general, increased. In 1890 the number of divorces was 55.6; in 1910, 87.4; in 1930, 173.9; in 1950, 231.7; and in 1956 it was 259.[23] The increase in divorce rates in the past sixty years is no evidence that marital unhappiness has increased to the same extent, for there are other variables. Divorce laws have become increasingly liberal during this time, and the grounds for divorce have been broadened. South Carolina, for example, did not permit divorce for any reason until 1949. Moreover, there has been a decided change in public opinion about divorce. Many persons who formerly continued unsatisfactory marriages, or separated, or were deserted, now secure a divorce. Formerly a divorce was often a matter of family disgrace, but now public attitudes are more tolerant. These changes in public opinion seem to reflect more fundamental transformations in values and norms relating to the nature of marriage and divorce.[24]

FACTORS IN DIVORCE RATES

Monahan lists three categories of factors which influence the divorce rate. First, there is the historical trend. People who marry this year are more likely to become divorced than those who married twenty or thirty years ago because the attitudes and expectations of married couples, as well as the change in values, make divorce more acceptable. Second, situational factors, such as depression, affect the divorce rate at particular times. During the last depression the divorce rate dropped over 20 percent in three years. Finally, the last category concerns biographical aspects, or the time at which the marriage was contracted, as during wars, when there are many hasty marriages.[25]

In the United States considerable differences in divorce rates depend largely on area, religion, education, occupation, and number of children. In urban areas there is a much higher divorce rate than in rural areas, and Cannon has concluded that the rural-urban differential is the greatest single factor affecting divorce rates.[26] The rural divorce rate is not markedly below the urban rate in all states, however, and some suggest that since

---

[23] *Ibid.*, Table 3, p. 406.

[24] See Elliott and Merrill, *op. cit.*, Chap. 17; S. Kirson Weinberg, *Social Problems in Our Time* (Englewood Cliffs, N.J.: Prentice-Hall, Inc., 1960), p. 442; and Goode, "Family Disorganization," *loc. cit.*, pp. 412–413.

[25] Thomas P. Monahan, "The Changing Probability of Divorce," *American Sociological Review*, 5:536–545 (August, 1940).

[26] Kenneth Cannon, "Marriage and Divorce in Iowa, 1940–47," *Marriage and Family Living*, 9:81–83 (February, 1947).

1940 the rural rates have shown a tendency to catch up with the urban rates. In Wisconsin, for example, the rural divorce rates have been about as high as the urban rates since World War II.[27]

Divorce rates are also higher in western than in eastern states. The higher divorce rates for western states may be due in part to differences in religious concentration and in legislation concerning divorce, as well as to the greater mobility of the population. In the northern and eastern states which have large Catholic populations, although divorce rates tend to be low (as an average of 1.3), the number of desertions contributed by these states appears to be markedly in excess of the national average.[28] Divorces and desertions are lowest for Jewish groups from 1937 to 1950; divorces were more frequent among Protestants but desertion was highest among Catholics, exceeding the Protestant rate by about 100 percent and the Jewish rate by about 500 percent.[29]

Differences in divorce rates exist between occupational groups. One author has indicated, for example, that available evidence demonstrates an inverse relationship between divorce rate and socioeconomic rank; thus, professional groups which are highest in socioeconomic rank, have the lowest divorce rate, whereas service workers and laborers which occupy the lowest socioeconomic ranks, have the highest divorce rates.[30] However, Monahan found that farm laborers in Iowa had the lowest divorce rates. Whatever the precise relation between divorce and occupation, data relating to these variables must be interpreted with caution. In the first place, before assessing the divorce rate, it is necessary to know how many persons within a given occupational category *marry*. In the second place, if we are examining the relative degree of family disintegration in various occupational groups, then it is necessary to know how many families in given occupational groups are broken by means other than divorce.

Divorces are most likely to occur early in marriage, the majority before the fifth year, and most frequently in the third.[31] Although slightly over half of the couples who are divorced in the United States have no children, many children are affected by divorce. In 1955, about 343,000

---

[27] E. E. LeMasters, *Modern Courtship and Marriage* (New York: The Macmillan Company, 1957), p. 571. See also Jessie Bernard, *Remarriage* (New York: Holt, Rinehart and Winston, Inc., 1956) for a review of urban and rural trends in divorce.

[28] See Monahan and Kephart, "Divorce and Desertion by Religious and Mixed Religious Groups," *loc. cit.*

[29] *Ibid.* Also see Paul Glick, *American Families* (New York: John Wiley & Sons, Inc., 1957).

[30] William J. Goode, *After Divorce* (New York: The Free Press of Glencoe, 1956), p. 46 and Chaps. 4 and 5. For contrasting views, see also Thomas P. Monahan, "Divorce by Occupational Level," *Marriage and Family Living*, 17:322–324 (November, 1955); and William M. Kephart, "Occupational Level and Marital Disruption," *American Sociological Review*, 20:456–465 (August, 1955).

[31] Harold T. Christensen, *Marriage Analysis* (New York: The Ronald Press Company, 1950), p. 13. See also Jacobson, *op. cit.*, pp. 144–147.

children were involved in divorce and annulment cases, or an average of slightly less than two children per couple.[32] The proportion of children involved in divorces has continued to increase during the past twenty or thirty years. Between 1922 and 1932 the average number of children affected by a divorce was 0.68; in 1955 the number was 0.87. This suggests that children are no longer as great a deterrent to divorce as they once were. The woman usually files for the divorce, either for reasons of chivalry on the part of the husband, or because he may be unwilling to sever relationships with his children, whose custody the wife usually retains.

Likewise, the legal grounds used in the divorce proceedings are seldom the real grounds for the proposed separation; the law permits divorce only for certain reasons and these reasons often do not fit the circumstances of a particular couple who wants a divorce. Usually the couple agrees on one of the generally "fictitious" legal grounds permitted by the state in which the pair resides. The grounds agreed upon are generally those least socially injurious to the other partner, and yet the most effective, legally. Divorce is not regulated by a national law, and there are consequently great differences in state divorce laws. Some states require a minimum residence (six weeks in Nevada and Idaho) and allow a wide variety of grounds. This leads to migratory divorce from those states which have exceptionally severe grounds, such as, for example, South Carolina, where no divorce was permitted until 1949, and New York, where at present divorce is permitted only on grounds of adultery. Consequently, many persons in some states who desire a divorce and have sufficient money to finance it, migrate to states with shorter residence requirements and less stringent grounds.[33]

A large proportion of divorced persons remarry, and there is evidence that this remarriage rate is increasing. In general, about one out of every five marriages in the United States is a remarriage. About two thirds of divorced women remarry, and about three fourths of divorced men remarry. The median length of time between the divorce and subsequent remarriage is 2.7 years, for both men and women. About one half of all brides aged thirty-five to forty-four are divorcees, and about one half of all grooms aged forty to forty-nine are previously divorced men. Of brides aged twenty-five to twenty-nine about one fourth have been divorced as compared to about one eighth for grooms aged twenty-five to twenty-nine.[34] About two thirds of the total remarriages are between persons who

[32] Bernard, *Remarriage*, pp. 301–303. See also Goode, "Family Disorganization," in Merton and Nisbet, *op. cit.*, p. 454.

[33] For a discussion of some of the legal and social problems which this presents for those seeking a divorce, see Herbert F. Goodrich, "Migratory Divorce," in *Conference on Divorce* (Chicago: The University of Chicago Law School, February, 1952), pp. 82–87.

[34] Elliott and Merrill, *op. cit.*, p. 437.

have previously been divorced. One study found that divorced women generally have a more successful remarriage than those who have never been divorced.[35]

Conflicting Roles and Role Expectations in the Family

Marriage and family relations, like all group relations, involve role playing, and deficiencies and conflicts over role playing in the family situation play a leading part in breaking down relationships.[36] Marital partners and other members of the family may each have different aspirations and evaluations of the roles which they play and expect of others in marriage and family relationships.[37] Conflicts in marriage and family roles may occur between marital partners over their duties and obligations.[38] There are also conflicts between family roles and roles outside the family: conflicts, particularly with parents, in the roles of children, and conflicts in marital roles and those of other relatives.

Difficulties in role playing on the part of husband, wife, and children have been accentuated by the changes which have taken place in the family and in urban living over the past century. This is due to the fact that the roles of family members, but particularly of the wife, are ambiguously defined in contemporary American society. In the American rural family of the past, roles were well defined, with the father being largely a patriarchal figure. Women played a subordinate role and were largely concerned with household duties. Families were large, and children were expected to perform household duties and to be obedient to parents and to family traditions.

ROLE CONFLICTS BETWEEN MARITAL PARTNERS

Until quite recently a woman was dependent upon her family prior to her marriage; thereafter she relied upon her husband for support. Today about three fourths of all women work before marriage. In 1890 only 4.6 percent of married women were gainfully employed. In 1940 this

---

[35] Locke, *op. cit.,* p. 301.

[36] If conflicts do result in marital unhappiness they may not always precipitate divorce or other forms of marital breakup. It is probable that many marriages do endure, despite conflict and unhappiness. There is little knowledge of the extent of unhappy but enduring marriages.

[37] One study has measured differences between role performances and role expectations of husbands and wives and constructed an index of marital strain. See Nathan Hurvitz, "The Measurement of Marital Strain," *American Journal of Sociology,* 65:610–615 (May, 1960).

[38] See, for example, a study of husbands' and wives' expectations regarding their roles in the sexual relationship: Paul Wallin and Alexander Clark, "Cultural Norms and Husbands' and Wives' Reports of Their Marital Partners' Preferred Frequency of Coitus Relative to Their Own," *Sociometry,* 21:247–254 (September, 1958).

percentage was 15.2, and by 1951 it was 26.7 percent, or one in four married women. Women's ability to work has made marriage for the sake of economic "security" less frequent; yet today a woman's lifetime chances for social status are still associated with marriage.[39] Divorce may not present the same difficulties that it once did, because more women today have had employment experience prior to marriage. Yet divorce does introduce problems, usually of both an economic and a social-psychological sort. In the first place, the great majority of men and women in our society have different expectations about their future and their roles. For men, work or a job becomes the focus of self-identity and emotional investment, as well as of social status. On the other hand, women's socialization experiences are such that self-identity and emotional investment are intimately linked to successful wifehood. Thus, employment prior to marriage is regarded by most women as only temporary; after marriage it may serve other purposes.[40] The different societal attitudes which men and women incorporate in their own work roles are today reflected in societal practices which allocate differential salaries and statuses to male and female workers performing the same duties.[41]

The larger number of women employed today, which is in part a reflection of the "emancipation" of women occurring largely in this century, does not mean that women are no longer socialized differently from men. But the so-called emancipation of women has introduced additional roles for women. This does not mean that the old role of wife-mother is obsolete, but rather that today the wife-mother is subtly forced by social pressures to play additional roles. Some women may resist these pressures; others may regard them as a signal to abdicate the "drudgery" of wife-motherhood and become a full-fledged "careerist." Women today may feel ambivalent concerning their marital roles.[42]

Moreover, contrasted with the relatively limited education given women formerly, women today frequently go beyond high school, either to college or to business or secretarial school. This greater amount of education makes the wife a different kind of mate: she will tend to define her role in such a relationship differently; she does not respect her husband's position to the same extent; and she is more able to discuss things on an equal basis with her husband. The college-trained girl sets higher standards for her mate, and is less likely to accept a man with an education inferior to hers. As a result of both work experience and education,

[39] See Parsons, "The Social Structure of the Family," in Anshen, op. cit.; and David Riesman, "Permissiveness and Sex Roles," Marriage and Family Living, 21:1–11 (August, 1959).

[40] Riesman, "Permissiveness and Sex Roles," loc. cit.

[41] See Eli Ginsberg, Woman Power (New York: Columbia University Press, 1957).

[42] See Nora Johnson, "The Captivity of Marriage," Atlantic Monthly, 207:38–42 (June, 1961).

a woman is less likely than formerly to leave all decisions to her husband; more probably she will demand an equal share in this activity.

Some role conflicts involve the pattern played by the marriage partner in his marital and familial responsibilities. In some families, members may play their roles in a way which deviates markedly from that generally prescribed, so that any organization of roles becomes difficult. Sometimes, deviation in role playing in marriage is due to role expectations, as in the case of many adolescents, which are not even the same as those normally required for the marriage role.[43] The popular explanation that "neither was prepared to assume marriage and family responsibilities" probably best applies to these cases.

In other situations the role of one marital partner may be derived from a patriarchal or a matriarchal tradition, whereas the other partner may come from a more equalitarian or democratic background. One of the partners may then wish to assume entirely the major decision-making functions, such as the expenditure of money and the disciplining of the children. For example, a husband who was raised in a patriarchal family, and has expectations of playing a similar role in his own marriage, may marry a girl who has been supporting herself and making her own decisions. The husband can refer to families where the husband makes decisions, and the wife can refer to other families in which decisions are made on a democratic basis. In general, it has been shown that marital happiness and stability are more probable if the marital partners are from similar social backgrounds.[44]

A reverse situation may occur where "the woman plays the authoritative roles, ruling over her husband and children despotically. A man who has grown up in such a family will perhaps expect his wife to dominate him, but she may have had a family experience which prepared her for a submissive and dependent role. If such a man married such a woman, a struggle arises which is won by the person who forces the other to make decisions for the pair." [45]

It appears that in general the roles played by the marital partners largely reflect the marital roles played by the parents or other persons with whom each of the partners was intimately associated in childhood. The reason is that the parents or other "significant persons" are merely the "instruments" through which societal attitudes, norms, and values regarding sex-associated roles are communicated to children. "Married adjustment may be regarded as a process in which marriage partners attempt to re-enact certain relational systems or situations which obtained

---

[43] See Marie S. Dunn, "Marriage Role Expectations of Adolescents," *Marriage and Family Living*, 22:99–111 (May, 1960); and Alvin Moser, "Marriage Role Expectations of High School Students," *Marriage and Family Living*, 23:42–43 (February, 1961).

[44] See Robert F. Winch, *Mate Selection* (New York: Harper & Row, Publishers, 1958).

[45] Waller, *op. cit.*, p. 285.

in their own earlier family groups." [46] The reaction to such role playing may cause tensions in the family. One husband said:

> "I'm naturally a 'Little Caesar.' I want my way all the time. Mother has the 'old' idea of a husband's role in the house. She thinks the husband should be the lord and master of the household. I usually get my way by insisting strongly." [47]

A wife said this about her husband, who was critical of her housekeeping role:

> "His mother was a perfectionist as a housekeeper. I do the best I can. When he comes home he will rub his white handkerchief over the top of the piano. He will not believe me when I tell him that I dusted the room only that morning, and that the city is notorious for its smoke and dirt." [48]

ROLE CONFLICTS BETWEEN MARRIAGE AND OTHER ACTIVITIES

Role-playing difficulties may represent a conflict among family roles and those required in various outside activities. There may be a degree of incompatibility between the role of a man as a husband and father and the demands of his occupation, or between the role of a wife and mother and outside interests, whether connected with a job or social activities. These difficulties which the family faces in meeting other role demands have been accentuated in American society by an urban way of life. In some instances these numerous demands may not represent conflict so much as the necessity for playing too many different roles; that is, the behaviors required of different roles may not actually be incompatible, yet the necessity of shifting to several roles during each twenty-four-hour period may seriously impede a person's skill in the playing of a single role.

Even when certain goals and conceptions of roles to be played are decided upon, society may make them difficult to carry out. The goal of becoming a professional man is highly rewarded by society; yet it makes early marriage difficult. A community may feel that having two or three children is desirable; and yet in housing and participation in social life it often rewards those without children. Parents may feel that their children have too much freedom; yet they offer them little "controlled" recreational facilities and permit commercial establishments to fulfill their recreational needs. A wife and husband may agree on the roles each is to play—for instance, companionship roles—but for economic reasons

---

[46] Leonard S. Cottrell, Jr., "Roles and Marital Adjustment," *Publication of the American Sociological Society*, 27:107 (May, 1933). Also see Ernest W. Burgess and Leonard S. Cottrell, Jr., *Predicting Success or Failure in Marriage* (Englewood Cliffs, N.J.: Prentice-Hall, Inc., 1939).

[47] Burgess and Wallin, *op. cit.*, p. 628.   [48] *Ibid.*, p. 630.

move to a small rural town which does not approve such roles. Thus, even if there is agreement as to the roles to be played in marriage, societal frustrations may prevent their being performed. If in the marital situation there is a failure to accept alternative conceptions of roles and goals, the potential unity is not realized.

Society has established, for example, no definite status for the working wife. It is undecided whether to reward or punish her for her emancipated form of living, especially the working wife in the middle classes.[49] As a result of his reaction to the uncertainty of others and the internal uncertainty he has learned, the husband is often ambivalent about his wife's working, particularly when it is not necessary. When the woman works from necessity there may be other difficulties in her role in the marriage.[50] This situation may be especially acute when the family lives in a community where many of the wives do not work. One study of married veterans on a college campus found that the employment status of wives was the most significant difference in the roles of husband and wife. The women who worked full time tended to have authoritarian conceptions of marriage, whereas those who worked only part time leaned toward the companionate conception of marriage.[51]

Differences about the need for children are reflections of conflict in the role playing of husband and wife. The husband may be influenced by his image of the traditional family, with the satisfactions derived from having many children around the house. If the woman has an occupation in which she is interested she may not want to give up her position in order to raise children. The man, on the other hand, may not want the obligation and expense which children bring.

ROLE CONFLICTS BETWEEN PARENTS AND CHILDREN

There may be conflicts between the roles of children and parents. Such conflicts have been intensified by the democratic and individualistic training now given children in an urban world, training which increases the adolescent conflict with a generation having different values and a different conception of the family roles. It has become increasingly difficult to impose authoritarian traditions of the last century on children of the present generation:

---

[49] See Riesman, "Permissiveness and Sex Roles," *loc. cit.*, for a discussion of how younger persons incorporate these societal attitudes toward their own working roles. See also Ginsberg, *op. cit.*, for a discussion of how, in salaries and status, society reflects a differential attitude toward male and female workers.

[50] See *Work in the Lives of Married Women* (National Manpower Council Conference; New York: Columbia University Press, 1958); and Lee Rainwater, Richard Coleman, and Gerald Handel, *Workingman's Wife: Her Personality, World, and Life Style* (New York: Oceana Publications, Inc., 1959).

[51] Motz, "Conceptions of Marital Roles by Status Groups," *loc. cit.*

"My mother is always picking on me or nagging at me constantly. I'm sure getting sick and tired of it all, but I realize that, if I ran away from home, I would never be able to live, dress, and eat as I do now. Besides, if I did go away, it would break my mother's heart, so I guess I will stick it out as long as possible. They never let me do what I want to do, so I do it anyway and tell them afterwards. Then it's too late to deprive me of my fun, and I can stand my punishment easily enough." [52]

Parents' expectations for their children frequently conflict with the children's desires. In an urban society children are often presented, through peers and others, with conflicting norms and values. As a result, younger persons may acquire attitudes which conflict with those of the parents, for the former have closer contacts with these emerging patterns and are more adaptable in learning them.[53]

ROLE CONFLICTS BETWEEN MARITAL PARTNERS
AND OTHER RELATIVES

Relations of members of a family to other relatives may be still another source of difficulty arising from role playing. In particular, the adjustment of satisfactory relationships with the "in-laws" of both families presents a difficulty in many marriages.[54] Patterns of respect for parents may conflict with the desire for freedom from them, and feelings of affection and obligation toward them may place the partner whose parent is in the home or living nearby in a peculiarly difficult position.

Family difficulties may start between parents and their son or daughter as the former attempt to continue or to reassume the familiar protective role. The presence of in-laws may magnify difficulties which would normally be temporary. Koos cites a case in which a wife's mother was taken into the husband's home. Trouble resulted because the mother immediately began to "side" with her daughter against the son-in-law in small matters which would have been resolved under other circumstances.[55] There is, consequently, an increasing tendency in America to escape involvement with parents and in-laws, as indicated by the plots of many of our motion pictures: "American films tend to picture both hero and heroine unbound by family ties. Homeless, in the main jauntily self-sufficient, they make their way through city streets, night clubs, lunch wagons, and hotel rooms until they find each other. . . . More than half of the heroes and half of

---

[52] Case document in Ernest W. Burgess and Harvey J. Locke, *The Family: From Institution to Companionship* (2d ed.; New York: American Book Company, 1960), p. 531.

[53] Kingsley Davis, "The Sociology of Parent-Youth Conflict," *American Sociological Review*, 5:523–535 (August, 1940).

[54] See Burgess and Wallin, *op. cit.*, pp. 603–608.

[55] Earl L. Koos, *Families in Trouble* (New York: King's Crown Press, 1946), p. 76.

the heroines have no relations. If they do have any, they are not likely to have more than one." [56]

Conflicts Involving Cultural Background and Interests

When members of a marriage or a family have backgrounds and social norms which are drastically different, this difference can be a source of a great deal of conflict and tension. In former rural societies in America, where the population within an area was quite homogeneous, an individual generally married someone who had grown up in the area and accepted the ideas and norms of the community. The marital situation offered little opportunity for a conflict of fundamental norms and values.

Conflicting definitions of the marital situation, and especially of the relation of the marital group to outside group activities, have developed within modern urban society. One study has shown that residence in rural areas during childhood is a favorable factor in marital adjustment, whereas residence in a city is unfavorable.[57] Moreover, spatial and vertical class mobility have increased the possibilities of the marriage of persons with diverse backgrounds and interests. Cultural differentiation appears to occur when a family or an individual goes up or down in the scale of occupation or of social class.

In a comparative study of happily married and divorced couples, Locke has pointed out the importance of agreement between marital partners on certain fundamental activities. He cites in particular the importance of always, or almost always, agreeing on "handling finances, recreation, religion, demonstration of affection, sexual relations, ways of dealing with in-laws, amount of time spent together, table manners, conventionality, and aims or objectives of the family." [58] These factors conform to common sense, for they refer to the general areas of interaction in marriage.

Similarity of family and cultural background is an important favorable factor in marital adjustment; a pronounced difference is unfavorable: "One may safely predict conflicts in a union where a rural person dominated by orthodox religious values and attitudes marries a cosmopolitan person characterized by unorthodox religious views and by Bohemian or other radical ideas and practices." [59] It has been suggested that marital adjustment is easier for persons who have similar social backgrounds, and that marriage stability and success is more probable if both partners are

---

[56] Martha Wolfenstein and Nathan Leites, *Movies: A Psychological Study* (New York: The Free Press of Glencoe, 1950), p. 101.

[57] Burgess and Cottrell, *op. cit.*, pp. 253–254.   [58] Locke, *op. cit.*, p. 85.

[59] Ernest W. Burgess and Harvey Locke, *The Family: From Institution to Companionship* (New York: American Book Company, 1945), p. 566.

from backgrounds with a strong set of values against divorce or other forms of disruption. Actually, the process of mate selection serves to bring together persons with similar backgrounds, for persons do tend in general to associate with, and to marry, others of similar social class, status, education, or religion.[60]

Some interests bind a marriage together, but others appear to have less effect. One study found that sports and games have little or no binding effect; friends, reading, and dancing have some effect; music, theater, and the church have considerable; and professional interests, active community service, and a common cause have great binding effect.[61] It is probable that agreement on a single factor or area of marriage interaction would not be of great significance in contributing to marriage success unless it were the outward expression of some more fundamental agreement —such as that concerning life values and goals.

Psychological Characteristics and Marital Interaction

The bulk of evidence on marital selection strongly suggests that similarity (or homogamy) of social characteristics is conducive to marital happiness and stability. Some have suggested, however, that whereas homogamous social characteristics may contribute to marriage stability, perhaps persons are happier if certain of their psychological characteristics are *not* alike, but "complementary." [62] Some feel that successfully married persons generally are those who have chosen partners whose traits tend to complement, at least emotionally, their needs. For example, as Winch has stated, aggressive persons sometimes appear to marry shy and retiring individuals:

> There is no evidence that persons with similar need patterns tend to marry. In the absence of evidence an explanation must depend upon theories of personality and of social psychology, and upon the implications of these theories. As we shall point out, there are strong theoretical reasons for believing that within the field of eligibles people tend to mate with those whose need patterns generally *complement* their own, rather than with those whose need patterns are *similar* to their own.[63]

In a test of this theory, Winch studied twenty-five married couples, all college undergraduates. The "needs" included dominance, submissiveness, receptiveness, and nurturance. "Nurturant" is the tendency or need to give support, aid, or care to a supposedly weak or helpless person. A

---

[60] Goode, *op. cit.*, pp. 525–526. For a partial bibliography of studies on "social homogamy" or common characteristics of marital partners, see Winch, *Mate Selection*, pp. 5–7.

[61] Burgess and Wallin, *op. cit.*, p. 442.   [62] Winch, *op. cit.*

[63] Robert F. Winch, *The Modern Family* (New York: Holt, Rinehart and Winston, Inc., 1952), p. 463. Italics added.

woman who behaves maternally toward her husband, whom she regards as a "little boy" needing to be looked after, would be nurturant. The following are Winch's complementary need types: Ibsenian (husband dominant and nurturant; wife receptive and submissive), Thurberian (husband nurturant and submissive; wife receptive and dominant), Master–Servant Girl (husband receptive and dominant; wife nurturant and submissive), and Mother-Son (husband receptive and submissive; wife nurturant and dominant).[64] Sixteen of the twenty-five couples could be classified satisfactorily in one of these types, with nine couples being exceptions.

At present the evidence on psychological characteristics does not definitely support the notion of either complementariness or of homogamy in mate selection. It is possible, of course, that there are general psychological characteristics and that some persons will be happier with mates who have dissimilar characteristics, whereas others would prefer mates with similar characteristics. The kind of mate a person seeks may depend upon his social background, which would tend to orient him toward one type of mate or another. It might be more appropriate to use the terms "expectations" or "role orientations," which clearly involve situational referents, rather than such static concepts as "trait" or "need." [65]

Terman has made one of the most complete and extensive studies of psychological factors in marital happiness.[66] It was based chiefly on the examination of the differences between 300 couples scoring high on the happiness index he used, and 150 who scored relatively low. More specifically, Terman found that one of the marital partners in an unhappy marriage is characterized by such symptoms as being grouchy, irritable, critical of others, dominative in relation to members of the opposite sex, and resentful of discipline. In general Terman found that happiness and emotional stability are closely related, though it is difficult to say which is the cause and which the effect.

There are a few studies which have attempted to "test" the consistency of psychological characteristics by obtaining couples' responses in many different situations. One study examined the characteristics "sympathy" (or empathy) and "adaptability," since previous researchers had suggested that positive marital adjustment was highly related to these factors. It was found that no general traits conforming to these factors could be observed. Instead, marital partners seemed to behave "sympathetically" or "adaptably," according to situational role demands. In some instances, it was found that the situation prescribed "sympathetic" role behavior

[64] Winch, *Mate Selection*, pp. 212–233.

[65] See Nelson N. Foote and Leonard S. Cottrell, *Identity and Interpersonal Competence* (Chicago: The University of Chicago Press, 1956).

[66] L. M. Terman, *Psychological Factors in Marital Happiness* (New York: McGraw-Hill Book Company, Inc., 1938).

for the wife, but not for the husband. In other situations, the role demands were reversed. These researchers concluded that the characteristics examined were not general factors, but that they must be interpreted in terms of situational norms governing sex roles.[67] Other studies have found no relation between marital happiness and personality characteristics, as measured on personality tests, such as the Minnesota Multiphasic Personality Inventory and the Edwards Personal Preference Scale.[68]

Social Participation and Marital Happiness

Since the family is a social group, one might well expect that the extent of social participation prior to marriage is related to marital happiness. According to some evidence, the number of friends, including those of the opposite sex, and the frequency of participating in social organizations are related to marital happiness.[69] The possession of many friends need not, of course, be related to marital happiness, but the presence of some satisfying relationships with other persons is probably a reflection of the manner in which an individual interacts with others. To the extent that a mode of interaction results in satisfying relationships prior to marriage it should also be conducive to later marital happiness.

Both American and British researchers have shown that the character of family friendship systems may contribute to marital stability or instability. In this case, it has been shown that it is not the number of friends which is significant so much as their similarity (in terms of values, goals, and so forth) to the particular family involved. Where friends of a family are similar, family disruption is much less frequent than when they are dissimilar.[70]

[67] Jack V. Buerkle, Theodore R. Anderson, Robin F. Badgley, "Altruism, Role-Conflict, and Marital Adjustment," *Marriage and Family Living*, 26:20–26 (February, 1961). For other studies relating to this, see Jack V. Buerkle and Robin F. Badgley, "Couple Role-Taking: The Yale Marital Interaction Battery," *Marriage and Family Living*, 21:53–58 (February, 1959).

[68] See Dorothy T. Dyer and Eleanor B. Luckey, "Religious Affiliation and Selected Personality Scores as They Relate to Marital Happiness in a Minnesota College Sample," *Marriage and Family Living*, 26:46–47 (February, 1961). See also Charles F. Bowerman and Barbara R. Day, "A Test of the Theory of Complementary Needs as Applied to Couples During Courtship," *American Sociological Review*, 21:602–605 (October, 1956).

[69] Burgess and Cottrell, *op. cit.*, and Locke, *op. cit.*

[70] See Bott, *op. cit.*, and Zimmerman and Cervantes, *op. cit.* The social characteristics referred to here included the proportion of kindred among the friend-families, the social backgrounds, as evidenced in region of origin, religion (ethical and moral views), income, and tastes. For further discussion of how the friend matrix of the family may operate as a means of social control, see Eugene Litwak, "Occupational Mobility and Extended Family Cohesion," *American Sociological Review*, 25:9–21 (February, 1960), and his "Primary Group Instruments for Social Control in Industrial Society: The Extended Family and the Neighborhood." Unpublished doctoral dissertation, Columbia University, New York, 1958.

Marital Happiness, Companionship, and the Sexual Relation

Some older studies have suggested that marital happiness and the degree of companionship in marriage were positively associated. One study reported marital happiness to be related to close association as demonstrated by always or nearly always talking things over, by joint participation in all or almost all outside activities, equality in accepting the judgments of the other, shared cultural activities, democratic relationships in making family decisions, and frequent kissing.[71] This shift in emphasis from a marriage based on status to one based on companionship is not easy, and the new emphasis has undoubtedly had a great deal to do with contemporary marital difficulties and divorce:

> First the right selection of a partner is much less easily accomplished for marriage as a companionship relation. Furthermore, the companionship marriage is sustained primarily by the happiness and satisfaction which husband and wife secure from it. If either partner concludes that the marriage is not offering these returns, divorce may be considered with the hope that another marriage may prove to be more rewarding.[72]

More recent investigations by both British and American sociologists have not supported the assertion that the degree of companionship in marital role relationships and happiness are necessarily correlated.[73] Instead, marital happiness occurs with about equal frequency in both the traditional and companionship types of marital role relationships. There was a tendency toward greater stability in the traditional type, and for expression of somewhat greater happiness.

Sexual incompatibility may in some cases create tensions in the marital relationship and may even contribute to the possibility of extramarital relationships. Burgess and Wallin conclude that "the problem of sexual maladjustment appears to spring most often from a divergence between husbands and wives in their attitudes to sexual intercourse and the frequency of their desire for it," with women more likely to have a negative attitude and to desire sexual relations less frequently.[74] Terman's findings indicate that such incompatibility is mainly expressed through the orgasm capacity of the wife and lack of similarities in sexual drive. He found that the orgasm capacity and similarities in sexual drive are correlated highly with marital happiness, whereas little or no correlation is reported for frequency of coitus, reported duration of coitus, or use of contraceptive techniques.[75]

An Indiana study found the following attitudes favorably related

---

[71] Locke, op. cit., pp. 266–267.

[73] See, for example, Bott, op. cit.

[75] Terman, op. cit., pp. 372–373.

[72] Burgess and Wallin, op. cit., p. 30.

[74] Burgess and Wallin, op. cit., p. 695.

to satisfying sexual relations: [76] the same degree of interest in sex; the rating of sex relations as enjoyable by men and enjoyable by women; rare or infrequent refusal of intercourse when mate desired it; no desire for intercourse with others during the marriage; no belief, knowledge, or suspicion that mate has had intercourse with others during marriage; no fear of pregnancy; and no jealousy on the part of mate if the other danced, talked, or associated with members of the opposite sex.

The relation of sexual enjoyment to marital difficulties is sometimes close and at other times remote. Sexual factors in marriage appear to affect men and women differently. An unsatisfying sexual relationship is more likely to affect the views of men about the success of the marriage, whereas with women there may be a low or a high degree of marital success regardless of the quality of the sexual relationship. Burgess and Wallin found that women enter marriage with a low sexual expectation, or that their sexual response may be a more general, rather than specific, expression of affection for the husband. Among men there are high sexual expectations, with the sexual factor being dependent on the wives' sexual expression. It is likely, of course, that marital happiness is the "cause" of sexual compatibility, rather than the reverse, as many have supposed.[77]

Sexual factors probably never operate in isolation and rarely of themselves break down a marriage. Burgess and Cottrell, as well as Terman, found that sexual difficulties were secondary expressions of conflicts arising from personality and cultural factors. Terman concludes that "sex factors combined are far from being the one major determinant in marriage." [78] Burgess and Locke concluded that "the sex factor was secondary to personality and cultural factors in influencing marital adjustment." [79] When sexual difficulties do seem to be a primary cause they may be an expression of tensions diffused from other conflicts or unresolved differences concerning the way each believes other conflicts should be settled. Burgess and Wallin found that "sexual adjustment can . . . be treated as being, to a large extent, an effect or a reflection of success in other areas of the marriage relationship." [80]

Economic Problems and Marital Stability

Contrary to many statements of married couples, economic factors do not appear to be the real reasons for disturbances in family unity. The

---

[76] Locke, *op. cit.*, pp. 156–157.

[77] Goode, "Family Disorganization," in Merton and Nisbet, *op. cit.*, pp. 433–434. Goode suggests that sexual expectations of persons entering marriage are probably not as great as they were following the decline of Victorianism and the emancipation of women. He suggests that young people today are better prepared for sex in marriage, and that their expectations are likely to be more realistic.

[78] Terman, *op. cit.*, p. 373.   [79] Burgess and Locke, 2d ed., *op. cit.*, p. 437.

[80] Burgess and Wallin, *op. cit.*, p. 696.

economic relationship, like the sexual relationship, is secondary in comparison with other factors, such as social roles, cultural backgrounds, social participation, and affection. The attitude of the marital partner toward economic factors appears to be dependent upon other factors.

Burgess and Cottrell found these economic factors related to marriage stability: (1) those occupations which tended to require more stable personalities and little mobility, (2) employment of the wife before marriage, (3) moderate income, (4) regular employment of the husband before marriage, and (5) some savings.[81] The last two items, as has been indicated, are probably more expressions of certain social roles rather than merely economic factors. Burgess and Wallin state that a number of economic circumstances constitute a major adjustment difficulty in marriage including "the unemployment of husband, living within a small income, disposal of income, to save or not to save, and the wife working after marriage." [82]

As was previously stated, members of a family play more than one role. Often tensions engendered in other roles express themselves in the family relationship. The family is often a vehicle for tensions arising in other parts of the society. Business and industry, for example, may encourage "supervisor anxiety." [83] This anxiety is often carried home from the plant or office, and the marital partner may be used as a scapegoat.

Loss of earning power may also serve to create family tensions. Often a man's salary is part of the image a woman marries, and with a loss in earning power due to illness or depression, a part of this image disappears, weakening the affectional bond between the two members. Numerous studies have shown that both depressions and unemployment sometimes tend to increase family problems.[84]

Marital Stability and Social Structure

Throughout this chapter, it has been emphasized that the family unit is part of a larger social matrix. There are great differences in family structure by class, occupation, and ethnic and religious groups. There may also be marked differences in the family roles played by persons of different ethnic groups, religions, or occupations. A marriage counselor who is helping with any crisis situation in the family must be aware of them.

Catholics, Jews, Mormons, and Quakers, to cite but a very few, have different expectations and must be understood in terms of them. The concepts

[81] Burgess and Cottrell, op. cit., pp. 136–138.

[82] Burgess and Wallin, op. cit., p. 609.

[83] John J. Honigmann, "Culture Patterns and Human Stress: A Study in Social Psychiatry," Psychiatry, 13:25–34 (February, 1950).

[84] Ruth S. Cavan and Katherine Ranck, The Family and the Depression (Chicago: The University of Chicago Press, 1938).

of the good husband and good wife are variously defined by these groups, and the marriage counselor needs to know these definitions when dealing with members of these groups. For example, Jews, especially Orthodox Jews, tend to define the good husband more in terms of the good provider than do, let us say, the Quakers, who lay greater store by psychological factors. The counselor might minimize the importance of the economic function and instead emphasize, say, romantic roles. It is difficult for a Protestant Anglo-Saxon counselor to appreciate the weight attached to this economic factor by an Orthodox Jewish wife. The problem of the marriage counselor is made even more difficult by the fact that there are types of Jews, Quakers, Catholics, and so on. There are Orthodox Jews, Conservative Jews, and Reform Jews; and there is considerable variation within each subculture. Religion is, moreover, only one social factor among many and has to be viewed in the light of the total constellation of causes. . . . When we turn to the influence of occupational factors on family behavior, we note that members of different professions, even those belonging to the same social class, religion, and ethnic group, may define proper family behavior differently. For example, the college professor's wife usually expects her husband to spend more time with her than does the doctor's wife. The minister's wife is expected to help her husband with his work more than the doctor's wife or the college professor's wife. The requirements of the professional lead to different expectations.[85]

As the character of American society has changed during the past century, so has the nature of family life been altered. Patterns which were once well adapted to the former type of society have become a source of marital conflict as ways of life have become more urbanized. As a result of the transfer of economic functions, the social and economic independence of women, and changes in the ideologies concerning marriage, the nature of the family has changed under urban conditions.

The modern urban family has lost many of its functions which formerly strengthened the unity of the group. The economic, religious, educational, and recreational functions of the family have diminished, and it has lost much of the protective functions with the development of various social services furnished by the state.

One of the greatest changes in family structure, brought about not only by the Industrial Revolution but by urban life, was the shift of economic functions from the family to other institutions. In contrast to the self-sufficient family of early rural America, the modern American family virtually produces nothing of its own. It now buys most of its clothes, household necessities, furniture, and various services. Most of its food is produced entirely outside the home and generally is even ready for serving. Thus the family has become primarily a consumption and distribution center, surrendering nearly all its productive functions to commercialized institutions. This function of consumption and distribution is important, however, and a failure to manage the family budget judiciously, especially

---

[85] Meyer F. Nimkoff, "Contributions to a Therapeutic Solution to the Divorce Problem: Sociology," in *Conference on Divorce*, p. 59.

in view of the numerous inducements to spend, may contribute to family instability.

> The family has become increasingly a unit of consumption, through which goods and services are purchased for money and within which they are consumed. Most of the making, canning, preserving, washing, clothes-making, and similar operations formerly performed by the family have been assumed by specialized agencies outside the home. Even the outside consumption of meals has increased in recent years, as evidenced by the growing number of restaurants, waiters and waitresses in proportion to the population as a whole. Bakeries and delicatessens have grown more rapidly than the population in recent decades.[86]

The religious activities of the family, which at one time included daily religious services at home, the saying of grace, and considerable religious instruction of the child, have been taken over by the Sunday school and the church. Training of the child in matters of moral conduct, hygiene, home economics, manners, and skills used to be done mainly in the family household. Beginning with five-year-old children, in most communities, these functions have increasingly been taken over by the school. The teacher has become the substitute parent in many ways. In school the young child is taught how to read and write, as well as how to get along with others, how to use a toothbrush, and how to do many other things formerly taught exclusively in the home: "The school has thus taken over those elements in the social heritage which relate to practical knowledge, in addition to those less utilitarian elements which are assumed to make life more meaningful. The relative importance of the home and the school in the broad function of education has undergone a considerable change, with the home perforce the loser." [87]

Recreation has also moved toward largely nonfamily and commercial types. The increase in leisure time in urban areas has been followed by more demands for recreational facilities and opportunities, and the marked differences in the recreational interests of the children and even of the husband and wife have resulted in more individualized recreation, often of a commercial nature. Many of the activities of family groups, such as motion pictures or television, offer little opportunity for communication and social interaction.

The family has been modified in this urban setting. This new family no longer operates as a separate economic unit, and its role as a socializing agent, including its educational, religious, and character-building functions, has diminished. In addition, the family has largely lost its ability to confer status on the individual by reason of his simply being a member of it; nor is status now as easily acquired by marriage into another family.

This change in the nature of the family has definitely represented seri-

---

[86] Andrew G. Truxal and Francis E. Merrill, *The Family in American Culture* (Englewood Cliffs, N.J.: Prentice-Hall, Inc., 1947), pp. 330–331.

[87] *Ibid.*, p. 351.

ous maladjustment to those who believe that the traditional functions of the family are its only real functions.[88] The traditionalists believe that it is necessary to reinstate many of these activities of the family so that it will be a large cohesive unit with a number of important functions, as it was in an agricultural economy.

Others regard these changes in the modern family as improvements because it is not the family as a functional unit which is important but rather the development of individual happiness.[89] If the position is taken that a new function, that of providing affection and companionship, is the chief integrative mechanism of the contemporary family, the loss of certain former functions does not constitute maladjustment but rather value conflicts over the success of the contemporary family and how it is achieving its new role.[90] Table 15.3 lists the distinctions between the former family of the rural type and the modern urban type:

Table 15.3. The Nature of Marriage

Former Rural Life Conditions	Modern Urban Life Conditions
1. Marriage a status of reciprocal rights and duties.	Marriage an interpersonal relation of compatibility.
2. Marriage largely arranged by parents (or by young people in accordance with parental standards of mate selection).	Freedom of young people in choosing a mate (ranging from predominance of romantic love to predominance of companionship as motives).
3. Separation of children and youth of the different sexes before marriage or only formal relations under strict chaperonage.	Increasing freedom of social relations before marriage with decline of parental supervision and control.
4. Love after marriage.	Love and companionship before marriage.
5. Emphasis upon the economic and legal aspects of marriage.	Stress upon the primacy of personal relations.
6. Evaluation of children as potential workers and economic assets.	Appreciation of children as persons and interest in their personality development.
7. Marriage relatively indissoluble.	Divorce resorted to if marriage regarded as failure.

SOURCE: Adapted from Ernest W. Burgess and Paul Wallin, *Engagement and Marriage* (Philadelphia: J. B. Lippincott Company, 1953), p. 31.

[88] Carle C. Zimmerman, *Family and Civilization* (New York: Harper & Brothers, 1947).
[89] Burgess and Locke, 2d ed., *op. cit.* and Joseph K. Folsom, *The Family and Democratic Society* (New York: John Wiley & Sons, Inc., 1947).
[90] For a discussion of the changes in the family, see Arthur W. Calhoun, *A Social History of the American Family* (New York: Barnes & Noble, Inc., 1945), and Zimmerman, *op. cit.*, pp. 610–634.

In general, the urban family has tended to become an affectional companionship and democratic unit. There is considerable evidence that the nature of interpersonal contacts of urban life results "in the urge to find love, affection, security and acceptance in a familial relationship." [91] One study of equalitarian, patriarchal or matriarchal patterns in family decisions, for example, found no significant difference in the relative dominance of husband and wife among the families of white professors, white skilled workers, Negro professors, and Negro skilled workers. Equalitarian patterns predominated in all of these groups. Nonworking wives, however, tended to be more dominant in decisions than working wives.[92] Some studies, however, have shown wide variations among social classes and occupational, educational, religious, and other groups. A British researcher, for example, found that the traditional type of marital role relationship was more frequent among working-class families, whereas the companionship type was more frequent among those of higher social status. Yet the correlation was not perfect, for the companionship type was observed in some working-class families, and the traditional type in some of higher social status.[93] "If both husband and wife are highly educated, they are likely to have a common background of shared interests and tastes, which makes a [companionship] relationship easier to conduct." [94]

Today in the United States there seems to be greater emphasis on what has been called the "romantic complex." [95] Probably the "romantic complex," which involves an emphasis on love and personal satisfaction as the sole justification for marriage, is in part a consequence of the decline of Victorianism occurring especially during the last half century.

Modern urban society has probably served to increase this romantic emphasis, because of the greater "individualism" of the family within the urban setting. As some have noted, the urban family is not necessarily "isolated," for members do retain many relationships with groups and families outside the family unit. But these groups and families are less likely, in the urban setting, to be connected or linked in some fashion with one another. Thus, although each group or family may exert control on some aspect of the family's activity, the social control of the entire family unit may be divided among many different sources. The result of this is that the urban family is often given greater freedom of individual choice and privacy in regulating its own activities. Hence, in cases such as these, marital partners are thrown more directly upon one another for emotional satisfaction and for carrying out family tasks. Yet this situation cannot be

[91] Winch, *Mate Selection*, p. 479.

[92] Russell Middleton and Snell Putney, "Dominance in Decisions in the Family: Race and Class Differences," *American Journal of Sociology*, 25:605–609 (May, 1960).

[93] Bott, *op. cit.*   [94] *Ibid.*, p. 112.

[95] Parsons, "The Social Structure of the Family," in Anshen, *op. cit.*

described as applying to *all* urban families. It merely appears that urban living increases the probability of its occurrence.[96]

Rather than being conceived of simply as a status relationship, the family is now coming to be regarded as a unit in which the roles of husband, wife, and children are companionship roles which emphasize the personal needs of all and are more nearly equal in the assumption of responsibilities. Moreover, the greater amount of social freedom given to each member is far different from that accorded in the traditional rural type of family. It is essentially a democratic orientation toward marriage, and involves equal participation in the privileges and obligations incurred in the family situation.

Summary

Divorce rates appear to have increased rapidly in Western society, although the rate varies greatly among different groups within a society. Most divorces occur early in marriage, the legal grounds for divorce being rarely the real reasons. A large proportion of divorced persons eventually remarry.

Role conflicts play a particularly important part in marital and family problems. They represent conflicts between marital partners over their duties and obligations; conflicts between family roles and roles outside the family; conflicts in the roles of the children, particularly with parents; and, finally, conflicts between marital roles and those of other relatives.

Conflicts of cultural background and interests are another area which may produce marital instability. Disagreements over values and goals in the marriage are the most significant. Similarities in norms are important in marital stability. The mutual expression of affection and satisfactory sexual relations are important factors in marital happiness. Sexual and economic difficulties in marriage appear, however, to be largely an expression of incompatibility in other areas of the marriage.

A new type of family which is more related to modern urban life is emerging. Although it has lost many of the economic, religious, educational, and recreational functions of the former rural family, the new urban family tends to be more democratic and puts more stress on affection and companionship.

Selected Readings

BOTT, ELIZABETH. *Family and Social Network*. London: Tavistock Publications Limited, 1957. A study of urban British families, which examines the relation-

---

[96] See Zimmerman and Cervantes, *op. cit.*; Litwak, "Occupational Mobility and Extended Family Cohesion," *loc. cit.*; and Talcott Parsons and Robert F. Bales, *Family, Socialization and Interaction Process* (New York: The Free Press of Glencoe, 1955), Chaps. 1 and 2.

ships between family roles and norms and the social matrix in which the family functions. The manner in which the social matrix acts as a medium of social control is thoroughly described.

BURGESS, ERNEST W., and LEONARD S. COTTRELL, JR. *Predicting Success or Failure in Marriage*. Englewood Cliffs, N.J.: Prentice-Hall, Inc., 1939. One of the major prediction studies in which difficulties in role playing are emphasized. A study of 526 Illinois couples primarily from Chicago. There is extensive case material.

BURGESS, ERNEST W., and HARVEY J. LOCKE. *The Family: From Institution to Companionship*. Rev. ed. New York: American Book Company, 1960. A comprehensive analysis of marriage and family relations emphasizing the shift from an authoritarian to a democratic family system.

BURGESS, ERNEST W., and PAUL WALLIN. *Engagement and Marriage*. Philadelphia: J. B. Lippincott Company, 1953. A detailed study of 1000 engaged and 600 married couples. In addition to statistical material there are numerous quotations from interviews and personal documents. The book also includes an extensive analysis of nearly all similar studies.

FOOTE, NELSON N., and LEONARD S. COTTRELL, JR. *Identity and Interpersonal Competence*. Chicago: The University of Chicago Press, 1955. An examination of family and marriage from a symbolic interactionist view. Theoretical issues in family study are discussed and a new approach to family research is suggested. Such concepts as "compatibility," "adjustment," "maladjustment," and many others are critically evaluated.

LOCKE, HARVEY J. *Predicting Adjustment in Marriage*. New York: Holt, Rinehart and Winston, Inc., 1951. A comparative study of divorced and happily married persons. In contrast to other studies which have generally studied college-educated persons, the sample is more representative of the general population.

WINCH, ROBERT F. *The Modern Family*. New York: Holt, Rinehart and Winston, Inc., 1952. An analysis of marriage and family relations with a sociopsychological emphasis. Chapter 15 deals with the theory of complementary needs.

ZIMMERMAN, CARLE C., and LUCIUS F. CERVANTES. *Successful American Families*. New York: Pageant Books, Inc., 1960. A study of over 9000 American families representing a cross section of social classes, ethnic and religious groups, and regions of the United States. The authors examine family friendship systems and find that the character of this system is one of the main determinants of family success or failure.

Chapter

16

Role and Status Conflict
in Old Age

The social roles of older people today are ambiguously defined. They have little place in our modern social structure, for there are few regular, institutionally sanctioned opportunities for full participation in an urban society. There is conflict between the role aspirations of older people and the actual role accorded them by our contemporary society. In this sense their difficulties in role adjustment are similar to those of the adolescent. Among both groups there is often a feeling of not being useful, participating members of society as well as a feeling that their desires are not fully recognized.

Age and aging have been defined in various ways by different researchers. Some have regarded aging as a period of physiological deterioration; others have viewed it as simply the advancement of years, and still others have emphasized that aging involves a restriction on cultural roles.[1] What, then, is the nature of aging, and what does it involve?

Physiological Changes

Aging is accompanied by certain physiological changes which are not necessarily the result of any disease. There is generally cellular atrophy and degeneration, as well as the more readily observable aspects of graying hair, baldness, wrinkling of the skin, stiffness, and changes in bodily form. These general progressive changes due to age can be listed as follows:

1. Gradual tissue desiccation. Recent studies of electrolyte (salt) concentrations in the tissue cells have cast some doubt as to the reliability of older experiments which formerly appeared to have established gradual tissue drying as part of the aging process.
2. Gradual retardation of cell division, capacity of cell growth, and tissue repair. This involves also a decline in capacity to produce the products of secretion, whether they be known substances such as pepsin or thyroxine or the less well identified antibodies involved in immunity.

---

[1] Leonard Z. Breen, "The Aging Individual," in Clark Tibbitts ed., *Handbook of Social Gerontology* (Chicago: The University of Chicago Press, 1960), p. 147.

3. Gradual retardation of the rate of tissue oxidation (lowering of the speed of living, or, in technical terms, the metabolic rate).

4. Cellular atrophy, degeneration, increased cell pigmentation, and fatty infiltration.

5. Gradual decrease in tissue elasticity, and degenerative changes in the elastic connective tissues of the body.

6. Decreased speed, strength, and endurance of skeletal neuromuscular reactions.

7. Progressive degeneration and atrophy of the nervous system, impairment of vision, of hearing, of attention, of memory, and of mental endurance.

8. Gradual impairment of the mechanisms which maintain a fairly constant internal environment for the cells and tissues (a process known as homeostasis). It is evident that sufficient weakening of any one of the numerous links in the complex processes of homeostasis produces deterioration.[2]

These physiological criteria, however, must be properly interpreted, for they cannot be applied to all members of a given age group, such as some chronological age like sixty-five. No longer is the concept of aging based on "an assumption of general organic, functional and psychological deterioration beginning in middle life and proceeding rather rapidly until it becomes disabling and finally incapacitating." [3] Physiological aging is a gradual process which varies tremendously among individuals. Contrary to popular opinion, for example, sexual activity does not suddenly decline among males, for the decline is so gradual that it is not until the late seventies or eighties that there is complete impotency, and exceptions occur even then. In some activities one function may decline while another increases, as in the case of physical speed as contrasted with endurance.[4] Some have expressed the view that the physiological changes associated with age are not significant unless they affect either the older person's ability to maintain relationships with others, or unless they alter his appearance in such a way as to affect society's judgment of him.[5]

The physiological deterioration of the aged is real in some cases, but it has probably been overemphasized for the total group. There is no question that certain conditions, such as heart disease and cancer, increase with age. For the year 1958, heart disease caused 747 deaths per 100,000

---

[2] Anton J. Carlson and Edward J. Stieglitz, "Physiological Changes in Aging," *The Annals*, 279:22 (January, 1952).

[3] Clark Tibbitts and Henry D. Sheldon, "Introduction: A Philosophy of Aging," *The Annals*, 279:6 (January, 1952). See also Breen, in Tibbitts, *op. cit.*, p. 146, and Hans Selye, "The Philosophy of Stress," in Clark Tibbitts and Wilma Donahue, *Aging in Today's Society* (Englewood Cliffs, N.J.: Prentice-Hall, Inc., 1960), p. 118.

[4] For example, the records for the 100-yard and 220-yard dashes are held by men from eighteen to twenty-two years of age, but the records for the long grind of the marathons are held by men between thirty-eight and forty-five.

[5] Robert W. Kleemeier, "Behavior and the Organization of the Bodily and the External Environment," in James E. Birren ed., *Handbook of Aging and the Individual* (Chicago: The University of Chicago Press, 1959), pp. 400–447.

persons between the ages fifty-five and sixty-four years; the cancer deaths for this age group were 392 for the same base population.

Chronological age is an unsatisfactory criterion for "old age" because of the great individual variation in the rate of physiological aging. Some people are relatively young at seventy or older, whereas some are quite aged physically at fifty. Some men have children in their eighties, some play golf in their eighties; Bernard McFadden, for example, made a parachute jump when he was over eighty. Many farmers past seventy can outwork a younger man in the field. As Stieglitz has pointed out, one of the more important concepts in the study of aging is that "physiologic age or biologic age is not the same as chronologic age. . . . Often biologic age is greater than chronologic age; sometimes it is less." [6] The attitude toward chronological age is well expressed by an eighty-year-old retired Army officer who had volunteered at the age of seventy for Army service and was rejected because of age.

> Comes 1942 and World War II. I still held a hold-over commission as Captain in the United States Army, inactive reserve. I wrote a letter to the powers that be at the War Department asking that I too may be ordered to active duty. Come back instructions to present myself to the regular Army examining board in session at Fort Sheridan, Illinois for complete and final examination for active duty. . . . Could not imagine why I seemed to be the main attraction there, but I later learned that it was due to my age, only 70 and that I made the various tests with flying colors. I did not feel a day older than I did when I first enlisted in the Army 48 years ago. At the conclusion of the exam the commanding officer had me call at his office to congratulate me on the almost perfect score, and asked me the question asked me several times that day. This usually was, "What do you do to keep in such perfect physical trim?"
>
> Now I waited from day to day hoping, with each mail, to receive that order directing me to report to the commanding officer at so and so for active duty. But alas a letter came OK but it simply said that my physical condition was quite perfect but that due to my age I would not be allowed to serve my country. A nice letter of appreciation was enclosed. Thus ended my military career forever. Again I had the pain of completely separating myself from the military service. I have discovered this. That as we age we do not feel our hurts, both physical or emotional pains, as keenly as we do in our younger days. This is because we are no longer as much alive. It is a melancholy fact that man begins to die the day he is born.[7]

It is clear that physiological age is not determined wholly by chronological age, but that these two variables are partially independent. Yet physiological deterioration alone does not define aging, for in addition

---

[6] Edward J. Stieglitz, *The Second Forty Years* (Philadelphia: J. B. Lippincott Company, 1946), p. 10. See also Selye, "The Philosophy of Stress," in Tibbitts and Donahue, *op. cit.*

[7] From a personal document.

there must be a societal reaction to such deterioration which defines it as symptomatic of aging. When a person's bodily functions become altered to such an extent that he begins to "look" old, the chances are great that he will increasingly withdraw from groups with which he has been formerly associated.[8] To the extent that he does withdraw, his social and psychological adjustment will be affected, and he will validate society's judgment of a relationship between chronological age and deterioration. Shock has further clarified the relationship between the behavioral and physiological aspects of aging. Although aging brings bodily changes such as a gradual "loss of cells," these changes do not account for the sudden behavioral changes or "breakdowns" noted in older persons following such events as retirement or widowhood. The latter are "imposed by society." [9]

Psychological Changes

Psychological changes in aging relate to differences in sensory and motor functions, learning ability, memory, and to changes in performance on intelligence tests.[10] Sensory and motor functions of the aged show some marked differences. Hearing difficulties, particularly for the higher tones, increase with age, and there is less visual acuity where there is speed and poor contrast or dim illumination. Motor responses requiring speed generally decline. In fact, soon after maturity there is a decline in the swiftness of dealing a blow, in simple reaction time, and in strength of grip. Older persons generally may not be as fast in a given task, but they make fewer errors than younger persons. If an older person has retained his mechanical skill, however, he may be able to keep up with the speed of younger workers. A number of studies have shown that older persons are more expert at tasks which stress accuracy rather than speed.

There is some uncertainty about changes in learning abilities with old age. It would seem that learning *speed* declines slowly past the age of thirty and more rapidly past the age of fifty. However, studies in learning *power*, i.e., grasp or comprehension, show that it declines at a much slower rate, with some persons showing no apparent decline even in their eighties.[11] It is difficult to draw definite conclusions because of the artificial nature of many of the experiments on speed of learning and age. According to Kaplan, the continuance of an occupation or interest and motivation probably affect learning ability a great deal.[12] One of the primary dif-

[8] Breen, "The Aging Individual," in Tibbitts, *op. cit.*, p. 152.

[9] Radio address by Nathan W. Shock, Director of the Michigan Institute of Gerontology, in a radio address on "Aging," June 20, 1961, University of Wisconsin Station WHA.

[10] Oscar J. Kaplan, "Psychological Aspects of Aging," *The Annals*, 279:32–42 (January, 1952).

[11] Irving Lorge, "Intellectual Changes during Maturity and Old Age," *Review of Educational Research*, 17:326–332 (1947).

[12] Kaplan, *loc. cit.*, pp. 35, 36.

ficulties in drawing conclusions from studies dealing with the relationship of age and learning stems from the fact that factors such as motivation, speed of performance and physiological status are intimately correlated with age, and exert a definite influence on learning task performance.[13]

Loss of memory, particularly the ability to recall present events, is often part of the popular characterization of the aged. Unfortunately, the evidence is not too clear on the extent of this loss. In Kaplan's words, these memory changes appear to "vary with the complexity of the task, loss being smallest on simple memory tests such as one dealing with visual memory for digits. There is a tendency for those of superior intelligence to sustain less memory loss than those who are mentally dull." [14] Since memory is related to personality, the role of motivation should play an important part. The decline on memory tasks may be due to perceptual speed in "grasping" the material to be recalled, rather than to an actual "loss" of memory.[15] There is no evidence that loss of memory is essentially a biological function.

At present, no definite conclusions can be drawn from studies dealing with the relationship of intelligence test performance and aging. In general, these studies have shown lowered performance with aging, yet this decline is particularly prominent on those test items which require visual acuity and motor agility.[16] This would suggest that the apparent intellectual deterioration of the older person may be partially due to sensory impairment rather than to decline of intelligence. Moreover, the lowered performance of the older person may be partially due to changes in schooling that have taken place and that may make him less able to perform at a high level on present-day intelligence tests. Also the older person may not be interested in the items on an intelligence test, and thus not be motivated to respond to them.[17] In addition, the speed factor, which is involved in all intelligence tests, creates a handicap for the older person.

Changes in Social Roles and Status

Neither the physiological nor the psychological characteristics of old age seem adequately to explain the differences in the status and role of older persons in various types of societies. Likewise, they do not sufficiently explain the difficult adjustment problems of older persons in contemporary society. Actually old age is a sociological process which is only partly de-

---

[13] Edward A. Jerome, "Age and Learning—Experimental Studies," in Birren, *op. cit.*, p. 696.

[14] Kaplan, "Physiological Aspects of Aging," *loc. cit.*

[15] Harold E. Jones, "Intelligence and Problem-Solving," in Birren, *op. cit.*, p. 732.

[16] George K. Bennett, "Relationship of Age and Mental Test Scores among Older Persons," in Clark Tibbitts and Wilma Donahue eds., *The New Frontiers of Aging* (Ann Arbor: University of Michigan Press, 1957), 153–157.

[17] Jones, "Intelligence and Problem-Solving," in Birren, *op. cit.*, p. 722.

termined by age; yet it occurs in the middle years in other cases. As a sociological concept, it may be regarded as "that point in an individual's life at which he ceases to perform all those duties, and enjoy all those rights, which were his during mature adulthood, when he begins to take on a new system of rights and duties." [18] This new system of rights and duties, or the status and role of the older person, is largely determined by the societal definitions of the nature of age and of the older person. From this point of view, aging is understood and interpreted "in terms of the behavior characteristics of persons designated by the society as aged." [19] The adjustment of the older person, which is the degree to which his behavior corresponds to the societal role expectations, depends upon the clarity with which his roles are defined, the compatibility of the roles, the degree of preparation for assuming the roles, the consistency with which other persons allow them to play these roles, and the extent to which motivations of older persons can be realized.

The process of sociological aging does not arbitrarily begin at any set age. Unlike chronological and biological aging, which takes place fairly continuously throughout life, sociological aging varies with societal definitions of age and the responses of individuals to changed age status. In this sense, chronological and physiological age are independent of the societal reaction, whereas sociological age is not. Thus, the aged person may not regard himself as aged, as was indicated when 499 men and 759 women, whose median age was 73.5 and 71.7, respectively, were asked whether they considered themselves middle-aged, elderly, old, or aged.[20] Only a small proportion regarded themselves as "old" or "aged." About half the men defined themselves as middle-aged, and in the age group sixty to sixty-four, two thirds put themselves in this category. In fact, not until they reach the seventies do most men and women have a conception of themselves as elderly. One woman in her eighties remarked, "I feel old only when I look at myself in the mirror."

Several factors account for the lowered status and undefined role of the aged. In a sense it is the result of urbanism, with its rapid social change and the tendency to emphasize youth and activity. Urbanized societies seem to regard older persons as having already had their turn at living and experiencing the gratifications of life. Old people no longer have the claim on kin for role, support, and social participation that they formerly did. Rarely is their advice given consideration, even if proffered, because their experiences and values are often out of line with those of the modern urban world. Some have therefore described the fundamental problem

---

[18] B. Hutchinson, *Old People in a Modern Australian Community* (Melbourne: Melbourne University Press, 1955), p. 1.

[19] Breen, "The Aging Individual," in Tibbitts, *op. cit.*, p. 149.

[20] Robert J. Havighurst, "Social and Psychological Needs of the Aging," *The Annals*, 279:16–17 (January, 1952).

of the aged as involving role transition to a socially nonfunctional role which is only ambiguously defined.[21]

In an urban society as a whole, and in the family group as well, the aged are often marginal people. The smaller family unit no longer has a place for the aged person, for the modern democratic family is organized around the interests, wishes, and activities of its young and active members, who are more highly valued in the urban culture. The older persons may be pampered, protected, or left to their own devices, but rarely are their wishes given equal consideration with those of others.

In urban areas today "what was good enough for father is not good enough for me." Present-day vertical class mobility has meant that the son may acquire more material goods, education, and status than his father had. The older person is thought to have lost his close touch with the dynamic occurrences and changes in everyday existence and undoubtedly he has to some extent. But this depends, of course, upon the older person himself. In times of rapid social change, each generation, in a sense, becomes a sort of subculture with its own set of values and motivations. This situation creates social distance between age groups. In rural communities social change is less rapid, and there is less friction between generations. The old person has met most of the problems which his progeny face. This picture is often reversed, however, in urban areas, where the tempo of life is so accelerated that an older individual has increased difficulty adapting to the pace. New norms are constantly appearing, and what mother said ten years ago about the "correct" way to bring up children, handle money matters, and run the household is often almost as dated as last year's top tunes. At the same time, attitudes and patterns of behavior are often extremely rigid among older persons. Habits are difficult to alter at any time in life, but this statement is especially true of old age.

This general characterization of the status of older people is by no means equally applicable to all classes or to all occupations, for there are many individual exceptions. The tendency for older persons to play a reduced status role is undoubtedly greater among the lower socioeconomic groups than among the upper classes, whose position and wealth continue to give them status even into advanced age. Likewise, in certain professions, such a law and medicine, an elderly person may even have increased status.

Many immigrants to America, in particular, have experienced conflicts upon reaching later maturity. With their predominantly rural back-

---

[21] See B. S. Phillips, "A Role Theory Approach to Adjustment in Old Age," *American Sociological Review*, 22:212–217 (1957), and H. L. Orbach and D. M. Shaw, "Social Participation and the Role of the Aging," *Geriatrics*, 12:241–246 (1957). For a discussion of a general theory of role change see Arnold M. Rose, *Theory and Method in the Social Sciences* (Minneapolis: University of Minnesota Press, 1954), p. 23. Also see the section on old age in S. Kirson Weinberg, *Social Problems of Our Time* (Englewood Cliffs, N.J.: Prentice-Hall, Inc., 1960).

ground, they have a heritage of strong family ties and high status for the aged. Not receiving the status and care which their early training led them to anticipate in their old age, they feel resentful and neglected. Old age often becomes a trying existence for them, especially because of the difficult relations with their children.

The basic difficulty seems to be the conflict between the behavior patterns which older people are supposed to display in urban society and the aspirations of older persons themselves.[22] They still have the same wishes and motivations as other persons for response, recognition, security, and new experience; yet there is increasing evidence that contemporary urban society and the newer rather undefined cultural definitions of the status and role of the aged are unsatisfactory to them and their peer generation. Consequently, personal adjustment among the aged appears to be the exception.

In modern society old age has become associated with a feared loss of physical attractiveness. Strenuous efforts are made to preserve this physical attractiveness on the assumption that to most people "to look young is to be young." Some observers have remarked that styles of clothing and other apparel are geared primarily to the youthful and not to the older person. Havighurst has recognized this fear in his discussion of the social and psychological needs of the aged person.

> Most of us, men as well as women, learn to place a high value upon our beauty and our strength. At the very least, we value highly our physical and mental vigor, our ability to do a hard day's work. In addition, most of us value our manliness or womanliness—the things that make us attractive to the other sex. Against these values the advancing years wage war. They rob a woman of her ability to have children, usually before she is fifty. Many women interpret this as a sign that they have lost much of their worth as women. Men do not fare much better. Already in their forties most of them lose much of their hair, grow fat in awkward places, and have to wear bifocal glasses. Both sexes lose the smooth skin that they value highly as a sign of youth. Then as the years go on, there is a real decrease of enjoyment of the physical aspects of love between the sexes, and finally the external sense organs of hearing and sight begin to lose their acuity.
>
> These insults to the self usually strike us in vulnerable places. We express it by saying that we do not like to grow older—but what we really mean is that we have invested a great deal of emotional capital in our physical attractiveness, and this investment is going bad on us.[23]

---

[22] Ruth S. Cavan, Ernest W. Burgess, Robert J. Havighurst, and Herbert Goldhamer, *Personal Adjustment in Old Age* (Chicago: Science Research Associates, Inc., 1949), pp. 18–29.

[23] Robert J. Havighurst, "Social and Psychological Needs of the Aging," *The Annals*, 279:11 (January, 1952). Reprinted by permission of *The Annals* of the American Academy of Political and Social Science. Whereas there has been intensive study of physiological changes associated with aging which affect bodily form and appearance, the effect of

One study found that a large proportion of older persons had feelings of unhappiness which seemed, on the whole, to increase as they grew older.[24] Older people vary considerably, however, in their responses to their changing situations. Riesman has suggested three different responses.[25] There are those who have psychological resources of self-renewal, lose little of their ability to enjoy life, and are relatively independent of the attitudes of the larger society. The majority have few resources of self-renewal, but at the same time do not decay because of their previous attitudes derived from work and other activities. Their adjustment, however, can be disturbed by a considerable change in their social situation. Others have neither inner resources nor the background of adequate social experiences and simply decay with old age and its problems. Which of these responses an individual makes seems to depend upon his past experiences and the social context surrounding transition to the aged role.

EMPLOYMENT AND OLD AGE

Work has more function and meaning than simply a source of income.[26] It also represents an expenditure of time and energy devoted to doing something and thus helps to prevent boredom. Work provides identification and status through a definition of role and a way of achieving recognition or respect from others. Association with others at work means having friends and contacts with members of one's peer or age group generation. According to the nature of the work, it may provide a source of meaningful life experience through creativity, new experience, or service to others. The findings of some recent studies have shown that work in American society has lost some of its function as a central life activity, and that its value has shifted somewhat from being an end in itself to a means.[27] Yet these studies also show that work continues to be a primary focus of self-identification and role conception. These latter factors may

---

these changes on the self-concept of the aged has not been studied.—Kleemeier, "Behavior and the Organization of the Bodily and the External Environment," in Birren, *op. cit.,* pp. 413, 447. Kleemeier poses the following questions for future research: What is the relationship of body size, self-concept, and acceptance of age roles? Are small size and youth associated in the formation of "age stereotypes"? Do body form and size affect adjustment to aging? Is selection of clothing related to these variables?

[24] Cavan *et al., op. cit.,* pp. 58–59.

[25] David Riesman, "Some Clinical and Cultural Aspects of Aging," *American Journal of Sociology,* 59:379–384 (January, 1954).

[26] Eugene A. Friedmann and Robert J. Havighurst, *The Meaning of Work and Retirement* (Chicago: The University of Chicago Press, 1954), pp. 1–9.

[27] See Robert Dubin, "Industrial Workers' Worlds," in E. Larrabee and R. Meyersohn eds., *Mass Leisure* (New York: The Free Press of Glencoe, 1958), pp. 215–228; David Riesman, "Leisure and Work in Post-Industrial Society," in Larrabee and Meyersohn, *op. cit.,* pp. 363–385; R. S. Weiss and R. L. Kahn, "On the Definition of Work among American Men" (Mimeographed; Ann Arbor: University of Michigan, Institute for Social Research, 1959).

explain why loss of work, as occurs at the time of retirement, is associated with problems of adjustment.

Many workers look forward to the time when, at sixty-five, there will be no more clock punching, when they can engage in activities of their choice or travel if they wish. Retirement, however, may not be a pleasant experience, even when social security or retirement payments are adequate.[28] For a person who has worked eight or more hours a day, five or six days a week, for thirty or more years, enforced idleness and the loss of opportunities to use developed skills often produce a crisis situation. Such an individual finds himself with little to do that is constructive, day in and day out; he has lost many companions, particularly those with whom he has worked; and with the additional loss of other social contacts he becomes bored and lonely. New habits must be developed, and this is difficult at any age. Just as students often soon tire of long-awaited summer vacations and wish for a return to the "grind" or routine of the college year, so the older person may at first be delighted by the "vacation," but in time fervently desires to return to some socially useful role. Riesman suggests that it is not work, but having a job, which is important to the individual.[29] Many authorities are now of the opinion that the concept of "retirement" is perhaps unfortunate and that most persons should be retained indefinitely at some work, even in an industrial society.

Older people without jobs need more than just leisure or a satisfactory income. As important, from the standpoint of personal and social adjustment, as the loss of employment or household duties is the loss of certain social roles which a person has played during the greater part of his mature life. A person's job determines many of his extrafamilial associations, and may offer opportunities for satisfaction of needs not met within the family. For men, earning a living is regarded in our society as the most appropriate mode of life. The job is the basis of status in the eyes of the family and associates. It is also a source of reference groups which come to function as an anchor of self-identity.[30] Thus, when they are unable to maintain an independent existence in an urban society, the aged tend to lose self-respect. They are often forced to relinquish authority in the family because they no longer contribute to its economy. If they live with their children, the latter often become head of the households, and the older persons no longer, as they once did, have the status of head of an economic unit. Since the aged person seldom owns a farm or other property of consequence he cannot maintain status through the possibility of transmitting it. Thus, for a man or woman who has always been a self-

[28] Clark Tibbitts, "Retirement Problems in American Society," *American Journal of Sociology*, 59:301–309 (January, 1954).

[29] Riesman, "Leisure and Work in Post-Industrial Society," in Larrabee and Meyersohn, *op. cit.*

[30] Wilma Donahue, Harold L. Orbach, and Otto Pollak, "Retirement: The Emerging Social Pattern," in Tibbitts, *Handbook of Social Gerontology*, p. 377.

470 Role and Status Conflict in Old Age

supporting, solid citizen, old age may become a fate often to be feared rather than anticipated.

The role of the retired old person is especially difficult where no other roles carrying equal status are available. The loss of the social function, through loss of jobs and forced or voluntary retirement, usually brings with it lowered social status and a diminution of self-esteem. Where the individual has been prepared to accept the new status, however, and has developed hobbies, interests, and a new and self-embracing image to fit the new roles and status, the situation may be different.

One of the most striking differences between rural society and an urban industrial economy is the fact that many of the urban aged are not gainfully employed. Although the proportion of those sixty-five years and over has increased greatly since 1890, by 1954 there was a marked reduction in the proportion employed. (See Table 16.1.) In 1890, 68.2 percent

Table 16.1. Percentage of Population Aged 45 Years and over in the Labor Force, 1890–1954

Age and Sex	1890 (June)	1900 (June)	1920 (June)	1930 (April)	1940 (April)	1950 (April)	1954 (Nov.)	1975 (est.)
Males								
45–54	93.9	92.8	93.5	93.8	92.7	91.7	96.7	94.6
55–64	89.0	86.1	86.3	86.5	84.6	82.9	88.8	82.3
65 and over	68.2	63.2	55.6	54.0	42.2	41.6	40.6	35.3
Females								
45–54	12.5	14.2	17.9	19.7	22.4	33.0	42.8	52.2
55–64	11.5	12.6	14.3	15.3	16.6	22.8	31.8	35.4
65 and over	7.6	8.3	7.3	7.3	6.0	7.6	9.5	11.8

SOURCE: *Trends in Gerontology* by Nathan W. Shock, with the permission of the publishers, Stanford University Press. Copyright, 1951 and 1957, by the Board of Trustees of Leland Stanford Junior University. Data from John S. Durand, *The Labor Force in the United States, 1890–1960* (New York: Social Science Research Council, 1948), Bureau of the Census, *U.S. Census of Population 1950*, Preliminary Reports, Series PC-7, No. 2; Bureau of the Census, *Current Population Reports, Labor Force*, Series P-57, No. 149 (December, 1954).

of the men in this group were employed, as compared with 42.2 percent in 1940 and 40.6 percent in 1954. In 1954, 96.7 percent of the men between the ages of forty-five and fifty-four were employed. This figure declined some 10 percent by the ages fifty-five through sixty-four, and among those over sixty-five the proportion was nearly one half as great. Although social security and other retirement benefits have had something to do with this change, the explanation is actually much more involved.

The trend in the employment of older women has differed from that of older men. As noted in Table 16.1 there has been an increase from 14.2 in 1900 to 42.8 in 1954 in the percentage of females aged forty-five to fifty-four who were employed. For females aged sixty-five and over, there has been a slight increase in the number employed from 1900 to 1954, whereas for men of this same age group, the trend has been consistently downward.[31] Considerable changes take place in the occupational distribution among persons as they grow older. In 1959, industries which hired greater proportions of workers forty-five years of age and older were agriculture, finance, insurance, and real estate. Those hiring the lowest proportions were construction, manufacturing, and trade. However, the greatest proportions of older women are employed in trade and service industries.

Increasing unemployment among older persons in an urban industrial world results from many factors, including their numbers, changes in skills, the growing emphasis on youth, and compulsory retirement at an arbitrarily chronological age. Their employment difficulties do not arise primarily from mere physical impairments due to age. The emphasis on youth and the arbitrary retirement at a certain age are partly a reflection of the impersonality of modern urban life and the categoric contacts between large numbers of persons. It is possible today to shelve people arbitrarily, irrespective of a particular individual's physical, mental, and social qualities. Rather than adjusting work speed and capacity to older persons, society asks the older person to adjust to the machine. Methods in industry change so rapidly that an older worker who has not been retrained often finds himself at a distinct disadvantage when competing with a new worker. There is increasing evidence that older persons, if given a chance, can adjust much better to industrial work than society thinks they can, and that they often have qualities, such as conscientiousness, carefulness, and precision, which younger workers do not have. This situation differs from that in many rural societies, where the young must learn from the older men the traditional ways of doing things. At no time in history have the skills of the aged been so rapidly discarded as today in urban society.

The consequences of a reduced income or of unemployment go far beyond mere figures. Between 1948 and 1957, the money incomes of older persons increased, although their incomes tended to remain below those of persons in the age groups from twenty to sixty-four. For example, the median income for men of sixty-five and over rose from $998 in 1948 to $1421 in 1957, or by 42 percent. Although this increase was substantial, it was nevertheless smaller than the 54 percent increase in the median in-

---

[31] Fred Slavick and Seymour L. Wolfbein, "The Evolving Work-Life Pattern," in Tibbitts, *Handbook of Social Gerontology*, pp. 322–323.

come of all men for this same period. Comparable figures for women of sixty-five and over for this period are $589 in 1948, and $741 in 1957.[32] Of the approximately 14.1 million persons aged sixty-five and over in July, 1957, some 3.9 million were employed, with this the chief source of their income. Approximately 6.7 million, or 47.3 percent, were supported principally by Old Age and Survivors Insurance benefits. About 10 percent, or 1,400,000, reported no income, or income only from public social insurance programs, or from other than earnings.[33]

The amount of money received from various outside sources is actually so small that it by no means makes up for the loss of regular wages.[34] Monthly payments under the 1958 amendments to the Old Age and Survivors Insurance program, for example, were between $33 and $127 for a retired worker, aged sixty-five and over, and between $49.50 and $190.50 for a retired worker and his wife. Women qualified at sixty-two rather than at sixty-five, although at a reduced benefit.[35]

OLD AGE AND THE FAMILY IN AN URBAN SOCIETY

Aged persons in the United States live under a variety of different family situations. About one third of the men sixty-five and over are married, as contrasted with only 18 percent of the women, who were generally younger when they married and who tend to outlive their husbands. Some of the others who live with their children have satisfying relationships, whereas others do not. Likewise, some who live apart from their children are happy, others unhappy.[36] The old and the young may work out a mutually satisfying relationship in the family group, but these adjustments, if any, are usually made in spite of the difficulties imposed upon the unity of the family rather than because of them. The following case illustrates some of the difficulties faced by the old person in working out satisfactory family adjustments as well as the difficulties faced by the younger members in making this adjustment.

> There is the case of elderly Mrs. Snow, who had been born and brought up in the country in very humble circumstances. Always there had been enough in a way, so that she and her family had preserved their dignity by self-support, but with little or no margin. The mother always was the accepted

---

[32] Current Population Survey of the Bureau of the Census, as quoted by Margaret S. Gordon, "Aging and Income Security," in Tibbitts, *Handbook of Social Gerontology*, p. 209.

[33] John W. McConnell, "Aging and the Economy," in Tibbitts, *Handbook of Social Gerontology*, pp. 490–491, and pp. 502–503.

[34] For a discussion of this problem see John W. Corson and John W. McConnell, *Economic Needs of Older People* (New York: The Twentieth Century Fund, 1956). Also see Gordon, *loc. cit.*, Table 9, p. 224.

[35] Gordon, "Aging and Income Security," in Tibbitts, *op. cit.*, p. 233.

[36] Ernest W. Burgess, "Family Living in the Later Decades," *The Annals*, 279:110–112 (January, 1952).

head of the family, for the father and husband was not much of a manager, although he worked hard as a gardener on a large estate. After the death of her husband, Mrs. Snow had very little cash, just as all through her life. With no near relatives in the country who would or could have her with them, she came to the city to live with a married daughter. The latter did not quarrel with this plan because she accepted it as her duty, even though at the time her home was crowded, for not only did her own children live there but one son had married and brought his young wife into the home. The old lady, moreover, was handicapped by very poor eyesight as well as by unfamiliarity with the neighborhood and had to stay indoors most of the time.

Friction was inevitable, and yet Mrs. Snow's record in the country as a neighbor, a worker, and a mother was a creditable one. She was crude and simple, but sternly Puritanical in her attitude toward family life and the duty of one's children toward their own. After a fairly exhaustive study of the family needs, it was decided that the mother—or grandmother—faced what for her was a pretty hard situation, and that the family friction between generations was the direct result of very crowded living conditions and limited income. A final source of conflict was the widely divergent attitudes of the two and three generations, one from the country and one from the present-day city, toward family, moral and economic standards.

The daughter was genuinely anxious to do what could be done, but was torn between the so-called respectability of the old-age assistance grant for her mother, whose physical limitations made it hard for her to get along in the city, and residence in a home for the aged in the country where all their former friends and neighbors would know that she had "put her mother away." The mother finally decided the matter for herself by choosing the home in the country. There Mrs. Snow has found a certain measure of contentment, because she is in familiar surroundings, and there is a certain freedom of activity because of the fact that she is out of the city; but she has also proved herself to be a very stubborn old lady. Her daughter now admits reluctantly that her mother was always the one at home who "told everyone else what to do and when to do it" and the yielding habit is so strong with this daughter, herself now a grandmother, that she will make any sacrifice rather than raise an issue with her mother over anything at all.[37]

The urban housing situation often limits the inclusion of aged persons within the household. If a family living in an apartment, which usually has no more than two bedrooms, includes an old person, it has the effect of reducing the number of children or it necessitates living under crowded conditions. Under crowded conditions, widely separated generations do not make good adjustments unless there are strong ties between the individuals and a feeling of mutual responsibility. On the other hand, urban housing situations have often been used as rationalizations for not including the aged in the household when actually there are other reasons, such as the

---

[37] Ollie A. Randall, "The Older Person in the World of Today—In the Family," in George Lawton ed., *New Goals for Old Age* (New York: Columbia University Press, 1943), pp. 61–62. Reprinted by permission of the publishers.

desire to maintain an independent household. In fact, Moore maintains that there is considerable crowding in rural housing, as "not all rural families live in large, rambling dwellings where aged parents may be given a room and a corner in a spacious living room. The spacious dwelling unit is a rarity in rural as in urban communities; crowding is common in both." [38]

ROLE AND STATUS OF THE AGED IN NONURBAN SOCIETIES

The lower status of aged persons in urban society today is not dependent upon chronological or physiological age; rather, it is a reflection of the values of the culture. In many cultures older persons occupy positions of high status. In a study of a large group of folk societies, Simmons has reported that almost without exception older people have such an enviable position that, rather than fearing old age, many look forward to it.[39] Among certain groups, such as the Palaung of North Borneo, who attribute long life to a person's virtue in a previous existence, the aging years of life are regarded as the best.[40] Although this is partly a reflection of the fact that few of these people ever reach old age, even though it is chronologically defined as younger than it is in urban society, social values appear to play the leading role in the status of the old.

In folk societies the old person usually has a fixed role to play. Among folk societies he is likely to be the dominant member of the family group, controlling its property and acting as leader for the kinship group. In fact, among many groups, such as the Australian aborigines, older males have preference in the selection of younger women for wives. This, in turn, enables them more effectively to continue their hold on family ties. Even very old people have a place in the family and community life. There is seldom idleness, but rather always a feeling of being useful, no matter how small the task. The following excerpt describes how the Hopi Indians of northeastern Arizona regard their aged:

> Old men among the Hopi tend their flocks until feeble and nearly blind. When they can no longer follow the herd, they work on in their fields and orchards, frequently lying down on the ground to rest. They also make shorter and shorter trips to gather herbs, roots, and fuel. When unable to go to the fields any longer they sit in the house or kiva where they card and spin, knit, weave blankets, carve wood, or make sandals. Some continue to spin when they are blind or unable to walk, and it is a common saying that "An old man can spin to the end of his life." Corn shelling is women's work

---

[38] Wilbert Moore, "The Aged in Industrial Societies," in *The Aged and Society* (Champaign, Ill.: Industrial Relations Research Association, 1950), p. 36.

[39] Leo W. Simmons, *The Role of the Aged in Primitive Societies* (New Haven, Conn.: Yale University Press, 1945).

[40] Leo W. Simmons, "Social Participation of the Aged in Different Cultures," *The Annals*, 279:43 (January, 1952).

but men will do it, especially in their dotage. Old women will cultivate their garden patches until very feeble and "carry wood and water as long as they are able to move their legs." They prepare milling stones, weave baskets and plaques out of rabbit weed, make pots and bowls from clay, grind corn, darn old cloths, care for children, and guard the house; and when there is nothing else to do, they will sit out in the sun and watch the drying fruit. The old frequently express the desire to "keep on working" until they die.[41]

One of the most important roles that old people play in folk societies is that of being the leading person in knowledge and decision making. Where there is no writing the old become the source of knowledge about many specialized techniques, religious rites, ethics, and physical ailments. Medicine men and priests are almost always old people. In fact, aged persons who have special qualifications in knowledge, wisdom, and experience find many opportunities to use their influence in the more formalized ceremonies, magical rites, and religious practices. Often they officiate at such events as child naming, initiations, weddings, funerals, and memorial ceremonies.

Old men in folk societies also exercise great political power: "Political, judicial and civil preferments and positions are often also the normal outcome of such personal growth in the lifetime acquirements of knowledge, wisdom, and sound judgment. The titles and often the offices tend to be lifelong. Old men may serve long and well as lawmakers, judges, and administrators of justice. Moreover, as leaders in exclusive societies and in initiating rites, the aging quite generally exercise the powers of discrimination and receive considerable deference." [42]

Role and status problems connected with old age rarely exist in those areas of the world, such as India, and many parts of Asia and Africa, where the family and not the individual is the unit of social status and action. It is axiomatic that wherever a predominantly traditionalistic social system flourishes, old age and aging are largely not problematic. The reason is that the role and status of aged persons are clearly defined by the traditional values. In addition, there are generally a series of preparatory roles preceding assumption of the aged role. In this situation, the aged generally occupy positions of high status. Peasant China of some years ago, when the large-family system still predominated, was a classic example of a society where aged people were an asset rather than a problem. Because of their Confucianist philosophical and religious orientation, others in the Chinese culture were obligated to care for, obey, and revere the old. Filial piety was a chief commandment in this culture and one which was part and parcel of the larger value systems. The longer one lived, the more

[41] Leo W. Simmons, "Attitudes toward Aging and the Aged: Primitive Societies," *Journal of Gerontology*, 1:79 (January, 1946).

[42] Simmons, "Social Participation of the Aged in Different Cultures," *loc. cit.*, p. 49.

he had to look forward to in the way of psychic and social gratifications.[43] Social change was at a minimum, and the old, as the bearers of the traditions and enforcers of the mores, had the highest status in the society. Far from being considered senile, the old, in fact, were the persons revered and cherished. A major goal in life was to reach old age. The aged controlled the lives and destinies of the family group. The old settled with the tax collectors upon the amount of the tax which the family contributed to the public treasury, contracted marriages for their children and great-grandchildren, served on the community councils, meted out the punishments, and gave their approval to certain types of behavior. The old conceived of themselves as having the highest possible status in the society and were so regarded by others.

Most older persons have a much more satisfactory status in rural societies than in urban. In the country almost everyone has a place in the cooperative activities of producing agricultural and household goods. The aged contribute in good measure, for they possess much of the rural society's technical skill and managerial experience. Furthermore, the integrated family system of rural areas gives the older person a continuing high place in the society. The individual is part of a group and rarely is in an individualistic setting. Old people are a part of this group, "the moving, directing, and controlling agents in this old rural type of collective entity. Because of this their status in such a society is greatly enhanced over that [which] they are privileged to enjoy in societies where familism does not persist." [44] In the larger rural families an extra person or two does not constitute the burden it may in an urban society. Moreover, the larger and more diverse rural household offers opportunity for much more interesting and productive work than does a household in the cities. The status of elderly persons in rural areas is also linked to the important roles they play as heads of households and in religious activities. Thus it is not likely that the older person's opinions and ideas will be scornfully disdained.

Increase in Aged Population

The magnitude of the problems of the aged in contemporary society which have been described can be more readily seen when it is understood that for the past hundred years the older age groups have continued to be an increasingly large proportion of the population. This situation exists not only in the United States but in most Western European countries as well.

Several European countries exceed the United States in the proportions of persons sixty-five and over relative to total population. The greatest

---

[43] Max Weber, *The Religion of China* (Hans W. Gerth, trans.; New York: The Free Press of Glencoe, 1951). Also see Olga Lang, *The Chinese Family and Society* (New Haven, Conn.: Yale University Press, 1946).

[44] Lynn Smith, "The Aged in Rural Society," in *The Aged and Society*, p. 46.

proportion of older persons in 1950 was to be found in France, with Great Britain, Sweden, and Germany following, in that order. The United States is fifth in rank, followed by Italy, Canada, and the Netherlands. (See Table 16.2.) In the United States, the proportion of those sixty-five and over has

Table 16.2. Percentage of Population 65 Years of Age and Over in Eight Western Countries

Country	1950	1900	1850
France	11.8	8.2	6.5
Great Britain	10.8	4.7	4.6
Sweden	10.3	8.4	4.8
Germany	9.3	4.9	—
United States	8.2	4.1	2.1
Italy	8.1	6.2	—
Canada	7.8	5.1	—
Netherlands	7.7	6.0	4.8

SOURCE: Reprinted from "Aging in Western Culture," by Ernest W. Burgess ed., *Aging in Western Societies,* Table 29, p. 15 and Table 2, p. 35, by permission of the University of Chicago Press. Copyright 1960 by the University of Chicago.

increased from 4.1 percent of the population in 1900 to 9.2 percent in 1960. (See Table 16.3.) Since 1900 there have been increases in all groups over thirty-five years. (See Figure 4.)

In 1960 the northeastern and midwestern states had the highest proportions of older persons, with percentages ranging from 10 to 12 percent.

Table 16.3. Population of the United States, by Age, 1960, 1950, and 1900
(In millions)

Age	Number			Percent		
	1960	1950	1900	1960	1950	1900
0– 4	20.3	16.3	9.2	11.3	10.8	12.1
5–19	48.8	35.1	24.5	27.1	23.1	32.1
20–44	58.2	57.1	28.8	32.4	37.7	37.9
45–64	36.1	30.8	10.5	20.0	20.3	13.8
65 and over	16.6	12.3	3.1	9.2	8.1	4.1
Total (all ages)	180.0	177.1	76.1	100.0	100.0	100.0

SOURCE: U.S. Department of Commerce, Bureau of the Census, *Current Population Reports:* Population Estimates, Series P-25, nos. 98, 114, 170, 187, 193, and 212. Figures given in mimeographed booklet, "Health, Education, and Welfare Trends" (Office of Program Analysis, Office of the Secretary, U.S. Department of Health, Education and Welfare; Washington, D.C.: Government Printing Office, 1961).

These proportions were lowest for the western states, with the exception of Oregon, and for the southern states, with the exception of Florida.[45] Some cities have a large percentage of older persons, for example, St.

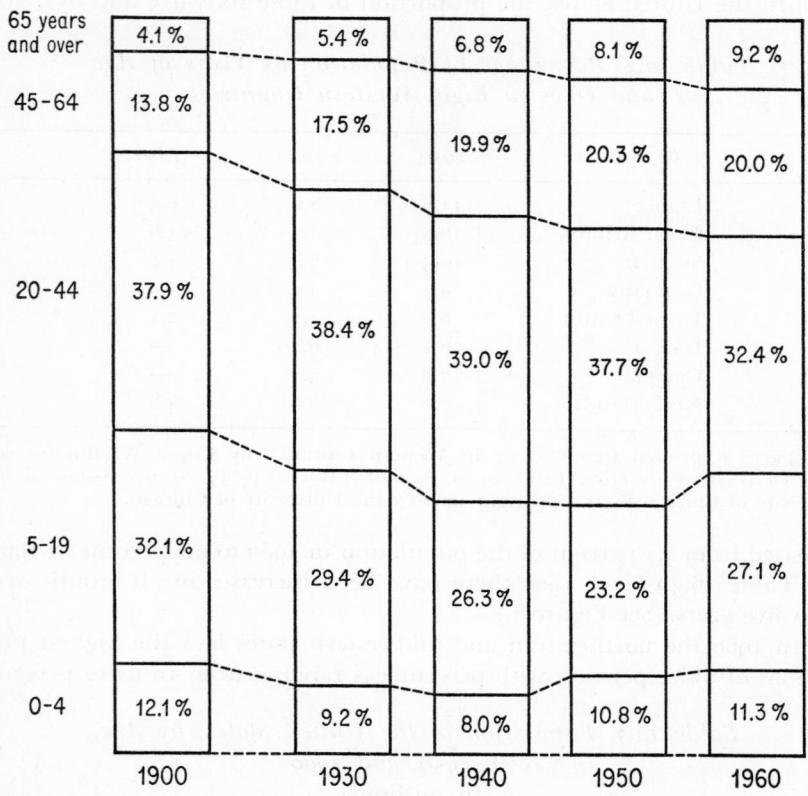

65 years and over	4.1%	5.4%	6.8%	8.1%	9.2%
45-64	13.8%	17.5%	19.9%	20.3%	20.0%
20-44	37.9%	38.4%	39.0%	37.7%	32.4%
5-19	32.1%	29.4%	26.3%	23.2%	27.1%
0-4	12.1%	9.2%	8.0%	10.8%	11.3%
	1900	1930	1940	1950	1960

FIGURE 4.—*Changing Proportion of Age Groups in the Population, 1900–1960*

SOURCE: U.S. Department of Commerce, Bureau of the Census, *Current Population Reports:* Population Estimates, Series P-25, Nos. 98, 114, 170, 187, 193, and 212. Figures given in mimeographed booklet, "Health, Education, and Welfare Trends" (Office of Program Analysis, Office of the Secretary, U.S. Department of Health, Education and Welfare; Washington, D.C.: Government Printing Office, 1961).

Petersburg, Florida, where 22.2 percent of the population in 1950 was sixty-five or over.[46]

There has been a continuous increase in the life expectancy of both

[45] From the 1961 White House Conference on Aging, *Chart Book,* published by the Federal Council on Aging, Arthur S. Flemming, Chairman, p. 15.

[46] William H. Harlan, "Community Adaptation to the Presence of Aged Persons: St. Petersburg, Florida," *American Journal of Sociology,* 59:332–340 (January, 1954).

whites and nonwhites. Generally white and nonwhite women live longer than men and therefore their percentage of the population increases with age. Life expectancy of white males under one year of age was 50.2 years in the period 1909–1911 and by 1958 had increased to 67.2 years. The corresponding life expectancy of white females increased during this period from 53.6 to 73.7 years. Nonwhite males do not live as long as white males, the expectancy for nonwhite males under one year in 1958 being 6.8 years less and that for nonwhite women being 8.2 years less than that for white women.

This increased life expectancy, with the consequent rise in the proportion of the population in the older age groups, has been largely attributed to the industrial development of Western civilization over the past hundred years. The application of industrial techniques to agriculture has increased and improved the food supply. Industrialization has also brought, as one writer has suggested, increased emphasis on the values of health and longevity.[47]

One reason for this increased life expectancy has been the success in combating infant mortality, the dread childhood diseases, including diphtheria and scarlet fever, and such youth-killing diseases as tuberculosis. This triumph of medicine has vastly extended the life span of the population and has added millions of persons to the older age groups. Of all children born at the beginning of the century, less than 60 percent would have lived to be fifty; but by 1948 this percentage had increased to 86.[48] Until recently little progress has been made in increasing the average life expectancy by reducing the death rate from certain diseases of old age. The average life expectancy of white males forty-five years and older has only increased from 23.9 years in 1909–1911 to 27.1 years in 1952. So far there has been little improvement since 1850 in the life expectancy of persons reaching sixty or seventy years.[49] Since 1940, however, the development of the antibiotic drugs has made it possible to pull many older persons through otherwise fatal illnesses, and if similar advances are made in the effective control of such characteristic ailments of old age as cancer and heart disease a longer life span may be expected.[50]

In 1960 life expectancy was continuing to increase faster for women than for men, with the result that the excess of females to males has also increased. At approximately age forty, the number of women and men was

[47] Moore, "The Aged in Industrial Societies," *loc. cit.*
[48] Tibbitts and Sheldon, "Introduction: A Philosophy of Aging," *loc. cit.*, p. 5.
[49] Nathan W. Shock, *Trends in Gerontology* (rev. ed.; Stanford University, Calif.: Stanford University Press, 1957).
[50] Even so, the only animal that normally lives longer than man is the giant tortoise. The longest that an elephant is known to have lived is sixty; fifty-four is the oldest for a parrot. Dogs of fourteen are about as old as an eighty-year-old man, and rats are old at four.—Carl V. Weller, "Biologic Aspects of the Aging Process," in Clark Tibbitts ed., *Living through the Older Years* (Ann Arbor: University of Michigan Press, 1949), p. 27.

about equal, but thereafter the number of women increasingly exceeded the number of men. Thus, for the ages forty-five to fifty-four, women exceeded men by about 5 percent, whereas for the group eighty-five and over, women were in excess by about 46 percent.[51]

Another factor of importance in producing this change in age composition has been the general decline in the birth rates throughout the Western European countries over the past century.[52] In the final analysis this decline in birth rate has been an expression of the increasing urbanization of the world.

Prior to the 1924 Immigration Act the United States received millions of immigrants, and for several years around the turn of the century the number was as high as a million a year. These newcomers were largely young, able-bodied persons in their teens and twenties when they came, but they are now in the older age groups and have had a marked effect on the composition of the population.

By 1975 it is estimated that there will be about 22 million Americans aged sixty-five and over compared with 16.6 million in 1960, even without further progress in medical science.[53] As of 1960 there were 34 persons aged eighty and over for every 100 persons aged sixty to sixty-four; by the year 2000 there will be 67. By 1980 a larger proportion of the aged will be women.

Old Age and Mental Disorders

The older person may often work out ways of dealing with his unhappiness which may be inappropriate in terms of satisfactory interpersonal relationships. When faced with difficulties old people often "respond by petulance, bitterness, exaggerated efforts to secure attention, and sometimes by hysterical symptoms." [54] Havighurst calls some of these symptoms "irrational defenses." [55] In some cases the aged person may retreat into a world of neurotic behavior, fantasies, and even psychoses, wherein the self is satisfied by past beauty or success in business or on the job. Another defense is loss of hearing, sight, and memory, a loss which is not genuine and which takes them, in the eyes of others, out of situations they wish to avoid. Some develop psychotic behavior but not all such behavior actually is psychotic. Havighurst explains why some old people escape through hallucinations:

---

[51] 1961 White House Conference on Aging, *Chart Book, op. cit.*, pp. 9–14.

[52] In recent years the birth rate in the United States has increased.

[53] Harold L. Sheppard, "Relationship of an Aging Population to Employment and Occupational Structure," *Social Problems*, 8:159–163 (Fall, 1960). See also McConnell, "Aging and the Economy," in Tibbitts, *Handbook of Social Gerontology*, p. 491.

[54] Stuart A. Queen and Jeannette R. Gruener, *Social Pathology* (New York: Thomas Y. Crowell Company, 1940), pp. 100–101.

[55] Havighurst, "Social and Psychological Needs of the Aging," *loc. cit.*, pp. 15–16.

Sometimes a woman who has lost her husband or a man who has lost his wife will go on talking to the absent loved one. Why not? It is a pleasure to have someone to talk to. So why not go on talking to the people one loved? If one listens carefully, one may hear them reply; and so a person living alone may converse a great deal with absent persons. Then when someone—a son or daughter—notices this, that person becomes disturbed and goes to a doctor and says, "My old mother (father) is having hallucinations." Yet when a child discovers what we call an imaginary playmate, which often happens with only children or first children, and carries on long conversations with that imaginary person, the parents are often quite proud, and they say, "My, what a good imagination that child has!" [56]

There are two major types of senile psychotic mental disorders. The first is probably strictly organic in origin, resulting, it is believed, from a shrinkage or "hardening" of the blood vessels in the brain, arteriosclerosis, which in extreme instances causes an almost complete destruction of brain tissue. Such physiological deterioration may not always be accompanied by a mental disorder, but where the latter does occur there is a sudden upset by convulsions or an epileptic seizure, severe headaches, emotional outbursts, instability, and varied episodic confusion.[57] There is the usual memory loss, particularly for recent occurrences. Some senile psychoses have an organic basis in that there is a shrinkage of the brain tissue, but they differ from arteriosclerosis in that there is no sudden onset. However, the evidence concerning the presence of arteriosclerosis and "shrinkage" of brain tissue is, in the majority of studies, based only upon hospitalized diagnosed cases, without an attempt to discover how frequently these same neurological changes occur in nonhospitalized and nonpsychotic cases. For this reason, the assertion that senile psychosis and arteriosclerotic degeneration and other brain changes are inevitably associated must be interpreted with caution.[58]

Although brain damage may produce psychotic behavior in older persons, there is considerable evidence that psychotic conditions in a large number of older persons are not proportional to the amount of brain deterioration. Lewis, for example, indicates that in most post-mortem examinations the pathologist can tell whether or not a brain is that of an old person, but cannot tell whether the person was normal or was mentally ill.[59] Many individuals who exhibited great mental deterioration in their

---

[56] *Ibid.*, p. 16. Reprinted by permission of *The Annals* of the American Academy of Political and Social Science.

[57] David Rothschild, "Senile Psychoses and Psychosis with Cerebral Arteriosclerosis," in Oscar Kaplan ed., *Mental Disorders in Later Life* (rev. ed.; Stanford University, Calif.: Stanford University Press, 1956).

[58] Rothschild, *loc. cit.*, p. 292. See also Eugene A. Confrey and Marcus S. Goldstein, "The Health Status of Aging People," in Tibbitts, *Handbook of Social Gerontology*, p. 183.

[59] Nolan D. C. Lewis, "Applying Mental Health Principles to Problems of the Aging," in Lawton, *op. cit.*, p. 94.

actions, which were thought to be due to biological old age, show little pathological changes of the brain at autopsy.[60] In addition, it should be pointed out that although diagnoses such as "senile psychosis" are frequently given to older persons referred for commitment to mental hospitals, such diagnoses are ordinarily given without conclusive evidence of senile neurological damage. Rather, there is a growing body of evidence which suggests that such diagnoses are given on the basis of the patient's *age* status, and not on the basis of specific organic changes associated with age.[61]

The functional disorders of paranoia, depressive behavior, and involutional melancholia appear to be common among institutionalized senile patients, although it is difficult to determine the precise extent. Functional mental disorders among the aged are probably an outgrowth of difficulties in interpersonal relations that characterize any such disorders regardless of age.[62] In this sense there are no truly "senile" functional psychoses; rather, there are functional disorders among the aged.

Manias and schizophrenic disorders are comparatively rare among senile patients, whereas depressions and paranoia are most common.[63] Perhaps the rarity can be explained by the hypothesis that the aged are too physically and socially feeble to revolt against an environment which they regard as oppressive. It is also possible and even probable that because of the wide breadth of experiences in the lifetime of the average person of later maturity he need not completely withdraw from the world of reality through schizophrenia, but merely retreats periodically to the recollection of those situations which have occurred during his lifetime and from which he has always derived satisfaction and can still do so.

Depressions among senile patients may result from excessive brooding over the lowered status, functions, and roles imposed upon them by our society, from the lack of satisfying outlets, and especially from the conflicts of the wish to quit living as against the desire to continue to live. Paranoid reactions are fairly common psychotic difficulties among older persons: "Depending on their previous modes of reaction, people may extrude the knowledge that they are growing older and their resentment of the younger generations which are making them aware of it, and attach their feelings to others about them. They become suspicious and even paranoid, feeling that they are persecuted and treated unfairly. There may be some truth in this at times, and they make the most of it." [64] Cameron has tried to show

---

[60] Robert B. McGraw, "Recoverable or Temporary Mental Disturbances in the Elderly," *Journal of Gerontology*, 4:234–245 (July, 1949).

[61] Evidence concerning the influence of sociological factors on commitment of older persons is given in the Technical Report, New York Department of Mental Hygiene, Mental Health Research Unit, 1958 (Albany: State Department of Mental Hygiene), p. 82.

[62] Moses M. Frohlich, "Mental Hygiene of Old Age," in Tibbitts, *op. cit.*

[63] Norman Cameron, *The Psychology of Behavior Disorders* (Boston: Houghton Mifflin Company, 1947), p. 572.

[64] Frohlich, "Mental Hygiene of Old Age," in Tibbitts, *Living through the Older Years*, p. 88.

that the proportionately higher commitment rates of paranoia in old age may partially stem from the fact that those close to the senile person find it easier to tolerate a sad and self-reproachful attitude than an aggressive and other-accusing one. On the other hand, the person who suffers impairment of his sense organs often tends to become suspicious and anxious. At the same time, restrictions are placed on the aged, and these, coupled with the sense organ handicaps of the old, are "optimal conditions for the development of paranoid reactions." [65]

However, there is considerable evidence that the higher rates of commitment of older persons to mental hospitals in recent years are related to structural changes in society. Among these changes are those affecting family organization, housing conditions, and concepts of family responsibility. According to some authors, children today are more willing to deal with the mental problems of older parents by placing them in mental hospitals.[66] A study in Syracuse, New York, analyzed the socioeconomic status of patients admitted to mental hospitals because of alleged senile psychosis or arteriosclerosis. It was found that the area of the city with the highest admission rate had the highest number of unemployed or disabled persons, the highest proportion of widowed and divorced, multiple-dwelling structures, tenant occupancy, and one-person households.[67] This would suggest that aside from any specific behavioral pathology, there are sociological factors which may condition or affect the societal reaction to the older person such as to result in commitment.[68]

In summary, psychic disturbances of the aged seem to be a product of cultural factors, a breakdown in customary channels of communication, and an interruption of routinized ways of living.[69] All of this is tied up with social changes in the status of the aged, their economic livelihood, and the nature of their family relations. Mental disorders of later maturity among males would appear to be at a minimum if the continuity between generations is maintained, spatial and social mobility is at a minimum, and if the person's status is not abruptly lowered.[70]

---

[65] Cameron, op. cit., p. 572.

[66] R. H. Felix, "Mental Health in an Aging Population," in Wilma Donahue and Clark Tibbitts eds., Growing in the Older Years (Ann Arbor: University of Michigan Press, 1951), pp. 23–44.

[67] Confrey and Goldstein, "The Health Status of Aging People," loc. cit.

[68] See also Robert H. Kleemeier, "The Mental Health of the Aging," in Ernest W. Burgess ed., Aging in Western Societies (Chicago: The University of Chicago Press, 1960), pp. 265–266; and George Rosen, "Health Programs for an Aging Population," in Tibbitts, Handbook of Social Gerontology, pp. 530–531; L. S. Rosenfeld, F. Goldmann, and L. A. Kaprio, "Reasons for Prolonged Hospital Stay," Journal of Chronic Diseases, 6:141–152 (1957).

[69] See H. Warren Dunham, "Sociological Aspects of Mental Disorders in Later Life," in Oscar Kaplan ed., Mental Disorders in Later Life (Stanford, Calif.: Stanford University Press, 1956).

[70] Ivan Belknap and Hiram J. Friedsam, "Age and Sex Categories as Sociological Variables in the Mental Disorders of Later Maturity," American Sociological Review, 14: 367–376 (June, 1949).

Social Participation of the Aged

There is evidence that social participation among the aged is related to satisfactory adjustment. Yet in contemporary society, opportunities for such participation are apparently difficult. A study of 499 men and 759 women primarily from large cities found that the companionship of friends decreases with increasing years.[71] Including their spouses, only about 50 percent of the males had a high degree of companionship at age sixty to sixty-four, and this proportion declined to about 33 percent in the subsequent years. There is a curious contradiction in the fact that although old age means increased leisure it also seems to mean decreased social participation. According to one study, the age group sixty to sixty-four had a low degree of social participation (28 percent), but this low degree of participation increased to 35 percent among those sixty-five to sixty-nine years of age.[72]

Recent evidence has shown that the number of friendships an older person has will be influenced by status changes, such as retirement or widowhood which affect his location in the age, sex, and class structure of a given community. For example, a comparison of friendships of older persons in two different communities revealed that either widowhood or retirement decreased a person's friendships *if* they placed the individual in a different position with respect to his peers. Yet neither widowhood nor retirement had a detrimental effect on friendships if both of these changes were also relatively prevalent among a person's peers.[73] These data suggest that aging as such does not necessarily adversely affect social participation, but that status changes which normally occur in the later years may adversely affect participation if they place an individual in a position different from that of his peers.

A recent development, somewhat different from the isolation from the community of "Old Folks' Homes" of the past, has been community situations which increase friendships among the aged. Although it is true, as Weinberg suggests, that loss of friends through death or dispersion is more probable with advancing age,[74] the creation of "retirement villages" and apartment communities for older persons both in the United States and

---

[71] Cavan *et al., op. cit.,* p. 48.

[72] *Ibid.,* p. 49. In this study nine types of participation were included: daily informal activities, hobbies, plans for the future, listening to the radio an hour or more daily, attendance at group meetings two or more times a month, holding club office, employment, attendance at church at least once a week, and voting in last election. High degree of participation indicated seven or more activities; moderate degree, five or six activities; and low degree, four or fewer activities.

[73] Zena Smith Blau, "Structural Constraints on Friendships in Old Age," *American Sociological Review,* 26:429–439 (June, 1961). See also Zena Smith Blau, "Old Age: A Study of Change in Status." Unpublished doctoral dissertation, Columbia University, New York, 1957.

[74] Weinberg, *op. cit.,* p. 515.

abroad, would seem increasingly to provide living arrangements which would offer significant opportunities for social participation among aged peers.[75] In addition, so-called Golden Age Clubs, where older persons get together at some community center, are becoming more common.[76]

A number of studies have shown that social participation among older persons is influenced by their social class. These studies show that in the United States, persons of upper and middle social classes generally participate more in both formal and informal associations than do those of lower-class status. This trend has been observed among the rural aged as well as among those in urban areas.[77] Some have suggested that lower-class status among the aged is associated with severe economic handicaps which necessitate a restriction of social participation.[78] In general, the evidence shows that economic and retirement status are more important than age in influencing social participation or withdrawal. Others do not participate because they never did so when younger and now are so socially isolated that they do not know how to go about it.

Studies of the social participation of European aged do not uniformly support the findings of American studies, which show a marked decline of participation with age. One study conducted in Sweden, for example, found no significant differences in the extent of participation in associations between those aged eighteen to fifty-six and those fifty-seven and over.[79] Havighurst suggests that older working-class people in Sweden participate more in mixed-age associations than is the case in the United States. In addition to mixed-age groups, there are in Sweden a significant number of "old peoples' clubs" whose membership consists predominantly of working-class persons. These clubs may foster some specific project or may exist primarily to promote informal social relations. Among the Swedish middle- and upper-class elderly people, traveling and visiting resorts are popular.

Although there is a general decline in the aged person's general social and community participation, some writers report that there is an increase in favorable attitudes toward religion, in religious activities, and in a belief in an afterlife. One study stated: "Apparently, as the prospect of an earthly future fades, the belief in a future after death replaces it." [80] There

---

[75] See Ernest W. Burgess ed. *Retirement Villages* (Ann Arbor: University of Michigan, Division of Gerontology, 1961) for a discussion of such living arrangements for older persons. See also I. L. Webber, "The Organized Social Life of the Retired: Two Florida Communities," *American Sociological Review*, 59:340–346 (November, 1954), for data showing the greater participation among older persons living in retirement communities.

[76] See Chapter 22.

[77] Philip Taietz and O. F. Larson, "Social Participation and Old Age," *Rural Sociology*, 21:229–238 (1956).

[78] Blau, "Structural Constraints on Friendships in Old Age," *loc. cit.*, and Peter Steiner and Robert Dorfman, *The Economic Status of the Aged* (Berkeley: University of California Press, 1957), pp. 146–147.

[79] Cited by Robert J. Havighurst, "Life beyond Family and Work," in Burgess, *Aging in Western Societies*, pp. 305–306.

[80] Cavan *et al.*, *Personal Adjustment in Old Age*, p. 57.

is conflicting evidence, however, on this point. More recent studies have suggested that religious feeling and religious participation do not necessarily increase with age.[81] It was found, for example, that women in all groups attended church much more often than did men, whose attendance declined with age. Among Protestants, only Negro men showed an increase in attendance with advancing age. Among Roman Catholics, attendance for men decreased with age, whereas for women it showed no change. Jews were the only group showing an increase in attendance for both men and women with increasing age. In addition to denominational and sex differences, religious participation seems definitely to be influenced by the type of community. Barron suggests that research data in general show greater religious feeling and church attendance among the aged in smaller communities but not in larger communities. This trend would probably also apply to other age groups.[82]

Social Adjustment of the Aged

The problems of adjustment which older persons in our society face stem largely from the fact that aging involves a *change of roles as well as of the statuses associated with these roles*. Adjustment, or conformity to changed role expectations, is complicated if the new role is poorly defined, or if there is inadequate preparation for it. Unfortunately, in modern urban society, in contrast to folk societies, both of these complicating factors are present in the case of older persons.

Several factors seem to be related to more adequate adjustment among older persons; yet the evidence concerning them must be interpreted with caution. For one thing, what is defined as "adequate adjustment" will vary for different subcultures, as will the factors which are taken as indices of "adjustment." [83] Some earlier studies suggested that such factors as these were conducive to adequate adjustment: new friends, new interests in civic and community affairs, new leisure-time activities and hobbies, and the avoidance of too much reminiscing over the past.[84] From adjustment scales,

---

[81] Harold L. Orbach, "Aging and Religion: Church Attendance in the Detroit Metropolitan Area," a paper read at the Annual Gerontological Society Meeting, Philadelphia, November, 1958. Also see H. Lee Jacobs, *Churches and Their Senior Citizens* (Grinnell, Iowa: Congregational Christian Conference of Iowa, 1957), p. 2.

[82] Milton L. Barron, *The Aging American* (New York: Thomas Y. Crowell Company, 1961), p. 177. For a further discussion on religious participation among the aged see Delton L. Scudder, *Organized Religion and the Older Person* (Gainesville: University of Florida Press, 1958).

[83] Raymond G. Kuhlen, "Aging and Life Adjustment" in Birren, *op. cit.*, p. 890.

[84] Havighurst, "Social and Psychological Needs of the Aging," *loc. cit.*, pp. 16–17. See, for example, Ethel Shanas, "The Personal Adjustment of 388 Cases of Recipients of Old Age Assistance." Unpublished doctoral thesis, University of Chicago, 1940; and John F. Schmidt, "Patterns of Poor Adjustment in Persons of Later Maturity." Unpublished doctoral thesis, University of Chicago, 1950.

these studies found that good adjustment among older persons was associated with "the fields of good health, the maintenance of marital and family relations and of friendships, leisure-time and other activities, membership in at least one organization, no discrimination or unhappy period in life, conception of oneself as middle-aged rather than elderly, old, or aged, feeling of permanent economic security, no lowered social status, plans for the future, church attendance and belief in an after-life." [85]

One of the most extensive recent studies of adjustment and old age found that certain factors may be positively related to adjustment in one socioeconomic group, and negatively related to another.[86] In this study, a measure of "morale" (adjustment) was used, and persons of high, medium, or low morale were compared on a number of variables, after they had been divided into high and low socioeconomic groups. On the variable "health," the morale of those in the high socioeconomic group tended to be high whether their health was "good" or "poor." Yet surprisingly, the morale of those in the low socioeconomic group tended in the low direction for those with "good" and those with "poor" health. On self-image, the same relationship appeared, with those of high socioeconomic status tending toward high morale, whether their self-image was "positive" or "negative," and those of low socioeconomic status showing the opposite tendency. In general, similar relationships were observed for the variables "social isolation," "visiting with children," and "visiting with friends," with those of high status tending toward high morale, whether socially isolated or not, and regardless of the frequency (or absence) of visits with children and friends.[87]

These findings raise questions concerning the universality of factors previously assumed to indicate good adjustment. Although the married tended to have higher morale than the divorced, widowed, or single, this may vary by social class. In addition, greater income was associated with an increase in morale only among those who were employed. Among those retired, greater income was not associated with a rise in morale.

There is some evidence that a conception of self as "younger" is associated with more favorable adjustment.[88] Some have suggested that identification with a younger age tends to "insulate" the aged individual against

[85] Ernest W. Burgess, "Personality and Social Adjustment in Old Age," in *The Aged and Society*, p. 147.

[86] B. Kutner, D. Fanshel, Alice M. Togo, and T. S. Langner, *Five Hundred Over Sixty: A Community Survey on Aging* (New York: Russell Sage Foundation, 1956).

[87] This study, unlike previous ones, was based on an adequate sample of older persons, and the measure of morale avoided circular reasoning in the definition, as the indices employed in the measurement of morale were independent of the attributes included in its definition.

[88] Kuhlen, "Aging and Life Adjustment," in Birren, *op. cit.*, p. 890; Burgess, "Personality and Social Adjustment in Old Age," *loc. cit.*, p. 147; and Zena Smith Blau, "Changes in Status and Age Identification," *American Sociological Review*, 21:198–203 (April, 1956).

the impact of role transition.[89] There is evidence, however, that self-conception is conditioned by situational or social factors. Blau found, for example, that socially isolated aged persons tended to regard themselves as "old" more readily than did those aged persons who were not socially isolated. Aged persons who participated in friendship cliques tended to conceive of themselves as more youthful than did nonparticipants.[90]

Many studies suggest that retirement entails greater adjustment problems for men than for women.[91] However, as one writer notes, "evidence is not consistent as to which sex is generally happier and better adjusted in old age." [92] Some data show that widowhood may pose especially difficult adjustment problems for women, but not for men.

These findings concerning sex differences in the response to circumstances associated with aging raise many significant questions which bear on the problem of *role change*. It is possible that, for either sex, an event or circumstance will not complicate adjustment to aging unless it deprives the individual of his primary role: that role which serves as an anchor of self-identity, status, and is the pivot of an entire "way of life." It may be that for most men in our society, work, or making a living, constitutes a primary role, whereas for women generally, being a wife has similar value.

When we consider each sex separately, however, we find that retirement or widowhood has a different impact, depending upon social class. For example, it was shown that widowhood has more consistent *adverse* affects on friendship participation among lower-class women than among middle- and upper-class women.[93] This is due, apparently, to the fact that the latter have developed social ties independent of their husbands prior to widowhood. Thus, by drawing upon these resources, the upper- and middle-class women are more readily able to find significant substitute roles following widowhood. This again seems to emphasize that the impact of the change of roles associated with aging will be eased if there are available satisfying substitute roles for which there has been some previous preparation.

Summary

The aged are in a deviant position in contemporary American society. As a group, the aged in modern urban society are deprived of former tradi-

---

[89] Kuhlen, in Birren, *op. cit.*
[90] Blau, "Changes in Status and Age Identification," *loc. cit.*
[91] Kutner *et al.*, *op. cit.*; Blau, "Social Constraints on Friendship in Old Age," *loc. cit.*; Steiner and Dorfman, *op. cit.*, pp. 148–152.
[92] Kuhlen in Birren, *op. cit.*, p. 890.
[93] Blau, "Structural Constraints on Friendships in Old Age," *loc. cit.*, p. 439. The greater tendency of middle- and upper-class women to foster associations was also pointed out in Robert L. Havighurst and Ruth Albrecht, *Older People* (New York: David McKay Company, 1953).

tional roles and statuses. They are poorly integrated into the social structure. The shift to the ambiguous role and lowered status of old age is the result of social change during the past few decades. Our society has no series of "role gradations" which precede the aged role, thus serving to prepare the aged individual to assume his new role and status. This situation differs from that of older people in folk and rural societies, where the aged have generally occupied well-defined roles associated with high statuses.

The number and proportion of old people in Western European society have greatly increased over the past hundred years. During that period the proportion of those over sixty in the United States has grown, largely because of technical advances which have increased the food supply and have improved the nation's health. Infant mortality and childhood diseases have declined, thus increasing life expectancy. There are indications that recent improvements in medicine will also be reflected in an increase in life expectancy among older persons. The decline in the birth rate has also contributed to the proportion of older persons, and in some societies a large number of immigrants has tended to age the population.

Although physiological and psychological changes occur in old age, these changes in themselves do not account for the position or the behavior of aged persons. Old age is a sociological phenomenon which reflects the manner in which the social roles of the aged are defined, the amount of compatibility in these roles, the degree of preparation for assuming the roles, and the consistency with which other persons allow these roles to be played.

Selected Readings

BIRREN, JAMES E., ed. *Handbook of Aging and The Individual: Psychological and Biological Aspects.* Chicago: The University of Chicago Press, 1959. A collection of articles dealing with physiological changes associated with age and suggestions for their possible effects on the social and psychological adjustment of the aged.

BURGESS, ERNEST W., ed. *Aging in Western Societies: A Survey of Social Gerontology.* Chicago: The University of Chicago Press, 1960. Reviews the trends in the phenomenon of aging in a number of Western European countries and Great Britain. Offers a wider perspective and basis of comparison of aging in the United States. Includes articles by leading authorities on social gerontology.

CAVAN, RUTH S., ERNEST W. BURGESS, ROBERT J. HAVIGHURST, and HERBERT GOLDHAMER. *Personal Adjustment in Old Age.* Chicago: Science Research Associates, Inc., 1949. One of the first sociological studies of the aged. There are extensive case materials.

FRIEDMANN, EUGENE A., and ROBERT J. HAVIGHURST. *The Meaning of Work and Retirement.* Chicago: The University of Chicago Press, 1954. A study of adjustment to retirement in a number of different occupations.

KAPLAN, OSCAR J., ed. *Mental Disorders in Later Life*. Revised edition. Stanford University, Calif.: Stanford University Press, 1956. A collection of articles by scholars from medical and social science fields, reviewing present research on the problems of mental illness among the aged, and suggesting important problems for future research.

POLLAK, OTTO. *Social Adjustment in Old Age*. New York: Social Science Research Council, Bulletin 59, 1948. A comprehensive analysis of the definitions of old age and of the psychological and sociological aspects of aging.

SHOCK, NATHAN W. *Trends in Gerontology*. Stanford University, Calif.: Stanford University Press, 1951, 1957. This book is a series of articles dealing with a number of aspects of aging.

SIMMONS, LEO W. *The Role of the Aged in Primitive Societies*. New Haven, Conn.: Yale University Press, 1945. A study of the social position of aged persons in a large number of folk societies. In nearly every society they were found to have an important position.

TIBBITTS, CLARK, ed. *Handbook of Social Gerontology: Societal Aspects of Aging*. Chicago: The University of Chicago Press, 1960. A series of articles dealing with research on the phenomenon of aging as it relates to the changes in roles and status occurring with age, and the effect of these on behavior and adjustment.

Chapter

17

Minority Groups

Human rights have been a matter of debate for centuries, but it was not until a historic session of the General Assembly of the United Nations in 1948 that there has been anything like a universal declaration of these rights. On December 10 of that year the General Assembly adopted thirty articles setting them forth in some detail. This declaration stated: "All human beings are born free and equal in dignity and rights" and "Everyone has rights without distinction of race, color, sex, language, religion, political or other opinions, national or social origin, property, birth or other status." Among the rights to which all persons are entitled are the following:

1. "Life, liberty and security of person"
2. Equal treatment before the law
3. Opportunity to take part in the government, directly or through freely chosen representatives who are elected by universal and equal suffrage
4. Opportunity to work, equal pay for equal work, and an adequate standard of living
5. Freedom of thought, conscience, and religion
6. Participation in the cultural life of the country [1]

Admittedly these are general statements which do not apply to all citizens in many countries today. On the other hand, they are statements which come as close as any to being universal norms of rights. For that reason they serve as a vantage point from which to examine "The American Creed."

The American Creed

A classic study of the American Negro has been aptly titled *An American Dilemma,* the dilemma being the contradiction between the American creed of democratic values and the actual treatment of the Negro.[2] The

---

[1] United Nations Department of Public Information, *These Rights and Freedoms* (New York: United Nations, 1950), pp. 170–176.

[2] Gunnar Myrdal, *An American Dilemma* (New York: Harper & Row, Publishers, 1944).

American Creed gives expression to certain humanitarian ideologies and includes these fundamental beliefs, which apply regardless of race, creed, ethnic background, or any hereditary status: (1) the right of political equality, (2) the right of due process of law and of equal justice before the law, (3) freedom of opportunity to achieve economic and political success, and (4) the right to express one's religious beliefs.

These beliefs permeate the American social scene, regardless of social class or geographic location. They are found expressed in such venerated documents as the Declaration of Independence, the Constitution, and the Bill of Rights, and, more explicitly, in countless Supreme Court decisions. The Creed is taught in schools and churches, and is regarded as a basic guiding principle by the Boy Scouts and the Girl Scouts of America, the YWCA and the YMCA, and many other similar organizations. It is symbolized in such national songs as "America," in the Statue of Liberty, and in countless stories, books, and plays dealing with the oppressed who sought freedom in America. Even those groups who experience discrimination believe in our American Creed, for, as Myrdal has written, "They, like the whites, are under the spell of the great national suggestion. With one part of themselves they actually believe, as do the whites, that the Creed is ruling America." [3]

SOURCES OF THE AMERICAN CREED

The American Creed appears to have been derived from a number of sources, including the Philosophy of the Enlightenment, Christianity, English law, capitalism, and the nature of American nationalism itself. The so-called Philosophy of the Enlightenment, with its emphasis on the sacredness of the individual, came out of the English, American, and French revolutions and the writings primarily of Locke, Rousseau, and Voltaire. These beliefs were probably best expressed by Thomas Jefferson in this country. Such philosophical and political writings from earliest times have been important factors in the development of this basic heritage. Another and somewhat similar source of the American Creed has been the tradition of justice contained in English law, upon which the law of this country is based. These traditional beliefs in statutory enactments, fair trial, due process of law, and judicial interpretations expressive of humanitarian principles have time and again met conflict in such behavior as lynchings and the third degree.

Individual opportunity for economic success, regardless of race, creed, ethnic origin, or class position, is the cardinal principle of capitalism, success being presumed to be based on individual initiative, hard work, and private savings. Nothing in the capitalist ideology implies that success

---

[3] *Ibid.*, p. 4.

shall go, largely, to American citizens of the white race. Christianity, another source of these values, emphasizes the brotherhood of man and the essential dignity of the individual. Although in practice "brotherhood" frequently means one's own religion, from a strictly Christian point of view it includes Jew and Christian, Protestant and Catholic, and all races, regardless of the color of their skin.

Finally, American nationalism probably emphasizes the diversity of its people more than do most other countries, where common cultural or religious ideals, tribal separativeness, or military history is more often stressed. Many historians have pointed out that Americans have generally stressed their racial and ethnic diversity and have been proud of their nation's being a refuge for those discriminated against in other countries. In fact, the diversity of the American people is probably their most important distinguishing characteristic. Regardless of their skin color, religious heritage, or ethnic background, all Americans believe that America is made up of people drawn from the ends of the earth and that there is true equality for all. A Negro leader has put it this way: "Every man in the street, white, black, red or yellow, knows that this is 'the land of the free,' the 'land of opportunity,' and 'cradle of liberty,' the 'home of democracy,' that the American flag symbolizes the 'equality of all men' and guarantees to us all 'the protection of life, liberty and property,' freedom of speech, freedom of religion and racial tolerance." [4]

DISCRIMINATION AND THE REINTERPRETATION OF
THE AMERICAN CREED

Along with the American Creed there has always existed another series of social norms and values which have reflected racial ideas and the superiority of certain groups over others.[5] Consequently, these two series of norms and values have existed simultaneously, the American Creed generally permitting some degree of discrimination. The basic rights of minorities have been interpreted and modified according to circumstances; even slavery was at one time reconciled by many with this creed. This struggle between the American Creed and racism is strong in certain parts of the United States where racial doctrines are supported by state laws. The simultaneous presence of contradictory norms within the same person has resulted in a situation which has been described as follows: "Although many Southerners today will agree that segregation is wrong in principle, the vast majority still fiercely defends it as right in practice. A mass of state laws and city ordinances enforce it. But Southerners seem to know in their hearts that it is not really defensible, and that the tide of events is against

---

[4] Ralph Bunche, as quoted, *ibid.*, p. 4.
[5] Robin M. Williams, Jr., *American Society* (New York: Alfred A. Knopf, Inc., 1954), pp. 438–440.

it. The result is a war in the South's own soul which many Northerners, who see the South only as stubborn and narrow-minded, fail to understand." [6]

The American Creed cannot, therefore, be thought of as a stable system of norms, for, like the interpretations of the Constitution by the courts, the Creed has also undergone continuous interpretations. Not only have the "rights" of minority groups changed from one generation to another; within the population at a given time and in a given place there are pronounced differences of opinion as to what behavior on the part of a given minority should be approved or disapproved and still be in line with the Creed. Some of the conflict between the older and newer generations represents an outgrowth of these systems of differential norms.

This frame of reference has been termed the "race relations cycle." [7] In this cycle successive stages of social interaction take place between subordinate and superordinate groups, and in each of them a series of temporary balances is established to avoid conflict. These levels become disturbed by new norms, and further new levels of adjustment arise among groups. More specifically, the parts of the race relations cycle are referred to as *conflict,* or the awareness of mutually exclusive ends; *accommodation,* or the establishment of a working arrangement in which reciprocal relations based on higher and lower status are accepted; and, as a final goal, *assimilation,* or the disappearance of accommodation and the establishment of an unconscious process of consensus or common norms. These processes are occurring simultaneously at various levels during the continuous process of conflict and redefinitions in a variety of areas. The following discussion will present, more or less specifically, the former conception of the American Creed at the outbreak of World War II, the new emerging definition, and possible future interpretations.[8] These statements should be regarded as only general comparisons.

Former Interpretation of the American Creed. For some time before the outbreak of World War II most Americans of the majority group, as well as many of the minorities themselves, were in fairly general agreement about the following minimum "rights" and obligations of Americans in terms of the American Creed. Many of these rights were actually not in full agreement with the American Creed. Some of these limited rights, moreover, had been achieved after a long and arduous struggle.

---

    [6] "The U.S. Negro, 1953," *Time,* 61:55 (May 11, 1953).

    [7] Robert E. Park, *Race and Culture* (New York: The Free Press of Glencoe, 1950), pp. 149–151. Also see Brewton Berry, *Race and Ethnic Relations* (2d ed.; Boston: Houghton Mifflin Company, 1958).

    [8] Negroes, mainly from the West Indies, have come in considerable numbers to Great Britain since 1942. There have been conflict and some accommodation, processes which have been analyzed by Anthony H. Richmond in *Colour Prejudice in Britain* (London: Routledge and Kegan Paul, Ltd., 1954).

1. Approval of segregated but "equal" education and other facilities as being in line with the American way of life.
2. The right to a job, an unskilled or semiskilled one at the least, with adequate relief if no jobs are available.
3. The right to vote, except in certain areas of the South.
4. Some elementary school education for every American, including members of the lowest minority group.
5. Decent health standards for all minority groups and the reduction of their high infant mortality rate and the incidence of such diseases as tuberculosis.
6. The elimination of substandard housing, the agency not agreed upon.
7. Condemnation of lynching and the protection of minorities from such un-American practices.

Emerging "Rights." The issues involved in granting full "rights" to minorities are now on a higher status level and many are of a different character from those accepted before World War II:

1. The elimination of the concept of "separate but equal" in education and in public facilities of an interstate nature.
2. The right to vote even in most of the South; the right to full participation in public housing facilities, public recreational facilities, and professional athletics such as baseball, and in the armed forces.
3. The right to higher jobs, such as those of foremen and junior executive positions, as in personnel work.
4. Elimination of discriminatory provisions in union membership and in employment.
5. The right to membership in professional groups.
6. The right to social participation in fraternities, sororities, and general club organizations in most parts of the country.

Future "Rights." Most people today would probably say that once conflict over the foregoing rights has been resolved, minority problems will have reached a stage of permanent accommodation. On the contrary, in terms of the American Creed, other issues involving new norms and values can be expected to arise. Some of these future "rights" include the elimination of segregation in municipal facilities within a state, full political equality, attainment of important positions in business and finance, and election or appointment to positions of leadership in professional and other formal organizations:

1. The elimination of all forms of segregation including intrastate and municipal public facilities and in living areas.[9]

---

[9] The elimination of segregation presents a problem for the Negro business and professional classes whose short-term status is based on being Negro businessmen, doctors, lawyers, teachers, or ministers. Negro enterprises, separate Negro churches, and higher status among the Negro group are endangered by the elimination of segregation.— E. Franklin Frazier, "Human, All Too Human," *Survey Graphic*, 36:75, 99–100 (January, 1947).

2. Full political equality in terms of both the appointment and the election of minority group members to high positions. This far transcends merely the granting of full suffrage. It would mean the election of qualified Negroes, American Orientals, Spanish-speaking Americans, Indians, and others to municipal, state, and national offices and the possibility of minority group members becoming governors, senators, cabinet members, Supreme Court members, Vice-President, or even President.
3. Right to position of high status in business and finance either as officers or as members of boards of directors. In America such a strategic position in the economy would bring with it important power considerations.
4. Position of leadership and not merely membership in professional and other formal organizations.

These trends merely represent a reinterpretation of rights or norms, new conflicts, and new accommodations. They do not constitute the final goal of the social and cultural process, which is the elimination of superordination and subordination. In such a situation social relations, as well as political and economic activities, are conducted largely without regard to racial, ethnic, or religious status. In the earlier history of the United States certain groups, such as the Germans, and later to a large extent the Irish, were discriminated against. These groups have now largely reached a state of assimilation. In Brazil the Negro, once a slave, has now reached a stage where he is identified largely as a Brazilian and not commonly as a Negro Brazilian.[10] A great deal of assimilation has taken place in the so-called racial laboratory, Hawaii.[11] Here live over half a million persons of diverse ethnic and racial groups—203,455 Japanese, 69,070 Filipinos, 38,197 Chinese, 4943 Negroes, 472 Indians, and 114, 405 "others," including Hawaiians. There are 202,230 white persons, and 430,542 nonwhites.[12] These people of Hawaii, who are even more racially mixed than the figures would indicate, live in a situation, even if not perfect, of harmony. Schoolteachers and principals are of all races. There are no racial restrictions in accommodations or employment. Hawaii in 1961 had an

[10] Donald Pierson, Negroes in Brazil (Chicago: The University of Chicago Press, 1942). A later study has challenged some of Pierson's findings. See Roger Bastide and Pierre Van Den Berghe, "Stereotypes, Norms and Interracial Behavior in São Paulo, Brazil," American Sociological Review, 22:689–694 (December, 1957).
[11] Andrew W. Lind, Island Community: A Study of Ecological Succession in Hawaii (Chicago: The University of Chicago Press, 1938). These nearly harmonious race relations, almost unique under the American flag, are the result of a long history of amicable race relations going back to the days before 1898 when Hawaii was a united self-governing stopover on voyages across the Pacific. Formerly Hawaii, as an independent nation with a cultural pattern of harmonious relationships between races, was in a position to require white persons who desired to trade or live there to accede to a pattern of respect and nearly equal treatment. Subsequently, the introduction of many racial groups resulted in a blending of cultures and in racial hybrids which served to perpetuate the original situation of race contacts.
[12] United States Bureau of the Census, General Population Characteristics (March 30, 1961), Bulletin PC (A2)–13.

elected Caucasian governor, both a Chinese and a Caucasian senator, and a Japanese congressman.

Segregation and the American Creed. Since to a minority group, the forced segregation of one group from another is probably one of the most important discriminations, the changing definition of segregation necessitates detailed discussion. Before 1941 there was consensus among the majority groups, as expressed through the Supreme Court, that, in general, segregation, at least for the Negro and similar groups, was in line with the American Creed. In pre–Civil War days the southern churches sanctioned segregation in the form of slavery, even citing Biblical passages in support of this practice. In the famous Dred Scott decision of 1857 the Supreme Court decided that Negroes were property, not citizens, and if freed they had no rights. Although segregation has a long history dating from the Negro freedmen group, it did not appear in the form of a real separation of the races until the 1890's and in the decades to follow, when more and more laws separating the races were enacted. Many of the laws relating to segregation, such as taxis and sports, were actually enacted much later. A city ordinance requiring Jim Crow taxis, for example, was adopted by Atlanta in 1940. After surveying the laws of segregation Woodward has concluded that most laws of segregation are neither as old nor as "natural" as some think. Racism as a legislative doctrine, to secure legal white supremacy and power, distinct from the inferior social position of Negroes, is much more recent.

> In a time when the Negroes formed a much larger proportion of the population than they did later, when slavery was a live memory in the minds of both races, and when the memory of the hardships and bitterness of Reconstruction was still fresh, the race policies accepted and pursued in the South were sometimes milder than they became later. The policies of proscription, segregation, and disfranchisement that are often described as the immutable "folkways" of the South, impervious alike to legislative reform and armed intervention, are of a more recent origin. The effort to justify them as a consequence of Reconstruction and a necessity of the times is embarrassed by the fact that they did not originate in those times. And the belief that they are immutable and unchangeable is not supported by history.[13]

Segregation in schools was maintained until recent years, sometimes unofficially, in communities in many northern and border states such as Illinois, Indiana, Missouri, Delaware, and West Virginia. Kansas did not completely abolish segregation until 1952. The Supreme Court had affirmed the belief that separate facilities constituted no violation of the American Creed, and in 1896 the Court, in a case involving segregation in transportation, stated: "We think the enforced separation of the races, as applied to the internal commerce of the state, neither abridges the immu-

---

[13] C. Vann Woodward, *The Strange Career of Jim Crow* (New York: Oxford University Press, 1957), p. 47.

nities of the colored man, nor denies him the equal protection of the laws, within the meaning of the 14th amendment." [14] Segregation was not a badge of servitude nor did it mean the inequality of races. Public education and transportation were "social" rights and not rights of citizenship and, therefore, could be segregated. Such segregated facilities, however, must be "equal."

The belief of the Court in segregation as "right" and "natural" in terms of the American Creed is clearly indicated by this statement: "Legislation is powerless to eradicate racial instincts or to abolish distinctions based on physical differences." This 1896 decision did indicate, however, that there were some unreasonable limits to segregation. A city, for example, could not require white persons to walk on one side of the street and Negroes on another.

The Supreme Court redefined this interpretation in 1914, stating that these segregated facilities in interstate commerce must be "equal," as in the case of railroad coach travel. This belief in segregation but equality was approved by many, but by no means all, of the leaders of minority groups, such as Booker T. Washington. How "equality" was to be maintained in various services, living accommodations, and social interaction was not clearly stated.

An example of some of these controversial issues was the question of higher education. In 1938 the Supreme Court ordered the state of Missouri to provide Lloyd Gaines, a Negro, with an education in law which would be substantially equal to that given white students.[15] In similar cases brought before the Court the ruling had favored "segregated but equal" facilities. Since few southern states provided graduate or professional training for Negroes, this redefinition of legal rights was extremely important.

In 1948 the Supreme Court ruled that if states did not provide equal separate facilities they must admit Negro students to white schools. In a desperate effort to avoid this step, some states set up makeshift separate facilities, and other southern states attempted to set up regional graduate schools to which Negroes from various southern states would be sent under a system of joint state expense. Others decided to admit a few Negro graduate students, but with various barriers to full participation. In Oklahoma,

---

[14] Plessy v. Ferguson, Supreme Court of the United States, 1896, 163 U.S. 537, 41 L. Ed. 256, 16 S. Ct. 1138. The only dissent from this decision was that of Justice Harlan, who maintained that "our Constitution is color-blind and neither knows nor tolerates classes among citizens." He also felt that segregation would create distrust and misunderstanding between the races. For a detailed discussion of the various Supreme Court decisions on segregation as well as the actual court decisions see Herbert Hill and Jack Greenberg, *Citizens' Guide to De-Segregation* (Boston: The Beacon Press, 1955) and Benjamin Munn Ziegler editor, *Desegregation and the Supreme Court* (Boston: D. C. Heath & Company, 1958). Also see Jack Greenberg, *Race Relations and American Law* (New York: Columbia University Press, 1959).

[15] Missouri ex rel. Gaines v. Canada, Supreme Court of the United States, 1938, 305 U.S. 337, 83 L. Ed. 208, 59 S. Ct. 232.

for example, one Negro graduate student was seated in an anteroom off the main classroom, and later in the same school had a small railing erected around his desk as a way of meeting the legal requirement of segregation. This was the situation existing in 1950, when the Supreme Court made a drastic redefinition of American rights.

The elimination of the concept of "separate but equal" facilities is probably one of the most important recent developments in race relations in the United States. Not only has actual "equality" been challenged as a fiction, but the maintenance of two types of facilities is thought to indicate second-class citizenship and to be harmful to the full dignity of the individual's personality. This is well illustrated in interstate travel. Before 1941 Negroes often had to ride in chair cars on trains because it was impossible to furnish separate Pullman cars for them. In a 1941 Supreme Court decision interstate railroads were ordered to provide first-class rail travel for everyone, which meant the admittance of Negroes to Pullman cars. A 1946 decision ordered segregation eliminated on buses in interstate travel. An important symbolic barrier was removed from interstate rail travel in 1950, for then dining cars no longer could require the segregated seating of Negroes and whites at opposite ends of a dining car or utilize a curtain to screen one race from another.

The barrier of "partial equality" of higher education was also torn down by the Supreme Court in 1950. The Court unanimously agreed in the McLaurin and Sweatt cases that the universities of Oklahoma and Texas must accept graduate students on the same basis as whites.[16] In the Oklahoma case a Negro graduate student named McLaurin was segregated in seating and eating arrangements from the white students, and the Court ruled that this denied him equal protection before the law and that he must be admitted under the same conditions of participation as white students. The Supreme Court stated that the setting apart of a student impairs and inhibits "his ability to study, to engage in discussions, and to exchange views with other students."

Previously the Court had implied that a makeshift separate law facility provided by Texas in downtown Austin was suitable, but now it argued not only that this segregation was contrary to the rights of an American citizen but also that "equality" was an impossible fiction. In regard to Sweatt's petition to enter the University of Texas Law School rather than the separate Negro school the Supreme Court said:

> What is more important, the University of Texas Law School possesses to a far greater degree those qualities which are incapable of objective measurement but which make for greatness in a law school. Such qualities, to name but a few, include reputation of the faculty, experience of the administration,

---

[16] McLaurin v. Oklahoma State Regents, Supreme Court of the United States, 1950, 339 U.S. 637, 94 L. Ed. 1149, 70 S. Ct. 851. Also Sweatt v. Painter, Supreme Court of the United States, 1950, 339 U.S. 629, 94 L. Ed. 1114, 70 S. Ct. 848.

position and influence of the alumni, standing in the community, tradition and prestige.

The Supreme Court also felt that Sweatt, as a practicing lawyer, could not function in a setting in which most Texas lawyers were not the products of a segregated school.

> This law school to which Texas is willing to admit petitioner excludes from its student body members of the racial groups which number 85% of the population of the state and exclude most of the lawyers, witnesses, jurors, judges, and other officials with whom petitioner will inevitably be dealing when he becomes a member of the Texas Bar. With such a substantial and significant segment of society excluded, we cannot conclude that the education offered petitioner is substantially equal to that which he would receive if admitted to the University of Texas Law School.

Few Supreme Court decisions have been more drastic than that of May 17, 1954, which stated that segregation in public schools is unconstitutional. The decision affected about 48 million persons, including some 10 million Negroes. It was a culmination of the series of previous decisions on higher education, but in its philosophy and effect was far more drastic than any one of them. In a unanimous decision the Court repudiated completely the "separate but equal" doctrine. The decision took into account the changes in the importance of education and the findings of psychological studies of children made since 1896. All children, to succeed, must have opportunities for equal education, and segregated but equal physical facilities are not "equal" in actuality.

> Education is perhaps the most important function of state and local governments. . . . It is the very foundation of good citizenship. . . . In these days, it is doubtful that any child may reasonably be expected to succeed in life if he is denied the opportunity of an education.
> To separate them [Negro children] from others of similar age and qualifications solely because of their race generates a feeling of inferiority as to their status in the community that may affect their hearts and minds in a way unlikely ever to be undone. . . . Separate educational facilities are inherently unequal.[17]

In 1955 the Supreme Court included recreation as a right of all citizens, ordering the end to segregation in public parks, playgrounds, and golf courses.[18] Each year since then additional desegregation decisions by the Supreme Court and other federal agencies, such as the Interstate Commerce Commission, have affected other facilities, such as bus travel and waiting rooms. In 1962 the Supreme Court ruled that *all* racial segregation in transportation facilities was unconstitutional. In the decision the Supreme Court said: "We have settled beyond question that no state may

---

[17] 347 U.S. 483.   [18] 350 U.S. 879.

require racial segregation in inter-state or intra-state facilities. The question is no longer open: it is foreclosed as a litigable issue."

Many forces operating in our society today have brought about some basic changes in American life leading to desegregation, particularly in the field of education. These forces include the increasing urbanization and industralization of the South, which make the maintenance of many forms of segregation difficult. The cost of maintaining separate school systems, theaters, and other facilities, for example, is becoming too difficult a financial burden. Desegregation in the Armed Forces, which took place after the Korean War, has had much effect upon the South, where there are a large number of military installations on which both Negro and white military and civilian personnel work and live without segregation. The policy of the industrial type of labor union to incorporate members of both races in the South is affecting many social relationships formerly based on segregation. The integration of the schools will, in the long run, as the present-day generation grows up, affect other forms of segregation. The insularity of the Deep South has been broken by the more rapid desegregation in the border states, the mobility of Southerners and Northerners, and such media as television, on which Southerners see, for example, Negroes participating in sports and political life. Finally, the whole picture of segregation is one which increasingly has been recognized as affecting adversely the international relations of the United States. Incidents like this have hurt the appeal of American democracy, particularly in Asia, Africa, and parts of South America:

> A Hindu dance team canceled an appearance at Centenary College here [Shreveport, La.] today after a spokesman said that two nearby restaurants had refused to serve two dark-skinned members of the troupe. Tom Burrows, manager of the troupe, Indrani and her Hindu Dancers, said that the Indian embassy was studying whether the entire Southern tour should be canceled. . . . Mr. Burrows said that the group had previously been refused service in Charlotte, N.C. To avoid an incident in Bossier City, the troupe explained at two restaurants that two of the musicians were "dark-skinned." . . . The dance team appeared before President and Mrs. Kennedy earlier in its tour. The tour is supported and encouraged by the State Department.[19]

The Concept of a Minority Group

A minority group is simply a group of people who, because of their racial, ethnic, or religious origin, are discriminated against, are given lower status, and thus in a sense are "second-class citizens." Louis Wirth has defined a minority as a "group of people who, because of their physical or cultural characteristics, are singled out from the others in the society in

---

[19] *The New York Times,* November 21, 1961, p. 32 C.

which they live for differential and unequal treatment, and who therefore regard themselves as objects of collective discrimination." [20]

More specifically, a minority group situation is characterized by (1) discrimination against a certain *group* of people; (2) the clash of this discriminatory treatment of the minority group with other norms and values in the culture, such as the American Creed, which would tend to give the groups equal status; (3) the recognition of this treatment as discriminatory by both minority and majority groups; and (4) an organized effort by the minority group to remove the discrimination.

As used here, a minority group should not be confused with a colonial problem, a separate cultural minority, or simply any group which is numerically in the minority. Although the native group in a colonial society may occupy a more or less inferior status, these "natives" are usually regarded as distinctly different from the ruling citizens. A separate status system exists for each. The American Indian of fifty years ago constituted a colonial problem rather than a minority problem. Within the past twenty-five years the 6 million natives of South Africa have been rapidly becoming transformed into a group which aspires to equal treatment instead of being segregated by the 2 million European whites of the dominant group.

In other parts of the world certain cultural groups may be referred to as minority groups, because they have often been denied opportunities to maintain a separate culture, to preserve their own language, and to exercise a degree of political autonomy.[21] Minorities of this type, however, may actually not even desire to have equal status within the larger society. The Negro in the United States well illustrates the fact that a minority is not the same as a distinct cultural group. Most authorities agree that among American Negroes there are practically no vestiges of African culture,[22] and that they desire to be Western Europeans as much as do members of the white population.

A minority group cannot necessarily be regarded as smaller in number than the majority. In many counties of the South the Negro population greatly exceeds the white population. (See Figure 5.) Nearly 1 million Negroes live in Mississippi, or about one in every fifteen Negroes in the United States. Although the Negroes in Mississippi represent about 42 percent of the population of the state, most of the western counties along the Mississippi River or in the Delta country have Negro populations generally outnumbering the white populations, in some instances as much as four to one. The Spanish-speaking population of the Southwest, which for a

---

[20] Louis Wirth, "The Problems of Minority Groups," in Ralph Linton ed., *The Science of Man in the World Crisis* (New York: Columbia University Press, 1945), p. 347.

[21] United Nations Commission on Human Rights, *Definition and Classification of Minorities* (New York: 1950), pp. 2–3.

[22] A different point of view has been taken by Melville J. Herskovits, *The Myth of the Negro Past* (Boston: The Beacon Press, 1958).

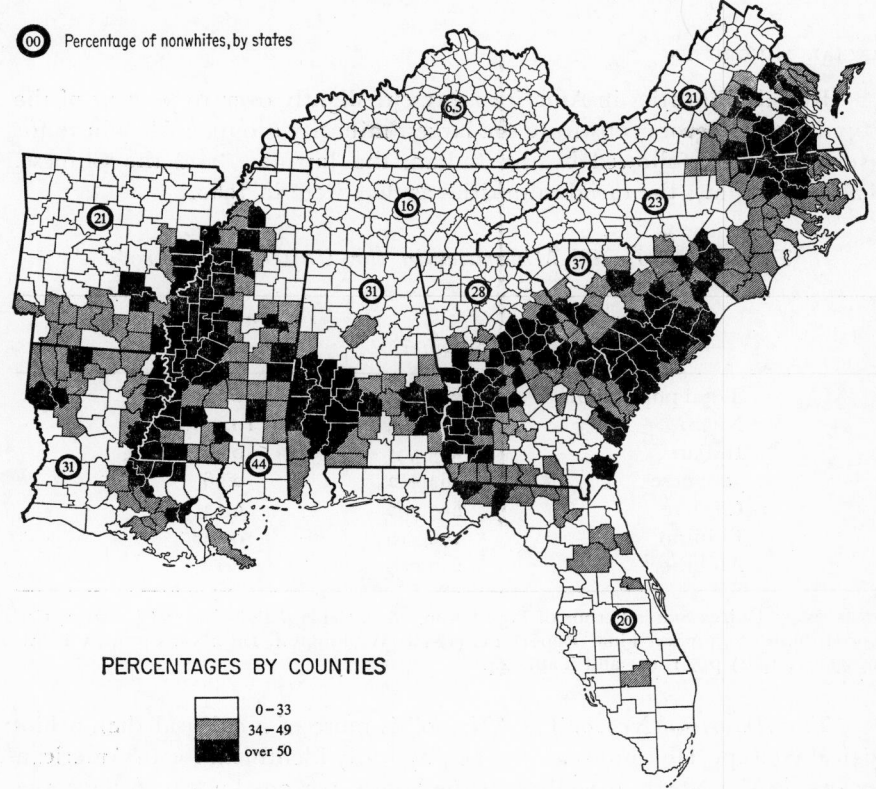

PERCENTAGES BY COUNTIES

	0-33
	34-49
	over 50

FIGURE 5.—Percentage of Nonwhite Population in Counties of Southern States

SOURCE: Adapted from "Next Steps in the South: Answers to Current Questions," *New South,* Vol. II, Nos. 7, 8 (July–August, 1956). Used by permission of the Southern Regional Council, Inc.

century had a status generally inferior to that of the so-called Anglos, was until recently the larger group, and still is in many communities.

Minorities in the United States

The United States has been called a "nation of nations." [23] It should more aptly be called a nation of races, nations, and religions. The heterogeneity of the population is so great that it is difficult to think of a stereotyped "typical American." Minority groups in the United States may be divided into three types, with primary emphasis on race, ethnic background, or religion.

[23] Louis Adamic, *A Nation of Nations* (New York: Harper & Row, Publishers, 1944).

RACIAL MINORITIES

Racial minorities in America represent slightly over 10 percent of the population. Negroes constitute the largest minority group, as they have for over a century, followed by the Indian, the Japanese, and the Chinese. Table 17.1 shows the racial minorities as they were in 1960.

Table 17.1. Racial Minorities in the United States, 1960

	Number	Percent of total population
Total population	179,323,175	100.00
Negro	18,871,443	10.5
Indian	523,591	0.29
Japanese	464,332	0.26
Chinese	237,292	0.13
Filipino	176,310	0.098
All other	218,087	0.12

SOURCE: United States Census of Population, 1960, General Population Characteristics, United States Summary, Final Report PC (1)-1B (Washington, D.C.: Government Printing Office, 1961) pp. 1–144 and Table 44.

The American Negro. The "Negro" is more of a cultural than a biological concept. He cannot always be physically identified, for in American society, in the North as well as in the South, persons known to have any Negro ancestry, no matter how small, are considered to be Negroes. United States census enumerators, for example, are given the arbitrary instruction that persons of mixed white and Negro "blood" should be classified as Negroes regardless of the proportion of Negro "blood." In some southern states this distinction has sometimes raised complicated legal questions. In those states where the question has been raised the courts have not been unanimous as to the proportion of Negro "blood" a person must have to be classified as a Negro.[24] In Virginia, for example, a person is considered a Negro for legal purposes if he is one sixteenth Negro, even though he is fifteen sixteenths white.

This cultural norm can be contrasted with that of Brazil, where there are also millions of Negroes but where status is not based to any extent on color. Whereas in the United States one drop of known Negro "blood" makes a person a Negro, many Brazilians whose grandmothers were Negroes of pure African descent are listed in the census as white and are so

---

[24] Charles S. Mangum, The Legal Status of the Negro (Chapel Hill: University of North Carolina Press, 1940), p. 1.

considered by others.[25] Thus many individuals are considered as white who have definitely Negroid physical features. Cultural norms define the Negro differently in the United States and in Brazil.

Beginning with the twenty Negroes who were first sold at Jamestown in 1619, the American Negro population has increased enormously as a result of natural increase and slave trade. Today there are 18,871,443 Negroes; or one in every ten Americans is a Negro. About one of every five Southerners is a Negro, whereas only one in twenty of the population in the Northeastern and North Central states and only one in thirty-three in the West are Negroes. (See Table 17.4.) The distribution of the Negro population in states with the largest percentage is shown in Table 17.2. In 1960,

Table 17.2. Number and Percentage of Nonwhite Population in Some Southern States and the District of Columbia, 1960

State	Number nonwhite	Percentage of total population
District of Columbia	418,693	54.8
Mississippi	920,595	42.3
South Carolina	831,572	34.9
Louisiana	1,045,307	32.1
Alabama	983,131	30.1
Georgia	1,125,893	28.6
North Carolina	1,156,870	25.4
Arkansas	390,569	21.9
Virginia	824,506	20.8

SOURCE: United States Census of Population, 1960, General Population Characteristics, pp. 1–164 and Table 56.

54.8 percent of the population of the District of Columbia was nonwhite, 42.3 percent of the population of Mississippi was nonwhite, as was 34.9 percent of South Carolina.

Although the Negro population has steadily increased, it has declined in proportion to the total population. The highest proportion of Negroes to whites occurred in the first census of 1790, when there were 757,000 Negroes, or 19.3 percent. The Negro population of the South has continued to decline, while that of the North and the Far West has increased. As late as 1910 almost 90 percent of the Negro population lived in the South, but during World War I the "Great Migration" of southern Negroes to the larger northern cities began. Manpower demands had increased in the North, as a result of war production, and at the same time immigration

[25] Donald Pierson, Negroes in Brazil (Chicago: The University of Chicago Press, 1942), pp. 127–128.

from other countries had decreased to almost nothing. The needed labor supply came, therefore, chiefly from southern Negroes.

The high prosperity of the 1920's continued this northward movement to the cities, and although the depression of the 1930's temporarily reduced it, World War II brought about a great increase in migration not only to the North but to the West and the industrial cities of the South. By 1940 the Negro population residing in the South had declined to 77 percent of the total Negro population; after the extensive population movements of World War II it continued to decline, reaching 59.9 percent in 1960. At that time nearly all the 6,474,536 Negroes in the North, and the 1,085,688 Negroes in the West, resided in large cities. Harlem, the largest Negro city in the world, has around a million people, and the so-called Black Belt of Chicago has over half a million in population. (See Table 17.3 for the nonwhite populations of the large cities of the United States.)

Table 17.3. Number and Percent of Nonwhite Population in Selected Large Cities, 1960

City [a]	Total Population [a]	Number nonwhite	Percentage nonwhite of total population
New York City	7,781,984	1,143,952	14.7
Chicago	3,550,404	837,895	23.6
Philadelphia	2,002,512	534,671	26.7
Detroit	1,670,144	487,682	29.2
Washington, D.C.	763,956	418,648	54.8
Los Angeles	2,479,015	416,475	16.8
Baltimore	939,024	328,658	35.0
St. Louis	750,026	216,008	28.8
Birmingham	340,887	135,332	39.7

[a] Data above refer to the 1960 census definition of "urban places." Roughly speaking, the area included in this definition corresponds to the central city and excludes the urbanized but unincorporated areas surrounding or lying adjacent to the city limits.
SOURCE: United States Census of Population, 1960, *General Population Characteristics*, pp. 1–176 and Table 63.

The migration of the rural Negro to the cities has brought many problems. He finds barriers at every turn, and he is shunted into the most disreputable areas of the city where he often lives under crowded, unhygienic conditions. This urban physical and social situation in which the Negro migrant finds himself has resulted in extremely high rates of death, particularly from tuberculosis, and in high rates of such forms of deviant behavior as delinquency and crime.

Because of these difficult conditions the majority often tends to view the Negro as if they constituted a single class. Negroes are socially stratified, and class relations within the group are important as well as those

Table 17.4. Location of the Negro Population, by Region, 1790–1960

Year	North [a]		South		West	
	Number	Percent	Number	Percent	Number	Percent
1790	67,424	8.9	689,784	91.9	—	—
1860	340,240	7.7	4,097,111	92.2	4,479	0.1
1910	1,027,674	10.5	8,749,427	89.0	50,662	0.5
1940	2,790,293	21.7	9,904,619	77.0	170,706	1.3
1950	4,246,058	28.2	10,225,407	68.0	570,821	3.8
1960	6,474,536	34.3	11,311,607	59.9	1,085,688	5.8

a Includes Northeastern and North Central states.
SOURCE: Bureau of the Census, *Historical Statistics* (Washington, D.C.: U.S. Government Printing Office, 1949), and *Characteristics of the Population*, Pt. I., 1960 Census, *op. cit.*

between its members and the majority group. For example, social class among Negroes is important in predicting the behavior in a given race-relations situation. The institutions and other activities of the Negro community can be understood only when studied in relation to the Negro class structure. Lower-class, middle- and upper-class Negroes differ markedly not only in social characteristics but in behavior as well. For example, delinquency, criminal behavior, and sexual promiscuity are comparatively rare among middle-class Negroes. The Negro class system of northern cities has been thus described by Frazier:

THE LOWER CLASS

At the bottom of the class structure in the Negro community in the northern city is the lower class, which comprises about two-thirds of the Negro population. In the lower class are found the great body of unskilled workers who earn a precarious living and those who subsist on irregular employment and relief. In this class are many of the most recent migrants from the South, especially those who have little education or are illiterate. However, this class is set off from the middle class not merely because of occupation and low income or even illiteracy. The lower class is distinguished from the middle class because of certain forms of behavior which are associated with lower-class status.

The shiftlessness and irresponsibility of lower-class Negroes are due partly to their lack of education and partly to the lack of economic opportunity for the great masses of Negro men. Since emancipation the masses of Negro men have constantly been drawn from the southern plantations into a fluctuating labor market. Because of the uncertainty and seasonal nature of work in lumber and turpentine camps, many of them have become footloose wanderers. In the towns and smaller cities of the South, they have provided the cheap and casual labor which was needed. Their position in northern cities

has scarcely been better except where there has been a demand for large numbers of unskilled workers. But usually the lower-class husband and father must
share the economic burden with his wife, who often finds more secure employment in domestic service.

In the northern city the lower class tends to be concentrated in those
areas where the Negro first gains a foothold in the city. In these areas the
lower-class Negroes are crowded into tenements and dilapidated houses
which are held for speculative purposes. In these deteriorated slum areas are
found second-hand clothing stores, taverns, cheap movies, and the lighter industries. Moreover, these areas are characterized by the absence of what
constitutes a real neighborhood. The public schools located in these areas
not only reflect in their physical appearance the general deterioration but
have scarcely any relation to the life of the residents. Even the church which
plays such an important role in the life of the middle class is absent or is
represented by the numerous "store front" churches. Consequently, the behavior of the lower class is free from the control of neighborhood influences
and the control of other institutions.

The absence of neighborhood controls is associated with a general lack
of participation in the institutions of the community. Various studies have
shown that Negroes of lower-class status are not affiliated with many forms of
organized activities. Even in their religious affiliations they tend to become
associated with the "store front" churches and churches outside the regular
denominations. In those churches they find escape from their poverty and
frustrations in a highly emotionalized type of religious service. But such
church affiliations have little influence on their morals and manners. The
shiftlessness and lack of ambition which characterize lower-class behavior are
generally associated with a lack of race pride. For the lower-class Negro, as
opposed to the middle class, tends to accept the estimation which whites place
upon the Negro's ability and racial characteristics.

There is an element among the lower class that is quiet and exhibits
good manners in public. There are lower-class families that struggle to maintain stable and conventional family life. They may humbly accept the fact
that they are poor in worldly goods as a part of God's plan but they believe
that even the poor may live righteously. Or they may believe that by living
honestly and justly and rearing their children properly, their children because of education will rise to a higher status.

THE MIDDLE CLASS

The emergence of a clearly defined middle class of any size and significance in the Negro community has coincided with the growing occupational
differentiation of the population. Consequently, it is in the large urban communities of the North that a fairly large, well-defined middle class has appeared. In the northern city there is a large group of clerical workers, skilled
industrial workers, responsible persons in the service occupations, and firemen, policemen, and other types of workers in protective service. There has
thus come into existence a relatively large group of workers with a background of stable family life, a good elementary or high school education,

and an income adequate to support a respectable way of living. Since the class structure in the Negro community is fluid, the upper layers of the middle class merge with the upper class, while the lower layers are hardly distinguishable from the lower class.

Because of their fairly secure and adequate incomes, Negroes of middle-class status are able to maintain what they regard as a desirable mode of life. This desirable mode of living includes, first, certain standards of home and family life. In the larger cities the middle class constantly struggles to escape from those neighborhoods inhabited by the lower class. This is often difficult because of rents and the restrictions upon the mobility of the Negro population. Nevertheless, the middle class endeavors to isolate itself from the environment of the lower class by moving into apartments occupied by people with similar standards. Since in middle-class families there is often a tradition of homeownership, which may have its roots in the South, Negroes of middle-class status endeavor to buy homes out of their savings. This ambition is generally thwarted because of the multiple dwellings in the large cities.

Even when Negroes of middle-class status cannot escape from an undesirable physical environment, they endeavor to maintain a stable and conventional family life. In the middle-class family, the husband and father assumes responsibility for the support of the family. He often takes pride in the fact that his wife does not have to aid in the support of the family. Both parents are usually interested in the welfare and future of their children. They are not simply interested in the physical welfare of their children but they want their children to conform to conventional moral standards. They want their children to avoid the behavior associated with lower-class status. Moreover, they want their children to take advantage of the educational opportunities which they themselves did not enjoy.

The stability of the middle-class family is often tied up with its affiliations with the institutions in the Negro community. The vast majority of Negroes of middle-class status are affiliated with the church. Although some of the more emancipated upper layers of the middle class may scoff at religion, they usually come from families which were closely identified with the church. But the religion of the middle class is different from that of the lower class. The middle class takes its religion seriously and believes that religion and morality are inseparable. At the same time Negroes of middle-class status believe that religious services should be decorous and that people should avoid the more extravagant forms of religious ecstasy. For the middle class the lodge also is an important form of associated activity. In the large cities the more secular Elks lodge becomes more attractive than the more sacred types of fraternal organizations. Likewise, for many of the middle-class families in the larger cities, affiliation with various social clubs where card playing and dancing are the chief forms of recreation represents a new outlook on life. But the middle class will seldom go in for "society," which is the prerogative of the upper class.

Just as the middle class looks down upon the ways of the lower class, it attempts to discover flaws in the behavior of the upper class. The flaws which it attempts to discover in the upper class are moral lapses. Perhaps the chief value of the middle class is respectability; and respectability in not only correct public behavior but moral conduct. The moral conduct and respectability of the middle class is bound up to some extent with its race consciousness. For the middle class is extremely race conscious. Failure to maintain respectability and moral conduct is a reflection upon the "race," i.e., the Negro. The race consciousness of the middle class is also tied up with the desire to rise in the world. Middle-class Negroes are ambitious for their children to get an education and rise in the Negro world. At the same time they are ambitious to prove the ability of Negroes to rise in the white man's estimation if not in the white man's world.

THE UPPER CLASS

In the northern cities, the Negro professional man, especially the doctor or dentist, figures prominently in the upper class. Members of these two professional groups find in the large Negro community in the North a rich source of income as well as a relatively free environment. Likewise, the Negro lawyer, the more successful at least, will be found in the upper class. It is in the border and especially the northern cities that the Negro lawyer will find the most fertile field for the practice of his profession. Moreover, the position of the Negro lawyer in the northern city is supported by the political power of the Negro, whereas in the South his practice is restricted because of the traditional status of the Negro. Public school teachers are likewise found in the upper class. Where the Negro public school teachers are not numerous, they gain a certain prestige by the uniqueness of their position. But as their numbers have increased, their class position has been determined by a complex of factors involving family, color, income, personal factors, and style of living. The same is true of the growing number of social workers. Negro public administrators who have recently made their appearance in the northern cities derive their social prestige partly from their occupations and partly from economic and social distinctions.

. . . The Negro businessman in the northern city has appeared in response to the varied needs of the large Negro communities in the North. . . . Although the more successful businessmen are at the top of the upper class, many of those in clerical occupations have gained admission to the upper class because their occupational status involves high educational qualifications and they are able to maintain certain standards of living. As among whites, in order to gain access to the upper class in northern cities, a Negro must have an income which will enable him to maintain a certain standard or style of living.

. . . The standards of consumption which the upper class regards as appropriate for its position in the Negro community are generally set by the wealthiest members of the upper class. They include the type of home which one should occupy or own and the manner in which it should be furnished. In the southern and border cities homeownership is high among the upper class. Ownership of homes in the northern city is determined, of course, to some extent by the general character of the city. But in recent years, even in New York City, the more prosperous among the upper class have bought homes outside the city. The furnishings of the upper-class homes generally reflect the desire for comfort and luxury, while taste in the selection of furnishings varies according to the general culture of the family. Likewise, in the matter of clothes, the cost of one's clothes and the amount of clothes which one possesses are regarded as an indication of upper-class status. Sometimes whites who work or associate in other ways with Negroes in professional and clerical occupations are at a loss to understand why their colored fellow workers dress better than they themselves. The same tendencies are apparent in the make of an automobile which a member of the upper class buys.

Since income and pecuniary valuations are beginning to play such an important role in upper-class status, there has naturally arisen a conflict between economic and social distinctions, as a basis of upper-class status. In Negro communities, especially in the North, there has appeared a class of Negroes who are eligible for upper-class status from the standpoint of income but who have gained their wealth through "rackets" or other unlawful means and lack the family or educational background associated with upper-class status. Shut out from the legal areas of competition, some of the more enterprising and intelligent Negroes find an outlet for their abilities in such outlawed activities as gambling. These so-called "upper shadies" engage in all types of conspicuous consumptions, involving expensive clothes and automobiles and luxury in food and drink, and expensively furnished homes. At the same time they are often conscious of their failure to achieve the respectability which would make them eligible for inclusion in the upper class. Some of them observe the social ritual, at least, which characterizes upper-class-status behavior.

Social ritual plays an important role in the life of the upper class. This social ritual, which is usually characterized as "social life," is focused upon entertaining and involves considerable expenditures. The numerous social clubs, in some of which there is much duplication of membership, are organized about cliques. These clubs are constantly breaking up and re-forming in order to eliminate members who do not represent the exclusiveness which they attempt to maintain. But most of these clubs are similar in that they undertake to provide lavish entertainment in expensively equipped homes. . . .

The social position of the upper class in the Negro community is indicated by its institutional affiliations. Its members are generally affiliated with the Episcopal, Presbyterian, or Congregational church. As among whites, the church affiliation of the upper class is due partly to the traditional association of their families with these churches, and partly to the tendency of Negroes of middle- or lower-class status to become affiliated with these churches when they achieve a higher status. Sometimes professional and businessmen maintain their membership in the Baptist and Methodist churches for economic reasons. Usually, the upper class prefers membership in the Congregational, Episcopal, or Presbyterian church because the sermons and mode of service accord with their general outlook on life and their ideas of decorum in public worship. For the same reason some members of the upper class have been turning to the Catholic Church in recent years.[26]

---

[26] Reprinted by permission of the publisher from *The Negro in the United States* by E. Franklin Frazier. Copyright 1957 by The Macmillan Company. Also see his *Black Bourgeoisie* (New York: The Free Press of Glencoe, 1957).

The Negroes' historical background of slavery and plantation living is different from that of other minorities. Both elements in this background have left a mark on contemporary race relations. In 1860, slaves constituted 89 percent, or approximately 4 million, of the Negro population, the ancestors of many of these having also been slaves. Many families in the South did not have slaves, and most of those who did owned only a few. For example, only one third of the southern families in 1850 had slaves, the average number of slaves being 8.6. In 1850, of the families who had slaves in the United States, about 17.4 percent had 1 slave, 29.5 percent had 2 to 5 slaves, 24.4 had 5 to 10, 17.4 had 10 to 20, and 11.3 had 20 or more slaves.

The position of the Negro in the United States cannot be understood without reference to the plantation, which, for centuries, was the home of nearly all members of this minority. In many ways the plantation was a forerunner of the present-day emphasis on mass production. With the use of a considerable amount of land, specialization in a commodity, a cheap labor supply, and an elaborate division of labor, it was possible to produce fairly cheaply certain agricultural products, chiefly for European export.

The complex division of labor on plantations involved the master or landowning class, the "poor-white" overseers, and the Negro slaves, who were divided into household or personal and domestic servants, skilled artisans, such as blacksmiths and shoemakers; and field hands, who were at the bottom of the social structure. The members of this biracial group lived a largely isolated existence on the plantation, but at the same time were in close physical proximity. In order to maintain a degree of separation, a system of social relationships developed, increasing social distance. These included beliefs about the racial superiority of the master class and the inferiority of the Negro, beliefs which were largely accepted by both groups, distinctive ways of addressing one another to indicate subservience on the part of the slaves, separate living quarters, a benevolence on the part of the master class toward the slaves, and legal penalties which, although infrequently employed, were there to guarantee obedience and the separation of the races. Each generation inducted the other into the philosophy of rule by the master class and subservience on the part of the young slaves born into slavery, new slaves from Africa taking from older slaves the patterns of being "good slaves." Slavery was upheld by institutional norms in the South and was supported by most organized religions as being natural and decreed by God. Since slaves were not allowed to read or write, were seldom allowed to gather in large groups, to leave the plantations at night, or to have their own ministers, it was evident, however, that this accommodation or acceptance of servile status was not complete. After the Reconstruction period harsh laws or "Black Codes" were put into effect in most southern states in order to guarantee the separation of the races and the segregation of the Negro.

This long history of slavery on plantations affected the Negro people in many ways. As an authority on the Negro has written, "The pattern of race relations which developed on the plantation provided the traditional basis of future race relations in the South." [27] Plantation life, which broke the Negroes into small groups and maintained close physical proximity to the whites, destroyed the African cultures of the slaves within a relatively short period of time. This process was aided by the diversity of backgrounds of the slaves and their lack of a common culture. Consequently, African cultures have almost completely disappeared among the Negroes. The languages, religions, and other customs are no longer there, and the Negro is fully "American." This has meant that, as compared with other minorities, the Negro has lost his cultural identity. He is not discriminated against because of his religion—practically all Negroes, for example, are Protestants—or because of his customs, but because of his biological background.

Life on the plantation affected Negro and white relations in other ways. It left patterns of speech and manners, "tones of command" on the part of the whites, and a tendency on the part of the Negro to be servile and dependent. A large part of the hostility of many southern poor whites to the Negro is a carry-over from plantation days. The plantation often had the best land, and the cultivation of land on plantations was more efficient as a result of the division of labor. To the poor whites the Negro represented a cheap competitive labor supply, household servants were often cared for better than they were, the artisan slaves often had mechanical skills which they did not possess, and the sick and aged Negro had a degree of security on the plantation. At the same time, the Negro, as a group, represented something for the poor white, despite a status lower than that of other whites, to look down upon.

The stereotype of the Negro as a poor, unskilled, superstitious, illiterate agricultural field hand came from plantation days and has been carried over today despite the large-scale movement of the Negro into industry. Finally, the slave and rural background of the Negro has handicapped him in his adjustment to urban life. He did not have experience with urban life. During slavery marriage was largely impossible, for as slaves Negroes could not make a legal contract. As a result, conditions of illegitimacy and sexual promiscuity were common, and the mother rather than the father was largely the center of what family there was. These patterns have been difficult to eliminate in modern society, imposed as they have been upon the instability of large-scale migrations. In 1959, for example, of the registered illegitimate live births in the United States, 134,100 were by nonwhite mothers, as compared to 74,600 for white mothers.

The Negroes in America have come a long way since plantation slave

[27] Frazier, *The Negro in the United States*, p. 44. Also see Edgar T. Thompson, "The Plantation: The Physical Basis of Traditional Race Relations," in Edgar T. Thompson ed., *Race Relations and the Race Problem* (Durham, N.C.: Duke University Press, 1939), pp. 180–218.

days and the largely penniless condition into which they were thrust after the Civil War. Practically all of the nearly 6 million Negroes of the North and West live under urban conditions and are engaged in industrial work. Approximately one half the southern Negroes now live under similar conditions. Between 1940 and 1944 alone a million Negroes moved from farming to urban industrial work. In 1960 over a million and a half Negroes belonged to labor unions, and increasingly they are moving from unskilled labor into positions of semiskilled and skilled employment. They are also making increasing use of the ballot. In spite of the fact that pressures from whites, apathy, lack of leadership, and low economic and educational status keep the number of Negroes who register smaller than it should be, legislative changes and other factors have made it possible for the Negro to participate in primaries and to vote in all elections in increasing numbers in the South. In Florida, for example, whereas only 5.5 percent of the adult Negro population was registered to vote in 1944, in 1956 37.5 percent had registered.[28]

Leading the spearhead of this rising Negro militancy are the general organizations of the National Association for the Advancement of Colored People (NAACP), which dates from 1909 and has over 350,000 members, and the National Urban League, established in 1910, which has as its chief goal the adjustment of Negroes to urban life.

The American Indian. America's half a million Indians have long captured the imagination of the world. They have been both heroes and villains in literature and song out of all proportion to their actual numbers. A majority of the Indians are still members of 200 reservations located in twenty-six states, most of them in the Far West. Half of them, however, live away from the reservation and are in the process of gaining title to land. Thirteen states, including Alaska, contain the bulk of the Indian population. Arizona has the largest number, with 83,387, Oklahoma second with 64,689, and New Mexico third with 56,255. (See Table 17.5.)

It is difficult to generalize about the American Indian. Some Indians are almost completely assimilated, whereas others, with their witchcraft, poor hygiene, and opposition to Western European ways, are almost as "Indian" in their customs as they were in 1870. Nearly all of them are still farmers or livestock raisers, eking out additional incomes by selling curios or acting as tourist attractions and guides. Most of their reservations are marginal lands, and the Indians on them must often be supported by special governmental appropriations and relief. This governmental help amounted to $87 million in 1953.

Most of the Indians are unbelievably poor, although a few tribes are well-to-do. The average family income of the Sioux on the Standing Rock

---

[28] H. D. Price, *The Negro and Southern Politics* (New York: New York University Press, 1957), p. 33.

Reservation in North Dakota was $767 in 1955; it ranged from $730 to $855 among the Navahos. During the same year the average national family income was about $5300. Living conditions and health standards among the Indians are also far below the national average. On the Turtle Mountain Reservation in North Dakota, for example, as many as fifteen people live in a one-room cabin. The life expectancy for Papago Indian children in southern Arizona is seventeen years, as compared with sixty-nine years for the United States as a whole.

Table 17.5. States with Largest Indian Populations, 1960

State	Indian population	Percentage of total state population
Arizona	83,387	6.4
Oklahoma	64,689	2.8
New Mexico	56,255	5.9
California	39,014	0.25
North Carolina	38,129	0.84
South Dakota	25,794	3.8
Montana	21,181	3.1
Washington	21,076	0.74
New York	16,491	0.098
Minnesota	15,496	0.45
Alaska	14,444	6.4
Wisconsin	14,297	0.36
North Dakota	11,736	1.9

SOURCE: United States Census of Population, 1960, *General Population Characteristics*, pp. 1–164 and Table 56.

The difficulties which many present-day Indians face result from past policies and past contradictions. The original policy that "the only good Indian is a dead Indian" found expression in campaigns to exterminate them in many parts of the country. The program to place Indians on reservations began about 1850, and Indians were removed, often by force, to certain specified areas, to which they were given title. When land- and gold-hungry whites wanted these lands, the Indians were often moved farther West, from one reservation to another, until, finally, most of them had such poor lands that they had to be partially supported by government subsidies.

In 1887 the Dawes Allotment Act was set up to make "white men" out of the Indians by giving each an individual allotment of 160 acres from the reservations which had previously been commonly held by the tribe. After a certain number of years this land was finally to become the Indian's property. There was a provision that surplus reservation land could be homesteaded by whites. The Indians often sold these individual land rights, usually for very little, and between 1887 and 1928 they lost title to 87 million out of 137 million acres of land.

In 1934 a new policy was instituted under the Indian Reorganization Act, which provided for the purchase of additional lands, for irrigation projects, and for self-government. Although these provisions strengthened the reservations, they continued segregation and expenditures of public funds for the special care of the Indians.

About 1950 a new program was begun which will eventually mean the discontinuance of federal supervision over Indians and the gradual assumption of necessary services by the states. In addition, efforts are being made to eliminate reservations entirely by granting them complete autonomy over a period of years and by assisting Indians to leave the reservation permanently and to relocate in other areas, particularly large cities. The Menominee Indians of Wisconsin, after some delay, were first to be affected by this program, federal supervision ending in 1961.

Two alternative ways of dealing with the Indian situation are available.[29] One aims at a quick and intensive attempt to break down the special status of Indians and integrate them into the mainstream of American life. The other aims at maintaining Indian tribal integrity and special rights until such time as the Indians are ready and willing to dispense with federal supervision and control.

On the whole, various Indian groups are so divided in their aspirations that they have not been too effective in working out a single national program. Some degree of pressure for an improvement in their situation, however, has been exerted on Congress and the general public through tribal representatives, the National Congress of American Indians, and an organization of persons interested in the Indian: Association on American Indian Affairs, Inc.

Japanese-Americans. Of the 464,332 persons of Japanese ancestry in the United States, 43.8 percent live in Hawaii and 33.9 percent life in California. Five states have 11.2 percent: in order, Washington, Illinois, New York, Colorado, and Oregon. The other forty-three states have only 11.2 percent.

These Japanese are immigrants or descendants of immigrants who came to the United States largely between 1870 and 1920. La Violette has divided the history of Japanese immigration into (1) the frontier period, from 1870 to 1908, (2) the family-building period, from 1908 to 1920, and (3) the second-generation period, from 1921 to 1941.[30] Although most of the immigrants were single, middle-class farmers who could afford the

---

[29] See Oliver La Farge, "Termination of Federal Supervision: Disintegration and the American Indian," *The Annals,* 311:41–46 (May, 1957).

[30] Forrest E. La Violette, *Americans of Japanese Ancestry: A Study of Assimilation in the American Community* (Toronto: Canadian Institute of International Affairs, 1945), p. 10.

passage, they first worked as laborers in this country. Between the period from 1908 to 1920 the general practice was to write home for a bride, "picture brides," as they were called. A so-called Gentleman's Agreement with Japan in 1907 had strictly limited the emigration of men to the United States, but some women were allowed to enter the country. The arrival of these women stabilized the Japanese family system in the United States.

The Japanese Exclusion Act of 1924 eliminated all immigration. Their exclusion was based on the erroneous belief that their industry, aggressiveness, and high birth rate constituted a threat to the numerically superior dominant group. One writer thus summarized this opposition to them.

> An anti-Japanese movement has been developing in the United States leading to differential race legislation. It has taken acutest form in the California Anti-Alien Land Law. Without attempting to characterize this movement adequately I may describe it as a movement partly economic, implicitly confessing fear of Japanese superior efficiency; partly racial, expressing scorn, disdain, and arrogance at the ambition and success of a people "instinctively" felt to be essentially inferior; partly political, furnishing opportunity to certain individuals and political groups to gain personal and party advantage by appealing to selfish interest and race prejudice against sections of the community politically helpless; and partly natural and inevitable, arising from numberless mistakes, misunderstandings, and misdeeds of individuals of different race groups speaking different languages and acting under different customs, ideas, and ideals.[31]

The Japanese in America have been characterized as having "a highly developed disposition of obedience and obligation, heavy self-demands involving the giving up of free impulse, a pride in name and the bringing of honor to one's family, an unusual cohesive organization of the group," and a generally dynamic aggressiveness.[32] In many ways, as Robert E. Park stated, the Japanese minority resembles the Jewish minority, for it is small in numbers, intimate, compact, and well organized. Both groups have great advantages in competition with a larger and less-organized community.[33]

The Japanese culture affects this minority group in different ways, according to whether its members are Issei, Nisei, or Sansei. The Issei are those born in Japan, who, prior to 1952, were aliens because laws prevented their naturalization and, in the past, in California their ownership of land. The Nisei and the Sansei, who make up about two thirds of all Japanese, are the children and the grandchildren of the Issei. Although they are a

---

[31] Sidney L. Gulick, *American Democracy and Asiatic Citizenship* (New York: Charles Scribner's Sons, 1919), p. 22.

[32] R. A. Schermerhorn, *These Our People* (Boston: D. C. Heath and Company, 1949), p. 206.

[33] See J. F. Steiner, "Some Factors Involved in Minimizing Race Friction on the Pacific Coast," *The Annals*, 93:117 (1921).

part of both Japanese and American cultures, their acculturation is generally not complete.[34] The social separation of the Issei from the Nisei is very great because of differences in the degree of language facility and in the extent of participation in American institutions. The Nisei, however, more than the Sansei, are a part of both cultures while not fully a part of either.[35]

At the time of World War II, nearly half of the Japanese in continental United States were engaged in agriculture.[36] Truck farming predominated, about 1600 farms being owned by Nisei, since the Issei were not then permitted to own land under California law. The Japanese produced about a third of all truck crops grown in California. About two fifths of the non-agricultural Japanese workers were in business, a like proportion of these being in personal and commercial services.

During World War II, the Japanese, most of whom were United States citizens, were subjected to one of the most extreme forms of discrimination in American history when they were ordered evacuated from the Pacific Coast and transferred to relocation centers. Several factors accounted for this action. The military officials in charge of the West Coast had a curious notion of the relations of race and culture; moreover, certain newspapers and politicians were opposed to the Japanese, many of whom were technically "enemy aliens." [37] These people were hurriedly uprooted and given only limited opportunities to protect their property, which many of them had to sell at a heavy loss when they could find no non-Japanese person to take care of it. The Japanese were incarcerated in camps behind barbed wire and under armed guards, in crowded institutional conditions and subject to tremendous psychological tensions.[38] During the war a large proportion were eventually released from the camps and relocated in states away from the Pacific Coast. After the war some 80 percent of them returned to the West Coast, three fourths of them to California. Actual income and property losses because of forced sales and damage during their absence have been estimated at $350 million.[39] Some 24,000 claims totaling $130

[34] Before World War II there was a small group of Nisei called the Kibei, American born Japanese who had been sent to Japan for part of their education and who were, therefore, often closer than the others to Japanese culture and traditions.

[35] Jitsuichi Masuoka, "Race Relations and Nisei Problems," *Sociology and Social Research*, 30:456–457 (July–August, 1946).

[36] Dorothy Swaine Thomas and Richard S. Nishimoto, *The Spoilage: Japanese-American Evacuation and Resettlement* (Berkeley: University of California Press, 1946).

[37] *Ibid.* Also see Morton Grodzins, *Americans Betrayed* (Chicago: The University of Chicago Press, 1949).

[38] Alexander Leighton, *The Governing of Men* (Princeton, N.J.: Princeton University Press, 1945).

[39] Leonard Broom and Ruth Riemer, *Removal and Return* (Berkeley: University of California Press, 1949), pp. 201–203. Also see Dorothy S. Thomas, *The Salvage* (Berkeley: University of California Press, 1952).

million were filed, and congressional legislation was passed permitting claims up to $100,000 to be settled without court litigation.

Since World War II a great many of the handicaps caused by relocation have been overcome, and Japanese-Americans are encountering less discrimination. The elevation of Hawaii to statehood in 1959 ended a long delay which was due, in part, to the many Orientals in its population.

Their chief organization is the Japanese-American Citizens League (JACL), a militant association which attempts to remove discrimination.

Chinese-Americans. Most of the Chinese now living in America are descendants of immigrants who came here from about 1850 to 1882, when the Exclusion Law barred further legal immigration. During the California gold rush few people would do the necessary menial tasks, and Chinese were imported as unskilled laborers. As the gold rush subsided and the whites returned to the cities, however, they competed with the Chinese for available jobs. As a result of a series of disturbances, the Chinese withdrew to segregated living in Chinatowns. This ghetto method of living kept the possibility of hostilities with the white population at a minimum, gave the Chinese certain limited specialized occupations, and enabled them to maintain their cultural unity. Their numbers were greatly increased from 1860 to 1882, when the western part of the transcontinental railroad was built and there was a need for cheap labor on the Pacific Coast. In some instances the Chinese laborers later returned to China. Although all immigration was officially banned until 1943, when a quota of 105 was permitted, some Chinese have illegally entered this country from Mexico and other places.

The number of Chinese in this country is still small, 237,292, as compared with 464,000 Japanese, largely because few Chinese women came here. Most of the Chinese immigrants came as young men, remained single, and often returned to China to live out their last years on the money made in the United States. Since they could not be citizens in California they, like the Japanese, were not allowed to own land there. Sixty years ago the Chinese population was considerably larger than it was in 1940. A large proportion of the Chinese in the United States is therefore American-born, as has been true of several generations.

With the passage of years Chinatowns appear to be declining. Several factors have accounted for this trend.[40] (1) Generally a Chinatown today must be part of a city of at least 50,000 people in order to exist. A smaller community could not support the different typical Chinese enterprises: restaurants, laundries, and curio shops. In 1940, 71 percent of the Chinese lived in the larger metropolitan cities. (2) The increasingly diversified employment opportunities for American Chinese, originally denied them through discrimination or legislation, have resulted in a decline in the

---

[40] Rose Hum Lee, "The Decline of Chinatowns in the United States," *American Journal of Sociology*, 54:422–433 (March, 1949).

number of persons living in Chinatowns. (3) In those smaller Chinatowns where there are extensive family and clan interrelationships, intermarriage in the community is difficult and thus many of the inhabitants move to larger Chinese communities. (4) Depressions and wars have weakened the economic structure of Chinatowns within cities and redistributed their population. (5) The movement of the central business districts is pushing Chinese inhabitants out and thus eliminating Chinatowns as distinct cultural entities. Probably only those in San Francisco and New York will remain. As Chinatowns disappear and the Chinese-Americans become acculturated, their dispersion will be much like that of other small minority groups who have become integral parts of the American society. Rose Hum Lee has summarized the situation as follows:

> In summary, Chinatowns go through various stages of development and decline: from an immigrant ghetto to a tourist-attracting centre, then to a shopping centre for the Chinese. While residents may live around it, more and more of them move outward and they return to it for special goods and services. The larger society's members travel there on special occasions. What distinguishes it from another community is its attempt to maintain a set of distinctive institutions, such as Chinese churches, *tongs* or Merchants' Associations, stores selling curios from various countries, shops handling the few items of Chinese merchandise they can import from "Free China," and restaurants catering to a dwindling clientele. Chinatowns have lost much of their exotic quality and uniqueness.[41]

With the exception of San Francisco's Chinatown, where generation after generation live in the same area and maintain their Old World culture, American-Chinese of successive generations live in a cultural setting which is more American than Chinese today.[42] The Old World culture gradually is lost, their ability to speak and write the Chinese language is usually lost by the third generation, and they become Americans in all but physical appearance. They want to be considered as Americans rather than as "marginal men" and assigned a minority status, but the possession of distinctive racial features adds to their difficulties. Because of these physical distinctions they may be treated as Chinese in one situation and as American in another. Thus they acquire a dual set of responses and are never wholly free from the possibility of differential treatment. Incidents of prejudice and discrimination, although perhaps not frequent, do arise, evoking feelings of marginality, resentment, and dormant fears.

---

[41] Rose Hum Lee, *The Chinese in the United States of America* (Hong Kong: Cathay Press, 1960, p. 68.

[42] *Ibid.* Lee points out (p. 410) that "the Chinese as a group are no longer economically depressed; their annual median incomes exceeded those of the Negro, Puerto Rican, Mexican, poor white, and those of other Asian groups, except Japanese, in 1950."

ETHNIC MINORITIES: SPANISH-SPEAKING AMERICANS

Most immigrants to the United States prior to 1890 were minority groups at one time, such as the Swedish and German groups in the nineteenth century, but they have now become part of the majority group. On the other hand, many of the groups in the New immigration, such as the Italians and the Poles, might still be regarded as ethnic minorities today. They are rapidly changing their minority status as they move into the second and even third and fourth generations. The status of these groups is chiefly dependent on their social class and on the part of the country in which they reside.

One ethnic minority, the Spanish-speaking Americans, has a unique position. This group includes Mexican immigrants and Puerto Ricans, who are American citizens, and those persons descended from them, as well as those persons of Spanish-American and Mexican descent in the Southwest who have been part of the United States for a century and whom one can hardly regard as immigrants. Their number has been estimated at about 3.5 million, as of 1950, or somewhat less than 2 percent of the total population of the United States.[43] This minority group thus comes after Negroes and Jews in size. Most of the Spanish-speaking minority is concentrated in five southwestern states, Texas, California, New Mexico, Arizona, and Colorado, but many are found in the Middle West and the Northeast, chiefly in such cities as Chicago, Detroit, Kansas City, and New York. (See Table 17.6.)

Spanish-Americans. The Spanish-Americans, or "Hispanos," are primarily descendants of the early Spanish colonists who settled mainly in what is now New Mexico, ceded to this country in 1848 after the Mexican War. They have lived in the Southwest for over three hundred years, and most of them are subsistence farmers in small communities. For the most part they have remained as Spanish in custom as many persons in Spain or in South America. They are unusually attached to the small, sleepy, isolated communities in the Southwest not only because of their cultural background and language but because of the discrimination on the part of Anglos. They are generally poor, and their illiteracy rates and death rates are very high. Some refer to them as the Forgotten People because so few Americans outside the Southwest have much knowledge of them or their problems.[44] Although most of them are still in these areas, there has been a recent movement to cities where, together with persons of Mexican an-

---

[43] Paul A. F. Walter, Jr., *Race and Culture Relations* (New York: McGraw-Hill Book Company, Inc., 1952), p. 325.

[44] George L. Sanchez, *The Forgotten People: A Study of New Mexicans* (Albuquerque: University of New Mexico Press, 1940).

cestry, they have generally set up a Spanish city within a city. Their adjustment to urban life has been a complicated one.

It is not the visibility of the Spanish-American minority that separates them from the majority group but their social and cultural differences. Although it is a heterogeneous group, it is largely a combination of a rural, folk way of life and a Spanish and sometimes an Indian culture. Between them and the Anglos or non-Spanish population there are a difference in language (the state documents in New Mexico are still being published in two languages), a difference in religion (the Spanish-Americans are nearly all Catholics), and frequently a difference in outlook on life. Their background is nonindividualistic, is family- and village-centered, and has a relatively low technological development.

Table 17.6. Estimated Spanish-Speaking Population of the Southwest, 1950

State	Total population	Spanish-speaking population	Percent Spanish-speaking
Texas	7,500,000	1,150,000	15.3
California	10,500,000	500,000	4.8
New Mexico	650,000	250,000	38.5
Arizona	750,000	160,000	21.3
Colorado	1,350,000	50,000	3.7
Total	20,750,000	2,110,000	10.2

SOURCE: By permission from *Race and Culture Relations* by Paul A. F. Walter, Jr., p. 329. Copyright, 1952, McGraw-Hill Book Company, Inc. Figures are approximate, to indicate roughly the proportion of Spanish-speaking people in each state. Since there are no precise statistics on the Spanish-speaking group, pretense at greater accuracy would be meaningless.

The world of the twentieth century is rapidly moving in on the Hispanos, who have found that their way of life of three hundred years ago cannot cope with it. The frequent feeling of futility is intensified by awareness of poverty, ignorance, poor diet, inadequate landholdings, and discrimination. Although they and government agencies are making efforts to improve this situation, the road will not be short or easy for a people who have resisted change for so long a time.[45]

Mexican-Americans. A hundred years ago, when the Southwest became part of the United States, it was peopled largely by Spanish-Americans and Mexicans. The descendants of those Mexicans and of many others who came later, together with Mexican nationals living in the United States, will be discussed here as Mexicans. The largest part of the Mexican migra-

---

[45] John H. Burma, *Spanish-Speaking Groups in the United States* (Durham, N.C.: Duke University Press, 1954).

tion came during the period of World War I to the time of the depression, and again during World War II, when there was a great demand for labor but little opportunity for European immigration. Over half the Mexicans and persons of Mexican descent in the United States live in Texas, but over 600,000 live in California and 100,000 in Arizona. Los Angeles has 120,000 Mexicans; Chicago, about 25,000.[46]

Although Mexicans are increasingly being employed in industry, they are still mainly migratory laborers, planting and harvesting beet sugar and cotton, and picking the fruit crops of the West. Most of them are unskilled laborers, few are in business or the professions. They are a comparatively poor and illiterate people, usually living in segregated and poor slum areas. As a source of cheap harvest labor, the Mexican migratory workers in one area have been described as being a "necessary evil."

> Generally speaking the Latin American migratory worker going into West Texas is regarded as a necessary evil, nothing more or less than an unavoidable adjunct to the harvest season. Judging by the treatment that has been accorded him in that section of the State, one might assume that he is not a human being at all, but a species of farm implement that comes mysteriously and spontaneously into being coincident with the maturing of cotton, that requires no upkeep or special consideration during the period of its usefulness, needs no protection from the elements, and when the crop has been harvested, vanishes into the limbo of forgotten things—until the next harvest season rolls around. He has no past, no future, only a brief and anonymous present.[47]

The discrimination against persons with a Mexican background arises from a number of factors. Although some of the Spanish-Americans and most Mexicans have a mixed Spanish and Indian ancestry—mestizos—this statement applies more to the Mexican group. As a result, they are often physically visible enough to be distinguished from the non-Spanish population. Many have dual nationalistic ties which Spanish-Americans do not have, and in the Southwest, particularly in Texas, they often encounter the latent century-old hostility of Anglos for Mexicans. Discrimination can also be explained by the fact that there is also often a difference in language, culture, and religion. Most of the Mexicans are poor. Many persons also tend to associate them with petty theft, personal violence, delinquency, and drunkenness, in all of which their rates are high but probably no higher than those for persons in a similar economic and cultural situation.

---

[46] During a year in the United States there are estimated also to be at least 40,000 "Wetbacks," Mexicans who enter illegally. Although they were for a long time a rural, agricultural people both in Mexico and in this country, over half of them now live, for at least part of the year, in urban areas. They often leave these urban areas for migratory agricultural work during the spring or summer.—*Ibid.*, p. 37.

[47] Pauline R. Kibbe, *Latin Americans in Texas* (Albuquerque: University of New Mexico Press, 1946), p. 176.

Several organizations set up by Mexicans and Spanish-Americans in recent years to help solve their problems have been concerned with discrimination against their group and other problems of adjustment which they encounter. The League of United Latin-American Citizens (LULACS), established in 1929, is their principal organization.

Puerto Ricans. By the end of 1956 there were an estimated 577,000 Puerto Ricans living in New York City, or about 95 percent of all Puerto Ricans in the United States. Nearly three fourths of them live in "Spanish Harlem." Most Puerto Ricans have emigrated in the last fifteen years because of overcrowding and poor economic conditions in Puerto Rico. But they have taken up residence in some of New York's worst housing areas. Although many Puerto Rican workers have improved themselves economically, most of them have a marginal existence and many come to the attention of the welfare authorities. Their background in language and culture is largely Spanish, but some, because of their mixed white and Negro racial background, encounter the same types of prejudice as do American Negroes. Consequently, these Puerto Ricans try to emphasize their Spanish language and customs. Their problems, particularly juvenile delinquency, will continue as long as the areas in which they reside contribute to deviant behavior and until, through cultural assimilation, they become more Americanized.[48]

Puerto Ricans on the whole are a youthful population, the median in 1950 being 24.3 years of age as compared with 35.0 years for New York City. The sexes are about equally divided as compared with previous migrant groups, and they tend to marry much earlier. Their birth rate is considerably higher than that of the general population of New York City. Their educational level is much lower than the level of New Yorkers in general, only one fifth of the adults over twenty-five having an eighth-grade education, as compared with three fourths of the New York population.

Unemployment among them is high. Generally they are employed as semiskilled "operatives," sewing machine operators or service tradesmen, and not as domestic servants. In fact, these first two classifications accounted for two thirds of employed Puerto Rican men as compared with approximately one third of all men. Four fifths of the women were "operatives" as compared with one third of nonwhite and one fourth of white women.

Despite these conditions, Puerto Ricans as a whole do not feel that they are discriminated against; in fact, in one survey only 5 percent thought so, and 98 percent thought their families had been treated fairly well in New York City.[49] There are several reasons for this rather unusual attitude:

---

[48] Burma, *op. cit.*, pp. 176–187. Also see Morris Eagle, "The Puerto Ricans in New York City," in Nathan Glazer and Davis McEntire eds., *Studies in Housing and Minority Groups* (Berkeley: University of California Press, 1960), pp. 144–177 and Clarence Senior, *Strangers Then Neighbors: From Pilgrims to Puerto Ricans* (New York: Freedom Books, 1961).

[49] Eagle, in Glazer and McEntire, *op. cit.*, p. 186.

(1) compared with wages, housing, and other living conditions in Puerto Rico, to them the situation is not too bad, (2) pride among Puerto Ricans prohibits them from admitting discrimination, (3) there is little contact with others than Puerto Ricans, and (4) they are so concerned with economic matters that discrimination means little to them.

RELIGIOUS MINORITIES: THE JEWS

The United States Census does not enumerate a person's religious beliefs any more than it does his political affiliation. Thus the only statistics on religious groups must be obtained through the religious denominations, generally from church memberships. These figures are often misleading, particularly in the case of the Jew, for some persons are regarded by others and by themselves as Jews even though they may not attend any church, or may even belong to some Christian denomination.

The Jews are classified here as a religious minority, although they are not clearly a religious group. Having been discriminated against for two thousand or more years, they are the classic minority group of Western civilization. Christ was a Jew and the Bible contains the history of the Jewish people and a large part of their traditional philosophy. Hence a Jewish author, Lewis Browne, wrote with irony, "How odd of God" to choose the Jews.[50] They have endured generations of persecution in many lands and under many rulers, from Herod to Hitler.

Many people believe it is impossible to speak of Jews as a group because of the diversity among them in the United States and throughout the world. No concept would include all Jews, even in the United States. They are certainly not a race. Most Jews are white and so mixed that they constitute no distinctive subgroup; there are also Negro Jews and Chinese Jews. Nor are they a religion. Many persons are called Jews who are not Jews at all; moreover, there is considerable variation within each religious group. Some people feel that Jews do not have a distinctive culture because of the cultural and linguistic variations which distinguish those from America, Germany, Iraq, Yemen, Algiers, India, and other countries. Studies of Israel, which has become a haven of Jews from all lands, indicate that it is one of the most diverse cultural groups existing today.[51] As one Jewish periodical has said: "We have not yet determined whether we are to use the term 'race,' 'religion,' 'nation,' or 'culture' to clarify the nature of our Jewish entity and identity." [52]

In sociological terms a Jew is simply a person who says he is a Jew or is considered by others to be a Jew. Several characteristics, however, give

---

[50] Lewis Browne, *How Odd of God* (New York: The Macmillan Company, 1936).
[51] Rafael Patai, *Israel: Between East and West* (Philadelphia: Jewish Publication Society, 1953).
[52] *Reconstructionist*, June 23, 1944, as quoted in Schermerhorn, *op. cit.*

some unity to the Jews as a group despite the many exceptions: the nature of the Jewish religion, the high regard for learning, the biculturality or dual culture of many Jews, their long ghetto existence, and their urban and commercial background.[53] Many of these characteristics, if considered individually, would apply equally to groups other than the Jewish.

1. The religion of the Jews has been at the same time different from and similar to that of the Christians, among whom they have lived since A.D. 70, when the people of Jerusalem were dispersed by the Roman legions. The Old Testament, on which their religion is based, is also a part of the Christian religion; yet in their belief that Christ was not divine they have been almost the only distinctive religious group residing in Western European countries. This denial of the divinity of Christ was one reason for their persecution.

2. Learning has always been highly regarded among Jews. A large part of Jewish education has been based on the study of the books of the Talmud, in which the role of the scholar has been stressed: "Turn all thou hast into money and procure in marriage for thy son the daughter of a scholar, and for thy daughter a scholar." As a result of this emphasis, the medical, legal, and teaching professions, as well as the ministry and philosophy, have probably meant more to Jews as a group than to gentiles.

3. Jews can frequently be characterized by their possession of a somewhat dual culture. While usually taking on the customs of the people with whom they have lived, the Jews retained some of the customs of ancient Israel. This biculturality has meant a dual set of customs of education and etiquette. Because they have long had a dual culture the loyalty of many Jews to a national state has often been doubted.

4. The Jews' long ghetto existence constituted a severe form of segregation which has affected even those Jews who have never been forced to live in a ghetto.[54] These areas in medieval days, and even recently, were surrounded by walls and gates which were closed at night. Armed guards watched the gates but only a few Jews ventured out even on weekdays to transact business. Inside the ghetto were the synagogue, the burial place, and the tenements. Often there were pogroms and other invasions of the ghetto in which the Jews were slaughtered:

> Forced by these circumstances to shun the Christians, the group within the ghetto became more provincial, narrow, ignorant, and superstitious, and the religion of the masses, as well as that of many rabbis, became more rigidly set than ever. The social effects of enforced segregation gave rise to an exaggerated cohesiveness and solidarity of the community (to outsiders, clannishness). It meant a temper of mind increasingly uneasy when too far from the organized forms of Jewish institutions and communal activities. Just as it has

---

[53] Schermerhorn, op. cit., pp. 381–387.
[54] Louis Wirth, The Ghetto (Chicago: The University of Chicago Press, 1928).

been remarked that one can take a girl out of the country but not the country out of the girl, so it would be equally true that it might be comparatively easy to take the Jew out of the ghetto but not the ghetto out of the Jew. In times of persecution—even though it affected their fellows in far distant lands—the lines within the Jewish community tightened so that an unbroken front was presented to the host society.[55]

Few other white Europeans have so suddenly in recent times been moved from segregation and economic and political subordination to freedom as were the Jews following their emancipation from the ghetto. Moreover, the Jew was probably the last such group to gain his freedom. Emancipation of the Jew followed the French Revolution and, beginning in France in 1806, was part of Napoleon's program in his conquest of Europe. This period of emancipation of only a century and a half is actually much shorter when one considers that it was not in effect in eastern European countries until fifty years ago. The ghetto was restored by Hitler in Germany and the occupied countries only thirty years ago.

This sudden change had a powerful and in some ways a disruptive effect upon the Jewish people as a whole. Even today the emancipation is only a century old, and for many members of the community less than that. The extent of the new-found freedom has been spotty and uneven. Late entrance into Western society has meant a sudden adjustment to the scientific and political revolutions which required centuries of adjustment to become assimilated into the thought patterns of the Christian world. Thus the full impact of the Copernican, Newtonian, and Darwinian world views struck the Jewish community at a single blow.[56]

A study of Jews in three small communities in the United States has revealed the effect of this past and the difficulties of acceptance by the gentile community which make the Jew "the eternal stranger."

As a group the Jews find it very difficult to break with their past nor are they ever quite accepted into the larger society. Thus they remain, par excellence, the eternal strangers. In general, they live in two worlds—a little disillusioned in both. They have no real world of their own because the ideological system of the ghetto, which was responsible for the survival of the Jewish world in the first place, fails to solve the intellectual and moral perplexities by which the modern American Jew is beset. On the other hand, the world of the larger community is not quite their own because despite the fact that it may admire and tolerate them, it feels eternally irritated at their stubborn persistence in being different and treats them, at best, as guests. Being loyal and neighborly has not helped, living together in the same town for a hundred years has not helped, speaking the same language and venerating the same national heroes and institutions have not helped. Even

---

[55] From R. A. Schermerhorn, *These Our People* (Boston: D. C. Heath and Company, 1949), p. 384. Extracts from this work are reprinted by permission of the publisher.
[56] *Ibid.*, p. 385.

when the lines between the Jewish and the Gentile communities become very thin, the Jews still find themselves far from constituting full-fledged members of the general community and their positions remain one of ambivalence.[57]

5. The Jews have traditionally been city persons from the time they left Israel, where they were pastoral nomads, until their present re-emergence as farmers in that country. Several factors account for this city background. During medieval times they were forbidden by law to own land, they could not take the oath of fealty, and their religious customs did not permit their serving in armies, service which might have enabled them to acquire land. Consequently, over the centuries the Jew has been limited to an urban, commercial way of life which has affected his approach to social relationships. Of all immigrant groups in the United States, he was not only the most urban; he was the only one with such an exclusively urban background. So pronounced has been this characteristic that Rose has tried to explain anti-Semitism as an outgrowth of everyone's unconcious dislike of the frustrations and problems of urban life.[58] Since he is the most closely identified with city life, the Jew has received the overt expression of this dislike for the city.

6. The proportion of Jews engaged in commerce is, and has been, probably larger than that of any other group, as would be expected from their urban background. Moreover, during medieval times Christians were generally not permitted to lend money at interest; hence it was logical that some Jews assumed the banking function. Aware of this commercial background of the Jew, anti-Semites have often charged that Jews dominate the economy. Several studies of the occupations of Jews in the United States, although not conclusive because of the difficulties of making such studies, do not support any general Jewish dominance of the economy out of proportion to their numbers.[59] A few occupations do have disproportionate numbers of Jews. They are not, however, occupations of any particular power, being largely in light industries, such as the manufacture and distribution of clothing. Jews do not occupy a strong position in newspaper publishing; banking and investment; rubber, chemicals, and petroleum; transportation; or public utilities.

The Jews have come to the United States in approximately four more or less distinct groups: the Sephardic Jews of colonial days; the German Jews, from about 1800 to 1880; the east European Jews, from 1881 to 1924;

---

[57] Benjamin Kaplan, *The Eternal Stranger: A Study of Jewish Life in the Small Community* (New York: Bookman Associates, Inc., 1957), p. 156.

[58] Arnold M. Rose, "Anti-Semitism's Part in City-Hatred," *Commentary*, 6:374–378 (October, 1948).

[59] William M. Kephart, "What Is the Position of the Jewish Economy in the United States?" *Social Forces*, 28:153–164 (December, 1949).

and the refugees from the Nazis and the effects of World War II from all over Europe from 1933 to the present.[60]

The Sephardic Jews, who came during the period before 1800, were largely the descendants of those Spanish Jews who had fled from Spain and Portugal after Ferdinand and Isabella had ordered their expulsion in 1492. During colonial times some of these Jews came to America, beginning in 1654 with the arrival in New Amsterdam (later New York City) of twenty-three Jewish men, women, and children who had been exiled when the Portuguese conquered the Dutch colony of Recife on the coast of Brazil. During the American Revolution a number of Jews achieved considerable status. Sephardic Jews have almost disappeared as an identifiable group.

There were proportionately few Jews in the United States until 1848, when they numbered about 20,000 in a population of 20,000,000. A few German Jews—in general, small tradesmen and peddlers—started emigrating between 1800 and 1848; in the years following the revolutionary movements which swept Germany in 1848, some 200,000 sought the political and economic freedom of the new land. They were chiefly political liberals as well as religious liberals who belonged to the Reform or liberal Jewish synagogue. On the whole, they did not tend to believe, as compared with Orthodox Jews, that kosher and other dietary laws were binding, that religious services need be conducted primarily in Hebrew, or that men and women need be seated separately during services.

Since these Jews had enjoyed considerable freedom in their home country, they thought of themselves more as Germans than as Jews. Their political, religious, and social liberalism, which was not as strongly opposed to intermarriage with gentiles, together with their largely middle-class, educated background, made the German Jew assimilate American ways more readily. Although some German-Jewish groups were traditionalists or German separatists, by the time the eastern Jews began emigrating they were well on the road to economic prosperity and a considerable degree of assimilation and amalgamation.

Eastern Jews from Poland and Russia began coming in large numbers in 1881, eventually numbering approximately 2 million immigrants and now with their descendants constituting the majority of the American Jews. As a result of the pogroms in Russia and Poland begun by the czarist government as a political policy, various European Jewish groups outside Russia and Poland arranged to bring thousands of Jews, mostly as family units, to this country. These eastern European Jewish immigrants differed greatly from the German Jews because they had been confined to an almost medieval ghetto existence. The majority were poor, Orthodox even

---

[60] Jews from Germany and eastern Europe entered the United States during all these periods.

in style of dress, and almost a quarter of them were illiterate. The German Jews had dispersed to the smaller cities and many to the Midwest, but the eastern Jews concentrated in New York City, which today has almost half the Jews in the United States. Many of the Polish and Russian Jews, although poor, had been skilled laborers—tailors, hatmakers, milliners, and shoemakers—and their services were needed in the garment industry in New York.

The eastern Jews, emancipated suddenly from the ghetto, have had tremendous difficulties in adjustment. Thrown into a large industrial metropolis after living in small cities and towns, many of them were able to move from extreme poverty to extreme wealth. These changes in economic status greatly strained their family system, which was traditionally closely organized and patriarchal, and produced friction between the generations. They also resulted in conflicts between German and eastern Jews, the former often tending to look down upon the eastern Jews and avoid them. Despite its problems, the eastern Jewish group, on the whole, has been able to maintain a considerable degree of solidarity through its organization and centers. Some modifications of the Orthodox Jewish religion have been made, members of this movement being called Conservative Jews. Their modifications, however, have not gone as far as those of the liberal or Reform group.

The last wave of Jews came with Hitler's persecutions and the subsequent postwar adjustment. In *Mein Kampf* Hitler set forth the battle cry of the Nazis against the Jews, who were regarded as a "race" personifying all evil.[61] The resultant Nazi purge reduced the Jewish population of Europe from 1939 to 1950 by two thirds, or more than 6 million. (See Table 17.7.) Most of the European Jews were killed, but some escaped to other countries, mainly to the United States and Israel. Between 1933 and 1944, about 160,000 to 200,000 Jews were admitted to the United States, almost all from Germany and Austria. In 1960 almost half of all the Jews in the world, 5,780,000, were in the United States and Canada, as contrasted with one third in 1939. (See Table 17.7.) The countries with the largest estimated Jewish populations in 1960 are the United States, 5,370,000; Soviet Union, 2,268,000; Israel, 1,880,000; Great Britain, 450,000; Argentina, 400,000; France, 350,000; Rumania, 220,000; Morocco, 200,000; Algeria, 135,000; and Brazil, 125,000. New York City and Los Angeles are the American cities with the largest Jewish populations, with 1,940,000 and 400,000 respectively. (See Table 17.8.)

The Jewish immigrants who fled the Nazis were largely older people with primarily a middle-class, skilled, or professional background. After

---

[61] For an account of the persecutions of the Jews under Hitler and of the results of the extermination policies, see William L. Shirer, *The Rise and Fall of the Third Reich* (New York: Simon and Schuster, Inc., 1960).

Table 17.7. Jewish Population, by Continents

Continent	1939	1950	1960	Percent increase or decrease, 1950–60
United States and Canada	4,965,620	5,198,000	5,780,000	+8.0
South and Central America	524,000	621,930	681,150	+9.5
Europe	9,739,200	3,550,000	3,714,300	+4.6
Asia (including Israel)	771,500	1,374,350	2,057,650	+46.7
Australia and New Zealand	33,000	44,000	68,500	+55.6
Africa	609,800	702,400	543,180	−21.5
World Total	16,643,120	11,490,680	12,836,790	+10.1

SOURCE: Figures for 1939 and 1950 secured from *Monthly Bulletin of Statistics,* Office of the United Nations, August, 1950. Figures for 1960 are from the Jewish Statistical Bureau, as presented in *The World Almanac 1962,* p. 258. (New York: New York World-Telegram and the Sun, 1962), p. 258.

the war another Jewish group of about the same size, principally displaced, poorer eastern Jews, came to the United States.

Because of these four distinct immigration periods, the American Jewish community has many differences, cultural and religious. An outstanding example of the latter is the division into Orthodox, Conservative, and Reform or liberal synagogues. The Orthodox membership, by families, is estimated to be 30,000; the Conservative, 250,000; and the Reform, 250,000.

Despite their differences in background and religious customs, Jewish groups are well organized. In fact, they are probably the most effectively

Table 17.8. Jewish Population by Cities of the World, 1960

City	Jewish population
New York City (greater)	1,940,000
Los Angeles (greater)	400,000
Tel Aviv-Jaffa	383,000
Philadelphia (greater)	330,000
Chicago	282,000
London (greater)	280,000
Paris	175,000
Haifa	174,000
Jerusalem	160,000
Boston	150,000
Montreal	102,000

SOURCE: Estimates given by the Jewish Statistical Bureau, as presented in *The World Almanac 1962,* p. 258.

organized minority group. Some of their associations are the American Jewish Congress, established in 1917 to defend the political rights of Jews and active among middle-class persons interested in militant Jewish efforts; the Anti-Defamation League of B'nai B'rith, organized in 1913 to oppose discriminatory articles in the press; the Jewish Labor Committee; Jewish Welfare Board; the Young Men's Hebrew Association; the Jewish War Veterans; the United Jewish Appeal; and many others devoted specifically to the aid of the Jewish state of Israel.[62]

Summary

A fully developed minority group is one which is discriminated against by a certain group. This treatment clashes with other values in the culture which would tend to give the group equal status. Both the minority and the majority group recognize this situation as discrimination, and the minority group organizes itself to remove the discrimination. On the basis of this analysis there are a number of minorities in the United States. Some are racial minorities, such as the American Negro, the American Indian, the Japanese-American, and the Chinese-American. Others are religious minorities, such as the Jew, and still others are ethnic minorities such as the Spanish-speaking American. The present status of all these groups can be understood only in terms of a long series of historic relations among various groups.

Selected Readings

BARRON, MILTON L., ed. *American Minorities.* New York: Alfred A. Knopf, Inc., 1957. A collection of readings in intergroup relations covering a wide range of topics.

BURMA, JOHN H. *Spanish-Speaking Groups in the United States.* Durham, N.C.: Duke University Press, 1954. A discussion of the background and problems of the Hispanos, Mexican-Americans, Filipino-Americans, and Puerto Ricans in the United States.

DAVIS, ALLISON, BURLEIGH B. GARDNER, and MARY R. GARDNER. *Deep South.* Chicago: The University of Chicago Press, 1941. A study of whites and Negroes in a southern city and their relations with one another.

DOLLARD, JOHN. *Caste and Class in a Southern Town.* New Haven, Conn.: Yale University Press, 1937. The relations of whites and Negroes in a southern town.

DRAKE, ST. CLAIR, and HORACE R. CAYTON. *Black Metropolis.* New York: Harcourt, Brace & World, Inc., 1945. A study of the Negro area of Chicago and in particular the differences in social classes.

---

[62] For further discussions of the social characteristics of American Jews, see Marshall Sklare, *The Jews* (New York: The Free Press of Glencoe, 1958) and Albert I. Gordon, *Jews in Suburbia* (Boston: The Beacon Press, 1959).

FRAZIER, E. FRANKLIN. *The Negro in the United States.* Revised edition. New York: The Macmillan Company, 1957. An analysis of the American Negro. Chapters 2 and 3 deal with slavery and the plantation as a social institution.

GREENBERG, JACK. *Race Relations and American Law.* New York: Columbia University Press, 1959. A comprehensive discussion of the legal aspects of race relations and their sociological implications.

KING, MARTIN LUTHER, JR., *Stride toward Freedom.* New York: Harper & Row, Publishers, 1958. A detailed chronological account of the steps and strategy used in the Montgomery bus strike by the leader of the Negro group.

LEE, ROSE HUM. *The Chinese in the United States of America.* Hong Kong: Cathay Press, 1960. An analysis of the Chinese in the United States today: their culture, social organization and personality, institutions, and their economic organization and social structure.

MYRDAL, GUNNAR. *An American Dilemma.* New York: Harper & Row, Publishers, 1944. Probably the best-known book on minorities in America. It is a detailed study of the Negro by a large staff under the direction of the Swedish economist Gunnar Myrdal. The first chapter deals with the American Creed.

SCHERMERHORN, R. A. *These Our People.* Boston: D. C. Heath and Company, 1949, Chap. 16. A discussion of the Jewish community and its bicultural status.

SHOEMAKER, DON, ed. *With All Deliberate Speed.* New York: Harper & Row, Publishers, 1957. Eleven members of the staff of the Southern Education Reporting Service, publisher of the *Southern School News,* analyze various aspects of the school-desegregation process. Particularly useful is the chapter dealing with communities where there was violent resistance to integration.

Southern School News. Southern Education Reporting Service, Nashville, Tenn. A monthly publication providing a comprehensive coverage of developments in the school integration picture in all the southern and border states. Its reporting is objective and factual. In addition to its regular reports, it reproduces some of the more important documents, speeches, and proposals relevant to public school segregation and desegregation. Extremely useful in following current developments.

These Rights and Freedoms. United Nations Department of Public Information. New York: United Nations, 1950. Contains the full text of the University Declaration on Human Rights adopted by the General Assembly of the United Nations in 1948 as well as the various drafts of this declaration.

WIRTH, LOUIS. *The Ghetto.* Chicago: The University of Chicago Press, 1928. A well-known study which traces the ghetto historically and shows its effect on the contemporary Jew.

WOODWARD, C. VANN. *The Strange Career of Jim Crow.* New York: Oxford University Press, 1957. An outstanding American historian shows that racial segregation in the South is of relatively recent origin and describes the social and political mechanism of its establishment.

Chapter

18

Discrimination and Prejudice

Discrimination can be defined as the denial of equality of treatment to an individual or to groups of persons who desire this equality.[1] Often it involves restrictions on social participation and on occupying positions of social status which give a degree of power in a society.

Although there can be many kinds of discrimination, such as by sex or social class, the discussion here will be limited to discrimination on the basis of race, ethnic background, or religion. Several forms of discrimination can be described and analyzed: (1) restrictions on general social participation, (2) discriminations affecting health and life expectancy, (3) exclusion from organized groups, (4) discrimination in public accommodations, (5) discrimination and segregation in educational facilities, (6) discrimination in employment and business, (7) discrimination in suffrage, public office, and immigration, (8) discrimination in administration of justice, and (9) other forms of discrimination.

Several rather widespread misconceptions exist about the nature of discrimination against minority groups. Many people associate discrimination only with lynching, "Jim Crow" or segregated seating arrangements in public transportation, poor housing, menial positions, and the poor quality of segregated education among the Negroes. Many other forms are less overt and thus there is less awareness of them. Although the exclusion of a member of a minority group from voting would generally be recognized as discrimination, for example, not so readily regarded as discrimination is the fact that even though that individual has a vote it might be virtually impossible for one of his group to be elected to public office.

Discrimination is often thought of chiefly as a problem of the Negro, whereas many other minority groups are subject to it. Another misconception is to think of discrimination in the United States as existing chiefly in the South. Actually there is frequent discrimination in many forms against nearly all minority groups from coast to coast and from North to South. As it has been observed more than once, "The Northerner is all for

[1] Gordon W. Allport, *The Nature of Prejudice* (Reading, Mass.: Addison-Wesley Publishing Company, 1954).

equality for the Negro, provided it is in the South." In 1960 more than half of the Negroes in the country lived outside of the Confederate states, primarily in the Negro ghettos of the large cities of the North. As one writer has stated, the second half of the twentieth century will find solutions of Negro discrimination in the United States primarily hinging on the success of integration in the northern and western metropolises.[2] So far Negro citizens largely live as second-class citizens in these cities.

Forms of Discrimination

RESTRICTIONS ON GENERAL SOCIAL PARTICIPATION

Probably the most serious forms of discrimination for a society are those restrictions which affect the general social participation of minority groups. They include a wide range of customs involving social conventions, segregated living, and media of mass communication. All of them represent restrictions on the full participation of certain minority members in the society.

Social Conventions. Certain social conventions may prohibit full social participation of members of minority groups. For example, they are often referred to as "nigger," "Injun," "Chink," "darkey," "boy," or "uncle." Children learn to associate degrees of acceptance with such verbal symbols which are considered "bad." Such words become categories of ideas with emotional effect and are difficult to overcome by later relearning or by contact with the real objects.[3] Frequently members of minority groups are called by their first names only and are not accorded such terms of formal address as "Mr." and "Mrs." Jokes about them also represent a subtle form of discrimination, for they tend to reinforce the social discrimination barrier.[4] Such characters as Rastus, Mandy, Abie, Ikie, and Mike are familiar examples of stereotypes.

Members of minority groups are often required to use rear entrances, to remove their hats in the presence of a member of the dominant group, and to use the term "sir" freely in speech. Numerous social taboos further restrict social participation. In certain parts of the South, Negroes and whites do not eat together, swim together, or participate in professional or nonprofessional sports together. One Negro has described what these restrictions mean:

---

[2] Harry S. Ashmore, *The Other Side of Jordan: Negroes Outside the South* (New York: W. W. Norton & Company, Inc., 1960).

[3] H. H. Smythe and Myrna Seidman, "Name Calling a Significant Factor in Human Relations," *Human Relations*, 6:71–77 (Autumn, 1958).

[4] Milton Barron, "A Content Analysis of Intergroup Humor," *American Sociological Review*, 15:88–94 (February, 1950). Also see John H. Burma, "Humor as a Technique in Race Conflict," *American Sociological Review*, 11:710–715 (December, 1946).

I recall a trip I made in the Deep South with a famous sociologist and his wife. We rode on that trip as conspirators in an enemy country. Each meal presented itself as a challenge, a battle to be fought, and each success was greeted by us as a victory over the enemy. As lunch time grew near we were all silent with a tension which descended over the entire car. Would we, under some pretext, be able to eat together? If not, could I find a Negro restaurant? If there were no Negro restaurants, should I go to the kitchen of the white hotel and pretend to be their chauffeur or should I remain in the car and have them bring sandwiches to me? At night came the question of finding a place to sleep. Should I again pretend to be their servant and attempt to get servant quarters at the hotel? Could I find a Negro family who might have a clean guest room? Should I sleep in the car or should we all travel on, in spite of fatigue, until we could find a city where I could obtain lodging?

Even normal body functions presented a problem. They could be performed, to quote Belden, "only with considerable opposition, delay, annoyance and irritation." Could I drink from the water fountain at the filling station? Would there be provisions for washing my hands or face? If a toilet is not marked "white" or "colored," dare I use it? [5]

There may also be restrictions on entertaining members of minority groups or inviting them to dances, parties, picnics, or other informal activities. Even more prevalent are restrictions on such social relationships as dating, courtship and marriage. In some states a member of a minority group seen in the company of a member of the majority group of the other sex may be arrested for disorderly conduct. There are more anti-miscegenation laws (laws prohibiting marriage between certain races), in fact, than any other kind of discriminatory statute.[6] Several states have only recently repealed such laws: Oregon, 1951; Montana, 1953; North Dakota, 1955; Colorado and South Dakota, 1957; and Idaho, 1959. The California Supreme Court held its antimiscegenation law unconstitutional in 1948. Such laws not only prohibit Negro-white marriages but often also forbid the marriage of whites with Mongolians, Malayans, Hindus, Koreans, and others, and often declare the marriage void, with criminal penalties which may be quite severe. The couple might be ordered to leave the state, and their children might be declared illegitimate.

Segregated Living and Inadequate Housing. Minority groups usually reside in poor housing and in segregated parts of towns, in "Niggertown," "Chinatown," or "Japtown," or on Indian reservations, or in Spanish-speaking areas. Housing, stores, motion-picture houses, taverns, and other facilities are often separate from the dominant group. One of the most

[5] Horace R. Cayton, "The Psychological Approach to Race Relations," *Reed College Bulletin*, 25:8–27 (November, 1946).

[6] Jack Greenberg, *Race Relations and American Law* (New York: Columbia University Press, 1960), p. 343.

difficult problems for a Negro, for example, is to try to live in a white neighborhood.[7]

Living in segregated areas has generally meant, for minority groups, poor housing conditions as well as high disease and infant mortality rates. Minority groups tend to live chiefly in the slums of such cities as New York, Birmingham, San Antonio, Phoenix, and San Francisco, or in shacks in rural areas. The 1950 census showed that 60 percent of all urban Negro families lived in substandard dwellings which were either dilapidated or lacked proper sanitary facilities. Only 20 percent of the white population lived in a comparable situation.

In addition to poor physical surroundings, the slum is often characterized by deviant norms, the presence of gambling, prostitution, and "honky-tonks," all of which create a hazardous moral atmosphere in which to raise families. Segregated living areas also interfere with free lines of conversation and social participation between minority and majority groups. One writer has described this restriction on social participation in reference to the Spanish-speaking people in Texas.

> It has been my observation that everywhere in the state the Spanish-speaking and Anglo groups have trouble in communicating with one another. It is an oversimplified but nonetheless accurate statement of the situation to say that Latins tend to talk mainly to other Latins and Anglos to other Anglos. There are many reasons why this is so. One is the "we" and "they" identification which I have already mentioned. All of us feel more comfortable with people like ourselves than we do with those we consider different. Another is the physical separation of the two groups resulting from separate residential and business sections, and, heretofore, separate schools. Still another is occupational separation which comes about because the Latins are channeled into relatively few occupations in which they make up the numerically dominant group. But whatever the reasons, it is an observable fact that, by and large, Spanish-speaking people tend to associate with other Spanish-speaking, English-speaking tend to associate with other English-speaking. There are few organizations in any community with mixed membership, few in which members of the two groups have an opportunity to talk across ethnic lines about matters of common concern. There are Anglo churches and Latin churches; Anglo Parent-Teachers Associations and Latin Parent-Teachers Associations; Anglo fellowship organizations and Latin fellowship organizations; Anglo veterans' groups and Latin veterans' groups.[8]

---

[7] Although minorities live in segregated areas because of low income and other reasons, there are also restrictive covenants of property owners, city zoning laws, and real-estate boards that seek to restrict the minority groups from living areas occupied by the majority group. The Supreme Court has outlawed restrictive covenants but the ruling has not put an end to their informal existence.

[8] Lyle Saunders, Address Delivered at the National Convention of the League of United American Citizens, San Antonio, June 11, 1949. (Report on the Study of Spanish-Speaking People, University of Texas.)

For minority group members whose education and income have improved it is often difficult to move into areas of better housing in suburban areas. Landlords will often not rent to them, and real-estate agents will not sell housing. In addition, the residents will often not welcome them. Although Jewish discrimination in housing is less a problem in suburbia than it was ten years ago and several hundred thousand Jews have moved into these areas, discrimination is still a problem.[9] A 1957 survey of the policies of the real-estate agents in suburban Detroit showed that one third indicated they did not wish to sell or rent to Jews and discriminated against them in one way or another.[10] The living situation in suburbia is partly a product of anti-Semitic attitudes and partly a product of Jews having their closest friendships among other Jews of the same community, class, synagogue, and organizational interests.

Such discrimination against the Japanese-Americans, an economically successful, highly educated, upwardly mobile group, is a constant source of unhappiness, irritation, and deprivation. One writer has said this about the California situation:

> Discrimination against the Japanese in California has diminished greatly since the end of the war. Partly as a result of this decline in discrimination, the economic and occupational status of the nisei has risen. Paradoxically, this economic progress has intensified the discriminatory situation in housing. For, before the war, very few nisei had the money or the inclination to seek independent housing. Most of them lived in the Japanese communities and many with their parents. The increase in income and in status of occupants have led many of them to search actively for better housing in better neighborhoods. And there they have often encountered discrimination.[11]

The situation is uneven in different cities, and among various minorities. For example, Negro housing is much better in Atlanta than in Birmingham.[12] In 1950, 17 percent of the Negro households in urban areas were classified as overcrowded, as compared to 4 percent of the white. Areas where Negroes live in Chicago, for example, which were built to house 20,000 persons per square mile now have 90,000.[13] It is common for several families to use the same toilet and kitchen facilities. In general, housing conditions of the Negro and Spanish-speaking minorities are

---

[9] Albert I. Gordon, *Jews in Suburbia* (Boston: The Beacon Press, 1959).

[10] Anti-Defamation League, *Reports on Social, Employment, Educational, and Housing Discrimination*, Vol. 2, No. 5 (January–February, 1959).

[11] Harry H. L. Kitano, "Housing of Japanese-Americans in the San Francisco Bay Area," in Nathan Glazer and Davis McEntire eds., *Studies in Housing and Minority Groups* (Berkeley: University of California Press, 1960), pp. 195–196.

[12] Robert A. Thompson, Hylan Lewis, and Davis McEntire, "Atlanta and Birmingham: A Comparative Study in Negro Housing," in Glazer and McEntire, *op. cit.*, pp. 13–84.

[13] Harry J. Walker, *The Negro in American Life* (New York: Oxford Book Company, 1959), p. 22.

similar to those which have been found for the Puerto Ricans in New York City.[14]

1. A very high proportion of families live in furnished rooms and apartments.
2. Families have insufficient space.
3. They live mainly but not entirely in the more deteriorated areas.
4. They live in old buildings in poor condition.
5. They have inadequate service and facilities.
6. They pay high rents, as compared with those paid by comparable groups.[15]

Media of Mass Communication. An important form of exclusion of minorities from participation in society is their relative omission from media of mass communication. Negroes, Spanish-speaking people, or those of Oriental descent are seldom cast as actors in motion pictures, television, or the radio except in stereotyped inferior roles. Magazine fiction also reflects majority and minority status. In an analysis of some two hundred stories, about 84 percent of the characters were identified simply as Americans, which usually implied white, Protestant, English-speaking, and Anglo-Saxon.[16] Of nine hundred identifiable characters, only sixteen were Negroes and ten were Jews. Typically, minority characters were described as the "amusingly ignorant Negro," "the Italian gangster," "the sly and shrewd Jew," and "the emotional Irish." Articles about Negro citizens who are not celebrities, or about Negro social gatherings, weddings, and other activities seldom appear in widely read newspapers, and advertisements seldom picture Negro families or individuals, except for an occasional Negro singer or athlete.[17]

Most school textbooks contain little deliberate bias, but there is often subtle discrimination through the omission of certain materials dealing with minorities. The history of America, at least in school textbooks, is largely the history of the majority group.[18] Although the situation is improving, this constitutes a basic form of discrimination.

HEALTH AND LIFE EXPECTANCY

Minority groups, such as Negroes, Spanish-speaking peoples, and Indians, generally have a higher death rate than has the white population

---

[14] Morris Eagle, "The Puerto Ricans in New York City," in Glazer and McEntire, *op. cit.*, pp. 144–178.

[15] *Ibid.*, p. 156.

[16] Bernard Berelson and Patricia J. Salter, "Majority and Minority Americans: An Analysis of Magazine Fiction," *Public Opinion Quarterly*, 10:168–190 (Summer, 1946).

[17] Consequently, some two hundred Negro newspapers and magazines are published whose contents, including advertisements, are almost exclusively Negro and whose advertisements usually show Negroes. One magazine, *Ebony*, has a circulation of over 500,000.

[18] Report of the Committee on the Study of Teaching Materials in Intergroup Relations (Howard E. Wilson, Director). *Intergroup Relations in Teaching Materials* (Washington, D.C.: American Council on Education, 1949).

in the United States. The higher death rate among Negroes is due to several factors, including poor health practices, insufficient medical care, poor living conditions, and their low economic level. In 1956 the death rate for whites was 9.3 (number of deaths per 1000 population) while the nonwhite rate was 10.1. The nonwhite death rate in 1930 was 16.3, as contrasted with 10.8 for the whites, which indicates the great health gains made by the nonwhites during the last two decades. Another indication of these gains is the fact that the life expectancy of the nonwhite population increased 5.7 years from 1940 to 1955, while the increase was 2.4 years for the white population. In 1959, the deaths under one year, per 1000 live births, were 23.2 for white babies, and 44.0—almost double—for nonwhite babies.

The higher death rate for the nonwhite population, which consists chiefly of Negroes, is predominantly in the communicable disease categories and nonmotor-vehicle accidents, primarily in industry. One example illustrates this differential. In 1959 in the United States approximately 30 percent of all deaths from pneumonia and influenza were among the Negroes.

Better hospital and health facilities are an obvious need to correct these conditions, but segregation and exclusion from hospitals is widespread in the South as well as in parts of the North. Hospital regulations, and even state laws which support them, often bar Negroes from medical association membership. Greenberg has written on this situation:

> Where there is discrimination in hospitals against Negro doctors they frequently must lose their patients to white physicians, for "white" hospitals are by far the best equipped. This bias is usually connected with medical society and hospital arrangements. Hospitals will admit only society members and the societies often will not accept Negroes, although this restriction has been waning in some places. Inability to participate in medical association meetings and to work in the best hospitals also impairs professional training. This discrimination has had a striking impact. Dietrich Reitze's study, *Negroes and Medicine,* reveals that while the Negro populations of New Orleans, Atlanta, and Nashville are increasing at a rapid rate the number of Negro doctors in these cities is decreasing substantially. This has been caused by the inability of Negro doctors to secure postgraduate training there along with their white peers and by the bar against Negro doctors' treating their patients in the best hospitals.[19]

EXCLUSION FROM ORGANIZED GROUPS

Nearly all organized groups have certain criteria for membership, such as occupation and education, and many persons who do not have these qualifications might often consider them discriminatory. The term "dis-

---

[19] Greenberg, *op. cit.,* pp. 168–169.

criminatory" will be restricted, however, to those members of racial, ethnic, and religious groups who are still not permitted to join even when they possess the necessary occupational or educational qualifications. Many organizations of a recreational nature have practiced discrimination, and some still do. Private golf clubs generally exclude Negroes, and often Jews.

A 1961 survey of 1152 clubs in forty-six states and the District of Columbia found that 781, or 67 percent, practice religious discrimination.[20] Of the 781 discriminating clubs, 691 excluded or limited Jewish membership, and 90 were Jewish clubs which excluded or limited Christian membership. The 1152 clubs represent a total membership of approximately 700,000 persons. Particular attention in the survey was paid to those clubs which were evaluated as enjoying maximum prestige in their communities. Of the 693 top American clubs, 60 percent practice religious discrimination, and of these discriminatory clubs more than 90 percent discriminate against Jews. The survey concluded: "If the thesis is accepted that many prestige clubs are factors in the power structures which influence greatly the political and economic life of the community, then the fact that 60 percent of the prestige clubs of the United States discriminate against Jews has serious implications for the Jewish group." [21] It was also pointed out that this type of discrimination against Jews is far greater than the levels of discrimination against them in other areas such as education, employment, housing, and public accommodations.

Although the situation is changing, many national college social fraternities and sororities exclude from membership those who are non-Christian or non-Caucasian. The exclusion may be explicitly stated in the constitutions; if there are no constitutional provisions, the exclusion is just as real—students from these minority groups are not asked to join.[22] Consequently, this is one reason why Jewish and Negro students have separate fraternities and sororities. Several universities within the past few years have taken a strong position against this discrimination, and it is becoming a subject of frequent discussion among fraternities and sororities. Occasionally a fraternity or sorority may defy the national organization and pledge a member of a minority group.

Many professional fraternities and associations either exclude certain minorities from membership or discriminate against them. In 1949 the American Bar Association had only 13 Negroes among its 41,000 members. Several national law fraternities exclude Jewish students as well. The American Medical Association and the American Dental Association has no national policy, but leaves the question of discrimination up to local

---

[20] "A Study of Religious Discrimination by Social Clubs," *Rights* (Publication of the Anti-Defamation League of B'nai B'rith), 4:83–86 (January, 1962).

[21] *Ibid.*, p. 86.

[22] See Alfred McClung Lee, *Fraternities without Brotherhood* (Boston: The Beacon Press, 1955).

groups, with the result that many qualified Negro doctors and dentists do not belong; hence Negroes have their own separate national medical, dental, and legal associations. Even where members of minorities are accepted in the organization they are seldom elected or appointed to positions of leadership. In 1949 the American Medical Association, for example, named a Negro to its policy-making body for the first time in its 103-year history.

About 98 percent of all Negroes attend exclusively Negro churches. Consequently, some Negro church organizations are very large, as is the African Methodist Church. Other Negroes may belong to separate Negro religious sects. Some of this separation is the choice of the Negroes and is a result of other forms of segregation, principally segregation in housing. In other instances separation in worship is the result of a church's not allowing Negro attendance, or failing to encourage it, or requiring separate seating arrangements. Various church groups have opposed these discriminatory practices and some have made a positive effort to end them.

The exclusion of minorities from formal organizations hinders general social communication with other groups. It may also mean exclusion from groups with high social status and consequently the denial of opportunities for "prestige" membership in the society. This exclusion often indirectly results in serious economic discrimination in certain occupations. Membership in certain social and professional fraternities, and even clubs, may mean associations and contacts which may furnish a definite business or professional advantage.[23]

PUBLIC ACCOMMODATIONS

Widespread discrimination against Negroes still exists in many parts of the South, as well as in some parts of the North, in the use of public accommodations—restaurants, hotels, resorts, and beaches, for example. Public facilities in the South, such as libraries, parks, drinking facilities, and toilets, are often marked "For Colored" and "For Whites," and in one state until recently there was even a law providing for separate telephone booths. Not only are these public accommodations segregated; in most areas of the South, where Negroes often outnumber whites, the

---

[23] "The exclusion of Jews from 'Greek letter' fraternities and sororities parallels their exclusion from social clubs and is similarly motivated [for social power]. It is silly to speak of college fraternities as though they were the end-product of some instinctive process by which like-minded individuals are sorted into special categories. Freshmen are rushed for the most specific and tangible reasons: social standing, wealth, family connections, special talents, athletic ability, and so forth. Fraternities, like clubs in later years, are the pools and generators of social power and prestige: those with it enter them, those entering them, heighten their potency. Social alliances formed in college naturally tend to carry over into adult life."—Carey McWilliams, "Does Social Discrimination Really Matter?" *Commentary*, 4:411 (November, 1947).

facilities for the white population exceed those for nonwhites. In 1952 nine southern states, for example, had 12 parks for Negroes, as compared with 180 for whites. In addition, most cemeteries in the South are segregated.

Before 1899 just three states required or authorized Jim Crow waiting rooms, but within a decade almost all aspects of rail travel in the South had come under segregation laws. Later, interstate busses followed in the 1930's, until, finally, only the airplane escaped. As one historian has written, "even to the orthodox there was doubtless something slightly incongruous about requiring a Jim Crow compartment on a Lockheed Constellation or a DC-6." [24] Busses, streetcars, and trains throughout the South have had separate seating arrangements for white and colored passengers; in addition, custom has also required that Negroes wait until all white persons have boarded a bus or a streetcar before they themselves could enter. In 1959 thirteen southern states had laws requiring or authorizing segregated travel. In 1961, however, the Interstate Commerce Commission ordered the elimination of all segregated facilities in waiting rooms and eating places in railway and bus terminals serving interstate passengers. Also within the last few years the bus companies of several southern cities, beginning with Montgomery, Alabama, and Tallahassee, Florida, have been forced, through widespread boycotting of the services by Negroes, to integrate passenger seating.[25]

Discrimination has also taken the form of prohibiting Negroes access to certain hotels, motels, restaurants, resorts, and the like, throughout most of the South as well as in parts of the North. Some of the self-styled better restaurants throughout the United States discourage the patronage of Negroes, Indians, Orientals, or Spanish-speaking persons. Discrimination may be accomplished by refusing admittance to these patrons, by asking them to leave, by refusing or delaying service, or by serving them unpalatable food. In the South Negroes may not be allowed to attend a public theater, a concert, or a motion picture or drive-in theater, or they are permitted to occupy only the least desirable section. Otherwise they must attend separate motion-picture theaters for Negroes, a discrimination which often represents a considerable financial burden to maintain in some of the smaller southern cities. In the South, and sometimes in the North, parks, playgrounds, swimming pools, and beaches are operated on a segregated basis. This discrimination is not limited to Negroes, for the Mexicans and Mexican-Americans in the Southwest encounter difficulties in such things as being refused

---

[24] C. Vann Woodward, *The Strange Career of Jim Crow* (New York: Oxford University Press, 1957), p. 103.

[25] See Martin Luther King, *Stride toward Freedom* (New York: Harper & Row, Publishers, 1958); and C. U. Smith and Lewis M. Killian, *The Tallahassee Bus Protest* (New York: Anti-Defamation League of B'nai B'rith, 1958).

service in barbershops, soda fountains, cafes, drive-ins, beauty parlors, hotels, bars, and recreation centers; segregation in housing, movies, schools, churches, and cemeteries, as well as in public buildings and public toilets; reluctant service in hospitals, colleges, social welfare offices, and courts; and even refusing to permit Mexican-American hostesses in USO's. Sometimes there will be signs "No Mexicans Allowed," "Mexicans Will Be Served in Kitchen Only," or "We Do Not Solicit Mexican or Negro Trade"; more often it is the less obtrusive but equally well understood "We Retain the Right to Refuse Service to Any Customer." [26]

Discrimination in vacation resorts may involve many minority groups, including Jews. Members of all these minority groups have even encountered difficulty in finding hotel or motel accommodations on the highways. The denial of the opportunity to take a vacation in a particular area or place because of an individual's or a family's race, religion, or ethnic background is a severe type of discrimination. A study of a midwestern vacation state has given us more specific information on at least one area. In this state a nationwide automobile association in 1946 listed 341 hotels, cabins, and tourist camps and houses as being restricted to gentiles only. According to a resort association official, in 1950 at least 80 percent of the state's resorts would not admit Jews or Negroes: "As for Negroes, I know of absolutely no top grade or even medium grade resort in the state which will accept a colored person." [27]

In 1959, twenty-six states had enacted laws forbidding bias in public accommodations, such as restaurants, hotels, and motels. These states are Alaska, California, Colorado, Connecticut, Illinois, Indiana, Iowa, Kansas, Maine, Massachusetts, Michigan, Minnesota, Montana, Nebraska, New Hampshire (covering advertising only), New Jersey, New Mexico, New York, Ohio, Oregon, Pennsylvania, Rhode Island, Vermont, Washington, Wisconsin, and Wyoming, as well as the District of Columbia.[28] Changes are taking place in other states also. In 1961, for example, Atlanta department stores' eating facilities, as well as many other restaurants, were opened to Negro patronage.

EDUCATIONAL FACILITIES

The accumulated knowledge of a culture is principally transmitted through its educational institutions, and discrimination in the extent and quality of any group's education may affect the cultural adjustment, social status, and personal enjoyment of its members. As groups, Negroes,

---

[26] John Burma, *Spanish-Speaking Groups in the United States* (Durham, N.C.: Duke University Press, 1954), pp. 107–108.

[27] Through the work of a state commission on human rights considerable improvement has been made in this situation since then.

[28] Jack Greenberg, *Race Relations and American Law* (New York: Columbia University Press, 1959), p. 101.

Spanish-speaking people, and Indians receive less education than members of the majority group, the dollar cost of their education is less, the quality of their school buildings is poorer, and their teachers are often less educated and more poorly paid than other teachers. Negro children in many parts of the South, as well as children of Spanish-speaking migratory workers, have fewer required days in school per year than do white children. This situation has improved considerably, and even more can be expected in the future because of the Supreme Court decision of 1954 ordering the end of segregation in education.

At the time of the 1954 decision seventeen southern and border states, in addition to the District of Columbia, had complete segregation in their elementary and secondary schools, with the exception of a few communities with only a few Negro children to educate. Four states outside this region—

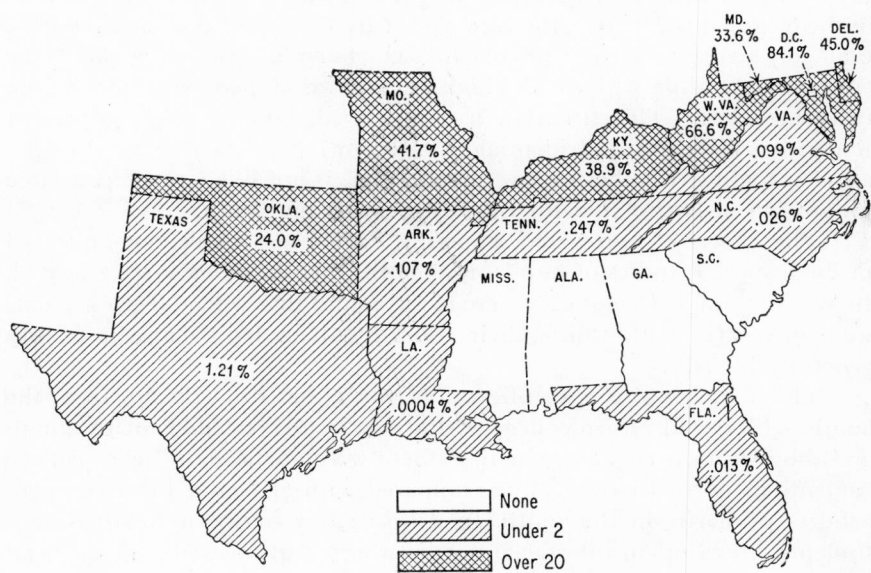

FIGURE 6.—*Percentage of Negroes in Schools with Whites, May 1961*

SOURCE: Southern Education Reporting Service, Nashville, Tenn., May 1961.

Arizona, Kansas, New Mexico, and Wyoming—allowed some local segregation contrary to law. Sixteen states prohibited by law any segregation, although not all of them enforced these statutes. Eleven other northern and western states had no laws on this matter. Figure 6 shows the present status of school segregation-desegregation in the southern and border states in May, 1961, exactly seven years after the Supreme Court decision.

As of May, 1961 in the southern region—that is, the states of Alabama, Arkansas, Delaware, Florida, Georgia, Kentucky, Louisiana, Maryland,

Mississippi, Missouri, North Carolina, Oklahoma, South Carolina, Tennessee, Texas, Virginia, West Virginia, and the District of Columbia—the Negroes in the 783 desegregated districts (out of a total of 6663 school districts) represented 22.9 percent of the region's total Negro enrollment. However, of these 706,163 Negroes in the desegregated districts, only 30.2 percent actually attended desegregated schools. The South in May, 1961, had 213,534 Negroes attending the same schools with whites, representing 6.9 percent of the region's 3,088,261 Negro students.[29]

Segregated schooling is not always a consequence of laws, however, for residential segregation in large cities generally means that, in both the North and the South, many schools are in fact segregated without laws. Since pupils are required to attend schools in the neighborhoods in which they live, the schools in Negro areas will virtually have all Negro pupils. Even Negro teachers are generally assigned in the North to schools located in the Negro areas. In 1959 the New York City Board of Education reported that 56.7 percent of the students in elementary schools throughout the city were attending segregated schools, defined as 90 percent or more from the same race.[30] This situation had improved, however, by 6.5 percent since 1957. Thus until residential segregation is markedly changed, segregated schooling, whether by law or otherwise, is not likely to affect a large proportion of Negro students in the North or the South.

The effects of segregated schooling have been amply demonstrated through special studies of pupils in schools which have been desegregated. In Washington, D.C. and elsewhere it was found that when Negro students were integrated with whites their educational level, in many cases, was generally inferior.

The majority of Negro college students, either from the North or the South, still attend Negro colleges. Although figures are difficult to obtain and the picture is changing, in 1948 there were about 3000 Negro college students in northern colleges, as compared with 75,000 at the 108 Negro colleges primarily in the South. In a 1957 study southern Negro college students attending an interracial northern university placed general social participation (Negro fraternities, sororities, dances, and so on) as the greatest asset of their college.[31] On the other hand, the greatest handicap was the inferiority of their college as measured by reputation, faculty, and their own performance at the northern university.

Another form of discrimination exists under the quota system by which only certain percentages of a given minority are accepted by an educa-

[29] "Statistical Summary of School Segregation-Desegregation in the Southern and Border States," *Southern Education Reporting Service,* Nashville, Tennessee, May, 1961, p. 3.

[30] Ashmore, *op. cit.,* p. 122.

[31] Marshall B. Clinard and Donald L. Noel, "Role Behavior of Students from Negro Colleges in a Non-Segregated University Situation," *Journal of Negro Education,* 27:182–188 (Spring, 1958).

tional institution. In a study of 10,000 high school seniors who applied for college admission, 72 percent of the applications of Protestant students were accepted, as compared with only 56 percent of the applications of Jewish students: "If we use the term 'discrimination' solely as an objective label for a difference in application success rates, leaving out any overtones concerning the social attitudes of responsible college admission officers, we can certainly say on the basis of these data that discrimination against Jewish high school students appears evident." [32] This study indicated, moreover, that the bright Jewish student was handicapped even more than those Jewish students whose grades were lower. A Connecticut study, involving 1381 questionnaires sent to students with equivalent grades, also revealed similar discriminatory college admission practices against the Jewish students. Some 41 percent of the Jewish applications, and 71 percent of the Protestant applications were accepted.[33] Quota systems also appear to apply to some professional and other graduate schools. The quota system is being abolished by many colleges and universities, because of public attitudes and the pressures of governmental agencies.

EMPLOYMENT AND BUSINESS

Members of the Negro, Indian, and Spanish-speaking minorities are disproportionately employed in such unskilled or semiskilled jobs as common labor, farm labor, housework, gardening, fruit picking, and shoeshining. Usually they do not receive equal pay for equal work, a white man often receiving more pay than a Negro, and an Anglo more than a Spanish-speaking person. On this subject Saunders remarked: "If one were to attempt to characterize the condition of the Spanish-speaking Texans, he would be forced to say that, in general, and for nearly any index of socioeconomic status that might be devised, the Spanish-speaking people are found to occupy a less desirable position than the Anglos or the population as a whole." [34]

Many unions have extensive restrictions on Negroes. Some discriminate by ritual and others by constitutional provisions, tacit agreement, or segregated auxiliary status. Certain unions bar Negroes from many positions. Although no constitutional provisions affecting Negroes exist, it is difficult for a Negro, for example, to become admitted to full membership in a union as a carpenter, painter, or bricklayer in many areas of the North and South. He may sometimes, however, become a member of a subordinate

---

[32] A. C. Ivy and Irwin Ross, *Religion and Race: Barriers to College* (New York: Public Affairs Pamphlets, No. 153. 1949), p. 11.

[33] Henry G. Stetler, *College Admission Practices with Respect to Race, Religion, and National Origin of Connecticut High School Graduates* (Hartford: Connecticut State Interracial Commission, 1949).

[34] Saunders, *op. cit.*, pp. 7–8.

affiliated union. It is equally hard for a Negro in the North or the South to become an electrician or a plumber. Some unions put Negroes in a sort of Jim Crow status by allowing them to pay dues but to have little voice in the organization.

This situation has improved with the advent of the industrial union, the short labor supply in some trades from the beginning of World War II, and the pressure of state Fair Employment Practices Commissions and the FEPC laws. In 1960 Negro union members numbered 1.5 million.[35] The average wages of nonwhite males have increased in the past twenty years from 41 to 58 percent of what white workers get. In this same period the percentage of Negroes in professional and skilled work doubled. These improvements, however, have not necessarily meant complete equality for the Negro workers, for one of the most persistent forms of discrimination in employment involves opportunities for advancement.[36] Sometimes advancement is contingent upon union membership, which cannot be secured; an example is a Negro brakeman who cannot become a railroad conductor. Discrimination may affect promotion to supervisor, foreman, salesman, buyer, or junior executive. According to Ashmore, in 1960 only six of the AFL–CIO unions had Negroes in positions of elected national leadership.[37]

Contrary to popular opinion, economic discrimination against non-whites increases systematically with their age and education.

> Many barriers to the education of non-whites will probably be taken down in the future, and this will increase their education relative to that of whites. This would also increase their income relative to that of whites if there were no discrimination; but, since discrimination rises with education, an increase in the education of non-whites may increase only slightly their incomes relative to those of whites. Hence it is important to investigate the cause of the greater market discrimination against older and better-educated non-whites.[38]

SUFFRAGE, PUBLIC OFFICE, AND IMMIGRATION.

Several million Negroes in the South are still restricted in their use of the ballot. Poll tax provisions still remaining in certain southern states curtail suffrage rights, for each voter must annually pay approximately $1.50 in order to vote, a large sum for low-income families. This voting prerequisite is also directed at poor whites and often serves to keep certain

---

[35] Ashmore, op. cit., p. 78.
[36] Robert C. Weaver, "Negro Labor Since 1929," Journal of Negro History, 35:20–38 (January, 1950).
[37] Ashmore, op. cit., p. 81.
[38] Gary S. Becker, The Economics of Discrimination (Chicago: The University of Chicago Press, 1957), p. 130.

social classes and political machines in power. Other restrictive devices have included registration requirements or literacy tests, the passage of which has often been subjectively determined by white poll workers, as well as various forms of intimidation at the polls or before elections.[39] Interestingly enough, large numbers of Negro voters were registered to vote in the various southern states before the turn of the century; the effectiveness of the various disfranchisement measures can be illustrated by what happened in Louisiana. Here 130,334 Negroes were registered voters in 1896, but there were only 1342 in 1904, after the passage of literacy, property, and poll tax qualifications. Also, in 1896 there was a majority of Negro registrants in twenty-six Lousiana parishes, but by 1900 there was a majority in none.[40]

There has been a tremendous growth in Negro voting during the past two decades. These advances have resulted from improved intergroup relations, state legislation, and various decisions of the United States Supreme Court. These decisions have outlawed a number of the various devices which had earlier been passed to prevent the exercise of the ballot. One of these devices, the so-called grandfather clause, stated that one's grandfather had to have been capable of voting; another, the exclusive "white primary" provisions, outlawed in 1944, kept a Negro from joining the Democratic party and thus virtually prevented him in some places from casting a meaningful vote. The poll tax is also gradually being removed throughout the South, although it is still in force in five states.[41] One study indicated that whereas in 1940 only about 2 percent of the total number of Negroes of voting age in twelve southern states qualified to vote, in 1947 some 12 percent, or more than 600,000, did so. In 1952 there were 1,200,000 Negroes registered to vote, and the number has been growing rapidly.[42]

Even if all minorities could vote freely, a wide and significant area of discrimination would exist if qualified members of minority groups could not be freely appointed to important governmental positions or run for political office without the possibility of discrimination. These positions are largely held by the older native white stock, and a relatively minor role in national and state politics is played by millions of citizens from minority groups. No Negro has ever been a cabinet member or a Supreme Court justice, but in 1961 Robert Weaver was appointed the first Negro to head a federal government agency, the Federal Housing and Home Finance Agency. Negroes have seldom held high subordinate positions in

---

[39] Ralph Bunche, "The Negro in the Political Life of the United States," *Journal of Negro Education*, 10:547–584 (July, 1941).

[40] Woodward, *op. cit.*, p. 68.

[41] These states are Alabama, Arkansas, Mississippi, Texas, and Virginia, although their poll tax laws are not uniform.

[42] Woodward, *op. cit.*, p. 127.

the federal government, although such appointments are increasing. Within recent years Negroes have been appointed directors of large state agencies in such states as Illinois and New York.

Members of minority groups are seldom elected to high state or national offices. In 1961 there were no Negro senators and only 3 Negro representatives. In 1956 there were but 1 senator and 2 representatives with a Spanish-American background, although this group is numerically large in several states.[43] Herbert Lehman, in 1949, was the first Jew ever elected to the Senate by popular vote, the last Jewish member having been appointed to the Senate in 1915. No person of American Indian ancestry occupies an elective position of political importance in the United States. Even the long opposition to Hawaii's statehood came, in part, from the fear that Hawaii might possibly be represented in Washington by Oriental senators and representatives, which is now the case.

At the local and state level of government, however, there has been increasing recognition of the right of minority members to be freely appointed or elected to public office. In 1949 a Mexican-American was elected for the first time since 1881 to the City Council in Los Angeles, and in 1950 for the first time in Chicago a Negro became a Cook County judge. Negroes are occupying an increasingly significant place in the local political communities, being appointed or elected to school boards in several southern cities, serving on the state boards of education, and securing places on city councils.

American immigration laws have almost consistently discriminated against some minorities: first, the Chinese Exclusion Act of 1882; later, the 1924 act, which outlawed Japanese immigration.[44] The 1952 immigration law, the McCarran Act, allowed the entrance of 185 Japanese annually; another act passed during World War II permitted the entrance of 105 Chinese, but it also provided for a total "Asia-Pacific triangle" quota of 2000 Orientals regardless of nationality. Laws also formerly prohibited naturalization of persons of Japanese or Chinese ancestry. This discrimination in immigration and naturalization reflects on immigrants of such ancestry and gives them the status of second-class and unwanted Americans.

ADMINISTRATION OF JUSTICE

It is a generally established fact that Negroes, as well as Spanish-speaking peoples, on the whole, are arrested, tried, convicted, and re-

---

[43] Some of these difficulties are described in Beatrice W. Griffith, "Viva Royal—Viva America," *Common Ground*, 10:61–70 (Autumn, 1949).

[44] This immigration act established quotas based on the proportion of the United States population which each country had in the 1890 Census, and thus discriminated against persons from Eastern and Southern Europe. The 1952 immigration act based quotas on the 1920 census instead of substituting the 1950 census, as advocated by many persons.

turned to prison more often than others who commit comparable offenses.[45] They appear to be more frequently subjected to the illegal "third degree" and other forms of police brutality. During 1949, for example, thirty-four Negroes were killed and thirty-three were injured while in police custody. A Negro or a Spanish-American offender may be dealt with more harshly by a judge than will a member of a majority group. Part of this situation in the past has stemmed from discrimination in the appointment of members of minority groups to police forces and the courts or in their limited service on juries.

Mob lynchings are still a blight on the American scene, but their extent has been exaggerated. From 1900 through 1960, altogether 1992 persons have been lynched. In the 1890's, when the population was only about 40 percent of what it is today, lynchings averaged 154 a year; in the 1930's, 13 a year; and in the 1940's, 4 a year. In some recent years no lynchings have been recorded: 1952–1954, 1956, 1958, and 1960. Many attempted lynchings still occur, and it has been estimated by Tuskegee Institute that lynchings of about 200 Negroes were prevented from 1937 to 1946.[46] Most lynchings occur in isolated rural areas, according to a 1930 study, which also found that most of the participants were young and unemployed, many with police records.[47]

Race riots involving Negroes and whites have occurred in several large cities, including Chicago in 1919 and Detroit and New York during World War II. During the last few years, as school integration has proceeded slowly in the South, there has also been some rioting and other acts of violence, but on the whole the fight against segregation throughout the South has been pushed largely by other means. Efforts to prevent rioting and violence have been made in several notable instances by the calling out of the National Guard, for example, in Clinton, Tennessee, and later in Nashville, Tennessee. By order of the President, federal troops were used in Little Rock, Arkansas to restore order.

In addition to rioting, many acts of vandalism have been directed against various minorities. Their property has been damaged or destroyed, and, in the case of the Jews, their cemeteries and synagogues have been defaced. In the first two months of 1960 there was an epidemic of 323 anti-Semitic acts directed against Jews in the United States.[48] About half of these acts involved the painting of a Nazi swastika, and other acts included, in order, anti-Jewish slogans, threats, physical damage, bombings,

---

[45] See, for example, Edwin M. Lemert and Judy Rosberg, "The Administration of Justice to Minority Groups in Los Angeles County 1948," (Publications in Culture and Society, Vol. 2, No. 1; Berkeley: University of California Press, 1948).

[46] President's Committee on Civil Rights, To Secure These Rights (New York: Simon and Schuster, Inc., 1947), p. 24.

[47] Arthur F. Raper, The Tragedy of Lynching (Chapel Hill: University of North Carolina Press, 1933).

[48] David Caplovitz and Candace Rogers, Swastika, 1960: The Epidemic of Anti-Semitic Vandalism in America (New York: Anti-Defamation League of B'nai B'rith, 1961).

Nazi flags, cross burnings, and ambiguous markings. Not all rioting and acts of vandalism have been directed against Negroes and Jews. One such example is the Los Angeles "Zoot Suit Riot" in 1943, which involved brutality to young adult Mexican-Americans.[49]

PAST DISCRIMINATION IN THE ARMED FORCES

Since World War II segregated service in the armed forces has largely been eliminated.[50] Even peacetime service in the army in any numbers, or on a nonsegregated basis, is a fairly new experience for the Negro. As late as 1949 California, Connecticut, Illinois, Massachusetts, Wisconsin, and Minnesota ended segregation in the National Guard. In 1939 there were 4500 Negro enlisted men in the United States Army and 5 Negro officers. Although, because of lack of racial identifications since complete integration, it is not possible at the present time to report the exact number of Negroes now in the armed services, it has been stated with some assurance that "for the total service personnel, approximately 2,500,000 for all the Services, ten percent are Negro." [51] The last tabulation of service personnel by race which was issued on a percentage basis as of July 1, 1954, gave the following percentages of Negro personnel against total personnel in the military services:

Army officers	3.0
Army enlisted men	13.7
Navy officers	0.1
Navy enlisted men	3.6
Air Force officers	1.1
Air Force enlisted men	8.6
Marine Corps officers	0.1
Marine Corps enlisted men	6.7

The highest ranking Negro officer in the United States Armed Forces in 1961 was Maj. Gen. Benjamin O. Davis, Jr., Chief of Personnel, Office of the Deputy Chief of Staff for Operations, Headquarters, United States Air Force. He was confirmed as a major general by the Senate in 1959, thereby becoming the highest ranking Negro ever to serve in the Armed Forces. His father, Brig. Gen. B. O. Davis, when he retired after fifty

---

[49] Carey McWilliams, *North from Mexico* (Philadelphia: J. B. Lippincott Company, 1948), pp. 244–258. Also see Ralph H. Turner and Samuel J. Surace, "Zoot-Suiters and Mexicans: Symbols in Crowd Behavior," *American Journal of Sociology*, 62:14–20 (July, 1956).

[50] Lee Nichols, *Breakthrough on the Color Front* (New York: Random House, Inc., 1954).

[51] This information was obtained, in a letter to the author, from the Manpower Office, of the Office of the Assistant Secretary of Defense in Washington, D.C., July 20, 1961.

years of Army service, served as a member of the American Battle Monuments Commission.[52] The highest ranking Negro line officer in the navy in 1960 was a lieutenant commander, although there have been full commanders in such professional specialties as medicine and engineering. In 1962 a Negro was appointed, for the first time, to be the commander of a United States warship.

Although West Point was established in 1802, the first Negro was graduated in 1877; five had been graduated by 1942; twenty-two by 1953; and thirty-eight through 1960. During the year 1959–1960, nine were attending the Military Academy, and two were graduated in 1961. The first Negro was graduated from Annapolis in 1949, the year in which the first Japanese-American entered the Naval Academy. From 1949 through 1959, fourteen Negroes were graduated from the Naval Academy, and three were graduated in 1961. For the academic year 1959–1960 three Negroes were enrolled at the Air Force Academy. Until recently, Negroes have been assigned chiefly to the transportation and engineering corps rather than to the combat infantry. As a result, they have not generally been associated with military traditions either as units or as officers and, of course, this fact has an important bearing on their national military status.

Relation of Discrimination to Prejudice

Thus far minority groups have been described and the extent and nature of the discrimination against them analyzed. To complete this discussion the basic sources of prejudice toward minority groups must be understood. As it is used here, prejudice is a negative emotional attitude of prejudgment toward a group of people. The "prejudgment" aspect of this definition means that prejudices exist only when they cannot be changed by new knowledge.[53] It is the quality of prejudgment and rejection of contrary evidence which indicates the emotional nature of prejudice.

Although prejudice and discrimination are generally associated, one can have prejudice without showing it by discrimination, either because there is no opportunity or because other attitudes may prevent the free expression of prejudice. Also, some people practice discrimination without necessarily being prejudiced, simply because the situation may call for it. This is particularly true in parts of the South, where a relatively unprejudiced person may still generally follow the discriminatory pattern. In fact, there are some five possible relations of prejudice and discrimination:

---

[52] "The Negro Officer in the Armed Forces of the United States of America," Memorandum for James C. Evans, Civilian Assistant Office, Assistant Secretary of Defense (Manpower, Personnel and Reserve) from Lt. Col. John T. Martin, Executive to the Civilian Assistant, Washington, D.C., June 30, 1960.

[53] Allport, *op. cit.*, p. 9.

1. There can be prejudice without discrimination.
2. There can be discrimination without prejudice.
3. Discrimination can be among the causes of prejudice.
4. Prejudice can be among the causes of discrimination.
5. Probably most frequently they are mutually reinforcing.[54]

In fact, as Rose has indicated, the history and process of change in intergroup relations involving discrimination and segregation may be quite distinct from prejudice.[55] Since 1940, for example, intergroup relations between majority and minority groups have drastically changed, but prejudice has not necessarily done so. The explanation appears to be in the differences in the legal, economic, political, and social forces that are operating.

Thus it can readily be seen that prejudice is not a simple concept. It is a complex social psychological state involving various degrees of negative attitudes toward minority groups. One does not, for example, have a single attitude toward Negroes, Jews, and foreigners, but one's opinions vary with respect to their social, political, and economic rights and aspirations. The same individual, too, may hold different kinds and degrees of prejudice toward the various minority groups.[56]

Prejudice is not limited to members of the majority group. Minority groups also have their prejudices. Negroes in America may be prejudiced against whites. Some white people may be prejudiced against Indians, but the latter also have strong dislikes for many whites. Many Jews are prejudiced against gentiles, and some Jews even have anti-Semitic attitudes toward other Jews.

Three sources of prejudice are analyzed here: the cultural heritage, the personality needs of the individual, and the extent to which economic factors exclude a minority group in a certain way. Finally, the effect that members of minority groups have on prejudice among the majority will be discussed.

Cultural Factors and Prejudice

Studies of infants and preschool children indicate that they typically do not exhibit prejudice toward racial or ethnic groups. This finding is of great significance, for it was at one time believed that human beings were by nature negatively disposed toward those who were biologically different. Prejudice is learned and appears to develop when definitions of the nature of subgroups (racial, ethnic, and religious) become more precise. Although

---

[54] George E. Simpson and J. Milton Yinger, *Racial and Cultural Minorities* (rev. ed.; New York: Harper & Row, Publishers, 1958), p. 21.

[55] Arnold M. Rose, "Intergroup Relations vs. Prejudice: Pertinent Theory for the Study of Social Change," *Social Problems*, 4:173–176 (October, 1956).

[56] Brewton Berry, *Race Relations* (2d ed.; Boston: Houghton Mifflin Company, 1958), p. 375.

some studies have reported finding marked prejudice against Negroes in children of five,[57] others indicate that children do not begin to withdraw from Negroes until about the fourth grade, do not think of themselves as a separate group until the fifth grade, and even in the eighth grade have many associations across race lines.[58]

Prejudice in its early stages of development is quite vague. The child begins with a rather undefined awareness of racial and religious differences, then develops hostility and avoidance of certain groups which later become more specific, and he may even, by ten or eleven, totally reject a minority group. Later this total rejection may be modified by democratic and other pressures in the society.[59] The child acquires prejudice in a gradual and subtle manner, so gradual that when he later finds he has antipathetic feelings toward certain groups he does not know why he feels in this way. From his culture the child learns many things which are related to prejudice, and he acquires from his culture beliefs about the nature of race and racial characteristics or marks. He learns the ways in which members of minority groups are supposed to act and what they are permitted and not permitted to do. He likewise learns that members of minority groups are supposed to exhibit fairly uniform negative characteristics or stereotypes. He early learns linguistic tags such as "nigger," "kike," "Jap," "Chink," and "greaser" which carry with them the idea of power for him and rejection and avoidance of members of minority groups. Lasker has stated that the pressures which mold the child's prejudicial beliefs are those which make for social conformity, namely, the attitudes of the parents, playmates, and such social institutions as the school and the church.[60] The child learns that certain groups, such as Negroes, have a lower status, that he should not play with them, and that there are other restrictions on their social participation. This lower status is often indicated to the child by the shabby appearance of members of minority groups, their poor housing, and their relative absence from white-collar positions in stores, banks, and similar places. He also notices that members of minority groups are not invited into the intimacy of the family. These patterns of minority and majority group behavior soon become accepted by the child as "natural," and even by the age of ten or eleven he may ascribe all favorable qualities to whites and none to Negroes, although at a later age he may modify this exclusiveness somewhat.[61]

---

[57] E. L. Horowitz, *The Development of Attitudes toward the Negro* (New York: Archives of Psychology, No. 194, 1936).

[58] Joan H. Criswell, "Racial Cleavage in Negro-White Groups," *Sociometry*, 1:81–89 (1937).

[59] Allport, *op. cit.*, pp. 297–310.

[60] Bruno Lasker, *Racial Attitudes in Children* (New York: Holt, Rinehart and Winston, Inc., 1929). Also see Mary Ellen Goodman, *Race Awareness in Young Children* (Redding, Mass.: Addison-Wesley Publishing Company, 1952).

[61] Allport, *op. cit.*, p. 309.

CULTURAL STEREOTYPES

Many things that the child learns about minority groups are learned through stereotypes, which are accepted as evidence that all members of any group have the same characteristics. Some of the common stereotypes which are culturally transmitted are these: "Certain minorities are lazy, irresponsible, and immoral"; "Certain minorities are more hard working and shrewd and get ahead too fast [e.g., Orientals and Jews]"; "People of minority groups are incapable of holding important positions in our society without the risk of a decline of our civilization"; "Negroes are Africans at heart, are a 'primitive, childlike people,' and expect to be treated as inferiors"; "Orientals are by nature crafty and cruel and cannot be trusted"; "Jews control business, banking, the press, motion pictures, and other important segments of our society"; "Jews cannot be trusted like other people, for they crucified Christ"; "Jews are noisy, vulgar, and aggressive in behavior."

Some cultural stereotypes are mutually exclusive, although this fact does not prevent some prejudiced persons from believing both. For example, the cultural stereotypes that Jews are Communists and at the same time "international capitalist bankers" are mutually exclusive. Some minorities are also looked down upon because they are thought to be indolent and incapable of full participation in our society, whereas others, like the Jews, may be discriminated against because they are all thought to be excessively aggressive. Merton has referred to this illogical approach to ingroup values as the "damned-if-you-do and damned-if-you-don't process of ethnic and racial relations." [62]

Although some aspects of a stereotype may be supported by facts, they are largely unscientific. In reality, they cannot be applied to all members of a minority group for a number of reasons, outlined by Simpson and Yinger:

1. The stereotype gives a highly exaggerated picture of the importance of some few characteristics—whether they be favorable or unfavorable.
2. It invents some supposed traits out of whole cloth, making them seem reasonable by association with other tendencies that may have a kernel of truth.
3. In a negative sterotype, personality tendencies that are favorable, that would have to be mentioned to give a complete picture, are either omitted entirely or insufficiently stressed.
4. The stereotype fails to show how the majority of other groups share the same tendencies or have other undesirable characteristics.
5. It fails to give any attention to the cause of the tendencies of the minority

[62] Robert K. Merton, "A Social Psychological Factor," in Arnold M. Rose ed., *Race Prejudice and Discrimination* (New York: Alfred A. Knopf, Inc., 1951), p. 515.

group—particularly to the place of the majority itself, and its stereotypes, in creating the very characteristics being condemned. They are thought of rather as intrinsic or even self-willed traits of the minority.

6. It leaves little room for change; there is a lag in keeping up with the tendencies which actually typify many members of a group.

7. It leaves no room for individual variation, which is always wide in human groups. One does not deal with a group average, but with specific individuals. One of the functions of stereotypes is shown by this failure to adjust to individual differences—to do so would be to destroy the discriminatory value of the stereotype.[63]

CULTURAL MISCONCEPTIONS ABOUT RACE

Racial beliefs and stereotypes are extremely important, for they not only give rise to prejudice and discrimination against minority groups, but also help to support both. These beliefs and stereotypes are of a number of types and include the concepts that the majority group must defend its values, that subordination to the majority group is natural, that the minority has some biological or other inferiority, and that discrimination against members of the minority is in their best interests.[64]

Such rationalizations to help one avoid subjective conflict are extremely powerful instruments for maintaining prejudice and discrimination. The individual can call on a ready-made stockpile of rationalizing beliefs which the culture provides. If one erroneously believes that Negroes innately have a body odor he can also believe that any close social contact or intermarriage with Negroes is impossible. If a minority group is believed to be mentally inferior, it would be only a mockery to place persons belonging to it in places of political or economic power where they would endanger American society. If a minority group, on the other hand, is believed to have a higher intelligence and to be excessively competitive, it would be detrimental to society if educational quotas and other restrictions were not imposed.

A major source of prejudicial attitudes are the numerous culturally transmitted misconceptions about race. As the child grows up in a culture he is certain, sooner or later, to hear frequently many such statements as the following: "Racial prejudice is innate"; "Certain races are pure, ordained by God, and should not be mixed"; "Races are distinct groups and over the years have not changed"; "All mixtures of racial groups result in biologically and socially inferior human beings"; "Certain peoples are markedly inferior in their native intellectual qualities"; and "Certain peoples are more or less emotional than others." These beliefs, and many

---

[63] George E. Simpson and J. Milton Yinger, *Racial and Cultural Minorities* (rev. ed.; New York: Harper & Row, Publishers, 1958), pp. 166–167. Reprinted by permission of the publishers.

[64] Berry, *op. cit.*, p. 118.

similar ones, represent folklore which has been transmitted in our culture without scientific evidence and largely below the level of conscious understanding. They often arise out of scientific half-truths or the misinterpretation of some actual historical facts. The evolution of man, for example, is expanded to include the false belief that the Negro is closer to the ape than is the white man. The historical fact that in many parts of the world slaves have been chiefly Negroes rather than Indians or Asiatics is enlarged to the belief in the world-wide natural inferiority of the Negro peoples.

Most of the beliefs about minorities are based on a misunderstanding of the scientific relation of race and culture. Race refers simply to biological subgroups distinguishable by certain physical characteristics, whereas culture refers to social norms and values which are nonbiological. There are Caucasian, Negroid, and Mongoloid races and various subgroups under each of these races.[65] Racial groups have few clearly distinguishable race marks, for there are no sharp and stable lines of demarcation. Rather, each race is a hypothetical average of certain physical features, including skin color, head shape, facial angle, nasal index, lip form, body proportions, and other characteristics. Although skin color is of great cultural importance, it is one of the most unreliable indices of race. Many "white men"—for example, most of the people of India and Pakistan—are actually not white in skin color at all.

Strictly used, the term "race" refers to biological processes and is distinct from culture. The two differ not only in terms of process but also in unit, transmission, method of change, and product, as indicated in the following outline.

	Race	Culture
Unit	genes and chromosomes	norms and values
Transmission	fertilization	communication
Method of Change	by mutation or amalgamation	by invention and diffusion
Product	biological individual	person (personality)
Examples	hair color, eye color, skin color, height, etc.	attitudes toward objects and ways of believing

Today there are no "pure" races. Through thousands of years, and as a result of trade, wars, and migrations, there has been a constant mixing of the races. Linton pointed out in his *Study of Man* that it seemed "slightly ludicrous" for the main exponents of the theory of superiority of pure

---

[65] "A race is a sub-group of peoples possessing a definite combination of physical characters, of genetic origin; this combination serves, in varying degree, to distinguish the sub-group from other sub-groups of mankind, and the combination is transmitted in descent, providing all conditions which originally gave rise to the definite combination remain relatively unaltered; as a rule the sub-group inhabits, or did inhabit, a more or less restricted geographical region."—W. M. Krogman, "The Concept of Race," in Ralph Linton ed., *The Science of Man in the World Crisis* (New York: Columbia University Press, 1945), p. 49.

strains to come from Europe which is one of the "most thoroughly hybridized regions of the world." "Tribes have marched and countermarched across the face of this continent since before the dawn of history, and the ancestry of most of the present population is not even pure white. . . . The result of all this has been an extreme mixture of heredity in Europe and a perfect hodgepodge of varying physical types." [66]

By varying one or the other of these components in different situations it is relatively easy to show that racial and cultural characteristics are independent of one another, and not correlated.[67] On the one hand, there are situations where the culture is fairly homogeneous but the racial groups constituting the culture are quite diverse. This is the case in the United States and in Brazil where, in addition to the white race, there are large Negro groups and an Oriental population.

On the other hand, there can be *relative* homogeneity of biological type and great cultural diversity. Before his Europeanization, the American Indian, who is biologically a subtype of the Mongoloid race, exhibited enormous cultural differences. The variations ranged from the Arctic and sub-Arctic culture of the Indians of northern Canada to the tropical culture of the Amazon jungles, and from the culture of the Plains and Forest Indians to the stone houses of the Pueblo Indians of the Southwest. Finally, there were the great cultures of the Aztecs, Mayas, and Incas, which were undoubtedly more advanced than those of the Britons and Gauls of the time of Caesar's *Commentaries.* Today in nearly every continent of the world the Negro exhibits enormous cultural diversity. There are American, British, Spanish, Portuguese, French, Belgian, and Dutch Negroes, besides those who belong to a host of native African cultures. Another example of cultural diversity is found in the white race, which exhibits considerable cultural variety in Western Europe; moreover, the Arabs, the Egyptians, and the people of India and Pakistan, all of whom are white men, also have greatly differing cultures.

In other situations the racial group can remain relatively constant while great changes take place in its culture. The difference between the type of culture of Japan at the time of Commodore Perry's visit a century ago and modern Japan, with its Western industrial type of culture and its fondness for baseball, is an example. Furthermore, although no culture ever really dies out completely, there are a number of instances where the racial group has continued even though there has been little or no understanding of the meanings of the previous culture. Until certain scientific discoveries were made, neither modern Egyptians nor Mayans could read the hieroglyphics on their ancient buildings. The descendants of the Car-

[66] Ralph Linton, *The Study of Man* (New York: Appleton-Century-Crofts, Inc., 1936), p. 35.
[67] See Edward B. Reuter, "Race and Culture" in Robert E. Park ed., *An Outline of the Principles of Sociology* (New York: Barnes & Noble, Inc., 1939), p. 188.

thaginians, Babylonians, and Assyrians live on; their cultures are largely dead.

The cultural misconceptions of racial characteristics have made it possible to associate all types of cultural factors with certain biological features. Sometimes a group is even defined as a race when it is not a race at all biologically. The Jews, for example, are generally referred to as a separate race when actually they are members of the white race. They may have had more physical homogeneity when they inhabited ancient Israel, but it is impossible to tell today, in a large proportion of cases, whether a person is a Jew.[68] The so-called Jewish nose existed among non-Semitic peoples and only a relatively small proportion of Jews today have such a nose. Today there are so many variations in measurable characteristics among Jews in various parts of the world that they have no racial identity. In parts of Germany, for example, as much as half the Jewish population have blue eyes and appear as fair as their neighbors.[69]

A culture defines certain physiological traits as being superior or inferior, in addition to defining certain supposed biological marks as constituting a "race." Actually a hooked nose is not inferior to a straight nose, thin lips are not superior to protruding lips, and wavy hair has no natural advantage over kinky or straight hair, although many societies may think so. A white skin is not "better" than a black or yellow skin, the Mongolian slanting eye, which is actually only a fold of skin over the eye, is just as good as the straight Caucasian eye, and a narrow head is neither inferior nor superior to a round one.

Beauty and ugliness are also seen in terms of the culture, for there is nothing "natural" about the aesthetic qualities of certain physical characteristics. Gleaming black skin and kinky hair, almond eyes and fat, tubby bodies are all regarded as being beautiful in particular cultures.[70] Livingstone is said to have remarked once, after having resided in Africa for some time among black-skinned people, that he felt almost ashamed of the paleness of his white skin.

Through the centuries various peoples have boasted of their biological superiority over others. Greeks, Egyptians, Romans, Arabians, Chinese, Incas, Tibetans, Vikings, Teutons, Anglo-Saxons, and Slavs have all pro-

---

[68] A recent book on race relations concluded that "Jews are a mixed people derived originally from Caucasoid stocks in the eastern Mediterranean area. Insofar as the original stock remains the basis of their inheritance, they can sometimes be identified as eastern Mediterranean peoples, but not as Jews. Since there are very few eastern Mediterranean peoples in the United States except Jews, their identification with this wider stock is not usually made."—Simpson and Yinger, op. cit., p. 59.

[69] R. A. Schermerhorn, These Our People (Boston: D. C. Heath and Company, 1949), p. 32.

[70] A Malay story of creation illustrates this point. In the beginning, so the story goes, man was created out of dough and baked in an oven. The first one was cooked too much, and he was a Negro. The second was pale and not done enough, and he was a white man. The third was cooked just right, a golden brown, and he was a Malayan.

claimed their superiority. There are a number of reasons, however, why no race or ethnic group can be shown to be superior over another.

1. No one has yet been able to demonstrate the innate mental, temperamental, or emotional superiority of one racial group over another, even though many of the results have indicated a lower intelligence for Negroes and American Indians.[71] This comparative testing has usually been based on a biased unrepresentative sample of the minority group with its differences in socioeconomic backgrounds, schooling, language, motivation, and rapport.[72] All groups have superior and inferior individuals. The differences among groups as a whole can probably be explained in terms of social and educational opportunities.

2. Superiority would have to be defined. Does it mean physical strength, military power, technological development? Or does it mean human happiness and the relative absence of social deviations? Does superiority imply the development of great religious philosophy, art, and literature? Although many nonwhite races cannot equal the development of machines and public sanitation, they may still have developed an emphasis on moral values, art forms, and cooperative living that may excel the technological developments of Western European civilization. The question of superiority in itself is an issue involving value judgments which, by their nature, may be incapable of solution. Can modern machines be compared with the complex system of reckoning kinship among the so-called inferior Australian aborigines? Can religious beliefs or art forms be compared in terms of any universal standards?

3. Superiority cannot be considered without regard to time. In different historical periods every racial group and most European national groups have excelled in warfare. At other times the Mongoloid peoples have been technologically superior to the white people. In fact, the idea of the superiority of a people is based on the belief that a given race actually produced all its culture. This assumption is contrary to the scientific position that most culture has been borrowed and spread by diffusion. As Linton has indicated, little of the average American's daily activity is exclusively a Western European invention or development.[73]

Prejudice and Personality Needs

Various attempts have also been made to explain prejudice almost exclusively in terms of personality needs. These explanations have taken two forms: that prejudice arises from frustrations and aggressions; and that

---

[71] Otto Klineberg, *Characteristics of the American Negro* (New York: Harper & Row, Publishers, 1944), p. 35.

[72] Otto Klineberg, *Race Differences* (New York: Harper & Row, Publishers, 1935), pp. 167–168.

[73] Linton, *The Study of Man*, pp. 325–327.

there is a general prejudiced personality pattern, often referred to as a "conformist" or "authoritarian personality." Although some of these explanations appear useful if accompanied by proper emphasis on the cultural heritage, they are not complete explanations of prejudice.

According to the first explanation, feelings of hostility arising within the individual may be freed at one level or all three. First, the individual may exhibit hostility in the form of free-floating aggression toward anyone or anything. Second, he may attach his hostility to the behavior of specific individuals and attribute his own inadequacies to their behavior. A common way to release hostilities is, however, the third type, wherein the aggression is deflected toward certain larger social categories, usually minority groups.[74] Dollard has probably developed this explanation more than anyone, particularly with reference to Negro-white relations in a southern town.[75] The frustrations of whites, arising out of the repressions placed by their culture on their free social and sexual relations, for example, serve to make them overtly and psychologically aggressive toward the Negro.

One form of the frustration explanation of prejudice, the "scapegoat theory," has had wide support among many writers on anti-Semitism who have sought to explain the centuries' old hatred for the Jew as a product of the frustrations of the gentile world. The Jew has been blamed for political failure, economic misery, and religious strife. In various historic periods other "safe goats," as Carey McWilliams has called them, have been scapegoats. According to Allport, a good scapegoat should have five characteristics: (1) The group should be highly visible in physical appearance, manners, or customs. (2) It should not be a weak group; yet (3) it should be an accessible one which is not strong enough to retaliate. (4) There must be some latent hostility toward the group. Finally, (5) the group should represent some ideological principle which the people resent.[76]

The frustration-aggression theory sounds extremely plausible, but it is too simple an explanation for minority prejudice in general. The political, economic, and social positions of some groups, such as the Indian and the Spanish-speaking peoples, are so inferior that it would be difficult to attribute prejudice toward these minorities as a scapegoat mechanism. Likewise, as one author has indicated, the Negro's social and economic status has been historically so inferior that one could hardly blame our troubles on him.[77] Many cultural and competitive factors other than frus-

---

[74] Robin Williams, Jr., *The Reduction of Intergroup Tensions* (Bulletin 57; New York: Social Science Research Council, 1947), p. 52.

[75] John Dollard, Neal Miller, Leonard Doob, *et al.*, *Frustration and Aggression* (New Haven, Conn.: Yale University Press, 1939), and John Dollard, *Caste and Class in a Southern Town* (New Haven, Conn.: Yale University Press, 1937).

[76] Gordon W. Allport, *ABC's of Scapegoating* (rev. ed.; New York: Anti-Defamation League of B'nai B'rith, 1948), pp. 42–43.

[77] Bohdan Zawadski, "Limitation of the Scapegoat Theory of Prejudice," *Journal of Abnormal and Social Psychology*, 43:127–141 (April, 1948).

tration and aggression enter into the explanation of prejudice. Aggression may well intensify prejudice, but this is not the same thing as saying that it causes prejudice. This theory, moreover, does not adequately explain why one group rather than another is the object of prejudice. Most prejudice has a long cultural history independent of the frustrations of given individuals or of historical situations. Simpson and Yinger have concluded that even though this theory helps to explain some of the forces behind prejudice, the "need" for it, it does not explain the "direction" prejudice takes.[78]

A somewhat different approach in terms of personality needs is the more recent work by psychologists and psychiatrists in the field of racial and religious discrimination which has sought to discover the general personality characteristics of prejudiced persons. This new approach has been based on the hypothesis that a certain constellation of personality traits characterizes the prejudiced person and that there is a "prejudiced personality." In 1938 Murphy and Likert reported that prejudiced college students tend to be prejudiced toward all minorities, and that these students were usually conservative and reactionary about other social issues.[79]

The most comprehensive attempt to discover a basic prejudiced personality pattern is reported in *The Authoritarian Personality* by Adorno, Frenkel-Brunswik, Levinson, and Sanford.[80] The purpose of this study was to reveal the characteristics of the "authoritarian personality," i.e., a specific syndrome which includes anti-Semitism, general ethnocentrism, and political-economic conservatism. Their sample consisted of 2099 persons, primarily professional, middle-class people. The total sample included, however, a mixed group from West Coast service clubs, patients of psychiatric clinics, inmates of San Quentin Prison, men at the Merchant Marine Officer School, parent-teacher association members, university students, and working-class men and women. A smaller group of the most prejudiced and the least prejudiced was then selected for comparative study. They were given an elaborate set of questionnaires consisting of a scale to measure anti-Semitism, one to measure ethnocentricism, and one to measure conservative and fascist tendencies. Approximately 80 of the highly prejudiced were chosen for intensive interviews and projective testing.

This research study revealed marked differences in the characteristics of the least and the most prejudiced persons. The least prejudiced were liberal, whereas the most prejudiced tended to be authoritarian and conservative. The former were cooperative, permissive, and flexible in social relationships, whereas the latter were power-oriented, looked up to the strong, disclaimed the weak, and had a conventional rigid fear of new situa-

[78] Simpson and Yinger, *op. cit.*, p. 84.
[79] Gardner Murphy and Rensis Likert, *Public Opinion and the Individual* (New York: Harper & Row, Publishers, 1938).
[80] T. W. Adorno *et al. The Authoritarian Personality* (New York: Harper & Row, Publishers, 1950).

tions. The least prejudiced had had an affectionate childhood and had an equalitarian marriage, whereas the most prejudiced had had an exploitative parent and had a dependent attitude toward their wives.

This theory of a prejudiced personality pattern may be useful if it is interpreted only in terms of the possible intensification of group prejudice. It has limitations, however, if it is suggested as a universal or basic explanation of all prejudice. The few such studies which have been made have been almost entirely concerned with anti-Semitism, and they have been based largely on samples of prejudiced persons who are probably unrepresentative of the general population.

Such theories have also not dealt sufficiently with the differential exposure to cultural norms concerning minority groups. It is possible that "authoritarian" and "liberal," rather than simply representing basic personality trait structures, actually denote certain norms which groups of persons display. It is likely that in many cases it is no more necessary to use psychological factors to explain prejudice toward Negroes than it is to explain certain habits in eating or dress. Even the selection of groups for prejudicial treatment has a cultural explanation and may vary from society to society. It is likely that many persons with an "authoritarian personality" or something resembling it are not excessively prejudiced. Conversely, in instances of excessive prejudice where such psychological theories may contribute an understanding, all such persons need not be explained in this way. Exposure to extremely anti-Semitic attitudes in the family or in other intimate social groups, with no unique psychological traits being present, could probably make a person a Jew-baiter.

> Before we can explain antiminority feelings in terms of a harsh, capricious, and unloving childhood, we must be aware of group structure and of variation in values among the subcultures of a society. If residents of Mississippi have a higher anti-Negro score than those of Minnesota, this does not prove that they are more authoritarian—i.e., more intolerant of ambiguity, more cynical, more rigid, less self-accepting. It may be that they simply express different cultural influences. Differences in agreement with the idea that there are two kinds of people in the world, the weak and the strong, may simply indicate differences in actual experience.[81]

Prejudice and Economic Factors

The previous discussion has emphasized the cultural and personality factors in prejudice. Attempts have also been made to attribute prejudice

---

[81] George E. Simpson and J. Milton Yinger, "The Sociology of Race and Ethnic Relations," in Robert K. Merton, Leonard Broom, and Leonard S. Cottrell, Jr., *Sociology Today* (New York: Basic Books, Inc., 1959), p. 379. Also see William J. MacKinnon and Richard Centers, "Authoritarianism and Urban Stratification," *American Journal of Sociology*, 61:610–620 (1956).

and the minority problem exclusively to economic competition and class conflict. It has been suggested that prejudice arises from unfair competition or the tendency of one group to exploit another.[82] One writer has stated that American history and our contemporary life clearly reveal the "stark, material profit-seeking core from which all of the varied forms of anti-Negro discrimination and oppression emerge." [83] Another Negro writer has concluded, after a lengthy study, that race prejudice is a social attitude engendered by certain classes who stigmatize a group as inferior in order that they might justify their exploitation of the group or its resources.[84]

There can be little doubt that economic competition does intensify prejudice. History has demonstrated that for centuries prejudice has been used as a weapon in religious and political struggles in Europe, including particularly the numerous anti-Semitic purges and pogroms. At various times there have been groups in America who have sought to eliminate certain minorities from economic and social competition. They have included the Native American party of the 1830's, the Know-Nothing Order of the 1850's, and a variety of more recent groups.

The great differentiation of groups and social roles in our modern society has made possible extensive areas of conflict over social and economic status. Under these conditions, therefore, it is sometimes possible for one group to try to restrict the economic position of another group entirely, or even to eliminate it. These intergroup tensions are more likely to develop in situations where there are more rapid and far-reaching social changes, changes that have resulted in increased culture conflict between groups. Migrations of groups with different physical and social characteristics often increase prejudice, for these newcomers exert pressures on housing facilities, transportation, schools, jobs, and even general social status. The pressures vary according to the size of the migration in relation to the existing population and the rapidity of the influx of the migrants. This type of pressure, with the resulting tensions, appears to have been an important factor in the famous Chicago race riot of 1919 and the Detroit race riot during World War II.

Open conflict between groups also seems to vary according to how direct and successful the minority competition is for wealth and prestige. The prejudice toward the Japanese exhibited in California by certain vested farming interests is an illustration of this point, and it contributed greatly to their removal from the West Coast at the outbreak of World War

---

[82] Alexander Lesser, "Anti-Semitism in the United States," *Journal of Negro Education*, 10:545–556 (July, 1941). See also Oliver C. Cox, *Caste, Class and Race* (New York: Doubleday & Company, Inc., 1948).

[83] Doxsey Wilkerson's Introduction to Herbert Aptheker, *The Negro People in America* (New York: International Publishers Co., Inc., 1946), pp. 8–10.

[84] Oliver Cox, "Race Prejudice and Intolerance—A Distinction," *Social Forces*, 24:216 (December, 1945). See also his *Caste, Class and Race*.

II.[85] Much of United States immigration policy has been directed toward excluding first the Chinese, then the Japanese, later people from Southern and Eastern Europe, and, finally, the Mexicans from competition with various groups in the society.

Certainly minorities experience discrimination in employment, wage scales, and occupational opportunities. The generally low status of unskilled labor, held at one time or other by most minority groups, has added to the prejudices against them, and interferes with their social participation in society.

This role of the competitive and individualistic nature of modern society in prejudice cannot be overlooked. An economic explanation of prejudice is far too simple, however, for such an explanation does not consider the varied role of cultural definitions nor the possible role of personality factors. Actually it does not explain prejudice; it only suggests an explanation of intensity in some cases. More specific arguments against such an explanation can be cited. As they grow older, children, for example, often exhibit prejudice under circumstances where there is little competition. Likewise, individuals of all groups may exhibit prejudice toward a given minority, whereas only a small number are in direct competition with the group. Upper-class southern whites, for example, may be prejudiced toward Negroes with whom they are in little competition, although they may benefit from having Negro servants. There may even be prejudice where there is almost no competition, as demonstrated by the attitudes of the whites of Australia toward the native aborigines. Simpson and Yinger have indicated the limitations of the competitive theory of prejudice as follows:

> Many contradictory forces are at work in any given expression of prejudice. Which one will predominate depends upon their relative strength and the setting in which they work. The "economic" element in prejudice is *least* likely to predominate where traditional definitions of roles are most stable, where economic classes are least self-conscious and organized, where the "intellectual climate" encourages the interpretation of individual frustrations in terms of personal opponents. The "economic" element in prejudice is most likely to predominate where traditional definitions of roles are being challenged, where large-scale organizations along class lines are most highly developed, and where group differentiation tends to correspond with differences in economic functions. The careful student will not accept a blanket statement of the *general* role of group conflict in prejudice, whether it be a statement that stresses or one that minimizes that role. He will, rather, seek to find the role of group conflict in *specific* situations as it interacts with the other forces at work in those situations.[86]

---

[85] Carey McWilliams, *Prejudice—Japanese-Americans: Symbol of Racial Intolerance* (Boston: Little, Brown & Company, 1944).

[86] Simpson and Yinger, *Racial and Cultural Minorities*, p. 148. Reprinted by permission of Harper & Row, Publishers.

Prejudice and the Minority

Prejudice can be related to the minority group as well as to the majority group. In the first place, it is likely that some relation between the behavior of the minority and prejudice exists. To many who are prejudiced this is a satisfactory explanation of their prejudices, and Allport has referred to it as the "earned reputation" theory.[87] Although it is far too simple an explanation, one writer has suggested that pronounced differences in behavior may cause prejudice and that prejudice is much more a product of interaction than solely a result of majority attitudes.[88] As yet there has been little research in this direction, but the approach looks feasible provided that proper weight is given to the likelihood that the majority attitudes are far more important in establishing prejudice.[89]

More evident is the effect of prejudice and discrimination on the behavior of minority members. First of all, prejudice and discrimination are interpreted by members of minority groups in different ways according to the nature of the contact, the cohesiveness of the minority, the region of the country, and the education, income, occupation and social class, personality, skin color, and the individual's early training for minority-majority relations.[90] In general, discrimination results in a feeling of inferiority on the part of the individual minority member, but may be expressed in other ways as well.

Minorities may deal with prejudice and discrimination by acceptance, avoidance, or aggression.[91] Some minority members may avoid difficulties by accepting their lot in life completely, as have "folk" or subservient Negroes.[92] They do not challenge their role and may look with disfavor on those who do. Such acceptance may arise from a real feeling of inferiority or it may give the person a feeling of security, acceptance, and pride in the approval with which he is received by an employer or other member of the majority group.

Avoidance can come in a number of ways. The member of the minority group may simply withdraw from it as do some mulattoes who pass as white persons or some Jews who hide their identity. There are indications that there even exists self-hatred among minority members, particularly anti-Semitism among some Jews.[93] Upper-class members of a minority —as do some Negro professional people—may simply isolate themselves

---

[87] Allport, *The Nature of Prejudice*, p. 217.
[88] Zawadski, "Limitation of the Scapegoat Theory of Prejudice," *loc. cit.*
[89] Allport, *op. cit.*, p. 217.   [90] Simpson and Yinger, *op. cit.*, p. 189.
[91] *Ibid.*, pp. 229–258.
[92] Charles S. Johnson, *Patterns of Negro Segregation* (New York: Harper & Row, Publishers, 1943), pp. 256–257.
[93] Kurt Lewin, *Resolving Social Conflicts* (New York: Harper & Row, Publishers, 1948), pp. 186–200.

from the problems of the lower-class members of their group. Another way to avoid some forms of discrimination is by living, for example, in all-Negro or all-Jewish communities. This withdrawal is only partly successful, simply because Harlem and similar segregated parts of a city are not completely self-contained and the minority member encounters prejudice in the outer world. Migration is a similar way of avoiding difficulties. Others may simply go out of their way to avoid contacts or incidents with members of the majority group.

Adjustment to prejudice and discrimination may take a pattern of aggression and hostility. Some may become aggressive group leaders who try in various ways to achieve equal status with the majority. Sometimes these attempts may involve physical aggression on the majority, but this is more apt to occur among children, as in juvenile gang warfare. Others may show their defiance of an accepted role by adopting the style of dress and acquiring the accouterments, such as an expensive automobile, of the majority. Some minority members may withdraw their patronage from business concerns operated by one of the majority group or refuse to patronize some individual belonging to it.

Summary

Discrimination is the denial of equality of treatment to an individual or group of persons who desire this equality. Discrimination may take several forms, including the following: (1) restrictions on general social participation; (2) health and length of life; (3) exclusion from organized groups; (4) segregation in public accommodations; (5) segregated and unequal educational facilities; (6) unequal opportunities in employment and business; (7) denial of the right to vote, to hold public office, to enter the country; (8) biased administration of justice; and (9) other forms of discrimination.

Prejudice is a negative emotional attitude of prejudgment toward a group of people. Although prejudice and discrimination are generally associated, one may be prejudiced without discriminating or discriminate without being prejudiced. There are three sources of prejudice: the cultural heritage, the personality needs of the individual, and, to a limited extent, the need for competitive advantages. The cultural source is basic to prejudice, and personality needs, as well as competitive advantage, appear merely to intensify it. Prejudice tends to affect the personality of minority members, but more research is needed to determine the extent to which their response accounts for the existence of prejudice in the majority.

Selected Readings

ADORNO, T. W., ELSE FRENKEL-BRUNSWIK, DANIEL J. LEVINSON, and R. NEVITT SANFORD. *The Authoritarian Personality.* New York: Harper & Row, Publishers, 1950. The most important study which has attempted to show that prejudice is primarily a result of a certain type of personality. The methodological sections are particularly good.

ALLPORT, GORDON W. *The Nature of Prejudice.* Reading, Mass.: Addison-Wesley Publishing Company, 1954. A comprehensive analysis of the group differences and psychological and sociocultural factors dealing with prejudice. Part V discusses the manner in which the child acquires prejudice.

ASHMORE, HARRY S. *The Other Side of Jordan: Negroes Outside the South.* New York: W. W. Norton & Company, Inc., 1960. It is the thesis of this writer and journalist that in the second half of the twentieth century the race problem in America is approaching its final focus in the great cities outside the South —New York, Detroit, Chicago, and San Francisco—where more than one third of the Negroes now live.

BARRON, MILTON L., ed. *American Minorities.* New York: Alfred A. Knopf, Inc., 1957. A collection of readings in intergroup relations covering a wide range of topics.

BERRY, BREWTON. *Race Relations.* Rev. ed. Boston: Houghton Mifflin Company, 1958. An analysis of the concept of race and race differences as well as an excellent critique of the various theories of prejudice.

BOYD, WILLIAM C. *Genetics and the Races of Man.* Boston: D. C. Heath and Company, 1950. A discussion of race and racial differences.

GREENBERG, JACK. *Race Relations and American Law.* New York: Columbia University Press, 1959. A comprehensive discussion of laws affecting race relations and their sociological implications. Includes public accommodations, interstate travel, elections, earning a living, education, housing and real property, the criminal law, and domestic relations laws.

JOHNSON, CHARLES S. *Patterns of Negro Segregation.* New York: Harper & Row, Publishers, 1943. A study of the different ways in which Negroes react to discrimination and segregation. Contains material from personal documents.

LEE, ALFRED MC CLUNG. *Fraternities without Brotherhood.* Boston: The Beacon Press, 1955. A study of racial and religious prejudice among fraternities.

ROSE, ARNOLD M., ed. *Race Prejudice and Discrimination.* New York: Alfred A. Knopf, Inc., 1951. A collection of readings on intergroup relations. Particularly good is the section dealing with prejudice and discrimination.

SIMPSON, GEORGE E., and J. MILTON YINGER. *Racial and Cultural Minorities.* Rev. ed. New York: Harper & Row, Publishers, 1958. Chapters 3–5 deal with the cultural, competitive, and personality functions of prejudice.

WILLIAMS, ROBIN, JR. *The Reduction of Intergroup Tensions.* New York: Social Science Research Council, Bulletin 57, 1947. A general survey of research on prejudice and discrimination and the techniques for their reduction.

The Effect of War on
Deviant Behavior

War today affects the incidence and nature of several forms of deviant behavior. Some forms decrease whereas others increase when a country is at war, and if these changes can be anticipated a country should be able to plan its national programs more adequately. Before discussing the effects of war on deviant behavior, however, it is important to understand the effects of modern warfare on a nation's economy and the relationship of war to social change.

In order to distinguish it from a number of other forms of armed conflict, war is usually defined as a conflict involving armed force between two sovereign nations.[1] War involves the use of force to subdue a nation or nations to the point where they will either surrender unconditionally or agree to concessions. As "instruments of national policy," wars have become a part of cultural mechanisms. War actually is a massive game conducted according to certain prescribed procedures which embrace the methods adopted, the instruments employed, and the rules governing its conduct.[2]

Modern warfare differs greatly from wars of a century or more ago. Instead of being largely a conflict of armies and navies with some demands on the civilian population, contemporary wars can now be characterized as "total war." Today entire nations mobilize for war, for the destruction of an enemy's military potential behind the lines has become as important for victory as the destruction of its armed forces. A nation's fighting strength depends upon how well and to what extent its entire resources have been mobilized and managed toward the ends of war.[3]

President Wilson once said that it is not an army that must be shaped

---

[1] Alvin Johnson, "War," *Encyclopedia of Social Sciences* (New York: The Macmillan Company, 1934), VIII, 331–342.

[2] James Wilford Garner, "Laws of Warfare," *ibid.*, p. 359. These rules include declarations of war, white flags of truce, the care of the wounded and prisoners, treatment of spies, the powers of an occupying commander, and even the outlawing of certain weapons such as the dumdum bullet and poison gas. An 1868 international agreement on war stated: "There are technical limits at which war ought to yield to the requirements of humanity."

[3] United States Bureau of the Budget, *The United States at War* (No. 1 of the Historical Reports on War Administration; Washington, D.C.: Government Printing Office, 1946), p. 3.

and trained for war but a nation. This complete mobilization of manpower and resources for war thus has great consequences for all the people of a nation. A wartime economy cannot rely on voluntary military or industrial manpower. Men are drafted for the armed services. Industrial plants are told what goods must be produced and how much, and the earnings and hours of workers in essential industries are controlled. In addition, heavy taxes must be levied to pay for the tremendous wartime expenditures, and efforts must be made to control dangerous wartime inflation.

War and Social Change

War creates a crisis situation which is favorable to social change. When a nation is fighting for survival, changes in the political, economic, and social framework are more likely to occur. An important aspect of war, and one which must be understood in relation to the changes which come about, is the way in which the inventive genius of the people is stimulated in order to overwhelm the enemy.[4] War has brought forth enormous advances in technology, in industrial development, and in such physical sciences as chemistry and physics.

During World War II total war mobilization produced a crisis situation which resulted in great changes in American society. Millions of new jobs meant the incorporation into the working force of many persons who had not previously participated in industrial production, and millions of men and women entered the armed services and government employment. These expanded opportunities for employment and positions with higher status meant increased social mobility. Between the summer of 1940 and April, 1944, the number of persons employed either as civilians or as members of the armed forces increased by 16 million. This number consisted of 7 million previously unemployed and 9 million additional persons, mostly young people, women, and older persons.

War also increases the number of families broken by temporary separation, desertion, and death. During World War II an estimated 3 to 4 million families were temporarily broken, chiefly because the man in the home had been taken into the armed forces. Hasty and often ill-considered marriages contributed to a postwar divorce rate nearly twice the usual one. Family tensions frequently developed, in part because of the shift of family roles. When women suddenly became independent wage earners or had to assume the role of both father and mother it was sometimes hard to reestablish a former and perhaps more compatible family role.

Millions of civilians and soldiers move to new residences during wartime. During World War II 27 million such moves were made, the most extensive shift of population in a short time in our entire history. The

---

[4] Waldemar Kaempffert, "War and Technology," *American Journal of Sociology*, 46:431–444 (January, 1941).

Bureau of the Census estimated that in March, 1945, 12 percent of the civilian population (15,300,000) were living in a county different from their residence at the outbreak of World War II. The white population in ten major war production areas increased 27 per cent. The Detroit–Willow Run industrial area increased 250,000, or 10.3 percent, in its resident white population; Hampton Roads, Virginia, 91 percent; and San Diego County, California, 110 percent. Much of this migration was from the farms to the cities, in some cases thousands of miles away. People from small towns and farms, between one fourth to one half of them from southern states, constituted the majority of the population that came to work in the bomber plants at Willow Run.[5]

This migration of millions of people, who would probably not have moved otherwise, meant the increase of impersonality, individualism, and norm conflicts. The loss of relatives and friends, in addition to housing difficulties, further increased the various tensions of people living under wartime conditions. As people moved to areas of insufficient housing, the crowded, congested conditions became more or less typical of wartime housing in many areas. Trailer housing developed in boom towns, and families often doubled up in tenements, thereby adding to already existing tensions.

Any wartime period produces other broad social consequences. So many have referred to these positive benefits of war in establishing common values that William James suggested the need for a "moral equivalent for war" to give people a common purpose. The conflict of war usually increases consensus among all groups in a society and consequently means less antagonism among various segments of the social structure. Intergroup tensions between majority and minority groups generally decline in the face of a common enemy, thus increasing the participation of minorities in wartime.[6]

Wars tend to unite the continuity of a nation in time by linking together its past, present, and future historic values. Even suicide seems to decline under such feelings of identification. During wartime many more groups and individuals are concerned with social issues which affect the general welfare of the people than are in time of peace.

War and Social Deviation

The waste of human life, natural resources, and civilian goods during war and the miseries of the vanquished are so obvious and have been enu-

---

[5] Lowell Juillard Carr and James Edson Stermer, *Willow Run: A Study of Industrialization and Cultural Inadequacy* (New York: Harper & Row, Publishers, 1952).

[6] In certain areas, however, where there has been a rapid increase in a minority group and limited housing and other facilities, there may be increased tension and in some cases even outbreaks of violence.

merated so often it is unnecessary to go into them here.[7] Instead, the discussion will deal with the effect of war on juvenile delinquency, ordinary and white-collar crime, prostitution and sexual promiscuity, mental disorder, suicide, family maladjustment, and discrimination. War affects the incidence and nature of these various forms of deviant behavior; yet it actually does not "cause" them. Rather, social trends present in a society become intensified and shifted during war. Social change and mobility, which are characteristic of an urban society, are simply increased by a war situation. Writing about World War II, one writer has stated: "Many of the social problems arising from wartime maladjustments were thus much the same as those apparent in peacetime, with their severity enhanced by accelerated wartime change." [8]

WARTIME JUVENILE DELINQUENCY

War brings with it a great increase in the number of children who get into trouble. In Great Britain, for example, during the first year of World War II, delinquency among children increased 41 percent in the under-fourteen age group, and 22 percent in the group aged fourteen to seventeen.[9] At the same time the crime rate of those over twenty-one decreased 12 percent. The high rate for the under-fourteen age group may have been the result of evacuation from their homes in areas under bombing attack, for all British children of this age were eligible for removal.

In the United States juvenile court cases increased 67 percent between 1938 and 1945. Cases disposed of in 56 counties serving areas with populations of 100,000 or more increased from 47,816 in 1938 to 79,748 in 1945. (See Table 19.1.) Boys' cases increased by the large figure of 65 percent in this period, but girls' cases increased by the even larger figure of 79 percent. Wartime delinquency among girls was chiefly related to sexual promiscuity.

A number of reasons for this increased wartime delinquency can be mentioned. Merrill has suggested the many dislocations—population, community relationships, economic relationships, employment relationships, educational opportunities, and family life.[10] The wartime dislocation of population and community relationships has already been referred to in our general discussion. Carr has stated that during wartime "in general, the greater the disruption of normal living and ordinary familial and other

---

[7] See, for example, Quincy Wright, *A Study of War* (Chicago: The University of Chicago Press, 1942), and L. L. Bernard, *War and Its Causes* (New York: Holt, Rinehart and Winston, Inc., 1944).

[8] Francis E. Merrill, *Social Problems on the Home Front* (New York: Harper & Row, Publishers, 1948), p. 10.

[9] Victor H. Evjen, "Delinquency and Crime in Wartime," *Journal of Criminal Law and Criminology*, 33:138 (July–August, 1942).

[10] Merrill, *op. cit.*, pp. 151–159.

*Table 19.1. Number of Juvenile Delinquency Cases Disposed of by
56 Courts Serving Areas with Populations of
100,000 or More, 1938–1945*

Year	Total cases	Index	Boys' cases	Index	Girls' cases	Index
1938	47,816	100	40,149	100	7,667	100
1939	52,800	110	44,981	112	7,819	102
1940	50,700	106	42,355	105	8,345	109
1941	55,064	115	45,474	113	9,590	125
1942	59,316	124	47,675	119	11,641	152
1943	78,692	165	63,972	159	14,720	192
1944	76,058	159	61,813	154	14,245	186
1945	79,748	167	66,047	165	13,701	179

SOURCE: Computed from United States Department of Labor, Children's Bureau, *Juvenile Court Statistics, 1945,* Preliminary Statement (Division of Statistical Research; Washington, D.C.: March 8, 1946). It is often difficult to compare statistics on juvenile delinquency because of changes in official policies and reporting. See, for example, Peter P. Lejins, "American Data on Juvenile Delinquency in an International Forum," *Federal Probation,* 25:18–22 (June, 1961).

social controls, the greater will be the amount of deviant behavior per unit population of youth exposed." [11]

There is evidence that delinquency increased more in areas of increased population than in those with decreases in population. Where areas had increased in population, juvenile cases had increased 55 percent, as compared with a 44 percent increase in areas of decreased population.[12] The movement of rural children into heavily urbanized wartime areas meant their exposure to different, and often deviant, values. It has also been pointed out that the rapid dislocation of economic relationships has an effect on children.[13]

During wartime many juveniles are employed who otherwise would be in school. It has been estimated that in April, 1944, 2.8 million boys and girls aged fourteen to nineteen were new to the work force. This rapid increase in employment was often correlated with the disruption of regular school programs, crowded schools, and shortages of teachers in heavily populated war areas. In addition, many of these adolescents were employed in activities which were not always inherently desirable.

War conditions produce tensions under the most normal family conditions. Few families can maintain their prewar status; hence tensions are increased at this critical period. Many fathers enter the armed forces or

[11] Lowell J. Carr, *Delinquency Control* (rev. ed.; New York: Harper & Row, Publishers, 1950), p. 116.

[12] Merrill, *op. cit.,* p. 164.

[13] David Bogen, "Trends in Juvenile Delinquency," *Federal Probation,* 9:25–28 (January–March, 1945).

go into defense work in other areas, and millions of mothers are engaged in full-time industrial or other work. As a result, children are given less supervision than usual. During World War II, such terms as "doorkey children" or "latchkey children" were frequently used to describe these youngsters.[14] Young boys, expecting to be drafted into military service, became more restless, more anxious about their future, and probably less concerned about the restrictions of traditional norms on their behavior. All these factors were added to the normal situations which tempt young people to engage in delinquent behavior.

WAR AND ORDINARY CRIME

Ordinary crime decreases during wartime. Sutherland studied criminal convictions during World War I in England, Germany, and Austria and to some extent in other countries. He concluded that the absolute number of convictions for crime in civilian courts decreased in all countries he studied except Canada, and that the absolute number of convictions of the male population decreased in all countries at war.[15] During World War II in the United States there was a decline in the rate of crimes reported to the police, arrests, and commitments to correctional institutions.[16] Even the large new industrial community around the bomber plants at Willow Run had little crime.[17]

This general decrease in crime appears to have been due primarily to the entrance of millions of young men into the armed forces. In the United States, from 1941 to 1944, arrests of men from eighteen to twenty-one, charged with all crimes, decreased 33.7 percent. This decline should not be attributed to any great increase in anticriminal norms or to the decline of criminal norms generally in our society. Since most ordinary crime is committed by persons in the younger age groups, their removal from the civilian population would obviously result in the decrease of wartime property offenses. One writer has stated that we should look for the effects of war "to be strained through intervening changes in conditions, regulations, and policies, and we should not expect war to have a predetermined or a direct effect on criminal and delinquent behavior."[18]

In the past, wars have had such different effects that it is often impossible to generalize about their relation to certain types of crime.[19] During World War II, property crimes in general decreased in the United

---

[14] Henry L. Zucker, "Working Parents and Latchkey Children," *The Annals*, 236:43-50 (November, 1944).

[15] Edwin H. Sutherland, "Crime," in William F. Ogburn ed., *American Society in Wartime* (Chicago: The University of Chicago Press, 1943), p. 186.

[16] Merrill, *op. cit.*   [17] Carr and Stermer, *op. cit.*, pp. 273-274.

[18] Walter C. Reckless, "The Impact of War on Crime, Delinquency and Prostitution," *American Journal of Sociology*, 48:378 (November, 1942).

[19] Hermann Mannheim, *War and Crime* (London: C. A. Watts & Co., Ltd., 1941).

States. There was a 13.2 percent decline in the rate for robberies reported to the police from the 1939–1941 average to 1944 as well as a decrease in larceny of 13.3 percent.[20] Burglaries during 1944 had declined 8.9 percent over the prewar average. Automobile theft, however, increased by 15.2 percent, largely because of the scarcity of cars. After the first few months of 1942 few new automobiles were produced, and they became increasingly valuable commodities worth, at times, over twice their original cost. The automobile had become almost indispensable to some people, and thus there was a better market for them than before the war.

Personal offenses, as a group, increased during World War II, but individual offenses varied greatly. The rate for rape increased by 27 percent over the previous average, and assault went up 19.9 percent. On the other hand, manslaughter by negligence remained about the same and, curiously, murder and nonnegligent manslaughter declined during the war by 7.5 percent. The increase in rape, largely statutory, that is, relations with girls under the legal age with or without consent, was due in part to what appears to have been a general increase in promiscuity. The greatest increase in rates occurred in those areas with the largest increase in population where there may have been more wartime public awareness of these offenses and thus more careful reporting.

The prison population appears to decrease markedly during a war. Between 1940 and 1944 the number of prisoners in American correctional institutions declined from 180,002 to 127,076, and new admissions to prison declined by 25 percent. A similar decline occurred in Canada and Great Britain. The decrease in prison population during wartime is almost immediate. Although there was an increase in the prison population of the United States from 1937 to 1939, beginning with the defense period, there was a decrease in 1940 of about 4.0 percent and in 1941 a decrease of 6.0 percent.[21]

This decline in the prison population seems to result from a number of other factors in addition to the general decline in the crime rate. Since over half of the men committed to prison are under thirty years of age and a large proportion of them are single, there is a tendency during a war situation for the courts to be more lenient and to consider the national interest in additional manpower. Consequently, probation is used more extensively, particularly if the offender is subject to draft and enlists voluntarily in the armed forces. During the last war, for example, the Army did permit the enlistment of men who had committed even two felonies, if the crimes were not of certain types. The public generally approved this practice because it felt that a person should not be allowed to avoid mili-

---

[20] Merrill, *op. cit.*, pp. 184, 186.
[21] Marshall B. Clinard, "Wartime Trends in the Prison Population," *Proceedings of the American Prison Association, 1942* (Boston: The Association, 1942), pp. 359–360.

tary service by committing a crime. As a result, many men were released from prison to enlist in the armed forces. More than one warden and reformatory superintendent complained that it was difficult to operate their institutions properly because the number of new admissions declined and other prisoners were paroled to the armed forces.

WAR AND WHITE-COLLAR CRIME

Although most ordinary crime appears to decline during a time of war, there is evidence that white-collar crime increases. This might be expected because opportunities for such violations increase during a total war. Laws regulating a much larger part of the economy are enacted, including production and labor controls as well as price and rationing laws, and there is an increase in the possibility of illegal activities in connection with government contracts and income tax regulations.

War Contract Frauds. War contracts provide a fertile field for illegal activities. War frauds and illegal profiteering were so extensive in World War I that for as long as fifteen years after the war Congressional committees continued to expose them. Similar large frauds on war contracts occurred during World War II. A postwar report of the United States Comptroller General stated that overpayments or frauds were involved in more than 5 percent of all war contracts. The investigations of the Truman Committee,[22] later the Mead Committee,[23] revealed that there were extensive violations, although by no means were all concerns at fault. Committee reports revealed that many substandard and defective products were manufactured, expense accounts were padded, and public officials were bribed.

Allocation of Scarce Materials. During World War II, there were serious violations of the War Production Board's orders on the allocation of priorities on scarce materials. During 1944, for example, in a total of 26,434 investigations the board found violations in three of five cases. In one case, for example, a concern used the scarce nylon allocated for military parachutes to make nylon hosiery. Another corporation was convicted of securing on false grounds a scarce material, an air-conditioning apparatus, ostensibly for its company hospital. The corporation in question claimed that its hospital was the only one in the community and that it could not be kept clean without the air-conditioning apparatus; but this equipment was actually installed in an exclusive country club of which many of the com-

[22] *Investigation of the National Defense Program,* S.R. 10, Additional Report of the Special Committee Investigating the National Defense Program Pursuant to S.R. 71, Pts. 1–14, 78th Cong., 2d Sess., 1943; and Pts. 15–20, 78th Cong., 2d Sess., 1944 (Washington, D.C.: 1944).
[23] *Investigation of the National Defense Program,* S.R. 110, Additional Report of the Special Committee Investigating the National Defense Program Pursuant to S.R. 71, Pts. 1–4, 79th Cong., 1st Sess., 1945; and Pts. 5–8, 79th Cong., 2d Sess. (Washington, D.C.: 1946).

pany's officers were members. This same corporation also fraudulently obtained such scarce items as ornamental stair rails, plumbing fixtures, and a new kitchen for the pampered country club.

Tax Violations. In spite of generally increased profits, some business concerns attempted to avoid their heavy wartime taxes. One popular method of avoidance was the submission of padded reports of costs in order to reduce taxable profits. Others were the excessive increase of salaries and bonuses for executives, the inclusion of interest on investments as costs, the placing of fictitious values on raw materials, the manipulation of inventories, the increase of reserves for depreciation, and the concealment of profits by intercompany transactions.[24] Taxes were also avoided through the manipulation of financial data.

Many income tax violations were revealed in connection with the government's efforts to deal with the black market in price-fixed and rationed commodities during World War II. Black-market profits were often not reported, or prices paid in black-marketeering transactions were allowed as a business expense in computing taxes, even though this was prohibited by the income tax laws. The government often could not collect other wartime taxes because of the illegal practice of keeping false accounts of transactions to avoid prosecution by government investigators trying to discover price and rationing violations.[25] These false bookkeeping practices were also violations of internal revenue laws. In 1947 revenue agents were still seeking persons who had not reported wartime black-market profits. "These include black-market deals on automobiles, liquor, textiles, sugar, poultry, meat and many other products. One man was found to have bought 3,900,000 pounds of rationed sugar for a fictitious candy manufacturing company. He resold the sugar at a huge black-market profit. Agents recently assessed him $310,000 for taxes, interest, and penalty on those profits." [26]

Black-Market Violations. The black market which existed throughout the United States in World War II is a good example of white-collar crime. It covered a wide range of violations of laws regulating the prices of commodities, the rationing of supplies of certain commodities, and the control of rents. Congress labeled violations of these laws as socially injurious, constituting a serious threat to our national security, and specified certain punishments by the state. Uncontrolled prices and rents could easily result in inadequate production of war commodities and facilities, profiteering from abnormal wartime market conditions, dissipation of defense appro-

---

[24] Federal Trade Commission, *Report on Wartime Profiteering*, Sen. Doc. 248, 65th Cong., 2d Sess. 1918 (Pt. 2 of the Nye Committee's Report; Washington, D.C.: 1935).

[25] Marshall B. Clinard, *The Black Market: A Study of White-Collar Crime* (New York: Holt, Rinehart and Winston, Inc., 1952), pp. 24–27, 272.

[26] "Hunt for Income Tax Evaders," *U.S. News & World Report*, 23:23–24 (December 5, 1947).

priations by excessive prices, undue impairment of the standard of living of persons on fixed incomes, and a possible postwar collapse of economic values. Compulsory rationing was necessary to avoid the unequal distribution of commodities in limited supply, such as meat, canned foods, gasoline, shoes, and tires. With millions of men in the armed services and unable to produce for themselves, and with many of our allies in need of large quantities of our supplies, rationing became a wartime necessity.

Price and rationing violations occurred in almost all commodities, from heavy industrial materials to such items as clothing, gasoline, potatoes, onions, cigarettes, and alcoholic beverages.[27] These actions involved mainly manufacturers, wholesalers, and retailers, and, in the case of rationing, consumers. There were also violations of rent regulations by landlords. Serious black markets occurred in the following: coffee, meat, poultry, potatoes, onions, sugar, grains, cigarettes, liquor, apparel, lumber, wastepaper, consumer durables, gasoline, fuel oil, used cars, tires, building materials, industrial materials, and scrap metal.

Black-market violations consisted of several types of activities: (1) over-ceiling price violations, (2) evasive price violations, (3) rationing violations (including the theft and counterfeiting of ration currency), (4) violations of rent ceilings, and (5) record keeping and reporting violations. Most of them were evasive in nature, and nearly all were subject to criminal prosecution because of the definite element of willfulness. There were "cash-on-the-side" payments, payments for goods which were never delivered, tie-in sales, short shipments, and quality deterioration. Sometimes cash payments above the legal price were treated as "loans" which the person making the sale never repaid the buyer. Illegal profits were secured by making an invoice for goods and simply not delivering them. In other cases a bill might be made out for a certain weight of goods—for example, a hundred pounds—but only part of it would be delivered. Desirable commodities often were sold "tied" to another and undesirable one. For example, when onions were scarce it was quite common for buyers of onions to have to purchase another item which was plentiful, in much the same way wholesalers sold beef to retailers only if they agreed to purchase such hard-to-sell items as hearts, tripe, and the like. Commodities were upgraded beyond their true value to secure extra illegal profits. Black-market beef graded "good" was often upgraded and sold as "choice," thus adding several cents a pound to the cost to the consumer. In other instances the size or the quality of a commodity was reduced without a change in the price, as when heavy "sizing" was added to cheesecloth to make it look like broadcloth. Violations of rent control orders included not only charges in excess of the legal rent ceilings but violations through side payments and through charges for rental services which were not provided.

---

[27] Clinard, op. cit., pp. 39–48.

For the first time in its history the United States government undertook the tremendous task of equalizing the distribution of goods in scarce supply through a compulsory rationing program. The rationing of goods for a large civilian population is indeed difficult. During a single year of World War II, for example, there were 30 million applications for gasoline, 18 million for tires, and 17 million for sugar for canning. Ration currency was similar in many ways to regular money, for it constituted a demand on a certain available supply in the nation-wide "bank." The violations of these rationing regulations constituted one of the most serious aspects of the black market.

The most common rationing violation involved illegal use of ration stamps and coupons, but there were also falsifications of applications for rationed goods based on need and previous use. In particular, there were widespread cases where invalid currency was used or valid stamps were not collected when they should have been. In some cases consumers did transfer their ration currency illegally to others, but in general the major violations consisted of the purchase by dealers of counterfeit and stolen currency from individuals and then the sale of a rationed commodity without requiring currency. Professional counterfeiters made, in most cases, the forged currency; other persons, many with criminal records, stole coupons from war rationing boards. Illicit gasoline coupons, selling from eight to fifteen cents a gallon, were easy to sell. A sheet of five-gallon coupons worth several thousand dollars could be carried in an overcoat pocket. In 1944 the Administrator of the Office of Price Administration reported that there had been over 650 robberies of local rationing boards in which coupons for 300 million gallons had been stolen. At least one in sixteen filling stations had severe sanctions instituted against it for accepting such currency during the war, although the figure was probably much higher because violations reported by investigators ran as high as 60 percent of such concerns. While our armed forces were burning 25 million gallons of gasoline a day during 1944, the black market in gasoline was also using up an estimated 2.5 million gallons a day, an amount which would have increased legitimate civilian supplies by 25 percent.[28]

Estimates of the extent of these black-market activities varied widely; yet, strangely enough, business estimates exceeded those of government agencies. One government estimate stated that "unofficial figures place as much as 20 percent of the meat supply going into black markets," and the OPA estimated that some 5 percent of the gasoline supply in 1943 and early 1944 was passing in illegal channels through the trafficking in counterfeit or stolen gasoline coupons on the part of filling station operators. In 1945 the Greater Cincinnati Meat Packers' Association estimated that 50 to 75 percent of all civilian meat was passing in black-market chan-

---

[28] Clinard, *op. cit.*, pp. 163–165.

nels, and in 1946 the American Meat Institute, after a survey of eleven major cities, concluded that five in six stores were in the meat black market. In March, 1944, a random sample group of 145 food retailers interviewed in Washington, D.C., revealed that at least one fifth (21 percent) of them believed that wholesalers did not observe their ceilings.[29]

Some estimate of the extent of the black market can be gained from a study of the actions taken by the Office of Price Administration. From the beginning of the OPA in 1942 until its termination on May 31, 1947, a period of slightly over five years, the limited OPA staff conducted over 1 million investigations and turned up 259,966 cases which resulted in the institution of some action leading to possible serious punishment.[30] By March 31, 1947, action had been completed on 170,708 of these cases, of which only 8465 were lost by the government, while 31,469 were withdrawn.[31] Approximately 1 in 15 of the 3 million business concerns in the country was punished by some serious sanction. Between 1943 and 1947, price, rent, and rationing civil cases amounted to as much as 54.2 percent, and criminal cases, 12.8 percent, of all cases brought before the federal courts.

In addition to these actions—the formal sanctions of the OPA—volunteer citizen price panels handled thousands of violations at the retail level; moreover, tens of thousands of actions were taken under local ordinances against the black market, ordinances which were similar to the national law in the five states and seventy-five municipalities which had them. In New York City alone, for example, there were 18,875 prosecutions of retailers and 4000 prosecutions of wholesalers in 1944. Uncounted black-market cases were also dealt with by other federal agencies. During the three years from June, 1942, to June, 1945, the OPA received a total of 784,147 tenant complaints which resulted in adjustments and settlements of some form, many, of course, being minor difficulties. In 1944 alone, a total of 6855 serious rent cases were referred to the Enforcement Department for formal action.

Large as the numbers of these cases are, they are mostly cases involving fairly serious action and barely scratch the surface of the total violations. In general, less than a fourth of the cases where the government found violation resulted in any serious action. In other cases warnings were sent, informal adjustments were made, or the case was dismissed with no

---

[29] "Grocer Experiences with the Price Control System," Special Memorandum No. 113, Surveys Division, Bureau of Special Services, Office of War Information, May 10, 1944, p. 11.

[30] For all its investigative work the government investigative staff consisted, on the average, of less than 3000 investigators and some 600 attorneys.

[31] The large number of cases withdrawn, for the most part, were those in which the defendants made a settlement or adopted some other compromise action, or they were cases in which the government suspended action in the closing days of price and rationing controls.

action. Consequently, a conservative estimate of serious violations during the five-year OPA period, instead of being 259,966 cases, should probably be at least three times this figure.

PROSTITUTION AND SEXUAL PROMISCUITY

Wars have generally been associated with increased prostitution and sexual promiscuity. One could hardly expect anything else when large numbers of unmarried young men are away from home in the armed forces at an age when sexual tensions are greatest. In addition, industrial workers, many of whom are married but away from home, are often well paid and living in congested areas, conditions which are sometimes conducive to sexual promiscuity.

Table 19.2. An Analysis of 1912 Studies Made by the American Social Hygiene Association, January 1, 1940, to March 31, 1945, in Communities Adjacent to Military Installations

Year	Percentage "good"	Percentage "bad"
1940 (82 communities)	36.6	32.9
1941 (364 communities)	44.5	24.9
1942 (517 communities)	44.7	12.7
1943 (401 communities)	47.4	9.0
1944 (415 communities)	46.8	6.2
1945 (First quarter, 133 communities)	47.3	3.8

SOURCE: "Social Protection—A Summing Up," *Journal of Social Hygiene,* 31:304 (May, 1945). *Journal of Social Hygiene,* copyright 1945, American Social Hygiene Association.

During World War II, however, the armed services, as well as national and local committees, worked so hard on this problem that organized prostitution was kept under more effective control than it had been in World War I. "Red-light" districts were closed in 650 communities during the war. The American Social Hygiene Association made 1912 studies of communities where there were large numbers of military and naval personnel, and classified conditions as "good" or "bad." [32] A community was "bad" if there was public solicitation by prostitutes; if bellboys, bartenders, taxicab drivers, and others worked as solicitors; and if hotels, taverns, and other places allowed prostitutes. Between 1940 and 1945 "good" communities increased from 36.6 percent to 47.3 percent, and the percentage

[32] "Social Protection—A Summing Up," *Journal of Social Hygiene,* 31:303–307 (May, 1945).

of "bad" communities declined phenomenally from 32.9 in 1940 to 3.8 in 1945. (See Table 19.2.)

Sexual promiscuity presented a different problem. Although prostitution decreased in World War II, sexual relations on an unorganized and noncommercial basis increased. As has been indicated, delinquency among girls increased by 79 percent during the war. Likewise, cases of rape, primarily statutory, reported to the police went up by 27 percent. In both instances the evidence suggests that an increase in sex relations with girls was characteristic of the last war. Some 50 to 75 percent of all women held for sex offenses in 1944 were under twenty-one years of age, and in one state 41.5 percent of all hospital cases of venereal disease involved girls under nineteen.[33] Arrests of girls under eighteen reported to the FBI increased 117.8 percent between 1941 and 1944. Arrests of all girls under twenty-one during this same period increased 134 percent. All the evidence —local observations, studies of various communities, Army and Navy findings, and juvenile court cases—indicated that the problem generally concerned the promiscuous and inexperienced young girl rather than the experienced prostitute.

Communities near service camps and other boom towns were particularly high in the incidence of promiscuity. Young girls were attracted to these areas for adventure, and there were few possibilities of social control because so much of the male population consisted of strangers. The reasons for this increase in sexual promiscuity during wartime, in communities within fifty miles away from service camps, have been summarized as follows:

> Among these conditions were the tendency of young persons to take less interest in their school work, especially the young girls who were subject to the attentions of the soldiers on leave; the tendency of many such young people to condone or accept new standards of behavior, particularly in the field of sex relations; an inordinate increase in the social activities of young girls of high school age who were "drafted" by local committees for dances and other entertainments; and finally the interchange of veneral disease between the youth of the local community and the military personnel, with uniformly unfortunate results.

> The effect of such modifications in the customary relationships of young persons was most clearly evident with the girls. Many of the problems of sexual promiscuity on a nonremunerative basis were the most obvious results of the changed community relationships. . . . As one high school superintendent remarked, with commendable understatement, "I must say that the near-by camp for more than 30,000 men has made this a very undesirable place in which to bring up boys and girls." [34]

---

[33] Eliot Ness, "Sex Delinquency as a Social Hazard," *Proceedings of the National Conference of Social Work, 1944* (New York: Columbia University Press, 1944), p. 280.

[34] Merrill, *op. cit.*, pp. 152–153.

WAR AND MENTAL DISORDER

War may be expected to affect the rate of mental disorder of various sections of the population differently. Children, women, adolescents, industrial workers, and those in the armed forces face war situations under different stresses.[35] Likewise there are differences when a civilian population is under attack and evacuations are necessary, and when it is not under attack.

There is no evidence of any marked increase in neuroses among the civilian population in World War II, although there was a marked increase in psychoses. First admissions of psychoneurotics to hospitals for mental illness increased from 4423 in 1939 to 5809 in 1944. Although the number so hospitalized constitutes only a minor part of neurotic behavior, it is still possible to use it as some sort of index. After studying neuroses during World War II, Merrill concluded that, for whatever they were worth, the figures did not indicate a widespread increase in neurotic behavior during World War II.[36]

This general mental state, as far as neuroses are concerned, was due in large part to the general participation in the war by all parts of the population, the mentally stable and the unstable. Those with neurotic behavior had an opportunity to divert their anxiety into a common, unified, and, to some, ideologically satisfying cause. Individual sentiments were replaced by national ones.

Of course, not all potentially neurotic persons shared these goals, and some experienced difficulties if they could not measure up to the expectations of others or if they could not develop sufficiently aggressive patterns to meet wartime conditions. As a result, some developed a "civilian war neurosis." [37] Some of these difficulties also appear to have been associated with fears about members of the family in service.

Psychotic behavior took a different trend during the war and increased, at least as measured by hospital first admissions. Schizophrenia appeared to account for the greatest increase. In 1939, there were 20,876 first admissions, or 22.4 percent of total admissions; by 1944 this number had increased to 29,010, or 26.1 percent of the total. However, this figure probably should be even larger because of the millions in the armed forces.

Mental disorder of a psychotic nature develops over a long period of time, and it is likely that these additional breakdowns were borderline cases and would have occurred in any event. The accelerated pace of life and

[35] H. Warren Dunham, "War and Personality Disorganization," *American Journal of Sociology*, 48:387–395 (November, 1942).
[36] Merrill, *op. cit.*, pp. 207–208.
[37] Felix Deutsch, "Civilian War Neuroses and Their Treatment," *Psychoanalytic Quarterly*, 13:300–312 (July, 1944).

more intense personal relationships during wartime probably widened, for example, the gap between the schizophrenic and other persons. In fact, it is likely that war simply aggravates in a society certain conditions which result in schizophrenia.[38] The wider opportunities for social participation in the war may account for the fact that the manic-depressive psychoses did not increase greatly. Between 1939 and 1944 there was a national increase of only 679 new cases committed to mental hospitals. The trend was considerably different from that of the schizophrenic cases.

It is difficult to determine whether the incidence of neuroses and psychoses would increase if the civilian population of the United States were subjected to heavy bombardment. There are indications, however, that mental illness did not materially increase in Great Britain under the German air attacks of 1940 and 1941. One British psychiatrist has written that "one of the most striking things about the effects of war on the civilian population has been the relative rarity of pathological mental disturbances among the civilians exposed to air raids. . . . The patients who do come, with few exceptions, present mainly the same problems as in peacetime." [39]

So far the discussion of mental disorder has been with reference to the civilian population. From 1942 to 1945 over 1,000,000 neuropsychiatric cases were admitted to Army hospitals, or between 6 and 7 percent of all hospital admissions.[40] Undoubtedly many of these cases were repeaters, and thus the figures probably were not quite this high. Neuropsychiatric disorders accounted for about half of all the discharges from the Army during the war, or a total of 545,000.

This high rate of mental breakdown, some of brief duration and others for a long period, appears to have resulted largely from a number of factors influencing a soldier's life. These included the demands of a new life, discipline, the lack of privacy, uncertainty, separation from home, privations, fatigue, danger, and difficulties in interpersonal relations—for example, inequalities in privileges, barracks life, and anxiety about problems at home.

There is no indication that particular factors in the previous background of soldiers made them more liable to mental disorders. On the contrary, it appears that group factors rather than individual inadequacies were the most important determinants in explaining variations in susceptibility to mental illness. The quality of leadership was particularly important, as well as the degree of group motivation and identification with a military group, whether it was a platoon, a company, or a bomber crew. The loyalty and the gripes that a man shared with his fellow members, no

[38] H. Warren Dunham, "War and Mental Disorder: Some Sociological Considerations," Social Forces, 22:137–142 (December, 1943).

[39] R. D. Gillespie, Psychological Effects of War on Citizen and Soldier (New York: W. W. Norton & Company, Inc., 1942), pp. 106–107.

[40] William C. Menninger, Psychiatry in a Troubled World (New York: The Macmillan Company, 1948), pp. 58–72. Menninger was Chief Consultant in Neuropsychiatry to the Surgeon General of the Army, 1943–1946.

matter what the danger and privation, and his confidence in leadership were important elements of his mental health.

SUICIDE AND WAR

Durkheim noted some sixty years ago that suicide tends to decline during wartime.[41] This same trend occurred during World War II, when the suicide rate per 100,000 declined by about one third, from 15.3 in 1938 to 11.2 in 1945. The number of suicides per year decreased to 14,782, which meant that many more failed to take their lives, possibly as many as 25,000 during World War II. Moreover, there was a steady decline from year to year until the postwar years, when the rates increased. (See Table 19.3.)

Table 19.3. Suicide Death Rates per 100,000 Population, United States, 1938–1947

Year	Rate per 100,000	Year	Rate per 100,000
1938	15.3	1943	10.2
1939	14.1	1944	10.0
1940	14.4	1945	11.2
1941	12.8	1946	11.5
1942	12.0	1947	11.5

SOURCE: "Mortality from Suicide," *Epidemiological and Vital Statistics Report* (Geneva: World Health Organization, 1956), IX, No. 4, 250–253.

Several factors probably accounted for this decline. The feeling of unity in wartime is the opposite of the social isolation of the typical suicide. National solidarity and the "we feelings" of wartime probably make personal difficulties of less importance to the individual. War also brings increased economic opportunities, and it has already been indicated that the rate of suicide is related to the business cycle. Wartime is a period of full employment, as well as high wages and profits, and thus less economic insecurity. Perhaps it would not be facetious to add that many persons would like to live to see the outcome of a war. At least, following the war there was a slight increase in the suicide rate.

WAR AND MARITAL CONFLICTS

Wars bring a number of changes in family relationship. The separation of wives and husbands, the new role suddenly assumed by some work-

[41] Émile Durkheim, *Suicide* tr. by John A. Spaulding and George Simpson (New York: The Free Press of Glencoe, 1951). Durkheim's original book was published in Paris in 1897.

ing wives, the movement of families to new locations, and the frequent crowded living conditions strain family relationships. In addition, hundreds of thousands of marriages are contracted in wartime without adequate preparation or understanding. In spite of these situations, the divorce rate did not increase much during the war years. The rate per 100 marriages increased only 10 percent: from 17.3 in 1942 to 27.5 in 1944.

The divorce rate did not increase appreciably during the war years for several reasons. Some persons solved their marital difficulties by entering the armed forces or moving to war industries in other areas in what might almost be termed desertion in peacetime. Others delayed divorce action until after the war because of the dependency checks which wives and children received while the husband was in the armed services. As Burgess has stated: "Wives who might otherwise sue for separate maintenance or divorce postpone such action until after the war, a prudential course in view of compulsory allowances to dependents of men in the service." [42] In June, 1944, 2,485,908 wives were receiving benefit checks from the Army.

The divorce rate remained stationary for two other more subtle social psychological reasons, morale and emotional factors. It was generally considered unpatriotic even to threaten to divorce a man who was defending his country, for if the individual soldier's morale were undermined the morale of the armed forces in general might be affected. It was considered a patriotic duty in wartime to retain family ties; consequently, many divorces were temporarily postponed. Probably some wives wanted a divorce, but were unable to obtain it because of the legal difficulties involved in divorcing a soldier who did not also want one. A soldier was not required to answer a divorce summons.

In the dangers of wartime for soldier and civilian alike marriage gave some sense of emotional security to both partners. There was a tendency even to idealize the absent partner: "The same deep desire for human assurance that increases the marriage rate in wartime helps also to maintain the solidarity of the family once it is established. In the immensity of war, men and women often hesitate to break the one human relationship which promises to give them sanctuary in a chaotic world. They may cling desperately to the form of the relationship, although the substance may long since have departed." [43]

On the other hand, war may have increased difficulties in postwar adjustments between persons who had been separated. Separations and other requirements of the wartime situation, with its interruption of established continuity, bring out conflicts and tensions between wives and husbands which had previously been covered up by the conventions of their immediate environment: "It often happens that a man realizes only in wartime what he did not notice in the routine of settled bourgeois exist-

---

[42] Ernest W. Burgess, "The Family," in Ogburn, op. cit., p. 25.
[43] Merrill, op. cit., p. 43.

ence, that his wife cannot or is unwilling to participate in his life. In the army he may need help he did not need before. Several men realize with shock that their wives loved their prestige, their social standing rather than themselves as persons." [44]

After the war all this changed. Divorces temporarily postponed were obtained. Many of the hastily contracted marriages did not last when the marriage was resumed under more normal, peacetime conditions. These divorces, added to the usual divorce rate, meant a steady postwar rise, with 1946 having the highest rate in history. In fact, it was not until 1952, seven years after the war, that the divorce rate became comparable with that of the prewar years.

DISCRIMINATION AND WAR

Now that wars have become world-wide in scope, discrimination against minorities has taken on even greater ideological significance than formerly. Media of mass communication make it possible to use discrimination within a country against some racial, religious, or ethnic group as a device for winning the support of other countries whose relation to the discrimination is only one of indirect identification.

If one were to choose one of the most positive results of World Wars I and II it might well be the general advancement of the position of minority groups in the United States. In a total war of today three things accounted for this advance: the urgent need for all available manpower, regardless of the racial, ethnic, or religious background of the person; the movement up the socioeconomic scale of the minority group due to the expansion of production and the opportunities in other areas for advancement; and, finally, the threat of a crisis situation in which the possibility of defeat made it possible and even desirable to grant more equality to certain groups than could be done in peacetime. Unfortunately, there were exceptions in discrimination against identifiable minorities who were closely associated with the belligerents, such as persons of German origin in World War I and of Japanese origin in World War II.

It would be impossible to describe the improvement of each minority group's position during and after World War II. Instead, the discussion will be limited here to the position of the Negro. At the beginning of the defense preparations his position in industry was weak in comparison with that of the white man. There was still a disproportionate amount of unemployment among Negroes, who were generally employed as unskilled or semiskilled labor. Many industries observed a color line in hiring and in making promotions.

[44] R. C. Anderson, "Neuropsychiatric Problems of the Flyer," *American Journal of Medicine*, 4:637-644 (May, 1948).

The first defense efforts helped the white industrial workers considerably, but did so little for the Negroes that their leaders organized a protest march on Washington in 1941. Discrimination in hiring continued to exist in many communities, even where there were labor shortages. Conditions improved in 1942, partly because of the upgrading of whites and the general labor shortage, but mainly because of the creation by executive order of the Fair Employment Practices Commission (FEPC) in 1941.[45] This order, issued by President Roosevelt, stated that discrimination because of "race, creed, color or national origin" was to be abolished in defense industries, and it forbade the granting of government contracts to those who did not obey it. Although the order could not be completely enforced, a large part of industry faced with shortages of labor honored it.

As the war progressed, another large migration of Negroes to industrial centers took place. This was similar, in general, to the urban migration during and after World War I; but this time there was also a movement of rural Negroes to the cities of the South where industrial production had increased. An estimated one million Negroes moved from the farm to industrial positions between 1940 and 1944. During this period the proportion of Negro labor in the skilled positions—as well as in the unskilled and semiskilled—doubled, and the income of Negroes increased materially.[46] They also entered new industries where they were able to demonstrate new skills, some of which had been acquired in expanded vocational training programs.

All this progress was reflected in the wider participation of Negroes in the armed forces, in improved public housing, and in attempts to remove other forms of discrimination. The Negro became militant in his demands for more social action. So much has changed in Negro-white relations since 1940 that some speak of it as a "Revolution." Perhaps these changes would have occurred anyway, but the war greatly accelerated them. In fact, the changes were so rapid and the Negro influx so fast that in certain areas during the war there was increased resentment, particularly because of pressures on limited housing. In several areas, such as Detroit and New York, there were brief race riots of considerable violence.

Summary

Modern warfare between industrial societies is referred to as total war and is accompanied by extensive social change, the regulation of all aspects of the economy, the separation of families, the movement of populations, a large increase in the labor force, and the organization of the

[45] Louis C. C. Kesselman, *The Social Politics of F.E.P.C.* (Chapel Hill: University of North Carolina Press, 1948).

[46] Robert C. Weaver, "Negro Labor Since 1929," *Journal of Negro History*, 35:20–38 (January, 1950).

members of a society into a force with a common purpose of increased nationalism and morale. It brings about many changes which are, however, largely a reflection and an intensification of trends already present in a society: an increase in the rates of juvenile delinquency, in white-collar crime, in sexual promiscuity, and in the psychoses.

On the other hand, during a war there appears to be a decrease in the incidence of ordinary crime, in the neuroses, in suicide, and in discrimination against minorities. Marital conflict during a war, as measured by divorce, does not increase materially, but during the postwar period divorce rates are far greater than those before the war. Whether these trends would occur in a nuclear war is another question. Large parts of the civilian population would be under attack, and there would probably be evacuation of large numbers of urban people to other areas, with different norms and values and at the same time an increase in impersonal relationships.

Selected Readings

CARR, LOWELL J. *Delinquency Control*. Rev. ed. New York: Harper & Row, Publishers, 1950, Chap. 5. This chapter deals with a survey of available information on the relation of war to juvenile delinquency.

CLINARD, MARSHALL B. *The Black Market: A Study of White Collar Crime*. New York: Holt, Rinehart and Winston, Inc., 1952. A study of price and rationing violations in the United States during World War II.

MANNHEIM, HERMANN. *War and Crime*. London: C. A. Watts & Co., Ltd., 1941. A study of the effect of war on crime by probably the leading authority on this topic.

MERRILL, FRANCIS E. *Social Problems on the Home Front*. New York: Harper & Row, Publishers, 1948. The most comprehensive analysis of the relation of war to various forms of deviant behavior, using primarily data from World War II.

OGBURN, WILLIAM F., ed. *American Society in Wartime*. Chicago: The University of Chicago Press, 1943. A series of essays by leading sociologists on the relation of war to various aspects of American life. Edwin H. Sutherland discusses the relation of war and crime.

PART
III

Deviant Behavior and

Social Control

The Reduction of Deviant
Behavior: General Programs

Over a period of time a society may adopt a number of alternative ways of dealing with negatively regarded deviant behavior. Sometimes social deviations may produce continuous tension in a society. In other cases the society may come to accept the deviations, establish an uneasy equilibrium, or, in the more usual cases, try to eliminate the deviations by increased pressure.

It might be argued that reduction of deviant behavior must be delayed until the nature and causes of deviations have finally been scientifically established, and ways of dealing with them found. Yet in a democratic society this is not feasible, for both policy and action depend ultimately on public decision, and when practical problems present themselves, public decision cannot always await the scientist. There is generally a period in which public action takes the form of trial-and-error efforts to combat the perceived threat of deviancy, a belief that "something must be done." But this action, however "unscientific" its foundation, ties in directly with the efforts of scientists. It is through such action, regardless of its success or failure in reducing deviation, that public interest and concern are aroused. One notable consequence of this is that funds for scientific research are often made available to scientists concerned with deviation. Eventually, the results of such scientific study may contribute to the fabric of understanding with which legislators and citizens arrive at more adequate policy decisions.

On the other hand, within a social system there may ultimately be acceptance of deviations, as has occurred countless times in Western European society. Women's use of cosmetics and their smoking and drinking a century or less ago among certain social classes were almost infallible signs of immorality, and for many justified the assumption that a woman who indulged in any of these practices was a prostitute.

Deviations may constitute a condition of equilibrium such as exists with regard to certain deviant sex practices or gambling in the United States. Although many people may realize that gambling, for example, is an expensive and, for society, an unproductive form of behavior, their attitude is complicated by the fact that most people have, at some time or other, gambled. "Drawing up legislation which will penalize the unwarranted deviation without jeopardizing the status of the numerous casual participants is exceedingly difficult." [1]

Societies may try energetically to eliminate deviations. Such a reaction more often occurs "when the norms violated are highly compulsive and universal in the culture." [2] Such deviations as incest, witchcraft, and adultery, for example, have almost always been treated harshly among primitive societies. On the other hand, in frontier days of a century ago horse stealing was regarded as a much more serious crime than is automobile theft today. In modern societies there is strong reaction against brutal murders, kidnaping, and sex crimes of violence, particularly those involving children.

One method by which strong societal action can be taken against deviation from norms is to cut the deviant off from communication with the group. Generally, this takes the form of rejection and decreased interaction, denial of privileges which the group controls, lowering of status, and, eventually, ostracism. As a result of this action, the deviant may leave the group voluntarily, or the group will collectively push him out. [3] Thus the individual who, as a member of a group, develops ideas or engages in behavior at variance with the group norms may be ostracized if initial communications directed at him are not successful in causing him to conform. If the individual perceives the group as at least as satisfying as his deviant ideas, and if he believes that the group will reaccept him if he renounces his ideas or behavior, he may do so. [4]

In a complex society, even though communication among members is not as direct and personal, there is still a considerable amount of collective hostility expressed toward deviants. Some of this is evidenced by societal stereotypes concerning deviants, such as the "delinquent," "sex deviate," "ex-convict," "chronic drunk," "dope fiend," "criminal," or "insane" person. These stereotypes are also communicated through newspapers, radio, television, and movies. For example, newspaper accounts seize upon such terms in their headlines, and mass media, in effect, play up the societal image of the deviant or law violator as one with defects of character, mentality, or intelligence. These stereotypes reflect societal attitudes concerning deviation, and the tendency to reject, label, ostracize,

---

[1] Edwin H. Lemert, *Social Pathology* (New York: McGraw-Hill Book Company, Inc., 1951), p. 60.

[2] *Ibid.*, p. 63.

[3] Stanley Schacter, "Deviation, Rejection, and Communication," *Journal of Abnormal and Social Psychology*, 46:190–207 (April, 1951).

[4] For further discussion of this process, see John W. Thibaut and Harold H. Kelley, *The Social Psychology of Groups* (New York: Holt, Rinehart and Winston, Inc., 1959), especially Chap. 13, and George W. Homans, *Social Behavior: Its Elementary Forms* (New York: Basic Books, Inc., 1961), section on conformity, pp. 116–119 and 339–358.

and isolate the deviant. These same stereotypes form the base of many traditional methods of dealing with deviants. This is evident from the manner in which deviants are "cut off" or isolated from respectable society through consignment to prisons, mental hospitals, treatment institutions for drug addicts or alcoholics, reformatories, or other "protective" institutions.[5] In some instances, of course, deviants are not physically isolated, but are socially isolated through relegation to a degraded status. When this occurs, the deviant's opportunities for finding employment and enjoying other societal privileges are markedly limited. He may, at this point, feel forced to seek the support of a deviant organization or subculture. Some suggest that this is one reason underlying the development of deviant groups, such as subcultures.[6]

If deviations become a subculture the difficulties of controlling such behavior are increased. Deviants of this type communicate knowledge among themselves about disapproved ways of conduct, and there is rapport among them. The members develop their own set of norms, distinct social roles, and a status system apart from that of the larger society. Some systematic deviation may have less organization, as is true of many delinquent gangs, than that of others, for example, organized and professional crime or traffic in drugs. Some types of deviant behavior—professional pickpocketing, begging, or prostitution, to name a few—have a long history. Many forms of professional crime, such as the techniques and language of pickpockets, can be traced back to Elizabethan times and earlier. Among such highly organized forms of deviant behavior "a definite professionalization of conduct by deviant group members develops, along with craft pride similar to that found among integrated occupational groups." [7] It is easier for members of such groups to indoctrinate others and more difficult for society to deal effectively with behavior which is supported by a highly organized subculture.

Some people feel that efforts to reduce deviant behavior should be concentrated, not on specific programs, but on broader attacks on a society's excessive mobility, impersonal relations, individualism, materialism, and norm conflicts. However, the general attack can be effective only if it is implemented by specific programs. The extensive spatial mobility of the American population, for example, may be reduced by a number of indirect measures. Some legislation, usually enacted for other purposes, has

[5] Lemert, *op. cit.*, pp. 44–47. These will be discussed in the next chapter.

[6] *Ibid.* See also Austin L. Porterfield, "The We-They Fallacy in Thinking about Delinquents and Criminals," *Federal Probation,* 21:44–47 (December, 1957). Also see Harold Garfinkel, "Conditions of Successful Degradation Ceremonies," *American Journal of Sociology,* 61:421–422 (1956). He points out that criminal judicial processes may be regarded as "status degradation ceremonies" from the prisoner's point of view. Two aspects of such ceremonies are the destruction of the person's identity, and the assignment of a new identity that is lower in the social scheme.

[7] Lemert, *op. cit.*, p. 44.

helped to keep people from moving to other areas. The government has attempted to stabilize the economy through measures to prevent depressions and inflations, and through unemployment insurance, social security legislation, and minimum-wage laws. More adequate housing has probably kept some persons from desiring to move, and mental hygiene clinics, as well as counseling agencies, family and individual, have kept others from changing their residences because of difficulties in interpersonal relations. Finally, the gradual elimination of racial discrimination is keeping certain people from migrating to other areas in the hope of removing inequalities in citizenship. A reasonably stable population would make it possible to deal more effectively with the norm conflicts of groups and reduce difficulties in interpersonal relations.

Moral and Ameliorative Problems

Difficulties in dealing with deviant behavior are often complicated by the lack of public agreement over whether certain deviations constitute a problem and also by disagreement about the norms and values involved in the solution. In this connection Fuller and Myers have distinguished between ameliorative and moral problems.[8] Ameliorative problems include deviations such as the conventional crimes of robbery, burglary, and murder, as well as drug addiction, mental illness, and alcoholism. The existence of an ameliorative problem implies that if the situation were eliminated the deviant behavior would be "ameliorated" or made better. Although in ameliorative deviations there is more general agreement that the situation is undesirable, there is disagreement as to the value of the corrective means or proposed solutions. This situation exists because the corrective means either interfere with other values of individuals or groups, or are believed to be inefficient. The solutions proposed frequently involve habits and attitudes which might have to be altered, and which currently provide a source of satisfaction for the individuals concerned. For example, few would say that mental illness or such ordinary crimes as burglary and larceny are other than "bad." The solution to these problems, however, presents a different issue entirely, for it might mean changing, for example, some aspects of urban life.

In moral problems there is not only disagreement over the proposed solution to the problem but there is disagreement as to whether or not the situation is undesirable and should be changed. There may be disagreement over whether such "moral" conditions as divorce, discrimination against minority groups, white-collar crime, gambling, and political cor-

---

[8] Richard Fuller and Richard R. Myers, "Some Aspects of a Theory of Social Problems," *American Sociological Review*, 6:24–32 (February, 1941). Also see John F. Cuber, Robert A. Harper and William F. Kenkel, *Problems of American Society: Values in Conflict* (3d ed.; New York: Holt, Rinehart and Winston, Inc., 1956).

ruption actually constitute social problems. To some, divorce is a serious moral transgression; to others, it is a solution to a problem which would be infinitely more serious if divorce were not permitted. Racial and religious discrimination is not "bad" to some people. They see the protection of vested interests, and preservation of so-called biological superiority or white supremacy, "natural law," and a host of others as reasons why it is, if not necessarily a good thing, certainly not a social problem. Others believe that it is a serious contradiction of the American Creed of human rights, democracy, and freedom of opportunity. Some people regard white-collar crime as real crime and a serious form of deviant behavior in society, whereas others do not. Gambling and political corruption have been similarly looked upon by some; by others they are regarded not as social problems but as "normal" situations in contemporary urban life. Obviously there are similar difficulties about solutions when there is disagreement over the existence of a problem.

Organized Public Education

Many people feel that public education is basic to any program dealing with certain types of deviant behavior. The underlying factors which account for the problems confronting modern society must be sought and dealt with on a broad basis. As some have noted, in order to find ways of combatting crime and delinquency, a necessary first step is to provide the public with more information about present problems and the successes and failures of methods used to deal with them.[9] Since in a democratic society operation of correctional and preventive measures rests ultimately on public support, it is imperative that the public be adequately informed. This information may be communicated not only through radio, television, the press, films, pamphlets, and books, but also through discussion. It is the type of education which seeks to provide such information which will be discussed here.

DELINQUENCY AND CRIME

The public has been educated about delinquency and crime through those national, state, and local conferences and various legislative commissions or committees which have wide publicity. In 1959, for example, the investigating subcommittee authorized by the Senate Judiciary Committee conducted widely publicized public hearings on the problem of juvenile delinquency. The objectives of the investigation were to examine: (1) the extent of delinquency, its causes and contributing factors;

---

[9] Hugh P. Reed, "The Citizens' New Role in Combatting Crime," *Federal Probation,* 24:31–36 (December, 1960).

(2) the adequacy of existing laws; (3) sentences and correctional action employed by federal courts; and (4) the extent of juvenile violation of federal narcotics laws.[10] The committee focused public attention upon the problems it brought to light, and recommended measures considered to be helpful both in preventing juvenile delinquency and in rehabilitating delinquents and youthful offenders. The publicity which the findings of this subcommittee have received helped to arouse the public about the gravity of existing conditions and the difficulty of dealing with them.

One of the most famous of all Congressional investigations of crime was the Special Committee to Investigate Organized Crime in Interstate Commerce, which was headed by Senator Estes Kefauver and which held nation-wide hearings during 1951.[11] These public hearings, the first senatorial hearings to be televised, enabled millions of Americans to see members of the Senate committee questioning organized criminals and their political allies about their activities.

In the past thirty years several Congressional investigations have influenced public opinion about white-collar crime: the investigation of the Teapot Dome scandals of the mid-twenties; the various committees investigating business ethics during the 1930's; and the Truman Committee, which investigated graft and corruption in connection with war contracts during World War II.[12] Senator Paul H. Douglas headed a well-known committee which, in 1951, went into the question of preventing graft and corruption in government. This committee made several proposals to avoid corruption in government, including the disclosure of income and other transactions by government officials, the definition of improper or unethical conduct, and the imposition of specific penalties. Douglas also proposed that a commission on ethics in government be set up.[13]

Congressional investigations which have received much attention within recent years have dealt with unethical conduct in the labor and management field, and with manipulation of prices by business executives in a number of major industries. The Senate inquiry of 1956 into labor corruption revealed the penetration into manufacturing concerns of racketeers and gangsters known to be connected with several large labor unions. Further inquiry documented a succession of collusive arrangements between business organizations and some unions. In addition, numerous improper and illegal activities were revealed in some labor unions, including collusion with organized criminals, violence and beatings, pay-offs, black-

---

[10] Senate Report of Juvenile Delinquency Hearings, 86th Cong., 1st Sess., S.R. 54, *Investigation of Juvenile Delinquency in the United States* (Washington, D.C.: Government Printing Office, February 12–13, 1959). See also reports dated during subsequent months.
    [11] See pp. 274–283.   [12] See p. 577.
    [13] Report of the Commission on Ethics in Government, Committee on Labor and Public Welfare, to accompany Senate Joint Resolution 107, October 9, 1951. Also see Paul H. Douglas, *Ethics in Government* (Cambridge, Mass.: Harvard University Press, 1952).

mail, padded expense accounts, speculation in gambling, and other forms of vice.[14] These investigations led to the passage of laws requiring labor unions to make full reports of their administrative and financial affairs, and to hold fair election proceedings with secret ballots. Also, these laws restrict the use of union funds by providing criminal penalties for their misappropriation. Yet one of the most significant results of these investigations was the arousal of public attention and concern, and the recognition by lawmakers of the need for legal restrictions as well as their adequate enforcement. As Attorney General Robert F. Kennedy has noted, an active interest on the part of citizens in public affairs is necessary: "Crime, corruption, and delinquency will continue to spread as long as people remain disinterested and lax and apathetic." [15]

In more general terms, people appear to need to be educated to realize that a democratic society rests fundamentally on the premise that laws are to be obeyed. This concept differs somewhat from the currently accepted idea that it is the responsibility of government to force the citizens to obey the law through fear of being apprehended if they disobey it. Organized crime, for example, cannot be successfully controlled unless there is some agreement on the immoral consequences of widespread commercialized gambling by the public and its relation to the bribery of public officials and police officers. The public's definition of a criminal needs to be changed so that it will include not merely those who violate the criminal law but those who violate any law. Society cannot expect to control ordinary crime with one set of standards while at the same time allowing violations of law such as organized or white-collar crime to take place under another set of standards. The citizen's responsibility for society's laws can be strengthened through his wider participation in neighborhood, community, and welfare activities which will help him to understand social objectives.

An important area in the control of white-collar crime is the development of more effective ethics among the professional groups and various organizations.[16] More ethical standards need to be developed among politicians and government officials as well as among professional men and businessmen. There needs to be some agreement among the various groups in society as to what is proper conduct, how new members are to be indoctrinated with such a code of ethics, and how deviations are to be treated. This relationship of ethics to white-collar crime is illustrated by the difficulties encountered in controlling "sharp" practices in business:

---

[14] Robert F. Kennedy, *The Enemy Within* (New York: Harper & Row, Publishers, 1960), pp. 17–25.

[15] *Ibid.*, p. 300.

[16] Marshall B. Clinard, "Corruption Runs Far Deeper than Politics," *The New York Times Magazine*, August 10, 1952, pp. 20–21. Also see the special issue entitled "Ethical Standards in American Public Life," *The Annals*, Vol. 280 (March, 1952).

Control of sharp, evasive, and fraudulent practices in business will have to develop externally, that is, by boycotting and the reporting of white-collar violators by their victims (other businessmen, buyers, and consumers) as well as internally, that is, within the world of business and its various organizations and associations. The reporting of white-collar violations and bringing of action in the regular law enforcement channels rather than through investigations and action of administrative commissions and regulatory bodies is a matter of vital concern to crime control. Crystallized public sentiment against white-collar crime would be more of a preventive force, since one of the reasons that so much white-collar violation in the business world exists is that the public is really not vitally interested in the ethics of its businessmen just so long as it gets good service from them. Businessmen, through their own organizations and associations, must also become vitally concerned with the ethics of doing business and the ways of rendering service to the public. In several quarters of well-established and highly organized business, strong internal controls over members by associations are developing, whereby businessmen through their own collective pressure can hold their colleagues in line. Ethical business practices are what is needed to combat white-collar crime, although it is realized that this is difficult to bring about in some highly competitive enterprises, in wildcat operations, and in businesses that have not developed a strong association.[17]

EDUCATION ABOUT MENTAL DISORDERS

During the past decade, great strides have been taken toward educating the public about mental disorder. Such education is carried out largely through the mass media and through the efforts of three agencies—citizens' mental health organizations, federal and state agencies, and professional groups. The National Institute of Mental Health, an agency created by an act of Congress in 1946, is responsible for coordinating work dealing with mental disorder, including the dissemination of information to the public, community programs, research, and training of psychiatric personnel. State agencies generally function to assist public education through community services.

Voluntary citizens' organizations are chiefly concerned with educating themselves and other members of the public about mental health. The work of these groups consists of such activities as gathering and documenting information about conditions affecting mental health, encouraging research on mental health, and trying to improve the number and quality of personnel in the field of mental health.[18] Much of their work is done through public speakers, motion pictures, radio and television programs,

---

[17] Walter C. Reckless, *The Crime Problem* (2d ed.; New York: Appleton-Century-Crofts, Inc., 1955), pp. 678–679.

[18] George D. Stevenson, "Citizens Mental Health Movement," *The Annals*, 286:92–99 (March, 1953).

and pamphlets. The professional organizations of certain applied disciplines, such as social work, medicine, and psychiatry, have assumed some of the responsibility for informing the public about mental disorder.

Despite such efforts as those described above, research evidence shows that the public generally continues to associate mental disorder with the stigma of public disgrace. A two-year poll of Americans' opinions of their own mental health showed that although one in four believed they had problems serious enough to seek help, only one in seven sought such help.[19] A 1960 study, for example, found that relatives of former mental patients tend to expect that friends and neighbors will respond to them with rejection and disapproval.[20] Other studies and national opinion surveys have revealed similar attitudes.[21]

There is also evidence that public ideas about mental disorder are highly stereotyped. To the public, the term "mental disorder" often connotes bizarre, highly disturbed behavior.[22] Some suggest that such stereotypes may be fostered by mass media information which tends too often to present an oversimplified, distorted view of the subtleties involved in mentally disordered behavior.[23] It has also been shown that information distributed to the public about mental disorder is biased in the direction of middle-class values and norms, and that the picture the public receives may not represent the norms of mental disorder or mental health in the other social classes.[24]

One of the most significant proposals of the Joint Commission on Mental Illness and Health (which was authorized by Congress in 1955 to conduct a five-year study on aspects of mental health in the United States) was for public information of a *specific* kind on mental illness.[25] The commission noted that the continuing lag in treatment of the mentally ill reflects a basic pattern of social rejection. It stated that information to

[19] Gerald Gurin, Joseph Veroff, and Sheila Feld, *Americans View Their Mental Health* (New York: Basic Books, Inc., 1960). Also see Charles D. Whatley, "Social Attitudes toward Discharged Mental Patients," *Social Problems*, 6:313–320 (Spring, 1959), and Howard E. Freeman and Ozzie G. Simmons, "Feelings of Stigma among Relatives of Former Mental Patients," *Social Problems*, 8:312–322 (Spring, 1961).

[20] Freeman and Simmons, "Feelings of Stigma among Relatives of Former Mental Patients," *loc. cit.*

[21] Charlotte Green Schwartz, "Perspectives on Deviance: Wives' Definitions of Their Husbands' Mental Illness," *Psychiatry*, 20:275–291 (August, 1957); and Robert H. Felix, "Social Psychiatry and Community Attitudes," *World Health Organization Technical Report* (Series 177; Geneva: World Health Organization, 1959).

[22] Shirley A. Star, "The Public's Ideas About Mental Illness." Paper presented to the annual meeting of the National Association for Mental Health, November 5, 1955.

[23] John Clausen, "Mental Disorders," in Robert K. Merton and Robert R. Nisbet, *Contemporary Social Problems* (New York: Harcourt, Brace & World, Inc., 1961), pp. 127–180.

[24] Orville R. Gursslin, Raymond G. Hunt, and Jack L. Roach, "Social Class and the Mental Health Movement," *Social Problems*, 7:210–217 (1960).

[25] Report of the Joint Commission on Mental Illness and Health, *Action for Mental Health* (New York: Basic Books, Inc., 1961), pp. 275–282.

the public should aim specifically to counter this societal pattern of rejection of the mentally ill. Such information should focus on the major difference between physical and mental illness, e.g., the differences in the reactions and attitudes toward the person by *others*. The commission report further stated that there is a tendency for persons to react to the mentally ill person with revulsion and ridicule. Public information should therefore make clear that public stereotypes of mental illness, as characterized by violent behavior, represent an exceedingly small proportion of all those who are mentally ill, and that these stereotypes inaccurately represent the overwhelming majority of the mental patients.

MARRIAGE AND FAMILY EDUCATION

Extensive work is being done now to dispense scientific information about marital and family relations. Many schools, particularly those dealing with higher education, have introduced courses in family relationships. High school courses are generally not designated as courses in family problems, but the subject is treated in health, home economics, and social science subjects. The first college course on marriage was given in 1926 at the University of North Carolina; marriage and family courses are now a regular part of the curriculum of many colleges and universities.

Numerous national and local organizations are interested in family relationships—so many, in fact, that it is sometimes referred to as "the family life movement." Some are interested only in education, whereas others include counseling and discussion of proposed legislative changes in their programs. Utah, for example, has passed legislation requiring marital counseling for couples who have filed for divorce. Most national organizations have a large number of local chapters. Some work is done by the YMCA and the YWCA and by many church groups.

The National Council on Family Relations, organized in 1938, is probably the best known of the national private family organizations. Other national private organizations not affiliated with religious groups include the American Association of Marriage Counselors, the American Eugenics Society, the American Social Hygiene Association, the Family Service Association of America, and the Planned Parenthood Federation of America.

ALCOHOL EDUCATION

Some of the most effective work in public education has already been done with alcoholism.[26] The accomplishments made in this area have

---

[26] Marty Mann, "The Challenge of Alcoholism," *Federal Probation*, 24:18-23 (March, 1960).

been fairly recent but they have encouraged similar work in other areas of deviant behavior. Considering that extensive scientific efforts in this field are hardly more than twenty years old, the progress has been remarkable. As early as 1949 a study found that nationally about one in five persons had come to believe that alcoholism is a "sickness" and that alcoholics should not be punished.[27] There are indications that this belief is held even more widely today. Some suggest that this indicates progress in the field of alcohol education. This change in attitude on the part of the public has been largely due to the work of Alcoholics Anonymous, state bureaus of alcoholism, Yale University's Section on Alcohol Studies (now at Rutgers University), the National Committee on Alcoholism, which has many local chapters, school educational programs, industrial in-plant programs, as well as the fullest cooperation of all types of media of mass communication.

Since the work of Alcoholics Anonymous will be discussed in the last chapter the remarks on alcohol education will be limited here to a few other programs. In 1956 there were state programs on alcoholism in forty-one states and the District of Columbia, many of which helped coordinate work in this area, furnished information on the subject to the public, and developed treatment and education programs. Practically all the states and the District of Columbia now require the teaching of alcohol education at some level in their school programs. More than sixty cities have information centers dealing with the problems of alcoholics, but many more are needed. Trained persons staff these centers, which are sources of information on alcoholism, including data on available treatment facilities—hospitals and sanatoria, medical specialists, Alcoholics Anonymous groups, and so on. Staffs not only help alcoholics work out some sort of treatment program but also help other persons who are interested in the problems of the alcoholic. Manuals devised for the use of schoolteachers cover many of the important aspects of what has been learned about alcohol and alcoholism.[28] These school manuals have adult counterparts in a large number of books, pamphlets, and audiovisual programs, which have been developed for the adult citizen.

The public attitude, held increasingly by many, that alcoholism is a "sickness" may enable the alcoholic to receive sympathy and social support for his temporary occupancy of a "sick role." [29] To this extent, the alcoholic's rehabilitation may be enhanced, since his compulsive drinking

---

[27] John W. Riley, Jr., "The Social Implications of Problem Drinking," Social Forces, 27:301–305 (March, 1949).

[28] See, for example, Joseph Hirsh, Alcohol Education: A Guide Book for Teachers (New York: Abelard-Schuman Ltd., 1952). For a general discussion of these programs see Raymond McCarthy and Edgar M. Douglass, Alcohol and Social Responsibility (New York: Thomas Y. Crowell Company and the Yale Plan Clinic, 1949).

[29] Lemert, op. cit.

seems to be due largely to perceived social rejection, ostracism, and isolation stemming from experiences of drinking of a noncompulsive nature.[30]

EDUCATION ABOUT DRUG ADDICTION

Recent information on the extent of drug addiction among young people has so disturbed the general public that immediate frontal attacks on the problem, including educational programs, have been instituted. Teaching concerning narcotics is required by New York State law. On the other hand, it is argued that information about the use of drugs may pique the curiosity of some teen-agers to the point that they will desire to experiment themselves.

There are some doubts as to the value of public information now distributed about drug addiction. For the most part, this information is communicated in a sensational manner and with heavy moralistic overtones which create an erroneous conception of the drug addict.[31] Like some of the information on mental disorders, this information tends to reflect and exploit public stereotypes concerning drug addicts. Ideally, educative efforts should be directed at what some suggest is the basis of the addiction problem in America—namely, public attitudes toward addiction and the drug addict. So long as addicts are ostracized, rejected, stigmatized, and isolated from respectable society, their rehabilitation and the reduction of the drug problem is impeded. As the experience of Britain suggests (see the discussion in Chapter 11), reduction of drug addiction will be possible only when the response of the public to addiction is directly approached.

DISCRIMINATION

Efforts to reduce discrimination are now so extensive that it is possible to do little more than to list them.[32] Educational methods include such a variety of approaches as intergroup education in the schools, community self-surveys on the extent of discrimination, and work camps where

---

[30] See Edwin H. Lemert, "Alcoholism and the Sociocultural Situation," *Quarterly Journal of Studies on Alcohol*, 17:306–317 (June, 1956) for some comments relating to the above. Also see David Mechanic and Edmund A. Volkart, "Stress, Illness, and the Sick Role," *American Sociological Review*, 26:51–58 (February, 1961).

[31] H. J. Anslinger and William F. Tompkins, *The Traffic in Narcotics* (New York: Funk & Wagnalls Company, 1953). These authors suggest (see p. 213) that information in the form of articles, speeches, discussions, pictures, and programs have bombarded the public in the last few years, yet by and large this information has fostered an image of a "dope fiend" and has tended to present inaccurately the picture of drug addiction.

[32] For a more detailed discussion see the special issue of *The Annals*, "Controlling Group Prejudice," 244:1–182 (March, 1946) and George E. Simpson and J. Milton Yinger, *Racial and Cultural Minorities* (rev. ed.; New York: Harper & Row, Publishers, 1958), Chaps. 22, 23.

members of different racial groups can associate freely, as they do in the well-known camps conducted by the American Friends Service Committees. These camps bring together young people from various racial, religious, and national groups around a task—such as building a new rural school-house or repairing housing in a slum area—not primarily concerned with majority-minority relations but which often influences them indirectly in a marked way.

An increasing number of workshops in intergroup relations have been held since the end of World War II. Most of these workshops are held on college and university campuses, with the cooperation of such agencies as the National Conference of Christians and Jews or the Anti-Defamation League, the city community relations boards, state agencies, the American Jewish Committee, the American Jewish Congress, and a number of the colleges and universities themselves. These workshops have averaged be-tween thirty to forty students, who are often community leaders, and they have varied in length from one day to a summer term of six weeks or longer. In April, 1957, one report listed sixty-six workshops in twenty-five states for the summer of that year.

Many church groups, labor unions, and similar groups have been active in developing an interest in discrimination and its consequences for American society. Most colleges now have a course in minority prob-lems, and many secondary schools deal with this topic in their social science or civics courses.

In 1956 there were 491 public or private national, regional, state, and local agencies, with paid staffs, exclusive of agencies of the federal government, working in the area of intergroup relations: 61 national private agencies, 63 regional agencies, 23 state public agencies, 48 state private agencies, 30 municipal agencies, and 266 local private agencies. In addition there were a large number of other groups with voluntary staffs.[33]

Of the national private agencies working in this area the most im-portant are the American Friends Service Committee, the American Jewish Committee, the American Jewish Congress, the Anti-Defamation League of B'nai B'rith, the Japanese-American Citizens League, the Jewish Labor Committee, the National Association for the Advancement of Colored People, the National Community Relations Advisory Council, the National Conference of Christians and Jews, and the National Urban League.

Most significant of the post–World War II developments in inter-group relations have been not only the enactment of state laws against discrimination in the fields of public accommodations, employment, hous-ing, and education but the creation of governmental civil rights agencies to administer these laws. According to the latest information available,

[33] Material furnished by the Research Department, National Association of Intergroup Relations Officials.

twenty-eight states have enacted laws prohibiting discrimination in one or more of these fields. Twenty-five of the states have public agencies with authority ranging from purely advisory powers, as in Kentucky and Florida, to full-fledged regulatory powers, including the issuance of enforceable orders, as in sixteen of the northern states. The public accommodations laws of some states, such as Massachusetts, date back to the post–Civil War period.

New York and Wisconsin were among the first states to enact fair employment practices (FEPC) laws in 1945. In 1961 Illinois passed fair employment practices laws to become the twenty-first state with such legislation. The first state fair-housing laws prohibiting discrimination in the sale, lease, and rental of dwellings were adopted by such states as New York, New Jersey, and Wisconsin in the late 1940's. All of these early laws applied only to public or publicly assisted housing. In 1959, Colorado, Connecticut, Massachusetts, and Oregon passed the first fair-housing laws applicable to private housing as well. Similar comprehensive fair-housing legislation has been enacted by three of the fifteen states which had such bills before their 1961 legislatures.[34]

Depending upon many complex factors, such as the population make-up and the climate of opinion toward human rights, state civil rights agencies vary considerably in organization, powers, functions, and budgets. The Wisconsin Governor's Commission on Human Rights, for example, with thirty governor-appointed nonsalaried commissioners, a civil service director, and a staff of two, was created by the legislature in 1947 with a broad mandate: ". . . to disseminate information and to attempt by means of discussion as well as other proper means to educate the people of the state to a greater understanding, appreciation and practice of human rights for all people. . . ." Without specific administrative responsibility or regulatory powers, the commission's program includes fact finding, education, community organization and relations, the handling of cases of discrimination, and recommendations of needed legislation. A broad approach utilizing existing agencies and resources and "tailor-made" techniques is employed to remedy specific problems and to promote a climate of opinion favorable to equal opportunity for all disadvantaged groups, such as Negroes, Indians, and migrant workers. The commission also has initiated and/or supported legislation which is now law, relating to non-discrimination in public accommodations, the National Guard, public housing, employment, migrant camps, and Indian affairs.

Twenty states also have private agencies in intergroup relations. About twelve of them are councils on human relations in southern states or-

---

[34] "State Laws and Agencies for Civil Rights: A Comparative Study of 28 States," (mimeographed; Madison, Wisc., Governor's Commission on Human Rights), February, 1960.

ganized through efforts of the Southern Regional Council to help particularly with tension growing out of school desegregation.

There are over thirty municipal intergroup relations agencies with paid staffs located in twenty-seven cities. Some have fair employment practices responsibilities, and others work for the improvement of relations between various groups through education, persuasion, and consultation. Most are in larger cities, such as Boston, Chicago, Cincinnati, Cleveland, Denver, Detroit, Kansas City (Missouri), Los Angeles, Milwaukee, Minneapolis, New York City, Philadelphia, Pittsburgh, Toledo, and St. Louis. In addition, there are 117 cities with local private agencies.

It is difficult to say how effective these public and private programs of public education actually are. The very organization of these official and unofficial bodies is an indication that more citizens are assuming a larger share of the responsibility for these problems. This widespread awareness of group prejudices is evident in the results of surveys and in the extent to which the subject of racial and cultural relations has been featured in the press, television, the radio, and motion pictures. "The fact that discussion of these problems is increasingly open and frank is in itself an indication of a more wholesome state of affairs." [35]

Preventive Agencies

It is often difficult for the public to see that it is easier and less expensive, in the long run, to prevent the development of deviant attitudes and antisocial behavior than to try to modify them later. In preventive work it is necessary to get to a situation before the person has been organized in a certain manner and a deviant conception of self has been formed. Several different types of preventive agencies have been, or are in the process of being, established. Some represent a general approach and apply to many problems, whereas others deal only with one.

LOCAL COMMUNITY PROGRAMS OR NEIGHBORHOOD COUNCILS

One of the most promising efforts to deal with the unsatisfactory features of urbanization and to reduce social deviation has undoubtedly been the greater citizen participation in attempts to change the local community. Local community programs or neighborhood councils, as most of these groups have been called, are becoming increasingly widespread and appear to have a sound theoretical basis, both in accomplishing group redefinitions and situations and in giving the individual a feeling of belong-

[35] Louis Wirth, "The Unfinished Business of American Democracy," *The Annals*, 244:6–7 (March, 1946). Also see Robin M. Williams, Jr., *The Reduction of Intergroup Tensions* (New York: Social Science Research Council, 1947).

ing in the larger social structure. They are used not only in the United States but also in many countries, including Great Britain and even India.[36]

This approach stresses the neighborhood as an important area of first-line action in combating deviant behavior. It is an attempt to deal with conditions in the environment which contribute to delinquency. An impressive amount of evidence in certain areas of social deviation indicates that often the neighborhood, rather than the individual or the family, is the locus of the problem. Research by social scientists in a number of cities has revealed that some neighborhoods have higher rates of deviations than others. This does not mean that deviations are nonexistent in some areas, but rather that if they are controlled in certain selected areas the total incidence can be materially reduced. As has been indicated, the rate of delinquency may be as much as five times greater in certain neighborhoods than in others. There are great variations in the rates for ordinary crime. Likewise, the amount of sexual promiscuity and family maladjustment may vary with neighborhoods. Similar variations have been found in the amount of suicide, discrimination against Negroes, and anti-Semitism. Although alcoholism and certain forms of mental illness have not been characterized by such wide ecological differences, the incidence of mental illness may be several times greater—and the chances of getting early treatment much less—in certain areas.

"Problem neighborhoods," as those areas generally characterized by high rates of deviant behavior are often termed, appear to exhibit a number of social characteristics. They are areas of great diversity in social norms and values, considerable spatial mobility, and little stability of the population. People migrate there from rural and urban areas, and from other countries and cities. Social contacts in the entire area are often less numerous or intimate, and although there is more tolerance, there is less concern for the welfare of neighbors. Shared activities of the entire neighborhood are less frequent and seldom involve common problems.

The neighborhood is an area in which the family functions. To a large extent the kind of neighborhood determines the type of family life which will develop. Often what a middle-class neighborhood claims as the personal virtues of the family are the reflection of groups of families and other institutions surrounding it. Conversely, there is a limit to what a single family with one set of norms can do if it is surrounded by other families with deviant norms and is in an area where the institutions also cater to

[36] Arthur Hillman, *Neighborhood Centers Today* (New York: National Federation of Settlements and Neighborhood Centers, 1960), and B. Chatterjee and Marshall B. Clinard, *Organizing Citizens' Development Councils* (Delhi: Delhi Municipal Corporation, 1961). Also see Marshall B. Clinard and B. Chatterjee, "Urban Community Development in India: The Delhi Pilot Project," in Roy Turner, ed., *India's Urban Future* (Berkeley: University of California Press, 1962), and Marshall B. Clinard, "Perspectives on Urban Community Development and Community Organization," *Social Welfare Forum*, 1962.

deviant norms. The family may come to reflect neighborhood approval or disapproval of conditions of marital infidelity, excessive drinking, or discrimination against certain groups. Neighborhoods and the children of neighbors help, more than is realized, to raise one's children.

The neighborhood is the child's world. It is largely the area of his social participation during afternoons, evenings, week ends, holidays, and vacation periods. His informal neighborhood education is frequently at odds with his more formal school education. There is often conflict between the neighborhood and the school in the definitions of what constitutes proper use of leisure time, sportsmanship, and moral codes.[37] Often the neighborhood play group can enforce more conformity than the school, and school programs which attempt, for example, to deal with juvenile delinquency cannot be effective without the active cooperation of the neighborhood. If there is a cleavage between school norms and neighborhood norms, the problems of dealing with delinquency are greatly increased. Similarly, child guidance clinics and law enforcement must depend on neighborhood support. The people of a neighborhood can support or ridicule the work of psychiatrists and police officers. What their neighbors think is often the really important thing to people. Where they have no neighbors only formal agencies are able to influence them.

Neighborhood programs usually involve a symbiotic relationship between local leaders and professional personnel, usually social workers or sociologists, who serve as catalysts for stimulating local desires for social reintegration. These professionally trained people generally do not carry out the programs and do not desire to do so. Rather, they find the leadership and suggest various possible ways in which to execute the programs, but they leave the decisions to local leadership.

> Outside leaders have a definite but limited role. This approach to area reorganization places principal emphasis on the role of natural community leaders who are carriers of conventional conduct norms. Not only do such leaders serve as nondelinquent models for emulation by youngsters attracted to programs offered by projects of this type, but because these indigenous leaders have prestige in the local area, they easily attract adults, as well as children and youths, to project programs in the first instance. It is around natural community leaders, then, that legitimate social structures can be germinated and multiplied in delinquency-prone areas. And it is in relationship with such leaders and within such structures that youngsters can develop the close and intimate attachments with conventional models, achieve the satisfactions, and acquire the sense of personal worth and purpose necessary to counter the drift toward delinquency characteristic of their life situations.[38]

---

[37] Henry D. McKay, "The Neighborhood and Child Conduct," *The Annals*, 261:33 (January, 1949).

[38] John M. Martin, "Three Approaches to Delinquency Prevention: A Critique," *Crime and Delinquency*, 7:23 (January, 1961).

The so-called Area Project work in Chicago has been one of the best known of these efforts. This neighborhood approach began a few years before 1934 and was incorporated in that year as the Chicago Area Project. Although primarily organized to counteract delinquency, it has indirectly stimulated many efforts to solve other problems. Initially the project was instituted to reduce the high delinquency in three areas of the zone in transition in the city; since then the work has been expanded to include seven other areas. The Area Project has the same purpose as have other agencies—the control of delinquency—but its methods are different:

> (1) It emphasizes the development of a program for the neighborhood as a whole. (2) It seeks to stress the autonomy of the local residents in helping to plan, support, and operate constructive programs which they may regard as their own. (3) It attaches special significance to the training and utilization of community leaders. (4) It confines the efforts of its professional staff, in large part, to consultation and planning with responsible neighborhood leaders who assume major roles in the actual development of the program. (5) It seeks to encourage the local residents to utilize to the maximum all churches, societies, clubs, and other existing institutions and agencies, and to coordinate these in a unified neighborhood program. (6) Its activities are regarded primarily as devices for enlisting the active participation of local residents in a constructive community enterprise, for creating and crystallizing neighborhood sentiment on behalf of the welfare of the children and the social and physical improvement of the community as a whole. (7) It places particular emphasis upon the importance of a continuous, objective evaluation of its effectiveness as a device for reducing delinquency, through constructive modification of the pattern of community life.[39]

More specifically, programs of this type try first to develop a civic pride in the activity of its residents. The degree of participation in community activities seems, in part, to be a product of the individual's conception of his responsibility for improving social conditions. Second, the local committees try to develop recreational programs for the neighborhood children and to reach natural groups of children, such as gangs. Being citizen-led, members of these groups often have the advantage of knowing the delinquents personally, and they can enlist the support of persons with similar racial and ethnic backgrounds. Third, community groups assist in the rehabilitation of delinquent and criminal offenders by encouraging them to adopt conventional norms. This is often done by asking such people to serve on community committees: "By this method the parolee or ex-offender is introduced into a conventional group, his role in

---

[39] Clifford R. Shaw and Jesse A. Jacobs, "The Chicago Area Project: An Experimental Community Program for Prevention of Delinquency in Chicago," "Mimeographed; Chicago: Institute for Juvenile Research, undated). Also see Anthony Sorrentino, "The Chicago Area Project after 25 Years," *Federal Probation:* 23:40–45 (June, 1959); and Solomon Kobrin, "The Chicago Area Project—A 25-Year Assessment," *The Annals,* 322:19–29 (March, 1959).

the community is thus redefined, which, in turn results in a redefinition of his own conception of himself. The vigor with which parolees and others with criminal records have worked to improve their own communities and to keep boys out of delinquency has been one of the most encouraging aspects of the Area Project program." [40] Programs of this type have now been developed in a number of communities in Illinois, patterned after the Chicago project. In Quincy, for example, such programs have been set up in five low-income neighborhoods. Variations of these projects, some with less citizen responsibility and more direction by the professional staff, have been adopted in other parts of the country.[41]

In an evaluation of the Chicago Area Projects by Witmer and Tufts, these conclusions were enumerated:

1. Residents of low-income areas can organize and have organized themselves into effective working units for promoting and conducting welfare programs.
2. These community organizations have been stable and enduring. They raise funds, administer them well, and adapt the programs to local needs.
3. Local talent, otherwise untapped, has been discovered and utilized. Local leadership has been mobilized in the interest of children's welfare.[42]

Some area projects go beyond a single neighborhood and become an association of neighborhoods, as in the Southside Community Committee in the large Negro area of Chicago. Between 1934 and 1940 eighteen in every hundred boys in this highly deteriorated area were brought before the court, a rate almost four times that of the city as a whole. In an attempt to reduce this high delinquency rate and to develop closer community integration, the local citizens set up committees, organized community centers and summer camps, and planned a variety of other programs. They have written about their work: "Each neighborhood organization attempts to deal with these problems as vigorously as possible. . . . Police were exceptionally cooperative with the neighborhood organizations, responding eagerly, and in some cases with ill-concealed surprise, to the novel spectacle of residents in vice-ridden neighborhoods taking action against disreputable elements in the community." [43]

---

[40] "Report of the Chicago Area Project, 1947–48" (Mimeographed; Chicago: Institute for Juvenile Research, 1949), p. 6.

[41] See Hillman, op. cit.

[42] H. L. Witmer and E. Tufts, The Effectiveness of Delinquency Prevention Programs, Children's Bureau, U.S. Department of Health, Education, and Welfare, Publication 350 (Washington, D.C.: Government Printing Office, 1954), p. 15.

[43] Southside Community Committee, Bright Shadows in Bronzetown (Chicago: South Side Community, 1949), p. 104. See Julia Abrahamson, A Neighborhood Finds Itself (New York: Harper & Row, Publishers, 1959), for a detailed description of how other Southside citizens in Chicago united in an effort to save their neighborhood from deterioration into a slum.

Martin has summarized the importance of a local community approach to delinquency prevention:

> Students of delinquency are becoming increasingly aware of the necessity of reaching out beyond the child and his family in their efforts at prevention. It is submitted that the most efficacious approach for modifying the operating milieu of the bulk of our delinquents is through the widespread establishment of community-centered programs of prevention. Supported by continued improvement in the collective welfare—particularly in terms of the successful assimilation of low-status groups—and incorporating the best of "corrections" and individual treatment, the community-centered approach offers the most hope for reducing law-violation by our children and adolescents.[44]

STREET CORNER PROJECTS

Another type of preventive program involves semiparticipant work with a group of deviants. This approach has been used particularly with delinquent gangs by various groups, such as the Boys Club of New York City and, more dramatically, by the Central Harlem Street Clubs Project of the Welfare Council of New York City. This project worked intimately with four Harlem street gangs from 1947 to 1950 in an effort to divert their activities into legitimate channels. The gangs varied from thirty-five to over a hundred boys, ranging in years from nine to nineteen, all of whom had been engaging in such behavior as fighting in gangs, stealing, committing sex offenses, smoking marihuana, drinking liquor, and gambling:

> The boys tended to see adults as authorities, hoodlums, or suckers. Authorities pushed them around, told them what to do and what not to do, moralized, made demands, threatened, condemned, and meted out punishments. Some boys regarded their parents and teachers in this light. According to the boys, the cops chased them from the streets in which they played, picked them up without reason, and subjected them to humiliating verbal abuse and brutal beatings. (On several occasions the workers observed actual instances of mistreatment on the part of the police.)
>
> According to the boys, hoodlums were the smart guys who got along in the work by exploiting, cheating, and outwitting the other fellow. The numbers man, the pimp, and the racketeer were outstanding examples. They were admired because they were "in the know," knew the "ins" and "outs," and could get around the law. One always had to be on guard with an adult because any adult might be a hoodlum at heart. The boys were especially suspicious of "nice" adults.
>
> The boys had little, if any, community identification. They hated living in Harlem. They hated the filth, the lack of decent places to play, the overcrowding. They felt that the community had no place for them. They were pushed around by the janitor. They were chased out of the candy store

---

[44] Martin, "Three Approaches to Delinquency Prevention," *loc. cit.*, p. 24.

by the store-keeper. They were hounded off the street by cruising patrol cars. As far as they were concerned adults had no use for them and this feeling was mutual! Many boys felt that their fellow club members were the only persons in the world for whom they cared or on whom they could count.[45]

A project worker was attached to each gang. As the project workers established relationships with the boys in the gang, gradually won their confidences, and became accepted by them they played several roles. One was a neutral role of observing and seeking information without displaying approval or disapproval; another was that of stimulating changes. They used such techniques as example-setting, delaying antisocial acts, and insight-inducing to make the boys aware of feelings they did not recognize. Through their associations they tried to encourage self-direction along the lines of new programs. They used various means to divert the boys' activities:

1. They organized baseball and basketball teams, obtained the use of school and church gyms for practice sessions, and participated in tournaments with the teams of former enemy gangs.

2. They held a number of dances and block parties at which they sold refreshments and raffled off gifts. With the profits from these ventures some of the clubs were able to buy uniforms and equipment for their teams.

3. They organized a series of movie programs for their members and friends. The Project supplied the movie projector, but the boys ran the shows themselves—choosing the films, setting up chairs, collecting tickets at the door, and cleaning up afterwards.

4. They went on a number of overnight hikes, camping trips, and fishing and crabbing outings.[46]

A more recent project has been the study of street corner groups and patterns of delinquency in connection with the program for detached workers of the YMCA of metropolitan Chicago.[47] Workers are assigned to make contacts with, and to try to change the delinquent patterns of, juvenile gangs. A preliminary report has stated that "we can say with a big degree of confidence that *gang fighting* virtually has been eliminated on the part of gangs with which the program has worked intensively. We want to know a good deal more about *why* this is true, however, and why other forms of delinquent behavior apparently are much more resistant to change than is gang fighting." [48]

[45] Paul L. Crawford, Daniel I. Malamud, and James R. Dumpson, *Working with Teen-Age Gangs*, A Report on the Central Harlem Street Clubs Project (New York: Welfare Council of New York City, 1950), pp. 18–19.

[46] *Ibid.*, pp. 39–40.

[47] James Short, Jr., "Street Corner Groups and Patterns of Delinquency," A Progress Report from National Institute of Mental Health Research Grant, M-3301 (Mimeographed; March 1, 1961).

[48] *Ibid.*, p. 28. Italics in the original.

THE SCHOOL

More and more schools have been recognizing that their duties extend beyond the transmission of knowledge. As the schools have taken over many responsibilities for character development which were formerly left entirely to the family and the church, some families have tended to attribute to them the difficulties which their children develop. Teachers can have a beneficial effect on children. The training of teachers has increasingly emphasized problems of mental health, and they have learned to recognize many incipient behavior difficulties of children in the classroom situation.[49] Such children are referred to the counseling staff for guidance if the school has one, or to any other appropriate community agency.

> Few would deny that the family is the best of all possible settings for the promotion of mental health. Here are concentrated the crucial influences and relationships that shape the development of the child and young adult, for better or for worse. Unfortunately, the family is a rather isolated unit of modern society; its members go forth from the home as individuals but may return to it as components of a different group. The family is not readily accessible to outside help, except as it seeks it, and society has no pervasive mental health resources that encompass the family within their structure.
>
> The school, however, comes remarkably close to achieving this relationship with the family. At least it is in a position to do so. In an era of universal compulsory education, the school is one institution of society through which each of us must pass. During our formative years we are influenced to varying degrees by this educational experience, which takes place against the background of the family, yet apart from it. Here, then, is a ready-made setting with a potentiality for directing, reinforcing, or correcting mental health. The school may not only guide, strengthen, and even treat the mental health of the pupil but also, through the role of the pupil as a family member, seek means of improving home situations for the sake of all members of the family.[50]

In some localities, schools have also done some work in antidiscrimination programs. The best known of such programs has been the Springfield Plan, where for many years in this Massachusetts community the school has attempted to teach a constructive program of intergroup relations from the lowest grades.[51] At the same time there are similar programs in adult classes, PTA's, churches, labor unions, and teachers' training courses to change the attitudes of adults.

---

[49] For a discussion of these issues see Wesley A. Smith and G. W. Goethals, *The Role of the Schools in Mental Health* (in preparation), as cited in *Action for Mental Health.*

[50] Joint Commission on Mental Illness and Health, *Action for Mental Health* (New York: Basic Books, Inc., 1961), pp. 123–124. Reprinted by permission.

[51] Alexander Alland and James Waterman Wise, *The Springfield Plan* (New York: The Viking Press, Inc., 1945).

Unfortunately, some school situations add to behavioral difficulties and to intergroup tensions, and may even contribute to truancy and to more serious delinquency. Many professional educators agree that schools are often places where juveniles, during the school day, are bored, subjected to monotonous routine, crushed when they try to express any individuality, or thrown into needless competition with others instead of learning how to cooperate with them.[52] In many urban areas the relation of teacher and pupil is impersonal. Nevertheless, the school situation is one of personal interaction, and too frequently those selected to educate others are themselves uninspiring and may even be seriously maladjusted. Teachers too often silence inquisitive, creative students by demands for obedience. As a result, "it is no wonder that part of the function of juvenile gangs engaging in delinquency is to furnish new experience, the thrill of the cleverly executed act of vandalism or auto theft." [53]

The National Education Association recently sponsored a project in juvenile delinquency which was initiated by the question, "What can the school do to prevent and control norm-violating behavior of children?" The project committee offered suggestions as to how the school may more effectively serve as a preventive agency from which the following were selected.[54]

1. The classroom teacher assumes the major responsibility for early identification of the potential norm-violating youngster. He maintains records and anecdotal reports of every pupil he teaches, thus ensuring that accurate and up-to-date information about individual students and their backgrounds will be readily available to himself and to other professional personnel.

2. The teacher maintains an attitude toward all his students which recognizes and upholds the dignity and worth of every individual, including that of the norm violator. As an instructional motivator and guide in the learning experience, he makes every effort to enable each pupil to achieve a level commensurate with his ability, despite norm-violating behavior arising from emotional or cultural problems.

3. The school develops an integrated system of special services, adequately and professionally staffed, to help the norm violator. These services generally are designed to assist the individual classroom teacher as she works with any pupil needing help. The school periodically assesses its unique needs for such services in the present and future, and it adopts long-range plans for meeting these needs.

---

[52] "Education for Our Time," Special Issue of *Survey Graphic*, 36:565–653 (November, 1947).

[53] Marshall B. Clinard, "Secondary Community Influences and Juvenile Delinquency," *The Annals*, 261:45 (January, 1949).

[54] See William C. Kvaraceus, *Delinquent Behavior: Principles and Practices*, Vol. II; and *Delinquent Behavior: Culture and the Individual*, Vol. I (Washington, D.C.: National Education Association, 1959).

4. For the extremely disturbed or disturbing youngster the school provides special facilities with special personnel in which remedial and rehabilitative services are available. The special class or center should be conceived of as, or allowed to become, a custodial or a hospital facility.

5. The school recognizes and accepts the fact that the family is one of the most important influences in the life of an individual, that few parents are willfully negligent or have any wish to raise a delinquent youngster, and that parents are in a strategic position to understand and evaluate the growth and development of their own children. The school, having recognized and accepted the responsibilities of identifying potential or actual delinquent behavior in the school situation, works with the family in a common endeavor to achieve what is best for the youngster.

6. The school and law-enforcement and court personnel develop a coordinated and cooperative program in all common areas related to juvenile norm-violating behavior.

7. The school recognizes that delinquency prevention and control is a community problem and requires action on the part of all citizens. The school studies, evaluates, understands, and makes use of the peer, ethnic, racial, and religious systems at work in its community. Utilizing and working with the resources of all available agencies and institutions, the school has a leadership role in the formation and continuation of a community-wide effort for the prevention and control of norm-violating behavior.

THE CHURCH

Churches of all types are increasingly recognizing their community responsibilities for attempting to improve interpersonal relations. Like the medical doctor, the clergyman is in a favorable position to detect potential problems in the early stages. A recent study found that 42 percent of Americans turn for help for problems to clergymen, 29 percent to physicians in general, 18 percent to psychiatrists or psychologists, and 10 percent to social agencies or marriage clinics.[55] Numerically there are far more clergymen than psychiatrists in the United States. Many theological students are now receiving training in counseling persons with problems of various types. In 1960 there were 343 programs in clinical pastoral training, counseling, or psychology offered by 212 Protestant seminaries; training is also provided in Catholic and Jewish theological schools. It is estimated that between 8000 and 9000 clergymen have taken formal training courses in clinical pastoral training.[56] Some even spend some time studying the problems of patients in mental hospitals and clinics. This study enables them

---

[55] Gurin et al., Americans View Their Mental Health.
[56] R. V. McCann, The Churches and Mental Health (in preparation) as cited in Action for Mental Health, pp. 132–140.

to supplement the work of the limited number of psychiatrists by counseling their parishioners.[57]

It has been suggested that clergymen's efforts in the area of mental health should be chiefly those of prevention. In particular, the clergyman can provide intervention during times of crises, partly by the use of religious rituals and partly by direct support and action. In order to accomplish this the clergyman should be readily accessible to his parishioners. "Finally the effectiveness of clergymen as psychological counselors appears to depend much more on their capacity for understanding human behavior and on the warmth of their personalities than it does on their professional training and orientation. This may also apply to mental health personnel, and with more cogency than many of us in the field are willing to admit." [58]

A similar development has been the increasing activity in pastoral premarital and marital counseling. Traditionally the church has also been the refuge of the aged in their loneliness. For many years there has been a large interdenominational program to deal with discrimination. This has included particularly the work of the National Conference of Christians and Jews. Programs to make the church a center for community activities, particularly youth programs, have also helped to deal with many of the problems created by urbanism. For example, the boxing programs of the Catholic Youth Organization (CYO), founded in Chicago in 1930, have been particularly effective in the zones of transition of larger cities. Some suggest that churches can play a more important role in forestalling juvenile delinquency. This might be accomplished through the church's effort in providing "education for living" and in providing social activities with other young persons or with families.[59]

CLINICAL AND COUNSELING FACILITIES

Many difficulties in interpersonal relations which might eventually lead to more serious problems have been treated in the early stages by outpatient clinics of various types, the chief ones being mental health clinics, child guidance clinics, alcoholic clinics, and marriage and family counseling agencies. Mental health facilities provide outpatient services with a full- or part-time psychiatrist and usually a psychologist and a social worker who help with diagnosis and treatment. In 1956 there were only 1294 such facilities in the entire United States; 750 for children and adults, 400 for children only and 144 for adults only. Of this number one third were in

---

[57] Thomas A. C. Rennie and Luther E. Woodward, *Mental Health and Modern Society* (New York: The Commonwealth Fund, 1948), p. 239.

[58] Joint Commission on Mental Illness and Health, *Action for Mental Health* (New York: Basic Books, Inc., 1961), p. 140. Reprinted by permission.

[59] Robert and Muriel Webb, "How Churches Can Help in the Prevention of Delinquency," *Federal Probation* 21:22–25 (December, 1957).

New York and Massachusetts alone. In the entire country during 1956 there were only 379,000 mental health clinic patients, 182,000 of these being adults. With the present staff in many cases the facilities were often unable to give treatment or to do follow-up work.

Child guidance clinics are of several types.[60] Some are general clinics which take all types of children with behavioral disorders. Some are affiliated with hospitals; others in larger urban areas are often set up in connection with school programs. There are few adequate evaluations of clinics such as these, and their effectiveness in reducing deviant behavior is not definitely known. However, one of the few studies evaluating the effect of such clinics on reducing delinquent behavior concluded that there was no indication of any effect.[61]

Special facilities for the treatment of alcoholics have been established in many cities. Some of the first clinics for alcoholics were established in Connecticut by Yale University in 1944. Although for most of the patients alcoholism has been a long and persistent difficulty, many are helped before it can become even worse. The recommended staff consists of a part-time psychiatrist, two full-time psychiatric social workers, an internist, and a psychologist. Such a clinic can deal with about 350 cases annually at a cost which represents but a fraction of the cost of untreated alcoholism in most communities.[62]

The first marriage clinics were established in Austria in 1922 and about eight years later in this country in New York City, Los Angeles, and Philadelphia. Today there are many such counseling centers which deal with problems of marriage and family relations. In general, their work is diagnosis and treatment, and they use the services of such specialists as psychiatrists, psychologists, sociologists, urologists, and gynecologists. Many other agencies, such as family service, are performing similar work along with their other activities.

COMPREHENSIVE PROGRAMS

Several attempts are now being made to deal with deviant behavior through more comprehensive programs. One of the largest, which began in 1962, involves an expenditure of $12.6 million to deal with juvenile delinquency on the lower East Side of New York City.[63] The project area of 107,000 persons has one of the worst juvenile delinquency records in the city despite recent public and private housing for 60,000 residents. The three-year project, called Mobilization for Youth, involves community de-

---

[60] George E. Gardner, "American Child Psychiatric Clinics," *The Annals*, 286:129–135 (March, 1953).

[61] H. Warren Dunham and LeMay Adamson, "Clinical Treatment of Male Delinquents: A Case Study in Effort and Result," *American Sociological Review*, 21:312–320 (June, 1956).

[62] McCarthy and Douglass, *Alcohol and Social Responsibility*, p. 114.

[63] *The New York Times*, June 1, 1962, pp. 1, 14.

velopment, recreation, school programs, clinical facilities, and the creation of new jobs for youths.

The community development and recreation programs include: neighborhood councils to create and guide the programs; neighborhood service centers, or helping stations, to offer casework facilities for families with special problems; coffee shops, furnished and staffed by young people, to serve refreshments and feature folk music, art, sculpture, and other cultural activities; and an adventure corps, for boys 9 to 15, to provide marching bands, educational programs, athletics, and vocational training.

Another phase of the project will be to meet the problems of "slum children in slum schools" through these programs: home visits by teachers; a planning committee to develop a curriculum for slum schools; reading centers in all elementary schools and reading clinics in two elementary schools; experimental classes for retarded children; and a homework helper program, with 300 good high school students being paid to tutor failing elementary school pupils.

One other phase of the project will seek to create new jobs and find existing work through these special programs:

1. Urban Youth Service Corps, to hire about 1000 unemployed, out-of-school youths and pay them $1 an hour for up to 35 hours a week. They will repair tenements, construct playgrounds, manufacture toys, repair furniture, beautify the neighboring areas, and serve as aides in public and nonprofit private institutions.

2. Youth Jobs Center, a central employment agency for counseling and job placement.

3. Exploratory work course, to be offered in junior high schools to inform students of job possibilities and requirements.

Summary

There are a number of ways to deal with negatively regarded deviations, including acceptance, a condition of equilibrium, and the elimination of the deviation, particularly through social isolation of the deviant. Norm and value conflicts are involved not only in the definition of various forms of deviant behavior but in proposals for their solution. Much can be done through public education to develop consensus on deviations. Agencies to prevent deviant behavior include local community programs or neighborhood councils, street corner projects, the school, the church, and clinical and counseling agencies.

Selected Readings

Action for Mental Health. Joint Commission on Mental Illness and Health. New York: Basic Books, Inc., 1961. Includes a detailed discussion of the role of public education in the prevention of mental disorder. Also a discussion of the part the school, church, and clinical and counseling facilities can play in the prevention of mental disorder.

Annals, The. Usually each year *The Annals* of the American Academy of Political and Social Science devotes one or more issues to some form of deviant behavior, considering it not only from theory but from social action as well.

BARTON, REBECCA CHALMERS. *Our Human Rights.* Washington, D.C.: Public Affairs Press, 1955. A detailed description of how a governor's Commission on Human Rights in a midwestern state operates to reduce discrimination. Contains numerous case materials.

CRAWFORD, PAUL L., DANIEL J. MALAMUD, and JAMES R. DUMPSON. *Working with Teen-Age Gangs.* A Report on the Central Harlem Street Clubs Project. New York: Welfare Council of New York City, 1950. A description of an attempt by the Central Harlem Street Clubs Project to change the behavior of delinquent gangs. Contains case materials.

CUBER, JOHN F., ROBERT A. HARPER, and WILLIAM F. KENKEL. *Problems of American Society: Values in Conflict.* Third Edition. New York: Holt, Rinehart and Winston, Inc., 1956. A discussion of the role of value conflicts in defining certain behavior as deviant. Includes a discussion of the distinction between ameliorative and moral problems.

DEAN, JOHN P., and ALEX ROSEN. *A Manual of Intergroup Relations.* Chicago: The University of Chicago Press, 1955. A manual of principles and techniques for reducing racial and religious discrimination in a community.

DOUGLAS, PAUL H. *Ethics in Government.* Cambridge, Mass.: Harvard University Press, 1952. A series of lectures given at Harvard University by the chairman of the Senate Commission on Ethics in Government. Contains proposals for the improvement of government ethics.

KOBRIN, SOLOMON. "The Chicago Area Project—A 25-Year Assessment," *The Annals,* 322:19–29 (March, 1959). An evaluation of the work of Chicago Area Projects in preventing juvenile delinquency.

Law and Contemporary Problems. "Narcotics," Vol. 22, No. 1 (Winter, 1957). Contains articles dealing with public attitudes and different methods of dealing with drug addiction.

MC CARTHY, RAYMOND G., ed. *Drinking and Intoxication.* New York: The Free Press of Glencoe, 1959. Discusses public attitudes toward problems arising from the use of alcohol, programs of alcohol education, and alcoholic clinics.

RECKLESS, WALTER C. *The Crime Problem.* Third ed. New York: Appleton-Century-Crofts, Inc., 1961. Chapter 21 is a discussion of delinquency prevention measures, including psychiatric clinics, the Chicago Area Project, the New York City Youth Board, and detached workers for street-corner groups.

SUTHERLAND, EDWIN H., and DONALD R. CRESSEY. *Principles of Criminology.* Sixth ed. Philadelphia: J. B. Lippincott Company, 1960. Chapter 29 is a discussion of the prevention of crime and delinquency, including the use of local community organizations, organized recreation, case work with near delinquents, group work with near delinquents, coordinating councils, and institutional reorganization.

The Reduction of Deviant
Behavior: The Use of Institutions

Many people think that, in order to deal more effectively with certain deviant behavior, it is necessary to build more and better institutions to which delinquents, criminals, mentally ill persons, and alcoholics can be sent to be "cured." Actually, institutional treatment has limited possibilities. In the first place, the sheer size of the deviant population is so great that the cost of institutionalizing more than a fragment of all deviants would be prohibitive. For example, the prisoner population of state and federal institutions, on December 31, 1959, was 213,709 (206,013 males and 7696 females), with about 97,000 new admissions each year. Yet in most cases the facilities in prisons were overcrowded.[1] This prison investment, antiquated as it often is, represents a capital outlay of hundreds of millions of dollars and a large annual operating cost. Second, it is difficult to change the attitudes of a human being in a setting as artificial as those an institution provides. Moreover, the mere fact that a person has received institutional treatment, in a prison or a mental hospital, for example, may be sufficient to stigmatize him for life and make ultimate rehabilitation even more difficult.

Prisons

Although many people think that prisons are the only way to treat law violators, prisons as they are known today are a relatively recent invention, being hardly more than a century and a half old. Serious offenders— thieves, burglars, and robbers—except for those sent to the galleys, were formerly not imprisoned. Either they were executed or they were punished by being subjected to physical torture, branded, maimed, sent to the pillory, or transported to a penal colony, usually in another hemisphere. Penal servitude in the galleys was used from about 1500 until early in the eighteenth century.

---

[1] U.S. Department of Justice, *National Prisoner Statistics* (No. 25; Washington: February, 1961).

Many factors affected the development of prisons—imprisonment in castle dungeons, the use of cell confinement by the church, houses of correction, and, most significant of all, the attitudes of the Quakers toward capital punishment. A few persons were held for periods of time in castles or fortress structures, but they were chiefly noblemen or persons awaiting trial or punishment. The Catholic Church, whose clergy could not be punished by the state by the use of the death penalty for criminal offenses, used confinement in cells. It also maintained institutions in which the sick, aged, and the mentally ill, as well as delinquents and criminals, sought refuge. Houses of correction, which came into use in several European cities during the sixteenth century, were used for petty offenders, including vagabonds, family deserters, prostitutes, and some juveniles.

In America toward the end of the eighteenth century the Quakers of Pennsylvania became appalled at the brutal methods being used on ordinary criminals, particularly the use of capital punishment for hundreds of crimes. The Pennsylvania legislature reduced the number of capital offenses to four, substituting fines, hard labor, and a relatively new idea for serious offenses—imprisonment—for all other offenses. The Walnut Street Prison in Philadelphia, built in 1790, was used for these offenders, who served their sentences in solitary confinement. This concept of using imprisonment as a punishment for crime spread throughout the world, and although there have been many modifications of the original idea, a sentence to prison is still one of the chief means of dealing with criminal offenders.

Today prisons are widely used in every country in the world. In 1959 there were approximately 230 state and federal prisons, for adult offenders, in the United States.[2] This number of prisons and reformatories does not include other places of incarceration, such as prison camps, workhouses, or farms, nor does it include the number of prisons in Alaska and Hawaii. There are also approximately 1500 municipal jails, workhouses, and farms for offenders convicted of misdemeanors and 2500 county jails, workhouses, farms, and camps for misdemeanants. There are also 177 juvenile correctional institutions, of which 117 are state, 30 county or municipal, 4 federal, and 25 private.

OBJECTIVES OF IMPRISONMENT

Originally the Quakers believed that meditation in prison would bring about reformation, but today public attitudes are extremely con-fused about the purpose of incarceration. Prisons seem to exist for such widely divergent purposes as retribution, deterrence, incapacitation, and rehabilitation. Some people regard the function of prisons as one of exacting retribution, *lex talionis,* "An eye for an eye and a tooth for a tooth."

---

[2] Of the approximately 214,000 prisoners confined in state and federal prisons and reformatories, about 25,000 are federal prisoners, under the Federal Bureau of Prisons.

This principle, based on the concept that an individual is completely responsible for his actions, presumes that the punishment of an offender is in proportion to the injury to society that he has committed. Those who hold such an attitude regard prisons as places in which society may exact vengeance upon the wrongdoer.

Many persons regard prisons as places whose very existence deters others from committing crimes. They assume that the knowledge that some are imprisoned for their crimes deters other citizens from committing crimes. Tappan has raised a number of objections to any belief that the mere threat of punishment has a uniform effect on individuals: (1) The restraining influences on crime are not as rational as punishment would suggest. (2) Deterrence from crime is not merely the result of punishment but also of many other factors, such as prestige in the community, moral training, attitudes toward authority, and the like. (3) The threat of punishment is probably greatest before a person is first convicted or incarcerated and declines thereafter. This is because the stigmata and ostracism associated with conviction and incarceration destroy the basis of this threat—a person's status as a "respectable citizen" or his self esteem. (4) The certainty and speed of punishment seem to have a more deterrent effect than merely the fact that punishment exists. (5) Finally, in many offenses of a circumstantial type the threat of punishment has slight deterrent effects.[3]

Still other persons look upon prisons as methods of getting offenders out of the way. Being imprisoned, they are unable to inflict further injury on society. This belief has two main flaws. Most of the people sentenced to prison not only are not dangerous but in all probability need more community participation rather than social isolation. A small proportion of men generally in prison, perhaps as little as 5 and not over 25 percent, are serious offenders. In the second place, nearly all prison inmates today are now released within from five to ten years, and it is highly unlikely that society would tolerate any incarceration for the actual life of many offenders, particularly since so many are committed when they are relatively young men. Thus prisons can only temporarily incapacitate persons from continuing their criminal activities.

For those who believe that the purpose of prisons is to rehabilitate, and these include practically all persons scientifically trained in correctional work, the idea of punishment is felt to be inconsistent. These people believe that prisons should be places where—after the social and psychological characteristics of prisoners have been studied by specialists, such as psychi-

---

[3] Paul W. Tappan, "Objectives and Methods in Correction," in Paul W. Tappan ed., *Contemporary Correction* (New York: McGraw-Hill Book Company, Inc., 1951), pp. 8–9. For further discussion of this problem, see Donald R. Cressey, "Limitations on Organization of Treatment in the Modern Prison," in *Theoretical Studies in Social Organization of the Prison* (New York: Social Science Research Council, March, 1960), pp. 78–110.

atrists and psychologists, sociologists, and others—offenders are classified into various types and a program is devised for their institutional treatment. Confusion in the minds of the public, the nature of prisons as they exist after a century or more of punitive methods, and, in fact, the whole idea of incarcerating men like animals, however, have all worked against much success in this direction. Here and there can be found examples of an effective use of prisons as instruments of rehabilitation. Even in those rare places where theory is applied to practice, however, there are often so many negative factors present, including the artificial nature of prison life and the stigma of society, that much progress in reformation would appear difficult. Probably prisons should serve primarily to prevent repetition of crime, by attempting to change prisoners' attitudes toward crime and their self-conceptions. The programs of such institutions should be directed toward changing offenders from law-violating to law-abiding persons, rather than providing custodial care as the majority of prisons presently still do.

Most prisons today do not appear to rehabilitate a very large proportion of their prisoners, although they may perform some other functions more effectively. Between 40 and 70 percent of most prison inmates have been previously incarcerated in some correctional institution, the national average being about one in two men. Leading prison officials are almost unanimously skeptical about the failure of the contemporary prison to rehabilitate, as are scientific observers and ex-inmates. There is abundant evidence that prisons are, in fact, excellent places for tutoring in crime.

CHARACTERISTICS OF PRISON LIFE

Prisons provide little or no freedom comparable to that of the civilian life to which nearly all the inmates return. A prisoner cannot generally go where he wants to go, eat what and when he pleases, tune in on as many radio or television programs as he desires, or even take a bath at any time, let alone when he needs one. Although there is some choice of work, it is limited, and where a man is fortunate to have full-time employment his pay is rarely more than from ten to fifty cents a day. Few opportunities are given him to make decisions, and permission to go anywhere is granted on much the same terms that it is granted a closely supervised child. In most prisons, inmates are marched everywhere, at night they are confined in cells hardly as large as lions' cages in the zoo, and at all times men on gun towers have lethal weapons ready to shoot. The attitude of some guards is impersonal, for they often operate almost mechanically in terms of the rule books and are interested in their work only for the security the jobs bring. Where the custodial officers are ignorant, untrained political appointees, their relationships with the inmates are likely to be even worse. Life for the inmates becomes dull, monotonous, and often a bitter, repetitious experience.

What particularly lengthens the social distance between prison officials and the inmates and negates rehabilitation are the endless prison rules which have been built up in the history of prisons. Once a rule has been put into effect, it is changed only with difficulty. Some of the rules result from the incarceration of thousands of men under maximum security in our larger prisons. The numerous rules of most prisons completely circumscribe the inmate's behavior, prescribing such things as the care of cells, personal hygiene, eating, going to chapel, respect for officers, and obedience. Many of these rules interfere with essentially human behavior and cause particular resentment among young men—rules about not talking in the dining room, from cell to cell, and in the corridors, or those regulating what is called "boisterous conduct." Most rules are so petty that they could not be generally enforced in a free society, in an industrial plant, or even in a military establishment. A few are necessary for the maintenance of order in any institution, but most prison rules are for the sake of rigid discipline or a display of authority, or are due to some situation the need for which may have disappeared a long time ago. Guards may display unwarranted authority over inmates because of the vague nature of many rules and the wide latitude with which they may be interpreted.[4]

In modern institutions infractions of rules largely result in the withdrawal of certain privileges, in counseling, and in rare cases, in the use of solitary confinement. Some institutions, however, use more severe methods to secure compliance.

The artificiality and social isolation of prison life and the multiplicity of rules are great hindrances to any program which attempts to deal with criminal attitudes. As long as prisons in general do not allow more social relations with the outside world it is unlikely that institutional treatment can achieve much in the way of attitude changes or satisfactory emotional adjustment. To change attitudes there must be opportunities to assimilate conventional cultural attitudes. Prison confinement allows only rare outside social contacts; visits from the outside are infrequent and rigidly supervised, the general practice being only once a month; letters are limited in number and censored; and often choices of reading materials, radio programs, and movies are restricted. The one-sex nature of prison communities results in great mental suffering and excessive discussion of sex, and the impossibility of heterosexual intercourse encourages homosexual practices among some inmates. The difficulties connected with the sex problem in prison communities make it one of the most serious and demoralizing features of prison life.

---

[4] See Vernon Fox, *Violence behind Bars* (New York: Vantage Press, 1956); and John Bartlow Martin, *Break Down the Walls* (New York: Ballantine Books, Inc., 1954).

The institutional system is not the only reason why it is difficult to rehabilitate inmates through imprisonment. Even if prisons were more successful, it would still be necessary to contend with the public's "convict bogey."[5] The public holds against a man not so much the crime for which he was convicted as the fact that he has been in prison. Perhaps if prisons were not the places they are, the public's reaction to imprisonment would not be as negative as it is. It is the prison experience which sets men apart and changes them, in the eyes of the public, into "dangerous convicts." Society vents its indignation against crime not on criminals but on "convicts." Once a man has been in prison the public attitude today is to stigmatize him in much the same way as a person who had been in a tuberculosis sanitorium was often formerly stigmatized. Ex-inmates frequently find it so difficult, after having left prison, to help their families face the stigma of the neighborhood, to get and hold a job, to participate in community activities, and even to have the right to vote again, that even those who at one time had intended to go "straight" return again to criminal activities, thanks to their post-prison experiences.[6]

THE PRISON SOCIAL SYSTEM

The prison community and the prison code also work against reformation. Every prison has its subculture and a complex social system of officers and inmates; within the latter group is a social structure in which some inmates have higher status than others.[7] For example, some have found that prisoners and staff members differ markedly in whom they consider to be a "leader."[8] This inmate subculture exists alongside the formal prison system. The informal rules which reflect this subculture generally exert a greater effect on the prisoner's actual behavior than does the system of formally prescribed rules. "The value system of the prisoners commonly takes the form of an explicit code, in which normative imperatives are held forth as guides for the behavior of the inmate in his relations with fellow

[5] Harry Elmer Barnes and Negley K. Teeters, New Horizons in Criminology (Englewood Cliffs, N.J.: Prentice-Hall, Inc., 1951), pp. 420–422.

[6] For further discussion, see Donald R. Cressey ed., The Prison: Studies in Institutional Organization and Change (New York: Holt, Rinehart and Winston, 1961), Chaps. 1–3.

[7] Donald Clemmer, The Prison Community (rev. ed.; New York: Holt, Rinehart and Winston, Inc., 1958), and S. Kirson Weinberg, "Aspects of the Prison Social Structure," American Journal of Sociology, 47:717–726 (March, 1942). For a general article and bibliography, see Morris G. Caldwell, "Group Dynamics in the Prison Community," Journal of Criminal Law, Criminology and Police Science, 46:648–657 (January-February, 1956). Also see Edwin H. Sutherland and Donald R. Cressey, Principles of Criminology (6th ed.; Philadelphia: J. B. Lippincott Company, 1960).

[8] Clemmer, op. cit., pp. 134–137, and Clarence Shrag, "Leadership among Prison Inmates," American Sociological Review, 19:37–42 (February, 1954). Also see Erving Goffman, "On the Characteristics of Total Institutions: The Inmate World," in Cressey, The Prison, pp. 15–67.

prisoners and custodians." [9] Violation of these norms, or informal rules, by any inmate evokes sanctions ranging from ostracism to physical violence. Some of these informal inmate rules are described in the following general maxims:

a. Don't interfere with the interests of inmates. Concretely, this means that inmates "never rat on a con," or betray each other. It also includes these directives: "Don't be nosey," "Don't put a guy on the spot," and "Keep off a man's back." There are no justifications for failing to comply with these rules.
b. Keep out of quarrels or feuds with fellow inmates. This is expressed in the directives, "Play it cool," and "Do your own time."
c. Don't exploit other inmates. Concretely, this means, "Don't break your word," "Don't steal from the cons," "Don't welsh on debts," and *"Be right."*
d. Don't weaken; withstand frustration or threat without complaint. This is expressed in such directives as, "Don't cop out" (cry guilty), "Don't suck around," *"Be tough,"* and *"Be a man."*
e. Don't give respect or prestige to the custodians or to the world for which they stand. Concretely, this is expressed by "Don't be a sucker," and "Be sharp." [10]

In addition to these informal rules of behavior, inmates share a prison argot which expresses their code or value systems. By means of this argot, they communicate to one another stereotypes of prison officials and of the prison world. Guards are known as "hacks" or "screws," and are to be treated with distrust and suspicion. Inmates who conform to the values of the prison officials (by accepting the ideal of hard work and of submission to authority) are labeled "suckers." In addition, there is great preoccupation with "rats" who "squeal" on another inmate to gain favors. The "yard" serves as a place to talk about prison life, about crime, and about the vagaries of society. The inmate who tries to be part of the inmate subculture and at the same time tries to benefit from the professional and administrative staff generally finds himself playing contradictory social roles.[11] The control of the inmate subculture, as one writer has described, is in the hands of "politicians" and "right guys."

> The prison population is largely in the control of a small group of men which has two divisions. There are the "politicians," "shots," or whatever they

[9] Gresham M. Sykes and Sheldon L. Messinger, "The Inmate Social System," in *Theoretical Studies in Social Organization of the Prison* (New York; Social Science Research Council, 1960), p. 5.
[10] Sykes and Messinger, *loc. cit.*, pp. 6–8. See also Gresham M. Sykes, *The Society of Captives: A Study of a Maximum Security Prison* (Princeton, N.J.: Princeton University Press, 1958); and for a more recent treatment of this same problem, see Goffman, "On the Characteristics of Total Institutions: The Inmate World," *loc. cit.*
[11] Lloyd E. Ohlin, *Sociology and the Field of Corrections* (New York: Russell Sage Foundation, 1956), pp. 34–37.

may be called in varying institutions, who hold key positions in the administrative offices of the prisons. They wield a power to distribute special privileges, to make possible the circulation of special foods or other supplies. They in frequent instances become "racketeers" and use their positions to force money and services from less powerful inmates. These men are seldom trusted by the top level of the prison hierarchy, are frequently hated by the general population because of the exclusiveness and self-seeking behavior characteristic of them. Yet the fact remains that in their position they are able to demand adherence to the behavior code of the community.

The other section of this controlling power is held by the so-called "right guys." These men are so known because of the consistency of their behavior in accordance with the criminal or prison code. They are men who can always be trusted, who do not abuse lesser inmates, who are invariably loyal to their class—the convicts. They are not wanton trouble-makers but they are expected to stand up for their rights as convicts, to get what they can from the prison officials, to never permit an opportunity to pass from which they might secure anything from a better job to freedom. . . . These men, because of their outright and loyal behavior, are the real leaders of the prison and impose stringent controls upon the definitions of proper behavior from other convicts.[12]

In recent years, studies of prison social structure have initiated interest in the possibility of harnessing informal inmate groups in modifying prison culture. As yet, there is insufficient knowledge of the kinds of social interactions occurring among prisoners, or of the specific mechanisms by which prison life alters inmate attitudes and loyalties.[13] In order to reintegrate offenders effectively the informal system of relationships and controls needs to be utilized and directed toward conformity with conventional norms.

Some rudimentary beginnings toward modifying prison culture have been made in creating "honor systems," a kind of prison self-government in which prisoners are given responsibility and allowed to make choices. Honor systems have been used in prison camps for smaller groups of prisoners, and are presently used in the California Institution for Men, a minimum security, honor type of institution.[14] Evidence suggests that prisoners released from such institutions have lower recidivism and parole violation rates; yet this may be due in part to the careful selection of prisoners for such institutions.[15]

Programs which effectively utilize all aspects of the inmate social sys-

[12] Hans Reimer, "Socialization in the Prison Community," *Proceedings,* American Prison Association, 1937 (New York: The Association, 1937), pp. 152–153. In order to make this study, Reimer, a sociologist, arranged to have himself voluntarily committed to prison.

[13] Sutherland and Cressey, *op. cit.,* p. 497. See also Clemmer, *op. cit.*

[14] Walter C. Reckless, *The Crime Problem* (3d ed.; New York: Appleton-Century-Crofts, Inc., 1961), pp. 524–528; Sutherland and Cressey, *op. cit.,* p. 492. Also see Kenyon Scudder, *Prisoners Are People* (New York: Doubleday & Company, Inc., 1952).

[15] Sutherland and Cressey, *op. cit.*

tem have not yet been devised, and promising programs which have been suggested have not been adequately applied. Some suggest that penal institutions, by their disciplinarian character, obviate the success of any such programs. Others suggest that though there are many obstacles to such programs, they are nevertheless possible, provided bold and imaginative steps are taken toward restructuring the formal system in such a way as to utilize the informal system. Cressey's "group relations approach," using programs involving groups, suggests a possible way of accomplishing this.[16]

THE FUTURE OF PRISONS

The predominance of certain bad features in prisons today raises questions about their future. Unfortunately, it appears that, because of society's attitude toward the offender, prisons will continue to exist for a long time. Meanwhile the main effort needs to be concentrated on keeping people out of prison by preventing delinquency and crime and by the wide use of adequately supervised probation. It is generally agreed that, from the standpoint of crime prevention, it is much wiser to concentrate on the widespread and effective use of probation than to attempt to change an offender's attitudes within the artificial confines of a jail or prison. Probation is a suspension of sentence after conviction in which the offender is allowed, with some restrictions, to remain in free society rather than being imprisoned. Probation, of course, should be well supervised and administered by a trained staff. If this situation exists it would be wise even to place an offender several times on probation rather than incarcerate him in a jail or prison. Not only is well-supervised probation likely to be more effective than prison treatment in preventing further crime; it is far less expensive even if carried out by well-paid professional persons. It is estimated that one probation officer carrying a recommended case load of fifty cases can adequately supervise this number at about the cost of maintaining three or four men in a prison for a single year.

Prisons generally would be more effective, however, under these conditions: [17]

---

[16] For discussions of prison social structure and group-centered programs, see Sykes, *The Society of Captives: A Study of a Maximum Security Prison;* Johan Galtung, "The Social Functions of a Prison," *Social Problems,* 6:127–140 (Fall, 1958); Lloyd E. Ohlin and William Lawrence, "Role of Inmate Systems in Institutional Treatment Procedures," *Proceedings,* National Association of Training Schools and Juvenile Agencies (1958), pp. 115–136; and Oscar Grusky, "Organizational Goals and the Behavior of Informal Leaders," *American Journal of Sociology,* 65:59–67 (July, 1959).

[17] See, for example, Marshall B. Clinard, "Prevention of Crime," *Journal of Correctional Work* (India), 7:1–12 (1960). Also see Marshall B. Clinard, "Prison Systems," *Encyclopedia of Criminology* (New York: Philosophical Library, Inc., 1949), pp. 384–385. See also Sutherland and Cressey, *op. cit.,* Reckless, *op. cit.,* and Richard R. Korn and Lloyd W. McCorkle, *Criminology and Penology* (New York: Holt, Rinehart and Winston, Inc., 1959).

1. An institutional setup is directed at a program of changing norms so as to make the offender into a law-abiding person. Wider use of group therapy should be promoted with a small group of offenders of similar type, discussing such topics as the nature of criminal behavior and how it might be changed, a technique which will be discussed in the next chapter. In a limited number of cases there should be individual therapy in the form of case work.

2. Institutions should be so diversified that the treatment program of a correctional institution can concentrate largely on offenders of a similar general type. Within each type, institutional treatment programs should be worked out for specific types of offenders. There should be institutions for the ordinary type of offender, for the more hardened and sophisticated type, for those with markedly inferior intelligence, and for others.

3. Correctional institutions should be of such size that an intensive treatment program can be worked out and the impact of the staff can be personal. The smaller the institution the fewer rules are necessary and the less rigorous the discipline. Generally a correctional institution should not be larger than 100 inmates although, if that is financially too difficult, the prison population might be as large as 500.

4. If correctional institutions are to be effective in changing a prisoner's attitudes, they should be relaxed and as much like normal living as possible. Less emphasis should be placed on discipline, rules, military programs, and an artificial institutional setting. Often the conceptions of themselves of persons subjected to this become even more criminal.

5. One new type of approach which has great promise is a combination of an institutional program with participation in free society. Nearly all offenders sooner or later return to free society, most of them, in fact, after less than five years. In prisons and jails criminals should associate with noncriminals. Relations with their families must also continue to be as normal as possible if they are not to become even more isolated and bitter against society. These objectives might be secured in several ways: (1) A program of home furloughs might be instituted. (2) Another way to encourage the outside contacts of the offender is to confine him to the institution during the evenings and week ends but allow him to work in free society during the day. This would mean that the noncriminals with whom he works would have a greater effect in changing his attitudes and criminal self-conception than his former criminal associates. This type of program is being tried in a number of countries. (3) Some kind of work camps might be set up for young persons, primarily nonoffenders, but judges could allow offenders to join them in place of institutional treatment. This procedure was used during the 1930's in the United States by the Civilian Conservation Corps camps, which carried out work in forests and on road construction programs.

6. In any institutional setup the staff should be stressed. The members

should be selected primarily in terms of how effective they can be in changing the attitudes of offenders. Of all the persons in authority in a correctional institution, probably the guard plays the most strategic role in that he is more frequently in contact with the offender. The guard is too frequently thought of as a custodial officer rather than as potentially a highly effective member of the treatment staff. Since his social background is generally much like that of most offenders he has an advantage in communicating with them that a more highly educated officer does not have. In any event, all the staff members of the correctional institution should have had training in criminology and in their role of changing the attitudes of prisoners. Those, of course, in higher administrative and welfare posts should have had college training that included advanced courses in the behavioral sciences.

7. Finally, there should be an effective selection of persons for parole and effective parole treatment.

California has developed a number of modern correctional programs in its Youth and Adult Authority, its forestry camps, and particularly its program at the California Institution for Men at Chino.[18] Here about 1500 men, of all ages and convicted of almost all types of offenses, have been in a rather unique program since 1941. The inmates of this farm-ranch of several thousand acres are carefully selected minimum security risks with good potential rehabilitative qualities. The institution has a trained staff and offers extensive educational and vocational programs. The inmates are housed in open dormitories having no walls or guns, they wear no uniforms, they do not march to the dining room, and they are allowed to take more leisurely meals than are permitted in most correctional institutions. Informal receptions for groups of inmates are often held at the superintendent's home, and an inmate council participates in the administration of the institution. Mail is not censored, except on an occasional sample basis. A most significant rehabilitative feature is the three-hour family picnic allowed each Saturday, Sunday, and holiday in a designated area.

After discovering that traditional methods did not work, Sweden in 1945 adopted a new comprehensive program including small correctional institutions of usually not more than a hundred inmates in order to promote a high degree of group interaction with the staff, something that is virtually impossible in larger prisons.[19] Most institutions are open, with

[18] Scudder, op. cit.
[19] Almost all these features have been included in the Swedish Prison Act of 1945. See Thorsten Sellin, Recent Penal Legislation in Sweden (Stockholm: Isaac Marcus Book Publishers, 1947). Thorsten Sellin, "The Treatment of Offenders in Sweden," Federal Probation, 12:14–18 (June, 1948). Also see Wilfred Fleisher, Sweden: The Welfare State (New York: The John Day Company, Inc., 1956), Chap. 11; Ola Nyquist, "How Sweden Handles Its Juvenile and Youth Offenders," Federal Probation, 20:36–42 (March, 1956); Torsten Eriksson, "Postwar Prison Reform in Sweden," The Annals, 293:152–162 (May, 1954); and Gösta Rylander, "Treatment of Mentally Abnormal Offenders in Sweden," British

no walls, armed guards, or gun towers. In addition, the Swedes allow most offenders short furloughs home every four months, in addition to special emergency furloughs and frequent visits and contacts with the outside world in order to change attitudes and reduce sexual tensions.[20]

Since men in prison spend a great deal of time in their cells or rooms, Swedish inmates are allowed to furnish their rooms in a homelike way, with rugs, drapes, pictures, bedspreads, individual radios, as well as many flowers, plants, paintings, books, electric hot plates, and cups and saucers for coffee. Swedish inmates work in diversified and skilled employment and are paid a fairly adequate wage, amounting to between 80 cents and $2.50 a day. All members of the staffs of correctional institutions are highly trained.

Mental Hospitals

Mental hospitals appear to have two functions: the treatment of patients so that they will recover sufficiently to return to normal society and the provision of custody and care so that both patients and society are protected. Too often the function of custody appears to take precedence over treatment in public mental hospitals.

The custodial aspect of mental institutions primarily serves to protect the patient from those of the outside world who might not understand him and his problems and also to protect him from harming others or himself. Most patients have not constituted a public menace. More often they are merely persons who have bizarre ideas, depressions, or suspicions of others. Few patients will actually harm others, in spite of the societal stereotype that mental patients are dangerous and to be feared. Some patients who have become accustomed to institutional life feel happier in custody than in free society because decisions are made for them, and life is routine. Where their care is good, they are often better fed and are cleaner and neater in dress and manners than they would be outside, and they usually do get some recreation and entertainment in institutions. In fact, it is these very features of custody which some people consider sufficient. Moreover, some patients become so accustomed to the hospital routine that it is difficult to prepare them for the changes in their interpersonal relationships which are necessary for a return to normal society.

EXTENT AND COST OF MENTAL HOSPITAL CARE

Today almost 88 percent of all patients are in state and local mental hospitals. Nearly 10 percent are in veterans' hospitals, and slightly over

---

Journal of Delinquency, 4:262–268 (April, 1955). During 1954 the author studied delinquency and crime and their treatment in Sweden.

[20] In Wisconsin, many jail prisoners, under the Huber Law, are allowed to work in private employment during the day.

2 percent are in private hospitals. Whereas admissions to state and local mental hospitals have increased during the past few years, releases have also increased, reflecting a shortened length of stay for many patients. From 1955 to 1960 there was a consistent decline in the resident population of these hospitals. (See Table 21.1.) In 1960 there were 235,231 admissions

Table 21.1. Resident Patients by Type of Hospital, 1955–1959

Year	All hospitals	State, county, and city hospitals	Veterans' hospitals	Public Health Service hospitals	Private hospitals
1955	632,551	557,969	57,991	2,001	14,590
1956	626,567	550,456	60,080	1,935	14,096
1957	620,544	545,796	59,240	1,965	13,543
1958	620,289	544,008	59,855	1,955	14,471
1959	616,964	540,662	60,779	1,827	13,696

SOURCE: Department of Health, Education, and Welfare, *Trends* (Washington, D.C.: Government Printing Office, 1961), p. 27. These are hospitals for long-term psychiatric care.

to state and local hospitals, 192,351 releases, and 49,846 deaths.[21] One study has concluded that this decline is not reflected in other types of hospitals, that it only represents a "shift in the flow and whereabouts of mental patients, possibly reflecting in part the readily accepted conviction that, if at all possible, it is better for the patient and his prospects to keep him out of State hospitals" and also represents a policy of increased discharge rates, which is in part a reflection of savings in maintenance costs.[22] Much of the increase in discharge rates has been possible through the use of tranquilizers.

The cost of caring for the mentally ill is enormous. During 1950 state governments spent, in tax funds, about $520 million on capital costs and maintenance of their state mental hospitals and about $45 million for other mental health services. Yet the amount spent for patients in state mental hospitals is meager when compared with the amount spent for care in general or private hospitals. In 1961 the Joint Commission on Mental Illness and Health reported that the average amount spent for patients in state hospitals is $4.44 daily, whereas the average daily amount for patients in community general hospitals, largely private, is $31.16, and for those in veterans' psychiatric or tuberculosis hospitals, $12.00.[23]

[21] Department of Health, Education, and Welfare, *Trends* (Washington, D.C.: Government Printing Office, 1961), p. 27.

[22] *Action for Mental Health,* The Final Report of the Joint Commission on Mental Illness and Health (New York: Basic Books, Inc., 1961), p. 20. This commission was appointed by Congress to make a five-year study.

[23] *Ibid.,* Chapter 1.

The Joint Commission reported in 1961 that overcrowding characterizes state hospitals in the United States today. Most state hospitals have from 2000 to 4000 patients.[24] They also found that the ratio of personnel to patients in state mental hospitals today is 0.32, as compared to a ratio of 2.1 for community general hospitals. In general, there is a shortage of psychiatrists in public mental hospitals. Although in 1956 there were 8713 psychiatrists in the United States, only about 1400 were employed full time in public mental hospitals.[25]

METHODS OF HOSPITAL TREATMENT

Because of their large size, it is extremely difficult for state hospitals to give effective treatment to their patients. Thus, the majority of patients receive either no treatment, or receive somatic treatments, usually in the form of drugs or electric shock. These latter treatments can be administered to large numbers of patients in a minimum of time and with little effort on the part of the staff.[26] These treatments help to reduce anxiety and the symptoms of the illness, but rarely deal with the "causes." Group psychotherapy, psychodrama, individual counseling, and occupational therapy, on the other hand, require a much greater effort on the part of the staff. The 1961 report of the Joint Commission on Mental Illness and Health concluded that 80 percent of the 277 state hospitals in the United States today are seriously lagging in the use of modern advances in the treatment of the mentally ill, and were providing custodial care rather than treatment. In only 20 percent of these hospitals was there evidence of some effort to take advantage of these new techniques. The commission found that more than half of all patients in state mental hospitals receive "no active treatment of any kind designed to improve their mental conditions." [27]

The use of the shock therapies, electric and insulin, has been largely a development of the past fifteen to twenty years. Electric shock therapy, which produces temporary convulsions or coma, can be administered to many patients in a relatively short period of time. Although various

---

[24] The Commission strongly recommended that present state hospitals of 1000 patients or more "add not one" additional patient, and that no additional hospitals of more than 1000 beds be built. The Commission further recommended a major reorganization of the existing method of treating the mentally ill, rather than simply increasing the size and population of hospitals, as has been customary in the past.

[25] *Action for Mental Health*, pp. 8–9, 144. In 1960 the American Psychiatric Association had 11,787 members, which, although insufficient for the demand, were nearly three times the 4000 members in 1946.

[26] M. Greenblatt, D. J. Levinson, R. H. Williams, *The Patient and the Mental Hospital* (New York: The Free Press of Glencoe, 1957). Also see Alfred H. Stanton and Morris S. Schwartz, *The Mental Hospital* (New York: Basic Books, Inc., 1954), p. 69, and S. Kirson Weinberg and H. Warren Dunham, *The Culture of the State Mental Hospital* (Detroit: Wayne State University Press, 1960).

[27] *Action for Mental Health*, p. 23.

theories, biological and psychological, have attempted to explain what happens in the shock therapies, so far none has been generally accepted. It has been difficult to come to a general theory in view of the fact that the results of this type of therapy vary greatly. The original claims of high success have been revised in more limited terms. Some patients do recover after a series of shock treatments and others are greatly improved. Most recoveries, however, are only temporary, and the relapse rate is high.

In general, relapse is greater where there is little follow-up treatment with individual psychotherapy. In one study of 380 patients who were given electric shock over a six-month period, 64.8 percent improved or recovered and 35.2 were unimproved.[28] Other studies which have used well-matched experimental and control groups and have employed rigorous research designs have found a much smaller percentage of improvement.[29] Studies of treatment methods in hospitals have found that the choice of treatments for given patients by the physician in charge is not related to the patient's diagnosis so much as it is to his social characteristics, principally his social class. It was found that upper-class patients were much more likely to receive psychotherapy, whereas somatic or physical treatments were used primarily with the lower-class patients.[30] One sociological study has suggested that the extent of prior social participation is favorably associated with this treatment.[31]

Beginning in 1953, tranquilizing drugs, including chlorpromazine and reserpine, have been widely used to relieve some of the symptoms of mental illness. In 1961 it was estimated that as many as one third of all public mental hospital patients received these drugs. One report, in fact, refers to the present situation in treatment as "the tranquilized hospital." [32] Being used to tranquilize those patients who are excited, hyperactive, unmanageable, highly disturbed or highly disturbing, these drugs have changed somewhat the management of psychotic patients in mental hospitals. They have helped to reduce shock treatments and have given more freedom to the patients. In addition, they have made possible greater communication and, consequently, closer relations between staff and patients.

The debate still continues, however, regarding the physiological and

---

[28] S. Kirson Weinberg, *Society and Personality Disorders* (Englewood Cliffs, N.J.: Prentice-Hall, Inc., 1952), p. 435.

[29] See George H. Alexander, "Electroconvulsive Therapy: A Five-Year Study of Results," *Journal of Nervous and Mental Diseases,* 117:244–250 (March, 1953) and Ugo Cerletti, "Electroshock Therapy," *Journal of Clinical and Experimental Psychopathology,* 15:191–217 (July–September, 1954).

[30] See Eugene B. Gallagher, Daniel Levinson, Iza Erlich, "Some Sociopsychological Characteristics of Patients and Their Relevance for Psychiatric Treatment," in Greenblatt *et al., op. cit.,* pp. 371–373.

[31] Malak Guirguis, "Interpersonal Relationships as a Prognostic Factor in Electric Shock Therapy of the 'Functional Psychoses.'" Unpublished doctoral dissertation, University of Wisconsin, Madison, Wisconsin, 1951.

[32] *Action for Mental Health.*

sociological results of these drugs. Some have predicted they would empty mental hospitals, while others have called them "clinical strait jackets." [33] A four-year study in New York State of the use of tranquilizers in state public hospitals between 1955 and 1959 gives some partial, but by no means complete, answers.[34] It was concluded that restraint and seclusion of patients decreased markedly, and that, by 1959, 60 percent of all cases were given freedom of the grounds, or ten times the number who had this freedom in 1956. Whereas first admissions had in previous years exceeded discharges, there was a reversal in 1959. About half of the patients continued on drug therapy after leaving the hospital. The relapse, or rate of return to the hospital, was 35 percent, which was no higher than that of predrug days. The greatest gain in the release of patients was in the age group twenty-five through forty-four; there was little change in the rate of release of those over sixty-five. The drugs had little effect on the senile psychoses, which is the primary cause for admission to mental hospitals. Schizophrenic patients showed far greater benefit than did patients with other types of psychoses or organic brain disease, and these drugs may help to reduce chronic schizophrenic cases.

THE SOCIAL STRUCTURE OF THE MENTAL HOSPITAL

The social structure of mental hospitals may work for or against success in treatment, for a mental hospital is a unique community with its own special social structure in terms of status and power to make decisions. (See Figure 7.) It is organized with the superintendent and professional staff, including psychiatrists, psychologists, occupational therapists, social workers, and similar personnel at the top of the prestige hierarchy. Next come the clerical staff and, following it in social status, the attendants and utility workers. The patients make up the "lowest" group. One of the major difficulties of this social system of status and power relationships is that in the treatment of the mental patient there is often a breakdown in formal and informal communication between staff members and between staff and patients.[35] This breakdown in the communication of information may lead to misunderstanding and interfere with the recovery of a patient.

Patients may be classified behaviorally in terms of the expectations of hospital staff members that they will or will not recover. "Hopeful" patients

[33] Ibid.

[34] H. Brill and R. E. Patton, "Analysis of Population Reduction in New York State Mental Hospitals during the First Four Years of Large-Scale Therapy with Psychotropic Drugs," American Journal of Psychiatry, 116:495 (1959). According to the authors there was no change in the methods or standards for admitting or discharging patients during this period. Unfortunately, a control group was not used, so that their findings cannot be accepted as conclusive.

[35] Alfred H. Stanton and Morris S. Schwartz, The Mental Hospital (New York: Basic Books, Inc., 1954), pp. 193–243.

are those whom the staff regards as having high chances of recovery and discharge. "Chronic" patients are those assigned lower chances of discharge, and who are expected to remain in the hospital for a long time. "Agitated" patients are those regarded as temporarily preoccupied with their illness and in need of special care, usually custodial. Patients may vacillate from "hopeful" to "agitated" and, conversely, from "chronic" to "agitated." [36]

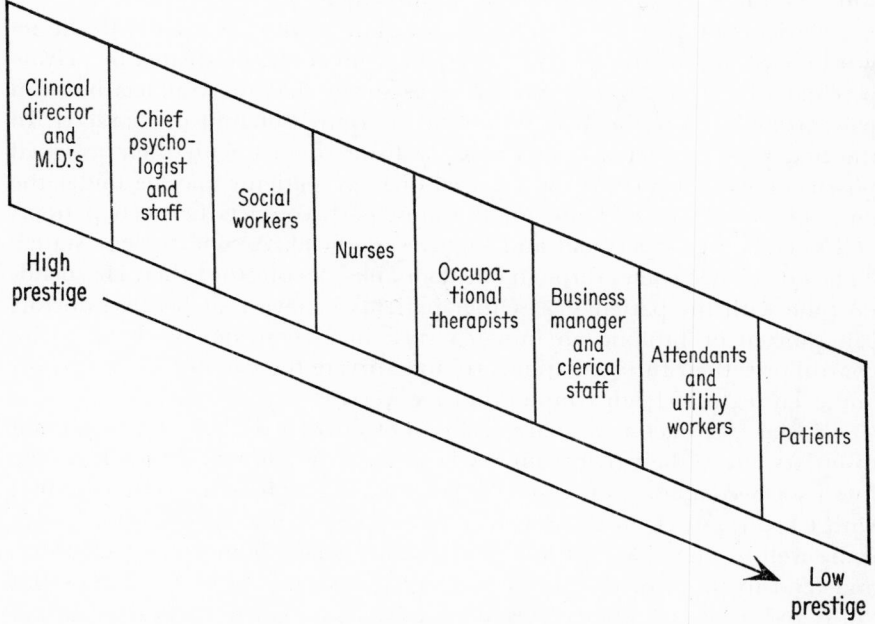

FIGURE 7. Hospital Status Hierarchy

SOURCE: Derived from Martin B. Loeb and Harvey L. Smith, "Relationships among Organizational Groupings within the Mental Hospital," in Milton Greenblatt, Daniel J. Levinson, and Richard H. Williams, *The Patient and the Mental Hospital* (New York: The Free Press of Glencoe, 1957), p. 16.

Patients of these three types are generally assigned to a ward with others of the same type. Each of these wards—the hopeful, the chronic, or the agitated—has its own culture, with a set of norms and values which differs from those of other wards. For example, for patients in the hopeful ward, "going home" is a value highly esteemed. Thus, the ward norms prescribe behaviors which will achieve this value. There is great disapproval of patients who show childish or disturbed behavior, but approval of those who

[36] S. Kirson Weinberg and H. Warren Dunham, *The Culture of the State Mental Hospital* (Detroit: Wayne State University Press, 1960).

give evidence of "making it on the outside." On the other hand, patients in the chronic wards (called the "back wards" by patients) often seem resigned to remaining in the hospital for the rest of their lives. Many, after numerous disappointments and setbacks, have given up hope of achieving some life on the outside. In the chronic wards, therefore, behavioral norms are directed toward accepting and making the best of hospital life. This involves keeping out of trouble with attendants or other patients, doing their work, and making some sort of life *within* the hospital.[37]

Patients in mental hospitals may not have quite the same attitude toward the professional staff as have patients who are being treated by private psychiatrists or in public clinics. The reason is that the contacts between patients and staff in the mental hospital are quite different in character. In the first place, patients have relatively little contact with their assigned physician, since as many as a hundred or more patients may be under the same physician's care. Thus, for the most part, contacts between patients and doctors are impersonal and highly superficial. As one patient stated, "The doctor just comes through one door and goes out the other. He spends no time with the patients." [38] Other patients believe that because doctors can shorten or prolong an inmate's stay, in a sense doctors have entire control over their future. Patients try to cultivate the friendships of doctors and even learn to feign symptoms of recovery.

Social class factors also are related not only to the etiology of mental disorders but to their treatment.[39] Class IV and V patients—those from the lower socioeconomic groups—are generally not as cooperative, as compared with Class I and II, in their treatment and not as highly motivated to become well.[40] They have little scientific knowledge about mental disorders and tend to think of them as a physical illness, wanting not therapy but "pills and needles." They are even secretive about giving knowledge about mental illness in the family, associating it with "bad blood," "a bump on the head," "too much booze," or some physical defect. On the other hand, Class I and II patients stress fatigue and overwork, which tend to make them more amenable to treatment.

Even more important, Class V patients tend not to think in the terms used by the psychitarist and other professional workers, who are middle and upper class and frequently have middle- and upper-class family origins. Frequently these difficulties even involve differences in indicating the meaning of what is said because of the differences in the language used. To the psychiatrist such patients with limited education often appear to be dull and stupid. They are worlds apart socially, and it is difficult for the profes-

---

[37] Weinberg and Dunham, *op. cit.*   [38] *Ibid.*, p. 41.

[39] August B. Hollingshead and Frederick C. Redlich, *Social Class and Mental Disorders* (New York: John Wiley & Sons, Inc., 1957). A partial replication of this study revealed a similar finding.—Robert H. Hardt and S. J. Feinhandler, "Social Class and Mental Hospitalization Prognosis," *American Sociological Review*, 24:815–821 (December, 1959).

[40] See pp. 396–398.

sional to think of them as friends in the same manner in which he might regard patients from Class I or II. Psychotherapy becomes difficult, and shock therapy often seems to be the simplest form of treatment. When the lower-class patient fails to cooperate he is regarded as a "bad patient," particularly when he displays lower-class violence. Whether or not a patient is a "good patient" depends on the sensitivity, intelligence, and the social and intellectual standards of the psychiatrist.

Much has been written about some of the attendant staffs of public mental hospitals: the inadequacy of their numbers, the frequent lack of proper motivation, insufficient training, and extensive turnover, largely because of poor pay. Fortunately, this situation has been improving. By far the greatest amount of contacts of patients is their contact with attendants. The relationship of many attendants to patients, unfortunately, appears still to be largely a custodial one. The patients learn to comply with the demands of the attendants and to know which ones are friendly or unfriendly. The patient who stands up for his rights is all too often likely to be classified as an "agitated person."

Sometimes attendants have favorites who are given preferred treatment: "These favorites may include the informal 'ward leaders,' the functionaries, or the 'stool pigeons.' Generally, the favorites are disliked by the other patients, although the exceptions are those who remain 'loyal' to the patients." [41] Strict enforcement of rules is often defended on the ground that the staff is too limited in size for other methods. One study found that resistance to the introduction of reform measures within a mental hospital came primarily from the attendants. Despite in-service training, unscientific rationalizations and beliefs about patients and mental disorders persisted. They included, for example, the belief that patients are "children" and in reality are happy, and that female patients are wilder and stronger than male patients.[42]

Too frequently much of the mental patient's life in a public mental hospital is spent either in aimless boredom in the wards or in performing menial tasks around the institution, tasks which have no connection with therapy. Although there may be some therapy in it, most of the maintenance work around a public hospital is done by patients, whether or not it is good for them. Some resent this subordinate role, but others become so habituated to it that they become incapacitated for the outside world. As one patient said: "This hospital has been home to me for eleven years. I'm used to it. The work isn't hard and I know how to get along. It wasn't easy the first two years, but after being in and out three times, I can call this home." [43]

[41] Weinberg and Dunham, op. cit., Chaps. 3 and 4.
[42] Thomas J. Scheff, "Control over Policy by Attendants in a Mental Hospital," Journal of Health and Human Behavior, 2:93–105 (Summer, 1961).
[43] Weinberg, Society and Personality Disorders, p. 430.

THE FUTURE OF THE MENTAL HOSPITAL

In spite of these various limitations, mental hospitals would be more effective in treatment if patients had more visitors, more letters, and other social relationships. Often, in fact, a patient's chance of discharge does not depend on the state of his "illness," but on whether there is someone interested in him—and willing to help him—on the outside.[44] Visits particularly mean a great deal to mental patients; yet generally the longer a patient stays in a mental hospital the less likely is he to have many visitors. Visiting appears to vary according to the type of ward, those on the hopeful ward receiving the most. The patient who has few visitors often loses prestige on the ward, feels he is forgotten, and misses this way of breaking up the hospital routine. One patient has written:

> Many patients are thrilled to have visitors. It takes their mind off the drabness of the hospital and off their own thoughts. It brings them closer to the world of which they so anxiously want to be a part. Pleasant conversation with company brings an assurance to patients that they may be treated affectionately and warmly by their family and friends.[45]

The trial home visits of hopeful patients before release are crucial experiences for most mental patients. This is the test period of adjustment in the interpersonal relations of the patient with his family, friends, and neighbors, and unless they and the patient have been sufficiently prepared by the professional staff, particularly the psychiatric social workers, a relapse may occur. The readjustments necessary because of institutional living and the stigma of having been in a mental hospital are often too much for the patient unless he has help from others.

The stigma of having been in a mental hospital presents one of the most serious difficulties. Many released mental patients are conscious of this stigma, and it interferes with recovery because it makes them feel that a barrier exists between themselves and others. To the public institutional treatment often implies that the patient is different from others. The past reputation of public hospitals has not helped the conception that "insane persons" are confined much as prisoners are. Consequently, few persons wish to admit confinement in a mental hospital, although people may increasingly admit, without too much fear of the stigma, having been under treatment, outside a mental hospital, by a psychiatrist or a psychoanalyst. It may be some time before a person feels like talking as fully about hospitalization for mental difficulties as about hospitalization for some operation.

---

[44] See Simon Dinitz, Mark Lefton, Shirley Angrist, and Benjamin Pasamanick, "Psychiatric and Social Attributes as Predictors of Case Outcome in Mental Hospitalization," *Social Problems*, 8:322–328 (Spring, 1961).

[45] Weinberg, *Society and Personality Disorders*, p. 445.

Although there is no question that the long-term goal of society must be largely one of prevention and early treatment of mental illness rather than extensive reliance on mental hospitals, the present plans of state mental hospitals, where most patients are treated, need to be altered. In this connection, the Joint Commission on Mental Illness and Health in 1961 made the following recommendations which are designed to reorganize our present system of dealing with the mentally ill:

1. Doubling federal, state, and local expenditures for public care of mentally ill within the next five years (1961–1965).
2. Ending the present state mental hospital program, and replacing it with specialized intensive treatment hospitals and community clinics. This would involve:
    a. Establishing a community mental health clinic for every 50,000 population.
    b. Establishing regionally located, non-isolated, intensive psychiatric treatment centers of 1000 beds or less.
    c. Discontinuing addition of patients to state mental hospitals of 1000 or more, and discontinuing construction of hospitals of more than 1000 beds.
    d. Converting existing state hospitals of 1000 beds or more into centers for long-term treatment of physically ill as well as some mentally ill.
3. Extensively expanding after-care and rehabilitation services.
4. Using non-medical hospital personnel with aptitude (attendants, nurses, etc.) to do psychotherapy since this essentially involves listening to patients talk about their troubles. Physicians would be given priority with specifically medical tasks, such as neurological examinations.
5. Greatly increasing the amount of money spent for research into human behavior. As compared to the amount spent on biological problems, such as polio, research on mental illness is in the 1908 era.
6. Increasing aid, in the form of loans, scholarships, etc., to persons entering the mental health field.[46]

An unusual program to prevent admissions to mental hospitals has been developed in Amsterdam, as a municipal government service, and involves the treatment of patients in their own homes wherever possible.[47] Prospective admissions are seen by a city psychiatrist immediately, or within twenty-four hours, after a patient has been reported as disturbed by such persons as the family doctor or the police. By seeing the patient in his own home the psychiatrist can better determine the circumstances and assess the contributing causes more effectively. If clinical observation is necessary the patient may be sent to one of the psychiatric wards in Amsterdam. Amsterdam is divided into four sectors, and a "team," consisting of a psychiatrist and several social workers, is responsible for supervision in

[46] *Action for Mental Health,* pp. vii–xxiv.
[47] A. Querido, "Social Psychiatry and the Legal Issue," *International Journal of Social Psychiatry,* 1:3–8 (Autumn, 1955).

each sector. Supervision is carried out by visits to patients' homes, the frequency of the visits depending on the particular case. The number of cases per team is about four hundred. In addition, the psychiatrist visits clinics about four times weekly and mental hospitals less frequently. Each team is part of the "Consultation Bureau," a sort of central agency with a personnel of about forty-five. It may also give advice to other public agencies, such as public assistance departments, and may give other help, including aid in finding jobs. About 8000 patients are dealt with by this Bureau each year.

It is reported that the program has succeeded in reducing the Netherlands mental hospital population. At present the program meets the needs of about a third of all patients who would otherwise require hospitalization. Dr. Querido, who has done much to develop the Amsterdam program, points out the extreme importance of the patients' *first* contact with societal representatives. Because of the nature of the program he has felt that it has had an effect in changing the public's attitudes toward mental illness and also in changing the psychiatrists' approach to the nature of mental disorder.

Summary

Institutions treat individuals who have developed some type of deviant behavior. It is difficult, however, to treat deviant behavior adequately through institutions because of the large number of those needing treatment and its cost, the limited professional personnel available, the artificiality of institutional life, and the stigma associated with institutional confinement.

Selected Readings

Action for Mental Health. The Final Report of the Joint Commission on Mental Illness and Health. New York: Basic Books, Inc., 1961. This report contains an analysis of the state of mental hospitals, with recommendations for improvement. The Joint Commission on Mental Illness and Health was set up by Congress to make a five-year study of the United States and make necessary recommendations.

Annals, The. "Prisons in Transformation," Vol. 293 (May, 1954). This issue presents various aspects of the problem of prisons and some suggestions for possible solutions.

CLEMMER, DONALD. *The Prison Community*. New York: Holt, Rinehart and Winston, Inc., 1958. A study of the prison as a social system, with particular emphasis on the inmates and their social relationships.

CRESSEY, DONALD, ed. *The Prison: Studies in Institutional Organization and Change*. New York: Holt, Rinehart and Winston, Inc., 1961. A series of articles on the organization of the prison, particularly its social system.

SCUDDER, KENYON J. *Prisoners Are People*. New York: Doubleday & Company, Inc., 1952. The story of the California Institution for Men, one of the most advanced prisons in the United States, by its first superintendent.

STANTON, ALFRED H., and MORRIS S. SCHWARTZ. *The Mental Hospital*. New York: Basic Books, Inc., 1954. A study of the mental hospital as a social system by a psychiatrist and a sociologist.

SYKES, GRESHAM M. *The Society of Captives: A Study of a Maximum Security Prison*. Princeton, N.J.: Princeton University Press, 1958. A sociological study of a prison, particularly the way informal rules of the inmate subculture control the behavior of its members.

TAPPAN, PAUL W., ed. *Contemporary Correction*. New York: McGraw-Hill Book Company, Inc., 1951. A series of articles on various aspects of modern correctional work by some of the leading men in this area.

WEINBERG, S. KIRSON, and H. WARREN DUNHAM. *The Culture of the State Mental Hospital*. Detroit: Wayne State University Press, 1960. A sociological study of a large midwestern public mental hospital. Contains much case and interview material.

The Group Approach to
Social Reintegration

Throughout the previous chapters the importance of the group in the development of deviant behavior has been emphasized. The group has been related to the acquisition of deviant norms and to difficulties in interpersonal relations, self-concept, and role conflicts. It has been seen that the deviant is a member of various types of social groups; that he plays a certain role in each of these groups; and that role conflicts may arise if participation in these groups exposes the deviant to competing demands and obligations. In addition, the deviant develops certain desires and attitudes through his group experiences which may conflict with the demands of the larger group, or "society." This recognition of the importance of group relationships is not confined to sociologists:

> The group factor in our civilization is receiving increasing attention. During the past decade there has been much interest in, and more understanding than previously of, the impact of the group on the individual, on the community, and on problem solving. The group in its various attributes— educational, therapeutic, recreational, and actional—is the object of study not only by social group workers but by educators, psychologists, and psychiatrists. Anthropologists and sociologists who have long been interested in the group as an institution are gaining new insights into the power of the group factor in present-day culture.[1]

The importance of group relationships was revealed, for example, in studies of neuroses among members of the armed services during World War II. It was learned that integrating or nonintegrating forces in the immediate social environment of the soldier were far more important than either his personality make-up, his family structure, or his previous history of personal maladjustment. The presence or absence of group supportive

---

[1] Dorothea F. Sullivan ed., *Readings in Group Work* (New York: Association Press, 1952), p. v. Also see Louis Wirth, "Clinical Sociology," *American Journal of Sociology*, 37:60 (July, 1931); Stuart A. Queen, "Social Participation in Relation to Social Disorganization," *American Sociological Review*, 14:252 (April, 1949), and his "The Concepts of Social Disorganization and Social Participation," *American Sociological Review*, 6:307–316 (June, 1941).

elements in the army, particularly identification with a group under conditions of stress, was found to be one of the most important keys to the development of mental disorder even among those who were supposed to have few tendencies in that direction.[2]

One commission of civilian psychiatrists who studied combat neuroses during World War II found that when "an individual member of such a combat group has his emotional bonds of group integration seriously disrupted, then he, *as a person,* is thereby disorganized. The disruption of the group unity is, in the main, a primary causal factor, not a secondary effect of personal disorganization." [3] William Menninger stated: "We seemed to learn anew the importance of the group ties in the maintenance of mental health. We were impressed by the fact that an individual who had a strong conviction about his job, even though his was a definitely unstable personality, might make remarkable achievement against the greatest of stress." [4] Such information, although limited, has suggested that neurotic symptoms may occur among ordinarily stable persons if the group situation is disturbed and that it might be well to analyze similar situations in civilian life which cause mental breakdowns.[5]

Primarily during the past twenty years numerous developments have recognized the importance of the group and have applied group methods in the prevention and treatment of social deviation. Still other work has combined theory and application in the study of group dynamics in problem areas.[6] Although some group psychotherapy existed as early as 1906, much of the recent increase in this work resulted from its use during World War II, when the number of civilian and military neurotic and psychiatric casualties, as well as the need to rehabilitate military offenders, made it impossible to treat cases on an individual basis.

The group approach differs sharply from the relationship of a pro-

---

[2] See Arnold M. Rose, "Factors in Mental Breakdown in Combat," in Arnold M. Rose (ed.), *Mental Health and Mental Disorder* (New York: W. W. Norton & Company, Inc., 1955), pp. 291–313. It was found that the rate of neuropsychiatric casualty in army units during World War II was higher in units with low morale, and lower in units with high morale.

[3] L. H. Bartemeir *et al.,* "Combat Exhaustion," *Journal of Nervous and Mental Diseases,* 104:370 (October, 1946). In order to minimize mental breakdowns among members of the armed forces in Korea an army psychiatrist in 1952 suggested that squads rather than individuals be rotated. The loss of a squad leader or disruption of friendships contributed to the breakdown of members left behind.

[4] William C. Menninger, "Psychiatric Experience in the War, 1941–1946," *American Journal of Psychiatry,* 103:581 (March, 1947). Also see his *Psychiatry in a Troubled World* (New York: The Macmillan Company, 1948), Chaps. 5–6.

[5] See S. Kirson Weinberg, "The Combat Neuroses," *American Journal of Sociology,* 54:465–478 (March, 1946).

[6] See Kurt Lewin, *Resolving Social Conflicts* (New York: Harper & Row, Publishers, 1948). See also Dorwin Cartwright, "Achieving Change in People: Some Applications of Group Dynamics Theory," *Human Relations,* 4:381–392 (1951) and J. Douglas and Marguerite Grant, "A Group Dynamics Approach to the Treatment of Nonconformists in the Navy," *The Annals,* 322:126–135 (March, 1959).

fessional person with an individual patient: the psychiatrist, for example, the clinical psychologist, and the social worker and their clients, where the emphasis is on a person-to-person relationship rather than on a group-person therapy. Moreover, not all forms of "group work" can be described as applying a *group* orientation to the treatment of social deviation. Many forms of so-called "group work" are actually *individually* oriented and are based upon the assumption that deviation is a consequence of a personality trait which is unique to an individual and not a kind of behavior developed in group relationships. Since this is assumed, the individual approach attempts to correct psychological malfunctions, believing that they, and not self-other relationships, are the causes of deviation.[7]

It is not the objective of the group approach merely to assist or supplement other forms of treatment, however. In essence, in the group approach, it is the *group* which is the instrument of change. The group approach views the *individual* as part of a broad stream of human relationships and within a complex network of roles and statuses. In a sense, any deliberate action which alters the relation of the individual to others in this network in an effort to change his behavior is an example of the group approach.[8]

There is evidence of growing recognition that the group approach is not distinguished by the number of persons involved, but by its particular perspective and theory.[9] There are today several variations of the group approach to social reintegration, all of which conform to our definition above. One type consists of group therapy, or group discussion sessions, which are usually employed with from four to twenty deviants, such as a group of prison inmates, in an effort to change attitudes and other behavior. This method has been employed both with deviants in institutions and in communities. In some cases role-playing techniques, such as psychodrama and sociodrama, have been used. Another type consists of activity or interest groups which have been employed primarily with delinquents and older persons. In some instances, groups in their "natural settings," such as delinquent street groups, have been the focus of reintegrative efforts.[10] Still other forms of the group approach include community reorganization,

---

[7] See Donald R. Cressey, "The Nature and Effectiveness of Correctional Techniques," in *Law and Contemporary Problems* (Durham, N.C.: Duke University Press, 1958), pp. 754–771.

[8] For further discussion of this approach, see Edwin H. Sutherland and Donald R. Cressey, *Principles of Criminology* (6th ed.; Philadelphia: J. B. Lippincott Company, 1960), pp. 322–327.

[9] This concept of the group approach agrees with our definition of the group in Chapter 1, page 4. See also Dorothy Fahs Beck, "The Dynamics of Group Psychotherapy Seen by a Sociologist, Part I: Basic Processes," *Sociometry*, 21:98–125 (June, 1958).

[10] See M. Stranahan, C. Schwortzman, and F. Athens, "Activity Group Therapy with Emotionally Disturbed Delinquent Adolescents," *International Journal of Group Psychotherapy*, 7:425–436 (1957); Walter B. Miller, "The Impact of a Community Group Work Program on Delinquent Corner Groups," *Social Service Review*, 31:390–406 (December, 1957); Lloyd W. McCorkle and Albert Elias, "Group Therapy in Correctional Institutions," *Federal Probation*, 24:57–63 (June, 1960).

of which the Chicago Area Project is a classic example.[11] The essential features of a "therapeutic community" have been applied to a number of institutions, such as mental hospitals.[12] Reports of these attempts suggest that they hold considerable promise.

Another type of group approach is the assumption by citizen groups of the major responsibility for dealing with a common problem with which the members are personally concerned. They are known by such names as Alcoholics Anonymous, Narcotics Anonymous, Recovery Incorporated, and Golden Age Clubs. Such groups have been formed to aid in the rehabilitation of the alcoholic, the drug addict, former mental patients, and delinquents, and to overcome the loneliness of old age. In each instance the group helps to integrate the individual, to change his conception of himself, to make him feel again the solidarity of the group behind the individual, and to combat social stigma.[13] These group processes, it is felt, replace the "I" feelings with "we" feelings, give the individual a feeling of being a member of a group, and redefine certain norms of behavior.

Group Approaches to Alcoholism

ALCOHOLICS ANONYMOUS

Alcoholics Anonymous is probably the most widely known and presumably the most successful of all informal group approaches to social reintegration. There are more than 7000 chapters—groups of alcoholics or "arrested" alcoholics—in the United States, in addition to chapters in many other countries. The total membership in the United States consists of about 300,000 persons; in the approximately 700 foreign groups there were 15,000 members. "In 1957 there were 257 hospital groups with 6000 members and 296 groups with 15,000 members holding meetings in jails, reformatories, prisons, and workhouses. Approximately 1000 seamen and 'lone' members in remote areas maintain a contact with each other by mail." [14]

Alcoholics Anonymous was founded in Cleveland less than thirty years ago by two alcoholics who felt that their mutual fellowship helped both of them with their drinking problems.[15] It is not an association or society in

---

[11] See Solomon Kobrin, "The Chicago Area Project—A 25-Year Assessment," *The Annals*, 322:19–29 (March, 1959).

[12] C. E. M. Harris, L. B. Brown, J. E. Cawte, "Problems of Developing a Group-Centered Mental Hospital," *International Journal of Group Psychotherapy*, 10:408–418 (October, 1960); and F. Knobloch "On the Theory of a Therapeutic Community for Neurotics," *International Journal of Group Psychotherapy*, 10:419–429 (October, 1960).

[13] Marshall B. Clinard, "The Group Approach to Social Reintegration," *American Sociological Review*, 14:257–262 (April, 1949).

[14] Harrison M. Trice, "Alcoholics Anonymous," *The Annals*, 315:111 (January, 1958).

[15] For a history of this organization see *Alcoholics Anonymous Comes of Age: A Brief History of A.A.* (New York: Alcoholics Anonymous Publishing, 1957).

the accepted sense of the word, for it does not have a formal organization with officers or dues. However, it maintains a central office in New York and publishes a journal called *A.A. Grapevine.*

It is difficult to ascertain definitely the degree of success of Alcoholics Anonymous, but there is considerable evidence that there has generally been a high rate of recovery among the members.[16] One writer, for example, has stated that A.A. claims it has a recovery rate of 75 percent for those who really try their methods.[17] Such statements are impossible to verify, for A.A. has no complete set of records, many A.A. members have a number of "slips" during the program, and many persons associate themselves with A.A. who are totally unsuited for it. There are also indications that those who associate themselves continuously with the A.A. program view their problem somewhat differently from those who have been exposed to A.A. but did not join it. In a study of 111 A.A. members compared with 141 non-members, a significant difference was found in that A.A. members tended to regard themselves, even before they ever attended a meeting, as persons who often shared their troubles with others. They tended less frequently to have known persons whom they "believed" stopped drinking through will power. They had lost longtime drinking companions, and they had had exposure to favorable communications about A.A.[18]

Alcoholics Anonymous is run by members only. No psychiatrists or other professional persons are directly associated with it. A potential new member must seek the help of the organization by admitting that he cannot deal with his drinking unaided. If he has been drinking unusually heavily for some time attempts are made to get medical help for him and to tide him over the aftereffects of his excesses.

The emphasis is on mutual help. When norms and values conflict there is a tendency to achieve some unanimity as to the goals and purpose of life and the relationship of alcoholism to them. The routine nature of life is diminished by participation in an outside activity in which the human element is stressed. Finally, and most important of all, the individual has a place to go and a group with whose members he can talk, where he can give and receive support.

The A.A. program breaks down the alcoholic's social isolation that

---

[16] Oscar W. Ritchie, "A Socio-historical Survey of Alcoholics Anonymous," *Quarterly Journal of Studies on Alcohol*, 9:149 (June, 1948); and J. Alexander, "Drunkard's Best Friend," *Saturday Evening Post*, 222:17–18, 74–79 (April 1, 1950).

[17] H. M. Tiebout, "Therapeutic Mechanisms of Alcoholics Anonymous," *American Journal of Psychiatry*, 100:468–473 (May, 1944). For a discussion of the use of A.A. techniques in correctional work, see Joseph A. Cook and Gilbert Geis, "Forum Anonymous: The Techniques of Alcoholics Anonymous Applied to Prison Therapy," *Journal of Social Therapy*, 3:9–13 (First Quarter, 1957). See also H. M. Tiebout, "Alcoholics Anonymous—An Experiment of Nature," *Quarterly Journal of Studies on Alcohol*, 22:52–68 (March, 1961).

[18] Harrison M. Trice, "The Affiliation Motive and Readiness to Join Alcoholics Anonymous," *Quarterly Journal of Studies on Alcohol*, 20:313–321 (June, 1959).

has resulted from the stigma of his excessive drinking, by drawing him into a group in which he is accepted on face value as a past drunkard. This group is an intimate, primary one in which members can more easily reorient themselves. An alcoholic feels at home with other alcoholics who, like himself, have known degradation and the stigma of being an alcoholic.[19] The life stories told at meetings are helpful to the members, as well as is the reading of their basic book, *Alcoholics Anonymous,* which contains many stories of ex-alcoholics. The organization even has a common argot, including, for example, words like "slip" to describe a person who has returned to drinking, "twelfth-stepping" for working with other alcoholics, and "dime therapy" for a member who uses the telephone to help someone in the group avoid a "slip." [20]

Each new A.A. member is assigned to a sponsor, perhaps an old friend or drinking companion, although more often a complete stranger, who refers to him as his "baby." This sponsor is someone who has been successfully coping with an alcohol problem, and is ready at all times to help his charge. He often asks the man's wife or his employer to give their support and understanding to the new A.A. member, and he may even visit persons to whom the alcoholic may have given worthless checks or from whom he may have borrowed money, asking them to give the alcoholic an opportunity to get back on his feet.[21]

As soon as possible the sponsor will take his "baby" to A.A. meetings several nights a week. These meetings are of two types, the open meetings which family, friends, and other outsiders may attend, and the closed ones attended only by alcoholics. At open meetings a number of alcoholics may speak of their experiences and of their rehabilitation; in closed meetings experiences and problems are told in a more intimate situation. In these meetings the alcoholic takes up separately the so-called twelve steps which are discussed and interpreted by other alcoholics. These twelve steps are briefly outlined as follows:

Step One: We admitted we were powerless over alcohol—that our lives had become unmanageable.

Step Two: Came to believe that a Power greater than ourselves could restore us to sanity.

Step Three: Made a decision to turn our will and our lives over to the care of God "as we understood Him."

Step Four: Made a searching and fearless moral inventory of ourselves.

---

[19] John F. Lofland and Robert A. LeJeune, "Initial Interaction of Newcomers in Alcoholics Anonymous: A Field Experiment in Class Symbols and Socialization," *Social Problems,* 8:102–111 (Fall, 1960).

[20] Simon Dinitz, "The Therapeutic Effects of Alcoholics Anonymous." Unpublished master's thesis, University of Wisconsin, Madison, 1948.

[21] See H. S. Ripley and J. K. Jackson, "Therapeutic Factors in AA," *American Journal of Psychiatry,* 116:44–50 (1959), for a discussion of the roles of "sponsor" and "baby" and their importance. Sometimes the word "pigeon" is used in place of "baby."

Step Five: Admitted to God, to ourselves and to another human being the exact nature of our wrongs.

Step Six: Were entirely ready to have God remove all these defects of character.

Step Seven: Humbly asked Him to remove our shortcomings.

Step Eight: Made a list of all persons we had harmed, and became willing to make amends to them all.

Step Nine: Made direct amends to such people wherever possible, except when to do so would injure them or others.

Step Ten: Continued to take personal inventory and when we were wrong promptly admitted it.

Step Eleven: Sought through prayer and meditation to improve our conscious contact with God "as we understood Him," praying only for knowledge of His will for us and the power to carry that out.

Step Twelve: Having had a spiritual awakening as the result of these steps we tried to carry this message to alcoholics, and to practice these principles in all our affairs.[22]

These twelve steps, which are greatly emphasized in the program, can be roughly summarized in four principles: (1) reliance on a power greater than themselves, (2) making an inventory of their problems, (3) making amends to others, and (4) carrying the message to others. The "power greater than themselves" is not specifically related to a particular religion, for A.A. accepts men of all faiths and does not tolerate discussion of religious doctrines. However, such a belief tends to reduce the isolation of the alcoholic, which has involved building all sorts of glass houses filled with rationalizations.[23] This "something" helps the individual to identify with the group, in fact, so great is the identification that "the so-called religious emphasis in A.A. may be explained in terms of Durkheim's thesis that religion represents essentially the group and the feeling of getting outside of one's self by identification with others."[24] The concept of a greater power constitutes a symbol of future resources and hope for the individual.

The moral inventory of the twelve steps represents a sort of self-analysis and is closely related to the procedure of making amends to others for things done while drinking. The inventory helps alcoholics discover some of the sources of their problems: making amends is a way to resolve problems because it helps to bring about their reacceptance into society. Relating their life stories at meetings enables the alcoholics to review their past experiences in the presence of the group. In this way they are able to assert their new role as nondrinkers.[25]

---

[22] *Alcoholics Anonymous* (13th ptg.; New York: Works Publishing Company, 1950), pp. 71–72.

[23] Tiebout, "Therapeutic Mechanisms of Alcoholics Anonymous," *loc. cit.*

[24] Clinard, "The Group Approach to Social Reintegration," *loc. cit.*, p. 262.

[25] For an excellent discussion of the group processes in A.A., see Sutherland and Cressey, *op. cit.*, p. 496.

In addition to these meetings, the alcoholic spends a great deal of time with other A.A. members, in the evenings or during lunch hours, in the late afternoon, and during week ends. Special programs are arranged for long week ends and holidays when the temptation to drink may be extreme. Coffee and "cokes" are served in the clubhouse, where card games and other recreational activities are common. There are also picnics for the families and sometimes auxiliary group meetings for the wives.

Carrying the message of A.A. to others is particularly important. In fact, Bales considers it the most important therapeutic aspect of the program. The relation of sponsor and "baby" and that of one member to another tends to create a series of reciprocal obligations toward others which result in greater solidarity or identification with the group. Alcoholics Anonymous involves a network of personal relationships and in this network each person is a focal point of interpersonal relations. This network of obligation is strengthened by the "carrying of the message." Bales has described it in this way:

> Further, his relationship to those whom he has brought into the group is strengthened by the expectation of each of his converts that he, who persuaded them that the program would work, will remain abstinent. He is, in fact, under obligation to each of these converts because of their dependence upon him. If he fails in his example to them, they may fail also. His failure cannot be a matter of purely personal concern, but involves the repudiation of accepted obligations. The success of each is to a peculiarly high degree contingent upon the success of the others in the group.[26]

The A.A. program allows the sponsor to see himself as he was before, in the image of the recently drunken "baby," or "pigeon," as the new members are sometimes called. Each is an image to the other, and the "baby" can call on his more successful sponsor for help on a twenty-four-hour basis. The "baby" is not only integrated into the group, "but he is integrated in a sympathetic but nevertheless strongly 'anti-alcohol' group in which status is clearly assigned according to the amount of anti-alcohol behavior which is exhibited." [27] In this way the attitudes and motives of the alcoholic about the use of alcohol are replaced with new attitudes and motives, for "A.A. redefines self and role as that of an ex-alcoholic who cannot stand liquor." [28] By associating with other teetotalers the member is not under pressure to drink alcohol. The frequent stories told in A.A. meetings of the alcoholic binges of others remind the alcoholic of his former self and role. The

[26] Robert F. Bales, "Types of Social Structure as Factors in 'Cures' of Alcohol Addiction," *Applied Anthropology*, 1:8 (April–June, 1942) and his "Therapeutic Role of A.A. as Seen by a Sociologist," *Quarterly Journal of Studies on Alcohol*, 5:267–274 (September, 1944).

[27] Sutherland and Cressey, *op. cit.*, p. 496.

[28] Edwin M. Lemert, *Social Pathology* (New York: McGraw-Hill Book Company, Inc., 1951), p. 367. Alcoholics Anonymous does not take any stand on the general consumption of alcohol by others, but it does as far as alcoholics are concerned.

A.A. Grapevine, their national official publication, contains chiefly stories and cartoons relating to the problem of alcoholics, and they serve as constant reminders of success and the dangers of failure. Mottoes supply additional social pressures to conform and include the "24-Hour Plan" of keeping sober only for the day, and such clubhouse slogans as "But for the Grace of God," and "This Clubhouse Keeps Us on the Beam."

The group therapy of A.A. appears to help overcome the forces which produced and reinforced the continuance of alcoholic drinking. As has been indicated, the alcoholic, through his drinking experiences, has built a conception of himself as a compulsive, uncontrolled drunkard. He has lost his self-respect, his friends have avoided him, and he himself has avoided groups except possible drinking groups. He wants acceptance, but conventional groups will not accept him. The A.A. member, through others' acceptance of him as he is, is offered an opportunity to learn new skills in interpersonal relationships. In addition, he acquires new goals: to keep sober and to reform other alcoholics. Thus, "the member sees in his prospective convert himself as he once was, and by teaching the other, becomes his own therapist." [29]

To turn again to the problem of why some persons become affiliated with A.A. and others do not, Trice found initial experiences at the first meetings to be important.[30] The chances were greater if the problem drinker had a clear understanding of what the meetings would be like, if he had a sponsor and group ties to keep in touch with him, if he had firm convictions about his drinking, and if he was not unduly sensitive to the social class differences found in A.A.[31] The effectiveness of these factors is increased if after a few weeks he finds that he can adjust to small informal and spontaneous groups, if his wife or his girl friend goes along with the program, and if he is aware of the symptoms of alcoholism.

RESIDENTIAL TREATMENT CENTERS

Hospitals have long been used for alcoholics. However, they are not of primary interest here, for their approach has often been typically individualistic and physiological. The type of center which is of interest here is generally called a "halfway house." The first were established several years ago in New York City, Long Island, and Boston. At present there are twenty such programs in different sections of the United States.[32] Halfway houses were begun in an attempt to rehabilitate the allegedly hopeless Skid Row type of alcoholic. These houses were established on the premise

[29] Cook and Geis, "Forum Anonymous," *loc. cit.*
[30] Trice, "The Affiliation Motive and Readiness to Join Alcoholics Anonymous," *loc. cit.*
[31] One study reports that initial activity is greatest where the A.A. group is relatively high and the newcomers are relatively low in social class.—Lofland and LeJeune, "Initial Interaction of Newcomers in Alcoholics Annoymous," *loc. cit.*
[32] E. Rubington, "The Chronic Drunkenness Offender," *The Annals,* 315:65–72 (1958).

that the deviant subculture of the Skid Row alcoholic and its meanings to him must be considered if rehabilitation were to succeed. The halfway house was thus seen as a social milieu offering social support halfway between the deviant subculture and conventional society.

After entering a halfway house the alcoholic is expected to get a job, pay for his room and board, assist with maintenance tasks, and to stay sober. The staff, which frequently consists of recovered alcoholics, conducts counseling sessions with new residents. Perhaps the most powerful rehabilitative force is the group pressure from both staff and group members. In the halfway house group pressures operate to produce sobriety, whereas on Skid Row they operate to produce inebriety. The halfway house is a good example of the modification of the alcoholic's system of social relationships in an effort to change his behavior.[33] Preliminary reports of the reintegrative success of the halfway house program suggest that it provides an essential transitional period that allows the alcoholic to prepare to abandon his old ways of life for new ones. Yet complete success seems to depend upon the opportunities he has of being reaccepted into conventional society.

GROUP PSYCHOTHERAPY

Other group methods, such as group psychotherapy, have been employed with alcoholics. They have involved group discussions of a small number of alcoholics, usually led by a professional person.[34] Group therapy has also been used with the wives of alcoholics.[35] Some persons have suggested that "therapeutic communities" or changes in hospital orientation, such as have been developed for mental patients, be organized in institutions for alcoholics.[36] (See pages 660–661.)

Group Methods with Drug Addicts

NARCOTICS ANONYMOUS

Narcotics Anonymous was established in 1948 by Danny Carlson, a former drug addict. Similar to Alcoholics Anonymous in both its activities and its structure, it uses an informal organization in combating drug addiction.

---

[33] *Ibid.*

[34] E. M. Scott, "A Special Type of Group Psychotherapy and Its Applications to Alcoholics," *Quarterly Journal of Studies on Alcohol*, 17:288–290 (1956).

[35] D. E. MacDonald, "Group Psychotherapy with Wives of Alcoholics," *Quarterly Journal of Studies on Alcohol*, 19:125–132 (1958); and W. W. Igersheimer, "Group Psychotherapy for Non-Alcoholic Wives of Alcoholics," *Quarterly Journal of Studies on Alcohol*, 20:77–85 (March, 1959).

[36] See Lorant Forizs, "Therapeutic Community and Teamwork," *Research Conference on Problems of Alcohol* (New Haven, Conn.: Laboratory of Applied Biodynamics, Yale University, 1958), pp. 591–595; and Florence Powdermaker and Jerome D. Frank, *Group Psychotherapy* (Cambridge, Mass.: Harvard University Press, 1953), pp. 62, 67–69.

Carlson was fully aware of the difficulties faced by former addicts in keeping off drugs, and he founded Narcotics Anonymous in the belief that addicts would be more likely to stay off them if they could join some sort of group comprised of ex-addicts who could understand and help each other in dealing with their difficulties.[37] The strength gained from the mutual support of those interested in keeping away from drugs was felt to be the best answer to the problem of addiction.[38] During the first year there were eighty members in this group. Although handicapped by financial problems, due to minimal outside support, it has grown in size. At present branches exist in most large cities in the United States and Canada.[39]

Members of Narcotics Anonymous hold meetings twice a week. New members are recruited by getting in touch with addicts while they are hospitalized for withdrawal of the drugs, or while they are still in prisons or reformatories. As in Alcoholics Anonymous, new members are assigned to an older member upon joining the group, and the new member can call upon his "partner" when he is having a difficult time.[40]

The process in Narcotics Anonymous is similar to that of A.A., in that norms and attitudes favoring the use of drugs are replaced by norms and attitudes opposed to their use. This is evidenced by the fact that members who are actively on drugs are not retained in the group. They are given the assurance, however, that once they are off the drugs, they will be accepted. In this way group processes operate to change behavior from that of an addict to that of an ex-addict. In addition, N.A. members adhere to a set of prescribed steps similar in content to those of A.A. The first step, for example, requires that members admit that they are addicts and reads as follows: "We admit that we were powerless over drugs—that our lives had become unmanageable." [41] The N.A. steps, like those of A.A., seem to provide members with a kind of formal "guide" which assists them in making the difficult transition from addiction to postaddiction.

In general, Narcotics Anonymous has not been as successful as A.A. in terms of effecting permanent change. However, this group is still not highly developed, and accurate judgment of its potential value must await systematic investigation. Some believe that the comparative ineffectiveness of N.A. is due to the absence of public and community support. Others suggest that the public attitude toward addiction in the United States is responsible for the tremendous handicaps an addict faces in being reac-

[37] Marie Nyswander, *The Drug Addict as a Patient* (New York: Grune & Stratton, Inc., 1956), p. 144.
[38] See Jerome Ellison, "These Drug Addicts Cure One Another," *Saturday Evening Post*, 227:22–23, 48–52 (August 7, 1954).
[39] Nyswander, *op. cit.*
[40] *Ibid.* Also see John M. Murtagh and Sara Harris, *Who Live in Shadow* (New York: McGraw-Hill Book Company, Inc., 1959), pp. 178–179.
[41] Murtagh and Harris, *op. cit.*, p. 178.

cepted by society.[42] There is no doubt that the public attitude toward drug addiction is much more negative than it is toward alcoholism.

OTHER GROUP METHODS

Doubt has been expressed by some persons as to whether the kind of group therapy afforded by N.A. would have a permanent or even a marked effect on drug addicts.[43] Such skepticism is probably due, however, to the prevailing view among many authorities that the drug subculture and the "personality traits and psychological needs" of the drug addict make change by informal methods difficult. Yet the findings of one study definitely show that group-oriented methods were effective in reforming drug addicts.[44] In this study the prodrug subculture of the treatment ward was significantly changed to an antidrug subculture by reorganizing the status system and by reassigning prestige to those showing signs of abandoning drug use. As a result, addicts on this ward reformed, in contrast to other treatment wards where reorganization was not attempted.

This method has thus far been employed on a small scale; yet it is possible that its use will increase. Some persons, in fact, believe that drug addicts present special problems which may be resolved by changes in hospital orientation rather than by changes in individual addicts. One therapist reports a situation where the creation of a "therapeutic community" in a hospital for drug addicts resulted in a noticeable change in patients' attitudes.[45]

Group psychotherapy has been employed to some extent with addicts.[46] Generally, however, such attempts have used an individual approach, so that the effect of the group, if any, has been incidental. Until specifically *group*-oriented psychotherapy is attempted on a wider scale, a definitive evaluation of its effectiveness will not be possible.

Group Methods in Reintegrating the Mentally Disordered

Until recently the only major form of group treatment of mental patients was group psychotherapy. Within recent years there has been a fertile expansion of group approaches to reintegrating psychotic and neurotic deviants.

---

[42] See Nyswander, *op. cit.*, pp. 145–146 and Murtagh and Harris, *op. cit.*, pp. 179–181.

[43] Walter C. Reckless, *The Crime Problem* (2d ed.: New York: Appleton-Century-Crofts, Inc., 1955), p. 376.

[44] James J. Thorpe and Bernard Smith, "Phases in Group Development in the Treatment of Drug Addicts," *International Journal of Group Psychotherapy*, 3:66–78 (January, 1953).

[45] See Arnold H. Zucker, "Group Psychotherapy and the Nature of Drug Addiction," *International Journal of Group Psychotherapy*, 11:209–218 (April, 1961).

[46] Nyswander, *op. cit.*, pp. 143–144.

RECOVERY, INCORPORATED, AND OTHER
INFORMAL ORGANIZATIONS

In existence at the present time are a number of informal groups which function to assist former patients in becoming socially reintegrated. One of these organizations, called Recovery, Incorporated, was founded in 1937 by thirty recovered mental patients of the Psychiatric Institute of the University of Illinois Medical School to help mental patients adjust to society in a satisfactory manner after their release from the hospital.[47] This organization emphasizes self-help, and the members mutually support each other in the problems of their daily lives. Most of the social activities of the ex-patients are of an informal nature. Families of the recovered patients often become closely identified with each other, and there are group visits, picnics, and other activities.

Formal group meetings are usually scheduled three times a week. On Monday, discussion sessions are held at the headquarters; on Wednesday, subgroups have neighborhood meetings in private homes; Saturdays are set aside for open meetings which patients, relatives, and friends attend. These meetings help the families to become familiar with the symptoms and behavior of mental illness, and learn how they can help the ex-patients. Since no formal meetings are held during four days of the week the new member is then alone without group support. If he should suffer a setback, however, he is instructed to call a veteran Recovery member, who will come to help him at any hour. If the illness becomes worse a neighborhood panel leader is summoned, and if he cannot help, psychiatric help may be suggested. In order that they will not be overly concerned, former patients are instructed not to indulge in self-diagnosis of their symptoms.

Clubs whose membership is composed of former mental hospital patients, sometimes known as "social therapeutic clubs," have been established in many sections of the United States in recent years, and are growing in number and variety.[48] Such organizations provide patients with an opportunity to gain confidence in social situations through participating in group activities with others who have similar problems. In this way groups such as these function as "steppingstones" to permanent community reintegration. This type of organization is much more common in England, where these groups have been in operation for many years.[49]

---

[47] A. A. Low, "Recovery, Incorporated: A Project for Rehabilitating Postpsychotic and Long-Term Psychoneurotic Patients," in W. H. Soden ed., *Rehabilitation of the Handicapped* (New York: The Ronald Press Company, 1949), pp. 213–226.

[48] Milton Greenblatt, "The Rehabilitation Spectrum," in M. Greenblatt and Benjamin Simon eds., *Rehabilitation of the Mentally Ill* (Washington, D.C.: American Association for the Advancement of Science, 1959), p. 19. See also pp. 229, 243.

[49] See J. Bierer ed., *Therapeutic Social Clubs* (London: H. K. Lewis, 1948).

GROUP THERAPY

Group therapy became generally recognized as an acceptable method of treatment during World War II, and since then the number of persons who have experimented with various forms of group therapy has increased. The success of the armed forces with group treatment of neuropsychiatric patients, the greater awareness of the overcrowding in mental hospitals, the shortage of psychiatrists, and the high cost of individual therapy resulted in the adoption of group therapy as a part of the general treatment program. In addition, many feel that group therapy methods are more effective with many mental patients than individual therapy.

There are several different types of group therapy. In some cases lectures dealing with difficulties of adjustment are given to the patients, and are often followed by discussions. In the usual method of group therapy, however, a psychiatrist and from four to twenty patients hold frequent discussions as a group in which all participate and in which there is group sharing of experiences. Sometimes additional tools are employed, for example, the psychodrama in which conflict situations are acted out by a group on a stage.[50]

In some instances, hospitals have found it advantageous to provide special group therapy sessions for close relatives of their patients.[51] These group sessions are held for about an hour or two once or twice a week, and are limited to approximately ten people. Such relatives often have a feeling of isolation, disgrace, hopelessness, and even guilt, and the purpose of group therapy is to discuss such feelings and to provide a more positive approach to the problem. Some therapists take a passive role, encouraging the relatives to talk about their feelings and at the same time allowing relatives of the other patients to discover the resemblances to their own feelings. As a group, the relatives of mental patients often try to help one another and sometimes develop strong feelings of group identification. Other therapists, however, take a more active role, explaining the principles of psychiatry to relatives and talking about the care given to the patients.

Psychodrama is somewhat similar to discussion therapy, but it is carried out in a different setting. It had its origin in Vienna in 1922, when Moreno founded the psychodramatic theater to treat various mental disorders. As a result of his establishment of a psychodramatic institute later at Beacon, New York, this technique has been increasingly used in mental

---

[50] Powdermaker and Frank, *op. cit.*, pp. 4, 5.

[51] W. D. Ross, "Group Psychotherapy with Psychotic Patients and Their Relatives," *American Journal of Psychiatry*, 105:383–386 (November, 1948). Also see H. P. Peck, R. D. Rabinovitch, and J. B. Cramer, "A Treatment Program for Parents of Schizophrenic Children," *American Journal of Orthopsychiatry*, 19:592–598 (October, 1959); and Erika Chance, *Families in Treatment* (New York: Basic Books, Inc., 1959).

hospitals.[52] The essence of psychodrama and sociodrama [53] is the acting out of behaviors in imaginary situations which have previously proved difficult for patients. In this sense both psychodrama and sociodrama are role-playing techniques, which offer an opportunity to acquire the social skills necessary to cope with certain situations. These techniques have been used in mental hospitals by both staff and patients, as means of fostering communication and understanding. They have also been used to assist patients in acquiring social skills, both in relation to the hospital group and in relation to anticipated real-life situations with friends, family, and employers.[54] The usual procedure employed in psychodrama is to have patients and staff—usually but not always a small group—meet together and choose a problem situation to enact, members of the group assuming the necessary roles. The group may be seated in a semicircle, with or without a stage, and usually there is a "leader" appointed to take charge of the meeting. The problem situation may be drawn from some past or anticipated hospital occurrences: the recovering mental patient may be urged to re-enact some of the episodes leading to hospitalization. By re-enacting these experiences the patient is able to anticipate new behaviors which will enable him to cope more effectively with the recurrence of such experiences. A patient may have walked away from his work assignment, for example, and this incident may be enacted. Or a new staff member may have arrived on the ward, and the feelings of patients toward his reception might be dramatized.

In psychodrama various imaginary scenes with family, friends, and employers may also be enacted, so that the patient may be able later to cope with difficult situations outside the hospital. After the initial enactment of the problem the roles may be reversed, with the patients assuming the roles of staff members and staff members the roles of the patients. The audience in attendance acts as a sort of "jury" or "discussion panel," for after the enactment, criticism and comments are invited. These comments may suggest how the problem might have been more adequately dealt with, and how the skills of the role players could have been improved. Frequently, these criticisms are difficult for both staff and patients, yet they seem to be helpful in enabling staff members to overcome professional blind spots and in assisting patients to grapple with situations which previously they have met with psychotic or neurotic deviation.[55]

[52] Jacob L. Moreno ed., *Group Psychotherapy* (New York: Beacon House, Inc., 1945).
[53] There is no clear distinction between these concepts in the literature.
[54] M. Greenblatt, Richard H. York, Esther L. Brown, *From Custodial to Therapeutic Patient Care in Mental Hospitals* (New York: Russell Sage Foundation, 1955), pp. 180–183.
[55] See Greenblatt, York, and Brown, *op. cit.*, pp. 180–190, and Knobloch, "On the Theory of a Therapeutic Community for Neurotics," *loc. cit.* Also see Robert H. Hyde and Richard H. Williams, "What Is Therapy and Who Does It?" in M. Greenblatt, D. Levinson, and Richard H. Williams, *The Patient and the Mental Hospital* (New York: The Free Press of Glencoe, 1957), pp. 173–196.

Evaluations of group methods have challenged the traditional psychoanalytic view of the treatment of mental disorders. It has been suggested that the role of the therapist does not call for special medical or psychiatric training, that the therapist's role may be assumed by nurses, aides, and attendants.[56] Indeed, it has been suggested by some that the social distance between psychiatrists and patients creates a barrier to therapy of a nonorganic sort. In addition, it has been pointed out by others that group therapy can, and does, result in changes in attitudes, motives, and self-concepts. A sociologist has described group psychotherapy as the "deliberate creation of an artificial subculture and the manipulation of a special social system" to effect changes in behavior patterns.[57] The key to effectiveness of group therapy is seen sociologically to result from experience in playing new roles, and learning to deal with situations previously met with inappropriate role behavior.[58]

Although few really carefully controlled experiments have as yet been made of the results of group therapy in mental disorders, there is almost unanimous opinion among those who have been engaged in this work that group therapy is effective. Little fundamental research has been done on what takes place in such group sessions, but it seems possible that the encouraging results are explained not by the theoretical scheme of the group analysts but by the process of informal group adjustment. In group therapy with mental patients, "should an individual member express misgivings about his prospects of improvement, or about the need for resolving his problems, or about the worth of the group itself, he will be resisted by other members, for any group that strives to survive evolves a set of objectives. . . . In effective group psychotherapy the identity of the collectivity and its survival center around the improvement of its members." [59]

In group psychotherapy mentally disturbed patients appear to develop an identification with one another and a degree of group integration; sometimes the opinion of the group appears to change the personality pattern and attitudes of one of its members; and each member secures an opportunity to play new roles and to acquire a new conception of himself. In the light of the problems of others it is possible for the patient to see his own difficulties and to relieve his feelings of social isolation. As one psychiatrist states the problem, "It is the group itself that becomes the therapeutic agent as a result of the interaction between the individuals who form

---

[56] Hyde and Williams, "What Is Therapy and Who Does It?" *loc. cit.*

[57] Beck, "The Dynamics of Group Psychotherapy . . . ," *loc. cit.*

[58] *Ibid.*, Also see George Psathas, "Phase Movement and Equilibrium Tendencies in Interaction Process in Psychotherapy Groups," *Sociometry*, 23:177–194 (1960) and "Interaction Process Analysis of Two Psychotherapy Groups," *International Journal of Group Psychotherapy*, 10:430–445 (October, 1960).

[59] S. Kirson Weinberg, *Society and Personality Disorders* (copyright, 1952, by Prentice-Hall, Inc., Englewood Cliffs, N.J.), p. 343. Reprinted by permission of the publisher.

the group." [60] Weinberg has summarized the result of such a treatment program in this way: "He finds that other persons have problems somewhat similar to his own, that all want to be socially accepted and all want to improve. The collective morale and identity that emerge encourage the isolated and timid person to increase his confidence, to become more socially active, and to feel that the therapeutic context is more real than in individual therapy." [61]

OTHER GROUP METHODS

Certain other methods, such as dance and music therapy, have been used to engage otherwise isolated patients in group activities. Often square dancing and other group dances are used. It has been found that even catatonic patients, who were given special rhythmic exercises if they were seriously withdrawn, would stay together and participate in the program if they held hands in a circle, but would scatter immediately if they dropped their hands. Music therapy has involved singing and similar activities involving rhythm. It is felt that songs have personal meanings, are an outlet for self-expression, revive memories, and are therefore useful in the treatment of mental patients. Patients may be given wooden blocks or sticks and encouraged to clap them together in time with a march music in two-four time. The music sessions also include the singing or humming of the national anthem, folk songs, or familiar new songs. Group discussion often goes along with these activities. These methods seem to have had some success. It has been suggested that whatever value these activities have depends on their ability to foster interpersonal relationships, and that there is little intrinsic value in the activities themselves.

THERAPEUTIC COMMUNITIES

In recent years several mental hospitals both here and abroad have attempted reorganizing their social structure in an effort to create what have been called "therapeutic communities" or "group-centered hospitals." The rationale behind these attempts has been that the social environment or the system of social relationships imposed by the hospital structure is so overwhelming that therapy of any kind cannot succeed in reintegrating patients unless this environment is itself "therapeutic." Thus, the general changes attempted have been to "level" the rigid hierarchical status structure by giving patients more responsibility for themselves, giving attendants and other lower-status personnel greater status-giving roles, redefining the

    [60] Bruno Solby, "Group Psychotherapy and the Psychodramatic Method," in Moreno, op. cit., pp. 50–51.
    [61] Weinberg, op. cit., p. 357.

roles of doctors and psychiatrists so as to give them less power in making decisions for patients, creating "patient governments" and establishing hospital-wide discussion meetings, and introducing greater use of psychodrama, for both staff and patients, and group therapy sessions led by nurses, attendants, and other nonmedical personnel. Important corollaries of these changes have been greater interaction between staff and patients and between patients, and greater ease of communication.[62]

In general, creation of a therapeutic community changes the hospital into a more "democratic" organization, where all may participate in what goes on. This contrasts to the highly authoritarian climate of the great majority of mental hospitals, where power of decision is vested in the few at the top of the prestige hierarchy.

In an Australian mental hospital, for example, reorganization took place after community group discussions were introduced.[63] In these discussions patients and staff of all levels were expected to suggest changes to improve hospital functions and relationships. If people were able to defend their suggestions these were tried out experimentally in the hospital. When it became recognized that changes could be initiated by people at all levels, a change in the rigid hierarchical role and status system of the hospital became necessary. Such changes were implemented, to some extent, in later staff policy meetings. Some of these changes consisted of allowing patients of both sexes to mix, beginning group therapy sessions led by attendants and nurses where patients were allowed to answer their own questions, and increasing interaction between patients, and between staff and patients.

FAMILY CARE AND HALFWAY HOUSES

Some procedures have attempted to reintegrate the mental patient under more "normal" group situations. The treatment for the mentally ill in Gheel, Belgium, for example, consists chiefly of incorporating mental patients into a small city. Here they are allowed, in the majority of cases, to live as part of the community rather than under the general scheme of institutionalization.[64] The people of Gheel have cared for the mentally ill since the medieval ages, when a shrine there became the object of frequent visits by mentally ill persons. A government mental hospital was

---

[62] See Greenblatt, Levinson, and Williams, *op. cit.*, Chaps. 4 and 36.
[63] D. Barker, L. B. Brown, J. E. Cawte, J. Riley, "Revising the Patients' Day in a Mental Hospital," *Medical Journal of Australia*, 45:700–702 (1958); and C. E. M. Harris, H. L. Brown, and J. E. Cawte, "Problems of Developing a Group-Centered Mental Hospital," *International Journal of Group Psychotherapy*, 10:408–409 (October, 1960). Also see H. Wilmer, *Social Psychiatry in Action* (Springfield, Ill.: Charles C Thomas, Publisher, 1958).
[64] See John D. J. Moore, "What Gheel Means to Me," *Look Magazine*, May 23, 1961, pp. 24–39 and Marvin E. Opler ed., *Culture and Mental Health* (New York: The Macmillan Company, 1959), pp. 4–5. The author visited Gheel in 1955.

established later. Among the 22,000 inhabitants of Gheel there are today over 2000 patients living with foster families. The town is divided into four wards, each with medical and nursing facilities, and the physician calls on the patients generally in the home. The mental hospital in the town is usually only a last resort. The objective of this plan is to absorb patients into both the home and the community. In addition, patients often perform various types of work, such as the care of children or farm work. Families receive a small remuneration for this patient-care from the Belgian government. It is believed that the value of this type of treatment lies in integrating patients into a normal, useful life, and freeing them from the social isolation of hospital wards. In addition, because Gheel residents are accustomed by tradition to caring for them, they are able to accept patients without fear or mistrust. This latter fact is believed to remove the stigmata of mental illness so that patients can be reintegrated.

This method of placing patients in individual homes has been practiced in several other European countries extensively for some years. In Denmark, for example, there are as many patients living outside the hospital at Aarhus as within it. The United States does not have a history of family care programs comparable to those of Europe, and generally, when employed, they have been used only for chronic patients. At present family care programs are in operation in Maryland, Massachusetts, and a few other states.[65] Experience with family care programs in this country indicates that they have great, but unexploited, potential.

Halfway houses for mental patients are similar to those described for alcoholics. The objective of such houses is to provide a transitional living unit for ex-patients who need an opportunity to regain the social and vocational skills necessary for "life on the outside." Such houses as these are more common in Europe than in the United States, and in 1960 there were less than ten such houses.[66] Houses differ in the degree to which they are autonomous: some are run almost wholly by the former patient residents, and others are dependent on hospital or social agencies. In 1956 a hospital in Vermont established a halfway house for 35 women, all chronic schizophrenics who had been hospitalized on an average of four years.[67] A housemother and a case worker were appointed, but the greater portion of responsibility for house maintenance and care was given to the patients themselves. Patients were able to make their own decisions and, as a group, were permitted to deal with the problems that arose. Many patients were

[65] M. Greenblatt and T. Lidz, "Some Dimensions of the Problem," in Greenblatt, Levinson, Williams, op. cit., p. 515. Also see Greenblatt and Simon, op. cit., p. 242.

[66] Greenblatt and Lidz, "Some Dimensions of the Problem," loc. cit., p. 514, and Greenblatt and Simon, op. cit., p. 240.

[67] George W. Brooks, "Opening a Rehabilitation House," in Greenblatt and Simon, op. cit., pp. 127–139, and Donald M. Eldred, "Problems of Opening a Rehabilitation House," Mental Hospitals, 8:20–21 (September, 1957).

assisted in finding employment. In addition, they were encouraged to participate in community social functions, in this way gradually regaining their place in the "outside." At the time of the study, twenty-seven of the thirty-five patients initially in the house were out of the hospital. Of them, eleven were completely free of psychotic symptoms, were employed and socially active, and were thought to be making a superior adjustment. Another ten were making a satisfactory adjustment, were employed, less active socially, but retaining some delusions and other symptoms. Five patients were making marginal adjustments, most of them living with their families. Only one patient was reported to be relapsed, but living in the community.[68]

These various group treatments of mental disorders seem to suggest that mental illness cannot be adequately explained by individualistic theories which attribute mental illness to early childhood experiences, such as those often advanced by psychiatrists and psychoanalysts. Rather, mental illness may develop out of difficulties that arise in relating to groups in adult life without necessarily having experienced exceptional difficulties early in life. One psychiatrist, in discounting the individual or personal problems of the patient, has stated that "since he [the patient] worked up his psychosis in the group, he can never be cured until he has worked out his recovery in a group." [69] As a research statement on the relation of mental disorder to socioenvironmental factors indicated, "the possible existence of group character structures, the stresses put on many by changing conditions or by the excessive demands of the culture, the sources of and the effect of loneliness and social isolation, and the techniques and effects of social esteem and social punishment on personality, these and many other problems need careful and continued investigation." [70]

Group Methods in Reintegrating the Aged

OLD PEOPLE'S CLUBS

One of the most prominent group approaches to reintegrating aged persons consists of informal groups or social clubs. Many clubs run by and for older persons have been organized within the last twenty years. Some, such as the Townsend Clubs, grew out of the depression and the need for

---

[68] Brooks reports that the thirty-five patients in this house had formerly been "dilapidated derelicts on the disturbed and semi-disturbed wards of the hospital—denuditive, smearing the walls of the seclusion rooms." He also reports that, as a result of this experiment, there had occurred in the hospital a marked increase in the status-value of the diagnosis "chronic schizophrenia," many hoping that they might be candidates for the halfway house.

[69] L. Cody Marsh, "Group Treatment of the Psychoses by the Psychological Equivalent of the Revival," *Mental Hygiene*, 15:341 (April, 1931).

[70] R. H. Felix and R. V. Bowers, "Mental Hygiene and Socio-Environmental Factors," *The Milbank Memorial Fund Quarterly*, 26:134 (January, 1948).

political organization to secure larger pension grants, but now they emphasize social relationships among old people. Some groups have originated around social activities, such as Golden Age Clubs or Three-Quarter-Century Clubs, and for the most part they have been concerned with group activities for the aged. Some but not all of the Golden Age Clubs are directed by professional workers and financed by Community Chests or other groups.

Regardless of the original purpose of the clubs, they provide a place for old people to gather, to meet others of their own age, and to enter into activities in which they are mutually interested. They play games, talk, sing, or sew, and, in the case of the Townsend Clubs, have engaged in political activities to promote their interests. All these activities give them something to do, a feeling of belonging, and also help to change their conception of themselves and their own problems because they see themselves through the eyes of others with similar, and perhaps even greater, difficulties.

Group Methods with Delinquent and Criminal Offenders

Although sociologists have used the group approach in their explanation of delinquents and criminals in criminology perhaps more than in any other field, the verification of the findings through the practical manipulation of the social world of offenders, using group methods, has not been as extensively investigated. The use of group therapy in correctional programs has increased in recent years.[71] Yet most of these programs are of relatively recent origin and have not been adequately evaluated as to their effectiveness.

Individual clinical methods of treating potential or actual offenders, although quite commonly used, are often assumed to be effective, in spite of the fact that their success has not been demonstrated. One study of the effectiveness of clinical treatment with male delinquents in Detroit found, for example, that there was no significant difference in percentages of arrest for those receiving psychiatric treatment as compared with those not receiving such treatment. These researchers concluded that "psychotherapeutic treatment of juvenile delinquents in varying degrees does not serve to prevent them from becoming adult offenders." [72] In view of the question about the ineffectiveness of clinical and individual methods, some persons have suggested that rehabilitative efforts in correctional institutions should be more on a group basis.

---

[71] Lloyd W. McCorkle and Albert Elias, "Group Therapy in Correctional Institutions," *Federal Probation*, 24:57 (June, 1960).

[72] H. Warren Dunham and LaMay Adamson, "Clinical Treatment of Male Juvenile Delinquents: A Case Study in Effect and Result," *American Sociological Review*, 21:320 (June, 1956).

INFORMAL GROUPS IN CONVENTIONAL SETTINGS

As yet little on the order of Alcoholics Anonymous or Recovery, Incorporated, has been developed for juvenile and criminal offenders. Efforts have been made to work on problems of deviant attitudes on an informal group basis, incorporating, for example, an entire delinquent group within a conventional framework. In one of these attempts the California Youth Authority, in cooperation with the War Department, in 1944 placed two groups of about 150 seriously delinquent boys in Army arsenals to work side by side with several thousand civilian men and women. The Army furnished barracks and provided otherwise for the boys. Efforts were made to change their roles by incorporating them into the norms and objectives of conventional society. The program seems on the surface to have made marked changes in the work habits of the boys, in their conception of themselves, and in group objectives.[73]

In India a similar though community-based approach has been used in an effort to achieve social reintegration of the formerly "criminal tribes" of India. These groups consist of people who for centuries have lived by criminal means such as stealing, robbery, and some types of pickpocketing. Frequently they sell women for prostitution, make alcohol illicitly, and fight with knives. Children born into the tribes acquire the deviant behavior patterns of their elders, with the result that the criminal traditions have been perpetuated. In recent years the Indian government has undertaken a rehabilitative program with these tribes. This program was begun when it was recognized that traditional methods, such as imprisonment, were largely ineffective. The objective of the present program is to achieve change in the behavior of these tribes by placing them in communities where they may gradually acquire noncriminal attitudes and norms. This is done by relocating groups within noncriminal villages or communities, and arranging special services to foster social interaction between local community members and members of the formerly criminal tribes.[74] A new experimental program has been started near Lucknow, India, where young children of these tribes are placed in a resident school on a voluntary basis. Here they receive a normal school program and have frequent associations with school children in the nearby noncriminal community. An effort is made to change not only attitudes but also self-conceptions by insulating them from their former associates.

---

[73] Described in John R. Ellingston, *Protecting Our Children from Criminal Careers* (Englewood Cliffs, N.J.: Prentice-Hall, Inc., 1948), pp. 95–118. Also see J. Douglas and Marguerite Grant, "A Group Dynamics Approach to the Treatment of Nonconformists in the Navy," *The Annals*, 322:126–135 (March, 1959).

[74] B. H. Mehta, "Ex-Criminal Groups in India," *Indian Journal of Social Work*, Vol. 16 (June, 1955); and P. N. Saxena, "Rehabilitation Work among Ex-Criminal Groups in India," *Social Welfare in India* (New Delhi: Planning Commission of the Government, September, 1955), pp. 505–516.

In Wisconsin, inmates of the county jails are permitted, under the Huber law, to work in free society during the day, as "day parole," returning to the jail in the evenings and on week ends, and deductions are made for their "lodging." The 1772 prisoners employed outside the jail during 1956 under this law earned $364,282.[75] In the Model Prison at Lucknow, India, a similar program is followed.

GROUP THERAPY

During World War II group therapy of a more specific nature was used with British military offenders. Later it was used in the United States at the Service Command Rehabilitation Center at Fort Knox, where the necessity for rehabilitating large numbers of persons far exceeded the supply of professional men available. In this group therapy work the "belligerent, over-assertive, anti-social rehabilitee is brought into line by his fellows and the asocial, shy, withdrawn person is drawn into the conversation." [76] Since World War II, more and more civilian correctional institutions have established group therapy as an aid to rehabilitation. For example, group therapy is extensively used at present in New Jersey prisons and reformatories as well as in many other states. In California, a group counseling program has been in operation since 1944.[77] Although there has been some use of sociodramas and psychodramas, for the most part the therapy has been mainly of the discussion-group type. These discussions may be guided by either a professionally trained leader, such as a sociologist, a psychologist, a social worker, or a psychiatrist, or by nonprofessional personnel with some in-service training. In New Jersey group therapy in correctional institutions is called "guided group interaction" in an effort to avoid confusion with group therapy as practiced by psychiatrists, as well as the implication that inmates are "mentally abnormal." The following excerpt is taken from a discussion in a New Jersey correctional institution in which an inmate comes to see that his difficulties in living in various cell blocks are primarily from his own actions and not from those of other inmates.

S: Well, I might. But he wants me to adjust myself to the people in A Wing [cell block] and learn to get along in A Wing.
J: Why can't you get along in A Wing?
S: Because I can't.

---

[75] Sanger B. Powers, "Day-Parole of Misdemeanants," *Federal Probation*, 22:42–46 (December, 1958).

[76] Joseph Abrahams and Lloyd W. McCorkle, "Group Psychotherapy of Military Offenders," *American Journal of Sociology*, 51:458 (March, 1946).

[77] Sutherland and Cressey, *op. cit.*, pp. 492–493; Norman Fenton, *A Brief Historical Account of Group Counselling in the Prisons of California* (Sacramento: State Department of Corrections, 1957); and G. Sterna, "The Correctional Officer as a Treatment Figure," *Group Counseling Newsletter*, California Department of Corrections, June, 1958, pp. 9–10.

J: What makes you think you can get along in another wing?

S: Because I'd be by myself then.

A: Can't you be by yourself in A Wing?

S: No.

J: Why can't you make those fellows leave you alone? You want to stay by yourself.

S: That is not the point. The point is they'll turn around and bother you anyhow. At least in one of the lock-up wings, if you don't want nobody around, you go in your cell and lock the door, and the hell with them. Right?

O: Sure.

B: Do you mean to tell me people bother you, S_____?

S: Yeah.

J: I think S_____ bothers people if I know S_____. I locked with you for three and a half months. If you come over to E-2 and pull the s_____ you pulled on B-3.

S: Well, anyhow, that's what he said. I am just stating what he said, that's all.

Leader: Well, I think S_____ made a point. He said that really what determines whether or not a guy is ready to go out depends on his ability to get along in any kind of situation.[78]

Such therapy seems to set in operation group forces directed toward socially accepted goals, and which partially counteract the antisocial group conniving that goes on so extensively in correctional institutions. This process does not occur automatically; and it extends over a long period of time. If the group atmosphere is one of true acceptance, respect, and noncensure, offenders seem to feel free to express their feelings and to share experiences of which conventional society would disapprove. Group acceptance of mutual feelings thus enables offenders to examine their experiences and the reasons for their confinement. In addition, if in the therapy group the offenders are trusted and expected to abide by anticriminal norms, they may come to regard themselves as nonoffenders, or at least as potential nonoffenders. If such changes in self-concepts do occur, it is probable that offenders will then aspire to the lives of "respectable" law-abiding persons. If this point is reached, criminal attitudes and motives will have been replaced by noncriminal attitudes and motives.[79]

. . . . there seems to be an assumption that free discussion of an inmate's problems and personality characteristics by and with an inmate group and a therapist will both enable him and force him to "face the facts" of his case. . . . Inmates who have had experiences similar to his will not let him lie,

---

[78] F. Lovell Bixby and Lloyd W. McCorkle, "Guided Group Interaction in Correctional Work," *American Sociological Review*, 16:458–459 (August, 1951).

[79] Sutherland and Cressey, *op. cit.*, pp. 494–496. Also see Richard R. Korn and Lloyd W. McCorkle, *Criminology and Penology* (New York: Holt, Rinehart and Winston, Inc., 1959), Chaps. 23 and 24.

bluff, or provide *ex post facto* justification for his criminal behavior. Presumably, the inmates . . . will accept his fellow inmates' friendly denunciations of his behavior and rationalizations more readily than he would accept the rejections and denunciations of the same behavior and rationalizations by an outsider.[80]

A variation of group therapy which has been employed in some correctional institutions consists of "role training" or role playing as part of the therapeutic technique. One institution conducted an experiment in "role training" as a means of preparing inmates for the problems which would be encountered after release from the institution.[81] According to these experimenters, if an offender upon release is to play the role of a nonoffender and a law-abiding citizen, he must have experienced (1) knowledge of the expectations of the role, generally through intimate contact with nonoffenders which allows identification with persons occupying the role; (2) rehearsal in the role, either imaginal or incipient; and (3) actual practice in the role.[82] Results indicated that role training was successful in improving role-playing skills and attitudes. There were highly significant differences when these offenders were compared with a control group.

It is unfortunate that, instead of changing the attitudes of the inmate about various *social norms,* most correctional group therapy work is still directed at attempts to modify personality traits and allowing the individual to release some of his aggressions. The approach used may, of course, help the inmate adjust to the frustrations of prison life, but often it does not get at the basis of his criminal behavior. Because the inmate's attitudes are derived from the social groups to which he has belonged, and because he has not had normal relationships with more conventional groups, it is important that group therapy programs be based on a group, rather than on an individual, theory of criminality.[83]

---

[80] Sutherland and Cressey, *op. cit.,* p. 494. In a rather unusual experiment in group therapy, two small groups of incorrigible prisoners in a North Carolina prison, one from security isolation and the other from the yard, were selected for discussion therapy.—Richard McCleery, *The Strange Journey* (Chapel Hill: University of North Carolina Extension Bulletin, Vol. 32, No. 4 [March, 1953]). A more recent study of fifty prison "rats," or prisoners at odds with their fellow inmates, has examined some of these circumstances.—Elmer H. Johnson, "Sociology of Confinement: Assimilation and the Prison 'Rat,'" *Journal of Criminal Law, Criminology and Police Science,* 50:528–533 (January–February, 1961).

[81] Martin R. Haskell and H. Ashley Weeks, "Role Training as Preparation for Release from Correctional Institutions," *Journal of Criminal Law, Criminology and Police Science,* 50:441–452 (January–February, 1960).

[82] *Ibid.,* p. 441.

[83] Donald R. Cressey, "Contradictory Theories in Correctional Group Therapy Programs," *Federal Probation,* 18:20–26 (June, 1954); also his "Changing Criminals: The Application of the Theory of Differential Association," *American Journal of Sociology,* 61:116–212 (September, 1955) and his "The Nature and Effectiveness of Correctional Techniques," in *Law and Contemporary Problems.*

One interesting recent group experiment in dealing with juvenile delinquency is known as the Provo (Utah) Experiment.[84] A group of habitual offenders, aged fifteen to seventeen, is assigned by the local court to join twenty others in daily group discussions. A control group is either placed on probation or sent to a correctional institution. The group discussions assume that delinquency is primarily a group phenomenon and the task of rehabilitation is one of changing shared delinquent characteristics. It involves discussions which (1) permit delinquents to examine the role and legitimacy of authorities in the treatment system; (2) give them the opportunity to examine the ultimate utility of conventional and delinquent alternatives for them; (3) provide the opportunity to declare publicly a belief or disbelief that they can benefit from a change in values; and (4) make peer group interaction the principal rehabilitative tool because it permits peer group decision making and grants status and recognition, not only for participation in treatment interaction, but for willingness to help others.

RESIDENTIAL TREATMENT CENTERS

A well-known experiment in a residential treatment center has been carried out at Highfields, which is part of the New Jersey correctional system and makes extensive use of group therapy and informal associations between staff and inmates in a fairly permissive, nonauthoritarian atmosphere.[85] It is a short-term detention facility located on the former estate of Charles Lindbergh in New Jersey, without bars or walls. The impact of the guided group interaction sessions, which are held five nights a week, appears to be reinforced by the group living experience.[86] In both guided group interaction and the living experience, the influence of the group is directed toward freeing the boys from delinquent associations and changing their conceptions of themselves from lawbreaking to law-abiding persons.

An evaluation made of the Highfields Project indicates that the delinquent boys aged sixteen and seventeen sent to Highfields have a lower rate of recidivism than those in the control group sent to the Annandale Reformatory.[87] In this study a control group of offenders, matched as to age, previous commitments, and so on, was sent for more conventional treatment to the New Jersey Reformatory at Annandale. A much lower percentage of boys from Highfields became delinquent after returning to

[84] LaMar T. Empey and Jerome Rabow, "The Provo Experiment in Delinquency Rehabilitation," *American Sociological Review*, 26:679–695 (October, 1961).

[85] Lloyd W. McCorkle, Albert Elias, and F. Lovell Bixby, *The Highfields Story* (New York: Holt, Rinehart and Winston, Inc., 1958).

[86] H. Ashley Weeks ed., *Youthful Offenders at Highfields* (Ann Arbor: University of Michigan Press, 1958).

[87] *Ibid.*

the community than did the boys from Annandale, even when such factors as age, parents' marital status, race, parents' occupation, residence, and so on, were held constant. Also, comparison of Annandale boys with the Highfields boys on a number of scales designed to measure attitudes and value orientations reveal favorable changes among the latter. The conclusion of the evaluating committee was that Highfields had demonstrated greater success than the traditional type of institution in reintegrating delinquents.[88]

Summary

Since evidence shows that deviant behavior is developed through group processes, group methods should help to bring about the social reintegration of deviants. Primarily during the past fifteen years, several different applications of group methods have been developed to treat mental disorders, delinquency and criminality, alcoholism, and old-age adjustment. These group methods have included more group therapy limited though it is; group counseling and discussion sessions; psychodrama and sociodrama; clubs for former deviants in communities; and, more recently, the creation of therapeutic communities in some mental hospitals and some correctional institutions. There have also been many informal applications through Alcoholics Anonymous and similar informal groups of mental patients, narcotic addicts, and old people who are working out their problems more successfully together than they can alone.

Group methods appear to be more effective in reintegrating many social deviants than the individualized approach. The group approach to social reintegration affects the deviant in a number of ways which can be summarized as socialization into nondeviant behavior patterns through taking the role of a nondeviant person, sharing feelings and examining problematic past experiences in a permissive, noncensuring group setting, identifying with others who are beginning to regard themselves as nondeviants, establishing loyalty and allegiance to new group norms and values, and eventually reorienting attitudes and overt behavior. As the individual is socialized, or resocialized, a network of new interpersonal relations is established. Group identification is enhanced and a "we" feeling is developed by noting that others have similar problems. The group becomes an important link in helping its members to adjust. The individual is thus enabled to gain a new conception of himself through group interaction. Finally, the operation of social pressures aids the establishment and mainte-

[88] The Highfields Project actually is not evaluating group therapy alone, but is also evaluating the difference between a small treatment institution with a permissive atmosphere and a reformatory. Although this study has shed some light on the value of group therapy, a more specifically directed research project is needed which would take inmates in the same institution and compare results in a group under such therapy with a control group which does not have such therapy.

nance of new social norms and values. This approach to the treatment of deviant behavior appears to offer unlimited possibilities for reintegrating deviants.

Selected Readings

Alcoholics Anonymous. New York: Works Publishing Company, 1950. This is the basic book used by members of Alcoholics Anonymous. It contains the stories of the founders, the general program, including the twelve steps, and a series of personal stories.

BALES, ROBERT F. "The Therapeutic Role of A.A. as Seen by a Sociologist," *Quarterly Journal of Studies on Alcohol*, 5:267–274 (September, 1944). The dynamics of Alcoholics Anonymous as seen by a sociologist who has studied it.

BIXBY, F. LOVELL, and LLOYD W. MC CORKLE. "Guided Group Interaction in Correctional Work," *American Sociological Review*, 16:455–459 (August, 1951). A theoretical analysis of the use of "guided group interaction" in the New Jersey correctional institutions. Contains several extracts from actual sessions.

CLINARD, MARSHALL B. "The Group Approach to Social Reintegration," *American Sociological Review*, 14:257–262 (April, 1949). An analysis of the entire area of group approaches to reintegration. Indicates the theoretical implications of this work, particularly for sociology.

CRESSEY, DONALD R. "Contradictory Theories in Correctional Group Therapy Programs," *Federal Probation*, 18:20–26 (June, 1954). A criticism of the present use of group therapy in prisons as placing too much emphasis on modifying personality traits and not enough on changing the attitudes and social roles of criminal offenders.

KORN, RICHARD R., and LLOYD W. MC CORKLE. *Criminology and Penology*. New York: Holt, Rinehart and Winston, Inc., 1959, Chaps. 23 and 24. Contains a discussion of group methods in prisons.

MC CORKLE, LLOYD W. "Group Therapy," in Paul W. Tappan ed., *Contemporary Correction*. New York: McGraw-Hill Book Company, 1951. A general statement on the use of group therapy in correctional institutions by one of the leaders in this area.

MC CORKLE, LLOYD W., ALBERT ELIAS, and F. LOVELL BIXBY. *The Highfields Story*. New York: Holt, Rinehart and Winston, Inc., 1958. A description of the plan, procedure, and operation of the experimental project for the group treatment of youthful offenders at Highfields.

POWDERMAKER, FLORENCE B., and JEROME D. FRANK. *Group Psychotherapy*. Cambridge, Mass.: Harvard University Press, 1953. A research study of the therapeutic effect of group therapy on neurotic and schizophrenic patients of the Veterans Administration hospitals. Contains extensive material from actual group therapy sessions.

VON MERING, OTTO, and STANLEY H. KING. *Remotivating the Mental Patient*. New York: Russell Sage Foundation, 1957. A description of efforts to treat patients by restructuring the social milieu of the hospital, with discussions of results in terms of patient improvement.

Author Index

Subject Index

Drugs (*continued*)
  stimulating, 293, 295
Drunkenness, 21–22, 26

Economic factors, deviant behavior and,
  99–105
Economic problems, marital stability and,
  452–453
Education, public, and reduction of de-
  viant behavior, 397–407
Educational facilities, discrimination and,
  544–547
Ego, 128
Electra complex, 133, 134
Embezzlement, 25, 132, 164, 268
Emotional security, family and, 199–200
Employment, discrimination and, 547–548
  old age and, 468–472
Endocrine glands, 43
Equality, 9
Ethnic groups, 520–525
  excessive drinking and, 357–359
  Mexican-Americans, 522–524
  Puerto Ricans, 524–525
  Spanish-Americans, 521–522
Excessive drinking, class differences in,
  352–353
  companions and, 349–352
  defined, 26
  ethnic differences in, 357–359
  false assumptions concerning, 36
  occupation and, 354–356
  personality traits and, 346–347
  religious differences in, 356–357
  See also Alcoholism
Exhibitionism, 210, 241, 245
Experimental group in scientific method,
  33

Family, as a social institution, 7, 8, 430
  conflicts within, 29, 430–459
  distintegration process, 433–435
  emotional security and the, 199–200
  interpersonal relations within, 431
  public education concerning, 602
  source of criminal attitudes, 196–200
  structure, changes in, 454–456
  traits, 42
  urban life and the, 454–458
Federal laws, crime and, 159–160
Federal Narcotics Control Act (1956), 293
Feeble-mindedness and deviant behavior,
  116–119

Felonies, defined, 153–154
Forgery, 120, 132, 205
Formal controls, 148–152
Fraud, 92, 120, 164
Free association, 127
Frustration, deviant behavior and, 16, 17
Functional mental disorders, 362–402
Functional psychoses, 27, 376–379
Funds, misappropriation of, 161–162

Gambling, 25, 92, 169, 170, 205, 209, 276–
  281, 593–594
  subgroups and, 24
Gangs, delinquent, 17, 186–196
Glands and deviant behavior, 42–43
Gonads, 42
Gossip, 149
Government, as a social institution, 7
Groups, attitude development and, 54
  based on interests, 6–7
  characteristics of, 4
  control, 33
  defined, 4
  dependence on, man's, 5
  ethnic (*see* Ethnic groups)
  experimental, 33
  membership, 54
  organization of, 6
  peer (*see* Peer groups)
  primary, 54
  racial (*see* Racial minority groups)
  reference, 54, 57
  religious (*see* Religious groups)
  secondary, 55
  social differentiation and, 9–13
  social norms and, 9–10
  social reintegration through, 644–671
  teen-age, subculture of, 11, 23
  See also Minority groups

Halfway houses, 662–663
Happiness, marital, companionship and,
  451
  psychological characteristics and, 448–
  450
  sexual relationship and, 451–452
  social participation and, 450
Health, antisocial behavior and, 43
  mental, problems of definition, 363–367
  minority groups and, 539–540
Heavy drinkers, 26
Heredity, alcoholism and, 40–41
  criminals and, 40–42

CHANGING AMERICA

CHANGING AMERICA

Blueprints for the New Administration

THE CITIZENS TRANSITION PROJECT

Edited by Mark Green

WITH WADE GREEN, JOHN SIEGAL, OLIVIER SULTAN,
AND MICHAEL WALDMAN

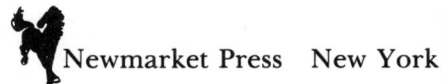

Newmarket Press   New York

92 93 94   10 9 8 7 6 5 4 3 2 1

Library of Congress Cataloging-in-Publication Data
Changing America : blueprints for the new administration / edited by Mark Green . . . [et al.].
    p. cm.
"A Citizens Transition Project."
ISBN 1–55704–162–8 (hc). — ISBN 1–55704–161–X (pb)
    1. Administrative agencies—United States. 2. Executive departments—United States. 3. United States—Politics and government—1993– 4. United States—Economic policy—1993– 5. United States—Social policy—1993– I. Green, Mark J. II. Citizens Transition Project (U.S.)
JK421.C26 1993
353.7'2—dc20   92–43972
                                    CIP

Quantity Purchases

Companies, professional groups, clubs, and other organizations may qualify for special terms when ordering quantities of this title. For information, write Special Sales, Newmarket Press, 18 East 48th Street, New York, N.Y. 10017, or call (212) 832-3575.

Manufactured in the United States of America
First Edition
Book design by Cassandra Pappas

To Phil Stern, for an exemplary life dedicated to democracy.

Acknowledgments

Thirteen months before the 1992 national election, several dozen advocates, scholars, authors, and officials came together to form the nonprofit Citizens Transition Project. Our aim was to draft a government-wide, agency-by-agency transition report on the long-odds bet that (a) there would be an interested new President in 1993 and (b) no one else would bother.

The dice came up seven.

This book is the successor of the 1989 Democracy Project volume, *America's Transition: Blueprints for the Nineties,* which benefited from the keynote presentation by Arkansas Governor Bill Clinton at the Project's June 1988 transition retreat in Washington, D.C. *Changing America* is the result of thousands of hours of effort by civic leaders who assumed that candidates focus more on campaigning than governance and that any President-elect would need the best ideas on how to budget and program the whole executive branch in the eleven weeks between the Election and Inauguration.

We would like to thank first and foremost Chuck Blitz, a true public citizen, for helping to conceive, conceptualize, and implement this project from its inception. And without Wade Greene's substantive and organizational contributions, the project and volume would never have existed. Joining Wade were editors John Siegal, Olivier Sultan, and Michael Waldman, whose quality enriched the volume.

Our deepest appreciation goes to Executive Director Deni Frand, and to Ophira Herman, for their good humor and long hours as they together shepherded fifty-eight chapters, seventy-eight authors, and 280,000 words to completion. Still, essential to the Project's existence and success were the generosity and confidence of a small group of dedicated backers, including: The Samuel Rubin Foundation, Alida Messinger, Hugh Westbrook & The Hospice Foundation, Joshua Mailman, John Goodman, Fred Howard, The Ploughshares Fund, Robert Stein, Matthew Gohd, The Harman Family Foundation, Jon Landau, Adele Simmons, Stanley Sheinbaum, Jeffrey Neuman, The Tides Foundation, The Angelina Fund, Smith Bagley, Charles H. Revson Foundation, Ron Feldman, Nancy Brown, Jonathan Rose, Ralph Alpert, Katrina vanden Heuval, and various members of the Social Venture Network.

There was also the faith and commitment of our supportive advisory board: Ira Arlook, Smith Bagley, Samuel Berger, Heather Booth, Robert Borosage, Roscoe Brown, Jr., Henry Cisneros, Joan Claybrook, Ben Cohen, Robert Coles, Patricia Derian, Chris Desser, Marian Wright Edelman, Peter Edelman, Mike Farrell, Jeff

Faux, Joseph A. Fernandez, Robert Fuller, Danny Goldberg, Lisa Goldberg, Lawrence Goodwyn, Stanley Greenberg, Wade Greene, Ellen Haas, Kirk Hanson, Gary Hart, Barbara Jordan, Elaine Kamarck, Robert Kennedy, Jr., Eleanor LeCain, Amory Lovins, Joshua Mailman, Pamela Meyer, Arnie Miller, Ralph Nader, Karen Nussbaum, Robert Peterkin, Esther Peterson, Jan Pierce, Drummond Pike, Letty Cottin Pogrebin, Robert Reich, David Saperstein, Marc Sarkady, Derek Shearer, Stanley Sheinbaum, Ron Silver, Adele Simmons, Theodore Sorensen, Marge Tabankin, Linda Tarr-Whelan, Cora Weiss, Cornel West, Hugh Westbrook, Geralyn White, and Harriett Woods.

Finally, we are deeply indebted to Esther Margolis and everyone at Newmarket Press for their confidence in and commitment to this project.

Mark Green, Chair
Harvey Gantt
Madeleine Kunin
Executive Committee,
December 1992

Contents

CHANGING AMERICA

Introduction

DEAR MR. PRESIDENT . . .

MARK GREEN

The Idea of Progress

W HAT DO WE DO NOW?"
The amusing yet apt last line of *The Candidate*—asked by
a senator-elect on election night of his campaign manager—is
the classic formulation of how campaigns are all about politics, not policies.
But the inability to focus on what happens after a heated election is not so
amusing when the winner has just seventy-eight days to appoint, budget,
program, and take over the $1 trillion-plus executive branch of the U.S.
Government. "For the last four years," lamented John Kennedy shortly
before his 1960 victory, "I spent so much time getting to know people who
could help me get elected president that I didn't have any time to get to
know people who could help me, after I was elected, to be a good president."

Consequently, while millions were understandably focusing on the *campaign* of '92 for the past year, the Citizens Transition Project concentrated
instead on the *government* of '93. For after two straight presidential races
that produced campaigns without content and victories without vision, America seemed ripe for a new approach in this new post–Cold War era.

Indeed, the reason there's such a huge, pent-up public hunger for
"change"—to use the buzzword of '92—is precisely because America itself
is changing. The U.S. is moving rapidly from an industrial-based economy
to a service/information-based one in a multi-polar (not bi-polar) world where
North-South relations are at least as significant as East-West ones. Three
fourths of us identify as environmentalists. A third of all children live apart
from their biological father, double the percentage of as recently as 1970.
While a fifth of all women worked in 1950, now three fifths do. A young

---

*Mark Green is the New York City Commissioner of Consumer Affairs. The
1986 U.S. Senate nominee from New York, he is author or editor of fifteen
books, including* Winning Back America *(1982),* Who Runs Congress *(4th
edit., 1984), and* America's Transition: Blueprints for the 90s *(1989).*

1

family with children earns *one third less* (in real dollars) in 1992 than it did in 1973. If Brazilian farmers burn their tropical rain forests or Japanese banks decide to sell their U.S. bonds, the personal and economic health of Americans is dramatically affected. And, of course, the major international threat today is not the Soviets militarily but the Japanese and Europeans economically.

But if America is changing, Washington isn't. It has instead given us a decade of avoidance when it came to critical questions of economics, environment, AIDS, housing, crime, poverty, and race. Presidents seemed to be like the generals at Gallipoli in World War I, who, far from the field of battle and basing their decisions on outdated tactics, kept sending waves of boys out of the trenches to die. Similarly, some national leaders keep talking about capital gains taxes and TV sitcoms as the reasons why boys in the ghetto shoot each other over $150 sneakers.

A frustrated public wants better answers, not the same platitudes. In fact, polling data indicate not only that most Americans believe we're headed in the wrong direction but also that there's majority support for dramatic alternatives—stronger environmental standards, radical campaign finance reform, national health insurance, strict handgun controls, reproductive choice, tax surcharges on the most wealthy, and increased spending on education and AIDS research. There appears to be a progressive mandate for change . . . but is there a progressive *program* for change?

Changing America: Blueprints for the New Administration provides one by pooling the best ideas from the most experienced advocates who have worked in creative exile for the past decade. We offer a menu, not a catechism, so that different authors suggest differing proposals in the interest of being inclusive. This volume, then, contains hundreds of reforms—large and small, short-term and long-term, legislative and administrative—for a better America.

But what's the *big* idea? True, the progressive side does not have the thematic clarity of a Heritage Foundation/Ronald Reagan in 1980, whose guiding lights were the twin premises of Soviets-bad and government-bad. So what is our version of the sled in *Citizen Kane*?

Simply, progress.

If Reagan and Thatcher proved anything, it was that a search for a "universal theory of the world," in Vaclav Havel's belittling phrase, was a futile ideological illusion. Instead, the only intelligent ideological observation may be simply that capitalism and democracy need each other, the first to produce wealth, the second to referee market competition and protect its losers. "Government without business is tyranny," a businessman once said, "but business without government is piracy."

Between laissez-faire ideologues and statist ideologues, however, is a large terrain where progressive pragmatists can search for new solutions in the spirit of both the poet of democracy, Walt Whitman, who said that "America is always becoming," and of the New Deal's FDR, when he said in 1933, ". . . take a method and try it; if it fails, admit it frankly and try another. But above all, try something." This notion of progress clashes with the new conservative "law of unintended consequences," which warns that every reform will be not only futile but also counterproductive. (My favorite is their argument that seat belts and air bags don't work because they lull drivers into taking more risks.)

This "law" is not only foolish—if adhered to in 1776, we'd still be British subjects—but it also collides with the idea of America, which is that we can always do better. And we have. There was no unintended consequence when Social Security largely eliminated old-age poverty, when the auto safety law saved two hundred thousand lives, and when the 1965 Voting Rights Act enfranchised millions of blacks throughout the South.

But even if lacking an "ism" other than progress, the contributors to *Changing America* are guided by five shared values that should help shape the next Administration's policy. These include *democracy, growth with fairness, family security, racial harmony,* and *reinvented government.*

Values for Democracy

• *Renew democracy.* Democracy is our "civic faith," writes William Greider in his *Who Will Tell the People?*, a system of continuous self-correction that compels officials to hear citizens and then make decisions in their interest. But a growing army of special pleaders with big money has instead perverted Washington into a "democracy for hire," Greider continues, where "government decisions on matters people care about intensely, from taxation to environmental protection . . . are cloaked in reassuring rhetoric but driven by favoritism and manipulation on behalf of monied interests."

We are living globally in a decade of democracy, as country after country benefits from a prodemocracy movement—except our own. Other societies produce a Walesa, a Havel, a Mandela, patriots who go literally from jail to leadership, while in America it's more likely that people go from leadership to jail. Instead of a prodemocracy movement, we've seen an antidemocracy movement that has spawned frustration and cynicism: While 28 percent of the public in the 1960s was convinced that "the government is pretty much run by a few big interests looking out for themselves," now two thirds of us hold this view. And as favoritism and PAC giving go up, voting and participation go down.

Instead, a functioning democracy should rest on two foundations: *citizen participation* and *reciprocal responsibility*.

First, you can't have democracy without citizenship. So long as most Americans are more spectators than participants—willing to be couch complainers rather than citizen activists—our democracy will exist in name only. Right now, people who earn over $50,000 a year vote on average twice as often as those who earn $5,000 a year, a de facto wealth test found nowhere in the Constitution. Instead, we need to aspire to a "civic society" where individual citizens are empowered to reach and sway official decisionmakers, whether in the voting booth or on the factory floor and whether in Peoria or Poland. For if powerful interests continue to drown out citizen voices— in Congress, in business, in court—then all reform will be stymied. How can we expect to reduce spending on unnecessary weapons systems or strengthen the Clean Air Act or enact national health insurance if military, business, and medical PACs can in effect dictate policy to committee members who operate on the principle of not biting the hand that funds them?

So a primary value for the next President and Congress is to seek a *new democracy* where constituents count more than contributors. At the least that means enacting two on-the-shelf reforms that Congress already passed in 1992 and President Bush vetoed. A campaign finance bill would help even the playing field between challengers and incumbents by reducing the power of proincumbent PACs and by assuring candidates access to the airwaves even if they lack a big war chest; and a "motor-voter" bill would increase voting by facilitating registration; a century ago the present system was devised, in part to make it harder for minorities and immigrants to exercise the franchise. Today, although conservatives object to easier registration because it might lead to "more fraud" (it hasn't in the states where it's been tried), what they really fear is more voters.

Second, as President Kennedy famously said in his inaugural address, a successful democracy means that citizens have not only rights but also responsibilities to each other. To sit on juries. Pay taxes. Obey laws they don't like. And, especially in an era of tight budgets, reciprocal responsibility also means meeting reasonable conditions if receiving a public or private benefit—from students paying back loans out of future earnings or national service, to corporations not fleeing communities that induced them to locate there, to CEOs whose incomes shouldn't rise when their firm's profits and jobs and salaries fall, to welfare recipients who should accept training and jobs. Sociologist Amitai Etzioni found it odd that "Americans demand the right to be tried before a jury of their peers, but are very reluctant to serve on one. They favor more government services of many kinds but tend to oppose the measures required to pay for them."

• *Generate growth with fairness*, since we've recently seen neither. Population has grown faster than jobs over the past four years, meaning that the per capita GNP has actually fallen. And all studies document what MIT economist Paul Krugman called "a big unprecedented jump [since 1980] in inequality to Great Gatsby levels" as the top 1 percent now own more than the bottom 90 percent.

The U.S. economy has been suffering both long-term and short-term assaults. Steady growth from 1950 to 1973 has been followed by stagnation from 1973 to 1992 because of low productivity, an OPEC oil tax, and the depressing effect of low-wage imports. More recently, the experiment in supply-side economics—tax cuts for the rich, wage cuts for working families, and program cuts for the poor—has provided nutrition for the top bracket but empty calories for everyone else.

While the budget and trade deficits have attracted the most attention, the real ball and chain around the ankle of the economy has been a little-acknowledged *investment deficit*, which has reduced profits, jobs, and revenues. Over the past fifteen years, Japan has averaged net domestic investment ratios of 18 percent of GNP; Western Europe, 10 percent; and the United States, 6 percent.

After years of underinvesting and redistributing wealth upward, the best economic strategy is *public investment in human capital* and *a new social contract in the workplace*, as several authors in this volume's economics section explain in detail. If the private sector won't invest, the public sector must—by investing in education, retraining, and infrastructure. Contrary to the prevailing orthodoxy, public investment in capital goods can produce new net wealth, as massive public investments after World War II demonstrated. And instead of the workplace friction that leads to six times more days lost to strikes in the United States than in Japan, a new President could try to be an honest broker for a new collaborative relationship in the workplace: If management agreed to more training, security, and stock for workers, who in turn agreed to more flexibility and productivity, all Americans could benefit from increased growth with equity.

The issue is not whether the economic pie should grow, but how it can grow so it benefits working families. Since a Trojan Horse trickling down on the middle class didn't work, it's time to try a trickle-up approach that invests more in workers than in the after-tax profits of owners. For ultimately, with goods and money and technology so transferable among nations, our greatest asset is a skilled workforce trained for the twenty-first century.

• *Provide family security*. Previously, security usually meant protection from possible foreign assaults. But especially as international threats recede, Americans now deeply desire personal security from exorbitant health care

costs, from pollution, from unemployment, from crime. Whatever the public's antipathy to government in general, there is widespread support for
specific government activism to make people feel safe in their homes and
on the streets and when illness and joblessness occur. As previously noted,
our political system should correct the shortcomings of our economic system:
While capitalism is based on *in*security (competition for sales and jobs),
democracy should provide security by means of a real safety net (health care
as a right, adequate unemployment benefits). Nor is it sufficient to talk about
family values and then oppose those actions government can take to make
families more economically secure, such as programs to provide for parental
leave, prenatal care, child care, child immunization, and parenting education.

A major way to advance family security is to stress the ethic that *prevention is preferable to repair.* Whether in environmental or health or economic policy, America has encouraged short-term calculations that produced
huge long-term costs. But it's cheaper and healthier to prevent cancer than
to try to cure it, avoid pollution rather than treat it, spend on roads and
minds rather than repair the consequences of collapse and ignorance later,
and convert many military facilities to civilian use rather than just lay off
workers.

A series of questions makes the point that often we can either pay now,
or pay later. Why does 25 percent of our $800 billion health care budget go
for overhead/administration while only 10 percent goes for preventive medicine and health promotion (as compared to 30 percent in many European
countries)? Since every dollar invested in Head Start is worth $4.75 in averted
spending, remedial education, welfare, or jail, why are two thirds of eligible
poor children not covered? Because air bags in cars are like a vaccine that
cost-effectively will save nine thousand lives a year, why did Detroit and
Washington take twenty years finally to get them in new car models? Should
society spend $2,000 once to teach an adult to read, or $8,000 a year for
welfare, or $50,000 for a year in jail?

In other words, to paraphrase a Consumer Product Safety Commissioner,
it makes more sense to build a fence at the top of a cliff than station an
ambulance at the bottom—a lesson that can have numerous applications for
government policy once Washington understands it.

• *Seek racial harmony*, even if politically hazardous. For years, our
national leaders have too often divided us by region, gender, class, and,
especially, race. Without having to be prodded by riots in South-Central Los
Angeles, we need a President and policies that remind us we're a *United*
States of America.

Yet as analyses from Myrdal and Kerner to Hacker and Terkel have documented, we remain two nations that fail to provide minorities with skills and opportunities from which we can all benefit. "From slavery through the present," writes Professor Andrew Hacker in *Two Nations*, "the nation has never opened its doors sufficiently to give black Americans a chance to become full citizens." So over a century after the Civil War and a generation after the Civil Rights acts, many still live in segregated housing and go to segregated schools. "The question for white Americans is essentially moral: Is it right to impose on members of another race a lesser start in life and then expect from them a degree of resolution that has never been demanded from your own race?"

But what's a President to do? At the least, do no harm. That means not pandering to white backlash by trying to give tax deductions to whites-only private schools (as Reagan did) and not appointing only 2 blacks out of 115 court of appeals judges (as Reagan and Bush did). Use the power of the White House pulpit, as President Johnson did, to repeat that it's evil to make legal or business judgments based on racial stereotypes. Enforce the civil rights laws vigorously—the dramatic growth of a black middle class shows how impressive the dividends can be. And seek universal programs that help all in need—for housing, prenatal care, child health, student aid, job training—and that disproportionately help citizens of color excluded from the mainstream economy.

Finally, only national credible leadership can make it acceptable to be frank about race in America. Senators Bill Bradley and John Kerry, for example, have courageously and candidly discussed three continuing sources of racial tension: a lack of training for high-skilled jobs; racial intolerance perpetuating segregation and isolation; and a poverty culture that defeats excellence. Would that be "blaming the victim"? Not if it's done by a President committed to broadening economic and civil justice for all and to requiring all Americans to live up to our mutual obligations, which include respect for others, obeying the law, and a sense of personal responsibility. "The only viable solution [to racial tensions]," writes poverty expert Christopher Jencks, "is to ask more of both the poor and the larger society."

Without such leadership, the continuing costs in despair, drugs, crime, and poverty—and the risks of civil strife caused by racial and ethnic tensions—remain high. Especially with half the new workforce this decade being either minority, foreign, or female, even beyond the sheer immorality of racism, we literally can't afford to hate.

• *Reinvent—and restore faith in—government*, to paraphrase author David Osborne. The greatest slander on democracy, from Reagan's inaugural, is that government *is* the problem.

But it is fundamentally un-American to tell people they can love their country yet hate its government. Of course government can mess up (does each military service need its own air force?), but so can business (S&Ls, Boesky, silicone breast implants). Since laissez isn't always fair, we need a vigilant public sector policing the private sector, helping the destitute, and enhancing our quality of life. Not even Ronald Reagan succeeded in reversing major New Deal or Great Society programs, for the simple reason that efforts from Social Security to Head Start work and are popular.

But those who believe in cooperative action helping people must restore public faith in discredited government, or new government initiatives will be rejected out of hand. And if you doubt that government has been discredited, you haven't recently tried to defend it in front of a talk show audience. There's something very wrong, however, writes E. J. Dionne in *Why Americans Hate Politics*, "when constituencies who had gotten jobs, gone to college, bought houses, started businesses, secured health care and retired in dignity because of government decided, all of a sudden, that 'government was the problem.'" So even though government helped win two world wars, end the Depression, and organize the moon landing, people focus more on recent failures to defeat poverty, pollution, and homelessness, which apparently are harder to lick than Nazis or gravity.

This is not only profoundly troubling but also ironic. For it's been anti-liberal government actions such as the Vietnam War blunder, the Watergate blunder, the Iran-contra blunder, and the read-my-lips blunder that have done so much to undermine government, the leading instrument of liberal activism. Just as corporations have had to restructure and get closer to customers to survive, government, too, has to restructure and be more result-oriented, which in the nineties means *spending less* and *flattening the bureaucracy*.

With few exceptions, the public rejects ideas that seem to have big price tags. Like it or not, Reagan's super-Keynesian deficits, probably as planned, now hamstring even desirable federal spending as interest payments exceed defense spending. Because the public wants government to spend less and do more, there's a rebuttable presumption against ideas that entail "more spending" *unless* proponents can demonstrate that they are (a) self-financing, (b) proven investments that yield long-term dividends, or (c) funded by user fees that tax those who benefit or those who can afford it.

Also, bureaucracy is a four-letter word that must be trimmed or flattened, which is more feasible given great advances in communications and computerization. And, whenever possible, government should strive to come up with nonbureaucratic solutions. Remember that some of the greatest reforms of this century—collective bargaining under the Wagner Act, the Freedom of Information Act, auto safety performance standards, JFK's Peace Corps, and Carter's human rights policy—largely involved the government-as-catalyst empowering people to protect themselves, rather than entailing more spending and bureaucracy.

The Veto by Elites

FOR BILL CLINTON, the political planets appear to be in alignment. Unlike Eisenhower and Nixon, there's no inherited war to distract him from his goals. He won by the largest margin (five points) of any newly elected Democrat since FDR in 1932. And he has substantial Democratic majorities in both houses of Congress.

But with all this, he will still face an obstacle course no less challenging than Indiana Jones in *The Temple of Doom*, who also thought he was home free merely by arriving at his long-desired address.

President Clinton on January 20 will immediately face vetoes by the unelected economic elite, a permanent government of special-interest groups who are hardly about to surrender a decade of redistribution of wealth upward because someone they didn't support may temporarily live in the White House. So the tobacco, banking, auto, medical, weapons contractor, securities, and tax-loophole lobbies will let him know the sources of their power—which is that money talks and that capital is mobile while countries are not.

If the new Administration's tax program, health plan, or environmental agenda are too rambunctious, we may see some "capital flight" from the States to abroad (which afflicted French President François Mitterrand after his initial election) as factories close and the new President is blamed. Backed by millions in PAC funds, the permanent government will also cite the deficit obstacle and the high-wage obstacle to frustrate Democratic initiatives. "You can't add to the deficit!" (which they helped engineer). "You can't have a high-wage strategy or a strict environmental strategy!" because firms (their firms) will move plants to Mexico or Taiwan.

Since America elects only two people to govern nationally, however, the new President and Vice President must call the bluff of the policy blackmailers.

That means, first, cutting the gordian knot of PAC power strangling Congress. With proven majorities in both houses for public financing reform, an early initiative would be both essential and successful. If members, however, think they have more to gain from PACs than from the President, he may as well pack it in.

Second, threats about "capital flight" shouldn't stop the new President from pursuing a high-wage, high-skills, smart-regulation strategy for American workers. Since we can never pay our workers so little to compete with $2-an-hour Koreans or pennies-an-hour Chinese, there's no practical alternative to announcing that we'll strive to bring the world up to our wage and environmental level rather than go down to theirs.

Third, the deficit obstacle can be hurdled in several ways. Many proposals in this volume entail *reforms without revenues*, such as creating a system of private certified toxic auditors; limiting big donor influence; establishing international minimal wage and safety standards under GATT; challenging big horizontal mergers; providing women the choice to terminate unwanted pregnancies; and choosing justices and judges more because of their integrity than their ideology. Other proposals can be funded with "earmarked revenues" or "mandated benefits" that don't add to the deficit. For example, a speculator's tax on resales and a limit on mortgage interest deductibility on mansions or second homes could generate revenues earmarked to low-interest loans for first-time homebuyers; or companies over a certain size could provide child care services. Finally, big-ticket items—such as the billions needed to expand drug treatment or replace decaying infrastructure—must be funded by a variety of tax reforms (costed out by Robert McIntyre subsequently) and savings from military and agribusiness subsidies.

Fourth, the only way to discourage the veto *by* elites is the veto *of* an elite. Any political or business leader has to let his or her natural adversaries know that he or she stands for something and won't be rolled. So a progressive president needs to choose a major moment to stand on principle and stand up to a big interest. Irrespective of the merits of their actions, it was invaluable to their anti-inflation efforts when President Kennedy forced the steel industry to roll back its announced price increases in 1962 and when President Reagan fired striking air traffic controllers. And it was disastrous for President Bush's agenda when he taunted Congress to read his lips about new taxes and then approved some. Once President Clinton articulates his priorities, he should let an opposing interest know his intentions and then win an exchange of his choosing to send a signal to future opponents.

Hats in Space

SINCE HECTIC NOMINEES LOOKING FOR VOTES in the fall can't be diverted by the concern that there are only eleven weeks between the election and the inauguration to name a cabinet, prepare a legislative program, write an inaugural address, and revise the outgoing president's budget,

Changing America hopes to help the new President get a fast start on day one to take over and shake up Washington. For the new resident at 1600 Pennsylvania Avenue probably has only three months after January 20 to launch themes and proposals that can plausibly be enacted in his first term.

Ultimately, the real "transition" is not seventy-eight days or three months or even the famous "Hundred Days" but probably a decade long. Dropout rates of 40 percent in the inner city, annual $300 billion deficits, the depletion of the ozone layer, and a "make my day" nastiness to the poor took years to accomplish; their solutions may take no less. Appreciate that some of the most significant public policy innovations in this era, such as integrated schools and the federal securities law and national environmental standards, all took a decade or two of great effort. "Reform," wrote Justice Arthur T. Vanderbilt of the New Jersey Supreme Court, "is not for the short-winded."

The way to start the process is an aggressive legislative program with a few priorities. Here, Ronald Reagan got it right but Jimmy Carter didn't. Inheriting a weak economy, Reagan's White House focused almost exclusively on his economic program—not his divisive social agenda but his popular economic agenda. When Secretary of State Alexander Haig attracted competing headlines in February 1981 by hinting at an invasion of Cuba, he was quietly told to shut up, and he did. The result: Reagan got his supply-side program enacted largely intact. But because Carter seemed unfocused and all over the map, he got little enacted, notwithstanding Democratic majorities in both houses of Congress. Presidents who try to do everything early may be remembered for little later.

The model here is President Kennedy when he "threw his hat over the wall of space" by announcing in 1961 that Americans would land on the moon by the end of the decade. What, then, are those few, large, concrete goals that President Clinton thinks really matters, thinks are part of his "mandate," and believes can be actually accomplished in either, say, the first year or in the first term? With so much to do—and undo—in 1993, the problem is not what to attempt but how to choose among alternatives.

Candidates for the first-year agenda include a public-investment-led economic recovery; affordable, accessible, universal health care; bold campaign finance reform; prenatal care for all pregnant women and a fully funded Head Start program for all eligible children; a 1993 version of Food for Peace for the former Soviet Union to generate exports here and democracy there; scholarships for all in need, paid back over time via payroll deductions or national service; a technology extension service to help convert advanced technology into commercial uses; and the Freedom of Choice Act. One way to bundle several of these ideas together is to state that the early goal will be *"health*—how to improve both the personal and economic health of all Americans by universal care and reinvestment in America."

First-term or first-decade goals could include annual world environmental summits to coordinate policies; a program to rebuild families by providing for the health and schooling of poor children; a ban on handguns; an electric car to clean the air and save energy; a GATT for minimum wages worldwide; shelter and services for the growing homeless; a new "social contract" in the workplace that produces more security, training, and productivity; an economic conversion plan for a million out-of-work employees of military contractors; a shift in the war on drugs from interdiction and arrests to prevention and treatment; and an end to world hunger.

While several of these short- and long-term initiatives can be announced early, only a few can be pursued early. But then, early successes can generate more political capital to be spent on yet more initiatives, in the way President Johnson used his extraordinary mandate from 1964 to keep enacting successive Great Society reforms in the 1965–66 congressional session. President Clinton, too, needs some early legislative victories in the 103d Congress to generate the momentum and muscle for later, larger efforts—which means avoiding such a legislative behemoth of a loser as Carter's energy bill. In such a sequence of success, political capital is not chips to be hoarded but candles to light other candles—so the more it's used, the more it multiplies.

Transition Prospects and Pitfalls

BEYOND THE EARLY NEED TO FACE down the unelected elites and to choose a few winnable legislative initiatives carefully, any President-elect must learn from the transitions of his recent predecessors. With the exception of George Bush's "friendly takeover" in 1989, to use John Sununu's useful metaphor, the transitions of Ike-JFK, LBJ-Nixon, Ford-Carter, and Carter-Reagan all involved a shift not only in presidents but also parties, as will occur in 1993. Assuming he wants to pursue his mandate for change aggressively, what lessons could Bill Clinton learn from these parallel experiences? Ten come to mind:

• *Woo—and rewoo—the Hill.* Congressional barons preceded President Clinton, will survive him, and quietly wonder why *they're* not at 1600 Pennsylvania Avenue. And since part of his mandate is to end the "gridlock" between branches and parties, the new President should again and again call and confer with key committee chairs. When Eisenhower failed to touch base with incoming House Ways and Means Committee chairman Daniel Reed of New York, Reed caused much trouble and delay for the administration's antideficit program. But if Ike could win over Senator Taft and Bush work well with Senator Dole (both former opponents), there's no member Bill Clinton can't talk to. (Okay, Bob Dornan doesn't count.)

Jimmy Carter said he tried but "it seemed that Congress had an insatiable desire for consultation." Given, however, his well-known aversion to schmoozing and the novice Georgians on his White House lobbying staff, he didn't try hard enough. If a new chief executive wants to leave a legislative legacy, what Mark Twain said of bourbon is also true of White House calls, cuff links, and dinner invitations: Too much is never enough.

• *Reach out for diversity.* Ike and Nixon had all-white, all-male Cabinets dominated by businessmen. Despite his populist outsider rhetoric, Carter's cabinet had Establishment written all over it. But because his party has been out of power for twenty of twenty-four years, President Clinton has the luxury of picking from a huge universe of hundreds of women and men— black, brown, Asian, and white and in their thirties, forties, fifties, sixties— who have formed a de facto shadow government while serving as congressional staff or in advocacy groups, universities, state houses, state governments, law firms, or think tanks. While personnel outreach needn't go as far as the way Richard Nixon's transition indiscriminately sent a solicitation letter to all sixty thousand in *Who's Who in America* (including LBJ!), a personnel search should go beyond the usual network of known, connected insiders to find a combination of experience and new faces reflecting the rich diversity of America. After all, the same old faces may come up with the same old policies rather than "change." Anything even close to all-white and all-male are today about as relevant as James Watt's ethnic humor.

• *Don't rush appointments.* There is immense pressure, especially for a President-elect promising change, to choose top staff quickly. Invariably, Clinton's pace will be compared to Ike's (who finished his cabinet on the twenty-seventh day after his election), JFK's (fortieth day), Nixon's (thirty-seventh), and Carter's (fiftieth). But in Jefferson's immortal words, "delay is preferable to error." Yes, make a few key picks early, as George Bush chose James Baker as secretary of state the day after his election. But especially given new ethics laws—and given the cost of selections not thoroughly vetted, like John Tower as defense secretary—President Clinton can afford to endure a few articles on his deliberateness to avoid having to endure the weight of a few potential albatrosses. "I must make the appointment now," said President Kennedy to John Kenneth Galbraith of one premature pick, "[though] a year hence I will know who I really want to appoint."

• *Fight for—and bond with—your cabinet.* To inspire loyalty *from* them, the President needs to demonstrate loyalty *to* them. At the first sign of serious congressional opposition to a cabinet pick, a new president must rally around him or her or reveal a fickleness that invites repetition. The way Carter let CIA director Ted Sorensen suffer petty attacks and then withdraw sent a damaging signal to other appointees and to Congress that Carter would jettison people and policies under pressure. Also, once in place, the new President should take a long weekend—as Eisenhower and Carter did—to socialize with his cabinet-level secretaries and to share his values and vision with them. Clinton needs to convey his sense of purpose and mission to them personally—and in exchange ask for a commitment of at least four years. Since policy change requires continuous effort, resignations after two years can sabotage a major initiative as effectively as a defeat on the Senate floor.

• *Share subcabinet picks with the cabinet.* Jimmy Carter allowed cabinet secretaries so much leeway to choose their own subcabinet appointees that departments became baronies faithful to secretaries but not Carter, which in turn persuaded influential members of Congress to bypass the White House with requests. Yet Ronald Reagan, overlearning from Carter's mistake, so centralized appointments from his White House that what he gained in ideological discipline he lost in diversity: Perhaps a *few* non-Reaganites could have helped avoid the debacle of a 95-0 vote against his proposed Social Security cutback in 1982 or, even, the Iran-contra scandal. President Clinton should ideally seek a more balanced approach based on a mutual consent on subcabinet choices between White House and secretaries.

• *Recover fumbles.* Carl Bauer, in his excellent book *Presidential Transitions: Eisenhower Through Reagan,* concluded that "it is important to bear in mind that all presidents make serious mistakes. That is guaranteed by the sheer speed of events, the difficulty of the job, and human fallibility." The difference between successful and failed administrations (and football teams) is whether they can recover their fumbles—or at least learn from them. The best reaction to a disaster, to quote John Kennedy after the Bay of Pigs, is "How could I have been so stupid?" Indeed, JFK responded so well and so quickly to that debacle, by accepting full responsibility in a forcefully delivered TV address, that his popularity actually rose. And within two days of the Senate's humiliating rejection of Senator John Tower as defense secretary, President Bush adeptly and quickly chose someone of competence and stature, Richard Cheney, who was quickly confirmed. End of story.

• *Visit Reagan.* Americans love leaders to display magnanimity and bipartisanship. Kennedy visited Nixon in Key Biscayne two weeks after the election and chose two Republicans to high posts who had even contributed to Nixon—Douglas Dillon to Treasury and McGeorge Bundy to the National

Security Council. But 1992 isn't 1960. Appointing Republicans to a change-oriented Administration after twelve years of Democratless cabinets might be a mixed metaphor. Instead, President-elect Clinton could visit Ronald Reagan as a generous gesture to learn from Reagan's successful transition—indeed, from his politically successful first year.

   • *Visit the FTC, HHS, EPA, etc.* After four straight presidential campaigns where the winner ran *against* Washington, the forty-second President could pull a shocker—visit not Korea but the bureaucracy. Presidents can't govern well without a skilled and loyal career civil service that alone has the institutional memory to know what not to do. But if civil servants are made to feel like aliens rather than patriots, why would they return ridicule with loyalty? President Clinton, contrary to Reagan's assertion that "government is the problem," obviously highly values public service. Visits to key agencies to spread his belief not in bigger government or smaller government but in smarter government can help motivate the troops who make Washington work.

   • *Focus on ethics.* When General Motors chairman Charles Wilson was nominated as defense secretary by Eisenhower, he initially refused to sell his stock in General Motors, even though the firm had extensive dealings with the Pentagon. Since then, actual or potential ethics conflicts have bedeviled several appointees. And since so many Reagan appointees were caught feathering their nest at taxpayer expense or taking literally their constitutional oath to "*execute* the laws faithfully," President Clinton should only appoint people who meet the strictest standards of ethics. He should make it clear that any appointee who failed to comply faithfully with a law's letter and spirit would be out on his or her ear the next day, which contrasts with a Ronald Reagan who never once reproached his dozens of derelict appointees. Such an integrity test means the consideration of people more interested in making history than money—people such as FDR's Frances Perkins, Truman's George Marshall, Kennedy's Stewart Udall, LBJ's John Gardner, Ford's Edward Levi, and Carter's Cy Vance.

   • *Deliver a brief inaugural address.* To avoid four more years of ridicule, Bill Clinton should make it short, sweet, and soaring. As both Kennedy and Nixon understood (their inaugurals were each some nineteen hundred words), such moments are *not* convention speeches or state of the union addresses which must touch all bases. If ever Mies van der Rohe's axiom applied to politics—"less is more"—it's on January 20. The key is to find the theme and metaphor that captures the historic moment.

Symphony of America

ONCE HE'S ELECTED AND HAS APPOINTED top people and articulated priorities and won a major fight, a progressive President still will always have to contend with the government-is-evil crowd, who are more eloquent than insightful but have access to the media beyond their numbers. These are the people who opposed child labor laws as violations of free enterprise, who, in the words of the famous *New Yorker* cartoon, used to go to the Trans-Lux "to hiss Roosevelt," who thought that Earl Warren should be impeached, and who believe that welfare payments create poverty. Basically, from ex-presidents Reagan and Bush to members like Newt Gingrich and Phil Gramm to advocates such as the Heritage Foundation and the Hoover Institute, this group will try to disparage all reforms as just more wasteful government.

The best answer to those who insist on shoehorning new solutions into old fights over individualism vs. state action is to talk about the larger community. Who among us when in need—of a scholarship, of Medicare, of a first-home loan—hasn't gotten a helping hand from others, including all others through a mechanism called government? The forty-second President, then, should advance the idea of the *Symphony of America*, where everyone should practice hard to develop her or his own individual skills and then come together to work in concert. America should mean bringing out the best in each of us, for all of us.

PART I

ECONOMIC POLICY

OVERVIEW: ECONOMIC POLICY

JAMES K. GALBRAITH

AND

MICHAEL MANDLER

U NTIL THE 1980S, American economic growth always raised the incomes of rich and poor alike. As John F. Kennedy liked to say, "a rising tide lifts all boats." Until Ronald Reagan. The Reagan era enriched the 1 percent at the top, who took home more than half of the fruits of growth. Meanwhile, the poor got poorer and the middle class lost ground.

Under George Bush, the tide itself ceased to rise. Economic growth under Bush was below that of any administration in fifty years. Yet the years of stagnation failed to serve any long-term purpose, such as the elimination of inflation risk or the restoration of strong productivity growth. They have instead created a trap that has paralyzed policy even as hardships and inequalities deepened.

The next Administration therefore faces a triple challenge. It must find a way to break out of the current slump and to sustain growth into the future. It must set in motion a program of structural reforms: public investment in infrastructure and education, and a health care system that will cover every American at a reasonable cost. Finally, the next government must turn to the deeper problems of poverty, low wages, rising inequality, and the splitting apart of America along economic and social lines. These are separate problems that cannot be solved entirely by economic growth.

James K. Galbraith, formerly Executive Director of the Congressional Joint Economic Committee, is Professor at the Lyndon B. Johnson School of Public Affairs at the University of Texas at Austin. Michael Mandler is Assistant Professor of Economics at Harvard University.

What We Should Have Learned from the Recession

TIGHT POLICY CAUSED THE RECESSION IN 1990, just as it had done in 1970, 1974, 1980, and 1981. In each of these cases, policymakers felt that circumstances had produced, or threatened to produce, an unacceptably high rate of inflation. In each case, tight fiscal and especially tight monetary measures were imposed in a deliberate effort to slow economic growth and to get the inflation rate down.

The most recent episode differs only slightly. First, though it was rising after 1987, the inflation rate by 1990 was still much lower than it had been in previous episodes. Second, the Federal Reserve intervened only gradually this time, slowly strangling the economic expansion from 1989 forward. It did not wait, as it had in the past, to declare a crisis and move in dramatic fashion.

Third, and most important, this episode was the one that was not supposed to happen. According to conservative doctrine, Paul Volcker and Ronald Reagan were supposed to have laid the framework for a stable expansion that would not be inflationary and that would therefore not ever require another strangulation. Slow and steady monetary policy would wring out inflation, preparing the way for stable and sustained growth. The deep recession of 1981–82 was deemed necessary, some conceded, to establish that the Federal Reserve was indeed committed to monetary restraint. Unemployment and the loss of output were the prices that had to be paid. But only once.

For a while, and particularly through the mid-1980s, when the American economy recovered strongly and with low inflation, it appeared that the modern conservatives had provided a powerful, safe, and effective formula for noninflationary economic growth. But two pieces of troubling evidence contradicted this view.

The first overlooked fact was the dog that didn't bark: the absence in the 1980s of a significant oil price shock. This was partly luck, in consequence of which the 1980s escaped the destabilizing experiences of 1973 and 1979.

The second overlooked fact was the role played by the high dollar and cheap imports in keeping inflation down. Driven by tight money and big deficits, the high dollar held down inflation mainly through the harshly corrosive effects of cheap import prices and cheap foreign labor costs. In the lower reaches of the industrial system, among the textile workers and producers of toys, sporting goods, watches, jewelry, and similar products, wages were compressed by the rapid rise of extreme low-wage competition. In export-competitive heavy industries such as industrial machinery and construction and farm equipment, markets collapsed, bankruptcies soared, and workers who had been America's wage leaders came under equally intense pressure.

These phenomena tell a radically different story of what really happened to inflation. Part of the 1980s' price stability was just luck. Insofar as government policy can take credit, the key features were the direct effects of deep recession and unemployment, followed by the indirect effects of huge trade deficits. Together these forces put a double vise on the wages of American production workers—good for as long as luck and the high dollar held.

If so, the Volcker-Greenspan monetary policies were never a sustainable solution to America's inflation problem. Ultimately, a devaluation of the dollar would be needed to stanch the growing trade deficit. But that would relieve, at least in part, the anti-inflation pressure. Higher costs and prices would follow—unless rising unemployment staved them off. And so a move toward trade balance necessarily entailed a choice: higher inflation or yet another recession, deliberately imposed.

A move toward inflation began with dollar devaluation in the mid-1980s. Other channels also contributed, especially the unchecked rise of health care costs. The inflation rate began to rise—quite slowly, but by enough to convince Alan Greenspan that the economic growth rate had to come down. A 35 percent jump in fuel prices in 1990 reinforced the sense of danger, although by that time the policy choice had already been made. A full-blown inflation crisis would not erupt; tight policies would prevent it. And the recession came.

The recession itself posed some tough new policy problems. The evident object was to knock down the inflation rate, but then to have the recession end in a smart recovery leading up to the election. But the usual policy instruments for this purpose were impaired. The size of the budget deficit, which was already soaring under the influence of the savings and loan bailout, seemed to preclude the decisive tax cutting that had so availed Ronald Reagan in 1983–84. The volume of private debts accumulated in the 1980s introduced the risk of a full-scale credit crunch and debt deflation, and raised doubts whether an easier monetary policy would work as it had in the past.

After a series of small interest-rate reductions that did not work, a recovery strategy finally crystallized. Just before Christmas 1991, Alan Greenspan delivered a full-point cut in the discount rate. In January 1992, Bush ordered income-tax withholding rates slashed, thereby adding to income growth in 1992 much of the fiscal stimulus normally required to end a recession. The administration launched into the usual election-year acceleration of domestic capital spending projects, and interposed no objections when Congress acted to delay proposed military spending cuts. By midyear, economic growth had resumed, though very slowly—much more slowly than policymakers had hoped for.

Even if recovery continues, how strong and durable will it be? Bush's tax stimulus will be neutralized in 1993 by the offsetting reduction of tax refunds on 1992 tax liabilities. Spending projects accelerated to 1992 will reduce spending in 1993. Delayed military cuts may also then take effect. Debt burdens remain heavy in the household sector. Finally, while short-term interest rates are low, the future course of monetary policy remains uncertain. For all these reasons, the future of the recovery remains a matter of doubt.

Breaking Out of Stagnation

MANY OBSERVERS WRITE AS IF ECONOMIC growth will resume in 1993 at a 3 percent rate or better whether policy acts or not. But the present evidence does not support this view. Rather, continued economic stagnation may well confront the next Administration, and may well be its first and most urgent economic policy challenge.

How can policy make recovery happen? First, a new President can act directly to create new jobs. The fastest and most efficient way to do this would be to follow the recommendations made by one hundred prominent economists in March 1992 and enact an emergency program of capital grants to states, cities, and towns. Such new spending would create jobs immediately, by forestalling budget and investment cuts already in prospect. Because it would be one-time and therefore self-limiting, this program is the ideal catalyst to pull the economy out of recession, and would not have long-term effects on the federal budget deficit.

Next, a tax cut should be considered. Of the proposals made so far, conversion of the personal exemption for children to a refundable credit is the most attractive, because it channels relief most effectively to middle-class and lower-income families. But this measure would be costly, and it would be permanent. Any program of permanent tax relief runs the risk of generating too much consumer demand, and too much import demand, at a later stage of the recovery. It is therefore imperative that such relief be counterbalanced by higher taxes on the wealthy—those who received so much tax relief in the past twelve years, as Robert McIntyre documents. Such progressive taxes should be enacted at the outset to establish their credibility, but the effective dates can be phased in, so that net stimulus is large at first but declines as the recovery proceeds.

Second, the new Administration needs to plan a recovery with balanced trade. Exports can provide the continuing stimulus that sustained economic growth will require. Recovery from the recession inevitably will increase import demand; only strong and deliberate policies can assure that exports also expand in order to avoid the trade deficit from exploding, as it did in the Reagan boom. To keep the dollar competitive, we need low interest rates both short- and long-term, and a new monetary policy that will get interest rates down and keep them down. As discussed more extensively in James Galbraith's later chapter, the Federal Reserve should send a clear signal of its intent to maintain stable and low short-term interest rates, so that long-term interest rates will fall. To reinforce this signal, the Treasury should cease the issue of long-term bonds until rates have fallen, and the Federal Reserve should use its open-market powers to buy back some of the high-yield issues that are outstanding.

We have had, and could again have, important new markets in the developing countries. But these now remain blocked, in part by the continuing debt crisis. The United States needs to get its hemispheric house in order. This means settling the remaining Latin debt on better terms than previously agreed, and it means creating new channels for development finance and for expanded trade within the Americas. Equally, the opportunities in Eastern Europe, in Russia, and in the other successor states to the Soviet Union are enormous. But they will not be and cannot be realized without planning and money. As a first step, the next President should appoint energetic advocates of global economic diplomacy in the top ranks of the State and Treasury departments, people who share Walter Russell Mead's thesis that global economic growth must be our main international objective.

The United States neither needs nor would benefit from a return to strict budget balance—not now, not in five years or even in ten. But the Federal Government does need to be on a course of financial stability in the long run, to assure sustained low interest rates and balanced trade. For this purpose, policy should bring the rate of growth of the national debt below the growth rate of the nominal Gross Domestic Product. For this objective, additional reductions, especially in unneeded military spending, may eventually be required. And if the economy grows too rapidly under the proposed program, even more aggressive direct reduction of the fiscal deficit will be necessary.

Public Investment and Health Care Reform

THE 1992 PRESIDENTIAL CAMPAIGN TURNED LARGELY around programs for long-term structural reform of the economy. Progressives coalesced around a program with three major elements: public investment, education, and reform of the health care system.

Public investment expenditures—in roads, bridges, mass transit, water and transport, communications systems, and environmental controls—are among the largest casualties of the Reagan-Bush era. The results are apparent around us, in decrepit highways, clogged airports, and dirty water and air. Jeff Faux and Robert Kuttner later show how increased investment in these areas will bring direct consumption benefits to American consumers and lower costs to American businesses. Research also suggests that there is no conflict between such projects and private investment; new public investments will stimulate, not depress, private investments.

Education reforms are similar. Primary and secondary public schools can and should be brought up to the highest world standards. A program that makes higher education accessible to all who qualify will help propel our work force into the next century. And some of the benefit of better education accrues to all Americans, directly and indirectly, in the fuller enjoyment of life.

Health care reform is an economic and a social issue. At present more than 10 percent of national income goes to health care, yet tens of millions of people—who work part-time, for small businesses, or who are unemployed—are not covered. Runaway health care costs are a drag on the competitiveness of American products, while the threat of losing coverage deters workers from seeking new jobs or from returning to school. Universal health care coverage with cost controls can powerfully improve economic efficiency and performance.

Large increases in education and infrastructure investment can be paid for out of reductions in unneeded military expenditure—John Steinbruner argues that the shift could total $211 billion over five years—although the planning for this transition is so far very underdeveloped. An advanced infrastructure program should be designed to take advantage of the technological and engineering talents that will be released from the national security sector. But all this requires a deep federal commitment to steer the conversion process, which, as John Tepper Marlin shows, has been absent in recent administrations.

The Squeeze on Wages: A Critical but Neglected Issue

IN THE 1980s, REAL WAGES REMAINED ROUGHLY constant on average. But a split developed in the wage structure: Those of the most skilled workers went up, while the wages of the less skilled went down. For example, while the weekly wage of a young male college graduate rose almost 11 percent, the weekly wage earned by a newly employed high school graduate fell by more than 15 percent.[1]

The problem of declining wages for the poor and much of the middle class is deep-seated, but it has taken on a new dimension in the past ten years. Ever since 1950, the manufacturing sector as a proportion of national output has not been growing. Continued productivity growth for forty years has therefore had the consequence of decreasing the demand for industrial labor, putting pressure on the relative wages of the less skilled. This is roughly parallel to the effect that that the mechanization of agriculture had on the farm population in the 1920s and 1930s.

The problem became a crisis in the early 1980s, when the high dollar wrecked exports and fostered rapid growth in manufactured imports from low-wage countries. Wages and employment in the low-skilled, labor-intensive branches of American manufacturing were sharply undercut, and over half a million well-paid jobs in heavy industry disappeared. And many millions of workers who kept their jobs found their wages falling under the pressures of the new competition.

In this harsh new environment, the link between falling wages and rising poverty has become direct. While every recession brings a rise in poverty, during most of the post–World War II period the recoveries that followed brought the poverty rate back down. In the 1980s, however, official and unofficial poverty rates at the peak of the expansion were *above* the poverty rate of the recession years of the 1970s.

The sharp falloff at the lower end of the wage scale is at the heart of our most pressing social problems. Many lower-income working families, who were always struggling, are now poor. For many poor families, the fall of wages means that work is not a clear route up from poverty even when full-time work can be found.

Solutions will not come easily. Structural change will not be reversed, and the United States cannot retreat from the global economy. Increases in productivity, however valuable for other reasons, do not create new jobs and do not address the problem of an increasingly divided income distribution.

As a first step, we favor a modest and gradual increase, and then indexation, of the minimum wage. This measure will raise the wages of the working poor in the service sector, at only minor costs to employment and trade. Equally important, this step will send a signal of determination to put wage fairness back on the agenda.

In the larger economy, progress will come along two paths: New sources of employment must develop, and the labor force must acquire new and greater skills. Robert Kuttner describes how a new social contract in the workplace, to provide labor with more security, skills, and flexibility, can help alleviate our low-wage, low-skill problem.

The promotion of new manufacturing industries provides a source of new jobs, both in those industries directly and in service industries that grow up around them. The measures already discussed, to promote exports and assure trade competitiveness of industry, are the single most effective way to create new high-wage employment. But they are not the only way. Historically, the Federal Government has fostered many of the industries with the best wage and trade performance—aerospace, communications, electronics, and chemicals—through regulation, directed purchases, subsidy, and protection. The military has often been the key element here, and its role cannot be allowed to disappear without a civilian replacement.

In the case of industries whose existence is threatened by trade, technological transformation may help maintain the level of manufacturing employment—as was the case of cotton textile production in the early 1970s. The recent revival of American motorcycle production demonstrates that industries need not follow irreversibly the path of decline, and that limited trade protection is not always harmful. The government does need, and does not now have, a systematic capability to seek and implement policies of industrial transformation where the opportunities exist.

Government regulations, far from being a hindrance to the progressive forces within industry, seem in fact to have often played a constructive role in establishing technological standards, maintaining reputations for purity and quality, and otherwise promoting advanced industries. So though "regulation" is a four-letter word politically, there may be a general rule that well-designed regulation can be technologically transforming, while repeatedly acceding to industry demands for regulatory relief—as in the case of automobiles—is a mistake.

The road to higher skills lies through education and training. A program to finance a college education for any qualified student through deferred repayment out of income or national service has the immense merit of democratizing access. To meet the needs on the supply side, the capacity of the state university systems, currently suffering acute financial crises, will have to be expanded.

To protect workers who are already working, training and retraining are part, but only part, of the answer. Training can usefully advance the careers of workers who receive training, but it cannot carry alone the burden of transforming uncompetitive industries into competitive ones, for the critical variable in many cases is not education and not skills but simply wages. Most American workers are as hardworking and productive as they ever were, but they cannot offset foreign wages that are a small fraction of their own. It is not logical to believe that better training can offset a tenfold wage gap for jobs that do not require advanced skills to begin with.

Where the opportunity for renewal is not present, sensible transition policies will be needed. Besides training, a good transition policy means retirement incomes, new jobs, and community redevelopment and reconstruction.

In such cases, it is less costly and more humanly decent to acknowledge the inevitable. Federal policies should provide adjustment assistance or early retirement to workers whose jobs are lost to trade. We should particularly recognize that older workers in our garment trades, overwhelmingly female, heavily poor, and undereducated, with relative wages falling in the past decade, are not going to move to Silicon Valley. Nor should they; we should as a matter of public policy treat them to an honorable retirement and give them a break.

The same is not true of younger workers, whose lives lie ahead. For these younger workers especially, jobs will be replaced, if often at lower wages. But other major costs occur in the decline of communities, in the lost value of housing, in the decay of infrastructure, in the forced migrations that follow—and these are not recuperated. This is what makes it so difficult for families and neighborhoods trapped in declining regions to adjust and recover. So urgent measures also include steps to stabilize communities and to maintain roads and schools so that our cities and towns can be reborn. We have successful experience with this sort of redevelopment in our Lowells and Pittsburghs, models to study and to learn from.

In all of these matters, common sense dictates prudent assistance to those displaced by trade and technological change. Assistance should be temporary where workers have long productive lives in front of them, and more permanent where they do not. The final principle should be: People who work full-time, or who have worked full-time for a lifetime, should not be poor.

A Program for Fairness and Growth

THE RECESSION, THE WEAK RECOVERY, AND their consequences have been fundamental symptoms of the state of economic policy under Reagan and Bush. The compelling policy issues facing us now are (1) how to restore and sustain growth; (2) how to reestablish competitiveness and productivity; and (3) how to keep American society from splitting apart along economic lines.

This section of *Changing America* presents a program for recovery with balanced trade, for good jobs at decent wages, and for a more fair economy. It has three main elements:

• A macroeconomic agenda, starting with public capital investment and some tax relief, but continuing primarily on the strength of growth in exports, through changes in the exchange rate and growth and reform in the world economy as a whole. With a program for phased expansion, and a timely shift once recovery is under way from reliance on new spending and low interest rates to deficit reduction, the U.S. economy can again grow solidly and for a long time.

• A public investment agenda, centered on major increases in long-term public capital formation and major reforms in the education system and in the delivery of health care.

• A fairness agenda aimed at easing transitions for people and communities and in narrowing the gap between the rich and everyone else. In a society with a more equal wage structure and a better safety net, changes will come more readily and be accepted more easily, because people will have less to fear.

A society "free from fear" has been a progressive ideal for six decades, and it is now surely time to take decisive steps in that direction.

NOTE

1. Lawrence F. Katz and Kevin M. Murphy, "Changes in Relative Wages: 1963–1987: Supply and Demand Factors," *Quarterly Journal of Economics* (February 1992): 35–78. The change is from 1979 to 1987.

Department of the Treasury

TAX POLICY

ROBERT S. McINTYRE

Summary

THE IRRESPONSIBLE SUPPLY-SIDE TAX POLICIES of the late 1970s and early 1980s put our government and our nation into a deep hole. Over the past fifteen years, incomes have stagnated or fallen for most family income groups, while their federal taxes have risen. Yet mainly because of huge tax cuts granted to the very richest Americans, annual federal budget deficits have soared and our accumulated national debt has more than doubled as a share of our national output.

In 1992, the average income of the richest 1 percent of the population will be $567,000—almost twice what it was in 1977 (in constant dollars). But the members of this elite group will pay $71 billion less in 1992 taxes than they would owe had the federal tax code remained as progressive as it was before the supply-side tax shift. Adding the interest on the national debt built up to pay for previous high-income tax reductions brings the current annual cost of the rich's tax cut to $137 billion. That's more than enough to explain the increase in the current structural budget deficit since Ronald Reagan first took office as president.

We will not solve our problems by repeating the mistakes of the past. In particular, our leaders should reject special-interest pleas to reenact discredited tax loopholes for capital gains or business investment. The record is clear that such costly tax breaks lead only to bigger deficits, economic distortions, and tax shelters, not growth and jobs.

Nor should we impose a regressive new national sales tax that would soak the poor and the middle class while leaving the wealthy almost unscathed. To be sure, the whole purpose of deficit reduction is to shift our resources away from spending and toward investment, both public and private. But the real issue is: *Whose* consumption should be reduced? Those

Robert S. McIntyre is director of Citizens for Tax Justice in Washington, D.C.

who push for sales taxes want to curb spending by poor and middle-income families. Those who push for progressive tax changes want to curb consumption by the wealthy. That, in a nutshell, is the choice that our nation faces.

Rather than adding to the burdens of ordinary American families, our tax policy goals for the 1990s should be to take back the Reagan-era tax cuts for the wealthy and put an end to the borrow-and-squander policies that characterized the past decade.

We should build on the progress toward tax fairness and economic common sense reflected in the path-breaking 1986 Tax Reform Act. By shutting down remaining tax shelters and loopholes and by increasing the top personal and corporate tax rates, we can promote fairness and achieve real efficiency gains for the economy—all while raising the revenues we need to cut the deficit and pay for needed government programs. This chapter describes eighteen specific reforms a new Administration could pursue in 1993, including:

- Increase the top tax rate on corporations and the best-off 1 percent of individuals to 36 percent; impose a 10 percent surtax on tax attributable to individual taxable income above $500,000 and corporate taxable income above $1 million; and add an additional 10 percent surtax on personal income above $1 million; five-year revenue gain: $144 billion.
- Reform the taxation of multinational companies; five-year revenue gain: $23 billion.
- End tax breaks for mergers and acquisitions; five-year revenue gain: $9 billion.
- Close loopholes in the Alternative Minimum Tax and raise the minimum tax rate on otherwise low-tax wealthy people and profitable companies; five-year revenue gain: $22 billion.

How Supply-Side Tax Policies Redistributed Income Upward

ADAM SMITH WAS THE APOSTLE OF MODERN CAPITALISM, but he mistrusted capitalists. "The interest of the producer ought to be attended to only so far as it may be necessary for promoting that of the consumer," Smith wrote in 1776. "People of the same trade seldom meet together, even for merriment and diversion, but the conversation ends in a conspiracy against the public." But in 1981, America's tax policy was taken over by a "supply-side" cabal whose members, despite their Adam Smith neckties, loved capitalists but had little faith in capitalism.

The result was the infamous 1981 Reagan Tax Act. At the time, its backers touted the act's radically lower tax rates on the rich and its unprecedented array of new tax loopholes and corporate tax breaks as the sure cure for lassitude by wealthy individuals and lackluster industrial performance. The supply-siders promised that when America's richest people got a break, everyone else would benefit as well. Incomes, it was said, would rise for all Americans. Our international competitiveness and a positive trade balance would be assured. Savings and investment would surge. Most strikingly, the Reagan administration predicted that its tax cuts would actually generate huge new revenues for the Treasury—enough to balance the federal budget and pay for an enormous increase in defense spending at the same time.

In truth, of course, exactly the opposite occurred. Rather than rising, incomes stagnated or fell for most family income groups. America's national savings rate hit record lows. The trade deficit ballooned to previously unheard-of levels. And far from a balanced budget, federal budget deficits soared almost beyond comprehension.

The supply-side program actually came in two installments: the 1981 Tax Act and its precursor, the 1978 capital gains tax cut (passed over the objection of President Jimmy Carter). Since 1977 (the year before the supply-side tax shift began), the median family income has been virtually stagnant. Incomes for the bottom 40 percent actually fell (by more than 10 percent for the lowest fifth). Even families in the fourth highest 20 percent of the income scale saw less than 0.5 percent annual increase in their average income.

"How can this be?" some may ask. "Didn't the economy grow over that period?" Yes, it did, albeit modestly by historical standards. But most of the benefits of that growth were concentrated on a tiny sliver of the population: the richest 1 percent. That elite group's inflation-adjusted average income has skyrocketed from $306,000 in 1977 to an estimated $567,000 in 1992—a jump of 85 percent.

Adam Smith maintained that a chief goal of taxation should be "to remedy inequality of riches as much as possible by relieving the poor and burdening the rich." But the supply-siders believed just the opposite. Although the 1990 deficit reduction act finally rolled back the remaining supply-side tax increases on the poorest Americans, three of four families—all but the poorest fifth and the richest 5 percent—now pay more in federal taxes than they would owe if the tax code had remained as progressive as it was in 1977.

The very rich, however, pay 29 percent less of their incomes in taxes than they would owe had the tax code remained as progressive as it was before the supply-side tax shift, for an average tax cut of $66,000 each in 1992. As a result, the average after-tax income of the wealthiest families grew even faster than their pretax income, vaulting by 105 percent from 1977 to 1992. The top 1 percent's *share* of total after-tax income rose by 81 percent. Perhaps most astonishing, 55 percent of the total growth in per-family after-tax income from 1977 to 1992 went to the richest 1 percent of the population. (See the tables at the end of this chapter.)

The $66,000 average tax cut for the top 1 percent translates into a total of $71 billion in lost revenues for the federal Treasury in 1992 alone. Adding the interest on the national debt built up to pay for the high-income tax reductions over the 1980s brings the current annual cost of the rich's supply-side tax bonanza to a total of $137 billion. That's more than enough to explain why, despite huge cuts in non-Social Security federal domestic programs, the structural annual budget deficit is $104 billion bigger (in GDP-adjusted dollars) in 1992 than it was when Ronald Reagan first took office.

To be sure, not all tax legislation in the past decade was destructive. On the contrary, almost every tax act after 1981, most notably the 1986 Tax Reform Act, moved in the direction of restoring fairness and fiscal responsibility.[1] But much more remains to be accomplished.

False Path 1: Another Round of Loopholes?

AT LEAST SINCE THE EARLY SIXTIES, every ten years or so, our politicians have come up with the bright idea that the government ought to help businesses and rich people decide how to invest. Then within a half decade or so, horror stories have surfaced about no-tax corporations or high-income tax avoiders, and Congress has done an about-face.

The Reagan era was the apotheosis of this cycle, starting with the loophole-laden 1981 Tax Act (and its soulmate, the 1978 capital gains tax cut) and finishing with the monumental 1986 Tax Reform Act. But the same sequence can be seen in prior decades. Nixon's 1971 Revenue Act was a potpourri of corporate "incentives"; the 1976 Tax Reform Act mainly went the other way. John F. Kennedy's 1962 tax bill, although reformist in most respects, enacted the investment tax credit; the 1969 Tax Reform Act eliminated the credit and closed other loopholes, too.

Now we again hear calls from those who want to lead us down the supply-side, loophole path again. (In fact, that's the entire Bush economic program.) This forces us once again to address a basic question: Are tax breaks for particular kinds of investments good for the economy? Does a supposed tension between tax equity and economic growth condemn us to lurch continually from focusing on one to concentrating on the other? No. Tax fairness and sound economic policy go hand in hand.

Let's start with capital gains. George Bush said that a capital gains tax cut will create "jobs, jobs, jobs" and will pull the economy out of recession. But look at what happened when capital gains taxes were cut in the past.

The 1978 Revenue Act cut the maximum capital gains tax rate from 39 percent to 28 percent. Over the twelve months prior to enactment of that change, the real gross domestic product grew by 5.8 percent. But after the 1978 capital gains tax cut was approved, the economy faltered. In fact, the GDP dropped by 1 percent over the next year and a half. The annual growth rate for the two years following the 1978 capital gains tax cut was only 0.3 percent; this was 5.5 percentage points lower than the growth rate for the year prior to the cut. Unemployment rose from 5.8 percent at the time of the tax cut to 7.3 percent two years later.

August 1981 saw another cut in the capital gains tax, this time lowering the top rate to 20 percent. Over the twelve preceding months, the economy had grown by 3.5 percent, but in the twelve subsequent months the GDP *fell* by 2.8 percent. In the two years after the 1981 capital gains tax cut was enacted, the annual growth rate was only 1 percent, which was 2.5 percentage points below the growth rate for the year prior to the cut. The unemployment rate ballooned from 7.3 percent to 9.3 percent.

Controverting supply-side assertions, tax laws that *increased* the capital gains tax typically have been followed by improved economic growth. After the 1976 Tax Reform Act was enacted, for example, the economy's growth rate jumped from 3.9 percent in the preceding twelve months to 5.2 percent over the next two years. Likewise, following enactment of the 1986 Tax Reform Act, the growth rate rose from 2.2 percent in the previous year to 3.8 percent over the next two years. Likewise, the jobless rate fell notably after the 1976 and 1986 capital gains tax hikes were enacted.

Does this mean that capital gains tax cuts cause recessions? Not exactly, although you can make a good case that the loose fiscal policies—big deficits—that capital gains tax cuts have usually abetted have led to tight money actions by the Federal Reserve Board that have precipitated economic downturns. Jimmy Carter has said that he wishes he had vetoed the 1978 tax bill because it fueled inflation and led to Paul Volcker's monetary crackdown.

The checkered history of the investment tax credit is also instructive. Originally adopted in 1962, it was beefed up in 1964, temporarily suspended in late 1966, brought back in early 1967, repealed in 1969, reenacted in

1971, increased in 1975 and 1978, expanded again in 1981, reduced in 1982, and repealed again in 1986. A 1978 analysis of the 1962–76 experience by economists Lawrence Summers and Alan Auerbach was almost totally negative. They found that the credit didn't increase the total amount of business investment but instead changed the composition and timing of investments— away from what the marketplace otherwise would have demanded. After sixteen years, they said, the investment tax credit had led to economic distortions, higher interest rates, more than half a million fewer housing units, fewer jobs, heightened inflation, and a general "undesirable effect on the economy."[2]

When Congress repealed the investment tax credit in 1986, it wasn't just tax fairness that was on its collective mind.[3] It also was thinking about economics. "As the world economies become increasingly competitive, it is most important that investment in our capital stock be determined by market forces rather than by tax considerations," said the official explanation of the 1986 Tax Reform Act. The House Ways and Means Committee report on the 1986 tax bill focused on the failure of the various tax breaks to deliver as promised: "Proponents of massive tax benefits for depreciable property have theorized that these benefits would stimulate investment in such property, which in turn would pull the entire economy into more rapid growth. The committee perceives that nothing of this kind has happened."

Indeed, the record of investment tax incentives in the first half of the 1980s was a typically sorry one. We didn't get more investment, we just got more tax shelters. From 1981 to 1986, total real business investment grew by only 1.9 percent a year, and far too much of that investment went into excessive, tax-motivated commercial office construction—leading to the "see-through office buildings" phenomenon all across the nation. Investment in industrial factories and equipment actually *fell* over that period, while there was a wave of corporate mergers and acquisitions. Companies that got the biggest corporate tax breaks actually had the poorest record when it came to investment growth and job creation (but they sharply increased dividends and executive pay). Likewise, 1981's sharp reduction in the top personal tax rate on capital income, hugely expanded tax shelter opportunities, and new gimmicks such as expanded individual retirement accounts did not produce the promised surge in personal savings. Instead, savings were merely shifted into tax-favored areas, while the beneficiaries of the tax breaks had more money to spend. The personal savings rate fell to record lows in the mid-eighties, while reported tax-shelter "losses" skyrocketed to $149 billion by 1986.

But after many of the loopholes were closed in 1986, money flowed out of tax shelters and business investment rebounded. Led by a resurgence in industrial investment, real business capital spending grew by 2.7 percent a year from 1986 to 1989—42 percent faster than the 1981–86 growth rate. In other words, tax reform worked exactly as advertised.

Some of the more recent proposals for bringing back investment tax breaks are purported to be more sophisticated than past efforts. Senator Dale Bumpers (D.–Ark.), for example, wants to target lucrative capital gains tax breaks to investments that are considered particularly fraught with danger. The underlying premise—that we want the wealthy to invest in projects that otherwise make the very *least* business sense—is hard to fathom.

Others call for an "incremental" investment tax credit for business equipment purchases. The idea is that companies would get the credit only if they invested more than they used to. This might sound good at first—after all, why do we want to reward investments that would have been undertaken anyway?—but the "incremental" credit actually exacerbates some of the worst economic problems of the investment credit in general. First of all, credits would be largest during strong growth periods when the economy and, therefore, business investment are expanding. But in economic downturns, when investment contracts, the credit would go way down. Thus the incremental credit would be what economists call "procyclical," too big and too costly when it's not needed, and too small when it might provide a fiscal stimulus.

An incremental credit would encourage all kinds of leasing deals, corporate reorganizations, and other tax-avoidance schemes as companies tried to maximize their advantages by lowering the base against which "new" investment is measured. It also would produce some crazy advantages for carefully timing investments. A business that invested $25 million a year for four years would get no tax break. But one that invested nothing for three years and then $100 million in the fourth year would get a big credit. It's hard to tell how much this would affect actual business behavior, but it clearly doesn't make any sense to favor sporadic investment patterns over steady ones.

The truth is that paying people and corporations to make investments that otherwise make no business sense is *not* a rational policy. Supply-side/trickle-down economics was a colossal flop. We don't need to repeat those mistakes again in the 1990s.

False Path 2: A National Sales Tax?

THERE ALSO ARE THOSE WHO RECOMMEND big increases in federal excise taxes or adoption of a new European-style national sales tax (or "value-added tax") as the solution to our government's revenue problem. They argue that we need tax policies that will shift our priorities more toward investment and less toward current consumption. Of course—that's the whole point of reducing the budget deficit.[4] But virtually all tax increases—and many kinds of budget cuts, for that matter—will have that effect. The real issue is: *Whose* consumption should be reduced?

Do we want to make it a bit more difficult for wealthy people to buy their second Mercedes-Benz, or do we want to put Plymouths and Chevrolets out of reach for many ordinary American families? Do we want to make it even harder for first-time homebuyers to achieve their dreams, or do we want to put a crimp in the style of people who buy fifty-thousand-square-foot mansions?

The hard truth is that those who push for sales and excise taxes want to curb spending by poor and middle-income families. Those who push for progressive tax changes want to curb consumption by the wealthy. When all is said and done, that is the choice our nation faces.

Make no mistake about it: Sales and excise taxes are inherently regressive. Table 5 shows the distributional impact of a 5 percent national sales tax, modeled after the value-added taxes in place in most European countries and which are roughly similar to the sales taxes in most American states. Even with the exceptions these countries provide for many food items, some clothing, health care and certain medicines, and most housing, the poor would pay five times more of their income in added sales tax than the rich would. The tax would cost middle-income families close to three times as much of their earnings, proportionally, as the rich.

Existing federal excise taxes are even more regressive than a national sales tax. Table 6 shows the impact of doubling federal excise taxes on gasoline, tobacco, and alcoholic beverages. As can be seen, the burdens as a share of income would be far higher on poor and middle-income families than they would be on wealthy people.

Since the mid-sixties, the rest of the industrialized world has moved sharply away from consumption taxes and toward higher corporate income taxes as a principal source of government revenues. In the United States, however, the trend away from consumption taxes has been far less pronounced and far from rising; U.S. corporate income taxes have *fallen* dramatically.[5] The difference is most striking between the United States and Japan. In 1965, Japan relied more on consumption taxes than did the United States, and corporate income taxes were about equal shares of the GDP in both countries. But by 1989, Japan's consumption taxes had fallen well below those in the United States, while Japanese corporate income taxes had risen to almost *triple* those in the United States as a share of GDP. If we want guidance from abroad about what to tax, then increased reliance on consumption taxes is exactly the opposite of the lesson we should learn.

Principles and Proposals for Progressive Tax Change

FORTUNATELY, REPEATING THE LOOPHOLE-BASED tax policy mistakes of the past or adopting regressive new consumption taxes are not the only options open to us. Instead, we can and should continue in the spirit of the 1986 income tax reforms, by closing unwarranted loopholes that remain in the law and by establishing income tax rates sufficient both to pay for the cost of government and to stem the rise in inequality in our country. Rather than adding to the burdens of ordinary American families, we can address the deficit by reversing tax cuts previously granted to the very richest people—those who can most afford to pay. Three principles should apply:

PRINCIPLE 1: TAKE BACK TAX GIVEAWAYS TO THE RICHEST 1 PERCENT
Since 1977, supply-side tax cuts for the richest 1 percent of the population have added more than $1 trillion to the national debt. In 1992 alone, the cost of those tax cuts will be almost $140 billion. After a decade and a half of tax cuts for the very wealthy, it's only fair to ask more from those whose after-tax incomes have more than doubled over the past fifteen years.

PRINCIPLE 2: PROTECT MIDDLE- AND LOW-INCOME FAMILIES
After-tax incomes for middle- and low-income families have been stagnant or declining since the late 1970s. Why should people who didn't benefit from the borrow-and-squander eighties foot the deficit bill?

PRINCIPLE 3: PLUG TAX LOOPHOLES
Despite several tax reform acts since 1981, business and investment tax breaks are expected to cost the Treasury $291 billion in corporate taxes and $285 billion in personal income taxes from fiscal 1992 to fiscal 1996. By shutting down remaining tax shelters and loopholes and by increasing the top personal and corporate tax rates, we can promote fairness and achieve real efficiency gains for the economy—all while raising the revenues we need to cut the deficit and pay for needed government programs.

Here are eighteen approaches a new Administration could adopt:

1. *Increase the top tax rate on the best-off 1 percent to 36 percent.* Counting employee payroll taxes (and a 1990-enacted offset for itemized

deductions), the marginal tax rate on wages now goes as high as 37 percent. But those at the top of the income scale face a marginal tax rate of only 32 percent on their wages, interest, and dividends, and only 28.8 percent on their capital gains (including the itemized-deduction offset).

Raising the top marginal tax rate to 36 percent would correct this anomaly. It would affect only the best-off 1 percent, generally people with a total annual income greater than $200,000. (The new tax bracket would kick in at $140,000 in taxable income for joint returns.) Hardly a radical move, it is the same proposal approved by Congress in March 1992 but vetoed by President Bush. *Five-year revenue gain: $53 billion.*

2. *Impose a 10 percent surtax on tax attributable to taxable income above $500,000, and an additional 10 percent surtax above $1 million.* This is an expanded version of the "millionaires' surtax" approved by Congress in March 1992 but vetoed by the President. Together with the rate increase, the surtax would extend progressivity and bring the top tax rate on the very, very rich to a maximum of about 43.5 percent. *Five-year revenue gain: $25 billion.*

3. *Increase the top corporate income tax rate to 36 percent and add a 10 percent surtax* on taxes attributable to corporate taxable income above $1 million, so that corporate rates will be comparable to the new individual rates. *Five-year revenue gain: $66 billion.*

4. *Tax capital gains the same as other income.* One of the greatest achievements of the 1986 Tax Reform Act was to tax capital gains at the same rates as wages, dividends, or other income. (Previously, capital gains had been 60 percent tax-exempt.) But in 1990, Congress reinstated a relatively small capital gains preference, capping the rate at 28 percent while putting the top regular income tax rate at 31 percent. This special break for capital gains should be repealed before it grows any larger. *Five-year revenue gain: $22 billion.*

5. *Tax capital gains on inherited property.* Currently, heirs can sell inherited property and pay no tax on gains that accrued prior to the time they inherit. Treasury analysts estimate that as much as two thirds of all capital gains escape taxation entirely due to this loophole—which will cost $27 billion in fiscal 1992 and close to $150 billion from fiscal 1992 to fiscal 1996. These built-up capital gains should be subject to tax at the time of inheritance. (Exceptions could be made for farms and closely held businesses by delaying the tax until inherited property is sold.) *Five-year revenue gain: $17 billion.*[6]

6. *Reform estate and gift taxes.* Estate and gift taxes (which only apply to the very largest estates) can often be avoided through trusts, partial-

interest gifts, and other complex arrangements. These kinds of tax-avoidance schemes should be curbed. *Five-year revenue gain: $8 billion.*

7. *Curb excessive depreciation write-offs.* Businesses write off the cost of their equipment considerably faster than it actually wears out. This loophole—expanded in the 1986 Tax Reform Act—has proven much more expensive than originally anticipated; it's now estimated to cost $144 billion from fiscal 1992 to fiscal 1996. Equipment "depreciation" write-offs should be scaled back to reflect better real wear and tear and obsolescence. *Five-year revenue gain: $24 billion.*

8. *End tax breaks for mergers and acquisitions.* The deductibility of corporate interest payments, even in the case of "junk bonds" and other types of debt that are more like stocks than real borrowing, helped fuel a wave of leveraged buyouts and other debt-for-stock transactions in the 1980s. From 1985 to 1990, more than $1 trillion in new corporate indebtedness was incurred, accompanied by $54 billion in corporate stock retirements— now costing the Federal Treasury some $20 billion to $30 billion a year in lost corporate taxes. The deals that were struck then cannot be undone, but strict curbs on interest deductions on debt used to finance acquisitions and other limitations on companies' ability to characterize equity as debt are needed to keep this problem from resurfacing and making the revenue hemorrhage even worse. In particular, interest on debt incurred to purchase stock (in excess of $5 million) should no longer be deductible, thereby stopping this perverse tax incentive for corporate debt.

In addition, many companies that made acquisitions in the eighties have taken extremely aggressive positions on their tax returns, in attempts to write off what they paid for "goodwill" and similar "intangible" assets. Billions of dollars in back taxes are at stake in litigation. Pending legislation would actually allow these deductions, which would reward past acquisitions and encourage future ones. If enacted, that law should be repealed. Instead, the law should be clarified to make crystal clear that *no* goodwill write-offs are allowed. *Five-year revenue gain: $9 billion.*

9. *Tax multinational corporations.* Multinational corporations, whether American- or foreign-owned, are supposed to pay taxes on the profits they earn in the United States. But our tax laws often fail miserably to achieve this goal. IRS data show that foreign-owned corporations doing business here typically pay far less in U.S. income taxes than do purely American firms with comparable sales and assets. At the same time, the loopholes that foreign companies use are also utilized by U.S.-owned multinationals, and even provide incentives for American companies to move plants and jobs overseas.

The problems in our taxation of multinational companies stem mainly from the complicated, almost unworkable approach we use to try to determine how much of a corporation's worldwide earnings relate to its U.S. activities. In essence, the IRS must try to scrutinize every movement of goods and services between a multinational company's domestic and foreign operations and attempt to assure that a fair, "arm's length" "transfer price" was assigned (on paper) to each transaction. But companies have a huge incentive to have their domestic operations pay too much or charge too little to their foreign operations for goods and services (for tax purposes only), thereby minimizing their U.S. taxable income. A May 1992 Congressional Budget Office report found that "[i]ncreasingly aggressive transfer pricing by . . . multinational corporations" may be one source of the shortfall in corporate tax payments in recent years compared to what was predicted in 1986.

We need to overhaul our rules governing international allocation of profits, to protect our tax base and our workers. The complex "transfer pricing" rules should be replaced with a much simpler formula approach, allocating profits based on the share of a company's worldwide sales, assets, and payroll in the United States. *Five-year revenue gain: $23 billion.*

10. *Limit meals and entertainment deductions to 50 percent.* Currently, 80 percent of business meals and entertainment are deductible—a subsidy that costs more than $10 billion a year. The percentage that can be deducted should be lowered to a maximum of 50 percent. *Five-year revenue gain: $16 billion.*

11. *Curb tax breaks for runaway plants.* Current tax rules allow companies to "defer" indefinitely U.S. taxes on unrepatriated income earned by foreign subsidiaries and allow companies to use foreign tax credits for taxes paid to nontax-haven countries to offset U.S. tax due on repatriated profits generated in a low- or no-tax foreign tax haven. These tax breaks, which encourage companies to move business activity overseas, should be disallowed, as provided in H.R. 2889. *Five-year revenue gain: $1 billion.*

12. *Curb oil and gas loopholes.* Oil and gas companies continue to be allowed to write off many of their capital costs immediately, and many can take deductions for "percentage depletion"—which has no connection with actual expenses. These special tax subsidies should be repealed. *Five-year revenue gain: $9 billion.*

13. *Tax foreigners' interest at 5 percent.* Interest earned by foreigners in the United States (on loans to American companies and the U.S. Government) was exempted from U.S. tax in 1984. Typically, this interest income is not reported to foreigners' home governments either. As a result, the

United States has become a major international tax haven. A 5 percent tax should be imposed on interest earned in the United States by foreigners. The tax could be waived if a foreign lender supplies the information necessary to report the interest income to the foreign home government. *Five-year revenue gain: $13 billion.*

14. *Curb farm tax shelters.* Unlike most other types of "tax shelter" losses, farm "losses" can often be deducted against nonfarm income, if a lenient "material participation" condition is met. Farm "losses" should not be allowed against unrelated income. *Five-year revenue gain: $7 billion.*

15. *Tax real estate "like-kind exchanges."* Currently, someone wishing to sell business real estate can put off paying capital gains taxes indefinitely by "exchanging" the property for other real estate. Tax deferral for these "like-kind exchanges" should be eliminated. (The change would not affect sales of personal residences.) *Five-year revenue gain: $2 billion.*

16. *End a real estate refinancing loophole.* Owners of business real estate can cash in their capital gains without tax by refinancing their properties. This is an enormous tax shelter that benefits wealthy real estate speculators. The rule should be that if real estate is refinanced for more than its original purchase price, the excess would be treated as a taxable event. (This would not apply to homes.) *Five-year revenue gain: $4 billion.*

17. *Conform book and tax accounting for securities inventories.* This was proposed by President Bush in 1992 and passed by Congress (but vetoed by the President). *Five-year revenue gain: $2 billion.*

18. *Reform the corporate and high-income Alternative Minimum Tax.* The Alternative Minimum Tax is supposed to assure that all companies and wealthy individuals pay some significant federal income tax. But there are a number of weaknesses in the AMT that should be corrected.

The AMT base should be broadened by eliminating deductions for interest payments to foreign lenders in tax havens, mortgage interest on second homes and on more than $200,000 in mortgage debt, and "company cars" (with minor exceptions). Executive fringe benefits should be subject to the AMT, and exceptions to the "at risk" antitax-shelter rules should be eliminated. And any of the reforms outlined earlier that are not dealt with in reforming the regular income tax should be adopted at least for AMT purposes.

In addition, the AMT rate should be increased from its current 20 percent on corporations and 24 percent on high-income individuals. The individual rate was originally set to be three quarters of the top regular personal income tax rate. In conjunction with increases in the regular tax rates, the minimum tax rates should be increased to 28 percent on individuals and 25 percent on corporations. *Five-year revenue gain: $76 billion.*

These eighteen suggested reforms are not intended to be exhaustive. But they illustrate that closing loopholes and taxing corporations and the wealthy at higher rates can raise the revenues we need to pay for government, and at the same time reduce economic distortions that sap productivity and long-term growth. Deficit reduction will indeed require sacrifice. But it should come primarily from those who benefited so greatly from the mistaken policies of the past.

TABLE 1.

Average Income Before and After Tax, 1977 and 1992
(in constant 1992 dollars, adjusted for changes in family size*)

Family Income Group	Pretax Incomes			After-tax Incomes		
	1977	1992	% Change	1977	1992	% Change
Lowest 20%	$9,216	$8,274	−10%	$8,356	$7,555	−10%
Second 20%	$20,445	$19,686	−4%	$17,288	$16,609	−4%
Middle 20%	$31,243	$31,973	+2%	$25,161	$25,705	+2%
Fourth 20%	$43,808	$46,909	+7%	$34,245	$36,452	+6%
Next 10%	$57,648	$64,542	+12%	$43,816	$48,707	+11%
Next 5%	$73,842	$85,835	+16%	$55,212	$63,317	+15%
Next 4%	$104,884	$132,036	+26%	$76,584	$96,217	+26%
Top 1%	$305,772	$566,674	+85%	$197,164	$403,402	+105%

Source: All figures are from the Congressional Budget Office, December 1991 and May 1992.

*The 1977 income figures were adjusted downward, using CBO data, to reflect the decline in average family size (in every income group) from 1977 to 1992.

TABLE 2.
Actual 1992 Federal Taxes Compared to
Taxes Under a Tax Code as Progressive as in 1977

Family Income Group	1992 Tax Rate	1992 Tax at 1977 Rate	% Change	Average $ Change	$ Change in billions	Change/ Income
Lowest 20%	8.7%	9.1%	−4%	$−33	$−0.7	−0.4%
Second 20%	15.6%	14.2%	+10%	+280	+6.0	+1.4%
Middle 20%	19.6%	18.8%	+4%	+247	+5.1	+0.8%
Fourth 20%	22.3%	21.8%	+2%	+208	+4.3	+0.4%
Next 10%	24.5%	24.4%	+1%	+112	+1.2	+0.2%
Next 5%	26.2%	25.9%	+1%	+315	+1.7	+0.4%
Next 4%	27.1%	28.2%	−4%	−1,473	−6.5	−1.1%
Top 1%	28.8%	40.5%	−29%	−66,130	−70.8	−11.7%

Source: Figures for 1992 are from the Congressional Budget Office, December 1991. Figures for 1992 taxes at 1977 progressivity are from Citizens for Tax Justice, June 1992.

TABLE 3.
Shares of Total Income Before and After Tax, 1977 and 1992

Family Income Group	Shares of Pretax Income			Shares of After-tax Income		
	1977	1992	% change	1977	1992	% change
Lowest 20%*	4.3%	2.7%	−38%	4.9%	3.1%	−38%
Second 20%	11.0%	9.3%	−15%	12.0%	10.2%	−15%
Middle 20%	16.2%	14.6%	−10%	16.9%	15.3%	−10%
Fourth 20%	22.7%	21.3%	−6%	22.9%	21.6%	−6%
Next 10%	15.7%	15.5%	−2%	15.5%	15.2%	−2%
Next 5%	10.1%	10.3%	+2%	9.7%	9.9%	+1%
Next 4%	11.7%	13.0%	+11%	11.1%	12.3%	+11%
Top 1%	8.3%	13.4%	+63%	6.9%	12.5%	+81%
Total	100.0%	100.0%	—	100.0%	100.0%	—

Source: All figures are from the Congressional Budget Office, December 1991 and May 1992. The 1977 income shares were adjusted to reflect changes in average family size (by income group) from 1977 to 1992.

*Includes families with incomes less than zero.

TABLE 4.
Shares of Total Growth in
Per-Family After-Tax Income,
1977–1992

Family Income Group	Growth Share
Lowest 20%*	−10%
Second 20%	−3%
Middle 20%	3%
Fourth 20%	11%
Next 10%	13%
Next 5%	11%
Next 4%	21%
Top 1%	55%
Total:	100%

Source: Based on data from the Congressional Budget Office, December 1991 and May 1992. The 1977 total incomes were adjusted to reflect reductions in average family sizes (by income group) from 1977 to 1992 and put in terms of the total 1992 number of families.

**Includes families with incomes less than zero.*

TABLE 5.
Effects of a 5% European-Style National Sales Tax in the United States as Shares of Income for Families of Four

Family Income Group	Tax/ Income
Lowest 20%	4.5%
Second 20%	3.2%
Middle 20%	2.6%
Fourth 20%	2.2%
Next 15%	1.9%
Next 4%	1.4%
Top 1%	0.9%

Source: Citizens for Tax Justice, 1991.

TABLE 6.
Doubling Federal Excise Taxes as Shares of Income for Families of Four

Family Income Group	Tax/ Income
Lowest 20%	2.3%
Second 20%	1.4%
Middle 20%	1.0%
Fourth 20%	0.8%
Next 15%	0.6%
Next 4%	0.4%
Top 1%	0.1%

Source: Citizens for Tax Justice, 1991.

NOTES

1. By the mid-eighties, even President Reagan had second thoughts about his earlier program. "I just didn't realize that things had gotten that far out of line," he reportedly told his Treasury Secretary after hearing about the outrageous level of corporate tax avoidance his 1981 tax changes had produced.

2. Summers, who went on to become a consultant to numerous corporations and is now chief economist for the World Bank, has since changed his opinion somewhat. Auerbach, now deputy chief of staff of the congressional Joint Committee on Taxation, generally sticks by his earlier views.

3. Well-publicized studies by Citizens for Tax Justice had shown that the investment credit had played a key role in the large number of large, profitable corporations that were able to escape all or almost all of their tax liability, year in and year out, in the first half of the 1980s.

4. Clearly, deficit reduction needs to be coordinated carefully with monetary policy to avoid making the cure worse than the disease. Without lower interest rates from the Federal Reserve Board as part of the deal, cuts in the budget deficit could easily lead to both reduced consumption and reduced investment. See the later chapter on Monetary Policy by James Galbraith.

5. In the 1960s, corporate taxes, at 3.8 percent of the GDP, amounted to 20.8 percent of total federal revenues. In the 1970s, corporate taxes were 2.7 percent of the GDP and 14.5 perrcent of total revenues. But in fiscal 1992, corporate taxes will be only 1.7 percent of the GDP and only 8.9 percent of total revenues.

6. The revenue estimate is low in the early years, because it will take a number of years for the reforms to be phased in fully. The same is true for several of the other revenue figures shown here.

Department of the Treasury

PUBLIC INVESTMENT-LED GROWTH

JEFF FAUX AND ROBERT KUTTNER

Summary

O N ITS CURRENT PATH, the U.S. economy faces years of slow growth and high unemployment. Even if the current recovery continues, private and government forecasters are predicting that the unemployment rate in 1997 will still be above its prerecession level. The result will be a cumulative loss of about $1 trillion in output and millions of jobs over the next five years.

Without faster growth, we cannot hope to reverse the long-term slide in real earnings—and in living standards—that the majority of working Americans are now experiencing. Nor can we hope to support fundamental social values such as equal opportunity, a fairer distribution of income and wealth, and ecological sanity unless we can generate a sustained rise in real income.

Economists and historians may disagree over the specific causes of our current economic stagnation. But there is a virtual consensus among observers of different philosophic persuasions that raising the rate of public and private investment is essential for curing it. Investment in plant and equipment is necessary to provide workers with the tools required to produce high-quality goods efficiently. Investment in people is necessary to provide them with the skills needed to make effective use of new technologies. Investment in transportation, communication, and environmental infrastructure is necessary for the smooth and safe working together of the millions of enterprises that make up the U.S. economy.

Today, America is considerably behind its major industrial rivals in the

Jeff Faux is President of the Economic Policy Institute in Washington, D.C. Robert Kuttner is coeditor of American Prospect *and a syndicated economics writer.*

share of its economy being reinvested in both public and private sectors. America's private capital stock is aging, its closed factories are not being replaced, and its public sector is deteriorating. In effect we have been living off of the capital investments made in earlier post–World War II years by previous generations. There is obviously a limit to how long one can sustain this behavior, and it is increasingly apparent that we are reaching that limit.

Neither monetary policy nor increased exports can jump-start faster growth. Over the next few years, the economy needs more fiscal stimulus to put idle labor and capital back to work. In the longer run we need to improve productivity to regain national competitiveness.

The only serious strategy available to satisfy these short- and long-term goals, including the acceleration of needed *private investment*, is to expand public capital spending on education, training, infrastructure, and civilian technology.

A minimum of roughly $300 billion above current spending levels is needed over the next five years to begin to redress the recent neglect of such public investments. This would still leave us investing considerably less than our major international competitors.

The investment should be financed by a combination of:

1. a peace dividend;
2. capital budgeting, which would permit borrowing dedicated for investment;
3. taxes, which should be raised as we approach full-capacity production, both to avoid future inflation and to raise net national savings.

Such a strategy requires Democrats to reject the failed macroeconomic theories of the recent past. By implicitly accepting conservative conventional wisdom that savings is more important than investment, that deficit reduction is more important than economic growth, and that investment is exclusively a private sector phenomenon, Democrats have for the past decade been unable to offer a positive dynamic economic program to reverse the slide in income among America's working families. They now have a chance to make the case that public spending for education, training, infrastructure, and civilian technology is essential for the nation's future living standards.

The Private Investment Gap

ON OUR PRESENT ECONOMIC PATH there is little possibility that the United States will close the private investment gap with our major rivals. Indeed, during the first five years of the 1990s, U.S. business investment in nonresidential plant and equipment is projected to grow at less than half the rate of the 1980s, which had slowed down from the 1970s, which had in turn slowed down from the 1960s.

This performance will not be improved by cutting the marginal tax rate on business income or capital gains. Differential tax rates can influence the *choice* among investments, but there is no evidence that under the conditions that now presently exist in the U.S. economy, such tax change will produce a rise in overall investment. *The obstacle to raising the rate of private investment is not the tax rate.*

Nor is the obstacle the cost of capital. Since the mid-1980s, capital costs have been cut in half for U.S. businesses, and there is now no difference between the cost of capital in Japan and in the United States.

Nor is it the cost of labor. American workers make less than workers in most of our European competitors and are almost even with Japanese workers.

Nor, as we shall examine below at greater length, is the major obstacle to private investment the low U.S. savings rate. Under conditions of less than full employment, investment is not primarily driven by the savings rate but by expectations of profit from expanding sales, which are a function of overall growth. Moreover, without the prospect of rising sales, capital is often diverted into asset speculation rather than put in productive plant and equipment. This occurred in the 1980s, when the corporate sector borrowed $1.3 trillion to "invest" in leveraged buyouts, junk bonds, and other forms of paper entrepreneurship that left them weakened by a huge debt burden with no increase in productivity to show for it.

This is not to deny that higher savings would be an important long-term factor in accommodating higher levels of investment once the economy is operating close to full capacity. But today, with the economy running roughly $250 billion below capacity, savings is not the problem.

Under conditions that now prevail in the U.S. economy, the business sector as a whole will increase investment primarily for two fundamental reasons: (1) when it expects that the market for goods and services will expand, or (2) when it sees opportunities to increase the efficiency of production. The reason why there will not be sufficient private investment in the U.S. economy in the near term is that the markets for American-made goods will not be expanding fast enough. The reason why there will not be sufficient private investment in the long run is that the rate of technological progress and innovation is below that of our competitors.

Raising the rate of private investment will therefore require a comprehensive strategy aimed at both the demand and the supply side—in the short run, generating customers, and in the long run, improving our ability to make better products more efficiently. Obviously, investment is what drives growth, but if investors are sitting on their checkbooks because of a depression in purchasing power and a perceived shortage of customers, and bankers have raised the hurdle defining qualified borrowers because of the same asset deflation and the damage to their own balance sheets, then there is only one reliable way to repair this economic short circuit: Government must spur investment directly rather than offering futile and costly carrots to private investors.

This strategy may violate some idealized notion of the superiority of markets at allocative efficiency. But after the hundreds of millions of economically useless square feet of commercial office space, shopping malls, and condos generated by the allocative judgments of private entrepreneurs, the claim about markets alone leading to efficient allocations of capital investment has lost some of its luster.

The Shrinking Public Investment Sphere

IN ECONOMIC TERMS, public investment programs are those that increase the nation's future capacity to produce goods and services—in either the public or the private sector. Like private investments, public investments create human and physical assets that generate new income streams and thus ultimately additional revenue to justify the initial outlay.

There is room for debate over what should or should not be included in a public investment menu. But let us start with a conservative, economic definition that limits it to civilian spending for: (1) human resources—education, training, and selected children's programs; (2) nondefense physical capital—highways, bridges, water systems, pollution control, airports, schools, etc.; and (3) nondefense R&D.

This is a narrow definition. For example, a sound economic argument can be made for housing assistance; it is cheaper to keep people housed than to rehouse them once homeless. Similarly, spending for any children's programs—from Medicaid to foster care—could logically be defined as investment. However, as any new income streams generated by these programs are more difficult to track, none of these investments is included in the following discussion.

Today, the rate of public investment in both physical and human capital is clearly inadequate. Between 1950 and 1970, the civilian public physical capital stock grew at an annual rate of 4 percent. Since 1970 it has averaged 1.6 percent, reflecting substantially lower rates of growth at federal, state, and local government levels. While the United States was cutting back on its public capital investment, our major competitors have been increasing theirs at a higher rate. Japan, for example, invested 5.1 percent of its GNP in public physical infrastructure between 1973 and 1985, while the corresponding figure for the United States was 0.3 percent.

The record on investment in human resources is equally grim. As the world market has become more competitive in the 1980s, the United States has responded with a less prepared work force. A 1990 study by the Economic Policy Institute revealed that the United States ranks fourteenth out of sixteen industrialized nations in per capita expenditures for grades K to 12. When limited to federal spending but expanded to include higher education and job training outlays, the data show that national investment in the work force has clearly been in retreat since 1981. Federal investment in education and training between 1976 and 1981 averaged 0.9 percent of the GNP. It dropped to 0.5 percent over the next decade and in 1994–96 is expected to fall further as a result of the current budget agreement between Congress and the Bush administration. The share of federal investment in children has dropped during the 1980s and is projected to drop further.

Finally, U.S. investment (public and private) in civilian research and development has long trailed that of our major competitors. In 1978, national expenditures for nondefense R&D as a share of GNP were: Japan, 2.0 percent; West Germany, 2.1 percent; and the United States, 1.6 percent. By 1988, the gap had widened: Japan, 2.9 percent; West Germany, 2.7 percent; and the United States 1.9 percent.

States and localities have not been able to pick up the slack. Education spending by states rose somewhat during the 1980s, but not enough to compensate for the federal cutbacks. Moreover, the increased state and local spending seems to have been less targeted on the disadvantaged, whose needs for resources are greatest. At any rate, the United States ended the decade spending proportionately less on grades K to 12 than its major international competitors. State and local spending for infrastructure actually declined over the period, and there was virtually no effort to raise state and local spending for training and civilian R&D, which have traditionally been federal functions.

Serious economists have always understood the critical contribution public investment makes to healthy economic growth. But this relationship has been obscured by the ideological shifts of the past decade, in which all government spending has been labeled "consumption." Recent research by economists David Aschauer, Alicia Munnell, and others has confirmed that there are direct links between spending on public infrastructure and the growth of private investment, productivity, and profits. Aschauer, for example, found that in the long run each additional dollar of public infrastructure investment raises private investment by forty-five cents.

If, since 1970, the United States had maintained the 1950s and 1960s share of GNP for core infrastructure (roads, bridges, airports, water and sewer systems, etc.), productivity growth would have been 50 percent higher; the average profit rate would have been 22 percent higher; and the rate of private investment would have increased by 19 percent.

Returns from human capital investment are also high. There is solid evidence that education and training lead to higher achievement, higher job productivity, and reduced social costs to the nation. The list of such benefits is long and the evidence is clear. Statisticians may quibble with the precise estimates, but we know that the relationship between public investment and long-term growth is positive and strong.

How Much Should We Spend?

ONE WAY TO MEASURE THE EXISTING GAP between our present level of public investment and the level needed to support a more prosperous economy is through historical reference. Federal investment as a share of the GNP was cut by a third between 1976 and 1990. Restoring the 1976 share to the 1990 budget would have required about $50 billion in additional investment in that year.

The 1976 investment share of the GNP is a relatively modest standard. It was not a peak year for federal investment as a whole nor for any particular investment category, and was below the average for 1975–81. But it does represent an investment level that the nation once found the means to support, even in the midst of the Cold War. It was also a time when the United States faced a much less competitive world economy and therefore had less reason to be concerned about reinvesting to maintain its international economic position.

A more up-to-date estimate can be calculated from the range of recent expert analyses of unmet needs in specific sectors. In addition to providing insight into actual needs, these estimates capture some of the cumulative effects of neglect of investment in previous years. For example, roads neglected since 1976 cannot be returned to their 1976 standard merely by returning highway investment to its earlier level. Instead, sustained spending well above the 1976 level will be required until the "backlog" is overcome.

As the following table shows, the investment gap, measured by adding the expert assessments, ranged from $63 billion to $126 billion, or from 1.1

to 2.2 percent of the GNP. The sums of the experts' estimates presented here are obviously rough approximations of the investment gap. They are probably conservative, as they often seek to achieve a standard less lofty than that of 1976. Indeed, many of the estimates of specific program needs are biased downward by the estimators' perception of what is politically realistic in an era of fiscal constraint and resistance to public spending, rather than a full assessment of need.

FEDERAL INVESTMENT GAP—EXPERT ESTIMATES

(outlays in billions of dollars)

	Needed Increase for Full Funding
HUMAN RESOURCES	
Education and training	23.3– 45.0
Children	6.1– 12.5
PHYSICAL CAPITAL	22.7– 54.8
R&D	10.8– 13.5
TOTAL INVESTMENT	62.9–125.8

Source: Jeff Faux and Todd Schafer, *Increasing Public Investment* (Washington, D.C,: Economic Policy Institute, *1991*).

A final estimate of need comes from the macroeconomic side. In March 1992 a group of one hundred economists, including six Nobel Prize winners and several from Wall Street firms, estimated that the United States economy needed a stimulus—largely in the form of public spending—of about 1 percent of the GNP in order to give a noninflationary boost to growth.

Thus, by almost any measure, the Federal Government should be spending an *additional* $60 billion per year for the next five years on public investment. Again, this is the level of investment needed just to keep the United States Treasury from further disinvestment. Even this level of investment will still leave us considerably behind Germany and Japan.

Capital Budgeting

JUDGMENTS ABOUT THE ADEQUACY of public investment are obscured by the way the Federal Government keeps its books. If the Federal Government's budget were kept in a more "businesslike" manner—one that reflected the economic realities underlying financial management—it would separate its operating deficits (profit and loss) from its capital account. Investments would be carried as assets and depreciation charges would be levied against the operating budget.

There are technical problems in coming up with a comprehensive capital budget for the United States Government, but there is general agreement that many expenditures of the U.S. Government do generate future income streams and should be interpreted as capital investment. Highways, education, training, and civilian research and development would clearly fall into that category. Investments in defense hardware and structures last for several years and would be considered capital in an accounting sense, but they do not increase future income and therefore would, from our standpoint, be excluded from a capital budget.

Although many industrialized countries and most U.S. state and local governments use capital budgeting, establishing a formal capital budget process for the U.S. Government will take years. But given the crisis in public investment, budgetary policies can be altered now to reflect more accurately the economics of capital budgeting. Specifically, the new Administration should present to Congress, along with its conventional budget, a proposal for a five-year Special Investment Program that would raise spending on human resources, physical investment, and research and development a minimum of $300 billion above the 1992 "current services" baseline (i.e., the real level of investment spending in that year).

At the same time, the new President should establish a bipartisan commission of government, business, labor, and academics to recommend a strategy for developing a permanent capital budget.

Financing Public Investment

MANY HAVE ASSUMED THAT THE PEACE dividend from cutbacks in military spending could be available to pay for much of it. But recent budget projections suggest that this may be a utopian assumption. The 1993 budget passed by Congress has dashed hopes that major shifts from defense to the civilian sector can be accomplished in the near term. Moreover, the high range of peace dividend proposals in the Congress seems to be roughly $150 billion in budget authority over five years. (See, e.g., proposals by Senators Sarbanes, Sasser, and Kennedy.)

It would take a cut in military spending considerably beyond that to generate sufficient revenues for investment. Only the large cuts proposed by John Steinbruner of the Brookings Institution, which come to $211 billion in current-dollar budget authority over five years, would provide the magnitude of investment funds needed. However, because of the considerable shutdown costs involved in realizing a peace dividend, outlay savings would be sufficient to finance the needed investment increase only in the later years.

Undoubtedly, some additional savings can be made by cutting other domestic spending. But domestic discretionary spending has been sliced thin, and, after almost twelve years of conservative government, there are not very many cuttable programs that would yield large savings. In terms of entitlements, the biggest program, Social Security, already pays for itself and has the support of the overwhelming majority of Americans. Medicare and Medicaid are part of the problem of the overall health care system that must be completely overhauled just to prevent costs from further draining the U.S. Treasury. In 1970, health care, education, and defense each claimed about 6 percent of our GNP. Today, while education and defense each take about 5 percent or our GNP, health care has ballooned to 14 percent. Failure to attain comprehensive health care reform has crowded out government's ability to invest in other sectors.

Thus we must face the brutal fact that if we want to increase investment in, and spur the growth of, the U.S. economy, funds will have to be borrowed or taxed—or both.

Sensible rules of both accounting and economics would suggest that the government should borrow for its investment programs in a time like the present when unemployment is high and the economy needs a net stimulus. But as the economy moves toward full capacity and inflationary pressures develop, more of the investment budget should be supported by taxes.

Raising taxes is not appropriate when the economy is suffering from weak demand, as it is now. But over the long run, higher taxes will be needed. And they are clearly justified. Compared with its competitors, the United States as a whole is undertaxed. If the U.S. tax share were equal to the average share of OECD nations, we would be raising more than $400 billion in additional federal, state, and local government revenues.

The major components of the Special Investment Fund could be financed in somewhat different ways. Physical infrastructure could be primarily supported through special borrowing by having the U.S. Treasury buy long-term no-interest bonds issued to it by state and local governments for specific projects. State and local jurisdictions would pledge specific revenue sources—fees, taxes, etc—to pay off the bonds. Different projects might require some minimum private investment share to help assure financial viability.

Human resources investments at the beginning would have to be supported by general borrowing, but once economic growth accelerates, they would be financed with dedicated tax revenues, such as proceeds of a surtax on incomes.

Similarly, expansion of civilian R&D would in the 1990s be financed by savings from defense spending and be part of a general plan to convert defense technology to civilian uses. Over the longer run, dedicated taxes from some appropriate source (e.g., a securities turnover tax) would be necessary.

New outlays for the Special Investment Fund would begin at the rate of $60 billion a year—the minimum needed to keep the nation from adding to its investment gap. The stimulus to spending would quicken economic growth beyond that now projected by CBO and other forecasters. As the unemployment rate dropped and industry began to approach capacity, it would then be appropriate to raise steadily tax revenues that would be dedicated to the investment spending. We would also expect that tax revenues would increase as a consequence of economic growth. These additional revenues could be used for investment or to begin to reduce the deficit in the latter part of the decade.

Rethinking Macroeconomics

IT IS NOT ENOUGH TO RESORT to a tactical shot of public investment in the hope of jump-starting the economy. A public investment-led plan must become an ongoing economic strategy, which in turn requires a rethinking of macroeconomics. In the years since John Maynard Keynes died in 1946, the popular and even the scholarly perception of the Keynesian insight about what drives economic growth has been badly bastardized by the conservative neoclassical story about how the economy works.

The standard story begins with the familiar accounting identity of "savings equals investment." It then leaps to the assumption that the rate of savings is what drives the rate of investment. In this account, America's economic performance is suboptimal because our private savings rate, already below OECD average, was further depressed by government "dissavings" in the 1980s. The urgent challenge, therefore, is to get the savings rate up, both by encouraging private savings and by reducing the public deficit.

Until very recently, this consensus was almost universal, running from moderately liberal neo-Keynesians to virtually all conservatives except extreme supply-siders.

The conservative version of this standard story has stressed private savings and investment. In theory, by increasing the after-tax rewards to savings and investment, public policy could increase the incentives to save and to invest. The more centrist view of this story has stressed the importance of reducing public deficits. For the most part, editorial opinion came to side with the latter view, and has chided both political parties for refusing to grasp the nettle of deficit-reduction: Politicians presumably knew as a matter of economics what needed to be done but lacked the political courage to do it. Even most liberal politicians, lacking a clear dissenting economic theory on which to base policy, have felt rather guilty about their cumulative failure to deal with the deficit. This premise, however, has crippled any serious discussion of additional public spending.

The standard story was wrongheaded economics from the inception, but there was no real political opening to challenge it until the bubble of speculative excess broke in the late 1980s, giving way to stagnation and recession. Suddenly it became respectable to acknowledge that a slow-growth economy is unlikely to recover its health by trying to raise its savings rate, which can only lead to further deflation.

As the one hundred economists organized by James Tobin and Robert Solow wrote in their open letter of March 30, 1992, "Since the economy has idle resources of labor and capital available to meet additional spending with appropriate production and the threat of inflation is minimal, it is appropriate to let these expenditures add to the deficit financed by borrowing, and it would cancel most or all of the needed stimulus to aggregate demand if they were financed otherwise."

The economists' statement suggests that we are finally openly acknowledging the underlying Keynesian insights that still accurately describe the modern economy. It is important, however, to understand what those insights were.

For Keynes, what ultimately drives growth is primarily on the investment side of the ledger. In some circumstances, it is sensible to use public deficits to restore aggregate demand, which will then induce entrepreneurs to increase investment to meet that increased demand for goods. High aggregate demand assures that all factors of production are fully employed—but they may be employed doing efficient tasks or silly ones. Keynes wrote, in a famous passage, that burying bank notes and paying people to dig them up would be better than nothing, but productive economic activity—building homes, streets, factories, etc.—would be better still. Over the long term, investment generates technical progress, and the resulting increased productivity is the real driver of long-term growth. This is the connection between the macro and the structural sources of growth that has been largely neglected in the conventional conversation.

In the popular caricature of Keynesianism, the action is all on the demand side. And even worse, "Keynesianism" has come to be seen mainly as a countercyclical exercise—incurring deficits or cheapening interest rates when economies are sluggish, and then "taking away the punch bowl just when the party gets going," as Federal Reserve chairman William Mc-Chesney Martin once described countercyclical monetary policy. But central bankers did this long before Keynes, and this was not what Keynes believed. Rather than seeing macroeconomic management as leveling the peaks and filling in the valleys, Keynes argued that when a boom was in progress and the economy is at or near full employment and full production, economic managers *ought to endeavor to keep it going.*

In this sense, the Japanese until recently have been the world's most effective Keynesians, for their entire postwar growth machine has been driven by very low interest rates. They have kept the financier in his place, and made sure that productive industry has access to all the capital it could use, at the lowest possible costs. This, in turn, allowed industry to live with relatively low rates of return and to have relatively long-time horizons. The strategy entailed certain policy tricks anathema to most laissez-faire Western governments, such as allocation of capital, interlocks to preclude any "market for corporate control," low and even negative interest rates for savers, and tax subsidies for small savings—but it had the result Keynes would have appreciated. Americans have had scant success exporting products to Japan's managed economy, but they did manage to export ideology. Japan's recent adoption of U.S-inspired financial market liberalization may turn out to be the ultimate poison pill, for it has wrecked Japan's ability to have high price-earnings ratios and hence low capital costs without destabilizing speculation.

The key point here is that the growth/productivity payoff is on the investment side, not on the savings side. And the key insight is that while savings may technically equal investment as an accounting identity after the fact, it is fallacious to presume that savings are what drive investment. Indeed, it is equally plausible that the causality works the other way around. A high rate of investment leads to a high rate of real economic growth, which makes it possible for people to enjoy increased real earnings, and to save. Conversely, if "liquidity preference"—a reluctance to invest risk capital—increases in a deflated economy because of fears about the future, government can tax the idle savings of the wealthy and invest the proceeds in growth-enhancing activities that will also increase growth and make any accumulated public debt less of a future burden on economic output. Alternately still,

government may also increase public borrowing to increase public investment, which is an alternative way of channeling idle private savings into
productive use.

Viewed in this sense, the problem with the policies of the 1980s was
not mainly that deficits were increased. To a large degree, the problem was
the composition of that increase. Deficits grew because the government
decided to collect fewer taxes from the rich—which, despite claims, did
nothing to stimulate investment. Had the government increased deficits to
increase investment directly, the deficits would have been far more benign.

Moreover, by viewing savings as nothing but the residual that is left over
after consumption, the usual accounting identity sets up perverse incentives
for policy. Given a savings rate perceived as too low, the only way to improve
it within the conventional assumptions is to depress consumption. But depressing consumption during a "debt-deflation depression" will only retard
output, intensify the deflationary spiral, slow growth, reduce the incentive
to invest, and thereby make the burden of past debt all the more disabling.

The standard story about inadequate savings is also open to challenge,
on grounds of faulty national income accounting. There are, in fact, at least
three distinct accounting challenges to the statistical claim of inadequate
national rates of savings. The first, associated with the work of Robert Eisner,
argues that when adjusted properly for inflation, the public debt is rather
less fearsome than generally claimed. Still, because the debt is being financed
out of current income, at interest rates that are high by historic standards,
the current level of debt, even when properly deflated, has relatively high
real costs.

A second adjustment has been suggested by Robert Blecker, who has
noted that most of the measured fall in private savings can be accounted for
by an increase in economic depreciation—that is, if changes in the nature
of technical progress has led to a shortening in the useful lives of productive
assets, these show up in the national income accounts as a charge against
savings. This insight is very persuasive. It suggests that if any savings/in-
vestment problem exists, it is because the high-tech/short product cycle
economy requires a faster consumption of assets and hence more savings to
finance it, and not because the real rate of private savings out of income has
declined. Blecker also suggests that the slowdown in growth itself accounted
for the slowdown in investment; this suggests that the usual analysis has the
cause and effect backward. Higher growth engenders more investment, not
necessarily vice versa.

A third revision on the national income accounts comes from recent
work by Fred Block, who notes that the official Commerce Department
measure of savings omits a key savings source: realized capital gains.

As Block observes in his most recent article, written with Robert L. Heilbroner and published in the Spring 1992 issue of *The American Prospect*, capital gains rose from $21.3 billion, or 3 percent of disposable income in 1970, to a 1986 peak of $295.8 billion, or 9.8 percent of personal income. As Block and Heilbroner comment: "No plausible measure of the national saving rate should ignore this immense addition to the financial investment power of households, or more accurately, to the households at the apex of the income pyramid."

Since the well-off save disproportionately, total national savings could hardly have dropped during a period when the well-to-do reaped enormous capital gains windfalls. During the 1980s, middle-class incomes stagnated, and saving by the middle class probably did drop. But the decline in the relatively modest savings of the middle class was more than offset by the increase in the capital gains income (and savings) of the well-to-do.

When the figures are adjusted for capital gains, Block and Heilbroner find that total savings for the years 1984–88 were significantly higher than during the early 1980s, despite Department of Commerce statistics that show savings plummeting. If capital gains are counted, they more than double the official measure of savings. For example, the 1988 supply of savings would be $300 billion rather than the paltry $145 billion that was reported. With this revised measurement, savings went up in the 1980s.

Conclusion

THE REVISIONS TO THE CONVENTIONAL framing of the problem of savings, investment, and growth is only the latest in a series of potent assaults on the reigning paradigm of the past decade and a half. On intellectual grounds, both the macro- and the microeconomic themes of the standard story are being discredited in the mainstream of serious economic thought. First, mainstream economics is inching toward redefining the present macroeconomic challenge; it is to raise the rate of investment, not to reduce the deficit. Second, after more than a decade of research comparing the structural advantages and disadvantages of different forms of capitalism, a surprising number of quite mainstream economists now agree that "structure" matters—that is, that public policy can successfully intervene in the basic process of bringing together the factors of market production. These factors include the nature of the system of education and training and its relation to production; the way labor interacts with management; the way the financial economy interacts with the real economy; how business interacts with government; and how government policies and public investments influence and diffuse technical learning.

The implication is that public spending for education, training, infra-structure, and civilian technology should not be seen as simply an effort to promote employment by stimulating demand. Such investments are essential to developing the nation's longer-term competitiveness and productivity, thereby shifting long-term economic growth to a higher trajectory.

Unfortunately, politics has not caught up with the shifts in economic thought. Despite the clear case for giving the economic goal of expanding investment priority over the accounting goal of balancing the budget, the Bush administration and Congress continue to fall over themselves to prove their zeal as budget cutters. Not only does this lack of honesty and clarity mislead the public, it also has utterly failed to reach its objective of reducing the budget deficit. In the end, the deficit problem cannot be solved in an economic vacuum. Under conditions of slow growth and idle capacity, attempting to cut budget deficits is self-defeating. In the long run, the deficit will come under control only when an administration committed to reaching and sustaining higher rates of economic growth comes to Washington.

Department of the Treasury

FISCAL POLICY

LEE SMITH AND LAWRENCE CHIMERINE

Summary

T HE NATION'S EXTENDED PERIOD of economic stagnation, marked by falling living standards, weak growth, and lagging competitiveness, is unlike any economic slowdown experienced in the post–World War II period. To be successful, the new President will need a program of new macroeconomic policies and structural reforms designed to foster strong, sustainable growth, an upturn in living standards, and a long-term reduction in the federal budget deficit. In fact, these objectives are closely linked: Strong, sustained growth will lower unemployment and lift wages and incomes; higher purchasing power will help generate the consumer spending necessary for continued growth; economic growth and rising incomes will spur private investment as well as cause tax revenues to rise, making it easier to finance needed public investments and reduce the federal budget deficit; and long-term deficit reduction will cut interest costs on the national debt, thereby freeing resources for new public investments, and bring down long-term interest rates, making new private investment more affordable.

The new economic strategy will be sharply different from the supply-side economic policies of the past twelve years. Lowering marginal tax rates and deregulating the economy did not increase investment, improve our competitiveness, or sustain economic growth.

Though supply-side failed, it would be a mistake to return to the policies it supplanted, the Keynesian policies of the 1960s and 1970s. Instead, America needs a new economic strategy based on the emerging consensus that

Lee Smith is Executive Director of New York Governor Mario Cuomo's Commission on Competitiveness and Director of Economic Policy and Research for the New York State Department of Economic Development. Lawrence Chimerine is Senior Economic Adviser to DRI/McGraw-Hill and a Fellow at the Economic Strategy Institute.

economic policy must give equal attention to the demand-side issue of growth, and to such structural problems as inadequate levels of public and private investment, short-time horizons, ineffective corporate governance, lack of cooperation between employees and managers and between business and government, faltering educational and social institutions, and urban poverty. In short, America needs a new strategy of investment-led growth that will encourage the structural reforms and new investment that will help raise productivity, improve our competitiveness, and increase economic growth.

One linchpin of the investment-led growth strategy is a new multiyear federal fiscal policy that will unbuckle the straitjacket of the 1990 budget agreement and support new priorities. Above all else, our fiscal policy must support increased public and private investment in the factors of production that are essential for lasting economic strength and rising living standards: modern public infrastructure, trained and educated workers, state-of-the art business capital stock, advanced technology, and development-oriented social policies.

The second linchpin is a new way of formulating and implementing economic policy. Instead of the current policymaking process, relying on a weak advisory agency—the Council of Economic Advisers—and competing cabinet secretaries, the new Administration should borrow from the model of the National Security Council and establish an Economic Security Council, headed by a cabinet-ranking adviser reporting directly to the President. This innovation would help the President integrate domestic and international interests as well as coordinate demand-side macroeconomic policies with structural policies. The economic security adviser would work in cooperation with the key cabinet secretaries, especially the Secretary of the Treasury.

A reinvigorated Treasury Department can play several key roles. It can be a major force in the new policymaking process, including working with the OMB to plan a new federal capital budget to account for federal expenditures more accurately. It will continue to be the lead agency for international economic policy. It can devise a means to finance new public investments and implement incentives for private investment. Finally, it can develop a long-term program to reform capital markets and revitalize the financial sector.

National Economic Strategy

THE ULTIMATE GOALS of any administration's economic policy should be to raise living standards and expand opportunity and, by so doing, significantly improve prospects for future generations. To achieve these goals the next Administration will have to confront the macroeconomic problem of inadequate demand that has worsened unemployment and virtually halted the growth of the economy over the past four years, and the structural problem of the lagging productivity and diminished competitiveness of American industry. Together, inadequate growth and lagging competitiveness have contributed to a gradual erosion of living standards and a widening of inequality.

FIRST PRINCIPLES

Stronger growth, improved competitiveness, and reduced deficits will not be achieved without a national economic strategy grounded in a new understanding of the operating principles needed to succeed in today's global economy.

First, the national interest in a strong economy cannot be left to private market forces alone, as the policymakers of the 1980s tried to do. The Federal Government has a clear responsibility for the performance of the economy and can play a constructive role in its improvement.

Second, the guiding principle underlying our domestic policies that "what's good for the consumer is good for the economy" should be revised, because in a global economy the key to consumption is the level of real wages and employment. Now our policy should aim for an economy of high-paying jobs that give consumers the ability to buy a wide range of goods, not merely an economy flooded by the cheapest products.

Third, economic considerations can no longer be secondary to political, national security, and other factors in setting the international policy of the United States.

Fourth, we need to focus on productivity growth, for it is the key to raising living standards for the vast majority of the population, and consequently significantly improve prospects for the next generation.

Finally, what we *make* as a country is important. We reject the idea that there are no differences among wood chips, potato chips, and semiconductor chips. Therefore, it is extremely important to make certain that the United States has a major presence in those industries that: (a) represent the growth markets of the future; (b) have high multiplier impacts on the rest of the economy; (c) generate high value-added products and thus provide high-paying jobs; and (d) are leaders and drivers of innovation and therefore are critical to technological progress.

Together, these five principles provide a basis for policies that will improve our economy's performance. The first step for the next Administration is to reach agreement with Congress on a new fiscal policy.

National Fiscal Policy

AT THE SAME TIME, despite the political difficulties, our huge structural deficits must be addressed. And the deficit is now so large that it cannot be eliminated by spending cuts alone. We also need to raise revenues by enacting selective tax increases and by promoting faster growth, which in turn will generate greater tax revenues.

The deficit must be brought down slowly, however, and not as quickly as Ross Perot and Paul Tsongas suggested. Because the deflationary impact of rapid deficit reduction will take effect much sooner than the favorable effects of higher investment, their policy would likely put the nation back in recession, which in turn would cause the deficit to increase.

INVESTMENT-CREATING POLICIES

• *Public infrastructure investment.* To help jump-start the economy and to keep pace with our competitors, we must return to our two-hundred-year-old tradition of public investment in infrastructure. Substantial new investments in the key infrastructure networks—transportation, water and wastewater, and telecommunications—are critical to the new progrowth economic agenda. Specifically, the Federal Government should substantially increase investment in infrastructure to $40 billion more in 1993 and $50 billion more per year from 1994 to 1997. These increases will not meet all our needs, but would reverse much of the deterioration and start the process of building the infrastructure of the twenty-first century, and in so doing, provide a much-needed boost to economic growth. Spillover from public infrastructure investment can also help lead to the development of new products, technologies, and even industries. Projects to be considered include high-speed trains, such as the Maglev project; new waste disposal and environmental cleanup; alternative energy production systems; and fiber-optic and other advanced telecommunications systems.

• *Human capital investment.* The nation needs to increase its investment in human capital. We recommend a $20 billion increase in federal spending in 1993 for education and training. These expenditures should be combined with reforms that better connect education and training systems to the needs of the private sector.

• *Public investment in technology and research.* The Federal Government should support a five-year plan to increase R&D significantly in critical technologies, either with new funding or by redirecting existing technology projects. It should also organize technology policy to coordinate our efforts better, encourage private industry, and institute intelligence and licensing systems for foreign technology. We should budget these programs at an average of $9 billion per year over the next five years.

- *Competitiveness programs.* Washington must also improve America's international competitiveness in strategic markets, which David E. Shaw discusses in greater length elsewhere in this section. Among the initiatives we support are a "national quality in manufacturing" initiative, with a special emphasis on helping smaller manufacturers attain high-quality standards. Such a comprehensive competitiveness agenda will cost an average of $8 billion per year over the next five years.

- *Social development investments.* To reduce poverty, the new President and Congress should support a new national public employment program for targeted urban areas. We propose $3 billion in new spending for public employment and programs to promote human development reforms in our educational and social policies.

- *Export growth/import reduction.* America must launch a serious national effort to open foreign markets, provide competitive financing for U.S. trade, encourage the export efforts of small and midsize companies, and encourage economic growth in our key overseas markets, especially Latin America. Such an effort could cost $5 billion in 1993, increasing to $10 billion in 1997. Even with such funding, export growth will take a long time to develop. A more immediate boost to growth can come from a reduction of imports in those markets where American producers are competitive, such as by reducing Japan's share of the U.S. auto parts market. A positive policy to bring about a large increase in the use of domestic parts in foreign-owned plants must be put in place as soon as possible.

- *Tax reform policies.* In addition, some significant changes in the basic structure of the economy and corporations will also be necessary to spur more private investment in the years ahead. It is vital that we begin to make the long-term investments that are needed to improve productivity and increase capacity, rather than the short-term, speculative, financial-type investments that were so prevalent in the 1980s.

- *Sliding capital gains tax.* Many conservatives and business leaders suggest that increased private sector investment can be accomplished by cutting the capital gains tax rate. However, capital gains tax changes by themselves simply do not influence fixed investment significantly, in part because reductions in the capital gains tax rate have a relatively small impact on the cost of capital. And it's fixed investment that's needed to help the economy off its back and begin the process of boosting productivity and competitiveness. A straight reduction in capital gains tax rates will simply provide a windfall on investments already made (and thus raise the budget deficit in the long run).

Changing capital gains taxes can, however, help shift the pattern away from short-term, financially oriented, speculative-type investments to badly needed longer-term investments if there is a much larger difference between the rates on short-term and those on long-term gains than would be necessary. This can best be accomplished by enacting a sliding-scale capital gains tax structure, incorporating an increase in the rate on short-term gains, with the rate declining the longer the asset is held (to perhaps near zero after five years or longer). Furthermore, the relatively low long-term rate should apply only to investments in productive assets, not to vacation homes, art, etc.

• *Investment tax credit.* Restructuring of the capital gains tax should be combined with enactment of more effective investment incentives. In particular, the investment tax credit, which has had an excellent track record in stimulating new investment in the past, should be restored. We suggest that a large credit (e.g., 20 to 25 percent) be implemented, but only on incremental investment over and above a base period, in productivity-enhancing equipment. For any company, the base can be calculated as the average of investment during the past several years. Dramatically accelerated depreciation, or total expensing, on incremental investment would work just as well. Not only would both provide a big incentive at the margin, but also revenues would not be lost for investments that were previously planned. Thus, if they do not stimulate new investment, there would be virtually no revenue loss to the Treasury; if they do, the increase in economic activity will generate enough added revenues to pay for part of the credit.

On a static basis, a net investment tax credit to encourage private firms to make new investments in equipment would cost up to $10 billion in the first year, rising to $15 billion in the second year. The capital gains reform proposed above would be revenue-neutral.

• *Tax on higher-income individuals.* There should also be an increase in the top marginal tax rate, or creation of a third rate (perhaps at about 38 percent) on relatively high incomes (over $200,000 per year). While this would not only restore some fairness to the tax system, such an increase would also be proinvestment. Coupled with a decline in the capital gains tax rate on long-term, productive investments, it would encourage relatively high-income individuals to shift some of their safe investments into riskier, long-term investments when combined with the lowered long-term capital gains rates suggested above.

As a further inducement, the low rate on long-term capital gains should be available only on new investments, further encouraging those now holding securities to shift to new investments, since they would not be eligible for the lower rate unless they did so. This would also have the advantage of unlocking a lot of existing investments, thus creating a short-term tax windfall.

Financing the Strategy

THE TOTAL COST OF THIS PROGRAM of new spending initiatives would be $93 billion in the first year, rising to $123 billion in year two, and remaining at $120 billion in years three through five. This is, of course, a huge sum, but it's far smaller than the cost of our flat economy for the past several years. The spending proposals outlined above—private investment incentives, infrastructure and human resource investments, and industrial competitiveness policies—reflect our conviction that spending priorities must match national goals for investment and productivity growth. In the long run, the growth that these initiatives stimulate will help provide some additional revenues. In the short run, to reduce the impact on the deficit, there are several financing strategies to fund this new national economic plan.

First, with the end of the Cold War, the United States can now shift more resources away from military spending. According to a recent Brookings study, and others, the defense budget can be safely reduced by at least $75 billion per year. The current budget agreement calls for only modest cuts in defense, but clearly some added Peace Dividend savings are feasible, as is explained in more detail elsewhere in this book.

Second, resources can also be shifted away from other spending categories so that spending priorities better match national goals. For example, a shift of only 5 percent of federal spending would free $70 billion for new priorities. A variety of reductions in public consumption are possible—for example, elimination of the space station; modest decreases in entitlements; and scaling back some tax expenditures, such as the home mortgage interest deduction on second homes.

Third, new revenues will also be needed. A program to privatize federal assets could raise up to $25 billion over two years. As mentioned earlier, the top income tax rate should rise to 38 percent for taxpayers making over $200,000 per year, effective in fiscal year 1994. And a new Congress and Administration should seriously consider a $30-per-ton carbon tax. Together these two tax measures will raise almost $42 billion in new revenue in the first year, rising to almost $66 billion in the fourth year, as Table 1 shows. These measures need to be passed, with the public investment spending, as

TABLE 1.
New Initiatives (excluding health care)
(in billions of dollars)

	1993	1994	1995	1996	1997
Additional spending					
Infrastructure investment	$40	$50	$50	$50	$50
Education and training	20	25	25	25	25
Strategic technology (R&D)	5	10	10	10	10
Total public investment	$65	$85	$85	$85	$85
Additional other spending					
Investment tax credit	$10	$15	$15	$15	$15
Competitiveness programs	10	10	7	7	7
Export market development	5	10	10	10	10
Public employment programs	3	3	3	3	3
Total spending	$28	$38	$35	$35	$35
Total	$93	$123	$120	$120	$120
Sources of additional funds: additional Peace Dividend savings	$20	$40	$50	$60	$70
Privatized federal assets	10	15	—	—	—
Income tax rate of 38% over $200,000 income	—	7	7	8	10
Reduced entitlements	4	5	5	6	7
Increased taxation of Social Security benefits	4	10	10	10	11
Space station, tax enforcement, misc. savings	18	25	28	28	29
Carbon tax: $30 per ton	—	35	36	45	56
Total funds	$56	$137	$136	$157	$183
Net cost of new initiatives	$37	$–14	$–16	$–37	$–63

part of a comprehensive package, so the bond markets do not react negatively to the temporary increase in the deficit.

Table 2 shows how the proposed initiatives will effect the federal deficit. These calculations begin with the projections of the deficit, under current policies, from the Congressional Budget Office. Now the deficit is expected to decline for the next two years, reaching a low of $244 billion in fiscal year 1993, and then to rise again, swelling to $290 billion in fiscal year 1997. To the extent that growth is even slower than the 3.5 to 2.5 percent growth that the Congressional Budget Office projects, the deficits will be even wider.

The initiatives proposed here provide an additional $37 billion in fiscal stimulus in fiscal year 1993 to help stimulate a strong recovery. In the following fiscal years, however, the savings from the Peace Dividend and the new revenues from a carbon tax will help drive to the deficit down to $227 billion, $63 billion below the projected baseline.

The Treasury's Role

THE TREASURY DEPARTMENT has always played a major role in the Federal Government by virtue of its responsibility for raising the revenue and managing the debts of the government. In addition, it oversees the banking and financial system and carries out the nation's international economic policy. As a result of these myriad responsibilities, Treasury secre-

TABLE 2.
Effects of Initiatives on the Deficit
(in billions of dollars)

	1993	1994	1995	1996	1997
CBO baseline total deficit°	$331	$268	$244	$254	$290
Additional public investment	65	85	85	85	85
Additional other spending (exc. health)	28	38	35	35	35
Additional funds (exc. health)	56	137	136	157	183
Deficit	368	254	228	217	227
Change from baseline deficit	37	−14	−16	−37	−63

*Includes on-budget and off-budget expenses and revenues.

taries—from Alexander Hamilton to Henry Morgenthau, Jr.—have often played a pivotal role in helping the nation meet its challenges.

Because of historical circumstances, the next Secretary, too, will have a great opportunity to help shape the future of the country. The nation is undergoing a transformation of its economic and social institutions. The system of the past sixty years—what has been called New Deal capitalism— is faltering under the relentless pressure of competing systems, specifically Japan's corporatist capitalism and Germany's social market capitalism. Their success not only challenges our share of world production and profits, but it also raises questions about how well our institutions work and how well our system organizes the factors of production—capital, labor, government, markets, etc—to produce a dynamic, growing economy. In these circumstances, the next Treasury Secretary will have the opportunity to make a major impact on the future of the nation.

One of the first things the new Treasury Secretary should do is help the President reorganize the way economic policy issues are handled within the Executive Branch. By moving within the first hundred days to establish the new revenue sources and spending priorities appropriate for investment-led growth, the next Administration will signal its commitment to rebuilding our economic strength and expanding opportunity. Yet, if history is any guide, six months into the term the initial excitement created by the new government will subside, the choices will become more difficult, and the policy debate will become entangled in traditional interest-group politics. To keep its momentum from dissipating and to improve its ability to implement its program, the new Administration should put in place a new policymaking process.

Today the President relies on a small advisory agency—the Council of Economic Advisers—and the Economic Policy Council, chaired by the Treasury secretary. This system diffuses responsibilities among competing agencies and cabinet secretaries. Economic policy is thrashed out in department-against-department turf battles, with the President playing the role of arbitrator, not the leader of an effective, coordinated strategy.

In contrast to the way economic policy is developed, the President has a very effective policy process for national security issues. For the past four decades, Cold War political and military priorities commanded much of the president's attention, not only because of their political importance but also because the president had an effective policymaking forum: the National Security Council (NSC). Established by President Truman, the NSC developed our national security strategy and coordinated its implementation with the relevant cabinet agencies, especially the Defense and State departments.

To give the President a comparably effective mechanism for dealing with economic policy, we should borrow the model of the NSC and establish a national Economic Security Council (ESC). The staff person in charge of the ESC, the economic security adviser, would report to the President and work in cooperation with the key cabinet secretaries, especially the Secretary of the Treasury, to integrate the many elements of a comprehensive economic policy. Given the primacy of the Treasury Department in economic policy matters, the ESC would enhance the role of the Treasury Department, not undermine it, by reducing agencies' competition and agencies' efforts to get their way by going directly to the President.

To start, the ESC would be a forum for the process of setting national targets for various measures of economic performance, such as rates of saving, investment, nonmilitary R&D, average SAT scores, health care inflation, productivity growth, and overall economic growth, for the next ten years. It would monitor these goals on a year-by-year basis, and if trends are unfavorable, policy changes should be considered to increase the chance of achieving them.

Of course, one of the essential targets the new Administration must address is the federal budget deficit. The next President should ask the Treasury Secretary and the director of the Office of Management and Budget to work together, and with Congress, to develop a set of objective and honest projections of future deficits, using realistic economic assumptions based on current policies. The President must decide on a targeted level for the deficit, and a time period to reach it—perhaps targeting a balanced budget in a seven- to nine-year time frame in order not to impede investment and growth.

In addition to developing fiscal goals, the Treasury Department should work with the economic security adviser and the director of the Office of Management and Budget to change the budgeting system used by the Federal Government. Because the Federal Government, unlike most states and the private sector, lacks a capital budget, it neither has a grasp on the amount of public investment nor on the differences among different types of government spending and debt. This system often encourages policymakers to underestimate the need for new investment. It also tends to undermine support for new investment by focusing attention on the total amount of spending, not on the composition of spending. Washington needs a new capital budget system to help policymakers and the public distinguish between investment and consumption.

But as the experience of state and local governments has shown, it is not always easy to classify expenditures. The obvious examples of investment are traditional public infrastructure expenditures—roads, bridges, airports, schools—whether financed on a hard-dollar basis or through bonds, with or without a dedicated revenue source for repayment. But what about borrowing to pay for current maintenance, or for expenditures to pay the costs of training programs, with or without a revenue stream consisting of future training loan repayments?

The Treasury Department should take the lead in formulating proposals for a capital budget. Since the question of how much money to spend on public investment cannot be separated from the question of how to finance it, and since the Treasury Department has primary responsibility for financing all government spending, Treasury is the logical agency to take the lead in capital planning. It has the expertise to recommend how much of the new public investments be financed on a pay-as-you-go basis and how much by borrowing. Treasury would develop a proposed capital budget, which it would then submit to the OMB, which would reconcile the proposed capital budget with the proposals for the government's operating account budget.

The Treasury Department will also be the focal point for implementing the investment parts of the new economic strategy. It will have to develop recommendations to the President about which new revenue streams and what amounts should be dedicated to new investments and how much should be used for deficit reduction. The President and Congress will also need guidance on the best way to increase public investment quickly while avoiding unnecessary projects. The Treasury Department should also delegate implementation and planning to the states to some degree through the use of revolving loan funds that will create a partnership with state and local governments.

Treasury will also face a number of complex issues on the private investment agenda. It will have to design the incremental investment tax credit so as not to reward investments that would have been made anyway, yet still provide an effective incentive. It will need to make a judgment on the various steps in the sliding-scale capital gains tax. Shortly after taking office, the Treasury Secretary should start work in cooperation with the private sector and Congress on a program of structural reforms to change the relationship of the capital markets to the manufacturing sector in order to lengthen investor time horizons, encourage more effective corporate governance, and provide more capital. This will necessarily involve discussion with institutional investors on how they can be encouraged to seek out investments that are essential for manufacturing and technological leadership and other economic priorities.

Finally, there are a number of critical international issues facing the Treasury Department. The Administration will likely want to keep the dollar stable at its current relatively low level but not let it fall further. It will need to develop a policy on foreign direct investment that will serve our interest in regaining technological leadership and increasing our competitiveness yet keep the United States relatively open to foreign capital. If we are to restore growth at home, we will have to restore growth abroad. International lending and development institutions can play a role in restarting global growth in the lesser-developed regions that represent important export markets, especially if Congress were to appropriate $5 to $10 billion for spurring global growth and the Treasury Department devised a way to leverage those funds.

FISCAL POLICY

ROBERT J. SHAPIRO

Summary

THE DEBAUCH OF THE NATIONAL BUDGET is a central failure of the presidencies of the 1980s and early 1990s. General recognition of this failure provides the next President and the next Congress with a singular opportunity to set a new course of progressive fiscal discipline, shifting resources to public investment while reducing the growth of other federal spending.

Progressive fiscal discipline rejects the budget policies of neglect that, since 1980, have curtailed federal investment in the common economic resources that can make a society more productive and competitive. It also goes beyond the politics of entitlement, which accepts large, fixed deficits as the price of preserving spending and tax subsidies for selected industries, rapidly rising spending for health care, and disproportionate transfer payments for affluent people.

The next President should begin by acknowledging the grave costs of large, fixed deficits. In contrast to the stimulative effects of small and periodic deficits, the large, permanent deficits of recent administrations have not helped to propel vigorous economic growth. While the government tripled the national debt in the 1980s, the economic prospects and prosperity of most Americans eroded. The stark facts are that, adjusted for inflation, the U.S. economy grew by less than 1 percent a year in the 1990s and by less than 2.7 percent a year through the 1980s—as compared to average annual growth of about 4 percent in the 1950s and 1960s, and 2.8 percent in the 1970s. Similarly, the average weekly earnings of most U.S. workers—every-

Robert J. Shapiro, who is Senior Economics Adviser to Governor Bill Clinton, is Vice President of the Progressive Policy Institute. He served as Deputy National Issues Director in the Dukakis-Bentsen campaign, as Associate Editor of U.S. News and World Report *and as Legislative Director to Senator Daniel P. Moynihan.*

one but the top quarter who work as supervisors, managerial, or professionals—fell by 3.6 percent in the 1980s and by another 1 percent in the first years of the 1990s.[1] As a result, the share of Americans with the means to finance their children's college education, own their own homes, and maintain health-care coverage fell, and the distribution of Americans' incomes and wealth grew less equal—while the federal tax burden on average-income families actually increased.

Large, fixed deficits also generate enormous servicing costs on the national debt that today claim more than $200 billion a year in scarce public resources. These deficits also limit sharply the government's ability to ease or end business downturns, as demonstrated in the 1990–92 recession. Finally, ever-growing deficits have paralyzed the political will of the national government, undermining its ability to undertake needed, long-term changes.

The next President should reject the fiscal policies of neglect and entitlement and adopt a new budget strategy based on principles of national investment and common responsibility.

• First, the budget should be divided into separate accounts for investment spending and consumption-related spending. Over time, all non-investment spending should be financed as it is spent, and deficits should be limited to no more than the government invests.

• Second, the government should commit a larger share of its resources to the common economic investments that help make people and firms more productive: sound education and training, state-of-the-art research and development, and world-class infrastructure.

• Third, the next President should relieve the burden of national debt by limiting the annual growth of all consumption-related federal spending so that it grows, year after year, more slowly than the economy.

• Fourth, the government should redesign many long-standing spending and tax policies so they are more effective and efficient, and end programs that do not generate national benefits justifying the attendant tax burden on average taxpayers. Every spending program in government should be subject to periodic review under sunset provisions, and the President should have and use a line-item veto to carry out these principles.

• Fifth, the next President should revolutionize the administration of the federal establishment so it can operate as flexibly and productively as a well-run business and can absorb 3 percent annual reductions in administrative budgets as well as substantial cuts in the federal work force.

The Source of the Problem: Spending or Taxes?

IF, AS NEARLY ALL ECONOMISTS AGREE, fiscal policy in the 1980s and early 1990s has hindered the government's basic capacity to promote prosperity, should a new policy of progressive fiscal discipline focus on spending restraint or tax increases?

When it comes to a large deficit's impact on a country's underlying economic prospects, the crucial element is not so much its absolute size as its scale and economic burden. In this context, the first question for fiscal-policy reform is whether the large, permanent deficits of recent presidencies reflect declining revenues and modestly rising spending, or spending that increased faster than the economy's capacity to support it.

The data show that while real federal spending actually grew much faster in the 1950s and 1960s than in the 1970s and 1980s, the faster spending growth in the earlier decades coincided with rapid economic growth. As a result, spending increases in the 1950s and 1960s entailed a lesser economic burden than later, when less-rapid spending growth claimed more of a slower-growing economy. Moreover, much of the spending increases of the 1950s and 1960s were targeted to public investments in education and public works that helped raise the underlying growth rate of the economy; the spending growth of more recent times, however, has been driven by the consumption-related spending of entitlement programs, defense, and interest payments.

As a result, although real spending grew faster in the 1950s and 1960s than later, its rate of increase as a share of the Gross National Product was twice as great in the 1980s as in earlier decades. Moreover, this dynamic persisted through the 1980s and the early 1990s, even as successive tax increases and tax reforms annulled the large revenue reductions approved in 1981.

The lesson is that the economic burden of federal spending comes not so much from whether spending continues to grow, but whether it grows faster than the economy.

As the economic burden of federal spending has increased, the distribution of federal taxes also has shifted: from corporations to workers, from excise taxes to payroll taxes, and from direct taxes to borrowing. The share of all spending covered by taxes on corporate profits has declined steeply and steadily, while the portion covered by payroll taxes has increased sharply. Excise and estate taxes now play a minor revenue role rather than a major one, while borrowing has grown from an incidental factor to a fundamental one. The only constant element has been the role of income taxes in providing

TABLE 1.
The Growth and Burden of Federal Spending

Decade	Average Annual Growth Rate of Real Spending	Share of GNP, Annual Average	Spending as a Rate of Increase in the Share of GNP Claimed by Federal Spending
1950s	5.7%	18.0%	5.6%
1960s	5.0%	19.0%	6.0%
1970s	3.0%	20.5%	7.4%
1980s	3.0%	23.1%	12.8%

Source: Calculations based on Budget of the United States Government, *Fiscal Year 1992,* "Historical Tables," *Table 1.3.*

TABLE 2.
Source of Funds for Federal Spending
(average annual shares)

Decade	Personal Income Tax	Corporate Income Tax	Payroll Excise/Tax	Borrowing	Estate
1950s	42.0%	26.9%	11.5%	17.2%	2.5%
1960s	42.0%	20.4%	18.4%	14.9%	4.4%
1970s	40.3%	13.3%	27.7%	11.3%	11.1%
1980s	38.0%	7.7%	29.2%	8.2%	17.7%

Source: Calculations based on Budget of the United States Government, *Fiscal Year 1992,* "Historical Tables," *Tables 1.1 and 2.2.*

a basic revenue base: The share of spending covered by revenues from the personal income tax has remained relatively stable for forty years, even with regular income-tax-rate cuts.[2]

Following deep tax cuts in 1981, persistent deficits created powerful pressures to find new revenues, relieved chiefly by seven successive increases in the payroll-tax rate. For this purpose, the payroll tax offered two advantages. First, most taxpayers consider the payroll tax more of a "contribution" than a tax. And second, most of the income of very affluent people—all wage or salary income exceeding about $55,000, and all dividends, interest, rent, and gains from capital assets—is exempt from payroll taxes. The result is that the federal tax burden on most working people increased in the 1980s even as the deficit grew, while declining for the highest-income households.[3]

For most people, therefore, large, permanent deficits have not brought lower tax burdens. Rather, recent presidents and congresses have persistently chosen both to tolerate large deficits and to raise payroll taxes as ways of paying for both spending increases and reductions in corporate, excise, and estate taxes.[4]

The impact of the tax policies of recent presidents, in short, has proved to be no more progressive than their deficit-spending policies. In effect, both approaches have drawn on the same political disposition, whether it assumes the form of promising to deliver more benefits and services for the same price, or the same benefits and services for less.

Progressive Restraints on the Growth of Spending

ECONOMISTS HAVE NO WAY OF DETERMINING what level of federal spending would promote the richest, the most civil, the most free, or the most equal society.[5] But this difficulty does not invalidate the sound economic reasons for limiting how quickly public spending can grow. The crucial judgment is that the share of national income used for public consumption should, under normal conditions, increase no faster than the economy, lest it slow private investment and growth. The same idea from a taxpayer's vantage could be stated as follows: As long as two thirds of the federal budget is financed directly from the income of ordinary households, federal spending should expand no faster than an average taxpayer's ability to pay for it.

From this conclusion the next President can derive a new rule to replace arbitrary deficit targets: The growth rate of public-consumption spending should not exceed the growth rate of per capita personal income in the preceding year. Nearly all spending under the control of Congress and the President should be subject to this limit—entitlements and discretionary spending, civilian and military expenditures, "on budget" and "off budget" programs. The only spending not covered would be national investments that can raise the trend-growth rate of the economy. The limit would be enforced every year, except during recessions and wartime, or other grave national emergencies.[6]

To enforce this restraint, a majority vote should be required before any congressional committee or either house of Congress can consider legislation that would increase an appropriation or authorization faster than the rate of income gain the year before, or that with already enacted legislation would breach the overall limit. If the President submits proposals for noninvestment expenditures that would increase spending faster than last year's income, he should be required to offer either offsetting consumption-spending cuts or a finding of national emergency. If at the end of the year consumption spending exceeds the legal limit, the excess should be deducted from the ceiling on consumption spending permitted for the following year.

This reform would moderate the growth of federal spending according to the pattern of ordinary people's economic lives, avoiding both a straitjacket on public commitments or license to run large, persistent deficits. It would allow spending to grow slowly when Americans are making small income strides and more rapidly when average people are enjoying greater gains.

Year after year, modest reductions in spending growth based on per capita income gains could revolutionize fiscal policy. Had Congress adopted this rule in 1980, nominal, noninterest spending would have grown at an average annual rate of 6.9 percent through the decade, as compared to the average of 7.6 percent a year actually recorded.[7] This modest difference would have been sufficient to all but eliminate the deficit by 1989 and reduce the $2.2 trillion publicly held national debt at the close of that year by more than $850 billion.

The reason is that under normal economic conditions, revenues will grow modestly faster than per capita income. First, revenues are based on (net) national income; and however rapidly national income grows, per capita income will grow more slowly because the population is increasing. Under progressive spending restraint, therefore, expenditures would increase more slowly than revenues on their natural course.[8] And second, when public spending grows at a slower rate than national income, the share of national income available for investment, that in turn can produce future revenue spending, increases. These relationships support the choice of per capita income growth to limit increases: so long as most of the burden of providing for the increase falls on private households and the private economy, most of the increase in national income should remain in private hands.

How to Restrain Spending and Promote Economic Growth

THE TASK OF RESTRAINING OVERALL SPENDING while promoting growth through private and public investment will entail, to begin, basic reforms in four budget categories: subsidies for selected industries; transfer payments and supports; the administration of the Federal Government; and defense spending.

These reforms should rest on two basic economic principles. First, competition is the spur to the innovation and flexibility required to compete successfully in a global economy. Therefore, fiscal policy can promote growth by reducing subsidies that insulate U.S. industries and firms from competition. Second, in a global economy, many nations share access to basic resources such as capital and technology. Fiscal policy's role in promoting competitiveness, therefore, should focus on public investments in the resources that the country has to itself—principally America's work force, economic infrastructure, and research and development.

REDUCE SPECIAL-INTEREST SUBSIDIES

In the old economy of a generation and two ago, American prosperity depended mainly on competition among domestic producers, primarily over who could produce a standard product or service at the lowest cost. With few exceptions, foreign competition was secondary, and the American market provided most of the resources needed for this domestic competition.

Today our prosperity depends on the outcome of competition among U.S. and foreign producers, especially those from the other advanced economies of Japan and members of the European Community. The share of the Gross Domestic Product accounted for by trade increased from about 10 percent in the 1960s to 20 to 25 percent in the 1980s and early 1990s. And more often than not, competition today turns on the capacities of firms and workers to create or adapt a service or product to meet changing demands in particular markets, and not merely on the relative cost of different products to meet the same demand. The firms, workers, and countries that win this global competition are the ones that are best at identifying new sources of materials, design, process, financing, marketing, technology, and demand from around the world, and best at putting these factors into production quickly.

The world economy, therefore, puts less value today on what America traditionally did best—produce standard goods and services more cheaply than anyone else by doing it on a larger scale and more efficiently. In the new economy, prosperity depends as much on the innovative capacities of a country's workers and firms to identify new markets and create new inputs and products for them. In short, a nation's economic success today depends as much on its firms' and workers' flexibility and adaptability to change as it does on managers' abilities to cut costs.

National fiscal policy, therefore, has to play a crucial but different role than the one many believed it should play in the 1970s and 1980s. In the old economy, government proliferated tax, spending, and credit subsidies for selected industries, as government's way of promoting U.S. competitiveness by helping firms to cut certain costs. In a globalized economy, most of these subsidies undermine innovation and efficiency by making many corporations too comfortable to change. National economic success in the 1990s will require that government turn away from industry subsidies and protections of almost every kind, and toward national investments in the common economic resources that help promote innovation and flexibility, principally education and training, research and development, and advanced communications and transportation systems among our markets.

The new Administration should reexamine all current spending and tax subsidies. To be sure, some embody strategies for correcting market failures, and their repeal could reduce economic growth. However, many more represent special tax or spending largess for influential interests. And eliminating these special-interest provisions could produce large savings: Industry-spending subsidies total an estimated $30 billion a year, and industry-tax subsidies cost substantially more.

REFORM ENTITLEMENT PROGRAMS

Fiscal policy in the 1990s should reduce the budgetary role not only of industry subsidies but also of transfer payments. These fiscal reforms should focus on those transfers that are both large and growing rapidly—health and retirement payments—and on their aspect which nearly everyone would consider unfair—using taxes to support disproportionate benefits for high-income persons.

The next President should offer the American people a new understanding governing direct transfers. Under this compact, everyone is *entitled* to certain basic goods, including access to basic health care and a decent retirement after working for a lifetime, and to a share of these goods that reflects at least what he or she has contributed to finance their general availability. In return, everyone is expected to work to help provide these goods for themselves, and to provide a fair share of the cost of guaranteeing their general availability by paying payroll and income taxes. But everyone also would be obliged not to claim a *disproportionate* share, and high-income people who can afford to provide for themselves should not receive a greater share of benefits than those who cannot afford to provide them themselves.

Put another way, fiscal policy in the next Administration should restrain the growth of transfer programs by ensuring that the share of entitlement benefits received by high-income people does not exceed their share of the population.

Most Americans have resisted restraints on entitlement programs because they consider these programs to be essentially fair. And the data show that, overall, transfer payments are distributed in a roughly flat pattern: Each income group receives spending benefits roughly equivalent to its share of the population. However, the distribution of benefits in the fast-growing retirement and health-care programs—Social Security, civilian and military pensions, and Medicare and Medicaid—modestly favors high-income persons. Moreover, the distribution of retirement and health-related tax expenditures—the value of tax deductions for IRA and Keogh contributions, and of the tax exemptions for all or part of Social Security income, for the insurance value of Medicare, and for employer contributions to pension and health-care plans—strongly favors the affluent. Combined, federal spending and tax benefits for retirement and health care are today distributed disproportionately to higher-income households.

The data demonstrate that federal tax and spending supports for retirement and health care provide a disproportionately small share to low-income households and a disproportionately large share to households with annual incomes above $75,000, especially to those with annual incomes above $200,000. As a matter of fairness, the new President should introduce reforms restraining the growth of taxpayer-supported retirement and health-care tax or spending benefits for very affluent people. Since these supports (along with interest on the national debt) are the fastest-growing elements of the federal budget, restraining their growth will steadily reduce future deficits.

TABLE 3.
Retirement-Related Federal Spending and Tax Benefits

Taxable Income Amt.	% U.S.	Spending Outlays (in billions)	Share	Tax Benefits Benefits (in billions)	Share	Total Value (in billions)	Share
Below 10K	21.9%	$51.2	17.5%	$2.4	2.8%	$53.5	14.2%
10K–20K	20.4%	$64.5	22.1%	$9.8	11.5%	$74.3	19.7%
20K–30K	16.3%	$50.8	17.4%	$14.3	16.7%	$65.1	17.3%
30K–40K	12.1%	$36.4	12.5%	$12.9	15.1%	$49.4	13.1%
40K–50K	9.0%	$26.0	8.9%	$10.9	12.7%	$36.8	9.8%
50K–75K	12.2%	$34.6	11.8%	$14.9	17.5%	$49.5	13.1%
75K–100K	4.2%	$12.3	4.2%	$6.0	7.0%	$18.2	4.8%
100K–200K	2.8%	$11.0	3.8%	$7.5	8.8%	$18.5	4.9%
Over 200K	1.1%	$5.3	1.8%	$6.7	7.8%	$12.0	3.2%
Total	100.0%	$292.1	100.0%	$85.4	100.0%	$377.5	100.0%

TABLE 4.
Health-Related Federal Spending and Tax Benefits

Taxable Income Amt.	% U.S.	Spending		Tax Benefits		Total	
		Outlays (in billions)	Share	Benefits (in billions)	Share	Value (in billions)	Share
Below 10K	21.9%	$26.8	25.9%	$0.6	1.2%	$27.4	18.0%
10K–20K	20.4%	$25.3	24.4%	$5.4	11.1%	$30.7	20.1%
20K–30K	16.3%	$17.2	16.6%	$8.6	17.7%	$25.8	17.0%
30K–40K	12.1%	$11.2	10.8%	$7.6	15.6%	$18.8	12.3%
40K–50K	9.0%	$7.3	7.1%	$7.1	14.5%	$14.4	9.4%
50K–75K	12.2%	$9.1	8.8%	$11.2	22.9%	$20.3	13.3%
75K–100K	4.2%	$3.0	2.9%	$4.3	8.8%	$7.3	4.8%
100K–200K	2.8%	$2.5	2.4%	$2.1	4.3%	$4.6	3.0%
Over 200K	1.1%	$1.2	1.2%	$1.9	3.8%	$3.1	2.0%
Total	100.0%	$103.6	100.0%	$48.8	100.0%	$152.4	100.0%

Source for Tables 3 and 4: Calculations based on data compiled by the Congressional Budget Office and the Joint Committee on Taxation.

INCREASE THE PRODUCTIVITY OF THE NATIONAL GOVERNMENT

The next President can also slow fast-growing federal spending by promoting the operational efficiency of the federal establishment. The federal bureaucracy today claims more than $200 billion a year for personnel and administration. Moreover, this figure continues to rise when it could be falling, if government were committed to finding ways of becoming more productive.

Under normal conditions, a healthy business can achieve 3 percent annual gains in productivity. The next President should require every federal office, agency, and department to meet the same standard by cutting its operating expenses. Such cuts are an established technique in business for motivating each unit to put together its own strategy for raising productivity and getting more for less—and no more than what governors from Virginia to California have done recently to help address state-budget shortfalls. Moreover, cutting federal administrative costs by 3 percent a year could reduce the growth of government spending by $6 billion to $7 billion in the first year and by tens of billions of dollars over four years—and without affecting any federal supports on which people depend. And this estimate does not include productivity reforms in the uniformed military, where substantial savings also could be achieved.

This strategy is intended not only to slow the growth of federal spending but also to coax federal managers and workers into approaching their missions more creatively. Most federal employees are committed public servants, often working for less pay than their private-sector counterparts; but the system in which they work is outdated. In nearly every other sphere, large private organizations have reduced layers of bureaucracy so that information can flow more easily to those directly involved in decisions and operations. Cutting the budgets for administration can help drive the search for new ways of delivering federal services and encourage a more entrepreneurial attitude in federal workers.

REDEPLOY EXCESS DEFENSE SPENDING TO PUBLIC INVESTMENT

With the end of the Cold War, national defense is the fourth category of consumption-related spending that a new government can reduce without impairing the national interest. Substantial defense cuts can provide resources needed to expand national investment in the common economic resources that promote growth and productivity.

The precise level of defense cuts, however, should be determined not by the scale of the country's domestic needs but by the difference between what is now required to preserve national security and what was earlier projected based on the presence of a Soviet military threat. (See, e.g., the discussion by John Steinbruner in this volume.)

While reforms of current industry subsidies, disproportionate transfer payments, and inefficient government operations are the chief means of slowing the growth of consumption-related federal spending, defense savings should be committed to expanding public investment in the nation's common economic resources. U.S. economic growth has been substandard in part because the government drastically slowed real federal investment in education and training, in the communications and transportation infrastructure that binds our markets and our businesses together, and in the research and development that provide an edge in global competition. A program of progressive fiscal discipline, therefore, should increase spending in these vital areas, as other spending described earlier is reduced.

The Fiscal Program for the Next President

TO ESTABLISH A NEW POLICY OF PROGRESSIVE and productive fiscal discipline, the next President should undertake six basic changes in the budget policies and politics of the national government.

1. The budget should be divided into three parts, reflecting the country's responsibilities and ambitions: a *past budget*—covering interest payments and the costs of the savings-and-loan bailout; a *future* or *investment budget*—covering spending for education, training, research and development, and infrastructure; and a *present* or *consumption-related budget*—covering all other government operations and transfer payments. The next President should commit himself to financing federal spending on the *present* and the *past* in the present, raising the revenues to cover past obligations and all current public consumption, and limiting future federal borrowing to no more than is invested in the nation's common *future* through programs that produce direct economic returns for the country.

2. We should increase public investment in the country's economic future and discipline spending on the present, reversing the priorities of public spending in the 1980s. Over four years, the share of the federal budget dedicated to national investment should double, financed chiefly by cutting excess defense spending. At the same time, the forty-second President should limit how rapidly other spending can increase, based on how rapidly Americans' per capita incomes grow. In this way, the government's consumption-spending ambitions can no longer outstrip the average person's ability and willingness to pay for them. And if we respect this democratic principle, the federal deficit could decline by more than half by 1995 and be effectively eliminated by 1999—without increasing an average family's tax burden.

3. The next Administration should provide America a more effective, efficient, and productive government by introducing to the federal bureaucracy the productivity-enhancing strategies and standards of a successful business. The federal work force can be reduced by at least a hundred thousand positions, and the government's administrative expenses—both Congress and the Executive Branch—can be cut by 3 percent a year, across the board.

4. Every policy and activity in the budget should be subject to a sunset provision requiring that every program and tax expenditure be reauthorized at least once every ten years or expire. In this way, both branches of government could have a systematic way of reexamining existing spending on a continuing basis.

5. The new President should use sunsetting—and a line-item veto—to establish a new standard for both tax expenditures and spending: Do a program's achievements justify the tax burden on average families required to pay for them? Or could the same results or better ones be achieved by reforming the program or by transferring its responsibilities to the private sector or to state or local governments—where most policy innovation has occurred in the last ten years?

6. The new Administration should apply this standard to reduce federal subsidies for special interests and fast-rising benefits for affluent people in the largest and fastest-growing federal programs: retirement, and health-care-related entitlements and tax expenditures. Federal payments to industries that use them to enrich their stockholders and insulate themselves from competition should be phased out. And future, additional benefits for affluent people who today claim a disproportionate share of the support from government retirement and health-care programs should be restrained.

A generation ago—when federal spending was moderate, tax burdens were low, national investment was robust, and the capital markets were not globalized—periodic, modest deficits provided supports for average people. Today, when a typical family's taxes are high, federal spending is higher still, and capital markets are globalized, large, chronic deficits that threaten both the upward mobility of most Americans and government's ability to help chart the nation's course.

Federal policies must leave behind the twin, failed fiscal politics of neglect and the status quo, and help move the nation forward with a new strategy based on progressive fiscal restraint, a relationship of mutual responsibility between people and their government, and a genuine commitment to investing in the country's future.

NOTES

1. *Economic Report of the President*, February 1990 (cited as *Economic Report*), Tables C-2, C-44.

2. The appearance of large, fixed deficits in the 1980s coincided with a historic slowdown in the growth of Americans' personal income. It is reasonable to suppose that the slow income growth intensified public demands for income-tax cuts, while also reinforcing the government's normal inclination to spend more.

3. The total federal income and payroll tax burden for a two-parent family at the national median income rose slightly in the 1980s, from 23.7 percent in 1980 to 24.1 percent in 1988; in contrast, the comparable federal tax burden for a family in the top 5 percent of taxpayers fell over the same years, from 28.9 percent in 1980 to 25.7 percent in 1988. Moreover, the share of all spending paid for by direct taxes on individuals—federal income and payroll taxes—rose steadily from 53.5 percent in the 1950s to 60.4 percent in the 1960s and 67.5 percent in the 1970s. In the 1980s, with payroll tax increases on moderate- and average-income Americans offsetting income-tax cuts for all income groups, the share of spending paid for by direct federal taxes on individuals stabilized at 67.2 percent.

4. Stated another way, the share of spending paid for by payroll taxes grew much faster than did the share of spending paid for by borrowing.

5. Even if such a calculation were possible, it does not take account of changes in public spending at the state and local levels, or of related private spending. It is not surprising,

for example, that when the growth of federal expenditures slows, spending by state and local governments often accelerates, to pick up functions being pared by the Federal Government.

6. On a decade-by-decade basis, the average annual growth rate of federal spending exceeded the average annual growth rate of per capita income consistently through the postwar period. Once the data are adjusted to exclude years following recessions, so that the government's ability to respond to a downturn is not crippled, and to exclude the wartime emergency buildups of the Korean and Vietnam conflicts, the average annual rate of spending growth exceeded the average annual rate of income growth, on a decade-by-decade basis, only in the 1980s. On an annual basis, the reform would probably have restrained the growth of federal spending in fifteen of the past forty years: 1989, 1988, 1985, 1984, 1979, 1977, 1976, 1971, 1964, 1962, 1961, 1957, 1956, 1955, and 1951. These calculations are derived from data reported in *Economic Report*, Tables C-26 and C-27; and *Budget*, "Historical Tables," Table 1.1.

7. If interest is counted, the average annual growth rate of spending would have been 7.1 percent under the reform, as compared to the 8.8 percent actually recorded. Note also that the simulation assumes that the limit would have been suspended in 1982 and 1983 as a result of the 1981–82 recession.

8. For example, if national income increases from $5 trillion to $5.4 trillion, and the population grows from 240 million to 245 million, the growth rate of national income will be 8 percent while the growth rate of per capita income would be 5.8 percent. Revenues would naturally increase by 7 to 8 percent, while spending increases would be limited to 5.8 percent. The modestly progressive character of the tax system provides a secondary reason why revenues naturally grow faster than the growth rate of per capita income. For example, a modest increase in income will push some taxpayers into higher tax brackets, as from zero to 15 percent, 15 to 28 percent, or 28 to 31 percent. In addition, many people's effective tax rates rise with income, even if their marginal tax bracket is unaffected, because the value of some deductions or credits does not increase. For instance, a couple with a $20,000 combined income and $6,000 in deductions and exemptions would pay income tax of $2,100 (15 percent of $14,000), or an effective rate of 10.5 percent. If their income rose 10 percent to $22,000, while the value of their deductions increased by only five percent—if, for example, they could not further increase their IRA deduction—they would pay income tax of $2,355 (15 percent of $15,700), raising their effective tax rate to 10.7 percent.

MONETARY POLICY

JAMES K. GALBRAITH

Summary

THE RECESSION THAT BEGAN IN 1990 and the failure of interest rate cuts to generate a strong recovery by the end of 1992 ought to trigger a new movement for reform of the Federal Reserve. This chapter describes the failure of the Volcker-Greenspan monetary regime and makes the case for comprehensive reform.

Monetary policy has remained outside politics in recent years, as critics of the Reagan-Bush economic policies focused on deficits in budgets and trade. But the recession was largely triggered by tight money from 1987 to 1990, and from 1991 to 1992 the Federal Reserve assumed the main responsibility for bringing on a recovery, by lowering interest rates.

It failed. Not only did past accumulations of debt block demand for new loans, but also interest rate cuts came too late, were too gradual, and were too hesitant. As a result, the Federal Reserve—having spent a decade fixated on the disappearing threat of inflation—never gained credibility as an agent of economic growth. Short-term interest rates fell, but long-term and real interest rates remained high, and a strong credit-based recovery never took hold.

In these circumstances, restoring sustainable economic growth will require a balanced program involving all of economic policy, including a monetary policy that assures low and stable interest rates. To establish the credibility of this new policy will require reform of the monetary policy-making process, as well as personnel changes at the Federal Reserve.

Specifically:

• Because sustained low interest rates are essential to economic growth, the new President and the Federal Reserve chairman should publicly commit

James K. Galbraith is Professor at the Lyndon B. Johnson School of Public Affairs at the University of Texas at Austin. His 1989 book, Balancing Acts, presents an in-depth discussion of the problems of inflation control that are mentioned in this article.

to a policy of keeping short-term interest rates low and bringing long-term rates down.

- To make the Federal Reserve more publicly accountable, Congress should: (a) require it to announce all Federal Open Market Committee (FOMC) directives and (b) pass the Hamilton-Sarbanes proposal to remove the five banker-influenced regional Federal Reserve Bank presidents from their voting role on the FOMC.

The End of the Conservative Monetary Era

IF IN 1993 THE AMERICAN ECONOMY finally recovers from its longest postwar recession, the Federal Reserve will surely deserve the credit. From the summer of 1991 forward, Alan Greenspan cut interest rates relentlessly, to the point where short-term rates fell to twenty-nine-year lows. A prudent epigone, Paul Volcker's successor and shadow during his first three years as Federal Reserve chairman finally made his own mark—as a rate cutter.

In the perhaps equally likely event that there is no strong recovery, one may argue that Greenspan's own caution, his discomfort in this new role, tripped him up. Because the rate cuts were gradual and not dramatic, because they were late and indecisive, Greenspan's Federal Reserve failed to become a credible agent of economic growth. It failed to persuade the markets that short-term interest rates would stay down once recovery began. As a result, long-term interest rates hardly came down at all. The recovery that resulted was slow, uncertain, and anemic, and if it was intended to place President Bush's reelection beyond challenge, it obviously failed in that objective.

But whether it was politically motivated or not, Greenspan's policy from 1987 onward was a fundamental departure from the rulebook that was supposed to have been established for monetary policy eight years before. It was the final end of the Volcker era, the final failure of the conservative monetary policy dream, and it ought to open a new debate over what has been since 1979 a politically closed subject.

To recall: In October 1979 Paul Volcker imposed his anti-inflation shock therapy: supertight money and superhigh interest rates. That "October Surprise," even more than the other one, ruined the Democratic Party. It contributed to President Carter's reelection defeat and set the stage both for the deep recession of 1981–82 and for the strong, noninflationary, but debt-ridden recovery that carried Ronald Reagan to his reelection triumph in 1984.

Despite these political consequences of his actions, Volcker was never accused of political motivation. To the contrary, even his sharpest critics gave him credit for a deeper purpose, based in part on the advanced academic economics of that time. This was to use a temporary bout of very tight money not only to cut the rate of inflation but also to change the image of the Federal Reserve, to establish once and for all that inflation would not be tolerated, and so to drive inflation expectations out of the system. With inflation expectations tamed, the theory went, sustained growth without renewed inflation would again be possible, and the pain would be justified by benefits over the long run.

As late as 1986 or 1987, one might have believed that Volcker had succeeded. Inflation did fall, and even with recovery stayed below half its former peak. U.S. economic performance was good, especially in international perspective. The United States had apparently reconciled real economic growth rates of 3 to 4 percent per year with stable inflation of about the same amount. We had also reduced unemployment from 10 to 6 percent, creating 13 million new jobs (by 1987). Eventually the expansion became the longest since World War II.

But could it continue? Had inflation truly been driven out of the system? Or were the gains merely temporary, provisional, an interim of stability at the price of chaos later? The conservative theory held that permanent stability had been reached. Today we know better. Volcker's expansion could continue only as long as the government chose to tolerate an overvalued dollar and an unsustainable deficit in the balance of trade. When the dollar came down, consumer price inflation gradually edged up, reaching 6.1 percent in 1990 (with help from Saddam Hussein). Greenspan's monetary policy reacted to this rising inflation in the old style, with tight money and high interest rates leading inexorably to recession. It thus abandoned, in deed though not in word, the pretext that the Volcker formula had been successful.

In reality, then, the gains from Volcker's war on inflation were not once and for all. Rather, the battle must be waged again and again, over the same scarred terrain of unemployment, human misery, industrial dislocation, and social decay. Greenspan's recovery—if there is a recovery—will be from Greenspan's own recession, and the only prospect it holds out is for yet another recession later.

The Deficit and Monetary Politics

OF COURSE, THROUGHOUT THE 1980s many people believed that economic policy was on the road to ruin. But attention focused mainly on the budget deficit and not on the Federal Reserve. In this view the Federal Reserve was mainly an innocent bystander; the real villains were big spenders and antitaxers who together tolerated deepening budget imbalance. Investment bankers, politicians, foreign central bankers, business journalists, and some professional economists formed a Greek chorus on the irresponsibility of it all. They insisted that the prosperity was merely borrowed and warned sternly that cutting "entitlements"—a code word for Social Security—or raising taxes would be necessary to avoid national financial ruin.

This argument virtually exempted the Federal Reserve from responsibility for any eventual debacle. It also overlooked two facts: that interest on the public debt, an item not insensitive to high interest rates, was the fastest-growing element of public expenditure, and that tight monetary policy constricted both private income and tax collections. Given these facts, it is not surprising that the deficit diversion drew support from Volcker himself, for whom it could serve as a scapegoat if (more likely, when) things went wrong.

The budget deficit also obscured another and more important phenomenon: rapid economic globalization. With rising trade in manufactured goods, a veritable flood of imports rolled in after 1983. It was easy to correlate deficits in budgets and trade, but to do so was fundamentally misleading. The "twin deficits" argument, of which Volcker was especially fond, ignored the role of tight money in generating a high dollar and trade deficit. It also both underplayed the structural role of the trade deficit and misstated the appropriate cure.

It was globalization that really delayed inflation during the 1980s expansion. Cheap foreign labor costs in low-technology industries split apart the wage structure. Cost competition held down wage increases in vulnerable industries, in particular labor- and materials-intensive sectors, from textiles to cars. At the same time, the high dollar killed export markets in more advanced sectors, holding down wage increases in industries such as aerospace and communications that would ordinarily have little trouble competing.

The effect was to substitute a large trade deficit and rising international debt for rising inflation. In the policy arena, trade issues tended to crowd out discussion of inflation. Yet it remained true that when policy finally moved to reduce the trade deficit, with dollar depreciation after 1985, a rising rate of inflation would eventually follow as long as the economy was to be allowed room to grow.

Paul Volcker seems to have suspected that his miracle was unsustainable when he resigned in the summer of 1987, as I wrote then, "in the nick of time." And thus it was that Alan Greenspan, the man who wanted in the worst way to be a central banker, got his wish. Since the economy at the moment of his appointment was not yet in crisis, he could hardly have called for a state of emergency and the draconian measures on which central bankers build their legends. But neither could Greenspan hope to sustain a noninflationary expansion through the whole of his term in office. Once policy set out to reduce the trade deficit, Greenspan's only choice was between a recession before an inflation crisis, or after.

Greenspan's Choice

GREENSPAN CHOSE TO SLOW THE ECONOMY, raising interest rates and tightening money to hold inflation in check. By 1989, real economic growth was less than the growth of population, and the economy was stagnant. By mid-1990, stagnation had turned into recession, and by late 1991 hopes for recovery, once quite strong, had actually faded. They did not return until heroic end-year cuts in interest rates brought them back in the spring of 1992—only to fade again by summer. There would be no inflation crisis for a simple reason: The fire fighters flooded the house before the fire began. Meanwhile, the trade balance had, of course, improved.

Thus the 1990–92 recession punctured the myth, the Reagan-Volcker myth, that sustained stable growth without inflation can be achieved by the magic of monetary policy alongside laissez-faire in all other domains. If the recovery does take hold, then either rising prices or a rising trade deficit are expected. And neither can be tolerated for very long.

As the Federal Reserve sought recovery in 1991 and 1992, short-term interest rates were repeatedly cut. But the spread between short- and long-term rates, nearly the highest in memory, tells us that the financial markets did not believe in the recession "cure." Rather, the markets appeared to be convinced that short-term interest rates would go up again once recovery was solidly established—or perhaps, merely after the election.

Is this the only way to live? Is there no way to keep this grim cycle from repeating? Might we not prefer a monetary strategy that was less disruptive, that destroyed fewer lives and livelihoods, that maintained a higher average standard of living? If so, we had better get serious about fundamental reform.

Projects for Reform: Straitjackets or Democratic Accountability

MONETARY REFORMERS ON BOTH THE LEFT and the right call for stable growth fueled by low real interest rates. They often argue that institutional reform of the role and structure of the Federal Reserve is a necessary means to this end.

Monetarist economists still led in spirit by Milton Friedman argue that the road to monetary stability requires getting the Federal Reserve on automatic pilot. They propose a fixed rule to dictate the rate of money growth. But with technical monetarism in even more disarray than usual (over, as ever, how best to define the concept of money), this idea has now gone somewhat out of fashion.

In its place we now have proposals to give the Federal Reserve a clear and single-minded mandate to seek a zero-inflation *outcome.* These proposals are rooted in the new classical economics, which has displaced monetarism in academic life. They have strong support from Governor Wayne Angell and even a perfunctory endorsement from Chairman Greenspan.

A zero-inflation policy would free the Federal Reserve from obligations even of lip-service to the Humphrey-Hawkins goals of full employment and full production. It is therefore a prescription for a return to the shock therapies of 1979–81, with a vengeance. A new recession would, with luck, eliminate the remaining market power of workers—labor markets would be made truly competitive by the simple device of crippling the industries that are presently competitive, in the other sense, on world markets. Meanwhile, construction and other cyclical workers would lie idle, and those in open competition with Third World products would see their wages fall even more. And as inflation rates fell while interest rates rose, business bankruptcies, mortgage foreclosures, and bank failures would rise. It is easy to see why the call for a zero-inflation policy remains somewhat hypothetical and why even conservatives, if they are wise, remain wary.

Progressives and populists, from the money radicals of the late nineteenth century to Representative Wright Patman to modern populists such as William Greider, have coupled calls for easy money and low interest rates with demand for a more democratic and politically accountable central bank. They make this link for the plausible reason that the structure of the Federal Reserve System now reflects, as it has since 1914, the power of creditors who prefer "sound" money and slow growth to any risk of inflation or increased bargaining power of workers.

This community suggests what are really two separate ideas. One is to rationalize the process of monetary policymaking by making it more responsive to and better coordinated with the other economic policies of the Executive Branch. The other is to make monetary policy more open and accountable to the people, in part by improving oversight procedures in Congress, and in part simply by making monetary policymaking more transparent.

Small "d" democrats can find plenty of flaws in the Federal Reserve's structure. The composition of its principal decisionmaking body, the FOMC, is probably unconstitutional, since the five regional Federal Reserve Bank presidents who rotate on and off this committee are not "officers of the United States" under the appointments clause of the Constitution. The Federal Reserve's own budget remains uniquely immune from congressional appropriations. And the FOMC and the Board of Governors are unusually shielded from normal federal sunlight requirements.

Fixing these defects would on many grounds be a good thing. But the question must be: What difference would it make for policy? Some reformers have championed the subordination of the Federal Reserve to the Treasury Department. Details vary from placing a Treasury representative on the Board (the Treasury secretary once sat there *ex officio*), to moving the whole institution into the Executive Branch. The argument for this is quite baldly that an "integrated" central bank would tend to pursue an easier policy, accepting higher inflation on average and achieving a lower rate of unemployment.

But is there really a divergence of interest or a failure of policy coordination between the Federal Reserve Board, or the FOMC, and the administration?

At best the answer is not clear. For Republican administrations, as well as for Democrats of the late Carter stripe, there may be no fundamental conflict between Federal Reserve policy and administration desires. On the contrary, the nominal independence of the Federal Reserve is often a political convenience. It enables the president to pretend both to insulate himself from the fallout of tight policies and to suggest an easier monetary policy than in fact he favors.

Putting the Federal Reserve under the Treasury would force an administration to invent another bogey (for a model, see the role now played by the German Bundesbank in, say, France or Britain). But it is doubtful that the independence of the Federal Reserve has fooled voters much; they remain resolutely willing to punish an incumbent administration for stagnation (1970, 1974, 1980, 1982) and to reward it for growth (1964, 1972, 1984). Republican presidents know this (Democrats have been known to forget) and therefore do not allow the Federal Reserve to escape from partisan control. The main merit of putting the Federal Reserve under the Treasury would be simply to assure that monetary policy changes course when an administration changes hands.

Proposals to make the Federal Reserve more accountable to Congress reflect a slightly different argument, namely that sometimes there are strong reasons why the institutional interests of the Federal Reserve and the Executive Branch differ from those of Congress. Congress, compared with the

Executive Branch, is a stable institution that likes a stable economy. Representatives make careers of their jobs; they face their constituents every weekend and their voters every two years. Therefore they don't like recessions, especially not off-year recessions patently geared to producing reelection booms two years ahead. There are no regular "off-year" elections to Congress.

Increasing Federal Reserve exposure to Congress thus has the practical effect of turning up the volume of congressional criticism of the Federal Reserve during recession years, and this is generally a stabilizing influence on policy. Increased congressional oversight was the purpose of a series of actions beginning in 1975 and continuing through the Federal Reserve Act amendments in the Humphrey-Hawkins Act of 1978. In that case, and not by accident, Congress framed regular reporting requirements to encourage a more stable demand policy. The design of the oversight was flawed and the implementation weak, but the intent did reflect a true congressional desire for stability that actual Federal Reserve policy has not displayed.

Today, the single most useful reform on behalf of congressional and public accountability would require immediate public announcement of all Federal Open Market Committee directives, which make monetary policy. The practical effect of these directives is almost always largely transparent to the markets, and their concealment has only one real purpose: to blunt their impact as news and therefore their vulnerability to criticism from the public and Congress. The present practice of releasing an old directive only after a new one has replaced it kills the news value of the FOMC's decisions and makes it all but impossible for Congress to make monetary policy a subject of current policy debate. Milton Friedman himself long ago suggested the proper procedure: Make and implement the Open Market decision on Friday, releasing the directive itself to the papers on Monday morning.

Even so, the generic difficulty with congressional oversight of monetary policy would remain, which is that it offers little political mileage, and at least some political risks, for members of Congress. Someone has to care enough to ask the questions. Henry Reuss, chairman of the House Banking Committee until 1981, was such a person, but monetary oversight in the House has since fallen on hard times. In the Senate, oversight has suffered from the departure of Senator William Proxmire.

The more tractable structural issue therefore may be not whether the Federal Reserve system can be brought *under* the control of the Treasury and Congress, but whether it can be more effectively detached *from* the present institutional influences of the largest banks. These influences ar now built into the system, and a reform package could do worse than take them out. For example, Congress could pass the Hamilton-Sarbanes proposal to remove the five banker-influenced regional Federal Reserve bank presidents from their voting role on the Open Market Committee. (The regional presidents often take strongly conservative ideological positions, and inside rumor has it that the board in Washington would not be unhappy to see them go.) To achieve true regionalism without the present nominal private bank ownership of the regional Federal Reserve banks, the boards of directors of those regional Federal Reserve banks, which now include local bankers by statute, could be reconstituted as state government appointments. The budget of the whole system should be brought into the federal budget. These actions would abolish the visible symbols of bank domination that the system now has. They might make it easier to pursue fundamental reforms of the way in which deposit insurance, regulation, and the lender-of-last-resort functions now work, so that the necessary business of supporting the banking system is not held hostage to the fate of particular private banks. An unbiased discussion of such reforms may become especially urgent if the difficulties of the banking system prove to be as serious as sometimes rumored.

It should be clear, though, that institutional changes in the Federal Reserve are at best necessary but insufficient. Under a progressive Administration committed to high growth and structural reform, subordination of an uncooperative Federal Reserve Board would be essential. But what exactly does a high-growth path require of monetary policy?

Sustaining Low Interest Rates

NOBODY DOUBTS ANYMORE that the Federal Reserve does control short-term interest rates. Long-term rates are another story, and without lower long-term interest rates recent easings have remained only partly effective. Low short-term rates do lower the dollar and help to relieve business debt burdens. But only low long-term rates can unleash the kind of capital spending essential to a major rebuilding of America's manufacturing capacity and infrastructure.

The key problem is that old conservative bugbear *policy credibility*. If long lenders believed, as they do not at present, that short rates were going to stay down, so that a series of short-term borrowings could plausibly substitute for a single long bond issue, then long-term rates would have to come down. The question is: How is this result achieved?

On the Administration's side, a strong precommitment to reducing the budget deficit in the long run, such as through higher tax rates enacted in 1993 on wealthier Americans but effective in 1995 or 1996, may be necessary—perhaps more for political than for economic reasons. This, coupled with an equally strong economic recovery and public investment program, will put the burden on the Federal Reserve to act to reduce long-term interest rates if markets by themselves do not bring them down.

Another part of the problem may be that Alan Greenspan cannot achieve the required result. For long rates to come down, investors must believe that short rates will stay down. But this belief is something that a right-wing, antigrowth, rentier-dominated, "stagnationist" board, committed to reacting to every twitch in the inflation rate, cannot deliver. Even with a new fiscal policy, it may be that only a changed Federal Reserve Board can make the credible public precommitment to sustained low interest rates that a climate of low long-term interest rates will require.

When this new accord is finally struck, policy itself could take certain practical steps to reinforce its resolve. For instance, the Treasury could suspend the issue of long-maturity bonds pending an interest rate drop. And the Federal Reserve could act to buy back long bonds in the open market, raising their price and reducing their yield.

With an across-the-spectrum fall in interest rates, borrowing for long-term capital investment would return to the American scene. (It may also be necessary to stabilize lending institutions, recognizing that the condition of the banks may actually be hurt by reductions in their lending rates relative to their present low cost of funds.) In most respects, a capital investment boom would be a very good thing. Alongside new public investment, the nation needs houses and an accelerated renewal of its industrial capital stock. In recent years the construction sector has substantially downsized. Construction equipment, farm equipment, and machinery manufacturing of all kinds took a vicious beating in the early 1980s. A good capital boom (though it might have to rely on imports at first) might help to restore these sectors.

The middle classes would benefit mightily from a reduction in interest on their consumer and mortgage debts. While there might be some losers among the rich, the really big losers would seem to be foreigners with relatively liquid claims valued in dollars (the dollar would fall), and perhaps a few institutional entities such as bond trading firms that specialize in speculative movements in bond markets.

A low interest-rate policy would also cut government expenditures and raise revenues. Every macroeconomic model verifies that lower interest rates would work powerfully to rectify the financial problems of the government. (Indeed, artificially projecting lower future interest rates has been for years a favorite trick of budgeteers who wished to disguise the size of future deficits.)

Yet there are also risks. The main one is that a simple credit boom is inherently unstable. Borrowers who fear that the low-rate environment will not last may borrow in advance of their own needs; lenders who hope it won't last will try to stay in liquid short-term assets. Speculative movements in credit demand and supply, which tend to grow if expectations of a rate rise increase, can put immense strain on a low-rate policy.

For this reason, such a policy presupposes renewed regulatory safeguards on credit flows to discourage speculative moves against the policy itself. Even quick examination of sustained low-interest policies in other countries, such as Japan and France from the 1950s through the 1970s, reveals that such quantity safeguards were almost always in effect. Without such regulation, the ability of a low-interest policy to withstand speculation is very doubtful.

But assuming that political obstacles and speculation can be overcome, a more progressive Federal Government must also be prepared to meet by other means the main economic contingencies that might cause its low-interest-rate policy to be abandoned. Chief among these, once again, is the eventual return of inflation.

Inflation is not an immediate risk. Excess capacity, foreign imports, and the generally cowed character of the labor markets will keep inflation at bay. But it is likely that the move toward sustained low interest rates will trigger dollar devaluation, raising import prices in advanced product lines (those imported from industrial countries against whose currencies the dollar would fall) and strengthening the bargaining hand of the strongest elements of American labor. Asset and commodity prices would also tend to rise. Over three to five years, it is likely that a low-interest policy would modestly accelerate the rise in inflation that had already been under way in the late 1980s.

Granted, some inflation can be tolerated, and some occurs as the result of external shocks that cannot always be avoided. But some inflation risks— two in particular—can and must be managed. These are: (1) wage-push inflation resulting from higher growth, increased labor bargaining power, and the spillover of wage increases from high- to low-productivity growth sectors; and (2) the spillover from asset-market speculation into the prices of currently produced goods. Dealing with these risks could require measures of credit regulation and a wage-price policy—a return, in short, to the unpleasant politics of inflation control. To make this politics work will, again, be no easy task. Indeed, we might as well face the reality that a low-interest-rate policy must be imbedded in a larger project of reform.

Comprehensive Progressive Reform (CPR)

COMPREHENSIVE PROGRESSIVE REFORM is consistent with much of the low-interest-rate and democracy/accountability programs, but it goes far beyond them. It demands not only a reconsideration of the Federal Reserve's structure and responsibilities but also a systematic integration of international and domestic economic policies.

The larger program for sustained growth is discussed in the "Overview: Economic Policy" and several other chapters in this section. It begins with an immediate emergency recovery program based on capital grants to states and localities and perhaps tax relief. It continues with an export growth and public investment strategy to sustain growth and competitiveness over the long term. It must, as noted above, include the design of new policies to stabilize growth and to reduce inequality (as argued in the overview chapter). Taken together, the hope is to reconcile three economic objectives that have been in increasing conflict for twenty years: high growth, balanced trade, and reasonably stable prices.

Once the broad strategy is defined, the role of monetary policy virtually follows. The Federal Reserve must establish the credibility of a sustained program of low and stable interest rates. It must commit to the competitiveness of the dollar, and so support both private investment and export demand. And it must return to the business of restoring order and discipline to the financial system.

Above all, the Federal Reserve needs to cooperate with the new Administration. It cannot continue to arrogate to itself, as it has for thirteen years, sole and independent responsibility for fighting inflation. Nor can the Administration afford to cede this responsibility to the Federal Reserve. A program of comprehensive economic reforms will not work unless the Federal Reserve cooperates by keeping interest rates low. A low-interest-rate policy can be sustained only when other policies for growth and financial stability are in place. In a program of comprehensive progressive reform, the Federal Reserve had better accustom itself to playing on the team.

Department of Commerce

ECONOMIC COMPETITIVENESS

DAVID E. SHAW[1]

Summary

B Y CARRYING A DISPROPORTIONATE share of the free world's defense burden and by failing to exploit the results of its own basic research commercially, America continues to subsidize its most able economic competitors. Moreover, our competitors have actively and successfully promoted the international economic viability of their companies and workers, while the cabinet department charged with principal responsibility for our own country's "international trade, economic growth, and technological advancement"[2] —the U.S. Department of Commerce—is currently budgeted at about 1 percent of the level of the Defense Department, and has thus far been allowed to play only a token role in advancing U.S. competitiveness.

To provide American companies with the resources necessary to compete within the world economy, and to arrest a secular decline in the number of high-wage, high-skill, high-value-added jobs available for American workers, the new Administration should seek a substantial reorganization of the Commerce Department, a significant increase in funding for several of its existing programs, and the introduction of two new initiatives. Specifically, we recommend:

David E. Shaw is the Managing Partner of D. E. Shaw & Co., a group of financial companies based in New York, and the Chairman of the National Economic Council. Earlier, Dr. Shaw served on the faculty of the Computer Science Department at Columbia University, and as a Vice President at Morgan Stanley & Co.

- Merging the Commerce Department, the Department of Labor, and the Small Business Administration.
- Removal of the National Oceanic and Atmospheric Administration from the purview of the resulting department.
- A ninefold increase in the combined budgets of the Advanced Technology Program, the Manufacturing Technology Centers, and the State Technology Extension Program.
- Strengthening certain internal laboratories of the National Institute of Standards and Technologies, and eliminating others.
- Provision of advanced information retrieval and large-scale technical document translation services by the National Technical Information Service.
- Resolution of various disparities between U.S. and foreign patent and trademark systems that place American firms at a competitive disadvantage.
- Certain modernization efforts aimed at improving accuracy and reducing costs within the Census Bureau and the Bureau of Economic Analysis.
- Increased funding for the Economic Development Administration, and certain changes within the Minority Business Development Administration.

The new President should also create a National Research and Development Agency to support long-term, industry-led research on precommercial, generic, economically critical technologies and to facilitate the effective transfer of these technologies to American industry.

Finally, he should propose establishing a network of 240 national industrial facilities, which would serve as centers for the low-cost, low-volume, rapid-turnaround prototyping of high-value-added, internationally competitive, noncommodity products. Housed within academic institutions and national laboratories, each facility would serve as a locus for research and development, technology transfer, education and training, incubation of new businesses, regional economic development (including defense conversion), creation of highly compensated skilled jobs, promotion of flexible manufacturing methodologies, and generation of investment and product royalty revenues for government and academia, without asking the Federal Government to "pick winners."

Introduction

DURING THE ADMINISTRATIONS of Presidents Reagan and Bush, the United States experienced two changes that dramatically altered the premises underlying its policies and plans: the end of the Cold War and a decline in economic competitiveness. The latter has been associated with the elimination of large numbers of relatively highly paid skilled jobs and their replacement by lower-wage jobs in which less value is added by the worker. Despite an increased prevalence of dual-income households, many American families have begun to experience a material erosion of their standard of living.

In view of these changes, most observers would probably agree that the greatest threat to American security during the remainder of the twentieth century is likely to be economic, and not military. The U.S. Defense Department, however, still has a budget approximately one hundred times as large as that of the cabinet department charged with primary responsibility for the nation's "international trade, economic growth, and technological advancement"[3]—the Department of Commerce. Admittedly, such comparisons are biased by the fact that the Pentagon is itself a major purchaser of goods and services, while the Commerce Department only facilitates the sale of goods and services to third parties. The fact remains, however, that the United States was allocating 5.4 percent of its GDP to defense expenditures in 1990, while Germany spent about 2 percent, and Japan a mere 1 percent.[4]

Although international political stability is an essential precursor of international trade, America's assumption of a disproportionate share of the free world's defense burden has effectively subsidized its most able economic competitors, allowing them to allocate a larger fraction of their budgets to the advancement of their relative positions within the world economy. The governments of these competing nations typically nurture their respective civilian economies through various forms of private/public partnership, including investments in human capital (e.g., in the form of education and training) and physical infrastructure; incentives and direct support for long-term research, development, and technology transfer focusing on generic, precommercial, economically critical technologies; and the active promotion of exports.

While remaining a world leader in basic research, America has in recent years enjoyed less success in the production and export of products based on that research. After laying the intellectual groundwork for the fabrication of semiconductor devices, the production of industrial robots, and the development of numerically controlled machine tools, for example, the United States quickly ceded control of the commercial markets for these important technologies to foreign competitors. Once again, America's recent failure to focus on the bottom line has resulted in an unintentional subsidy of precisely those nations that have posed the most formidable challenge to its economic security.

Notwithstanding the introduction of a few small-scale programs and superficial changes in organization and nomenclature, the Commerce Department is for the most part no better armed to face this challenge than it was in 1975, when a twenty-seven-year-old business strategy consultant named Ira Magaziner—later to emerge as an influential expositor of the dynamics of contemporary international competition—returned from visits to Japan and West Germany, where he was told of government/industry programs that would soon help to alter the balance of world economic power. Comparing what he had learned in West Germany and Japan with his experiences in the United States, he would later write:

> Back home in America, by 1975 I'd had more than a dozen talks with U.S. Commerce Department officials. I'd found them to be skilled at special requests, like helping a company get foreign customs to clear goods, but there was no larger vision of how American firms could adapt to a global economy. I certainly heard no one in Commerce speaking about an overseas car threat. No one was warning about a steel threat, either. But both threats were unfolding: Foreign companies were coming at us with the support of their governments. Our companies, meanwhile, were being left to face this new competition on their own.[5]

History of the Commerce Department

BY THE EARLY TWENTIETH CENTURY, most of the world's industrialized nations had already organized government agencies for the promotion of industry and international trade, both of which were then enjoying rapid growth. The agency that was proposed in 1903 by a trust-busting, square-dealing Theodore Roosevelt, however, was charged not only with promoting the nation's business but also with regulating business activities to protect workers and consumers, and absorbed the formerly independent Labor Department, along with a number of other existing entities. Staff members affiliated with labor, however, were vastly outnumbered within the department by those associated with business. As the nascent American labor movement began to gain strength, unions were able to lobby effectively for an autonomous representative in the Executive Branch. In 1913, the Department of Labor was spun off as a separate cabinet-level department, and the Commerce and Labor Department was renamed the Department of Commerce.

While the Commerce Department has served a number of functions since its inception, the most significant from the perspective of economic competitiveness has probably been its role in the development, promotion, and regulation of new inventions and technologies, including electrical devices, radio and television, automobiles, and aircraft. The Department of Transportation, the Federal Aviation Administration, and the Federal Communications Commission, for example, all arose from programs initiated within the Commerce Department, and internal research programs in a number of areas are still conducted within the Commerce Department's National Institute of Standards and Technology.

The Reagan/Bush Commerce Department

UNDER THE REAGAN AND BUSH ADMINISTRATIONS, the White House has sought with varying degrees of success to eliminate or eviscerate a number of the major functional units of the Commerce Department. Both presidents attempted to disband the Economic Development Administration (EDA), for example, arguing that any assistance that might be provided for economically distressed (rural or urban) areas should come from the affected states or localities, or from private investors.[6] Recognizing that such areas were unlikely (by definition) to have the resources necessary to pull up their own bootstraps, and worried that those businesses and individuals most capable of alleviating local economic problems would leave for better opportunities, Congress was able to block the outright elimination of the EDA. Over time, however, the Reagan and Bush administrations succeeded in reducing the EDA's budget from a peak of $6.59 billion in 1977 to $256.8 million in 1992.

Most of the progress made by the Reagan/Bush Commerce Department toward enhancing American competitiveness was initiated by Congress. While Congress created the Advanced Technology Program, the Manufacturing Technology Centers, and the State Technology Extension Program, White House competitiveness policy has been limited to such acts as the establishment of the Malcolm Baldrige National Quality Award, the curtailment of antitrust enforcement, and the elimination of federal environmental regulations. Testifying before the Senate Banking Committee, Dr. Ian Ross, director of AT&T's Bell Laboratories, called the Reagan administration's reception of the report of the President's Commission on Industrial Competitiveness "rather disappointing and frustrating. . . . At that time the main response we got was 'there isn't a problem.'"[7]

It seems clear that the relative inaction of Presidents Reagan and Bush in the face of declining U.S. competitiveness has arisen not from neglect but from deliberate policy decisions based on an optimistic belief that American business would thrive if left to its own devices within an environment of lower tax rates (especially in the case of high-income taxpayers) and a less active Federal Government. The outcome associated with this strategy has been disappointing, to say the least.

Changes to Existing Programs

IN THIS SECTION WE WILL FIRST PROPOSE changes to the overall, agency-level composition of the Commerce Department and then briefly review those programs currently overseen by the department that have the greatest relevance to questions of economic competitiveness, suggesting various changes in content and funding level.

AGENCY-LEVEL REORGANIZATION
The new President should ask Congress for authority to reorganize the Commerce Department in two ways:

1. Transfer the National Oceanic and Atmospheric Administration (NOAA), which now accounts for over half of the Commerce Department's budget, into either the Department of the Interior or the Environmental Protection Agency, or divide its constituent programs between the two.

2. Merge the Commerce Department with the Department of Labor and the Small Business Administration to form a new "inner cabinet" department charged with lead responsibility for ensuring that America's companies are internationally competitive, technologically competent, and capable of providing high-wage, high-growth, high-value-added jobs for American workers.

The NOAA's current mandate, which includes mapping the oceans, predicting the weather, conducting oceanic and atmospheric research, and monitoring and managing various aspects of the environment, is peripheral to what we believe should be the central focus of the Commerce Department and much closer to those of the two agencies identified as its possible new home.

Apart from not insignificant issues of cost savings and communication efficiencies, the proposed reunification of Commerce and Labor reflects our belief that the interests of companies and their workers are more nearly congruent today than was the case when the two departments were separated in 1913. If America is to remain a world economic power, business and labor will have to cooperate "to increase the potential value of what its citizens can add to the global economy," as Robert Reich puts it, "by enhancing their skills and capacities and by improving their means of linking those skills and capacities to the world market."[8] A similar argument underlies the proposal to absorb the Small Business Administration, eliminating substantial and costly programmatic redundancy and enhancing the opportunities for a fundamental attack on those problems now confronting both large and small firms.

NATIONAL INSTITUTE OF STANDARDS AND TECHNOLOGY

Three of the programs now administered by the NIST—the Advanced Technology Program (ATP), the Manufacturing Technology Centers (MTCs), and the State Technology Extension Program (STEP)—speak directly to the country's industrial competitiveness but are currently funded at a level insufficient to have any significant effect. While none of these programs has been operational long enough for their cost-effectiveness to be assessed accurately, the available evidence justifies a substantial increase in the funding of all three.

Indeed, it would appear that such an increase could be justified solely on the basis of expected increases in future corporate and personal tax revenues, quite apart from the substantial private benefits accruing to American citizens. In any case, it seems clear that the expected marginal return on investment for each of these programs is dramatically higher than those of, for example, the $8 billion Superconducting Supercollider, NASA's $30 billion space station, or most of the defense research and development projects whose putative civilian spin-offs are frequently offered by way of justifying even larger expenditures. By way of contrast, the federal budget for fiscal year 1992 included only $47 million for the ATP program, along with $15 million for the seven regional MTCs and a token $1 million for the STEP program.

The Office of Technology Assessment estimates that "current industrial extension programs, state and federal, reach only a small fraction—probably less than 2 percent per year—of the nation's small manufacturing firms."[9] While the Federal Government now allocates about $400 million annually for the Agricultural Extension Program, the MTCs and STEP, which were modeled after this program, currently receive about 4 percent of this amount. This discrepancy is particularly alarming in view of the fact that manufacturing represents approximately 20 percent of our GNP, while agriculture now accounts for only 2 percent. Indeed, the Pentagon's research and development budget is about a hundred times larger than that of the ATP program, despite the fact that America now seems far more vulnerable to economic competition than to military threat.

In the short term, funding for the ATP, MTC, and STEP programs should be increased from about $64 million in fiscal 1992 to about $250 million in fiscal 1994, and assuming subsequent evaluation confirms their effectiveness, to about $550 million in fiscal 1995. In the long run, however, we recommend integrating the ATP and MTC programs within the framework provided by two new initiatives—the National Research and Development Agency and the national industrial facilities—both of which are described later in this chapter.

The NIST's own internal laboratories, which currently account for the majority of its budget, should be reviewed with an eye toward strengthening certain internal programs and facilities and eliminating others in favor of competitively awarded contract research. The National Technical Information Service (NTIS) should assume an expanded role in collecting, translating, and distributing foreign research results to U.S. firms. The NTIS should also make full text information (as opposed to abstracts or bibliographic data) available to American clients, both on CD-ROMs and through on-line information retrieval, for most of its documents by 1996.

PATENT AND TRADEMARK OFFICE

The international competitiveness of American inventors is compromised by a number of disparities between U.S. and foreign patent laws. While the United States is currently participating in international negotiations aimed at eliminating these disparities, other countries have indicated that they are unlikely to approve such standards unless the United States agrees to switch from a "first to invent" system for establishing patent priority (a convention we share with only one other country) to the more commonly employed "first to file" system.

In view of the competitive disadvantages now suffered by American inventors because of asymmetries among the intellectual property laws of different countries, Congress should enact the Patent System Harmonization Act of 1992, which would lay the groundwork for an international treaty whose overall effect would be beneficial to American industry. In a similar vein, the United States should modify its trademark laws to gain inclusion in the Madrid Agreement for International Registration of Trademarks. Participation in this agreement would allow American firms to make a single filing for trademark protection in all member countries, avoiding the time and cost now required for separate filings in each country.

CENSUS BUREAU AND BUREAU OF ECONOMIC ANALYSIS

The Commerce Department's two "statistical agencies," the Bureau of the Census and the Bureau of Economic Analysis (BEA), are responsible for the collection, processing, analysis, and dissemination of a wide range of information about the United States, its citizens, and its businesses. It should be noted that neither the familiar decennial census nor the economic surveys conducted more frequently by both the Census Bureau and the Bureau of Economic Analysis in fact succeed in capturing all data on which they are nominally based. Millions of Americans, for example, either cannot be located for, or refuse to participate in, the national census process and are thus excluded from the resulting statistical summaries. Because census statistics are used in the congressional reapportionment process, and because certain groups (e.g., homeless individuals, poor inner-city residents, and the members of certain minority groups) are believed to be undercounted systematically, this phenomenon has considerable practical significance.

Given that it is impractical to sample all members of the underlying population, it is natural to ask whether it makes sense even to attempt such an exhaustive enumeration, or whether statistical survey techniques might be used to compute a "best unbiased estimator" from a restricted but more deliberately chosen sample set. It is possible that such an approach might produce better estimates of the quantities to be measured, and in the case of a survey sample of significantly smaller size than the whole population, might do so at a dramatically lower cost. The feasibility of such an approach should be evaluated as part of a more general study aimed at the improvement of statistical information and the control of collection and analysis costs.

ECONOMIC DEVELOPMENT ADMINISTRATION AND MINORITY BUSINESS DEVELOPMENT ADMINISTRATION

Given the current strain on America's state and municipal budgets, distressed communities in the United States have little alternative but to look to the Federal Government for help in building the infrastructure necessary to attract, retain, and expand local businesses, thus creating new employment opportunities. In many cases, our real choice is not whether to provide financial assistance to the residents of these communities but whether to provide such assistance in the form of carefully targeted investments aimed at making such residents self-sufficient, or in the form of unemployment insurance or other entitlements.

During a period in which defense cuts and factory closures are generating significant pockets of regional unemployment, a particularly strong case can be made for the latter alternative. As a stopgap measure, the EDA's overall funding should increase to approximately $1.5 billion per year. Such a sixfold increase would still result in a lower level of support than was maintained during the Carter administration, but would provide immediate employment opportunities with vital public works projects and help to arrest the downward economic spiral that currently threatens a number of America's most desperate communities.

Because a substantial share of the EDA's resources are targeted at the inner cities, the major increase proposed here should prove especially beneficial to minority businesses. Such a "transfer of opportunity" seems reasonable, however, given that minorities now represent approximately 25 percent of the American population but own only 6 percent of America's operating businesses and account for only 1 percent of its aggregate business revenues.[10] The Minority Business Development Administration, whose operations have been allowed to deteriorate under the Reagan and Bush administrations, must also be overhauled if it is to provide management and technical assistance to minority firms effectively, and to coordinate the minority business procurement efforts of other federal agencies.

New Competitiveness Initiatives

NATIONAL RESEARCH AND DEVELOPMENT AGENCY

Although the United States was spending approximately the same fraction of its GNP on research and development as Japan as of the end of the Reagan administration, defense accounted for nearly two thirds of America's government R&D expenditures, compared with approximately 5 percent in Japan. Research and development expenditures targeted at industrial development, on the other hand, amounted to 4.8 percent of all Japanese R&D expenditures and 14.5 percent of those in West Germany but accounted for only 0.2 percent of the American R&D budget.[11]

In light of recent changes in the relative importance of economic and military factors as determinants of American security, the Federal Government should reverse the Reagan-era trend toward the militarization of American research and development. Such a change would appear to have considerable support within the general public: A total of 77 percent of all respondents in a poll conducted by Louis Harris & Associates in April 1992 said they favored redirecting military research and development funding toward civilian R&D.

As a vehicle for commercial and industrial research and development, the next Administration should create a National Research and Development

Agency (NRDA), a principal focus of which would be support of research and development aimed at increasing America's economic competitiveness. The agency would be funded at a level that would rise to $11 billion per year within four years, but all such funds would be obtained by means of a reallocation of current government R&D funds, with no overall (constant-dollar) increase in federal R&D expenditures. Specifically, support for the NRDA would be derived from a $9 billion annual reduction in defense R&D (to a level that would still be 15 percent higher in inflation-adjusted dollars than the corresponding figure at the end of the Carter administration), along with smaller cuts in the research and development budgets of the Department of Energy (representing a substantial cut in the defense-related portion of its budget, partially offset by increases in funding for civilian energy research) and of NASA.

Like the Defense Advanced Research Projects Agency (DARPA), Japan's Ministry of International Trade and Industry, and the research agencies of a number of other industrial nations, the NRDA would have a long-term focus and would provide support for high-risk, high-payoff investigations offering the prospect of substantial "upside" benefits. Funding would be provided for the industry-led development of widely applicable, precompetitive, critical technologies that might ultimately lead to economically significant products manufactured by American firms, with special emphasis on the promotion of exports. The agency would invest heavily in programs capable—in fact, and not simply in theory—of facilitating the effective transfer of such technologies.

Among the NRDA's most important programs would be a national manufacturing research initiative, which would promote research on, and the training of researchers and educators specializing in, both the technological and organizational aspects of contemporary manufacturing.

NATIONAL INDUSTRIAL FACILITIES

One element of the next Administration's program for strengthening America's industrial base should be the creation of a network of some 240 facilities for the low-cost, low-volume, rapid-turnaround prototyping of a wide range of economically important products. Housed within universities, two- and four-year colleges, and national laboratories across the country, these national industrial facilities (NIFs) would be designed not to "pick winners" but to provide the tools necessary for "natural" winners to prosper within America's free market system and within an increasingly competitive world economy. Each NIF would serve as a locus for:

- *Research and development* focused on new technologies having strategic importance to America's economic competitiveness.
- *Technology transfer*, through which such technologies would be translated into high-value-added, noncommodity, exportable products.
- *Incubation of new businesses* through the reduction of various barriers to the creation of entrepreneurial and "intrapreneurial" ventures.
- *Education and training* of students, workers and managers in flexible manufacturing and management techniques.
- *Regional economic development* through the creation of industry and jobs in economically distressed urban and rural areas.
- *Revenue generation* for the government and universities in the form of royalty income from and residual interests in new ventures.

We envision perhaps twenty geographically distributed NIFs of each of a dozen or so different varieties, each corresponding to a different type of "manufacturing," where that term is meant to include the production not only of electronic systems, metal and plastic products, and mechanical devices, for example, but also such products as specialized computer software and new organic molecules for pharmaceutical applications. Each NIF would include a suite of instruments and tools sufficient for the design, engineering, prototyping, and testing of a wide range of products within the class covered by that facility.

Research, product design, and prototyping would be conducted on an independent or collaborative basis by entrepreneurs, academics, and staff members of national laboratories, as well as by small and medium-size companies and innovative and autonomous "skunkworks" teams from larger firms. In some cases, an NIF might function as a well-equipped, specialized incubator for a new venture, creating business and employment opportunities within its local community. In others, it might offer an existing small firm shared access to often expensive state-of-the-art equipment that it could not justify purchasing for dedicated use and for which it had only intermittent need. On-site experts would be available for instruction and consultation in the course of product development, and would assist in the use of design and manufacturing equipment.

Charges would ordinarily be made for the use of equipment, materials, and services, but the activities of some users would be fully or partially supported by contracts or grants from the Federal Government or from state or local governments (including the National Research and Development Agency proposed above). Start-up firms might in some cases be permitted to pay for their use of an NIF in the form of product royalties, or, to mitigate early cash-flow pressures, by granting the NIF a nonvoting, equitylike passive residual interest, which would be convertible into common stock only for purposes of sale in the event of a public offering. To provide real incentives for technology transfer, professors, graduate students, and federal scientists would also share in any such financial rewards, as would their respective institutions—many of which are now under considerable financial stress.

Perhaps most important, the NIFs would be designed to serve a catalytic function in helping American industry make the transition from traditional mass production techniques to the new flexible manufacturing methodologies that have, perhaps more than anything else, been responsible for Japan's ascendance as a world economic power. Whereas classical mass production is exemplified by the performance of a single repetitive task on a highly specialized machine by a highly specialized worker, flexible manufacturing typically involves the use of reconfigurable, multifunctional manufacturing equipment, often operating under networked computer control, by broadly trained workers capable of performing more than one function.

The use of flexible, multipurpose production equipment makes feasible the rapid development of specialized products targeted at new and strategically important markets—a goal that has proven elusive for many American companies. This capability for rapid product evolution and differentiation will be essential if U.S. firms are to position themselves and their workers as high-value-added (and highly compensated) purveyors of novel, specialized products, rather than as "commodity" producers within mature industries that are destined to experience increasing competition from low-wage developing countries.

The NIFs would serve both as laboratories for the development of flexible manufacturing systems and as schools for training professionals and skilled laborers (including those facing layoffs attributable to defense cutbacks or the decline of local industries) in flexible manufacturing techniques. After serving as "interns" with entrepreneurial projects incubated with an NIF, some trainees might find employment with new ventures or business units arising directly from those projects, while others would gain the experience necessary to secure positions in other firms exploiting similar technologies.

In addition to their direct role in developing new products, the NIFs would provide a powerful stimulus to the development of new tools for such development. By ordering the most advanced flexible manufacturing equipment produced by American companies on an ongoing basis, the NIFs could play a role analogous to one often played by the Pentagon, acting as "early adopters" of strategically important civilian technologies and thus mitigating the financial risks assumed by innovative American tool-builders.

Working with the NIST to promulgate standards (both at the user and internal interface levels), the NIFs could also help to "modularize" many aspects of the manufacturing process, encouraging different vendors to compete for the best (e.g., the strongest, lightest, cheapest, or least polluting) realization of each module. The emergence of such standards would also aid in the transfer of new products from small-scale prototyping within NIFs to large-scale production in the "outside world." A developer might, for example, use a program developed for the low-volume, numerically controlled machine tools used to construct prototypes within the NIF to control the high-volume equipment later used by a large-scale manufacturer.

The total operating cost of a national system of 240 NIFs might be about $7 billion per year, an estimated half of which might be recouped directly from industry in the form of user fees, royalties on patents and product sales, and capital gains on the sale of passive residual interests in spin-off companies.

The net short-term operating cost of the NIFs would be paid for by corresponding reductions in weapons procurement, military staff reductions, and other defense expenditures, with special efforts made to mitigate the effects of defense and aerospace layoffs through the creation of new, highly skilled civilian positions directly or indirectly associated with the NIFs and their various commercial spin-offs. Moreover, the long-term return on such an investment would be expected to include additional tax revenues generated by increased productivity, expanded American market share, and new employment opportunities.

NOTES

1. In preparing this chapter, the author has made use of factual material and analysis generated in the course of ongoing research projects on the Commerce Department and on American technology policy, conducted under the auspices of the National Economic Council, a not-for-profit research and educational foundation. The author is indebted to Walt Burkley, Mike Russell, and Roger Stone of the National Economic Council's full-time staff, and to project researchers J. Eric Barnes, Geoffrey Best, Stephanie Brown, Christopher Butt, David Einhorn, Emily Feldman, Gerry Fifer, Andrew Frankel, Ada Frumerman, Mark Hulak, Marc Mehl, Linda Mischel, Dave Pretty, Rudy Scarito, Doreen Shulman, Marc Sussman, Dick Tihany, and Julius Wang for their substantial contributions to these projects. The opinions and recommendations presented herein are those of the author alone, however, and not of the National Economic Council or its staff or researchers. Thanks are also due to Dan Burton, Gary Feldman, Julie Franklin, Ted Jacobs, Laura Madden, Patrick Mulloy, Erik Pages, Skip Styles, and Len Weiss. Professors Alan Borning, Andrew Harris, Stephen Kline, Robert Reich, Derek Shearer, and Jeffrey Ullman, along with Dr. Robert Shapiro and Governor Bill Clinton, provided valuable feedback for which the author is especially grateful.

2. *The United States Government Manual*, 1991–92 (Washington, D.C.: U.S. Government Printing Office, 1991), p. 149.

3. Ibid.

4. International Institute for Strategic Studies, *The Military Balance 1991–1992* (International Institute for Strategic Studies, 1991), pp. 212–15.

5. I. Magaziner and M. Patankin, *The Silent War: Inside the Global Business Battles Shaping America's Future* (New York: Vintage Books, 1989), p. 10.

6. U.S. Congress, House of Representatives, Committee on Appropriations, *Subcommittee Hearings on 1993 Appropriations for Departments of Commerce, Justice, State, the Judiciary, and Related Agencies*, 102d Cong., 2d sess. (Washington, D.C.,: U.S. Government Printing Office), p. 101.

7. U.S. Congress, Senate, Committee on Banking, Housing, and Urban Affairs, *Summary of Oversight Hearings on the Condition of the U.S. Industrial and Financial Base*, 101st Cong., 2d sess. (Washington, D.C.: U.S. Government Printing Office, 1990), p. 25.

8. R. Reich, *The Work of Nations* (New York: Alfred A. Knopf, 1991), p. 8.

9. Cited in U.S. Congress, Senate, Committee on Banking, Housing and Urban Affairs, *Summary of Oversight Hearings*, p. 19.

10. U.S. Department of Commerce, *MBDA Annual Business Assistance Report*, fiscal year 1991 (Washington, D.C.: U.S. Government Printing Office, 1991), p. 2.

11. Council on Competitiveness, *Gaining New Ground: Technology Priorities for America's Future* (Washington, D.C.: Council on Competitiveness, 1991), p. 14.

The Office of the U.S. Trade Representative

TRADE POLICY

BRUCE STOKES

Summary

I N TODAY'S INCREASINGLY INTEGRATED GLOBAL economy, trade policy, much maligned and often ignored in the past, will be one of the foundation stones of U.S. economic recovery in the 1990s. In the next few years, federal initiatives regarding the regulation and promotion of exports will help shape the future of the American economy and the types of jobs and incomes Americans will have.

In the past, trade policy has been the handmaiden of diplomatic and security interests. If new economic priorities are to prevail, the Office of the U.S. Trade Representative and the other aspects of U.S. trade policymaking must be fundamentally restructured beyond a mere bureaucratic exercise.

The last major trade reorganization took place in 1979 after the completion of the Tokyo Round of multilateral trade talks, when, among other things, jurisdiction over dumping and countervailing duty cases was transferred from the Treasury Department to the Commerce Department. An effort to merge USTR and elements of the Commerce Department failed in the early 1980s, stifled by bureaucratic rivalries and turf fights.

To avoid such problems, and since trade is only one aspect of the country's international economic posture, the new President should early create a National Economic Council, staffed by a small team of high-ranking officials, to coordinate domestic and international economic policy on the model established by the National Security Council. At the same time, he should announce creation of a Department of International Trade and Industry (DITI), combining the functions of the U.S. Trade Representative's Office with trade and industry activities currently housed in the Commerce Department and other agencies. So the next time an administration decides

Bruce Stokes is the international economics correspondent for The National Journal. *A member of the Council on Foreign Relations, he is coauthor of the forthcoming book* The European Challenge *(1992).*

that some trade restraints must be imposed, the DITI, as a quid pro quo for additional costs to consumers, would require industry and labor to make sacrifices, too, such as limiting executive compensation, wage demands, workplace rules, and investment options.

Mounting tension between Congress and the White House over trade matters also dictates a new sorting out of authority and responsibility between the Executive Branch and Congress regarding trade policy. As trade becomes more central to the well-being of the economy, Congress, as a natural voice for the concerns of dislocated workers and communities, will inevitably demand to play a greater role in trade matters. To best be able to do that, the congressional leadership must take a more direct role in trade matters through creation of a Congressional Trade Office, comparable to the Congressional Budget Office.

In addition, trade reorganization at either end of Pennsylvania Avenue will fail if the restructuring is done with an eye on the past. Trade policymaking must focus on the problems of the twenty-first century—trade and the environment, competition policy, trade-related investment measures, work-related social policies—not the trade difficulties of the 1970s and 1980s. This will require not only a new degree of coordination within the government but also presidential leadership to prepare the United States to compete in world markets through a more proactive trade policy, backed by a comprehensive effort through industrial policy to improve the performance of U.S. companies.

A Legacy of Failure

USTR WAS CREATED IN 1962 AS a lean, noncabinet-level arm of the president, whose main job beyond negotiating tariff reductions was to act as an honest broker between or among government agencies in coordinating U.S. trade policy. Over the years USTR's role has changed as the importance of trade and international economic policy has evolved. The staff has grown to 155; the agency has achieved cabinet status and has become enmeshed in negotiations ranging from baseball bats to semiconductors.

The first U.S. Trade Representative was Christian Herter, a Republican, appointed by Democratic president John F. Kennedy as a symbol of the avowed bipartisan nature of U.S. trade policy. Since then the political clout of Trade Representatives has waxed and waned, reaching its height in the Carter administration, when Robert Strauss, former chairman of the Democratic National Committee, exercised widespread influence. But recent

USTRs—Clayton Yeutter and Carla Hills—have had less influence both within the Executive Branch and on Capitol Hill.

Rather than be the leader of trade policy, a bureaucratically weak and directionless USTR has often been at the mercy of political pressures around it. This reactive rather than proactive stance has often led to bad trade policy, and U.S. trade interests have suffered.

For example, in the early 1980s, the United States backed into managing trade for the beleaguered U.S. auto industry. Rather than impose formal U.S. trade barriers, the Reagan administration convinced the Japanese to cap voluntarily their exports to the United States. The price paid by the U.S. economy was enormous. At the peak of their impact, the United States was paying $2.2 billion dollars to Japan each year in the form of higher auto prices just for the privilege of having Japan withhold its exports. Restricted in what they could ship to the United States, the Japanese shifted their product mix to be able to sell more profitable large luxury cars and have gone on to capture a large part of that lucrative market. And trade barriers accelerated Japanese automakers' plans to build cars in the United States.

Managing auto trade in this ad hoc fashion—letting the Japanese impose their own restraints, with no attempt to manage the composition of trade and no attempt to manage the transfer of production—led to a U.S. automobile sector that is now even more dominated by Japanese producers than was ever feared possible in the early 1980s.

Conservatives and traditional economists decry such managed trade and maintain that, where it has happened in the past, it involves a system too susceptible to political pressure. But in a democracy trade policy should and always will be a political exercise, for its consequences involve the livelihoods of real workers and real communities.

And the pressures to manage trade will only increase in the years ahead. The completion or failure of the current Uruguay Round of multilateral trade negotiations is likely to open a Pandora's box of trade complaints that had been held in abeyance pending resolution of the trade talks. Faced with an avalanche of unfair trade practices cases filed by manufacturers and, for the first time, by service providers, USTR will be tempted to do what it has always done—strike market-sharing deals with foreign governments to avoid all-out trade wars.

The lesson of recent history is that managed trade is inevitable, even under the most free-market-oriented presidents. The challenge is to manage trade with a sense of purpose so that it enhances competitiveness, rather than merely protects weak industries.

New Issues

THIS LEGACY OF TRADE POLICY FAILURE is complicated by the rapidly changing nature of the international economy and the plethora of new issues that are emerging on the U.S. trade agenda. U.S. trade laws and institutions are based on the presumption that trade issues involve passing goods across borders. But increasingly the trade policy process will be called upon to deal with the adverse consequences of trade (pollution, income inequalities) as well as domestic policies (competition policy, labor standards) that threaten to distort trade. How to integrate these new issues into trade policymaking is a new and growing challenge.

Nowhere is this more apparent than with the politically charged issue of striking a balance between preservation of the environment and maximization of the economic benefits of freer trade. Although U.S. trade officials are sensitive to the importance of the environment and can draw on the expertise of the Environmental Protection Agency, environmental concerns are so far removed from trade negotiators' worldview that problems are inevitable.

For example, in negotiating food safety standards in the ongoing Uruguay Round of multilateral trade talks, U.S. trade officials failed to assess whether any existing U.S. standards might be deemed protectionist under the American proposals. Purely by coincidence, the Government Accounting Office (GAO) was doing a study relating to this topic. GAO didn't understand the significance of its results for the trade negotiations, and only by accident was its report brought to USTR's attention.

Similarly, USTR has consistently argued for a "sound science" basis for any trade barriers erected to achieve an ostensible environmental purpose. This stance reflects U.S. experience with the European Community's ban on the importation of hormone-laden beef. The Community had no scientific evidence to suggest such produce is harmful to human health, and USTR saw it as purely a protectionist measure designed to prop up European cattle raisers. But a "sound science" standard, which appeared reasonable to trade negotiators, waves a red flag in the eyes of environmentalists. DDT residue on fruits and vegetables has long been banned from U.S. grocery shelves. But the environmental community acknowledges that there is no solid scientific evidence for the U.S. DDT ban. Mexican farmers, soon to be part of a single North American market, still use DDT. Environmentalists worry that Mexican produce growers could successfully overturn the U.S. DDT ban by appealing to the "sound science" criterion, either through the new dispute resolution mechanisms in NAFTA (North American Fair Trade

Agreement) or through the GATT (General Agreement on Tariffs and Trade). Such an undermining of U.S. health and safety standards in the name of open markets would seriously weaken public support for free trade. In retrospect, USTR's advocacy of the "sound science" doctrine could prove to be a serious political error made by trade officials insensitive to the broader ramifications of the issues they are now forced to deal with.

Environment is not the only new, complex issue trade policymakers will be forced to wrestle with in the years ahead. The Commerce Department's recent decision to impose dumping duties on imports of flat panel computer screens is an example of the cost to the nation of the current bureaucratic diffusion of trade responsibilities. The department's narrowly focused dumping determination has driven Apple and other U.S.-based notebook computer makers to shift their assembly operations offshore to avoid paying the high duties. In this case, a fundamental decision was made about the shape of the economy through a narrow interpretation of trade law. No one had overall responsibility for thinking through the long-term implications of the move or for coming up with an alternative solution that might have both nurtured a U.S. flat panel display industry and ensured that U.S. computer makers had access to competitively priced displays.

Immediate Executive Branch Reorganization

THE ORIGINAL MISSION FOR USTR, THAT of coordinator of disparate departmental policies, is still an important function. But implicit in that role is a judgment that trade policy is a derivative of foreign policy or farm policy, not a coequal. With the emergence of the global market and the growing importance of trade to the domestic economy, trade policy needs an advocate in the halls of government.

But USTR is stretched too thin to deal with the complex of international commercial issues now facing the United States. Only six USTR officials focus on Japan at a time when Japan accounts for two thirds of the U.S. trade deficit. Two officials deal with service trade issues, one of the key negotiating points in the Uruguay Round. Especially on trade problems with Europe and Japan, where diplomatic and security concerns were involved, the State and Defense departments have often been able to outgun USTR, burying trade officials in a blizzard of reports, tying them up in meetings until they relent on proposed tough trade measures.

There can be no U.S. trade policy separate from agricultural policy or foreign policy. To guarantee that someone is responsible for balancing the nation's various needs, knitting them together into a coherent external commercial policy, a National Economic Council (NEC) should be created within the White House, as proposed by Senator William Roth, (R., Del.). Its task will be to coordinate domestic and international economic policy much as the National Security Council (NSC) balances competing diplomatic and military concerns.

Currently this coordinating role is played by the Policy Coordinating Group and by the long-standing Economic Policy Council (EPC). But the EPC merely represents the departments—including Treasury, Commerce, and USTR—that constitute it. And neither body has a staff comparable to the NSC. A NEC—to be staffed by ten to fifteen professional economists, trade and industry experts—will be big enough to fight the details. The NEC will also cast a wider net to ensure that in dealing with emerging trade issues, disparate voices—EPA, the Federal Trade Commission, NASA—get heard.

More important politically, an NEC will be responsible for knocking heads among all the bureaucratic players—the Treasury Department, the State Department, the Pentagon, and others—forcing them to resolve their differences. The President will thus be spared from always becoming the final referee on interagency trade disputes, a task both Presidents Reagan and Bush increasingly had to play due to USTR's weak-sister status within the bureaucratic lineup. Given their common lack of background on international economic matters, it is not surprising that they often sided with the nontrade departments or made trade decisions that were politically expedient but economically flawed.

An economically minded arbiter with White House clout is now sorely missed. In the Uruguay Round negotiations, for example, the Treasury Department has forced separate negotiations on liberalization of financial services, arguing that banks and the securities industry are so important that they should not be involved in the same bartering over access or be subject to the same range of retaliatory measures as other traded services. They won this fight, not necessarily on the merits of their argument but because of Treasury's traditional influence within the cabinet. An NEC could level the bureaucratic playing field on these issues to guarantee that decisions were based on the best economic interests of the United States, not on the parochial interests of one cabinet-level department.

To focus adequate bureaucratic resources on trade issues and to give these concerns greater bureaucratic clout, a Department of International Trade and Industry (DITI) should also be created. DITI would include USTR; the Commerce Department's International Trade Administration (with its country desk officers, product specialists, statistical analysts, and lawyers who administer trade law); the Export-Import Bank of the United

States; the Overseas Private Investment Corporation; and the U.S. and Foreign Commercial Service, which has responsibility for promoting exports. If it is politically feasible, the export promotion activities of the Department of Agriculture should also be included.

In addition, DITI should have responsibility for the technology-related functions within the Commerce Department as well as the national research laboratories and a newly created civilian equivalent of the Defense Advanced Research Projects Agency (DARPA), the Advanced Civilian Technology Agency, as proposed by Representative Sander Levine (D., Mich.) and Senator John Glenn (D., Ohio.)

With this mix of duties, DITI would be able to fashion trade policies in conjunction with industrial policies to make sure that both worked in tandem to improve American competitiveness. For example, if a DITI had existed in the 1980s, it could have worked with the U.S. auto industry and the auto unions to design a comprehensive American auto policy. DITI could have organized the international auctioning of the import quotas, to see to it that the economic rents generated by the restraints accrued to the U.S. Treasury and not to the Japanese automakers. Import restraints could have been designed to provide automakers with breathing room while they, in close conjunction with their workers and the communities where they had their facilities, invested and restructured to improve their productivity and quality. DITI could have provided pump-priming funding for needed new technologies, cutting through government red tape where necessary. DITI could also have acted as overseer, to guarantee that environmental or antitrust laws were not trampled on in the name of competitiveness. As a quid pro quo for the cost of import restraints to the consumer and to the economy, DITI could have required industry and labor to make sacrifices of their own, limiting wage demands, workplace rules, executive compensation, and investment options.

To complement this reorganization and to create a common identity among trade personnel, a Trade Corps of public officials should be created. In a different era, it was deemed necessary to create the Foreign Service, an elite group of public servants willing to devote their professional lives to statecraft. With the national well-being now as dependent on economic and trade matters as it is on traditional diplomacy, it is time to elevate the status of those who defend U.S. economic interests in the international marketplace.

This Trade Corps, first proposed by Representative Marcy Kaptur (D., Ohio), would cut across agency lines, including all officials involved in trade work above a certain level—GS-12, possibly—as long as they have a minimum (possibly two to three years) of experience dealing with trade matters. Most of these trade experts would work within the new DITI, creating a much-needed *esprit de corps* and sense of professionalism not always evident among some current trade officials. But some of the Trade Corps would be drawn from economics and commercial officers in the State Department, the Treasury Department, and elsewhere. Their membership will permit closer communication between and among departments and the development of common views on trade issues that transcend narrow departmental approaches.

In recent years, a growing number of trade policymaking jobs have been held by political appointees. Trade issues are far too complex and important to the nation's future to be left to people who, experience shows, are likely to come and go in less than two years. For trade reorganization to work, the new Administration must commit itself to staff key positions with Trade Corps members.

But Trade Corps officials will incur similar, reciprocal obligations. In the past, a disturbing number of U.S. trade negotiators have left government service to work for foreign interests. At times this has created a serious conflict of interest. As important, it has generated the impression among the public that those charged with defending U.S. international economic interests cannot always be trusted. In a free society there is a limit to what controls can or should be placed on an individual's right to sell his or her services. But the potentially damaging impact of a government trade negotiator crossing the table to advise the other side is so great that it justifies some restrictions. For a set period—say, five years—Trade Corps members should be prohibited from advising all interests, domestic or foreign, on issues that directly or indirectly relate to work done during their government service.

Congressional Restructuring

REORGANIZATION OF TRADE POLICYMAKING WITHIN the Executive Branch is a necessary but hardly sufficient prerequisite for improving Washington's ability to deal with the trade issues likely to face the nation in the decade ahead. Without a radical restructuring of congressional handling of trade matters, the new Administration will be hamstrung in its efforts to strike a new trade posture.

It has become fashionable in Washington in recent years to attribute congressional–White House tension over trade matters to partisan politics. The Democrats' hold on Congress and Republican control of the White

House have obviously been sources of ongoing friction. But twelve years of divided government clouds the lesson of the Carter administration, when Congress and the White House struggled mightily over such trade issues as domestic content for automobiles and the Tokyo Round of multilateral trade negotiations. Trade discord along Pennsylvania Avenue, however, is not a partisan issue but a systemic, institutional problem. And it only promises to be worse for the new Administration. In the wake of the end of the Cold War, as economic competitiveness issues supplant military security concerns on the national agenda, members of Congress, irrespective of their parties and ideologies, will increasingly involve themselves in trade problems because these once remote issues now have an economic and political impact in nearly every congressional district.

This problem was already apparent during the crafting of the 1988 Trade Act. While the House Ways and Means Committee and the Senate Finance Committee had lead responsibility for the legislation, twenty-three congressional committees were involved in the final drafting. The recent debate over renewal of fast-track trade negotiating authority—in which environmental and labor concerns dominated the discussion—only highlighted the manifold domestic economic complications attendant with America's growing integration into the global economy. And any Executive Branch reorganization in the new Administration will only create additional jurisdictional squabbles on Capitol Hill, where the House Energy and Commerce Committee, for example, would be loath to give up its jurisdiction over the trade components of the Commerce Department.

Such congressional jurisdictional problems distort trade policy. In 1991 the United States spent $2.7 billion on export promotion. Thanks to the power of the House and Senate Farm committees, which have responsibility for the foreign agricultural service of the Department of Agriculture, three quarters of that money was spent to promote farm exports, which account for only 10 percent of the nation's sales overseas.

America can ill afford to continue shoehorning trade problems into existing congressional committee jurisdictions simply to avoid bruising the egos of congressional barons. Yet, a frontal assault on the trade prerogatives of the powerful Senate Finance and House Ways and Means committees would be doomed to failure.

Moreover, separate House and Senate committees solely devoted to trade are not the answer. As in the Executive Branch, it makes little sense to take the international aspects of environmental problems, antitrust issues, and so many of the other future trade concerns, and lump them together in a single committee. Trade issues are increasingly not severable from domestic concerns and trying to do so in some arbitrary manner would only make for bad policy.

Increased coordination of trade-related legislation by the House and Senate leadership is the only way to overcome the balkanization of responsibility for trade created by existing congressional fiefdoms, while maximizing the expertise inherent in the existing committee structure. Moreover, the congressional leadership needs to take a more active role in trade issues to counterbalance the power of the Senate Finance and House Ways and Means committees, which have traditionally given the administration free rein on trade.

In addition, as the pendulum of influence over trade policy shifts back down Pennsylvania Avenue toward Capitol Hill, the old accommodations between Congress and the White House designed to make trade policy work are breaking down. In recent years Congress has granted the administration fast-track negotiating authority, forgoing the right to amend a trade pact by promising to have a simple up or down vote on legislation implementing trade agreements. This arrangement has enabled the Executive Branch to provide foreign trading partners with some assurance that deals they strike with the United States are final and will not have to be renegotiated because of congressional tinkering. But it is the consensus in Washington among trade experts that once fast-track negotiating authority expires in mid-1993, Congress will not agree to renew it in its present form. Faced with that prospect, some means must be found to accommodate congressional desire to have greater influence over trade relations while recognizing the continuing need for the United States to present a coherent front in dealing with its trading partners.

Congress needs a Congressional Trade Office (CTO) modeled on the Congressional Budget Office to help committees on Capitol Hill better assess Administration action on trade. The CTO, composed of two dozen or so economists and regional and product-specific experts, could act as Congress's trade think tank, providing comprehensive analyses of everything from the effectiveness of our negotiators in the Structural Impediments Initiative talks with the Japanese to what the rule of origin should be for autos and computers receiving duty-free treatment in the North American Free Trade Agreement. Most important, CTO representatives, as surrogates for not just one committee but also for the congressional leadership, could sit in on trade negotiations, providing Congress with up-to-date information on progress in the talks. Involved in back-room discussions with U.S. trade negotiators when compromises must be made, they could advise the Administration against concessions that Congress won't swallow, while implicitly committing Congress to deals deemed acceptable.

Any administration—Republican or Democratic—will oppose this reform as an encroachment on Executive Branch prerogatives and as a needless additional layer of consultation and coordination. The Senate Finance and the House Ways and Means committees are likely to put up a stiff fight, because a CTO would be a competing power center.

But failure to effect congressional trade reform will stymie the effectiveness of Executive Branch reforms. Moreover, inaction would implicitly endorse the current, confused system, which is clearly not working. Finally, congressional trade reorganization guarantees that Congress, the elected representatives of those most affected by the consequences of trade policy, plays an effective role in policymaking.

Conclusion

THE UNITED STATES CANNOT HAVE A trade policy totally separate from its foreign policy, its monetary policy, its farm policy, or its environmental policy. But for too many years this tautology has been used as an argument by the State Department, the Treasury Department, and others to keep the trade policymaking apparatus weak. But trade policy has refused to take a backseat. And an anemic USTR has merely assured that America is saddled with bad trade policy. The new President has a chance to make a new beginning with trade, rather than depending on the weak organizational lineup of the past.

Department of Agriculture

AGRICULTURE POLICY

MARK RITCHIE AND KRISTIN DAWKINS

Summary

THE AGRICULTURE INDUSTRY and the people of rural America stand at a crossroads. While there are a number of significant positive trends developing across rural America—such as more environmentally sound farming practices and growing ties between rural and urban communities—they are outweighed by serious economic and environmental problems. The White House and the U.S. Department of Agriculture (USDA) have yet to address these problems effectively:

- Net income for farmers and farmworkers has declined for a decade.
- Government-set farm prices are below the cost of production.
- Occupational health and safety in agriculture and the food industry have deteriorated significantly.
- Poverty among rural farming communities is at record levels, especially among women and children, leading to growing hunger and malnourishment.
- Food quality has deteriorated due to excessive processing and packaging.
- Cutbacks in federal inspection have resulted in a decline in food safety.
- Taxpayer costs remain unacceptably high.
- Rural infrastructure (including roads, bridges, and schools) is in serious disrepair, hampering economic recovery.

With more than 110,000 employees and an annual budget greater than $50 billion, the USDA is the second-largest federal agency, surpassed only by the Department of Defense. The USDA has responsibility for almost everything relating to farming, forestry, and the food industry.

To reinforce the positive trends while addressing the problems noted

Mark Ritchie is the Executive Director of the Institute for Agriculture and Trade Policy, Minneapolis, Minnesota. Kristin Dawkins is a Senior Fellow at the Institute.

above, the next President and Secretary of Agriculture must tackle two major interrelated tasks.

First, they must make a number of important specific domestic and international agricultural policy decisions, including:

- Changes in current domestic food and farm policy as shaped by the 1990 Farm Act and the 1990 Budget Reconciliation Act to address the serious economic, ecological, and social problems created and exacerbated by these pieces of legislation.
- Rejection or acceptance of the agricultural provisions of the North American Free Trade Agreement (NAFTA) and the General Agreement on Tariffs and Trade (GATT), both of which have been accepted by the Bush administration but are strongly opposed by farmers, consumer groups, and environmentalists.

Second, and equally important, they must pursue the redefinition, reorientation, and reorganization of the USDA. New visions, missions, goals, and ethical considerations are needed to rebuild economically and ecologically sustainable family farms and rural communities, for while the USDA in the past has focused primarily on individual farm units, its mandate must be expanded to include the entire rural community—small towns and nonfarming rural residents in addition to family farms.

Historically, the USDA has concentrated its research and educational activities on maximizing per-acre or per-worker crop and livestock production, without regard to net profit, food quality and safety, or ecological consequences. Now, the USDA must expand its goals to promote human health, protect the environment, and provide adequate net income to efficient and sustainable farming families. The USDA must also expand its mission to include the widest possible range of new farm-related products such as biofuels, industrial raw materials, medicines, and new services, including wildlife conservation, ecological protection, and agri-tourism.

State of Our Family Farms and Rural Communities

POSITIVE TRENDS

Despite the tough economic times across rural America, there are a number of important positive trends in agriculture. The USDA must commit the resources necessary to reinforce, support, and extend these. Here are some of the most important:

- *Environmental progress.* Farmers are reducing their dependence on expensive chemicals, fossil fuels, and other capital-intensive methods of production through expanded use of sustainable farm practices, leading to greater economic resilience and improved protection of the environment. In addition, there has been a sharp increase in the use of agricultural and forestry products for pollution prevention and cleanup. The increased use of biofuels such as ethanol and recent breakthroughs in the development of truly biodegradable plastics made from plant matter are examples of new technologies that are both ecologically sound and economically productive.

• *Rural and urban links.* A large number of individuals and groups are working to build links between rural and urban people. Farmers' markets, community-supported agriculture, city–country dialogues, and church exchanges are examples of a new promising relationship that bridges the economic divide and promotes cultural understanding and cooperation.

• *Adding value.* There is a slow but steady shift toward activities that are adding more value to our raw crops and livestock products. These include more local processing and direct marketing by producers themselves through their cooperatives and collective-bargaining organizations.

• *Consumer expectations.* Consumers have ever greater expectations for their food, including higher standards for safety, nutrition, and quality. Changing consumer preferences are translating into new opportunities for producers.

NEGATIVE TRENDS
The following trends, however, are harming family farmers, consumers, or the environment. The next Administration must design and implement political and policy strategies to reverse them.

• *Economic crisis for farmers and farmworkers.* Federal farm policy has set commodity prices at levels below the average cost of production, creating an economic crisis for rural America. In real terms, there has been a decade-long decline in net income for farmers, wages for farmworkers, and return on investment for owner-operators and tenant farmers. As a result, small and moderate-size family farms are being forced out of business, and their land is being consolidated into ever larger units, far beyond the size that can be farmed in an ecologically sustainable way. About thirty-one thousand farm families are being forced to leave their land each year.

• *Negative impacts on farm-related businesses and rural communities.* As a direct result of this farm income crisis, the industries and businesses that provide production inputs and other goods to farm families continue to be in economic crisis as well. The worst year ever for tractor sales was 1991, but it appears that 1992 may be even worse. This economic turmoil has led to a significant depopulation of many rural areas, a trend compounded by the "graying" of rural America caused by the disproportionate exodus of young people unable to find employment. Both the economic crisis and outmigration have caused serious reductions in tax revenues, making it impossible for many communities to maintain the physical infrastructure of roads, schools, and hospitals necessary for economic recovery.

• *Hunger and malnutrition.* Due to the overall economic crisis, the number of hungry people in the United States today is greater than at any time since the 1930s. Although food stamp rolls are at a record level of nearly 26 million people, the number of new recipients continues to rise by about 100,000 each month. Women and children in particular are extremely hard hit.

• *Food quality, safety, and security concerns.* The nutritional value of many foods has been lowered through excessive processing, packaging, transportation, and storage, as well as because of the addition of excessive additives and preservatives. As a result, consumer confidence is down, particularly in regard to the safety of specific foods such as meats, seafood, fruits, and vegetables. At the same time, U.S. reserve supplies of some critical food items are often below necessary levels, resulting in shortages in our school lunch and elderly nutrition programs, and in unnecessary rises in retail prices.

• *Economic concentration in agribusiness and the food-processing industry.* The Bush administration's failure to enforce antitrust laws and its manipulation of price, credit, and subsidy policies has led to an unprecedented level of monopoly and economic concentration in agriculture. Four or less firms control almost all major food items, including poultry, pork, beef, flour, breakfast cereals, and many others. As a result, farmers have fewer options for where they can sell, while consumers pay higher oligopolistic prices.

• *Dangerous working conditions.* Occupational health and safety factors for farmers, farmworkers, and food industry workers such as meatpackers have deteriorated significantly. There has been a sharp rise in toxic chemical poisoning, machinery accidents, and stress-related illness.

• *Taxpayers' burden.* Federal budget costs for USDA-administered farm programs remain at unacceptably high levels. Over the past decade more than $150 billion have been spent, virtually all of which subsidizes exporting corporations and their overseas buyers.

The Reagan/Bush Record

CURRENT DOMESTIC FOOD and farm policy is dictated by two pieces of legislation: the traditional Farm Bill, now slated to run until 1995, and the Budget Reconciliation Act of 1990. Covering everything from food stamps and the WIC (Women, Infants, and Children) program to farm commodity programs, these two pieces of legislation largely determine the economic possibilities for rural America.

When President Carter left office, the U.S. agricultural community was enjoying relative economic stability. Under Presidents Reagan and Bush, there has been a decade-long depression in rural America.

- Farm commodity prices in 1990 averaged half of their levels in 1980 in both real terms and in purchasing power.
- From 1980 to 1990, the value of farm exports fell more that 50 percent—from $40 billion to less than $20 billion in adjusted dollars.
- The cost of diesel gasoline in 1980 was 55 cents per gallon; today it's more than $1 per gallon.
- More than 600,000 families lost their farms over the past decade, causing a 24.1 percent decline in overall farm population.

Almost every person in this nation, both rural and urban, knows that our family farms have been through one of their worst decades since the 1930s. Hollywood movies, rock concerts, books, and thousands of newspaper articles have chronicled the crisis. But current farm policy has not only been bad for family farmers, it is also a disaster for taxpayers. Annual costs soared to as high as $47 billion in 1987, compared to $5 billion in 1980, with most of this money going directly to agribusiness in the form of export or storage subsidies.

A New Domestic Agriculture Policy

THE CURRENT BUSH FARM POLICY needs to be overhauled completely to balance supply with demand, eliminate farm subsidies, and encourage rather than discourage more sustainable farming practices. Major provisions of this new domestic policy should include the following:

- *Changes in farm commodity programs.* There are two central economic elements in every farm bill. First, Congress sets minimum prices— now only about half the cost of production—that must be paid to farmers by domestic and foreign buyers. This is accomplished through a USDA-administered price-support mechanism called the Commodity Credit Corporation nonrecourse loan program. Second, Congress sets a "target" price for farmers that is above the minimum price but still below the average cost of production. To cover part of the farmers' losses between the loan rate and the target price, the government makes deficiency payments that are often called "farm subsidies," although they primarily benefit domestic and overseas buyers by holding prices at unrealistically low levels.

The new Administration must use its discretionary authority as granted in the current Farm Bill to set the loan rate of the Commodity Credit Corporation at the cost of production, thereby enabling farmers to sell their produce at fair prices and eliminating expensive deficiency payment programs.

Simultaneously, supply management programs must be strengthened to make certain that supply and demand stay in balance, protecting soil and water resources and wildlife habitats while maintaining reasonable reserve stocks and stable prices.

• *New environmental protection provisions.* A wide range of policies is needed to encourage the deintensification of production in agriculture and to ensure that basic procedures for protecting soil, water, and air resources are followed throughout the entire food chain. The new Administration should preserve existing programs, such as the Conservation Reserve Program, which have served to protect wetlands, prevent nonsource point water pollution, and reduce soil erosion. In addition, it should develop new programs that encourage farmers to adopt new production methods, including improved soil testing and more carefully adjusted equipment, to ensure that chemicals are not being used excessively or unnecessarily.

• *Farm credit.* Government-provided credit should be used primarily to help young and returning farmers get started and to help existing farmers make new investments to boost environmental protection and productivity. Credit programs should not be used to cover year after year of financial losses due to government-set low prices. Once policies are in place to guarantee remunerative prices, the new Administration can also ensure that sufficient credit is available to help farmers get back on their feet, to bring young farmers into the business, and to generate investment on a nondiscriminatory basis at affordable rates of interest.

The new Administration must also eliminate major abuses, such as the denial of credit on the basis of race and outright corruption, through proper oversight and regulation. There are roles to be played by all elements of the farm credit system, including private lenders, the Federal Government, state governments, and the cooperative farm credit services. Affirmative steps would include strengthening local control and encouraging credit unions and cooperatives—steps that make sure the rural community will not suffer the credit strangulation of the Bush era.

• *Food stamps, WIC, and other food security programs.* Poverty, especially among women and children, has increased dramatically during this past decade. It is increasingly difficult for poor people to find healthful food at affordable prices. The new Administration must expand successful programs, such as WIC and food stamps, to provide for all eligible families desiring this assistance. Efforts by the USDA to deny emergency benefits, as it is doing in South-Central Los Angeles, need to be reversed immediately.

International Policymaking: GATT, NAFTA, and the FTA

U.S. INTERNATIONAL AGRICULTURE POLICYMAKING has been dominated during the past decade by three major negotiations: the General Agreement on Tariffs and Trade (GATT), the North American Free Trade Agreement (NAFTA), and the U.S.-Canada Free Trade Agreement (FTA). The new Administration will face major decisions on all of them.

GATT: THE GENERAL AGREEMENT ON TARIFFS AND TRADE

GATT is by far the most important international trade agreement, covering 107 countries and 90 percent of the world's trade. Because U.S. agriculture supplies about half of the world's total supply of feed grains, GATT policies have an enormous effect on U.S. farmers, rural communities, and the rural economy.

There are three primary concerns with existing GATT rules. The first is the failure of GATT to enforce key provisions of the agreement. Second, there is a need to clarify some existing rules to deal with confusion and misunderstandings that have resulted from imprecise or ambiguous language. Third, there are several new rules that would be important to add to GATT to reflect changed and changing ecological and economic circumstances.

Failure to Enforce Existing Rules. Two key GATT rules affecting agriculture are essentially ignored. In Article VI, GATT defines the cost of production as including "the cost of marketing and a reasonable return"; exports priced at lower rates are considered "dumping." Yet almost all major producers, including the United States, allow companies operating within their territory to engage in export dumping, causing chaos in world markets. Dumping has a detrimental impact on small farmers and food security in both the United States and developing nations of the Third World. As small farmers are often unable to compete, even in their own local markets, with underpriced, highly subsidized dumped exports, they are driven off the land, and more and more of a region's food supply must then be imported at increasingly higher cost.

In Article XI, GATT requires countries using import controls to link them with internal production controls. This linkage, which depends on supply management to generate a balance between production and consumption, is intended to guarantee nondiscriminatory treatment for all producers and fair trade. Yet almost all major countries ignore this rule. The next Administration must work to ensure that all GATT member nations comply with these existing rules.

Clarification and Updating of Existing Rules. The new Administration should carefully review the current GATT and a number of recent GATT rulings to determine those with potentially negative impacts on U.S. consumer, farm, or environmental interests, and push for clarification or reestablishment of historic interpretations. For example, in a recent dispute between the United States and Canada, a GATT panel ruled that our Federal Government must do everything within its constitutional power to overturn or preempt state laws that are designed to help small wineries and breweries by exempting them from special excise taxes. This GATT ruling included the demand that all state and local laws inconsistent with GATT rules must be brought into compliance or preempted by Federal Government action. This is a complete reversal of previous interpretations and could lead to federal preemption of an incredibly wide range of current state and local laws, covering everything from environmental protection and food safety to credit law and restrictions on the ownership of farmland by corporations.

Also, while the original GATT oilseeds panel interpreted GATT rules in a way that threatens numerous existing U.S. Government farm programs that are not targeted directly to producers, a second oilseed panel ruled that all countries, including the United States, are prohibited from introducing or expanding farm programs to assist producers of any crops where the tariff on that item has been "bound"—a term that refers to an agreed maximum tariff. Under this interpretation, numerous U.S. farm programs could be subject to challenge by GATT in the near future.

Another recent GATT panel ruled that in order to be eligible to control imports of agricultural products under GATT Article XI, nations must have in place supply management programs that are quantity-based. This ruling excludes supply management based on land set-aside programs, such as we now have in the United States. If, as a result of this panel decision, the United States loses (or gives up) our current waiver allowing import quotas in Section 22 of the Farm Bill, many of our current programs will immediately be in danger.

Most of the current GATT was written more than forty years ago—long before certain issues, such as the dangers of global environmental degradation, the role of global corporations, or the need for global food reserves, were even considered. It is essential that the next Administration take the lead in bringing these new issues out into the global debate, and push to see specific measures added to the GATT agreement to address some of these concerns.

For example, at present the world's emergency grain reserves are stored mostly in the United States, at great expense to U.S. farmers and taxpayers. Every few years these global food stocks become too large. When this happens, it is again the U.S. farmers and taxpayers who end up shouldering most of the burden of reducing production enough to bring stocks back to normal levels.

The new Administration should insist that GATT rules be amended to include a "world food reserve" provision requiring all nations to share the cost of maintaining world food reserve stocks, and requiring all major producers to share equally in the process of reducing excess production and stocks when this reserve becomes too large.

The Uruguay Round. The problems afflicting farmers and the rural economy could be rectified as part of the current renegotiation of GATT known as the Uruguay Round. Although these talks are currently stalled, the United States is in a powerful position to reestablish them and to create a great deal of momentum for real change.

Before these talks can begin to be productive, however, the new Administration must dismiss the current "Dunkel draft" text, which was endorsed by the Bush administration. The Dunkel draft fails to address most of the negative trends, and it contains numerous new provisions that would be even more devastating to U.S. agriculture.

NAFTA: THE NORTH AMERICAN FREE TRADE AGREEMENT

An analysis of the NAFTA text drafted by the Bush administration indicates that it contains numerous provisions that will aggravate the decline of agriculture in all three countries—Mexico, Canada, and the United States. Producer and consumer groups from all three countries have put forward a powerful joint critique of the current draft. In addition, producer leaders from the three countries have been meeting to draft language for the kind of positive "win-win" policies needed in any final agreement.

The new Administration should reopen negotiations to make sure that the language developed by the producers themselves forms the basis of a new North American Free Trade Agreement.

FTA: THE U.S.-CANADA FREE TRADE AGREEMENT

Although the FTA was completed and implemented in 1988, it has been in a constant state of flux due to the large number of trade disputes it generated. The new Administration must correct numerous flaws in the FTA and its implementation:

1. Meat and food inspections at the U.S.-Canada border were discontinued, resulting in some shipments of contaminated meats and other foods. The new Administration must reestablish inspections to guarantee that unsafe food is prevented from crossing the border in either direction.

2. The Bush administration has put U.S. farmers, especially wheat producers, at a competitive disadvantage by its interpretation of the FTA. The new Administration should hold public hearings to determine the full extent of the problems that must be addressed and to find solutions that are mutually agreeable with the Canadians.

3. The FTA has not yet prevented the dumping of products at prices below the cost of production in either direction across the border. The new Administration needs to address this immediately, reexamining the import and export of wheat, corn, pork, and beef in particular.

4. The FTA has jeopardized environmental protection measures on both sides of the border. "Harmonization" of standards under the FTA, for example, led to a lowering of Canadian pesticide standards that now require Canada to allow the import of foods with greater concentrations of pesticide residues. The FTA has also been used to challenge local legislation in the United States requiring recycled fiber in newsprint. The new Administration must ensure that the FTA cannot be used to undermine existing environmental standards in either country.

5. Finally, the new Administration should conduct a general review of all current rules in the FTA. This review should lead to the elimination of those provisions that could harm the public interest and to interpretations of the FTA that reinforce the positive trends occurring in rural America.

Reorientation and Reorganization of the USDA

WITH A BUDGET GREATER THAN $50 billion and more than 110,000 employees, including those in support offices in almost every county throughout America, the USDA is the second-largest federal agency, second only to the Department of Defense. With jurisdiction over forestry as well as agriculture, USDA policies have a tremendous impact on our nation's natural resources and environmental quality. The USDA is also one of the most diverse of all Federal Government agencies. To make sure that this decentralized structure leads to positive changes for rural communities, the new Administration must transform the agency beyond its historically narrow focus.

First, it should expand the mandate of the USDA to include the entire rural community—small towns and rural, nonfarming residents in addition to farming families. Similarly, the mandate should be expanded to promote human health, protect the environment, and provide adequate net income to efficient and sustainable farming families.

The new Administration must expand the mandate of the USDA to include basic scientific research that benefits the public at large. Over the past decade its programs have been directed toward simply fulfilling the commercial research needs of a few giant corporations, such as creating special herbicide-resistant plants. Economic and policy research has likewise been directed away from basic analysis to providing statistical alibis for the increasingly indefensible policies of the Bush administration. Recent research and education, for example, have emphasized the maximization per acre or per worker of crop and livestock production without regard to net profit, food quality and safety, or ecological consequences.

The new Administration must make a number of changes in the massive USDA bureaucracy to reorient the agency's mission and reduce budget costs while improving services. The following are key areas needing immediate attention:

1. National food safety and inspection services are now scattered among different federal agencies and departments, including the USDA, the Food and Drug Administration, and the Environmental Protection Agency. The new Administration should consolidate these agencies under one umbrella-style Food and Nutrition Department to end wasteful and costly competition and duplication among competing agencies.

2. Timber and forestry issues are also scattered among the Department of the Interior, the Department of Agriculture, and, to a lesser extent, the Environmental Quality Board and the Environmental Protection Agency. The new Administration should also consolidate these agencies under one umbrella-style Timber and Forestry Department to reduce costly duplication and enable sound, sustainable management through coordinated policy.

3. There are four major overlapping agencies with the USDA: the Agricultural Stabilization and Conservation Program (ASCS), the Soil Conservation Service (SCS), the Farmers Home Administration (FmHA), and the Extension Service. The new Administration should house these agencies

together where feasible, and better coordinate their functions for increased efficiency.

We must forge entirely new farm and food policies to regenerate a sustainable, family-based farming system—a system designed to increase employment, reduce urbanization, protect our water and air quality, provide more nutritious food, conserve wildlife and natural resources, and provide greater food security for all nations, both rich and poor.

To accomplish this shift in policies, the next Administration will need to change some of the underlying values and assumptions that now shape our nation's farm policies, especially the idea that our land and water resources can be used and abused endlessly. It is a shift every bit as crucial and enormous for the natural environment as the abolition of slavery was for the human environment, for just as today we act as if our natural resources are cheap and endless, so in the nineteenth century were similar assumptions held about the human resources of those who happened to be black.

Today we face a task much like that of the nineteenth-century abolitionists. We must lay to rest the idea that the Earth's natural resources can be enslaved, despite any economic dislocation that may result. We cannot delay. The very survival of hungry people today, and in future generations, depends on our success in achieving a more sustainable farming system, one that carefully balances the economic and ecological relationships between people and the land.

TRANSPORTATION

JOAN B. CLAYBROOK[1]

Summary

T RANSPORTATION IS A PIVOTAL FACTOR in defining the quality of life in America. It affects our economic viability, environment, and public health. Without technologically advanced systems for the movement of people and goods in the twenty-first century, America will continue to lose its productivity and vitality.

In recent years the Federal Government has steadily decreased real federal transportation spending, transferring much responsibility to state and local governments, which have little or no means of absorbing the costs. This is a policy of "first the shift, then the shaft."

The government's laissez-faire policies have failed to maintain our transportation systems, disinvesting in our now deteriorating infrastructure. We have not formulated long-range plans, a necessity for heavy capital investments such as transportation systems and for related business decisions. And little effort has been made to alter ongoing federal transportation subsidies that distort market pricing signals.

The consequences of these policies are frightening. Economic studies by David Aschauer and others show that as much as half of the U.S. decline in national productivity can be attributed to the shortfall in infrastructure investment, and the environmental effects of motor vehicle pollutants cost at least $10 billion each year. For airways and highways, it is now likely that the economic costs of congestion and delay exceed the amounts we spend on building and maintaining adequate facilities. The economy will continue to underperform and productivity will slump as workers spend too much

Joan B. Claybrook is President of Public Citizen. She served as Administrator of the National Highway Traffic Safety Administration of the U.S. Department of Transportation under President Carter. Her publications include Freedom from Harm: The Civilizing Influence of Health, Safety, and Environmental Regulations *(Public Citizen and Democracy Project, 1986).*

time commuting instead of working. Congestion in the transportation network delays goods so that efficiency innovations such as "just in time" delivery for manufacturing are not possible in many industries.

The most important government action in the short term is to implement the landmark 1991 Intermodal Surface Transportation Efficiency Act (ISTEA).

For the longer term, the basic concepts underlying ISTEA are a model for all transportation investments. A national long-range plan must include the following:

- Creation of a capital budget to fund long-term investments adequately.
- Adjustment of user-fee and tax schedules to moderate current subsidies and distorted market pricing.
- Evaluation of a unified trust fund, merging trust funds for specific transportation modes.
- Increased intermodal connections through planning and funding.
- Federal investment in innovative technological research and development for the next century, while avoiding esoteric *Star Wars*-type pet projects and political pork.
- Strong enforcement of the federal antitrust and deceptive-practices laws to prevent monopoly pricing and other fraudulent activities in a deregulated marketplace.
- Issuance of new mandatory motor vehicle safety standards in ISTEA and new auto fuel economy standards to reach 40 mpg by the year 2003.

Introduction

TRANSPORTATION AFFECTS EACH OF US in our daily lives, whether through time and money wasted in traffic, the timely delivery of goods to the supermarket or the manufacturing plant, the wrenching death or injury of loved ones in transportation crashes (over five hundred thousand serious injuries occur each year), or the pervasive effects of air pollution on our health and landscape.

Overall, transportation expenses eat up about eighteen cents of every consumer dollar—the largest single expense after housing. Total federal funding in fiscal 1993 will exceed $36 billion, with over 80 percent financed from user fees. Over 50 percent of these funds are for the highway program.

Transportation is also one of our largest employers. Railway, aviation, water transportion, mass transit, and trucking industries employ 3.5 million workers. Related vehicle manufacturing, highway building, and the associated service industries employ many millions more. Jobs, economic development, productivity, and growth depend heavily on the transportation sector.

Highway travel and public funding for it dominate all other modes even though overall for both people and goods it is often the most costly method of travel, the most dangerous, and the most damaging to the environment. The lack of effective long-range planning and investment in the most efficient transportation systems, as well as lack of connections among various transportation modes, impedes speedy delivery, creates social inequities, and increases consumer and business costs and congestion. The enactment of the landmark ISTEA legislation positions America to reinvest in transportation policy to bring substantial benefits to our economy, environment, and social health.

The Department of Transportation was created in 1966 in response to President Lyndon Johnson's request to Congress to consolidate various transportation programs housed in different parts of the government. Ultimately the Department of Transportation included programs taken from the Commerce Department, the Treasury Department, the Interstate Commerce Commission, the Civil Aeronautics Board, the Public Health Service, and the Department of Housing and Urban Development. Also brought under the DOT was the independent Federal Aviation Administration. "In a nation that spans a continent," President Johnson said, "transportation is the web of the union."

Recent Legacy

DURING THE PAST DOZEN YEARS, transportation policies have been skewed by ideological barriers that have undermined sensible, scientifically based, and cost-effective decisionmaking. For example:

• There has been a refusal to recognize the safety and service damage done to the nation's air transportation system after some eleven thousand highly trained air traffic controllers were fired during a 1981 union strike. Replacements took years to hire and train.

• Resistance to issuance of safety, environmental, and cost-saving regulations in all transportation modes has caused tens of thousands of deaths and injuries and billions of dollars in economic waste. Revocation of the automatic restraint (air bag) standard in 1981, and the six-year delay before the standard was reissued by order of the U.S. Supreme Court, will probably ultimately have caused more than forty thousand deaths and nearly one million unnecessary injuries.

• There has been a failure to enforce the law, such as not requiring timely recalls of defective vehicles, and not ensuring compliance with antitrust and deceptive-practices laws during a period of economic deregulation in the airline and trucking industries.

• Reluctance to invest federal dollars in innovative research on new technologies, despite studies that show that private investment increases with public investments, by ten to forty cents for each public dollar, has slowed economic growth and our international competitiveness.

• There have been cutbacks in federal funding for general infrastructure repairs and long-term capital investments from 3.1 to 1.9 percent of the Gross National Product since 1968, an overall reduction of 38 percent. By 1989, a total of 70 percent of peak-hour urban travel took place in congested conditions, up from 55 percent in 1983. Motorists lose over 700 million hours of travel time in stalled vehicles, wasting 3 billion gallons of gasoline (about 4 percent of U.S. consumption). According to the FAA, air travelers experience about 20,000 hours of flight delays annually, costing passengers and carriers more than $5 billion a year.

• We have not engaged in long-term transportation planning and investment while our trading partners overtook us. During the 1990s, Japan will invest $3.1 trillion and Germany an estimated $1.5 trillion while developing sophisticated transportation systems and rapid communications technology that may someday reduce the need for commuter travel. The U.S. plans call for just over $1 trillion, although our population and size far exceed those of Germany and Japan combined. By any measure we are far behind.

Transportation Priorities and Initiatives

ALTHOUGH EACH TRANSPORTATION MODE faces unique crises, limitations, and challenges, several key cross-cutting issues should attract the attention of the new Administration during its first hundred days.

SAFETY
As Lyndon Johnson said in 1966, "No function of the new department—no responsibility of its secretary—will be more important than safety. We must insure the safety of our citizens as they travel on our land, in our skies, and over our waters."

While no transportation secretary has repudiated this pledge, during the past dozen years the National Highway Traffic Safety Administration (NHTSA)—the DOT agency whose programs save nineteen thousand lives each year—has seen the largest percentage cut in its budget and staff, revocation of key safety standards, and failure to act on a long-needed agenda of unfinished standards (see the chapter on the NHTSA by Clarence Ditlow).

Large trucks are a major and increasing safety concern as nearly five thousand people, mostly car occupants, are killed each year in large truck crashes. Although the ISTEA froze use of longer combination vehicles (long double and triple trailers) effective June 1, 1991, except in the twenty states where they could then operate, these vehicles should be banned altogether, an option reserved by the law for the states.

In 1991, more than five hundred people were killed in crashes at railroad grade crossings. Railroads have successfully exempted themselves in most cases and placed liability on state and local governments. As a result, these unnecessary and predictable deaths and injuries continue to occur year after year.

Several initiatives to enhance transportation safety include:

• Implementing the mandatory rulemaking actions set forth in the ISTEA, which could save eleven thousand additional lives a year, with key deadlines occurring in 1993. Priority should be given to issuance of effective standards on head injury, rollover, upgraded side impact protection, and child booster seats.

• Issuing key truck safety standards requiring antilock brakes, energy-absorbing rear underride guards, on-board recorders, and improved occupant restraint systems.

• Improving container strength, operator qualifications and training, limits on hours, and conditions and routing of travel for vehicles containing hazardous materials; addressing the current industry efforts to secure weakened federal rules for hazardous-materials routing that could preempt stronger standards in some states.

• Initiating a cooperative program to investigate options to reduce the number of deaths at railroad grade crossings.

• Increasing significantly the air traffic control staff to handle current and anticipated levels of air traffic safely, without overworking controllers, whose jobs require great attention to detail as they make life-and-death decisions.

ENVIRONMENT

Transportation and the environment are inseparable. Cars and trucks are the major sources of air pollution, in many communities causing 90 percent of carbon monoxide pollution, 40 percent of nitrogen oxide (NO) emission, and 50 percent of volatile organic compounds (VOC) emission. NO and VOC react photochemically, causing ozone pollution, or smog. About half of the greenhouse gas emissions causing global warming come from burning fossil fuels. Although oil consumption has been down significantly for buildings, industries, and utilities since the 1973 embargo, it has increased 21 percent for transportation. Vehicles release some 350 million tons of carbon each year. All transportation sources account for about 30 percent of the U.S. carbon dioxide emissions.

The pollutants caused by motor vehicles create huge costs in damage to health, to crops and forests, and to materials and lost labor in productivity, amounting to $9 billion (in 1989 dollars) according to a Federal Reserve study, and to $10 billion to $200 billion (in 1989 dollars) according to a University of California at Davis study.

The rising number and increased use of motor vehicles make transportation emissions a steadily worsening problem, undermining three generations of clean-air acts. And federal transportation policy has systematically exacerbated this disaster. With low fuel taxes, our gasoline price is one half to one third the price in Europe and Japan, strongly promoting vehicle use. And federal fuel excise taxes have been devoted to creating a network of highways and interstates no other country approaches, and correspondingly a pattern of land use that has limited successful mass transit development to a few urban areas. Thus our federal highway subsidies have created a society addicted to its unparalleled mobility—a dependency that reaches deep into the American life-style.

To improve the environment, transportation policy should:

• Begin a long-term gradual increase in the gas tax. While difficult politically, such a move would help to offset highway subsidies.

• Upgrade the 1985 standard (27.5 mpg) by issuing vehicle fuel economy standards of 40 mpg by 2003, as directed in pending legislation of Senator Richard Bryan (D. Nev.). Higher CAFE standards will reduce fuel emissions and could save nearly 30 percent of the projected costs of foreign oil imports by the year 2010.

• Permit tolls on federally funded highways.

INTERMODAL TRANSPORTATION SYSTEMS
The Department of Transportation is divided into multibillion-dollar modal administrations, each supported by powerful constituencies. Not surprisingly, they usually operate independently of each other, resulting in minimal plan-

ning for timely, efficient, and cost-effective intermodal connections such as rail systems that run to airports or ports. Further, investments should be preceded by intermodal plans under the firm and guiding hand of the secretary to bring together highly independent transportation sectors. Experience in other countries, especially in Europe, reinforces the critical role the government must play in developing an aerial vision of national transportation networks.

INFRASTRUCTURE: PLANNING, FUNDING, PARTNERSHIP

The Organization for Economic Cooperation and Development (OECD) reports that U.S. net investment in infrastructure is an anemic 0.3 percent of GNP, compared with 5.7 percent in Japan and 3.7 percent in Germany. This shortfall is largely a response to short-term budget concerns, but the consequences of these decisions have long-term implications. Not only are we not generating the kinds of innovation that spur rapid economic growth, we are also not preparing for the future with development of technologies such as high-speed transportation, light rail, "smart" highways focused on improving safety, congestion, and the environment, and even better communications to reduce transportation needs. While there is debate over the specific magnitude of the problem, the need to double our overall rate of investment as recommended by the National Council on Public Works Improvement has not been seriously challenged.

Reversing our infrastructure shortfall must start with a strategy for increased financing and refocused policy goals. Merely pouring money into construction is not efficient, but revising programs without increased investment is not effective either. Future capital investments should be weighted toward transportation technologies that best reduce congestion, pollution, and safety hazards, such as light rail.

The new Administration should pursue several funding and policy initiatives to enhance infrastructure investment:

• Assure all funds now collected for transportation infrastructure are made available for that purpose rather than bottled up to make the deficit look smaller.

• Create a long-term transportation capital investments budget to avoid the continual sacrificing of investments needed for future growth to fund current domestic projects.

• Make a conscious effort to limit the "pork barrel" flavor that often pervades public works projects, particularly large ones. Such an effort is necessary to restore faith in government expenditures for these important nation-building activities.

• Examine the pros and cons of merging the existing transportation trust funds so that transportation needs, and not available funds, drive funding decisions. To increase trust fund revenues that are inadequate to meet national goals for the twenty-first century, adjust user fees and excise taxes so that all users pay their fair share, taking into account the full environmental, social, and maintenance costs.

• Develop partnerships among federal, state, and local governments, citizens' groups, and business for effective transportation planning and implementation, as recognized in ISTEA, which allows local flexibility in setting projects to assure national goals of long-term planning, economic health, environment, energy, and social equity.

• Coordinate capital investments to assure that they meet the needs of related states and connect modes of transportation.

Long-Term Goals for Major Transportation Systems

HIGHWAYS AND TRANSIT

The Federal Aid Highway Act of 1956 initiated construction of the nationwide 44,849-mile Interstate and Defense Highway System (only now being finished), with grant-in-aid funds by formula to states for primary, secondary, and urban road construction (total federally supported mileage, 851,714). Funded out of the Highway Trust Fund with ongoing revenues from a modest gasoline excise tax (ten cents for cars; trucks pay somewhat more), this program has dominated federal transportation programs since 1956.

America as a result has the best highway system in the world. It has contributed mightily to our economic prosperity as well as to environmental and economic crises facing many cities and the decline of nonsubsidized competitors. In recent years, the highway system also has been allowed to deteriorate. Over 40 percent of the nation's interstate highways need immediate attention over the next three to five years to prevent the substructure from collapsing.

Between 1983 and 1991, authorized levels for highway funding hovered between $10 billion and $13 billion. The fiscal year 1993 increased request of $19 billion was spurred by the Intermodal Surface Transportation Efficiency Act (ISTEA), a $151 billion program over six years for highways, bridges, transit systems, and highway safety. Labeled "veto bait" only weeks before being signed by President Bush in November 1991, it suddenly was justified as a "jobs" program. Job creation is expected to be forty thousand to seventy-five thousand for each $1 billion spent.

ISTEA is a remarkable legislative initiative. It designates a National

Highway System consisting of existing interstate mileage and some primary highways to focus federal resources on the roads most important to national transportation needs. It fundamentally changes the way the Federal Government, the states, and local government will set transportation policy, determine priorities, and select the best projects to fit community needs.

ISTEA places planning responsibility at the local rather than the state level; the local level is arguably more sensitive to local needs and land-use problems, while encouraging statewide coordination of planning that complies with clean air and other environmental laws and land-use considerations. This process replaces the previous project-by-project approach. The new law's flexible funding will be made available for a mix of surface transportation programs developed to meet state and local community needs: from mass transit, to high-occupancy vehicle lanes, to new construction, to demand management. Highway spending will no longer be automatic, ending the previous favoritism for new highway construction at the expense of other transportation alternatives.

Urban transit policymaking at the federal level originated at the Housing and Urban Development Department and was transferred to the DOT in 1968. ISTEA puts the highway and urban transit programs on an equal footing for the first time. For the past twelve years urban transit funding has been severely restricted. While the Reagan and Bush administrations tried to eliminate all operating subsidies, Congress regularly funded them. Urban Transit funding for capital investments is significantly increased by ISTEA, which authorizes $31.5 billion over six years, or 64 percent over 1991 levels. But even these increased authorization levels remain far below urban transit funding in European countries. Nevertheless, the administration's 1993 appropriations request was only $3 billion, not the $5 billion authorized.

RAILROADS

The Federal Railroad Administration is a small agency, transferred from the Interstate Commerce Commission and responsible for a mixture of safety, efficiency, customer service, financial assistance, and technology research programs. Its proposed 1993 budget request is $429 million, which includes a $343 million grant to Amtrak, $40 million for safety and $26 million for research and development. Of this, $15 million is devoted to safety, environmental, technical, and economic assessments as to the viability of magnetic-levitation high-speed rail, which the administration and Congress suggest are necessary before any commitment is made to proceed with development of prototypes.

Amtrak was a product of federal law, creating a national railroad passenger network to replace the failing passenger service provided by for-profit railroads that were driven under following the construction of the interstate highway system and the development of reasonably priced airline service. But Amtrak had weaknesses from the outset. Its route system was designed by Congress and riddled with political compromises. Amtrak has spent many years developing a more rational system that more closely correlates with transportation demand. Amtrak also had to replace obsolete and deteriorated equipment, inherited from its private railroad predecessors, with modern cars and engines.

With surprising perseverance, Amtrak has overcome many of the problems that plagued its private railroad predecessors, especially heavy competition from airlines and highways. It has steadily cut back its operating funding requests from the government with employee cooperation and support, in a demonstration that productivity improvements can be obtained from government-created entities. Amtrak is actually doing more with less. With improving service quality and on-time performance, it can now consolidate its tourist travel markets in the rest of the country. It also may be able to branch out to provide commuter service in a number of metropolitan areas facing environmental and congestion problems in work travel, now that flexible surface transportation funds are available to support such alternatives.

Still, Amtrak is facing two financial problems. First, its capital budget has shrunk and cannot meet the need to replace and install new, quality equipment. Second, the federal program to upgrade the Northeast Corridor route between Boston and Washington, D.C., to a high-speed rail line is floundering. Improving this strong rail corridor would generate new ridership, as well as revenues that could be reinvested to strengthen other parts of the national rail system. A federal investment in high-speed rail travel would be modest, prudent, and considerably cheaper than expanding the area's interstate highways and airports. Funding for Amtrak capital investment, the Northeast Corridor, and advanced technology research, particularly for bullet trains, should be the priorities. France transports 5 million passengers each year in its 185-mph trains. Germany and Japan have invested $1 billion each for research in magnetic levitation technology.

FREIGHT SERVICE

Bankruptcies, deteriorating service, and line abandonments plagued freight railroads during the 1970s. The freight rail crisis was not unexpected. Railroad track was laid for nineteenth-century needs, before there was competition from trucks and barges, and by the late twentieth century there was too much track for the railroad's dwindling share of freight traffic to support. Government deregulation in 1979–80 permitted failing railroads to disappear and the surviving ones to shrink their plants. These steps were painful, particularly in the overbuilt Midwest and Northeast, which had to absorb major service reductions. But they were necessary to reach a more rational system base, enabling the surviving carriers to earn a return on their investment that would justify staying in the business.

However, freight rail remains at an insurmountable competitive disadvantage. While railroads own and maintain their tracks, the Federal Government systematically subsidizes the trucking industry, the railroads' main competitor, by paying for its plant—the highway network—through federal excise taxes. Trucking firms do pay fuel and other taxes, but overwhelming evidence from federal, state, and private studies shows that they do not pay their fair share and that a disproportionate burden of the highway infrastructure tax falls on cars. Another competitor to railroads, the barge industry, is likewise a beneficiary of major federal subsidies, through continuing federal expenditures on the vast inland waterway network. As long as this pattern of subsidy continues, railroads will continue to lose marginal traffic to the other modes, which each year obtain a higher share of the transportation market. Railroads are increasingly limited to carrying only captive traffic— goods that for reasons of geography, bulk, or weight cannot practically travel by other modes.

Since railroads are cleaner, safer, and more fuel-efficient than alternative modes of freight transportation, the new Federal Government should level the playing field by revising the old patterns of federal subsidies that distort transportation market decisions.

AIRLINES

Two units of the Department of Transportation are responsible for setting and administering the nation's aviation policy. First, the office of the secretary oversees the commercial aspects of the aviation industry, with the exception of proposed mergers, which since 1989 have fallen under the jurisdiction of the Antitrust Division of the Justice Department. These responsibilities were inherited from the disbanded Civil Aeronautics Board.

Second, air safety has been the province of the Federal Aviation Administration (FAA) within the Department of Transportation ever since the DOT was created in 1966. The FAA's wide array of responsibilities include operating the air traffic control system, certifying that aircraft and pilots are competent, monitoring airline safety records and performance, and assisting the nation's airports to expand and modernize to meet anticipated growth in the years to come. The FAA has a proposed 1993 budget of more than $9 billion, with about half for operations and half for capital investment, 85 percent of which would be funded from the Airport and Airway Trust Fund, financed by taxes on air passengers, airlines, and airport users. The fund has an accumulated balance of $7 billion.

More than a decade after Congress deregulated airline routes and fares, the airline industry is in trouble, suffering a loss of $6 billion in the past two years. Eastern and Pan Am, industry bulwarks for decades, have recently gone out of business. Today TWA, Continental, and America West are struggling to emerge from Chapter 11 bankruptcy proceedings. Air traffic congestion, outdated equipment, and understaffed government air traffic controller stations threaten the safety and efficiency of our airways. The government needs to set the industry back on track with a strong agenda that places equal and forceful emphasis on safety and economic competition.

The 1978 decision by Congress to deregulate airline routes and rates has produced savings for consumers that total several billion dollars each year. The state of the airline industry today, however, is the result of the "do nothing" government policies of the past decade. During the 1980s the U.S. Department of Transportation rubber-stamped an unprecedented number of airline mergers, reducing competition and setting the stage for higher fares and dissatisfactory service for passengers in the future.

Congress, in deregulating routes and rates, meant for the Department of Transportation to retain a strong federal presence in areas such as antitrust, consumer protection, safety, and small community service. But the DOT has dragged its feet when it comes to regulating, even in areas that require intervention to keep this industry competitive. For example, two major airlines, American and United, own the two principal airline computer reservation systems, which have been manipulated to favor those two airlines to the detriment of competitors. Because the DOT has not effectively curbed abuses in this area, in the near future these two airlines and one or two others may dominate the American market, and with fewer competitors it will be easier to boost ticket prices and eliminate discounts.

Air traffic has surged over the past decade under deregulation, with its highly competitive ticket prices. But the FAA, which runs the air traffic control system, has not been able to handle traffic on a timely basis since eleven thousand controllers were fired in 1981. "Flow control" restrictions now keep many aircraft parked at the gate until the understaffed system can absorb another flight. As passengers waste twenty thousand hours annually sitting on runways, the FAA has stubbornly insisted that the system is adequately staffed and working efficiently. The number of full-performance controllers in August 1991, according to the General Accounting Office (GAO), was still 16 percent below 1981 levels (two thousand fewer controllers), even though air traffic increased 30 percent during that decade.

The most important of the FAA's modernization programs—the advanced automation system, computer technology used for radar display by air traffic controllers to guide aircraft in and out of airports and track their progress—is years behind schedule. The inadequacies of the current, outdated system puts unnecessary stress on controllers, but the new system may not be in place for a number of years.

Prodded by the Aviation Safety Research Act of 1988, FAA research and development has jumped 30 percent in four years, with more spending on safety, security, and the interface between controllers and traffic control systems, as well as at least 15 percent on long-term efforts required by the law. However, the agency continues to be criticized by Congress and the GAO for not complying with the statute's requirement to publish resource estimates for long-term projects in its research plan.

The new Secretary of Transportation should consider these initiatives:

• A tough antitrust policy must closely scrutinize big mergers that reduce competition. It is now common for weak airlines to sell their assets (such as international routes) to larger, healthier airlines or to affiliate with foreign airlines.

• Barriers to entry that limit the gate, takeoff, and landing "slots" for smaller scheduled airlines at crowded airports need to be removed to encourage competition.

• Abuses in airline computer reservation systems must be stopped. Today, travel agents are limited to signing up with one of only four airline computer reservation systems, and the two largest systems—which control 70 percent of the reservation market—were developed by American and United, the two largest airlines. A number of studies document various biases in these systems that have the effect of steering unknowing passengers to book on the airline that owns the system and away from smaller airlines that might provide better service.

• The nation's airports must match anticipated growth in air travel. Successfully meeting new demands will require better usage of existing facilities as well as creation of new capacity in the system. The $7 billion now hoarded in the Airport and Airway Trust Fund should be used productively for infrastructure improvement and development.

• Comprehensive guidelines regarding deceptive practices in this industry need to be issued, and a joint federal–state program created to police abuses when they occur. As an adjunct to this policy, Congress should enact a federal law allowing states and consumers to challenge an airline's anti-competitive and deceptive practices directly in court.

MARITIME

The Maritime Administration facilitates the development, promotion, and operation of the American merchant marine, including direct financial assistance to the maritime industry as well as port development technology assessment. It also maintains the National Defense Reserve Fleet. Its proposed 1993 budget is $312 million. A total of 75 percent is allocated to the Ready Reserve, comprised of ninety-six government-owned U.S.-flag merchant ships to provide sealift in a national emergency.

The U.S. maritime industry's success last year in supporting Operation Desert Shield/Desert Storm belies an industry in a crisis of its own. The nation's fleet of privately owned merchant ships continues to erode. Today there are fewer than four hundred ships in the fleet, and by the year 2000 about three quarters of these may be in mothballs. In the past decade we have lost roughly two thirds of the U.S.-flag liner companies, and two of the remaining six are threatening to withdraw unless the government radically reforms the rules of U.S.-flag operations.

Foreign-flag vessels now carry more than 80 percent of this nation's liner cargo, and by the year 2000 some predict that domestic-flag vessels may vanish. As more of our cargo is handled by foreign-flag ships, jobs for U.S. merchant seafarers have declined. In 1990 there were about twenty-seven thousand active seafarers, fewer than one third of the number active in 1960.

The maritime industry is a valuable national asset. Besides its role in the national security—ocean vessels handled 95 percent of the total cargo for Desert Shield/Desert Storm—it is a significant component of the nation's economy. According to the Secretary of Transportation, the U.S. maritime industry generated nearly $21 billion in total revenues and more than $12 billion in balance of payments receipts, including more than $4.2 billion in export freight and charter hire payments to U.S. carriers by international companies.

Washington should also ensure that our ports and harbors will continue to support national economic and military interests with adequate ship repair and sealift capability. The Federal Government must work even more closely with ports, steamship lines, and the ship repair industry to prepare for these needs. Initial steps should include: establishing a vessel contingency retainer program, funded by the Defense Department, to supply military needs in emergencies and help rebuild the U.S. merchant fleet; preparing an inventory of maritime industry facilities to help rationally allocate federal resources; providing marketing support to promote U.S. ship repair capability in the world marketplace; and committing to preserve military cargo preference for U.S.-flag operations.

Federal policy should also create a unified federal approach to port and harbor maritime issues, using the combined resources and ingenuity of the Maritime Administration, the Federal Maritime Commission, and the Military Sealift Command.

COAST GUARD

The U.S. Coast Guard was established in 1915 but traces its origins to the Lighthouse Service in 1789 and the Revenue Cutter Service in 1790. Its responsibilities include promotion of safety of life and property at sea; safety and security of vessels, ports, waterways, and their facilities; maintenance of aids to navigation; enforcement of federal laws on the seas; and icebreaking assistance. As a specialized service of the U.S. Navy, the Coast Guard also maintains military readiness. The agency's proposed 1993 budget is $3.7 billion, of which about $200 million is funded by the Department of Defense.

During the past twenty years, new statutes have assigned the agency significantly expanded tasks, including responsibility for preventing and responding to polluting oil spills, controlling hazardous materials on waterways, enforcement against illegal drug transportation, and preventing ocean dumping as well as pollution from ships. The agency also is responsible for standards to ensure safe construction and operation of fishing vessels, recreational boats, and tankers (such as requiring double hulls or other designs to carry and contain polluting or hazardous materials safely).

The Coast Guard is the principal maritime agency responsible for enforcing federal law and treaties on navigable coastal waters and the high seas. This responsibility covers fisheries, drug smuggling, illegal immigration, hijacking of vessels, and marine environmental protection. Enforcement is the agency's largest single operating expense. Increased enforcement of regulations and law is needed to assure compliance, yet the Coast Guard has been particularly lax in maintaining enforcement records and conducting analysis of enforcement measures in the pollution prevention program, actions essential to assure enforcement is active and effective. From available data, the DOT inspector general found that reports of pollution spills are often ignored.

Drug interdiction uses 20 percent of the agency's operating expenditures, yet the House Transportation Appropriations Subcommittee found that this task has been only marginally effective in reducing illegal drug availability and use, even though cocaine seizures have increased from six thousand pounds in 1985 to thirty-three thousand pounds in 1991. The subcommittee found that most officials believe reduction in demand, not supply reduction, is an essential change in priorities, as Mathea Falco argues in more detail in her chapter on national drug control policy.

The new Administration should consider these initiatives:

- Increase recreational boating safety/injury prevention efforts in cooperation with states, focused on alcohol and drug use and safety procedures.
- Establish more stringent oversight of enforcement responsibilities, including record-keeping, investigation, and penalty assessment for violations of marine law.
- Establish a mandatory vessel registry system, and prohibit vessel abandonment.

NOTE

1. In preparing this chapter, Joan Claybrook received indispensable help from Mortimer L. Downey, Executive Director and Chief Financial Officer, Metropolitan Transportation Authority, State of New York; Jackie Gillan, Deputy Executive Director, Advocates for Highway and Auto Safety; John Hassell, Transportation Consultant, Linton, Mields, Reisler and Cottone; Con Hitchcock, Attorney with Public Citizen and Legal Director, Aviation Consumer Action Project; Victoria Nugent, Assistant to the President, Public Citizen; and Jim Smith, Tom Dawson, and Greg Andrews, partners at Smith, Dawson, Andrews, a Washington, D.C., public affairs firm.

The Case for a New Social Contract

LABOR POLICY

ROBERT L. KUTTNER

Summary

IN A GLOBAL ECONOMY, a high-wage society requires workers who are well trained, highly motivated, and empowered. In the heyday of the postwar era, America existed in splendid isolation as our economy lived off the immense capital investment of World War II. The industrial labor movement delivered job security and decent wages. The old industrial relations system offered a very limited three-way social contract in which government was a player but only as arbiter of collective bargaining under the Wagner Act framework. Government's function was to allow labor and management to bargain for shares of a growing pie in an economy whose institutions were, in retrospect, remarkably stable.

Today the economy is necessarily undergoing radical restructuring, but the benefits and costs are very unequally distributed. The few mechanisms available to ease the pain are minimal and defensive, and there are even fewer mechanisms or resources to convert the turbulence into opportunity. Instead, the new President should help persuade labor and management to agree to a new social contract to enhance America's competitiveness. Such a new arrangement—where workers would get more training and security while management would get a more flexible and productive work force—would be based on a broad new set of workplace policies:
- Unemployment compensation as our principal form of labor market subsidy should give way to a comprehensive system of lifetime learning and retraining.
- Long-delayed labor law reform should be enacted, to allow unions to contest representation elections without reprisal, to bargain collec-

---

Robert L. Kuttner is coeditor of The American Prospect, *economics columnist for* Business Week, *and the author of four books on political economy, including* The End of Laissez Faire.

tively when they win such elections, and to prohibit the permanent replacement of striking workers.

- Government should promote an incomes policy as part of a commitment to noninflationary full employment.
- Pension funds should be immune from management raids and should be a source of capital for new, more democratic corporate forms.
- Government should promote codetermination in corporate governance, both to improve the efficiency of the enterprise and to help incubate a more effective and durable form of trade unionism.
- Public policy should promote other new forms of employee empowerment and ownership.
- Government should systematically seek to convert low-wage, dead-end jobs into paraprofessional jobs with career ladders.
- Wage subsidies to breadwinners should be used to assure that a worker with a full-time job earns enough to keep a family out of poverty.

Introduction

IT HAS BECOME CONVENTIONAL to observe that Americans can function in a global economy either by "working cheaper" or by "working smarter." That is, American workers can compete against the hundreds of millions of underemployed and desperately poor workers of the Third World either by working at Third World wages or by demonstrating the productivity that justifies premium wages. If American workers expect ten times the wages of workers in Bangladesh, then they need to generate ten times the hourly output per worker.

American wages have been declining in real terms in recent decades. Not only is the average nonsupervisory wage today back to the level of the early 1960s, but the distribution of income has also been growing more unequal. Many of the remaining good jobs are already taken by workers in their fifties, and when these workers retire, their jobs will be retired with them. A younger generation faces lower-paid jobs, with depressingly short career ladders.

Based on these trends, America needs better education and more worker training and retraining. But this formulation, though unobjectionable, tells only a small part of the story. A competitive, high-wage work force requires not only higher levels of worker skill but also more productive capital, smarter industrial organization, and an entirely different conception of the worker's role. This in turn requires a different politics.

In the competition to retain and create "good jobs at good wages," the

United States has been losing out to nations with a clearer sense of national purpose and a higher regard for labor. Increasingly, our problem is less a matter of how hard Americans work or even how much training they have than a series of structural differences between the American workplace and those of our advanced industrial competitors such as Japan and the European Community. There are differences in labor laws, in the structure of corporations, and in the power of unions. But the several differences boil down to a single crucial difference: the contingent nature of relationships in the American market economy. Here is where public policy can make a difference to assure workers that their efforts will be rewarded.

Contingent America

IN PURE LAISSEZ-FAIRE ECONOMICS, every relationship is a price auction in miniature—a one-night stand. In laissez-faire theory, economic actors need to be relentlessly free to choose a better supplier, a better worker, a better employer, a better investment—and on a moment's notice. The hallmark of the American economy is contingent relationships between suppliers and producers, between producers and customers, between investors and entrepreneurs, and above all between managers and employees. Unions once created a longer-term social contract, but unionism is everywhere under attack. This contingent approach to capitalism is at the heart of what has become a cliché about what ails America: the "short time horizon" that afflicts everyone from portfolio managers to product designers to corporate chief executives.

Japan, Germany, France, and Sweden, among others, have a much more social conception of capitalism. Owners of capital stick with investments for the long term and don't demand high financial yields every quarter. In return, managers can plan for the longer term. The hostile takeover is not permitted in Japan and is far less frequent in Europe. Japanese and German corporations cultivate long-term relationships with suppliers. That, in turn, makes it rational for the supplier to invest in expensive, long-lived equipment and process technology as well as in highly trained workers. And virtually every other advanced industrial economy has public policies to compensate for the market's notorious tendency to underinvest in human capital.

At the root of this institutional difference is a different conception of what makes for an efficient, socially sustainable economy. European corporatism and the Japanese tribal form of capitalism each in its own way tempers laissez-faire, but in a fashion that enhances economic performance as well as social solidarity. As Japan and Europe have demonstrated, there are strategies that enrich social comity, and by so doing improve economic performance. Far from compromising economic efficiency, the social imperative can complement the economic imperative.

In general, the forces that call for a more social conception of capitalism are weaker in the United States than in other developed nations. In Japan, the combination of a feudal history; a very strong, competent, and prestigious state bureaucracy; and religious teachings on the question of reciprocal social obligation all reinforce Japan's well-known group consciousness. In Europe, corporatism draws strength from a variety of factors: the greater class consciousness of workers; the greater strength of trade unions; the history of relatively stronger unitary states; the fact that small exporting states—say, Sweden or Austria—can't afford the luxury of social strife; the Burkean tradition of noblesse oblige conservatism that respects the value of established social structures and fears pure capitalism; and the influence of the Roman Catholic Church and of Christian Democratic parties, which made the social market economy respectable to conservatives.

In secular liberal America, however, the prevailing ethic is far more individualist to begin with. Redistributive policies, argue American conservatives, reward laggards and hold back the most enterprising; the race should be to the swift. Trade unions, historically, have been the most important force advocating a more social conception of capitalism and a more durable social contract between worker and employer. But unions were always relatively weaker in America, and in the 1980s unions came under attack from the Reagan and Bush administrations. The government ceased being a neutral arbiter and sided with management in labor conflicts subject to the National Labor Relations Board (NLRB), and labor policy intensified the ability of management to treat workers like just another disposable factor of production. Deregulation undercut the ability of workers to negotiate job security and predictable career paths in regulated industries. A conservative administration and allied courts made it easier for industry to raid pension funds, ratchet down wages and benefits in hostile corporate takeovers, reduce fringe benefits, and evade compliance with health and safety requirements.

However, in a nice ironic twist, there is today an opening to insist on a more social conception of capitalism and greater comity between manager and worker, not just because we value this approach as citizens but also because economic efficiency and competitiveness demand it. As in the 1930s, we must save a pure market economy from its own worst impulses. Labor policy serves both as an instructive case in point and as a metaphor for the larger problem.

When labor is cheap and expendable, managers will prefer cheap labor to smart capital. In the short run, cheap labor may produce cost advantages, but over the long term cheap labor does not increase the productivity of the enterprise. Paradoxically, the more expensive labor is, the more it is likely to be replaced with capital, which over time makes the entire economy more efficient and the wage earners better off. Paradoxically, too, the weaker that trade unions are, the more likely they are to define security in terms of a particular job classification, which retards the dynamic flexibility of the economy as a whole. For this alternative approach to benefit particular workers (who are at risk of losing particular jobs), the entire strategy needs to be anchored in a commitment to full employment, worker employment security, lifetime learning, and labor mobility.

Elements of a New Social Contract

LABOR LAW REFORM: BEYOND BUSINESS UNIONISM

The old system that lasted roughly from the late 1930s to the late 1970s is often called "business unionism." It offered a kind of crude social contract in which government guaranteed workers' rights to bargain collectively for wages and working conditions, and in turn unions refrained from challenging management prerogatives. Employees sought security in industrywide master contracts and in an elaborate set of job classifications and work rules. The old industrial relations system was a kind of armed truce, balanced by labor's ability to inflict damage, by industry's ability to live in a predictable competitive environment, and by government's willingness to enforce the ground rules.

The ability of American trade unions to deliver benefits to their members and the ability of government to broker a generation of social peace were covertly dependent on American economic preeminence internationally and on tacit toleration of oligopolistic industries at home. Without ruthless price competition in the basic industries, the economy created an umbrella under which unions could bargain for master contracts and regular raises, and industry could pass the cost along to customers.

But the postwar period of industrial stability is now history, and so is the old basis for labor power. The century-old slogan "Take wages out of competition," which has been the rock-solid principle of traditional trade unionism, is a dead letter in many industries. On the contrary, wages are back in competition, not only among firms but also among different plants within the same firm, and even, under "two tier" arrangements, among different generations of workers doing identical jobs in the same plant. So all the major preconditions of the old social contract have dissolved. Global competition and deregulation have ended oligopoly; the strike no longer has the force it once did; many companies are much more anti-union; and, if one more assault were required, the NLRB is no longer impartial. Some of this assault on unionism reflects changed historical circumstances. But some of it reflects deliberate strategy by management and government.

Labor law reform was nearly enacted under President Jimmy Carter, but fell two votes short of breaking a conservative filibuster in the Senate in 1978. Even before Reagan, an increasingly conservative NLRB eroded much of the Wagner Act. Because of the board's reluctance to punish employers and the rise of a new generation of fiercely anti-union corporations, a worker who signed a union card increasingly risked losing his or her job. Even when a union had a majority of cards, the fight had to begin all over again in preparation for an election, during which interim management could escalate its bare-knuckle tactics. Even when unions won elections, the task of negotiating a first contract became a protracted affair, leaving workers again vulnerable to reprisal. And when workers resorted to the ultimate weapon—the strike—management began the previously unheard-of tactic of hiring permanent replacement workers. All of this only became worse under the Reagan administration, which within a few months of taking office signaled its own intentions by firing striking air traffic controllers.

Following this desultory history, labor law reform, at best, should now shift to a Canadian system under which a union is certified as soon as half the workers in a bargaining unit sign cards. It would prohibit, as the original Wagner Act supposedly did, reprisals by employers. It would prohibit the practice of shutting down a plant to dodge a union. And it would make illegal the practice of hiring permanent replacements for striking workers.

The power balance between labor and management has shifted, except in one dramatic respect. Management may have more power today to weaken unions, but at the same time management needs labor's cooperation more than ever. At one time in the history of mass production it may have been possible to design machines to be idiotproof and to deploy human drones as one more interchangeable part. However, the very nature of the new technology demands smart, flexible, inventive human workers who can respond creatively to situations not anticipated in manuals or programmed into assembly lines. It is not enough to have brilliant engineers and dumb workers, if in fact it ever was.

BETTER TRAINING FOR BETTER JOBS

A new progressive Administration needs to devise an active labor market policy to provide, as industrial transitions occur, opportunities for lifetime learning, retraining sabbaticals, and job upgrading. This approach would also create a far more systematic strategy of technical training and certification, as well as a "second chance" system for young people who dropped out of school.

The American economy suffers from the mismatch between skills and jobs. As a whole, the United States needs a more highly skilled, better-trained work force. But too many of the available jobs still demand only minimal skills. Too many employers seem bent on reducing labor costs in the short run rather than creating high-wage, high-skill jobs for the long run. Society has no mechanism for steadily upgrading the quality of work and of the work force. Among corporate personnel officers in the service sector, the most common complaint is that they can't find high school graduates competent to read instructions, to do basic arithmetic, to show up on time, or to take jobs at $5 an hour—not that they have advanced training programs going begging.

It is a staple of the labor economics literature that firms generally underinvest in training, for the perfectly rational reason that a worker newly trained at company expense is entirely free to go to work for a competitor. This is a classic case of an "externality": The person called on to make the decision doesn't get the full benefit or suffer the full cost. So optimal social decisions are not always made by private actors. Society does have real shortages of workers in certain highly skilled craft occupations, such as machinists, but we have far too few mechanisms to train them. There is, of course, the obvious need for schools to do a better job equipping new workers with basic skills but also for the systematic upgrading of the work force throughout one's productive life.

Therefore it is necessary to overhaul drastically the system we have for sharing the costs of labor market transitions, and in the process use those outlays to upgrade the skills of the entire work force continuously. When a worker is laid off because of a restructuring or a downturn in the business cycle, the choice ought not be short-term unemployment compensation versus a lower-paid job elsewhere. If the worker is fifty-eight, perhaps an early retirement plan makes sense; but if he or she is thirty-eight, the worker should be a candidate for a retraining sabbatical.

At present we have small programs for helping to train disadvantaged young workers and for reemploying workers displaced by industrial transition. But about 80 percent of our total labor market outlays go for unemployment compensation. Other industrial nations invest much more heavily in subsidizing labor market transitions. Sweden's ratio of outlays is the reverse of ours: Less than 20 percent of manpower outlays go to pay for the cost of idleness, and more than 80 percent go to subsidize retraining and re-employment.

The Swedish system of labor market boards continuously upgrades the work force and allows workers to welcome rather than resist industrial re-structuring that improves productivity in the long run. When the Swedish unemployment rate rises, the national labor market board can declare that funds are now available for workers to take paid sabbaticals to learn new skills. This opens up jobs for other workers, reducing the overall unemployment rate and upgrading the productivity of the entire work force at the same time. The labor market board can also use labor market subsidies as tools of regional or sectoral industrial policies.

For example, if a town has lost a major employer—say, a shipbuilder—a local ad hoc tripartite committee of business leaders, labor representatives, and local government can get funds to conduct a study and determine what kind of new industry might be suitable, given the local labor force. The local committee can then submit a proposal to the national labor market board, which in turn can offer a prospective employer subsidies to pay for the cost of retraining and part of a few years' wages.

This system, in effect, uses a labor subsidy as a capital subsidy. Unlike the caricatures of economic planning that invariably feature some heavy-handed bureaucratic czar attempting to "pick winners and losers," this approach is locally based and relies on entrepreneurs to identify opportunities. It allows government and trade unions to play a constructive role, with the additional benefit of targeting development to localities with high unemployment, and continuously upgrading worker skills. It is far better than our characteristic system of enticing new development by means of bargaining away a community's needed local tax base.

Changing the emphasis of our labor market subsidies, from subsidizing unemployment to subsidizing reskilling and reemployment, would accomplish several other goals that serve the broader objective of a more collaborative and competitive economy. First, by socializing part of the cost of training, it compensates for the tendency of managers to underinvest in upgrading the skills of their workers. It also can be part of a national strategy of constantly working to create good, high-skill, well-paid jobs rather than cheap ones.

Second, the existence of an active labor market policy makes it possible to negotiate new productivity-enhancing agreements because it creates a temporary place to put excess labor. Retraining sabbaticals and reemployment subsidies constitute one more element of the bargain for government to bring to the table, and one more benefit that can substitute for wage inflation.

The most elegant blueprint for an American active labor market policy is contained in the 1990 Report of the Commission of the Skills of the American Workforce, which was chaired by Ira Magaziner, Ray Marshall, and, interestingly enough, William Brock. In its report, "America's Choice: High Skills or Low Wages!,"[1] the commission observed that "America may have the worst school-to-work transition system of any advanced industrial country. Students who know few adults to help them are left to sink or swim." Former Republican and Democratic secretaries of labor agreed that a comprehensive system of skills training is needed. So should the next President.

UPGRADING LOW-WAGE WORK

According to the Census Bureau,[2] the proportion of year-round, full-time workers with low earnings ($12,195 per year or less in 1992 dollars) has steadily increased, from 12.1 percent in 1979 to 18.0 percent in 1989. Roughly half the jobs created in the 1980s pay an annual wage of less than $11,000. The cost-cutting strategy of too many employers is only making the problem worse. The policy challenge is the systematic upgrading of low-wage service sector work, and contingent work generally.

Contingent work, which includes temporary work, part-time work, and contract work, means work divorced from any job security or career ladder. Contingent jobs have exploded in recent years as employers have sought to insulate their labor costs from abrupt shifts in economic conditions. Unfortunately, this strategy puts all the burden of adjustment on employees and denies the economy the highly skilled, secure labor force it needs.

Nearly all workers in the contingent labor force have no health or pension benefits, no job security, no union representation, no access to career ladders. According to a study by Virginia duRivage,[3] nearly 30 million people, most of them not by choice, are in the contingent work force. Reforms should make sure that employers can't evade paying benefits that comparable full-time jobs carry.

The new Administration should seek a systematic strategy for upgrading low-wage, low-skill work generally. There are essentially two possible strategies for upgrading service sector work: wage subsidy and professionalization.

A number of academic experts, such as Robert Lerman of Brandeis University, David Ellwood of Harvard's Kennedy School, and Harvard sociologist Theda Skopol, have urged that the present welfare system be converted to a system of wage subsidy, using a revised version of the earned income tax credit (EITC). For example, if the head of a household earned $200 a week as a fast-food cashier, the Labor Department would make up the difference between that wage and the poverty level for that worker's family. There would have to be experiment and refinement of this approach, to make certain that employers did not lower prevailing wages in order to have the government make up the difference. Moreover, the fact of working would trigger a variety of social fringe benefits, such as child care, the opportunity for retraining sabbaticals, and comprehensive health insurance. This strategy represents a substantial improvement over traditional "welfare" approaches because it rewards the holding of a job with a higher standard of living. Author Robert Greenstein describes this new approach in more detail in his chapter on welfare reform.

There is also a need for the Labor Department to initiate pilot programs aimed at the systematic upgrading of work in human services, which is expected to be a major growth area. For example, home health care is both a more cost-effective and a more dignified alternative to nursing home care for the elderly. Yet home health care services are available only sporadically, and are notoriously underfunded. As a consequence, the work is a typically "secondary labor market" job—low-paid, without fringe benefits or career ladders, and subject to predictably high turnover. The system treats home health workers as comparable to housemaids.

A home health care worker, however, could just as logically be a para-professional, analogous to a visiting nurse. This would require greater training, higher pay, and the creation of career paths. But for society, the greater expense would be well worth the cost if it kept more people out of nursing homes. There are dozens of other service occupations where professionalization would be an avenue both to more productive provision of the service, and better-paid careers.

AN INCOMES POLICY

The usual textbook "trade-off" between inflation and unemployment is not an iron law of economics. Rather, it results primarily because we lack institutions of constructive social bargaining. In a laissez-faire economy, low unemployment gives workers the bargaining power to demand wage increases in excess of real productivity gains. Fearing inflation, the authorities then keep the money supply too tight and public spending too low, which slows the rate of economic growth. But with a serious social compact, we could run a high-growth, full-employment economy without wage-driven inflation. Workers could be assured job opportunities and lifelong training and retraining; industry would be assured a high-quality work force and labor peace. Government would invest in substantial upgrading of worker skills and restructuring of industry.

The broad and idealized appeal of this approach, however, tends to blind many advocates of quality-of-worklife strategies, who seem to believe that all moves in this direction are to be encouraged, regardless of who is ultimately in charge and regardless of how much authority is genuinely handed over to workers. In a highly competitive economy, where firms are under ruthless cost-cutting pressure, benign bargains in one firm tend to be scrapped as soon as the going gets rough, and one side—management— retains all the power. Consequently, unions have tended to resist the conventional version of an incomes policy as well as many quality-of-worklife experiments, viewing such proposals, in power terms, as a one-way street. A variation on the same theme is Professor Martin Weitzman's proposal for a "share economy" in which pay packets would be partly based on a share of the firm's total earnings rather than on a fixed wage.[4]

Weitzman's model claims, as a matter of technical economics, that helping labor markets and making firms operate with the marginal cost of labor lower than the average cost would reduce unemployment. And perhaps it would. But the share economy strategy fails to change the governance of the firm. In fact, it gives workers another downside risk associated with entrepreneurship—the opportunity to take pay cuts during downturns— without offering them the control that usually belongs to the entrepreneur.

Overseas, strong unions are generally willing to make wage bargains that hold wage increases to the real increase in productivity. They make these bargains precisely because there are government policies that enhance worker security and they are strong enough to contribute to the well-being of the firm, the industry, and the economy. A new social contract can make that happen in America.

PENSION FUNDS IN A COLLABORATIVE ECONOMY

Public policy ought to reform radically the structure of pension funds, their governance, their influence on capital markets, and their role in worker ownership. The present system, however, is perverse. Not only are most pension funds beyond the control of workers, but also the practice of tying pensions to individual firms allows pension assets to be raided in takeover attempts, often at the expense of workers. In capital markets, pension funds, which logically ought to be a source of stable, patient capital, instead are managed in the interest of short-term performance, which paradoxically fuels the very takeover game that harms workers. Many workers find themselves displaced by capital that represents their own deferred savings. Instead, pension fund capital, owned by workers, should help underwrite restructuring that truly benefits and empowers workers.

Pension funds are, of course, deferred wages. The present regulatory scheme fails workers on several counts, even on the narrow test of providing income for their retirement. Workers who change jobs lose benefits. Pension savings are often available to be raided, based on the fiction that they are "overfunded." And a firm with a generous pool of pension assets often finds itself the target of either a hostile raid or a preemptive raid by its own management. The Employee Retirement Income Security Act (ERISA) creates a labyrinth of regulations, but it fails to give workers the most elementary protections against the raiding, or termination, of pension funds.

In recent years, the fraction of workers enrolled in company-sponsored pension funds has declined, after peaking in 1980. The system of company-based pension funds took off during World War II because in a very tight labor market fringe benefits allowed companies to provide their workers with additional compensation that did not violate wage and price controls. During the postwar era of strong unions and stable firms, pensions became part of the standard benefit package. But as competition has intensified and unions have been ravaged, companies have resisted paying pension benefits. Tying pension entitlements to individual employers never made economic or social sense. ERISA is one of the most self-defeating pieces of legislation ever enacted, since it attempts to regulate an activity—pension benefits—whose very existence is voluntary to begin with. Not surprisingly, large employers have attempted to evade the strictures of ERISA in the most direct manner— by getting rid of their pension plans.

Ideally, private pension funds should be collapsed into a second, earning-based tier of Social Security. The present system of Social Security would continue, as a pay-as-you-go system. The second tier would be based on earnings histories and paid-in contributions, but funds would no longer be under control of corporate trustees, and the accrual of funds would follow the worker wherever he or she went. Only this degree of reform would permit full portability and full protection against either raiding or spurious or authentic bankruptcies. Failing that, there should be a drastic overhaul of the regulations permitting raiding and termination, and far tougher conflict-of-interest strictures to prohibit managers from using pension assets in corporate takeover contests. All firms should be required either to have pension plans that met a minimum standard, or to pay into a pool for workers in small firms without such plans.

CODETERMINATION AND MORE EFFECTIVE UNIONISM
In the 1980s, government became more hostile both to trade unions and to the idea that public policy needs to cultivate labor's constructive influence

on productivity. Yet these realms are linked, both as substance and as politics. Politically, in virtually every industrial democracy, trade unions provide the most reliable key electoral constituency for political parties that believe in a mixed economy. There is a close correlation between the strength of organized labor and the ability of progressive administrations to govern successfully. In nations with weak or fractious labor movements, the right is the usual majority party. In nations with strong, unified labor movements, the center-left party begins with a powerful ally. In the United States, a hostile national administration and a turbulent climate of industrial transition have combined to weaken trade unionism.

Substantively, labor's enthusiastic support for industrial transitions depends on some social guarantee that such transitions will benefit the work force rather than take place at labor's expense. A society grows more productive by substituting capital for labor and by applying new technologies. When workers have reason to view those transitions as sources of increased living standards and improved opportunity, rather than as threats to their livelihood, they won't try to block progress, and positive gains result.

Government needs to help the labor movement reinvent itself, both as a valid policy goal per se and to revive a political constituency for progressive politics and government. An authentic brand of codetermination can help accomplish that goal. Professor Paul Weiler, an architect of Canadian labor law and an adviser to the AFL-CIO, proposes mandating an American form of codetermination roughly modeled on German works councils. All workplaces with twenty-five or more employees would elect a committee that would enjoy real power to deal with wages, benefits, hiring and training, work organization, and technical innovation. The committee would also have access to company books.[5] Weiler sees such committees as enhancing the reach of unions in organized firms, and as functioning in nonunion firms as a kind of preunion, giving employees experience in collective representation and presumably paving the way for eventual unionization.

As generations of critics have observed ever since A. A. Berle and Gardiner Means wrote *The Modern Corporation and Private Property in 1933*, the corporation is not truly accountable to its shareholders. Today the hostile corporate takeover is currently the only serious form of management accountability; in extremis, shareholders take advantage of a raider's borrowed capital and tender their shares, reaping a windfall gain. Old management is displaced by new management, but workers seldom benefit; typically, many lose their jobs or suffer losses of wages and benefits in the crusade for greater "efficiency."

Codetermination is a far more useful and less disruptive ongoing brand of corporate accountability. Today shareholders are free to sell out at any moment, for financial gain; almost by definition, they are unlikely to care what happens to the company in the long term. By contrast, workers are the firm's most reliable and durable constituents. Yet, under our corporate system, the shareholder has all the power and the worker has none.

While the new economy cries out for more collaborative labor-management culture, the traditional social organization of the corporation resists it. And this suggests a related paradox: The current weakness of organized labor makes it easier for management to resist sharing authority in a meaningful way. For example, many quality-of-worklife experiments seem to show great promise, but, when a real crunch comes, management usually retains the real power. And next time, workers are far more wary of such experiments. Research by Maryellen Kelley of Carnegie Mellon University suggests that quality-of-worklife efforts bear much more fruit in unionized firms because workers there have more confidence that they can challenge inefficient systems of management without fear of retaliation. Employee involvement schemes in union settings, says Kelley, allow workers to articulate the "tacit knowledge" that they ordinarily fail to share with management.[6] Employee stock ownership plans, likewise, are gaining popularity, but only a small fraction of them have produced real participatory management and power-sharing as well as profit-sharing. In short, given the impact of heightened competition on industrial relations, genuine collaboration is all the more imperative—and all the more difficult to accomplish.

WORKER OWNERSHIP

In the recent past, corporations on the verge of bankruptcy have been willing to entertain worker buyouts. But because these are undertaken as a last resort rather than a deliberate goal, they operate in the most improbable circumstances and usually fail.

In the case of Eastern Airlines, for example, the prospect of bankruptcy in the early 1980s brought both labor and management to the very brink of a radically new form of social contract in which management gave workers partial ownership and shared authority both on the shop floor and in the boardroom, and workers departed from the adversarial tradition, began thinking like profit-maximizing managers, and agreed to a more flexible form of compensation in which wages were reduced and part of their pay was based on gross earnings. In its first year the new approach saved tens of millions of dollars, and Eastern was able to run in the black for the first time in years.

But this new bold bargain was snuffed out before it had time to mature because of the competitive pressures of deregulation, the old habits of traditional management, the inability of Eastern's several unions to pursue a common strategy, the fact that labor still was only a minority owner, and management's option to sell out to a new owner or to declare bankruptcy.

In the steel industry, the surviving integrated mills are in the throes of a long-term restructuring that will leave the United States with fewer mills, reduced production capacity, and a fraction of the workers it once had . . . but a far more productive and dynamic industry in what remains. Along the way, a much more collaborative industrial relations culture is struggling to be born.

For example, at LTV Steel, labor and management agreed to an experimental arrangement at one plant in Cleveland of the sort long advocated by industrial relations experts. The old book of job categories would be thrown out; workers would be paid according to one of three skill levels and made available to perform any of several jobs; most workers would be salaried; there would be job-security guarantees and new shop-floor authority for the work force.

Shortly after that agreement was struck, LTV went into bankruptcy—in part because the cost of pensioning off its workers exceeded the savings it achieved from closing excess capacity. The only institution we have for socializing some of this cost is the Pension Benefit Guarantee Corporation (PBGC), which has become a kind of back-door Ministry of Industrial Restructuring in a society that does not believe government ought to be in that business at all. So instead of facilitating collaboration, or spending public money to lubricate new bargains, taxpayer money goes only to mop up the cost of private failure and to ease a little of the pain inflicted on workers.

The Federal Government needs to play a far more affirmative role in bringing about codetermination and restructured arrangements, both as guarantor of the new bargain and as supplier of technical assistance and sometimes of public capital.

Labor-management collaboration during a period of heightened competition, technological change, and corporate restructuring requires more than better labor laws or training in participatory management. The new President and Congress should realize that it requires a new conception of the governance of the corporation, of the corporation as a social creature, of workers as stakeholders in that corporation, and of government as guarantor of an effective social contract. That, in turn, requires new institutions and new imagination. The payoff is immense: a more productive and competitive economy, a much better prospect of high-growth macroeconomics without inflation. That the payoff is also a more decent, defensible society should not blind us to the fact that this path is also sounder economics.

NOTES

1. *America's Choice: High Skills or Low Wages!* (Rochester, N.Y.: National Center on Education and the Economy, 1990).

2. U.S. Bureau of the Census, "Workers with Low Earnings: 1964 to 1990," P-60, No. 178 (Washington, D.C., 1992).

3. "Flexibility Trap: The Proliferation of Marginal Jobs," *The American Prospect* (Spring 1992), pp. 84–93.

4. Martin Weitzman, *The Share Economy* (Cambridge, Mass.: MIT Press, 1984).

5. Paul Weiler, *Governing the Workplace* (Cambridge, Mass.: Harvard University Press, 1990).

6. Maryellen Kelley and Bennett Harrison, "The New Industrial Culture: Journeys Toward Collaboration," *The American Prospect* (Winter 1991), pp. 54—61.

PART II

INTERNATIONAL
AFFAIRS

OVERVIEW: MILITARY AND FOREIGN POLICY

SAMUEL R. BERGER AND JANNE E. NOLAN

Introduction

T HE NEXT PRESIDENT WILL ASSUME OFFICE at a pivotal moment in history, for the crossroads we face today is no less consequential than the choices confronted by the United States earlier in this century, after World Wars I and II. In 1918 America chose to withdraw from the world, to turn inward. The consequences were tragic. The abdication of American leadership allowed dictators to advance, plunging us back into war.

By contrast, after World War II, under President Harry Truman, the United States chose to remain engaged in the world, with a burst of creative energy that produced institutions that have shaped the postwar peace, from NATO to the United Nations, from the IMF to the GATT.

Today there are voices from both the right and the left who again call for "America first." Indeed, the United States cannot remain affirmatively engaged in the world if we do not address our urgent domestic agenda. But it is equally true in today's global economy and disorderly post-Cold War era that Americans cannot be safe, prosperous, or true to our values if we are not engaged actively in the world.

America's leadership—in advancing freedom and democracy, resolving regional and ethnic tensions that can cascade into broader conflicts, re-

Samuel R. Berger is former Deputy Director of the State Department Policy Planning Staff (1977–81). He is the foreign policy director of the Clinton-Gore Transition and was previously engaged in international trade law at Hogan & Hartson in Washington, D.C. He is the author of Dollar Harvest *(Heath Lexington Books, 1971). Janne E. Nolan is a Senior Fellow at the Brookings Institution and the author of* Trappings of Power: Ballistic Missiles in the Third World *(Washington D.C.: Brookings Institution, 1991).*

straining the proliferation of weapons of mass destruction, and lifting the crushing burden of poverty from much of the globe—is essential, for our own sake as well as that of others.

For nearly fifty years, the containment of communism has been the guiding and largely unquestioned premise of American foreign policy. The visionary statesmen who crafted this framework could never have imagined the burdens it would be asked to bear, from the prevention of a nuclear holocaust to the defense of countries remote from America's shores. But after nearly three generations, containment has succeeded. The sacrifices borne by Americans in the effort to stem communist expansion helped nuture the nascent forces of freedom—courageous men and women who stood in front of tanks and on them as they achieved victory for human liberty and democratic change. Even five years ago, it seemed that no one could imagine that, with such swiftness, we would witness an end to the division of Europe, the emancipation of the populations of Eastern Europe from the control of the former Soviet Union, and the virtual elimination of the threat of U.S.-Soviet (now Russian) nuclear war. What should the next President do with this historic opportunity?

The world today bears little resemblance to conditions the United States has faced since the end of World War II. The Soviet Union and the Warsaw Pact literally have collapsed and, with them, the conceptual framework that served as the foundation for U.S. engagement in the world. The traditional objectives of American military power—to maintain sufficient forces to deter a Soviet nuclear attack on us or our allies, to defeat Soviet conventional aggression in Europe, and to counter Soviet adventurism in Latin America, the Middle East, and Asia—have become relics of the equally atavistic Cold War.

The new international environment challenges the next President to reevaluate and redefine America's role in world affairs in terms that Americans can understand and support. He cannot be propelled by Cold War thinking, simply on a smaller scale. Nor can we afford a government whose idea of foreign policy is driven largely by the pursuit of cordial relations with foreign elites.

In the past four years, Americans have come to believe that an activist foreign policy comes at the expense of sound domestic policies. But at a time of growing domestic unemployment, economic stagnation, and inadequate health services to those in need, it is not surprising that many Americans see foreign policy as an unwarranted and costly distraction from the pressing domestic agenda.

The first international challenge for the new President is to offer a vision of America's global role that American citizens can support and understand. This must be based on the clear and explicit premise that a sound domestic policy and a strong foreign policy are inseparable; indeed, they are mutually reenforcing. Americans must understand that we cannot be strong at home unless we compete successfully in world markets . . . unless we champion the values of democracy and freedom throughout the world . . . unless we work with others to address threats we cannot solve alone, such as preserving the global environment and halting the proliferation of nuclear weapons—in short, unless we take our leadership responsibilities seriously.

At the same time, America cannot exert decisive international influence without a vibrant economy at home; we will have neither the resources nor the political consensus to sustain our influence in the world if we are weak and insecure at home. The only foundation on which to build a new and enduring foreign policy is one that truly reflects Americans—their values, their interests, and their culture.

Central Challenges

SINCE THE UNRAVELING OF THE SOVIET EMPIRE, Americans have been offered a slogan without a strategy. The concept of a "new world order" is a sound bite, not a blueprint for America's future or a source of guidance for Americans trying to understand their place in this new international environment.

A genuinely new world order must be based on a set of rights and responsibilities that challenge not only other nations but the United States as well. Our foreign policy must draw strength from our most cherished values and beliefs, and we in turn must live up to the responsibilities we are asking others to bear—from higher standards for environmental protection, to agreements for military restraint, to genuine equity in trade relations.

A new security order for the 1990s should reflect several fundamental premises:

1. *Continued threats to American interests.* The end of the Cold War does not mean the end of danger in the world or threats to America's national interests. The demise of communism unfortunately has not brought an end to international conflict, armed aggression, political injustice, or regional conflicts that threaten to erupt into wider wars. Even as the great powers achieve unprecedented levels of accommodation, conflicts of decades or even centuries in duration persist throughout the world—conflicts often fueled by ethnic and religious divisions, poverty, and political repression. Increasingly these dangers are compounded by modern arsenals containing both

conventional and sophisticated weapons of mass destruction, as both John Steinbruner and Michael Klare discuss.

2. *America's global economic interests.* America is part of a *global economy* whose prosperity requires greater international engagement, not less. At a time when military power translates less easily into global influence, America's economic leadership must be at the core of our national security policy. Walter Russell Mead's chapter, "The New Global Marketplace," properly stresses that such a policy must ensure that we have free and fair access to foreign markets, that America's economy can compete on an equal footing with that of other countries, and that we invest in industries and people at home that give us the edge in technological innovation and commercial competitiveness.

3. *Promoting democracy.* The strength of U.S. foreign policy depends on the successful marriage of our values and our interests. It is in our national interest, both morally and pragmatically, to reinforce the powerful global movement toward democratization. How other governments treat their people is important to us as American citizens *and* because the world will be a more stable and peaceful place for our children if democracy prevails.

4. *A new concept of national security.* The traditional concept of national security must be broadened to accommodate new and emerging threats long overshadowed by the military confrontation between the United States and the Soviet Union. It must include challenges to our survival arising from the degradation of the global environment, from the proliferation of destructive technologies used to make weapons of mass destruction, and from the economic deprivation and political oppression that persist in much of the world. These are global threats that cannot be solved by America alone, nor without American leadership.

5. *A reemphasis on collective international action.* Many of the international institutions established after World War II—from the United Nations to NATO to the GATT—are seeking to evolve to meet new global challenges. These political and economic alliances capitalize on the shared strengths of friendly nations and can be instruments of more equitable burden-sharing. They provide mechanisms for the peaceful resolution of disputes, for aiding or intervening in countries in distress, and for devising new instruments of conflict prevention.

American leadership and resources are vital but not sufficient conditions to redress global problems. Multilateral efforts based on coalitions of like-minded states increasingly must replace unilateral initiatives. The collective security concepts designed by the founders of the United Nations, in particular, as discussed by Enid Schoettle, can serve as a foundation for a new security order whose aim is both to avert wars and to take decisive international action if diplomacy fails.

America's New Role in the Post-Cold War World

1. *Meeting new threats*. Despite the increased emphasis on cooperation over confrontation in East-West affairs, the United States still must be prepared to protect our national interests militarily—and if necessary unilaterally—if diplomatic measures fail. Saddam Hussein was a painful reminder of the persistence of violence in international relations. There are several potential sources of conflict and instability, including:

• *Continued disintegration of the former Soviet republics and Eastern Europe*: The collapse of the Soviet Union and the growth of nationalist and subnationalist movements throughout Eastern Europe and the former Soviet republics are persistent sources of instability and international tension. Conditions in divided states such as what was Yugoslavia may continue to deteriorate, threatening the peace in Europe and providing the basis for a return of authoritarianism.

The resurgence of ethnic and religious conflict can no longer be viewed as a threat confined within specific countries or regions, as the terribly destructive war in what was Yugoslavia clearly demonstrates. The new Administration must work with the international community to develop more effective means for collective intervention to bring an end to such crises, or we could forfeit freedom's victory in the Cold War to forces of chaos and violence.

• *The spread of weapons of mass destruction*: The continuing proliferation of weapons of mass destruction throughout the world may pose the greatest peril in the coming years to American and international security. If nuclear, chemical, and biological weapons become more widely available, along with the means to deliver them effectively and at longer distances, even minor regional conflicts could have grave international consequences.

In Northeast Asia and the Middle East, for example, the end of the Cold War has not changed security conditions dramatically. Reports that North Korea might be on the verge of developing its own nuclear weapons remind us that the antagonism between that state and South Korea did not disappear with the easing of relations between their respective major suppliers. Similarly, despite the victory of the international coalition over Iraq in "Desert Storm," the growing offensive military capabilities of Syria, the efforts of Libya to acquire nuclear and chemical weapons, and the continued willingness of Iraq to thwart international efforts to disarm it preclude any sanguine notions of imminent peace in the region.

• *Terrorism.* The specter of terrorism, with its often brutal effects on innocent civilians, may increase with resurgent ethnic rivalries and stockpiles of weapons moving through the underworld of international arms peddlers. Some states still use terrorism as an instrument of foreign policy, or tolerate its use by groups with which they sympathize. Terrorism shakes the confidence of states in their ability to assure their security, making it more difficult to restrain arms buildups and reduce military budgets.

2. *Restructuring our forces for the future.* Although the new international system may be more demanding and complex than the old order, the collapse of the Soviet Union gives the United States a historic opportunity to create a far more efficient and less expensive military posture.

The preservation of military readiness, a strong deterrent, the morale of our military personnel, and advanced technological capabilities remain essential. But with the significantly diminished threat from the former Soviet Union, we can terminate most of our costly strategic modernization programs and substantially cut our forces in Europe and Asia even while we fulfill our treaty obligations worldwide.

The NATO alliance remains a vital form of insurance to preserve stability in Europe. But the United States should encourage, not resist, greater military cooperation among European countries. Institutions such as the Western European Union, for example, can complement rather than undercut NATO. The unremitting hostility of the Bush administration to any form of European military collaboration has impeded the adaptation of NATO to post-Cold War European security challenges.

An effective military force for the coming decades must rest on five essential elements:

• *A new concept of deterrence*: The United States still requires a survivable nuclear force to deter any conceivable threat to the United States or its allies. This force can serve as a hedge against the resurgence of a nuclear threat in the former Soviet Union and to deter the use of nuclear weapons by any emerging regional power. However, as we continue to reduce reliance on nuclear weapons, negotiate further force reductions, and reorient our nuclear posture toward greater stability and safety, we must also think creatively about ways to eliminate the prospects for the use of nuclear weapons. This could include taking our nuclear forces off alert; eliminating elements of our deterrent that would have to be launched quickly in a crisis; improving our command, control, communications, and intelligence to prevent inadvertent or accidental launch of nuclear weapons; and improving our global intelligence capabilities to provide early warning of crises. An expanded program to help the former Soviet Union dismantle its arsenal and to strengthen safety measures would further reduce security threats to the West. And finally, as Peter Gray discusses in "Nuclear Weapons: Build Down/Clean Up," a new concept of deterrence must engage both declared and emerging nuclear powers in an effort to rid the world of weapons of mass destruction—building sound, verifiable, and universally applied arrangements that renounce the legitimacy of these instruments of war.

• *Power projection*: The United States must possess highly flexible, mobile, and technologically superior forces to project American power where it is needed to counter aggression that threatens our interests. The United States is the only country with the technology, personnel, and will to lead international coalitions against aggression that threatens our vital interests and those of our allies.

• *A technological edge.* The Persian Gulf War showed that America's technological advantages—in communications, space-based surveillance, tactical air power, and training—made it possible to conduct a short war with few American casualties. U.S. advantages in these areas can be used to deter conflict around the world. In a time of growing fiscal constraints, however, this will require establishing clearer priorities and devoting more serious attention to maintaining the manufacturing and technological vitality of our industrial base.

• *Intelligence.* In an environment where future adversaries may be less easily discernible, we will need to rely on more sophisticated intelligence and better understanding of social, political, and economic as well as military developments around the world. In addition to our investment in intelligence technologies such as satellite reconnaissance, we need highly skilled intelligence experts to distill information on the underlying conditions that fuel tensions and then to help avert crises before they escalate to full-scale conflict.

• *New security institutions.* The new Administration should exercise greater leadership in fostering institutions that can help prevent and mediate conflict, such as the Conference on Security and Cooperation in Europe (CSCE). A strong CSCE could enhance stability in Europe, create the foundations for a strong and more united Europe, and maintain an important role for the United States in European affairs.

The United States also should take the lead in strengthening the United Nations' capabilities for preventing crises, conducting peacekeeping operations, and devising new initiatives to promote cooperative approaches to security. Two proposals deserve strong U.S. support: (1) providing the U.N. Secretariat with an early-warning system that would enable it to monitor crises in their early stages; and (2) establishing a U.N. Rapid Deployment Force that would maintain a multilateral force, under the auspices of the United Nations, to be deployed in appropriate circumstances. These steps would strengthen and advance the vision of the United Nations' founders, who believed that a world of collective security and peaceful resolution of disputes is preferable to one driven by military ambitions and costly preparations for war.

3. *Promoting democracy*. As others have noted, the Bush administration was too often a status quo force in a revolutionary world. With the end of the Cold War, the animating principle of American foreign policy must be the preservation and advancement of freedom and democracy around the world.

Even as communist regimes were collapsing in Eastern Europe during the late 1980s, the current administration too often embraced these historic changes only reluctantly and often rhetorically. Similarly, in Latin America, Africa, Asia, and the Middle East, the East-West rivalry led the United States to embrace repressive regimes even if it meant soft-pedaling our opposition to the violation of human rights and basic political freedoms, or, in the case of Iraq, condoning the acquisition of a massive arsenal that eventually was used to attack its neighbor.

The new President should understand that democracy is the most enduring source of stability in the modern world. Democracy reduces the likelihood of conflict by providing nonviolent means for solving disputes. Democratic countries make better partners because they are more likely to observe international law, reject terrorism, and extend civil rights to their indigenous minority groups.

To the greatest extent possible, economic and security assistance must be used as an incentive for building indigenous democratic movements. Similarly, the United States must lend strong support to the effort by international financial institutions to link economic assistance to progress toward demilitarization, democratization, environmental protection, social justice, and respect for human rights.

4. *Restoring America's economic leadership*. National security in the post-Cold War world increasingly will be measured not by military arsenals but by the knowledge we possess as a people and how productively we work—our ability to develop and harness new technologies and compete in a world economy.

A program to restore our economic vitality is essential to American global leadership. An America that is underinvesting cannot credibly exercise leadership with other major industrial nations to achieve coordinated and concerted economic policies essential for sustained growth in a global economy. An America that is ridden with debt cannot marshal the international resources needed to preserve and advance the gains of democracy against the powerful forces that resist change and produce chaos or a return to authoritarian regimes.

Other portions of this book address what is needed to restore America's domestic economic strength. For these purposes, our point is this: Foreign policy and domestic policy can no longer be divorced—in our thinking or our decisionmaking as a nation. If we are weak at home, we cannot lead in the world. If we do not lead in the world, we cannot be strong at home. It is that simple.

5. *Preserving the global environment.* Today, the national security agenda must be expanded to include new threats to our collective survival. Section VI of this book tells how the clouds of environmental crises are gathering. They pose a challenge to all nations to work together as never before, because these threats know no boundaries, and cannot be solved by nations acting alone.

Man-made pollutants are changing the composition of Earth's atmosphere in a way never before seen. As global warming continues, the surface temperatures on Earth will increase, perhaps radically affecting climate patterns—and therefore life cycles—on Earth. Increased depletion of ozone due to the production of chlorofluorocarbons and other industrial gases can progressively destroy the ozone layer, stripping the earth of protection against dangerous ultraviolet radiation.

Just when most nations of the world are seeking the path of greater international cooperation to deal with these and other environmental crises, the Bush administration blocked progress and failed to assert leadership, putting us on the wrong side of history at the summer Rio summit.

The new Administration must place the United States at the forefront of leadership, not resistance, in the international battle against global warming. It should shape, not dilute, international actions to protect Earth's ozone layer and biodiversity and to save its forests from destruction. It should support developing nations in their efforts to preserve their environmental heritage. And it should work to control burgeoning population growth by coordinating our policies with those of private organizations and other industrialized countries in support of family planning programs.

The next President, finally, will define America's role in a new world. In a world where we can watch on our television at home as American planes descend on the Iraqi capital half a world away . . . where Iron Curtains and Berlin Walls are penetrated by fax machines and computer terminals . . . and where decisions made in the central banks of Europe and Japan can affect the cost of our home mortgage, we cannot hide from the world and still remain safe or prosperous. America must lead in the world, guided by our commitment to individual freedom and dignity and grounded on a revitalized national economy that gives us the confidence and the resources to help shape the new international era.

THE FORMER SOVIET EMPIRE

MARK GARRISON AND JAN H. KALICKI

Summary

THE COLLAPSE OF THE SOVIET EMPIRE and end of the Cold War give Americans the chance to shift vast resources to reviving our economy and tending to the needs of our people. But this golden opportunity can elude our grasp if we turn inward and leave the former Soviet republics and Eastern Europe to their own devices. For our own sakes we should help them build viable, nonmilitaristic societies on the ruins of communism.

The root problem throughout the area, and the key to achieving American goals, is economics. Economic desperation can be the undoing of young democracies, an effective tool of military juntas and demagogic dictators, and gasoline on the flames of destructive nationalism. Americans understand that it is in our own interest to help these countries get on their feet, but lose enthusiasm if that seems to mean we cannot now begin to meet our needs at home. Strong leadership is needed to make the case that if trillions were spent to win the Cold War, we can surely find the billions—from the Group of Seven, our Gulf allies, and ourselves—needed to secure the peace.

Nevertheless, Americans' concerns about jobs at home must be heeded.

Mark Garrison is director of the Center for Foreign Policy Development at Brown University's Thomas J. Watson, Jr., Institute for International Studies; in the 1970s he headed the State Department's Soviet office and was deputy chief of mission in the U.S. Embassy in Moscow. Jan H. Kalicki is senior vice president at Lehman Brothers, and senior adviser to the Brown Center; previously an adjunct professor at Brown and Georgetown universities, he has served as a member of the Policy Planning Staff under Secretaries of State Kissinger and Vance and as chief foreign policy adviser to Senator Edward M. Kennedy.

One way is through programs that provide aid in the form of U.S. goods. A program on the model of the P.L. 480 program could sell U.S. agricultural and manufactured goods for local currencies and use these "counterpart funds" for various purposes in the U.S. interest, thus helping recipient countries move to market economies while stimulating the U.S. economy and creating jobs here.

A significant security danger is balkanization, in both the historical and the current Yugoslav sense. Heading off that danger requires not only assistance toward economic recovery but also political and military steps carried out with the understanding of a psychologist and the precision of an acupuncturist. The leaders of each of these countries cannot lightly renounce the pursuit of military power, especially if their people perceive security threats from their neighbors. One way to unwind or prevent regional arms races is to offer alternative means of assuring security, such as credible international security guarantees. And in extreme cases, as in what was Yugoslavia, U.S. backing for international military action may be the only way to end local wars stemming from ethnic conflict.

The principles that guide Americans are clear: self-determination, democracy, free markets, human rights, nonuse of force. But we may find that in some cases our principles will be at cross-purposes. Democracy may not easily and everywhere accept free market ideas; self-determination may lead to human rights violations; the leaders best able to lead their countries away from confrontation and crisis may not be Jeffersonian democrats. We must keep our eye throughout on what should be our top priority: preventing crises and eliminating the underlying causes of conflict.

Unlike his predecessors, the next President will be expected to lead in a multipolar, not a bipolar, world, with less, not more resources, from a nation more concerned about its domestic than its foreign agenda. But lead he must—to help assure that the East never again presents a threat to our national survival, and to help achieve a historic transformation from a Soviet empire to a community of free, peaceful, and prosperous states.

U.S. Interests and Priorities

IT IS WIDELY ACCEPTED that the United States has a deep interest in what kind of countries emerge from the ashes of the former Soviet empire. Will they be democratically governed? Whether democratic or not, will they pursue zero-sum ethnic, religious, or ideological agendas at home and against neighbors? Will they seek military advantages over neighbors? Do nuclear weapons figure in their aspirations, either as bargaining chips for economic or political advantage or as threats against neighbors? Will they seek alliances that could eventually lead to another 1914 scenario?

Each of the fifteen countries carved out of the former Soviet Union, and each Central and East European country, will answer these questions for itself through its actions over time.

Democracy. Clearly, the U.S. interest is for these countries to develop strong and resilient democracies responsive to their people's needs and desires within the circumstances of each country. We want them to share our respect for individual rights and freedoms, although this is less clearly a vital U.S. interest. Ideally, democracy will not open the way to ethnic strife within or between countries on a scale that could lead a whole region down the path to war, with unpredictable consequences for the international community and specifically for the United States.

Orderly change, not status quo. "Stability" is often cited as a U.S. interest, in this as in other regions of the world. More precisely, we seek "process stability"—not the absence of change, but change that takes place through a process that responds to the needs and desires of the people of a country, adapts to changing circumstances, avoids violence, and accommodates the greatest number while treating individuals and minority groups fairly. In the international context, process stability means acceptance of changes stemming from self-determination while avoiding conflict and discouraging destructive nationalism. A guiding principle is freedom of choice tempered by rational calculations of self-interest and respect for others' interests.

Healing, not destructive, nationalism. It is in the tempests of nationalism that immature democratic institutions in the East may yet founder. Nationalism can be a positive force as a rallying point for a people struggling for their freedom and self-confidence. But it can become destructive when historical grievances, ethnic and religious animosities, and frustrated cultural heritages build to the point that groups of people try to do each other harm. Destructive nationalism can take on a life of its own and work counter to the economic interests of a people seized by its emotions. But there is no doubt that it can be greatly exacerbated by economic desperation, which magnifies the grievances and animosities.

The Crucial Arena: Economics

WHAT CAN THE UNITED STATES DO REGARDING DEMOCRACY, nationalism, or militarism in this region? Economic deprivation and desperation are likely to lead them in directions that are counter to U.S. interests. This is why the United States has already committed itself in principle to

help these countries get on their feet and establish working market economies. The issue is how much help to give and how to give it. The Bush
administration in April 1992 announced support for a $24 billion program,
but there was less to it than met the eye.[1]

MOVING TO THE MARKET

The objective is clear: to create a functioning market economy, a market
that sets prices based on supply and demand, thereby enabling producers
to produce, distributors to distribute, and consumers to consume. Unfortunately, reformers in these countries have found that the path to the market
winds through a minefield. Vast sectors of the economies will go bankrupt
when subsidies cease, adding to the unemployment and human suffering
already rampant. Continued subsidies feed the raging inflation that is pushing
tens of millions of people below the poverty line. This desperation creates
fertile ground for demagogues and political rogues of all stripes. The outside
world can help create conditions in which a market economy can emerge.

WHY SHOULD THE UNITED STATES HELP . . .

Effective political leadership is needed to convince Americans that helping
the new democracies get on their feet is a wise investment for the long run.
We can see in principle that the establishment of civilianized, democratic,
market-oriented societies in place of our former superpower opponent is
necessary for a true and lasting peace and for reducing U.S. military expenditures and keeping them down, thus permitting greater investment in
education, infrastructure, jobs creation, and other contributors to a healthy
economy and society in the United States. We can also understand intellectually that economic desperation in these countries is not only a human
suffering that should be relieved but is in fact a direct threat to our own
security and well-being.

. . . WHEN WE HAVE OUR OWN PROBLEMS AT HOME?

What is clear in principle becomes muddied when Americans face their own
economic stringencies. Our voters are not saintly. When so many needs
demand our attention at home, when resources are so strained, when taxpayers (fairly or not) feel much put upon, sacrifices for a distant goal are
not popular. Help to Russia or its neighbors in the former Soviet Union and
in Eastern Europe is easily depicted as help that should instead be channeled
to creating jobs, educating our children, feeding our hungry, and rebuilding
our cities and domestic infrastructure.

This is a challenge for strong leadership. The next President of the United

States must make the case for both a restored America and a revived world economy, within which Central and Eastern Europe and the former Soviet Union can be nursed back to economic—and thereby political—health. These are inseparable components of U.S. prosperity as well as security.

It was a similar watershed in history that led a Democratic president and a Republican congressional leadership to give their bipartisan support to the expensive reconstruction of Europe after World War II. The task in the East after the Cold War is much more difficult and complex, and financial resources alone will not solve it. But they will help, and a multilateral aid consortium of the Group of Seven (including those countries assisted by the United States forty-five years ago) and of the Persian Gulf states can make a critical difference. But the United States must help lead the way with substantial contributions. Fortunately, President Yeltsin's dramatic June 1992 visit to Washington, including his arms control concessions and assurances on American MIAs, have made those contributions more likely. In turn, U.S. aid to our allies in the past and to the post-Soviet republics today increases our ability to persuade the G-7 nations and our Arab allies in the Persian Gulf War to provide the majority of any future support.

HELPING OUR ECONOMY AND THEIRS, TOO

Because it is especially difficult to make the case, during a prolonged recession, that tax money or any "peace dividend" should be used to create jobs in the former Soviet empire, the next President should propose programs that provide aid in the form of American goods, both agricultural and industrial.

Priming the pump with American goods. A model for that kind of assistance is the P.L. 480 program, dating from 1954. In addition to grants of food aid, that program was designed to sell agricultural commodities to countries with nonconvertible currencies and balance-of-payments problems. The recipients pay with their local currencies, which are held by the U.S. Government and used for purposes agreed on by the two governments. The result is that the recipients obtain needed commodities without expending scarce hard currency reserves, local sales absorb surplus currency, and the proceeds can be used for worthy purposes.

In a new "U.S. goods for peace and progress" program, agricultural commodities would continue to be a natural candidate, but care would have to be taken to assure that no harm is done to emerging private agriculture in recipient countries. Consumer goods and medicines, which are in terribly short supply, would also be a good starting place, followed by equipment for producing them.

On the U.S. end, such a program would contribute to stimulating the economy and creating or protecting jobs. The long-term effect would be to create export markets for U.S. goods as the economies of Eastern Europe and the former Soviet republics get on their feet.

Detailed mechanisms for accomplishing U.S. purposes would have to be worked out with the recipient governments, and Congress would have to enact new legislation.

Here are some of the difficult issues, and possible ways to tackle them:

• *Who decides what commodities can be purchased?* In principle this should be decided by the market in the recipient country, with some control by economic authorities in that country to minimize damage to promising but fragile domestic producers and to promote efficiency. Perhaps joint ventures involving American partners could submit proposals for purchase of commodities relevant to the venture's future business. For example: A joint venture to produce and market widgets could initially import U.S. widgets and sell them in Russia, creating a distribution and sales network and generating profit that could be reinvested in the venture. The U.S. supplier would receive dollars from the U.S. Government for the widgets, and the joint venture would pay for them in rubles, which would go into a U.S. Government account to be used for stated purposes.

• *Who decides how the local currency proceeds are to be used?* Agreements with recipient governments would establish a mechanism for assuring that recipient country interests are not harmed in the process of pursuing purely U.S. aims, such as expanding U.S. markets. But most of the U.S. policy aims would also be shared by the recipient governments, including economic recovery, bolstering democracy, and moderating ethnic and regional conflicts within the recipient country. Examples of such "positive sum" applications: grants in dinars for reconstruction in Croatian, Muslim, and Serbian areas of Bosnia-Hercegovina, once peace is restored; credits in korunas for new enterprises in Slovakia; credits in rubles for economic development in Romanian, Gagauz, and Russian portions of Moldova, if the factions there resist the urge to go to war; a grant in rubles to establish an institute for national security studies and research in Kazakhstan; a grant in rubles to establish in Russia a research institute to design safe and environmentally sound nuclear power stations; and a program supporting U.S. teachers, managers, and Peace Corps volunteers throughout the region.

Turning on U.S. private investment. Much more can be done to spearhead the commitment of the private sector to invest in the countries of the former Soviet empire. Foreign direct investment can be a powerful vehicle for focusing capital, technology, and management expertise where they matter most—at local levels of entrepreneurial activity and private enterprise development. The Export-Import Bank and more recently the Overseas Private Investment Corporation have encouraged this private sector activity through credits and guarantees. But the next Administration and Congress should move to expand these mechanisms significantly. In addition, the President should propose that a new multilateral credit support facility be created to support Eximbank and other export credit agencies with the equity and subordinated debt required to attract higher investment flows to the post-Soviet republics and Central and Eastern Europe. Along with U.S. support, the President should seek funding by Japan as well as European and Persian Gulf states—with the focus of the new facility on private sector development not only in Europe but also in the Central Asian republics.

TUNE THE SPEED OF REFORM TO WHAT DEMOCRACY CAN BEAR

One final consideration as the United States looks for the best ways to help these economies get on their feet: A degree of caution, even humility, is in order in prescribing the shock therapy approach of instant marketization and privatization, particularly with regard to the former Soviet Union. A transition from a centrally planned economy based on huge state enterprises has never been done before. It is complicated immensely by the breakup of the country into independent, and in some cases antagonistic, units. And to try to make these wrenching changes through a democratic process that is itself just trying to get its bearings, requiring the newly enfranchised to vote for yet more self-sacrifice amid the rubble of their personal lives, accentuates the dilemma.

Therefore, the United States should exercise restraint, and urge restraint on the IMF and other institutions, in prescribing hard-and-fast timetables as prerequisites for assistance. The democratic process in each country must play a role in decisions on how long to continue subsidizing which state enterprises and how rapidly they should be allowed to sink if unable to swim into competition and privatization.

Political as well as economic impact statements. In 1991 and 1992, economic purists inside and outside of government were pressing for draconian measures to cut the budget and freeze the money supply, a course that would be politically intolerable anywhere in the world. This pressure has diminished somewhat as the political and social risks of these measures became more evident. The task ahead is to increase, or at least conserve, the domestic support needed to implement a credible program of economic recovery. In 1993 and beyond, the next Administration and Congress must insist on recommendations that weigh the political as well as the economic impact of new prescriptions so that the pursuit of free markets does not yield the bitter harvest of fascist dictatorships.

International guidance, domestic sensitivity. To get the most out of both outside pressure and on-the-ground judgments, it is worth exploring the creation of an international organization sponsored by donor nations, with some capital at its disposal and a body of trained managers and controllers who could work directly in certain key enterprises to achieve agreed-on objectives—whether the aim is to keep the enterprise ticking during a transition period to provide employment or essential output, or whether the aim is to make the enterprise viable for privatization. The foreigners in an enterprise would provide expertise, hard-nosed economic judgments, and control over expenditure of the foreign credits; local managers would run the enterprise; and the host government would make political assessments and establish its priorities.

We should remember that joint decisionmaking and management of funds were at the heart of the successful international partnership underlying the Marshall Plan in an earlier era.

Encouraging Peaceful Relationships

WHILE THE FIRST LINE OF DEFENSE against destructive nationalism is a functioning economy that effectively meets the needs of the people in each country throughout the region, that is not a realistic near-term expectation. And destructive emotions can easily override calculations of economic self-interest, especially if the economic payoff is speculative or in the distant future. The failure to demobilize the Red Army has led to the danger of independent action by military units within newly independent countries or within Russia itself; the specter of warlordism hangs over the entire region. How can the United States help to head off conflicts?

RESPECT FOR EACH COUNTRY'S HURTS AND HOPES
A basic principle in thinking about this problem is that we are dealing not just with sovereign states but also with states whose sovereignty is so new, whose self-centeredness is so strong, that outsiders who wish to draw them into a search for constructive and mutually advantageous solutions have to bend over backward to make clear that their interests are for them alone to define and that there is no intention to try to exploit differences between them and their neighbors. Every gesture must be a careful and respectful one.

At the heart of each country's view of its interests is security. Therefore, calls to eliminate military forces, or to desist from acquiring them, are more effective if combined with credible international military or political guarantees. Of course, the United States should not— indeed, cannot—unilaterally guarantee the security of any country that feels the need. But we and our allies can and should develop with each country a rich and multilayered relationship that encourages a feeling of security even without formal guarantees. A Western track record of supporting effective U.N. action against aggression can contribute to a feeling that small, weak countries do not have to face an aggressor alone.

THE UKRAINIAN EXAMPLE

The whole region is fraught with potential conflict situations, some with obvious implications for U.S. security and interests, others with none, and others that have no direct implications but have the potential in unpredictable ways to be transformed into threats. An example of a situation with great potential for involving U.S. interests involves relations between Ukraine and Russia, in part because of the size of the two countries, in part because of their location, and in part because of their military potential. The relationship is bedeviled by a history that linked the two Slavic nations in a rocky marriage in which Moscow was traditionally dominant. When divorce came, it turned nasty in some respects. Particularly ominous are arguments over military forces and over territory, such as the Crimea.[2]

What can the United States do other than try to remain on good terms with both contesting parties (whether Ukraine and Russia, Russia and Moldova, Armenia and Azerbaijan, or the Czech lands and Slovakia) and to help both parties regain their feet economically? We have to recognize that these nations have real differences to work out and that they are doing so in a context of emerging democracy that sharply limits the room for leaders to compromise even when they are inclined to, and in the presence of heavily armed factions that constrain local leaders even more.

In these circumstances, we must think through the priorities and principles that should guide our actions.

CRISIS PREVENTION FIRST

A top priority must be crisis prevention, specifically the avoidance of conflict in the whole region of Eastern Europe and the former Soviet Union, but particularly in those areas where conflict can lead to unpredictable escalation: north-central Europe and Russia, and Ukraine and the Caucasus.

Unfortunately, crisis prevention may present trade-offs against other priorities, including the promotion of democracy, protection of human rights, and support for privatized market economies. We should pursue all those principles as diligently and intelligently as our own democratic system permits. But we should be clear in our own minds that our first priority is the prevention of crises, including the elimination of underlying causes of conflict.

Security Issues

U.S. AND WESTERN DIPLOMACY DESERVE GREAT CREDIT for achieving the adherence of all states liberated from the "internal" as well as the "external" Soviet empire to the confidence-building conventional force and nuclear agreements negotiated with President Gorbachev. Because of growing conservative opposition in Russia, President Yeltsin deserves even greater credit for not only adhering to these agreements but also agreeing to eliminate the SS-18 heavy missiles, which have been at the core of U.S. strategic insecurities in the past. How can we build on these developments to advance process stability in each of the countries and within the region?

NUCLEAR AND CONVENTIONAL WEAPONS
Everyone's long-run interests clearly will be served by removal of nuclear weapons from three of the four former republics of the Soviet Union where they were deployed, leaving Russia as the sole nuclear state among them.

The approach used thus far—bringing the three destined to give up nuclear weapons into formal agreements with Russia and the United States— seems to be effective. It is in fact a useful model for using the yearning of newly independent countries for acknowledgment of their status as a tool for engaging them constructively. They are in effect trading a bargaining chip of dubious practical utility but tremendous symbolic importance in exchange for status recognition that may not endow practical benefits but is nevertheless symbolically beneficial to struggling new regimes.

A similar approach can be useful in tackling the issue of conventional military forces in the former Soviet Union. But that issue poses problems more complex than nuclear weapons. The leaderships of these countries cannot lightly renounce the pursuit of military power. It is a real, or strongly perceived, factor in their countries' national security and also an important psychological element in their self-image as independent national states able to provide for their own security. The need for security protection flows from perceived threats from neighboring former republics. Some (e.g., Ukraine) see Russia as a potential threat. Others (Armenia and Azerbaijan) see an immediate neighbor as a dangerous enemy, and may resort to external alliances (e.g., with Turkey or Iran). And others (Moldova and Georgia) face internal insurrection. Those former republics that would prefer to spend little on military forces may feel it necessary to spend more because their neighbors are doing so.

The countries of Eastern Europe are beset by concerns about neighbors, including Germany, and a felt need to be able to provide for their own defense. Although not now very evident, these pressures can lead in the future to militarization efforts, or to the pursuit of alliances that could eventually re-create a 1914 situation. Meanwhile, their efforts are in the direction of trying to come under the NATO umbrella.

NEW SECURITY STRUCTURE

Much of the pressure to build military power or to enter alliances, as well as legitimate concerns about security, could be dealt with by creating a security system that provides satisfactory guarantees to each country without the need to build its own powerful military force.

Such a system can only take form out of a process involving each potential member, taking into account the specific interests and concerns of each. But the outline of a process can be laid out. Essential principles are *inclusivity* and *mutual security*.

The most logical way to assure inclusivity is to base the process on the Conference on Security and Cooperation in Europe (CSCE). Initiatives now under way to create a peacekeeping operation under CSCE political control and NATO command, together with the Vienna-based European Security Forum for arms control, which includes all CSCE members, create a sound foundation. Under strong presidential leadership, the United States can help create a system to provide security against aggression and against threats of force directed at any participating country. Every possible path to that goal should be explored, including collective security arrangements as well as arms control agreements that emphasize defense and minimize offensive capabilities. Nuclear and missile nonproliferation accords would fit naturally into such a negotiating forum. The agenda could also include, by agreement, exploring collective arrangements for dealing with internal armed conflicts.

DISMANTLING THE SOVIET MILITARY/INDUSTRIAL COMPLEX

Considerable attention has already been devoted to the issues surrounding the Soviet capacity to design and produce nuclear weapons and to the broader question of the potential displacement or unemployment of scientists and engineers from the former Soviet military/industrial complex. A comprehensive U.S. approach to the problem should focus on three categories.

The first is nonproliferation of weapons of mass destruction and high-tech weapons know-how. Clearly, the United States would not want renegade states such as Libya to gain access to weapons, components, or know-how. Even proliferation to democratic countries such as India is not welcomed.

Already there are efforts to establish institutional arrangements to support Soviet scientists in constructive work at home.[3] Since the danger of proliferation can directly affect U.S. security, and since in any case the thrust of such programs would also contribute to the U.S. objective of helping get the Soviet economy on its feet, the next Administration should make, as a matter of high priority, a commitment of more than token resources. At the same time, resources should also be applied to prevent leakage of existing weapons and components. In implementing these programs, attention must also be paid to the danger that weapons research teams, if kept intact, could be the nucleus for an arms industry of a Russian military regime that conceivably might emerge.

The second category is the link between economic recovery in the former Soviet republics and the fact that one of the significant resources of those republics is the large body of trained and capable engineers and scientists in the military/industrial complex. They have the potential to contribute to a revival of civilian industry. We should support efforts to help put them to work through new multilateral and other programs.

The third category is U.S. business interests. This can cut many different ways. A U.S. corporation might benefit by commissioning research by a Soviet team, but this could disadvantage U.S. scientists and engineers. A U.S. corporation might profitably buy a surplus Soviet system, but this might undercut an American producer of similar systems. Or U.S. investors might enter into a joint venture relying in part on Soviet research and engineering that promotes new economic activity benefiting both countries' economies.

In each of these categories, and even more in their relation to each other, there are trade-offs among U.S. interests. Strong presidential leadership can assure that the most essential national interests—direct security threats and the indirect threat of a failed Russian reform movement—are given priority.

NOTES

1. The $24 billion figure was for a multilateral program that included $18 billion in financial support from G–7 countries, including an unspecified amount from the United States, and a $6 billion currency stabilization fund from the IMF, requiring no net U.S. budgetary outlay. Legislation submitted to Congress at the same time

gave good reasons for extending economic assistance and proposed a number of mechanisms but did not request any new appropriations to implement the plans. (The White House, "Multilateral Financial Assistance Package for Russia" and "Freedom Support Act of 1992: Fact Sheet," press releases [April 1, 1992].)

2. The Crimea, although separated from Russia by Ukrainian territory, has been part of Russia since the eighteenth century and is populated mainly by Russians and other nationalities, but was transferred from Russia to Ukraine in 1954 by Khrushchev for administrative convenience.

3. During President Yeltsin's summit visit to the United States in June 1992, agreements were reached on cooperation in space and on other cooperation in science and technology, and in a broad "Charter" linked "responsibility to prevent weapons of mass destruction," science and technology exchanges, and conversion of defense industries to civilian production. (The White House, "Joint Statement on Cooperation in Space," "Joint Statement on Science and Technology Cooperation," and "A Charter for American-Russian Partnership and Cooperation," press releases [June 17, 1992].) Earlier, the National Academy of Sciences, at the request of the president's science adviser, organized a study on dealing with Soviet research capabilities. The study concluded that preservation and reorientation of the basic science capability of the former Soviet Union is in the U.S. interest (A. Carter, F. Press, and G. Stever, workshop co-chairmen, *Reorientation of the Research Capability of the Former Soviet Union: A Report to the Assistant to the President for Science and Technology* [Washington D.C.: National Academy Press, 1992].)

THE NEW GLOBAL MARKETPLACE

WALTER RUSSELL MEAD

Summary

T HE GLOBAL ECONOMY HAS BEEN LOSING STEAM for twenty years—since the collapse of the Bretton Woods system. Growth was slower in the seventies than in the sixties; slower in the eighties than in the seventies and, so far, the nineties have been the worst decade for the world economy since World War II.

An effective agenda for global growth is the key to both the economic and the political objectives of the United States in the nineties. Without healthy rates of global growth, Eastern Europe cannot make a successful transition to democracy, East Asia cannot achieve democracy and stability, and the American economy cannot achieve the growth needed to raise the living standard of the American people and to bring the budget deficit under control. Rebuilding the world economy is the most important single objective of the new Administration, but this goal cannot be achieved without the cooperation of America's major economic partners. Fortunately, the new Administration has a unique opportunity to lead an international coalition for growth; Europe, Japan, and the developing world are prepared as never before to cooperate in a joint effort for economic growth that is grounded in two basic strategies.

• *An international public sector initiative for global growth.* The IMF and the World Bank have earned a reputation as the "debt police" of the world economy. During the past decade, these Bretton Woods institutions advocated programs of restructuring and austerity in debtor nations. After

Walter Russell Mead is Senior Fellow for International Economics at the World Policy Institute and a contributing editor at Harper's *and at the* Los Angeles Times. *He is currently working on book projects for Alfred A. Knopf and the Twentieth Century Fund.*

the collapse of European communism, they extended these policies to Eastern Europe. In the nineties, the Bretton Woods institutions can and should play a more stimulative role. Equipped with additional capital from the United States, Europe, and Japan, they can return to their original, expansionary role in the world economy. Additionally, joint action by the world's richest economies can support infrastructure investment, environmental programs, and basic medical and nutrition programs in the developing world and Eastern Europe. Soundly managed international institutions can leverage contributions from donor governments and combine debt relief with "positive conditionality" to stimulate an expansion of purchasing power in troubled economies while relieving human suffering. A relatively small investment of U.S. funds will improve the trade deficit and generate a major expansion of U.S. exports.

• *A new approach on trade.* U.S. trade policy has failed. The Uruguay Round of trade talks and the North American Free Trade Association proposals create a trading system that is fundamentally hostile to American interests. The United States is, by world standards, a high-wage, high-regulation economy. GATT, NAFTA, and other U.S. trade programs tilt the world trading system to favor low-wage, low-regulation producers. The Uruguay Round proposals provide no safeguards against systematic violations of international law by our trading partners and cannot serve as the basis of U.S. trade policy. While America—the world's largest exporter as well as the world's largest importer—needs an open international trading system, present U.S. policy leads inevitably to trade wars and closed markets.

The new Administration should base its trade policy on "free and sustainable trade." Its objective must be trade agreements aimed at raising wages and living standards in developing countries, rather than lowering them here. The world trading system must support important U.S. policy objectives—such as environmentally sustainable development—and not undermine them.

In pursuit of these objectives, the new Administration should reopen the Uruguay Round and NAFTA and should announce a systematic review of U.S. bilateral agreements and programs like the GSP [Generalized System of Preferences] and the CBI [Caribbean Basin Initiative].

Background

UNDER THE BRETTON WOODS SYSTEM, the United States was able to act as the locomotive of world growth. The Federal Reserve was in effect the world's central bank, and its growth-oriented policies set the pace for the global system. Since Bretton Woods collapsed, the United States and its principal economic partners have been unable to find an alternative method to stimulate growth. Germany and Japan have each tried and failed to replace the United States as the locomotive; persistent policy differences have made it impossible for the three countries to agree on joint action. Worse still, the post-Bretton Woods system rewards restrictive, growth-inhibiting policy while punishing countries that follow stimulative fiscal and monetary policies.

Meanwhile, the world trading system, despite the intentions of its creators, acts as a brake on the global economy. When production shifts from high-wage to low-wage economies, demand and ultimately economic growth begin to slow. Slow-demand growth leads in turn to protectionist pressures as the economic competition for inadequate markets intensifies. For twenty years, American administrations have deplored the resulting deceleration in growth and have suffered the economic and political consequences, but have failed to develop a new strategy for global growth that can win the support of our principal partners.

The Opportunity

THE NEXT ADMINISTRATION HAS A HISTORIC OPPORTUNITY to get the world economy moving again. For the first time in a generation, the three pillars of the world economy—Europe, the United States, and Japan—face a common set of problems that demand joint action for global growth. In Europe, the collapse of the Communist system and of Eastern Europe's economies creates a political and economic problem for Western Europe that cannot be ignored. Western Europe, and especially Germany, knows that economic failure in Eastern Europe will lead to deepening problems and widening wars. Yet the conventional prescriptions of bilateral aid and limited assistance from the World Bank and the International Monetary Fund are quite clearly inadequate for Eastern Europe's needs.

Meanwhile, Japan is suffering from its worst economic crisis since the oil shocks of twenty years ago. On the one hand, Japan's domestic economy has lost some of its magic. On the other, it faces mounting criticism and protectionism from its principal partners—from the European Community as well as the United States. Japan cannot maintain its growth rates in a stagnant world economy.

Now is the time for action: in the short term, to jump-start the global economy and, over the course of the next Administration, to lay the foundations of a new, growth-oriented global economic system.

Recommendations

PUBLIC SECTOR INITIATIVES FOR GLOBAL GROWTH

Joint action by the world's leading economies is necessary to open a new era of dynamic economic growth. It is no longer possible for one country to act as the "locomotive of world growth" and take on the burden of providing global economic stimulus. Europe, the United States, and Japan can, however, act together to return the world to the type of noninflationary growth experienced in the Bretton Woods (1945–73) era. The attempt to get this cooperative action should be a major thrust of U.S. diplomacy during the coming Administration. Economic success will improve the international climate; solidify an open international trading system; prevent the reemergence of hostile economic blocs; and, not least, stimulate rapid American growth in the next four years.

Failing the return to world economic growth, the Administration will face a deteriorating political situation in Eastern Europe, with the potential for Balkan-style conflict on a much greater scale. It is by no means clear that the United States could avoid being drawn into widespread European hostilities. Beyond the problems of Eastern Europe, slow economic growth will increase political tensions in the Middle East and East Asia. Governments around the world will find it more difficult to cooperate; national rivalries will emerge, and international order will be severely tested. Domestically, successful international economic policy will provide the new Administration with the political and economic breathing space required for domestic initiatives and reforms. Strong economic growth will control the budget and trade deficits and provide resources for selected new programs without cutting old ones or raising taxes. For all these reasons, *an international growth initiative needs to be at the top of the new Administration's priorities.* Because success depends on the cooperation of foreign partners, these policies will take time to implement—all the more reason to start early and to establish the Administration's position on growth in the public mind from January 1993. Some components of the new strategy are:

• *Joint action.* In the past, the United States acted alone to stimulate the global and domestic economy through expansionary fiscal and monetary policy. Our budget and trade deficits of the past twelve years are the legacy of this economic role. In the future, neither the United States nor any other country should assume the burden of global stimulus alone. Joint action by at least two of the world's leading economic zones—Europe, North America, and East Asia—will be necessary.

• *International horizon*. In addition to measures undertaken to stimulate their domestic economies, leading countries must work to stimulate economic demand in developing countries. Through bilateral aid, through expanded lending and money-creating activity by international financial institutions, and through a different policy mix by developing countries, the United States and its principal economic partners can prime the global pump. The joint use of international financial institutions to achieve national goals of the United States is an astonishingly effective use of funds. Assuming contributions from Europe, Japan, and the Arab world, each dollar of U.S. appropriations can create many times that amount of global economic stimulus.

Intelligently targeted global stimulus will achieve both political and economic goals for the United States. For example, an internationally funded child nutrition program will improve living conditions in poor countries and create a less confrontational global political climate. It will also, by increasing the world market for farm goods, improve U.S.-EC trade relations while tending to raise farm incomes in the United States and to improve our balance of trade. Similar programs to provide basic services around the world—clean water, effective sewage disposal facilities, mass transit in the rapidly growing metropolises of the Third World—will provide, directly and indirectly, customers for American producers and improvements in public health and pollution control.

• *Reform of the Bretton Woods institutions*. An increase in resources will allow the Bretton Woods institutions (the IMF and the World Bank) to return to a role more in keeping with their founding philosophy: being instruments for promoting growth and improving world living standards. Over the past twelve years these agencies performed a valuable function in helping—at times, prodding—developing debtor countries to shift away from failed development strategies. Privatizing state industries, opening the domestic economy to international competition, and dismantling wasteful subsidies of various kinds were important steps for these countries to take to lay the foundation for future growth.

Other aspects of IMF and World Bank policy in the past twelve years were less helpful. Economic reform too often became a never-ending round of austerity. Essential programs such as education and health care were slashed along with wasteful ones; real wages fell even as production for export increased; environmentally unsustainable development programs multiplied even as cash-strapped governments had to cut back or postpone environmental spending.

The costs of austerity were not limited to the developing world. The

United States itself suffered from this approach. Austerity in Latin America dramatically cut one of the world's best markets for American goods during the past twelve years. The United States lost tens of thousands of jobs and billions of dollars in tax revenue; the U.S. budget and trade deficits would have been consistently lower throughout the decade had another approach to Latin America been pursued.

American taxpayers should not and in the long run will not support international financial institutions that do not benefit the American economy. To retain American support and to win the increased allotments that they need to do their job, international institutions must take a more growth-oriented stance. Their job is to support sustainable consumption in developing countries, not to curtail it. Washington has a strong voice at the IMF, the World Bank, and a host of other international financial institutions. Beginning in January 1993, that voice must insist on a turn toward environmentally and socially sustainable growth-oriented policies by these institutions.

• *Positive conditionality.* The turn toward more growth-oriented policies involves many benefits for developing countries. It is both reasonable and, from the standpoint of maintaining political support for much higher levels of assistance, necessary that these initiatives require reciprocal action by recipient countries. Some of these obligations would be similar to those now enforced by the IMF and the World Bank; others would reflect the new realities created by new types of aid. Strict international audits, provision of matching funds, nondiscrimination agreements, enforceable agreements to abide by international human rights conventions, limitations on arms purchases, and adherence to the principles of sustainable development might all be part of the positive conditionality attached to these new forms of aid. This conditionality may well feel intrusive to some countries, but the new and radically more growth-oriented world economic policy behind these conditions will be welcome to countries that have suffered extensively under the policies of the past twelve years.

• *A new approach for Eastern Europe.* The formerly Communist nations of Eastern Europe will, in the nineties, be either the world's biggest growth opportunity or the world's biggest headache. A burst of economic development in this region could bring a generation of rapid growth in the world's most important market, or instability and war could threaten world peace and darken the prospects of the world economy. We are currently on the path to failure in Eastern Europe; almost three years after the fall of the Berlin Wall, not one single nation in Eastern Europe has maintained its Communist-era living standards. These countries now face the daunting prospect of a vicious cycle: their poor economic performance creates political uncertainty, and this in turn makes foreigners reluctant to invest. An urgent priority of the new Administration must be the development, with the G-7 nations, of an economic recovery initiative in Eastern Europe. This initiative will take advantage of the expanded resources and the new policies to be undertaken by the international financial institutions discussed above, and will also involve specific steps dictated by the special circumstances of Eastern Europe.

• *A dollar clearinghouse for East-East trade.* The collapse of trade among the former Communist countries has greatly exacerbated the difficulties of transition to the market system. A Western-funded dollar clearinghouse would provide "soft" credits to formerly Communist countries to promote increased trade among themselves. The "transferable ruble" system of trade had many flaws, but the failure to replace it with a transitional system is a principal cause of the growing economic problems of Eastern Europe. Longtime relationships among producers and customers have been disrupted at a time of unprecedented economic strain.

The dollar clearinghouse system will provide "soft" dollars for East-East trade to stimulate economic revival; once recovery is well under way, the emphasis will shift toward integration of the Eastern economies into the world market.

• *Expanded loan and investment guarantees.* Eastern Europe will need much greater support from Western governments and multinational institutions than it has yet received. One measure of the need: The eastern portion of Germany will receive an estimated $1 trillion in transfer payments and assistance from the former West Germany during the first decade of unification, but many observers believe that this aid will be insufficient. A total of $200 billion a year would be required to provide the rest of the East with one tenth the per-capita aid going to eastern Germany. Aid on this scale is simply not available, but an imaginative system of credits and guarantees would ease the aid gap, which may otherwise destroy Eastern Europe's experiments in democracy and capitalism.

Western governments and international financial organizations can provide a number of useful investment and loan guarantees to help attract more private capital to the East. A thoughtful program involving long-term mortgaging or pledging of royalties of such resources as Russian oil and gold can help relieve the acute liquidity problem of the East without undue costs or unacceptable risks. An expansion of loan guarantees and export financing will increase the East's purchasing power and provide a boost to U.S. companies.

A GROWTH-ORIENTED TRADE POLICY

U.S. trade policy is currently a mix of contradictory impulses and policies. On the one hand, the United States urges—even pressures—developing countries to adopt development strategies that depend on low-cost exports to, largely, the American market. On the other hand, the United States is itself seeking to replace its trade deficit with a surplus, and it takes vigorous action against developing countries whose export strategies are too successful. With part of its energy, the United States pursues an ambitious global free-trade strategy through GATT negotiations. Meanwhile, it simultaneously pursues a regional strategy—the current version of the North American Free Trade Area idea—that contributes to the Balkanization of the world economy.

Worse still, U.S. negotiators have made little effort to shape the new international trading system in ways that benefit American interests. The United States is a high-wage, high-regulation economy, and it is not in our interest to change. High wages in American manufacturing are, of course, a benefit to those who receive them, but they have an economic value that extends throughout the American society. The high wages paid to American workers are the bedrock of the U.S. economy. Our high standards of health, safety, and environmental regulations—despite occasional regulations that may be poorly conceived or outmoded by economic change—are vital to the well-being of the American people and the land we live in. The basic economic and social interests of the overwhelming majority of the American people are linked to the preservation and even the extension of this type of economy—but U.S. trade negotiators have taken an opposite tack.

At both GATT and NAFTA they have failed to resist—and have sometimes even encouraged—the development of trade rules that undercut American interests. GATT does not, for example, require companies wishing to participate in international trade to observe the most minimal safety, health, and environmental standards. Under GATT, for example, no trade sanctions may be leveled against goods made with child labor. Countries that offer no old-age social insurance to their work forces, that crush unions, that fail to enforce any health and safety standards in the workplace compete on equal terms with more enlightened countries. Under the perverse logic of GATT, the willingness of a country to use child labor or to deny elderly workers any retirement benefits whatever becomes a "competitive advantage" that it is GATT's duty to protect. This system not only forces the United States to compete with low-wage, low-regulation producers but also actively undermines the health of the world economy by exerting downward pressure on world wages—and therefore on consumer demand, and therefore on economic growth. Workers in the United States whose jobs go overseas lose income; under GATT, workers in other countries earn lower wages than they would if international trade laws supported their basic human rights.

This system is leading the United States and the world into a pattern of deepening economic difficulties, and the new Administration must begin immediately to work for constructive change in the global arena in the following areas:

• *Human rights and trade.* Present U.S. policy on trade assumes that liberalization, understood as the dismantling of tariff and nontariff barriers to trade, is the chief and almost the only method available to increase the volume of world trade. Attempts to impose high standards regarding method of production will, U.S. negotiators believe, slow the growth of trade, and therefore of the economy, because such attempts involve the growth of nontariff barriers to international trade.

The new Administration should take a somewhat different line, and view the adoption of environmental and labor rights safeguards as instruments for *increasing* trade and for *stabilizing* the open international trading system. Countries that respect basic human rights are better diplomatic partners because their governments are more stable and their objectives more rational. Similarly, countries that honor the economic and political rights of their workers are better trading partners. They have a better distribution of income and so are better customers; and their competitiveness reflects real natural comparative advantage, not the artificial suppression of wages and the tolerance of unsafe or inhumane working conditions. An American President who speaks sincerely and straightforwardly about the importance of international worker rights in world trade will strike a chord in many countries, increase U.S. prestige around the world, and reshape the world trading system in ways that work better for the citizens of all countries.

• *A new round for GATT.* The first concrete challenge for the next Administration will be the disposition of the Uruguay Round of international trade talks held under the auspices of GATT. The difficult history of the Uruguay Round illustrates vividly the shortcomings of past approaches to trade policy. While pursuing an aggressive program of trade liberalization at GATT talks, the United States and other countries as well moved toward increasingly protectionist economic policies at home.

Depending on circumstances in January, the new Administration should either reopen the Uruguay Round or call for a new round of GATT talks to take up the issues of the nineties. The integration of the formerly Communist countries of Europe, the rapid industrialization of Asia, and the continuing tendency of the world economy to split into competitive blocs must be addressed through international negotiations. Continuing technological change and the failure of the Uruguay Round to deal adequately with the social and environmental aspects of trade mandate a new round.

In the new talks, the U.S. position must reflect a broader domestic coalition than it has in the past. Senators and representatives from both parties must be more intimately involved in the elaboration of the U.S. position. Consumer groups, environmentalists, human rights organizations, and labor unions must participate in the development of the U.S. position.

The new Administration should present a U.S. position that is more consonant with U.S. interests than the ideologically motivated stance of recent years. The United States in GATT must fight to defend the existence of the high-wage, high-regulation economies of the West. Countries that wish to participate fully in the world economy must be prepared to assume the obligations that such participation inevitably involves—although the United States will recognize its own responsibility to take steps to help developing countries harmonize their production standards upward. Ideally, the new U.S. position will offer much more sweeping access to U.S. markets for countries that harmonize up. The initiatives for global stimulus and substantially increased aid discussed above must be linked with the new trade initiative so that developing countries enjoy, on balance, equally favorable treatment under the new system.

• *A new approach to NAFTA.* A similar change in philosophy needs to be applied to the North American Free Trade Area. The integration of the U.S., Mexican, and Canadian economies can be made to work for all three countries, but in its present form the U.S. position in NAFTA is both too generous and too niggardly. It is too generous in the indiscriminate way it opens U.S. markets to competition from low-wage workers denied many of their basic human rights in what remains a corrupt one-party state in Mexico. Furthermore the United States places no pressure on the Mexican regime to democratize and to establish effective means of safeguarding the political and human rights of domestic critics. It is too niggardly in that it fails to provide Mexicans sufficient help in overcoming their domestic economic problems and their crushing burden of foreign debt.

A somewhat different policy mix is needed, one that borrows from the experience of the European Community in its approaches to countries such as Portugal, Italy, Spain, Turkey, and Greece. The EC was more forthcoming than the United States has been on questions such as aid, and was more demanding than the United States has been on questions such as democracy. The colonels in Greece and the one-party regimes in Portugal and Spain had to step down before EC membership was even possible.

The idea of NAFTA is too important for the three countries to rush into an ill-considered agreement. As the history of the European Community shows, economic integration takes time; it also takes a more thoughtful approach than the present text exhibits. The new Administration should continue NAFTA talks and press for a comprehensive agreement in the context of these concerns.

 • *Bilateral agreements.* The new Administration should announce a comprehensive review of all existing U.S. bilateral and regional trade agreements and concessions. Trade agreements must be better designed to promote genuine comparative advantages and to smooth the transition of developing countries to a higher wage system. While the mix of carrots and sticks will differ in some cases from existing arrangements, the new system should not on balance be more restrictive than the old. Countries that accept basic worker rights and wage protection will get increased freedom from limits on their trade—for example, through a liberalization of the MFA system that limits textile exports from developing countries. Loan guarantees, debt relief, and other incentives would also form part of a new system of bilateral trade agreements.

Conclusion

INTERNATIONAL ECONOMIC AND TRADE POLICY OFFERS the new Administration some of its most critical choices—and some of its greatest opportunities. The American people know that the policies of the past twelve years have not worked, and they are hungry for new approaches. A fresh start, a commitment to global growth, and a trade policy that serves American interests through a renewed commitment to human rights and fair play will put U.S. economic policy on a firmer foundation while responding to the electorate's mandate for change.

The President of the United States should make absolutely clear to the American people and to our economic partners in the rest of the world that a healthy, growing, high-wage, socially and environmentally responsible economic system—here and abroad—is the principal goal of American economic and trade policy. The Administration's position in international trade negotiations, in G-7 meetings, and in dealings with the formerly Communist countries of Eastern Europe should visibly support these key economic objectives. In this way, the Federal Government will enjoy the continued confidence of the American people while it builds an international constituency in support of these core American policy objectives.

HUMAN RIGHTS

HOLLY BURKHALTER AND ARYEH NEIER

Summary

T HE WORLD TODAY IS VASTLY DIFFERENT than it was when Ronald Reagan took office as president, yet many of the destructive and cynical policies from that era linger in the conduct of foreign affairs today. The end of the Cold War permits and requires a new approach to American foreign policy in which protection of human rights plays a preeminent role. For that to happen requires that the President and his appointees demonstrate a consistent commitment to human rights, which would include taking the following steps:

Revitalize and reinvigorate the State Department's Human Rights Bureau with the appointment of top diplomats who command the respect and the attention of the bureaucracy. Provide the bureau with expanded resources, and have it carry out a systematic review of U.S. human rights policies, with an eye toward enhanced compliance with U.S. human rights laws. Expand the appointment of human rights experts to the staff of the National Security Council, and create a credible and informed labor rights working group within the office of the U.S. trade representative in order to use the leverage of trade to advance human rights. Review and revamp foreign aid and trade programs so that aid to gross human rights abusers is curbed and democratic developments are rewarded. Develop human rights initiatives within the international community.

Holly Burkhalter is the Washington Director of Human Rights Watch. She is coauthor of With Friends Like These *(New York: Pantheon, 1985) and contributor to* The Human Rights Reader *(New York: New American Library, 1989). Aryeh Neier is Executive Director of Human Rights Watch and previously was the National Executive Director of the American Civil Liberties Union (1970–78). He has authored many books and articles, including* Only Judgment *(Middletown, Conn.: Wesleyan University Press, 1988).*

Appointing human rights leaders to key posts within the foreign-policy-making institutions and enhancing participation in international human rights initiatives is only part of a successful human rights policy. The President and his appointees can raise the profile of human rights everywhere by addressing abuses forcefully and publicly, distancing the United States from the abusers, and seeking ways to relieve the suffering of the victims of repression. Former president Jimmy Carter is still revered around the world for the attention he personally gave to the human rights cause.

The post-Cold War era has witnessed dramatic human rights gains, with the end of decades-long armed conflicts and the establishment of democracies where tyrannies once reigned. But this period has also witnessed some of the worst atrocities of the twentieth century, as in such cases as Somalia, Iraq, and Yugoslavia. The Bush administration has been capable of supporting human rights when other interests did not compete, but has failed to make human rights a major focus of U.S. foreign policy. After the gross politicization of human rights during the Reagan years and the neglect of the Bush era, the world needs a forceful and impartial human rights advocate in the White House.

Revitalizing the State Department's Human Rights Bureau

THE STATE DEPARTMENT'S HUMAN RIGHTS and Humanitarian Affairs Bureau was established in 1977 as a result of the efforts of an activist Congress determined to change the State Department's historically cozy relationship with abusive regimes that happened to be allies. The first assistant secretary of state for human rights, Patricia Derian, appointed by President Carter, set an unmistakable tone at the bureau. Derian identified with the victims of abuse, loathed those who abused them, and did everything in her power—diplomatically and sometimes not so diplomatically—to signal U.S. concern and stigmatize repressive regimes.

Derian and the Human Rights Bureau won some battles at State and lost others. But there was one thing that never occurred on her watch: The Human Rights Bureau was never a defender or an apologist for violative governments. That kind of "clientitis" certainly existed in the Carter administration, but it did not emanate from the one bureau whose sole function is to promote respect for human rights. Things changed when Elliott Abrams assumed the office in December 1981. Abrams immediately embroiled himself in the most significant foreign policy debate of the early 1980s by becoming the sturdiest proponent of U.S. aid to the Salvadoran military and the Nicaraguan contras. In so doing, he routinely defended atrocious military forces, misstated their human rights records, and slandered their victims. The Human Rights Bureau was transformed from being the in-house watchdog at the State Department and its public defender of victims, to being the cheerleader for the Reagan administration's worst excesses and an apologist for its favorite clients.

Richard Schifter succeeded Abrams as head of the Human Rights Bureau. During his seven-year tenure there, which ended in 1992, Schifter tended to play a nonadversarial role within the State Department. Though he did not publicize his grievances, it is widely understood that Schifter was disgusted with the Bush administration's coddling of China and, within the corridors of the State Department, was critical of this policy. He often spoke out publicly as well on human rights matters in China and elsewhere. Among the bureau's positive contributions during Schifter's tenure was its institution of a regular series of human rights training sessions for Foreign Service officers, where State Department critics were invited in to lecture. And the bureau has significantly upgraded reporting on human rights by the State Department, to the point that its annual volume, *Country Reports on Human Rights*, has become a highly useful resource in most—but not all—of the 173 countries and territories it covers.

Sometimes, however, Schifter squandered the bureau's moral capital by associating himself publicly with misguided policies or by failing to address desperate human rights problems publicly.[1] In one case—that of Israel—Schifter proved himself incapable of disinterested judgment on the government's record of abuses against Palestinians, and even went so far as to water down the country report on Israeli violations as submitted to his bureau by the U.S. staff in Jerusalem and Tel Aviv.[2] And human rights monitors were scandalized when, in December 1991, the Human Rights Bureau issued the preposterous—and dangerous—pronouncement that supporters of ousted Haitian president Jean-Bertrand Aristide did not face political persecution. The opinion was significant because it was used by asylum adjudicators of the Immigration and Naturalization Service in assessing Haitian claims to be fleeing political persecution.[3]

Though it is difficult for outsiders to judge its role within the State Department, the perception of the human rights community has been that the Human Rights Bureau is either not in the bureaucratic loop on some of the most important human rights questions of the day, or that its voice is not heeded. (Schifter is said to have resigned in April 1992 because he was tired of fighting losing battles.)

The weakness of the bureau may well be as much a reflection of the low priority placed by the Bush administration on human rights generally as it is on the quality of its leadership. But there are some occasions where the bureau has not appeared even to *want* to play an activist role. For example, in 1992 a number of human rights groups formally requested that the bureau seek to be represented at the U.S. trade representative's inter-agency working group on labor rights, which evaluates petitions filed under the Trade Act alleging violations of the rights of association and other labor rights.[4] Currently the State Department is represented at the working group by its Economics Bureau, whose officials appear neither to know about nor to care about labor rights and have proven themselves hostile to the very idea of linking rights issues with U.S. trade. Yet the Human Rights Bureau's response to appeals that it also be represented at the working group received an indifferent shrug, and apparently the matter was dropped.

The Human Rights Bureau's lack of interest in the U.S. trade repre-sentative's labor rights review process is troubling because it suggests that the bureau's leadership is either not interested in playing a policymaking role with respect to compliance with an important human rights law, or is unwilling to challenge the Economics Bureau's hegemony here. The bureau's failure to insist on representation in the USTR interagency group has had important (and undesirable) consequences for human rights. Without the expertise and advocacy that the Human Rights Bureau could bring to it, the working group is a little-noticed backwater with almost no expertise in the field of worker rights. And it has squandered a significant opportunity to exercise U.S. leverage through trade benefits.

At this point, the Human Rights Bureau requires a transfusion and an oxygen tent. Its most immediate need is for a President and a Secretary of State who care about human rights and intend to incorporate the issue into all aspects of U.S. foreign policy. This fresh approach would allow the bureau to start to play the role envisioned for it at its creation.

Evaluate Foreign Aid

THE FIRST THING THE NEW HUMAN RIGHTS BUREAU secretary should do is institute a high-level mechanism for evaluating U.S. foreign aid, U.S. votes on loans from the multilateral development banks, and other forms of U.S. assistance to regimes with poor human rights records. A body of human rights laws enacted since the mid-1970s formally prohibits military and economic aid (with the exception of humanitarian assistance) and licenses for the commercial sale of military equipment to regimes that engage in a consistent pattern of gross violations of internationally recognized human rights. U.S. human rights laws also instruct the American representatives to multilateral development institutions such as the World Bank to vote against loans to gross violators. Though these laws have failed to prevent aid to some of the worst abusers in the world, they remain the standard by which U.S. foreign assistance should be measured.

During President Carter's tenure, the Christopher Commission, chaired by Under Secretary of State Warren Christopher, played the role of evaluating the human rights records of foreign aid recipients. The commission included representatives of the State Department, Treasury Department, and Agriculture Department as well as other agencies involved in foreign assistance. It concentrated on those cases where foreign aid was controversial and evaluated the human rights performance of the proposed recipient and the implications of the aid. The Christopher Commission was by no means successful in ending all aid to gross violators of human rights, which it should have done to comply with U.S. human rights laws. But it did provide a high-level forum for resolving differences between the Human Rights Bureau and other State Department fiefdoms, and the results were frequently good.

The Human Rights Bureau may have been consulted within the State Department bureaucracy during the Reagan and Bush presidencies on questions of foreign aid to governments with poor records, but it is hard to know what effect those consultations had over the years. During the 1980s the United States supplied abundant quantities of military and economic assistance to many governments with terrible human rights records, including such African disasters as Chad, Kenya, Sudan, Somalia, Zaire, Liberia, and the vicious Angolan rebel group, UNITA.[5] In Latin America, the top aid recipient of the 1980s, of course, was the government of El Salvador, which managed to murder some fifty thousand of its own noncombatants in a decade. Given such a record, it is hard to imagine that the bureau's advice—if solicited—was heeded. An alternative possibility—that the bureau might have agreed with such foreign aid decisions—is even worse to consider.

A New Commission

A NEW COMMISSION LIKE THE CHRISTOPHER COMMISSION could enhance the role of the Human Rights Bureau and promote human rights generally if it were to issue a public human rights certification for all aid recipients. Once that report was made public, it would be possible for nongovernmental human rights groups to join in the process by evaluating the report and criticizing or concurring. Members of Congress would be interested as well, and the entire process would be an ideal way to breathe life into human rights laws that are now largely ignored.

The public reporting process alone would make an enormous contribution to human rights by embarrassing abusive regimes and making it more difficult for assistance to be given over the objection of the Human Rights Bureau or human rights advocates outside of government. If the Administration should decide to go forward with a controversial sale or aid program to a government engaged in abuses, it should be prepared to defend its choice and at the same time describe actions to be taken to raise human rights concerns forcefully and publicly.[6]

More openness generally in the conduct of foreign policy can be very helpful to the human rights cause. With respect to arms sales, for example, current law requires congressional notification only if the contract is larger than $14 million in "major defense equipment" or $50 million in defense articles or services. This level is so high that Congress is seldom informed on anything but the biggest-ticket items (such as sophisticated aircraft). Most weapons sales to repressive regimes are never reported. Similarly, congressional monitoring of nonmunitions sales to police forces is virtually nonexistent because there is no requirement in law that such sales be reported. Thus the United States sells quantities of equipment to repressive police forces, but they generate no controversy because these sales are generally not known.

Congressional involvement in monitoring arms sales may be irksome to the executive branch, but it offers the human rights community the opportunity to hold up the human rights record of the proposed recipient for scrutiny. If the sale cannot stand the light of day from a human rights perspective, it should not go forward.[7]

The spreading "Iraqgate" scandal, wherein the Reagan and Bush administrations supplied one of the most vicious regimes on earth—which engaged in genocidal practices against its Kurdish minority—with billions of dollars in Export-Import Bank and agricultural commodity credits suggests that these forms of assistance should also be subjected to formal human rights review and certification. Though there are no human rights prohibitions in U.S. law on commodity credits or Export-Import Bank credits, these credits should nonetheless be reviewed. It is hard to imagine that President Bush would have felt as free to funnel aid to Saddam Hussein as late as 1989 if he had been forced to face the kind of public uproar that would have ensued when an interagency human rights review panel had issued its findings on Iraqi practices.

Human Rights Bureau participation in foreign policy decisions should not be limited to foreign aid, sales, and other benefits. Much of human rights policy is nonmaterial: It consists of representations by our ambassadors and their staffs in the field; it is in the public utterances of the President and his spokespeople at the White House and the State Department; it is manifest in the foreign visitors received at the White House, and the things said and unsaid when U.S. officials visit foreign capitals.

Perhaps the most glaring example of an atrocious public signal from the Bush administration was the December 1989 visit to Beijing by National Security chief Brent Scowcroft and Deputy Secretary of State Lawrence Eagleburger. With the blood barely dry on Tiananmen Square, Scowcroft, a former general, toasted the Chinese leadership with these words as television cameras rolled: "We extend our hand in friendship and hope you will do the same." He then went on to say, in a callous slap at the Chinese democracy movement: "In both our societies there are voices of those who seek to redirect or frustrate our cooperation. We both must take bold measures to overcome these negative forces." In view of the fact that much of the Chinese democracy movement had been killed, jailed, or driven underground, one wonders what further "bold measures" against them Scowcroft was proposing.

Clearly, symbolic acts have enormous significance for human rights policy. A toast like Scowcroft's sets back the cause of human rights. (Indeed, the political import of the general's remarks eclipsed the impact of the economic sanctions that President Bush had invoked against China after Tiananmen Square, and undid the best efforts of those in Congress seeking to isolate and stigmatize the Chinese leadership.) On the other hand, positive symbolic actions can do a great deal to promote the cause of human rights around the world. When an ambassador such as Smith Hempstone, the Bush administration's envoy to Kenya, denounces human rights abuses and makes common cause with Kenyan democrats and human rights advocates, it makes an incomparable contribution to the human rights cause.

The Human Rights Bureau can and must be involved in diplomatic strategy at every level of the foreign policy process. The bureau must be consulted about public speeches on foreign policy matters at home and abroad, and must be included and heeded in devising a human rights focus for foreign visits, summit meetings, U.N. matters, and trade rounds. Its reports should be the basis for making decisions about foreign aid and other benefits, as noted above, and its representatives should be included in overseas missions.

At this time, the Human Rights Bureau cannot play such a role because of the low priority the Bush administration has placed on human rights generally and because it does not have the resources that the role demands. Regular attention to human rights matters and regular consultation with the

Human Rights Bureau's secretary by the President and the Secretary of State would go far to raise the stature of the bureau. But significant resources—including additional staff—are required if the bureau is to play a watchdog role within the bureaucracy, visit the scenes of grave abuses abroad on a regular basis, upgrade training in the field for human rights reporting officers in our overseas embassies, and organize cooperative human rights efforts with our closest allies. (It should be noted that the cost would be trivial in comparison with the sums now misspent on aid to abusive governments; such aid should be terminated unless carefully earmarked for basic human needs.)

Currently, the Human Rights Bureau only has one staff member per region. Its budget is so low that its regional officers seldom even visit the countries they are expected to cover. As an indication of the new role envisioned for the bureau, the new Secretary of State should immediately enhance the bureau's budget, and give it the status that would attract the best talent in the Foreign Service to serving there.

The Human Rights Bureau has an essential but awkward role to play. It must be the watchdog and in-house critic of U.S. policy. Others within the foreign policy bureaucracy will deal with competing concerns, but the Human Rights Bureau must be the internal advocate of human rights concerns above all others. The bureau can also play an important public role by speaking out about abuses and defending victims. It can only play its proper role and attract seasoned and respected diplomats to its ranks if working for the Human Rights Bureau is perceived to be career-enhancing as well as a signal honor. The only way for the bureau to achieve that high stature within the bureaucracy is for it to be abundantly clear that the President and the Secretary of State energetically back the bureau and the values embodied in the laws establishing the bureau.

NOTES

1. For example, at an important congressional hearing in September 1991, Schifter testified in favor of a U.S. antinarcotics military aid package for Peru. He strongly defended the government's human rights record and minimized human rights problems. In February of the same year, Schifter publicly congratulated the Indian government for its respect for human rights when in fact that government's human rights record is abysmal.

2. At congressional hearings in May 1990, Schifter would not even publicly repeat the criticisms of Israeli abuses that were included in the State Department's country reports on human rights. It was not until he encountered intense questioning from committee members that he reluctantly uttered a word of criticism.

3. In the months leading up to the Human Rights Bureau's opinion that no one was persecuted because of his or her support for Aristide, over a thousand Haitians— many of them supporters of Aristide—had been killed by the armed forces and their paramilitary allies, and hundreds jailed and tortured. Virtually every popular group in Haiti had been destroyed or driven underground, their leaders and supporters arrested or terrified into silence.

4. The labor rights petitions are filed pursuant to Section 502(b)(8) of the Trade Act, which links Third World governments' trade benefits under the Generalized System of Preferences with their performance on labor rights.

5. In his 1991 book *Free at Last?: U.S. Policy Toward Africa and the End of the Cold War* (New York: Council on Foreign Relations), Michael Clough notes that until 1989 the top five foreign aid recipients in sub-Saharan Africa were dictatorial regimes in Sudan, Somalia, Zaire, Liberia, and Kenya. Of the five, Liberia's Doe, Sudan's Nimeiry (and later Sadiq), and Somalia's Siad Barre have departed the scene altogether, leaving chaos, death, and mass starvation in their wake; Zaire's Mobutu and Kenya's Moi are barely hanging on to power as their societies collapse around them.

6. Indeed, human rights law already requires that the Executive Branch report to Congress if it decides to waive human rights considerations on national security grounds. Section 502B(A)(2) of the Foreign Assistance Act states that the human rights limits may be waived only if "the President certifies in writing [to the Congress] . . . that extraordinary circumstances exist warranting provision of such assistance and issuance of such licenses." To our knowledge, the provision has never been invoked, and there has never been a public report indicating the national security considerations that justified a waiver of human rights standards and the provision of aid or commercial sales to violative regimes.

7. A proposal for reviewing commercial arms sales on human rights grounds was made by the Lawyers' Committee for Human Rights in their 1992 publication *Human Rights and U.S. Foreign Policy*.

Department of State

THE UNITED NATIONS

ENID C. B. SCHOETTLE

Summary

THE NATIONS AND PEOPLES OF THE UNITED Nations are fortunate in a way that those of the League of Nations were not," said U.N. Secretary-General Boutros-Ghali in his report "An Agenda for Peace."[1] "We have been given a second chance to create the world of our Charter that they were denied."

With the end of the Cold War, the United Nations can begin to serve as a vital element in a new world order. Indeed, if such an order has any meaning, it must build on the world's only universal political organization. Whether this "second chance" for the United Nations can succeed, however, depends mainly on the United States. As the sole remaining superpower and the predominant country among the five permanent members of the Security Council, constructive American leadership is necessary if the United Nations is to achieve its promise while serving U.S. interests. To state this is not chauvinism or "unipolar" hubris. For the time being, other countries cannot—and in any event will not—take the lead in furthering peace, security, human rights, democracy, social progress, and economic development around the world without the active participation of the United States. Equally important, America also stands to benefit hugely if these goals are successfully pursued. The United States, therefore, has a responsibility to the American people and, indirectly, to the rest of the world for the success of the United Nations.

Among twenty concrete steps to strengthen the United Nations, the new Administration should:

Enid C. B. Schoettle is Director of the Project on International Organizations and Law and Senior Fellow, Council on Foreign Relations. She has published, among other works, Postures for Non-Proliferation: Long-Term Arms Limitation and Security Requirements for Minimizing the Proliferation of Nuclear Weapons *(1979).*

- Ask Congress to treat U.N. peacekeeping costs as a national defense cost, shifting budget authority and funding for some portion of U.S. peace-keeping contributions from the Department of State budget to the Defense budget while leaving policy oversight in the Department of State.
- Link, wherever possible, U.S. arms control and disarmament policies more closely to the U.N. Security Council, and give maximum support to the U.N. Special Commission's ongoing efforts to disarm Iraq.
- Persuade Congress to meet U.S. financial obligations to the United Nations through full and prompt payment of current assessments and the immediate repayment of all arrearages.
- To put the United States in the front rank of human rights observance, sign and submit to the Senate for ratification the International Covenants on Economic and Cultural Rights and the Elimination of all Forms of Racial Discrimination, and the Conventions on the Elimination of Discrimination Against Women and the Rights of the Child.
- Work to establish an International Criminal Court, where individuals accused of international crimes such as terrorism, international narcotics trafficking, hijacking, crimes against humanity, war crimes, and attacks on international civil servants and peacekeepers could be tried.
- Use the fiftieth anniversary of the United Nations in 1995 as the target date for these reforms.

History of U.S. Policy Toward the United Nations

TWICE IN THIS CENTURY—in 1919 and 1945—the United States led the world in drawing lessons from horrific global wars. The chosen alternative in each case was a universal organization to maintain the peace. In 1918, while World War I still raged, President Wilson began to design an international organization built on the principles of internationalism, the rule of law, and collective security. The Senate's rejection of the Versailles Treaty and the Covenant of the League of Nations—reflecting long-standing tenets of isolationism and unilateralism in American foreign policy—contributed substantially to the subsequent failure of the League of Nations, since other states would not act while America remained outside the international system.

From the outset of World War II, President Roosevelt was determined to design a postwar security system that could prevent repetition of the mistakes of the interwar period. The attack on Pearl Harbor had transformed U.S. isolationism into widespread support for "an international order. . . that would never again tolerate aggression from which the Americans would have to rescue Europe."[2] In 1942, the Advisory Committee on Postwar Foreign Policy was created. Soon an international agency—"the United Nations authority"—was envisioned through which states would jointly agree to keep the peace and, if necessary, enforce it by sanctions and force of arms. Unlike in 1919–20, this departure from traditional American foreign policy was supported not only by Democrats but also by important Republicans—above all, Senator Arthur Vandenberg. By the end of the war, the United Nations, the Bretton Woods institutions, the International Court of Justice, and several U.N. specialized agencies had already been designed.

The United Nations is in no way a world government. Rather, it is an intergovernmental organization of sovereign states whose success "depends on the common ground that they create between them" to cooperate in their longer-term self-interests.[3] The U.N. Charter—written by senior statesmen schooled in two world wars and a disastrously flawed interwar peace—is a visionary but practical document, designed to address the broad causes of war as well as to manage the peace. It sets forth revolutionary objectives:

- Maintenance of international peace and security through the peaceful resolution of disputes, the rule of law, sanctions, and, finally, joint military action to suppress aggression or other threats to the peace.
- Decolonization of colonial peoples, based on equal rights and self-determination.
- Economic development, including social, cultural, and humanitarian development.
- Promotion of human rights and fundamental freedoms without distinction as to race, sex, language, or religion.
- Harmonizing the actions of nations to attain the above objectives and develop common approaches to global issues such as drugs and the environment.

The United Nations was designed for continued postwar cooperation among the wartime allies but was soon engulfed by the Cold War. Thus, with the accidental exception of the Korean War, the United Nations was unable to address the core differences between East and West and became a forum in which the two sides struggled over a wide array of security, political, and economic issues.

Even during the Cold War, however, the United Nations was effective in several ways. In the field of international peace and security, it helped the superpowers avoid direct confrontation in potentially explosive areas. It invented the concepts of unarmed military observation missions and lightly armed peacekeeping forces under the command of the U.N. secretary-general. These were interposed between conflicting parties as a third-party presence to observe cease-fires, contain conflicts, and maintain a local peace. In Jerusalem and Kashmir in the 1940s; in the Sinai in the 1950s; in the Congo and Cyprus in the 1960s; in the Sinai, on the Golan Heights, and in Lebanon in the 1970s, the United Nations mounted indispensable operations that averted escalation into East-West conflict. But the Cold War placed sharp limits on what U.N. peacekeeping could do: Unless the superpowers concurred, their rivalries remained off-limits for the Security Council.

The United Nations also effectively managed the process of decolonization. As testimony to the world's commitment to self-determination of colonial peoples, it grew from 51 founding members in 1945, to 100 members in 1960, 127 members in 1970, and 154 members in 1980. This effort had the strong support of the United States, often against the interests of close European allies.

Having achieved independence, however, these new countries—mostly poor and nonwhite—sought alternatives to Western economic, social, and political arrangements. With their growing majority in the General Assembly, they pressed for institutions and programs to serve their special interests, such as the United Nations Industrial Development Organization (UNIDO), the Center on Transnational Corporations (CTC), the New International Economic Order (NIEO), and the New International Information Order (NIIO). These initiatives were often supported by the Soviet Union, China, and their allies, thus adding North/South divisions to the East/West confrontation within the United Nations.

By the 1970s, the United States had become widely skeptical of the capacity of the United Nations to serve U.S. foreign policy interests. As one indicator of its increasing isolation within the organization, the United States cast its first veto in the Security Council only in 1970. By 1990 the United States had cast 69 vetoes, second only to the Soviet Union. By contrast, of the Soviet Union's 114 vetoes, only 11 were cast after 1970, reflecting the shift away from U.S. and Western dominance within the United Nations.

In addition to these limits on U.N. effectiveness, competing U.S. approaches to foreign policy undercut multilateralism as an organizing principle. Traditional isolationism, unilateral interventionism, and selective engagement with like-minded states, such as NATO, the G-7, or close clients in the developing world, each had its proponents as the foreign policy most likely to serve American national interests. All three approaches avoid the requisites of multilateralism: action in conformity with universal standards and respect for international law. Often multilateralism entails action through the United Nations or appropriate regional organizations. However, even if at a particular juncture unilateralism or selective engagement is deemed necessary and preferable to working through the United Nations, multilateralism suggests acting "inside the Charter," to use Senator Vandenberg's useful distinction. In short, multilateralism requires a commitment to respect international norms and to take consistent actions across a wide spectrum of political, economic, social, and security issues not necessarily limited to specific current interests of the United States. For many Americans, these requirements have seemed onerous and uncompelling.

Moreover, various aspects of American domestic politics also undercut the U.S. commitment to multilateralism. First, by the 1970s, overt racism in American politics had been largely discredited. At the same time, the U.N. General Assembly was largely non-European. As the U.N. Secretariat grew, it also reflected a geographic distribution among an increasingly diverse membership. Thus the United Nations became an easy target for those Americans tempted to displace their racist views onto new objects. Often disguised as criticism of "bloated bureaucracies" and "preening diplomats" drawing huge salaries, the undercurrent of racial disparagement was obvious, rendering motivations suspect.

Second, the growth of single-issue constituencies in American politics has had a particularly negative impact on the United Nations, which requires support across a wide range of issues. For example, increasingly bitter domestic controversies over family planning, abortion, and population policy led the Reagan and Bush administrations to withhold all funds from the U.N. Population Fund (UNFPA), which the United States itself had helped found in 1967. This reversal was based on the allegation that UNFPA "comanaged" China's population program, which, in turn, but without any UNFPA funds, utilized coercive abortion and sterilization.[4] As another example, those in American politics particularly sympathetic to Israel have not only opposed actions in the United Nations hostile to Israel—such as challenges to Israel's credentials and the egregious 1975 General Assembly resolution condemning "Zionism as racism"—but have also attacked the United Nations as a whole. Enjoying a powerful presence in crucial congressional committees dealing with the United Nations, these forces over time have played a significant role in minimizing overall support for the United Nations in the Congress, the media, and the public at large. The welcome rescinding of the "Zionism as racism" resolution in 1991 has not yet had a noticeable impact on this sector of opinion.

Recent Legacy: U.S. Policy Toward the United Nations, 1981–92

IN NO AREA OF RECENT PUBLIC POLICY are there such sharp swings as in U.S. policy toward the United Nations. The period began with a Reagan-appointed ambassador commenting sarcastically that the United Nations was free to leave New York if it felt mistreated and gleefully offering to ". . . be at dockside bidding [the United Nations] a farewell as it set[s] off into the sunset."[5] It ended with the U.N.-authorized victory in the war against Iraq and a ringing call from President Bush at the United Nations for a ". . . new partnership of nations . . . based on consultation, cooperation, and collective action, especially through international and regional organizations. . . ."[6] These twelve years of U.S. policy toward the United Nations have left a confused legacy.

In 1981, Cold War disillusionment, endemic North-South disputes, and the marked absence of domestic political support for the United Nations provided fertile ground for the administration's posture toward the organization. The Reagan administration seemed to assume that the United Nations could do nothing to advance American foreign policy interests: the United Nations was at best a nuisance and at worst a menace, threatening the United States and Israel with hostile rhetoric and repugnant ideas. Jeane J. Kirkpatrick, the U.S. permanent representative to the United Nations, conducted the administration's policy of verbal counterattack. In Washington, the International Organization Bureau in the Department of State was led by some of the administration's most zealous Cold Warriors and United Nations-bashers.

In the early 1980s, the administration thus disrupted U.N. activities wherever the United States had leverage: rejecting the laboriously negotiated Law of the Sea Convention; withdrawing from UNESCO; postponing in 1981 the payment of U.S. assessments to the United Nations by one year, thus putting the United States permanently in arrears and the United Nations permanently in financial straits; and, in 1984, withdrawing from the compulsory jurisdiction of the International Court of Justice. By 1984–85, U.S. policy toward the United Nations was unrelievedly hostile. Echoing the administration's rhetoric and practice, Mayor Edward I. Koch of New York City, a Democrat, was emboldened to call the United Nations a "cesspool." Public support for the United Nations hit a forty-year low.[7]

In 1985, with administration support, Congress passed the Kassebaum Amendment, which required a unilateral cut of 20 percent in U.S. assessments for the United Nations' regular budget and for the specialized agencies until some kind of weighted voting on budgets was instituted. Subsequent revisions of the Kassebaum Amendment imposed further requirements on the United Nations: 15 percent reductions in U.N. Secretariat staff; reduced secondment of nationals from any member state to the Secretariat; and implementation of consensus-based budgeting.[8] These withholdings contravened the fact that full payment of assessments is obligatory under international law, and sent shock waves through the U.N. system.

Some positive reforms indeed were carried out. Agencies where real abuse was extant were reined in and reformed. Developing countries recognized that their ideological rhetoric had lost credibility with donor countries and had failed to elicit much-needed help. Thus they began to adopt more pragmatic policies and agreed to U.N. reform. In 1985–86, the General Assembly established the high-level "Group of 18," which worked with the Secretariat to institute budget ceilings, program priorities, and consensus-based budgeting.[9] Beginning in 1985, the new U.S. permanent representative to the United Nations, Vernon A. Walters, began moving the administration toward a more cooperative, less confrontational policy.

This incipient change in U.S. policy received an indispensable boost after 1985 from Mikhail Gorbachev's dramatic changes in Soviet foreign policy. "New thinking" made it possible for the superpowers to work through the U.N. Security Council to resolve outstanding regional conflicts that had long been sustained by Cold War rivalries. The July 1987 resolution demanding a cease-fire in the Iran-Iraq War was the turning point: For the first time in history, the five permanent members of the Security Council worked together to coauthor a resolution.[10] This action was followed by a succession of Security Council decisions addressing other long-standing conflicts: the withdrawal of Soviet troops from Afghanistan in 1988;[11] the cease-fire and transition to independence in Namibia, with the accompanying withdrawal of Cuban troops from Angola in 1988;[12] and the cease-fire and military demobilization in Nicaragua in 1989.[13]

With the collapse of communism in East/Central Europe and in the Soviet Union, the Security Council accelerated its work on disputes left over from the Cold War. It authorized peacekeeping operations in the Western Sahara;[14] in El Salvador;[15] in Angola;[16] and in Cambodia.[17] Most dramatically, the Security Council authorized enforcement action by the United States-led coalition against Iraq in 1990–91, and imposed intrusive conditions on Iraq at the termination of hostilities.[18]

Freed of Cold War shackles, the United Nations has begun to play the central role it was designed to play in international politics. Yet despite the new opportunities to pursue American objectives through the United Nations, the administration has not fully exploited them. Indeed, despite ringing speeches by President Bush at the United Nations, and strong declarations by G-7 summits pledging support for the United Nations, U.S. policy has lagged far behind the rhetoric.

This gap is most apparent with regard to U.N. financing. As of December 31, 1988, America's debt had mounted to $308 million for the regular budget and $95 million for various peacekeeping forces, totaling 54 percent of all arrears owed the United Nations. That year, President Reagan pledged to resume essentially full funding of U.S. assessments. President Bush pledged in 1989 to repay U.S. arrearages over a five-year period. Despite these commitments, Congress continues to appropriate less than the full amounts of current assessments, and as of August 1992 has appropriated only two installments of arrearages. In 1992 the administration has pressed hard for payment of U.S. peacekeeping assessments of the large new peacekeeping forces in Cambodia, what was Yugoslavia, and El Salvador, and Congress has appropriated most of these assessments. With this exception, however, the administration has not fought for full, prompt payment of America's financial obligations to the United Nations. As of July 15, 1992, the United States owed $555 million for the regular budget and $202 million for peacekeeping, or 43 percent of all arrears owed the United Nations, only slightly lower than in 1988. As a result, the financial crisis confronting the United Nations remains as bad as it has ever been.[19]

Moreover, ever since the one-year "slippage" in paying U.N. assessments in 1981, the United States has routinely paid its annual 25 percent assessment to the United Nations' regular budget *after* the subsequent U.S. fiscal year begins in October, rather than in January, when U.N. payments fall due. This "technical problem" keeps the United Nations in a financial choke collar for at least three quarters of every year, since the United Nations is explicitly forbidden to borrow to cover these United States-caused deficits. In addition, since the early 1980s, the United States has increasingly micro-managed U.N. financial and administrative arrangements, withholding funds for particular U.N. activities it does not like and using its delayed and reduced payments to force U.N. compliance.

To escape the growing financial crisis, in November 1991 former secretary-general Javier Pérez de Cuéllar suggested several businesslike ways to reform the United Nations' hand-to-mouth finances. These included: (1) charging interest on all U.N. assessments unpaid for over sixty days; (2) increasing the United Nations' working capital fund; (3) granting the secretary-general authority to borrow commercially; (4) establishing a $50 million peacekeeping reserve fund to meet start-up expenses and deploy forces quickly; and (5) eventually establishing a U.N. peace endowment fund to enable the secretary-general to cover the costs of unanticipated peacemaking efforts and the start-up expenses of peacekeeping operations.[20] Except for the $50 million peacekeeping reserve fund, the United States has criticized all these proposals.

In addition to the continuing financial crisis, since 1989 the Bush administration has advocated *zero real growth* in the U.N. regular budget and the budgets of the U.N. specialized agencies. This has meant that any new U.N. initiative must be financed by reductions in other ongoing activities throughout the U.N. system. Only new peacekeeping operations—by definition, emergency and thus unpredictable actions—are exempt. While all major donor countries are committed to cost-effective U.N. budgeting, the constraint imposed by zero real growth inevitably suppresses U.N. initiatives at a time when the world is demanding them.

Perhaps the most glaring omission in the administration's policy toward the United Nations has been its lack of serious post-Cold War planning for utilizing the United Nations in the new world order. In stark contrast to Presidents Wilson and Franklin D. Roosevelt—who, during wartime, undertook comprehensive planning for the new international organizations that the peace would require—President Bush has conducted an ad hoc, reactive foreign policy at the end of the Cold War. Even his transitory label for the new era—"the new world order"—was an accidental *bon mot* rather than a summary worldview, such as Wilson's Fourteen Points or Roosevelt's Four Freedoms.[21] This lack of conceptual thought and institution-building at a time of revolutionary change has left the United States open to the charge that, as the sole remaining superpower, it reserves the right to do anything it wants in foreign policy. This lack of serious commitment to multilateral organizations is doubly unfortunate, since the United Nations as an institution is now more popular in the United States than at any point in the past forty years.[22]

Initiatives for Practical Multilateralism

THE TIME IS AT HAND TO ORGANIZE U.S. FOREIGN POLICY along more practical, multilateral lines through the United Nations, regional organizations to which the United States belongs, and international law. Despite the fact that strengthened international institutions could in specific cases limit our freedom of action, their long-term benefits outweigh their costs.

Why should the United States rely more on multilateral organizations, mainly the United Nations? First, the United Nations reflects the world as it is. With 179 members, the United Nations is the planet's universal political organization and includes all of the newly recognized independent states of East/Central Europe and the former Soviet Union as well as most of the world's small states and microstates.[23] The major regional organizations are also tending toward regionwide scope.

An obvious advantage of the United Nations is that, by definition, it serves as a viable forum for *all* countries potentially party to any controversial issue. For example, through the United Nations, Iran—valued by Armenia and Azerbaijan as a potential mediator—can cooperate actively with the CSCE on Nagorno-Karabakh, despite the fact that Iran is not a member of the CSCE. Many other warring parties have taken advantage of the United Nations' universal umbrella.

A second advantage is that at a time of constrained public budgets and huge federal deficits, the United Nations and the regional organizations to which the United States belongs offer automatic burden-sharing mechanisms. Thus America need not pay all the costs of important policy objectives. Since 1972 the United States has been assessed 25 percent of the United Nations' regular budget, which is calculated as being roughly equivalent to the U.S. share of the global national product, corrected for population.[24] Since 1973 the United States has been assessed 30.4 percent of the costs of U.N. peacekeeping operations, reflecting the special Charter obligations of permanent members of the Security Council to maintain international peace and security and the privilege of the veto. Thus the rest of the world is obligated to pay 69.6 percent or 75 percent of the United Nations' peacekeeping and regular budgets, respectively. At a time when the United States does not feel financially able to undertake major unilateral initiatives, and given the difficulties of negotiating contributions from others ad hoc, as we did in "Desert Storm," prenegotiated burden-sharing arrangements are attractive.

A third advantage is that America clearly benefits from maintaining an international environment of stability and orderly change. The United Nations is a universal forum in which, by discussion and broad exchanges of views, international norms are articulated and over time accepted by most U.N. members. Broad conformity with such international norms serves as a stabilizing factor in promoting world order.

Finally, as the U.N. Charter astutely foresaw, peace and security can be maintained only if justice and human rights, economic and social development, cultural pluralism, humanitarian cooperation, and the rule of law are respected and furthered. Conversely, poverty, massive deprivation of human rights, refugee flows, and environmental disasters endanger peace and security. With its broad and inclusive policy agenda, the United Nations permits bargaining across issue areas, accommodates states with varying interests and priorities, and, in this most general sense, promotes world peace.

Initiatives for the New Administration

WHAT SHOULD THE NEXT PRESIDENT DO in his first hundred days and throughout his term to strengthen U.S. policies toward the United Nations and other multilateral arrangements?

PEACE AND SECURITY

1. Endorse Secretary-General Boutros-Ghali's report "An Agenda for Peace" on strengthening the United Nations' capacity for preventive diplomacy, peacemaking, and peacekeeping.

2. Announce "peacetime collective engagement" as a major national security mission of the United States.

Specifically, the President should:

- Establish high-level functional units in the Department of Defense to promote U.S. participation in U.N. peacekeeping, humanitarian assistance, and disaster relief operations.
- Authorize more U.S. military planning billets at the United Nations, and assist the United Nations in other ways to make peacekeeping capabilities more standardized and compatible.
- Identify standby U.S. forces for U.N. military observation and peacekeeping operations. The United States should typically provide intelligence, airlift, sealift, logistics, communications, engineering, and motorized capabilities, all U.S. comparative advantages.
- Reverse the long-standing practice that the United States does not contribute peacekeeping units to U.N. operations.

3. Ask Congress to treat U.N. peacekeeping costs as a national defense cost, shifting budget authority and funding for some portion of U.S. peacekeeping contributions from the Department of State budget to the Department of Defense budget, while leaving policy oversight in the Department of State.

4. Order an urgent, high-level study of the enforcement missions proposed in "An Agenda for Peace." The President should remind domestic critics that since the United States has a veto in the Security Council, U.N. forces could never be used against U.S. interests.

5. Link U.S. arms control and disarmament policies more closely to the U.N. Security Council, and continue to give maximum support to the U.N. Special Commission's ongoing efforts to disarm Iraq.

6. Announce a return to the bipartisan policy that prevailed from 1946 to 1984, and accept, with suitably modified reservations, the compulsory

jurisdiction of the International Court of Justice (ICJ) and pledge to make fuller use of the ICJ in international dispute resolution.

FINANCING

1. Promise to meet U.S. financial obligations to the United Nations and other international organizations through full and prompt payment of current assessments and the immediate repayment of all arrearages. The President should then announce that the United States will keep current, stressing that these assessments are international legal obligations, not discretionary domestic political choices.

2. Announce that the fiscal year 1994 budget will include payments to international organizations in the fiscal year in which they fall due, as was U.S. practice prior to 1981.

3. Pledge U.S. support for various reforms in U.N. financing, including:
- Charging interest on all U.N. assessments unpaid for over sixty days.
- Increasing the United Nations' working capital fund.
- Granting the secretary-general authority to borrow commercially.
- Establishing immediately a standby peacekeeping reserve fund and establishing by 1995 a U.N. peace endowment fund to cover the costs of unanticipated peacemaking efforts and the start-up costs of peace-keeping operations.
- Exploring nontraditional ways to raise funds for the United Nations, such as levying taxes on arms sales and international air travel, or borrowing from the World Bank and the International Monetary Fund.

HUMAN RIGHTS AND DEMOCRATIZATION

1. Strengthen U.N. capabilities in the fields of human and minority rights and democratization. Specifically, the new President should call for the following:
- Reform the U.N. Trusteeship Council, which has virtually completed its work, into the Council for Human and Minority Rights. Its job would be to represent the interests of nonsovereign religious, ethnic, and national minorities, and indigenous peoples.
- Strengthen the Center for Human Rights, the U.N. Human Rights Commission, and the Electoral Assistance Unit.

2. Give maximum support to the 1993 World Conference on Human Rights.

3. To put the United States in the front rank of human rights observance, he should sign and submit to the Senate for ratification the International Covenants on Economic and Cultural Rights and the Elimination of all Forms of Racial Discrimination, and the Conventions on the Elimination of Discrimination Against Women and the Rights of the Child.

4. Work to establish an International Criminal Court, where individuals accused of international crimes such as terrorism, international narcotics trafficking, hijacking, crimes against humanity, war crimes, and attacks on international civil servants and peacekeepers could be tried.

ECONOMIC AND SOCIAL ISSUES

1. Utilize the multilateral economic agencies of the U.N. system—the U.N. Development Program, the regional economic commissions, the Bretton Woods institutions, etc.—to promote growth-oriented economic development. Together with other donor governments, the United States should further reform the economic and social programs of the United Nations to make them as efficient as possible, and then provide them additional funding so that world poverty can be reduced.

2. Use the U.N. Conference on Environment and Development as a basis for further international action, from adding national targets/timetables to the Framework Convention on Climate Change to providing the best possible representation in the new U.N. Commission on Sustainable Development.

3. Increase support for coordinated U.N. efforts in humanitarian assistance, including assistance to refugees and other displaced persons. Since the U.S. military has the greatest capability to act quickly in such global emergencies, humanitarian assistance and disaster relief should be important parts of the Defense Department's mission of "peacetime collective engagement."

4. Link U.S. domestic drug control programs more closely to the U.N. International Drug Control Program, and shift a fraction of current federal spending on domestic drug programs to this multilateral effort.

5. Resume full U.S. contributions to the U.N. Population Fund, first withheld by the Reagan administration in 1985.

U.S. GOVERNMENT DECISIONMAKING

1. Upgrade the status of international organizations and multilateral diplomacy in the Department of State and the U.S. Foreign Service by:

- Designating a senior official to oversee U.N. and other international organizations affairs in the Department of State, and integrating multilateral policy more closely with individual regional and functional bureaus.
- Appointing a distinguished ambassador to the United Nations—either a respected political figure like an Adlai Stevenson or a Henry Cabot Lodge, or the best senior ambassador from the U.S. Foreign Service.

2. Use the fiftieth anniversary of the United Nations in 1995 as the target date for these reforms.

NOTES

1. General Assembly/Security Council Document A/47/277 (S/24111), "An Agenda for Peace: Preventive Diplomacy, Peacemaking, and Peacekeeping: Report of the Secretary-General" (June 17, 1992), p. 22, para. 75–76.

2. L. Bloomfield, "Collective Security and U.S. Interests," paper at Brown University (May 14–15, 1992), pp. 10–11.

3. See "An Agenda for Peace," p. 1.

4. See J. Tessitore and S. Wolfson, eds., *A Global Agenda: Issues Before the 46th General Assembly of the United Nations* (Lanham, Md.: University Press of America, 1991), p. 141.

5. See *The New York Times* (September 20, 1983), p. A1.

6. Statement by President Bush to the U.N. General Assembly (October 1, 1990).

7. See A. Kay, H. Henderson, F. Steeper, and S. Greenberg, "Perceptions of Globalization, World Structures and Security," *American Talk Issues* (March 1992), p. 9. See also letter of Edward Koch, *The New York Times* (June 12, 1992).

8. José E. Alvarez, "Legal Remedies and the United Nations: À La Carte Problem," *Michigan Journal of International Law* (Winter 1991): 236–39.

9. Ibid. See also General Assembly Resolution 41/213 (December 19, 1986).

10. Security Council Resolution 598 (July 20, 1987).

11. Security Council Resolution 622 (October 31, 1988).

12. Security Council Resolution 435 (September 29, 1978), Security Council Resolution 632 (February 16, 1989), and Security Council Resolution 626 (December 20, 1988).

13. Security Council Resolution 644 (November 7, 1989).

14. Security Council Resolution 690 (April 29, 1991).

15. Security Council Resolution 693 (May 20, 1991) and Security Council Resolution 729 (January 14, 1992).

16. Security Council Resolution 696 (May 30, 1991).

17. Security Council Resolution 717 (October 16, 1991) and Security Council Resolution 745 (February 28, 1992).

18. See U.N. Document DPI/1104/Rev. 3 (December 1991).

19. See General Assembly Document A/46/600/Add. 1 (November 19, 1991) and U.N. Press Release SG/SM/4748 (May 13, 1992).

20. General Assembly Document A/46/600/Add. 1.

21. See Thomas Friedman, "Bush's Roles on World Stage: Triumphs, but Troubles, Too," *The New York Times* (June 26, 1992), p. A1.

22. See A. Kay, H. Henderson, F. Steeper, and S. Greenberg, "Perceptions of Globalization, World Structures and Security."

23. See U.N. Press Release ORG/1148 (July 31, 1992).

24. General Assembly Resolution 2961 B (XXVII) (December 13, 1972).

Department of Defense

CONVENTIONAL AND NUCLEAR DEFENSE

JOHN STEINBRUNER

Summary

A REVOLUTION IN WORLD POLITICS has fundamentally altered the security problems of the United States. There is no immediate prospect of major conventional aggression. Nuclear deterrence is not politically contested and at any rate is easily assured at projected levels of U.S. forces. The most serious threats are emerging from the potential disintegration of the former Soviet military establishment, from weapons proliferation, and from spontaneous civil violence.

To respond effectively to this new era, the security policy of the United States that was developed over the four decades of Cold War must also be fundamentally altered. Military confrontation must be subordinated to *cooperative regulation* as the primary method of international security. Common standards can and should be set for the size of all national force deployments, the character and rate of their technical development, their operational practices, and above all the information they convey to the international community.

The case for an international security arrangement of this sort is powerful. It faces no ideological barriers. It would produce better security with less uncertainty at lower cost. And if such an arrangement is not achieved, the United States must expect eventually to lose its current military advantage as weapons proliferation inexorably progresses. But to create such an arrangement, the United States will have to reduce its now clearly superior military establishment more than is currently intended and will have to

John Steinbruner has been Director of Foreign Policy Studies at the Brookings Institution since 1978. He has authored a number of books and monographs, including Decisions for Defense: Prospects for a New Order (1991).

develop credible means of limiting its use to circumstances that command international consensus.

Over the long term, the creation of a cooperative security arrangement or any other viable replacement of the Cold War confrontation will require that the United States subject its military establishment to more disciplined planning and spending. Currently projected U.S. force levels are higher than can realistically be maintained, and they could safely be reduced by $211 billion over five years. Controls on weapons exports and on relevant technical trade must be consolidated, redesigned, and integrated into a general cooperative security arrangement.

Introduction

IN EVOLVING ITS NATIONAL SECURITY POLICY over the next several years, the United States unavoidably encounters the most fundamental questions it has faced since the origins of the Cold War.

Beginning in the 1950s, U.S. conventional forces were mandated to contain the threat of a large-scale ground offensive originating from the Soviet Union's alliance system and simultaneously to prepare for lesser contingencies elsewhere in the world. U.S. nuclear forces were directed to maintain a continuously available capability to deliver a decisive number of nuclear weapons against the Soviet alliance system in instantaneous reaction to any strategic attack.

In the course of forty years those instructions became matters of solid national consensus, and they commanded large resources. From 1950 through 1990, the United States spent a total of $11.4 trillion in constant 1992 dollars to create and maintain a military establishment whose primary purpose was to perform these two basic missions—an average of $279 billion in today's dollars for each of those forty-one years.[1] These sums represented 7.8 percent of the total economic product of the period (GNP).[2] They included approximately 25 percent of the nation's total technical investment and more than 50 percent of the Federal Government's contribution.[3] They created globally deployed military forces and a base of industrial support, both of which are now clearly superior to any in the world. They inspired a commensurate level of political, conceptual, and emotional support within the United States.

Standing now at the apex of its accomplishments, the military establishment of the United States remains a source of national pride and a focus of national resources. It no longer fits the circumstances, however. With the dissolution of the Soviet Union and the resulting reconfiguration of its military establishment, the prospect of large-scale conventional aggression has absolutely disappeared. Moreover, the residual nuclear weapons the Russian Federation is maintaining could not be used for the sudden attack or political intimidation that were traditionally feared. Deterrence and containment are both readily accomplished, so much so that reassurance is now the more demanding problem. For friends and former foes alike, too much power concentrated in any nation's hands is unsettling—an aversion enshrined in our own political system. Precisely because we have succeeded so well, the new President in this new era needs to redefine the purposes of U.S. military forces and to tailor their capabilities to those purposes.

The necessary redefinition, moreover, will have to involve much more than a simple redirection of established military capabilities away from Russia and against other potential opponents. Immediate threats of conventional invasion or of massive strategic bombardment do not emanate from any other source in anything like the same magnitude. There is no serious prospect of a rapidly developing military engagement that would demand the resources currently maintained by U.S. military forces. Their currently projected size, technical evolution, and operational posture cannot be justified in traditional terms, despite some continuing political sentiment to do exactly that.

The most serious security problems that have emerged in the new situation have a very different character. Caught up in a process of radical economic and political reform, the command system of the former Soviet military establishment is subject to serious deterioration. The strict control it exercised over large inventories of nuclear and conventional weapons is in jeopardy, as is the industrial establishment that created those weapons. The fate of that command system and its industrial base will inevitably affect the prospects for controlling the general process of weapons proliferation. And it is this process of proliferation, fueled by the inexorable internationalization of relevant technology and motivated by surging ethnic antagonisms, that poses the most serious longer-term threat to the United States.

These externally imposed imperatives to redefine our security posture will be a difficult problem for the U.S. political system. The pressures are too strong to be resisted indefinitely, but the commitment to traditional programs is so deeply entrenched that one cannot expect the Defense Department to initiate a fundamental redesign. The next President will have to issue fresh instructions to military planners for the unavoidable transition to occur effectively and coherently. That, in turn, requires that a new political consensus be formed to replace the Cold War formulation.

Problems of Sustaining Confrontation

SINCE U.S. MILITARY PLANNERS HAVE NOT BEEN GIVEN a new security policy to guide their preparations, they are operating, inevitably and appropriately, within the old one. Lacking an assumed opponent in the league of a Soviet Union, official accounts refer instead to possible threats they cannot yet imagine. In the words of the Joint Chiefs of Staff chairman, General Powell: "We can still plausibly identify some specific threats—North Korea, a weakened Iraq, perhaps even a hostile Iran. But the real threat to our security is the unknown, the uncertain. In a very real sense the primary threat to our security is instability."[4]

The overall level of military forces that are intended to be sustained have been reduced by about 25 percent from the 1990 base—the last year of the Cold War.[5] These reductions, scheduled to be completed by 1997, are expected to reduce defense spending about 28 percent in constant dollars below the levels that would have been required to sustain the 1990 force structure.[6] Within that reduced base, investment and training proceed much as they did before.

CONVENTIONAL FORCES

In response to a general sense of uncertainty, U.S. conventional forces at their reduced levels are still being designed to respond on short notice— unilaterally, if necessary—to a threat arising anywhere in the world. As summarized in Table 1 at the end of this chapter, they are projected to retain 88 ground-force brigades of standard size (including 12 Marine), 30 tactical air wings (including 4 Marine), 12 aircraft carriers, and 831 aircraft plus 205 ships for carrying military personnel and equipment over long distances.[7] There is no serious possibility that these forces would be needed at the land borders or sea approaches of the United States itself. They were constructed and are being maintained for global power projection—that is, to defend the United States by means of engagement in other parts of the world.

The performance of U.S. forces in the Persian Gulf War gave new meaning to the capacity for global power projection. Although Iraqi forces did not provide competitive opposition and the feats of precision were not perhaps as frequent or decisive as press coverage implied, the tactical air operation nonetheless gave an instructive glimpse of the future. The integrated combination of remote sensing, information processing, rapid communication, operational coordination, and precision delivery are giving advanced conventional munitions an intrusiveness and potential decisiveness that is unprecedented in the history of warfare. It appears that ground force movements can be stopped, that fixed defenses can be breached, and that critical social assets can be selectively destroyed. The resulting ability to conduct military operations is extraordinary, as is the potential to engage in remote coercion. Images of this potential, now generally labeled reconnaissance/strike capability, will heavily influence defense planning throughout the world.

It has required fifteen years of intense investment for the United States to develop reconnaissance/strike capacity to the extent that was displayed in the Persian Gulf War. While that accomplishment fell well short of the full potential, it is nonetheless at least a decade ahead of any other military establishment's mastery of the relevant technology and operational practices. The core technology on which it is based is inherently available in commercial markets and cannot be controlled unilaterally. The investment required to match it is very difficult, however, since it does not involve any single weapons system but rather the integration of many different things.

This set of circumstances poses some obvious problems. The inclination is naturally very strong to retain a major military advantage that has been so laboriously acquired. To make that an explicit objective of defense planning, however, would predictably inspire general mistrust and would incite competitive investments from a number of military establishments. Although it would be difficult for any of these to match the U.S. capability fully, many could reasonably aspire to negate it in local areas and/or to offset it with precision delivery systems that could reach the United States and thus pose a countervailing deterrent in kind.

General mistrust may seem to be an abstraction; but if it developed to the point that global operations of U.S. forces could not be routinely sustained, much of the value of those forces would be lost. Similarly, the political will and technical ability of competitors may be discounted, but it would be unwise to test that with a stark challenge. In the critical area of advanced electronics, U.S. military programs are already lagging a decade behind the leading edge of commercial markets, and they are not likely to escape the weight of design regulations and procurement procedures that retard their adaptation to new technology. If sufficiently stimulated, smaller countries with less entrenched military establishments might prove to be more adroit in applying commercial technology to military purposes. Unrestrained national competition in the development of advanced conventional weapons capability is not an attractive prospect, even for the acknowledged leader.

These considerations have been appreciated well enough within the United States to produce a decisive rejection of an explicit policy to sustain military superiority. When defense planners drafted such a policy as guidance for preparation of the 1993 defense budget,[8] the political reaction was so negative that the president was immediately induced to repudiate the draft. The replacement, as publicly reported, avoids any direct claim to preserve military superiority but does not provide a replacement rationale that reasonably justifies the size and operational focus of the conventional forces that the current defense plan proposes to maintain.[9]

NUCLEAR FORCES

The START treaty signed on July 31, 1991, and the subsequent U.S.-Russian framework agreement signed on June 17, 1992, will reduce the active deployments of nuclear weapons substantially below their peak levels. Once these agreements are implemented, the United States is expected to have 3,500 strategic warheads carried on slightly over 1,000 delivery systems plus an additional 1,600 tactical weapons. Russian forces are expected to have somewhat lower inventories but comparable destructive potential. Historical deployments were in the range of 11,000 to 13,000 strategic weapons on each side, with total active inventories exceeding 20,000 nuclear weapons each[10] and total weapons production exceeding 60,000 weapons for each of the two forces over the course of the Cold War.[11]

The large scheduled reductions will not have a major effect on underlying deterrence capability. The number of targets that might reasonably be associated with the idea of deterrence does not exceed 2,000 in either society. If the highest-priority targets were to be included in an attack of that size, the resulting damage to basic economic and social functions would be near the maximum effect that could be produced by an attack of any size.[12] Even after the nuclear forces have reached their lowest contemplated end state— now scheduled for the year 2000 or 2003 under the framework agreement yet to be completed formally—they will still retain destructive power against any industrial society that is functionally comparable to what they currently have.

Full implementation of the framework agreement will have a substantial effect on the capacity to attack fixed ICBM launchers, a matter that has been a major focus of political contention for the past two decades. By requiring the complete elimination of the SS-18 missile—the most efficient hard-target attack weapon in the Russian arsenal—and by generally prohibiting multiple-warhead missile systems based on land, the agreement will significantly reduce the vulnerability of American missile silos as calculated by standard analytic methods. Since the American Trident II missile (also widely known as the D-5) can still be deployed with up to 1,750 warheads, and since 400 of these are to be of the high-yield W-88 warhead design, Russian missile silos have not been relieved of potential threats to the same extent, but the Russian force is expected to place primary reliance on the SS-25 system, which conducts mobile operations on land. The difficulty the United States had in attacking mobile missile launchers in Iraq during the Persian Gulf War suggests that the Russians can be quite confident of the safety of their SS-25 force, and, at any rate, the difficulties of executing a hard-target attack have always made missile silo vulnerability much greater in calculated assessment than it is in operational practice. The reduction and reconfiguration of strategic forces projected under the framework agreement will remove this problem of apparent ICBM vulnerability and will thereby reinforce a constructive change in attitude.

Changes in political attitudes about nuclear weapons and their deterrence missions have in fact been more substantial and more meaningful than the changes in the degree of physical threat. With the emotions of the Cold War rapidly receding, it is now widely assumed that the core deterrent mission is not difficult to achieve and that the credible extension of that threat to cover traditional allies or conventional threats of otherwise unmanageable size is also far less of a burden than once supposed. The latter problem at any rate has been vitiated by the transformation of political and military circumstances in Central Europe. The force reduction agreements consolidate this change in attitude and stabilize what has all along been largely a problem of perception. That is an important accomplishment.

That does not mean, however, that the problem of strategic security has been acceptably resolved. Even when total nuclear weapons deployments are reduced to the 3,000 to 3,500 range and even if the trend toward more relaxed operational postures continues, an inherent underlying danger will remain. Both the United States strategic force and the one that the Russian Federation has inherited are acutely aware that their command systems are vulnerable to severe disruption in the course of a nuclear attack of any size exceeding a few tens of weapons. As protection against this circumstance, both have prepared to launch retaliatory strikes within minutes of receiving definitive evidence that they are being attacked with nuclear weapons. This is a very demanding procedure requiring special preparations at the point of crisis when the possibility of an attack is judged to be greater than normal. There is some chance, presumably low but essentially unmeasurable, that these ingrained alert procedures and rapid-reaction inclinations might trigger an inadvertent nuclear engagement. This problem will not be removed by the scheduled reductions.[13]

It is possible to improve operational safety without meaningfully reducing the core deterrent effect, but it is unlikely that a truly systematic effort of this sort would be undertaken without reversing the principle of active confrontation so essential to the Cold War formulation. Measures that would provide the most effective protection require a commitment to fairly intimate cooperation, and that in turn requires a fundamentally different basis for security policy.

The issue of ballistic missile defense is also an unresolved problem of strategic security. It is now conceded nearly universally that the Reagan administration's aspiration to force a decisive shift to a defensive configuration of strategic weapons by means of a unilateral technical initiative (i.e., "Star Wars") is not remotely feasible. There is an active question, however, about whether some more limited evolution of defensive technology could be undertaken that would provide meaningful protection against accidents or small-scale deliberate attacks. This idea is currently a matter of dispute within the United States, and it is perhaps the most serious unresolved problem of security policy between the United States and Russia.

In the June 1992 summit meeting between Presidents Bush and Yeltsin, an agreement was signed to develop the concept of a global protection system—the more expansive and less realistic Russian formulation of the idea. That agreement was a procedural response to substantive disagreements, such as whether to restrict cooperation to the sharing of early warning information (the Russian inclination) or to enable deployment of missile defense technology (the stated American intention) and whether to allow deployment of missile defense on the basis of shared financing and technology (the only option feasible for Russia) or as a matter of national initiative (the unstated American intention).

Resolution of these issues is primarily a question of fundamental security policy. Even under the most limited objective, the deployment of a strategic defense system could not rely on technical performance alone. To have any sustained viability and to avoid perverse effects on the broader strategic interactions, any defensive deployment would have to be subjected to detailed mutual consent. The rule that there is to be no strategic defense except by mutual consent is the principal element of the 1972 ABM treaty between the United States and the Soviet Union, and, as the principal strategic successor, Russia would have to be a cooperating partner in any deployment. So also as a matter of practical politics would the other nuclear weapons states. Though the main proponents of ballistic missile defense do not acknowledge the point, and indeed resist it, any serious prospect for deployment almost certainly depends on shifting the basis of policy from confrontation to cooperation.

The Promise of Cooperation

UNDER THE PRESSURE OF EXTERNAL EVENTS, the unresolved problems of conventional and nuclear defense strongly encourage the United States to make this fundamental revision in its central principle of security. Cooperative engagement was the principle very successfully used to deal with the German and Japanese military establishments after World War II. The result internationalized their security and our own and effectively removed any serious expectation that we would again become enemies. It also prevented any active preparation for such an event.

Although the relationships with Germany and Japan were developed in a larger context of confrontation with the Soviet Union, that does not now appear to be a necessary condition. In fact, cooperative relationships have been gradually evolving with the former Soviet and the Chinese military establishments even before the political revolution that unfolded after 1989. The CSCE (Conference on Security and Cooperation in Europe), Paris Charter of November 1991, and formal treaties such as START and CFE (Conventional Forces in Europe) seek to make cooperation the organizing principle of security and provide some portion of the institutionalized procedure required.

The distinction between cooperation and confrontation cannot be settled by means of any bureaucratic exercise or even by an authoritative declaration of policy from the newly elected President. Within the United States political system, fundamental policy results from the accumulation of specific actions. It must be validated through congressional votes on the defense budget as well as sustained by public opinion. Because the next Administration will not command an established consensus on these central questions, it will face an unusually demanding problem of policy leadership. To initiate the process of adjustment, the new President must formulate the issues directly and explicitly in a fundamental review of security policy.

Immediate Actions

SINCE CONGRESS APPROPRIATES BUDGETS on an annual basis and since the budget cycle provides the primary context for making decisions, it is notoriously difficult for United States defense planners to deal coherently with major issues that are visible only with longer-term perspective. There are, however, at least two prominent exceptions: the reconfiguration of the former Soviet military establishment—particularly its arrangements for controlling nuclear weapons; and the civil violence that has accompanied the dismemberment of Yugoslavia. Both subjects have commanded attention despite the recent surge of concern for domestic priorities.

STABILIZING THE SOVIET MILITARY STRUCTURE

The formal dissolution of the Soviet Union occurred before any definitive structure of constitutional authority could be established to replace it, which left unanswered urgent questions about control over nuclear weapons. All nuclear weapons of the former Soviet Union are still apparently managed by the single integrated command system that historically controlled those weapons, and all will be located on the territory of the Russian Federation. A protocol to the START treaty has been signed by the United States and the four Soviet successor states whose territories contain active nuclear weapons deployments that makes each of the four responsible for implementing the treaty's obligations, but also commits Belarus, Kazakhstan, and Ukraine to compliance with the Nonproliferation Treaty as states without nuclear weapons. The United States has offered financial and technical assistance for the transportation, storage, and ultimate dismantlement of the weapons that are being removed from active inventories.

There are important ambiguities in these arrangements, as well as practical difficulties in their implementation. The START protocol confers international legal standing on the three non-Russian states for the management of nuclear weapons but does not set a specific date for their adherence to the Nonproliferation Treaty. That appears to leave open the question of who owns the weapons still deployed on their territory during the seven-year process of reduction, and it tempts them to obstruct the process to enhance their standing. Given the degree of political strain in the relationships among the Soviet successor states, the seven-year duration taken over from the original bilateral negotiation is clearly hazardous, and efforts should be immediately made to accelerate it. The preferred way would be to detach the warheads from all strategic launchers scheduled for removal under the START treaty and to hold them in jointly monitored storage. A supplemental agreement to accomplish this objective is an immediate imperative for the next President of the United States.

Moreover, it is probably not possible to accomplish the intended reduction and consolidation of nuclear forces without simultaneously providing some international context for the massive transformation that conventional forces of the former Soviet Union are destined to undergo. Nuclear and conventional forces were sufficiently integrated in traditional Soviet military operations that arrangements to stabilize the nuclear component are inherently at risk if the Red Army disintegrates because of its financial and constitutional crisis. Talks on how to engage with the Soviet successor states on the management of nuclear weapons will probably have to be extended to military forces generally if those talks are to succeed. The urgent need to do so fundamentally requires working out arrangements for association with NATO that the successor military establishments could reasonably accept as equitable—that is, something more integral and more reliable than the observer status that has been allowed to them.

INTERNATIONAL RESPONSE TO CIVIL VIOLENCE

So far the general transformation under way among the Soviet successor states has been remarkably peaceful, given the magnitude and difficulty of what is involved. It would be foolish not to recognize, however, the potential for civil disorder and ethnic conflict. There is a serious possibility that spontaneously generated conflicts might overload the already burdened relationships between Russia and the other nominal members of the Commonwealth of Independent States. In addition, it would be irresponsible not to apply the somber lessons of Yugoslavia—notably, that early and forceful international intervention is necessary in some circumstances to prevent an unmanageable conflagration, and that the international community does not have the mechanisms for timely and effective action. There are no established principles to determine when international intervention is legitimate and necessary. There are no direct precedent or operational plans for an international force to control civil violence, as distinct from reinforcing a peace that provisionally exists.

Prevailing sentiment in the United States is clearly not inclined to support any international intervention, which makes systematic preparation unusually difficult. But more systematic preparation is an immediate requirement of security policy, even if there is not an immediate political mandate. Again, current U.S. forces have all the firepower and operational readiness they are likely to need. Their deficiencies have to do with the political and organizational context in which they might have to operate.

Longer-Term Actions

THE INERTIA ASSOCIATED WITH MILITARY PROGRAMS is considerable. Major weapons development programs frequently extend for twenty years, from initial conception to full operational mastery. The service life of the products involve similar spans of time, as do the normal careers of the officer corps. Production and training cycles are of shorter duration but nonetheless operate on multiple-year schedules. Under normal circumstances, therefore, it is not possible to make rapid changes in the size, technical configuration, or operational posture of U.S. forces. Established commitments to individuals and institutions generally preclude such changes, and the exceptions have nearly always been due to the beginning or ending of a major war.

This means that desired changes of security policy imposed by new circumstances and the necessary reconfiguration of military forces will almost certainly have to be accomplished gradually. A particularly decisive new Administration should make immediate changes in policy even though the outcomes would have to evolve over five to ten years.

DISCIPLINED DEFENSE PLANNING

For the past decade, in the estimation of most independent observers, the defense planning process has not operated with the strong integrative direction necessary to make major changes in conventional and nuclear forces. Budget decisions have been made largely within the separate military service organizations, where institutional commitments tend to prevail over general national security considerations. After the Goldwater-Nichols Defense Reorganization Act of 1986,[14] which enhanced the powers of the chairman of the Joint Chiefs of Staff, coordination among the military services has improved, but the broader dimensions of security—bilateral and regional diplomacy, arms sales, and the various forms of international organization, for example—have not been systematically related, as was reflected in the Persian Gulf War. U.S. logistical movements during that episode and the eventual combined arms assault were highly successful against an outclassed opponent, but the need for the operation was created by the failure of preventative policies.

Disciplining the planning system to define better-integrated outcomes and to move systematically toward them over five- to ten-year durations is the primary procedural requirement of the new security situation. In meeting this requirement, there are also a number of substantive changes, described below, that certainly must be considered and in all probability implemented.

ADDITIONAL FORCE STRUCTURE REDUCTIONS

First, the size of U.S. forces will almost certainly have to be reduced below their currently projected end state. There is no plausible opponent whose containment would require active forces in the amounts that the existing defense plan proposes to maintain. Even with indefinite continuation of the more polite form of confrontation that is the underlying logic of current U.S. security policy, competing domestic priorities and international sensitivities are very likely to induce further reductions. The next President of the United States should lead the formation of a cooperative international security arrangement to enable a more extensive reduction of U.S. forces and a more favorable overall security outcome.

Setting appropriate force levels is not an exact science and is a matter of differing political preference. Table 2 at the end of this chapter provides illustrative possibilities corresponding, in the first instance, to the continuation of traditional policies but with forces more appropriately tailored to the circumstances and, in the second, to the systematic development of cooperative arrangements. The latter would involve comprehensive ceilings on all of the significant military establishments and would reduce operational uncertainty. These two options define a range of reasonable outcomes within which substantial budget savings can be achieved.

The two options differ largely in terms of the number of ballistic missile submarines and tactical air wings they would preserve. The traditional security option would complete the currently projected program of eighteen Trident boats and would retain a total of thirty land-based tactical air wings. The cooperative security option would reduce the ballistic missile submarine force to ten boats, which would not maintain continuous alert patrols, and would retain twenty-one tactical air wings. Both would retain forty-five ground-force brigades—the equivalent of fifteen standard-size divisions. Since the lower levels of the cooperative security option would be accompanied by corresponding restraints on other military establishments, the two options would confer comparable net capacity. In both cases U.S. forces could readily perform basic deterrence, could defeat any attempted conventional invasion, and would provide a superior base for responding to a breakdown of the arrangement and a renewed buildup of forces.

The more systematically organized cooperative security option clearly offers more efficient security. It would save $211 billion in constant 1992 dollars over five years and potentially some $640 billion over ten years. More than two thirds of these savings can be achieved, however, through the unilateral tailoring of forces under the traditional collective security policy.

BETTER ALLOCATION OF DEFENSE RESOURCES
Second, whatever the ultimate size of U.S. force deployments proves to be, it will be necessary to adjust the internal allocation of resources among people, activities, and equipment. After an extraordinary surge in weapons procurement during the 1980s, in which replacement and technical upgrading occurred at a faster rate than could be sustained, the current defense plan projects a period of underinvestment. That might indeed be a prudent

adjustment for the moment, but it is eventually desirable, even imperative, to set the process of investment at efficient, sustainable rates.

A particularly important element of this allocational adjustment involves the balance between technical development and weapons procurement. Throughout the period of the Cold War, technical development has been embedded in programs designed for large-scale procurement. The system has operated with a sense of time urgency, believing that the United States was locked in a race with the Soviet Union.

All the original conditions that shaped this pattern have now changed. Technical investment is now much more expensive, and real improvements in military performance are much more difficult to achieve. The United States is reducing forces rather than building them and has large inventories of relatively modern, long-lasting equipment. It is not locked in a technical development race with the Soviet successor states or as yet with any other country. Under these altered conditions, the organization and financing of technical development will have to be made more independent of large-scale production or it will seriously degrade. That in turn probably requires a consolidation and restructuring of the supporting industry and a substantial change in the categories of congressional appropriations—tasks whose difficulty rivals that of economic reform in Russia.

CONTROLLING PROLIFERATION

Third, since the general process of weapons proliferation is now a more serious threat to the longer-term conventional and nuclear defense of the United States than any immediate military operation could realistically be, the regulation of weapons exports and of trade in related technology is a commensurately more important area of security policy. Here again, some radical changes will have to be considered to adjust to new circumstances. Given the internationalization of economic activity and the fact that commercial applications are leading to the development of some of the most significant technologies, established export control policies are being overwhelmed. The facts that the legal and institutional arrangements are different for different categories of weapons and that the major suppliers are not cooperating in all of these categories compound the problem. Consolidated weapons export control arrangements relying primarily on all the major weapons suppliers enforcing disclosure rules have become a security imperative.

OPERATIONAL SAFETY OF NUCLEAR WEAPONS

Fourth, to improve the safety of nuclear weapons operations, there must be some very substantial changes in prevailing practices. In particular, we need to eliminate the rapid-reaction inclinations of the U.S. and Russian strategic forces. Cooperative arrangements can assure that no nuclear weapon could operate without some significant and observable period of preparation. If the required period were on the order of a week or even a few days, existing pressures on the command systems would be substantially alleviated without meaningfully reducing the core deterrent effect. Arrangements of this sort would most probably involve a systematic separation of nuclear warheads from strategic launchers and a fitting of all warheads with tags that would enable the fact of separation to be verified remotely.

FORMALIZING COOPERATION

Fifth, cooperative arrangements must be developed to set common international standards for force deployments, to preclude offensive configurations, and above all to require substantial transparency in all aspects of military development. There are no longer impenetrable ideological barriers preventing these arrangements from including all of the major military establishments. Achieving that result would produce better, more efficient security for all in a manner that does not have overtones of national hegemony. The effort to accomplish this would itself be a major benefit to the United States; its success, even more of a benefit. The next President of the United States must act to institutionalize international security.

TABLE 1.
Conventional Force Structure: Administration Plan

Major Forces	1990	1996
Ground-force brigades		
Army		
Active	59	45
Reserve	60	31
Marine		
Active	9	9
Reserve	3	3
Total	131	88
Land-based wings		
Air Force		
Active	24	15
Reserve	12	11
Marine		
Active	3	3
Reserve	1	1
Total	40	30
Aircraft carriers	14	12
Carrier wings	15	13
Other ships and subs	488	405
Airlift	831	831
Sealift	205	205

Sources: "Statement by John D. Steinbruner Before the Senate Committee on Appropriations, February 19, 1992," attached tables; "Department of Defense Annual Report, 1992" (GPO); Assistant Chief of Naval Operations (Air Warfare), "Future of Naval Aviation Brief" (August 1991).

TABLE 2.
Collective and Cooperative Security: Force Structures and Costs

Major Forces	Traditional Collective Security		Cooperative Security	
	1996	2002	1996	2002
Budget Authority (051, billions of 1992 dollars)				
Strategic nuclear	26.5	23.6	20.0	14.7
Theater nuclear	0.7	—	—	—
Ground (Army and Marines)[1]	43.7	30.1	40.1	30.1
Land-based tactical air[2]	49.1	43.9	41.5	32.0
Naval (incl. carriers)	45.3	39.0	47.2	39.0
Airlift and sealift[3]	13.4	13.4	13.4	13.4
National intelligence and communications	19.2	19.2	17.9	17.6
Total (051)	197.9	169.2	180.1	146.8
Force Size and Composition				
ICBMs	400	100	210	100
Bombers	124	41	69	40
SLBMs	312	432	336	240
Theater nuclear (warheads)	1,556	—	—	—
Ground (brigade equivalents	57	45	54	45
Land-based tactical air (wings)	33.3	30	24	21
Naval (ships and submarines)	268	247	307	231
Airlift	831	831	831	831
Sealift	205	205	205	205

Source: "Statement by John D. Steinbruner Before the Senate Committee on Appropriations, February 19, 1992," attached tables.

1. *Includes reserve as well as active-duty forces.*

2. *Includes Marine air wings.*

3. *Airlift includes intertheater as well as intratheater; sealift includes 72 active and 183 ready reserve ships. National Defense Reserve Fleet not included.*

NOTES

1. Steven Kosiak and Paul Taibl, "Analysis of the FY93 Defense Budget Request" (Defense Budget Project, March 11, 1992), Table 4; 050 outlays were converted from FY93 to FY92 dollars using DOD deflators. Office of the Comptroller of the Department of Defense, "National Defense Budget Estimates for FY93" (March 1992), Table 5–9.

2. Office of Management and Budget, *Budget of the United States Government, FY92* (Washington, D.C.: U.S. Government Printing Office, 1992), Part VII–66, Table 6.1.

3. National Science Board, "Science and Engineering Indicators" (Washington, D.C.: U.S. Government Printing Office, 1991), Appendix Tables 4–17, 4–26, 4–27; Bruce L. R. Smith, *American Science Policy Since World War II* (Washington D.C.: Brookings Institution, 1990), pp. 49–50, 80.

4. "Statement of General Colin C. Powell, Chairman of the Joint Chiefs of Staff, Before the Senate Committee on Armed Services, January 31, 1992," p. 5.

5. "Statement of Secretary of Defense Dick Cheney Before the Senate Committee on Armed Services with the FY93 Budget of the Department of Defense, January 31, 1992," p. 1.

6. *Budget of the United States Government, FY92*, part VII-55, Table 5.1; *NDBE*, FY92, Table 5-7; DOD, "Complete Set of Briefing Charts on the FY93 Budget."

7. "Statement by John D. Steinbruner Before the Senate Committee on Appropriations, February 19, 1992"; Carl Conetta and Charles Knight, "U.S. Army Base Force 1995: Active Combat Maneuver Units with Brigade Count" (Project on Defense Alternatives Briefing Memo, June 3, 1992); OSD, *Annual Report to the President and the Congress, February 1992* (Washington, D.C.: U.S. Government Printing Office, 1992), Appendix C.

8. See Patrick Tyler, "Pentagon Imagines New Enemies to Fight in Post Cold War Era," *The New York Times* (February 17, 1992).

9. See Patrick Tyler, "Pentagon Drops Goal of Blocking New Superpowers," *The New York Times* (May 26, 1992); Barton Gellman, "Pentagon Abandons Goal of Thwarting U.S. Rivals," *The Washington Post* (May 27, 1992).

10. OSD Press Conference (January 29, 1992).

11. See Ray Hall, "Total Quantities and Costs of Major Weapons Systems Procured" (1974–93); and past years of Office of DOD Comptroller, "Procurement Programs (P-1): DOD Budget," latest issue (January 29, 1992).

12. Michael May et al., *Strategic Arms Reductions* (Washington, D.C.: Brookings Institute, 1988), Chap. 4.

13. Bruce Blair and John Steinbruner, *The Effects of Warning on Strategic Stability* (Washington, D.C.: Brookings Institution, 1991).

14. Public Law 99–433 (October 1, 1986).

Department of Defense

MILITARY CONVERSION

JOHN TEPPER MARLIN

Summary

THE COLD WAR IS OVER, the Soviet Union has crumbled, and military expenditures are declining all around the world. Yet the United States seems unwilling to adjust fully to these changes and realize the potential of a peace dividend. The Bush administration defense budget request for fiscal year 1993 was more than $291 billion, roughly comparable (in constant dollars) to the rate of U.S. defense spending during the Vietnam War. If current world trends continue and the U.S. defense budget were to follow the slow downward glide proposed by the Pentagon, the United States would account for *45 percent* of world military spending by 1997. Clearly, a sharp cut in U.S. military spending is in order. We need to implement a large-scale "conversion" to a peacetime economy.

We have done it before. After World War II, American defense contractors, backed by deliberate government programs, went back to what they were doing before the war; they "reconverted." Building a peace economy has become more difficult with the permanent defense-industry establishment that grew up in the Cold War. It promises to be painful unless there is concerted preparation, which is certainly feasible. Some significant successes have already occurred. There would unquestionably be more if not for the lack of presidential leadership.

In the late 1980s, when military spending began to fall back to normal Cold War-levels after the Reagan buildup, the Bush administration paid little attention to conversion. In 1990, Congress stepped into the leadership void and appropriated $200 million to the Departments of Labor and Commerce for local conversion programs. But the administration for two years blocked implementation of the law; choosing instead to increase licenses for foreign

---

John Tepper Marlin has served as Director of the Conversion Information Center of the Council on Economic Priorities. He is currently Chief Economist for the Comptroller of the City of New York.

arms sales.[1] The administration also opposed the more than $1 billion in conversion outlays passed by Congress in October 1992, even though control of the funds is left with the Defense Department.

The new President should act quickly to assist communities suffering from defense cuts, by concentrating existing federal programs on communities that are hardest hit. Upon his election, the President should announce his intention to develop a peace economy program (PEP) and make it a top priority. He should promptly convene the statutory (since 1990) Economic Adjustment Committee, and inform members of the committee that he will personally chair the first meeting. He should then weave the more promising proposals into a broader program for reinvesting in America.

Introduction: The Global Context

IN THE DEPARTMENT OF DEFENSE'S 1992 annual report, Secretary of Defense Dick Cheney measured U.S defense sufficiency with little regard to the dramatic reduction in external threats. He argued that cuts deeper than the 2 percent-a-year downward glide proposed by President Bush would leave the American military dangerously undernourished and pointed out that "as a share of America's GNP, DOD outlays are expected to fall . . . well below those at any time since before World War II."

But Cheney's base for historic comparison is inappropriate. In the years before World War II, Europe was arming to the teeth while the United States was pursuing an isolationist policy. By contrast, in the early 1990s the Warsaw Pact countries' military budgets are in a free fall and Europe is rapidly scaling down its military spending. The Reagan-era buildup—five years of spending above $300 billion (in 1991 dollars)—was the longest sustained period of high U.S. military spending in this century. World War II exceeded that figure for only four years and the Korean and Vietnam wars for only two years each. The U.S. military budget catapulted 50 percent in these five Reagan years, and the U.S. share of world military spending rose from 22 percent in 1980 to 28 percent in 1985.[2]

Assuming that other countries continue to reduce their levels of military spending[3] and projecting U.S. spending based on the Bush proposals,[4] a startling picture emerges. By 1997 the U.S. share of the world's total military spending would be almost 45 percent.

Our military budget is looking increasingly unreasonable both in relation to the rest of the world and also to core U.S. interests. A large military budget makes it harder to address domestic threats such as the decay of our inner cities and the unaffordability of health care. It also makes it harder to find the money to help stabilize newly democratic states. We need to pursue an alternative course. "Conversion" of our heavily military economy into a normal peacetime economy must be a high priority of the next Administration.

Past U.S. Conversion*

AMERICAN MILITARY SPENDING FOR WORLD WAR II peaked in 1945 at $804 billion. It dropped dramatically to $78 billion immediately after the war. Yet well before World War II ended, business leaders became concerned about adjustment in the postwar period. If the stimulative effect of wartime spending—military Keynesianism—worked to pump up the economy, many feared it could work in reverse as the defense engine slowed down.

So a blue-ribbon Commission on Reconversion was created to plan for peace by analyzing transitional needs for every industry. It was properly called "reconversion" because most defense contractors had been making civilian goods only a few years before. For example, Detroit's car manufacturers switched to making tanks, then went back to making cars. Manufacturers of lipstick cases switched to making bullet cartridges, then switched back.

The commission and its allies engaged in a massive community-based planning effort tied to national policies. In the end, the worst fears of U.S. leaders—that we would plunge into a postwar recession—did not come to pass. One major reason was the planning efforts of the Roosevelt and Truman administrations, which encouraged steps both to stimulate demand and to provide transitional educational programs for laid-off defense workers and mustered-out military personnel.

Studies of defense cuts in the early 1960s showed that as the Cold War persisted, weapons became more and more complex, thereby increasing the structural immobility of the industry. Subsequent studies confirmed that defense-contractor cuts would become increasingly difficult to absorb. For example, few civilian uses are likely for products designed to withstand nuclear blasts or to burn holes in metal from several miles away.

---

*"Conversion" is used here in the broad, community- or economywide sense of the term, meaning a move from military production to civilian production in a coordinated way. A narrower use of the term, implying retooling at the plant level, is becoming less common. Conversion advocates undermined their cause in the 1970s and 1980s with the narrower concept: There were too few examples of success, which reduced the chance of getting conversion legislation so defined through Congress.

But there is still considerable potential for conversion. According to a 1991 survey of high-level defense-industry executives undertaken by the Winbridge Group, corporate America seems to have learned something from conversion shortcomings in the 1970s. Of executives responding, 48 percent reported "strategic and financial success" in selling their products in commercial markets. Even two thirds of those *opposed* to conversion because of past failures said their firms had technology with commercial potential. But positive defense-industry action is still the exception.

The keys to company success are:

• Recognizing cuts and planning ahead: Healthy lead time is essential.

• Keeping conversion projects small: It is easier to convert for small companies, or for small projects within companies. Groups of people working in small teams with the active support of top management have been effective. In nature, transplanting large trees has been shown to be difficult, while smaller trees take root more easily. The same applies to converting business enterprises. Small works.

• Focusing on alternative uses for familiar technology. Some military technologies are too specialized to have any commercial applications, but generally, technology transfer should become easier and less costly now that the Pentagon has backed away from pursuit of "recoupment" charges.

• Integrating people familiar with commercial production and markets into product development teams.

• Assuming little or no innate marketing skill or cost-awareness within military divisions.

Impact of Defense Cuts on States and Localities

AS DEFENSE SPENDING HEADED DOWNWARD AGAIN in the late 1980s, a general optimism about absorbing cutbacks prevailed. But 1990 turned out to be a precursor of future defense-cut pain, for two reasons: (1) While in aggregate the cuts might not be severe, at the local level they were highly disruptive; and (2) a national recession was under way by the second quarter of 1990.

The Council on Economic Priorities (CEP) in 1990 made a detailed analysis of the relative impact of defense cuts by developing measures of potential state, local, and industrial dislocation. For testimony to Congress's Joint Economic Committee, CEP developed a Vulnerability Index that combines a state's defense dependence with the state's unemployment rate, in the same way that the "misery index" combines the unemployment and inflation rates. The number ranged in 1990 from a high of 17.2 in Virginia and Puerto Rico to a low of 4.8 in Nebraska.

To take account of the amount of defense spending at risk—that is, the amount likely to be cut—and to measure the cumulative effect of specific defense cuts on each state, CEP developed the Defense Dislocation Index. Likely cuts were determined for each state by calculating the value of prime contracts in every state for each weapons system at risk. The measure showed how severely defense cuts were likely to affect the economy of a state. These cuts are occurring now. In the absence of adequate planning and support for stimulative domestic economic activity, transitional educational programs, and incentives, they are very disruptive to local employment, revenues, and social services.

Nationwide, the Congressional Budget Office estimates a direct gross military employment loss of 1.1 million workers between 1991 and 1995, composed of 400,000 direct jobs lost in the private military industry, another employment loss of 200,000 suffered by military-industry supplier firms, 360,000 active-duty personnel cuts, and 130,000 federal civilian jobs lost.[5] The Office of Technology Assessment estimates 1.4 million direct jobs lost by 1995.[6] If one factors in a plausible overall multiplier of 2, the net job loss could be more than 2 million over five years.

By 1991—at best midway through the recession—half the states were so hobbled by budget deficits that they could not adequately cope with existing problems, let alone the transitional retraining and development needs created by defense cuts. Most northeastern states fall into this category. Implementation of federal economic-adjustment legislation, passed in late 1990, was seen as essential for the hardest-hit communities.

The Conversion Law of 1990 provided a modest $150 million for local job training through the Department of Labor and $50 million for infrastructure financing through the Economic Development Administration (EDA) in the Department of Commerce. It also doubled the budget of the Office of Economic Adjustment (OEA), created in 1963 by Secretary of Defense Robert McNamara. By funding the OEA, the law unquestionably smoothed the way for the hardest-hit communities, such as St. Louis and Fort Worth. Unfortunately, the transfer of money to the Department of Labor and EDA took nearly a year and occurred only upon application of intense congressional pressure.

President Bush had reportedly vowed to veto any conversion legislation that crossed his desk. Because the 1990 Conversion Law passed as a rider to the defense spending bills, it slipped by. But the Defense Department held up the $200 million appropriated for conversion in a minisequester that lasted until late 1991.

EDA, entrusted with administering $50 million of the conversion money, engaged in its own minisequester that lasted until January 1992,[7] and did not announce how to apply for grants until March 10, 1992. In the interim it solicited grant requests from communities surrounding Pease Air Force Base, New Hampshire, and Groton, Connecticut, after they emerged as politically important during the primary challenge to President Bush.

When in January 1992 President Bush announced his cuts in the defense budget, he said nothing about helping those who are affected by the cuts, counting on the threat of job losses to keep workers and Congress behind his efforts to sustain defense spending.

The conversion provisions of the 1992 Defense Authorization and Appropriation Acts (which set spending for fiscal year 1993 and were approved in October 1992) are commendable as far as they go. The final bill authorizes $1.5 billion for conversion programs and features several improvements over the 1990 law. Among the 1992 provisions are:

- an additional $50 million for Department of Labor worker-relocation and training programs under the Job Training Partnership Act (JTPA);
- an additional $80 million for EDA;
- $50 million above the $4.9 million requested for planning grants to be issued through the Office of Economic Adjustment;
- $405 million divided among several manufacturing-technology and industrial-base programs.

These provisions were passed over the objections of the Bush administration, but the president will probably refrain from vetoing the legislation because to do so he would have to veto the whole defense bill. While the 1992 bill is a significant improvement over the 1990 Conversion Law, the 1992 bill still sets aside only about 0.5 percent of the overall appropriation to facilitate conversion.

Arms Exports

THE ONLY ALTERNATIVE TO CONVERSION the Bush administration has substantially supported is increased licensing of arms sales abroad. U.S. disbursement of foreign and military aid has been indiscriminate—witness Iraq's use of U.S. agricultural credits to build up the Iraqi arsenal. The Foreign Assistance Act demands that the United States withhold weapons and aid from countries that fail to meet internationally recognized human rights standards, yet we regularly give and sell weapons to countries that not only fail to meet recognized international standards but fail even by State Department accounting.[8]

Industry observers are predicting that U.S. companies will account for more than 50 percent of the world's arms export market over the next five years. To help give American firms an edge, the Pentagon went so far as to pay for the exhibiting of planes at foreign air and trade shows, reversing our longtime policy of charging these expenses to the firms on whose behalf they were incurred. This subsidy cost taxpayers millions before it was rescinded under pressure. A complementary initiative in the Senate threatened to use the Export-Import Bank to finance weapons sales. Fortunately it was struck down under public pressure.

A Peace Economy Program

RATHER THAN CONTINUE TO WASTE RESOURCES and play arms merchant to the world—with unpredictable and potentially dire consequences—we need to acknowledge the overdevelopment of our defense economy and address with a concerted effort the economic woes caused by this distortion. The next President should initiate a peace economy program, the aim of which should be to address the jobs impact of defense cuts *without* encouraging continued arms races.

In the short term, the incoming President should address the restrictions of the 1990 Budget Enforcement Act "fire wall," which allocates savings from the military budget solely to deficit reduction. (The Senate in March 1992 turned back a motion to end the fire wall.) Appropriate attention to the definition of defense items by OMB can reduce some of these restrictions. The fire wall expires in October 1993.

The President should immediately apply the lessons to be gleaned from conversion successes and take advantage of programs that can be implemented administratively, without legislative approval or breach of the fire wall. At the same time the President should identify legislative initiatives and rally congressional allies for more significant changes. The incoming President should undertake both short-term and longer-term measures.

SHORT-TERM MEASURES

1. *Review the 1990 Budget Enforcement Act.* The next President should meet with congressional leaders and end the restrictions of the 1990 Budget Enforcement Act "fire wall," which allocates savings from the military budget solely to deficit reduction. As noted, the fire wall expires in October 1993 but is enforced at the President's discretion by the Office of Management and Budget.

2. *Energize the EAC.* The 1990 Conversion Law and the 1992 law just passed by Congress give the President considerable latitude and funding to

undertake conversion activities. The Economic Adjustment Committee (EAC) would be a good mechanism for coordinating these activities. The EAC was created in the 1960s as the steering group for the Office of Economic Adjustment, was given formal status as a presidential committee by President Carter in 1978, and was upgraded to a statutory body in the 1990 Conversion Law. The EAC is formally composed of cabinet secretaries, with representation in 1990 from the Agriculture, Commerce, Defense (including the three services and Defense Logistics), Education, Energy, Health and Human Services, Housing and Urban Development, Interior, Justice, Labor, and Transportation departments, the Council of Economic Advisers, the Office of Management and Budget, the Arms Control and Disarmament Agency, the Environmental Protection Agency, the General Services Administration, the Small Business Administration, and the Office of Personnel Management.[9] But it has never met at the cabinet level. The President should be inclusive in soliciting ideas from EAC members, the Defense Conversion Commission that Congress created in 1991, and nongovernmental organizations such as the Council on Economic Priorities, the Center for Economic Conversion, the National Commission for Economic Conversion and Disarmament, and Business Executives for National Security. He should recognize communities (e.g., St. Louis) and companies (e.g., Hughes and TRW) that are attempting to diversify away from military production, by inviting their leaders to come to the White House to address the EAC.

3. *Hold the Economic Development Administration accountable for implementing its portion of the 1990 Conversion Law.* This should be done by requiring regular reports on the publicizing of conversion-related programs and the disbursement of funds.

4. *Review agency roles.* Through the EAC, the President should review the conversion roles of government agencies, including the Department of Commerce, especially EDA and the assistant secretary for technology; the Department of Defense, especially OEA; the Department of Labor; and the Small Business Administration.

The Department of Labor should be given leeway in creating experimental training programs. In the 1970s it funded the National Society of Professional Engineers (NSPE) to undertake a skills conversion program for aerospace workers; NSPE formed committees that surveyed major employers to identify job prospects for technical personnel and then designed and administered reorientation courses in regions affected by defense cuts to qualified laid-off workers. Virtually all who were enrolled were rehired before their courses were completed.[10] Similarly, the National Tooling and Machining Association has created several effective apprenticeship programs, including one that brings with it an associates degree from a community college. The Clearinghouse on Technology and Production Initiatives has also committed R&D money to Ohio, New York, Pennsylvania, Michigan, and Minnesota to help small businesses bid on defense and civilian contracts and initiate job training. It should be asked to report on such promising programs as a local training initiative in the Florida Panhandle, industrial networks in Denmark and Maine, and initiatives in the German Lander region and northern Italy.[11]

The Small Business Administration should examine existing loan and loan-guarantee programs that could be used to help small businesses with their capital needs for conversion. Representative Mary Rose Oakar (D., Ohio) recommended in the 102d Congress (1) more funding for small-business transition loans, half devoted to export activities, (2) a major effort to restructure and enhance the small-business venture capital process, and (3) a 50 percent increase in the successful Community Development Loan and Small Business Innovation Research programs.

Agencies with international responsibilities, such as AID, could be invited to EAC meetings to consider the applicability of lessons learned in U.S. conversion programs to conversion problems in the former Soviet Union.

LONGER-TERM MEASURES: SEVEN IDEAS

1. *Use military resources to address domestic needs.* Put the military to work on environmental cleanup of defense bases, as recommended by Senator Sam Nunn (D., Ga.), or reforestation, a task that would put many people to work and, if handled appropriately, would generate enormous environmental dividends. Contractors are already profitably diversifying into environmental cleanup technologies. The next President should appoint a high-level Administration official, perhaps the Vice President, to coordinate and spearhead environmentally oriented research, conversion, and cleanup initiatives. This official should be provided with a budget and a staff. Additionally, from underemployed, former military contractor employees, America could use a Healthcare Corps, a Teaching Corps, a Childcare Corps, and a Conservation Corps.

2. *Assist businesses and localities in expanding civilian employment.* Increased aid to state and federal programs targeted to create jobs in hard-hit areas would help save local jobs in both the short term and the long term, where structural readjustment is urgently needed. Examples of alter-

natives to military spending follow; in parentheses are funding levels suggested in the bill of Representative Sam Gejdenson (D., Conn.), which deserves presidential support in 1993:

- solar and renewable energy R&D ($2.1 billion);
- energy conservation ($600 million);
- pollution control and abatement ($1.2 billion);
- historic preservation ($600 million);
- maglev, high-speed rail development ($1.5 billion);
- increased mass-transit funds ($4.2 billion, including $1 billion for the Intelligent Highway Vehicle System);
- community development grants ($1.2 billion);
- EDA grants ($1.2 billion);
- increased JTPA Title III (Department of Labor) funds ($1.2 billion), and export enhancement programs ($1.2 billion).[12]

Additionally, technology transfer and training programs administered by DOD, NSF, and the Department of Commerce should be expanded to provide more manufacturing and marketing help to small defense suppliers. Encourage small-business technology development by extending the one-stop industrial services centers for small businesses, modeled on those established by some states. Create an extension service for defense contractors, especially small ones, and workers to link with commercial work.

3. *Extend employee training programs.* Extend training and related incentives for defense-industry employees to prepare them for civilian work. The 1992 law calls for the Secretary of Defense to announce in January which programs will be cut, which information must be relayed to affected workers at the plant level within two weeks. These employees will then be eligible for retraining programs prior to layoffs. But because Congress often significantly alters the Pentagon's request, the secretary's list will not necessarily identify the correct programs; some workers destined to be laid off will not benefit from these provisions. Multiyear defense budgets and broader eligibility for retraining programs, generally, would be better.

4. *Redirect the National Labs.* The National Labs should play a much larger role in carrying out environmental, public transportation, energy generation, and conservation research programs. The current program of developing Cooperative Research and Development Agreements (CRADAs) between the National Labs and private businesses should be encouraged and expanded.

5. *Launch a new national infrastructure project.* Example: Build high-speed railway lines as a flagship infrastructure development program. Trans-

portation experts are widely agreed on the viability and desirability of high-speed passenger rail in densely populated corridors of the East Coast, the West Coast, and the South. But more ambitious projects may also be viable. Americans went to war in Panama to protect U.S. troops guarding an obsolescent waterway—too narrow for modern supertankers and large cargo ships. The canal might be replaced by modern U.S. transshipment facilities on both coasts, connected by high-speed container-carrying trains. Creating such facilities—with essential private-sector guidance and involvement to ensure commercial viability—would be a challenge equal to Eisenhower's National Defense Highway System and the St. Lawrence Seaway. It should be undertaken with private-sector financing, but it surely won't happen without leadership from Washington. The current emphasis on tilt-rotor and supersonic planes that have dubious commercial prospects should be redirected to trains.

6. *Encourage business investment*. Senator Joseph Lieberman (D., Conn.), in his bill S. 2075, promotes assistance to defense-dependent firms (i.e., firms more than 35 percent dependent on defense contracts) through a business equivalent of the IRA—a tax-free deposit by which a company can accumulate money to use for investment in new nondefense plant and equipment, and for employee retraining.

7. *Contain arms exports*. U.S. conversion efforts should be explicitly linked to multinational efforts to reduce arms exports and a national policy for guiding civilian R&D to encourage civilian innovation. This would reduce the chance of the "new world order" turning into new world orders for advanced weaponry—and slowing our conversion to a peacetime economy. A program to reduce arms exports should be linked to reduced arms production.

These conversion-related proposals raise a broader issue. We must scrap the hidden military-dominated industrial policy of the Cold War era and substitute an open West European-Japanese-style civilian industrial policy.

NOTES

1. Not until July 30, 1992, did President Bush start talking about conversion of military research and retraining of aerospace workers. See *Newsday* (July 31, 1992), p. 17.

2. Information for 1979–89 is taken directly from the annual report of the U.S. Arms Control and Disarmament Agency, *World Military Expenditures and Arms Transfers, 1990*, table 1.

3. The basis for the projections is described in John Tepper Marlin, "Tell the Pentagon: The Cold War Is Over," *Challenge: The Magazine of Economic Affairs* 35 (4) (July–

August 1992): 25–26. Military spending in Russia is projected to drop steadily as a percentage of its GNP down to 6 percent; its GNP in 1990–93 is projected to drop 10 percent, 15 percent, 20 percent, and 10 percent, respectively, and in 1994–97 is projected to start growing by 4 percent a year. Other Warsaw Pact nations are projected to follow the Russian model, but with the percentage of their GNP devoted to the military dropping to 4 percent. For Europe outside the Warsaw Pact we project an average decline in military spending for 1990–97 of 10 percent a year; for the Middle East, Asia, Africa, and Latin America, of 5 percent a year.

4. For administration proposals we rely on three 1992 Congressional Budget Office (CBO) sources: (a) Actual 1990 and 1991 figures from its *The Economic and Budget Outlook: Fiscal Years 1993–97* (January 1992), table D–8, p. 120, with information from pp. 50 and 53; (b) *CBO Study: The Economic Effects of Reduced Defense Spending* (February 1992), showing a path down to $225 billion (1992 dollars) by 1997; (c) for 1993–97; projections and the "050" defense-budget line, see CBO, *An Analysis of the President's Budgetary Proposals for Fiscal Year 1993* (March 1992), table 4–2, p. 64; table 4–6, p. 75; and table 2–2, p. 20.

5. U.S. Congress, Congressional Budget Office (CBO), *The Economic Effects of Reduced Defense Spending* (Washington, D.C.: CBO, February 1992), p. 22.

6. U.S. Congress, Office of Technology Assessment (OTA), *After the Cold War: Living with Lower Defense Spending* (Washington, D.C.: U.S. Government Printing Office, February 1992), p. 59.

7. The basis for this minisequester was unquestionably political. See John Tepper Marlin, "Written Testimony Presented to the Joint Economic Committee," U.S. Congress (March 20, 1990), pp. 30–31.

8. Federation of American Scientists, *Arms Sales Monitor* (May–June 1992), p. 1.

9. Lall and Marlin, p. 24.

10. Mary Rose Oakar, "Statement Before the House Committee on the Budget" (February 19, 1992).

11. The Office of Technical Commercialization is in the Technology Administration of the Department of Commerce. John Heiser heads the Clearinghouse at the Springfield, Virginia, office of the Department of Commerce.

12. Office of Representative Sam Gejdenson, "Reps. Gejdenson, Reed Tell Leadership Funding for Jobs for Defense Workers Must Be Included in Final Budget Package," press release (February 27, 1992); Gejdenson, "Support the Industrial Reinvestment and Defense Diversification Act of 1992," letter to colleagues (February 26, 1992).

Department of Defense

CONVENTIONAL WEAPONS PROLIFERATION

MICHAEL T. KLARE

Summary

U NTIL RECENTLY, the control of international trafficking in conventional arms has been a low priority for the U.S. Government, which has traditionally viewed arms transfers as a convenient tool for promoting U.S. security objectives in Third World areas.

As a result of the Iraqi invasion of Kuwait, however, it is now obvious that uncontrolled arms exports contribute to military buildups in troubled areas and aggravate existing regional tensions. In the aftermath of the Persian Gulf War, therefore, American policymakers pledged to make control of the arms trade a major diplomatic priority. President Bush subsequently announced a "Middle East arms control initiative" (MEACI) in May 1991 and helped to launch a new set of arms control negotiations by the five permanent members of the U.N. Security Council (the "P-5"). On October 18, 1991, the P-5 announced a set of proposed guidelines for controlling arms transfers.

Despite announcement of the MEACI and the P-5 guidelines, the Bush administration has continued to boost U.S. arms exports to the Middle East. As a result, a new arms race is in full swing in the area, and progress toward a regional peace settlement has made little progress. In justifying its actions, the administration has clung to traditional arguments regarding the security benefits of arms transfers. On close inspection, however, these arguments shrivel.

Michael T. Klare is an Associate Professor of Peace and World Security Studies at Hampshire College in Amherst, Massachusetts, and the author of many articles and studies on the arms trade, including American Arms Supermarket *(Austin: University of Texas Press, 1984).*

If we are to make genuine progress toward global peace and security, the next President must repudiate the obsolete export policies of the Bush administration and impose meaningful controls on the conventional arms trade. Such efforts should include the adoption of multilateral restraints in accordance with the proposed P-5 guidelines, along with unilateral initiatives intended to eliminate all vestiges of a prosales orientation in the U.S. Government.

Introduction

THE PERSIAN GULF WAR OF 1991 and the many subsequent revelations regarding foreign involvement in Iraq's military programs have focused an unprecedented degree of attention on the problem of global arms proliferation. Most of this attention has been concentrated on issues arising from the proliferation of *unconventional weapons*—that is, nuclear, chemical, and biological munitions, plus the missiles used to deliver them. However, the Persian Gulf War has also called worldwide attention to problems arising from the proliferation of *conventional* weapons—the tanks, guns, planes, bombs, and missiles that constitute the basic instruments of modern warfare.

Long neglected by policymakers and arms control experts, the global trade in conventional weapons has emerged as a major world security issue. Because the ethnic and regional conflicts now engulfing many regions are largely fueled by conventional arms, it is becoming increasingly evident that any long-term progress toward regional peace and stability will require multilateral curbs on the munitions trade.

Although the need for conventional arms transfer restraints has been acknowledged by senior U.S. policymakers, the Bush administration has moved very slowly in this direction. In the immediate aftermath of the Persian Gulf War, President Bush indicated that conventional arms transfer control would be a major goal of U.S. foreign policy in the post-Persian Gulf War period. Subsequently, beginning in the summer of 1991, U.S. officials have participated in a series of Great Power talks aimed at adopting controls on the flow of conventional arms to areas of conflict. But the administration has also authorized billions of dollars' worth of new arms exports to the Middle East, including the sale of seventy-two F-15 fighters to Saudi Arabia. And because other major military suppliers are likely to greet such sales with increased marketing efforts of their own, we are likely to witness an intensified arms race in the Middle East and in other troubled areas.

The United States is faced, then, with two clear policy options: Either we move toward the adoption of tight international constraints on the arms trade, or we allow restoration of an essentially unregulated arms market. Our choice is crucial, for with the Cold War over, the greatest threat to world peace and security that we face today is the increasing frequency and intensity of regional conflicts. In this situation, the relative tempo and scale of international arms trafficking will prove critical: If the arms flow expands, we are almost certain to see an increase in the intensity and duration of regional and ethnic conflicts; if we can bring this trade under control, we will have a better chance at curbing the virulence of these engagements.

Unfortunately, the proliferation of conventional arms has tended to receive less attention from U.S. policymakers than has the proliferation of nuclear, chemical, and missile technology. This discrepancy reflects the perception that transfers of the latter are more dangerous than transfers of the former, and the belief that transfers of conventional weapons can, under certain circumstances, enhance U.S. security interests abroad. But while it is certainly true that the proliferation of unconventional weapons poses a substantial threat to world security, it is essential to recognize that conventional-arms trafficking is a key part of the global proliferation problem and that our failure to bring this trade under tight control will seriously undermine U.S. efforts to promote peace and stability in areas of conflict.

The Global Impact of the Arms Trade

AN EXPANDED FOCUS ON CONVENTIONAL ARMS transfer control is essential for several key reasons:

1. The military might of likely regional aggressors is composed largely of modern conventional weapons acquired through international sales channels. Recall that Iraq did not use its chemical arms and missiles to invade Kuwait—such acts of aggression can only be conducted by conventional forces. Similarly, the primary threat to Israel consists of the large conventional armies of its Arab neighbors. Thus, if we are to diminish the threat of regional conflict and aggression significantly, we must seek to limit and downsize the conventional force of potential belligerents.

2. There is a close relationship between conventional arms transfers and the risk of nuclear and chemical escalation in regional conflicts. It is precisely because so many Third World countries have acquired large quantitites of modern conventional weapons that some among them have acquired unconventional weapons as a hedge and a deterrent. The greater the flow of conventional arms to areas of conflict, therefore, the greater the risk that

existing nuclear and chemical powers will seek to preserve and to expand their supplies of unconventional weapons. And should any of these powers face catastrophic defeat in some future conventional conflict, they are certain to consider the actual use of their nuclear or chemical munitions—indeed, this is *the most likely way* in which a regional nuclear war might erupt in the post-Cold War era.

3. The diffusion of technology to make conventional arms is proceeding at an even more rapid pace than the spread of nuclear, chemical, and missile technology. According to the Stockholm International Peace Research Institute (SIPRI), some forty Third World countries now manufacture small arms and artillery, while a dozen or so produce tanks, aircraft, ships, and missiles.[1] Many of these countries plan to expand and to upgrade their military production efforts in the years ahead.

4. There is a high correlation between arms transfers and human rights abuses in countries ruled by authoritarian regimes. In many such countries, the military is used more for internal policing and repression than for external defense, and the weapons acquired by these countries are often used in the suppression of dissident groups and movements. Thus, arms provided by Germany to Turkey have been used to suppress Kurdish separatists, and arms provided by the United States to Thailand have been used to suppress prodemocracy forces in Bangkok. The use of imported arms for repressive purposes is a recurring feature of international arms traffic and suggests the need for strict human rights restrictions on all foreign military sales.[2]

5. The growth in conventional arms sales to Third World countries is being accompanied by—and contributes to—a growing black-market arms trade with insurgents, terrorists, separatist groups, and other *nonstate* entities. No matter how rigorous our export controls and those of our allies, it is inevitable that a certain percentage of state-to-state military sales leak into the black-market trade; with the growing privatazation of weapons production in both the East and West, this leakage appears to be growing larger all the time.

6. Finally, there is a risk that U.S. forces committed to peacekeeping or contingency operations abroad will be confronted by capable Third World armies equipped with large numbers of sophisticated weapons. We clearly faced such a threat in the Persian Gulf War; fortunately for our side, Iraqi forces lacked the training and leadership to employ their high-tech weapons in an effective manner. We cannot assume, however, that such will be the case in all future encounters of this sort; sooner or later we are likely to face a modern, well-trained Third World army, and then the diffusion of so-

phisticated arms will pose a significant threat to the success of our efforts and to the lives of our soldiers.

For all of these reasons, it should be evident that uncontrolled arms sales represent a significant threat to U.S. and international stability. If there was any question about this before 1990, the Iraqi invasion of Kuwait and the resulting Persian Gulf War should have dispelled any doubts.

The Persian Gulf War and Its Aftermath

BETWEEN 1980 AND 1990, Iraq conducted the most ambitious buildup of conventional arms ever undertaken by a Third World country, and this undoubtedly contributed to the self-confidence with which Saddam Hussein ordered the attack on Kuwait. In addition, the evident ease with which he was able to acquire sophisticated arms from the major suppliers—all of which sold arms or technology to Baghdad in the 1980s—must have persuaded him that the major powers had no real objection to his hegemonic aspirations.

In the wake of this conflict, President Bush and his senior advisers acknowledged the threat posed by unconstrained arms sales and affirmed the need for new controls. "The time has come," Secretary of State Baker told the House Foreign Affairs Committee on February 6, 1990, "to try to change the destructive pattern of military competition and proliferation in [the Middle East] and to reduce the arms flow into an area that is already overmilitarized."[3] In his first press conference after the war's conclusion, President Bush also spoke of the need for conventional arms trade restraint. "Let's hope that out of all this there will be less proliferation of all different types of weapons, not just unconventional weapons," he declared on March 1, 1991.[4]

Subsequently, on May 29, 1991, President Bush announced a "Middle East arms control initiative" aimed at curbing the spread of ballistic missiles, weapons of mass destruction, and "destabilizing" conventional arms. As part of this effort, he called for meetings of the five permanent members of the U.N. Security Council (the P-5) to consider the adoption of mutual "guidelines" for the control of conventional arms transfers.[5]

In response to this proposal, representatives of the P-5 met over the summer and early fall of 1991, and, at a meeting in London on October 17–18, adopted draft guidelines for the control of conventional arms transfers. In signing the London document, the P-5 promised to consult with one another regarding the flow of arms to particular regions and to "observe rules of restraint" when deciding on major arms exports. They further pledged to avoid arms transfers that would be likely to: (a) prolong or aggravate an existing armed conflict; (b) increase tension in a region or contribute to regional instability; (c) introduce destabilizing military capabilities in a region; (d) contravene embargoes or other relevant internationally agreed-on restraints to which they are parties; or (e) be used other than for the legitimate defense and foreign security needs of the recipient state.[6]

The adoption of these guidelines suggests a strong commitment by the United States to the principle of conventional arms transfer restraint. If followed up with appropriate regulatory and enforcement measures, the London guidelines could provide the foundation for an international arms transfer control regime akin to the existing regimes for the control of nuclear, chemical, and missile technology. But Bush administration officials appear to view the guidelines as little more than a hedge against some future repetition of Iraq's mammoth arms buildup of the 1980s.[7]

The Bush Administration's Backtracking on Arms Sales

THE BUSH ADMINISTRATION'S RELUCTANCE to interpret the London guidelines as a call for significant arms transfer restraint is undoubtedly a product of the administration's continuing belief in the efficacy of arms transfers as a tool of foreign and military policy. This view of arms exports first arose during the early Cold War era, when both superpowers used such transfers as a device for winning and retaining the loyalty of Third World countries, especially in the Middle East. Later, during the Nixon era, such transfers were also seen by U.S. policymakers as a means for strengthening the defenses of pro-Western states in order to diminish the potential requirement for direct U.S. military intervention on their behalf.[8]

This inherited view of the political and military efficacy of arms transfers is clearly evident in statements by senior Bush administration officials. Thus, in response to queries regarding the desirability of arms transfer restraints, Secretary of Defense Dick Cheney told Congress on March 19, 1991, that while he might be willing to entertain some such controls, the continuing supply of arms to U.S. allies in the Middle East should remain America's top priority. "I think our first concern ought to be to work with our friends and allies to see to it that they're secure," he asserted.[9]

This, in essence, represents the core of the Bush administration's position on conventional arms transfers: America will pursue moderate restraints at the international level while continuing to satisfy the military requirements of key allies and clients in the Third World. It is a position that appears to satisfy competing pressures and demands: on one hand, the pressure to follow through on pledges to establish multilateral constraints on global arms trafficking; on the other, the pressure to preserve long-standing military relationships with friendly foreign governments.

But while a compromise position of this sort is undoubtedly attractive to U.S. policymakers, it is not a stance that can be sustained indefinitely. Any increase in U.S. military sales to its allies and clients abroad will inevitably be seen by other suppliers as providing justification for an increase in their own arms exports. This point was made with particular clarity by Andrei Kokoshin, a senior Russian military official, in early 1992. "I think if other countries would have started reducing arms deliveries, this would have had some effect [on Russian arms export policy], but it turned out that most democratic countries are not stopping arms sales, but increasing them," and thus Russia feels no obligation to reduce its sales.[10]

It is also important to recognize that what is viewed as a "defensive" weapon by one country is often seen as potentially offensive to another, and thus increased U.S. military sales to any country in a region—no matter how "defensive" we may consider the equipment to be—will inevitably stimulate a desire for additional arms by that nation's neighbors and rivals. Hence, U.S. sales of tanks and multirole fighters to Egypt, Turkey, and Saudi Arabia will inevitably be viewed by Iran, Israel, Syria, and other Middle Eastern countries as a potential threat, thus justifying additional arms acquisitions of their own. The result of such behavior, inevitably, will be an intensified arms race with an increased risk of miscalculation and conflict.

That appears to be happening. According to published accounts of the administration's arms export plans for 1992—the "Javits list" of pending arms transactions—the Executive Branch is contemplating some $35 billion in new foreign military sales agreements, with the majority of these agreements involving sales to Saudi Arabia and other buyers in the Middle East.[11] Sales of this magnitude will undoubtedly stimulate an appetite for equivalent items in neighboring countries, and thus the flow of arms into what Baker called an "already very overmilitarized" area will surely increase.

Dissecting the Case for Arms Sales

DESPITE THIS PROSPECT, proponents of arms transfers in government and industry will continue to argue for a relatively relaxed policy on military exports. The arguments used to advance this position are well known.[12] By strengthening the defensive capabilities of America's allies, it is argued, we help to deter attacks on them by aspiring regional hegemons and thus diminish the likelihood that American forces will be required to repel such aggression in the event that deterrence fails.[13]

Arms sales are also described as a means of preserving a "warm production base" in the U.S. defense industry—that is, of maintaining in operation various weapons production lines that would otherwise be shut down for lack of domestic orders. With the end of the Cold War and the decline in U.S. military spending, many such lines—including those for the M-1 tank, the F-16 fighter, and the AWACS radar patrol plane—are facing imminent closure. To keep these lines open—and thereby preserve thousands of high-paying jobs in the military sector—many government and industry leaders are calling for a substantial increase in U.S. military sales abroad.[14]

These arguments have a certain amount of merit but must be set against the challenges of the post-Cold War era—an era characterized by the breakdown of traditional alliances and recurring conflicts at the regional level. In this new environment, each delivery of arms into a region is likely to aggravate local tensions and prompt further weapons acquisitions by other regional powers—thereby placing all countries in the vicinity at greater risk.[15]

It is also risky, as repeatedly demonstrated by events in the Middle East, to assume that today's friendly regime will remain loyal to Washington in the future, or that it will successfully resist efforts by hostile factions to overthrow it. The Nixon administration poured billions of dollars' worth of sophisticated arms into Iran when we thought that the reign of the shah would last forever; it didn't. Today, those same weapons (or at least those for which Iran has been able to obtain spare parts) are being used by the shah's successors to threaten stability in the Persian Gulf area.

Nor can we have any confidence that substantial U.S. arms transfers to threatened allies will significantly reduce the need for U.S. intervention should a key ally come under attack. "The Gulf War proved that, no matter how well [America's allies] are armed, the United States still is the ultimate guarantor of their security," former Arms Control and Disarmament Agency (ACDA) head Paul C. Warnke testified in 1991. "We simply cannot arm Saudi Arabia or Israel or Egypt enough to ensure their physical safety, especially if we are arming their neighbors as well."[16]

The argument that arms sales can rescue the U.S. defense industry and provide stable employment to American workers is also fallacious. No Third World country or combination of countries can spend enough on U.S. arms to compensate for the United States' long-term decline in domestic military spending. Given this fact, the only prudent course for U.S. defense contractors at this time is to diversify their production into nonmilitary fields for which there is a demand in the civilian economy, as discussed by John Tepper Marlin elsewhere in this volume.

Consequently, America's long-term security interests—and those of its friends and allies—would best be secured by constraining the flow of conventional arms to areas of conflict and by persuading the nations of these areas to join in regional peace talks aimed at reducing regional tensions and lowering the levels of regional arsenals.

An Action Plan for the Next President

IN ACCORDANCE WITH SECTION 402 of the Foreign Relations Authorization Act, the next Administration should commit itself to a program of *conventional-arms transfer restraint*. Such a program should rely primarily on multilateral measures, but—in recognition of America's role as the world's number one arms supplier—should also include prudent unilateral measures. The goal, in every case, should be to diminish the destabilizing impact of arms sales on regional conflict situations, and to advance the other foreign policy objectives of the United States—particularly the promotion of democratic forms of government, human rights, and sustainable economic development.

THE FIRST HUNDRED DAYS

The establishment of an effective international system for the control of arms transfers will take months and possibly years to complete. There is a great deal, however, that the President can do in the first hundred days after taking office:

• Declare a six-month *renewable* moratorium on arms sales to the Middle East pending adoption of international constraints in accordance with the P-5 London guidelines of October 17–18, 1991.

• Create a new position of assistant secretary of state for arms export control, whose responsibility shall be to review all U.S. arms transfers to ensure that they accord with the arms control and foreign policy objectives of the United States. Also, require that this official consult with the Director of the ACDA regarding the arms control implications of every transfer over a certain level (say, $25 million), and report these findings to Congress.

• Change the name of the Center for Defense Trade (CDT) in the Department of State back to its original name—Office of Munitions Control (OMC)—and instruct the staff of this agency to view international arms control as its principal responsibility.

• Rescind the Eagleburger directive of July 1990 instructing U.S. embassy personnel abroad to "support the marketing efforts of U.S. companies in the defense trade arena." Instead, order U.S. personnel to refrain from such trade promotion activities.

- Issue a presidential order prohibiting the Department of Defense from supplying equipment or personnel for military trade shows or "arms bazaars" in the United States or abroad.
- Abolish the 3 percent fee imposed by the Defense Security Assistance Agency (DSAA) in all foreign military sales cases and used to subsidize DSAA operations (thus providing an internal incentive for higher levels of arms exports).

LONG-TERM OBJECTIVES

Simultaneously with enactment of the measures described above, the next President should initiate a long-term effort to establish a global regime for the control of conventional arms trafficking. In constructing this regime, the following control systems should be established:

1. *Multilateral supplier restraints.* The President should elevate the P-5 negotiations into a major international arena for the adoption of rigorous multilateral controls on arms transfers. Such controls should include some combination of *technology controls* (i.e., limits on the introduction of highly destabilizing weapons such as ballistic missiles and deep-penetration bombers) and *volume controls* (i.e., monetary limitations on the annual value of military transfers from any given supplier to any recipient or region).

Because the P-5 will require a certain amount of time to gain experience and confidence in the implementation of such restrictions, it would be appropriate for them to adopt a slate of interim restrictions and then proceed progressively to more rigorous controls. As a start, the P-5 might ban the sale of deep-penetration bombers to the Middle East and South Asia, and set a limit (say, two hundred) on the number of tanks that could be delivered to any country in a given year. Additionally, or alternatively, they could set a limit (say, $500 million) on the total value of all weapons that could be supplied from one country to another.

2. *Unilateral initiatives.* In support of these multilateral measures, the next President—in cooperation with Congress—should adopt a number of unilateral initiatives designed to slow the tempo of U.S. arms exports and to prompt similar action by the other suppliers. Such measures should begin with a six-month moratorium on arms sales to the Middle East, as proposed by many in Congress. The President should also ban sales of arms and military technology to nations that refuse to place their nuclear facilities under the nonproliferation safeguards of the International Atomic Energy Agency (IAEA) or that are suspected of producing chemical and/or biological weapons.

As a further demonstration of U.S. resolve to curb the arms traffic, the President should eliminate all government programs or policies that facilitate or encourage such sales. As noted, this should commence with a ban on government participation in military trade shows and on the loan of military equipment to U.S. defense contractors for this purpose. With the cooperation of Congress, the President should also phase out the foreign military sales credit program and other federal subsidies for arms purchases by foreign governments.[17] Effective organizational machinery should also be established in the Department of State to ensure that all U.S. arms transfers—whether conducted as foreign military sales or commercial sales—are in accord with U.S. policies regarding arms control, democratization, and human rights.

3. *Promote regional arms control agreements.* Because supply-side restraints can go only so far in reducing the flow of arms and military technology to areas of tension, the President should make the adoption of regional arms control agreements—entailing mutual restrictions on the importation of conventional weapons—a major diplomatic objective. Secretary of State James Baker provided a useful precedent in this regard with the "shuttle diplomacy" he conducted in 1991 to launch Middle East peace negotiations. A major priority of the new President, therefore, must be to reenergize these talks and to assist in the establishment of similar talks in South Asia and the Far East.

4. *Suppress black-market trafficking.* To curb the black-market trade in conventional weapons, the President should tighten U.S. export procedures and encourage and assist other governments to do likewise. Such efforts should be supplemented by increased intelligence-sharing among the major military suppliers, and by combined intergovernmental efforts to identify, monitor, and suppress international arms-smuggling syndicates.

5. *Promote economic conversion.* Finally, to soften the impact on U.S. industries and communities of any reductions in American arms sales and to alleviate pressures to sell abroad, the President should initiate a program of federal support for local conversion efforts. Such support should include government grants for community-based conversion planning efforts, for job retraining, and for research on civilian applications of military technologies.

NOTES

1. Michael Brzoska and Thomas Ohlson, *Arms Production in the Third World* (London and Philadelphia: Taylor and Francis, 1986), p. 16. See also Stockholm International Peace Research Institute, *SIPRI Yearbook 1990: World Armaments and Disarmament* (Oxford and New York: Oxford University Press, 1990), pp. 299–308.

2. For further discussion of this point, see Michael T. Klare and Cynthia Arnson, *Supplying Repression: U.S. Support for Authoritarian Regimes Abroad* (Washington, D.C.: Institute for Policy Studies, 1981).

3. Statement of Secretary of State James Baker before the House Foreign Affairs Committee, Washington, D.C. (February 6, 1991) (State Department transcript).

4. From the transcript of Bush's remarks in *The New York Times* (March 2, 1991).

5. "Fact Sheet: Middle East Arms Control Initiative," *U.S. Department of State Dispatch* (June 3, 1991), p. 393.

6. "Meeting of the Five on Arms Transfers and Nonproliferation: London, 17/18 October 1991."

7. For an analysis of the Bush administration's interpretation of the P-5 guidelines, see *BASIC Reports on European Arms Control* (British-American Security Information Council, February 19, 1992).

8. For discussion, see Michael T. Klare, *American Arms Supermarket* (Austin: University of Texas Press, 1984), pp. 39-53.

9. Quoted in *The New York Times* (March 20, 1991).

10. Quoted in *The Washington Post* (February 23, 1992).

11. The estimates for 1992 are drawn from the "Javits list" of proposed arms sales, provided to Congress each year in accordance with Section 2765(a) of the Arms Export Control Act (see Associated Press wire story by Jim Drinkard of February 26, 1992).

12. For articulation of these arguments, see Paul Y. Hammond et al., *The Reluctant Supplier* (Cambridge, Mass.: Oelgeschlager, Gunn & Hain, 1983); and Roger P. Labrie et al., *U.S. Arms Sales Policy: Background and Issues* (Washington D.C.: American Enterprise Institute, 1982).

13. In justifying a 1986 arms shipment to Saudi Arabia, for instance, the State Department said that "our willingness to support Saudi self-defense has served as a deterrent to Iran," then considered the major threat to U.S. interests in the Persian Gulf. Moreover, "it will also reduce the chances that we would have to take emergency action later to protect our interests." ("U.S. Proposes Arms Sales to Saudi Arabia," *Department of State Bulletin* [May 1986], p. 77.)

14. See David C. Morrison, "Saudi F-15 Sales: Jobs, Jobs, and Jobs?" *National Journal* (April 18, 1992): 947–48.

15. Prepared statement of Paul C. Warnke before the Permanent Subcommittee on Investigations, Senate Governmental Affairs Committee (Washington, D.C., June 12, 1991), p. 3.

16. Ibid.

17. I am indebted to William D. Hartung of the World Policy Institute for these two suggestions. See Hartung, "Curbing the Arms Trade: From Rhetoric to Restraint," *World Policy Journal* (Spring 1992): 239.

NUCLEAR WEAPONS: BUILD DOWN/CLEAN UP

PETER GRAY

Summary

THE SCALE AND COST of the U.S. nuclear weapons industry—born half a century ago as the Manhattan Project—realized a 1939 prediction by Nobel physicist Niels Bohr that building atomic bombs would require "turning the country into a gigantic factory."[1] The laboratories, factories, and test sites, known as the "Nuclear Weapons Complex" by the Department of Energy (DOE) that manages it, occupies 3,300 square miles, typically employs more than 100,000 people, and costs about $13 billion in federal money per year.

The environmental, economic, public health, and social harm from nuclear weapons work began to emerge in the mid-1980s. The manufacture of more than 60,000 nuclear weapons has generated about 125 million cubic feet of radioactive waste—more than 1 billion curies of radioactivity. Radioactive and toxic material was released, often deliberately, into the air, water, and soil, and continues to migrate beyond site borders. People living near plants such as Hanford were exposed to many times the radiation doses believed safe—even in the 1940s. Atmospheric nuclear testing contaminated the planet with radioactive fallout, some of which will remain in the biosphere for millennia, potentially causing hundreds of thousands of cancer fatalities.

Nuclear weapons work has also poisoned democratic processes and public trust. The government suppressed data on radiation and health, subverted legal and legislative actions, and denied compensation to injured parties. A

Peter Gray is a senior science and policy writer for the Nuclear Weapons Production Project at Friends of the Earth in Washington, D.C. Gray is a contributing editor of The Washington Monthly *and the editor of* Facing Reality: The Future of the U.S. Nuclear Weapons Complex *(May 1992).*

program charged with defending democracy has used secrecy and immunity from oversight to defend itself *from* democracy.

The United States cannot persuade or compel other countries to forgo nuclear arms if it continues to develop, test, and manufacture new weapons itself. While no country is in a better position to call for verifiable global bans on nuclear testing and on production of "fissile materials" for weapons, the Bush administration has been virtually alone in its opposition to these and other proliferation control measures.

The country faces exciting opportunities to capture the benefits of the Cold War's end—and a dismaying cleanup project that might be as long and costly as the nuclear arms race itself. There could be no better time to reform an entrenched nuclear weapons bureaucracy; the missing ingredient has been presidential leadership. The new Administration's top priorities in this area should be to:

- Save tax dollars and reduce risk by insisting that DOE plan for a future arsenal in the realistic range of zero to three thousand weapons.
- Strengthen confidence in a reduced-arsenal world by agreeing to verifiable warhead dismantlement and inspection.
- Reduce the proliferation threat through verifiable multilateral agreements to end fissile material production.
- Ease the transition to a peacetime economy by giving nuclear arms workers choices between environmental restoration work and quality job training.
- Promote worker and public health by releasing epidemiologic and radiation effects data.
- Improve site restoration efficiency by giving cleanup authority to an agency not responsible for weapons production.
- Gain public trust by ordering DOE to comply with environmental, health, and safety laws, accept citizen participation, and operate as openly as possible.

Facing Reality

ALTHOUGH SOME DIFFERENCES REMAIN, Presidents Bush and Yeltsin agreed in 1992 to reduce strategic nuclear forces to thirty-five hundred or fewer weapons each for the United States and the Commonwealth of Independent States within about ten years. Including reductions in tactical nuclear weapons, the United States and the Commonwealth of Independent States are on the way to cutting their arsenals by about 80 percent from 1990 levels. Successful arms control treaties and initiatives, and withdrawal of strategic forces from alert, have reduced the risk of all-out nuclear war.

So why worry about the nuclear weapons industry? Unfortunately, the bureaucracy that built more than sixty thousand nuclear weapons during the Cold War cannot reform itself. For four decades, DOE officials have prepared for every contingency—*except* the end of the Cold War. During the 1980s, while total DOE funding stayed roughly constant, the proportion devoted to nuclear weapons more than doubled, reaching about 70 percent by 1988. DOE managers and contractors are ill-prepared to carry out what should be their new missions of nuclear facility cleanup, verifiable warhead dismantlement, proliferation control, and victim compensation.

As the Cold War wound down in the late 1980s, citizen pressure exposed environmental devastation from nuclear weapons production. Yet DOE did not search for alternatives to business as usual, nor did it begin a genuine effort to clean up old messes before creating new ones. Instead, it asked the country for a vast spending program to build an array of new plants it calls "Complex 21" for warhead development and production through the middle of the twenty-first century. Although some independent oversight is now in place, so are three ingredients of disaster present since the 1940s:

• *Conflict of interest.* Careers and fortunes of DOE managers and contractors have depended on endless development and manufacture of new nuclear warheads.

• *Lack of oversight.* The extreme secrecy of the Manhattan Project spread a "national security" shield over every aspect of nuclear arms work. Weapons plants are not subject to the regulations and accountability that govern the rest of society.

• *Extremely hazardous materials.* When nuclear weapons factories operate, they produce and process many of the most deadly substances ever identified—with inadequate concern for where the materials go. Huge quantities of radioactive isotopes have been emitted through routine operations, test explosions, and accidents.

DOE secretary James Watkins attempted, rhetorically, to break with the past. Watkins criticized DOE's "management culture" and promised to reform it. He finally conceded a lack of need for more "fissile materials" (plutonium and highly enriched uranium) for weapons. Watkins dropped the assumption that the nuclear stockpile must contain twenty thousand warheads, and he slated several obsolete facilities for decommissioning. Meanwhile, however, DOE:

• lobbied to restart unneeded plutonium operations at Rocky Flats, Colorado;

- resisted a verifiable multilateral ban on making fissile materials for weapons;
- pushed to operate obsolete, risky reactors at Savannah River, South Carolina, and poured billions of dollars into an attempt to build an oversized new production reactor—to make new tritium that will not be needed for at least twenty years;
- fought for development of new warheads that have no military mission;
- obstructed progress toward a comprehensive test ban treaty;
- opposed legislation requiring DOE to comply with environmental, safety, and health statutes.

The industry is in a rut, unable to anticipate change or respond to it effectively. For example, the administration's vision of "Complex 21" assumed a future arsenal of three thousand to seventeen thousand warheads. This plan implies an industry built to support the upper stockpile limit. Although weapons manufacture has been stalled for several years, the annual research, development, and production budget still exceeds $7 billion.

But DOE's nuclear negligence, especially in light of the diminished international threat, cannot be allowed to continue. Here's a sample of its deadly legacy:

- The Fernald Feed Materials Production Center in Ohio emitted between 600,000 and 3 million pounds of toxic uranium dust into the air and water. Known drinking water contamination was kept secret for years during the 1980s.
- Plutonium processing at the Rocky Flats Plant in Colorado has contaminated the region's air and water. Serious plutonium fires, and plutonium accumulation in ventilation ducts, have endangered plant workers and neighbors.
- Hanford Reservation in Washington State has released massive quantities of radioactive isotopes into the air, soil, groundwater, and Columbia River. Dozens of huge tanks are filled with waste of unknown composition; some have generated compounds that risked causing a disastrous explosion.
- Los Alamos National Laboratory in New Mexico has one of the world's largest radioactive dumps, containing more than 12 million cubic feet of radioactive waste, and is still adding about 180,000 cubic feet per year. Cleaning up more than 2,000 known contaminated sites is expected to cost at least $2 billion.
- When a DOE biologist at Oak Ridge National Laboratory in Tennessee discovered extremely high levels of mercury in the local environment, he was reprimanded for "failure to perceive bureaucratically positive solutions." DOE later admitted emitting more than two million pounds of mercury.

• Waste at the Idaho National Engineering Laboratory (INEL)—including nearly 1,000 pounds of plutonium, more than 200 tons of uranium, and 90,000 gallons of organic solvents—was dumped into shallow trenches. This material is seeping toward the Snake River Plain aquifer. From 1957 to 1963, scientists at INEL knowingly released 6 million curies of radioactivity into the atmosphere.

• Since 1960, Lawrence Livermore Laboratory in California has emitted tritium-contaminated water and more than 750,000 curies of tritium into the air.

• In 1988, when workers at Knolls Atomic Power Laboratories in New York complained about radioactive contamination, General Electric, the site contractor, issued a "security newsletter" to all employees, threatening termination, $100,000 fines, or life imprisonment if they spoke to outsiders about the plant.

• In 1989, at the Pantex warhead assembly/disassembly plant in Texas, 40,000 curies of tritium were released, exposing five workers. The Advisory Committee on Nuclear Facility Safety reported: "confusion, misread instruments, and uncertain actions. . . . It is still unclear that effective control of the situation by an adequately prepared response team ever took place."

The Administration Needs to Keep the Public Involved

FEW BUREAUCRACIES WILL REFORM merely because they are obsolete. Unless DOE's $13 billion (including "cleanup") annual budget is actively monitored and redirected, it is likely to overlook precious opportunities and ominous hazards.

Congress has helped open federal agencies to outside scrutiny, especially with the 1966 Freedom of Information Act, permitting citizens to obtain secret documents unless a document satisfies one of several explicit exemptions. It has also imposed some constraints on DOE, preventing it from continuing all-out weapons development into the 1990s. In 1992 Congress passed a nuclear testing moratorium to match the Russian and French initiatives. But pork barrel politics has hindered legislation. Billions of dollars have been spent trying to build new tritium production reactors or restart risky old ones at Savannah River, although the need for new tritium is decades away. In Nevada, where most citizens oppose nuclear testing, the state's entire federal delegation has supported the program—for the sake of test site jobs.

DOE's nuclear weapons laboratories, primarily Lawrence Livermore and Los Alamos, have wielded inordinate political clout, partly based on an image of pure, clean research. The labs have in fact produced substantial contamination from their R&D operations, not to mention from nuclear testing. Lab scientists have adapted to the end of the Cold War by concocting fresh excuses for undiminished funding. Their schemes include farfetched proposals for generating electricity with thousands of underground nuclear explosions, and building gigantic thermonuclear bombs to fend off asteroids.

A Congress and an Administration acting in the national interest could quickly realign "Complex 21" through mandates and budget requests. Since a strong majority of voters supports ending nuclear weapons testing and production, the next President should promote democratic processes that strengthen citizen involvement. This would include permanent oversight structures, tight limits on secrecy, and a requirement that nuclear weapons work be publicly justified.

Controlling nuclear proliferation and cleaning up after the Cold War are daunting prospects. However, the United States has applied hundreds of times more money and ingenuity to the arms race than to the "disarms race." More than cash, the missing ingredients are political will and a positive long-term vision of a U.S. role in creating a safer, healthier world.

New Initiatives

THE NUCLEAR WEAPONS INDUSTRY should be subject to these constraints:

1. The nuclear weapons plants and labs should be designed to support a stable future arsenal in the range of zero to three thousand warheads at most, instead of three thousand to seventeen thousand. A much-reduced industry should have a maintenance mission of safety monitoring, weapons security, and minimal remanufacturing of a "finite deterrent" stockpile. The new Federal Government should treat near-total elimination of nuclear weapons as a serious possibility.

2. Nuclear weapons activities must comply with state and federal environmental, health, and safety regulations. The environmental impact statement process should be used to ensure that all practicable alternatives are considered, including the "no-action alternative" to construction projects.

3. All research toward weapons with new military characteristics should halt. Research, development, and testing must be limited to safety and other modifications to prepare for a comprehensive test ban within three to four years.

A testing moratorium would demonstrate U.S. willingness to join Russia, Kazakhstan, and France—saving hundreds of millions of dollars and providing time to consider seriously the need to continue the program.

The implications of acknowledging that the United States needs no more than a small fraction of its present arsenal are profound:

- There is no need to "preserve the option" of making more fissile materials for weapons. The country can endorse a verifiable global production ban.
- Plutonium recycling and fabrication are unnecessary for at least five to ten years.
- Tritium production can be delayed at least twenty to forty years.
- Warhead remanufacture can be delayed at least five to ten years.
- Many billions of dollars can be saved by canceling unnecessary construction and production projects.

The next Administration should chart a positive course for DOE or other agencies that might take its place. The highest future priorities should include:

1. *Nonproliferation.* While the chance of a massive nuclear attack is now remote, the threats of regional nuclear war and nuclear terrorism are growing. Nuclear weapons development conflicts with nonproliferation efforts. Scientists at the national labs should therefore be directed away from designing exotic new weapons and toward strengthening the treaty obligations, intelligence analyses, export controls, and U.N. inspections that are the world's real hope for avoiding catastrophe.

2. *Warhead dismantlement.* If the thousands of surplus weapons from planned arms reductions are not dismantled verifiably, and their components securely stored, the risk of clandestine reassembly, sale, or theft will grow, and confidence in arms treaties will be undermined. Existing agreements have no verification provisions and no way for the United States to monitor the fate of thousands of former Soviet warheads.

Obsolete nuclear warheads should be disassembled and made inoperable as quickly as possible, and their critical components safely stored. The new Administration should first announce that all its withdrawn warheads will be dismantled. Dismantlement could be accelerated by retiring and disabling more weapons than can be disassembled each year at the Pantex plant in Texas. Weapons should be separated from missiles and aircraft, rendered inoperable, sealed in special containers with tamperproof tags, and stored in facilities open to international inspection.

3. *Waste disposal.* While spending billions of dollars, DOE has developed no safe and politically acceptable disposal site. This failure stems from heavy-handed political tactics and a lack of candor that continues to inspire opposition to waste sites. The present system of waste handling is poorly founded in science and economics.

Radioactive waste should be categorized according to its physical characteristics rather than by the process that generated it. Realistic estimates of eventual disposal costs should be included at the "front end" of every nuclear waste generating process, rather than being passed on to taxpayers and future generations.

4. *Environmental mitigation, compliance, and cleanup.* Decommissioning and decontamination of closed plants will be a long and costly process. DOE has not developed a coherent plan to minimize the risk of catastrophic accidents—such as high-level waste tank explosions—as well as to control injury to future generations.

The clash between cleanup and DOE's traditional functions of nuclear weapons production and nuclear power promotion may require that the department be subdivided, or that cleanup be assigned to another agency, such as the Environmental Protection Agency (EPA). Whoever does the work, all cleanup costs must be paid from the nuclear weapons budget; the burden should not be shifted to state or local governments. "Cleanup" funds should be monitored to ensure that they do not support future production.

5. *Environmental restoration leadership.* For the country to neglect its accumulated nuclear waste and contamination and to forgo the profit that could come from developing and exporting better technology would be doubly shortsighted. Instead, the United States should strive to be the world leader in toxic and radioactive waste technology, a growing market that could provide economic and human health returns.

6. *Worker and community peacetime transition.* Worker retraining, site restoration, and other peacetime activities conflict with managers' desire to resume weapons production. DOE has often used the threat of layoffs as a political lever to maintain production funding, even though the labor needed for cleanup could exceed previous production employment for many years.

The Administration should strive to minimize economic hardships for nuclear workers and surrounding communities when weapons plants close. Former plant workers should have preference on retraining for cleanup work, but their health and safety must be given the highest priority.[2] At the very least, the DOE budget should immediately include a fund to continue health and life insurance for former plant employees. The GI Bill following World

War II was a very successful investment—in social justice as well as in productivity. That example should be reexamined as a prototype for fair treatment of the workers and citizens who served on the front lines of the Cold War.

7. *Comprehensive health effects studies.* Secrecy shields not only the design, manufacture, and testing of nuclear weapons but also data on radioactive and toxic emissions and on workers' exposures and health. Independent scientific studies of illness and death among workers and nearby communities have often been stymied by a lack of data.

More complete, less biased, publicly accessible radiation health effects studies are needed. The best available epidemiological results should be used to determine who should be compensated for illnesses that may have come from exposure to toxic and radioactive substances.

8. *Victim compensation.* The communities and workers exposed to hazardous DOE emissions have not received the fair compensation that citizens would expect if private companies had exposed the public or work force to danger. But DOE is essentially immune from the damage claims of citizens. The next Administration should reverse this Reagan-Bush legacy and acknowledge the true costs of the arms race by dealing fairly with those who paid far more than their share to "win the Cold War."

9. *Public oversight and regulation.* The costs of excessive secrecy are written in the mismanagement and disregard for safety that were themes of nuclear weapons programs since the 1940s. In 1991 the Congressional Office of Technology Assessment recommended that DOE be regulated by the EPA or the Nuclear Regulatory Commission. Unfortunately, there has been no legislative response.

Effective oversight also requires adequate funding. Yet the administration has requested only 0.63 percent of the total defense and energy cleanup budget for EPA oversight activities. By contrast, private corporations restoring commercial waste sites pay an average of 2 to 4 percent of total cleanup costs for EPA oversight.

Independent agency control will be necessary to avoid the problems caused by DOE regulating itself. Citizen participation must also be accepted as a fact of life for any agency charged with the public interest. To complement outside involvement, DOE and its contractors must be subject to effective whistle-blower protection laws.

10. *Gaining public trust.* A profound lack of public confidence in DOE's nuclear programs could hinder post-Cold War work such as site cleanup. DOE secretary Watkins has complained about the "litigious mis-

chief" of states and citizens groups, apparently failing to understand that litigation is almost inevitable when a program has serious compliance problems, and that lawsuits are often the only way the public can influence DOE decisions. Administrators need to understand the perspectives of people who have had no choice but to live with the hazards imposed by nuclear weapons activities.

Conclusion

POLITICIANS AND CITIZENS WHO HAVE CHAMPIONED PEACE and environmental causes have been viewed by nuclear arms workers as the enemy, simply because one of the immediate consequences of ending excessive weapons production can be the loss of thousands of jobs. Contractors and DOE officials have exploited this animosity.

The short-term economic effects of shutting down an obsolete industry will always tempt politicians to opt for the status quo to minimize controversy. The Administration should make the peacetime transition as smooth as possible for affected workers, as John Tepper Marlin writes elsewhere in this volume, but it should also aggressively pursue reform. Public support can be assured if the President articulates the benefits of getting over the country's Nuclear Weapons Complex:

- reduced environmental and health hazards;
- a diminished threat of nuclear proliferation and terrorism;
- resources freed to improve life for everyone;
- a stronger, more open democracy.

NOTES

1. Richard Rhodes, *The Making of the Atomic Bomb* (New York: Simon & Schuster, 1986). p. 500.
2. Congress has begun to address the problem with legislation such as the Wirth Bill, to create a workers' superfund, but these initiatives have received little DOE or administration support.

PART III

JUSTICE POLICY

OVERVIEW: JUSTICE

STEPHEN GILLERS

I S LAW MERELY POLITICS IN ANOTHER FORM? If so, what is justice? If not, how shall we recognize the difference?

The approach the next President and Attorney General take to those questions will largely determine the quality and nature of justice policy and law enforcement during America's next four years.

Justice in America suffers most when government officials treat its institutions as nothing more than instruments for acquiring and maintaining political power. When politics and justice are both perceived as forms of power, the law becomes subservient and responsive to the goals of politics, its tradition of independence is weakened, its authority is depleted, and the rights and security of Americans are more easily imperiled.

The propensity to politicize the administration of justice has been found in both Democratic and Republican administrations. It reached its apex, to be sure, under Attorneys General John Mitchell and Edwin Meese, yet many others have found themselves caught between the presidents they served and the law they swore to uphold.

Blame, however, must go mainly to their presidents. The White House is inevitably and understandably tempted to make the Justice Department an instrument of its political agenda and little more. But the temptation must be resisted, for the Justice Department is not just another agency, nor is justice just another political chit to be apportioned according the demands of constituency politics.

To signal his commitment to integrity and independence in the administration of justice, the next President must appoint as the next Attorney General a woman or man of great prominence and unquestioned character, both as a lawyer and a citizen. Merit is a must, although few attorneys general

Stephen Gillers is Professor of Law at New York University School of Law. He has authored many articles and books, including most recently Regulation of Lawyers: Problems of Law and Ethics *(3d ed., Boston: Little, Brown, 1992).*

in the past forty years have satisfied this seemingly self-evident criterion, and some have roundly mocked it.

But merit without independence will not be enough. The next Attorney General must also be a woman or man with whom the next President does not have a close personal relationship. Given our recidivist experience with a politicized Justice Department, a rather unfamiliar and formal relationship between the President and Attorney General might be a helpful balance against the inevitable political pressures. In any event, the appointee must be someone who would rather pack up and go home than tolerate inappropriate political imposition.

It was a mistake for President Kennedy to appoint his brother as attorney general. It was a mistake for President Carter to appoint Griffin Bell, given their close relationship. It was a mistake for President Nixon to appoint his campaign manager. And it was a mistake for President Reagan to appoint the family lawyer. These things are true regardless of the qualities of the individual appointees, which ranged widely. The next President has an unfortunate tradition to undo. But he can undo it, and set a commanding precedent, with a single, thoroughly inspired choice.

Similar considerations should inform selection of all other Justice Department personnel subject to Senate confirmation, particularly the Solicitor General.

While the Attorney General sets the tone for the work of the Justice Department, most policies are developed and executed by deputies and assistants. The kind of Attorney General the next President should appoint will not permit the Administration to choose his or her subordinates. He or she will give the transition team due regard, will consider its candidates, and will consult with respect. But of all cabinet members, the Attorney General most needs to be free to pick the people who will run the department and fashion its policies, for the loyalty of the Attorney General's subordinates must be to the same goals of enlightened law enforcement and constitutional liberty that will command the loyalty of the Attorney General. The independence of the department cannot be limited to its leader. It must run deep within the staff.

True, the boundary between justice, on the one hand, and politics, on the other, is not self-evident. But the fact that the boundary can be ambiguous or elusive does not mean there is none, for justice must not be the handmaiden of politics, and the path to probity requires constant vigilance. As a minimum, the next Attorney General should never tolerate the likes of the 1989 incident in which a White House lawyer made direct calls to a federal prosecutor in Atlanta to inquire about a politically sensitive and possibly embarrassing criminal investigation.

But the independence of the Justice Department requires more than a minimal principle of nonintervention into the investigation and prosecution of specific cases. It also requires the willingness and capacity to assert America's constitutional tradition despite short-term political inconvenience, even in instances when the President, or his political posture, might be on the other side of an issue.

Consider a clear and instructive example. In 1987 the U.S. Supreme Court held, 5–4, that Georgia could execute a black man convicted of killing a white man notwithstanding powerful statistical evidence that "defendants charged with killing white victims were 4.3 times as likely to receive a death sentence as defendants charged with killing blacks." According to the study, "black defendants . . . who kill white victims have the greatest likelihood of receiving the death penalty" in American courts. Yet because the defendant in *McCleskey* v. *Kemp*[1] could not show that his particular death sentence was the product of racial bias—a virtually impossible burden—he lost.

Although the United States was not a party to *McCleskey*, it was free to argue as a friend of the Court. Instead, it remained mute—and its silence meant a denial of justice. As Justice William Brennan wrote in dissent, the most important consideration in whether McCleskey lived or died was whether his victim was white or black.

Regardless of the Administration's stand on the death penalty, the *Justice* Department never should have supported the proposition that a state may maintain a capital punishment regime where the persuasive evidence reveals a pattern of capital sentencing bias against black defendants who kill white victims. Its support for that proposition might have swayed one vote and changed the outcome. While it may not have been politically expedient for the President to make that particular argument, that's not the test. An independent Attorney General should be a person who can tell the Chief Executive that the traditions of American justice required it—even if it might upset the President, even if it might open the Administration to political attack, even if it might make the Attorney General subject to misguided criticism as being "soft on crime."

Simply put, the U.S. Justice Department cannot sit quietly by and accept that a criminal sanction—especially the ultimate sanction—is being applied in a blatantly discriminatory fashion.

Similarly, in a case that foreshadowed the recent Los Angeles riots, Lyons, an African American, lost consciousness and suffered physical injury when a Los Angeles police officer restrained him with a certain kind of chokehold after stopping him for a traffic infraction. Lyons had "offered no resistance or threat whatsoever," according to his federal civil complaint.

This allegation was not specifically challenged and had to be accepted as true in deciding the legal issue before the Court.

Lyons sued for money damages on the ground that the use of the particular chokehold violated his constitutional rights. But he also sought a court order stopping use of the chokehold against anyone who was not threatening the use of deadly force. He alleged that its continued use against nonviolent persons would violate the Constitution. The danger of death or injury was especially pronounced for black males. The chokehold had caused sixteen deaths between 1975 and 1981. Twelve of its victims—75 percent— were black men. Only 9 percent of the Los Angeles population at the time were black males.

The Supreme Court said that Lyons did not have "standing" to seek to stop the use of the chokehold because he could not show that he would ever again be subject to one. In other words, he had no right even to present the question to the federal court for decision; its doors were closed to him. The fact that the chokehold had been used against Lyons and that he had a real fear of recurrence was not sufficient to grant Lyons the right to seek protection.

City of Los Angeles v. *Lyons*[2] was a 5–4 ruling that could have been decided differently if the U.S. Department of Justice had chosen to side with Lyons and emphasize the importance of keeping the federal courts open to decide these questions. Instead, the Justice Department remained mute—and justice was denied.

The next President should appoint as Attorney General, Solicitor General, and their immediate subordinates, men and women sufficiently independent and alert to the traditions of American justice to declare that the principles articulated in cases like *McCleskey* and *Lyons* are at war with the proudest standards of our constitutional heritage.

It is no accident that I have selected as examples two Supreme Court cases concerning race and law enforcement. For over a generation after *Brown* v. *Board of Education* and more than a century beyond the Emancipation Proclamation, racial fault lines still run deep through our society. Moreover, the highest risk zone remains where the state meets the people most forcefully—namely, law enforcement.

The next President, and those who staff his Department of Justice, must affirm the kind of thinking in the Bush administration that led to the selection of John Dunne as assistant attorney general for civil rights (an excellent choice in his own right who especially shines when compared to William Bradford Reynolds, his Reagan administration predecessor), support for the Americans with Disabilities Act, and the filing of Voting Rights Act and Fair Housing Act cases.

But above all, the next Administration must never again succumb to the Bush administration's tendency toward the corrosive divide-and-conquer strategy that produced the reprehensible "Willie Horton" ad and misrepresented as a "quota" bill the Civil Rights Act of 1990, which merely codified the reasonable and widely accepted burden-shifting presumption of *Griggs v. Duke Power Co.*[3]

It must be the policy of the next Administration to make it clear at once, and repeatedly throughout its tenure, that appeals to bias based on race or religion, national origin or sexual orientation, whether sophisticated or crass, will be instantly condemned, whenever, wherever, and by whomever they are made. That message must go out as a moral dictate, an incontrovertible principle, that will brook no compromise, no matter how great the political reward. It must be repeated and its import demonstrated frequently through proclamation and policy.

The authors of the chapters in this section of the book offer a cornucopia of suggestions for depoliticizing justice, deescalating the rhetoric and reality of racial division, and enhancing public safety.

For example, Penda Hair details pragmatic policies that will advance America's civil rights agenda by dealing with the lasting, though changing, legacy of racial division in the America described by Professor Henry Louis Gates in his essay "Two Nations . . . Both Black."

David Vladeck and William Schultz recommend the reversal of government efforts that block the ability of litigants like Lyons to present their cases in federal court. They propose an agenda for the Justice Department's oft-overlooked Civil Division that emphasizes independence and professionalism.

And Mark Gitenstein and Ron Klain make specific proposals for improving the selection of federal judges through a process, insulated from rank political abuse, that will result in less emphasis on ideology and more on merit and diversity. Deserving of special attention is their recommendation that "the selection process for the District Courts and the Courts of Appeals is better located in the Justice Department" than in the White House, where it tends to become more politicized and where "factors like distinction and excellence play a [lesser] role."

By emphasizing independence in the administration of justice, the authors and I do not claim that law and politics are entirely separate spheres. The President must make or approve many decisions that affect daily life at the Department of Justice and in other law enforcement agencies. The Administration's antitrust policies, the proper allocation of scarce resources to combat crime, and the broad standards for identifying the women and men who will be nominated for federal judgeships are a few examples of decisions to which the Chief Executive has substantial claim. But even here, an Attorney General should consider it within his or her legitimate authority to lobby hard on such issues to ensure that their resolution honors American traditions of justice and fairness.

Independent justice—based on merit and constitutionalism—can co-exist quite comfortably with the dictates of political necessity as long as the President and Attorney General are committed to the principles of integrity and restraint, and communicate that commitment, in word and deed, to White House and DOJ staff.

The next Administration will have to struggle most diligently with the clash between political considerations and an enlightened and just policy in confronting the twin scourges of crime and drugs, for nowhere is the tendency toward rhetoric and demagoguery greater, and in no other area is the need for sensible reform and hard choices more acute.

Mathea Falco, who ran the international antidrug program in the Carter State Department, reports in her essay that even though President Reagan doubled the federal antidrug budget, and President Bush doubled it yet again—so that it is about $12 billion today—most of the increase has been spent on the supply side, in a futile effort to stop importation of drugs into the United States. Little attention has been paid to reducing demand through treatment and education, even though no treatment whatsoever is available for over two thirds of America's heavy drug abusers, and students of the subject agree that reduction of demand, not interdiction of supply, is the best strategy to attack this scourge.

The forty-second President must face a stark truth: Despite successive "wars" on drugs, interdiction efforts have not succeeded. Ms. Falco reports that a 1991 Government Accounting Office study, like prior GAO studies, concludes that despite the massive effort, the government has not reduced drug flow into the United States. With resources scarce, and drug abuse remaining a chronic drag on American families, workers and businesses, the best contribution the next President can make is to right the imbalance—in spending, attention and rhetoric—between enforcement policies that haven't worked well and treatment and education approaches that seem as if they will. It's a big decision, one that will draw political fire from those whose sights have been trained on interdiction and "tough" solutions, but it is a decision that will make a real difference.

Reducing demand also promises to reduce crime. As Ms. Falco writes, more than three fourths of state prison inmates are drug abusers, though only a tenth receive help. And the help is often nothing more than random counseling. Lee Brown, a former New York City, Atlanta, and Houston police commissioner, reports similar statistics: A total of 54 percent "of the violent male offenders in state prisons in 1986 admitted being under the influence of drugs or alcohol at the time of their offense."

Commissioner Brown, who has spent his life in the trenches of law enforcement, concludes that "the plague of drug abuse and substance abuse . . . may comprise the single greatest threat to our communities and to our way of life."

Locking up a drug dealer for a decade costs society $300,000. Meanwhile, someone else will have taken his or her place. As long as there are buyers, there will be a market. As one St. Louis cocaine dealer told *The New York Times*: "They could lock up a thousand brothers, even ten thousand brothers. There's always going to be someone new out here selling."

The job is to remove the buyer by removing the demand. Interdiction and enforcement, by themselves, won't do that. Treatment and education must be an essential part of the policy. Unfortunately, because of a lack of political leadership, those who advocate fighting drugs with education and treatment are often perceived as favoring programs that coddle abusers. "Drug education and treatment have gained a name as a wimp activity," said Congressman John Conyers. "If you favor these things, you're a softy."

A locked prison cell or confiscated planeload of cocaine sends a tough but inadequate—and, ultimately, ineffective—message. But while a hospital bed, treatment center, or school program may now send a "wimpy" message, it is a message that offers the promise of reducing demand, which in turn will reduce supply.

The next President must exert the leadership and ingenuity to unscramble these false signals, to right the balance and priorities in the area of drug policy, and to ensure that the "drug czar" and the myriad federal agencies and offices that touch on drug policy are in step with the policy shift. It is an administrative and communications challenge, to be sure, but above all, it is a policy choice that only the President can execute.

A new Administration must take the message of prevention to communities and schools across the country. And it must apply that message not only in the area of drug abuse but throughout its entire law enforcement program as well.

For decades, local law enforcement has been reactive; "just the facts, ma'am," was its motto. Today, law enforcement professionals are realizing that investigation and prosecution after the fact is only half the job. So from New York to Los Angeles, local police departments are struggling to redefine their mission and reform their methods in an attempt to prevent crime as well as punish it.

Commissioner Lee Brown, who has preached the gospel of community policing across America while implementing it in three of the nation's largest and toughest cities, proposes a new federal role in reforming policing. Just as the Law Enforcement Assistance Administration brought high-technology hardware to local police departments in the 1960s and 1970s, so the next Administration must work on the software of America's local law enforcement agencies by providing training and technical assistance for municipalities ready and willing to do the hard work of reorienting the relationship between the police and the people.

The Los Angeles riots may be quickly forgotten, but the roots of that rebellion run deep into the American soil. It should be obvious to all that police-community relations remains the flash point that can ignite racial conflagration. Thus it should be agreeable to all that the Federal Government must now play a catalytic role in reforming that relationship.

To the extent that we have made progress in dealing with racial divisions, it has been due in large measure to the principled participation of the U.S. Justice Department in the struggle for equal rights and equal justice.

That is a tradition and role that the Justice Department must affirm and update: by advocating prevention in drug policy and law enforcement; by standing on the side of constitutional principle, even when it is publicly controversial or politically risky; and above all else, by maintaining an impeccable and unimpeachable commitment to independence and integrity in the administration of justice.

Despite the deficit, the recession, or any other challenges we will face, justice can flourish in Washington. Making that happen, though, begins and ultimately ends in an unflinching, unwavering commitment by the next President to America's most basic values, which surely include the "rule of law."

NOTES

1. *McCleskey* v. *Kemp*, 481 U.S. 279, 287 (1987).
2. *City of Los Angeles* v. *Lyons*, 461 U.S. 95 (1985).
3. *Griggs* v. *Duke Power Co.*, 401 U.S. 424 (1971).

CIVIL JUSTICE

DAVID C. VLADECK AND WILLIAM B. SCHULTZ

Summary

THE CIVIL DIVISION OF THE DEPARTMENT OF JUSTICE represents the Federal Government in a wide array of cases, many of which directly affect the lives of every American. The division's main job is to defend the policies set by other agencies when they are challenged in court, which it has done uncritically over the past decade.

But the Civil Division sets and implements its own policies as well, including, during the past twelve years, fighting to limit citizen access to the courts, restricting the public's right of access to government information, protecting the "right" of anti-abortion protesters to block access to abortion clinics, and urging the radical restructuring of the civil justice system in the United States to make it more difficult for those who have been injured to get full compensation. At the same time, the division has largely ignored its mandate to bring enforcement actions to vindicate our nation's health and safety laws and to recoup the monies stolen during the savings and loan debacle.

The next Administration must take a fresh look at the Civil Division's "win at all cost" approach to litigation. There must be a renewed commitment to the principle that the most important value is achieving justice, not simply zealously defending any policy of any federal agency without regard for the ramifications. Because there is a need to reorder the division's focus fundamentally, a policy planning office must promptly be established to imple-

---

David C. Vladeck is an Attorney at Public Citizen Litigation Group and has written monographs in various publications, including Litigation Under the Freedom of Information Act *(ACLU, 1978–92). William B. Schultz is Counsel to the Subcommittee on Health and the Environment of the House Committee on Energy and Commerce.*

ment new policies relating to access to the courts, access to government information, real reform of the civil justice system, and enforcement of federal health and safety laws.

The new President and the Justice Department should implement the following recommendations:

• *Reverse the Reagan/Bush attack on access to the courts by consumers, environmentalists and members of Congress.* Civil Division lawyers must be instructed to avoid raising standing and other justiciability arguments that seek narrow litigation victories but defeat the broad interests of justice.

• *Revise the Reagan/Bush policies regarding access to government information.* The next President should issue an executive order affirming the principle that all government information is presumptively available to the American public, and establishing a fixed policy that no agency may withhold records unless it can demonstrate that a significant, identifiable harm will flow from the records' release.

• *Enforcement of the health and safety laws must be given a higher priority.* An important task for the Civil Division is to assist in revitalizing the role of government in enforcing consumer protection laws administered by the Consumer Product Safety Commission, the National Highway Traffic Safety Administration, the Food and Drug Administration, the Occupational Safety and Health Administration, and other regulatory agencies. Civil Division lawyers must play a leading role in formulating consumer-protective litigation.

• *The division must step up its efforts to combat fraud, waste, and abuse.* The past twelve years have seen the government increasingly victimized by fraud—from the savings and loan criminals who stole or wasted $500 billion, to defense contractors who routinely bilked the government of millions. The Civil Division must step up its efforts to go after those who engage in such white-collar waste, fraud, or abuse.

• *Reverse the Bush Administration's assault on the civil justice system.* The Civil Division should issue model state legislation that proposes realistic reforms to break the logjam that is now crippling our civil justice system without denying citizens prompt, fair, and full redress for their injuries.

• *Withdraw the Civil Division's support for the anti-abortion movement.* The next government must not only reverse its policy of denying women reproductive choice, but also Civil Division lawyers must be directed to cease litigation activities supporting such anti-abortion forces as Operation Rescue.

Introduction

THE CIVIL DIVISION OF THE DEPARTMENT OF JUSTICE is unlike any other litigating arm of the Federal Government because its posture in court is typically defensive. Attorneys who work there represent the Federal Government in cases involving matters as diverse as the personal injury claims of shipyard workers exposed to asbestos; suits by members of the public for access to documents under the Freedom of Information and Privacy acts; challenges to Executive Branch actions brought by members of Congress; and cases brought by both industry and public interest groups against regulatory agencies. Because the work of the Civil Division touches the lives of most Americans, its approach has a significant impact both on whether justice is achieved and on the public's perception of whether we have a just government.

Unfortunately, at least since the Reagan administration, the attorneys who have set policy for the Civil Division have undervalued the importance of seeking justice while overemphasizing the importance of narrow litigation victories. Having conducted interviews with more than twenty lawyers who have either litigated against the Civil Division or been employed by it, we were struck by the consistent theme that the division's lawyers approach litigation in much the same way as a private practitioner. They perceive their mission as winning each case at any cost, without any special appreciation that, as representatives of the U.S. Government, they are obligated to factor in the public interest in their decisions.

Attorneys in the Civil Division routinely raise an array of technical and jurisdictional defenses such as standing, mootness, ripeness, and failure to exhaust administrative remedies. The practice is so notorious and the division's attorneys are so aggressive in making their arguments that lawyers who litigated against the division sometimes joke, only half in jest, that Civil Division lawyers believe that they have lost a case if the court reaches the merits.

General rules about when it is appropriate to raise technical defenses are not possible. In our view, however, these defenses should be used sparingly, and then only with the permission of the most senior lawyers within the division. If the Federal Government wants to deny citizens who seek redress against the government their day in court, that act should be a solemn one taken only on the basis of clear, long-settled, and specific precedent. To reverse the current Civil Division practice of pressing hard on every imaginable jurisdictional defense, the new head of the Civil Division must send an unmistakable message to the division's attorneys that defending the government is different from defending private parties: The ultimate goal must be justice, not necessarily winning.

These procedural and jurisdictional motions are being made by attorneys who are among the most talented in government. What is more, during the Bush administration, the division has been managed more professionally and less politically than many other divisions within the Justice Department. With an able staff in place, what the Civil Division needs now is leadership and a new direction.

Overview and History

THE CIVIL DIVISION IS THE LARGEST litigating unit within the Department of Justice, employing more than five hundred lawyers and nearly four hundred support personnel. It handles the Federal Government's general civil litigation in both district and appellate courts, except the Supreme Court. The nature of the litigation is as diverse as the activities of the government itself.

The Civil Division is headed by an assistant attorney general and five deputy assistant attorneys general. Historically, the deputies were principally career lawyers, but that changed during the Reagan/Bush administrations, when most deputies have been political appointees. The division has six major litigating units: Federal Programs, Torts, Commercial Litigation, Consumer Litigation, Immigration Litigation, and the appellate staff.

FEDERAL PROGRAMS BRANCH

The Federal Programs Branch, with approximately ninety lawyers, litigates on behalf of about a hundred federal agencies, the President and cabinet officers, members of Congress, and other government officials. Its principal role is to defend challenges to the constitutionality of federal statutes and attacks on the legality of federal programs and policies. Among its principal responsibilities are:

• *Regulatory enforcement.* The branch is responsible for bringing affirmative litigation to ensure compliance with federal statutes such as the National Highway Traffic Safety Act or the Employment Retirement Income Security Act. It is also responsible for defending the positions federal agencies take in formulating regulations or other policies.

• *National security and foreign relations.* In the course of its representation of the President, the Defense Department, the State Department, and the CIA, the branch is involved in highly visible national security and foreign relations litigation. This includes litigation stemming from press censorship during the Persian Gulf War, the administration's noncompliance with the War Powers Resolution, and political asylum requests.

• *Freedom of information and privacy.* This unit represents the Federal Government in litigation under a number of open record and meeting laws, including the Freedom of Information Act, the Privacy Act, the Government in the Sunshine Act, and the Federal Advisory Committee Act. Until 1983, the Civil Division also was in charge of formulating and coordinating the government's policies regarding the Freedom of Information Act and the Privacy Act, through the Office of Information and Privacy. However, those functions were transferred to the Office of Legal Policy, which was created in 1981 principally to assist in the selection of judges. We recommend that the Office of Information and Privacy be transferred back to the Civil Division, which conducts all of the government's litigation under the two acts.

TORTS BRANCH

The Torts Branch, with 130 lawyers, represents the interests of the United States, including its employees who are sued individually, in suits where money judgments are sought for damages resulting from negligent or wrongful acts. The Torts Branch's major work falls into three categories:

• *General torts claims.* This category includes traditional problems in tort law such as personal injury and medical malpractice. Among the important emerging issues are radiation claims brought by those alleging injury from the government's testing and production of nuclear weapons and materials, and Agent Orange litigation brought by veterans claiming injury from exposure to the defoliant in Vietnam.

• *Environmental and occupational disease litigation.* Increasingly, the government is involved in litigation involving hazardous substances. The lion's share of these cases involve the use of asbestos in ship construction during World War II, although there are mounting numbers of cases alleging environmental contamination from the use and disposal of toxic substances on and around U.S. facilities—particularly nuclear sites such as Savannah River, Rocky Flats, and Fernald, nonnuclear arsenals, and military bases.

• *Constitutional tort litigation.* Prompted by the Supreme Court's 1971 decision in *Bivens* v. *Six Unknown Agents of the Federal Bureau of Narcotics*, federal officials are now often the targets of tort cases alleging violations of constitutional, statutory, and common-law rights. These cases run the gamut from one alleging a conspiracy among federal law enforcement officials in the Greensboro Ku Klux Klan shooting in 1979 to others involving issues of national security. These cases can be highly sensitive, often involving top-level federal officials and key federal operations.

COMMERCIAL LITIGATION BRANCH

The Commercial Litigation Branch, with over 170 attorneys, is the largest unit within the Civil Division. It prosecutes claims for the recovery of monies fraudulently secured, enforces the government's contract and patent rights, and defends the country's international trade policy. Among its major responsibilities are:

• *Civil fraud.* The Commercial Litigation Branch is responsible for bringing suits to recover losses resulting from fraud in federal programs and contracts and the bribery and corruption of federal officials. These cases can involve mischarging, false claims for payment, substitution of substandard goods, multimillion-dollar loan frauds, employee embezzlement, and abuses involving federal grant monies. Although this work is important and extremely cost-effective (this litigation more than pays for itself), its staff is still far too meager to tackle the mammoth job at hand.

• *Debt recovery.* Branch lawyers handle suits for money and property on behalf of the government. Much of this work is to protect the government's interest in bankruptcy proceedings, where the government often has a multimillion-dollar stake in the outcome.

• *Customs and international trade.* Branch lawyers represent the United States in customs and international trade matters before the International Trade Court and the Court of Appeals for the Federal Circuit. These cases often involve significant issues including dumping, countervailing duties, and international trade agreements.

OFFICE OF CONSUMER LITIGATION

The smallest unit within the Civil Division, the Office of Consumer Litigation, is responsible for the enforcement of federal consumer protection statutes through civil and criminal litigation. Among the office's clients are the Food and Drug Administration, the Consumer Product Safety Commission, the Federal Trade Commission, and the National Highway Traffic Safety Administration.

OFFICE OF IMMIGRATION LITIGATION

This office was created in 1983 to conduct civil trial and appellate litigation under the immigration laws. With thirty attorneys, the office handles litigation arising under the Immigration Reform and Control Act of 1986, including the new employment authorization and sanction provisions. The office also handles cases brought by individual aliens challenging orders of deportation and exclusion, denials of political asylum, and class actions challenging immigration policy and enforcement actions by the attorney general.

APPELLATE STAFF

The appellate staff, with fifty five lawyers, is responsible for the appellate work of the entire Civil Division. Its caseload includes matters from all of the division's branches and offices, as well as cases that are brought in the Court of Appeals directly from administrative agencies. By giving the appellate staff this broad jurisdiction, the division retains centralized control over the government's vital litigation in the appellate courts.

Policy Changes That Work

ALTHOUGH THE DEFENSIVE NATURE OF THE WORK done by the Civil Division limits the kinds of policy changes that realistically can be implemented, there are a number of directives that should be issued to advance the public interest and to make the division work more efficiently.

The Civil Division Should Not Routinely Raise Standing and Other Technical Defenses That Deny Citizens Access to the Courts.

A lawsuit against the government must often overcome several hurdles before the court can reach the merits. The plaintiff must first show that the federal court has jurisdiction over the case. Next, the government will typically raise a number of other defenses—for example, standing, sovereign immunity, statute of limitations and ripeness—in an effort to persuade the court that it should dismiss the case rather than reach the merits of the plaintiff's claim.

Invocation of these doctrines can delay justice and deny the courts the ability to resolve claims. For example, the Bush Justice Department repeatedly used the standing doctrine—the principle, based on Article III of the Constitution, that the federal courts will hear only actual "cases" or "controversies" in which the plaintiff has been injured—to close the courthouse door to those with legitimate grievances, including environmentalists who seek to challenge adverse environmental decisions, members of Congress who seek to challenge Executive Branch abuses, and citizens seeking to challenge regulatory programs that directly touch their lives.

This excessive resort to standing defenses has troubling constitutional implications. It is basic separation-of-powers doctrine that the rough balance of power among the branches was designed to assure that each branch checked the potential excesses of their coordinate branches. This system of checks and balances—which is fundamental to our Democracy—is thrown off kilter if the federal judiciary is stripped of its power to review executive action. Yet the Reagan and Bush administrations, often through the Civil Division, advocated precisely such a withdrawal of judicial authority.

Perhaps the best illustration of the harshness of the Bush administration's position is *Lujan* v. *National Wildlife Foundation*. This case was brought by a national environmental organization to challenge a decision by the Bureau of Land Management (BLM) to open up a tract of federal land in Wyoming to mining activities. The environmental organization sought to use this case to challenge the BLM's overall policy of opening up vast parcels of land in eleven western states to mining.

To demonstrate standing, the environmental group presented several affidavits from members who claimed that they used the Wyoming tract for recreational purposes. But, adopting the position developed by the Civil Division, the Court found that these affidavits were insufficient, because no member said that he or she used the exact area that would be used for mining activities, even though the court recognized that the mining activity would necessitate the construction of roads, would be noisy, and would generally degrade the area around the mine. Worse, the court held that the National Wildlife Foundation would have to challenge *each* of hundreds of separately issued decisions.

The decision in *Lujan* v. *National Wildlife Foundation* places enormous obstacles in the path of those who would challenge agency actions. In environmental cases, for instance, a plaintiff would have to show that he or she used the precise parcel of land or stretch of waterway at issue, and demonstrate precisely how he or she would be injured. The fact that the land, water, or air will be somewhat more polluted might not be enough; the plaintiff would have to show how the increased pollution caused or threatened imminent harm. And even if the plaintiff prevailed, the government would not have to change its underlying *policy*, if for no other reason than environmental groups do not have the resources to bring the literally dozens of lawsuits that would be needed to challenge the government's action effectively.

Freedom of Information Act Cases Should Be Litigated Only Where There Is an Identifiable Governmental Interest in Withholding Documents.

For the past twenty years, Congress has engaged in a sustained effort to make government accountable by enacting a number of statutes granting broad access to government records and opening government meetings to the public. Yet the Reagan/Bush administrations waged a systematic assault on these laws.

The attack on the Freedom of Information Act (FOIA) has taken a number of forms. For example, the Reagan administration rescinded the policy announced by former attorney general Griffin Bell that the Justice Department would oppose FOIA requests only where there was a showing of "demonstrable harm" to the government.

As soon as Reagan took office, however, the Bell memorandum was replaced with an antidisclosure policy requiring the department to defend all suits challenging an agency's decision to deny a request submitted under the FOIA unless the agency's denial completely lacks a substantial legal basis or the defense of the agency's denial presents an unwarranted risk of adverse impact on other agencies' ability to protect important records. The Bush administration has retained this antidisclosure standard.

As is evident under this standard, unless an agency's position is clearly frivolous, it will be defended by the Justice Department. Compounding the problem, the Bush administration, through the Civil Division, has pressed hard in the courts to narrow substantially the types of records that must be released. For example, in *Critical Mass Energy Project* v. *NRC*, the Civil Division has asked the U.S. Court of Appeals for the District of Columbia to overturn a seventeen-year-old decision interpreting the "commercial information" exemption to the FOIA to allow the government to withhold records companies say they customarily keep secret. That position, if it prevails, will mean that most safety information submitted to the government—concerning drugs, medical devices, consumer products, nuclear power plants, and automobiles—will no longer be made public, reversing over twenty years of practice.

The Reagan administration's opposition to the dissemination of any information relating to national security culminated in its withdrawal of Executive Order 12065 governing classification and its replacement by Executive Order 12356, which makes it virtually impossible to gain access to allegedly classified information. The Bush administration has retained this highly restrictive order. The executive order has great significance under the FOIA, since under Exemption 1 only information properly classified in accordance with the executive order may be withheld. While there are many differences between the executive orders, two changes have had profound effects.

First, Executive Order 12065 provided for balancing the public interest in disclosure against the injury to national security in determining whether to disclose certain classified materials. Yet the present order discards this balancing test and categorically forbids disclosure of classified material regardless of whether there might be an overriding public interest in the material.

Second, under the prior executive order, classification could not be restored to documents once they had been declassified and released to the public. The rescission of this provision in the new executive order has led to a number of ugly incidents, including books being seized off library shelves because the books contain newly reclassified information, and scholars threatened for publishing information gleaned from once-declassified sources.

Executive Order 12356 must be withdrawn. It should be replaced with an Order directing that classification and declassification decisions take into account the age of the documents and the public interest in disclosure and prohibiting, or at least restricting, the reclassification of formerly declassified materials.

The Civil Division Should Initiate More Enforcement Actions.

The Civil Division has the authority both to defend and to prosecute regulatory cases on behalf of agencies such as the Consumer Product Safety Commission, the National Highway Traffic Safety Administration, and the FDA. Historically, these cases have been developed and referred to the division by the relevant agencies, but the Justice Department has the authority to initiate such actions on its own. Of course, as a practical matter, the agency with jurisdiction over the matter would have to be consulted prior to initiating any litigation, but there is no reason why the Civil Division should remain passive in the process of developing cases.

Greater emphasis also needs to be placed on the prosecution of civil fraud cases in the government contracts area. While the Commercial Litigation Branch of the Civil Division has been expanded from the thirty-five lawyers it had in 1988, its resources are still too meager to handle all of the government's civil fraud litigation, encompassing all of the savings and loan thefts, defense contracting abuse, procurement cases, and fraud in federal grant programs cases. Indeed, every one of the dozens of major corporate law firms that specialize in government contract or savings and loan work has more lawyers engaged in this litigation than the entire Civil Division. This drastic imbalance in resources cannot be allowed to persist.

The Civil Division Should Reconsider Its Appropriate Role in the Formulation of Political Policy.

Historically, the Civil Division's involvement in political matters was quite circumscribed; while it *defended* the political decisions made by other governmental entities, the division itself had little or no involvement in the decisionmaking process. Increasingly, however, the Civil Division has been drawn into the political fray on issues as diverse as funding for abortion counseling and proposed sweeping "reforms" of the civil justice system. This trend must be reconsidered because there are strong arguments for separating the policymakers from the lawyers who defend the policy.

When lawyers do not participate in the formulation of a policy, they have no "ownership" interest in it and can be more dispassionate about its merits. Indeed, the policy battles over which the Civil Division appears to have had influence seem to prove our point. Most well known is the *Rust* v. *Sullivan* litigation, which involved a challenge to the government's efforts to ensure that federal family planning funds were *not* used even to inform women of abortion as an option. The strategy designed by the Civil Division—arguing that the government has no obligation to subsidize any type of speech—prevailed in the Supreme Court, even though the effect is to force the doctors and nurses who staff these clinics to tell half-truths to their patients by informing them about adoption but not abortion options.

Equally troubling is the Civil Division's role in leading the administration's attack on the civil justice system, although this is a subject on which the division has expertise, and thus its participation is more appropriate. These attacks are based on the mythology that there has been an explosion in the volume of civil litigation and that runaway juries are imposing punitive damage awards crippling to big business. To place a brake on this process, the administration proposes "reforms" that would reverse two hundreds years of American tradition and virtually shut the courthouse door on the ordinary citizen.

For example, the administration says that the loser in a lawsuit should pay the winner's attorney's fees. That might make sense when Exxon sues IBM. But what about a suit brought by someone who was injured by a large corporation? The rule would chill any litigation, no matter how meritorious.

The administration also wants a cap on punitive damages, no matter how egregious the conduct and no matter how serious the injury. The only damages the administration would permit would be medical expenses and lost income. Under this proposal, gross misconduct that, for example, causes the quick death of an infant, would effectively go unpunished, since there would be few medical expenses and no lost earnings.

The administration also urges the retention and expansion of the gag orders that are prevalent in civil discovery and that big corporations routinely support. These orders squander resources, since they prevent other similarly situated plaintiffs and the public from learning the truth about potentially harmful products; they also drive up the costs of litigation considerably by forcing each plaintiff to go through the same exacting discovery process.

The Civil Division Should Adopt a Formal Policy of Working with the State Attorneys General.

One positive fallout of the Reagan/Bush administrations' policy of not enforcing regulatory laws is that state attorneys general have become much more aggressive in bringing consumer protection litigation. The work of state attorneys general offices is federalism at its best. The Civil Division should adopt a policy of formally encouraging appropriate enforcement by state attorneys general and of working with states where federal and state interests overlap.

The Civil Division Should Create a Policy Section to Implement Significant Policy Changes, Such as Those Recommended in This Chapter.

The Civil Division should establish a policy planning component that would work directly under the assistant attorney general. The purpose of this component would be to consider significant policy changes, such as those recommended in this chapter. Once policy shifts are adopted, this office could then participate actively in their implementation. For example, if the new Civil Division decides to curtail the current practice of reflexively raising justiciability defenses, the Policy Section would then review briefs raising justiciability arguments to ensure that the new directive is being fully implemented.

The Civil Division Should Review The Following Additional Issues.

• *National security cases.* The Civil Division handles virtually all of the highly sensitive civil cases involving national security issues. These include cases (a) to enforce secrecy agreements that forbid security agency employees from publishing information acquired during their employment (such as the case against Frank Snepp); (b) brought by former government employees who have been stripped of their security clearances and/or fired because they allegedly present a security risk; or (c) filed by journalists, scholars, or public interest organizations seeking alleged national security information under the FOIA.

The government has a need to protect sensitive information. However, in the national security cases that have been litigated over the past twelve years, the Civil Division has too often uncritically accepted the agency's representations about the potential for harm, no matter how strained those representations may have been.

To ensure that the national security claims the Civil Division raises in court are well founded, the head of the Civil Division should issue a directive to staff lawyers stating that in cases implicating national security issues, staff attorneys must make a reasonable inquiry into the basis for the agency's claims of potential harm and must be satisfied that such claims are grounded in fact. Lacking an adequate factual basis, the Civil Division should decline to make the assertion urged by the agency.

• *Homosexual rights cases.* Over the past twelve years, the Civil Division has handled a number of highly controversial cases involving the rights of homosexuals to retain their jobs in the military and national security agencies. The Civil Division has vigorously defended these restrictive practices. In our view, and in the view of many of the judges who have reviewed these cases, this all-out attack on the rights of gay men and lesbian women is unwarranted and unlawful. A task force, which would include the assistant attorney general in charge of the Civil Division and representatives from the military and the security agencies, should be formed to review and revise existing policies regarding the treatment of homosexuals in the federal sector.

• *Immigration cases.* The past decade has seen an explosive growth in the number, importance, and visibility of immigration cases. The influx of enormous numbers of Haitian refugees has raised serious questions about the fairness of the asylum process, since Haitians are invariably denied asylum even though the country has been faced with repeated political upheavals. Similar charges have been raised with respect to the asylum policy for other peoples.

Immigration policy is set principally by the Immigration and Naturalization Service, not by the Civil Division. Yet, increasingly, the Civil Division is taking an unusually aggressive role in trying to ensure that these policy decisions may not be challenged in court. In the typical case, the division throws up every conceivable justiciability argument that can be raised, even to the point of arguing unsuccessfully to the Supreme Court that certain *constitutionally* based claims may not be litigated. Equally troubling, the division routinely practices widescale "nonacquiescence" in immigration cases—that is, it refuses to be bound by an adverse ruling by one court of appeals while the issue is being litigated elsewhere, throwing the law, and the ability of immigrants to comply with the law, into disarray. These tactics should cease. The Civil Division must not erect needless obstacles to review of immigration decisions that have such profound effects on the most vulnerable of all litigants.

Criminal Division, Department of Justice

CRIME

LEE P. BROWN

Summary

IMPELLED BY PERCEPTIONS THAT CRIME RATES continue to rise, that our streets are increasingly unsafe, and that criminals are becoming more vicious, Americans are demanding that government restore order and reduce fear. The result is a crisis of public confidence, both in the criminal justice system and in the ability of our political process to protect individual rights and public order.

As a result, the next Administration and Congress must act emphatically to restore public confidence in the credibility and effectiveness of the criminal justice system. To combat this crisis of public safety and public confidence, the new President must proactively address the myriad social issues that underlie crime and permit it to flourish.

Our national crime problems are not limited to street crime. Rather, the insidious issues of drug abuse, traditional and nontraditional organized crime, corporate or "white collar" crime, and governmental corruption must be on Washington's crime control agenda.

The social costs of the drug epidemic, for example, are inestimable in terms of human misery, the lives lost, and the opportunities inhibited. The drug epidemic is a public health crisis, particularly in terms of its role in the spread of AIDS and HIV through intravenous drug use.

And drug abuse is an economic issue as well: A recent White House report estimated that in 1990 American drug abusers spent approximately $41 billion on illicit drugs, and the tax-free billions in profits that drug dealers realized from these sales are typically reinvested by the drug criminals in

Lee P. Brown, a Distinguished Professor at Texas Southern University, is former Commissioner of the New York City Police Department. Dr. Brown has written extensively on police management, community relations, crime, and the criminal justice system, and is coauthor of the book The Police and Society: An Environment for Collaboration and Confrontation.

other illegitimate enterprises, which siphon off additional billions of dollars from the economy.

Despite the complexity of the criminal justice crisis, no major inquiry into the nature and causes of crime in America has yet been conducted, and no extensive inquiry into the state of the criminal justice system has been attempted in a quarter of a century. The findings of the last comprehensive study—the 1967 President's Commission on Law Enforcement and the Administration of Justice—are dated, largely because it achieved success in alleviating many of the major systemic problems and issues present at the time it was conducted.

The president's commission, for example, was directly responsible for the Omnibus Crime Control and Safe Streets Act of 1968 and the creation of the Law Enforcement Assistance Administration (LEAA). The LEAA annually devoted hundreds of millions of dollars over the course of its fourteen-year history to modernize and improve the criminal justice system by raising police and law enforcement education levels and standards, providing equipment and training to a multitude of criminal justice agencies, and generally wresting the law enforcement component of the criminal justice system from its traditional stagnation and inertia into the twentieth century.

Despite its success, many of the findings and recommendations developed by the president's commission are obsolete. A new presidential commission is needed to address *today's* public safety crisis, which includes drug crime and an entrenched and economically immobilized criminal underclass. Traditional organized crime has matured and moved into new spheres of exploitation, while newer nontraditional organized crime groups are filling much of the void they left behind; also, white collar "crime," corporate crime, and government corruption threaten our democratic values and free enterprise system; and a fairly small percentage of "career criminals" are responsible for the vast majority of street crimes.

The evolving philosophy and practice of "community policing" has already proven its effectiveness in addressing citizens' concerns and in reducing crime, and its full potential is as yet unrealized. Technology and science have also revolutionized the criminal justice system through such new investigative techniques as DNA testing and computerized fingerprint identification systems, as well as the use of electronic home monitoring as an alternative to incarceration. These and an array of other potential solutions require an orchestrated plan of study and action, incorporating the results of recent research and utilizing them in a coherent set of policies that will form the philosophy and program for America's next generation of criminal justice professionals.

Dynamics of the Contemporary Criminal Justice Crisis

TO DATE, OUR NATIONAL RESPONSES TO crime issues have been relatively unfocused, with the Federal Government and state and local governments implementing limited and largely parochial policies on an ad hoc basis; as a result, our fragmented approach lacks both the quality and the strength of a real national agenda.

Government must act forcefully to combat crime through determined enforcement efforts. At the same time, it must foster and reward the initiative of individual private citizens and community groups who offer their time and resources to allay the criminal justice system. Only with this two-pronged approach, with leadership coordinating the application of large-scale government programs and the individual resourcefulness of citizens, can we hope to diminish the crime crisis.

This spirit of partnership is at the core of the community policing philosophy, which departs from the traditional view of police as an isolated and monolithic entity whose role and responsibility are confined primarily to the enforcement of criminal laws. Community policing involves neighborhood residents in the process of identifying and resolving the problems confronting their communities. It allows police officers to be more creative and more versatile in their approach to police work by establishing a working partnership between the police and the law-abiding public to prevent crime, to arrest offenders, to recognize and achieve realistic and permanent solutions to chronic neighborhood conditions, and generally to enhance the quality of life of neighborhood residents.

Community policing is premised on a philosophy that citizens can no longer look solely to the police to redress the problems they confront or to restore a deserved sense of public order; they must become individually and collectively involved in the problem-solving process to enable law enforcement to exercise its crime control and peace keeping roles fully. The potent effect of community involvement and "community policing" has been dramatically illustrated in New York City, where the nation's largest police agency has embraced its philosophy. For the first time in thirty-six years, in 1991, New York City realized a significant across-the-board decline in every category of reported index crimes.

Despite this progress, we must not expect that enforcement efforts, typically conceived of in terms of arrest and criminal sanction, will unilaterally accomplish a reduction in crime. By their nature, arrest and criminal sanction are responses to crime that are brought to bear when other and less intrusive means of control have failed.

All too often, individual citizens as well as government officials ignore the other components of the criminal justice enterprise and look solely to the police for solutions to immediate and long-term crime problems. While police have the ability to improve vastly the quality of life in the communities they serve, their impact on macro-level problems is extremely limited. Police officers and agencies, particularly those subscribing to the philosophy of community policing, can often prevent further social deterioration or dislocation at the local or neighborhood level, but it is unrealistic to expect that law enforcement alone can stem the social disorder rising from a national tide of social and institutional degeneration.

A paucity of affordable housing, the failure of primary and secondary schools adequately to educate or provide our youth with marketable job skills, unemployment and institutionalized poverty, inadequate health care and mental health care, and a host of other indicia of social breakdown are hardly within the immediate purview of the local police. Police can achieve their potential effectiveness only when government acts to reform these institutions, and when it provides each component of the criminal justice system—the police, the courts, corrections, prosecution, and probation and parole subsystems—with the legislation, resources and support they require.

Crime Control: Rhetoric and Reality

DESPITE THE BOASTFUL "TOUGH TALK" FROM the Bush administration about responding aggressively to crime, our national crime control and crime reduction policies have not been buttressed by the leadership or resources required to reform this nation's criminal justice system. The rhetoric has largely functioned to sidetrack the American public from the true issues and to divide further an already too stratified society.

Such diversionary rhetoric occurred in reaction to the Los Angeles riots when the Great Society social policies and programs of the mid- to late 1960s were attacked as having created the basis for the disorder that specifically beset Los Angeles and the antipathy that now generally characterizes our nation. Nothing, in fact, could be farther from the truth. Before they were curtailed, the Great Society programs cut this nation's level of poverty in half; the anger and indignation expressed by the poor and by disenfranchised minority citizens is the result of cynicism and frustration at having opportunities offered and then withdrawn.

PROACTIVE VERSUS REACTIVE POSTURES
In the decade between 1980 and 1990, our prison population increased by almost 130 percent. As a result, Americans are now confined at a higher rate than in any other industrialized nation. The National Council on Crime

and Delinquency estimates that by 1994 the combined population of state and federal prisons will reach 1 million, more than double the prison population in 1980. However, the current rhetoric of "getting tough" on crime by sentencing increasing numbers of inmates to increasingly lengthy terms in already overcrowded prisons is infinitely myopic and ultimately self-refuting. The rhetoric does, however, serve a diversionary political end and clearly satisfies the retributive urges of a frustrated and poorly informed constituency, which is itself caught up in and blinded by the emotion-laden rhetoric they espouse. These policies cost much but do little to deter inmates from further criminality once they are released; to reintegrate them as productive members of society; or, most importantly, to deter others from following in their footsteps.

Moreover, demographic analyses of state and federal prison populations have repeatedly pointed out that male inmates are disproportionately African American or Latino (African-American males accounted for 46.9 percent of the total male state prison population in 1986, Latino males 12.6 percent), that they are poorly educated with few marketable job skills (61 percent of all male state prison inmates have less than twelve years of schooling, about 40 percent are unable to read, and only one third were employed full-time at the time of their arrest), and that a large percentage have histories of substance abuse (54 percent of the violent male offenders in state prisons in 1986 admitted being under the influence of drugs or alcohol at the time of their offense).

Many contend that our correctional systems serve primarily to create and maintain an American underclass, relegating to prisons and jails those who comprise the rabble and the human detritus of a withering society. No democratic state worthy of the name has the right to conceive of its constituents as social debris, much less to sanction or impose on them a system of justice that is a subterfuge for the creation or maintenance of an underclass.

It is time for a fundamental shift in our national approach to criminal justice matters. To resolve the problems we confront, the transition must include a commitment to address the individual and environmental factors that lead to criminality and the social and economic conditions that allow it to flourish. Setting aside our political differences and putting divisive rhetoric to rest, we must establish a lucid reality-based agenda to implement strategies that resolve rather than exacerbate the formidable crime issues and crime problems confronting the nation.

FEAR OF CRIME, AND COMMUNITY POLICING
It is an undeniable fact of contemporary American life that crime rates are at an unacceptably high level. Similarly, it is perceived that violent crime in

particular continues to increase nationwide, although empirical evidence demonstrates that in sharp contrast to the skyrocketing levels of crime during the 1960s and 1970s, the actual number of violent crimes and property offenses, as well as their per capita rate, have remained fairly static in the past decade. Although crime levels continue to rise and although the current volume and rates of crime *are* at unacceptable levels, the public perceives the type and kind of crime occurring around them to be much more prolific and much more violent than the empirical data can account for. These heightened public perceptions are directly attributable to the level of disorder that exists in our society.

The data suggest that a significant proportion of Americans have altered their life-styles and regularly avoid certain areas or certain behaviors because they fear victimization. Researchers point out that while fear of crime exists to some extent throughout society, it is most heavily concentrated among those groups who see themselves as most vulnerable to victimization—specifically, the elderly, women, the poor, African Americans and other minorities, and those who reside in urban areas. At least two immediate social costs of fear of crime are pointed out by Mark H. Moore and Robert C. Trojanowicz, who note that "if the inner city populations are afraid of crime, then commerce and investment essentially disappear, and, with time, the chance for upward social mobility." If Hobbes is correct in asserting that the most fundamental purpose of civil government is to establish order and protect citizens from the fear of criminal attack that made life "nasty, brutish, and short" in the "state of nature," then the current level and distribution of fear indicate an important governmental failure.[1] Moore and Trojanowicz go on to note that while levels of fear are related to actual levels of victimization, a host of intervening variables, including a general individual sense of vulnerability, signs of physical and social decay, and intergroup conflict also contribute to the equation.

Many of the quality-of-life issues that people associate with crime and disorder are not criminal offenses, and even those legally proscribed behaviors that do constitute criminal offenses are irregularly enforced at the local level and are not included in national crime figures. As James Q. Wilson and George Kelling pointed out in their brilliant and highly influential 1982 *Atlantic Monthly* article "Broken Windows,"[2] the public associates the physical deterioration of their neighborhoods and disorderly behavior within their communities with crime and with the subversion of public order. This article illustrated that when disorderly conduct or physical deterioration are left unchecked, residents lose interest and pride in maintaining their homes and take no steps to prevent or repair their neighborhood's physical or metaphorical broken windows.

Absent public attention and public action, disorder and further deterioration flourish, and fear of crime is compounded. Ultimately, the synergistic cycle of decay and degeneration is criminogenic—criminals assume ownership of the streets left vacant by the fearful and demoralized citizens who have tacitly ceded control to them.

The fact that fear of crime continues to spiral upward despite empirical proof that the numbers and rate of actual crimes occurring have moderately declined points to a failure by federal, state, and local law enforcement to communicate adequately with the citizens they serve. This failure is a lingering artifact of the traditional style of law enforcement, in which police agencies were isolated, largely autonomous, and monolithic bureaucracies imbued with little concern for achieving effective interaction with the community. Community policing, which emphasizes and practices a high degree of police-community interaction and which has great concern for mobilizing neighborhoods to join with the police to address local problems, holds tremendous potential to relieve unrealistic levels of fear of crime.

Community policing can reduce citizens' fears by creating feedback mechanisms to convey accurate information that reduces excessive or unrealistic fear while maintaining a healthy respect for avoiding or preventing crime hazards. A high level of police-citizen interaction and an ongoing, well-informed dialogue are part and parcel of the community policing philosophy.

Moreover, the important role of foot patrols in densely populated areas and the reassuring presence of a neighborhood beat officer who knows and is known by the community have a potent effect on reducing residents' fears. Thus one collateral benefit to be gained by the implementation of community policing is the reduction of unrealistic or excessive fear within the neighborhoods where it is practiced.

The onus for reducing unwarranted fear of crime is not solely borne by local agencies, however. Federal and state agencies can help to reduce fear as well as to achieve an array of additional benefits within our nation's neighborhoods by facilitating and encouraging the continued growth of community policing. Federal and state law enforcement agencies can reduce fear of street crime by enhancing the assistance and resources they currently provide to local agencies (typically through formation of innovative multijurisdictional task forces that have had a proven effect on street-level and midlevel drug distribution networks) as well as by adopting aggressive programs to communicate the realities of crime to citizens. Cooperative and holistic programs such as the "Weed and Seed" initiative—which impact the critical nexus of fear, commerce, and quality of life referred to by Moore and Trojanowicz by pulling the "weeds" of crime and planting the economic and social "seeds" of community viability—are illustrative of an appropriate federal role. Such a program should not, however, place a disproportionate emphasis on "weeding," to the detriment of "seeding."

There exists a particular role for the Federal Bureau of Investigation in reducing fear of crime. With the end of the Cold War, the FBI's emphasis on counterespionage investigations should be reduced, and the FBI should devote even more of its considerable resources to the abatement of street crime and the implementation of joint federal, state, and local street crime task forces.

SETTING THE PRIORITIES OF A NATIONAL COMMISSION ON CRIME AND JUSTICE

To establish a comprehensive and coherent crime control agenda as well as to demonstrate commitment to crime reduction, the next Administration should create a national Commission on Crime and Justice modeled after the 1967 President's Commission on Law Enforcement and the Administration of Justice. The commission must examine a host of social, individual and economic variables, assessing their collective and particular impact on the crime equation; and it must be eclectically comprised of nonpartisan scholars and practitioners recognized as leaders in their respective fields.

The commission must also play a catalytic role in providing guidance for and direction to the activities of the nation's myriad law enforcement agencies. The commission should advance cooperative arrangements to encourage harmonious and synergistic relationships between and among agencies, such as the multijurisdictional task forces mentioned throughout this chapter. The tremendous resources we devote to law enforcement efforts at the federal, state, and local levels can be made more effective by refining and focusing our currently fragmented and often parochial approaches to crime reduction.

In determining the comprehensive national agenda to reduce crime, the commission should consider the following specific issues:

• *Federal commitment to cities.* For more than a decade, the Federal Government has devoted one quarter of its budget to military expenditures, but less than 1 percent to aid for our cities. Because our urban areas face a crumbling infrastructure, the commission must examine and redress the effects of inadequate roads, highways, bridges, and mass transportation systems on the local and national economy and thus on employment and crime.

• *The needs of children.* One of the few areas of consensus with regard to crime control is the almost universal agreement on the need to ensure that today's youth and the young people of succeeding generations are raised in stable, loving, and supportive families from which they can draw the strength and the values to resist the potent lure of a criminal life-style. Yet the capacity of the American family to transfer values and to socialize young people properly is being eroded by the untenable burdens of economics and social decay.

We must also provide our youth with equal access to quality education so that every young American can enter the job market armed with essential skills and prepared with the education necessary to participate fully and productively in our society. Our current crisis in education contributes to our criminal justice crisis—over one fifth of our students fail to graduate from high school, and they face severely limited job opportunities. It is not difficult to imagine how alluring the benefits of a criminal career appear to a young man or young woman whose opportunities are limited by lack of education or job skills; neither is it difficult to imagine how despairing and unemployable youth succumb to the false euphoria of drug abuse. Additionally, we must recognize that adult literacy is crucial to the strength of our families, to the health of our economy, to the reduction of crime, and to the stability of democracy; we must also implement literacy and job training programs today if we hope to save future generations.

• *Juvenile justice*. Our juvenile justice system requires a comprehensive review so that it may practice more effectively the preventive and protective roles for which it was established. Specifically, this review and reconstitution must be conducted with a view toward expanding delinquency prevention programs. Children and juvenile first offenders who are identified as being at risk of entering the juvenile justice system must be redirected into carefully structured individualized intervention programs that address the particular issues putting the child at risk. By providing support, services, and skill development, troubled children can be redirected onto the path toward a productive and law-abiding adulthood.

Partially as a function of public misperceptions concerning juvenile crime (overall, juvenile arrest rates declined modestly over the past decade), misguided legislative efforts since the 1970s have eroded many of the traditional protections extended to juveniles, and the juvenile justice system's emphasis has concurrently shifted away from the goal of rehabilitation to the ideology of retribution. In many jurisdictions, the statutory age for prosecution as an adult has been lowered, and young people are increasingly exposed to the procedures and inappropriately harsh sanctions of the adult system. The incarceration rate for our nation's young people has increased substantially within the past decade, particularly among minority youth, resulting in overcrowded juvenile detention facilities that cannot provide the level of security and safety for which they were designed and to which juveniles are reasonably entitled.

Our national agenda must recognize the special needs of delinquent youth by taking specific remedial steps to restrict adult court jurisdiction to only those minors who are accused of serious and violent offenses, and only after judicial hearings have established that these juveniles are not amenable to rehabilitation in the juvenile system. The national agenda must provide the juvenile justice system with the resources it needs to assess and treat juvenile offenders, particularly those high-risk youth whose offenses demand institutionalization. We must also recognize that the application of the death penalty to juvenile offenders has no demonstrable deterrent effect and that such a penalty is prohibited by both the Geneva Convention and the International Covenant on Civil and Political Rights. A credible national agenda based on respect for human rights and human life must therefore oppose the recent U.S. Supreme Court decisions permitting states to apply the death penalty to those individuals whose offenses were committed at age sixteen or older.

• *Employment opportunity*. Perhaps the most essential ingredient in changing the crime equation is the availability of employment opportunities, particularly for young people. Employment opportunity can help to break the cycle of poverty and hopelessness in which so many Americans seem inextricably caught, and that contributes so greatly to crime causation.

This aspect of the national crime control agenda is of utmost importance because the relationship between unemployment and crime has long been recognized. The research that has consistently shown a direct link between unemployment and crime in the United States has shown the same in other countries as well. The research findings point toward a wide range of crime control theories and also fit the commonsense notion of who goes to prison. Consistently about half or more of the local jail and state prison inmates have not held full-time jobs at the time of their arrest. Furthermore, in a Rand Corporation study, prison inmates listed economic reasons as the primary motive for committing crime.

• *Handgun violence*. The Commission on Crime and Justice must give priority to the proliferation of handguns across the nation. The extent and viciousness of firearm violence are illustrated by the fact that of the 23,000 homicides nationwide in 1989, 60 percent (14,000) were committed with firearms; between 1979 and 1987, handguns were involved in about 27 percent of the total violent crimes. A nationwide gun control policy restricting access to guns through a mandatory waiting period and criminal history

check, coupled with stricter sentences for those convicted of the possession
or sale of illegal firearms, will diminish the number of deadly weapons in
the hands of criminals.

The availability of cheap, deadly handguns contributes greatly to the
handgun homicide rate and to the total crime picture, but the impact of
handguns is not limited to urban areas alone. Nationwide, 3,662 law enforcement officers were assaulted with firearms in 1990, and 48—almost 74
percent of the total of 65 officers murdered—were killed with handguns. A
recent study by the federal Bureau of Alcohol, Tobacco and Firearms revealed that the three leading brands of cheap handguns, each retailing for
less than $100, account for 27 percent of the total number of handguns
recovered by American police agencies, and this proliferation of cheap handguns shows no sign of abating. One company will soon introduce a powerful
9mm pistol that will retail for $155, while another recent introduction to
this deadly market is a 25-caliber handgun made to resemble a toy and
advertised at $45.

The manufacture and sale of relatively inexpensive handguns is only one
facet of the problem. An allied issue is the lack of a comprehensive national
gun control policy: Individual state laws regarding the purchase and registration of handguns vary tremendously, facilitating the activities of rings
involved in illegal gun transshipments across state lines. A recent study
revealed that in New York City, which has one of the nation's most restrictive
gun control and licensing laws, about 40 percent of the illegal handguns
seized by police had been legally purchased in Virginia, where gun purchase
and registration requirements are relatively lax. These data clearly illustrate
the need for more stringent federal statutes to ban interstate smuggling of
firearms, as well as the need for interdiction by federal law enforcement
agencies.

Law enforcement officials have recognized and begun to address this
illegal gun running. We need joint federal, state, and local task forces to
investigate and interdict the interstate flow of handguns and other deadly
weapons, such as the seminal, multijurisdictional Firearms Task Force, which
recently began operation in New York City and which recovered about four
hundred illegal firearms in its first year of work. Such task forces unify and
focus the resources, the investigative talents, and the criminal intelligence
capabilities of the agencies that comprise them, aggressively bringing these
qualities to bear against the organized gun running rings that threaten our
collective and individual safety.

The national crime control agenda must, therefore, include the Brady
Bill, which enjoys the support of America's leading law enforcement officials

and organizations and which would impose a national mandatory seven-day waiting period and require a background check on individual purchasers prior to handgun sales.

The national agenda must also include support for the Firearms Violence Prevention Act to bar the acquisition or transfer of the cheap and easily concealed handguns favored by many criminals, as well as support for the federal assault rifle legislation introduced by Senator Dennis DeConcini (D., Ariz.) to make it unlawful to transfer, import, ship, receive, or possess any assault rifle not possessed lawfully before the effective date of the law's enactment. The scope of the National Firearms Act of 1986, which required federal registration of machine guns, should be expanded to include handguns, and the essential information contained within its national registry should be made available to law enforcement agencies to aid them in illegal-weapons tracing and investigations. These legislative initiatives, combined with the aggressive enforcement strategies outlined above and the creation of antiviolence education programs, will help to stanch the deadly flow of illegal handguns and will undoubtedly result in saving precious lives.

• *Police training.* Like its historic predecessor, the national Commission on Crime and Justice's agenda must also encourage enhanced training and education for police officers; at present, only about 6 percent of the nation's 17,000 law enforcement agencies require recruits to have some college education, and only about 20 percent of the police agencies serving populations of 250,000 or more have college requirements for recruits. A bill establishing a federally funded Police Corps was approved by the 101st Congress, but no funds were ultimately allocated. This worthy proposal would provide education loans and basic police training for college students interested in a career in policing; after four years of police service in a federal, state, or local law enforcement agency, the loans would be forgiven.

Similarly, a National Center for community policing, funded by the Bureau of Justice Assistance, can provide police agencies and officers with the training, the technical assistance, the consultant services, and the other help necessary to achieve a fundamental and permanent transformation of American policing.

• *Community policing.* Finally, as discussed previously, our national crime agenda must facilitate the adoption of community policing throughout the nation. Conventional police tactics and conventional policing strategies simply cannot cope with the massive social displacement and social dysfunction that have come to define our contemporary crime picture. Proactive, problem-solving police officers and police agencies, forming partnerships with the community and marshaling all the available resources residing in the community, have already demonstrated their potent effect on crime and on the quality of life in neighborhoods.

Conclusion

THE FORMULATION OF A COMPREHENSIVE ANTICRIME AGENDA can best be achieved by appointing a national Commission on Crime and Justice and equipping its diverse staff of expert personnel with broad powers of inquiry.

The need is unequivocal: Large-scale public fear, cynicism, and disillusionment, born of a too-stratified society that does not deliver the equality and opportunity it promises, are the prime contributors to our criminal justice crisis. Such fear, cynicism, and disillusionment are particularly pernicious and pronounced among minorities, the poor, and the disenfranchised, whose access to the benefits and promise of the American Dream has been effectively denied, and government's failure to redress these issues threatens its very foundations and our way of life.

Crime in America can be reduced. Crime in America must be reduced. Turning the tide of crime and ending the cycle of poverty, violence, and despair in which it flourishes will require leadership possessed of the courage, the knowledge, and the resources to act quickly and dynamically.

We have heard time and again the drumbeating rhetoric of a "war on crime," but to this point leadership has consistently failed to supply the troops, the strategy, or the materiel required to win that war. History confirms that such protracted "wars" or "conflicts," bereft of commitment and action and discernible enemies, are inevitably doomed to failure. At this juncture we are presented with the possibility and the opportunity to win that war and to vanquish the insidious enemy within. Only by striking peremptorily and aggressively, and by tenaciously maintaining our vigorous attack on the root causes of crime until victory is achieved, can we end our internecine conflict and ensure our citizens the level of domestic tranquillity they rightfully demand and expect.

NOTES

1. Mark H. Moore and Robert C. Trojanowicz, "Policing and the Fear of Crime," *Perspectives on Policing* 3, (Washington, D.C.: National Institute of Justice and Harvard University, June 1988), p. 2.
2. James Q. Wilson and George Kelling, "Broken Windows," *Atlantic Monthly* (March 1982), pp. 29–38.

Antitrust Division and the Federal Trade Commission

ANTITRUST POLICY

ELEANOR FOX AND ROBERT PITOFSKY

Summary

THE CHALLENGE OF THE 1990S will be to restore credibility to fundamental antitrust enforcement and, at the same time, adjust antitrust policies to take into account the new realities of global competition.

During the Reagan administration, antitrust enforcement was reduced to a bare minimum. It consisted of vigorous enforcement against small-business cartels, a few cases challenging horizontal mergers between exceptionally large firms, and a stated intention to challenge "predatory conduct" (although the Reagan administration never found any instances worth challenging). All the rest of antitrust was consigned to a nonenforcement oblivion.

During this period, the administration changed the terms of analysis. It gutted the concept of antitrust as a policy against private power. It vowed not to challenge any transaction unless the antitrust enforcement itself would improve efficiency in the allocation of resources. Because enforcers assumed that what private business does is per se efficient, not surprisingly they could seldom find an antitrust victim.

The Bush administration moved in the direction of restoring the legitimacy of antitrust regulation and the credibility of antitrust as a deterrent, but enforcement levels remained relatively low.

Immediate reinvigoration of antitrust calls for the following steps:

1. Restore the soul of antitrust. Recognize antitrust as a tool against unrestrained anticonsumer private power and as a policy designed to pre-

Eleanor Fox is Professor of Law at New York University and coauthor of Corporate Acquisitions and Mergers. *She served on the National Commission for the Review of Antitrust Law. Robert Pitofsky is Professor of Law at Georgetown University Law Center and a former Commissioner at the Federal Trade Commission. Each was a co-author of the recently published* Revitalizing Antitrust in Its Second Century.

serve the dynamic rivalry that itself promotes technological progress and efficiency.

2. Reestablish the antitrust agenda. That means law enforcement against at least some vertical and conglomerate mergers, as well as horizontal mergers, anticompetitive boycotts, vertical distribution arrangements (particularly vertical minimum resale price maintenance), and enforcement of Section 2 of the Sherman Act against manipulations by dominant firms to hurt competition and consumers.

3. Expand the staff of the two decimated federal agencies so they are adequate to handle antitrust business.

4. Rescind the permissive enforcement guidelines adopted during the 1980s that depart from existing law.

5. Improve coordination of enforcement efforts between the Federal Government and state attorneys general, and solidify enforcement coordination with foreign governments.

Examined against a longer time horizon, there are two essential goals that need to be addressed during the 1990s.

1. *Adjust U.S. law to global competition.* Examine U.S. antitrust policy in the context of global needs, including the strength of foreign competition as well as broader trade goals of the United States. The United States stands virtually alone among industrialized nations in failing to take international trade considerations into some account in enforcing its antitrust law. Appropriate areas for reform of U.S. antitrust enforcement include: (a) Permit introduction of an efficiency offset in merger enforcement where the merger occurs in a moderately concentrated market and when firms can prove efficiency "by substantial evidence"; (b) allow more sensitive antitrust treatment for firms that are "failing" or operate in a "distressed industry"; (c) allow more sensitive treatment for transactions where it can be demonstrated that collaboration is necessary to permit research and development.

2. *Worldwide harmonization of antitrust.* While complete procedural or substantive harmonization of antitrust is not feasible at this time, some steps can be taken in cooperation with countries that are moving in the direction of more vigorous antitrust enforcement. These steps include: (a) Adopt as a principle international hostility toward cartels; (b) seek international cooperation in antitrust investigations; and (c) negotiate toward the development of international "safe harbors"—that is, agreements that certain kinds of arrangements will be legal or presumptively legal in all jurisdictions.

Introduction

IN MANY RESPECTS, the past twelve years have been the worst of all times for American antitrust laws. The core ideas and values of antitrust have not only been challenged by administration officials assigned to enforce the law, but also antitrust has often been blamed by those same nonenforcers for difficulties American firms have encountered in competing in global markets. Meanwhile, there has been virtually no effort to adjust American antitrust enforcement to the new realities of global competition.

The leading example of wasteful economic behavior encouraged by lax antitrust enforcement is the "merger mania" that dominated American financial markets in the 1980s. In 1980 the total reported value of U.S. corporate acquisitions and takeovers was $33 billion; by 1988 that figure had risen to almost $250 billion. During the decade of the 1980s, over $1 trillion in assets changed hands in a frenzy of merger activity. There were thirty-one thousand mergers and acquisitions in the United States—many of enormous size—amounting to about six times the annual average in the late 1970s. Many mergers reflected paper manipulations designed to make financiers rich; few had even a remote connection with the goal of enhancing productivity or efficiency.

Gigantic mergers between competing companies—in steel, chemicals, oil, and the airline industry—sailed through with government blessings. The five largest mergers in U.S. history occurred during the 1980s, all involving oil companies. These included Chevron-Gulf ($13.2 billion); Texaco-Getty ($10.1 billion); Dupont-Conoco ($8 billion); British Petroleum-Standard Oil ($7.6 billion); and U.S. Steel-Marathon Oil ($6.6 billion). Also, Campeau took over Federal Department Stores for $6.6 billion, and R. J. Reynolds acquired Nabisco for $4.9 billion. There were twenty-four mergers in the airline industry during the 1980s, not a single one challenged as a result of administration policies. Among the airlines swallowed up were Eastern, People's Express, Frontier, Western, Republic, and Ozark—with the result that many areas or city pairs are now served by only one or two airlines. In 1985 alone, at the height of this merger binge, there were thirty-six mergers involving assets of more than $1 billion—more than five times as many as had occurred in the entire period prior to 1980. Meanwhile, Federal Government enforcement people largely sat on the sidelines.[1]

The antitrust laws should be enforced more vigorously in the 1990s. Many of the areas where Reagan (and to a much lesser extent, Bush) enforcers virtually repealed congressional statutes—for example, vertical and conglomerate merger enforcement under Section 7 of the Clayton Act, and monopolization enforcement under Section 2 of the Sherman Act—deserve to be reinvigorated. An appropriately revitalized antitrust policy would neither abandon antitrust enforcement (on the Chicago school theory that almost everything the business community does must be "efficient"), or enforce the laws in a way that is insensitive to the needs of American firms to improve productivity and efficiency in order to compete in global markets.

The nature of competition in the United States and the world is changing rapidly. To succeed, U.S. firms must successfully cope with the challenge of increasingly aggressive foreign competition and also sell successfully in global markets. Some indication of the growing impact of international trade on American markets is the fact that general imports into the United States grew from $40 billion in 1970 to $495 billion in 1990.[2] The new President and the Antitrust Division should pursue more vigorous antitrust enforcement because the best way to enhance the ability of American firms to compete effectively in global markets is to ensure that the markets in which they compete at home are highly competitive.[3]

Recent History

THE ANTITRUST LAWS ARE A SET OF regulatory statutes designed to curb the accumulation of private economic power and ensure fairness in the marketplace—all without unnecessarily discouraging innovation and efficiency.

The main antitrust laws are the Sherman Act and the Clayton Act. Section 1 of the Sherman Act prohibits contracts, combinations, and conspiracies in restraint of trade. Section 2 of the Sherman Act prohibits monopolization and attempts to monopolize. The Clayton Act declares illegal certain price and service discrimination (the Robinson-Patman amendment to Section 2), certain restrictive arrangements such as exclusive dealing and tie-in sales (Section 3), and anticompetitive mergers (Section 7). The two statutes are enforced at the federal level by the Department of Justice and the Federal Trade Commission. The Department of Justice can enforce these statutes both in civil and criminal proceedings, while the Federal Trade Commission has only civil enforcement authority; in all other significant respects they have coordinate jurisdiction. The two agencies have worked out an adequate program for coordinating investigation and enforcement so that their efforts do not conflict or overlap.

From the late 1930s through 1980, American antitrust was a largely bipartisan program designed to protect free markets from exploitation through the accumulation of monopoly power or through conspiratorial behavior among competitors. There were ups and downs in enforcement levels and priorities during those decades, but antitrust was accepted as sound and important policy.

Partly in response to some earlier excesses, the Nixon and Ford administrations in the early 1970s and the Carter administration in the late 1970s rejected some of the more interventionist positions of the Warren U.S. Supreme Court, accepted some (though by no means all) of the teaching of economists, and began to develop a more sophisticated antitrust program.

This period came to an abrupt end with the election of Ronald Reagan in 1980. A new band of nonenforcers curtailed antitrust activity to the point where it concerned virtually nothing other than hard-core horizontal cartels (i.e., mostly price fixing conspiracies in the electrical and highway construction industries) and mergers likely to lead to monopoly.

The decline in enforcement activity was accompanied by, and reinforced by, a steady and drastic reduction in staff. In 1980 the Antitrust Division of the Department of Justice had a total of 939 authorized professional positions, but that number had dropped to 549 by 1988. Only 515 staff members were actually on board at the end of fiscal year 1988.[4] As of June 1989, there were only 220 lawyers and 40 economists on the staff of the Antitrust Division.[5] Similarly, the Federal Trade Commission staff declined from 1,700 employees in 1979 to 1,011 by the end of the 1987. Thus agency staffs were cut almost in half during the Reagan years, during a period when the economy was expanding, new industries were becoming subject to the antitrust laws (as a result of "deregulation"), and certain kinds of potentially anticompetitive transactions such as mergers were vastly increasing.

The overall decline in Antitrust Division investigations and enforcement activity is demonstrated in the following tables:

Tables 1 and 2 show a sharp decline in investigations in all significant areas, with the virtual disappearance of investigations of monopolizing behavior under Section 2 of the Sherman Act. Thus restraint of trade investigations fell from 225 in 1979 to 77 in 1991; monopoly investigations from 20 in 1979 to 5 in 1991; and merger investigations from 152 in 1979 to 82 in 1991.

The decline in investigative activity in the merger area is demonstrated in Table 3.

The data in Table 3 are stunning when viewed against this background fact: In the 1980s there were about six times as many mergers per year—many involving extremely large companies—than in the late 1970s.[6] Similarly, there was a decline in district court cases filed on the civil side of the Department of Justice's activities. The one area where enforcement activity held up is in the filing of criminal cases—mostly price fixing and bid rigging—where the Department of Justice in the 1980s was exceptionally active.[7]

While this activity was commendable, the enforcers used the statistics—the number of cartel cases they brought, which were mostly against very small local firms—to divert attention from the fact that they did little else, and big firms were left to do virtually anything they chose.

Levels of Nonenforcement

IT IS HARD TO APPRECIATE THE EXTENT of nonenforcement of antitrust during the 1980s without examining particular areas.

TABLE 1.
DOJ Investigations*

By Type of Conduct	1979	1980	1981	1982	1983	1984	1985	1986	1987	1988	1989	1990	1991
Sherman Act, Sec. 1 (restraint of Trade)	225	219	169	120	116	106	107	137	96	92	81	71	77
Sherman Act, Sec. 2 (monopoly)	20	65	34	12	9	3	5	8	3	3	5	4	5
Clayton Act, Sec. 7 (merger)	152	59	84	83	76	97	102	101	109	74	83	83	82

*Data for 1979–81 are from 1988 authorization hearings. Data for 1982–91 are from Antitrust Division work load statistics, fiscal years 1982–92, reprinted in 62 BNA Antitrust and Trade Reg. Rep. 79 (Jan. 1992). According to the work load statistics report (note 1), the numbers for 1979 through 1981 may be inflated because of the prior practice of counting investigations each time they went into a different phase, which could lead to some double counting.

TABLE 2.
District Court Cases Filed*

By Type of Conduct	1978	1979	1980	1981	1982	1983	1984	1985	1986	1987	1988	1989	1990	1991
Civil cases	27	31	28	25	18	16	14	11	6	15	11	6	14	17
Criminal cases	31	27	55	71	94	98	100	47	53	92	87	86	75	81

*Data for 1979–81 are from 1988 authorization hearings. Data for 1982–91 are from Antitrust Division work load statistics, fiscal years 1982–91. According to the work load statistics report, the numbers for 1979 through 1981 may be slightly inflated because of the prior practice of counting investigations each time they went into a different phase, which could lead to some double counting.

TABLE 3.
DOJ Merger Enforcement*

By Type of Conduct	1982	1983	1984	1985	1986	1987	1988	1989	1990	1991
Pre-merger notification:										
Received	1204	1101	1339	1604	1949	2533	2747	2883	2262	1529
Investigations initiated	55	62	79	106	85	89	56	64	59	67
Cases filed	8	4	5	7	6	6	6	5	11	4

Antitrust Division work load statistics comparable data for 1979–81 not available.

1. *Price fixing and cartel behavior.* As Tables 1 and 2 indicate, criminal cases filed under Section 1 of the Sherman Act—the principal source of enforcement against price fixing, bid rigging, output restrictions, and market division—increased in number during the 1980s and early 1990s. The Antitrust Division handles all criminal enforcement; its selection of hard-core cartels as an enforcement priority is appropriate. The division sought and obtained increasingly substantial prison sentences and fines.[8]

The problem with this enforcement program, particularly in the Reagan years, was that the target of enforcement was almost entirely a "hapless, economically insignificant" group of small businesses—generally asphalt suppliers, small bakeries, construction firms, obscure trade associations, and others.[9] This is because the Reagan Justice Department was looking for clear, unambiguous cartels; small firms usually cannot cooperate with competitors without clear cartels; big firms can.

Clearly, during the 1980s, *Fortune* 500 firms had little to fear from federal antitrust enforcement, even when price fixing and bid rigging was at issue.

2. *Monopoly behavior.* The Sherman Act provision outlawing monopolization and attempt to monopolize is the centerpiece of antitrust, designed to prevent strong firms from driving weaker competitors or new entrants out of the market. Traditionally, monopolization cases often involve predatory pricing, refusals to deal, tying arrangements, and similar market behavior. It is increasingly recognized that monopolization cases must be carefully selected so as not to punish firms simply because they have competed suc-

cessfully and so as not to chill aggressive competitive behavior,[10] but that hardly justifies virtual abandonment of the field. Amazingly, the Reagan administration initiated just two monopoly or attempt to monopolize cases during eight years, both rather oddball situations that were impossible for government enforcers to ignore. One involved an attempt by American Airlines to initiate a price fixing scheme with Braniff where the Antitrust Division was given the taped transcript of the conversation containing the effort to collude.[11] The other involved predation involving the institution of phony lawsuits.[12]

Under the Bush administration, both the Antitrust Division and the FTC were more active in initiating investigations,[13] but as Table 2 shows, case levels did not change much.

3. *Merger enforcement.* The 1980s witnessed an extraordinary burst of merger activity. However while total government challenges to mergers averaged about twenty per year during the period 1970 to 1980, they fell to less than ten per year during the 1980s.[14]

A striking feature of 1980s nonenforcement in the merger area was the widely perceived failure of the Reagan administration to enforce its own guidelines. Reagan enforcers published merger guidelines in 1982 and 1984 that were more permissive than those that previously applied, indicating, absent countervailing factors, that they were "likely to challenge" a merger in a moderately concentrated market that increased concentration by a significant amount, and would challenge substantial mergers in highly concentrated markets in all but "extraordinary cases."[15] In fact, there were many mergers in highly concentrated markets with great increases in concentration that were not challenged[16] and only a few instances of challenges in moderately concentrated markets.[17] During most of the Reagan years, all merger enforcement was against horizontal mergers; during the Bush administration there were a few investigations of, and cases against, vertical and conglomerate mergers.

4. *Vertical contractual arrangements.* The Reagan administration acted as if it simply repealed the law with respect to vertical restraints. There were no cases during the Reagan years against resale price maintenance, territorial and customer allocation, tie-in sales, and exclusive dealing contracts. There was one set of cases challenging price discrimination under the Robinson-Patman Act.

The most striking example of administrative nullification relates to the refusal to enforce the law against resale price maintenance—agreements between manufacturers and dealers (often coerced into the agreement) to set a minimum price on sales to consumers. The U.S. Supreme Court declared this practice illegal in 1911[18] and has maintained that position consistently even in recent years. Conservative economic theory argues that such arrangements that eliminate price-cutting and discounting practices help consumers by ensuring that the full-service retailers will not be undercut by discounters of the same brand. It is indefensible for administrators simply to nullify clear Supreme Court doctrine and congressional will by nonenforcement of the law.

The Bush administration restored enforcement against vertical restraints to the antitrust agenda. The FTC voted out complaints based on theories of boycott, tie-in sales, and resale price maintenance; the Department of Justice opened a cluster of investigations of resale price maintenance, refusal to deal, and exclusive dealing arrangements.[19]

5. *State enforcement.* In the early 1980s, exasperated by the inactivity and default of federal enforcement authorities, state attorneys general often maintained the only credible antitrust presence. The only government cases filed in the Reagan years against resale price maintenance, territorial allocations, and boycotts were by state enforcers; the states also filed important price-fixing and merger cases.[20] As a result of several cases, such as a vertical price-fixing case against Panasonic, millions of dollars of rebates were paid to consumers.[21]

Proposals for Immediate Revival of Antitrust

THE MOST IMPORTANT ENFORCEMENT TASK for the 1990s is to reassert the presence, credibility, and integrity of federal antitrust enforcement by (a) carefully selected and sensible enforcement initiatives and (b) policy statements that undo the damage of a decade of trivializing and blaming antitrust.

A number of short-term steps should be taken:

1. *Policy directions.* Through speeches or policy statements, a new Antitrust Division should reassert the government's intention to address previously ignored anticompetitive arrangements. There is nothing wrong with focusing on hard-core price fixing and large horizontal mergers as priority enforcement objectives, but some vertical and conglomerate mergers raise competitive problems, and there are instances in which dominant firms set out to achieve monopoly power by driving rivals out of business. There are many examples of vertical price fixing designed to inhibit the ability of discounters to pass low prices on to consumers. In short, a major challenge

facing the next Administration is to restore the antitrust enforcement agenda.

2. *Staff*. As noted earlier, the antitrust enforcement staffs of both enforcement agencies were cut by almost 50 percent from 1981 through 1989 and then increased by about 10 percent in the past four years. Given the vast increase in the size of the economy since 1980, and the increase in areas where antitrust oversight is essential—particularly pertaining to international mergers, joint ventures, and cartels—a further restoration of staff is essential. If the staff of each agency were to be expanded another 10 percent, that would still leave each agency a leaner operation than in 1980 but more capable of carrying out its core mission.

Since the combined budget for antitrust enforcement at the Antitrust Division and the FTC is under $100 million, that would mean a total budget increase of about $10 million.[22]

3. *Guidelines*. The Reagan administration weakened antitrust enforcement in part through the publication of some extremely permissive guidelines. While it is essential not to dislocate capital markets unnecessarily or impair corporate planning by wholesale rejection of existing guidelines, a new assistant attorney general should identify particular guideline provisions that are perverse, and eliminate them. One set of guidelines, dealing with vertical contractual restraints, abandoned existing law and introduced exceptionally conservative, ideological notions of market effects. In December 1985 Congress enacted a joint resolution calling on the attorney general to withdraw the division's vertical restraint guidelines, in part because they were a misleading statement of existing law. For example, they adopt lenient enforcement positions on all distribution arrangements as long as only one brand is affected—a position rejected by the U.S. Supreme Court in its 1992 *Eastman Kodak* case.[23] It would make sense to announce promptly that this set of guidelines has been rescinded.

The Federal Government's 1992 revision of its merger guidelines presents a more complicated case. The 1992 DOJ/FTC horizontal merger guidelines introduce some intelligent new thinking about merger analysis but generally indicate a more relaxed government posture than applied even in the 1980s. The 1984 guidelines, for example, stated that the department would be "likely" to challenge a substantial merger in a moderately concentrated market; the 1992 guidelines note only that such a merger may "potentially raise significant competitive concerns."[24] Similarly, the 1984 guidelines indicated that substantial mergers in concentrated markets would be challenged except in "extraordinary cases"; the 1992 guidelines describe comparable mergers as "potentially [raising] significant competitive concerns." The 1984 guidelines more accurately reflected existing law.

One controversial aspect of the new guidelines deserves immediate attention. Even at high levels of concentration (e.g., where a merger produces a combined market share of 20 percent or more in a three- or four-firm industry), the 1992 guidelines fail to reflect fully Supreme Court teaching that such mergers are usually anticompetitive and should, except in extraordinary circumstances, be challenged by the government.[25]

4. *Coordination with state attorneys general.* When the Reagan administration's neglect of antitrust became most severe, state attorneys general stepped into the breach. Federal officials regarded the state attorneys general as unwelcome and unprincipled intruders, calling them "political opportunists." Although Bush administration officials have done a good deal to repair the damage done, a prompt statement that coordination makes sense and collaboration is invited will set the right tone for future dealings among enforcement authorities.

Long-Term Proposals

1. *Enforce the antitrust laws.* Despite considerable antagonism during the past twelve years, particularly from the Department of Justice under Attorney General Edwin Meese, the core of antitrust remains intact. A few U.S. Supreme Court decisions curtailed antitrust exposure in some areas (e.g., distribution restraints and predation), but in general the Supreme Court moved cautiously in the direction of easing the law. All that is needed to restore credibility to antitrust enforcement, therefore, is the will and political backing from the White House to enforce the law.

The goal should not be to return to the all-out warfare of the 1950s and 1960s (which incorporated a dose of bias against big business) but rather to enforce the antitrust laws in a pragmatic and thoughtful way.

2. *Legislation.* With one exception, little in the way of new legislation is required. The exception is a bill, the Consumer Protection Against Price Fixing Act, that has passed both the House and the Senate (but got bogged down—among other reasons—because of the threat of presidential veto), which would reaffirm the traditional antitrust rule that retailers may not agree with or coerce suppliers into cutting off other retailers who offer lower prices to consumers. This traditional prodiscounter rule was undermined in the 1980s by several Supreme Court opinions, making it difficult to prove agreement or coercion.

3. *Antitrust Reforms—U.S. response to global competition.* Overall, the antitrust laws should be enforced more vigorously. Still, a new assistant attorney general in charge of antitrust should review the law and economic realities and determine whether some selective modifications would contribute to international competitiveness.

Following are three examples of such possible modifications. They relate to efficiencies, financial failure, and research and development. These examples are not proposed as a vehicle to drive a hole through the body of antitrust. Quite the contrary; these initiatives are proposed as a way to preserve the integrity of antitrust. Efficiencies, firm survival, and technological progress are quite properly recognized by courts and the public as having high social value. Our proposal would simply place on the table factors that judges do in fact consider, and then circumscribe the appropriate role for these concerns.

a. *Consideration of efficiencies in merger enforcement.* According to the U.S. Supreme Court, efficiencies are not a relevant defense to an anticompetitive merger. The United States is one of the few countries in the industrialized world that does not authorize efficiency considerations to be taken into account, at least as one factor, in determining the legality of mergers. We believe efficiencies proved by substantial evidence (with the burden of proof on the party asserting the efficiency claim) should be an admissible factor, and perhaps should be a persuasive factor where the market is not highly concentrated.

This proposal would change the result in only a few merger cases, but it would prevent the merger law from standing in the way of mergers whose dominant effect is to improve the ability of American firms to compete successfully abroad. Also, the modification should lead firms to seek mergers and joint ventures that could be defended on a dynamic efficiency basis, which itself could have a salutary influence on U.S. competitiveness.

b. *Failing companies and distressed industries.* United States antitrust law provides only a narrow exception for failing companies and no exception for firms operating in a distressed industry. Even when industries are beset with chronic overcapacity and financial weakness, frequently as a result of increasing imports, the enforcement authorities and the courts have not seen fit to permit any exceptions. But this approach may be inconsistent with the intent of Congress as well as good policy.

c. *Research and development.* Merging parties sometimes offer as a justification the prospect of improvements in R&D. Ordinarily no special exception for mergers is necessary because R&D can be conducted through less restrictive arrangements—cross-licenses, joint ventures, etc. But there are occasional situations in which the expense of engaging in R&D in particular product markets is so great and the synergies in expertise are so great that the benefits are unlikely to be achieved without merger. Although that situation is rare, we believe that flexibility to allow such mergers by proof again of "substantial evidence," where several other competitors are active in the field, is justified.

4. *Globalization of antitrust.* An increasing number of nations have antitrust laws that are similar but not identical. In our globalized economy, the laws of several different nations may apply to the same transaction, leading to inefficiencies in enforcement and exacerbating the problem of substantive differences in law. The United States should take the lead in seeking to minimize the inefficiencies and unnecessary inconsistencies.

The most immediately feasible option would involve sharing of information and frequent communication, including notification of all enforcement initiatives that affect the interests of another nation and notification of all complaints against other governments or their nationals based on interference with competition. Basic harmonization can also include bilateral or multilateral agreement on formal or procedural matters, such as conforming merger notification information requests; and it can include attempts to arrive at common principles regarding extraterritorial reach of national antitrust laws.

Going farther, the United States should explore with other nations possible agreement on the following principles or in the following areas:
• Nations shall adopt and implement the principle of freedom of movement of goods and services, freedom of enterprise, and freedom of trade.
• Nations shall not tolerate cartels, including export and import cartels.
• Nations shall not prohibit transnational research joint ventures of firms accounting for no more than, for example, 40 percent of any relevant market, nor prohibit short-term exclusive dealing contracts that account for no more than 20 percent of a market. (Other safe harbors may be devised. Our purpose here is to introduce the concept of transactions that are clearly permissible because they are permitted under consensus world principles and because freedom to engage in such transactions is important to world welfare.)
• Nations shall exchange information and consult on matters involving the interests of one another; shall aid one another in discovery and enforcement against persons within a nation's jurisdiction; and a nation shall hospitably consider requests by another nation to enforce its law against persons in its jurisdiction who are harming the interests of the requesting nation (as per the recent U.S./European Community Executive Agreement).
• Finally, the new Administration should initiate a major conference

with representatives of the United States, Canada, the European Community, Japan, and perhaps East European nations to discuss harmonization of procedures in antitrust enforcement and harmonization of substantive provisions where possible.

NOTES

1. See generally, E. Fox and L. Sullivan, "Retrospective and Prospective: Where Are We Coming from? Where Are We Going?" in H. First, E. Fox, and R. Pitofsky, *Revitalizing Antitrust in Its Second Century* vol. 2 (Westport, Conn.: Quorum Books, 1991).

2. Department of Commerce, Bureau of the Census, *Statistical Abstract of the United States* (1991), p. 804.

3. For an elaboration on this theme, see M. E. Porter, *The Competitive Advantage of Nations* (New York: The Free Press, 1990), pp. 662–164.

4. Oversight and Authorization Hearings into the Policies and Enforcement Record of the Antitrust Division (DOJ): Hearings Before the Subcommittee on Monopolies and Commercial Law of the House Committee on the Judiciary, 100th Cong., 1st and 2d sess. (1988), p. 614

5. Report of the American Bar Association Section of Antitrust Law, Task Force on the Antitrust Division of the U.S. Department of Justice (July 1989), p. 6 n. 2. (hereinafter "ABA Task Force Report").

6. See T. Krattenmaker and R. Pitofsky, "Antitrust Merger Policy in the Reagan Administration," *Antitrust Bulletin* 33, (1988): 211–13.

7. Similar statistics concerning enforcement are not available for the FTC, but the overall patterns of decline in enforcement, especially during the Reagan years, is roughly the same. See R. Pitofsky, "The Renaissance of Antitrust," *Record of the Bar of the City of New York* 45 (1991): 851.

8. ABA Task Force Report, p. 33.

9. E. Kovacic, "Federal Antitrust Enforcement in the Reagan Administration: Two Cheers for the Disappearance of the Large Firm Defendant in Nonmerger Cases," *Research in Law and Economics* 12 (1989): 173.

10. In 1945, the courts came close to adopting a "nofault" antimonopoly position, punishing all monopolies that engaged in mildly exclusionary conduct. See *United States v. Aluminum Co. of America*, 148 F.2d 416 (2nd Cir. 1945). That stringent policy has given way in more recent cases to an approach that allows competitors to compete vigorously and fairly to protect their legally acquired monopoly positions; see, e.g., *Texas Corp. v. IBM*, 510 F.2d, 894 (10th Cir.) *cert. dismissed*, 423 U.S. 802 (1975); *Olympia Equipment Leasing Co. v. Western Union Telegraph Co.*, 397 F.2d 370, 376–77 (7th Cir. 1986).

11. *United States v. American Airlines, Inc.*, 743 F.2d 1114 (5th Cir. 1984).

12. *In re Amerco*, 109 FTC 135 (1987) (consent order).

13. See Krattenmaker and Pitofsky, "Antitrust Merger Policy," n. 6.

14. Calkins, "Developments in Merger Litigation, *Antitrust Law Journal* 56 (1988): 86,974.

15. See U.S. Department of Justice Merger Guidelines, Trade Reg. Rep. 4 (CCH), sec. 13,103 (June 14, 1984), at sec. 3.1.

16. ABA Task Force Report, p. 27.

17. House Subcommittee on Monopolies and Commercial Law, Federal Merger Enforcement (1979—87), repr. in *Antitrust and Trade Reg. Rep.* 54 (BNA) (1988): 476–77. Krattenmaker and Pitofsky, "Antitrust Merger Policy," n.5.

18. *Dr. Miles Medical Co.* v. *John D. Park & Sons Co.*, 220 U.S. 373 (1911).

19. See Krattenmaker and Pitofsky, "Antitrust Merger Policy," n.6.

20. L. Constantine, "The Mission and Agenda for State Antitrust Enforcement," *Antitrust Bulletin* 36 (1991): 835, 840–41.

21. *In re Panasonic Consumer Elec. Prod. Antitrust Litigation*, 89 Civ. 0368 (SDNY 1989).

22. A substantial increase in antitrust enforcement resources is needed. See ABA Task Force Report, pp. 19–20; Report of the American Bar Association, Section of Antitrust Law, Special Committee to Study the Role of the Federal Trade Commission, 56 ATRR S-1, S-28 (1989).

23. *Eastman Kodak* v. *Image Technical Services, Inc.* S.Ct. (1992).

24. 1992 guidelines, sec. 1.51(B).

25. Law and policy is discussed in IV P. Areeda and D. Turner, *Antitrust Analysis* (1978).

CIVIL RIGHTS

PENDA D. HAIR

Summary

THIS NATION NEEDS LEADERSHIP on civil rights issues to educate the public about the continued pervasiveness and perniciousness of racism. We need a leader who will forcefully repudiate the prior administrations' use of buzzwords and symbols to stir up racial fears for political advantage. The Reagan/Bush administrations have not only vigorously attacked laws and court decisions that provided effective remedies for racial discrimination, but they have also spent the past twelve years using the "bully pulpit" afforded by the White House to portray reverse discrimination, "quotas," and black-on-white crime as America's only racial problems. Government policy over the past decade strongly contributed to the feelings of rage and isolation that resulted in the recent uprising in Los Angeles.

The new Administration should immediately embark on an aggressive, highly publicized enforcement program to discover and remedy racial discrimination in voting and political participation, employment, housing, education, and other areas of public life. This program should include the following short-term actions:

1. Issue a strong statement to all federal agencies and employees involved in civil rights enforcement, instructing them immediately to start applying the "effects" definition of discrimination to Titles VI, VII, and IX of the Civil Rights Act of 1964, the Fair Housing Act, and other appropriate federal civil rights statutes.

2. Announce the Administration's support of increased federal funding for testing (undercover audits of housing providers and employers) as a major investigative and enforcement initiative.

3. Immediately revoke the prior administrations' opposition to voluntary and court-ordered affirmative action.

Penda D. Hair is Director of the Fair Housing Program of the NAACP Legal Defense and Educational Fund, Inc.

4. Endorse legislation to overturn the U.S. Supreme Court's decision in *Presley* v. *Etowah County.*

The new program of enforcement should also include these longer-term steps:

- Pursue a litigation strategy to convince the federal courts to apply the Civil Rights Act of 1991 to pending claims.
- Pursue a litigation strategy to convince the U.S. Supreme Court to rule explicitly that the "effects" definition of discrimination applies to the Fair Housing Act.
- Reinvigorate HUD's enforcement of the Fair Housing Act.
- Implement a litigation strategy to apply the Voting Rights Act to judicial elections and to legislative procedures that dilute the political power of African Americans and other minorities.

The Message

THE NEW ADMINISTRATION MUST BE AWARE that at least in the short term, its public message may be the most important contribution it can make to combat racism and enforce civil rights. Over the past twelve years the White House has used the media to distort and inflame. The Reagan and Bush administrations have publicly denounced and battled against measures such as minority-targeted scholarships, affirmative action, and school desegregation that are designed to eliminate the vestiges of America's legacy of discrimination.

The healing must start with a new message designed to give hope to victims who feel ignored and devalued, to educate the public about our history of racial oppression and the continuing need for affirmative remedies, and to warn those who may be inclined to discriminate that such conduct is illegal and will be discovered and severely punished. This message must begin with the proclamation that blatant racial discrimination still pervades our society and our governmental institutions and that it continues to heap disadvantages on every single African American living in this country today. This new message will assure African Americans and other oppressed groups that the Federal Government is no longer engaged in a "blame the victim" strategy but is genuinely seeking solutions.

Comprehensive Strategies

CIVIL RIGHTS AND ANTIDISCRIMINATION ENFORCEMENT cuts across many different government agencies, such as the Departments of

Justice, Labor, and Housing and Urban Development, as well as the Equal Employment Opportunity Commission and the Commission on Civil Rights. It also cuts across many subject areas, including fair housing, fair lending, equal employment, voting rights, educational opportunity, and criminal justice. However, there are major policy initiatives that should be applied across-the-board.

THE "EFFECTS" STANDARD

The "effects" definition of discrimination was incorporated into federal civil rights law twenty-one years ago in a unanimous U.S. Supreme Court decision written by former Chief Justice Warren Burger. In *Griggs* v. *Duke Power Co.*, the Court held that an employer's use of selection devices that disproportionately disadvantage African American candidates constitutes discrimination under Title VII of the Civil Rights Act of 1964, unless the employer demonstrates that the devices are job-related and justified by business necessity. The Court in *Griggs* invalidated the employer's requirement that candidates for positions in departments that had previously been designated only for white workers either possess a high school degree or pass a standardized intelligence test. The Court in *Griggs* held that Title VII prohibits not only *intentional* discrimination but also practices that are "fair in form but discriminatory in operation." The Court concluded that "good intent or the absence of discriminatory intent does not redeem employment procedures or testing mechanisms that operate as 'built-in headwinds' for minority groups and are unrelated to measuring job capability . . . . Congress directed the thrust of the Act to the *consequences* of employment practices, not simply the motivation."

The *Griggs* decision is a landmark of civil rights law akin to *Brown* v. *Board of Education*. The effects standard provides a partial remedy for the past discrimination against African Americans, by prohibiting employment practices that " 'freeze' the status quo of prior discriminatory employment practices." The effects model also serves to prohibit practices that are probably motivated by discriminatory intent that cannot be proven because of the difficulty of producing evidence of a malicious motive. In *Griggs*, for example, the employer's conduct raised a strong suspicion of discriminatory intent. By shifting the focus from intent to the consequences of the employer's actions, the effects standard removes the divisive moral question and instead focuses attention on systems that discriminate.

In the employment area, the *Griggs* definition of discrimination was subsequently extended to selection devices, such as height and weight requirements, that have an adverse impact on women or members of certain ethnic groups. The concept of discrimination as adverse impact also has been extended by Congress and the courts beyond the employment context. Nine federal courts of appeals have held that the disparate impact definition of discrimination applies under the Fair Housing Act to prohibit a variety of types of conduct. For example, in *Betsey* v. *Turtle Creek Associates*, the court for the Fourth Circuit held that a landlord's policy of evicting families with children from one of its apartment buildings, which had the effect of evicting almost 75 percent of the minority tenants and only about 25 percent of the white tenants, violated the Fair Housing Act unless the landlord could show that "business necessity" compelled this policy. And in *Huntington Branch NAACP* v. *Town of Huntington*, the court for the Second Circuit struck down a zoning ordinance that perpetuated segregation by restricting multifamily housing to areas where minorities were already concentrated.

Congress also adopted an effects test in 1982 amendments to Section 2 of the Voting Rights Act. This "results" test explicitly looks at the interaction of the challenged practice with social and historical conditions to determine whether, in the totality of the circumstances, minorities have equal opportunities to participate in the political process and to elect representatives of their choice. This variation of the effects test is explicitly designed to remedy a history of official discrimination in the political process.

Despite virtually universal acceptance and the practical effectiveness of the effects test, the Reagan/Bush administrations have carried out a fierce campaign to eliminate this standard from our civil rights laws. Their campaign came to a head in the battle over the Civil Rights Act of 1991. Although a twenty-year history of implementation of *Griggs* in the workplace revealed no tendency toward use of quotas, the Bush administration branded the effort to restore *Griggs* as a pernicious "quota bill."

The Bush administration's attack on *Griggs* is not limited to employment issues. The Department of Justice has taken the position that no effects standard applies to claims brought under the Fair Housing Act. This repudiation of the *Griggs* test in the housing area has severely undermined the enforcement effort.

The new Administration should make across-the-board implementation of the effects standard a top civil rights priority. This initiative should include strong advocacy of interpretations of the provisions of the Civil Rights Act of 1991 that would truly restore the *Griggs* principle. The new Administration also should engage in a campaign designed to convince the Supreme Court to rule that the *Griggs* principle applies to claims brought under the Fair Housing Act. The Administration should make clear that the effects test applies to all programs covered by Titles VI and IX of the 1964 Civil Rights Act, particularly in the education and housing areas.

SUPPORT AND FUNDING FOR "TESTING" AS AN INVESTIGATIVE TECHNIQUE

"Testing" is a brilliant investigative technique that was first used in the civil rights area by fair housing organizations. Testing is undercover investigative work. For example, investigators pretend to seek housing to "test" whether the housing provider treats black and white "testers" the same. This type of investigation provides powerful evidence of *intentional* discrimination, the most difficult type of discrimination to prove.

An ABC Television *PrimeTime Live* episode videotaped undercover testing in St. Louis, Missouri, in 1991. The resulting report, which aired on September 26, 1991, documents blatant racial discrimination. For example, a white official at an employment agency offered courteous service to the white tester while lecturing the black tester on laziness. The black tester was quoted a down payment for a car that was $1,000 higher than that quoted to the white tester for the purchase of the identical automobile from the same salesman. The black tester was repeatedly told by a dry cleaning establishment that there were no jobs available, while the white tester was told that positions were available. The black tester was told that no apartment was available, after the white tester had been given a tour of a vacant apartment five minutes earlier.

Litigation using testing evidence has been enormously successful. As stated by John Dunne, assistant attorney general for civil rights, "fair housing testing has become the most effective investigative tool and evidence in fair housing cases."

Despite the effectiveness of fair housing testing, the availability of this enforcement technique is severely limited by two factors. First, fewer than fifty private fair housing organizations with the capacity to perform testing currently exist nationwide. These organizations generally are concentrated in the Midwest, the Northeast and the West. In large portions of the country, especially the South, testing organizations are extremely rare.

Second, HUD has adopted restrictive guidelines on the types of testing that can be performed with federal funding. Under the Fair Housing Initiatives Program (FHIP), Congress in 1987 authorized the department to make grants to private organizations to engage in testing and other enforcement activities. However, the department adopted guidelines that allow testing only after receipt of a "bona fide" allegation of discrimination. Since the victims of housing discrimination rarely become aware of the violation, the most effective testing programs use random checks in addition to testing actual allegations. The Bush administration has recognized the value of testing, and the Department of Justice has recently announced that it will implement its own housing testing program. While it is too early to ascertain the effectiveness of the department's testing program, most fair housing advocates believe it is preferable to have testing conducted by private, non-profit organizations, since it is not clear whether Justice Department testers could sue for damages, which is crucial to the effort to deter housing providers from engaging in discrimination.

Testing also could be extremely valuable in investigating lending and credit discrimination. Data recently made available reveal sharp disparities in the rates at which white and black applicants with identical incomes are granted mortgage loans. These data strongly suggest either intentional discrimination or the use of arbitrary criteria that have a severe adverse impact on African American access to mortgage loans. Testing could ferret out the precise cause or causes of this roadblock to home ownership.

Another extremely promising development is employment testing. Over the past few years several organizations have worked to adapt testing techniques to the employment area. Although this technique is still in its infancy, several lawsuits have been brought based on tester evidence. The Equal Employment Opportunity Commission has accepted tester evidence in employment discrimination cases. The use of testers to detect employment discrimination, particularly hiring discrimination, offers the potential to open huge numbers of entry-level jobs to African Americans, Latinos, women, and other minorities.

The new Administration should recognize that testing is possibly the most potent weapon available in the war to detect and remedy discrimination. It should encourage and provide funding for massive testing programs in all areas of public life. In the housing area, as a supplement or alternative to the Department of Justice's in-house testing program, the new Administration should support an increase in FHIP program funding from the current $8 million to $26 million per year. The eventual goal of the FHIP program should be to provide "seed" money to start hundreds of new private fair housing organizations in unserved or underserved areas and to provide on-going support for existing organizations. The FHIP budget should gradually increase as new organizations are created each year. The new Administration also should immediately revoke the "bona fide" allegation requirement and should consult with private fair housing groups and advocates to develop fair and workable testing guidelines.

In the employment area, the Executive Branch should engage in a legal campaign to convince the federal courts, including ultimately the Supreme Court, to give the same respect to employment testing that has been given to housing testing. This includes the availability of damage remedies for testers and private testing organizations. The Administration should also support federal funding of private employment testing efforts by developing the employment equivalent of the FHIP program, with an initial annual budget of $10 million.

AFFIRMATIVE ACTION
Despite a well-orchestrated campaign by the Reagan/Bush administrations to remove affirmative action from our landscape, affirmative action is not dead. The U.S. Supreme Court has generally approved both court-ordered and voluntary affirmative action, including goals and timetables, to remedy past discrimination or to achieve other important objectives. The only recent Supreme Court setback on the issue of affirmative action is the invalidation of the City of Richmond's minority business set-aside program in *City of Richmond* v. *J. A. Croson Co.* However, even this decision left open the possibility that a more carefully crafted minority-business set-aside would be upheld. Most recently, in *Metro Broadcasting, Inc.*, v. *FCC*, the Court upheld explicit minority preference policies used by the Federal Communications Commission in awarding broadcast licenses.

Numerically based affirmative action remains one of the most effective tools to remedy the effects of current and historic discrimination. Affirmative action has been generally accepted and, in many instances, enthusiastically implemented by businesses and by state and local governments.

The new Administration should immediately announce, in a major public address by the President, its strong commitment to both voluntary and court-ordered affirmative action, including appropriate goals and timetables. The Administration should reinvigorate enforcement of executive order 11246, which requires affirmative action by government contractors. This Executive Order has been constantly threatened by the Reagan/Bush administrations but still remains on the books. The Justice Department should pursue numerical remedies in appropriate court cases and should reassure employers that they will not be prosecuted for voluntary use of appropriate affirmative action plans. The Administration should apply affirmative action principles to itself in filling all federal government positions, starting with the cabinet, and the President should fill any vacancies on the Supreme Court with jurists who are not ideologically opposed to affirmative action.

Programmatic Recommendations

FAIR HOUSING

Housing patterns in this country remain incredibly segregated. The vast majority of African Americans, Latinos, and Asians are locked into segregated neighborhoods. Very frequently these neighborhoods afford few jobs, poor schools, and inferior public services.

It is unlikely that the recent civil unrest in Los Angeles would have transpired if housing in that metropolitan area were not segregated, for in a desegregated community, the jury probably would have included one or two African Americans who could have explained the realities of police brutality and racial discrimination to their colleagues. In a desegregated community there would not have been a racially isolated and oppressed south-central neighborhood.

Segregation is not the result of chance, of differences in income levels, or of mere private choices. Persistent patterns of racial segregation are the legacy of a host of official actions of federal, state, and local governments and of discriminatory and segregative policies followed by the housing industry.

Recognizing the tremendous scope of housing discrimination and the need for bold and vigorous enforcement, Congress in 1988 enacted broad amendments to the Fair Housing Act. These amendments extended the act's coverage to discrimination against families with children and the disabled. The 1988 amendments established the most comprehensive governmental enforcement system ever included in a federal civil rights law. Under this system all complaints must be investigated by HUD. If HUD finds "cause" to believe that a violation occurred, the parties are then offered a choice of an administrative hearing before a HUD administrative law judge, or a federal court trial, usually before a jury.

According to a 1991 HUD report of testing audits in twenty-five American cities, African Americans encounter discrimination 59 percent of the time. Millions of African Americans are victims of housing discrimination each year. Although HUD and the Department of Justice have responsibility for eradicating this pervasive racial discrimination, these agencies have done little to bring about fundamental change in the housing industry. The Department of Justice's repudiation of the effects standard is one reason why. This policy requires expensive and time-consuming investigations in an effort to uncover intent and forecloses the department from bringing many cases.

HUD's statistics suggest that valid complaints are being wrongfully rejected with "no cause" findings. In its most recent report to Congress, HUD indicated that for all types of housing discrimination, it received 4,457 complaints and closed 4,138 complaints in 1990. Of those, 1,739 were "administratively closed," 1,709 were conciliations, 609 were "no cause" determinations, and only 81 claims resulted in "cause" determinations. HUD reached a "no cause" determination seven and one half times for each "cause" determination.

The statistics for claims alleging racial discrimination are even more disturbing. In 1990, HUD found "no cause" in 310 cases alleging race or color discrimination, and found "cause" in only 15 race claims *nationwide*. "No cause" was found twenty times more often than "cause" in race claims in 1990. While HUD's own testing survey shows that African Americans suffer discrimination 59 percent of the time, HUD finds "cause" in less than one half of 1 percent of all race discriminations claims filed with the Department. Either HUD is wrongfully finding "no cause" in huge numbers of cases, or HUD's educational efforts have failed to generate complaints from the millions of victims who are known to exist.

The low number of "cause" findings might be explained if HUD were obtaining substantial remedies for victims of racial discrimination through the conciliation process. But although HUD settled 1,709 claims in 1990, the average monetary damages in settled cases was only $826. In contrast, in *Secretary ex rel. Herron* v. *Blackwell*, a HUD administrative law judge awarded $65,592 in damages, and a civil penalty of $10,000, in the first racial discrimination case to go to administrative trial under the 1988 amendments. Private fair housing advocates routinely obtain six-figure damage awards in court cases. For example, a jury recently awarded $850,000 in compensatory damages to three plaintiffs in a housing advertising case. Large damage awards are important not only to compensate the victims but also to serve as deterrents to future discrimination.

Under the new Administration, HUD should adopt a much more aggressive approach to investigation and resolution of fair housing complaints. HUD and the Department of Justice should notify enforcement personnel that substantial damages are necessary in cases where there is a violation. HUD and the Department of Justice must send a strong message to the housing industry that discrimination will no longer be tolerated and that damage awards can no longer be written off as an ordinary cost of doing business. Off-the-record settlements should be strongly discouraged.

HUD should follow the definition of "reasonable cause" included in its own regulations and should not require absolute or indisputable proof before finding "cause." Investigators and other enforcement personnel should be retrained to make clear that detecting and remedying discrimination is more important than closing cases. HUD should modify its current quality control and personnel management systems, which give employees strong incentives to find "no cause."

The most efficient and effective way to investigate many complaints is testing. HUD should set up a system to refer appropriate complaints to private fair housing organizations for testing. As new fair housing organizations are started around the country, HUD could gradually attain the goal of referring all appropriate complaints for testing.

The Department of Justice also should implement an aggressive program of enforcement against localities that adopt zoning or other restrictions on low-income or multifamily housing or that limit such housing to neighborhoods with high concentrations of minority residents. The Department of Justice should promote the application of the effects test to such restrictions.

Finally, the new Administration should take immediate action to enforce fair housing and fair lending laws with regard to housing financing. Redlining of minority neighborhoods and blatant discrimination against minority applicants must be dealt with swiftly and forcefully. The enforcement responsibility, which is now spread among numerous agencies, including the Federal Reserve, the FDIC, the comptroller of the currency, HUD, and the Department of Justice, should be concentrated in one agency. Although the Department of Justice has begun an effort to coordinate such investigations, the department is severely limited by its refusal to apply the effects test. The department can prosecute lenders who use arbitrary and unjustified credit standards only if it finds evidence of an intentional racial motive. The new Administration should instead vigorously apply the effects standard to lending discrimination. It also should support legislation to force lending institutions and Fannie Mae and Freddie Mac to make more mortgage funds available to moderate-income home buyers.

VOTING RIGHTS

The Bush administration's record on voting rights is a definite improvement over the Reagan administration's. Some have claimed that the administration's positive actions in this area appear to stem from a Republican Party strategy to use the Voting Rights Act's redistricting remedies for its own partisan advantage. Nonetheless, regardless of motive, the Bush Department of Justice has generally supported the "results" test.

At least two crucial issues involving the scope of the Voting Rights Act remain to be resolved in the 1990s. First is the applicability of Section 2 of the Voting Rights Act to judicial elections. Of the approximately 12,000 state court judges in this country in 1991, only 465 (4 percent), were African

American and only 150 (1 percent) were Hispanic. The lack of a voice in the judicial system is directly related to the rage and despair that now exist in many African American communities. A recent poll showed that 81 percent of African Americans believe that the judicial system is racially biased.

The majority of state trial judges in this country are elected. Virtually all of these judges are elected from multimember districts that do not give African Americans or other people of color a fair chance to elect judges of their choice. Application of the Voting Rights Act to the judicial districting process offers a real promise of desegregating these elected state judiciaries.

Two cases raising the issue of the applicability of the Voting Rights Act to judicial elections were decided by the U.S. Supreme Court in 1991. The plaintiffs in both cases, representing African Americans and Latinos, argued that judicial elections should be treated the same as any other voting practice and that Section 2's "totality of the circumstances" test should govern. While proclaiming its commitment to the coverage of judicial elections, the Department of Justice took a more narrow approach, arguing that the Court should be required to give weight to the state's interest in its current exclusionary system.

The Supreme Court decisions were favorable. The Court held that judges are "representatives" under the Voting Rights Act. Therefore, judicial election districts may be challenged under the "results" standard in Section 2 of the act. The Court left it to the lower courts to determine, in the first instance, the nature and scope of Section 2's application to these elections.

The Supreme Court's decisions in these two cases leave open a valuable opportunity for the Department of Justice to influence the development of the law in the lower courts. The new Administration should take advantage of this opportunity by advocating strong application of Section 2 to judicial elections. The department should also use its power under Section 5 of the Voting Rights Act and refuse to preclear changes in judicial election schemes that do not comply with Section 2 of the act.

The Supreme Court's recent decision on another voting rights issue was not so favorable. In *Presley* v. *Etowah County*, the Court severely restricted applicability of the Voting Rights Act by holding that Section 5 does not apply to procedures that eliminate or dilute the powers of elected representatives.

In the mid-1980s, in two Alabama counties, African Americans won elections to county commissions that had previously been all-white. When the commissions were all-white, each commissioner had jurisdiction over the roads within a certain geographic area of the County. But as soon as African Americans had the potential to be elected, these commissions changed the rules and stripped the individual commissioners of power to allocate funds for street repair.

The Supreme Court held that Section 5 does not cover these types of discriminatory actions. The Court reasoned that the formal right of African Americans to vote is all that is required by Section 5, even if representatives chosen by minorities are deprived of the power to serve their constituents.

Largely because of gains brought about by the Voting Rights Act, African American and other minority officials have begun to attain elected office. However, structures and procedures in the legislative process in many jurisdictions are being used to dilute African American votes. Just as the votes of a cohesive African American community may be submerged and diluted in an at-large election scheme, the procedural rules used by a legislative body, combined with bloc voting by a white majority of representatives, can dilute the power of newly elected minority officials. These "third generation" barriers to equal political participation may be the most pernicious in the 1990s.

Congress is considering legislation that would overturn *Presley*. The new Administration should support this legislation, which is consistent with the history and purpose of the Voting Rights Act.

JUDICIAL SELECTION AND CIVIL LIBERTIES

MARK GITENSTEIN AND RON KLAIN

U NLIKE OTHER COUNTRIES, America's nationhood rests not on a common ethnicity, language, or culture, but on a common idea: the notion of personal freedom and individual liberty. Enshrined in our Constitution, it is the central duty of the federal judiciary to interpret the meaning of that charter, and it is the obligation of the President and the Senate that we have judges who appreciate and are able to uphold the American ideal of freedom.

Yet the federal courts, like all government institutions, are only as good as the men and women who comprise them. As a result, judicial selection represents a major challenge both to a President's political skills and to his statesmanship. Consequently, deciding how to handle judicial selections will be among the most lasting decisions of the new Administration. From the start, the President must be clear in his own mind about the role judicial appointments play in advancing his policy goals, with a due regard both for the politics of the moment and for the long-term national interest.

President Bush continued with President Reagan's use of litmus tests to appoint conservatives to the bench; by contrast, Presidents Kennedy and Johnson undermined their own policies by appointing anticivil rights nominees to the bench in the South. The next Administration should strike a balance between these two poles.

Specifically:

• The Administration must develop appropriate, specific criteria for choosing judicial nominees that emphasize qualifications as much as judi-

---

Mark Gitenstein, former Chief Counsel of the Senate Judiciary Committee, is a Partner at Mayer, Brown & Platt in Washington, D.C. Ron Klain, formerly Chief Counsel of the Judiciary Committee, was the Washington Issues Director for the Clinton-Gore campaign. He also served as a member of the President's Commission on the Appointments Process.

cial philosophy; the President must establish a clear-cut chain of responsibility, including broad-based consultations, for recommending potential nominees.

• The Administration must make greater diversity (more women and minorities) a priority in selecting nominees for the federal bench.

• The President should seek the Senate's advice (not only its consent) with respect to filling vacancies on the U.S. Supreme Court; if he does not, the Senate should be particularly vigilant in exercising its constitutional powers.

The Reagan/Bush Record

NEW JUDGES WILL JOIN A FEDERAL judiciary that has been radically transformed over the past twelve years since the Reagan and Bush administrations have made no secret of their agenda with respect to the courts: They have been openly engaged in a deliberate effort to stack the courts with conservatives who share the Reagan/Bush agenda, especially their social agenda. They have been equally candid about their intention to "lock in" their policy goals with their judicial nominations. Former attorney general Edwin Meese stated frankly that the Reagan administration aimed to "institutionalize the Reagan revolution so it can't be set aside no matter what happens in future presidential elections."

Over the past four years, President Bush has continued this same policy by deferring on matters of judicial selection to the far-right faction within his party. Reagan and Bush nominees now hold six of the nine seats on the U.S. Supreme Court; 105 of the 179 positions on the U.S. courts of appeals; and 374 of the 649 federal district court judgeships.

The impact has been evident. As recently as 1986, the U.S. Supreme Court invalidated most state restrictions on a woman's right to choose whether to have an abortion. Yet in 1992 the Court came one vote away from eliminating all constitutional protections of that right.

The Court's retreat on choice is by no means the only example of how our civil liberties have been devastated by the Reagan and Bush justices. The Rehnquist Court has issued rulings that have gutted the meaning of critical civil rights laws; ended strong protection for religious practices from governmental intrusion; shifted the balance in the courtroom to favor the state over the accused; and compromised historic freedoms from police searches and seizures.

Nor have the changes affected by the Reagan and Bush programs for judicial selection been seen at the Supreme Court alone. In district and appellate courts all across the country, civil rights plaintiffs are finding their cases harder to make; environmental groups are having more trouble challenging problematic governmental regulations; and criminal defendants are seeing their claims of errors in trial and sentencing largely ignored—even in capital cases.

Depending on which course it chooses, the next Administration will use its power of judicial selection to make this troubling trend an irreversible reality—or it will use its power to undertake the first steps in restoring our federal courts to their rightful role as the critical guarantors of our personal freedoms in a nation whose very purpose and meaning rest on those protections.

Ideology and Judicial Selection

SOME CRITERIA FOR A PRESIDENT TO APPLY in selecting judicial nominees are widely agreed on: The first trait to seek in any judge is open-mindedness and a willingness to review each case on its own merits, with due regard for precedent and without an ideological fixation about the result. Perhaps the next most important trait is the capacity for detachment. Without it, a judge's other qualities are meaningless, as Judge Learned Hand said: "[A judge] must approach his problems with as little preconception of what should be the outcome as it is given to men to have; in short, the prime condition of his success will be his capacity for detachment."

The forty-second President should also take into account other important criteria: intellectual capacity, competence, and temperament; good moral character; freedom from conflicts of interest; and acknowledged and proven integrity.

These criteria of personal and intellectual integrity are widely accepted; they are the cornerstones of merit selection. Nominees who lack them will clearly be rejected, and a President who takes them lightly will find failure in this area, and deservedly so.

More controversial, however, is the question of ideology in judicial selection. And here the U.S. Supreme Court and the lower federal courts should be considered separately.

THE LOWER FEDERAL COURTS
The selection of judicial nominees for these courts should neither overemphasize nor ignore the philosophies of the candidates for the bench. Judicial philosophy should matter less for these courts, because the judges on them are sworn to apply the law as discerned by the U.S. Supreme Court,

and not act in a manner contrary to that Court's precedents. Having said that, though, the role of ideology in judicial selection for these courts cannot be overlooked altogether.

The Reagan/Bush litmus-test approach, with its narrow emphasis on nominees with an ultraconservative perspective on legal and social policy, threatens to interrupt the philosophical evolution of American jurisprudence and therefore to deprive our courts of the confidence of the American people, on which they ultimately depend. The next President should not nominate men or women proposed solely on the basis of judicial philosophy, without regard to their excellence, for to do otherwise undermines his own credibility as well as his ultimate ability to pursue his own policy goals.

But while the President should put less emphasis on ideology in filling the lower federal courts than has the past three administrations, at the same time he must also pay attention to the philosophical balance of the courts in selecting nominees. In this regard, he should act with a view to redressing the imbalance that has arisen in the courts over the past decade. The future of our liberties and of our Constitution depends on it.

Hopefully, the next Administration will focus more on getting the best-qualified men and women for the lower courts—people with diverse experience in the legal profession, sound judgment, and a dedication to the law and the Constitution—above all else.

THE U.S. SUPREME COURT

The question of ideology and the High Court is more complex. Some presidents have made Supreme Court nominations without regard to ideology, preferring to choose candidates on the basis of "excellence" alone. Others have selected justices for crassly political reasons; this approach has produced some of our greatest justices—Hugo Black, Earl Warren, and William Brennan come to mind—but also, some of our worst.

Throughout history, many presidents have placed a high value on ideology and have tried to use their nomination power to reshape the Supreme Court in an effort to further their legal and political agendas. When the Senate shares a similar view for the country, these campaigns have often been successful, and justifiably so: The strong Federalist Court of the early republic, which laid the legal groundwork for our emergence as one nation, is a premier example; the same is true of the New Deal Court of the 1930s, which authorized the sweeping social legislation that provided the framework for the modern regulatory state.

Presidents Reagan and Bush have attempted the same sort of implementation of their social policies through the Supreme Court, but have pushed this agenda even though most Americans reject their vision—a rejection embodied in the Democratic majority found in the Senate since 1987. This conflict was the background for the epic struggle over the Bork nomination that year.

Even after the Bork defeat, the Reagan and Bush administrations continued to select conservatives for the Court: Anthony Kennedy, David Souter, and Clarence Thomas. Taken with Justices O'Connor, Rehnquist, and Scalia, these six nominees are among the most ideological choices for the Court in history. Even if the 1991 Court term suggests the emergence of a new center on the Court—composed of Justices O'Connor, Kennedy, and Souter—it is a conservative center, and the result of these choices has been a dramatic shift in the Court's jurisprudence.

The next Administration faces a difficult challenge: Ideally, it should temper the role that ideology plays in the selection of Supreme Court justices, but at the same time it cannot be oblivious to the need to balance the Court after a long series of conservative nominees. The most important long-run goal is to place men and women of excellence and distinction on the Court, to restore its prestige and its historical role. But in so doing, the new President cannot ignore the equally paramount need to replace the lost voices of a William Brennan, a Thurgood Marshall, or a Lewis Powell on the Court.

The two goals—the ideal of deemphasizing ideology in judicial selection while also consciously working to counter the consequences of the Reagan/ Bush ideological packing of the Court—may be less at odds than they first appear to be. Though four justices have been replaced in the past six years, four *more* of the remaining members of the Court are over sixty-five and may well retire within the next President's term. Thus, Bush's successor will probably have an opportunity to select several men and women to serve on the Court—and in so doing, leave his most lasting legacy on our government and our law.

Who Staffs the Selection Process?

WHO IN THE NEXT GOVERNMENT will have the authority to propose and review candidates for the bench? Any model is a truly personal decision of the President and depends in large part on how the President staffs his Administration.

Under Presidents Reagan and Bush, the locus of the selection process has appeared to be ideologically driven—shifting back and forth between the White House and the Justice Department, depending on where the clique of legal conservatives are more powerful. Thus, in the first seven years of the Reagan presidency, the center of judicial selection was wherever Ed Meese was serving: When Meese was at the White House, the decisions were made there; when he became attorney general, the Justice Department assumed the dominant role.

When President Bush came to office, the White House counsel, C. Boyden Gray, and his conservative assistant, Lee Lieberman, appeared to play the dominant role in judicial selection, particularly when Richard Thornburgh was attorney general. More recently, with a return of conservatives to power in the Justice Department under William Barr, authority in judicial selection appears to be moving back to that agency.

This ideologically driven staffing of the selection process—particularly for the lower federal courts—is unhealthy and unwise. While it is obvious that the next President and his immediate advisers will be personally involved in the Supreme Court selection process, the selection process for the district courts and the courts of appeals is better located in the Justice Department, for two reasons.

First, as a general rule, the more the judicial selection process resides in the White House, and especially in the hands of White House staff, the more political it becomes—and the less that factors like distinction and excellence play a role. Second, the very limited staff of the White House counsel's office means that a decision to center the selection process there will inevitably lead to undue delays in that process. Thus, under President Bush, it has taken an average of almost fourteen months to name nominees for the lower federal courts—an absurd stretch, given that many vacancies can be anticipated months in advance due to retirements and early notification of resignations.

The selection process is, of course, "staffed" by officials outside the Executive Branch: By tradition, nominees for the district courts are selected by senators of the President's party from that state. While the efforts of the Carter, Reagan, and Bush administrations to assume more control over courts of appeals selections have been successful, efforts to do the same for the district courts have been largely fruitless. Whatever the merits or drawbacks of this system, it is very unlikely that the next President will be able to change it.

Thus, with respect to the district courts, the role of the Administration in judicial selection is something more of a veto power. Even accepting this limitation on the role, the next Administration can do a better job than this one in exercising it. First, the Bush administration has been almost exclusively ideologically driven in exercising its veto over senatorial candidates, rejecting potential nominees for failing a narrow, conservative litmus test. While ideology will and should play some role in the screening process, it should not predominate. Second, judicial selection should not be used as a bargaining chit with senators on other matters. Given the importance of these life tenure posts, such horse-trading is singularly inappropriate.

Finally, the Bush administration has done too little to use its power to push senators toward more merit-based means of selection—such as judicial nominating panels, or other screening devices aimed at excellence in trial court judges—or toward picking candidates who will provide diversity on the federal bench, which we discuss below.

Diversity Among Judicial Nominees

JUDGES ARE SUPPOSED TO TREAT ALL litigants equally, without respect to gender, race, or other factors. But when significant federal courts are all-male, or all-white, many Americans lose confidence that they are receiving "equal justice under law."

Of course, we do not believe that the next President should apply a "quota" system in selecting judicial nominees. But given the abysmal track record of the past twelve years, the new Executive Branch should launch a variety of affirmative measures to make sure that the federal bench looks more like America.

Stop and consider the statistics for a moment. Under Presidents Reagan and Bush, the percentage of African-American federal judicial nominees fell to 3 percent; the overall nonwhite percentage was just 7 percent. Several courts of appeals—including that for the Third Circuit, which is the home of one in ten blacks in this country—have become all-white benches. Hispanics and Asian Americans are similarly underrepresented in the federal courts. Thus the perception of equal justice is evaporating.

Under President Reagan, the percentage of women nominees dipped to 11 percent; while President Bush has gotten the percentage up to 16 percent (almost identical to President Carter's ratio), women now compose a much higher percentage of the experienced lawyers in this country. What was adequate fifteen years ago—if it was adequate fifteen years ago—can no longer suffice today.

To obtain more diversity, the next Administration should, first, engage in a broad "talent search" to identify qualified women and minorities to serve on the federal bench. Consultations with minority bar associations, associations of women lawyers, and civil rights groups would be a start. One or more officials in the Justice Department should be assigned to this task on a full-time basis.

Second, it should instruct senators that a significant percentage of their choices for the district courts should be women and minority candidates. The Administration should refuse to defer to senatorial nominations when senators fail to pursue the goal of increased diversity on the bench as vigorously as it does.

Third, it should seek more of its nominees from nontraditional types of lawyering—that is, from places other than private law firms. For example, recent studies have shown that among the partners at America's 250 largest law firms, only about 1 percent are black. If such law firm partners are the principal talent base from which nominees are drawn, then the current lack of diversity in the courts will never be corrected. Only by searching in a broader pool—among government lawyers and public interest lawyers, for example—will a sufficiently diverse number of candidates be found.

Consultation with Outside Groups

NO MATTER WHO IDENTIFIES and selects judicial nominations within the Administration, there will be and should be consultation with outside organizations on these choices. Such consultations make political sense, if for no other reason than to find out how a particular nominee is likely to fare with certain influential groups.

Yet this practical concern is by no means the only reason for such consultations. Local chapters of civil rights organizations, for example, may know whether a particular lawyer has some appreciation of civil rights issues. Or for specialized courts, like the federal circuit, specialized bars can advise the President whether a potential nominee has the requisite expertise.

Over the past forty years, the American Bar Association has played a predominant outside consultative role. Early in this period, this special role was attacked by liberals, who thought the ABA unduly conservative; of late, it is conservatives who have challenged the ABA's legitimacy, fearing its excessive liberalism. But through it all, the ABA's special role has continued, as it should.

Indeed, the ABA should be involved early in the process. The value of its assessment is, in the first place, that the ABA is the organization most likely to render a disinterested and nonpartisan *professional* judgment about a nominee. Moreover, the ABA procedure for evaluation avoids stalemate by not insisting on unanimity, and its rating system—ranging from "Exceptionally Well Qualified" through "Well Qualified" to "Not Qualified"—is helpful to evaluators at both ends of Pennsylvania Avenue. Finally, by working behind closed doors, the ABA evaluation system offers a chance for the

President to be warned of bad candidates who have slipped through his selection process—before the President becomes visibly, and publicly, committed to the nominee.

The Bush administration has attempted to make the ABA's role in judicial selection an exclusionary one. It has forbidden nominees from meeting with local bar associations, many of which traditionally evaluated such candidates for fitness. And it has attempted to cut out, altogether, the many women's groups, civil rights groups, and other public interest organizations who played an advisory role under President Carter.

The hypocrisy of this position was made plain during the Clarence Thomas nomination, when the same administration that forbade its *lower court* nominees from meeting with bipartisan local bar associations permitted its *Supreme Court* nominee to meet with a variety of civil rights groups, in an effort to garner their support.

The next Administration should, at the least, unequivocally remove the "gag" from nominees: Those who are willing to meet with local bar leaders, outside organizations, and concerned citizens should be permitted to do so. All such meetings should be disclosed to the Senate and the public.

Moreover, as a general proposition, all of these groups—the ABA, the National Bar Association and outside groups on both the left and right— ought to have a channel into the selection process, as a matter of common courtesy and common sense. Of course, none of these groups, including the ABA, should hold a veto over nominees. But the future Administrations would do better to run a more open selection process, and a more inclusive evaluation process as well.

Background Investigations of Nominees

THE TIME TO FIND OUT THAT a judicial nominee is ill suited for the bench due to his or her background is *before* that person is nominated, not after. Thus a practical warning for the next Administration is implicit in the demanding criteria judicial nominees must meet: By the time a judicial nomination is sent to the Senate, there should be no surprises lurking ahead for the President.

Once a nomination is made, the discovery of disqualifying information about a nominee—information that would have convinced the President not to nominate that candidate in the first place—is inevitably the subject of political wrangling. The President is embarrassed, the nominee is embarrassed, his or her supporters are embarrassed. A search for the truth about such charges is replaced by partisan posturing over them. Of course, the tragic story of Anita Hill's charges against Clarence Thomas are the most infamous example of this phenomenon—but by no means the only one.

As the Thomas nomination showed, whatever short-term victories the President can achieve by continuing to press a public fight for confirmation notwithstanding character problems, in the long run, the ultimate losers of such highly public fights are the President's prestige and public respect for our courts. Put another way, no matter which side wins a confirmation fight like the Thomas battle, in the end there are no real winners.

Prevention is the only cure for such conflagrations. The fullest possible inquiries should be made by the Justice Department and the FBI before a nomination is made. These investigations should not be undertaken as superficial efforts to produce clean bills of health for nominees but rather as a vital prophylactic to prevent the President from making a disastrous mistake; after all, at issue are lifetime appointments. The Justice Department does the President no favor when it tells him what he wants to hear about a nominee, instead of what he should—and must—know about that person before staking his reputation on the candidate's character.

In turn, the findings of these Justice Department investigations—as well as the recommendations of competent outside groups, such as the ABA—should be carefully reviewed before any nomination is made. The President's watchwords in considering these reports must be: When in doubt, don't.

Since the late 1970s, the White House has shared this background information with the Senate Judiciary Committee, and should continue to do so. The committee has a superb track record with respect to confidentiality, and the sharing of this information prevents needless duplication and tiresome delays in the confirmation process.

The Role of the Senate

WHAT ROLE SHOULD THE SENATE PLAY in the selection of or consultations about the nomination of federal judges and justices?

When the next President takes his oath of office, he will face a Senate that increasingly has taken its "advice and consent" function *very* seriously. With respect to the Supreme Court nominations, the Senate not only intends to exercise its "consent" role aggressively, but several key senators—especially after the Bork and Thomas imbroglios—have also said they expect to be asked their "advice" about selections.

Such an "advice and consent" role is consistent with that contemplated by the framers of the Constitution. The repeated considerations of the Constitutional Convention concerning the judiciary make it clear that the delegates intended the Senate to play a broad role in the appointment of judges.

The delegates' first conclusion was to lodge exclusive control over the judicial selection process with Congress and to leave no role for the president at all. As the debates proceeded, the convention twice more rejected the idea of vesting the selection of judges in the president. Indeed, even the ultimately adopted "advice and consent" language was once rejected by the convention, in favor of Senate selection of judges.

All told, there were four different attempts to include the president in the selection process, and four times he was excluded. It was not until the final days of the convention that the Special Committee on Postponed Matters reported the "advice and consent" compromise, which it ultimately adopted. It is difficult to imagine that after four attempts to exclude the president from the selection process, the framers intended anything less than the broadest role for the Senate. In dividing responsibility for the appointment of judges, the framers intended to prevent the president from encroaching on the integrity and independence of the courts. That is why it remains the Senate's constitutional obligation today.

History, too, supports a role for the Senate in shaping the selection of nominees. Consultations between the White House and the Senate over candidates for Supreme Court vacancies were commonplace throughout the nineteenth century. In our own century, President Hoover's selection of Benjamin Cardozo and President Reagan's selection of Anthony Kennedy were both heavily influenced by advance consultations with Senate leaders. In other instances, even where such consultations were not conducted, the president picked candidates who strode the ideological gulf between themselves and the Senate.

The value of such consultations—if taken seriously, and then put to use—is obvious. When Justice Powell resigned in June 1987, the White House consulted with Judiciary Committee chairman Joe Biden and majority leader Robert Byrd about a successor. The two Senate leaders were shown a list with more than a dozen names on it, and asked for their views. Both responded that one man was sure to provoke a national conflagration; the others would yield more mixed responses. That one man identified as a certain problem was the one man the president ultimately chose: Robert H. Bork. The consultation on the Bork nomination failed to avert controversy, but only because the administration failed to take advantage of the opportunity to do so.

The Bush administration has spurned consultations with the Senate, and the result—the brutal, searing confirmation fight over the Clarence Thomas confirmation—is one that must not be repeated. In rejecting consultations, the president cites his "constitutional power" to select nominees of his choosing; but the Constitution's text speaks of the Senate's role in *advice* and consent. In rejecting consultations, President Bush cites history and tradition; but the long practice in our history is of holding such consultations, not spurning them. In rejecting consultations, he cites the need to assume responsibility for the performance of duties assigned to him; but the fact is that the president consults—even defers—to senators on selection of lower court nominees, whose authority derives from the same source, Article III of our Constitution, as does the Supreme Court's.

The next President should consult with the Senate, well in advance of any vacancy, about candidates for Supreme Court vacancies. The Administration should make available to the Senate leaders any data it has about the nominees so that the senators' responses are as well informed as possible. While it may seem counterintuitive, such full disclosure is, ultimately, in the President's best interest: If the President selects a candidate who is the product of this consultative process but about whom information has been withheld from the Senate, the response from Capitol Hill and the country will be all the more negative when this adverse information is discovered, as it inevitably will be.

Did President Reagan help himself by ignoring consultations and selecting Robert Bork? Did President Bush help himself by rejecting consultations and nominating Clarence Thomas? Or were both presidents done far more damage by pushing ahead rather than yielding to compromise?

Since these questions answer themselves, the forty-second President must recognize that the American people want a moderate, balanced federal judiciary, not one that is perceived as being conservative or liberal. An honest and effective consultation process between the Senate and the President is probably the easiest way to achieve that goal. The Founding Fathers would have expected no less.

Office of National Drug Control Policy

TOWARD A NEW NATIONAL DRUG STRATEGY

MATHEA FALCO

Summary

AMERICANS RANKED DRUG ABUSE well ahead of the federal deficit, the environment, and the economy as the most important challenge facing the country, according to a 1990 Gallup poll. Yet they are increasingly pessimistic about the effectiveness of government drug policy. Despite $76 billion in federal tax money spent to combat drugs since 1981, drug addiction and drug crime have increased. At the same time, occasional marijuana and cocaine use has declined among better-educated Americans.

Federal drug policy has concentrated heavily on enforcement intended to reduce the supply of drugs. But demand-reduction programs—prevention, education, and treatment—received only 20 percent of the anti-drug budget during the Reagan administration and less than 30 percent during the Bush administration. Massive expenditures to cut off supplies have not helped: Heroin and cocaine are far more available at cheaper prices today than they were ten years ago. In 1991, the Office of National Drug Control Policy (ONDCP) reported that there were 1.8 million cocaine addicts, triple the number of earlier estimates, and 700,000 heroin addicts.[1] Within the criminal justice system, where more than half of all offenders have serious drug problems, treatment is even more scarce, despite evidence that it can reduce recidivism by as much as half.

Mathea Falco, a lawyer, is Director of Health Policy, Department of Public Health, New York Hospital-Cornell Medical Center. From 1977 to 1981 she was Assistant Secretary of State for International Narcotics Matters under President Carter. She is the author of The Making of a Drug-Free America: Programs That Work *(New York: Random House, 1992).*

358

The next federal drug strategy should reflect the hard lessons of the past decade and concentrate more on reducing demand than supply. What is needed is not more money, but a strategy that builds on what we know about what works. The new Administration should redirect resources away from futile efforts to eradicate drugs in foreign countries and stop them on the high seas and instead make treatment readily available. Prevention programs that have demonstrated their effectiveness should be implemented in every school and community. Law enforcement will still have an important role, but one that emphasizes community policing designed to drive dealers out of neighborhoods. To implement the new strategy, the director of the ONDCP should be restored to cabinet rank and given real authority over the dozens of competing federal agencies involved in combating drugs.

Historical Background

AMERICA'S SKEWED APPROACH to the drug problem is not new. Since the adoption of the Harrison Narcotics Act in 1914, which outlawed heroin and cocaine, Americans have viewed drug abuse primarily as a challenge to law enforcement rather than as a health or social problem. In the early decades of this century, drug use was associated with certain immigrant groups and racial minorities who were seen as potentially violent and subversive. Opium was linked to Chinese workers; cocaine to blacks, particularly in the South; and marijuana to Mexicans in the Southwest. To counter this threat, the public assumed that law enforcement was the best strategy.[2]

In addition, heroin, cocaine, and marijuana—the major targets of America's drug war—have traditionally been produced abroad. Americans have tended to blame other countries for being the source of our drug epidemics. As a result, efforts to cut off the supply of drugs have dominated U.S. drug policy. The operative assumption has been that stopping the flow of drugs as close to the source as possible will drive up prices, forcing American users to stop or seek treatment. In this view, increased prices also deter new users from trying drugs. Law enforcement, interdiction, and international initiatives play a key role in this supply-side strategy.

For much of this century, illegal drug use was not widespread, and the prohibitionist approach was generally accepted. However, in the late 1960s, drug abuse became a major national concern as marijuana gained popularity, particularly among young people. At the same time, large numbers of American military personnel stationed in Southeast Asia during the Vietnam War tried heroin, and many became addicted.

Although relying on tough "drug war" rhetoric to fight this epidemic, President Nixon changed the earlier policy emphasis on law enforcement to make demand reduction his primary focus. In 1971 he created a single, high-level agency, the Special Action Office of Drug Abuse Prevention (SAODAP), to supervise all federal prevention, treatment, and research programs. SAO-DAP was housed in its own building across the street from the White House, and the president often participated in meetings of the Strategy Council on Drug Abuse. From 1970 to 1975, prevention, education, and treatment programs received almost *two thirds* of the total drug budget ($1.92 billion out of $3 billion).

Under Presidents Ford and Carter, federal policy moved back toward enforcement, which received slightly more than half of total antidrug funding from 1976 to 1981. International efforts to reduce the supply of drugs were important, but not as central as they would become in the 1980s. Cooperative programs with Turkey and Mexico during the 1970s—which cost the United States about $150 million—succeeded in reducing the flow of heroin into the country for brief periods.

Drug policy during the 1970s was marked by considerable continuity in both Republican and Democratic administrations. All gave priority to reducing heroin addiction, targeting traffickers rather than users, and providing treatment on demand. By 1980, the heroin epidemic had been contained, with the numbers of addicts stabilized at an estimated five hundred thousand, down from about seven hundred thousand eight years earlier.

Recent Legacy

THEN CAME THE MOST RECENT "WAR ON DRUGS." In 1981, President Reagan radically changed the focus of drug policy, concentrating almost exclusively on law enforcement and interdiction. From 1981 through 1986, funding for drug enforcement more than doubled —from $800 million to $1.9 billion. During the same period, federal support for prevention, education, and treatment declined from $404 million to $338 million, while drug prevention programs received an average of $23 million a year.[3] The Reagan approach no longer linked supply reduction directly to demand reduction. Because of the drastic budget cuts, treatment was not available for many addicts, and prevention programs were nonexistent in most schools and communities. Drug enforcement became an end in itself.

The Reagan administration also gave new importance to border interdiction, especially at key entry points. Vice President George Bush chaired the South Florida Task Force of the National Narcotics Border Interdiction System, which included hundreds of officials detailed from the U.S. Customs Service, the Coast Guard, the Drug Enforcement Administration (DEA), and the Justice and Treasury departments. But the widely publicized interdiction campaign did not succeed. In 1983, the General Accounting Office (GAO) found that more drugs were entering the country than five years earlier; in 1985, another GAO study reported similarly discouraging results. Nonetheless, interdiction programs continued to expand, accounting for almost a third of the entire federal drug budget by 1988.

President George Bush has followed the policies of his predecessor. Supply reduction initiatives receive more than 70 percent of federal antidrug funding, which has doubled since 1988. With the collapse of the Soviet Union, the U.S. military has played an increasingly important role in interdiction. Funding for military antidrug programs jumped from $5 million in 1982 to $1.27 billion in 1992.

Bureaucratic Disarray

THE FAILURE OF A FEDERAL POLICY has been compounded by fierce competition among the dozens of federal agencies involved in combating drug abuse. The rapid expansion of law enforcement funding in the early 1980s worsened earlier problems of coordination. The press frequently reported on these struggles, particularly when the Coast Guard, the Customs Service, and the DEA all took credit for the same drug seizure.

At the same time, the Reagan administration weakened federal leadership in prevention and treatment programs both by cutting funding for them and by giving states wide discretion in how to spend these funds. Since 1973, the National Institute of Drug Abuse (NIDA) had set the direction of demand-reduction efforts nationwide; however, when the new block grant system was established, NIDA became essentially a research agency without operating responsibility or a significant voice in policy direction.

In response to mounting bureaucratic chaos, Congress in 1983 adopted legislation to concentrate responsibility for all federal antidrug efforts in one cabinet-level office. President Reagan vetoed the bill, despite its strong bipartisan support, in large part because Attorney General Edwin Meese did not want to cede the Justice Department's leadership role in drug policy. In 1988, despite continuing opposition from the administration, Congress created the ONDCP as part of the Antidrug Abuse Act of 1988.

President Bush appointed William Bennett as the nation's first "drug czar" (director of ONDCP) and accorded him cabinet rank. Bennett used the position as a highly visible platform to articulate the administration's goals as well as his personal views—declaring on network television, for example, that people who sell drugs should have their heads cut off. Despite

Bennett's pronouncements, the bureaucratic situation remained largely unchanged. In 1991, Bennett resigned, and Bush eliminated the cabinet rank for his successor, Robert Martinez, who had been defeated in his bid for reelection as governor of Florida in 1990.

Although ONDCP exercises a formal coordinating role and prepares a congressionally mandated annual strategy, the office has no authority to enforce policy direction. More important, it has little influence within the Administration in making strategic funding decisions. As a result, bureaucratic competition flourishes unchecked, with each agency fighting for its own resources both within the administration and on Capitol Hill.

The Failure of the Supply Side Strategy

THE CRITICAL FAILURE IS NOT simply a failure of bureaucratic organization but a failure of strategy as well. Our recent history has shown that supply-control efforts do not increase drug prices or reduce drug availability, the measures by which drug enforcement has traditionally been judged. Despite an estimated $15 billion in expenditures for interdiction, crop eradication, and international control programs from 1981 to 1992, illegal coca production in Peru and Bolivia more than tripled, while cocaine prices within the United States fell from $60,000 to $15,000 a kilo. At the same time, worldwide opium production has also tripled, and heroin prices are at historic lows. A series of GAO reports in 1991 concluded that the U.S. supply-side strategy has failed to reduce the flow of drugs into the country.

The largest profits from the drug traffic are made at the street level, not in foreign poppy or coca fields, or on the high seas. Even if the United States were able to seize half the cocaine coming from South America—an unrealistically optimistic prospect—cocaine prices in American cities would increase by less than 5 percent. Today, a vial of crack cocaine sells for $5, less than the cost of a single admission to the movies and well within the reach of every teenager. Even doubling the price would not substantially reduce consumption.

Moreover, a relatively small volume of drugs can supply our entire drug market. A twenty-square-mile field of opium poppies produces enough heroin to meet annual American demand. Four Boeing 747 cargo planes or thirteen trailer trucks can supply American cocaine consumption for a year. Even if the governments of Peru and Bolivia were able to curtail cocaine production—which is highly unlikely, given current economic and political conditions—neighboring Andean countries could rapidly replace these sources. Indeed, coca cultivation has already spread to Colombia, Ecuador, and Brazil.

The dominant political response to the failure of supply control initiatives is to call for even *more* resources and greater efforts to cut off the flow of drugs. Yet what is needed is not more money but an entirely different approach. Drug abuse is driven by demand, not supply, and we now know how to reduce the demand for drugs. The most promising approaches borrow heavily from our experience with alcohol and tobacco, and give prevention and treatment high priority. Law enforcement plays an important role in helping communities reclaim their streets, but as most police officers readily admit, it does not work as the primary means of defense.

The most promising strategies are coming not from Washington and state capitals but from communities working to find new solutions to their drug problems. They are moved by the simple but critically important discovery that the answers to America's drug problems lie here at home, not in foreign countries. They recognize, too, that no one can escape the myriad effects of drug abuse and that they must therefore "take ownership" of this problem.

Short-Term Priorities: The First Hundred Days

• *Adopt a new national drug strategy that concentrates on prevention, education, treatment, and community law enforcement.* The new strategy should reallocate resources from supply control, which now consumes roughly 70 percent of the federal drug budget, to demand reduction. As an initial step, resource allocation should be 50–50, which would mean shifting $2.5 billion from enforcement into prevention and treatment. (As suggested in the next recommendation, $1.5 billion of this could come immediately from interdiction and international programs. The remaining $1 billion would come from other supply-control programs.) Such a shift might well find support in Congress, which in the past has expressed frustration (intermittently) with the dominance of enforcement. In 1988, the Senate mandated that 55 percent of the federal drug funds appropriated under the Antidrug Abuse Act be allocated to demand reduction, but specific percentage allocations were dropped in the House-Senate conference. None has been proposed since then.

OMB currently estimates that drug abuse costs our country $300 billion a year, including government antidrug programs as well as the costs of crime, health care, accidents, and lost productivity. For example, the cost of keeping some one million Americans behind bars—more that half of whom are there for drug-related reasons—exceeds $20 billion a year.

What progress has been made against marijuana and cocaine use among better-educated Americans reflects increased health concerns and increasingly negative social attitudes about drugs. Extending these gains throughout society will require an intensive campaign to put into practice what we have learned about reducing demand.

Many of the most effective programs are not expensive compared to the costs of prison construction, high-tech interdiction equipment, and law enforcement hardware. For example, two of the most promising school prevention programs, Life Skills Training (LST) and Students Taught Awareness and Resistance (STAR), cost about $15 to $25 per pupil, including classroom materials and teacher training. They reduce new smoking and marijuana use by half and drinking by one third, and these results have been sustained for at least three years. Yet these programs have not been replicated nationwide, and many school districts continue to pour federal dollars into curricula that have failed to produce proven results.

As former commissioner Lee Brown argues in his chapter on crime, we have learned that community-based law enforcement that engages neighborhood residents can make a lasting difference. Breaking up street drug markets is more effective—and less costly—than massive interdiction efforts in making drugs expensive and difficult to find. The active presence of police officers in drug-infested neighborhoods increases the "hassle" factor that drug dealers and buyers face. Even if drug prices remain unchanged, increasing search time to make a deal can discourage drug use and drive dealers away. Citizen patrols reinforce police efforts, particularly when they are part of larger communitywide initiatives to organize residents and resources against drug abuse and dealing.

In cities across the country, new coalitions are encouraging citizen participation in the fight against drugs. For example, the Miami Coalition for a Drug-Free Community, which has a small professional staff and relies largely on volunteers, has an annual budget of $200,000. Yet it has leveraged over $6 million in contributed resources to launch a major antidrug media campaign, a special drug court and an intensive-treatment program for drug offenders, and other initiatives.

• *Bring the drug war home.* In 1992, the United States spent $3 billion on interdiction and international control programs, and plans to spend another $3 billion in 1993. These programs have not only failed to curtail the availability of drugs in this country, they have also contributed to political instability in countries where fragile governments are threatened by powerful drug interests, most recently Peru. By supporting police and military antidrug operations, U.S. programs often exacerbate human rights abuses and corruption among government officials.

As a first step, the new Administration should reprogram half the funds currently directed toward interdiction and international eradication programs to reducing domestic demand for drugs. (At current levels, interdiction receives about $2.4 billion and international eradication programs about $0.6 billion.) This would mean an additional $1.5 billion in 1993; this money could be spent to expand treatment, prevention, and community law enforcement. Within the first six months of the next Administration, ONDCP should commission studies from Rand and other independent groups to determine what proportion of the remaining $1.5 billion can usefully be spent abroad. Interdiction may still have a useful role, although at substantially reduced levels.

The United States will continue to play an important role internationally. However, rather than making bilateral narcotics control programs the centerpiece of policy, as has been the case, the United States should support multilateral cooperation through the United Nations and regional groups such as the Association of Southeast Asian Nations (ASEAN) and the Organization of American States (OAS). These organizations currently operate very limited programs to reduce illicit drug production, trafficking, and drug abuse. U.S. support for multilateral cooperation has been minimal: The U.S. contribution to the U.N. drug agencies has remained under $5 million a year on average since 1977.

Instead of making foreign drug production the major target of U.S. international programs, which is now the case, a more effective approach would be to attack the multinational financial organizations that support the traffic. This should be a top priority for U.S. drug enforcement efforts. The 1988 Convention Against Illicit Traffic established a framework for attacking money laundering and bank secrecy worldwide. It provides for seizure of assets, extradition of traffickers, and transfer of criminal proceedings. For the first time, the international community has agreed to work together to undermine the traffic profit structure, even though such efforts might expose corruption in major institutions. The United States should take a leadership role in going after drug kingpins and their bankers.

As part of its larger foreign policy concerns, the United States should consider whether assistance to drug-producing countries would strengthen democratic governments and advance American economic interests. Drug traffickers are often more powerful and better armed than the governments in a number of countries, such as Colombia, where drug lord Pablo Escobar

escaped from a Medellín jail in August 1992 despite the presence of an
Army brigade. But Americans should not delude themselves that our efforts
to help other governments will significantly reduce domestic drug addiction
and crime. Although President Bush described the 1989 seizure of General
Noriega as an important victory in America's drug war, cocaine traffic from
Panama has almost doubled since then. In the war against drugs—like so
much else on the nation's agenda—it is time to wage the battle at home.

• *Give the director of ONDCP (the "drug czar") cabinet rank and presidential support in setting drug policy.* To overcome the bureaucratic confusion and competition that now characterize the federal antidrug effort, the
ONDCP director should have cabinet rank and full authority to develop and
implement policy. The President should visibly support the Director, particularly in interagency arguments over funding, so that a new national drug
policy can be effectively implemented. And to enable ONDCP to implement
a new strategy, its budget, which currently is declining from $127 million
in 1992 to $79 million in 1993, needs to be restored to support innovative
research and demonstration projects as well as to strengthen its oversight
functions.

The potential powers of the drug czar and ONDCP are great, but as
yet unrealized. Every cabinet department has a substantial antidrug program,
ranging from a total of $4.3 billion in the Justice Department and $1.1 billion
in the Treasury Department to $45 million in the Department of the Interior
and $16 million in the Department of Agriculture. Within each department,
drug functions are fragmented among many agencies, such as in the Justice
Department, where thirteen agencies are involved. Since a new drug strategy
that concentrates on demand reduction will encounter massive bureaucratic
resistance from the enforcement agencies, presidential commitment and a
strong ONDCP will be critically important in implementing a major change
in policy.

Longer-Term Initiatives

• *Make treatment readily available.* Pessimism about society's ability to
deal with drugs is deepest when it comes to treatment. Most Americans
don't realize that treatment works—not always, and often not the first time,
but many people eventually overcome addiction. Success rates are higher
for people with stable families, employment, and outside interests, and lower
for those who suffer from serious depression and anxiety. National studies
that have followed tens of thousands of addicts through different kinds of
programs report that the single most important factor is length of time in

treatment. One third of those who stay in treatment longer than three months are still off drugs a year later. The success rate jumps to two thirds when treatment lasts a year or longer. And some programs that provide intensive, highly structured therapy report even better results.

Yet, treatment has been a low priority nationwide since the early 1980s, as drug enforcement dominated state and federal spending. In 1991, treatment received 14 percent of the $10.5 billion federal drug budget compared to 25 percent ten years earlier, well before the cocaine epidemic created millions of new addicts. The impact of this shift is painfully obvious in most cities, where addicts often face waits of six months before they can get help.

In an extensive review of treatment in 1990, the National Academy of Science's Institute of Medicine (IOM) reported that private programs receive 40 percent of all treatment spending but provide only one quarter of the nation's treatment capacity. Of the 5.5 million American drug abusers who require treatment, as many as 4.2 million must rely on public programs. Yet only 600,000 publicly funded treatment "slots" are currently available— which means that fewer than 15 percent of those who need treatment are able to get it at any one time.

The Institute of Medicine notes the importance of expanding treatment without sacrificing quality, which means providing intensive, structured, comprehensive programs. The Federal Government currently provides about half the support for all public treatment in this country. In 1993, the present Administration plans to spend $2.3 billion on treatment. As a first step in expanding capacity, $1.5 billion could be reallocated from supply control (equal to the amount proposed to be cut in the first year from interdiction and international eradication programs). Careful cost analysis should be done for subsequent budget years, including an assessment of how to convert private treatment capacity (which is often underutilized) to public use.

The AIDS epidemic in the United States is currently being spread most rapidly by intravenous drug users. In 1990, a report by the Office of Technology Assessment concluded that expanded treatment was essential "to break the chain of HIV transmission and stem this lethal infection from spreading further."[4]

As President Nixon discovered twenty years ago, providing adequate treatment is at the heart of an effective drug strategy. Making treatment a top priority will also require a firm commitment to encourage top professionals to work in the drug field. Erratic, diminishing funding over the past decade has severely eroded the ranks of treatment researchers, therapists, and clinicians. Sustained support will be required to ensure that qualified professionals are—and stay—engaged in treatment.

• *Concentrate treatment resources in the criminal justice system.* Criminal offenders are more deeply involved in drug abuse than any other group in the nation. Without treatment, nine out of ten return to crime and drugs after prison, and the majority will be rearrested within three years. Extensive studies have shown that treatment of drug offenders does work. Therapeutic communities inside prisons reduce recidivism by a third to a half after inmates return to society. The most effective programs are extremely rigorous, demanding far more from offenders than passive incarceration, and cost only $5,000 to $8,000 a year for each inmate.

Yet, treatment is still very scarce. The GAO reported in 1991 that only 364 of the 41,000 federal prisoners who have drug abuse problems are participating in intensive treatment programs. More than three quarters of all state prison inmates are drug abusers—at least 500,000 offenders—but only 10 percent receive any help. The GAO concluded that even these numbers are inflated, since most treatment, which consists of drug education and occasional counseling, is ineffective.

Within prisons, priority should be given to treating offenders with serious heroin and cocaine problems, since they are responsible for the largest proportion of predatory crimes. Intensive, residential drug treatment, which has proved effective in reducing recidivism among this group, is the most cost-effective approach according to the IOM, which estimates that there are at least 350,000 prison inmates and 750,000 offenders on probation and parole who need this kind of intensive treatment.

The Federal Government provides the bulk of funding for state prison treatment programs, both through small discretionary grants administered by the Departments of Justice and Health and Human Services and through block grants to state agencies. However, states must decide how to allocate these grant funds among a number of competing law-enforcement purposes, and treatment often loses out. A new federal strategy could make additional funds available to the states specifically for prison treatment programs.

A recent Rand Corporation study found that community supervision programs for offenders on parole or probation—regardless of their offense—will fail unless drug treatment is provided. The more intensive and structured the treatment, the more likely it is to be effective. But because treatment of any sort is woefully inadequate, offenders must compete with noncriminal addicts for limited treatment space. Some cities, such as Miami, have created special programs to provide immediate treatment for drug offenders; these programs have shown good results. The treatment cost per offender is less than $1,000. But in most cities, drug offenders do not get treatment, although most would participate if treatment were available.

In short, drug treatment remains our best hope for breaking the costly cycle of crime and addiction.

• *Support a massive media campaign to change attitudes about illegal drug use and underage smoking and drinking.* Advertising is a powerful force in shaping American attitudes about desirable behavior. The antismoking ads required by the Federal Communications Commission to counter cigarette advertising from 1967 through 1970 resulted in a decline in cigarette consumption of 10 percent, the first time in this century that smoking declined for more than two consecutive years. When cigarette and antismoking ads were removed from the airwaves in 1971, cigarette consumption resumed its upward trend.

The national advertising campaign launched by the Partnership for a Drug-Free America in 1987 has shown positive results in changing attitudes about marijuana and cocaine, particularly in locations where the ads are frequently seen. The campaign relies heavily on donated creative talent, print space, and airtime. Donations to date have exceeded $1 billion. However, in some areas, donated time has been limited and the ads have not achieved widespread coverage. In addition, the Partnership does not target alcohol and tobacco, largely because it depends for support from advertisers who benefit from the $5 billion those industries spend annually on promotion.

A national prevention strategy should build on the Partnership's efforts by providing incentives to attract additional contributions, particularly for prime-time advertising in all major media markets. Public-service announcements have generally failed to make an impact, often because networks donate less desirable time slots, and they are not frequently aired. Mechanisms should be explored to improve incentives for contributing as well as mandating a certain amount of prime-time antidrug advertising. Since youthful drinking and smoking are closely linked to drug abuse, antitobacco and antialcohol ads should be an integral part of the federal prevention campaign. As the antismoking ads in the 1970s demonstrated, a long-term commitment to advertising is required to maintain positive results.

• *Develop effective prevention programs that reach every American family, school, and community.* The federal strategy should make clear what we know about what works and what doesn't in prevention and provide current information and practical guidance to school districts in how their prevention dollars might most effectively be spent. (The Drug-Free Schools Act provides $500 million a year in federal funds to school districts with no strings attached.) The research is persuasive that every American school-child can benefit from the new prevention programs.

For the many children who do not attend school regularly, prevention must be provided through community organizations, such as the Boys and Girls Clubs, which provide supervised recreation, education, and prevention training. But these programs reach only a tiny fraction of the children who are at very high risk of becoming drug abusers. The Federal Government should provide prevention funding directly to local communities to develop their own programs and strategies through their churches, clubs, and other organizations.

   • *Make research a high priority.* Most of the policy decisions of the past decade have been based on political necessity rather than careful research. This is especially true in drug enforcement. Rand Corporation studies have illuminated the failure of interdiction to raise drug prices in the United States, and other scholars have examined the utility of street-level law enforcement. Funding has not been available to evaluate the relative effectiveness of various approaches, even though American taxpayers are now spending more than $9 billion a year on drug enforcement.

   Prevention and treatment research have also been very limited, with the result that rigorous evaluation is still scarce. What we have learned is based on very recent studies funded largely by foundations. New models of treatment are urgently needed to respond to changing patterns of drug abuse, and those that have been developed require solid evaluation. Recent studies indicate that matching patients with types of treatment can significantly improve the outcome for about 60 percent of the patient population, while 20 percent do not do well in any setting and are often the most dangerous. Greater understanding of matching could lead to a more efficient use of resources.

   Because research rarely produces immediate, highly visible results in the war on drugs, it has not received sustained political support. But without assured funding, long-term research cannot be undertaken. Billions more dollars will be wasted unless both demand reduction and supply control strategies are systematically evaluated.

Conclusion

U.S. DRUG POLICY IS DOMINATED BY the view that drug abuse is above all a law-enforcement problem best addressed by supply-control strategies. Unfortunately, experience demonstrates that these strategies usually do not work and probably can never work, even if additional billions of dollars are spent trying to wipe out drug production and seal the borders. Nevertheless, some progress has been made against occasional marijuana and cocaine use. We have learned that health concerns and negative social attitudes play a powerful role in changing behavior, and that media campaigns such as the Partnership for a Drug-Free America are making a measurable difference. We know that new approaches to prevention can substantially reduce new drug use among schoolchildren. We also know that three of four addicts can learn to live without drugs if treatment is highly structured, is sustained for a year or longer, and if meaningful alternatives are available. Within the criminal justice system, treatment can reduce recidivism among drug offenders by a third to a half.

We have learned that the answer to America's drug problem is here at home, in our families, churches, schools, and communities. But can we translate this knowledge into federal policy? Or will we remain prisoners of our past failures? It's up to a new President pushing a new strategy to kick America's worst habit.

NOTES

1. "What America's Users Spend on Illegal Drugs," Office of National Drug Control Policy Technical Paper (The White House, Washington, D.C., June 1991).
2. D. Musto, *The American Disease: Origins of Narcotic Control* (New York: Oxford University Press, 1987).
3. M. Falco, *Winning the Drug War: A National Strategy* (New York: Priority Press/ Twentieth Century Fund, 1989).
4. J. Sisk, "The Effectiveness of Drug Abuse Treatment: Implications for Controlling AIDS/HIV Infection," Office of Technology Assessment Background Paper (September 1990).

PART IV

SOCIAL POLICY

OVERVIEW: SOCIAL POLICY

MARY JO BANE

PRESIDENT FRANKLIN D. ROOSEVELT and the New Deal first defined the social policy mission of the Federal Government: to provide economic security to people unable to support themselves. Recognizing our shared responsibilities as a people—our social responsibility—the Social Security Act, one of the New Deal's major accomplishments, created several federal agencies to design and manage programs to support the elderly, the disabled, the unemployed, dependent children, and others.

President Johnson's Great Society defined an additional social policy mission: social investment. The decades since the 1960s have seen the development of programs that provide education, training, employment services, health services, and social services—programs that recognize society's responsibility to invest in its human and social infrastructure. Far from mutually exclusive, these two missions often reinforce each other, and programs such as the jobs programs connected with Aid to Families with Dependent Children (AFDC) or the rehabilitation programs for disabled recipients of Social Security often address both tasks of the nation's social agenda.

This dual mission—economic security and social investment—is at the core of the social policy system. We need to assess any new federal policy and administrative initiatives by how much they contribute to carrying out that mission effectively—whether they indeed provide economic security

Mary Jo Bane is Commissioner of the New York State Department of Social Services. She was previously director of the Malcolm Wiener Center for Social Policy at the Kennedy School of Government at Harvard University and is the author of many books on poverty, welfare, and social and public policy.

for those in need, and whether they help build family strength, healthy development, and productivity.

The Players

AT THE CENTER OF FEDERAL SOCIAL POLICY are the cabinet departments of Health and Human Services (HHS); Education; Housing and Urban Development (HUD); and Labor. These departments interact with a wide array of state and local government agencies and private and not-for-profit contractors and providers to carry out their mission. The system is labor-intensive and very large. There are, for example, more than 2 million teachers in the system, almost 4 million health care workers, and almost half a million social workers.

Apart from Social Security, for which it bears direct responsibility, the Federal Government is not a primary provider of services. The basic interactions with clients are carried out by millions of people in the states and the private sector who have considerable discretion in shaping both policy and service delivery.

The most important role of the Federal Government is to provide leadership to the system: articulating the common mission of the social policy system, specifying goals, and providing the means by which the goals can be achieved by the myriad players in the system. In particular, many of the services provided at the local level receive financial support from the Federal Government and are governed by federal regulations. In recent years, unfortunately, the Federal Government has largely abdicated its leadership role.

The Historical Legacy

THE MOST DRAMATICALLY SUCCESSFUL EXAMPLE of federal leadership in the social arena is, of course, the Social Security system itself. The Federal Government developed and passed the initial legislation in the 1930s, and has since solidified and extended benefits for the elderly and the disabled. The Federal Government's administration of the Social Security programs has been, with few exceptions, responsible and efficient. The program is, and is perceived to be, a highly effective, universal public system for ensuring economic security. It has essentially eradicated poverty among the elderly.

The Federal Government has also played a leading role in the area of higher education. The GI Bill, enacted in 1944, enabled millions of World War II veterans to attend college and spurred the development of a huge system of public higher education, which continues to provide subsidized higher education to large proportions of young Americans. In 1965 the Higher Education Act established federally funded grant and loan programs that, in turn, helped stimulate and reinforce the efforts of state and local governments to make higher education widely available. With the Federal Government in the lead, the higher education system has carried out its social investment mission at high levels of both access and quality.

In addition to the appropriation of financial resources, federal leadership can also manifest itself through law enforcement and the power of the White House—as in the opening up of public elementary and secondary education to historically discriminated-against groups. Both the moral leadership of Presidents Kennedy and Johnson and the judicial rulings of federal courts led to the dismantling of segregated school systems in the South. More recently, the Federal Government successfully pursued the inclusion of handicapped children in mainstream education and the provision of special services to children who encounter barriers to learning.

In these three arenas, the Federal Government led the social policy system to a new conception of its mission and to a new commitment to quality and service. In one instance—Social Security—the Federal Government developed, funded, and operated the system. In the other two, federal leadership influenced the operation of largely nonfederal systems through funding, regulation and, as important, moral leadership.

"Failed social policies of the past," that indiscriminating incantation frequently used to discredit government's role in our lives, seems hardly an apt description of these legacies from the New Deal and the Great Society. While not every program proved as successful as Social Security, the record clearly demonstrates that government can have a positive role in helping people improve the condition of their lives.

The Recent Legacy

IN RECENT YEARS, the Reagan and Bush administrations have focused on dismantling and discrediting the role of government rather than attending to the country's present and future needs. First, they cut funding for important social programs. Even more important failures of federal leadership occurred, however, outside the arena of budget negotiations. Through both rhetoric and action, the Federal Government has emphasized the ineffectiveness and even counterproductiveness of governmental programs and actions—and in the process contributed to destructive divisions in society around social issues.

Welfare provides one example. There has been a long and legitimate debate over the appropriateness of encouraging or requiring work-related activities by recipients of AFDC benefits. The congressionally initiated Family Support Act of 1988 reflected a developing consensus around the goal of self-sufficiency, requiring states to provide child support and employment services and, in exchange, requiring recipients to participate in them. Not content with the law's emphasis on self-sufficiency, however, the administration went on the rhetorical offensive, characterizing welfare recipients as being indifferent to or incapable of self-sufficiency. Both the administration's rhetoric and its policies have made it very difficult for states, localities, and social services agencies to run work/welfare programs that build on the strengths and desires of recipients to move toward economic independence.

Consider also the delivery of education and social services. Social policy officials, experts, and advocates have been vigorously debating how to organize and finance our education system, health care system, and social services. States and localities are experimenting with a variety of approaches to managing schools, to instruction, and to assigning children to schools and educational programs, and with greater reliance on private and not-for-profit agencies to deliver a variety of services, funding them through contracts or vouchers. These experimental approaches, many of which appear to be quite successful, try to debureaucratize service delivery and to make it more flexible and more responsive to customers—what David Osborne has dubbed "entrepreneurial government."

The Federal Government, however, has in many instances embraced this concept with a vengeance, pushing it to extremes that are destructive, even dangerous. It has tied the broadly supported interest in school choice to its own obsession with privatization. Rather than contributing to constructive problem-solving, this stance has tended to reinforce the public's distrust of government. By claiming that government cannot do anything well, it has undermined the system's capacity to respond to social needs and, in the process, has made the states' task of developing innovative and flexible programs more difficult.

A third arena in which the Federal Government has provided negative rather than positive leadership in recent years is that of abortion. I believe that the debate over abortion is necessary and serious, involving our most profound beliefs and most deeply held values. But the abortion debate has not occurred in an atmosphere of respect and of a search for common ground; instead, it has divided the society along religious and class lines—in no small part because of the White House's shrill support for one side of the debate. Rather than help society reconcile the beliefs and values at issue, the Federal Government has for the past twelve years used this issue to divide us further.

The Immediate Need: Federal Leadership

THE NEXT ADMINISTRATION MUST FIRST and foremost reaffirm the importance of the social policy mission and should lead a collective effort to articulate that historical mission in the context of twenty-first-century needs and capacities. Such a task will require attention to symbols and rhetoric as well as to actions and policies.

The first task is to rehabilitate government. The next Administration should work to turn around the public perceptions that nothing can be done to solve social problems and that government is ineffective in the social policy arena. Both clients of and workers in social policy agencies must believe that they can indeed attain their goals if they are sufficiently committed, innovative, and energetic. Public assistance clients and workers must believe not only that they *should* but also that they *can* move from public assistance to economic independence. Parents and teachers must believe that all children can indeed be educated, that schools can be safe, and that communities can be involved in educating children and supporting family strength. The public as well needs to believe in social policy goals and in the possibility of attaining them, through a combination of public and private actions, if it is to commit the resources and support to do the job. The only way to change the hostile public perception of social programs may be to present the public with programs that embody both governmental and individual responsibility and that *do* work—as many already do.

The next President should appoint highly qualified and visible leaders to the major social policy departments. He may want to reorganize some cabinet departments to emphasize the dual missions of Social Security and social investment, perhaps by merging the Education and Labor Departments and some "investment" activities from HHS and HUD; perhaps by moving food stamps in with the economic security programs that are located mostly in HHS. The President should consider convening a social policy summit, analogous to the education summit convened early in the Bush administration. Such a meeting bringing together the President and the governors could serve several purposes: It could emphasize the importance of the social policy mission; recognize the crucial partnership of the Federal Government with the states; and begin anew the process of articulating social policy goals for society.

The next Administration should put a high premium on making existing social programs work, starting with the programs that the Federal Government operates itself or in which it contributes significantly to operations. The Social Security Administration, for example, should put in place the most modern technology and workplace practices to make its operations a model of efficiency and customer responsiveness. The federal activities that provide operational support to child support enforcement should be expanded and modernized. The student assistance programs for higher education should streamline and modernize procedures for granting loans and for collecting debts. In general, federal social policy activities should set the example of being well-run and responsive, and be recognized as such.

The Federal Government should also examine carefully the division of labor among itself, states and localities, and the private sector. "Privatization" or "not for profitization" may be appropriate in many areas of service delivery. State and local operation of service programs needs to be supported, not duplicated or second-guessed, by the Federal Government. Making social policy work will require relentless attention to quality service delivery at all levels and relentless examination of who is best suited to do a particular job.

Finally, the next President needs to move quickly to heal the divisions that have so destructively torn society apart in recent years: divisions of race, class, and religion. Here, too, the President should rely both on policies and on the all-important bully pulpit. Two areas in particular are in desperate need of leadership: racial issues and the abortion debate, as Penda Hair and Estelle Rogers explain. In both these areas, the President needs to be committed strongly to healing the fissures that have appeared in the past decade, and to listen carefully to all sides of the issues.

The Policy Needs

IN ADDITION TO LEADERSHIP in articulating and institutionalizing the social policy mission, the next Administration needs to develop new policy approaches in a few key problem areas.

HEALTH

The first key area is health care, which is a top priority due to increasing costs and limited access for millions of uninsured. The new Administration needs to commit itself to a general approach that has real promise of providing access to quality care in a cost-effective way, and then begin the hard political work of fashioning an acceptable compromise.

But access to primary care is as much an issue as the ability to pay for it, especially for the low-income population. The new Administration should develop community-based, cost-efficient settings for delivering primary health care and for managing specialized care. While financing reform, through the structuring of financial incentives, will have some effects on the delivery of services, other measures are likely to be necessary: for example, incentives for physicians to enter primary care and support for community primary care clinics.

ECONOMIC SECURITY

The second early problem for the forty-second President is that of economic security for low-income families. This is a broader problem than "welfare reform," though many of the most important initiatives are often discussed under that rubric. Marian Wright Edelman, Robert Greenstein, and Elaine Kamarck tell how providing economic security for families requires a number of initiatives directed at ensuring that families who work are not poor: an increase in the minimum wage, expansion of the earned income tax credit, support for day care and health care, and refundable tax credits or children's allowances for families with children.

Providing economic security also requires special attention to the problems of single-parent families, who often experience very high poverty rates and great difficulty in escaping welfare. The best approach to providing economic security for single-parent families combines work with a strong child support enforcement and insurance program. Children are entitled to support from both their parents; the current child support system comes nowhere close to guaranteeing such support. Strong enforcement measures, combined with a government guarantee of a minimum level of child support, would enable single parent families to achieve economic independence.

Job and work force development is the third crucial piece of economic security policy. Many people are ready and eager to leave the public assistance rolls but lack the real job opportunities to do so. Creating good jobs should be an important priority of the next Administration—especially in the public and nonprofit sector, matching unmet service needs with the needs of disadvantaged workers for real employment. In addition, the next President must help the states develop a coordinated approach to job training and employment services that builds on the JOBS program and expands it to other needy populations.

EDUCATION AND SERVICES FOR CHILDREN

Finally, America in 1993 must start investing anew in education and services to families, children, and disadvantaged populations. The focus should be on children, whose needs have been neglected for too many years and whose healthy and productive development is crucial to the country. In particular, we must make our schools work again. We must figure out ways of radically modernizing and improving instruction as well as organizing other services around the schools or other community institutions.

In these areas, actual service delivery takes place at the community level—in millions of classrooms, offices, and service settings. Neither improved quality nor greater service integration—both of which are crucial—can be achieved in Washington. The Federal Government, however, can provide the impetus and the means for state and local governments to make such improvements, and can take the lead in developing the technology that communities could use to deliver instruction and services in radically different ways. For example, computer technology allows linkages among institutions—a kind of networked case management. The technology also exists for education and service provision to design a variety of outcome measures that can be used to see whether the system is doing a good job. The Federal Government could then provide incentives and technical assistance for communities to use in undertaking their own reform.

Nowhere are our deficiencies in these areas so clear as in the cities of our country. America needs a comprehensive national urban agenda to redress more than a decade of urban neglect by Washington. At a minimum, we need a national Administration that recognizes the cities' past, present, and potential contributions to our national strength, one that does not advise people, in times of difficulty, simply to walk away, to "vote with their feet."

While other areas will require attention from the next Administration, it is important to have a limited and focused agenda, and these three areas are not only extremely important but also ripe for innovative problem-solving.

Department of Housing & Urban Development

HOUSING

PETER DREIER AND JOHN ATLAS

Summary

THE UNITED STATES CURRENTLY SPENDS LESS on *direct* housing aid than any other Western industrial democracy. To guarantee every American an opportunity to live in decent, safe, and affordable housing, we have to change national priorities and spend more, but we also must spend better: reduce development costs, eliminate waste, and target assistance to low-income and middle-income consumers.

For over sixty years, federal housing policy has been characterized by its "stop and go" nature, its internal inconsistencies, and its lack of coordination among the many agencies involved. It has served to shape macroeconomic, social welfare, and community development policies, among others. As a result, government programs have had a "crazy quilt" quality to them, focusing on such varied—and mutually exclusive—programs and goals as:

- creating jobs and stimulating the economy in times of economic recession while driving up interest rates, and therefore depressing new housing starts, during periods of inflation;
- expanding homeownership, particularly among the middle class, and especially in the suburbs—as a result undermining the vitality of cities;
- revitalizing cities, focusing on downtown business districts—and in the process destroying low-income housing and working-class neighborhoods;
- improving inner city low-income neighborhoods, either by providing better housing for existing residents or by attracting new (often more

Peter Dreier, formerly Director of Housing at the Boston Redevelopment Authority, is E. P. Clapp Distinguished Professor of Politics at Occidental College and a board member of the National Housing Institute. John Atlas is President of the National Housing Institute and a public interest lawyer specializing in housing.

affluent) residents—and creating higher housing costs that displace
poor and minority families;

- providing the poor with low-cost housing—and isolating them in
  poorly designed and poorly managed public and subsidized housing
  projects;
- reducing racial segregation by increasing opportunities for minorities
  to live in predominantly white residential areas—but discriminating
  against minorities in the implementation of Federal Housing Administration (FHA) insurance programs and by failing to enforce the
  Community Reinvestment Act (CRA).

The Department of Housing and Urban Development (HUD) was created in 1965, but responsibility for *housing* has been diffused among many
agencies. Despite its name, HUD has had only a limited role in the formulation and implementation of *urban policy*, which involves many issues
outside its jurisdiction—including transportation, economic development,
capital flows, education and job training, and income assistance. Clearly, a
housing reform agenda must broaden its focus beyond HUD.

The overriding purpose of federal housing policy should be to guarantee
every American the opportunity to live in an affordable home in a desirable
community. The nation's current housing policies and institutions, however,
are failing in two specific ways:

First, the system that worked well for thirty years after World War II—
using government to target private credit—has been dismantled. As a result,
many young families are now shut out of the homebuying market.

Second, Federal Government efforts to assist the many Americans who
can't afford to rent an apartment or buy a house in the private market have
been both inadequate and inefficient.

To address these problems and strengthen America's social and economic fabric, the next President and Congress should focus on the following
five goals:

1. Expand homeownership opportunities, particularly among young
   families currently shut out of the American Dream of first-time
   homeownership.
2. Eliminate homelessness by providing poor Americans with direct
   rental assistance.
3. Restore the nation's inventory of public and subsidized housing
   by expanding resident participation and ownership.
4. Increase the supply of affordable housing, primarily by expanding
   the capacity of community-based nonprofit developers.

5. Rebuild and stabilize the economies and social fabric of urban neighborhoods by expanding job and homeownership opportunities and reinvigorating community self-help efforts.

History

IN THE LATE NINETEENTH and early twentieth centuries, housing reformers focused attention on the housing conditions of the poor who lived in tenements in the burgeoning industrial cities. They pushed through *local* laws to eliminate the evils of the slums—overcrowding, poor ventilation, lack of sanitation, and poor construction—by setting minimum safety and construction standards.

Attention by the 1930s turned to *federal* intervention. Spurred by massive unemployment and the collapse of the private housing finance and construction industry, various interested constituencies—homebuilders, the banking industry, trade unions, and unemployed workers—pushed Washington to establish the first home financing program and the first public housing program to help with both housing and jobs.

In 1932, Congress created the Federal Home Loan Bank (FHLB), owned and governed by member thrift institutions, to make the flow of mortgage funds more dependable and to create a national market for mortgages. The Housing Act of 1934 created the Federal Savings and Loan Insurance Corporation (FSLIC), which insured individual depositors' accounts from bank failures, and the Federal Housing Administration (FHA), which guaranteed individual mortgages against their default and gave banks the confidence to offer long-term (thirty-year) mortgages. The postwar Veterans Administration (VA) housing program offered similar help to veterans. These federal home finance policies, as well as the IRS's policy allowing homeowners to deduct local property taxes and mortgage interest from their federal income tax, led to an unprecedented postwar home construction boom and the steady rise in homeownership from 44 percent in 1940 to 62 percent in 1960 to 65 percent in the mid-1970s.

The Housing Act of 1937 created the public housing system. Local housing authorities were established to build and administer public housing, using proceeds from sale of their own tax-free bonds. Public housing advocates, like their European counterparts, initially envisioned it for the middle class as well as the poor, but the real estate industry, warning about the specter of "socialism," successfully lobbied to limit public housing to the poor.

The cross-purposes of postwar federal housing policy are obvious. FHA policies encouraged loans to whites in suburbs but not to minorities or in central cities. Thus, aided by the massive investment in federal highway programs, the FHA helped trigger the postwar exodus of business and residents to the suburbs, leading to the economic decline of core cities. Urban renewal, on the other hand, revitalized some core cities, but in doing so pushed out the poor at the expense of commercial development and market-rate housing. Other policies promoted low-income housing but gave priority to high-rise projects concentrated in existing low-income neighborhoods and removed from the commercial revitalization efforts.

The civil rights movement and the urban riots of the 1960s triggered a new round of federal housing initiatives. The major civil rights acts banned racial discrimination in housing and other areas of American life. The short-lived War on Poverty sought to improve ghetto life by raising the incomes of the poor, providing them with the means to improve their housing. HUD was formed in 1965. Its first major program, "Model Cities," combined both physical improvements and social services but lasted only a few years.

When the riots erupted, several presidential reports on urban problems were released in 1968 including that of the National Advisory Commission on Civil Disorders (the Kerner Report); all cited the condition of ghetto housing as a major problem and recommended a major new commitment to low-income housing.

In response, the Housing Act of 1968 established a housing production goal of 26 million units within ten years, with 6 million units for low-income households. But public housing was meeting increasing disfavor. Tenants were increasingly minorities and welfare recipients instead of the "working poor"; local public housing authorities faced rising operating expenses. Between 1968 and 1973 only 375,000 public housing apartments were added. So Congress turned to the private sector to build low-income housing. Several programs gave private developers low interest-mortgages, tax breaks and, later, rental subsidies. A low-income homeownership program (Section 235) provided low-down-payment, low-interest mortgages. Each program was later criticized as expensive "bribes" to lenders and developers, exceeding the per-unit costs of public housing. But eventually over 2 million units of privately owned subsidized housing were built—almost double the overall number of public housing units. New housing starts set records in the 1970s, even if far short of the 26 million goal.

In 1974 a number of urban-oriented programs were folded into community development "block grants" (CDBGs) distributed directly to cities under a needs formula, on the theory that mayors understood local needs better than Washington did. The funds could be used for capital improvements, human services, and housing. In 1974 Congress also created the Section 8 program to entice private developers to house the poor, with subsidies for new construction, rehabilitation, and rent supplements.

President Carter slightly expanded urban-oriented housing programs, including Urban Development Action Grants to stimulate private commercial and residential development. HUD's annual budget reached $25 billion to $30 billion, and the Federal Government added about three hundred thousand subsidized units a year.

The 1970s witnessed continued exodus to the suburbs, the steady growth of homeownership, and uneven housing construction trends. Several federal policy changes influenced lending institutions. Pressure from neighborhood groups led in 1977 to the Community Reinvestment Act, which required banks seeking to expand or move offices to prove they were not red-lining low-income neighborhoods. Congress in 1980 passed the first of many bank deregulation laws that would contribute significantly to the decline in home-ownership rates in the 1980s.

The Reagan-Bush Years

BREAKING WITH EVERY ADMINISTRATION since the New Deal, the Reagan administration launched a major assault on federal support for low-income housing. Seeking a "free and deregulated" housing market, President Reagan slashed funds for new housing from over $30 billion in 1981 to about $8 billion by 1987. Funds to cities were sharply cut. New construction of subsidized housing ended (except a small program for the elderly). In place of production programs for the poor, Reagan substituted a slightly expanded rent supplement program with enough funding for only a handful of eligible families. (In tight housing markets with few vacancies, the vouchers proved as useful as handing out food stamps while the grocery shelves are empty.)

The Reagan administration initiated a small "demonstration" program to sell off public housing to tenants, but without providing adequate subsidies to make it feasible. It also failed to address the problem of vanishing subsidized housing—the almost 2 million privately-owned, low-income, subsidized housing units that, due to an escape clause, allowed owners to charge market rents twenty years after the projects were built. Only congressional opposition stopped Reagan's efforts to penalize cities that had enacted rent control by withholding federal housing funds. In addition, HUD was decimated—more so than any other domestic-oriented agency.

Deregulation of the banking industry enabled the S&L industry to engage in commercial loans, undermining its role as provider of secure mortgages for homebuyers. Simultaneously, high inflation and FHA limits on home prices made it difficult for people who had not already bought a home to do so.

In 1981, federal tax reform created additional incentives for investment in rental housing, fueling a spurt in rental production, but the 1986 Tax Reform Act removed most of them. One exception was a "low-income housing tax credit," which provided corporations and wealthy individuals with tax incentives to invest in low-income apartment projects.

Soon after President Bush took office, two major controversies that had been brewing during the Reagan years—the S&L crisis and the HUD scandal—broke wide open.

• During the 1980s, Washington deregulated the banking industry. No longer restricted to making loans to homeowners, many S&Ls engaged in an orgy of real estate speculation, with few internal controls or government oversight. Mismanagement and corruption, as well as an overheated real estate market, led to the collapse of hundreds of S&Ls, especially in the Southwest, California, and New England. When they went bankrupt, the Federal Government, which insures deposits in S&Ls, was required to reimburse the depositors—a bailout that may eventually top $500 billion.

• As President Bush was taking office, the media belatedly uncovered evidence that the Reagan administration had used scarce HUD monies as a slush fund for politically connected developers, former Reagan Administration staffers, and campaign contributors. Implicated in the "HUD scandal" were Reagan's HUD secretary, Sam Pierce, many of his top aides, and other administration officials.

Bush's HUD secretary, Jack Kemp, spent much of his four years trying to "clean house" by instituting tighter controls on the allocation of funds. But his policy initiatives, such as privatizing subsidized housing and fostering enterprise zones in inner cities, were ignored by Bush until the Los Angeles riots.

In light of Presidents Reagan and Bush's neglect, Congress and housing activists stepped in. Following the recommendations of its housing task force, Congress in 1990 enacted the National Affordable Housing Act (NAHA), which slightly increased overall HUD funding levels for the first time in a decade and created a new "block grant" program, called HOME, that directs federal funds to each state, and to many cities and counties, by means of a formula based on need. A minimum of 15 percent of HOME funds is targeted for community-based, nonprofit organizations. The NAHA also included a version of Kemp's program to sell public housing to tenants—Homeownership and Opportunity for People Everywhere (HOPE)—funded at about $400 million.

The Legacy of Inaction: America's Housing Crisis

SINCE 1980, THIS WEALTHY COUNTRY has experienced a drastic decline in homeownership, rent increases far beyond inflation and a tragic epidemic of homelessness. A new comprehensive federal housing program must address the following key problem areas:

DECLINING HOMEOWNERSHIP

For the first time in the postwar era, the rate of homeownership declined in the eighties, from 65.6 percent in 1980 to 63.9 percent in 1989, especially among the young.[1]

These numbers are not surprising: A recent Census Bureau study, *Who Can Afford to Buy a House?*, found that 48 percent of American families could not afford to buy the median-price house in the region where they lived.[2] Why this crisis? The median price of a new single-family home climbed from $69,300 in 1982 to about $122,700 in 1990. In 1973, a young family with children spent about one quarter of its annual income to carry a new mortgage on an average-price house; today, over half of such a family's annual income is needed. Even in areas where housing prices haven't fallen, new homeownership remains low, mainly because of low wages, high unemployment, and high down-payment costs. Meanwhile, foreclosure rates during the 1980s were double those of the prior decade.

With a few exceptions, homes built by private homebuilders are geared toward the wealthiest third of the population. The average new home in 1991 cost over $120,000—higher in many parts of the country.[3] In the 1990s alone, over 1 million young families will enter the homebuying years but will be shut out of homeownership unless these barriers are removed.

RENT SQUEEZE

The 1980s witnessed a widening housing gap caused by several factors: Renter households are increasing, their real incomes are declining, housing costs are up, and low-rent units are disappearing. By 1991 at least a third of all renters in every state could not afford market-level rents. Millions of Americans live doubled up or tripled up in overcrowded apartments. Millions more pay more than they can reasonably afford for substandard housing— one emergency (rent increase, hospital stay, layoff) away from becoming homeless.[4]

Yet only 29 percent of the 13.8 million low-income renter households eligible for federal assistance receive any housing subsidy—the lowest level of any industrial nation in the world[5]—leaving the rest at the mercy of the private housing market, facing swelling waiting lists for even the most deteriorated subsidized housing projects.

GROWING HOMELESSNESS

The homeless are the most tragic victims of these trends. By moderate accounts their ranks have swollen to 600,000 on any given night and to 1.2 million over the course of a year. Shelters note that demand for their services increased by about 20 percent a year during the past decade.

The composition of the homeless population has changed, from the initial stereotype of an alcoholic or mentally ill middle-aged man or "bag lady," many of them victims of the "deinstitutionalization" policies of the 1970s, to now include families, even many with young children. A recent U.S. Conference of Mayors survey found that almost one quarter of the homeless work but simply cannot afford permanent housing. About one third of homeless single men are veterans.

Since the early 1980s, local groups (churches, local government, the United Way, foundations, and community groups) have assumed the brunt of providing the homeless with such basic survival services as soup kitchens, emergency shelters, and health clinics. But demand has outpaced available resources, requiring assistance from a Federal Government primarily responsible for the problem in the first place. In 1987 Congress enacted the McKinney Homeless Assistance Act (named after a Republican congressman), providing $355 million for emergency shelters, soup kitchens, health care and job training programs, mental health services, and other efforts.

Agencies that provide services for the homeless are increasingly frustrated with short-term "Band-Aid" solutions that ignore the underlying causes. No stopgap measure can eradicate the legacy of the policies of the 1980s: growing poverty and stagnant wages; cuts in "safety net" programs that provide a cushion for the poor; the impact of "deinstitutionalization," which virtually emptied mental hospitals of about half a million people but failed to replace them with community-based homes; and the deepening shortage of affordable housing available to the poor.

TROUBLED HOUSING INDUSTRY

The homebuilding industry is in its worst slump since World War II.[6] New starts (including single-family and multifamily housing) fell to a postwar low of 1.01 million in 1991, down from a high of 2.37 million in 1972.

The number of new homes sold has also plummeted. In 1991 only 509,000 new single-family homes were sold, the lowest figure since 1970 except for the 1981–82 recession. Many homebuilders and real estate brokers have gone out of business.[7] Unemployment in the building trades (construction) has soared.

DECAYING CITIES

For years, America's mayors warned about the "quiet riots" of poverty, violence, drugs, and neighborhood decay. Cities, they said, were ticking time bombs waiting to explode. The events in Los Angeles that followed the Rodney King trial reflect these anxieties. Federal policies that subsidized the exodus of businesses, jobs, and people are much to blame.

• Highway-building policies opened up cheap land in the hinterlands to real estate speculation and development, as Peter Calthorpe and Henry Richmond discuss in their chapter on sustainable growth.

• Federal tax policies promoted corporate flight over modernizing and expanding existing plants and equipment in cities. Since 1980, the *Fortune* 500 industrial companies have lost 3.9 million employees from their payrolls. As William J. Wilson points out in *The Truly Disadvantaged*, the urban poor—disproportionately people of color and young people—face a widening mismatch between their skills and available jobs in cities.[8]

• Red-lining by banks, insurance companies, and the FHA led to a self-fulfilling prophecy of decline. An October 1991 report by the Federal Reserve, for example, found that blacks and Hispanics were rejected for home mortgages more than twice as often as whites with similar incomes, yet federal bank regulators have failed to enforce the 1977 CRA—while the White House and Congress looked the other way.[9]

• The Pentagon has played a critical role in the flight of business, jobs, and people from cities. A new study by Employment Research Associates for the Boston Redevelopment Authority found that the Pentagon has sucked tax dollars out of cities. In 1990, for example, taxpayers in eighteen of the twenty five largest cities sent $24 billion more to the military than they took in from military contracts, salaries, and facilities.[10]

• Federal cutbacks to cities under Presidents Reagan and Bush exacerbated the crisis. In 1980, federal dollars accounted for 14.3 percent of city budgets; today, it's less than 5 percent. Some state governments helped fill the gap during the 1980s, but are now cutting local aid to the bone as they face their own fiscal crises. As a result, America's cities face a shrinking tax base and fiscal traumas. At the same time, the percentage of America's poor living in cities grew from 30 percent in 1968 to 42 percent today.

To avert fiscal collapse, many cities have been closing schools, hospitals, and police and fire stations; laying off essential employees; reducing basic services such as maintenance of parks, repairing roads and enforcing housing

and health codes; and postponing or canceling capital improvements. Increasingly, the urban poor and the working class are pitted against each
other for these shrinking resources, exacerbating social and racial conflict.

An Agenda for Change

IN 1949, CONGRESS PLEDGED A DECENT HOME for every citizen.
That promise has not been kept. As several decades of progress were reversed
during the 1980s, the country now faces the worst housing crisis since World
War II. The next President and Congress must address this issue with the
same resolve that President Truman applied to the Marshall Plan and that
President Kennedy applied to the space program. The following ten initiatives provide a basis for a progressive new national housing policy.

SHORT-TERM INITIATIVES

Set Clear Goals. The solution to the nation's housing crisis is to expand
the overall supply of housing and provide government assistance to the many
American families priced out of the private market. Soon after taking office,
the next President should announce a specific national goal for both new
housing starts and the rehabilitation of substandard housing, between 1993
and 2000—with a specific percentage targeted for low-and moderate-income
families. The President should also announce goals of steadily increasing the
number of homeowners and of providing direct rental assistance to all low-
income families who cannot afford market rents.

Fix HUD. After twelve years of neglect, HUD is broken, incapable of
implementing even the modest programs for which it is now responsible.
Secretary Kemp, busy cleaning up after his predecessor, did not improve
the day-to-day operation or clarify the overall mission of the agency. The
central office is still top-heavy with bureaucrats with little or no expertise in
housing or community development. Regional and local offices have no
agencywide mission. Programs are often inflexible or encumbered by complex and needless rules and regulations.

The next secretary should consolidate HUD programs into flexible block-
grant programs administered by state, county, and local governments, de-
centralize operations toward regional and local offices, and hire staff with
technical skills and experience in housing and community development.
He or she should appoint an assistant secretary for community self-help,
who would work with community-based organizations in urban neighborhoods.

Full Funding for the HOME program. Funding for the HOME program—which provides funds to state, county, and local governments to rehabilitate substandard housing, promote neighborhood revitalization, create new affordable housing units, and help low- and moderate-income families purchase their first homes—was limited to $1.5 billion for fiscal year 1992. Increasing it to at least $5 billion for fiscal year 1993 would not only increase affordable housing but also help put people to work.

LONGER-TERM INITIATIVES

Tenant Self-Sufficiency. HUD should give tenants a greater stake in their communities. There are currently about 3 million federally assisted apartments in developments across the country. Some 1.3 million units are in public housing, owned and managed by local housing authorities; another 1.7 million apartments are owned by private landlords or (through foreclosure) by HUD.

Congress has been reluctant to fund Secretary Kemp's pet HOPE program to help tenants in public and HUD-subsidized developments purchase their homes because it is unworkable and risks suffering the same fate as the Section 235 program of the late 1960s and 1970s, where many families bought deteriorated houses and, unable to make repairs and keep up payments, wound up losing their homes and their life savings.

Since the 1940s, the United States has made an investment worth about $75 billion in public housing. Once targeted to the working poor, public housing has increasingly become home to the extremely poor. In 1988, the average annual household income of those in public housing was $6,539, one fifth of the national average. Only about 40 percent of its nonelderly households have a wage earner. About 800,000 families are on the waiting lists of the nation's 3,060 local housing authorities.

Kemp's program is unworkable because even if tenants were handed the keys to their homes, free, their incomes are typically lower than the monthly costs of operating their apartments (utilities and taxes, not to mention repair and maintenance needs). In the few showcase resident-ownership projects that Kemp promotes, HUD poured huge subsidies (e.g., over $130,000 per unit at Kenilworth-Parkside in Washington, D.C.) to make them work. But under the HOPE program, HUD will only provide buyers with subsidies for five years. What happens then? Moreover, there are few safeguards to prevent the new homeowners from eventually selling their homes for a windfall profit, thereby reducing the housing stock available to the poor.

A successful program of resident management and ownership of both public housing *and* privately owned subsidized developments should work to strengthen families, catalyze a sense of community, and bring subsidized housing into the mainstream of urban neighborhoods. Toward that goal, under a new assistant secretary for community self-help, HUD should:

• Provide adequate funds so residents organize to address day-to-day concerns (e.g., crime or maintenance), and create resident management corporations to manage and eventually (if they desire) own their developments. Training funds to help residents become effective managers and owners are essential.

• Empower tenant groups to oversee and strengthen tenant screening and eviction guidelines to remove residents engaged in criminal or damaging activities. Revise income/priority guidelines to encourage working families to live in these developments.

• Working with tenant groups, repair these developments before they are sold. For $2 billion annually, distressed public housing complexes could be modernized within ten years.

• Sell developments only as resident-owned limited equity cooperatives, to guarantee that this housing will be available for low-income residents after initial owners have left.

• Offer owners of privately owned subsidized developments capital gains tax breaks to sell their developments to non profit organizations or resident-owned entities.

Target Private Capital and Credit. To encourage private capital and credit for housing and neighborhood development, the next President and Congress should:

• *Enforce the CRA.* Streamline enforcement of the CRA and the Equal Credit Opportunity Act by placing enforcement powers in HUD rather than (as currently done) four separate regulatory agencies.

• *Streamline disposition of federally-owned properties.* Merge the divisions of the RTC and the FDIC that dispose of residential property formerly held by lending institutions. The combined agency should dispose of these assets to community-based nonprofit organizations for affordable housing.

• *Target pension funds for housing.* Encourage pension fund investment in affordable housing with federal guarantees. A program would pool together housing development projects, and then issue bonds backed by the projects, guaranteed by the Federal Government. Pension funds would purchase these low-risk, fair-rate-of-return securities. The bonds would be a "prudent" investment overseen by a joint board of government, labor, and business. The cost to government would be nominal.

Expand Community Housing Partnerships. The next Administration should significantly increase the capacity of nonprofit, community-based development organizations to construct and rehabilitate affordable housing and establish two target goals: First, to increase the HOME program budget to at least $10 billion by 1996 and to $15 billion by the year 2000. Second, to increase the nonprofits' minimum share of HUD's production and rehabilitation efforts to at least one-third by 1996 and one half by 2000. Funds would be made available to state and local governments in a two-tier approach—an entitlement grant program and a matching grant program (based on an ability-to-pay formula).

Perhaps the only silver lining in the dark cloud of the Reagan administration's housing cuts was the emergence of many community-based nonprofit housing developers in cities across the country. Some 2,000 such grass-roots entities—churches, unions, community development corporations (CDCs), and tenant cooperatives—developed almost 320,000 units of housing and created (or retained) almost 90,000 permanent jobs. They have been responsible for most of the affordable housing constructed and rehabilitated during the decade. Cities with sophisticated nonprofits have formed umbrella organizations, often called "housing partnerships," to improve efficiency and expand the scale of development.

These nonprofit organizations would become the major delivery system for the creation of affordable housing. Family housing developments built with federal assistance should be of mixed income and provide long-term affordability, to avoid the problems we now face with the "vanishing subsidy" dilemma. High-rise developments would not be constructed, except for senior citizens.

Expand Rental Assistance to Eligible Families. When the budget allows, HUD should provide rent supplements to low-income renter households—currently about 9.7 million families—who receive no housing assistance and cannot afford market rents. This would cost about $20 billion a year.

Only about 1 million families receive assistance under the current program of rent vouchers (essentially, additional income support) favored by Presidents Reagan and Bush. The next Administration should begin to establish a universal rent subsidy program for families who cannot afford market rents, giving priority to homeless families and families at risk of becoming homeless (the 5.1 million households that HUD defines as "worst case" households). Recipients would be required to participate in job training programs or in a public works jobs program—provided child care and health insurance are available.

HUD and HHS must streamline their crazy-quilt approach to providing income subsidies to the poor. In addition to HUD's housing subsidies, HHS is responsible for matching AFDC benefits (which sometimes include small housing allowances) administered through state welfare departments. According to the Urban Institute, some 4.6 million households receive AFDC benefits but no housing subsidy—even though in no state does an AFDC grant alone come close to the amount needed to pay market-level rents.

Assist First-Time Homebuyers. To assist first-time homebuyers, the new Administration should implement the following:

• *Housing Development Bank for lower interest rates.* Create a Housing Development Bank, parallel to the Federal Reserve Bank, to offer interest rates, available to lenders, at two points below the prime rate for first-time homebuyers, and three points below the prime rate for first-time homebuyers in distressed cities.

• *Reduce down payments.* The FHA's mortgage limits have not kept pace with rising home prices, leaving many potential homebuyers ineligible. The FHA should (a) revise its limits to expand the potential for homeownership for many young families and (b) reduce its down-payment requirements to 3 percent for the first $50,000 of a home's value and 5 percent in excess of $50,000.

HUD should also create a down-payment revolving loan fund to help first-time middle-income buyers overcome down-payment obstacles, payable within five years. Any appreciation of the homes' value would be shared with the Federal Government, based on a formula that included the size of the loan, the income of the buyer, and the amount of appreciation. Those proceeds would be placed in the revolving loan fund to help future first-time buyers.

• *Stop snob zoning.* A task force appointed by Kemp identified "snob zoning," which communities (primarily suburbs) use to discourage inexpensive housing, as a major obstacle to developing affordable housing. Jurisdictions (states, counties, cities) that engage in exclusionary ("snob") zoning practices should be denied federal funds.

• *Mortgage revenue bonds.* The Federal Government should continue the mortgage revenue bond program, which allows state housing agencies to raise funds to provide below-market loans for low- and moderate-income homebuyers. Some states, such as Massachusetts, have utilized additional revenues to bring mortgage rates down several more points and require low down payments. All homes purchased through tax-exempt funding or additional mortgage assistance should incorporate deed restrictions to keep homes affordable for subsequent buyers.

Graduated Tax Credit for Homeowners. Demand for housing is more elastic among working-class and middle-class consumers than it is for the wealthy. As a result, a *graduated* tax credit will increase demand for home-ownership among households who could not otherwise afford it and stimulate homebuilding, which will help the housing industry. This approach is more fair, cost-effective, and probusiness than the current regressive homeowner deduction, which disproportionately benefits the wealthy and should be eliminated.[11] The vast majority of homeowners will continue to get the same or greater benefits, but the wealthy will receive less.

Community Self-Help Foundation. HUD should establish a foundation to help empower urban communities to improve their neighborhoods. The foundation would provide funds for the training and placement of leaders and organizers to work with community-based, nonprofit organizations and assist these groups in planning, coalition building, research, and leadership development.

NOTES

1. The homeownership rate from 1982 to 1989 dropped from 38.6 to 35.3 percent for twenty-five- to twenty-nine-year-olds, from 57.1 to 53.2 percent for those between thirty and thirty-four years and from 67.6 to 63.4 percent for those in the thirty-five- to thirty-nine-year-old category.
2. In terms of race, 43.3 percent of whites, 76.6 percent of blacks, and 74.2 percent of Hispanics are shut out of the home-buying market. In terms of age, 71.2 percent of families headed by a twenty-five- to thirty-four-year-old, and 47.2 percent of families in the thirty-five to forty-four age category cannot afford to buy a home. Over a third of existing homeowners—and 91 percent of all current renter families (including 98 percent of black and Hispanic families)—could not afford to buy a home if they wanted to purchase a house today.
3. Down-payment requirements of 20 percent dictate that would-be buyers have at least $24,000 up-front in addition to several thousand additional dollars for closing fees. This is simply beyond the means of most American families under forty.
4. In 1989, 85 percent of the nation's 7.5 million low-income renter households (5.1 million households) paid at least 30 percent of their income for housing. About half of all poor renters (3.5 million households) paid at least half of their income for housing.
5. According to HUD, in 1989 there were 13.6 million renter households eligible for federal housing assistance, but only 4.07 million (29 percent) eligible households received assistance. Of the assisted households, 1.36 million were in public housing units, 1.65 million were in private, government-subsidized developments, and 1.06

received housing certificates or vouchers. Among the 9.7 million households who do not receive assistance, HUD identified 5.1 million households with "worst case" housing problems—paying more than half of their income for housing or living in seriously substandard apartments.

6. President Bush recently told the national Association of Home Builders: "The old adage is coming true: As housing goes, so goes the economy." (*The Boston Globe*, May 19, 1992).

7. For example, membership of the National Association of Realtors declined from 794,000 in 1990 to 745,500 in 1991.

8. Between 1973 and 1989, the annual incomes of low-skilled white men in their twenties fell by 14 percent; for blacks, by 24 percent. Incomes for white male high school dropouts in their twenties fell by 33 percent; for blacks, by 50 percent.

9. The riot-torn areas of Los Angeles, home to more than 500,000 residents, has only 19 banks. Los Angeles County had 1,068 supermarkets in 1970 but only 694 in 1990; most of the boarded-up markets are in Los Angeles's minority areas.

10. In Los Angeles, taxpayers sent $4.74 billion to the Pentagon and received only $1.47 billion back—a net loss of $3.27 billion, or $3,000 per family. That translates into almost 100,000 jobs.

11. The existing deduction for mortgage interest and property taxes cost the Federal Government $47 billion in 1991 alone. Over 80 percent of these tax benefits goes to the 20 percent of taxpayers who earn over $50,000 annually; half of this subsidy goes to the 8 percent of taxpayers, with incomes over $75,000. About a third of this subsidy goes to the wealthiest 3.8 percent of taxpayers, with incomes over $100,000, and about 12 percent goes to the wealthiest 1 percent of taxpayers, whose incomes are over $200,000.

Department of Health and Human Services

HEALTH

THEODORE R. MARMOR

AND

MICHAEL S. BARR

Summary

THE UNITED STATES SPENDS MORE than any other nation on health care—some $800 billion this year—but more than 30 million Americans lack any health insurance, and even those with insurance are anxious about gaps in their protection. Yet for two terms the Reagan administration was unwilling to put forward serious proposals for reform, and the Bush administration only reluctantly presented a partial plan in the face of Democratic action and public outcry. Blaming spiraling costs on American patients, Reagan and Bush called for more of the same. They ignored the reality that our imperfectly competitive market in medical care has not led to cost restraint or wider access and that a perfectly competitive medical care market is impossible and in any event undesirable because it rations care by ability to pay.

The next Administration must distinguish badly designed "Band-Aids" from essential steps to reform, and focus on the following key questions: Who will be insured? What medical services will be insured? How will the financial costs be distributed? How will defensible borders be put on what we spend as a nation? How do we ensure democratic accountability, decent quality of care, and efficient administration?

A straightforward version of national health insurance is ethically and

---

Ted Marmor is Professor of Public Policy at the Yale School of Organization and Management and is coauthor of America's Misunderstood Welfare State. *He was on President Carter's Commission on the Agenda for the 1980s. Michael Barr is a recent graduate of the Yale Law School and coauthor of* "Making Sense of the National Health Insurance Reform Debate," Yale Law and Policy Review *10 (1992).*

financially desirable, politically feasible, and administratively implementable. It could provide publicly financed, comprehensive, universal insurance coverage at lower cost than America's current arrangements. This chapter highlights several transitional steps—among other desirable possibilities—that the new Administration might take toward the goal of genuine reform:

Step One
- A national health insurance program for prenatal and child medical care, publicly financed through earmarked, sliding scale premiums and other revenues.
- Reform of Medicare to fill obvious gaps in coverage and to simplify its administration.
- Universal protection against catastrophic medical costs through refundable tax credits.

Step Two
- A national health insurance program for hospital care, with rules for all payers and/or global budgets, publicly financed with earmarked, sliding-scale premiums and other revenues.

Step Three
- A national health insurance program for physician services, with a common fee schedule and/or global budget, again publicly financed.

Medical Care: Unaffordable, Inaccessible

AMERICA'S CURRENT MEDICAL ARRANGEMENTS are economically, socially, and politically unsustainable. Spiraling costs, incomplete coverage, and baffling insurance arrangements head the list of serious complaints. The United States spends more on medical care than any other nation, but dissatisfaction is rampant, and America's health outcomes are comparatively poor.[1] In 1991, total health expenditures were about $740 billion.[2] At the same time, 34 million Americans, most of whom come from families with a working parent, were without health insurance, and countless more worry about gaps in their coverage.[3] Some health insurance plans are collapsing, while others impose premium increases two to three times the rate of general inflation and rely on "managed care" policies that restrict patient choice of medical providers and alienate patients and physicians alike.

It is therefore no surprise that a majority of Americans are unhappy with the cost of medical care and uncertain about their economic security in the event of illness.[4] Contrary to the rhetoric of many medical interest groups, American values about medical care do not differ significantly from those of citizens in other industrial democracies. Large majorities of Americans believe that no one should be allowed to be bankrupted by high medical costs; that the poor and the unemployed should have access to the same quality of care as everyone else; that people with heart conditions or cancer should not pay more for health insurance than those who are healthy; and that government should ensure that all citizens get the medical care they need.[5] A recent survey reported that nine of ten Americans believe that "everybody should have the right to get the best possible care" and that two thirds think it is unfair that some people get more comprehensive coverage than others.[6] In another survey,more than 60 percent said they "favor making care more available to everyone who does not yet have it rather than lowering the nation's health-care spending" if such a choice must be made.[7]

History of Federal Health Care Policy

THE CONTEMPORARY WORLD OF AMERICAN MEDICINE reflects shifting bargains and unanticipated outcomes, none of them neat, simple, or satisfying. Administrative complexity, high cost, and inadequate coverage for those who need it most emerge from a confusing mélange of private and public health insurance. To name the components of our "system" is to understand both its complexity and its inadequacy.

A third of our expenditures are for private health insurance, organized largely through employment. A little less than a third are out-of-pocket expenditures: deductibles, copayments, coinsurance, and direct payments by the uninsured. The remainder—some 40 percent—is public expenditure: government insurance for the elderly and disabled (Medicare); federal/state financing for some of the poor (Medicaid); CHAMPUS for military families, the Veterans Administration's direct provision; health insurance for federal employees; and tax credits for private insurance.

In addition, the Federal Government has a wide-ranging role in subsidizing research; regulating the dissemination of drugs and medical equipment; and, in some prominent instances, directly providing care. The VA, for example, has as large a medical delivery system as most nations in the world. The Food and Drug Administration intervenes directly in determining what pharmaceuticals reach the market and what devices are deemed safe and effective. The Occupational Safety and Health Administration regulates work conditions for most Americans, and public health programs affect the care received by many groups, including Native Americans, selected poor mothers and infants, and migrants.

Yet the challenge in 1992 is not to attack all federal policy affecting health—a diffuse and daunting task. Rather, it is to reform the rules of medical finance so the major threats to our economic security are reduced and the most frustrating barriers to sensible care are lowered. The consensus for change has finally reached a level that fundamental alteration of the financial ground rules is possible, an unusual opportunity that must not be squandered. Therefore, the new President should focus on alteration of the *medical* status quo in its first year, and in the remaining years turn to the important task of improving federal policy affecting *health*.

The Legacy of "Promarket" Reforms

DESPITE THE "PROMARKET" RHETORIC of the Reagan and Bush administrations, it is clear that privately based controls have not and will not constrain overall medical-care expenditures. Over the past decade, the nation pursued a bewildering mix of private solutions—business coalitions at the local level, self-insurance by large firms, experiments in group practice (preferred provider organizations [PPOs], health maintenance organizations [HMOs]), case management, and consumer "cost-sharing" (deductibles, coinsurance). Private insurance firms spent large and rapidly increasing sums on utilization review and prior authorization arrangements in "managed care" plans and on marketing, billing, and other administrative overhead.

This staggering growth of organizational and managerial innovation— not to mention paperwork—has failed to restrain the relentless rise in national health expenditures and has actually decreased access to insurance protection.[8] "The increasing emphasis on competition and managed care has," in the words of one Canadian critic, "set many new places at the health-care feast. These administrative overheads, which, from the Canadian perspective, are just so much wasted motion, add $50–100 billion to American costs."[9] Astonishingly, the United States spends as much as a fifth of its health dollars on billing and other nonmedical administrative costs.[10] As Robert Evans has shown, "Canadians spend less per capita to administer universal comprehensive coverage than Americans spend to administer Medicare and Medicaid alone. . . ."[11]

Moreover, private insurance companies differentiate among their applicants on the basis of their expected health risk. Widespread screening increasingly leads to outright denials, exclusion of "preexisting conditions" from coverage, or substantially increased premiums. Small groups and individuals are the usual targets of these practices; they typically face experience-rated premiums (based on past sickness history) rather than community-rated premiums (based on the average per capita costs of insuring a larger group). Families in larger, employer-based insurance pools also routinely face experience-rated premiums. And because a lost job may mean the loss of health insurance, even employees with good coverage fear becoming "insurance hostages" to their current jobs.[12]

Equally counterproductive are "cost-sharing" plans that require copayments, coinsurance, and deductibles to encourage patients, the theory goes, to reduce utilization. First, cost-sharing is bad health policy. It reduces access to preventive care while having little impact on utilization of high-cost, high-technology, high-intensity services because the demand for such services is largely physician-determined and because the costs of such services vastly exceed almost all cost-sharing limits.[13] It also reduces the likelihood that those with serious medical symptoms requiring medical attention will actually seek such care.[14] Finally, cost-sharing leads to "similar reductions in both appropriate and inappropriate care."[15]

Second, cost-sharing is bad economic policy. OECD data "clearly contradict" the claims of microeconomic demand theorists "that higher consumer payments and cost-sharing—or more generally, more market-type pricing—would lead to lower health expenditures per capita or as a share of GDP."[16] So, too, does the American experience. If anything, the administrative expense associated with complex mixes of deductibles and copayments has added to our total health expenditures. And despite the highest level of direct patient payment of any OECD country, American utilization rates have continued to rise.[17]

Third, cost-sharing points the finger in the wrong direction. Increases in national health expenditures in the 1980s were attributable far more to rising medical prices than to increased utilization or population growth.[18] And finally, cost-sharing is bad social policy. It unacceptably rations medical care by ability to pay.

Far from rejecting cost sharing and managed care, promarket conservatives endorse more of both and blame spiraling health costs not on health insurers or providers but on the American "consumer." They ignore the reality that our imperfectly competitive market has not led to cost restraint or universal access and that perfectly competitive medical care is impossible in a market fraught with asymmetric information and biased risk selection. Medical care is not just another commodity like automobiles, and obtaining hospital care is hardly like shopping for a new car. It is more like looking for a tow truck and a mechanic at 2:00 A.M. on a deserted road in the middle of nowhere. You take what you can get, you do what they say, and you pay what they charge. At the same time, few would argue that a patient who needed a tumor removed should be denied care because he or she could not afford the hospital fees. Thus, even if a near-perfect market for medical care were possible, it would restrain consumption at an unacceptable price for most Americans.

Peddling "promarket" ideology, conservatives employ an antigovernment rhetoric that substantially distorts the available choices. Any new policy initiatives will have to take on these myths. And they will also have to take on those currently benefiting from our rapidly inflating health industry. The interests arrayed against national health insurance are powerful and well financed; they have obvious, concentrated stakes in avoiding financial losses. But public support, once aroused, can overwhelm such opposition, as the history of Medicare's enactment illustrates. And this year, a very unusual coalition of management, labor, and citizen groups has put national health insurance on the political agenda. Most employers, employees, unions, the unemployed, those locked into jobs, and retirees—and the growing number of doctors and hospital administrators who believe that the current system is economically and morally unacceptable—stand to gain. Notwithstanding the difficulties ahead, what is essential is that our political leaders take on the task.

National Health Insurance Reform

POLICY CHOICES

Medical care reform must assure cost containment, universal access to appropriate medical services, and quality medical care. Fundamental change in financing and administration—not tinkering—is required. Three substantial options exist. Each commits to universal coverage and to reasonably comprehensive medical-care provision. The key differences lie in their approaches to cost containment as a counterweight to the inflationary pressure that widened coverage necessarily brings.

1. The "modified competitivists," such as Alain Enthoven and Stuart Butler, recognize subsidization of universal coverage as a precondition for ethically defensible reform. Both are drawn to the presumption of neoclassical microeconomics that price competition is the best allocator of goods and services. Both adhere to the rhetoric of "consumer choice" among health insurers. While they differ with regard to out-of-pocket payments and how many insurance intermediaries there should be,[19] both ignore that choice of care-giver, not choice of insurance company, is what most Americans really value. And both ignore the crossnational evidence that government, not the private insurance industry, can straightforwardly provide universal health insurance at an acceptable price.

2. The second option is the so-called single-payer approach, modeled largely on Canada's universal health insurance program. While single payer refers only to the financial architecture, the core elements of this approach extend beyond financing. Sensible single-payer plans combine financial accessibility, countervailing buyer power, and political accountability in a way that expands access while restraining cost increases. Unlike current U.S. arrangements, everyone in a geographic area would be covered by the same plan. Insurance companies would not vie for premiums, but doctors and hospitals would compete for patients, fame, and regard. Overall budgets would be publicly set, in a process that is necessarily contentious. To borrow Albert Hirschman's expression, *voice* is its mode, where *exit* is key to the so-called competitive model.[20] The question about this approach that many policymakers raise, however, is its political viability.

3. The final major reform options—based largely on the German model—attempt to adapt all-payer rate-setting to the American employer-based insurance market.[21] Employer-based "play or pay" proposals seek to provide universal coverage by requiring employers either to provide health insurance to their employees ("play") or to pay a tax into a public fund that would cover the uninsured. If established properly at the outset, strict all-payer rate-setting may help constrain overall costs. Through community-rating and limits on preexisting condition clauses, employer-based plans may reduce job "lock-in." Each plan requires significant out-of-pocket payments (cost-sharing) by patients and retains a central role for private insurance. Financing comes from payroll taxes and other sources.

To avoid the appearance of taxation, the "play or pay" approach leaves in place a complex, costly administrative apparatus that diffuses accountability and drains billions of dollars each year from medical care itself. Employers are likely to "dump" the worst risks, with the highest per capita costs, into the residual governmental program. How could the government plan not be perceived as a failure under those circumstances? Moreover, "play or pay" will impose more medical costs on employers, in general, than they currently pay, especially for firms whose employees lack full coverage. The danger with such plans is that the continued explosion in medical-care costs may overwhelm the reform agenda before more serious steps forward can be made.

PRINCIPLES OF FUNDAMENTAL REFORM

Five principles should guide medical-care reform in the United States:
- Universal insurance coverage for all Americans, with no significant deductibles or co-payment obligations on patients.

- Comprehensive, broad coverage of all medically necessary medical care, comprehensibly formulated and described.
- Public administration and finance to promote accountability and control costs.
- Freedom to choose providers and provider-patient autonomy in medical treatment decisionmaking.
- Portable insurance coverage, not tied to a specific job or geographic location.

Universality. Insurance coverage for all Americans is essential for several reasons. First, all Americans have the same fears of financial ruin, the same need for decent medical care. No one should have to use the emergency room as "family practitioner." Second, and paradoxically, universality promotes cost control. It avoids the problem of "free riders"—uninsured patients who receive care others have to finance. If accompanied by some form of fee limits, broad coverage helps prevent cost shifting from patients who will not or cannot pay higher medical prices to patients who will and can pay higher prices, a practice that thwarts overall cost control. Third, universal protection in a common plan promotes democratic accountability. American voters would be able to concentrate their political attention on the cost, quality, comprehensiveness, and efficiency of the national health insurance program instead of dispersing it on the countless fragmented insurance organizations they now face separately.

Comprehensive benefits. Benefits must be both comprehensive and comprehensible. Even Americans with insurance worry that the fine print of their plans will rob them of insurance protection just when they need it most. Comprehensive plans also reduce wasteful bureaucratic hassle and promote individual choice in the doctor-patient relationship.

Political accountability. Political accountability is important in its own right, but international experience also shows that it is the sine qua non of effective cost control. Why does a publicly financed and publicly administered arrangement tend to constrain costs? Pressures to spend more on medical care exist in all industrial democracies. In fragmented finance systems, each payer is interested in his or her medical costs, not the overall costs of medical care. Any cost shifted represents a 100 percent gain to that payer. But like squeezing a balloon, efforts to control one's own costs by cost shifting to others spreads costs around rather than containing them. American companies, for instance, try to shift their costs either to patients, through cost sharing, or to government, through cutting benefits and turning employees into potential charity cases. Under this arrangement, total costs are discovered at the end of the year, not decided, and the results are predictably expensive.

Two forces appear to be at work in publicly financed systems that use countervailing buyer power to balance inflationary pressures in medical care. First, other public institutions compete for the tax funds that medical care claims. These competitors, whether departments of education, transportation, or finance, have obvious organizational incentives to voice the "opportunity costs" of medicine.

Second, concentrating political accountability for insurance powerfully constrains any cost shifting to patients and other payers. In the current medical market, bargaining and information imbalances—as well as the organization of providers and insurers into well-financed pressure groups—allow providers to drive up costs. The payer side must have a correspondingly concentrated interest to balance those stakeholders who regard expenditures as benefit, not cost. Under a publicly financed and publicly administered system, the health professions would face what amounts to a consumer's cooperative in bargaining over the annual health budget. Balancing these interests does not mean health expenditures will assume any particular level and stay there, but it is a necessary condition for constraining these costs.

Public financing through earmarked premiums and taxes makes Canadian health outlays highly visible to the public. Such financing in the United States may mean that individual citizens, instead of paying a mix of out-of-pocket expenses, premiums for health insurance, and direct and indirect taxes, would pay explicit, earmarked premiums to a trust fund for a universal health insurance program. In the aggregate, Americans could well pay less for a sensible national health insurance program than they pay under present arrangements. More important than the precise method of the levy is that government be held accountable for its financing and administration.

Free choice of providers. Most Americans want the freedom to choose their doctors and other medical-care professionals without interference, whether from HMOs, insurance companies, or the government. Moreover, U.S. doctors understandably want freedom to provide care without distracting second-guessing or preclearance procedures.

Portability. The lack of portable coverage locks workers into jobs some would rather leave, and makes others fearful that if they lose their job, they will also lose their health insurance. It also concentrates risks and costs in relatively small groups. Particularly in a context of low union membership and fewer long-term relationships between workers and employers, linking insurance to employment makes far less sense than in earlier decades.

Policy Recommendations

LONG-TERM OPTIONS: KEEPING THE GOAL IN MIND

A national health insurance plan could provide comprehensive, universal insurance coverage and quality care at lower costs than America's current arrangements. Every American citizen would be given a computerized health insurance card. Americans would be free to choose their doctor or hospital of choice. Patients would not have to file claims, much less deal with incomprehensible forms. Administrative costs would be significantly lower, and frustration levels would be reduced. Medical-care dollars would no longer be wasted on eligibility determinations, insurance marketing, or risk evaluations to set different premium rates. Physicians would not need to obtain approval from administrators for the treatment they recommend. They would bill the new insurance plan on a fee-for-service, per-capita, or other arranged basis.

Doctors who choose to remain eligible for reimbursement by the national health insurance plan would not be able to bill patients extra by charging a fee in excess of the health plan's negotiated rate. Private insurance plans would cover only those services not insured by the new insurance plan. The national health insurance plan would use its countervailing buyer power to negotiate fee schedules (uniform rates at which insurers reimburse providers) with physicians, and global budgets (including operating and capital budgets) with hospitals in full view of the public, and thus in a democratically accountable fashion. The insurance plan could be financed through earmarked taxes and administered, as Senator Tom Daschle has suggested, through an independent agency or agencies akin to the Federal Reserve Board.

The Federal Government need not prescribe the details of state administration. The plan could be partially financed and administered by state governments and could be adapted to reflect local preferences. To receive federal funding, however, the state programs should be required to fulfill the five principles outlined in the previous section.

The U.S. General Accounting Office has estimated that a universal health plan like Canada's, if implemented in the United States, could provide universal coverage without copayments or deductibles for less than we currently spend for medical care and could result in significant long-term savings.[22] Moreover, while spending less, Canadians are more content with their medical-care arrangements. A 1989 study, for example, showed that 56 percent of Canadians reported overall satisfaction, compared to 10 percent of the American sample.[23] Are the desires of Canadian and American patients really so different, or is it their systems?

Finally, to the degree that cost control works, it necessarily frustrates the income aspirations of at least some health professionals. Physicians' fees, for example, are an estimated 234 percent higher in the United States than in Canada, and the take-home pay of American physicians is on average more than 50 percent higher than that of Canadian doctors. The salaries of American hospital executives grew 8.5 percent in 1989, while the CPI increased by only 4.6 percent.[24] But even with the countervailing power of Canada's national health insurance, its doctors remain the highest-paid professionals in Canada.[25]

Cost control may, of course, also threaten the quality of care. But medical-care professionals can justifiably mobilize public support to make sure that cost restraints do not seriously lower the quality of care. These fights make the regular determination of hospital budgets, and especially doctors' fees, very contentious matters. It is essential to design formats, select negotiators, and employ modes of public explanation that do not worsen the pain that such struggles over budgetary goals entail.

SHORT-TERM OPTIONS: HOW TO GET THERE FROM HERE

A straightforward version of national health insurance is ethically and financially desirable, politically feasible, and administratively implementable. We suggest implementation based on the three building blocks outlined below. What is crucial is that any national health insurance plan begin with the proper structure, and that key financing and administrative choices are made clearly at the beginning of the process. In particular, cost-control mechanisms through physician fee schedules or per-capita rates, and hospital reimbursement rates or global budgets, need to be put in place at the outset. Access can be increased sequentially by population group or type of service.

Universal maternal and well-child insurance plus stopgap measures in Medicare reform and tax credits for catastrophic coverage. Lack of access to affordable prenatal and childhood care remains one of this country's largest moral failures. Such care is also often highly cost-effective. Because Americans in general and doctors in particular tend to be the most concerned about access for this group, the next Administration could begin a national health insurance plan by replacing private insurance arrangements with publicly financed *universal* insurance coverage for prenatal and well-child care. Such an effort would also set citizens down the road toward thinking about health insurance in the same way that we currently think about Social Security insurance—that is, as a universal program, not as a means-tested, targeted program for the poor. Earmarked premiums proportional to income would be paid into national or state trust funds. Doctors could be paid on a fee-for-service basis, and hospitals reimbursed through global budgets for such care, per capita, or on the basis of a predetermined rate for a given illness or treatment.

In addition, to expand coverage for the elderly—a group already largely covered for many essential procedures—Medicare reform is needed to fill gaps and simplify administrative procedures.

Finally, catastrophic protection with a high deductible (e.g., 15 percent of income) could then be provided for *all* Americans through refundable tax credits, but only as a stopgap toward fundamental reform. These steps admittedly would do little comprehensive about cost control or access. Yet they would increase access and financial security, begin moving the United States toward universal coverage, and refrain from adding more complicated layers of tinkering to the already muddied American medical-care scene.

Universal hospital insurance. The second step would replace private insurance coverage for hospital care with a universal hospital insurance plan paid through income-based premiums placed in a trust fund. Hospital care constitutes the most expensive and largest component of health expenditures (about 40 percent), but one third of our hospital beds are empty; there is clearly excess supply. Existing prospective payment systems used by Medicare and many private insurers can be expanded to establish rates to reimburse hospitals for the care of all their patients. Then, to make cost control even more effective, governmental bodies could negotiate global budgets for hospitals. Expanding access while setting global budgets probably would not add to present overall expenditures (since most hospital care is "paid for" in some way or another already). Financing universal hospital insurance would address problems of access, uncompensated care, and medical bankruptcy, particularly relieving the stresses now being placed on large urban hospitals.

Universal physician coverage. The third step—providing universal physician coverage—would likely cost government less, since physician services currently comprise less than 20 percent of total health expenditures. The United States could draw on its experience designing fee schedules for physician services in the Medicare program, or the experiences of HMOs in setting per-capita reimbursement rates. By negotiating with provider groups to set rates for all payers, government can constrain physician expenditures. Moreover, although doctors have an obvious hostility to price setting and budget limits, they are dismayed by the large number of uninsured patients, irritated by complicated and intrusive forms of utilization review, and burdened with massive paperwork. They thus may be more inclined to agree to such a plan than conventional wisdom would lead one to believe.

STATE EXPERIMENTATION

If the Federal Government fails to act decisively to address the health care crisis, states will likely continue to experiment on their own. Just as the province of Saskatchewan's hospital insurance plan led the way toward national health insurance in Canada, state experimentation with publicly financed universal health insurance may prove useful in this country to spur federal action. Similarly, just as the Canadian program itself is administered by its provinces and territories, so, too, could an American single-payer system be administered by state, regional, or local entities. Two elements of caution, though: First, the more buyers and levels of government involved, the more diffuse the countervailing power. Second, state plans face dim prospects unless they receive considerable financial and administrative assistance from the Federal Government.

Conclusion

IN 1992, universal health insurance moved to the top of the American political agenda, prompting furious debate and ideological name-calling in the presidential electoral campaign. For the forty-second President coming into office in January 1993, no other domestic question, save the overall state of the economy, can be more important. The status quo is unacceptable to a vast majority of Americans. On its present trajectory, the costs of medical care will not only continue to burden U.S. business and labor but also will consume all the marginal resources that recovery from the recession might bring to public finance. Reform of the fundamental ground rules of medical finance and accessibility, then, should be the centerpiece of the first hundred days in office.

Other health and medical care matters should await those reform proposals. Some of these programs—for example, health insurance for federal employees, and programs involving Veterans Administration hospitals—would be directly affected by the enactment of national health insurance and structural reform in the medical care economy. Others would need to be addressed as part of the discussion among government, health care providers, and the citizenry—for example, tort reform, and the availability of health care in rural areas and inner cities.

Finally, any attempt at reform must show sensitivity to the administration of health insurance in ways that too often get neglected. First, the system needs to be understandable to most Americans. And second, Americans must have channels to participate in the formulation and evaluation of medical policy affecting the most intimate features of our lives. Commentary, complaint, and suggestion—the voice of democracy—should not be left to interest groups and political theory. As the new Administration selects its course from among the available options, it should neither tinker with medical care nor tether the public. In the process of a fundamental restructuring of our health care system, citizens must be empowered to monitor the performance of a universal health insurance plan for which Americans have waited so long.

NOTES

1. In 1986, U.S. life expectancy of females was 78.3 years, and of males 71.3 years, compared, respectively, with 79.7 and 73.0 years for Canada, and 78.4 and 71.8 years for Germany. The U.S. infant mortality rate (deaths per 1,000 live births) in 1988 was 10.0 compared with 7.2 for Canada and 7.6 for Germany. *OECD Health Database* (1991).

2. *The New York Times* (December 30, 1991), p. A10. In 1990 the United States spent $666 billion, or 12.2% of GNP. Katharine R. Levit et al., "National Health Expenditures 1990," *Health Care Financing Rev.* (Fall 1991): 29.

3. *See* Emily Friedman, "The Uninsured: From Dilemma to Crisis," *JAMA* 265 (1991): 2491; *Canadian Health Insurance: Lessons for the United States* (Washington, D.C.: U.S. General Accounting Office, 1991), p.24.

4. Robert J. Blendon et al., "Satisfaction with Health Systems in Ten Nations," *Health Affairs* (Summer 1990): 185.

5. Humphrey Taylor and Uwe E. Reinhardt, "Does the System Fit?," *Health Mgmt. Q.* (Third Quarter 1991): 4.

6. D. Callahan, "Allocating Health Resources," *Hastings Center Rep.* (April/May 1988): 14, 15.

7. R. Blendon, "The Public's View of the Future of Medical Care," *JAMA* 259 (1988): 3587.

8. *See* William B. Schwartz, "The Inevitable Failure of Current Cost-Containment Strategies: Why They Can Provide Only Temporary Relief," *JAMA* 257 (1987): 220.

9. Robert G. Evans, "Tension, Compression, and Shear: Directions, Stresses, and Outcomes of Health Care Cost Control," *J. Health Pol. Pol'y & L.* 15 (1990): 101,115.

10. Amitai Etzioni, "Health Care Rationing: A Critical Evaluation," *Health Aff.* 9 (Summer 1991): 88, 91; Morris L. Barer et al., "Canadian/U.S. Health Care: Reflections on the HIAA's Analysis," *Health Aff.* 10 (Fall 1991): 229, 233–34 (average annual growth in real per capita costs for administering U.S. system, over 5 percent; in Canada, only 1.6 percent).

11. Robert G. Evans et al., "Controlling Health Expenditures—The Canadian Reality," *New Eng. J. Med.* 320 (1989): 571, 573.

12. Paul Cotton, *Preexisting Conditions Hold Americans Hostage to Employers & Insurance, JAMA* 265 (1991): 2451.

13. Nicole Lurie et al., "Preventive Care: Do We Practice What We Preach?," *Am. J. Pub. Health* 77 (1987): 801, 803–4; Emmett B. Keeler and John E. Rolph, "The Demand for Episodes of Treatment in the Health Insurance Experiment," *J. Health Econ.* 7 (1988): 337, 363. By reducing utilization, cost sharing also has a negative

effect on the health of children and pregnant women and reduces the life expectancy of poor individuals with high blood pressure. See Robert H. Brook et al., "Does Free Care Improve Adults' Health?," *New Eng. J. Med.* 309 (1983): 1426, 1431; Arleen Leibowitz, "Effect of Cost-sharing on the Use of Medical Services by Children: Interim Results from a Randomized Controlled Trial," *Pediatrics* 75 (1985): 942.

14. Martin F. Shapiro, "Out-of-Pocket Payments and Use of Care for Serious and Minor Symptoms," *Archives Internal Med.* 149 (1989): 1645–48. Cf. Martin F. Shapiro et al., "Effects of Cost Sharing on Seeking Care for Serious and Minor Symptoms," *Annals Internal Med.* 104 (1986): 246, 250.

15. Keeler & Rolph, "The Demand for Episodes of Treatment," 7:363; Kathleen N. Lohr et al., "Use of Medical Care in the RAND Health Insurance Experiment: Diagnosis and Service-Specific Analyses," *Med. Care* (Sept. 1986 Supp.): S1, S72; Albert L. Siu et al., "Inappropriate Use of Hospitals in a Randomized Trial of Health Insurance Plans," *New Eng. J. Med.* 315 (1986): 1259.

16. Martin Pfaff, "Differences in Health Care Spending Across Countries: Statistical Evidence," *J. Health Pol. Pol'y & L.* 15 (1990): 1, 14, 20.

17. Evans, "Tension, Compression, and Shear," 15:120. Experience shows that none of the Canadian provinces believes that cost sharing will save them money by reducing utilization. By law, "a province which imposed user charges would have its federal grant reduced by the amount of the charges, but it would still retain all savings from reduced utilization. No province now has user charges." Id.

18. Levit et al., "National Health Expenditures 1990": 30.

19. Butler advocates high copayments and deductibles to prod consumers into cost-conscious medical choices. Enthoven eschews out-of-pocket payments in favor of price competition for premiums among a limited number of insurers.

20. Albert Hirschman, *Exit, Voice & Loyalty* (1970).

21. In contrast to these "play or pay" proposals, in Germany government plays a powerful role in guiding negotiations among physicians, hospitals, and "sickness funds" to set all-payer reimbursement rates and underwriting rules. These nonprofit funds essentially function as agents of the government and cannot compete in any meaningful way for consumers.

    In the mid-1960s, Canadian provinces could, and some did, use preexisting health insurance firms as "post offices," intermediaries (for the flow of funds and the processing of claims) between the provincial authorities and physicians. (Medicare operates in a similar fashion in this country.) Contracting out financial tasks is certainly compatible with political accountability, as the Canadian experience demonstrates. Within a few years, however, the Canadians found such indirect management cumbersome and much more expensive to manage than direct administration. Moreover, this approach is incompatible with continued competition among insurance companies as medical underwriters. Playing that game means a continuation of the uneven insurance coverage and adverse risk selection of the 1980s.

22. *Canadian Health Insurance*, pp. 67–68. A similar program in Canada has provided its citizens with high-quality care at much lower costs than in the United States. Before fully implementing universal health insurance in 1971, Canada financed its medical care in roughly the same way that the United States did. At the time, Canada spent approximately the same proportion of its Gross National Product on medical care as the United States did, and its costs were increasing at about the same rate as U.S. costs. Since 1971, Canada's health expenditures in relation to its national income and population have essentially stabilized in real terms, while ours have

steadily increased. Canada now spends 30 percent less of its GNP on medical care than we do, and the difference is growing. See Evans et al., "Controlling Health Expenditures," 320:571; Barer et al., "Canadian/U.S. Health Care," 10:229.

23. Robert J. Blendon et al., "Satisfaction with Health Systems in Ten Nations," *Health Aff.* (Summer 1990): 185, 188.

24. Regina Herzlinger, "Healthy Competition," *Atlantic Monthly*, (August 1991), p. 74.

25. See generally Robert G. Evans, *Strained Mercy* (1984); Morris L. Barer et al., "Fee Controls as Cost Control: Tales from the Frozen North," *Milbank Q.* 66 (1988): 1.

REDUCING POVERTY

ROBERT GREENSTEIN

Summary

NEARLY 36 MILLION AMERICANS—one in seven—lived in poverty in 1991, the largest number in more than a quarter century. Two fifths of them—or 14.3 million—were children. In the world's wealthiest nation, one in every four children under age six is poor. The child poverty rate in the United States is about double the rate in Canada and four times the average in Western Europe. The next Administration's challenge is to design policies that avoid the pitfalls of the U.S. welfare system—and partially replace that system—while reducing poverty more substantially and promoting values of work, family, and personal responsibility.

Such policies can be built on several principles:

• *"Make work pay."* A family with a parent who works full-time should not be poor. Achieving this goal entails expanding the earned income credit, a tax credit for low-income working parents, and strengthening the minimum wage, now well below its historical level. The dependent care tax credit, the government's principal child care subsidy, should be made "refundable" to enable working poor families to receive a credit payment.

• *Strengthen the child support system to make both parents assume responsibility for children.* The child support system should be overhauled to strengthen paternity establishment and toughen collection procedures. At the same time, a custodial parent who helps secure the establishment of a child support order—so that an absent parent meets his or her responsibilities—should be assured at least a modest level of child support. Work requirements can be imposed on absent parents who persistently fail to make their support payments due to lack of earnings. Training programs should be made available to improve their employability.

Robert Greenstein is Executive Director of the Center on Budget and Policy Priorities, a public policy institute in Washington, D.C.

• *Reform the income support system to support work and marriage while reducing child poverty.* This can be done through improved child support collections that do not decline if a single parent works or marries; increased resources for welfare employment and training programs so more recipients are helped to secure and retain jobs; other welfare reforms; and, if resources permit, a children's tax credit that also does not decline with work or marriage.

• *Promote mobility by easing barriers blocking poor inner-city residents from job and education opportunities in the suburbs.* Most new jobs, especially low-skilled jobs, are in the suburbs. The Federal Government can help improve access to suburban job markets for inner-city residents through expanded housing certificates and vouchers accompanied by housing location services, and through modifications in job training and transportation programs.

The Underlying Trends

WHILE A LINGERING RECESSION has pushed poverty up since 1989, long-term trends have been raising poverty rates for more than a decade, especially among families with children. In 1989, the peak year of the longest peacetime recovery since World War II, the poverty rate was higher than during the worst recession years of the 1970s.

Four underlying trends have been pushing up poverty rates: declining wages, a weakening safety net, a growing number of female-headed families, and the tendency of the economy to distribute most of the gains from economic growth to those already better off.

1. *Wage trends.* The poverty rate for families with children in which the family head works was nearly 50 percent higher in 1991 than in 1979. In fact, about 60 percent of all poor families included a worker in 1990 (working an average of about 35 weeks during the year[2]), as did nearly two thirds of all poor families with children.

Moreover, a major study by economist Rebecca Blank, a former senior staff economist on President Bush's Council of Economic Advisers, found that employment among the low-income population rose *more* during the recovery of the 1980s than during the recovery of the 1960s, yet poverty fell less during the 1980s recovery. Why? Primarily because wages have been eroding since the 1970s, especially in low-skilled jobs. The average hourly wage for nonmanagement jobs in the private sector is now lower than at any time since 1967. And by 1990, nearly one of every five full-time year-round workers was paid wages too low to lift a family of four to the poverty line.

2. *A contracting safety net*. Government assistance now lifts out of poverty a smaller proportion of low-income families with children than in the late 1970s. The safety net has eroded in two principal areas: aid to the jobless and cash assistance to poor families. Following budget cuts at both federal and state levels, the proportion of the unemployed receiving unemployment insurance set a record low in five of the six years from 1984 to 1989, with only one third of the jobless receiving unemployment benefits.

The reductions are equally striking in the Aid to Families with Dependent Children (AFDC) program, the welfare program for very poor families with children. By January 1992, the welfare benefit in the typical (or median) state for a family of three with no other income had fallen 43 percent below the 1970 level, after adjusting for inflation. The total value of AFDC and food stamps *combined* for a family of four with no other income is, in the average state, back to the level of AFDC alone in 1960, before the food stamps program was created. The AFDC cuts aimed at working poor families have been even more severe; few such families still qualify for aid.

On a positive note, Congress and the president have expanded the earned income tax credit (EITC), a refundable tax credit that supplements wages for low-and moderate-income working families with children—although not enough to compensate for the loss in AFDC benefits. When wages, AFDC, food stamps, and EITC benefits are added—and federal income and payroll taxes subtracted—a mother with two children who works and earns wages equal to 75 percent of the poverty line had $3,000 *less* in real disposable income in the average state in 1991 than she would have had in 1972.

3. *Demographic changes*. The increase in the proportion of families headed by single mothers has also pushed up poverty rates. The poverty rate among female-headed families with children is nearly six times the rate among married-couple families with children. Close to half of all female-headed families with children are poor. About two of every five people in poverty live in a female-headed family.

4. *Growing income disparities*. The fourth factor, which rests in part on the first three, is the increasing tendency of the economy to distribute its benefits unevenly. An analysis by the Congressional Budget Office found that between 1977 and 1989, the average after-tax income of the bottom fifth of the population dropped 9.5 percent, while the average income of the middle fifth edged up 5 percent. At the same time, the top fifth gained

33 percent, and the average after-tax income of the top 1 percent of the population more than doubled, rising 104 percent. Among families with children, the trend toward growing income disparities was even sharper, with the bottom fifth suffering a loss of more than 18 percent in average after-tax income during this period.

The Challenge

TACKLING POVERTY IS NOT SIMPLY A SOCIAL or an ethical issue, but an economic one as well. Other Western nations have far lower poverty rates than we do. Our willingness to tolerate so much more poverty—especially among children, the work force of the future—could hinder our competitive standing down the road. Increasingly, corporate executives, organized through institutions such as the Committee for Economic Development, are urging stronger action to combat child poverty.

There is no "silver bullet." No single policy or program can turn things around by itself. Beyond the policy prescriptions recommended in the next section, two core principles should guide the new Administration's efforts against poverty:

First, there should be a reciprocal responsibility binding both poor families and the government. Parents should work if they are able, absent parents should pay child support, and custodial parents should help ensure that child support can be collected. The government, in turn, should provide effective education and training programs and employment opportunities, effective child support collection mechanisms, and adequate wage levels and fair tax and benefit policies so these families need not be poor.

Second, to the extent possible, new antipoverty initiatives should be race-neutral and operate outside the traditional welfare system. Policies that are viewed as race-specific or that are focused primarily on very poor, nonworking families become contentious. The poverty policies that have generated the broadest support in recent years are those that stress nonwelfare approaches, include working families in the $10,000 to $20,000 or $25,000 annual income range along with the poor, and that do not have a race-specific connotation.[3]

A key challenge is to overhaul the income support system in a manner consistent with these principles. The recent study that found much higher poverty rates in the United States than in Canada or Western Europe also discovered that these large differences in poverty rates do *not* stem from differences between the United States and the other nations in work effort or welfare dependence, or race or family structure. For example, poverty rates among non-Hispanic whites in the United States are substantially higher than the poverty rates for the entire populations of the other nations studied.

Rather, the study found that the single most important factor explaining the higher U.S. poverty rates is much weaker government benefit and tax credit policies here. The poverty rate *before* taxes and government benefits is about the same in the United States as in Western Europe. But the poverty rate *after* taxes and benefits is far greater here.

A central challenge is to develop policies that avoid the political and substantive pitfalls of the current U.S. welfare system—and partially replace that system—while offering stronger income support and promoting rather than undercutting the values of work, family, and personal responsibility.

Initiatives for a New Administration

STRONG POLICIES TO "MAKE WORK PAY"

Families that work full-time should not be poor. Hence, full-time work at the minimum wage should lift a family to the poverty line when other supports such as the earned income credit are counted and payroll taxes are subtracted. Policies to "make work pay" include reforms in the earned income tax credit and the child care tax credit, an adjustment in the minimum wage, and universal access to health care coverage so families who move from welfare to work do not lose health insurance.

Expanding the EITC. An increase in the earned income tax credit, widely supported by liberals and conservatives alike, is at the center of a reinvigorated "make work pay" strategy. The EITC is prowork and profamily, being provided only to parents who work and who live with their children. In addition, the credit is "refundable," meaning that families that earn too little to owe income tax still receive it. And unlike welfare payments that can drop a dollar for each additional dollar earned, EITC payments *rise* with earnings until a family's income reaches about $7,500, thereby encouraging employment among those who otherwise work little if at all. More than 13 million low-income working families with children now receive the EITC, nearly three times the number of families getting welfare.

To enable full-time working parents to raise their families to the poverty line, the EITC needs to be enlarged and adjusted to reflect family size more adequately.

Family needs increase with family size. The poverty line and welfare benefits do as well. But wages do not. As a result, as the number of children in a low-wage family grows, the family falls steadily farther below the poverty line—and wages become increasingly less competitive with welfare.

To help address this problem, Congress established two tiers to the earned income tax credit in 1990: a basic benefit for a family with one child, and a benefit about $150 a year higher for a family with two or more children. But the adjustment is too small—much smaller, in fact, than the increase in the poverty line or in welfare benefits for an additional child.

A restructured EITC would boost the benefit for families with two children and create a third tier for families with three or more children, as recommended in 1991 by the bipartisan National Commission on Children. Census data show that *60 percent* of all children in working poor families live in families with three or more children.

What About Food Stamps? When determining whether wages and benefits bring working families to the poverty line, should food stamps be included in the computation, along with the minimum wage and the EITC? It is preferable not to include food stamps, since only 32 percent of the working households eligible for food stamps receive them. In addition, a substantial fraction of working poor families are not eligible because they do not meet the outdated food stamp assets limits. As a result, including food stamps means that while policies can be developed under which working families appear, on paper, to be brought to the poverty line, many such families will actually remain poor. In addition, the preferred support structure is one under which a full-time working parent can lift his or her family out of poverty without having to go to the welfare office.

If food stamps are included in the calculation, however, strong steps need to be taken to enhance access to the program by the working poor. A recent Agriculture Department study found that working households who try to get food stamps often lose wages because they must take off from work to apply at the welfare office.

The Minimum Wage. Besides the EITC, the other central factor in determining whether a low-wage worker can raise his or her household to the poverty line is the minimum wage. The wage standard has eroded substantially in recent years: While full-time work at the minimum wage typically lifted a family of three to the poverty line in the 1960s and 1970s, it leaves such a family nearly $2,000 below the poverty line in 1992.

Most minimum-wage workers are not poor, usually because there are other earners in the household. But a Congressional Budget Office study found that in 1987, nearly three of every five poor workers paid by the hour had earnings at or below what the minimum-wage would have been had it kept pace with inflation during the 1980s. The erosion in the minimum wage during the 1980s clearly increased the ranks of the working poor.

The principal argument against raising the minimum wage is that doing so would result in substantial job loss. In part, this argument rests on studies of labor markets of the 1960s and 1970s. New research conducted by leading labor economists, however, shows that the minimum-wage increases instituted in 1990 and 1991 did *not* reduce employment and had positive effects on the incomes of low-wage workers[4]—probably because labor markets have changed and the minimum wage now appears to be so low that it can be raised modestly with at most a small effect on employment. A growing number of economists who previously opposed a minimum wage increase now are reconsidering their position. Examination of the new evidence and a willingness to rethink old views are in order here.

A modest minimum wage increase would help raise working families to the poverty line. It would also moderate the degree to which the earned income tax credit had to be increased, thereby making the EITC enlargement less costly.

The Dependent Care Tax Credit. If wages and income supports lift a working family to the poverty line but health and child care costs consume a sizable chunk of the family's income, the family will remain stuck in poverty conditions. On the child care front, a simple step should be taken: The dependent care tax credit, the government's principal child care subsidy, should be made refundable.

Through this credit, the government provides nearly $3 billion a year in subsidies to families for dependent care costs. But because the credit is not refundable, working poor families are ineligible while near-poor working families receive only a tiny credit. Only 9 percent of the subsidies provided by the credit go to the bottom 40 percent of households.

Making the credit refundable, a reform that passed the Senate with bipartisan support in 1990, would solve this problem. Internal restructuring of the dependent care credit can offset a portion of the costs.[5] (Making work pay also entails access to health insurance, an issue treated elsewhere in this volume, and reducing the penalties the welfare system now imposes on welfare mothers who go to work, a matter treated later in this chapter.)

REFORMING THE INCOME SUPPORT SYSTEM TO PROMOTE SELF-SUFFICIENCY AND REDUCE CHILD POVERTY

Just as important as "making work pay" is overhauling the income support system so it promotes work and parental responsibility and reduces child poverty more effectively.

Child Support Enforcement and Insurance. Some 16 million children—one in four—lived in a single-parent family in 1990. About half of all children born in the United States today will spend some of their childhood in a single-parent home.

Single parents often find themselves in a difficult position. They are responsible for the economic support of their children, with no second earner in the family to supplement their earnings. And they are solely responsible for childrearing, which often makes it difficult to work full-time. Even married mothers who share childrearing responsibilities with a spouse usually do not work full-time year-round; only one third do.

These constraints make the provision of child support payments by absent parents (typically the father) vital. In 1989, however, about three of every five single-parent families received *no child support at all* from the absent parent. One result: When fathers leave their families, the poverty rate among children in these families doubles.

Overhaul of the child support system should be a priority for the next Administration and Congress, starting with a thoughtful bipartisan proposal unveiled in 1992 by Representatives Tom Downey and Henry Hyde. The proposal would strengthen child support collections through federal guidelines to assure that adequate child support awards are established and updated over time and by federalizing child support collections, instituting more vigorous procedures to establish paternity, implementing broader mechanisms for withholding child support obligations from wages, and imposing stiff penalties for nonpayment. Federalizing collections will help surmount the problem of fathers moving to other jurisdictions to evade their responsibilities. An Urban Institute study found that total child support payments would *quadruple* if all custodial parents had adequate awards and all noncustodial parents paid their full obligation.

The proposal also would impose tough work requirements on absent parents who persistently fail to meet their child support obligations due to lack of earnings, accompanied by employment and training services to improve the employability of absent parents, along with some public service jobs.

In addition, the proposal would transform child support into an insurance program. This would address circumstances in which little child support is collected because the father is employed at a very low wage, temporarily unemployed, disabled, or otherwise unemployable. If a child support order was established against the absent parent, the government would guarantee a minimum payment of about $165 per month for the first child and smaller amounts for additional children. Then, if the absent parent earned too little to pay this much, the government would provide the difference. This would cushion children in middle-class as well as poor families from a sudden decline in the noncustodial parent's income, preventing many nonpoor children from slipping into poverty.

In addition, child support insurance would radically alter the employment incentives facing single parents and make it much more feasible for single parents to work—because the child support guarantee payments would not decline if a mother got a job or worked more hours. By contrast, AFDC penalizes mothers who try to work by ultimately reducing their AFDC checks by a dollar for each additional dollar earned.

Child support insurance also would substantially lessen welfare use, since a family's AFDC payments would be reduced by the amount of its child support payments. Some would leave the welfare rolls altogether. Furthermore, because child support payments would substitute for welfare benefits, single mothers would be better off than under the current welfare system only if they went to work.

The bottom line would be much stronger incentives for the custodial parent *both* to secure a child support order against the absent father and to go to work—and a clear message that there is no "free ride" in fathering a child. These bold reforms should spur large increases in child support collections, greater work effort, and reduced child poverty and welfare receipt. A major demonstration testing a variant of this approach in seven New York counties produced impressive results, including a 25 percent increase in earnings and work hours, a 50 percent increase in new child support orders, and higher family incomes among program participants than among a control group—with no increase in benefit costs to the state. The project increased work and parental responsibility and reduced child poverty without cost to taxpayers.

Reforms in Welfare. Improvements in these areas will lessen the need for welfare. But reform of the welfare system itself is also essential to help families leave welfare and support themselves at a level that enables them to escape poverty.

Some states are attempting to alter the behavior of AFDC families through changes in welfare benefits. Under "learnfare," for example, a family's benefits are reduced if a child in the family has too many school absences. The "family cap" approach eliminates additional benefits if a woman conceives a child after going on AFDC.

But there is no evidence that such approaches work. The only evaluation of a learnfare program, conducted in Milwaukee, found it failed to improve school attendance. In addition, most experts believe that "family caps" will have little impact, since research indicates that AFDC benefit levels have little effect on the number of out-of-wedlock births or the size of AFDC families. And even without a family cap, large families have been on the decline for some time among AFDC recipients. In 1969, one third of AFDC families had four or more children; today, fewer than one in ten do.

The sole innovation in AFDC that has been proven to help recipients become more self-supporting is the welfare-to-work approach embodied in the Job Opportunities and Basic Skills program (JOBS) established by the Family Support Act, the bipartisan welfare reform law enacted in 1988.

In April 1992, the first major evaluation was issued of a program fitting the characteristics prescribed by the Family Support Act—the GAIN program in California, which mandates education and training for AFDC recipients. The study found that after one year, AFDC single parents participating in GAIN had earnings 17 percent higher than AFDC recipients in control groups and received lower welfare payments as a result. The findings were even positive for long-term AFDC recipients, a group not helped by earlier welfare-to-work programs that placed less emphasis on education and training.

Despite these encouraging results, the JOBS program is not being fully implemented. The Family Support Act provides $1 billion a year in federal funds for JOBS programs as long as states provide the required matching funds. But due to budget pressures, only nine states drew their full federal allotment for JOBS in fiscal year 1991. As a result, only about one in ten AFDC family heads now participates in JOBS. This suggests that state matching requirements should be reduced—and the amount of federal funds made available to states for the JOBS program increased—to benefit a larger proportion of AFDC recipients.

The next President will also face proposals for welfare changes in several other areas: requests for waivers allowing states to override federal welfare standards, proposals to ease work and marriage penalties in AFDC, and calls to place limits on how long a family can receive AFDC benefits.

Waivers should surely be available for demonstration projects to test approaches that hold promise of improving the welfare system. But federal waiver authority should not be twisted out of shape to provide a back-door way for states to reduce AFDC benefits as a budget-cutting measure. For example, federal law prohibits a state from receiving federal Medicaid funds if it cuts AFDC benefits below the levels it paid in May 1988. Nevertheless, the Department of Health and Human Services has encouraged states to believe they can ignore this standard, reduce benefits further—even though the cost of living was 20 percent higher in mid-1992 than in May 1988—and receive a waiver for it. The next HHS Secretary should promptly reverse this policy. Otherwise, child poverty will increase further.

On another front, there is an emerging consensus to reduce the penalties for marriage and work now embedded in AFDC. An AFDC recipient and a low-wage worker can lose several thousand dollars if they marry, and AFDC recipients can become "worse off" if they work. States could be provided options not to reduce AFDC benefits a dollar for each dollar earned, to ease welfare rules that discriminate against two-parent families, and to modify how benefits are computed if a mother marries or remarries. Alternatively, the Federal Government could change these rules nationally. The child support insurance proposals outlined earlier also would make a large difference here.

Finally, should government limit the length of time a family can receive AFDC benefits? This approach has never been tried and raises several questions. What would be done to prepare recipients better to enter the job market before their benefits run out? What should happen to those still on AFDC at the end of the benefit period?

Even with a strengthened JOBS program that provides expanded employment services, a substantial minority of families are likely to remain on AFDC at the end of the benefit period—mostly those with the least education and employment experience and the most serious personal or family problems. Simply eliminating all benefits to them would likely lead to increased homelessness and child neglect.

Offering a guaranteed job to every AFDC recipient at the end of the benefit period would be more attractive but would cost billions of dollars. Without information on the impact of such a program on long-term recipients, it is not clear this is the best place to commit such large sums.

A third option—"workfare"—would continue to provide AFDC benefits but would require recipients to "work off" these benefits at unpaid employment. This is unlikely to make many recipients self-sufficient. Workfare participants are typically placed in temporary, low-skill jobs that do not provide training or enhance their ability to compete in the job market. Since those remaining on AFDC at the end of the benefit period are likely, by and large, to have the least education and the fewest skills, workfare is unlikely to improve their prospects significantly. Demonstration projects have shown that workfare fails to boost subsequent employment and earnings among long-term AFDC recipients and does not raise their skill levels.

What these participants appear to need is more education, job training, and other employment-related services. Rather than simply cutting off benefits after a time period or requiring all recipients to participate in workfare, continued receipt of benefits could be conditioned on participation in further education or job training programs or meeting other employment-related obligations.

Time-limiting proposals raise other issues as well. How would recipients who have young children and can work only part-time fare? Would they face a choice between full-time work and the loss of all income? To deal with this and other matters relating to time limiting, Harvard poverty expert David Ellwood—the originator of the time-limiting concept—has proposed tying a time limit on AFDC benefits to a series of other policy changes that would enable both two-parent families with a full-time worker and single parents who can only work part-time to escape poverty: child support insurance; a large EITC increase; minimum wage improvement; universal health care coverage; and both full-time and part-time public service jobs for recipients whose time on AFDC runs out and who do not find other employment. Ellwood has expressed strong reservations about instituting time limits without these policy reforms.

There are also questions about disabled AFDC recipients who do not qualify for the Supplemental Security Income program. More than 20 percent of female AFDC family heads are disabled. In addition, some single parents without a physical disability have psychological or other problems sufficiently serious to make it difficult for them to cope adequately with a job setting. What would happen to their families at the expiration of the time limit?

Because of the unanswered questions about time-limiting benefits, implementing such a policy immediately could have unforeseen consequences and lead to policy failure. It would be preferable if policymakers determined to pursue this concept tested it first through carefully designed demonstration projects to see which, if any, approaches to time limiting are effective in moving AFDC recipients into employment and to determine their overall impact on these families.

A Children's Tax Credit. Still another change in the income support system worth considering is institution of a refundable tax credit for children. In 1991, the National Commission on Children unanimously recommended converting the tax code's personal exemption for children into a universal tax credit of $1,000 per child. The tax credit would (a) close a long-standing policy gap between the United States and other Western industrial nations— virtually all of which have a children's credit or allowance; (b) improve tax progressivity; (c) significantly reduce child poverty while helping middle-class families as well; and (d) promote work, because the credit would not decline as earnings increased. A refundable children's credit could also ease the marriage penalties embedded in the welfare system.

The children's tax credit is highly desirable but also expensive. The commission's recommendation has a price tag of $40 billion a year, and even narrower versions of the program are costly. Considering the scarce funds available for new initiatives, other recommendations in this chapter should receive higher priority.

If, on the other hand, the new Administration finds the resources for, and wishes to propose, a "middle-class tax cut," then a refundable children's credit is, by far, the best tax cut option. There are two ways to design a children's credit at reduced cost. One is to reduce the credit to well below $1,000 and eliminate a substantial part—but not all—of the personal exemption for children. For example, the personal exemption for children could be reduced from $2,350 in 1993 to $1,000, while a $375-per-child tax credit was established. Taxes would be unchanged in the 28 percent tax bracket and raised marginally for those in the 31 percent bracket. For families in the 15 percent bracket, where the bulk of the middle class is found, a tax cut of about $170 per child would be provided. Poorer families would receive the full benefit of the new credit.

Another alternative would be to replace the personal exemption entirely with a tax credit of about $650, but only for young children (e.g., under six). Under either option, the credit eventually might be enlarged or expanded to older children if economic circumstances permitted.

Food Stamp Reform. Finally, the food stamp program, while well designed in most respects, has some serious flaws that call for reform.

The House of Representatives overwhelmingly approved a bipartisan package in 1990 that would correct features of the food stamp program that create disincentives for collection and payment of child support and also would equalize the program's treatment of elderly households and families with children with respect to housing costs. The food stamp program now takes into account all housing expenses of elderly and disabled households with very high housing cost burdens, but uses a more parsimonious formula for other households, most of which are poor families with children. The result is inadequate food stamp assistance for some families with children and who incur very high housing costs.

The bipartisan proposals to address these issues have not been enacted due to lack of agreement over how to pay for them. The next Administration should take the lead in breaking this logjam and should also restructure the troubled food stamp employment and training program.

"MOBILITY STRATEGIES" TO IMPROVE ACCESS TO JOBS AND EDUCATION

Because so many low-skilled jobs have moved from the cities to the suburbs over the past twenty years, the next Administration should develop "mobility strategies" to provide low-income city residents better access to job and educational opportunities in the suburbs.

Between 1980 and 1986, two of every three jobs added in metropolitan areas were located outside city boundaries. In Atlanta, 75 percent of the net new jobs created during this period were in the suburbs. In Washington, D.C., the figure was 91 percent; in Los Angeles, 95 percent; in Chicago, 100 percent. Inner-city residents often fail to learn of such job opportunities and, if they do, often have difficulty commuting to these job sites.

Enterprise zones and similar initiatives are unlikely to reverse these trends. As the Urban Institute has noted, "the record of attempts to halt or reverse the trend toward job decentralization is not encouraging. . . There are virtually no examples of success in restoring strong economic activity and job creation to an inner-city area the size of South Central Los Angeles. . . " This does not mean that development of inner-city areas should not be attempted. But as the Urban Institute cautions, development efforts are "no substitute for policies that open up access to the metropolitanwide job market."[6]

The Gautreaux program, which has operated in Chicago since 1976, offers one promising approach. Four thousand black families living in inner-city housing projects, all past or current AFDC recipients, were given rental subsidies and moved to private housing—some elsewhere in the city and others to the suburbs, as housing became available. Before the program started, the families who moved to the suburbs closely matched the families who moved within the city. But after moving, their experiences diverged sharply: the suburban-movers achieved much higher levels of employment; their children had substantially lower school dropout rates and higher rates of college attendance, sharply higher employment levels, and much higher average wage levels.

As the researchers noted, "This program revealed that these low-income people had capabilities that were not evident when they lived in the city. Adults were able to get jobs and youth were able to do much better in school, but these capabilities were hidden in the city." The more abundant job opportunities, especially for low-skilled individuals, and the superior educational systems in the suburbs appear to have made a large difference.

These results suggest that federal low-income housing resources should be much more heavily focused on providing certificates and vouchers that enable poor families to move to private housing in areas with better job and educational opportunities. This is a far cheaper alternative than costly programs that enable a tiny fraction of public housing residents to stay in and purchase their units (often at a cost to taxpayers of $50,000 or $100,000 per unit) or that construct large numbers of new public housing complexes in the inner cities.

The Gautreaux program also had another feature: It surmounted participants' fears of moving to unknown areas by enrolling supportive suburban landlords, as well as counselors who took families to visit the suburban communities. This paid off. The program did not involve either the construction of public housing complexes in the suburbs or the movement of large concentrations of inner-city families to particular suburban locations and did not spawn suburban backlash.

The next Administration should emphasize certificates and vouchers, linking them to housing location and counseling services. At the same time, means to improve access to suburban job markets for the many inner-city residents who will stay in the cities should also be pursued, by helping develop "reverse commuting" services in metropolitan areas; by encouraging locally administered employment and training programs to reorganize on a metro-wide rather than a county basis; and by orienting job training services provided to city residents toward suburban as well as central-city labor markets.

Of course, housing efforts are needed well beyond those than can be mounted through Gautreaux-like programs that provide location and counseling services. With 56 percent of all poor renters paying more than half their income for housing in 1989—and with 4 million fewer low-rent units than low-income renters—one of the next Administration's leading priorities in the poverty area should be major expansion of low-income housing assistance programs, principally through substantial increases in housing certificates and vouchers.

MAKING HARD CHOICES ON INVESTING SCARCE RESOURCES

Finally, Washington will have to make tough choices on where to invest resources. An Administration that announces an intention to rebuild the economy, improve public investment, reduce child poverty, or achieve other such goals will be faced with an onslaught of interest groups contending that their favored programs meet the Administration's goals. It will need to signal early on its determination to say "no" to many proposed domestic program and tax expenditure increases. Not every poverty program is a sparkling success or a priority for expansion, and some programs justified on grounds of their aid to the poor mostly benefit other groups whose claims for new resources are weak.

The next Administration should focus on what works and what doesn't. Expanding "early intervention" programs with a proven track record so they reach all eligible low-income children and youth—such as Head Start, the WIC nutrition program for pregnant women and young children, child immunization, community health centers, and the Job Corps—makes sense.[7] By contrast, decisions to raise benefits for Social Security "notch babies," expand the targeted jobs tax credit, or make school lunches free at all income levels, to name a few areas where organized constituencies are likely to push expansions and claim poverty-reducing effects, would represent unwise use of precious resources.

NOTES

1. This chapter benefited from comments by Kathryn Porter, Art Jaeger, Wendell Primus, Paul Leonard, Isaac Shapiro, Susan Steinmetz, and Edward Lazere.

2. The data showing that, on average, workers in poor households are employed during thirty-five weeks of the year are census data for 1987. More recent data are not available.

3. Recent policy improvements fitting this prescription include large expansions of the earned income tax credit, extension of Medicaid to substantial numbers of pregnant women and to children in poor and near-poor working families, creation of new child care programs, and expansion of the WIC program.

4. See research by David Card of Princeton, Lawrence Katz and Alan Krueger of Harvard, and Allison Wellington of Davidson College.

5. Under current law, the percentage of its child care costs a family can claim as a tax credit phases down from 30 percent to 20 percent over an annual income range ending at $28,000. A second phasedown, limiting the credit to 10 percent for families with yearly incomes over $100,000, could be added.

6. The Urban Institute, *Confronting the Nation's Urban Crisis* (1992), p. 17.

7. The need to expand these programs is covered elsewhere in this volume, as is the need for improvements in other areas key to poverty reduction such as education, training, child care, housing, and unemployment insurance.

CHILDREN

MARIAN WRIGHT EDELMAN

Summary

FOR TWO DECADES, declining wages and family incomes, rising housing and education costs, and falling marriage rates have battered American families and children. Key outcomes for children have stagnated or worsened. The American dream that each generation will be better off than the prior generation is in danger of dying.

But these results are not inevitable or unchangeable. They are a cause for action rather than paralysis. On some of the key indicators of children's well-being—such as child poverty, infant mortality, immunization, and teen birth rates—the United States has in the past achieved substantial and rapid improvements. Many other nations, some far poorer than we, have sharply lower infant mortality rates, at least in part because they ensure that all mothers receive prenatal care and support. They have held down their child poverty rates—even though their workers face the same international economic trends that have depressed the wages of less-educated American workers—by providing a safety net for all families with children.

The task of meeting our children's and our nation's urgent domestic needs has been too long deferred. Now the successful conclusion of the Cold War means that energy, attention, and funds exist to reverse the pattern of national neglect of families and children. We must take advantage of this historic opportunity to assure that no American child is left behind. The essential first steps are to make sure that every child receives a Head Start, a Fair Start, and a Healthy Start:

• *A Head Start*. Quality preschool, child care, and Head Start programs help keep children at grade level, help children get ready for school so they can become productive members of society, and prevent later costly special education and teen pregnancy. Over the next three years we must assure

---

Marian Wright Edelman is President of the Children's Defense Fund.

431

that all eligible children are able to participate in Head Start and have access to quality child care.

• *A Fair Start.* An unhealthy, homeless, or hungry child will not learn well. America's astronomical and self-defeating child poverty levels are far higher than those of other wealthy democracies. Families need basic economic security—starting with enough jobs at decent wages, a refundable children's tax credit, and assured child support.

• *A Healthy Start.* On many indices of child health, America ranks behind almost all of its competitors and economic peers. Federal law currently promises Medicaid health coverage to every poor child, but this will not be fully phased in until the year 2002. Children and mothers who need basic health care—including prenatal and maternity care, checkups, immunizations, and care for children who are sick or disabled—cannot wait another decade for health insurance and access to health care. They need access to health care now.

The Status of Children in America

FOR OVER A DECADE, America's children have become poorer, less likely to have health insurance or be properly immunized, and more likely to be homeless, neglected, or teen parents. Their parents have been battered by waves of recession, unemployment, wage stagnation, job insecurity, skyrocketing housing and health costs, and worries about crime-ridden neighborhoods. Surviving childhood, much less having the opportunities to develop as a healthy child, no longer can be taken for granted.

• More than 14 million children live in poverty in America—3 million more than in 1980. One in every five children in America is now poor; many more live in families with incomes only marginally above poverty. One in every four children under six years old is poor.

• In 1990 more than 25 million children—or 40 percent—lacked employer-based health insurance coverage. The majority are in working families. Of the 46 million children who did have private coverage, nearly 20 million will experience some period without health coverage by the end of 1992.

• Seven percent of all infants born in 1989 were born at low birth weight, the highest level in nearly two decades.

• In 1989, birth rates for teens aged fifteen to eighteen shot to their highest level in nearly two decades.

• Fewer of our children are vaccinated against preventable diseases such as like polio, measles, mumps, rubella, and pertussis than in the past. Measles epidemics are becoming common.

- More than 100,000 children are homeless in America every night.
- About 407,000 children are in foster family homes, group homes, or institutional settings—almost a 50 percent increase from the mid-1980s.

Our nation knows how to solve the problems of its children and families. A range of proven national, state, local, community, and private initiatives have helped in the past or in particular communities in the 1980s to reduce low birth weight births, infant mortality, child poverty, hunger, teen pregnancy, school dropouts, preventable diseases, and family breakup, and to increase children's school readiness, educational achievement and attainment, health status, hope, and self-esteem.

And we can afford to solve these problems. The extra tax breaks enacted by Congress and the president since 1977 gave just the wealthiest 1 percent of Americans an extra $39 billion in 1990 income alone. And with the Cold War over, many experts believe that our nation could reduce military spending this decade by as much as 50 percent and invest that money more wisely in our families, our schools, our health care system, and our economy. We have already wasted two years of this opportunity to rebuild our country's future. We can't afford to waste another day.

A Healthy Start

IN SPITE OF OUR WEALTH AND MEDICAL SOPHISTICATION, American children are perhaps the least healthy among children in affluent nations, due to poverty and lack of access to health care.

One in seven children—about nine million—has *no* health insurance at all. Even while general economic conditions improved over much of the 1970s and 1980s, workers and their children lost health insurance by the millions. Why? Most nonelderly adults and children get their health insurance through the adults' employer, who pays some or all of the premiums for a worker and, less frequently, for the worker's spouse and children as well. But employers have been cutting back dramatically on fringe benefits as well as wage levels.

By 1990 a total of 25 million children under age eighteen years—40 percent of all children—had no employer-based health policy. At the current pace, by the year 2000 half of American children won't have employer-based insurance. Medicaid, the Federal Government's insurance program for the poor, has only partly filled the growing void. Even middle-class parents often cannot afford to buy coverage on their own: a decent family health insurance package can cost upward of $6,000 a year. And medical care is so expensive that it is very hard for families to purchase without insurance. In addition,

Percentage of Children with Employment-Related Insurance

	1977	1987
All children	72.8	62.9
Poor children (family income below federal poverty level)	27.5	23.0
Moderate-income children (100–199% of federal poverty level)	63.4	47.0
Middle-income children (200–399% of federal poverty level)	83.6	79.0
Upper-income children (400% of federal poverty level and more)	85.4	86.9

millions of children in cities and rural areas don't have access to health services regardless of insurance status because there are few or no doctors, dentists or clinics—public or private—in their neighborhoods.

Due in significant part to growing poverty and the lack of access to health care, the proportion of pregnant women who get prenatal care in the first three months of pregnancy *fell* in the United States in the 1980s. One million babies a year are born to women who don't see a doctor in the first three months of pregnancy. The outcome of this dismal prenatal care record and of too much poverty and drug abuse? One quarter of a million babies are born at low birth weight each year, making the United States only thirty first in the world in 1990 in preventing low birth weight births.

The story is similar when it comes to infant mortality, in which the United States ranked twentieth in the world in 1990. And the United States now ranks seventeenth in immunizing one-year-olds against polio, and if we compare nonwhite U.S. child immunization rates to the overall rates in other nations, the United States would rank seventieth. In many of our cities, only one third or fewer of preschool children have gotten appropriate and timely vaccinations.

America's failing health care system wastes our children's potential and our nation's resources and inflicts unnecessary suffering, disease, and disability on far too many children and families. To provide all American children a healthy start in life, we must ensure that all children and families have financial access to health care; that all communities have enough doctors, clinics, and basic public health care services; and that all families can make use of the services they need to safeguard their children's health.

• We must join the remainder of the developed world in guaranteeing that all children and families have either public or private health insurance. Our health insurance system must cover all basic services for all children, parents, and pregnant women, including preventive as well as acute care.

• In addition, too many communities lack doctors, clinics, and basic public health services. The Federal Government should substantially increase support for community health centers, migrant health centers, health care for the homeless projects, and scholarships and loan repayment for the National Health Service Corps, and must fully fund the Title V Maternal and Child Health Services block grant.

• We must ensure that all children are fully immunized against preventable diseases. Like other countries, the Federal Government should establish a system of universal vaccine purchase and distribution to providers, whereby the government purchases enough vaccine for all children and distributes it free to doctors and clinics, who in turn immunize children without regard to their insurance coverage or family income.

• The government must put the supplemental Food Program for Women, Infants, and Children (WIC) on track to serve all eligible women, infants, and children by fiscal year 1996 to assure that every child entering school in the year 2000 will have received the prenatal care and nutrition assistance needed during the preschool years.

A Fair Start

IN A BIPARTISAN REPORT CALLED *The American Agenda*, addressed in the fall of 1988 to incoming President Bush, former presidents Ford and Carter urged that the needs of poor children be placed on the very short list of issues for "immediate decisions and actions":

> In the United States today, one child in five is poor. This is intolerable in history's richest nation. Children make up the biggest single segment of the 32 million Americans who live below the official poverty line. Children in poverty have a national economic impact as well, now and over the long term. The United States will need all of its children educated and trained for the tight labor market and increasingly complex skills of the 1990s and beyond. We believe that it would be imprudent to delay any longer on taking Federal action to begin the long process of assisting these children of poverty.

The nation has lost four years since this call for action. The situation has worsened: More than 14 million American children—more than one in five children—are now poor. This rate is two to fourteen times the rates in other wealthy countries that are our allies and economic competitors— Australia, Canada, Sweden, Germany, the Netherlands, France, and the United Kingdom. And it is destructive for our nation and the economy. Poor children are more likely to be born too small, to die, to be sick and hungry and malnourished, to fall behind in school and later to drop out, and to cost the nation billions of dollars in later remedial costs and lost productivity.

America's minority children are especially affected. Two fifths of black children and nearly two of five Latino children are poor, compared to one in six white children. But child poverty is truly an American problem that affects all, leaving 5.5 million white, non-Latino children, 4.4 million black children, 2.6 million Latino children, and 400,000 Asian American children poor in 1990. More than half of poor American children live in suburban and rural areas, small towns and cities.

How did this happen? From 1973 to 1990 the share of all income that went to the richest one fifth of Americans rose substantially, while the poorest one fifth of Americans saw their share of the country's total personal income fall by nearly one sixth. The middle class lost out as well. Families with children bore most of the brunt. Young families with children (with a family head under age thirty), in particular, saw their median income fall by one third over this seventeen-year period. Child poverty in these families more than doubled—most of the increase came in the eighties—despite increasing work effort.

Child poverty grew in the 1980s primarily because workers' wages dropped and because government programs failed to compensate for these labor market changes. The main cause was not more single-parent households or declining work effort among the poor. Work effort rose. The majority of poor families have at least one working parent, and many others could work if given the opportunity and modest support to do so. In fact, many young married-couple families have tried to compensate for lower wages and fewer benefits by sending a second worker into the work force. These second earners have softened (but not eliminated) the economic blow. But the growing number of young parents working longer hours or coping with two jobs has placed families with children under tremendous stress and generated new costs for the families, especially child care costs, that offset some of the second workers' income. Many families, moreover, have two jobs that together provide less security and less support and less access to health care than one good job did a generation ago. And this two-earner strategy is totally unavailable to the growing number of single-parent families.

What can government do? In Canada, Australia, and Western Europe in the 1980s, child poverty rates generally fell or stayed flat, even though they faced similar or worse macroeconomic problems than we did. But these other nations expanded rather than cut their antipoverty efforts. For example, in the United States the poverty rate in 1986 for children in single-parent families before counting income from government transfer payments was 58 percent. After government help was added, this poverty rate was reduced to only 54 percent. In that same year, the United Kingdom, with Margaret Thatcher as prime minister, had an even higher child poverty rate in single-parent families before government help was counted—71 percent. But after government payments, only 8.5 percent of single-parent families were left in poverty.

Unfortunately, our political leadership too often has used child poverty not as a cause for action but as an occasion to attack poor parents, using myths about their "values" and "behavior" and the role of welfare.

Welfare is not even an overwhelming share of the income of poor families with children; in fact, many poor families do not get government help. Earnings provide 54 percent of poor families' income. Child support, unemployment insurance and other such sources are 17 percent. All means-tested program income, including Aid to Families with Dependent Children (AFDC), is 29 percent of the income of poor families with children. Welfare also is not the cause of deficits: AFDC, the country's main welfare program, takes two cents of the state tax dollar in the average state, and less than one cent of the federal tax dollar.

And welfare is not destroying our society's values. Certainly teens should postpone sexual activity and pregnancy; people shouldn't have children until they are ready to support them financially and emotionally; parents should work to support their families; children should be born within the bounds of marriage; and children need two parents, although we must support and not stigmatize the often heroic efforts of single parents to raise children alone. These values are central, but welfare has not been the culprit in eroding them. There is strong evidence, for example, that welfare does not cause more teen pregnancy and teen births, does not cause women to have more babies to get welfare, and does not cause poor people to migrate to high-benefit states. For example, a U.S. Department of Health and Human Services study found no significant relationship between AFDC benefit levels and out-of-wedlock birth rates.

Instead of attacking welfare recipients, this nation must focus on eliminating child poverty, a goal well within our reach by the year 2000. We must both restore strong family values and, as a nation, again come to value helping those who either are trying to or cannot help themselves.

In their 1992 pastoral letter "Children and Families," the National Conference of Catholic Bishops captured this essential interplay of private and public values: "No government can love a child and no policy can substitute for a family's care," the bishops wrote, but "Government can either support or undermine families as they cope with the moral, social, and economic stresses of caring for children. . . . The undeniable fact is that our children's future is shaped both by the values of their parents and the policies of our nation."

Here are the essential first steps:

1. *A refundable children's tax credit.* As recommended by the National Commission on Children, the government should replace the personal exemption for children with a uniform and universal refundable credit—a modest $800 to $1,000 per child, available to every family with children either to reduce taxes or to be paid to the family if it has no tax liability to offset. The United States is the only Western industrialized democracy that does not have this type of children's credit, children's allowance, or other universal public benefit. The current personal exemption provides no assistance whatsoever to poor and moderate-income families with children (including millions of working families) that have no federal income tax liability, and gives middle-income families only half the help that it gives the wealthy.

2. *Child support assurance.* The government should assure that all children who are not living with both parents receive a minimally adequate child support payment from the absent parent through more vigorous federal and state enforcement efforts—to establish paternity, obtain support orders, and collect payments from absent parents.

And the government should establish a system of child support insurance for those cases when the amount of the child support order falls short or when payments cannot be or are not collected. The government would seek the funds from the absent parent.

Taken together, the children's tax credit and ensured child support benefit would provide a solid economic floor upon which families could build. If they were established at appropriate levels, a single parent with one or two very young children would be able to lift her—or his—family above the poverty line by working at least half-time at the minimum wage. Similarly, a married-couple family with two children and at least one worker employed full-time at the minimum wage would secure an income above the poverty line.

Currently, when a parent on AFDC goes to work, the family stands to lose most or all of the earnings as a result of increased taxes, reductions in benefits, and the costs of working. Instead, the combination of the children's tax credit and ensured child support could encourage and reward work effort, giving even the lowest-skilled or lowest-paid parents a base on which to build and stay out of poverty.

3. *Minimum wage.* Parents who can work should work, but in turn parents who work should not have to be poor or see their children suffering

in poverty. The efforts of parents to lift their families out of poverty will be successful only if the nation makes sure that the economic rewards of work are more adequate for family support. The government must revive its commitment to a "family wage" by moving to make up the ground the minimum wage has lost to inflation. In 1979 the national minimum wage for full-time work—forty hours a week, fifty two weeks a year—gave a family of three an income a little over the poverty line. In 1992 the same full-time, year-round minimum-wage job pays only three-fourths to the poverty line for the family.

4. *Earned income credit.* As a complement to a higher minimum wage, the federal earned income credit for low-income workers with children should be expanded, particularly for larger families, who typically suffer the most severe poverty, to ensure that no working family lives below the poverty line.

5. *Family leave.* The lack of even minimal assurances of parental leave from work at the time of birth, adoption, or family or medical emergencies forces working parents into a cruel choice between work and family responsibility. The next Administration should work with Congress to enact the Family and Medical Leave Act.

6. *Other initiatives.* The government can help AFDC families earn their way out of poverty by strengthening education and training opportunities— for example, expanding the successful Job Corps program to serve more severely disadvantaged youths. And it can reform AFDC by increasing financial incentives for recipients to work, by eliminating unreasonable asset limitations that keep poor families ineligible, and by removing rules that discourage two- parent families from participating. Establishing a true safety net also means reform of unemployment insurance eligibility rules to allow more low-wage and part-time workers to qualify for benefits, and an increase in AFDC benefits to compensate for cost-of-living increases in recent years.

Giving all children a Fair Start also requires reforming the child welfare system. Reports of child abuse and neglect skyrocketed in the 1980s. In 1990, an estimated 407,000 children were in foster family homes, group homes, or institutional settings, up from 270,000 in the early 1980s. Increasing numbers of infants and very young children are entering foster care. The dearth of treatment and rehabilitation options is also driving up the population of juveniles held in public detention, correction and shelter facilities. In the child mental health system, too, residential treatment has increased dramatically, despite the demonstrated effectiveness of community-based programs and estimates that 50 percent of youths in residential treatment receive inappropriate care. The reliance on out-of-home placements as a first response rather than a last resort not only overwhelms the system, fails to protect children, and tears apart many families unnecessarily, but also costs the taxpayers enormous sums of money.

Children who come to the attention of the child welfare, juvenile justice, and mental health systems often share many characteristics and have inter-related problems: histories of neglect, family violence, or family unemployment; low self-esteem; poor school performance; and unattended physical or mental health needs. They and their families generally need comprehensive, sustained, and individualized help to turn their lives around. They seldom receive it. Instead, they all too often are bounced from agency to agency, receiving partial, unrelated, and fragmented services.

Numerous successful programs have been developed over the past decade, based on two principles: that most families in crisis do want to be helped to protect their children better, and that most families can change when offered the right kind of help. Many of these family services must be developed at the state and local level, but the Federal Government can play an important role in strengthening services by:

• providing support for families whose children are at imminent risk of placement. The Federal Government guarantees federal matching money when states place children in foster care, but provides far fewer federal dollars to help states provide the types of services that could protect children and avert the need for foster care or prepare families to be reunited after separation;

• offering states help in building statewide networks of family resource and support programs, and family preservation programs.

A Head Start

IN 1991, a total of 67 percent of mothers with children younger than eighteen years, including 53 percent of women with a child younger than one year, were in the labor force. For many this was a matter of necessity— among them, single mothers without significant or reliable child support payment and women married to young men or with less than a college education, whose wages have decreased sharply over the past decades. As a result, about 10 million children spend a significant part of each weekday being cared for by someone other than their parents.

Every parent should have the opportunity to choose whether to combine parenting with work outside the home during a child's early years. Government can help mothers who prefer to stay at home by providing or mandating paid family leave, expanded income support, universal health coverage, a refundable children's tax credit, and child support assurance.

For families in which the mother has a job, whether by necessity or by choice, access to good, affordable child care is critical to the child's well-being. And for many groups of children, Head Start and other comprehensive child care programs go even farther in helping families. In addition to pre-school education, they provide health and nutrition services for children, social services for the whole family, and opportunities for parental involvement and support. And they are good investments: Every $1 spent on such programs saves an estimated $3 in future costs of school failure, teenage pregnancy, welfare, and crime.

In recent years the nation has made great strides toward ensuring that good-quality, affordable child care is more broadly available. In 1990 Congress passed the nation's first comprehensive child care legislation, which created two child care programs—the Child Care and Development Block Grant and the "At Risk" Child Care Program—and expanded the earned income credit to provide income support for low-income families with children.

Congress that year also approved a rapid expansion of Head Start to serve all eligible children by 1994. But appropriations have fallen short, so Head Start served only 30 percent of eligible children in 1992.

Too many American children still spend their days in unsafe child care, move frequently from one care arrangement to another, or do not receive the stimulation they need to get ready for school. For low-income children in particular, publicly assisted child care often remains extremely fragmented and uneven in quality.

While the funds flowing from the 1990 changes have helped hundreds of thousands of families, states still aren't able to come close to providing assistance for all families who need it. Moreover, low salaries make it difficult to attract and retain child care teachers, endangering the stable relationships children need. Teacher salaries declined by nearly one quarter between 1977 and 1988, after adjusting for inflation, even though teacher educational levels increased. And while child development experts recommend one caregiver care for no more than three or four infants, eighteen states allow child care centers to operate with five or more infants per adult.

The first national education goal adopted by the president and the governors in 1990 pledges that by the year 2000 every child will be ready for school. The most important step to reach that goal is a guaranteed investment in Head Start over the next three years to ensure that funds are available to serve *all* eligible three-, four-, and five-year olds (which would require

$6.1 billion in 1995 over current funding); to ensure that Head Start is available for families who need full-day, full-year services; and to continue to strengthen the quality of Head Start. The Federal Government must also fully fund the Child Care and Development Block Grant.

The welfare of children depends, of course, on many issues beyond those mentioned. In particular, improving the lot of American children will require significant reform in our education, housing, teen pregnancy prevention, and other policies, many of which are discussed elsewhere in this volume.

FAMILY POLICY

ELAINE CIULLA KAMARCK

Summary

WHILE THE DISINTEGRATION of family structure is most evident among the very poor, the crisis of the American family extends to the vast middle class and to their children as well. This chapter summarizes the important links between family structure and the well-being of America's children and communities. The chapter goes on to outline six approaches to a progressive family policy—approaches that stem from the proposition that the role of government is to support families as they go about raising the next generation. As Governor Bill Clinton says, "Governments don't raise children, people do."

The specific proposals begin with two tax initiatives: an increase in the personal exemption or a tax credit for families with children, and an expanded earned income tax credit program that allows the working poor to support a family and remain off welfare. This proposed children's exemption or children's credit is critical to giving those engaged in childrearing much-needed economic support. In the next section are several ideas about reform of the child support system, both to establish paternity and to increase payments to the custodial parent. It also includes proposed reforms in divorce law as it applies to couples with children. In addition, this chapter includes proposals to encourage parental responsibility and family-friendly workplaces. Finally, it ends with some family preservation strategies for families under the acute stresses associated with extreme poverty.

Elaine Ciulla Kamarck is a Senior Fellow at the Progressive Policy Institute. This chapter is an adaption and update of Putting Children First: A Progressive Family Policy for the 1990's *(Progressive Policy Institute, 1990) by Elaine Ciulla Kamarck and William A. Galston, with essays by Robert J. Shapiro and Margaret Beyer.*

Introduction

MOUNTAINS OF EVIDENCE FROM PSYCHOLOGISTS, educators, and sociologists—and our own common sense—indicate that children from healthy, stable families are likely to have far fewer problems themselves and create far fewer problems for society. Over the past decades, many American families have simply disintegrated. Most evident in high divorce rates and most acute among the urban poor, the crisis of the American family cannot be conveniently pushed aside as only a crisis of the poor or a crisis of minorities. It extends to the vast middle class and their children as well.

For years the right wing, quick to talk about values, ignored the economic pressures that had come to shape the modern American family, while the left wing emphasized economics and ignored values. In reaction, the past three years have seen a coming together of liberals and conservatives, Democrats and Republicans on a variety of family-related issues. Yet, the Bush administration, ever quick to give lip service to "family values," consistently refused to take seriously the task of formulating a full-fledged and uniquely American family policy.

This, then, should be the task of the new Administration: formulation of a family policy consistent with American culture and values that takes into consideration the divergent needs of all American families. A new family policy should first recognize that public programs cannot fully substitute for healthy families. With the exception of those children and families in severe crisis, the goal of government should be to support and compensate families as they carry out their critical social role—providing for the economic and moral well-being of children. This goal will require both additional resources and minimal bureaucratic cost, complexity, and intrusion, working instead to broaden individual choice and opportunity.

A progressive family policy should emphasize the goal of family preservation and address the needs of particular families in particular situations: for middle-class families, a package of tax cuts that includes a substantial increase in the personal exemption for young children and elderly parents; for the working poor, an increase in the earned income tax credit; for the poorest of the poor, early family preservation strategies; and for all families, reform of divorce laws, reinforcement of parental responsibility, and the creation of family-friendly workplaces.

The Importance of Family Structure

AT THE CENTER OF CONCERN OVER THE AMERICAN FAMILY is the question of family structure. A large body of evidence supports the conclusion that, in the aggregate, the intact two-parent family is best suited to the task of bringing up children as healthy participants in society. This does not mean that all single-parent families are bad or dysfunctional; nor does it mean that preservation of a two-parent family is always the best option. In cases of abuse, for instance, a two-parent family obviously does not serve the best interests of the children; and millions of single parents are struggling successfully against the odds to provide good homes for their children. At the level of statistical aggregates and societywide phenomena, however, significant differences emerge between one-parent and two-parent families. We should not be afraid to talk about these differences; they can and should shape our understanding of social policy.

The clearest consequence of raising children in one-parent families is economic. As David T. Ellwood, the author of *Poor Support: Poverty in the American Family*, has observed, "The vast majority of children who are raised entirely in a two-parent home will never be poor during childhood. By contrast, the vast majority of children who spend time in a single-parent home will experience poverty."[1]

In fact, changes in family structure over the past three decades—rising out-of-wedlock births and rising divorce rates—provide the most dramatic explanation for concomitant large increases in childhood poverty. In 1949 children in single-parent families were almost twice as likely to be poor as children in the general population; by 1979 children in these families were three and a half times as likely to be poor as children in the general population.[2] In a large statistical study using census data from the 1960s, two Penn State sociologists conclude that "child poverty rates would have been one third less in 1988 if family structure had not changed since 1960." Furthermore, "changing family structure accounted for nearly 50 percent of the increase in child poverty rates since 1980." Finally, they conclude that "child poverty and racial inequality cannot be separated from the issue of changing family structure in America."[3]

The economic consequences of a parent's absence (almost always the father's) are exacerbated by the psychological consequences, which include higher-than-average levels of youth suicide, low intellectual and educational performance, and higher-than-average rates of mental illness, violence, and drug use.[4] In a recent study, for example, Douglas A. Smith and G. Roger Jarjoura found that "Neighborhoods with larger percentages of youth (those aged 12 to 20) and areas with higher percentages of single-parent households also have higher rates of violent crime." The relationship between crime and one-parent families, in fact, is so strong that controlling for family configuration erases the relationship between race and crime and between low income and crime.[5]

Among the very poor, the scarcity of intact families and the resulting poverty and social pathology stem largely from the failure of families to form in the first place. This has led to new approaches to welfare reform that seek to remove obstacles to marriage and, in some instances, to provide outright incentives to marriage. Nonetheless, family structure turns out to be just as important to the middle class, which has experienced high divorce rates over the past few decades. In 1981, a study by John Guidubaldi, then president of the National Association of School Psychologists, found that the psychological consequences of divorce were significant *even after correcting for income differences*.[6] Guidubaldi's study has been confirmed and deepened by the work of Judith S. Wallerstein who studied sixty middle-class divorce families and concluded, "The effects of divorce are long-lasting. . . . Divorce is almost always more devastating for children than for their parents."[7]

It is hardly surprising, then, to discover what teachers and school administrators have known for some time: At the root of America's declining educational achievement is the disintegrating American family. During the 1980s per pupil spending in the United States increased and yet, at the end of the decade, test scores registered absolutely no gains.[8] John Ourth, principal of Oak Terrace High School in Highwood, Illinois, writes ". . . that a child who is in crisis cannot learn until school personnel recognize the crisis and take steps to ameliorate its effects. . . . Any major change in a child's family (and separation and divorce are among the most major) can spell crisis. . . ."[9]

A great deal of attention has been given to educational experimentation and to educational restructuring recently. But unless and until we recognize the centrality of the family to effective education, the most intensive reorganization efforts will come to naught. Ever since James S. Coleman and his coauthors published their seminal study on this topic over a quarter century ago, research has consistently reinformed the importance of family on student achievement.[10] In addition, there is an overwhelming body of evidence suggesting that the "hidden curriculum of the home," which is critical to the development of language skills, is directly related to children's later success in school.[11]

Untangling just what it is about family structure that makes for high or low educational achievement is a difficult task. Clearly economics plays a role: Children from poor families consistently do less well than do children from nonpoor or well-to-do families. But income is clearly not the whole story. In a study of 14,493 students conducted by the National Association of Elementary School Principals and the Institute for Development of Educational Activities, family structure had an important and significant effect on educational achievement above and beyond income level, especially for boys. Lower-income girls with two parents, for instance, score higher on achievement tests than higher-income boys with one parent. At the very bottom of the achievement scale are lower-income boys with one parent.[12]

In the past decade, schools have introduced many innovations to cope with the problems that children are bringing with them to the classroom. In some particularly poor communities, schools will have to turn into therapeutic entities if they are to educate their children effectively. But in the end government will never have the resources or the ability to replace what children lose when they lose supportive families. Thus the focus of public policy in the new Administration should be to look for ways to foster stable families.

Policy Proposals

GIVEN ALL THE MONEY IN THE WORLD, government programs will not be able to instill self-esteem, good study habits, language skills, or sound moral values in children as effectively as strong families can. Many of those in the best position to see the effects of family breakdown—educators— have responded to the family crisis with an admirable array of before- and after-school programs and curricula designed to do everything from bolstering self-esteem to teaching abstract values. But in the end, government cannot replace the family, nor should it try.*

Here are several desirable policies to meet the needs of particular families in particular situations:

INCREASING THE PERSONAL EXEMPTION
The United States is the only country among eighteen rich democracies in the world without a family allowance or some other sort of government subsidy per child.[13] From eighteen-month maternity leaves in Sweden to children's allowances in France, West European countries have acknowledged that if families are placed under so much stress that they cannot raise children effectively, the rest of society cannot make up the difference in later years.

---

*A similar conclusion is reached by other students of the social welfare state. Alan Wolfe, in his 1989 book, *Whose Keeper? Social Science and Moral Obligation,* argues that at some point, the expansion of the welfare state tends to erode family responsibility and solidarity: "The moral issues involved in the new welfare state are more serious than at first was realized. The Scandinavian welfare states, which express so well a sense of obligation to distant strangers, are beginning to make it more difficult to express a sense of obligation to those with whom one shares family ties."

In 1948 the United States had a profamily policy based on a simple notion: The government should not tax away that portion of a family's income that is needed to raise children. According to economist Eugene Steuerle, the 1948 personal exemption was $600, and median family income was $3,187.[14] A family of four at median income paid a minuscule 0.3 percent of their income in federal income taxes compared to today's 9.1 percent.[15] In 1964, Congress adopted a policy of increasing the minimum standard deduction but not the personal exemption. The result, according to Steuerle: "Tax-exempt levels for households without dependents have been moving closer and closer to tax-exempt levels for households with dependents."[16] The real value of today's personal exemption of $2,000 is far less than it was in 1948.

In addition, family incomes grew slowly in the 1970s and 1980s. Hardest hit by this conjunction of changes in the economy and tax policy have been the children of middle-class and moderate-income people whose income is derived entirely from wages.

To reverse decades of neglect, a new Administration should seek a substantial increase in the personal exemption of dependents only—from the current $2,000 to between $6,000 and $7,500 per dependent—to reflect the real costs of raising a child in today's world.*

A $6,000 personal exemption for all dependents in 1990 would have cost the government a whopping $43 billion. To be affordable as well as effective, the increase in the personal exemption should be limited to preschool children (under age four), who ideally require expensive one-on-one care out of reach of all but the most well-to-do families. Such a limited program would cost about $10 billion. Alternatively, the Joint Committee on Taxation estimates that a personal exemption of $4,000 for children under age five, phased down to the current level by age eight, would cost $2.8 billion in 1991, $5.7 billion in 1992, and a total of $27.1 billion in the years 1991–95.[17]

In addition, the proposal should avoid the mistakes of past attempts at family policy, whereby the tax code ended up subsidizing the well-to-do. (Originally day care credits were given to all families regardless of income.)

---

*Simply adjusting for inflation would put the 1948 personal exemption near $3,000. But we should also take into account both the rising costs of raising a child (in his or her first year, at least) and the growth in real income. *American Demographics* put the cost of raising a baby in his of her first year in 1990 at $5,774. That same publication put the cost of raising a baby in his or her first year in 1958 at $800. Whether coincidental or not, the personal exemption in 1958 was very close to the actual cost of raising a new baby in that year. When economists try to match the value of the 1948 personal exemption for today's families they come up with estimates between $6,000 and $7,500 per dependent—numbers that are coincidentally close to the actual first-year cost of raising a child in 1990.

Our suggestion: Begin phasing the $6,000 exemption per young dependent back down to the current $2,000 at some point near double median income (about $64,000 per year). An alternative means of achieving progressivity is to offer a substantial tax credit per child of $800, as advocated by Senators Al Gore and Jay Rockefeller and by Congressman Tom Downey—since tax credits, unlike tax deductions, are automatically progressive.

But even the creation of a larger children's exemption will not decrease the federal tax burden on median-income families with children to desirable levels. One reason is the enormous increases in the payroll tax used to finance Social Security, which have hit average-income families the hardest. Thus any change in the personal exemption needs to be coupled with a significant decrease in payroll tax rates.[18]

These steps will aid not only two-parent families, for whom the extra money might make it more feasible for one parent to stay home full time with small children, but also single parents who must work and who need help with the costs of day care. But there is another piece of tax law that must be changed to aid single parents. The tax code currently provides three filing statuses: single, married, and head of household. The latter is designed for single parents and is taxed at a rate that, as Larry Lindsay points out, is "roughly midway between those applied to single filers (which are higher) and those applied to married couples (which are lower)." This makes no sense, as Lindsay argues, since "Single-parent families have nothing in common with single people and everything in common with other families."[19] Single-parent families should have the same tax rate as married couple families.

These three steps, taken together, would move us toward the goal of giving parents greater choice. The mother who is forced to go back to work for economic reasons is as much a prisoner as the mother of an earlier era who was forced to stay at home for reasons of social pressure. Working mothers will have more money under this plan to pay for the kind of day care that every parent wants.

EXPANDING THE EARNED INCOME TAX CREDIT

Ordinary tax relief will not help working poor families, in whose ranks can be found more than half of all poor children. In 1988 there were more than 2.9 million poor American families, with children under age eighteen, headed by someone who was working.

A significant increase in the earned income tax credit (EITC) wage supplement, once tied to family size, would be the most efficient way of helping working, poor families—more so, in particular, than another increase in the minimum wage, since 85 percent of minimum-wage workers live in nonpoor households, and half of all poor workers hold jobs not covered by the minimum wage.[20]

The goal: to guarantee that any parent working full-time, year-round be able to support his or her family above the poverty line. Converting the current EITC program into a guaranteed "working wage" for poor families would require that the wage supplement be set at the level required to fill the gap between full-time, year-round minimum-wage earnings and the poverty line, given the size of the family. Therefore, the benefit would grow with the number of hours worked and the number of children being supported. Congress made an important step in this direction in 1990 when it passed a $12.4 billion expansion of the EITC. The new legislation also created an extra credit for children under one year of age.

DIVORCE LAW REFORM

Twenty years ago, the state of California enacted a much-heralded "no fault" divorce law to end the use of the courtroom as a battleground and to end some of the more humiliating and culturally obsolete grounds for divorce. Other states rapidly followed. No-fault divorce was and is a sensible and important reform for married couples without children. But for families with children, no-fault divorce has been, as the sociologist Lenore Weitzman shows, a driving force behind the feminization of poverty. "Divorce has radically different economic consequences for men and women. . . divorced men experience an average 42 percent rise in their standard of living in the first year after the divorce, while divorced women (and their children) experience a 73 percent decline."[21]

The real gap between husbands and their wives and children postdivorce is almost certainly larger than the already substantial gap Weitzman calculates, since she assumes that the father actually made his child support payments, which, of course, is far from universal.

Even after the limited federal and state reforms of the 1980s, the child support system is a mess. More than one third of all absent fathers simply ignore their legal obligation to support their children, and many others pay only a fraction of what they owe. The average annual payment for those who do pay is only $2,300, and many use delays or arbitrary reductions in support payments to achieve other bargaining objectives vis-à-vis the custodial parent. If a reasonable level of collections and payments were achieved, absent fathers would contribute at least $25 billion more each year than they do today.[22] And if the system were made less discretionary and more uniform, a major source of uncertainty, conflict, and distress for custodial parents would be removed.

Therefore, the new Administration should seek passage of the Downey-Hyde proposal currently in Congress, which would make the IRS the central collection agency for child support payments. Other steps toward reform are as follows:

• In the future, the Social Security numbers of both parents would appear on each child's birth certificate so that every child's father and mother can be identified.

• All absent parents would be expected to contribute a portion of their income, which would vary with the number of children they fathered or bore.

• Payments would be collected by employers, just like Social Security taxes, and remitted to the federal government, which would then send this money directly to the custodial parent. All absent parents would be included, not just delinquents. Failure to pay would be an offense comparable to tax evasion.*[23]

But we need to go beyond rigorous enforcement of child support decrees. Women enter marriage earning less than men for a whole host of reasons, including sex discrimination and employment in low-paying "female" fields. But if in the course of their marriage they have become mothers, they leave marriage earning substantially less than men. As Weitzman points out, "marriage—and then divorce—impose a differential disadvantage on women's employment prospects, and this is especially severe for women who have custody of minor children. The responsibility for children inevitably restricts the mother's job opportunities by limiting her work schedule and location, her availability for overtime, and her freedom to take advantage of special training, travel assignments, and other opportunities for career advancement."[24]

A principle of spousal equality is obviously appropriate in those divorces where the woman is childless. But in those cases where children are present, divorce law reform must take into account the impact of motherhood on a woman's earning capacity as well as the per capita expenses of the household with woman and children.

Finally, a thorough reform of divorce law must go beyond even questions of economic support. Because of the shattering emotional and developmental effects of divorce on children, it would be reasonable to introduce "braking" mechanisms that require parents contemplating divorce to pause

---

*States are experimenting with a variety of child support enforcement innovations. Arizona, like Massachusetts, is moving to tie the award of state professional licenses to punctual child support payments. Minnesota is beginning to accept other states' enforcement orders as is, without the traditional extra in-state hearings. Other jurisdictions are offering amnesty periods for overdue payments, followed by police roundups of tardy fathers.

for reflection. There is transatlantic precedent for such procedures. A report from Britain's Law Commission has recommended that such couples "notify the courts of their intention and then spend at least nine months resolving crucial details of the divorce. Their first obligation would be to decide the future of their children before settling questions of property and maintenance. Only then could couples return to court for a divorce." As one recent account notes, "By encouraging parents to look at the consequences of a family breakup rather than at the alleged cause or excuse for it, the commission hopes couples will improve their prospects of saving the marriage."[25]

Some efforts are under way in the United States to emphasize the importance of the children's well-being in the postdivorce family. An experimental program in the Atlanta court system requires counseling sessions for parents considering divorce; and courts in Washington state require that divorcing parents submit a "parenting plan" that provides for their children's physical care and emotional stability and that seeks to minimize the child's exposure to harmful parental conflict.[26]

ENCOURAGING PARENTAL RESPONSIBILITY

Obviously, the state has limited ability to make adults into good parents. Nevertheless, there are things in addition to economic support that can be done to reinforce the parental role. The Federal Government and state governments should evaluate the success of several new approaches to this problem described below.

Sometimes parents may have to be held responsible in civil law for the criminal actions of their children. California's STEP (Street Terrorism Enforcement and Protection) Act makes it a misdemeanor for parents knowingly to permit their children to be involved in gang activities. In other instances, parents may be fined for failing to provide the minimum standard of parental authority with regard to a child's education. Last year, for example, Arkansas enacted three new laws providing for civil penalties against parents whose children have excessive school absences and against parents who fail to attend school conferences at which a plan to help their child master basic skills is presented.

Nowhere, however, is the issue of parental responsibility more acute than with the thousands of mothers who use drugs during pregnancy, with disastrous consequences for their offspring and society. Most drug rehabilitation centers now refuse to take pregnant women.[27] In fact, pregnant women should be given *priority* in treatment centers and, when they do not seek treatment on their own, the state should be empowered to force them into treatment. Mandatory treatment on the front end, during pregnancy, is far preferable to prosecution and separation after the child is born. This strategy could improve significantly the health of these children and the parenting skills of the mother.

THE FAMILY-FRIENDLY WORKPLACE

Slowly but surely, businesses are learning that they are dependent on female employees, and that dependence will only grow as the composition of the labor force continues to change in the 1990s. Several studies have confirmed what employers have known for some time: A large number of personnel problems are related to child care problems that affect parents.[28]

Businesses are now realizing that they must develop family-friendly workplaces to recruit new employees and keep old and valued ones.* Many employers are now:

- developing family leave policies;
- making available flextime arrangements;
- offering dependent care plans either through on-site day care or through area day care providers which they subsidize;
- offering sick child care;
- offering time off to attend teacher conferences;
- making home-based employment possible for those employees whose jobs lend themselves to such arrangements.

This last suggestion (telecommuting) has great potential, especially in those businesses that employ hundreds of employees, the majority of whom are women, in repetitive data processing tasks. (Telecommuting also offers economic and environmental advantages for society by reducing the number of commuters.) The Federal Government, which as one of the nation's largest employers led the way in the use of flextime schedules, should begin to offer telecommuting options to qualified interested employees and should promote the use of such measures in the federal work force and through dissemination of information.

The opposition of the business lobby to the very modest proposal in the Family Leave Bill of 1990, vetoed by President Bush, is therefore incomprehensible—especially in view of a 1989 Government Accounting Office (GAO) report on the bill that states: "We believe there will be little meas-

---

*Aetna Life and Casualty found, for instance, that in 1987, 21 percent of the women who left technical positions did so because of family obligations. At American Bankers Insurance Group, the absentee rate for employees who use the company's on-site day care center is 7 percent, versus the companywide figure of 17 percent. *Challenges* (Washington, D.C.: Council on Competitiveness, May 1990).

urable net cost to employers associated with replacing workers or maintaining output while workers are on unpaid leave."[29] The new President should sign the Family Leave Bill as a minimum signal to business of the need to create a family-friendly workplace.

FAMILY PRESERVATION POLICIES[30]

The role of government *vis à vis* the vast majority of American families ought to be to support them in their critical role as parents. But government has no choice but to become deeply involved with the lives and choices of those families who live under the set of severe stresses associated with extreme poverty—such as crime, drug and alcohol abuse, and violence. Usually the state becomes involved only after the child needs to be removed from the home for his or her own safety—and who then enters the damaging world of foster care.

This system is now breaking down under pressure. The next Administration should follow the lead established by Congressmen Tom Downey and George Miller in the Family Preservation Act, which shifts the focus of child welfare from removal of the child after crisis to prevention. Delivery of home-based services to families at risk of ending up in the child welfare system, for instance, are much less costly in the long run than foster care. A GAO report looked at home visiting programs and concluded: "Compared to families who were not given these services, home-visited clients had fewer low-birthweight babies and reported cases of child abuse and neglect, higher rates of child immunizations, and more age-appropriate child development."[31]

Conclusion

ONCE WE UNDERSTAND THAT STABLE FAMILIES are the bedrock of stable communities, we can begin to look at all social policy with an eye toward strengthening and preserving families. In spite of their great diversity, all American families are both economic and moral units. When they are functioning well they take care of the next generation's psychological and moral well-being as well as their physical well-being. Some families need economic assistance from the government; others merely need the government to be on their side when it comes to helping them work and raise children. Still other families need large and substantial help, from social workers and therapists, just to function at all. The new Administration should recognize these differences in establishing a comprehensive family policy for the 1990s.

NOTES

1. David T. Ellwood, *Poor Support: Poverty in the American Family* (New York: Basic Books, 1988), p. 46.

2. Eugene Smolensky, Sheldon Danziger, and Peter Gottschalk, "The Declining Significance of Age in the United States: Trends in the Well-Being of Children and the Elderly Since 1939," (Madison, Wisconsin: Institute for Research and Poverty, 1987).

3. David Eggebeen and Daniel T. Lichter, "Race, Family Structure, and Changing Poverty Among American Children," *American Sociological Review* 56 (December 1991): 801–17. See also Victor R. Fuchs and Diane M. Reklis, "America's Children: Economic Perspectives and Policy Options," *Science* 255 (January 3, 1992): 41–45.

4. On youth suicide see K. D. Breault, "Suicide in America: A Test of Durkheim's Theory of Religious and Family Integration, 1933–1980," *American Journal of Sociology* 92 (1986): 651–52; and John S. Wodarski and Pamela Harris, "Adolescent Suicide: A Review of Influences and the Means for Prevention, *Social Work* 32 (1987): 477–84. On low intellectual and educational attainment see Sheila Fitzgerald Krein and Andrea H. Beller, "Educational Attainment of Children from Single-Parent Families: Differences by Exposure, Gender, and Race," *Demography* 25 (2) (May 1988): 221–34; Robert W. Blanchard and Henry B. Biller, "Father Availability and Academic Performance Among Third-Grade Boys," *Developmental Psychology* 4 (3) (1971): 301–05; Donald E. Carter and James A. Walsh, "Father Absence and the Black Child: A Multivariate Analysis," *The Journal of Negro Education* XLIX (2) (1980): 134–43; and Marybeth Shinn, "Father Absence and Children's Cognitive Development," *Psychological Bulletin* 85 (2) (1978): 295–324. On drug usage see Ted L. Napier, Timothy J. Carter, and M. Christine Pratt, "Correlates of Alcohol and Marijuana Use Among Rural High School Students," *Rural Sociology* 46 (2) (Summer 1981): 319–32.

5. Douglas A. Smith and G. Roger Jarjoura, "Social Structure and Criminal Victimization," *Journal of Research in Crime and Delinquency* 25 (1) (February 1988): 27–52; quote, p. 40.

6. John Guidubaldi, H. K. Cleminshaw, J. D. Perry, B. K. Nastasi and J. Lightel, "The Role of Selected Family Environment Factors in Children's Postdivorce Adjustment," *Family Relations* 35 (1986): 141–51.

7. Judith S. Wallerstein and Sandra Blakeslee, *Second Chances: Men, Women, and Children a Decade After Divorce* (New York: Ticknor & Fields, 1989), pp. 297–99.

8. See Peter Brimelow, "American Perestroika," *Forbes* (May 14, 1990).

9. "Children in One-Parent Homes: The School Factor," *Principal* (September 1980), p. 40.

10. James S. Coleman et al., *Equality of Educational Opportunity* (Washington, D.C.: Department of Health, Education, and Welfare, 1966).

11. See Dr. Samuel G. Sava, "Rescuing a Generation: Second Thoughts on Having It All," speech given to the National Association of Elementary School Principals (April 9, 1990), San Antonio, Texas.

12. Sally Banks Zakariya, "Another Look at the Children of Divorce," *Principal Magazine* (September 1982), p. 35. See also R. B. Zajonc, "Family Configuration and Intelligence," Science 192 (April 16, 1976): 227–36 and Ann M. Milne, David E. Myers, Alvin S. Rosenthal, and Alan Ginsburg, "Single Parents, Working Mothers, and the

Educational Achievement of Schoolchildren," *Sociology of Education* 59 (July 1986): 132.

13. See Harold L. Wilensky, "Common Problems, Divergent Policies: An 18-Nation Study of Family Policy," *Public Affairs Report* (Berkeley, Calif.: Institute of Governmental Studies, May 1990), pp. 1–3.

14. Eugene Steuerle, "The Tax Treatment of Households of Different Size," in *Taxing the Family*, ed. by Rudolph G. Penner (Washington, D.C., American Enterprise Institute, 1984), p. 76.

15. Ibid.; and Robert J. Shapiro, "The Tax Fairness Index: Who Pays for the National Government" (Washington, D.C.: Progressive Policy Institute Policy Report, July 1990), p. 4.

16. Steuerle, "Tax Treatment," p. 78.

17. Letter, Ronald A. Pearlman, Joint Committee on Taxation (June 12, 1990).

18. See Shapiro, "The Tax Fairness Index," and "1986 Tax Reform, the Sequel: Cutting Social Security Tax Rates Without Increasing the Deficit" (Washington, D.C.: Progressive Policy Institute Economic Outlook No. 5 [May 14, 1990]).

19. Larry Lindsay, op. *cit.*, p. 223.

20. The authors are indebted to Dr. Robert J. Shapiro of the Progressive Policy Institute for the analysis summarized here, which originally appeared in "An American Working Wage: Ending Poverty in Working Families" (Washington, D.C.: Progressive Policy Institute Report No. 3 [February 1990]).

21. *The Divorce Revolution: The Unexpected Social and Economic Consequences for Women and Children in America* (New York: The Free Press, 1985), p. 323.

22. Ellwood, *Poor Support*, p. 159.

23. Ibid., pp. 163–65.

24. Ibid., p. 342.

25. Marilyn Garner, "Putting Children First—the New English Precedent," *The Christian Science Monitor* (March 30, 1990).

26. See Revised Code of Washington Annotated, Title 26—26.09.184, Permanent Parenting Plan.

27. Susan Diesenhouse, "Drug Treatment Is Scarcer Than Ever for Women," *The New York Times* (July 7, 1990), p. E26.

28. For a review of these studies see *Employers and Child Care: Benefiting Work and Family* (Washington, D.C.: U.S. Department of Labor, 1989), p. 7.

29. "Parental Leave: Revised Cost Estimate Reflecting the Impact of Spousal Leave" (Washington, D.C.: U.S. Government Printing Office, April 1989), p. 2.

30. Credit for some of these ideas should go to Dr. Margaret Beyer, author of "Families Under Intolerable Stress" in *Putting Children First: A Progressive Family Policy for the 1990s* (Washington, D.C.: Progressive Policy Institute, 1990), p. 34.

31. *Home Visiting: A Promising Early Intervention Strategy for At-Risk Families* (Washington, D.C.: U.S. General Accounting Office, 1990), p. 3. See also "Keeping Troubled Families Together: Promising Programs and Statewide Reform," Family Impact Seminars (June 8, 1990).

Department of Education

EDUCATION

NICK LITTLEFIELD

Summary

THE AMERICAN SYSTEM OF EDUCATION IS IN CRISIS. Too many children are not ready to learn when they start school. Too many schools are unable to prepare their students for the challenges of the twenty-first century. Unless we act dramatically, America's competitiveness, America's standard of living, and ultimately American democracy itself will be in peril.

For twelve years, the Reagan and Bush administrations have in turn ignored the crisis and favored an agenda to privatize education that threatens to segregate educational opportunity by income group. Rather than this flawed strategy, the next President must pursue an integrated four-part approach to improving education, each part as vital to our success as the steps in a delicate medical operation.

• *Educational security for children.* Students who start school unprepared will never catch up to their peers. To ensure that every child starts school ready to learn, we must adequately fund Head Start and other programs designed to meet the health, nutritional, developmental, and educational needs of young children.

• *New common schools: elementary and secondary school reform.* Under the leadership of the next President, the Federal Government must stimulate local school reform by helping to create conditions for "new common schools" all across America. Educators have already reached widespread consensus on the essential elements of successful school reform. Now we need to provide federal incentives and support to encourage schools to

Nick Littlefield is Staff Director and Chief Counsel of the U.S. Senate Committee on Labor and Human Resources, chaired by Senator Edward M. Kennedy. This chapter is a collaboration among Mr. Littlefield and Ellen Guiney, Terry W. Hartle, Michael Iskowitz, Rick McGahey, and Chip Phinney, who are also members of Senator Kennedy's committee staff.

implement such plans. Second, the Federal Government should create a Fund for Teaching in America to place teachers at the center of efforts to restructure schools and teaching methods. Third, we must shift the emphasis in federal programs toward comprehensive school-based aid that gives schools more flexibility in deciding how best to serve students. Fourth, we must confront the problems posed by the enormous financial inequities that are all too common in education; the quality of a child's education should not depend on the property values in his or her school district. Fifth, we must strengthen technology in our nation's schools and create an American Schools Technology Highway.

• *School-to-work transition*. Unlike other industrialized nations, America does very little to prepare those who leave school and enter the work force directly. Either we make the investment in human capital necessary to become a nation of high-skilled workers, through high-quality training in the schools and in the workplace, or we consign America to a low-wage future with a declining standard of living.

• *Access to higher education*. All children who can profit from higher education should have the opportunity to participate at a high-quality institution. That will require providing them with adequate preparation in secondary school and the financial aid necessary to pay the bills. We must also improve the management of the Department of Education so that student aid programs are administered effectively. Also, we should help our nation's colleges and universities repair their deteriorating infrastructure.

Introduction

AS JOHN DEWEY OBSERVED IN HIS CLASSIC *Democracy and Education*, education is essential to the success of American society, not just because it prepares citizens for self-government, but also because it plays a vital role in fostering equality of opportunity. Dewey made another important observation: Education in a democracy must develop in its citizens the capacity for initiative and adaptation. "Otherwise," he warned, "they will be overwhelmed by the changes in which they are caught and whose significance or connections they do not perceive."

Beginning with the development of public "common" schools in the nineteenth century, American education has often fulfilled that role admirably. Initiative and adaptability have been the hallmarks of our society at its best. But an education system designed for an agrarian and manufacturing society, a society in which most women were not in the work force and in which minorities were systematically excluded from many jobs, cannot effectively meet America's needs in today's diverse, global, high-tech, information-based economy. The problems of our schools are well known. One of every four students leaves high school without a diploma. Twenty-three million Americans are illiterate. International surveys show American students consistently lag behind their counterparts in Germany, France, Japan, and other industrialized nations. Many Americans who enter college in the United States would not be admitted to college anywhere else in the world, and even the best schools admit students who require remedial courses in basic skills.

Employers find it more difficult to locate skilled employees. According to the Council for Economic Development, only 30 percent of employers said that students had "the ability to read and understand written and verbal instructions," while only 25 percent thought that students were capable of doing basic arithmetic. In the high-tech economy of the 1990s, this lack of basic skills and creative energy translates into reduced productivity and slumping wages. A high-school graduate now will make only as much in real dollars as a high school dropout could earn in the 1970s. In 1989, 20 percent of white and 40 percent of black males with only a high-school diploma did not earn enough to support a family of four above the poverty line, percentages two-and-a-half times greater than in 1969.

Our failure to solve these problems has brought our nation to the brink of one of the gravest social and economic crises in our history. At comparable times of crisis—during the Civil War, during the Great Depression and World War II, after the launching of *Sputnik* and at the beginning of the War on Poverty—American presidents have gathered the collective will, intellect, and persistence of the nation behind an expansion and rethinking of the federal role in education. Another such moment has arrived.

The Reagan-Bush Legacy

STATE AND LOCAL GOVERNMENTS are primarily responsible for American education; federal funds amount to only 6 percent of the money spent on education. However, throughout our nation's history, federal leadership has resulted in some of the most significant and positive changes in American education. The Morrill Act of 1862, for example, provided federal land grants to states to establish and expand what became many of our nation's finest public universities. And for almost three decades, the Federal Government has promoted equal opportunity by supporting education of the disadvantaged, promoting racial equality, bringing children with disabilities into our public schools, and developing specialized enrichment programs.

In the current crisis of our educational system, federal leadership has been absent. The Reagan administration tried to eliminate the Department of Education and many education programs. Although it failed in that effort, it succeeded in shrinking the federal share of education spending by 40 percent. America now ties for twelfth out of sixteen industrialized countries in spending per student on elementary and secondary education.

Educators hoped for more from George Bush, the self-proclaimed "education president." With the nation's governors, he defined six national goals for the year 2000: (1) all children will start school ready to learn; (2) the high-school graduation rate will increase to 90 percent; (3) all fourth-, eighth-, and twelfth-grade students will demonstrate competency in challenging subject matter and will be ready for responsible citizenship; (4) U.S. students will be first in the world in math and science; (5) all Americans will be literate; and (6) American schools will be safe and free of drugs.

These goals require dramatic changes in education policy, but President Bush was slow to act. Instead, the administration, under Secretary of Education Lamar Alexander, devoted its energies to promoting its America 2000 plan. The plan would effectively abandon public schools, where 88 percent of our children are educated, by diverting scarce federal funds from public schools to private schools in the form of vouchers for private school attendance. The plan also called for creation of a small number of new schools—to be selected by the Secretary of Education—perhaps sponsored by private, for-profit, or religious groups.

Implementing private school voucher plans and establishing private schools would accentuate the financial inequities that plague American education. As David Osborne has observed in *Reinventing Government*, an unrestricted voucher system "would be certain to produce inequitable outcomes because the affluent would add money to their vouchers and buy the best education they could afford. Most others would be unable to do this, and the education market would segregate by income group." And America 2000 simply ignores the staggering realities in American schools—the despair, drugs, street violence, and lack of health care and foundation for learning that mark so many inner-city children.

There is some evidence from New York City and elsewhere that choosing their schools improves students' performance. But choice among bad schools is not a reasonable choice. If school choice is to have any real impact on education, it must be coupled with a much broader reform in the nation's school systems.

Rather than giving up on free public education and letting the marketplace take over, we must develop a coherent, comprehensive plan to renew our public education system and to integrate it with the safety nets of health and social services. In the words of Brown University's Theodore Sizer, we need to "change the way we think about our schools: what they are and what they must do."

No one is better positioned to lead the American people to this new vision and to inspire them to realize it than the next President of the United States.

Educational Security for Children

ANY PLAN TO REFORM AMERICAN EDUCATION must begin with a strategy to achieve the nation's first education goal—that every child start school ready to learn. Marian Wright Edelman has written a blueprint for action to achieve this goal in her chapter on "Children" in this volume. Her proposals will not be repeated here except to emphasize that no matter how much we reform our schools, our efforts will have far less impact on student achievement if children are unhealthy and lack family support and early childhood education when they start school.

We know what to do: Programs such as Head Start and WIC are proven, cost-effective ways to support healthy early childhood development and save millions of dollars in later costs. But these programs are underfunded and fall far short of serving all eligible recipients. All children should be entitled to basic health care and nutrition, to immunization against disease, to comprehensive family services, and to participation in a program such as Head Start. The next Administration in its first hundred days should work with Congress to dedicate a specific revenue source, placing the funds in trust, to expand Head Start or similar programs by a total of at least $1 billion per year until all eligible children are served. Since the New Deal and the Great Society, senior citizens have been provided social insurance. The next President should assign his highest priority for education reform to providing educational security for children.

New Common Schools: Elementary and Secondary School Reform

SALARIES AND FACILITIES CONSUME 85 percent of education spending at the local level, leaving schools little money for innovation and improvement. As a result, federal dollars can be critical to supporting curriculum and management reform.

NEW COMMON SCHOOLS

The reforms of the past decade brought few gains in student learning but did establish how important it was to break fundamentally with past organizational and teaching practices. The traditional "factory model" schools, where students are alienated and failing and teachers are isolated and dissatisfied, must give way to a new common school built on a few tested ideas: school-based decisionmaking; better academic programs that set high standards but avoid tracking students in dead-end programs; extensive, school-based teacher renewal; smaller classes; longer, more flexible school days and years; increased learning time spent on important subjects, and instruction that connects subjects; social services, health services, and parental links to schools; investment in children *before* they fail; and performance-based assessments that more fairly assess what students have learned and what they can do.

Such changes will require strong leadership in the schools; teachers and staff who feel both committed to a clear mission and plan that they have formulated, and are empowered to use their best judgment and take risks; stable, well-trained teams that work well together; accountability for teacher performance; and good communication with parents, social workers, and medical staff. Good models abound, but we need national leadership to encourage all schools and communities to implement them.[1]

The Federal Government should provide incentives for school-based reform and support for implementation, and require accountability to ensure that our children are actually learning more as a result of these reforms. A relatively small amount of federal funds, allotted first to the states, and then awarded, on a competitive basis, to local schools based on a school's strategy for reform, can make all the difference in whether schools actually undertake to change themselves.

A FUND FOR TEACHING

Education reform must focus on the nation's 2.5 million public school teachers. They, not schools or school boards or superintendents, educate our public school children. Yet today many teachers are overwhelmed by enormous classes and unmotivated students and stifled by rigid rules and unimaginative teaching techniques. Unless there is a well-conceived and well-funded effort to revitalize American teachers, it will be impossible to meet new national standards or to make more than minor changes in our classrooms.

The next President and Congress should establish a Fund for Teaching in America to give teachers time, training, and resources to restructure their schools, reconceive their teaching methods, and attract talented Americans into teaching. As Deborah Meier, the principal of Central Park East High School and a MacArthur Award winner, has observed, "No public institution is more deeply entrenched in habitual behavior than schools. . . . [The changes needed] cannot be 'taught' in the best designed retraining program and then imported into classroom practice. What is entailed is changing the daily experiences of teachers, substituting experiences that will require them to engage in new practices and supporting them in doing so."

Until now, federal support for teachers has focused on enriching the practice of individual teachers only. The President's Fund for Teaching would focus instead on transforming the practice of groups of teachers as they interact in their daily lives in schools. Funding would go directly to these groups, not through local bureaucracies, and would be based on their own joint plans for restructuring and renewal. The requirements would be minimal: that at least 90 percent of the teachers in a school ultimately participate; that they demonstrate gains in student achievement by multiple performance measures; that the local union agree to grant waivers from contractual rules for tenured teachers if necessary to implement the plan; that the teachers work with an institution of higher education in planning and implementation; and that the teachers have their principal's support. Funds could be used to develop new materials and strategies to reach students and meet standards; to extend the day for planning or for students; for school- or university-based courses; to pay teachers to undertake extra responsibilities; or for other uses that are part of a coherent plan.

REEXAMINING "CATEGORICAL" PROGRAMS

Historically, federal education policy has targeted either specific student populations with special needs—for example, economically disadvantaged students, students with disabilities, or students with low proficiency in English—or high-priority areas such as science and math, drug education, or vocational education.

There is growing evidence that such "categorical" programs reinforce the status quo rather than stimulate change. "The major lesson of federally funded programs over the past quarter century," writes Gordon Ambach of the Chief State School Officers, "is that if they are maintained in separate categorical pockets, if they are managed through organizations or units which do not have central responsibility for education, and if they are not designed to implement school wide and comprehensive change, they will not be successful." The categorical approach also hinders efforts to create coherent approaches to meeting students' needs. Because these programs isolate students outside regular classrooms and provide remedial instruction, they are rarely integrated with the rest of the student's school day and may contribute to isolation of the child in school.[2] By contrast, the Accelerated Schools concept, based on work by Henry Levin of Stanford University, has proven across the country that at-risk students make more progress if their academic program is speeded up rather than slowed down.

The next President should look for ways in which the services provided by federal programs can be better integrated and schools can be given more flexibility to use these grants to benefit the students they are meant to help. If possible these programs should be combined and repackaged as single, multipurpose grants to individual schools, allowing schools to allocate and shift funding to meet their particular needs along with federal policy goals.

SCHOOL FINANCE EQUITY

In his book *Savage Inequalities*, Jonathan Kozol paints a compelling picture of the distressing disparities among America's schools. Students in poorer areas have fewer educational resources than those in wealthier areas, and there is evidence that this lack of resources depresses student achievement. Money alone is not the solution to poor student performance, but lack of money may well be one of its causes.

Most states underwrite local school financing by guaranteeing that each child will have a minimum level of per-pupil expenditure. The state sets a target tax rate for local school districts based on property valuations and, if needed, makes up the difference to meet the minimum per-pupil expenditure. Many children in poor areas are shortchanged because the per-pupil floor may be too low to be significant, or because cash-strapped states cannot fulfill their promises.[3] The importance of this issue grows as the country moves toward developing national standards for all students to meet. How can a student learn physics in a school with no physics teacher?[4] Financing scholar Henry Levin estimates the overall additional cost for a successful education at $2,000 per year per at-risk student.

The next President should appoint a Commission on School Financing Equity to examine the problem and consider such approaches as a "value-added" variation on the public school choice concept that would give poor children money for whatever public school they attend without affecting that school's regular federal funds; directing the Federal Government's block grant funds (Chapter II funds) only to states that have equalized funding for their students; targeting a percentage of federal education funds to property-poor districts or districts with an unusually high "municipal overburden" for other services for citizens; and providing incentives for states to shift from funding education through the property tax to other sources of earmarked revenues.

AN AMERICAN SCHOOLS TECHNOLOGY HIGHWAY

Just as the Federal Government connected America in the 1950s through the construction of a vast highway system that fueled economic growth and strengthened national defense, so in the 1990s the government should connect America's educational institutions through a national technology network. Few institutions or workplaces in America are as technologically underequipped as our schools, especially in America's poorer school districts. According to a September 1992 report in *MacWorld*, even when poorer inner-city and rural school districts have computers, "[these] districts lack the training and social support to use computers effectively." "In most cases," the report concludes, "computers simply perpetuate a two-tier system of education for rich and poor." Even in wealthier school districts, computer technology is often unavailable or used ineffectively.

The next Administration should upgrade technology in the nation's schools and lay the foundation for a national network linking the schools to one another and to key education resources such as libraries and laboratories. The Administration could use as a model the already authorized National Research and Education Network, which will link federal research laboratories and research universities via fiber-optic cable.

School-to-Work Transition

ACCORDING TO THE GENERAL ACCOUNTING OFFICE, about 50 percent of young Americans—the so-called "forgotten half"—do not participate in postsecondary education. And, as the Commission on the Skills of the American Work Force notes, "America invests little in its front-line work force. We do not expect much from them in school. We give them few job skills and training. And we let them sink or swim when they are the people we must count on to lead the way to a competitive and productive economy."

In comparison, occupational information and training programs are integrated with school in many European nations, starting as early as age twelve. In Germany, for example, students can enter one of over 350 formal apprenticeship programs. The European systems are a cooperative effort that involves schools, business, labor unions, and the local community. Coupled with strong basic and problem-solving skills, they provide our competitors with a highly trained, productive work force, giving them a major advantage in international competition.

OCCUPATIONAL STANDARDS AND CERTIFICATION

America's current occupational training is a hodgepodge of local programs with no recognized standards. And businesses, especially small firms, lack information on the training needed to achieve high quality and high productivity. One important exception is training in unionized construction and building trades. Employers and unions jointly develop recognized occupational standards and implement training to help participants meet those standards. Once an individual is certified in a nationally recognized building trade, he or she can go anywhere in the country and have these credentials accepted by an employer.

To achieve these standards in other industries and occupations, the next President should establish a National Board for Professional and Technical Standards backed up by advisory committees for major industries and occupations that include representatives from business, labor, education, and community groups. Their work should be undertaken in concert with the work of those developing education content standards in elementary and secondary subjects. The board would oversee the development and encourage the implementation of occupational proficiency standards, curricula, and competency assessments to measure student achievement. This will allow greater quality control and intelligent choice of programs by students, families and public funders.

COMPREHENSIVE SCHOOL-TO-WORK PROGRAMS

America must develop its own apprenticeship programs. The next President should encourage a development of a wide range of apprenticeship and career preparation projects. Students in the seventh through tenth grades would participate in career preparation programs to learn about a wide variety of possible careers. Students in the eleventh and twelfth grades should have the opportunity to enter apprenticeship programs that integrate academic and workplace instruction and lead to a high school diploma or community college degree along with a certification of occupational mastery.

The programs must be consistent with occupational and industry standards that will be developed simultaneously with the demonstration programs and should offer students the flexibility to switch among career options and move from occupational to educational paths without harm. Key elements include: clear-cut goals and objectives; structured wage increases during the program; systematic performance evaluations; and the involvement of private business, including commitments for summer employment during the program and for full-time employment after its completion. In addition, the Federal Government should provide leadership and start-up support to encourage communities to establish cooperative agreements that include businesses, labor unions, schools, and young people.[5] Similar training programs should be available to school dropouts through the establishment of youth opportunity centers.

Higher Education

HIGHER EDUCATION IS A MAJOR AMERICAN INDUSTRY (14 million students), an engine of economic growth and social progress and a source of admiration worldwide: more than 400,000 foreign students attend our colleges and universities each year, and foreign companies have begun to establish research centers and underwrite faculty chairs on American campuses.

But there are troubles on the horizon. Three issues in particular must be addressed: access, management of student aid programs, and the academic infrastructure.

ACCESS TO HIGHER EDUCATION

Between 1980 and 1992, tuition and fees facing college students jumped by more than 110 percent while the cost of living grew just 48 percent. Financially pressed states have begun to increase tuition sharply at public colleges, which serve 80 percent of American college students.

The federal Pell grants program was established twenty years ago to assure that the financially neediest students receive grant assistance before they are forced to borrow money. In the past decade, the maximum Pell grant has grown by just 33 percent—failing to keep pace even with increases in the cost of living. Not surprisingly, many college students have gone heavily into debt; some have abandoned their college dreams altogether. The next President should place a high priority on increasing grant assistance.

Student loans have become the dominant form of financing for higher education, especially for middle-income families. In 1992, several million college students and their families will borrow approximately $13 billion under the Guaranteed Student Loan (GSL) program. The current GSL program relies on costly subsidies to entice private sector lenders and is terribly complex and plagued by high default costs. Major revisions are needed to make student loans cheaper, more effective, and more efficient.

One promising possibility is the institution of direct loans to students from the Federal Government. While the details of direct-loan proposals vary, there are several common themes:

- *Universal eligibility.* Loans are available to any student, regardless of family income.
- *Direct lending.* Funds go directly to students from the Federal Government, through the schools, at interest rates that are wholesale, not retail, eliminating the costly subsidies to the middlemen—banks, guarantee agencies, secondary markets, and servicers.
- *Repayment options.* Students have a range of repayment options, such as income contingency or cancellation for community or national service.

Direct student loans would be substantially cheaper for the Federal Government over the life of the loans because they would eliminate subsidies, cut paperwork, and reduce defaults by providing for direct repayment through either Social Security withholding or the IRS. The General Accounting Office (GAO) recently estimated that a direct-loan program would save $4.8 billion over five years compared with the current program.[6]

Such a system would also offer flexible repayment. The Federal Government could adjust loan repayment to the borrower's income after leaving school. Students could pay off their debts through community or national service. The Commission on National and Community Service, established in 1990, has made an excellent start in identifying and testing a wide range of service models. The commission's work will be essential in implementing a vastly expanded service plan.

But student aid is not enough. Too many students do not know enough about the value of postsecondary education or the kinds of assistance that are available. Others are not given adequate preparation in high school. Many of those who fall by the wayside are minorities or disadvantaged. One promising solution is early intervention. Such programs promise students in elementary school that their college tuition will be paid if they stay in school, and offer counseling, mentoring, tutoring, and enrichment activities to support them. A successful program that helps prepare students for college is the federal Special Programs for Students from Disadvantaged Backgrounds, popularly known as TRIO, which help students overcome social and cultural barriers by providing them with information, counseling, academic instruction, tutoring, and assistance in applying for financial aid. Thanks to recent funding increases, there are more than 1,700 TRIO projects, serving more than 670,000 students. Even so, only 10 percent of eligible students are being served.

ADMINISTRATION OF STUDENT AID PROGRAMS
Only an effective, competent Department of Education can make the complex federal student aid programs work. Unfortunately, the Reagan admin-

istration cut staff and administrative resources to the point where the department could no longer fulfill its responsibilities. The results: Reviews of schools fell sharply in the past decade, and defaults skyrocketed—from $239 million in 1980 to an estimated $3.4 billion in 1992.

The Department of Education must be retooled to operate student loan programs effectively. A national student loan database should be established to facilitate program administration, and poor-quality schools must be eliminated and lenders and other participants carefully regulated.

REBUILDING ACADEMIC FACILITIES

Between 1950 and 1975, the physical plants of America's colleges tripled in size. Today, many of the facilities constructed during this period have become obsolete and require substantial renovation or replacement. A 1989 report by Coopers and Lybrand called these aging facilities a "time bomb" that places "at risk the ability of colleges and universities to fulfill their missions of teaching and research in an increasingly knowledge-based society." A generation ago the Federal Government helped to build many of these facilities through the Higher Education Facilities Act of 1963. But it largely stopped in the early 1970s.

The next Administration should adequately fund the Academic Facilities Modernization Program at the National Science Foundation, and the newly enacted Higher Education Facilities Act of 1992. The Administration should also eliminate the tax-exempt bond cap that limits private universities to $150 million in tax-exempt financing at any one time and that effectively forces institutions to borrow from more costly markets.

Funding: Investing in American Education

EXCELLENCE IN EDUCATION DOES NOT COME CHEAP. But as the saying goes, "If you think education is expensive, try ignorance." Indeed, we are already paying for our failure to invest adequately in education. Mark Tucker of the National Center for Education and the Economy estimates that 25 percent of higher education dollars are spent on remedial education. American businesses spend billions of dollars to provide entry-level workers with the basic skills they should have learned in high school. Like preventive medicine, preventive education costs far less than remedial education down the road. According to the Committee for Economic Development, $1 spent on high-quality early education saves $6 in future social costs for such needs as special education, public assistance, and crime prevention. Education truly is an investment in our nation's future, an investment that will pay dividends many times over in the long run in increased productivity and a growing economy.

What about funding? First, we must recognize that in the new world order, where economic power is as important as military power, a strong education system is a crucial ingredient in a strong national defense. As we gradually downsize our military forces, there is no more important place to invest the savings than in education. Second, we will obtain savings from the changes proposed in this chapter. For instance, implementation of a direct-loan program could save $1.5 billion a year. Third, if and when the federal budget is divided between current and capital expenses, as recommended in the Economic Policy section, many education expenses—for example, for school facilities and technology—could be included in the capital budget and amortized over the long term.

Finally, it may be necessary to earmark particular sources of revenue and create education trust funds to ensure that education spending is not subjected to the ups and downs of the annual appropriations process—for instance, a corporate tax that would approximate the money already being spent by corporations on remedial training for their employees, and or a Head Start and school reform trust fund. As many states have already demonstrated, citizens will support new taxes for education when they have confidence that the money is being well spent. But commitment and leadership from the next President of the United States are necessary to make any of these changes happen.

NOTES

1. In Kentucky, young children are ungraded until grade four. In several schools in Boston, all children, whatever their physical and mental disabilities, learn together. In Carrollton, Georgia, all teachers are well trained in technology and integrate it into their instruction. In East Harlem, the school day is reorganized with fewer courses but more content. In middle schools in San Diego, performance-based assessments have replaced report cards. In Hammond, Indiana, teachers identify their problems and initiate the solutions.

2. The Congressional Research Service points out some of the negative effects of these practices:

   . . . fragmentation of services to children, with challenges for coordinating special program instruction with their regular instruction; inefficient use of resources that may remain unused when not required by the special needs pupils; treatment of partial needs when a more coherent focus on the whole child might be more effective, especially with respect to children with multiple special needs; or instruction of pupils in separate settings, whether or not this is explicitly required by the legislation, when this might not be the most effective technique.

3. There are now education finance suits, challenging the distribution of educational resources, in thirty-five states.

4. Congress has introduced legislation in the past to involve the Federal Government in this issue. The Fair Chance Act of 1991 (H.R. 3850) sought to channel federal funds directly to local school districts when state efforts to equalize funding were lagging. The Neighborhood Schools Act of 1992 (H.R. 4323) provides for a thorough review of participating states' school finance programs and directs the National Academy of Science to develop model school finance programs to measure the equalization of each state's school funding system.

5. The Boston Compact, for example, has engaged schools, universities, business and labor in long-range efforts to help students get and keep jobs.

6. New estimates from the Office of Management and Budget are even higher. And these estimates are low because they assume that the loans would be collected as they are now, through private servicing and collection agencies. By collecting payments through the income tax system, additional tax dollars could by saved due to both reduced servicing costs and reduced defaults.

ARTS AND CULTURE

AGNES GUND

Summary

T HE ARTS, whether music, literature, drama, dance, media-based or visual, have long been of little consequence to the Federal Government, which has largely ignored its importance to the quality of our lives and our standing as a nation. It was not until 1965, with the creation of the National Endowment for the Arts (NEA), that Washington committed itself to support directly art and culture and to foster creation, access, and appreciation of the arts.

For the past twelve years there has been no real growth in the NEA's budget, and little has been done federally to develop the role of the arts in our society further. Worse, during the past four years, a few controversial grants have been used by Senator Jesse Helms and others as political fodder to undermine the almost universally accepted value of the arts and threaten the NEA's very existence.

The next President will need to show strong leadership to support the arts and the crucial mission of the NEA. In the short term he should reaffirm the government's commitment to the NEA, take politics out of grantmaking by returning that function to the arts community and stressing the importance of art as art, and make art part of the national agenda, emphasizing its formative role in education. A nonpolitical, nationally prominent appointee for the arts should be named to coordinate and promote arts and cultural policy for the NEA, the National Endowment for the Humanities, and other agencies, and a concerted effort should be made by the next Administration not to further decrease congressional appropriations, as well as provide increased tax incentives for private support of arts and cultural institutions by, among other things, making permanent tax deductions for the appreciated value of art.

Agnes Gund is President of the Museum of Modern Art in New York City and the founder and trustee of The Studio in a School Association.

History

THE IMPORTANCE OF ART AND CULTURE has never been fully recognized in the United States—possibly because of our Puritan background, the importance of the work ethic, our distaste for the aristocratic and the elite, or the stress on the practical, popular, and commercial rather than the beautiful and the cultivated. Whatever the reasons, it was not until the end of the past century, when America became wealthy and the wealthy had time to spare, that Americans turned to art and started collecting masterpieces of Europe and Asia. These collections are now the core of our great museums.

Unlike Europe and elsewhere, we have never defined ourselves by our art and culture, but rather by our political system and our industrial and military power. Even as a rich culture was developing here, until World War II, art and culture were largely thought of as something imported, something European. As a result, many of America's artists and writers traveled to Europe to study or pursue their careers.

In the nineteenth and early twentieth centuries, municipal art museums were founded in large part as the crowning glory to public education. Art was deemed to be morally uplifting and was to serve in improving the moral stature of the people —as well as to provide aesthetic pleasure (not too much), refine popular taste, and enhance education. Libraries, museums, and concert halls flourished under the patronage of individual benefactors, but it is often patronage provided by the state that insured the economic stability and vitality of such institutions as the Metropolitan Museum of Art founded in 1870 in New York, or the National Gallery of Art, which opened in 1941 in Washington, D.C.. Governmental support for the arts thus first manifested itself at the local level in concert with private philanthropies to build and maintain museums and other cultural institutions for the general public.

During World War I, the Federal Government itself got involved, at first indirectly by establishing charitable deductions in the federal income and inheritance tax laws to foster private philanthropy and help establish artistic and cultural institutions. The Federal Government first became directly involved in support of the arts in the 1930s, when it employed artists, writers, actors and musicians under the WPA arts programs.

In 1965, following President Kennedy's initiative, President Johnson and Congress established the National Endowment for the Arts to support the arts directly by encouraging artists, assisting artistic productions in areas where they might not otherwise be available, and helping to educate and encourage appreciation of the arts. The legislation was also intended to spur the development of similar statewide arts programs.

The NEA was founded on the principle that "the encouragement and support of national progress and scholarship in the humanities and the arts, while primarily a matter of private and local initiative, is also an appropriate matter of concern to the Federal Government." Congress further noted that "it is necessary and appropriate for the Federal Government to help create and sustain not only a climate encouraging freedom of thought, imagination, and inquiry, but also the material conditions facilitating the release of this creative talent."[1] The mission of the endowment is "to foster excellence, diversity, and vitality in the United States; and to help broaden the availability and appreciation of such excellence, diversity, and vitality." In advancing these purposes, a single aesthetic standard was not to be imposed and the content of works of art was not to be directed in any way.[2]

In the first eight months of its existence (in fiscal year 1966), the NEA received $2.5 million in appropriations and established a flurry of programs in music, dance, literature, visual arts, theater and education. Its first grant —$100,000 to the American Ballet Theatre—rescued the company from extinction. Twenty percent of the NEA budget was mandated to go directly to state arts agencies. Within two years every state had established its own arts agency. The endowment's annual budget stabilized at about $8 million during the Vietnam War. Contrary to expectations, the Nixon and Ford administrations proved strong supporters of the NEA. The endowment's budget quadrupled under President Nixon and reached $80 million in 1975 under President Ford. Numerous new programs were launched or expanded. As Nancy Hanks (Chair of the NEA from 1965 to 1972) noted, the NEA stimulated the arts "far beyond the modest federal funds expended. One federal dollar can generate three or four private dollars, and 75 percent of those private contributors are likely to contribute again."[3]

Under President Jimmy Carter, the NEA budget went from $100 million in 1977 to $149 million in 1979. Many established NEA programs enlarged and extended their focus—reaching out, for example, to the disabled and minority constituencies. Joint state and federal arts policy planning was developed and structured, and local arts agencies set up an association to represent their interests. From 1966 to 1979, state arts appropriations increased from $2.7 million to more than $80 million. The number of community arts agencies increased from about sixty in 1966 to more than three thousand today.[4]

Clearly, the endowment has been a vital stimulus to the growth and appreciation of the arts in America. The NEA helped develop artistic growth for artists, arts organizations, and audiences; improve the managerial capability and long-term stability of arts institutions; generate increased financial support from the private sector; and spawn steadily growing regional, state, and local networks of public sector arts support. The NEA's mandate that federal dollars be matched or surpassed has created an unprecedented public-private partnership for support of the arts. Each $1 in federal money awarded has attracted more than $6 in nonfederal matching funds. Audiences have grown as the arts —in all their variety—have been made more accessible through a variety of programs on local, state, and national levels. Overall, the arts in America have flourished since, and because of, the NEA's founding.

Unfortunately, government support for the arts has come in question ever since President Reagan first proposed to gut the NEA.

The Recent Legacy: 1980–92

THE RELIGIOUS RIGHT AND ANTIGOVERNMENT conservatives were the core of the Reagan revolution that swept the White House in 1981. The religious right took issue with the content of NEA grants and PBS programming, and antigovernment conservatives objected to the NEA and the Corporation for Public Broadcasting on the principle that government had no business funding art in the first place. As a result, since the early 1980s there has been an ongoing effort to cut funding for the NEA—at first under the guise of reducing the budget deficit and cutting big government, and later to cater to the religious right, which was outraged by the content of certain projects that received federal money, directly or indirectly. In his first budget, for fiscal year 1982, President Reagan proposed a 50 percent cut in the NEA budget. Congress agreed to only a 10 percent cut, for a budget of $143 million[5]. The NEA budget is now $174 million—less than what is annually spent on military bands, a fraction of what Americans spend on golf and fishing equipment, and an amount dwarfed by the nearly $600 million that the city of Berlin spends on the arts and the $1.5 billion spent by the French government on the arts.[6]

At the same time, several tax reforms enacted in the 1980s left a dramatic void in private support for countless cultural institutions. The Kemp-Roth tax cuts of 1981 reduced the maximum income tax rates from 77 percent to 31 percent. Because the maximum rate was cut so dramatically, so was the stimulus for tax deductions for charitable contributions. Arts organizations were among the most strongly (and negatively) affected.

The tax revisions of 1986 eliminated many tax deductions for not-for-profit and charitable organizations. In particular, the 1986 reforms effectively eliminated tax incentives for the donation of appreciated property, whether stocks or art. The change had a disastrous effect on gifts of art to museums, significantly reducing what to many museums is the only source of new art. It has been estimated that donations dropped by 33 percent nationwide. (It is ironic that those who call for the private sector to support and maintain art and cultural institutions and activities have at the same time removed incentives for the private sector to do so.) In 1991, the rule was suspended and art donations substantially increased. But even if the suspension is extended for the rest of 1992 and into the future, the sluggish economy has made fundraising for all arts organizations, from both individuals and corporations, more difficult than ever.

In recent years, the NEA has come under attack as elitist, charged with sponsoring art that some find repugnant or a threat to society's values—notwithstanding the overwhelming number of grants to unobjectionable and unquestionably worthy undertakings, from folk art to Mozart.

The controversy and turmoil began in 1989, when a traveling exhibition of works by winners of the Awards in the Visual Arts program of the Southeastern Center for Contemporary Art (SECCA) of Winston-Salem, North Carolina, arrived in Richmond, Virginia. Among the works was a photograph of a plastic crucifix submerged in urine by photographer Andres Serrano. Although the NEA had only funded SECCA, Donald Wildmon and his American Family Association began a campaign against the NEA for its indirect association with the award. (The NEA never funded Serrano directly or saw the photograph.) Further controversy erupted when the Corcoran Gallery of Art in Washington, D.C., canceled an exhibition of photographs by Robert Mapplethorpe, which, when later exhibited in Cincinnati, resulted in obscenity charges against the Cincinnati Art Center and its director.

These controversies erupted as Congress was considering funding and reauthorizing the NEA. Senator Jesse Helms of North Carolina introduced an amendment proposing sweeping restrictions on the content of works and projects funded by the NEA that focused on sexuality and religion that included a vague clause that would allow any offended party to take issue. The Helms amendment was defeated, but a symbolic cut—equal to the two controversial NEA grants—was made to the NEA budget. An antiobscenity clause was also attached which grant recipients were required to sign. Further efforts to curtail or abolish the endowment were defeated in Congress and, in January 1991, a federal judge ruled that the content restrictions placed on NEA grants in 1990 were unconstitutional.

In 1992, Patrick Buchanan, running his insurgent campaign for the

Republican presidential nomination, attacked George Bush for presiding over an NEA that supported "so-called art [that] has glorified homosexuality, exploited children, and perverted the image of Jesus Christ." Following Buchanan's initial success in the primaries, Bush's NEA chairman, John Frohnmayer, was forced to resign.

Anne-Imelda Radice, the woman appointed to succeed him, has done little to calm the arts community. She has cavalierly denied grants approved by peer panels and the presidentially appointed National Council of the Arts for the apparent purpose of avoiding controversy in the media and from conservative politicians—even though the grant-making process has been exemplary in its success. It has built-in checks and balances, such as peer panel recommendations; conflict-of-interest controls; and a presidentially appointed National Council, which reviews recommended grants with final review of those grants by the NEA chair. Further, in the critically important case of matching grants, what the NEA supports must also be supported by the private sector before funds are actually spent. The sole criterion for awarding grants should be conformity to the NEA's mission statement, mentioned earlier.

Instead, political pressures have upset the process. Changes have been made to broaden membership on grant-recommending panels and to limit their authority, as well as to increase the percentage of funds given to state arts councils or to small regional organizations—although, as in the case of SECCA, this will clearly not eliminate controversy.

It was only to be expected that, after a sustained assault on the NEA and government funding for the arts, the Bush administration and conservatives in Congress would turn their attention to public television and the Corporation for Public Broadcasting (CPB). And, indeed, the CPB came under attack in the course of the 1992 debate to reauthorize its funding. Public television was attacked as "an entitlement for the upper middle class." In fact, public television is one way by which music, theater, opera, and dance are made available to a wider audience—not to mention educational and public affairs programming. Commercial, market forces alone cannot be relied on to enrich cultural identity and nurture the spirit of a nation.

Public television was also charged with liberal bias. In fact, we live in a diverse society, and public television should broadcast a wide spectrum of views without fear for its existence—and it often does. One noteworthy aspect of *The Civil War* by Ken Burns, for example, was that it acknowledged and represented the black point of view as distinct from the Southern and Northern points of view. And as *The New York Times* noted recently, "Charges that public television's content leans too far to the left are less than compelling when its schedule includes, on a weekly basis, William F. Buckley, Jr., Morton Kondracke, and John McLaughlin, in addition to such periodic specials as *The Conservatives* and a forthcoming series with Ben J. Wattenberg as host."

A New Agenda for the Arts and Culture

DESPITE THE SUSTAINED ASSAULT ON CULTURE AND THE ARTS by the Reagan and Bush administrations and their allies in Congress, a recent Lou Harris poll, "Americans and the Arts VI," found that 60 percent of Americans favor federal financing of the arts, and that support cuts across regional, racial, gender, educational and income classifications with, for example, more than 63 percent of people with an annual income of $15,000 to 25,000. Eighty-nine percent supported the principle of pluralism and diversity, and endorsed the view that "good art is a reflection of the life and times of a nation and culture, including expressions which support as well as criticize existing values." In addition, 80 percent believed that "in order for the arts to come forth with their best and most creative efforts, the arts need to operate freely, and with a minimum of government control," and three quarters agreed that government should fund individual artists as well as programs, organizations, and institutions, and that "government should not dictate to the artist what the artist should create."

There is clearly broad public support for a renewed commitment of government to the arts and to pluralism and diversity in the arts. The next President, then, should move quickly to affirm his commitment to the National Endowment for the Arts and other cultural agencies of government, and take them out of the political football arena. The President must support a national agenda that overarches state and local initiatives. At the same time, the Administration and Congress must resist any impulse to interfere in actual content of arts projects and programs. In term of specific measures:

• The new President should establish a nonpolitical, appointed "office of cultural ambassador" to support and help promote the work of the NEA, the National Endowment for the Humanities (NEH), CPB, and other governmental agencies and institutions that involve the arts. The person appointed should have a national reputation in the area of arts and culture and be someone who can provide national leadership in the field.

• The income tax forms which provide a line item for commitment of $1 to the presidential campaign fund should also include a line item for the dedication of $1, $5 or $10 to artistic and cultural programs.

• The next President and Congress should restore tax incentives to donors by allowing ongoing tax deductibility of donations of works of art to public institutions. The 1991 suspension that allowed the deductibility of the appreciated value of donated works of art and other properties must be extended. There should also be increased incentives for private support of all of the arts, including, for example, a deduction for at least 50 percent of the value given to arts organizations.

• The Department of State and other federal agencies, such as the U.S. Information Agency, should coordinate their efforts to sponsor cultural exchanges to make America's art and cultural heritage available to the world and, similarly, to sponsor America's access to the art of the world.

• In the long term, the next President needs to foster a better understanding of the role of art and culture in the lives of individuals and communities through education—and, at the same time, the role of art and culture in education. The President should advocate a balanced education that encompasses visual arts, performing arts, literature, the history of the arts, and the media and design arts.

• At the same time, the President should encourage institutions to represent better the work of women and the diverse ethnic and cultural groups that are part of this nation.

• Finally, the next President must increase financial support for the arts and artistic institutions after twelve years with no real growth in spending. Certainly the next President will face a difficult fiscal situation, but he must also recognize that many cultural institutions have closed and others are at risk of closing and also that art and cultural institutions constitute a sound investment that attracts business and investment in their communities, an educated work force, and tourism.

NOTES

1. 20 U.S.C.A., sec 951 (West 1990 and Supp. 1992).

2. *Guide to the National Endowment for the Arts* 1992–1993 (Washington, D.C.: National Endowment for the Arts, 1992).

3. Milton C. Cummings, Jr., "Government and the Arts: An Overview," in *Public Money and the Muse, Essays on Government Funding for the Arts*, ed. Stephen Benedict (New York: W.W. Norton, 1991).

4. Op cit.

5. Op cit.

6. John Rockwell, "Arts Czar of Berlin: Power and Problems," *The New York Times*, (July 16, 1992) p. C15.

The Commission on National and Community
Service, ACTION and the Peace Corps

CITIZEN PARTICIPATION

MELANNE VERVEER, SUSAN ARMSBY,
AND MIMI MAGER

Summary

E MPOWERMENT" AND "CHANGE" have been much-discussed
in the 1992 presidential election because both the public and politicians understand that apathy, disconnection, and cynicism must
be replaced if America is to address the serious challenges confronting the
nation.

Community service has a long and rich history in America and irresistible
appeal because it promotes democratic values and civic responsibility—by
enabling Americans, particularly young Americans, to become more actively
involved in their own communities and other communities in need. Volunteers have been recognized as a national resource that needs to be nurtured
and supported. Three of the most popular and meaningful programs ever
offered by the Federal Government enabled Americans to give of themselves
while gaining important job skills and experience: the Civilian Conservation
Corps of the 1930s, VISTA, and the Peace Corps. President John F. Kennedy
proved beyond question that Americans can respond enthusiastically to the
challenge of contributing to the well-being of our nation. That ethic has
been lost as national leaders said that government is more problem than
solution and that personal self-gain in the marketplace is the highest good.
It's time to underscore once again that citizenship carries not only rights but
responsibilities. It's time for Americans to renew the contract between cit-

*Melanne Verveer is Executive Vice President and Susan Armsby is the former
Associate Public Policy Director of People for the American Way. Mimi
Mager, a former VISTA official in the Carter Administration and Executive
Director of Friends of VISTA, is currently Director of Congressional Rela-
tions with the Office of the Mayor of the District of Columbia.*

izenship and service that is essential to a free society. Here's how the next President can encourage, promote, and reward service at the national, state, and community levels.

• A revitalized ACTION agency would become the point agency in the Federal Government for promoting and supporting national and community service initiatives. It would administer, improve, encourage, and promote existing public service programs and voluntary initiatives currently scattered throughout the Federal Government either in ACTION, the Commission on National and Community Service, or in various other federal departments. The agency would launch a major recruitment campaign—similar to the public awareness campaigns of the Peace Corps and the military services— to raise the visibility of its programs and attract a broad spectrum of Americans.

• The next Administration should enact a new program to enable low- and middle-income Americans to attend college by borrowing money from a newly established Trust Fund. In return, the college graduates should have the option of repaying the loan through deductions from their paychecks or through loan forgiveness for national service—doing work our country urgently needs.

The Reagan-Bush Legacy

PRESIDENT NIXON created the ACTION agency with the approval of Congress in 1971 by bringing together, under one agency, all federal volunteer programs previously administered throughout the government. Volunteers in Service to America (VISTA), the Retired Senior Volunteer Program, the Foster Grandparent Program and other domestic programs, and programs of the Small Business Administration, such as SCORE (Senior Corps of Retired Executives) and ACE (Active Corps of Executives), along with the Peace Corps, were placed under its administration.

ACTION's primary purpose is to foster and expand voluntary citizen service in communities throughout the nation through activities designed to help the poor, the disadvantaged, the vulnerable, and the elderly. For example, the Foster Grandparent Program is recognized as the first intergenerational program model benefiting foster grandparents as much as the children they serve. Together, the foster grandparents and the children seek solutions to such personal problems as abuse and neglect, physical and emotional handicaps, drug and alcohol abuse, illiteracy, juvenile delinquency, and teenage pregnancy.

ACTION was more dramatically affected by the 1980 election of Ronald

Reagan than perhaps any other federal agency. Thomas Pauken, Reagan's first Director of ACTION, represented the antithesis of ACTION's leadership in the Carter administration. An avowed right-wing conservative ideologue, Pauken was determined to change what he viewed as ACTION's liberal philosophy and agenda. From the outset Pauken's tenure was mired in controversy. One of his first items of business was to attempt to "phase out" the VISTA program. Political background checks of former and potential ACTION program grantees became the norm. Longtime career employees of the agency were given notice, transferred, or reassigned to do-nothing jobs and, quickly, the agency became inundated with political appointees who shared Pauken's philosophy and agenda.

In response, Congress and the General Accounting Office investigated charges of illegal misappropriation of funds by the new leadership, questionable hiring and funding practices, and politicization of ACTION's programs and staff. As a result of congressional and GAO actions, attempts to misappropriate and divert funds were halted, and the VISTA program survived. To save the Peace Corps from politicization during the early Reagan years, Congress voted to separate it from ACTION. Pauken resigned after four years but, by then, Congress had taken steps to secure VISTA's survival though the remainder of the Reagan administration.

In stark contrast, George Bush dubbed community service "a thousand points of light" in his 1988 presidential campaign and has often said that "[f]rom now on, any definition of a successful life must include serving others." Public relations, however, rather than program, has been the mainstay of President Bush's work on community service. His White House Office of National Service has bestowed daily "Points of Light" awards to volunteers across the country and established the Points of Light Foundation.

The Bush administration did not attempt to reverse the Reagan damage to federal voluntary programs, particularly to VISTA, or to provide increased support for the existing service programs. Officials of ACTION, for example, have been limited to simply processing and monitoring grants. Its political leadership has shown a lack of vision, innovation, and commitment in exploring the full potential of the agency program.

The only major legislative initiative on community service during the Bush administration was sponsored principally by Senator Edward Kennedy (D., Mass.), the National and Community Service Act of 1990, which created a national youth service infrastructure and provides funding for school and campus-based community service, youth and conservation corps, and large-scale national service. President Bush proved more an obstacle than a leader in the passage of the Act. During congressional hearings, the Administration praised youth service but did not express support for the legislation. As a result, many Republican members of Congress attacked the bill as a waste of federal funds. The President requested no funds for the first or second program years, and also stalled nominating members to the Commission on National and Community Service (which administers the Act) from November 1990 to July 1991. As a result, a year of community service activities authorized by the Act and $57 million in appropriations were forfeited.

The Commission on National and Community Service has established itself as an innovative agency committed to its mission of promoting service and minimalizing bureaucratic barriers to good programing. In less than a year, the Commission has issued regulations to implement the programs, conducted grant competitions for the Act's four major programs, and awarded funds to over 150 state, local, and private agencies to conduct programs. The Commission is governed by twenty-one members appointed by the President to three-year overlapping terms and six ex-officio members, who are agency heads. The Executive Director is appointed, and may be removed, by the Board. Currently, the Commission operates with a small staff. It works closely with lead agencies and their advisory boards in forty-seven of the fifty states, Puerto Rico, and the District of Columbia.

The Commission's programs are:

• Serve-America, which provides funds to states to integrate community service into elementary and secondary education and increase the number of adult volunteers in schools. This program prepares youth for the responsibilities of citizenship and stimulates their interest in learning traditional subjects by promoting a "service-learning" approach that makes these subjects relevant to the real world.

• Higher Education Innovative Projects, which support campus-based service and train teachers at all levels of the educational system to integrate service into their classes.

• The American Conservation and Youth Service Corps Program, which offers opportunities for young people ages sixteen to twenty-four to engage in conservation and human service while they gain job skills, education, and scholarships. Based on the Depression-era Civilian Conservation Corps, these programs now operate in seventy-five locations across the country.

• The National and Community Service Demonstration Program, an experimental program which supports seven test sites for large-scale, full- and part-time national service. The 1992 programs are sponsored by Arkansas, Pennsylvania, Massachusetts, Oklahoma, Georgia, Maryland, and the Seneca Nation of Indians in New York.

The National and Community Service Act has made an important contribution in helping to channel the energy and idealism of young people into productive change. It has brought communities together to envision how service could help meet community needs, such as taking care of young children in day-care centers, teaching reading skills to people who cannot read, distributing food to the homeless at local shelters, helping in environmental cleanup activities, spending time with senior citizens in nursing homes, and participating in a neighborhood crime-prevention program.

By providing funding to schools, community organizations, and state and local governments, the Act strongly integrates service into our formal and informal educational process. By the end of the year, it will have reminded millions of Americans, young and old alike, that they are needed, and will have shown them what they can do to help.

New Priorities and Initiatives

THE NEXT PRESIDENT should lead by example in reaching out to all Americans to serve their nation and their communities, rolling up his own sleeves and joining in service projects throughout the country, encouraging his appointees, members of Congress, and federal employees to get involved in service projects, and recognizing service leaders for their accomplishments. But more than that, the next President must also promote national and community service to involve more Americans in service through schools, youth corps and full- and part-time national service.

1. *The Commission and ACTION should be merged, strengthened, and renamed "Serve-America," or another name emblematic of its role.* The revitalized agency would reach out to the American people by elevating public service in the life of the nation, encouraging Americans of every age to participate in the public life of their communities, and providing the opportunity for those who are willing to serve in a variety of programs. Neither government alone nor the voluntary sector can solve the needs of many of our fellow citizens, whether for environmental restoration and protection, care for the young and elderly, public safety, housing, food assistance, literacy education, etc. But together, government and citizen participation can provide much-needed resources and manpower to meet these national goals.

A renewed—and renamed—ACTION agency would become the point agency in the federal government for promoting and supporting national and community service initiatives. ACTION is uniquely positioned to take on such a role through its networks and longstanding community involvement in nearly every state. It would administer, improve, encourage, and promote existing public service programs and voluntary initiatives currently scattered throughout the Federal Government either in ACTION, the Commission on National and Community Service, or in various other federal departments. Opportunities to serve in the Peace Corps would be promoted by the new agency, but the administration of the Peace Corps would continue to remain a separate agency.

Appointing an outstanding director and deputy director of the revitalized ACTION agency is essential. Both should be eminently qualified, experienced, visionary, and committed to public service. The importance of community service in bringing citizens together in common cause must be understood. In addition, the most committed and experienced staff should be recruited for filling political and career positions in Washington and the field.

Program directors for VISTA, the Older Americans Programs, and the National and Community Service programs should report to the director. A formal partnership with the Peace Corps should be quickly established as well as high-level liaisons with the proposed Education Trust Fund, and the departments of Education, Labor, and Health and Human Services. An overarching board should be established to link all the programs. A review of smaller service projects in various departments, such as the Student Literacy Corps in the Department of Education, the Community Partnership Demonstration Grant Program in the Office for Substance Abuse, the Service Corps of Retired Executives Association in the Small Business Administration, and Tax Counseling for the Elderly in the Internal Revenue Service, should be undertaken by the director to assess whether the constituents would be better served if the program were transferred to the agency. It would make sense, for example, for Tax Counseling for the Elderly to stay at the IRS.

2. *The agency would launch and coordinate a national recruitment and public awareness campaign to raise the visibility of its programs and attract a broad spectrum of Americans.* The agency would address overall programmatic questions such as national recruitment, public awareness initiatives, benefits, training, and liability protection in all federal service programs. Because voluntary and service programs have been handled in a piecemeal fashion, Americans know very little about available opportunities, and in-service and post-service benefits and training vary greatly. For example, the availability and type of training to carry out programs under the National

and Community Service Act programs differ among themselves, as well as with VISTA programs.

3. *The revitalized agency would also coordinate the outreach begun by the Commission on National and Community Service to state and local officials, service leaders in all levels of the education community, unions, and the private sector.* Elementary and secondary-school teachers and administrators should be able to lead their students in service learning and provide information to students about higher-education community-service opportunities, available college loans linked to service, as well as programs for the non-college bound, such as full-time and summer conservation corps and YouthBuild. College graduates should be made aware of VISTA, the Peace Corps, VISTA Literacy Corps, and other national or state, public or private service opportunities. Employers, unions, civic associations, neighborhood associations, and religious institutions should encourage participation in service activities. To the extent practicable, employers should alert retirees to the Retired Senior Volunteer Programs, Foster Grandparent Program, and the Senior Companion Program.

4. *The National and Community Service Act programs should be continued and expanded in the next Administration.* The National and Community Service Act provides the foundation for a national service system that achieves the multiple goals of increasing access to higher education through community service, expanding service opportunities in elementary and secondary schools, involving more Americans in the solution of community problems, and stimulating increased civic participation.

The next President should adopt as his own the goals of the National and Community Service Act: to renew the ethic of civic responsibility in the United States; to encourage all citizens, regardless of age or ability, to engage in service; and to build an infrastructure for service opportunities based on existing agencies and organizations. Together with VISTA and the Peace Corps, the National and Community Service programs provide the foundation for a strong national service plan for the next President—the two education-based programs prepare youth for more intensive service experiences provided by the full-time programs. In addition, the full-time programs should serve as the primary placements for participants in the service-payback option for student loans discussed in the Education Trust Fund section.

5. *The agency's new recruitment structure should place an emphasis on attracting national VISTA volunteers, especially young people of diverse backgrounds and people with special skills.* VISTA is the federal government's only full-time domestic antipoverty volunteer program. VISTA vol-

unteers commit themselves to work for one year, full-time. They live within the low-income communities they serve and receive a sustenance level allowance. In 1965, VISTA volunteers were primarily nationally recruited volunteers, and overwhelmingly white, middle-class college graduates. During the early 1970s community VISTAs were recruited from the low-income communities served by VISTA. These volunteers worked side by side with nationally recruited volunteers with special skills, thus enabling VISTA to not only serve the needs of the poor, but also nurture local leadership capacity and community self-sufficiency.

Today, due to the Reagan administration's refusal and Bush administration's reluctant efforts to conduct national recruitment or public awareness campaigns in support of VISTA, there are far too few nationally recruited volunteers, especially young Americans. It is critical to expand opportunities for VISTA service. Nationally recruited volunteers should work side by side with locally recruited volunteers.

It is also very important to expand and revitalize the VISTA national headquarters staff, which has been drastically reduced. The VISTA leadership should develop and issue new VISTA guidance papers clearly outlining the program's mission, philosophy, and criteria for selection of projects and reemphasize the essential role of VISTA volunteers as catalysts and mobilizers of financial and volunteer resources, rather than as direct providers of services. VISTA needs visionary and inspired leadership that understands the program's potential and the importance of empowerment and community development.

6. *The Peace Corps should continue under its current administrative structure but efforts should be made for joint recruitment between the Peace Corps and other federal service programs.* Unlike VISTA, the Peace Corps escaped politicization during the Reagan years and maintained strong bipartisan support from large numbers of Americans who want to volunteer to serve their country abroad by helping to address poverty-related human, social, and environmental problems. Unfortunately, because of limited resources, the Peace Corps has not been able to accept the large numbers of potential volunteers who show interest. The next President should support increases in the Peace Corps budget to support more volunteers.

The Peace Corps' mission was and, after three decades, remains "to promote world peace and friendship." Its three statutory goals are 1) to assign volunteers to interested countries to help them meet their need for trained personnel; 2) to promote better understanding of Americans among the people served; and 3) to promote better understanding of people of other countries among American people.

The Peace Corps should also diversify its approach to assigning and supporting its volunteers overseas so that it will be able to field more volunteers in more countries.

7. *The next Administration should tap into the growing pool of older Americans for volunteer service.* As the number of older Americans expands, outreach to them is especially important. The Older American Volunteer Programs (Foster Grandparents Program, Retired Senior Volunteer Program, and the Senior Companion Program) have been the fastest growing programs in ACTION. The programs were initially perceived and developed with a focus on senior citizens as recipients. Over the years the emphasis has changed from seniors as recipients to seniors as resources to provide volunteer services to help address community needs. Collectively, these programs enable seniors to be both providers and recipients of volunteer services.

Each program should have its own experienced, committed, and visionary director. The directors should have demonstrated leadership capabilities and should serve as advocates for national and community service by older Americans. The programs should be viewed as models for national and community service initiatives for seniors.

8. *Other initiatives.* The agency could also launch several new efforts including support for a national service alumni association (similar to the Returned Peace Corps Volunteers) of citizens who have served in a service program. The Commission on National and Community Service should also consider establishing regional training institutes to train teachers to incorporate service into the curriculum and to train social service providers and others to use volunteer assistance effectively to supplement service provision.

Additionally, the revitalized agency will assist in the development of new initiatives, such as the proposed national service Education Trust Fund and any service opportunities for military personnel and bases in transition. ACTION should reestablish its former role in developing and evaluating innovative service programs.

Educators Trust Fund: The Service Payback Option

THE NEXT ADMINISTRATION should enact a new program to enable low- and middle-income Americans to attend college by borrowing money from a newly established Trust Fund. College graduates should have the option of repaying the loan through deductions from their paychecks or through loan forgiveness for national service—doing work our country urgently needs.

The Trust Fund should recognize that service opportunities must be structured in a way that provides real services to communities that would not otherwise be provided. By offering relief from student loan indebtedness, the Trust Fund would be a voluntary program, not a mandatory one.

Existing federal, state, and local public service programs—such as VISTA, Peace Corps, American Conservation and Youth Service Corps, National and Community Service Act demonstration programs, placements with nonprofit service organizations, and certified jobs related to human, educational, environmental, and public safety needs, especially those related to poverty where a labor shortage exists—could qualify under the loan forgiveness program of the Education Trust Fund. Work such as that targeted at addressing problems of inadequate education, child care, public safety, and health care would be emphasized. There should be an office within ACTION to provide a national database on service positions and to act as a certifying agent to ensure that service work undertaken to qualify for loan forgiveness meets the certification criteria and that there will be overall accountability in the service programs. The state agencies administering Commission-funded programs should be given responsibility to identify service slots that meet federal established criteria.

The Trust Fund should develop an outreach plan to ensure that there is broad awareness of the national service option. In addition, colleges should be encouraged to include in their recruiting materials facts on loans and repayment options, and existing national service programs should recruit more aggressively on college campuses. The Trust Fund should allow young people to participate in certified service programs before going to college or trade school, thereby earning credit to offset future debt.

Funding for Service Programs and Outreach

WITH SENSITIVITY to concerns about the federal budget limits and the cost-effectiveness of community service, the new agency should request funding that reflects a streamlined administration and additional service opportunities to meet the needs of Americans. To carry out the key ACTION, Commission, and other programs, a minimum of $350 million should be requested for fiscal 1994. This level of funding would allow for the recruitment, training, and outreach initiatives to be developed and launched.

In addition, the creation of an Education Trust Fund with a service payback option will require significant additional funding to expand service opportunities. This investment will continue to yield enormous dividends for meeting the serious challenges confronting the nation.

REPRODUCTIVE RIGHTS

ESTELLE H. ROGERS

Summary

THE 1992 U.S. SUPREME COURT DECISION in *Planned Parenthood et al.* v. *Casey* is a vivid reminder of the profound erosion of reproductive rights during the Reagan-Bush years. Indeed, one of the great ironies of the current debate is the myriad ways that a "conservative" administration has found to intervene in this most private sphere of personal choice.

But since there is no one agency where reproductive rights are enforced, stopping the unraveling of our reproductive freedom will require more than tinkering with a single agency. It demands a new President deeply dedicated to the basically conservative proposition that government should not interfere in the private decision of whether or when to bear a child. It demands a new President with the courage and resolve to pursue a reproductive rights agenda on several levels. And it requires that the new Congress recognize the national consensus that government does not belong in the bedroom. (According to a 1992 *Los Angeles Times* poll, for example, 78 percent of Americans believe that the abortion decision should be made by the pregnant woman.)

National leadership. For the past twelve years, the message from the top has essentially adopted the hysterical rhetoric of the far right. The next President should make it clear that *Roe* v. *Wade* struck the appropriate balance between competing rights and interests in the abortion debate. Contrary to the way it has been popularly portrayed, Roe is the compromise that many have been looking for.

Estelle H. Rogers, a lawyer and public policy consultant in Washington, D.C., coordinated all of the pro-choice "Friend of the Court" briefs in the U.S. Supreme Court's 1989–90 and 1990–91 terms. She is currently Director of Public Policy at the ACLU Reproductive Freedom Project. The author wishes to thank Gillian Thomas for her advice and research assistance.

Executive Branch reforms. The next President must rescind every executive order and regulation that has been promulgated to diminish reproductive rights. These include the "gag rule" in federally funded family planning clinics; the ban on aid to overseas family planning programs, which include abortion services; the rule prohibiting abortions in overseas military hospitals; and the ban on fetal tissue research.

Legislative agenda. The next President must urge the passage of the Freedom of Choice Act, which codifies the right to an abortion in federal law and prohibits the states from restricting the right before fetal viability, or thereafter if the abortion is necessary to protect the life or health of the woman. Other legislative priorities for the next Administration include the reauthorization of the Title X program, which gives federal funds to clinics providing family planning services; and passage of the Reproductive Health Equity Act, which restores public funds for abortions on the same basis that they are available for pregnancy-related services.

Judicial appointments. The next President must ensure that any nominee to the federal judiciary is committed to upholding the right of privacy and the right of reproductive choice that emanates from it. While the recent *Casey* decision did not explicitly overrule *Roe v. Wade*, it effectively repudiated the central holding of Roe that abortion is a fundamental right. It thus opens the floodgates to more restrictive state statutes whose validity will undoubtedly be litigated. Although judges will remain key players in this drama for the foreseeable future—and despite the remarkable success of the past three administrations in rolling back reproductive rights—much of the damage is reversible by a dedicated and aggressive new pro-choice President.

History

ABORTION WAS FAIRLY COMMON IN THE EARLY YEARS of the American republic, and no state regulated it until 1821. The common law permitted abortion until "quickening," generally in the fourth or fifth month of pregnancy, when fetal movement could be felt by the pregnant woman. After quickening, abortion was usually considered a misdemeanor committed by the doctor. The woman herself was immune from prosecution.

A Connecticut statute enacted in 1821 prohibited the inducement of abortion by the use of poison after quickening. Other early statutes seemed similarly geared to considerations of the woman's health, not religious or moral concerns, and generally did not affect her right to end her pregnancy at an early stage. Even the more restrictive statutes prevalent in the middle

of the nineteenth century were merely designed to protect the physicians'
monopoly on abortion services and prohibit competition from other practitioners. Gradually, however, both moral ambivalence and racist eugenic
concerns (because of a significant drop in the birth rate among white women)
fueled the doctors' increasingly successful movement after the Civil War to
criminalize abortion. More than forty statutes were enacted. Generally, they
permitted abortion only when necessary in the opinion of a physician (or
sometimes two) to preserve the life of the woman. Since many doctors
interpreted this "therapeutic" abortion exception broadly, by the early twentieth century abortions continued in large numbers, and criminal indictments
and convictions were relatively rare.

The modern debate on abortion really began in the 1950s. With medical
advances making pregnancy safer, doctors felt less justified in recommending
abortion. Hospital review boards subjected the decision to public scrutiny
and reduced the number of abortions precipitously. In the early 1960s,
however, the significant threat of birth defects from thalidomide and rubella,
as well as the increasing safety of abortion itself, caused the medical profession to rethink its restrictive stance. In 1967, the American Medical Association officially called for the liberalization of abortion laws. In the 1967
legislative session, twenty-eight state legislatures considered bills liberalizing
abortion; by 1970, twelve states had passed laws adding exceptions to their
strict statutes. In 1970, New York, Alaska, Hawaii, and Washington State
decriminalized abortion altogether.

On a parallel track, in 1965 the U.S. Supreme Court recognized the
right of marital privacy in *Griswold* v. *Connecticut*, striking down a Connecticut law that criminalized the use of contraceptives by married persons.
But no event was more pivotal to the history of reproductive rights than the
Court's 1973 decision in *Roe* v. *Wade*. This was a challenge to a Texas statute
that criminalized abortion except to save the life of the mother. The opinion
in Roe recognized the constitutional protection for a woman's decision to
end her pregnancy, but, equally importantly, *Roe* unleashed the passionate
and potent forces of the right-to-life movement. It was their well-orchestrated
campaign to unravel *Roe*, coupled with the fortuitous election, seven years
later, of the Reagan-Bush team, that have led us to the precarious state in
which we find reproductive rights today.

Following *Roe*, the abortion battle shifted to the Congress, where members under the leadership of Rep. Henry Hyde (R., Ill.) introduced a series
of initiatives designed to ban federal funding for abortion. They had the
support of President Jimmy Carter, who believed that government should
not be seen as encouraging abortion. Before 1976, almost three hundred

thousand or 33 percent of all legal abortions, were paid for by Medicaid. Prohibiting such funding was viewed as a significant step in dramatically reducing the number of abortions. Eventually a series of Supreme Court decisions deemed restrictions on state and federal funding to be constitutional.

The Reagan-Bush Legacy

THE GAUNTLET WAS LAID DOWN with the adoption of the Republican platform of 1980, supporting a "human life" amendment to the Constitution and pledging the appointment of judges who "respect traditional family values and the sanctity of innocent human life. . . ." (Actually, similar planks appeared in the Republican platform of 1976, but the Democrats won the election.) There was an explicit and deliberate strategy to use the multifaceted power of the presidency to roll back the gains attained by women under *Roe*.

With the election of Ronald Reagan, the right-to-life movement attained a powerful ally, not afraid to use the bully pulpit of the presidency to spur supporters to increasingly aggressive, even violent, methods of intimidating those seeking only to exercise their constitutional rights. Equally effective was his use of executive rulemaking authority to restrict the reproductive rights of those within the reach of federal power and his use of the veto to thwart the will of the pro-choice majority in Congress. But Ronald Reagan's most enduring legacy was the transformation of the federal judiciary, and ultimately the U.S. Supreme Court—the trump card the right-to-life movement was looking for.

Legal tests of *Roe* were frequent and largely unsuccessful until 1989, when the Supreme Court agreed to hear a clinic's challenge to a restrictive Missouri statute in *Webster* v. *Reproductive Health Services*. Among other provisions, the statute prohibited the use of public hospitals and public employees in performing or assisting nontherapeutic abortions, even when no public funds were expended. It also mandated expensive and risky viability tests to determine the weight, age, and lung maturity of a fetus believed to be twenty weeks or more in gestational age. The Reagan administration joined the state of Missouri in urging the Court to reconsider its ruling in *Roe*. By that time, four of the seven justices in the *Roe* majority (Burger, Stewart, Douglas, and Powell) had retired from the Court. A resounding reaffirmation of the rights enunciated in *Roe* was surely not in the cards.

In fact, what did result from the *Webster* litigation was legally inconclusive. No majority of the Justices endorsed a single opinion, but the

Missouri statute was upheld. However, if the Court's action was legally inconclusive, it was also politically explosive. The *Webster* decision, in the words of *Roe's* majority-opinion author Justice Blackmun, "invites every state legislature to enact more and more restrictive abortion regulations in order to provoke more and more test cases. . . ." And legislate they did. To date, more than six hundred bills have been introduced in the states and territories. This torrent shows no signs of abating.

One of the legislative proposals passed in the wake of *Webster* came from Pennsylvania, long an active venue for the right-to-life forces. This statute occasioned the much-debated 1992 Supreme Court ruling in *Planned Parenthood et al.* v. *Casey*. The law reads like a menu of abortion restrictions: husband consent, parental consent, a twenty four-hour waiting period, a state-prescribed litany of information about abortion, and onerous public disclosure and recordkeeping requirements for providers. (In fact, some identical provisions had previously been struck down by the Court—with a markedly different cast of characters—in the 1986 case of *Thornburgh* v. *American College of Obstetricians and Gynecologists*.)

Obviously, all such restrictions increase the cost and occasion delay in obtaining an abortion. A delay between the first trimester and late in the second, for example, can increase the cost tenfold and cause significantly greater health risks. The risk of complications from abortion, normally a safer procedure than childbirth, is estimated to increase 30 percent for each week of delay.

The momentous outcome of the case has been widely misunderstood by the press. Again, as in *Webster*, the Court issued several different opinions, none of which commanded a majority. However, it is patently clear that a 7–2 majority of the Court, some of whom professed support for *Roe*, have now abandoned its core principles: the trimester framework and the "strict scrutiny" standard of review for restrictions on abortions. This is tantamount to an outright overruling of *Roe*. States are now able to enact regulations designed to discourage abortion throughout pregnancy, and these regulations will be reviewed by the courts under newly relaxed standards. While a complete ban on abortion will probably be unconstitutional under *Casey*, the new latitude permitted to the states will undoubtedly result in increased costs and reduced availability of abortion services, thus making the "right" a hollow promise for many women, especially poorer women.

Apart from the activity in the courts, the Reagan and Bush Administrations have made persistent and effective use of executive power to thwart the exercise of reproductive rights. For example, the "gag rule" bans abortion counseling in any facility that receives *any* federal funds. Other anti-choice initiatives include similar conditions attached to grants of family planning

moneys abroad (the so-called Mexico City policy), restrictions on the reproductive rights of women in the armed forces, and a prohibition on federally
funded research using fetal tissue obtained from abortions.

The attempts of the pro-choice Congress to supplant these policies have
been stymied by a vocal minority sufficient to prevent the override of a
presidential veto. In addition to the ongoing gag rule fight, a veto even
prevented the District of Columbia's use of its own revenues for abortions
for indigent women. In a very real sense, the majority does not rule when
it comes to abortion rights. A "supermajority" is necessary.

Even beyond their power to promulgate rules, veto legislation, and
appoint the judiciary, the Reagan-Bush administrations have displayed a
more insidious tendency over the past twelve years to tolerate, and even
tacitly approve, the use of terror tactics to deter women from exercising
their constitutional rights. In fact, in 1991, the Justice Department argued
in federal court in Kansas that the court had no authority under the civil
rights laws to enjoin Operation Rescue from blocking abortion clinics in
Wichita.

The result? Dramatically diminished access to abortion services in recent
years. Eighty-three percent of the counties in the United States, where 31
percent of women of childbearing age live, have no clinic or hospital performing abortions. Not surprisingly, rural populations are particularly underserved. Many doctors and hospitals, particularly in more isolated areas,
simply will not endure the harassment involved in performing abortions.

Just as recent administrations have used these elaborate schemes to
factionalize the American community and to erode women's reproductive
freedom, a new leader who is committed to privacy rights and the rights of
women could bring us together. Only when women are free to make intimate,
personal decisions without governmental interference are cultural diversity
and individual autonomy truly respected.

Short-term Priorities

BECAUSE THE PAST TWELVE YEARS have been unmitigated disaster
for reproductive rights, there is a strong temptation to consider every re-
medial-action proposal a short-term priority. However, some steps can and
should be taken immediately, a few even before the inauguration.

A NEW MESSAGE

The very first step should be a major address by the President-elect designed
to recast the reproductive rights debate in new terms: the language of wom-
en's equality and autonomy, the need for comprehensive family planning

services as a central component of a national health care plan and the tradition of privacy in family decisionmaking. He should understand, when presented with compromising language or strategies, that choice *is* the compromise that recognizes and actualizes personal autonomy and religious diversity. A button at the April 1992 record-setting pro-choice march on Washington really said it all: "If you don't like abortion, don't have one."

There may be no aspect of the abortion debate in which national leadership is more urgently needed than on the issue of the reproductive rights of minors. The new President must articulate the necessity for young women to have access to safe, legal abortions without government-imposed parental involvement. The medical community has viewed confidential care for adolescents as essential to their health care since at least 1967, when the American Medical Association passed an official policy mandating treatment for suspected venereal disease without parental notification. Every state subsequently codified this policy in the interest of public health, and to encourage minors to seek medical care. Since that time, the AMA has passed several policies reaffirming the organization's commitment to confidentiality for adolescents, both in general and in the specific context of abortion.

Public opinion on this issue, though sharply divided, has been skewed by the failure of pro-choice advocates to present effectively the overwhelming evidence that teenagers voluntarily seek the help of their parents in all but the most dysfunctional families. In that minority of cases, including some where the pregnancy is the result of incest, *requiring* parental notice or consent has proven to have disastrous consequences. A 1986 report by the prestigious National Academy of Sciences found that requiring parental involvement in minors' abortion decisions delays their attempt to seek abortion and causes increased health risks. The report recommends the abolition of such laws, finding no empirical evidence to support special procedures for minors.

The factual record developed in the case of *Hodgson* v. *Minnesota*, which eventually found its way to the Supreme Court, is revealing. From 1981 through 1985, Minnesota's mandatory parental notification law affected over seven thousand pregnant teenagers between ages thirteen and seventeen. The trial court found that the law had the effect of raising the teenage birth rate, increasing the number of unwanted children with their attendant problems, increasing the number of more dangerous second-trimester abortions, and reducing the number of doctors willing to perform abortions on minors. Minnesota teenagers who availed themselves of the court bypass procedure (about half, or thirty-five hundred), whereby application is made to a state judge for a waiver of the parental notification requirement, have faced a traumatic set of hurdles that compromised sound medical practice and personal privacy. In fact, even the judges hearing the bypass cases testified in *Hodgson* that there was no legitimate interest to be served in burdening the minors' abortion decision with such obstacles.

While everyone wishes that young women would routinely seek parental involvement in such important issues, mandating it does not magically transform a troubled family into a happy one. Such laws merely reflect wistful, nostalgic fantasies about the American family.

SEEKING INPUT FROM THE EXPERTS

Even before the inauguration, the President-elect should convene a "summit" of state reproductive rights leaders, including abortion providers, to hear testimony on the scope of the problem of access to abortion services and on possible solutions to the stark geographic disparities that currently exist. This is obviously a complex issue, but certain causal factors are clear. First, the very effective campaign by the right-to-life movement against providers and their patients has deterred many, particularly individual medical practitioners, from continuing to perform abortions. In this connection, the next President must vigorously support passage of the Reproductive Freedom Protection Act, which imposes financial sanctions on states whose law enforcement officers fail to protect the civil rights of women seeking abortions.

The shortage of providers is undoubtedly compounded by the curriculum in medical residency programs. In a 1991 survey of 286 programs, it was found that 31 percent offer no abortion training at all; only 12 percent *require* training in first-trimester abortions and 7 percent in second-trimester abortions. As recently as 1985, almost 25 percent required such training. Clearly, a change in national leadership could provide the climate needed to increase the availability of this training; the feasibility of federal funding incentives to the schools that offer or require it should be investigated as well.

RIGHTING PAST WRONGS

Within his first hundred days of taking office, the next President must inventory and rescind every executive order and departmental regulation that has been promulgated to diminish reproductive rights. (This is one area in which the draconian policies of the recent past can be undone as easily as they were imposed.) These include, but are not limited to, the following:

• *The Title X "gag rule,"* promulgated by the Secretary of Health and Human Services in 1988, prohibits nondirective counseling and referral by barring all information about abortion at more than 3,900 family planning clinics that serve over 4.5 million women each year. These regulations transform a politically neutral counseling service, as intended by Congress in enacting the program in 1970, into a mechanism for distributing one-sided information in accord with the political viewpoint of an administration. (The Supreme Court upheld the constitutionality of the regulations in the 1991 case of *Rust* v. *Sullivan*.)

• *The "Mexico City policy,"* also known as the international gag rule, was announced at the 1984 Mexico City International Conference on Population by the Reagan-appointed delegate. It provides that foreign nongovernmental family planning programs must withhold all information and services relating to abortion in exchange for financial contributions from the United States.

• *The rule prohibiting abortion services in overseas military hospitals* was announced by the Department of Defense in 1988. It bars military women and their dependents from obtaining abortions in these facilities, even with their own funds.

• *The ban on federally funded research using fetal tissue*, in effect since 1987, prohibits the use of federal funds for research that uses tissue obtained from abortions, on the remarkable ground that such funding supposedly encourages more abortions. Since fetal tissue has proven invaluable to research into many diseases, including diabetes, Parkinson's and Alzheimer's, and since very limited amounts are available from miscarriages and ectopic pregnancies, this policy has proven particularly divisive even within the Republican party.

Of course, the most fundamental change to be sought from a new Administration is the restoration of the right to abortion itself, which the Supreme Court has done so much to undermine. While nothing can be done in the short term to reconstitute the Court, the new President must aggressively work with Congress to pass the Freedom of Choice Act with no restrictive amendments. This act is designed to codify *Roe* v. *Wade*, statutorily guaranteeing the same rights that are gradually being dismantled by the judiciary. It specifically prohibits the states from restricting the right of a woman to terminate a pregnancy before the fetus is viable, or after viability if an abortion is necessary to protect her life or health. (The original, expansive language of the Act has already been amended to allow great latitude to the states with respect to minors' abortions, public funding, and conscientious opposition to performing abortions.)

Long-Term Priorities

THE NEW ADMINISTRATION must also act on a continuing basis to promote equity in the delivery of health care, including abortion services, and to reduce the rate of unwanted pregnancies. Several programs should be initiated toward meeting these goals.

IMPROVING ACCESS TO SERVICE

Correcting the gross maldistribution of abortion services nationwide should be an ongoing priority. As in the period before *Roe*, a woman's access to abortion providers is again largely an accident of geography. The expected proliferation of new state regulations in the wake of the *Casey* decision will only make matters worse. Tax, medical school loan forgiveness, or other incentives to encourage clinics or doctors to locate in underserved areas should be investigated and, if feasible, implemented on an experimental basis.

The Title X program, which gives federal funds to clinics providing family planning (but not abortion) services, should be strengthened and reauthorized on a long-term basis. Recently this program has been funded year-to-year because it has been caught in the crossfire of the abortion debate in Congress. The need for comprehensive family planning services nationwide is patently clear, and this program should not be held hostage to extraneous issues.

PUBLIC FUNDING

After several adverse Supreme Court decisions and intense congressional activity in the mid-1970s, the issue of public funding of abortions was lost, it seems, never to be heard about again. For all intents and purposes, it has been ceded to the right-to-life movement. But why? For any right to be meaningful, whether it is constitutionally mandated or statutorily created, it must be available to all of the people, regardless of indigence. To hold otherwise is tantamount to granting the right to vote but allowing a heavy poll tax. And the ban on public funding has implications far beyond Medicaid alone. Women in prisons, women on Native American reservations, federal employees, and many others are affected by it.

The new President must lay the political groundwork to guarantee essential fairness. In this connection, he must work to secure passage of the Reproductive Health Equity Act, which legislatively restores public funding to abortion services on the same basis that government moneys are available for pregnancy-related services. In addition to the inherent philosophical value in restoring public funding, it would also have the concomitant effect of redistributing abortion services, since more doctors, clinics, and even public hospitals would find it economically feasible to perform abortions.

RESEARCH AND EDUCATION

Creating an environment hospitable to advancing research in new methods of family planning, thereby reducing the need for abortion, is also an important priority. Programs and funding for contraceptive research have been proceeding at a snail's pace; this country now lags far behind Western European countries.

The failure of the United States to allow the importation of the revolutionary French abortifacient RU-486 is perhaps the starkest evidence that public health has yielded to the pressures exerted by the right-to-life movement. The drug, though successfully used by over 100,000 French women, is currently under an "import alert," which bans its importation for consumer use. This ban should be lifted immediately, and everything possible should be done to encourage its testing and licensing by the Food and Drug Administration.

In addition to its proven effectiveness as a private, nonsurgical method of terminating pregnancy during the earliest stages, RU-486 may prove to be an effective monthly contraceptive and a natural weapon against breast cancer and other cancers and tumors. Nevertheless, the requests of two prestigious cancer research centers to explore this possibility were turned down by the Federal Government.

Pregnancy prevention programs and policies also deserve ongoing attention, as they are obviously the most effective ways to mitigate the need for abortion. Both improved sex education and more available methods of birth control would help to reduce the burgeoning teen pregnancy rate. The current administration, however, has insisted on hiding its head in the sand. In a recent but by no means unique move, for example, the federal Office of Personnel Management (OPM) has deleted a chapter titled "Adolescent Sexuality: Preventing Unwanted Consequences" from a medical guide that Blue Cross/Blue Shield sent to 275,000 federal employees. It was felt by a senior OPM official that the six-page discussion on contraception was "too controversial" for some parents.

JUDICIAL SELECTION POLICIES

Finally, we must recognize that the U.S. Supreme Court stands as a significant obstacle to even the most modest prescription for change. The constitutionality of each and every abortion-related congressional enactment and state law will undoubtedly be tested in the coming years in the federal court system, which has been remade over the past twelve years in the image of Ronald Reagan and George Bush. In fact, over 65 percent of the currently sitting federal judges, and five of the nine U.S. Supreme Court Justices, have been appointed during these administrations. (Eight of the nine justices were chosen by Nixon, Reagan, or Bush; and the ninth, Justice Byron White, is nonetheless part of the current Court's conservative majority.) On the circuit courts of appeals, Reagan-Bush appointees hold the majority of seats on eleven of the thirteen courts and a plurality on the other two.

Since roughly 5 percent of the federal bench turns over each year, the next eight years could radically change the face of the judiciary once again. Whatever one's attitude toward the legitimacy of ideological questions and "litmus tests," it *is* clear that the new President must at least determine that anyone under serious consideration for federal judicial appointment has a vision of the Constitution that comprehends a progressive, developmental notion of individual rights and liberties.

Conclusion

IT IS CLEAR THAT THE *WILL* TO MOVE an anti-choice agenda, coupled with the strategic use of presidential power, has resulted in one of the most dramatic policy successes of the Reagan-Bush years. Likewise, the will to move a reproductive rights agenda, and the willingness to use every legitimate method to do so, can achieve a similarly dramatic result in the next Administration. Much of the damage of the past twelve years is reversible; the lives and health of millions of women depend on its being reversed, and soon.

AIDS

OLIVIER SULTAN

Summary

F OR TWELVE YEARS, the Reagan and Bush administrations played politics with one of the worst public health crises of this century, the epidemic of AIDS. Since initially detected in 1981, AIDS has taken over 150,000 lives in the United States. Some 100,000 Americans are currently living with AIDS, and over 1 million are believed to be infected with HIV. The next President must confront AIDS as the public emergency it is.

• *Leadership*. The President must use the power of his office to mobilize and organize the nation against AIDS. He must designate one Cabinet-level person in charge of coordinating and implementing the Federal Government's action against AIDS, and establish better cooperation with state and local governments, community-based organizations, and international organizations.

• *Prevention and Education*. We can limit the spread of HIV if only we can encourage people to avoid high-risk sexual behavior. Therefore, the next President should lead a nationwide effort to educate all Americans, especially those most at risk, on safer behavior. In particular, the President should help lift the de facto ban on condom advertising on the airwaves.

The President should reallocate some of the War on Drugs monies to fund prevention education programs and drug treatment on demand, and encourage states to develop needle-exchange and needle-bleaching programs.

And government at all levels should encourage the distribution of condoms, especially to adolescents in schools and prisons.

Olivier Sultan, former Research Director of the Democracy Project, is a Yale Law School student. The author wishes to thank Dr. June Osborn, chair of the National Commission on AIDS, for her invaluable assistance.

- *Medical research*. Funding for HIV research must be increased. The health agencies must continue their efforts to open up clinical trials and make available safe experimental drugs, especially to groups who have been traditionally excluded.

Finally, planning for the distribution of an AIDS vaccine should start now.

- *Treatment and care of persons with AIDS or HIV*. Early intervention can help prolong the lives of people with HIV. The government should promote early detection through voluntary, confidential or anonymous testing, with pre- and post-testing counseling available. The next Administration and Congress should also renew their commitment to community-based organizations and fund the Ryan White CARE Act at authorized levels.

Finally, the next President must create a national health care coverage program.

The Reagan-Bush Legacy

IN THE SUMMER OF 1981 the first cases of what we now call AIDS were reported by the Centers for Disease Control (CDC), the chief surveillance arm of the U.S. Public Health Service. In 1982, the CDC officially classified the new collection of clinical conditions as a syndrome. Ten years later, AIDS has become possibly the greatest health crisis of our time, imposing a dramatic toll in human lives and on the nation's economy and health care systems.

- By the end of 1991, more people had died of AIDS in this country than in the combined Vietnam and Korean wars; and while it took almost ten years for the first 100,000 deaths from AIDS among Americans to occur, the next 100,000 deaths will occur in only two years. The death toll is projected to reach 350,000 by the end of 1993.[1]

- Some 100,000 Americans are currently living with AIDS, and over 1 million may be infected with HIV (the virus associated with AIDS), some already ill. The CDC estimates that some 50,000 to 60,000 Americans develop full-blown AIDS each year, while 40,000 to 80,000 get infected each year, including up to 2,000 babies.[2]

- The number of AIDS cases among teenagers has increased 70 percent over the past two years. AIDS is now the sixth-leading cause of death among 15- to 24-year-olds.[3] And as the rate of infection among gay men seems to be declining, it is rising for women and children—especially among African Americans and Latinos.

- By 1993 AIDS will clearly outstrip all other diseases in lost human potential. The annual loss in productivity attributable to illness and pre-

mature death due to AIDS was expected to reach an estimated $55 billion
by 1991.[4] And a federal study in 1991 estimated that the nation's medical
bill for treating people with AIDS and HIV carriers would jump from $5.8
billion that year to $7.2 billion in 1992, and to $10.4 billion in 1994.[5]

Yet President Reagan simply ignored the emerging epidemic until his
friend Rock Hudson died in 1985—by which time some 20,000 Americans
had died from AIDS-related causes. Until then he "apparently thought of
AIDS as something like a passing epidemic of measles."[6]

George Bush raised hopes that his administration would adopt a kinder,
gentler response to the crisis, with a landmark speech in March 1990 in
which he called for "compassionate care" for people with AIDS. That was
the last of the president's leadership on this issue. Funding for AIDS has
gone up only 113 percent under the Bush administration—from $2.3 billion
in 1989 to a requested $4.9 billion for 1993—but the majority of the money
is entitlement spending (e.g., Medicare, Medicaid, income support) that has
gone up only "because more and more Americans are dying of AIDS, and
they are eligible for basic safety-net programs because they are elderly,
disabled, veterans, or poor," as Representative Henry A. Waxman (D., Calif.)
points out.[7]

Funding for research has increased 33 percent since 1989—from $892
million to $1.19 billion—but is now barely keeping up with inflation.[8] An-
thony Fauci, director of the National Institute of Allergy and Infectious
Disease of the National Institutes of Health (NIH), admits that proposed
levels of funding for 1993 "certainly will slow down" work toward a cure.[9]

But the greatest failure of the Reagan and Bush administrations was
their unwillingness to address the AIDS epidemic as a public health issue.
There is little doubt that President Reagan would have responded with
greater urgency if the disease had not first struck gay and bisexual men and
injecting drug users (IDUs). And the Bush administration opposed measures
advocated by most health experts to make high-risk behavior less so. Example: more than 30 percent of AIDS cases can be linked, either directly
or indirectly, to intravenous drug use. Yet despite considerable empirical
evidence that needle-exchange programs help reduce HIV infection among
IDUs and do not increase drug use (quite the contrary), the President's drug
czar, Bob Martinez, opposed such programs as "wrong on moral grounds."[10]
At the same time, drug treatment programs remain grossly underfunded.
Example: the administration continuously fought against explicit educational
material in this country—for instance, putting together a $1.5 million ad-
vertising campaign that did not once mention the words "sex" and "condoms"—and opposed the distribution of condoms in schools, while spending

more than $3 million to distribute condoms abroad that are marketed "like Coca Cola."[11]

The Reagan and Bush administrations ignored the recommendations of commission after commission and failed to put together a comprehensive strategy to fight the epidemic—leading the bipartisan National Commission on AIDS to conclude, "President Bush and the Department of Health and Human Services have failed to meet fully their responsibilities in leading the national response to the monumental human suffering and economic loss from the HIV/AIDS epidemic."[12] Ten months after the President appointed him to the Commission, Magic Johnson resigned, expressing to Mr. Bush his disappointment "that you dropped the ball, and your administration is not doing everything that it must to fight this disease."[13]

Action Plan for the Next President

LEADERSHIP

AIDS challenges not only the ingenuity of our medical researchers but also the ability of our nation to rise above prejudice and ignorance. Only the President of the United States has the stature to lead these two struggles. The next President must use the power of the bully pulpit to combat discrimination against persons with AIDS and HIV, depoliticize the scientific response to the epidemic, and muster the resources needed to get the job done. In particular, he should address head on some of the more difficult issues tied to the epidemic, such as the mistrust of the role of government in the African American community; hostility from sections of the general public against homosexuals and drug users; the need for honest, explicit prevention efforts, especially for adolescents; people's irrational fear of people with AIDS; civil rights issues; the urgency and determination to find a cure; and the need for accelerated funding for education, research, treatment, and care for people with HIV.

Federal efforts have suffered from lack of coordination among the many departments and agencies who ought to play a role in the nation's response. AIDS raises challenges that go beyond the jurisdiction of the health agencies to a host of other departments as well—from the Department of Justice to the Department of Housing and Urban Development. The next President needs to designate one senior official, of cabinet rank, to coordinate the government's plan of action. Such a person could be the Vice President, a newly empowered head of the Domestic Policy Council, or an appointed "AIDS czar" with the necessary authority to act in coordination with other cabinet members. At the same time, the President should end the politicization of high-level appointments in scientific and technical agencies, tapping instead into the large pool of talent in the scientific and healthcare communities.

There must also be better coordination with, and assistance extended to, state and local governments and private and nonprofit agencies. Here the Federal Government can play an important role of oversight, guidance, and clearinghouse for worthwhile local initiatives that other communities ought to emulate.

The Federal Government should also reassert its role of leadership in the international community, leading the world's efforts in research and technical assistance to other countries, and avoiding the hostility of the international AIDS community by closing its frontiers to people with HIV. The Agency for International Development should cooperate with international bodies such as the United Nations and the World Health Organization to address the tragedy of AIDS in sub-Saharan Africa and the emerging epidemics in Asia and Latin America. Immediately, the Immigration and Naturalization Service should rescind immigration restrictions against people with HIV.

Once the federal apparatus is in place, the appointed coordinator of the government's efforts should bring together officials, experts, grass-roots activists, people with HIV, and others to conduct an honest assessment of the scale of the crisis and to devise a well-thought-out, comprehensive strategy. In that area, the President and his designee should take advantage of the numerous studies already conducted by federal agencies and commissions, such as the recommendations of the National Commission on AIDS in its 1991 report *America Living with AIDS*.

PREVENTION AND EDUCATION

As long as there is no cure or vaccine for AIDS, the only protection against the virus is prevention. The good news is that HIV is not casually transmissible through sharing kitchen utensils or handshakes, for instance. In fact, the health care community essentially knows the means of transmission of the virus—sexual contact, sharing of contaminated injection equipment, exposure to infected blood or blood products, and to an infant during gestation or at birth. In some rare cases, transmission may also happen through breast-feeding. Therefore, HIV infection is uniquely preventable through the avoidance of risk behavior.

But here again, politics has been the enemy of science. The Federal government should be at the forefront of a national effort to educate everyone, in particular the communities most affected, about the ways to protect themselves, and should lead state and local governments in establishing programs known to work to reduce high-risk behavior. But because HIV transmission involves such taboo subjects as sex and drugs, the administration has gotten mired into right-wing politics, opposing explicit measures that would save life and advocating a simplistic (and ineffective) "Just Say No" approach to both sexual conduct and use of drugs.

In the face of a crisis that has already taken many lives—and threatens to take countless more—the next Administration needs to set prejudices and moralizing aside and shape its response based on good social and medical science and a decade of programs that work. The new President should, within his first few weeks in office, present a national HIV prevention initiative comprising accessible and explicit education, drug treatment on demand, needle-exchange and needle-bleaching programs, and condom distribution.

Funding Social Science. The next Administration must base its efforts on good social science. There is a lot we don't know scientifically and medically concerning AIDS, but there is also a lot we don't know in terms of prevention—behavioral factors, for instance. Only government can fund such research—but unfortunately, the Bush administration in 1992 canceled a broad survey on sexual behavior after objections from far-right members of Congress and activists. Ignorance is not a plausible policy.

Education. The Administration must work with state and local governments and grass-roots organizations to educate people on the means of transmission of HIV and how to protect themselves. Education works. First, as the National Commission on AIDS pointed out, "[t]he discrimination that occurs against people with HIV disease results largely from fear and ignorance, and the best weapon against these is education."

Second, there is some evidence that the rate of new infections among urban gay white men has decreased in recent years, in part in response to efforts by members of this group to educate others about safer behavior. But educational materials must be carefully developed to reach those for whom they are intended—ideally, by members of their community—and be accurate, accessible, nonjudgmental, and frank: e.g., abstention *and* safer sex; drug cessation *and* safer drug injection. The Administration should work with Congress and the CDC to lift current content restrictions that block the very type of explicit education that is most needed.

Education should be targeted in particular at the most vulnerable groups—such as the poor and the homeless, prison populations, ethnic minorities, women (who often believe they are not at risk), and teenagers, among whom AIDS cases have jumped 70 percent over the past two years. The Secretary of Education should encourage state and local school boards to develop comprehensive AIDS curricula for the schools, starting with the early grades and including material relevant for each age group.

Various studies show that about half of sexually active teenagers do not use condoms. Yet the CDC in July 1992 vetoed some TV and radio ads as part of its much-touted, $1.5 million "America Responds to AIDS" campaign that included use of the words "sex" and "condoms."[14] The next Administration should end this Comstockian reluctance to promote the use of condoms aggressively, as is done in many European countries and in Mexico,[15] and should reach out to the TV networks to encourage them to accept ads and public service announcements promoting the use of condoms as an alternative to abstinence.

Drug use. But we need to go beyond education. Take the case of intravenous drug use. IDUs now represent more than 50 percent of new AIDS cases along much of the East Coast. The Bush administration opposed needle-exchange and needle-bleaching programs, preferring the "Just Say No" strategy made famous by Nancy Reagan—but yet repeatedly failed to fund drug treatment programs adequately for those eager to follow its advice. Drug treatment services are currently available to fewer than a third of the nation's estimated 5.8 million heavy drug users.[16] In no large city is the waiting period to be admitted in a program less than four weeks. The government spends $11 billion a year on the War on Drugs, but most of that money goes to interdiction and law enforcement efforts.

The new Administration should (a) reallocate War on Drugs money to assure treatment on demand, (b) lift the ban on federal funds for needle-exchange and needle-bleaching programs and (c) encourage states to develop such programs through War on Drugs matching grants. Many officials who initially opposed needle-exchange programs have reversed themselves in the face of overwhelming evidence from Europe, Australia, Canada, and the United States that these programs work. In August 1991, an eight-month-old New Haven program showed a 33 percent reduction in new HIV infections among participants.[17] And many of these programs serve as conduits to drug treatment as well.[18] Needle-bleaching programs have also proved successful to slow new HIV infection.

Sexual Transmission. Half of girls have sex by age seventeen and half of boys by age sixteen. Thirty-three percent of women with AIDS report being infected through heterosexual contact.[19] Clearly, the government needs not only to tell teenagers and others about abstinence but also encourage those who will engage in sexual behavior to engage in safer sex. Most importantly, the government needs to encourage the use of condoms—and, to the extent possible, make condoms available in schools. The concept may be less controversial than expected: A 1992 national Gallup poll found 68 percent support among adults, and only 25 percent opposed.[20] One important vehicle could be the Comprehensive Youth Service Act of 1992, which would provide resources to establish school-based comprehensive health and social service centers. The Federal Government should also distribute condoms in prisons, the public institutions with the highest rate of HIV infection. Also, an important element for prevention of HIV is the early detection and treatment of other sexually transmitted diseases, such as syphilis.

In addition, the government should encourage research for alternative means to prevent HIV transmission during sexual exchanges. In many cultures, it may be difficult (or even dangerous) for a woman to ask her partner to use a condom.

Finally, it is important to note one success of the Reagan administration: Because of systematic testing and voluntary deferral of individuals in high-risk groups, the blood supplies can be considered safe.

MEDICAL RESEARCH

Scientists have done an impressive job unveiling the mysteries of AIDS. By late 1983, Professor Luc Montagnier at the Pasteur Institute had isolated the human immunodeficiency virus. By mid-1985, American researchers had developed technology to screen blood supplies; and by 1987 the drug AZT was found to have certain antiviral properties against HIV. For people with HIV with access to available treatments, HIV need no longer be the short-term death sentence it once was.

But there is still a lot we do not know about the virus—for instance, the comparative efficiency of various means of transmission. And, of course, there is still no cure or vaccine.

Increased funding and resources for research. Funding for research, which increased rapidly after 1985 under congressional pressure, is now barely keeping up with inflation. The next Administration must renew our financial commitment in the search for a cure, for a vaccine and for treatment of the various conditions associated with AIDS and HIV (especially opportunistic infections). Besides the NIH (which conducts its own research) and the FDA (which reviews drug approval requests), the CDC is currently under heavy strain from AIDS and the emerging tuberculosis epidemic, but its spending has remained flat. Increased funding for surveillance of the epidemic to maintain the best information possible is simply essential.

Increased access to experimental drugs. The HIV epidemic has brought to the forefront the conflicting needs of scientists for rigorous research methods and of their experimental subjects whose lives are at risk. For people with AIDS or HIV whose conditions may have no known treatment or who are allergic to existing drugs, experimental drugs are often the only hope for survival. AIDS activist organizations such as ACT UP have achieved a small revolution in the scientific world by dramatically speeding up and opening up clinical trials, increasing patient access to drugs in trial, and gaining a voice on many decisionmaking bodies such as the NIH, the Food and Drug Administration, the Institute of Medicine, and institutional review boards. More progress is needed, and the AIDS czar should review the procedures of the various scientific agencies to that end.

In particular, the next Administration should build on the existing computerized database completed by the Department of Health and Human Services in July 1989 to make available information about ongoing clinical trials to patients and their doctors.

Second, the NIH and others must continue their efforts to open up clinical trials to groups that have been traditionally excluded, and actively seek out individuals in those groups. Programs for drug users, African Americans, women, children, prisoners, and other groups who have been excluded need to be developed similar to the "AIDS Clinical Trial Group Without Walls" concept that specifically conducts clinical studies for hemophiliacs. Pediatric research should be developed, with necessary precautions.

Third, many patients have gained access to promising new drugs through "compassionate use" investigative new drugs (INDs), which make potentially life-saving drugs under study available outside traditional clinical trials. The next Administration should quickly promulgate regulations under review since September 1990 for such "parallel track" distribution.

Fourth, the new President must sign the reforms to the 1983 Orphan Drug Act that Congress passed and President Bush vetoed in 1991. The act was initially intended to encourage pharmaceutical companies to develop drugs for treating small numbers of people with rare diseases, by providing them with financial incentives and a seven-year exclusive right to the drug's market. Unfortunately, companies have abused the act with such drugs as AZT and aerosol pentamidine. The National Commission on AIDS soundly suggests a cap on sales and profits that "would deny orphan status to a drug once it had proved very profitable."[21]

Early Planning for a Vaccine. It now seems unlikely that a vaccine will be available before the next century. But the new Administration should start considering the complex issues raised by development, testing, and distribution of a vaccine. For instance: How will the vaccine be tested in humans? Once approved, how will it be distributed in regions of the world lacking easy access and well-developed health care structures? And how should companies be encouraged to develop a vaccine in the face of potentially enormous liability risks?

TREATMENT AND CARE FOR PERSONS WITH AIDS OR HIV

Even if no additional person became infected with HIV, the number of people already infected is believed to exceed 1 million. They need and deserve compassionate and quality care and treatment.

The good news is that treatments now exist to delay the emergence of AIDS in people with HIV, and the progression of disease in persons with AIDS. Early detection and early intervention are critical. The CDC estimates that approximately 60 percent of individuals with HIV infection could benefit from early intervention. Unfortunately, it is believed that only 12 percent of people who are infected know of their serostatus.[22]

Testing. Early detection is the first priority. The Federal Government needs to encourage sound testing procedures at all levels of government.

The government should encourage broad voluntary testing by setting up strict requirements for mandatory pre- and post-test counseling, availability of confidential and anonymous testing, confidentiality rules, and protection against discrimination for persons with HIV or AIDS.*

Mandatory testing is probably one of the most inefficient forms of AIDS-related expenses. Both Illinois and Louisiana experimented with mandated premarital screening; both quickly rescinded their statutes as not cost-effective. In the first six months of the Illinois program, 70,846 applicants for marriage were tested; only 8 were found seropositive, half of them in high-risk groups. Cost of the program: $2.5 million, or $312,000 for each HIV-positive individual identified. At the same time, the number of marriage

---

*In particular, the Department of Justice should closely monitor implementation of the Americans with Disabilities Act, which bars private-sector discrimination in employment, public accommodations, transportation, and public services.

Regarding strict confidentiality rules, continued developments in the benefits of early intervention for people with HIV may warrant reconsideration of notification of sexual partners. Potential benefits should be weighed, however, against the risk of deterring people from being tested once confidentiality is no longer assured.

licenses fell 22.5 percent while increasing in neighboring states, costing
Illinois an additional $77,250.[23]

Recent consideration was given to mandatory testing of health care
personnel following the highly publicized case of Kimberly Bergalis, infected
by her dentist in Florida. The chance of getting infected during surgery
ranges from 1 in 41,000 to 1 in 416,000; during a visit to the dentist, from
1 in 263,000 to 1 in 2.6 million.[24] But the cost of mandatory testing for health
care personnel could add $1 billion to the annual U.S. healthcare budget.[25]
Again, it is a waste of money we can ill afford. Instead, the Federal Government should adopt guidelines to protect both patients and health care
personnel similar to those adopted by New York State's Department of
Health.

Case Management. People with HIV or AIDS face myriad challenges. On
the medical front, they have to get tested, undergo continued monitoring
of their condition, stay on top of clinical trials and new developments in
drug research, and plan for long-term care. In addition, they often require
comprehensive social service assistance, from housing to counseling to income. A physician cannot be expected to meet those needs. But local organizations are increasingly training case managers to help with all aspects
of the disease.

Community-based organizations (CBOs) and demonstrations projects
such as the "San Francisco Model" have played a crucial role in the struggle
against AIDS—for instance, helping patients avoid hospitalization for home
care or nursing homes, and significantly bringing down health care costs. In
1990 Congress enacted the Ryan White CARE Act to encourage the provision
of ambulatory care services to people with HIV, through federal grants. The
program was especially beneficial for underserved areas. But funding has
remained far below the authorized level of $850 million. The next President
should demand that Congress fully fund implementation of the act. In addition, the Federal Government should work with state and local governments to provide technical support to CBOs and others on the front lines
of the AIDS epidemic.

Availability of Health Care Personnel. AIDS has created additional pressure on a health care system already under stress. The Federal Government should encourage more health care providers to assist persons with
HIV or AIDS, by expanding the National Health Service Corps and by developing new programs such as the Disadvantaged Minority Health Improvement Act to attract minority health care workers. Specific HIV/AIDS

fellowships and training programs should be established, especially in underserved areas.

In addition, many doctors are reluctant to accept AIDS patients on Medicaid because reimbursement levels are very low—64 percent of the rates for Medicare. Reimbursement rates for Medicaid should be brought to par with Medicare.

Financing. As the National Commission on AIDS has pointed out, "[c]osts for HIV care presently and in the foreseeable future probably total no more than 2 percent of total U.S. health expenditures."[26] The burden of health care financing is therefore a burden not so much for society at large as for the individuals directly affected. Studies from 1991 estimated that the direct medical cost for treating a person with HIV was close to $6,000 a year, while the direct cost for a person with AIDS was $32,000 a year. These costs are especially daunting considering that most people with AIDS are either uninsured (29 percent) or underinsured.

Our health care system is in disarray. Thirty-seven million Americans lack health care insurance. The next President should heed the recommendation of the National Commission on AIDS and countless others and create a program of universal health care coverage that would include drug payments.*

Until such a program is in place, the new Administration should enact the following measures:

• Ninety percent of the cost of medical care for a person with HIV goes to high-priced drugs.[27] To bring the cost of drugs down, the next President should sign the Drug Orphan Act reform that President Bush vetoed and undertake a consolidated purchase and distribution of drugs for prevention and treatment of HIV diseases. Under a similar program for childhood vaccines, the government purchases large quantities from drug manufacturers at 40 percent below private-sector costs.[28]

• Forty percent of AIDS patients are insured through Medicaid. But too many are driven to extreme poverty to qualify, and many people with HIV do not qualify because they are not considered "totally disabled." The government should raise income eligibility levels and broaden requirements to include persons with HIV illness. Raising the income level to 100 percent of the federal poverty level, for instance, would expand coverage to an additional 70,500 people and cost the Federal Government $176 million (and state governments a total of $169 million).[29]

*See Theodore R. Marmor and Michael S. Barr's chapter on health care in this section.

In addition, the Federal Government should significantly raise the cap on total Medicaid expenditures for Puerto Rico, where the AIDS epidemic is intense.

• Twenty-nine percent of AIDS patients have private insurance that often is inadequate, or that they risk losing with their jobs. Under the COBRA program, disabled individuals can retain their insurance coverage for twenty-nine months after they leave their jobs. The government should help pay COBRA premiums for people with HIV, as eight states already do—and could actually save money by keeping individuals on private insurance rather than Medicaid.

• Finally, 2 percent of people with AIDS are on Medicare. Nonelderly disabled individuals must first qualify for Social Security disability insurance and then wait two years before being eligible for Medicare. The government should lift this two-year waiting period.

Poverty. HIV disproportionally hits the poor. And many *become* poor after contracting HIV, either because they cannot retain their job, because of the cost of drugs or to qualify for Medicare. As a result, many persons with HIV are homeless and lack a steady income. Lack of affordable and appropriate housing is an acute problem of those caught in the epidemic. The next President should direct his Secretary of Housing and Urban Development to make provisions for housing these people a priority.

NOTES

1. National Commission on AIDS, *America Living with AIDS* (1991), p. 3.
2. Eric Eckholm, "Aids, Fatally Steady in the U.S., Accelerates Worldwide," *The New York Times* (June 28, 1992), p. E5.
3. Report by the House Select Committee on Children, Youth, and Families, in "U.S. Response to Youth and AIDS Is Criticized," *The New York Times* (April 12, 1992), p. A27.
4. Anne Skitovsky, "Estimates of the Direct and Indirect Costs of AIDS in the United States" in Alan F. Fleming et al. (eds.), *The Global Impact of AIDS* (New York: Alan R. Liss, 1988), chap. 17.
5. Study by the Agency for Health Care Policy and Research in Malcom Ritter, "Price Tag of AIDS Reaches $5.8B," *Daily News* (November 29, 1992), p. 26.
6. Robert S. Walker, *AIDS: Today, Tomorrow* (New Jersey: Humanities Press International, 1991), p. 120, quoting interview with Brigadier General John Hutton, President Reagan's physician, in the *San Antonio Express News* (September 1, 1989), p. 1.
7. Hillary Stout, "Adequacy of Spending on AIDS Is an Issue Not Easily Resolved," *The Wall Street Journal* (April 22, 1992), p. A1.

8. Robert Pear, "As Bush Defends AIDS Policy, Its Critics See Flaws," *The New York Times* (October 18, 1992), p. A27.

9. Stout, "Adequacy of Spending On AIDS Is an Issue Not Easily Resolved," p. A1.

10. Robert Pear, "U.S. Drug Official Urges Mayors to Forgo Needle-Swap Programs," *The New York Times* (June 3, 1992).

11. Stout, "Adequacy of Spending on AIDS Is an Issue Not Easily Resolved," p. A1.

12. Philip J. Hilts, "National AIDS Panel Says Administration Has Not Done Enough," *The New York Times* (June 26, 1992), p. A18.

13. Philip J. Hilts, "Magic Johnson Quits Panel on AIDS," *The New York Times* (September 26, 1992), p. A5.

14. Philip J. Hilts, "U.S. Agency Is Criticized for Dropping AIDS Ads," *The New York Times* (July 1, 1992).

15. "Notes and Comments," *The New Yorker* (September 16, 1991), p. 23.

16. Joseph B. Treaster, "Candidates Seek Little Change in Antidrug Efforts," *The New York Times* (October 22, 1992), p. A22.

17. Mirey Navarro, "Yale Study Reports Clean Needle Project Helps Check AIDS," *The New York Times* (August 1, 1991), p. A1.

18. Olivier Sultan, "A Case for the City's Needle-Exchange Program," *The New York Observer* (December 19, 1988), p. 8.

19. National Commission on AIDS, *America Living with AIDS*, pp. 27–8.

20. Karen De Witt, "Poll Shows 68% Support Distribution of Condoms at School," *The New York Times* (August 28, 1992).

21. National Commission on AIDS, *America Living with AIDS*, p. 84.

22. Ibid., p. 74.

23. James F. Childress, "Mandatory HIV Screening and Testing" in Frederic G. Raemer, ed., *AIDS & Ethics* (New York: Columbia University Press, 1991), pp. 63–4.

24. Michael Kinsley, "Red Peril," *The New Republic* (August 12, 1992), p. 4.

25. Jessie Mangaliman, "How Much Will It Cost?," *New York Newsday* (September 21, 1992), p. 73.

26. National Commission on AIDS, *America Living With AIDS*, p. 68.

27. Ibid., pp. 70, 75. The cost of treating people with AIDS is expected to increase as IVUs become a greater percentage of AIDS patients, since they usually face other, simultaneous health care problems.

28. Ibid., p. 83.

29. Ibid, pp. 77–8.

PART V

REGULATORY POLICY

OVERVIEW: REGULATION

RALPH NADER

H OW MUCH STAMINA DOES THE LAW HAVE regarding corporate misbehavior and consumer safety standards when confronted by raw political power? One textbook answer could be seen in the Reagan/Bush determination to impair or destroy the various missions of the regulatory agencies to advance the health, safety, and marketplace rights of consumers and workers.

Even before the recent ideological assault on public health and consumer laws, regulation has been historically undermined. After the first wave of regulatory agencies—commencing in 1887 with the Interstate Commerce Act—was subjected to academic appraisal through the 1950s, the progressive view was that the regulatees were controlling the regulators. Studies documented how railroads, trucking companies, and airlines twisted the Interstate Commerce Commission and the Civil Aeronautics Board to be their legal price-fixers and promoters of their anticompetitive interests, rather than defenders of consumers and competition. Congressional hearings and other reports showed how industry lobbyists—routinely nourished by the revolving door of former regulatory appointees—shaped the agenda and output of these agencies. And then their influence on Capitol Hill blocked any corrective amendments. (The correlation of PACs and votes is illuminated by Ellen Miller and Phil Stern's chapter in this book.) Consequently, the learning curve of experience was not allowed to improve the consumer protection work of regulators who labored under a framework largely frozen in an early-twentieth-century format.

For decades, the supposed beneficiaries of these agencies—consumers—were neither encouraged, informed, nor empowered to participate in formal proceedings. Barriers of secrecy, lack of standing to petition or sue the agency, judicial deference to agency decisions no matter how insupportable, unavailability of experts, and the prohibitive cost to participate

---

Ralph Nader, the well-known consumer advocate, has started dozens of ongoing organizations advocating consumer and environmental interests.

combined to shut them out. The results: a cushy agency culture that embraced the purported regulatees.

Then, beginning with the Carter years, an elaborate network of antiregulatory think tanks, led by the American Enterprise Institute and the Heritage Foundation, produced torrents of reports purporting to demonstrate the failure of all kinds of regulations and the superiority of unrestrained markets (with the notable exception of federal programs designed to subsidize some businesses directly or through tax expenditures). The antiregulatory catechisms reached such a fever pitch that the nation's declining innovation, productivity, and "competitiveness" were even attributed to the stifling hand of regulation.

Since 1980, these trends have exponentially accelerated. With virtually no statutory authority to do so, the Reagan and Bush administrations took the existing statutes they inherited and let them operationally lapse. Almost whatever corporate lobbies wanted done or not done was what they received, if not from these regulatory agencies then through the secret back-door maneuvers of the Quayle Competitiveness Council and its patron/ally, the Office of Management and Budget (OMB).

As the following chapters demonstrate, agency budgets were routinely cut, standards were not issued, other standards were weakened or revoked, recalls were not ordered, information was withheld or not collected, and violations were ignored. For the most part, agencies were headed by presidential appointees who openly declared their resolve to dismantle their agency's lawful purposes in the name of deregulation. Secretary of Transportation Drew Lewis told an auto dealers' convention in early 1981, for example, that as far as he was concerned there would be no auto safety standards issued in the first Reagan term. Indeed, that department would issue no safety standards of any consequence to the end of the Bush term, except a modified passive restraint regulation known as the air bag standard, due to a U.S. Supreme Court order after Reagan unlawfully revoked the Carter standard in 1981.

Although these Reagan/Bush appointees all took an oath of office to enforce the laws of the land, their unbridled political discretion to negate these laws, to decline program implementation, and to do so with subsequent administrative impunity has raised, as never before, this question: Are these laws that direct the health, safety, and financial services and telecommunications industries mere exhortations at the whim of the "rule of man" over the "rule of law"? Beyond Reagan's sheer lawlessness, Bush's devolutionary contributions extended the brazenness of the Office of Management and Budget and the Quayle Competiveness Council to new lows—not just interfering with agency standards or rulemaking work at later stages but also censoring even preliminary proposed rulemaking in clear violation of the Administrative Procedure Act and other safeguards against ex parte pressures. For the most part, the agencies learned not to resist and behaved like the newspaper editors who decide to censor themselves before the advertising agencies have to make any move in that direction.

The ruling political ideology has also diluted the external enforcement mechanisms. Reagan/Bush judges possessed by this ideology refuse to hold agencies accountable to their statutory requirements, cutting a wide swath for "agency discretion." Increasingly, they are interposing "no standing to sue" obstacles to citizen groups and other intervenors who do not have "Inc." after their names. Intervenor funding for impecunious groups considered capable of making a worthwhile contribution to agency proceedings was eliminated in 1981 from the few agencies—for example, the Federal Trade Commission (FTC) and Auto Safety—where the Carter administration had moved to reduce economic barriers to access to one's Federal Government. Congressional oversight was shrugged off again and again by the White House and Executive Branch agencies and departments, notwithstanding occasionally visible and adverse publicity. After a while committee chairs realized that the media were not interested in covering oversight hearings, thereby reducing sharply the motivations for such initiatives. And the media themselves have a bias against reporting inaction, in contrast to action, which played right into the hands of the Reagan/Bush dismantlers. So if the Environmental Protection Agency (EPA) does very little under the Drinking Water Act or if the Occupational Safety and Health Administration (OSHA) is blocked by White House politicians from issuing long-overdue workplace standards against toxics, the media yawn at such inaction.

In an unusual display of frustration, Congress during the final days of its 1992 session passed an amendment banning one hundred or more employees of the Federal Aviation Administration from receiving any of the expected pay raises for government employees on January 1, 1993, until the agency issued an overdue final environmental impact statement (mandated by an earlier law) on aircraft noise along the East Coast.

The Federal Communications Commission (FCC) has looked permissively over the way some television stations have been complying with the new Children's Television Act, which was intended to raise the quality of children's programming. Broadcasters were actually telling the FCC that compliance with the act justified *Super Mario Brothers* (which builds self-confidence), *Leave It to Beaver* (which offers moral tales), *Teenage Mutant Ninja Turtles* (which teaches "nutrition and physical fitness"), and so forth.

These compliance reports were brought to the media's attention in the autumn of 1992 by a citizen group, not by the FCC, which seems little troubled by the mockery made of a law it never liked in the first place.

Despite the new Clean Air Act's clear requirement for public participation, the EPA issued a regulation that permits companies to increase their allowed emissions unilaterally, without the need to give public notice. Someday a court will declare that rule invalid, but officials may then try another ploy to vitiate the act, for there is no penalty imposed on these officials for violating the law of their agency's mission.

So where's the opposing party as regulations implode? Democratic passivity has allowed the Republican assault to go largely unchallenged. With the exception of Chairman Henry Gonzalez and several House Banking Committee allies, the Democrats demurred from turning the deregulation of the banks by Reagan/Bush and the savings and loan debacle into major financial reforms and political popularity. Tapping the same reservoirs of campaign money from banks and other companies as do the Republicans had some connection with such lassitude. The consequences were minimal public awareness, less public mobilization, and the further institutionalization of no-law laws at the obligated expense to the taxpayers of more than $500 billion.

Company lobbyists, lawyers, and publicists also have developed a skilled culture of control over these agencies at lower levels, where civil servants retain some interest in delivering for the public. At present, corporate lawyers have so many opportunities for tying up agencies in knots for interminable delays that they can wait out entire administrations of four or eight years. And then comes a new administration that drops the standards entirely or alters them in a way to start a whole new process of procrastination. The history of the air bag standard, the drug efficacy implementation, the fuel efficiency standards, and the occupational toxics standards illustrate different ways in which laws can be blocked for years turning into decades.

Emboldened by their license to anesthetize agency actions, the OMB-Quayle Competitiveness Council suppressors pursued theories so grotesque as to be comical. In a March 10, 1992, letter to Assistant Secretary of Labor Nancy Risque-Rohrbach, an OMB deputy administrator, James B. MacRae, Jr., was not satisfied that a watered-down set of permissible exposure limits (PELs) for toxics in the construction, maritime, and agricultural industries simply complied with rigged cost-benefit formulas. He demanded to know how compliance with these health standards would "affect workers' employment, wages and therefore, health." MacRae surmised that companies would pass on any compliance costs to either workers or consumers. In either case, he wrote, lowered incomes would lead these people to smoke and drink more and eat more junk food. He suspended review of the rule proposed until such an analysis convinced him otherwise. Or heads I win, tails you lose.

The chapters that follow—as well as the chapter on the EPA in the Environmental Policy section—depict in some detail the failures of the various regulatory agencies and the interferences of the OMB in their workings. The authors also make cogent agency-specific recommendations for change and implementation of the long declared but impaired objectives of these agencies. What is lacking is a program of transagency tools that citizens can use to reverse the nullification power that has assaulted the rule of law. The tools of a citizen-driven government are based on the principle that a regulatory agency should facilitate the organized representation of its intended noncommercial beneficiaries. For the National Highway Traffic Safety Administration, that means motorists and pedestrians; for the FCC, that means radio, television, and telephone consumers; for the SEC, that means stockholders; for the FTC, FDA, and Product Safety, that means consumers. Given the observed experience of regulatory agencies and the scholarship about them, this principle is the generic basis for all other mechanisms of accountability to enhance the optimal delivery of these institutions.

One can make strong arguments for citizen participation rights (e.g., freedom of information, citizen petitions, intervenor funding, fairer agency procedures, broader citizen standing to sue), a more capable agency research and testing base, better public information and disclosure, and a system of judicial sanctions on culpable political appointees and civil servants. But where is the civic power going to come from to accomplish such objectives? One key answer is legislated programs designed to empower citizens by facilitating their banding together in nonprofit advocacy and self-help groups.

The state government of Illinois, for example, now authorizes inserts in its mass mailings that invite residential ratepayers to join the Illinois Citizen Utility Board (CUB), a nonprofit consumer group empowered to participate in gas, electric, and telephone utility regulatory procedures, with a right to take the appropriate companies to court. CUB's full-time staff and grassroots members have saved consumers over $3 billion in higher rates since 1983 in addition to their policy and other reform achievements. Parallel groups could develop if banks, insurance companies, the Postal Service, and other regulated sellers or legal monopolies were obliged to have their billing envelopes or delivery systems include invitations to customers to band together. Such consumer organizations would constitute a community intelligence, not just to participate in legal forums where decisions are made but also to bargain privately with large corporate sellers.

If such efforts existed, they could help to countervail business advocacy before regulatory judges. Yet, now there are still often hearings where the regulatee side has all the lawyers, economists, and scientists, while the affected consumer community is either invisible or underrepresented. Would we allow criminal courts to hear only from the prosecution? Or only from the defendant? One cost-effective reform to balance the scales of regulatory justice would be the creation of a small Consumer Advocacy Office, which would intervene in other agency proceedings to argue, from a consumer perspective, why a particular proposal should be enacted or strengthened. Any president who created such an office would be justly remembered as a consumer pioneer as much as Teddy Roosevelt for beginning enforcement of the antitrust laws and John F. Kennedy for announcing his "consumer bill of rights" at Yale University in 1962.

Today, regulatory decisions are anticonsumer by default as often as by design. Should there be a lawyer in a Consumer Product Safety Commission proceeding representing mothers of children who are at risk of choking on small toys? Should there have been an independent consumer advocate telling the Federal Aviation Administration not to secretly allow McDonnell Douglas substantially more time to correct its cargo-door latch problem— after which 346 people died when a cargo door blew out of a 747 outside Paris? The answer is, of course, yes. Spending $30 million a year on an office composed of scientists, economists, and lawyers representing the public's interest would end the current corporate hegemony over regulatory proceedings that affect the health, safety, and economic well-being of millions. And if the Consumer Advocacy Office intervened successfully in even one such proceeding a year, it would pay for itself in saved lives and dollars.

Moving beyond consumer intervention, the levers of federal, state, and local procurement dollars can be pressed to stimulate safety, health, and environmental innovations. Together, their procurement dollars amount to some 18 percent of the GNP, or $1 trillion dollars a year. They purchase many of the same products and services that consumers buy—motor vehicles, paper, drugs, detergents, light bulbs, energy, telecommunications, and more. Successes in the use of government procurement have included some energy-efficient buildings, generic drugs, life-cycle costing, and the purchase by the General Service Administration of fifty-three hundred air bag-equipped cars in 1985 that brought Ford Motor Company, and later the rest of the auto companies, back into the air bag business. Procurement could quickly expand the market for recycled products and photovoltaic solar units. In an era of budget deficits and corporate control of regulators, directing the government purchasing dollar toward meeting established statutory regulatory goals should prove to be popular and economical to taxpayers and consumers alike.

Government services administrator Gerald Carmen, a staunch Reaganite and quite cool to regulation, had just such an enthusiastic response to the air bag procurement proposal when I placed it on his desk in 1982. At present, OMB, no less, is expressing more than a routine interest in expanding the utility of the government purchasing lever in response to the representations of our Government Purchasing Project.

Moreover, there is great potential in the Federal Government's adopting the principle of reciprocity to condition the corporate welfare programs that make up the tens of billions of annual dollars in business subsidies, guarantees, giveaways, grants, inflated contracts, and cheap leaseholds. Reciprocity means that these taxpayer assets can be utilized for private corporate profit only if conditions are met to further the health, safety, environmental, and competition laws. It is a matter of the taxpayers receiving a return on their investment. If auto companies are bailed out in various ways, from loan guarantees to import quotas, why not require faster progress in safer and more efficient motor vehicles, which, in turn, would improve their competitiveness? If banks are to be bailed out, why not bargain for more investment in moderate- and low-income housing mortgages, an end to redlining, and inserts being periodically placed in monthly bank statements inviting customers to join in statewide financial consumer associations to watchdog both their banks and the agencies that are supposed to protect their savings? What is wrong with the government representing the taxpayers' monies in a more "businesslike" fashion, which is to say a quid pro quo? After all, a workfare program in return for federal aid to dependent corporations should resonate among both conservatives and liberals alike.

The vacuum created by the federal abdicators has led many states to move to fill the void. Worker right-to-know laws regarding toxics in the workplace started at the state level. So did community right-to-know laws such as Proposition 65, which passed in California in 1986. Other examples include laws protecting nonsmokers from cigarette smoke in public places, child safety seat use laws, and the successful California initiative raising tobacco taxes for use in antismoking programs and health coverage for the indigent. Other state safeguards regarding banking services, radioactive waste transport, and nuclear power plants, to name a few instances, found the Reagan/Bush administrations moving to preempt them federally—a strange but unsurprisingly corporatist undermining of states' rights.

Finally, an imaginative competition policy that enforces the antitrust laws can unlock many of the wasteful practices that have come from (a) the merger and acquisition binge of the past decade and (b) certain joint ventures and other restraints of trade so wholly ignored by the FTC and the Justice

Department. More than enforcing the antitrust laws, an authentic competition policy would reduce the nonmeritorious competition known as corporate crime.

The hollow echoes from the drumbeats of the antiregulatory catechisms are reaching more and more of the American people as they begin to relate some of their losses, traumas, and illnesses to the antienforcement mania of the past twelve years. Satire is insufficient to describe the torrents of reports by the Reagan/Bush administrations and by right-wing think tanks that blamed modest regulatory standards and law enforcement for the nation's declining innovation, productivity, and "competitiveness." The reality behind these slides is fed by mismanagement of giant corporations, speculation, outright corporate crime, and the immensely wasteful merger and leveraged-buyout craze that displaced productive investment. Nor did the $3 trillion debt addition by Washington and a $200 billion annual interest payment on the national debt help matters.

Regulatory problem-solving must meet an empirical test, not a rhetorical abstraction. The actual benefits of regulation—as detailed in *Freedom from Harm*, published in 1986 by Public Citizen and The Democracy Project—must not be obscured. Laws can and have protected the physical and economic security of human beings. They light the way for a society seeking workable approaches where the rule of law can tame the dictates of power. The history of regulation is sufficiently rich in lessons both to caution and to guide us and the next President in this direction.

But beneath all these aspirations must emerge the new instruments of democracy. Fortunately, the mechanisms described earlier in this overview cost the taxpayer next to nothing and are universally usable by citizens who can choose whether to exercise such opportunities for membership. Presidents, even when well intentioned, are more prisoners than leaders in the White House. They are prisoners of powerful, omnipresent business lobbies from here and abroad. It is organized citizen energy that can turn them into leaders against what Thomas Jefferson called "the excesses of the monied interests."

Federal Trade Commission

CONSUMER PROTECTION

JONATHAN W. CUNEO

Summary

CONCEIVED IN AN OUTBURST of populist fervor, the Federal Trade Commission (FTC), an "independent" federal agency, possesses broad powers of investigation, administrative prosecution, public reporting, adjudication, and rulemaking with respect to unfair commercial practices. Yet the FTC has never lived up to its potential to be a national watchdog.

For many years it lived a quiet existence, never attempting to flex the muscles that Congress gave it at birth. After public criticism of the FTC's failures, the Nixon, Ford, and Carter administrations began an ambitious program of revitalizing the agency. But when the revitalized agency began to disturb powerful interests in the late 1970s, those interests exercised their political clout in Congress to defeat numerous important FTC initiatives through both the appropriations process and legislation. During the Reagan era, new "deregulatory" leadership abandoned entire programs and failed to enforce the law altogether in some areas. Although there has been a tangible increase in activity under the Bush FTC team, the FTC has yet to approach its potential.

Experience demonstrates two reasons why the FTC has not fulfilled its mission. First, lacking visibility, its programs lack popular support. Many Americans have no idea that the commission even exists. Therefore it has been politically defenseless against powerful opponents who seek to defeat its programs through congressional action as well as "deregulatory" ideologues who attack its initiatives from within. Second, its overly ambitious combination of functions has hampered its basic law-enforcement mission. Because it acts as prosecutor and judge in the same proceeding, the FTC must bend over backward to afford procedural fairness.

Jonathan Cuneo is counsel for the Committee to Support Antitrust Laws (COSAL). He formerly served as counsel with the Federal Trade Commission.

As trade and communications become more globalized, the need for an effective, consistent, and vigilant federal consumer law-enforcement agency grows. As currently structured, the FTC cannot do this. The new FTC should consider fundamental changes, including, among other things: (1) building political support by holding a series of meetings in locations across the country and vastly increasing its regional presence; (2) possibly seeking new legislation to transfer its adjudicative responsibilities to the federal courts, consolidating its decisional authority in a single administrator, and making the FTC an Executive Branch agency; and (3) increasing its investigative capabilities.

Historical Background

THE CIRCUMSTANCES OF THE FTC'S BIRTH were glorious. During the height of the Progressive era, antitrust policy and enforcement occupied center stage in American political theater. There was well-placed distrust of the huge industrial trusts that had emerged from the industrial revolution to dominate several major American industries.

As early as 1890, Congress recognized the need for legislation to ensure that the rapidly expanding force of American business did not gouge consumers or deny fair business opportunities to entrepreneurs. The powerful prohibitions of Sections 1 and 2 of the Sherman Act against restraints on trade and monopolization carried stiff penalties. But in 1911, the U.S. Supreme Court interpreted the Sherman Act as having an implied "rule of reason" standard in the *Standard Oil* and *American Tobacco* cases. These decisions, which had the practical effect of permitting the judiciary to allow some anticompetitive practices, set off a populist backlash.

Antitrust became a major issue in the 1912 presidential campaign. Congress's response to the perceived judicial nullification of the Sherman Act was twofold: First, the Clayton Act of 1914 defined certain specific practices to be illegal; second, contemporaneously with the Clayton Act, Congress created the FTC—to replace the Bureau of Corporations, largely a report-writing agency—as a regulatory agency with a charter to prevent "unfair methods of competition."

Then Boston lawyer and later U.S. Supreme Court justice Louis Brandeis championed these legislative responses to the trust problem. Supported by President Woodrow Wilson and encouraged by the perceived successes of the Interstate Commerce Commission, Congress created the FTC as the first federal agency of general jurisdiction with combined powers to enforce the law and adjudicate claims—in effect, to act as prosecutor and judge of the same action. In later years this combination of powers became controversial, leading to challenges from participants in agency proceedings and creating suspicion in the judiciary and doubts on Capitol Hill.

In 1915 the FTC came into existence as an independent administrative agency. Congress sought to assure the impartiality of the five presidentially appointed and Senate-approved commissioners by affording them staggered seven-year terms and providing that no more than three could be of the same political party. The legislative history makes clear that the agency was to be composed of neutral experts who could understand the complexity of modern business transactions and react with alacrity to evolving conditions and new abuses.

In addition to the controversial power to order unfair methods of competition to cease and desist, Congress gave the FTC power to investigate and issue reports on corporations—backed with the power to subpoena information. In 1938 Congress amended the FTC Act specifically to include a consumer protection mission—to prohibit "unfair or deceptive acts or practices in commerce"—within the FTC's jurisdiction.

In 1973 and 1975, to bolster the agency's powers, Congress confirmed and expanded the agency's rulemaking power, conferred an extremely limited private right of action for FTC Act violations, and expanded the FTC's ability to pursue injunctive relief in court through the Magnuson-Moss Act. In 1976, after years of requests by the FTC, Congress created a procedure in the Hart-Scott-Rodino Act under which merging companies had to notify the FTC and the Antitrust Division of the Department of Justice in advance of a merger.

Throughout its history, the FTC has had many illustrious chairs and commissioners. Joseph E. Davies, a statesman who later served as ambassador to the Soviet Union, was the first Chairman. President Roosevelt appointed James Landis, later Dean of Harvard Law School and SEC chairman, to the FTC. Other alumni include A. Leon Higginbotham, now a circuit judge on the U.S. Court of Appeals for the Third Circuit; Paul Rand Dixon, longtime chief counsel of the Senate Commerce Committee; Caspar Weinberger, later secretary of defense for President Reagan; and James C. Miller III, later director of the Office of Management and Budget for President Reagan.

The talent has not been confined to the leaders. Economist John Blair wrote a seminal report on the structure of American petroleum industry while at the FTC in the early 1950s, and twenty years later wrote the influential book *Economic Concentration: Structure, Behavior and Public Policy*. The brilliant organizational economist F. Michael Scherer served as

director of the Bureau of Economics in the 1960s. Robert Pitofsky, later
dean of Georgetown Law School, served as director of the Bureau of Consumer Protection and then as a commissioner. Political economist and author
Robert Reich, the economics director of the Clinton-Gore transition, served
as Director of the Office of Policy Planning in the late 1970s.

A broad mandate, strong regulatory powers, political independence, neutrality, and huge talent at the staff and commission level—these would appear
to be all the ingredients of a successful government program to protect
fragile markets and fair competition. Unfortunately, throughout its seventy-
seven-year history, the FTC has rarely if ever fully lived up to the circumstances of its hopeful birth.

For years it was colloquially known as "the little old lady of Pennsylvania
Avenue." Because few Americans know how FTC programs benefit them,
the FTC lacks political clout. When corporate representatives redubbed the
agency the "national nanny" in the late 1970s, they easily persuaded a Democratic Congress to curb the agency's "overzealousness" and to curtail specific
FTC activities (most notably the FTC's power to promulgate a trade regulation rule dealing with funeral industry practices, and the FTC's ability to
publish reports about insurance) by legislation. Although many of these
programs would have benefited Americans across the country, there was no
public hue and cry. And when President Reagan's ideologically conservative
chairman, James Miller—consistent with his own laissez-faire philosophy—
gutted program upon program (e.g., the FTC's merger enforcement program, the "line of business" reporting program, and the FTC's used-car
rule), there was scarcely a whimper of protest. Why?

With one exception—the landmark tetracycline case—it is difficult to
recall the "trusts" the FTC has "busted." A review of successful FTC-
adjudicated cases and consent orders reads like a catalog of small businesses
and inconsequential cases. When the FTC has sought to investigate or press
claims against economically powerful industries, those industries have frequently been able to thwart the FTC's efforts through complicated and
protracted cumbersome FTC proceedings or by nakedly applying political
pressure.

Examples of the difficulties of FTC procedure abound. Most involve
challenges stemming from the FTC's combination of prosecutorial and ad-
judicatory functions. In the 1970s, a case involving allegedly deceptive sales
of encyclopedias required a record of more than twenty thousand pages and
involved numerous federal court cases challenging FTC actions or appealing
the FTC's final order. One of the most significant challenges involved
whether the administrative law judge who tried the case should have been

disqualified because he had previously served as an adviser to a commissioner during the investigative stages of the case.

The FTC's "shared monopoly" cereal case took nine years from filing of the complaint to issuance of an initial decision, and became tangled in the FTC's attempt to rehire the administrative law judge in the case by contract after he determined to retire.

Similarly, the FTC has never developed anything approaching an administrative jurisprudence on the meaning of "unfair methods of competition" (Section 5 of the FTC Act) beyond the Sherman and Clayton acts; in fact, the FTC often looks to the courts' interpretation of the Sherman and Clayton acts in interpreting its own Section 5 mandate. And the FTC's Bureau of Competition is often regarded as a poorer, less threatening cousin of the Department of Justice's Antitrust Division.

Recent Legacy

BEFORE THE 1970S, the FTC performed its tasks somnolently, with occasional cyclical shifts in emphasis. The late 1960s brought a fire storm of public and congressional criticism over the FTC's lackluster performance. A group of "Nader's Raiders" published a scathing report on the Federal Trade Commission in 1969. Shortly thereafter, the American Bar Association, under the leadership of Miles Kirkpatrick, published a report reaching similar conclusions. Both of these efforts identified serious problems but laid the blame heavily on a perceived lack of quality among agency personnel.

President Nixon directed Chairman Weinberger to "revitalize" the agency. Weinberger reorganized the agency in 1970 in a manner that has survived without fundamental alteration since. Underneath the commissioners are three basic operating bureaus: the Bureau of Competition, with responsibility for antitrust enforcement; the Bureau of Consumer Protection, with responsibility for the FTC's consumer protection mission; and the Bureau of Economics, with responsibility for industry analysis and economic evidence. Working on the enforcement programs with the Bureaus of Competition and Consumer Protection are regional offices. As of 1992, the FTC maintains ten regional offices: in Boston, Massachusetts; New York, New York; Atlanta, Georgia; Cleveland, Ohio; Chicago, Illinois; Dallas, Texas; Denver, Colorado; Seattle, Washington; San Francisco, California; and Los Angeles, California. Significantly, because of the combination of functions, the FTC must maintain a dual staff, with some agency personnel and activities insulated from others because of the necessity of maintaining a wall between prosecutorial and adjudicative activities.

The "revitalized" and Republican FTC set about a program of stepped-up enforcement activities in the early 1970s in both the antitrust and consumer protection areas. These included:

• The "shared monopoly" cases against breakfast cereal companies, *In re Kellogg Co.*, and oil refiners, *In re Exxon Co.* In the late 1950s, economists observed that relatively few firms dominated a number of major industries in the vast postwar North American continental market. These firms, according to the theory, did not compete with each other vigorously on price and quality, but rather relied on relatively minor product differentiation and heavy advertising expenditures to sell essentially similar products at inflated prices. The end result would be poor performance, industry stagnation, and ultimately international competitive problems. Economists considered automobiles, steel, and several other major markets to exhibit this oligopolistic industry structure. The "shared monopoly" theory was controversial under Sherman Act analysis because neither an agreement nor a monopoly was involved; yet the FTC boldly pursued the "shared monopoly" theory.

• The Bureau of Competition began to challenge restraints among professionals, most significantly challenging the American Medical Association's professional rules prohibiting advertising.

• The FTC's new Bureau of Consumer Protection proposed new trade regulation rules dealing with such topics as door-to-door sales, used cars, octane ratings, funeral industry procedures, mobile home warranties, and credit practices.

• The Bureau of Consumer Protection enforced "advertising substantiation" requirements under which national advertisers had to support their claims or face "corrective advertising."

• The Bureau of Economics initiated "line of business" reporting. Through this program, conglomerate corporations reported their sales, profits, research and development costs, and other financial data by line of business. Resisted by some corporations, this program augmented the FTC's industrial concentration studies and made basic and important empirical information available to scholars.

In 1977 President Carter appointed Michael Pertschuk as chairman. Pertschuk had served as chief counsel of the Senate Commerce Committee, had been involved in the passage of the 1975 legislation strengthening the FTC's authority, and was an outspoken consumer advocate. Pertschuk pushed forward with the proconsumer initiatives of the Nixon and Ford administrations, added new ones, and turned up the rhetorical volume.

But many of the FTC's programs then began to draw criticism from

Capitol Hill, largely "inspired" by lobbyists for interests under fire from the FTC. Prominent among the controversial new initiatives during the Pertschuk years (in addition to those his predecessors commenced) were:

• The rulemaking proceeding examining the fairness of children's advertising practices. Controversy erupted over Chairman Pertschuk's public statements, and a district court disqualified him from further proceedings (again on combination-of-powers grounds) in a strongly worded opinion. By the time a court of appeals resoundingly reversed the district court (finding that rulemaking did not require the same appearance of neutrality as adjudication), lobbyists had used the district court's disqualification order to their advantage on Capitol Hill.

• A 1979 FTC report on the adequacy of disclosures on the costs and return of whole life insurance policies. This exhaustively researched report revealed that investors really received a low rate of return on the investment portion of their policies. The report inflamed the industry, and their lobbyists set about seeking a legislative "remedy."

• An industrywide investigation of the domestic automobile manufacturing industry. Although the FTC did not follow its investigation with a case, the investigation itself was controversial as Detroit struggled to meet federally mandated pollution requirements and as high gas prices boosted foreign car sales.

Beginning in late 1978, the FTC faced a barrage of criticism on Capitol Hill over its alleged "overzealousness." Difficult oversight hearings, threatened appropriations restrictions, and lack of reauthorization legislation marked the Commission's experience from 1978 to 1980.

Despite the Carter Administration's repeated interventions on the FTC's behalf, the Democratically controlled Congress bowed to the entreaties of the insurance, breakfast cereal, and funeral directors' lobbies. In May 1980, using its purse strings as a weapon, Congress allowed the FTC's funding to lapse repeatedly, passing only short appropriations as a bargaining tool with the president. On several occasions the FTC had to begin the wasteful process of shutting down. In the end, President Carter accepted a legislative veto over FTC rulemaking proceedings in exchange for reauthorization legislation—the so-called "Federal Trade Commission Improvements Act of 1980"—which profoundly weakened the agency.

The 1980 legislation contained new restrictions on the FTC's authority as well as narrow sections targeting specific FTC proceedings. The most important restriction barred the FTC from writing reports on insurance unless pertinent congressional committees approved. Other provisions terminated—or effectively ended—ongoing proceedings.

Although Pertschuk blamed the crisis on "some overzealous staffers," once again, personnel were not to blame. FTC staffers were in the main doing what the commissioners had directed them to do. The Commission, in turn, was carrying out the revitalization that President Nixon had directed years before. The FTC was damned if it didn't do its job, and damned if it did.

Swept into office in no small measure on an antiregulatory platform, President Reagan appointed economist James C. Miller III as chairman. Under Chairman Miller the FTC terminated proceedings, canceled programs, and reduced personnel. Pulled to and fro, agency staff morale was at an all-time low.

Miller, his colleagues on the commission, and his senior staff were not responding to corporate lobbyists. Rather, they were proud deregulatory advocates, aligned closely with the "Chicago School of Economics." The Chicago School places great faith on market mechanisms and strongly advocates a minimal governmental role in correcting marketplace abuses in both antitrust and consumer protection. Its advocates see little danger in corporate size, oligopoly, vertical restraints, or the conglomerate movement. For the most part, they believe that antitrust should be confined to preventing "horizontal" restraints (agreements between or among competitors)—and leave the supposedly self-correcting market to deal with other situations.

Accordingly, during the Reagan years, the FTC:

• Virtually abandoned its role in enforcing the law against major product defects.

• Eased national advertisers' responsibilities to substantiate their advertising claims and refrain from deceptive or misleading advertisements.

• Terminated the breakfast cereals (*Kellogg*) "shared monopoly" case, which had been of signal importance in challenging oligopolistic market practices.

• Adopted an extremely lax merger enforcement policy. The Subcommittee on Monopolies and Commercial Law documented that despite the Hart-Scott-Rodino Act's procedures to review mergers before they are completed, the Justice Department's Antitrust Division and the FTC made a "second" request for information in only a minute percentage of cases and challenged only a handful. The FTC challenged no mergers on vertical grounds or under conglomerate merger theory. The impact of this policy can hardly be overstated. As Eleanor Fox and Robert Pitofsky detail in their chapter in this book, the 1980s witnessed one of the greatest tidal waves of takeovers and mergers—complete with the largest securities fraud scandal in history.

• Expanded a procedure first developed during earlier years of effectively counseling merging parties on how to avoid an antitrust challenge.

• Failed to enforce the law against vertical price fixing, In stark contrast, in the past decade state attorneys general achieved successful settlements against Mitsubishi, Panasonic, Minolta, and Nintendo for supplier-dealer abuses.

• Reversed its prior policy of sharing Hart-Scott-Rodino Act data with the states, even though advance notification is an essential tool for preventing anticompetitive mergers locally.

Because the Justice Department's Antitrust Division prosecutes most horizontal price-fixing as a criminal offense and because the FTC has no criminal jurisdiction, the FTC's role in challenging horizontal restraints is limited. However, a significant positive role that the FTC played in the 1980s was its continued presence in challenging horizontal restraints among professionals.

Consistent with its "economic" (as opposed to law-enforcement) approach, the FTC gave a vastly expanded policymaking role to the Bureau of Economics in reviewing staff recommendations that the FTC commence proceedings. Some commissioners took one or more economists as "attorney advisers." Yet, in a curious twist, the FTC canceled the "line of business" reporting program, designed by and for economists, just as it was beginning to bear fruit. The FTC also canceled its economic concentration studies, long a staple of microeconomic literature.

The 1980 legislation and subsequent Reagan-era leadership particularly devastated the Bureau of Consumer Protection's enforcement program. The FTC brought relatively few cases, imposing new and almost insurmountable economic criteria for case filing. For example, the FTC delayed actions against defects in some life-threatening products because its economists maintained that the free market—that is, wrongful-death lawsuits—would take care of the problem (even though they hadn't previously).

During the 1980s, state attorneys general somewhat filled the enforcement vacuum in antitrust and consumer protection. For example, as mentioned, states initiated four vertical price-fixing actions against major manufacturers of household items. The states also brought—and are now prosecuting—a case against several large insurers and reinsurers alleging that their illegal boycott conduct was responsible for much of the 1986 liability insurance crisis. This titanic action is one of the largest and most significant consumer cases charging cartel conduct in history. On the merger front, in a number of instances (most prominently the merger between Lucky Stores and American Stores), states successfully challenged mergers that the federal antitrust authorities had let proceed.

Many states and localities have now established consumer hot lines and are vigorously pursuing consumer cases. These include consumer protection programs involving credit, utility shutoffs, landlord-tenant problems, home solicitations sales, and telemarketing, just to name a few. State attorneys general—most of whom are elected—have found that vigorous enforcement programs are popular and generate more in revenues and restitution than they cost.

The Bush Record

PRESIDENT BUSH APPOINTED Janet D. Steiger, a family friend, as chair of the FTC. While the Steiger FTC is substantially more active than its Reagan-era predecessor—bringing more actions, strengthening the rhetoric, and increasing staffing—the FTC is far from fulfilling its promise of eliminating unfair methods of competition and unfair business practices.

• The Bureau of Competition has maintained its focus of challenging horizontal restraints, particularly in the health care field and among professionals. In fiscal year 1990, the FTC authorized challenges to only seven mergers and issued only one adjudicated opinion holding one merger unlawful. It issued three other administrative complaints. The Steiger FTC has accepted two settlements in vertical price-fixing cases, including the Nintendo settlement in which the FTC joined the states.

• The Bureau of Consumer Protection has focused on a number of discrete areas, most prominently telemarketing fraud. Other areas include alternative investments (e.g., precious metals, rare coins), diet claims, and credit practices. The FTC has obtained a handful of consent orders and has obtained "consumer redress" in a few other instances. In 1991, however, New York City's Department of Consumer Affairs brought 320 cases against deceptive ads, versus only 25 for the national FTC.

Recommendations

THE FTC WOULD BE WELL SERVED by a broad rethinking of its relation to the public, its structure, its procedures, and its statutory authority. In an era of increased interstate trade and increased globalization of trade, there is a resounding need for a strong federal consumer protection presence. To fulfill the unmet promise of the FTC's original mission, the new President should give the new chair the mandate to change its orientation and structure fundamentally.

1. *Problem: Building political support*. The primary, short-term goal of a new FTC should be to build public support for its programs. As the previous discussion illustrates, throughout the last twenty five years the FTC has gone

in and out of favor with policymakers. Maintaining an effective law enforcement program amid wild political fluctuations is extraordinarily difficult if not impossible. The FTC's political weakness stems from its lack of a grassroots political constituency. Yet, as recent experiences of state attorneys general have proven, consumer protection programs should be popular and effective.

A new FTC under new leadership should promptly:

• Convene a series of meetings/hearings across the country chaired by its most senior officials to listen to problems, gather facts, and promote the goals of the agency. The schedule should include appearances in major cities and states. The FTC should publish the dates and locations and invite local consumers and government and business people to attend.

• Inaugurate a "consumer complaint" hot line through which consumers with problems speak *directly* with FTC attorneys. Consumer complaints have long been a source of FTC cases, yet consumer calls often go unanswered. Many state and local governments maintain such services, and the new FTC should explore ways to coordinate its activities with other governmental entities. Such calls can indicate patterns of abuse and yield major cases, as they do in such large local consumer offices as the Department of Consumer Affairs in New York City.

• Establish a program through which *all* mail is substantively answered *within one week* and all consumer complaints acted on within time limits.

2. *Problem: Making the FTC a law-enforcement power.* As noted above, the FTC is an independent agency that can investigate alleged violations and later prosecute them, act as judge at the conclusion of the investigation, and then issue industry wide trade regulation rules. This combination of functions dilutes the FTC's law-enforcement function, creates the need for a multimember commission, and has resulted in byzantine rules to ensure procedural fairness. The new FTC should appoint a bipartisan, expert panel to consider the desirability of legislation to transfer its adjudicative functions to the federal judiciary and consolidate its decisionmaking into a single administrator agency, like the Environmental Protection Agency.

If there is one EPA administrator and one head of the FDA and the NHTSA, should there be five FTC commissioners? Effective law enforcement requires a unified and consistent prosecutorial authority. Congress designed the current commission structure with five members with staggered seven-year terms for political insulation and adjudicative fairness, not prosecutorial consistency. Assuming no resignations, the President elected in 1992 would have to wait until 1996 before appointing a working majority with a new proconsumer philosophy. (The President cannot dismiss a sitting commissioner without cause.) A new structure with a single prosecutorial authority subject to the direction of the President might better suit the FTC of the future.

3. *Problem: Management improvements*. FTC investigations often take years. By the time the FTC acts, the problem it is addressing has frequently subsided. The new FTC should:

- Rearrange its staffing—particularly in the Bureau of Consumer Protection—to hire more trained consumer investigators and fewer economists.
- Place rigid time limits on its investigations.
- Share its expertise by intervening on behalf of ignored consumer interests before other regulatory agencies.

4. *Problem: Effective use of data collection efforts*. The FTC has broad information-collection and report-writing powers that have atrophied in the past decade. These powers have enormous potential for basic economic research as well as popular education. The FTC should revive the "line of business" and industry-concentration data-collection programs, refocus its report-writing program to concentrate on matters of interest to consumers, and issue reports that are hard-hitting and understandable by the press and lay people.

5. *Problem: Insurance jurisdiction*. The FTC has no jurisdiction even to report on competitive problems in the insurance industry. The FTC should press for *complete* repeal of the McCarran-Ferguson Act and of the portions of the 1980 FTC Improvements Act of 1980 that limited its reporting powers on insurance.

6. *Problem: Effective industrywide trade regulation rules*. The FTC's experiences with its trade regulation rulemaking proceedings on children's advertising, funeral industry practices, and used cars—to name a few— demonstrate the difficulty of agency rulemaking without sufficient political support. In each case, Congress intervened to curtail the FTC's ongoing proceedings.

The FTC should therefore use any new public "outreach" programs (see recommendation 1) as a tool both to learn what problems are sufficiently widespread and so severe as to require a rulemaking proceeding, and to build support for any such proceeding.

7. *Problem: Better public disclosure of key decisions*. Many FTC decisions not to challenge mergers have major consequences for entire industries. Yet, the FTC never explains why it does not challenge a merger. In every case in which the FTC issues a second request under the Hart-Scott-Rodino

Act, the FTC should issue a public explanation of why it issued the request and why it then did not challenge the merger.

8. *Problem: Enhanced private rights of action for violations of the Federal Trade Commission Act*. The Magnuson-Moss Act has cumbersome rule-making procedures and limited consumer private-action provisions. The FTC should seek legislation providing for multiple damages for willful violations, and removal of the procedural problems in the Magnuson-Moss Act.

PRODUCT SAFETY

ROBERT ADLER AND R. DAVID PITTLE

Summary

CONGRESS PASSED the Consumer Product Safety Act (CPSA) in 1972, establishing the Consumer Product Safety Commission (CPSC) as a five-member independent regulatory agency with a mandate to: (1) protect the public against unreasonable risks of injury associated with consumer products, (2) assist consumers in evaluating the comparative safety of consumer products, (3) develop uniform safety standards and minimize conflicting state and local regulations, and (4) promote research and investigation into the causes and prevention of product-related deaths, illnesses, and injuries. Among other things, the agency has the regulatory power to:

- set safety standards for consumer products;
- ban products;
- issue administrative "recall" orders to compel repair, replacement, or refunds for products that present substantial hazards; and
- seek court orders to require the recall of imminently hazardous products.

In addition to providing these powers, Congress imposed, under section 15(b) of the CPSA, a requirement that businesses under CPSC jurisdiction report to the agency all instances in which they obtain information indicating that their products contain defects that "could create" substantial product hazards. These "15(b) reports" rapidly assumed a major role in the agency's regulatory activities.

Robert Adler is Associate Professor of Legal Studies in the School of Business at the University of North Carolina. He formerly served as Counsel to the Subcommittee on Health and the Environment on the House Energy and Commerce Committee. R. David Pittle is Vice President and Technical Director for Consumers Union and served as Commissioner on the U.S. Consumer Product Safety Commission for nine years.

All of these powers form the necessary arsenal for an agency responsible for reducing or eliminating a significant portion of the current estimate of 22,000 product-related deaths and 28 million product-related injuries befalling American consumers each year. Yet, the CPSC has failed to fulfill its life-saving mission. Why?

Openly hostile to the existence of the CPSC, the Reagan administration first sought to eliminate the commission, but finding Congress unalterably opposed, the administration imposed enormous funding and staff cuts on the agency—the largest percent suffered by any of the federal regulatory agencies. In addition, the administration appointed a series of "reluctant regulators" to the CPSC, leading to halfhearted and ineffective enforcement of the agency's authority.

Although popular with the American public by virtue of its product safety mission, the agency needs new leadership, greater resources, and improved morale if it is to function properly. The new Administration and Congress should:

• Decide whether the agency should remain as an independent collegial body or should be transformed into a single-administrator agency. Restore a meaningful measure of agency resources lost under the Reagan/Bush administrations.

• Abolish the "gag rules" in current law that prevent the CPSC—alone among federal health and safety agencies—from releasing in a timely manner information about potentially defective products.

• Streamline CPSC rulemaking procedures so that its ability to write safety standards in the event that industry voluntary efforts prove unsuccessful becomes credible. End the self-imposed restrictions on product recalls foisted on the CPSC by its Reagan/Bush appointees.

History of the Agency

CONGRESS ENACTED THE CPSA during the "consumer decade," 1965–75, when it established or strengthened a multitude of agencies. The need for such legislation arose from the report of a study commission established in 1968 by President Johnson. This group, the National Commission on Product Safety (NCPS), estimated that consumer products injured 20 million Americans every year. Of these, 110,000 sustained permanent disabilities and 30,000 died, at an annual cost in the billions of dollars. The NCPS concluded that the exposure of consumers to unreasonable product hazards was "excessive" and recommended that Congress establish an agency with broad jurisdiction to address product hazards.

In rapid response, Congress enacted the Consumer Product Safety Act, which for the first time established federal administrative jurisdiction over enormous numbers of consumer products. Estimates range from 10,000 to 15,000 product categories; the number of businesses producing and distributing these products is well over 1 million. To get an idea of the agency's authority, visualize the products found in a large shopping mall. Except for guns, drugs, tobacco, food, and boats, the safety of virtually everything in the mall falls within CPSC jurisdiction.

FROM "MODEL AGENCY" TO "BASKET CASE"

Those involved in establishing the CPSC sought a "model agency." This meant that the CPSC must have strong regulatory authority, adequate funding, broad public participation (especially from consumers) in decisionmaking, widespread openness, and substantial independence from White House influence. With these features, it was expected that the CPSC would quickly establish a vast federal network of product safety standards through open, democratic procedures.

The CPSC initially tried hard to be a model agency. It tackled safety problems vigorously. Its openness policy required virtually all meetings between commission employees and outside parties to be open to the public. It stretched the Freedom of Information Act to include virtually all commission documents, including memorandums discussing legal weaknesses of agency rulemaking options. It actively solicited petitions from members of the public, using a policy that imposed virtually no formal requirements on petitions. It also provided funding for consumer participation in its rulemaking.

Conventional wisdom in the early 1970s held that the small CPSC was pound for pound the most powerful regulatory agency ever created. At the confirmation hearings of the first set of commissioners in 1973, one senator remarked that so great was the CPSC's authority that an honest person wouldn't want it and a dishonest one shouldn't have it.

By the time Jimmy Carter took office, however, conventional wisdom had taken a 180-degree turn: The image of the CPSC was now of an awkward body that gave good intentions a bad name. The agency's founders had expected the CPSC to promulgate fifteen to twenty safety standards per year, and were critical that only three standards had been developed under the CPSA between 1973 and 79—a wholly misguided criticism, given that the CPSC promulgated more than thirty safety regulations between 1973 and 1981 under all the statutes it administered. Moreover, the agency's openness policy drew criticism even from consumer groups, who, angered that the release of legal memoranda might enhance industry's challenge to agency rules, had accused the agency of confusing "openness with nakedness."

Both the rise and the fall of the agency's reputation were undeserved in many respects. Contrary to the views of many observers, the agency was hardly the most powerful regulatory agency in Washington. Although it possessed the power to ban products and set safety standards, so did most other health and safety agencies. And, unlike some other agencies, the CPSC's rulemaking authority was heavily weighted with procedural requirements that made it virtually impossible to set standards quickly.

From the low days at the beginning of the Carter administration to the arrival of the Reagan administration, the agency actually regained much of its lost luster. It did so not by churning out greater numbers of safety standards—on the contrary, under Chairman Susan King, the agency promulgated only eight regulations in three and a half years, fewer than under either of her Republican predecessors—but by successfully redefining the agency's role. The redefinition involved convincing the agency's critics in Congress, the White House, and the media that (1) successful regulation depended more on the quality of regulations than their quantity, (2) some alternatives to mandatory standards—such as product recalls—presented results equal, if not superior, to standards; and (3) within its limited resources, the agency actually operated fairly effectively and efficiently.

During the Carter years, the CPSC began to broaden its focus beyond mandatory standards. The agency began a number of initiatives to push industry groups to upgrade voluntary standards rather than writing mandatory standards itself. In the more successful cases, the key seemed to be that highly motivated industry officials were able to persuade their firms to develop voluntary standards to avoid mandatory action by the CPSC.

CRIPPLED BY THE REAGAN ADMINISTRATION

Shortly after President Reagan took office, OMB director David Stockman denounced the CPSC (and the FTC) in vivid terms, "They've created this whole facade of consumer protection in order to seize power in our society. I think part of the mission of this administration is to unmask and discredit that false ideology." Thereafter, until halted by determined congressional opposition, the Reagan administration sought to abolish the CPSC.

Although unsuccessful in its efforts to kill the commission, the Reagan administration was able to slash its budget and staff dramatically. In 1981, the White House obtained a 25 percent cut in agency funding and a 25 percent cut in full time staff, by far the largest-percentage reductions among all federal health and safety agencies. Thereafter, the administration, using its latitude to cut staff, forced further substantial reductions in personnel. Eventually Congress threatened to impose statutory personnel floors, leading the administration to moderate its attacks and settle for small but persistent staff cuts each year.

Although Congress protected the CPSC from total destruction by the Reagan administration, that administration interpreted the loss of many liberal incumbents in 1980 as a national mood for deregulation. In response, Congress passed a set of amendments in 1981 that trimmed the agency's authority substantially. Among other things, it:

- tightened restrictions on the ability of the commission to release information from which a consumer product manufacturer could be identified;
- imposed a virtual ban on the release of "15(b) reports" from manufacturers containing information about possible product hazards (other health and safety agencies, such as the NHTSA and the FDA, with analogous reporting requirements, may freely release such reports);
- added additional substantive and procedural requirements that must be met before the agency could promulgate safety standards or impose product bans; and
- established an advisory panel on chronic hazards; the panel must be convened and consulted before the agency can begin rulemaking with respect to products presenting a risk of cancer, birth defects, or gene mutations.

By far the strongest proponent of the Reagan deregulatory philosophy was Terrence Scanlon, CPSC chairman from 1985 to 1989. Scanlon was openly hostile to the agency's mission; his blanket refusal to consider mandatory standards and his efforts to cripple the agency's recall authority caused great consternation among consumer groups and in Congress.

Among the most hazardous products faced by the commission during Scanlon's term were All-Terrain Vehicles (ATVs). According to CPSC staff, as sales of these vehicles rose, the numbers of related injuries and deaths exploded. From 1982 through August 1987, roughly 790 people died and 300,000 suffered injuries while using ATVs, allegedly from their inherently unstable design. Yet at the end of a long negotiation with the manufacturers, the commission settled for a ban on future sales, but without a recall of any existing vehicles.

After years of controversy, Scanlon resigned in early 1989 to join the Heritage Foundation. Unfortunately, President Bush's appointees to the agency, although less confrontational, have proven to be equally unwilling to take action against hazardous products.

Recent Legacy

NO CURRENT COMMISSIONER has any product safety, consumer protection, or other technical background to prepare him or her for service on the commission. All came to the agency as a result of political connections having nothing to do with the mission of the agency. All tout themselves as generally opposed to government regulation, an odd qualification for a critical regulatory position.

AN UNCHANGED CPSC IN THE BUSH ADMINISTRATION
Little has changed at the CPSC during the Reagan and Bush years. The commission continues in a regulatory torpor, acting with vigor only when withdrawing or ending regulations. Since 1981, the breakdown of nonsafety-related regulatory actions is as follows:
- products exempted from child-resistant requirements of the Poison Prevention Packaging Act (an exemption means that the product need not comply with these requirements): 9
- proceedings or regulations terminated, withdrawn, or suspended: 8
- minor technical amendments or regulations (i.e., terms clarified or requirements relaxed): 6

In sharp contrast, the number of safety-related regulatory actions since 1981 is substantially less:
- substantive labeling rules: 1
- safety standards or bans promulgated: 6

Even these abysmal statistics overstate the commission's regulatory record because two of the safety standards were promulgated early in the Reagan administration by commissioners who were Carter holdovers, and most of the other regulations (such as the lawn darts ban and garage door openers standards) were grudgingly promulgated by the commission under intense pressure from the Congress.

The commission's complete deference to industry initiatives has not changed from the Reagan to the Bush administration. Although there is little dispute in the product safety community that voluntary industry standards can promote safety effectively, this general principle has been converted into blind dogma by the commissioners. They simply will not deal with hazards, no matter how severe, outside of a voluntary standards approach, no matter how little progress toward an adequate standard has been made by an industry group and no matter how unlikely it appears that the group ever will make progress.

THE CONSUMER PRODUCT SAFETY COMMISSION IMPROVEMENT ACT OF 1990

After the CPSC spent seven years surviving on continuing resolutions, Congress enacted the Consumer Product Safety Improvement Act of 1990. The act provides modest improvements. It:

- requires companies to report to the commission whenever one of their products creates an unreasonable risk of serious injury or death;
- requires that the President consider individuals with background and expertise in "consumer products and protection of the public from risks of safety" as appointees to the agency;
- imposes a set of procedural requirements designed to expedite rule-making and to force the commission to respond to citizen petitions;
- requires the commission to study, issue reports on, or continue rule-making proceedings on a variety of products such as those generating indoor air pollution, and automatic garage door openers;
- requires manufacturers, under certain circumstances, to report to the CPSC lawsuits concerning potentially dangerous products that have resulted in verdicts or settlements for plaintiffs;
- increases the amount of money that the commission can seek under the Consumer Product Safety Act, and establishes for the first time civil penalties under the Federal Hazardous Substances Act and the Flammable Fabrics Act.

Undoubtedly the most controversial portion of the legislation as it moved toward enactment was a provision that would have required manufacturers to notify the CPSC whenever a product liability lawsuit was filed against them. Unfortunately, it ran into a barrage of industry opposition and was watered down by its House sponsors to require reports only after the settlement or loss of three suits within two years on the same product. As enacted, it clearly fails to provide the commission with current news regarding emerging hazards.

CPSC FUNDING

The CPSC is a tiny agency—a regulatory speck compared to other federal health and safety agencies. It actually started much closer in funding levels to other agencies, but its parity ended abruptly with the arrival of the Reagan administration. As previously noted, once the administration failed to abolish the CPSC, it began starving it. OMB director Stockman freely admitted that the cuts "form an integral part of the administration's efforts to redirect regulatory policy." In other words, cripple the agency and it will do less.

Because the CPSC is so small, decisions regarding its budget are as much symbolic as financial. Just as abolishing the CPSC would have had no appreciable effect on the nation's deficit, doubling the agency's budget would similarly go virtually unnoticed. Budget decisions about the CPSC, however, do play a key role in sending a message about the President's views regarding consumer protection and product safety. Certain critical agency functions, previously choked off, desperately need more resources if the agency is to fulfill its mission. For example, the CPSC has cut substantially its National Electronic Injury Surveillance System (NEISS), a network of hospital emergency rooms that regularly report on product-related injuries. Resulting delays in gathering this information result in unnecessary deaths and injuries. Similarly, CPSC's field staff has been slashed so severely that the agency cannot truly be considered to maintain an adequate presence for critical activities such as investigating injuries and monitoring compliance.

It would be impossible to detail all of the hazards known to or suspected by the CPSC that have been either ignored or "back-burnered" in recent years because of the agency's limited resources. The list is large and growing, helped not at all by the antiregulatory attitudes of the current commissioners.

Priorities for Change

EXPRESS SUPPORT FOR THE AGENCY WITHOUT CREATING UNREALISTIC EXPECTATIONS

Although statutorily authorized to seat five commissioners, the commission has been barred from paying salaries for more than three for several years. Hence, given the rotation of slots at the agency, the new President may not be able to appoint a majority of appointees on the commission until 1996. One slot opens in October 1992, and, of course, one commissioner or more could resign. In any event, the President should voice strong objections to the direction of the commission under the Reagan/Bush administrations and point out the philosophy he thinks should govern agency actions. For example, he should convey his disagreement with the current commissioners' focus on trivia, their willingness to tolerate unconscionable delays in the development of voluntary standards, and their inability to provide a sense of direction to the product safety community.

Coupled with criticism of the current commission's approach, the next President should express strong support for the agency's product safety mission, without creating unrealistic expectations. Even a replenished and reinvigorated CPSC will have to make difficult choices about where to devote its scarce resources, virtually guaranteeing that some unnecessary risks will not be attended to quickly and that the agency could be criticized for inaction.

APPOINT COMMISSIONERS WITH A KNOWLEDGE OF AND A COMMITMENT TO PRODUCT SAFETY

As previously stated, the Consumer Product Safety Improvement Act of 1990 requires that the President consider individuals with background and expertise in "consumer products and protection of the public from risks of safety" as appointees to the agency. Not surprisingly, President Bush ignored this directive in the one CPSC appointment he made after the act's passage. The new President should give this directive great weight.

DECIDE WHETHER THE CPSC SHOULD REMAIN AS A COLLEGIAL, INDEPENDENT AGENCY OR BE TRANSFORMED INTO A SINGLE-ADMINISTRATOR AGENCY

Throughout the agency's existence, critics have suggested that the CPSC be transformed from its status as an independent collegial agency to that of a single-administrator agency. A single administrator, it is said, would operate more efficiently than a collegial body.

Those who favor retention of the CPSC's current status argue that better, more thoughtful decisions get made by collegial bodies. Since its decisions often involve complex judgments incorporating scientific data, engineering analyses, injury information, and economic calculations, a collegial body with diverse viewpoints reaches more balanced conclusions than a single individual would.

We make no specific recommendation about agency structure except to caution a new administration not to conclude that the agency's problems will be solved by either changing or retaining its collegial form. Far more critical to its success will be the quality of the appointees, their commitment to promoting product safety, the policy direction given them by the White House, and the resources provided them to carry out their mission.

REVIVE AN INTERAGENCY LIAISON GROUP

One of the most effective innovations under President Carter was the liaison group comprised of federal health and safety agencies, including CPSC, FDA, OSHA, and EPA. Under this arrangement, staff representatives regularly met to exchange information about products common to the jurisdiction of all agencies— for example, formaldehyde, vinyl chloride, and asbestos; to develop uniform procedures, such as reporting requirements;

to exchange information relevant to compliance activities; and to discuss other common problems. So successful was this organization at promoting thoughtful regulation that it was immediately abolished by the Reagan administration and replaced with a far less effective and more politically controlled group. The new President should reestablish this group promptly to share its members' best insights, data, and methodologies, rather than conspire about how to scuttle life-saving proposals—as the Quayle Competitiveness Council currently does.

ABOLISH UNNECESSARY RESTRICTIONS ON THE RELEASE OF ESSENTIAL PRODUCT SAFETY INFORMATION

One of the fundamental ingredients of an effective market is timely and adequate information. Unfortunately, the CPSC, unlike any other federal health and safety agency, operates under cumbersome, time-consuming restrictions that frustrate the release of safety information.

Under Section 6(b) of the CPSA, before the agency releases information from which the identity of a manufacturer could be ascertained, it must first notify the manufacturer of the contemplated release of information; permit the manufacturer to comment on the information to be released; and then take "reasonable steps" to assure (1) that the information is accurate, (2) that disclosure is fair under the circumstances, and (3) that disclosure is reasonably related to effectuating the purposes of the CPSA.

As implemented by the current commissioners, these "reasonable steps" require lengthy investigations, evaluations, product analyses, and consumer complaint confirmations. Manufacturers not satisfied with the agency's actions have the right to be notified of an impending information release and the right to sue to enjoin its release.

Not surprisingly, manufacturers often threaten lawsuits. Given the CPSC's limited resources, the agency understandably has been eager to avoid litigation over 6(b) matters, a fear that enables belligerent manufacturers to intimidate the agency into withholding information about serious product hazards.

To repeat: The CPSC is the *only* federal health and safety agency with such restrictions. Under the Freedom of Information Act, a requester at NHTSA, OSHA, FDA, EPA, or the FTC would have immediate access to most product hazard information.

In addition, information-processing costs at the agency have exploded. The agency currently spends over a dozen staff years and hundreds of thousands of dollars annually in direct costs to process information under 6(b) requirements. For a tiny agency charged with saving lives, this is absurd.

A new Administration committed to providing information to consumers so that the market can function freely should seek the complete repeal of Section 6(b). Its removal would add immeasurably to consumer protection while actually saving the government money.

ABOLISH RESTRICTIONS ON THE RELEASE OF SECTION 15(b)
REPORTS ABOUT POSSIBLE SUBSTANTIAL PRODUCT HAZARDS

Under Section 15(b) of the Consumer Product Safety Act, businesses that obtain information about defects in their products that could create a substantial product hazard are required to notify the CPSC. This is similar to requirements enforced by the NHTSA with respect to motor vehicles and by the FDA with regard to medical devices. Members of the public have access to reports of potential hazards at the NHTSA and the FDA as soon as they are filed—the CPSC is another story.

Until 1981, the public had access to Section 15(b) reports at the CPSC. However, capitalizing on the antiregulation mood that year, the U.S. Chamber of Commerce convinced Congress that, except for relatively narrow circumstances (e.g., if the agency brought an imminent-hazard lawsuit in court), the public should be denied access to these reports. The chamber's argument was that confidentiality would encourage manufacturers to file 15(b) reports. The chamber's argument proved dramatically wrong. The number of 15(b) reports, which had peaked at roughly two hundred in fiscal year 1979, dropped after the law was changed to only ninety-six reports in fiscal year 1982. (In recent years the number of reports has crept upward from the low of 1982, but never has matched the high of 1979.) Clearly, confidentiality has had no positive impact whatsoever.

On the other hand, the public has been denied access to important information about possible product hazards. Once again, manufacturers gained unfair leverage in negotiating recalls with the agency.

DIRECT THE CPSC TO STIMULATE GREATER REPORTING
OF POTENTIAL PRODUCT HAZARDS UNDER SECTION 15(b)

Although the CPSC recall program has been one of the agency's most successful, its successes have occurred more because of an energetic and committed staff than because of widespread compliance by industry with the CPSA. It seems inconceivable, with the CPSC's jurisdiction over 10,000 to 15,000 different products distributed by over 1 million businesses, that only 100 to 200 instances arise nationwide during a year that would lead a company to report a possible product hazard. When one considers that the FDA receives roughly 18,000 such reports from a much smaller universe of manufacturers or that consumers file roughly 60,000 to 70,000 product liability lawsuits annually, one unavoidably concludes from the handful of 15(b) reports that this section is being widely ignored by industry.

A particularly discouraging fact is that, with few exceptions, the severest hazards involved in CPSC recalls have been uncovered by agency staff from information sources other than 15(b) reports. Clearly, something must be done to enhance this program. Its potential benefit to consumer safety is immense.

STREAMLINE AGENCY RULEMAKING PROCEDURES

The Administrative Procedure Act (APA), 5 U.S.C. Sections 551–59, requires an agency that contemplates rulemaking to provide notice to the public of the proposed rule, take comments on its proposed rule, and promulgate a final rule if satisfied that no serious objections have been raised. Those aggrieved by an agency rule are free to challenge it in court if they feel it was not promulgated in accordance with the agency's legislative mandate or was not justified on the basis of available evidence.

Rulemaking at the CPSC must follow this basic model, as well as a host of requirements not contained in the APA—in particular, many added in the 1981 amendments. These amendments impose "paralysis by analysis" on the agency. Under the CPSA as amended, before the commission can promulgate a rule, it must issue a formal Advance Notice of Proposed Rulemaking and evaluate comments about whether it should even begin rulemaking. Should the agency conclude after making numerous statutory findings that rulemaking is appropriate, it must then conduct a preliminary regulatory analysis, including a comprehensive cost-benefit analysis. If the CPSC still concludes that action is warranted, it must then propose its rule together with its regulatory analysis and seek public comment. If, after reviewing the comments, the agency continues to believe that a regulation is warranted, it must publish a comprehensive final notice, including elaborate findings about alternative courses of action considered, costs and benefits, its reasons for choosing to promulgate a regulation, and specific findings that no adequate voluntary standards exist to deal with the problem.

The number and complexity of findings guarantee that the agency will rarely if ever undertake mandatory standards. But one must be clear about the effect of these requirements. Were there no formal requirements, the agency undoubtedly would engage in much of the same analysis called for in the law. The important difference is that these detailed legal requirements form a minefield. The burden on the commission to follow a torturous path strewn with technical potholes makes for extremely slow action. Knowing this, industry lawyers are quick to raise a host of objections based on these requirements every step of the way, knowing that the agency will be forced to document in excruciating detail its compliance with the statute.

The possibility of adequate safety standards being developed by the CPSC can be an invaluable stimulus to spur industry action—but it must be a credible threat in the CPSC's dealings with industry. Hence, the new administration should support streamlining the CPSC's rulemaking process. At a minimum, the requirement for an Advance Notice of Proposed Rule-making should be made discretionary, and some of the more irrelevant and burdensome requirements called for in the regulatory impact analyses should be abolished. Further, with respect to rules that simply require labels or specific instructions for products, all requirements not mandated by the Administrative Procedure Act should be abolished. Warnings and labels rarely have the economic costs associated with them that performance standards or bans do. Accordingly, the agency should be freer to consider and use this type of rule.

CLARIFY THE ROLE THAT VOLUNTARY STANDARDS PLAY IN CPSC ACTIVITIES

To paraphrase Will Rogers, the current commissioners have never met a voluntary standard they didn't like. Despite Congress's attempt in the Consumer Product Safety Improvement Act of 1990 to prevent the agency from blindly relying on voluntary standards to address product hazards, there is little that can be done to improve matters until new commissioners arrive. If the current commissioners want to look to voluntary standards even when industry has shown itself incapable of acting or unwilling to act, no amount of legislation or congressional prodding can move them.

The new Administration must restore proper balance to the commission's relationship with the voluntary standards community. Such a new balance need not result in large numbers of mandatory standards. But it must establish industry's obligation to cooperate with the agency fully in its voluntary standards activities and make clear that the agency must insist on meaningful and credible progress from industry. No particular legislation is necessary to do this. Rather, the agency must simply tighten its procedures for monitoring voluntary standards, establish deadlines for action, and move firmly to take mandatory action should it become clear that adequate voluntary action will not occur.

EXPAND THE AGENCY'S INJURY DATA CAPABILITIES

An indispensable element of injury reduction is knowing which products injure, kill, or sicken consumers. One of CPSC's most useful activities is the acquisition and dissemination of injury data. In many cases, merely knowing that a problem exists virtually ensures its solution. Many manufacturers do not have an accurate notion of a new product's potential for harm because they receive injury reports only for the products they manufacture. Because the CPSC can gather data nationwide, it can illuminate a risk that no one manufacturer could appreciate. Once aware of a problem, most manufacturers will attempt to fix it.

Unfortunately, as budget cuts have deepened, the CPSC has been forced to cut back severely on injury data collection. Yet, this information is vitally necessary for the agency to determine which products present the greatest risks.

The new Administration must meet two immediate needs with respect to the CPSC's injury data systems. First, it must provide sufficient resources to enable them to function properly. Second, it must direct the CPSC to expand data sources known to be useful that have historically been underutilized at the agency. In particular, the CPSC receives thousands of consumer complaints every year that are not used effectively. In part this is because the agency does not have the resources to receive or evaluate large numbers of consumer complaints. And, in part, this results from the CPSC's inability to share such information in a timely fashion with the public because of Section 6(b) restrictions. The CPSC is a small agency with an important task. Its successes often go unnoticed; its unfinished business is painfully obvious.

AUTO SAFETY

CLARENCE M. DITLOW

Summary

I N RESPONSE TO REVELATIONS about the auto industry by Ralph
Nader in *Unsafe at Any Speed*, Congress established the National Highway Traffic Safety Administration (NHTSA) in 1966 to stem the rising
tide of traffic fatalities. Since 1966, regulated improvements in vehicle safety,
highway design, and driver operation have indeed dramatically reduced
traffic fatalities, saving over two hundred thousand lives and preventing many
millions of injuries.

The first years of the agency were heady ones, with the issuance of over
fifty vehicle safety standards that required car companies to take known, but
unutilized, safety technologies such as shoulder belts and collapsible steering
columns off the shelf and put them into all cars. Auto safety regulation
became more difficult as NHTSA moved to adopt a second round of regulations that forced the development of new technologies such as the air
bag. Research programs became increasingly important as NHTSA ventured
into new safety areas where the availability of technology was not so clear.
By the end of the 1970s, the agency had made substantial progress in documenting novel regulatory solutions such as dynamic side-impact standards
to reduce head injuries and the design of the vehicle exterior to reduce
pedestrian injuries. Invaluable consumer information programs on tire quality and crashworthiness were started in 1980.

During the 1980s, safety progress slowed, with the primary gains coming
from the phase-in of safety features in new vehicles required by regulations
adopted in the 1970s. The automatic-restraint standard was issued in 1984
only because the U.S. Supreme Court overturned the Department of Trans-

*Clarence M. Ditlow is Executive Director of the Center for Auto Safety and
author of numerous publications on consumers, auto safety, air pollution,
and transportation, including* The Lemon Book *and* The Safe Road to Fuel
Economy.

portation's 1982 revocation of the standard. Research programs and enforcement efforts were cut to the bone. In the late 1980s, congressional efforts to enact an NHTSA authorization bill mandating new standards such as rollover prevention, dynamic side impact, and extension of all passenger car standards to light trucks and vans forced NHTSA to propose or adopt rules in many of these areas in 1990–91, just before the NHTSA authorization bill was passed in December 1991.

The demise of federal auto safety programs came at a time that consumer demand for auto safety improvements grew. Auto companies who had for twenty years opposed air bags found it hard to sell cars without them. Revitalized leadership at NHTSA could make enormous strides in dramatically reducing the social losses from auto crashes. NHTSA could utilize the rulemakings and safety research required by the 1991 Surface Transportation Act in combination with public support for auto safety to develop the safest and most efficient vehicles ever produced. Traffic fatalities could be cut by another 25 percent and fuel economy could be increased by 50 percent. The United States could regain world leadership in auto production by producing a safe "green car" for the twenty-first century.

History

OVER 1.6 MILLION PEOPLE had been killed in motor vehicle accidents in the United States before Congress passed the landmark National Traffic and Motor Vehicle Safety Act along with the Highway Safety Act in 1966. For the first seventy-five years of motor vehicle transportation, Americans did not have federal regulatory agencies to protect them from death and injury on the nation's highways. Without safety regulation, traffic casualties continued to rise, so that by 1966 a total of 53,000 people were killed and 1.9 million injured. If the 1966 fatality rate of 5.7 deaths per 100 million vehicle miles traveled had continued, over 130,000 people would have been killed in traffic accidents in 1991. Instead, the death rate was 1.9 and 46,000 were killed.

The 1966 legislation was enacted because of a number of converging factors—the work of safety experts such as Dr. William Haddon, the political leadership of Representative Kenneth Roberts and Senators Warren Magnuson and Abraham Ribicoff, the publication of Ralph Nader's *Unsafe at Any Speed*, and simple public outrage at the rising traffic toll.

Until Congress acted, Americans relied on the car companies to produce safe vehicles. That trust was sadly misplaced as the auto industry refused to adopt one safety feature after another. One of the earliest examples is the refusal of General Motors to use laminated safety glass in windshields when such glass was developed by DuPont in the 1920s. In the 1950s, auto companies opposed mandatory lap belts. In the 1960s, they opposed shoulder belts on the grounds that they could cause neck injuries.

The 1966 National Traffic and Motor Vehicle Safety Act established the federal role in auto safety. For the first time, the Federal Government had the responsibility and authority to set minimum safety standards for all motor vehicles used on the nation's highways. If vehicles were found to have defects after manufacture, the government could order their recall. NHTSA was set up with the specific mission of regulating motor vehicle safety, even having the power to order the recall of cars with defects. In enacting the National Traffic and Motor Vehicle Safety Act and its companion Highway Safety Act, Congress specifically noted the failure of the auto industry and its voluntary standards-setting organization, the Society of Automotive Engineers, to protect the public adequately.

As a result of the vehicle and highway safety regulation under the 1966 acts, over 200,000 lives have been saved and many millions of serious injuries prevented. Compared to the annual $100 billion cost of motor vehicle accidents and the personal costs of lives shattered in accidents, federal regulatory programs are the equivalents of inexpensive vaccines. Motor vehicle safety standards have added no more than $500 to the price of the average $15,000 new car. Every $1 spent on vehicle safety reduces accident and injury costs by at least $10.

From the issuance of the first standards in 1967, the federal motor vehicle safety standards have gotten increasingly sophisticated and effective. The first thirty standards were based on existing technology and used simple static tests to determine compliance. These required such basic safety features as laminated windshields, lap and shoulder belts, collapsible steering columns, interior padding, seat anchorages, and stronger door latches.

The second generation of safety standards, issued in the early 1970s, began to force innovation and utilized more advanced dynamic tests. A prime example is the gas tank standard, which specifies the amount of permitted fuel leakage when the vehicle is struck by a 4,000-pound moving barrier in a 30 mph rear impact. Others include windshield retention in frontal collisions.

The third generation of safety standards, now beginning to be implemented, require the use of test dummies to measure injury criteria in crashes. These standards are performance standards in the truest sense of the term, in that manufacturers must develop vehicles that will provide specified occupant protection levels as measured in vehicle barrier crashes at 30 mph.

These dynamic standards avoid problems seen with the earlier static standards, such as collapsible steering columns not collapsing in off-center crashes.

NHTSA has responsibility for some highway safety programs as well. The most visible and significant highway safety program has been the national 55 mph speed limit, which alone has saved 50,000 lives since its enactment in 1974. Two other major highway safety programs were developed in the 1980s. First, much tougher drunk driving laws were enacted with the strong support of new citizen groups such as Mothers Against Drunk Drivers (MADD). Congress required states, subject to loss of federal highway funds, to raise their drinking age to twenty-one, which reduces the alcohol involvement rate of the highest-accident-risk group. As a result of the tougher drunk driving laws, the proportion of fatally injured drivers who were legally intoxicated dropped from 50 percent in 1980 to 40 percent in 1990.

Second, beginning with New York in 1984, states also began adopting mandatory seat belt use laws (MULs). A driving force in this effort was the auto industry, which hoped to defeat mandatory installation of passive restraints by getting states with two thirds of the nation's population to pass MULs by 1989. In the forty-two states that have passed MULs since 1984, seat belt use rates have climbed to 50 to 60 percent. In all states with MULs, the lowest seat belt use is observed in the highest-risk drivers—those at night and young drivers.

In response to the Arab oil embargo in 1974, Congress passed the Energy Policy and Conservation Act (EPCA), giving NHTSA responsibility for fuel economy (CAFE) standards. From 1977 to 1980, NHTSA set CAFE standards through 1985, which resulted in the doubling of auto fuel efficiency and the saving of 2.8 million barrels per day of petroleum. Consumers saved more than $1,000 in gasoline operating costs over the life of their vehicle, while reduced gasoline demand lowered air pollution, stabilized gasoline prices, and reduced our need to import oil or produce it in fragile environmental areas.

The Reagan/Bush Legacy

Safety standards. From its first day in office, the Reagan administration conducted a full-scale assault on the safety programs of NHTSA, beginning with a freeze on all rulemaking and revocation of the passive-restraint standard, the 5 mph no-damage bumper standard, and tire treadwear ratings—three of the most popular and valuable standards NHTSA ever issued. But for a stunning reversal by the U.S. Supreme Court, which unanimously overturned the revocation of the passive-restraint standard, we would not have air bags in all new cars; because we will, this standard alone will soon save nine thousand lives per year.

Other rules that were delayed or killed by the Reagan administration covered improved side-impact protection, pedestrian protection, protection from battery explosions, rollover stability and protection, and upgraded light truck and van safety. The only new standard issued between 1981 and 1988 was high-mounted rear brake lights—one for which all the work had been done prior to 1981.

Although NHTSA promulgated several rules after President Bush took office in 1988, these were issued under pressure from Congress to include them in NHTSA's reauthorization bill if the agency failed to act. Other than extending long overdue passenger car standards to light trucks and vans (head restraints, side-impact protection, automatic restraints, and high-mounted rear brake lights), NHTSA required shoulder harnesses in rear seats and dynamic side-impact protection for passenger cars. However, the rule sets requirements only for the torso and pelvis and not for the head, a source of far more injuries.

While the Reagan-Bush NHTSA gives the illusion it is doing everything that needs to be done with rulemaking, in reality important, life-saving matters such as rollover and dynamic side-impact testing for trucks had not been proposed as rules until Congress required such rulemaking in 1991.

Defects and recalls. Vehicle safety standards are intended to build safety into new vehicles, but the recall program ensures that consumers get safety. If vehicles fail to meet a standard or contain a safety defect, the recall program forces manufacturers to take back the vehicles. NHTSA carries out its recall program through defect and noncompliance investigations. One of the most obvious safety failings of the past twelve years is the demise of the defect recall program. For every car or light truck recalled during the Reagan/Bush administrations, another car or truck went unrecalled, even though NHTSA asked the manufacturers to recall the vehicles. The backlog of defective vehicles has grown to 70 million and has resulted in at least 20,000 accidents, 7,000 injuries, and 500 deaths. In a September 1990 report, the General Accounting Office (GAO) confirmed that NHTSA had in fact closed thirty-seven defect investigations without obtaining a recall when the manufacturers refused to do a voluntary recall.

Recalls reflect the lax enforcement policy, averaging 225 per year for the past 12 years, versus the average of 300 per year from 1971 to 1980. Recalls are also down because investigations into defects continue to plummet, with fewer than ten formal investigations into defects opened in the past twelve years, whereas NHTSA used to open nearly that many in one year.

Since the Department of Transportation (DOT) became a toothless tiger that would not back up its recall requests with formal defect determinations and lawsuits to compel a recall, manufacturers simply refused to recall dangerous cars without fearing any adverse consequences. The only lawsuit that NHTSA filed to force a recall came in the case of brake lockup in GM X-cars only after two House hearings, two GAO reports, and front-page newspaper stories questioned NHTSA's inaction in the face of the mounting deaths, injuries, and accidents from this defect.

Research and development. The Reagan/Bush administrations have inflicted serious institutional damage on the technical capability of NHTSA to carry out its missions. Internal reorganizations and reassignments in the first two years of the Reagan administration resulted in the loss of more than two hundred professional staff. The total R&D budget was cut by 25 percent between 1980 and 1982. Three key research programs were eliminated altogether: the Experimental Safety Vehicle Program, which developed the basis for advanced passenger car rulemaking; heavy-duty-vehicle research; and auto industry and fuel economy research. Between 1980 and 1990, NHTSA's motor vehicle research budget dropped 39 percent and its staff 23 percent. In real dollars, the budget reduction was about 55 percent. At the same time that the NHTSA research budget was being cut, defense spending was doubling and federal R&D funding generally was being increased. In terms of years of life lost, injury prevention programs are stepchildren under the federal budget. Auto injuries represent more than 4 million years of life lost and get $112 million for research expenditures, while cancer costs 1.7 million years of life lost and gets about $1 billion in federal research money.

The nadir of the Bush administration's hostility to valuable R&D programs came in its wanton destruction of the last three research safety vehicles (RSVs). The culmination of a $30 million NHTSA R&D program, the RSVs demonstrated that safe, fuel-efficient cars could be built. Despite RSVs' being used in the graduate engineering program at the University of Virginia, the Bush administration had them destroyed in 1991 when they were cited to support pending legislation to raise fuel economy standards to 40 to 45 mpg.

The real damage from the reduced research in the 1980s will be seen in the 1990s, when the agency should be setting more advanced safety standards. In short, today's research is tomorrow's standard. And tomorrow's standard takes twelve years to get into all vehicles, since the average life of a vehicle is twelve years.

Fuel economy. Due to the Reagan administration's relaxation of fuel economy (CAFE) standards, the United States consumes an extra 1 million barrels per day of gasoline, or more than could be produced from the Alaska National Wildlife Refuge. In addition to making the nation more dependent on foreign oil, this bankrupt policy increases air pollution and global warming by emitting an additional 80 million tons of carbon dioxide (CO_2) annually. The increased use of gasoline results in an additional 100,000 tons of reactive hydrocarbons nationally, and 1,500 tons per year in cities such as New York and San Francisco.

Despite the dramatic benefits of CAFE standards, the Reagan/Bush administrations waged regulatory war against stringent CAFE standards and unsuccessfully tried to get Congress to repeal EPCA. These actions include:

- relaxing the 1986-89 statutory 27.5 mpg car CAFE standard;
- slashing the 1985 and later light-truck CAFE standards;
- relaxing CAFE test procedures to raise CAFE levels illegally;
- failing to enforce gas guzzler regulations stringently;
- terminating rulemaking to raise CAFE standards higher than 27.5 mpg for 1986 and later-model years.

Citizen access. The Reagan/Bush administrations have closed public access to many files and proceedings in order to carry out policies aimed to protect the auto industry, to the detriment of the consumer. Manufacturer requests for confidentiality are routinely granted where they once would have been rejected. Consumer requests for information on their vehicles take months where they once took days. Films of government crash tests that could review poor crashworthiness in new cars are no longer made widely available. Even essential information in consumer complaints was withheld from the public on the grounds that people who often complained to ten or more entities, including car companies, had an expectation of privacy.

Short-Term Priorities/Initiatives

THE AGENCY MUST USE ITS REGULATORY MEASURES to revitalize the U.S. auto industry by making it a technological leader in safety, emissions, and fuel economy rather than the follower it has been for the past decade. With increasing consumer demand for safety and environmental quality shown in the marketplace, relaxing standards heads the American auto industry in the wrong direction.

Within the first month, the next Administration should identify and inventory the agency actions dropped over the past twelve years, including every rulemaking, every closed defect or noncompliance investigation where a voluntary recall was requested, every enforcement program terminated, and every change in public information policy. Within its first three months, the next Administration should reverse those decisions identified as inconsistent with the agency's mission. Within its first six months, it should review the R&D program and identify research that should be initiated or expanded and research that should be terminated or reprogrammed. Based on the review and the needs of the agency to support rulemaking, a new R&D budget should be proposed with funding at least twice present levels. Within the next Administration's first nine months, the agency should identify new procedural and information programs that should be issued and carried out. Within the next Administration's first year, a three-year program plan should be developed so that notices could be issued and rulemakings carried out before the end of the forty-second President's first term.

VEHICLE SAFETY STANDARDS

NHTSA must immediately issue and revise those standards for which the basic research has already been done. The rulemakings required by the NHTSA Reauthorization Act of 1991 in the Intermodal Surface Transportation and Efficiency Act (ISTEA) should be carried out aggressively and every rule issued. The following is a list of immediate rulemakings for the next Administration.

Vehicle handling and stability (rollover). This standard is needed primarily for multipurpose passenger vehicles such as the Jeep, Suzuki Samurai, and Ford Bronco, and some small cars. The death rate from rollover crashes in sport/utility vehicles with their high center of gravity and narrow track width is more than double that for passenger cars. Rulemaking is required by ISTEA.

Head injury protection. Thousands of serious head injuries and brain damage occur each year from contact with the vehicle interior in crashes. Better management of crash energy in frontal crashes is possible with interior component improvements, such as eliminating hard surfaces on instrument panels, increasing the contact area and energy absorption of the front header and front A-pillar, improving windshields with glass/plastic designs to absorb more energy and further mitigate ejection, and upgrading the collapse and energy-absorption characteristics of the steering column and wheel. A very simple addition—just one inch of padding on the A-pillar and roof headers—could reduce head injuries by up to 50 percent at 20 mph impact speeds. These countermeasures would prevent 1,000 to 1,500 fatalities annually. Rulemaking is required by ISTEA.

Dynamic side-impact crash protection for light trucks and vans. Side-impact crashes cause 8,000 occupant deaths and thousands of injuries annually. About 1,000 lives could be saved each year with a dynamic side-impact standard to protect occupants in car-to-car crashes by reducing thoracic/abdominal injuries and preventing ejection with improved structure and door latches. This standard was finally issued for cars in October 1990, but over an unduly protracted schedule of 1994–97. This standard should also be applied to light trucks and vans. Rulemaking is required by ISTEA.

Antilock brakes. Large-truck crashes kill 4,700 and injure about 150,000 people annually. Most of these (4,000 deaths and 100,000 injuries) are occupants of other vehicles and pedestrians. One of every three tractor-trailers can be expected to crash every year—a rate far higher than for passenger cars. Heavy trucks need antilock brakes to stop in shorter distances and provide stability to avoid jackknifing. This standard should be reissued immediately. Antilock brakes also should be required on passenger cars, light trucks, and vans immediately to help reduce the 10,000 rollover crash deaths occurring each year. Rulemaking is required by ISTEA.

Child booster seats. Booster seats are used by children after they become too big for child seats but too small for seat belts, yet there is no safety standard governing these devices. NHTSA should issue standards for booster seats. Rulemaking is required by ISTEA.

Seat belt fit. Most seat belts are designed to fit the average-size male, with short adults and children being inadequately protected. Seat belts should be designed to fit the fifth-to-ninety-fifth-percentile adult, with adjustable shoulder anchorage points. Rulemaking is required by ISTEA.

Bumper standard. The first bumper standard of 5 mph was issued in 1973, in response to directions from Congress. It was upgraded to a no-damage requirement in 1980, but reduced to 2.5 mph by the Reagan administration in 1982. Since this reduction, repair costs have skyrocketed. The 1980 minimum standard of 5 mph should be reissued, with consumer information on performance at 10 and 15 mph.

Integral head restraints. The head restraint standard, issued in 1969, permits either adjustable or integral head restraints. Although a DOT evaluation of the standard a decade ago revealed that integral head restraints were 70 percent more effective and 50 percent cheaper, many companies still produce and sell adjustable head restraints; requiring head restraints would directly save auto manufactures costs and provide superior protection to occupants. If all cars instead of less than half had integral head restraints, we would eliminate over 100,000 injuries each year instead of just 64,000.

CONSUMER INFORMATION PROGRAMS

Vehicle standards set minimum performance requirements, which many vehicles exceed. Automakers could use this positive news to sell vehicles to the public if the government provided such information. When NHTSA began crash-testing cars in 1980, every single Japanese car tested failed the crash tests. In sharp contrast, domestic manufacturers had a wide range of models that passed the tests. Instead of criticizing the Japanese manufacturers for producing unsafe cars, the domestic manufacturers criticized the crash tests as unreliable, inaccurate, and misleading. The domestic industry lost a sales opportunity by not stressing and building on its safety advantage in the 1980s. As we enter the 1990s, the domestic industry ought to place safety, reliability, quality, and consumer protection at the top of its criteria. NHTSA can lead the way to improved performance beyond the minimum vehicle standards and toward increased competitiveness by establishing the following consumer information programs:

Higher severity for the crash test program. The New Car Assessment Program (NCAP), which crash-tests cars at 35 mph, should immediately start testing new cars, vans, and light trucks at speeds of at least 40 mph to show consumers the distinctions among the crash performances of various makes and models. With air bags in some vehicles, there will be clear differences between the protective quality of these vehicles compared to belt-only-installed cars, and consumers should be aware of the total performance capability.

Side-impact, rear, rollover, and child restraint crash tests. Crash tests covering the various directions of impact are needed to inform consumers fully of the safety performance of new cars, and also child restraints. As a first step this year, of NHTSA should begin issuing dynamic side-impact ratings for every car in the NCAP program.

Consumer information crash protection label. Consumer information labels should show the highest crash speed at which the vehicle meets the minimum injury criteria under the federal motor vehicle safety standards. The results of crash tests by manufacturers, monitored by the government, should be revealed to the consumer at point of sale, with information on the price label or beside it. Such information is truly effective only when consumers are given it at the time they purchase the vehicle. The NCAP program can be used as an enforcement tool to verify the accuracy of the manufacturer's tests.

Make and model fatality ratings. DOT should publish an annual report listing fatality rates per 10,000 registered vehicles by manufacturer, make, and model for overall and specific crash modes.

RESEARCH AND DEVELOPMENT

NHTSA's R&D budget has to be doubled to put it back to where it was ten years ago in terms of real dollars. Since costs to society from auto crashes in the United States now total over $100 billion, an R&D program of just increasing DOT's vehicle crash test program alone from 75 crashes per year to 250, or a crash per workday, would yield significant results in both consumer information and research data for advanced standards.

ENFORCEMENT

When it comes to recalls and standards enforcement, the message is simple: A new NHTSA administrator should enforce the standards and order recalls when defects are found. When an auto company refuses to do a voluntary recall, don't close the investigation but open a formal defect investigation, hold a public hearing, and seek an enforcement order in the courts if necessary. When noncompliance and willful refusals to recall are found, the agency must seek the maximum fine possible, of up to $800,000, versus the few thousands of dollars it now imposes.

Long-Term Priorities/Initiatives

VEHICLE SAFETY STANDARDS

Higher severity frontal crash protection standards. The motor vehicle safety standards have been set at 30 mph for two decades. Yet NHTSA demonstrated 40 mph protection with air-bag-equipped Volvos ten years ago, and 50 mph with its research Safety Vehicle. To assure greater occupant protection and also to push manufacturers to upgrade their automatic crash protection designs in the cars (using air bags or advanced belt systems), the standard should be set at 50 mph crash speed into fixed barriers.

Higher severity side-impact protection. Tests should be conducted at 40 mph to improve protection for older age groups from outside intrusion and interior impact. This requires door and side structure improvements and integration with improved seat designs.

Pedestrian safety. About 7,000 pedestrian fatalities and 150,000 serious injuries occur each year. Youths under age fifteen and seniors age sixty-five or over account for 25 percent of pedestrian fatalities and 40 percent of injuries. Pedestrians have a much higher probability of being injured than do vehicle occupants. Pedestrians are consistently involved in about 2 percent of highway crashes but account for 16 to 18 percent of fatalities. Striking vehicles can be made far more forgiving with such changes as soft pedestrian-friendly front bumpers, rounded leading edges and grilles, and elimination of frontal protrusions.

Improved fuel systems. Several hundred fatal crashes occur each year where fires and explosions kill and maim people. Existing Standard 301 for fuel tank integrity should be upgraded to require 50 mph front and rear impacts and 40 mph side impacts. The well-packed fuel containment design in the research safety vehicle is a model of what can be done for compliance at higher speeds.

Intelligent vehicle systems. The auto industry is pushing Intelligent Vehicle Highway Systems (IVHS) to reduce congestion and increase the number of vehicles on the road. Rather than emphasizing vehicle travel, IVHS can be used to improve vehicle safety. NHTSA should use its R&D to develop advanced standards such as detecting rollover conditions, oncoming objects and vehicles, crash severity, and road conditions to activate safety systems in the vehicle to avoid crashes or reduce injuries in the event of a crash.

RESEARCH AND DEVELOPMENT
For the last three years of its term, NHTSA's R&D program must develop the basis for long-term rulemaking and help the U.S. auto industry regain technological competitiveness in the global auto market. While NHTSA cannot fund basic research for the auto industry because that would cost tens of billions of dollars and is appropriately the role of the private sector, NHTSA can use its R&D funds to identify advanced technologies that our auto industry can pursue to its advantage. The priorities of the long-term R&D program must be biomechanics to identify injury mechanisms in crashes, intelligent vehicle systems, and advanced power plants. One of the best steps the next Administration can take is to restore the research safety vehicle programs of the 1970s to develop the generation of fuel efficient, safe cars needed for the twenty-first century.

FOOD, DRUGS, AND MEDICAL DEVICES

WILLIAM B. SCHULTZ

Summary

T HE FOOD AND DRUG ADMINISTRATION has the broadest jurisdiction of any federal regulatory agency, being responsible for the
safety of foods, drugs, cosmetics, and medical devices. Although
historically insulated from political pressures, there has been a major shift
in the focus of the agency during the past twelve years, as politics have
frequently been used to allow the interests of regulated companies to override
science and in some cases the clear requirements of the law. The Reagan/
Bush administrations accomplished this result by allowing the Department
of Health and Human Services, the Office of Management and Budget, and
the Council on Competitiveness to review, and at times veto, important
policy decisions of the FDA. During the next Administration, the commissioner of the Food and Drug Administration should be given full authority
to make decisions within the agency's jurisdiction, and serious consideration
should be given to making the FDA an independent regulatory agency.

The Reagan and Bush administrations have not given the FDA the
resources it needs to do the job that Congress has required it to do and that
the public expects. As a result, both consumers and the regulated companies
have suffered. Consumers suffer when the agency cannot expeditiously remove a dangerous product from the market, assure honesty and fair dealing
in the marketplace, or prevent fraud by prohibiting the promotion of a
product through unproved claims. Both consumers and the regulated industry suffer when the agency delays approving products that have been
fully tested and ultimately are found to be safe and effective. The regulated

*William B. Schultz is Counsel to the House Subcommittee on Health and
the Environment. This article does not necessarily reflect the position of the
subcommittee or the views of any of its members.*

industry suffers when inadequate funding causes the agency to take inconsistent actions with respect to competitive products. The next Administration should adequately fund the Food and Drug Administration.

The FDA operates under the authority of the Federal Food, Drug, and Cosmetic Act, which Congress enacted more than fifty years ago. Because its enabling statute is so old, the FDA often lacks powers that are routinely given to other administrative agencies today. For example, the FDA cannot subpoena evidence in connection with an investigation even though there are more than two hundred statutes in federal law giving subpoena authority to other federal administrative agencies. The FDA also does not have the authority to order a recall of most of the dangerous products it regulates, nor does it have authority to impose civil money penalties. As a result, the FDA is not able to protect the public from health hazards and from fraud adequately. The next Administration should support legislation that would give the FDA adequate authority to enforce the laws it administers.

Finally, the FDA is extremely slow in reaching decisions. It is not uncommon for it to take more than seven years to issue an important regulation. The agency has been reviewing the safety and efficacy of over-the-counter drugs for twenty years, and it still has not issued final regulations for many important categories of OTC drug products. During the next Administration, the FDA should adopt procedures that allow it to make regulatory decisions expeditiously.

History of the Office

THE FOOD AND DRUG ADMINISTRATION is our oldest consumer protection agency. It also has the broadest jurisdiction, being responsible for regulating products that account for twenty-five cents of every dollar spent by American consumers. In addition to human drugs, the FDA is responsible for regulating medical and radiologic devices, vaccines, serums, blood and blood products, biological products, cosmetics, and animal drugs. The agency also has jurisdiction over all food products, except for meat and poultry, which are regulated by the Department of Agriculture, and pesticides, over which it shares jurisdiction with the Environmental Protection Agency. The FDA carries out its mission with only eight thousand employees and an annual budget of approximately $765 million. This budget is smaller than that of an average-size hospital.

Congress adopted the first food and drug law in 1906. Perhaps because the agency is so old, it has never had the status of an independent regulatory agency such as the Federal Trade Commission or even a separate executive branch agency such as the Environmental Protection Agency. Instead, it has been a division of another agency since its creation, initially the Department of Agriculture, subsequently the Federal Security Administration, and in modern times the Department of Health, Education, and Welfare (HEW), which was restructured as the Department of Health and Human Services (HHS) and the Department of Education in the late 1970s. The FDA is directed by a single commissioner, who is subject to Senate confirmation but who also must report to the secretary of the department.

The agency is divided into sections that have been constantly renamed and reorganized in recent years. Currently the principal divisions are the Center for Food Safety and Applied Nutrition, the Center for Drug Evaluation and Research, the Center for Biologics Evaluation and Research, the Center for Devices and Radiological Health, the Center for Veterinary Medicine, and the National Center for Toxicological Research (the agency's research arm).

The FDA regulates products in two basic ways. For the vast majority of products, the statutes and other regulations promulgated by the agency set a standard that products must meet. Examples are the requirement that food not be "adulterated" and that over-the-counter drugs be "generally recognized by experts" as being "safe and effective." Products that are subject to this type of standard may be marketed without any prior review by the agency. However, products in violation of the standard are subject to injunction and seizure, as well as the criminal penalties provided for in the appropriate statute.

On the other hand, beginning in 1938, Congress has enacted a series of statutes requiring that products within the jurisdiction of the FDA also be subject to premarket review. This is essentially a licensing scheme under which the product may not be sold until it is first approved by the agency. In 1938 Congress imposed the requirement that "new drugs" be "safe," and in 1962 it added the requirement that they be proven "effective" as well. Effectiveness must be proven by "substantial evidence," which the statute defines as "well-controlled clinical investigations."

Congress also enacted laws requiring premarket approval of food additives in 1958 and color additives in 1960. Animal drugs were added to the list in 1962. Each of these three laws contains a "Delaney clause," prohibiting the FDA from approving these products unless the applicant has demonstrated that the substance does not cause cancer in humans and laboratory animals. In 1976 Congress adopted comprehensive legislation covering medical devices, although very few medical devices have actually been subjected to the premarket approval requirements.

During the 1980s Congress enacted the Orphan Drug Act of 1983 and the Drug Competition and Patent Term Restoration Act of 1984. The Orphan Drug Act was designed to create new incentives for drugs whose potential patient population is so small that companies were not willing to invest in their research and testing. The act provided tax breaks, a small grant program, and seven years of exclusivity for orphan drugs, which it defined as drugs for diseases and conditions that affect fewer than two hundred thousand people. In 1990 President Bush pocket-vetoed legislation to amend the Orphan Drug Act to allow competition by manufacturers of highly profitable orphan drugs, as measured by the willingness of two or more companies to invest in the product and to race to obtain the first approval.

In 1990 Congress also enacted the Nutrition Labeling and Education Act (NLEA) and the Safe Medical Device Act.[1] The NLEA is a comprehensive statute that by 1994 will require full nutrition labeling (information about fat, calories, salt, etc.) on all food. The only significant category of products excepted from the NLEA is poultry and other meats, which are within the jurisdiction of the U.S. Department of Agriculture. In addition, the NLEA will prohibit health claims (such as the claim that "fiber prevents cancer") until the FDA has determined that there is a strong scientific basis for the claim.

The Safe Medical Device Act provides the agency with a host of new tools to regulate medical devices such as breast implants and CAT scanners. The act will require hospitals to report information about injuries that may have been caused by medical devices. It will also require device companies to conduct studies on the experience with certain critical devices during the first years after they have been approved, and to establish tracking systems so that the FDA can identify the recipients of devices such as heart valves if it becomes aware of serious safety problems. Finally, the 1990 amendments give the FDA the power to recall devices that may pose a serious risk to public health and to impose civil penalties for legal infractions relating to devices.

Recent Legacy, 1981–92

WHEN THE REAGAN ADMINISTRATION TOOK OFFICE, it emphasized voluntary industry compliance instead of regulation and signaled that enforcement of the law was no longer a priority. One of the administration's first acts was to eliminate an FDA pilot program that would have provided patients information (called "patient package inserts") about prescription drugs. During the Reagan administration, the FDA did not initiate a single new regulatory program designed to protect the public health. In addition, enforcement actions at the FDA declined by 50 percent.[2]

These changes were the direct result of a major shift early in the Reagan administration about how decisions were made at the FDA. The Federal Food, Drug, and Cosmetic Act delegates all authority to the secretary of the Department of Health and Human Services, and, prior to the Reagan administration, the secretary of HHS had delegated that authority to the commissioner of the Food and Drug Administration. Because it was viewed as an agency charged with grappling with scientific issues, its decisions were rarely politically reviewed, much less overturned, by the secretary of HEW or of HHS.

This approach began to change in the Carter administration, although what started as an exception became the rule during the Reagan years. As one of his first official acts, HHS incoming secretary Richard Schweiker issued a regulation withdrawing the delegation for "highly significant public issues." Today the secretary of the Department of Health and Human Services reviews virtually every significant regulation issued by the Food and Drug Administration. In addition, the department (often through several of the assistant secretaries, the chief of staff, and the executive secretary) now participates in decisions about what enforcement actions the agency should bring, the types of educational information the agency should disseminate, all FDA press releases and other public communications, and even what the FDA may tell industry representatives at FDA-industry meetings.

Another important change made by the Reagan administration is the expanded role of the Office of Management and Budget (OMB). As a result of Executive Order 12291 and Executive Order 12498, all significant regulations and plans for future regulatory initiatives must be reviewed by the OMB in addition to HHS. In a number of cases, HHS and the OMB reversed the FDA on important policy decisions, to the detriment of public health. For example, when six color additives turned out to cause cancer in animals, the FDA, taking directions from HHS, reinterpreted the Delaney clause rather than remove the dyes from the market, as required by law. The agency's decision was reversed by a unanimous panel on the U.S. Court of Appeals for the District of Columbia Circuit, in an opinion written by Judge Stephen F. Williams, a judge appointed by President Reagan.[3]

The FDA's decision to ban the importation of unpasteurized milk in interstate commerce was reversed by HHS and the OMB until a federal court ruled that the agency was legally required to impose the ban.[4] Similarly, FDA action to require labeling on tampons to inform women about toxic shock syndrome (TSS) was delayed for four years (during which time hundreds of women contacted TSS, and a significant number of them died) until a federal court ordered to the agency to issue the regulation.[5] Finally, several hundred children died from Reye's syndrome because the OMB ordered the agency to delay issuance of a regulation to require a label on aspirin warning about Reye's syndrome and advising parents not to give aspirin to children who had flu or chicken pox.

During the mid-1980s, the agency reversed its policy on health claims and allowed claims to be made with no review or substantiation by the agency.[6] The competitive nature of the free market forced manufacturers to begin making deceptive and misleading claims or else lose market share. Meanwhile, the agency made no effort to adopt comprehensive regulations requiring nutrition labeling.

The public health suffered in other areas as well. Although the 1976 Medical Device Amendments directed the FDA to undertake a comprehensive review of devices on the market in 1976, progress during the 1980s was extremely slow. Fourteen years after the amendments were enacted, the FDA had required the submission of data for only 8 of the 140 types of devices that the agency placed in Class III, the category reserved for the most potentially dangerous devices, such as those used every day by heart surgeons and anesthesiologists.

During the Reagan-Bush years, increasing attention was paid to the question of whether fish are being adequately inspected. Nevertheless, the agency's 1992 budget allocated only $40 million to a fish inspection program. Although this is almost twice as much as the agency allocated toward fish inspection in 1990, neither the financial resources nor the program's structure are adequate to protect the public health. In contrast, the USDA's meat inspection program, which has also been subject to serious criticisms, was funded at a level of $473 million in fiscal year 1992. The USDA has approximately 7,000 employees to inspect meat and poultry facilities, which is just 1,000 less than the entire work force of the FDA.

During the 1980s little attention was paid to the regulation of over-the-counter drugs. In contrast to prescription drugs, a manufacturer may begin marketing an OTC drug without first receiving approval from the FDA. In 1972 the FDA began reviewing all over-the-counter drugs to determine whether they were safe and effective. At that time the agency announced that it would not enforce the legal requirement that OTC drugs be effective until it had completed the OTC review for that drug. By the early 1980s the FDA-appointed scientific panels had concluded that 66 percent of all OTC drug ingredients and claims were not supported by available scientific evidence. Yet the Reagan administration cut the staff responsible for reviewing OTC drugs by almost 50 percent, and by the late 1980s the agency had completed its review on only 20 percent of OTC drug ingredients. Today, final decisions (and enforcement actions as to efficacy) are still outstanding for more than 50 percent of OTC drug ingredient categories.

Finally, the agency in the 1980s was almost incapable of issuing major regulations. It took eight years to issue regulations required by the 1976 Medical Device Amendments, which required reporting by medical device manufacturers.[7] It has yet to issue regulations required by the Orphan Drug Act of 1983 or the Drug Competition and Patent Term Restoration Act of 1984.

In fact, the agency's ability to track regulations was in such disarray that as recently as 1991 it was unable to produce a list of pending regulations when asked to do so by the House Subcommittee on Health and the Environment. When the list finally was produced, it turned out that pending regulations had been under consideration for an average of nine years. Regulations designated as important took an average of five years to issue. There were two regulations that had been pending for twenty-nine years each.[8]

The generic drug program was brought to a virtual standstill when the Subcommittee on Oversight and Investigations of the House Committee on Energy and Commerce revealed that FDA officials had taken bribes and that a significant number of generic drug companies had submitted fraudulent data to the agency. Although the pace has picked up slightly, there is still a large backlog of generic drug applications at the FDA, and as a result many lower-priced generic drugs are not available to the public.

The year 1990 was a pivotal one for the FDA. Congress enacted two major pieces of legislation designed to address the abuses of the 1980s: the Nutrition Labeling and Education Act and the Safe Medical Device Amendments. In addition, Dr. David Kessler was appointed commissioner.

One of the bright lights of the Bush administration, Dr. Kessler has revitalized the agency's enforcement program, and as a result enforcement actions have doubled in most categories. Dr. Kessler has also improved the agency's record in issuing regulations; for example, it met the one-year deadline for proposed regulations to implement the NLEA.[9] Although it has missed a number of deadlines for regulations required by the Safe Medical Device Act, it has issued two important proposed regulations required by the law.[10]

One of the FDA's most important functions is to approve new prescription drugs. The law requires the agency to act on new drug applications within 180 days after they are filed. However, actual approval times are much longer, and in 1991 they averaged a little more than two years. The agency has been much more successful in approving important drugs, such as drugs designed to treat AIDS, cancer, and other serious or life-threatening diseases. The two most important drugs approved to treat AIDS in recent years, AZT and DDI, were both approved in less than six months after their new drug applications were filed.

Under Dr. Kessler, the FDA has also begun to reevaluate the testing requirements for medical devices and to tackle the backlog of devices that have never been approved for safety and efficacy. In one of the most highly publicized decisions it has ever made, during the spring of 1992 the FDA severely restricted the sale of silicone gel breast implants because of concerns about risks to the public health.

There is a dark side to the FDA's recent revival as an effective regulatory agency, and that is the emergence of Vice President Quayle's Competitiveness Council as a counterforce to the agency even beyond the continued presence of HHS and the OMB. Prior to Dr. Kessler's appointment, the FDA had drafted a bill that would have updated and modernized the agency's enforcement authority. For example, while there are more than two hundred statutes conferring subpoena authority on federal administrative agencies, the FDA has no ability to issue an administrative subpoena in connection with an investigation it is undertaking. Consequently the agency did not have authority to compel production of essential documents in the possession of the manufacturers of silicone gel breast implants, even though trial attorneys in product liability litigation with the companies had had access to the documents for many years.

Nor does the FDA have the authority to order the recall of foods, drugs, or cosmetics that are dangerous to public health. While other agencies can impose civil money penalties where there have been violations of law, the FDA must choose between criminal penalties or no penalties at all.

During the early months of his tenure, Dr. Kessler testified that he supported these new powers, and the secretary of HHS, Dr. Louis Sullivan, testified that he had approved the FDA enforcement bill drafted by the FDA giving the agency all this new enforcement authority, which had been supported by Democratic and Republican administrations going back to the early 1970s.

The regulated industry then did what it has done with increasing frequency in recent years: It took its case to the White House, which at the last minute prohibited Dr. Kessler from testifying in favor of his proposals. As a result, Republicans in Congress have opposed legislation to update the agency's enforcement authorities, and President Bush has opposed enactment of any new enforcement legislation in 1992.

The White House also has intervened to weaken the standard for measuring whether there has been substantial compliance with requirements for conveying nutrition information for fresh fruits, vegetables, and fish. Worse, the food industry has apparently succeeded in persuading the White House to pressure the FDA to grant a nine-month extension to the March 1993 implementation date for the requirements of the Nutrition Labeling and Education Act.

To date, the White House's most visible role in overseeing the Food and Drug Administration has been in the area of drug regulation. In November 1991, the Competitiveness Council forced the FDA to allow drug experimentation on human subjects before the FDA has even reviewed a testing proposal to determine whether the experiment is legally and ethically valid. Neither the White House nor the FDA has suggested that this proposal will significantly speed up the approval of drugs.

The Competitiveness Council also took credit for the FDA's policy statement on the requirements for genetically modified plants. The statement would give the food industry wide latitude in deciding whether a genetically engineered product is sufficiently different from food products currently being marketed to justify premarket approval by the FDA. If the regulated company decided that premarket approval was not justified, then the FDA would receive no information and would be unlikely to have any basis for taking regulatory action until a public crisis occurred. Newspaper articles published at the time of the announcement stated that the food biotechnology industry sought FDA involvement to bolster public confidence in genetically engineered products.

By the end of 1992 the FDA will be in far better shape than when Dr. Kessler arrived two years before. By bringing a relatively small number of enforcement actions, he has demonstrated that large portions of the industry can be brought into line. Despite interference from the Competitiveness Council, Dr. Kessler has largely succeeded in restoring the FDA's credibility with the public and in restoring the morale of the agency. Nevertheless, the FDA cannot survive as an effective agency as long as its discussions are subject to review and approval by the political operatives at HHS, the OMB, and the Competitiveness Council. As the Environmental Protection Agency's experience with the Clean Air Act demonstrates, the more important the issue, the more likely it is that the White House will require that the industry's self-interest override the agency's duty to protect the public health.

The FDA will also begin receiving additional resources in 1993. During its closing days, the 102d Congress enacted a bill that would generate $350 million in prescription drug user fees over the next five years. The money would be used solely to augment the agency's resources for the drug approval process, and, the FDA estimates, in five years would allow it to cut drug review times almost in half (to six months for breakthrough drugs and twelve months for all drugs).

Priorities and Initiatives

STRUCTURAL CHANGES

1. *Independence.* The commissioner of the FDA should be given authority to issue regulations and to make all other decisions within the jurisdiction of the agency. The FDA should also be removed from the Public Health Service (a division of the Department of Health and Human Services) so that the commissioner reports directly to the secretary of HHS. The 1981 withdrawal of delegation to the agency should be reversed, and Executive orders 12291 and 12498 should be revoked. Serious consideration should be given to making the FDA an independent regulatory agency. Its decisions should be based only on the law, its scientific expertise, and comments or information that it reviews on the record. The back door to overruling FDA decisions through HHS and the OMB should be closed.

2. *Funding.* The FDA should be funded at a level adequate to support the significant programs it is legally required to implement and to permit it to make timely decisions on the safety and efficacy of its regulated products. If it is not possible to obtain additional appropriations for the agency, the new Administration should support legislation to allow the FDA to charge fees for programs it administers and to use those funds to increase its budget.

3. *Enforcement.* The FDA and Congress should work to enact legislation that will give the agency adequate authority to monitor products under its jurisdiction and to bring enforcement actions where there have been violations of law. Such legislation should include administrative subpoena authority so the agency can obtain evidence essential to its investigations; record inspection authority to be used in connection with inspections of food, device, OTC drug, and cosmetic facilities (the agency already has this authority for drugs); temporary detention authority for foods, drugs, and cosmetics (the agency already has this authority for devices); and administrative and judicial civil penalty authority for all products.

DRUGS AND BIOLOGICS

1. *AIDS and cancer drugs.* The FDA should continue to give high priority to the review and approval of drugs and vaccines designed to treat

AIDS, cancer, and other life-threatening diseases. It should use all possible approaches to assist in the design of studies to determine if these products are safe and effective, and to ensure that applications to market these products are reviewed as quickly as possible.

2. *Generic drugs and other drugs that are not essential to treatment or prevention of life-threatening diseases.* The FDA should be adequately funded so that it can make timely decisions on applications for all drugs, including generic drugs and other drugs that are not designed to treat life-threatening diseases.

3. *Patient package inserts.* The FDA should develop an effective program for conveying information about prescription drugs to patients, including the use of patient package inserts.

4. *Over-the-counter drugs.* The FDA should expeditiously make final decisions on the over-the-counter drugs that have not been fully evaluated as part of the over-the-counter drug review, so that all OTC drugs will have to satisfy the statutory requirements of safety and efficacy. The FDA should also adopt a program whereby it can make timely decisions with respect to requests for a change in the status of OTC drugs.

5. *Drug advertising.* The FDA should reevaluate its rules pertaining to drug advertising and adopt standards that ensure that drug advertising, including the promotion of unapproved indications of prescription drugs, meets the requirements of law.

MEDICAL DEVICES

1. The FDA should expeditiously issue the regulations that are needed to implement the Safe Medical Device Amendments of 1990, including requirements for user reporting, tracking of implantable and certain other devices, and postmarketing surveillance of devices.

2. The FDA should allocate sufficient resources so it can evaluate data from manufacturers and medical device users (such as hospitals) on injuries caused by devices.

3. The FDA should adopt a plan for expeditiously requiring manufacturers of pre-1976 critical devices (such as heart valves) to submit data on safety and efficacy and for reaching decisions on whether to continue to permit the marketing of such devices.

FOODS

1. The FDA should implement the regulations for the Nutrition Labeling and Education Act as promptly as reasonably possible.

2. The FDA should work to ensure that the U.S. Department of Agriculture's regulations on nutrition labeling for meat and poultry are consistent with the NLEA and the FDA's regulations.

3. The FDA should be given authority (jointly with the Federal Trade Commission) to require that food advertising be consistent with the labeling requirements of the NLEA.

4. The FDA should review its regulation of unavoidable contaminants such as lead, aflatoxin, and mercury and establish procedures whereby safe levels are established through a process the agency can defend to the public.

5. The FDA should adopt a comprehensive program to ensure that fish products consumed in this country are safe; this should include enforceable standards for contaminants in fish, the authority to close contaminated waters, and public education about the risks of consumption of raw fish.

6. The FDA should revise its proposal on genetically engineered foods to require, for a limited period of years, premarket review of all such foods, to assure the public that genetically engineered foods are safe for consumption prior to being sold to the public.

NOTES

1. Public Law 101-535 (November 8, 1990); Public Law. 101–629 (November 28, 1990).
2. Public Citizen Health Research Group, *Decreased Law Enforcement at the Food and Drug Administration and the Occupational Safety and Health Administration FY 1981–1984* (1984); memorandum from FDA Office of Legislative Affairs to William B. Schultz (July 10, 1992).
3. *Public Citizen v. Young*, 831 F.2d 1108 (D.C. Cir. 1987).
4. *Public Citizen v. Heckler*, 653 F. Supp. 1229 (D.D.C. 1986).
5. *Public Citizen v. Commissioner*, 724 F. Supp. 1013 (D.D.C. 1989).
6. 6. See 55 Fed. Reg. 28,843 (August 4, 1987).
7. 49 Fed. Reg. 36,348 (September 14, 1984).
8. General Accounting Office, *FDA Regulations: Sustained Management Attention Needed to Improve Timely Issuance* (February 1992).
9. 56 Fed. Reg. 60,367 (November 27, 1991).
10. 56 Fed. Reg. 60,024 (November 21, 1991) (user reporting); 57 Fed. Reg. 10,702 (March 27, 1992) (device tracking).

WORKPLACE SAFETY AND HEALTH

MARGARET M. SEMINARIO

Summary

ON SEPTEMBER 3, 1991, the nation was shocked and horrified when twenty-five workers were killed in a fire, trapped behind locked doors, at a chicken processing plant in Hamlet, North Carolina. It seemed unthinkable that the same kinds of conditions that claimed the lives of 146 young women in a fire at the Triangle Shirtwaist Factory eighty-one years ago could exist in America today.

More than two decades after the passage of the Occupational Safety and Health Act, however, the promise of a safe and healthful workplace is far from a reality. Every year more than 10,000 workers are killed on the job, 6 million are injured, and 60,000 are permanently disabled. Tens of thousands more die prematurely from long-term occupational diseases. Occupational injuries are on the increase and now are at the highest level in the past decade.

After twelve years of neglect, the Occupational Safety and Health Administration (OSHA) has neither the will nor the resources to do the job. There are only enough federal inspectors to inspect even the most hazardous workplaces once every thirteen years.

It's time for a renewed national commitment to protect the health and safety of America's workers. There needs to be a new approach that both inspires greater efforts by employers and empowers workers to take action on safety and health hazards. OSHA standards and inspections are still

Margaret Seminario is Director of Occupational Safety and Health for the AFL-CIO. She is a member of the National Advisory Committee on Occupational Safety and Health and of the Federal Advisory Council on Occupational Safety and Health.

needed, but workers and employers must play the major role in preventing workplace injuries and illness. Here are several necessary steps:

• Comprehensive OSHA reform legislation that requires workplace safety and health programs and joint management-labor committees and that expands worker rights and OSHA's authority should be strongly supported and enacted.

• Standards must be set on key safety and health hazards such as ergonomic hazards, which have resulted in an epidemic of cumulative trauma disorders throughout American industry.

• Enforcement must be strengthened and data collection improved to better target OSHA inspections to hazardous workplaces and operations.

• Better cooperation and coordination with EPA, NIOSH, and state agencies should be sought to improve and expand worker protection efforts.

• OSHA's budget and staffing levels must be increased and new sources of funding sought to finance compliance assistance activities such as training and technical support. Current levels of funding are totally inadequate to meet even current responsibilities.

OSHA History

FEDERAL LEGISLATION GOVERNING WORKPLACE SAFETY and health was first enacted in the 1960s and 1970s as part of a broader congressional agenda to address growing environmental and public health and safety concerns. The Coal Mine Health and Safety Act, governing conditions in the nation's underground mines, was enacted in 1969 following a major disaster in Farmington, West Virginia, that took the lives of seventy-nine workers. The next year Congress passed the Occupational Safety and Health Act of 1970 (OSHAct), which applied to most nonmining industries.

The OSHAct federalized responsibility for workplace safety and health regulation and enforcement, which previously had been overseen by the states. OSHA was created at the Department of Labor to carry out the law's regulatory authority. Two other agencies, the National Institute for Occupational Safety and Health (NIOSH) and the Occupational Safety and Health Review Commission, were also established for the respective purposes of conducting research and adjudicating OSHA enforcement cases.

The OSHAct covers all private sector workplaces except for those hazards and situations that are subject to the regulation of another federal agency (e.g., radiation in nuclear facilities, farmworker exposure to pesticides, and mine safety). Eighty million workers and 5.9 million workplaces are subject to the act's requirements. State and local public employees are covered in those states that operate a state OSHA plan. (Twenty-one states operate state plans for both the private and the public sector, while two additional states have plans that cover only the public sector.)

The primary responsibilities and functions of OSHA are setting standards and enforcement. Ten regional offices and eighty-five field offices employing two thousand people are responsible for the inspection and enforcement activities. The remainder of the agency's staff, an additional four hundred people, are headquartered at the national office in Washington, D.C. Programs on training and education, compliance assistance, and the promotion of voluntary compliance have also been part of OSHA's activities.

The Occupational Safety and Health Administration has had a tumultuous history. Though the OSHAct was passed with bipartisan support by overwhelming majorities in both the House and Senate, the OSHA program soon became a target of political intervention and attacks.

In its early years, OSHA was opposed by the business community, particularly small business, as well as by the Nixon administration. With an inexperienced, unqualified staff and inadequate resources to do the job, it became an easy target of those who opposed the Federal Government's role in overseeing job safety. As a result, in the early 1970s little progress was made in establishing a meaningful national safety and health program.

During the Ford administration, OSHA began to make some progress under the direction of Dr. Morton Corn, a respected safety and health professional. Efforts were launched to improve and expand the staff through in-house training and the hiring of qualified safety and health professionals. Important occupational health problems such as lead, noise, coke oven emissions, and cotton dust were targeted, and regulatory action was initiated against these hazards.

With the Carter administration and the appointment of Dr. Eula Bingham, a toxicologist, OSHA continued to gain strength and credibility. Final standards were set on the chemicals lead, cotton dust, arsenic, acrylonitrile, DBCP, and benzene, and a policy for regulating cancer-causing substances was promulgated. And the agency stepped up its enforcement activities against employers who violated the law.

For the first time, the agency also directed significant resources involving workers in safety and health activities in the workplace. A major worker educational program, the New Directions Program, greatly expanded worker safety and health training through grants to unions, universities, and employer groups. Through regulations workers and their representatives were guaranteed the right of access to worker exposure and medical records. And the agency proposed a worker right-to-know standard on chemical hazard information. All these measures attempted to give workers more information and participation in safety and health activities at the worksite.

The significant achievements of the Carter administration did not come without opposition. Indeed, the more serious the initiative, the greater the opposition. Legal challenges by the business community seeking to overturn standards became routine. Legislatively, there were yearly attempts to limit OSHA's authority through appropriations riders, and in 1980 a major reform bill was introduced that would have limited the agency's inspection powers. For the most part, however, these efforts were unsuccessful, and by 1980, after a decade of struggle, the agency had finally established its legitimate role in the regulatory arena.

The Reagan/Bush Years

PROGRESS AT THE OCCUPATIONAL SAFETY and Health Administration came to an abrupt halt in 1981 with the inauguration of President Reagan. Like other government regulatory agencies, OSHA was subjected to the Reagan administration's philosophy of deregulation and voluntary compliance. Direction for OSHA's activities came from the President's Task Force on Regulatory Relief along with oversight from the Office of Management and Budget, which was given broad authority to review and approve all major proposed and final rules. Thorne Auchter, a Reagan campaign official with no safety and health expertise, was appointed head of OSHA and proceeded to carry out the administration's deregulatory policy.

In the early years of the Reagan administration the assault on OSHA's regulatory and enforcement programs was broad and unrelenting. Major OSHA standards, such as those on lead and cotton dust, were targeted for review and weakening. All work on new standards, such as those on confined-space entry and chemical hazard right-to-know, was suspended.

A concerted effort was undertaken to impose a cost-benefit test for setting OSHA health standards. Previously, OSHA health standards had been set on the basis of risk, taking into account technological and economic feasibility considerations. The effort to require cost-benefit analysis was sidetracked when the U.S. Supreme Court ruled in the cotton dust case that such a balancing was prohibited by the Occupational Safety and Health Act.

Similar initiatives were also undertaken to weaken OSHA's enforcement activities. Directives were issued that greatly reduced the scope of OSHA inspections and the severity of citations and penalties, the result being a 41 percent reduction in serious citations and a 74 percent reduction in assessed penalties during the first three years of the Reagan administration. The administration issued a series of policies exempting the majority of employers from routine safety inspections. Industries with lower than average injury rates were removed from the inspection targeting list, and individual employers were exempted if their injury log showed a lower than average injury rate. As would be documented in subsequent enforcement actions by OSHA, the result of these policies was to encourage widescale underreporting of injuries and illnesses by employers.

OSHA's budget and staffing levels were also reduced by the Reagan administration. From 1981 to 1983, the number of inspectors was cut from 1,300 to less than 1,000, and the overall OSHA staff was cut from 2,734 to 2,285. Even without changes in regulatory and enforcement policies, these budget and staffing cuts reduced OSHA's level of activity.

As with its sister agency the Environmental Protection Agency, the Reagan administration's deregulatory assault on OSHA generated a significant backlash from the public. The administration's deregulatory ideology could not withstand growing public concern and demands for government action to address serious safety and health concerns such as exposure to asbestos, benzene, and formaldehyde. Actions by unions and public interest groups and critical media attention stymied many deregulatory initiatives and forced OSHA to initiate new regulatory activities in a number of areas. Similarly, the Reagan administration's enforcement policies of inspection exemptions and weak penalties could not withstand public scrutiny, particularly when it became clear that extremely hazardous conditions were receiving little if any government enforcement.

Demands for increased action led to some changes and improvements in the OSHA program in the later years of the Reagan administration. Secretary of Labor William Brock appointed a safety and health professional, John Pendergrass, to head the agency. New standards on some major hazards were issued. And the agency scrapped its inspection exemption policy and initiated "an egregious penalty policy" assessing multimillion-dollar penalties against employers who willfully and flagrantly violated the law.

The first years of the Bush administration brought in large measure a continuation of late Reagan-years policies and programs. Gerard Scannell, a safety and health professional with previous service with OSHA, was appointed to head the agency. Scannell established good working relationships with labor, employers, and Congress and built support for the OSHA program. Under Elizabeth Dole, later to be secretary of labor, a few new regulatory and enforcement initiatives were undertaken, including a proposed standard on seat belt use. But with the arrival of Lynn Martin as secretary of labor, support for such initiatives diminished. In January 1992

Scannell resigned and was replaced by Dorothy Strunk, a longtime Republican congressional staff person on the House Education and Labor Committee, with no professional background in occupational safety and health.

Since January 1992 OSHA has once again suffered from a midstream change in leadership and election-year politics. Actions have been taken to delay or limit the application of new OSHA standards on chemical process safety management and bloodborne infectious diseases, regulations issued as a result of congressional mandates. OSHA's egregious penalty policy for flagrant violators has not been utilized. President Bush's regulatory moratorium has slowed or halted progress on other important OSHA standards, even though standards necessary to protect safety and health are supposedly exempt from the moratorium.

The administration has also announced its opposition to legislation to reform the Occupational Safety and Health Act (S.1622 and H.R.3160), introduced in 1991 by Congressman William Ford and Senators Kennedy and Metzenbaum. The OSHA reform legislation marked the first comprehensive attempt by Congress to update the Occupational Safety and Health Act since its passage in 1970. Except for a sevenfold increase in maximum OSHA penalties included in the 1990 Budget Reconciliation Act, the OSHAct has never been changed.

The OSHA reform proposal established a new approach to safety and health protection by requiring that employers establish worksite programs with the participation of workers through joint safety and health committees. Among other things it also strengthened workers' protection against retaliation and OSHA's civil and criminal enforcement authority.

The reform proposal largely embodied measures already adopted by several states, such as program and committee requirements, or present in other federal laws. Nonetheless, the Bush administration took the position that no improvements in the OSHAct were needed and threatened to veto the proposed OSHA reform legislation if passed by the Congress. The administration also opposed other legislative OSHA proposals, including a construction safety bill and legislation enhancing OSHA criminal penalties.

The Bush administration's treatment of the OSHA reform legislation is a prime example of the Reagan/Bush failures on workplace safety and health. The legacy of the twelve years of Reagan/Bush neglect includes:

• *Increased workplace injuries and illnesses.* Since 1983 there has been a steady increase in reported injuries and illnesses, which today are at the highest level in the past decade. In 1990 more than 10,000 workers were killed on the job, 6 million injured, and 60,000 permanently disabled. The annual cost of workplace injuries alone is estimated to be $83 billion a year.

• *Reduced staffing levels and budget to address growing problems.* OSHA has fewer people and less money in real dollar terms to carry out its statutory responsibilities than in 1980. Today, OSHA has an annual budget of less than $300 million and a staff of approximately 2,400, about 1,000 of whom conduct worksite inspections. OSHA has been unable to keep up with growing demands and new areas of concerns such as indoor air quality, infectious diseases, and VDT hazards.

• *Inadequate regulation of major safety and health hazards.* OSHA has failed to act on safety and health problems such as ergonomic hazards, indoor air pollution, confined-space entry, and exposure to methylene chloride, glycol ethers, and other solvents. Ergonomic hazards alone have caused hundreds of thousands of crippling repetitive strain injuries annually, with the incidence of these injuries reaching near epidemic proportions in meat-packing, auto manufacturing, and among some VDT operations.

• *Control of the OSHA regulatory process by the Office of Management and Budget.* The OMB interference in the regulatory process has grown to the point that it is almost impossible for OSHA to issue regulations in a timely fashion. OMB has misused its "authority" under Executive orders 12291 and 12498 to block work on important standards such as chemical process safety and ergonomic hazards and to weaken other rules. The OMB has tried to dictate new methodologies for risk assessment and cost analysis that are at odds with the requirements of the OSHAct.

• *Diminished commitment and competence at OSHA.* The lack of commitment to a strong worker safety program has seriously eroded OSHA. Talented staff have left, and it has been difficult to attract qualified people at all levels in the agency, including the assistant secretary. OSHA now has neither the leadership, professional expertise, energy, nor creativity to tackle serious safety and health problems.

• *Reduction in private sector initiatives.* The lack of federal leadership and of a strong OSHA program has also led to a reduction in private sector initiatives to address workplace hazards. Health and safety staffing levels in many corporations have been cut. Without mandatory requirements, corporate safety and health activities have not received the necessary level of financial and institutional support from top management.

Short-Term Priorities

THE NEXT ADMINISTRATION has the opportunity to provide renewed leadership and direction for the nation's safety and health program. With considerable public and congressional support for new workplace safety initiatives, the new Administration should, during its first hundred days:

• *Declare a renewed national commitment to protect workers' safety and health.* The next Administration should publicly recognize the nation's failure to fulfill the promise of a safe and healthy workplace made by the OSHAct in 1970 and should call for a new approach that empowers workers to have a voice in protecting their safety and health on the job.

• *Appoint a respected, strong agency head.* OSHA needs a strong leader who is well respected in the safety and health field. The next head of OSHA should be someone who can build support for the agency's programs, and someone who has a proven track record of getting things done.

• *Work with Congress on Administration-backed OSHA reform legislation.* OSHA Reform legislation will be a major initiative in the 103d Congress. The next Administration should move quickly to work with the Senate and House committees and other interested parties to draft an Administration-backed comprehensive OSHA reform proposal. Its centerpiece should be the empowerment of workers to have a greater voice in safety and health through the establishment of local and safety and health committees.

• *Clear out the backlog of standards and establish priorities for new standards.* As a result of inaction by the Reagan and Bush administrations, the rulemaking for many OSHA standards, including confined-space entry, methylenedianaline, and asbestos, has dragged on for years. The next administration needs to clear out this backlog and issue final standards for these and other hazards.

OSHA should also establish clear priorities for additional setting of standards, seeking the input of labor, management, NIOSH, and the states. If OSHA has a clear regulatory agenda and acts on these standards, petitions and lawsuits for new standards will be less likely.

• *Take immediate action on ergonomic hazards.* Cumulative trauma disorders (CTDs) caused by poor job design have reached epidemic proportions. Over the past five years, CTDs have increased at an alarming rate in many occupations, including meatpacking, auto assembly, and VDT operation. The agency has taken enforcement actions on ergonomic hazards in some industries, but there is no standard requiring preventive measures for this growing problem. OSHA committed to developing an ergonomic standard in 1990, but the OMB has blocked and delayed rulemaking. The agency should launch a major campaign on ergonomics hazards that includes a proposed standard, and enforcement and education initiatives.

• *Limit the OMB's interference in OSHA rulemaking.* OSHA standard-setting activity can proceed only if the OMB's role in the process is significantly altered. The executive orders granting the OMB review authority should be rescinded or altered to set strict time frames for review and to require that OMB communications be made part of the public record.

• *Establish an aggressive enforcement policy that is consistently applied.*
OSHA should revise its enforcement policy to make full use of the increase
in maximum penalties enacted by Congress in 1990. There should be an
aggressive campaign against employers who fail to abate cited hazards in a
timely fashion. A new oversight program should be initiated to assure consistent enforcement by OSHA's regional and area offices and state OSHA
programs.

Long-Term Priorities

THE MAJOR CHALLENGES FACING OSHA in the long term are to
improve and expand its regulatory and enforcement programs to meet growing demands at a time of severe budget constraints. Passage of OSHA reform
legislation will place new responsibilities on the agency but will also provide
new opportunities to launch new initiatives. To meet these challenges successfully, the next Administration should undertake the following:

• *Develop worksite safety initiatives that empower workers.* Whether
or not OSHA reform legislation is enacted, the next Administration must
establish a new approach to safety and health that fosters greater activity in
these areas at the worksite and that gives workers a voice in safety and health
matters. The old approach of setting and enforcing standards on particular
hazards is necessary but will never be sufficient to do the job. Federal OSHA
should require both worksite safety programs, as six states already do, and
joint safety committees to provide workers with the right to participate in
safety and health decisionmaking on the job.

• *Expand training education and technical assistance to employees and
employers.* Initiatives on safety and health programs and committees will be
effective only if OSHA supports and promotes training, education, and technical assistance for workers and employers.

The New Directions Training and Education Grants Program, virtually
eliminated during the Reagan/Bush years, should be expanded to support
increased training and education activities by unions and employers. OSHA
should develop materials and curricula that can be used to train workers
and safety committee members and supervisors, as well as be used in model
safety and health programs. Such materials would greatly assist employers,
particularly small businesses, to comply with OSHA requirements and help
ensure that workers receive adequate training.

The agency should explore alternate sources of funding to finance training and its compliance-assistance activities, including OSHA penalties or a
tax on employers with hazardous conditions; both approaches have been

used in several states to fund similar activities. Financing OSHA's voluntary programs off-budget would free approximately $25 million, most of it from the consultation program; this money could be directed toward enforcement activities.

• *Develop budget proposals that are sufficient to meet the agency's statutory responsibilities.* OSHA has never had sufficient resources to do its job, but the Reagan and Bush administrations cut OSHA staffing and refused to request the funds necessary to do the job. The new President needs to order an honest assessment of OSHA's resource needs, including resources necessary to implement any new legislation and develop budget proposals that more realistically reflect these needs.

Even if budget constraints are severe, honest information on the agency's budget needs should be presented to Congress so that informed decisions about OSHA's budget can be made.

• *Improve cooperation and coordination with other agencies.* OSHA's standard-setting activities could be strengthened through better coordination with NIOSH and EPA's Office of Pollution Prevention and Toxic Substances, which have better risk assessment capabilities than OSHA. Working together, the agencies should identify one or two rulemakings for joint activity. EPA and NIOSH can be given primary responsibility for risk and exposure assessment, while OSHA should develop the technical and economic feasibility information for the proposed rules.

Similarly, on the enforcement side, OSHA should make increased use of NIOSH and EPA in its enforcement programs and cross-train other federal agency inspectors, such as those at the Department of Agriculture, whose responsibilities bring them into workplace settings.

• *Increase the use of criminal penalties in enforcement cases.* Given limited resources, OSHA needs to continue its practice of enforcement actions and step up criminal enforcement activity. If enacted, OSHA reform legislation will give the agency expanded criminal authority. However, even without new legislation, OSHA should set up its criminal enforcement activities by working with the Justice Department to establish a more aggressive criminal enforcement program, including better investigations in fatality cases. OSHA should also explore working jointly with state and local prosecutors who have established criminal enforcement programs for occupational fatalities, such as those in Milwaukee, New York, and Illinois.

• *Improve performance of state plans.* Many of the state OSHA plans are deficient in performance. Staffing levels are low, standards are slow to be adopted, and enforcement is now much weaker than federal OSHA's, particularly with regard to willful situations and penalties.

OSHA needs to improve its oversight of state plans and move aggressively against those that are deficient. Federal standards should be imposed where states are delinquent in adopting standards. This means requiring states to adopt penalty structures and citation policies comparable to federal OSHA's to eliminate the discrepancies between federal and state enforcement.

• *Sharpen inspection targeting.* OSHA needs to target its inspections to hazardous worksites and operations and to employers who have poor records. OSHA must expand injury and illness reporting requirements so the agency has establishment level data on which to base inspection decisions. Better use should be made of OSHA's inspection database to identify employers with a history of violations. The agency needs also to explore utilizing the Toxic Release Inventory, state-based heavy metal registries, and other sources of toxic chemical and exposure information for targeting health inspections.

• *Improve injury and illness data.* The Department of Labor's data collection activities are failing to collect complete, accurate, or useful information on injuries, illnesses, and fatalities. Efforts to improve the data systems of OSHA and the Bureau of Labor Statistics (BLS) have been under way since 1984 but have been slowed by the OMB and changes in OSHA's leadership. OSHA should work jointly with the BLS and NIOSH to implement the recommendations of the National Academy of Sciences' Panel on Occupational Safety and Health Statistics and the Keystone Dialogue Group on Work-Related Illness and Injury Recordkeeping. These include the collection of establishment-based injury data and the use of nonemployer sources for collection of occupational illness information.

BANKING REGULATION

PAMELA GILBERT AND
SUSANNAH GOODMAN

Summary

T HE SPECULATIVE BOOM of the Roaring Eighties has been followed by the real estate and banking crash of the 1990s. This time,
unlike the Great Depression, the cost is being borne by taxpayers
through deposit insurance rather than by depositors through bank panics.
But the impact will be huge nonetheless. The S&L collapse—the product
of deregulation, speculation, and fraud—is expected to cost taxpayers $500
billion to $1.4 trillion over forty years. Commercial banks are heading for
their own bailout; already, the Bush administration has received authority
to borrow $70 billion to replenish the FDIC's Bank Insurance Fund. If the
banks cannot repay this "loan," as is likely, then taxpayers will have to make
up the difference.

The next President must grapple with the complete breakdown of banking regulation. As currently structured, our banking system privatizes profits
and socializes risk. That trade-off seemed agreeable when banks limited that
risk and made certain to serve the broad public. Instead, over the past two
decades, banks and S&Ls poured funds into commercial real estate, leveraged buyouts and takeovers, and ill-advised loans to less-developed countries.
Indeed, the biggest banks made the worst lending decisions and now pose
the biggest threat of huge bailouts. Now there needs to be a renewed
understanding between banks and the taxpayers.

This new banking order should revolve around two principal goals: (1)
limiting taxpayer exposure and (2) ensuring that the banking system channels

*Pamela Gilbert is Acting Director of Public Citizen's Congress Watch, a
consumer advocacy organization. Susannah Goodman is the banking policy
analyst at Public Citizen's Congress Watch. Tom Schlesinger, Director of the
Southern Finance Project, contributed to this chapter.*

589

capital to the productive economy rather than to renewed speculation. It must take account of the cyclonic change in the financial marketplace, which has been transformed by competition with new, unregulated sectors of the industry, but must keep in mind that the purpose of deposit insurance is to prop up not the banks but their customers and the underlying economy.

Measures to ease the recession and credit crunch. Banks have responded to the postbubble constriction by restricting lending to small and medium-size borrowers, who were not the cause of their distress. Several immediate steps can be taken to help jump-start the economy:

• A moratorium on deregulation by regulatory fiat. The Federal Reserve and other regulatory agencies have effectively repealed many safety-and-soundness rules by letting banks underwrite securities and insurance and expand across state lines, all without adequate safeguards. The new President should immediately issue an executive order halting such unilateral actions, or where necessary (as with the Fed) put pressure on independent agencies to refrain from such action.

• A moratorium on foreclosures and calling of small business and home mortgage loans by institutions under federal control (i.e., receivership or conservatorship).

• Capital requirements should be assigned to government securities to reflect interest rate risks. This will enhance the appeal of business lending and ease the credit crunch.

Increase deposit insurance premiums. So many banks have failed that the Bank Insurance Fund of the FDIC is in the red, and taxpayers are not currently protected from the coming commercial bank bailout. On September 15, 1992, the FDIC board exempted three quarters of the banking industry from paying an increase in insurance premiums to cover the cost of future bank failures. To prevent taxpayers from being stuck with another huge bank bailout, the next Administration should repeal this exemption and raise insurance premiums on all banks.

Restructuring the financial industry. An overhaul of banking laws should see the creation of a two-tiered banking industry. A network of public purpose banks would receive the public benefit of deposit insurance and would channel loans to relatively safe and socially useful investment areas (loans to small and medium-size businesses, residential mortgages, consumer loans, etc.). A second tier of money center banks would be empowered to enter riskier and potentially lucrative fields, but must do so without the taxpayer subsidy.

Restructure the Resolution Trust Corporation (RTC). The RTC—the agency that implements the S&L bailout—must be dramatically restructured. Currently the RTC seeks to dump its real estate assets on an already depressed market, thus losing money for taxpayers, hurting the economy, and dragging down the still-operating banks. (According to the most complete estimate, the agency loses forty cents on the dollar with each sale.) The RTC should shift its focus to encompass asset management, as necessary, to help the real estate market recover. Moreover, the RTC should offer "seller financing" to give the real estate market greater liquidity and to enable working families to buy RTC property. Funds for the RTC will be needed again in April 1993, so the next President will surely have an early decision to make.

Regulatory reform. Banks and S&Ls are regulated by a jumble of agencies with overlapping jurisdictions and inadequate resources. Moreover, these agencies are dominated by the industries they regulate. To prevent a recurrence of the S&L fiasco, regulation must be made to work by the chartering of a Financial Consumer Association (FCA) to monitor regulation and represent citizen interests; and by repealing the banking exemption to the Freedom of Information Act (FOIA).

Introduction: The Financial System in Crisis

THE NEXT PRESIDENT, like it or not, will be forced to grapple with a financial crisis of staggering dimensions. The speculative boom of the Roaring Eighties has been followed by the real estate and banking crash of the 1990s. This time, unlike the Great Depression, the cost is being borne by taxpayers through deposit insurance rather than by depositors through bank panics. But the cost of bank and S&L failures will be an economic ball and chain for decades to come. In short, recent banking regulation—or, more precisely, bank deregulation—stands as one of the most colossal failures in the history of American governance.

The S&L collapse will cost taxpayers $500 billion to $1.4 trillion over forty years. In 1991, the budget of the Resolution Trust Corporation (RTC), the bailout agency, was the third largest in government (behind Defense and Health and Human Services). The size of the scandal defies comprehension. Consider: In 1992, lawmakers fretted over where to find the $1 billion needed to clean up Los Angeles after the worst riots since the Civil War; by contrast, the cost of bailing out one S&L, Silverado, was $2 billion.

Now commercial banks—the financial titans whose headquarters adorn America's skylines—are in crisis, too. Of the nation's twelve thousand banks, some one thousand are on regulators' "problem list." Between the beginning of 1986 and the end of 1990, banks charged off some $75 billion in bad loans. The return on assets of all banks in 1990 was just fifty cents per $100. In April 1992, the Congressional Budget Office projected that future bank failures would cost $43 billion. Large "money center" banks are in the biggest trouble. Banks holding about one quarter of all banking assets failed to meet impending capital standards.

Taxpayers will almost certainly be called on to rescue the commercial banks. Indeed, the bailout may already have happened. In 1991, Congress authorized the FDIC's Bank Insurance Fund (BIF) to borrow up to $70 billion from taxpayers to pay for bank takeovers. Moreover, it is also likely that this taxpayer "loan" will not be paid back, meaning that at least a partial taxpayer bailout will have to be acknowledged.

Sadly, the boom period that preceded this crash was itself marked by a dramatic misallocation of resources—a capital flow steered by misguided banking regulation. Publicly insured funds flowed to high-stakes mergers and leveraged buyouts on Wall Street, not start-up ventures. Most dramatic was the real estate bubble, which priced the middle class out of the housing market. Banks and S&Ls poured so much money into commercial real estate that in 1992 the nation had enough vacant office space to last another twelve years, according to an analysis by Salomon Brothers.

In the post-crash period, banks have restricted lending to small and medium-size businesses that were not the cause of bank failures. Instead, banks have bought government securities. According to the FDIC, banks had more than 21 percent of their assets invested in Treasury securities in mid-1992, but commercial and industrial loans made up only 16 percent of assets. Government Treasuries are attractive because banks don't have to keep capital in reserve to back them up. In addition to depriving business of credit, this stockpiling of Treasuries may be creating potentially serious safety and soundness problems for the banks. These government bonds could plunge in value with a rise in interest rates likely to be caused by the first signs of inflation.

The prospect of rising interest rates also belies bankers' claims of renewed profitability. In 1992, banks' paper balance sheets have showed record profits. The primary source of this is the wide spread between the low interest rates they pay on deposits and the interest rates they collect on Treasuries and other "loans." This "profit," however, is transient and may disappear when interest rates rise and the spread thins.

Banking regulation, in short, has spun off its axis. A program that was designed to ensure that the savings of the middle class were protected was transformed into an entitlement for swindlers and speculators. The financial industry continues to push for more deregulation as the answer to its problems. But a bank is not a shoe store: Financial institutions are both too important for the economy, too prone to boom and bust, and too reliant on taxpayers for a safety net, ever to be deregulated. Thus the next President will need to deal with the immediate consequences of the current financial crisis, and to restructure banking regulation to advance both a strong industry and the economy.

The Origins of Current Regulation

AMERICA'S BANKING REGULATORY SYSTEM is, at its heart, a social contract. Banks and savings and loans received deposit insurance for their customers, thus ending the debilitating cycle of bank panics. In turn, they were heavily regulated to reduce risky behavior and to ensure that the financial system served the credit needs of the real economy. (For example, savings and loans were chartered to provide credit for home ownership.) Underlying this social contract is the realization that a sound financial system is necessary to provide the capital for economic growth and opportunity, and that it must be oriented toward supporting productive investment rather than speculation.

In the first days of the New Deal, banking laws were passed that continue to be the basis of the social contract. The Glass-Steagall Act of 1933 had two major elements. First, it instituted deposit insurance (then $5,000, now up to $100,000), provided by the newly created FDIC. Second, to prevent a recurrence of dangerous lending practices that occurred during the stock run-up of the previous decade, Glass-Steagall required separation between the commercial banking industry and investment banks. Savings and loans received deposit insurance in 1934, provided by the Federal Savings and Loan Insurance Corporation (FSLIC), along with their own set of regulations. Thrifts were required to lend primarily for home mortgages. Both types of institutions were limited in the interest they could pay; indeed, checking accounts could not pay interest at all.

In a time of relatively stable interest rates and inflation, this regime worked well. Commercial banks lent most heavily to corporations, and S&Ls to homebuyers. This functioning banking system was one major reason why 60 percent of the public eventually owned their own homes. Bank failures dwindled in number. Wrote historian Kenneth Davis, "Of all New Deal reform legislation, this was the most resoundingly and unqualifiedly successful, measured on its own terms."

Deregulation and Disaster: The Reagan-Bush Record

BEGINNING IN THE LATE 1970s, and greatly accelerated in the 1980s, policymakers inaugurated dramatic changes in the nature of financial regulation.

INTEREST RATE DEREGULATION

In the late 1970s, two trends brought enormous pressure on banks and S&Ls. First, the Federal Reserve reacted to oil-shock-induced inflation by radically hiking interest rates, over the objections of President Carter, in October 1979. By 1980, interest rates had hit 21 percent. The Fed kept interest rates at high levels throughout the 1980s, even as inflation receded. Depositors shifted in droves to money market accounts when interest rates soared above the amount that could legally be paid by banks and S&Ls. (The Fed had ruled that money market funds could pay unlimited interest.)

In 1980, Congress uncapped the interest rates that could be paid by banks and S&Ls. Coupled with the tight money policy of the Federal Reserve, this led to an interest rate war as banks, S&Ls, and their unregulated competitors bid for depositors. In the same legislation, deposit insurance was dramatically expanded, from $40,000 to $100,000 per account. The Reagan administration then encouraged the growth of "brokered deposits," in which investment firms placed investor deposits in insured bank and S&L accounts in $100,000 chunks—a subversion of the purpose of deposit insurance, since it let individuals earn high-yield returns on risk-free investments.

SAVINGS AND LOAN DEREGULATION

In 1982, Congress completed the decontrol of the savings and loan industry. Thrifts argued that they could not make money restricted to long-term, low-return home mortgages, even though that was their purpose for existing. The Garn–St. Germain Act deleted nearly all constraints on how S&Ls could invest their money, removed restrictions on who could own thrifts, and enabled them to operate with literally no capital. State legislatures, competing for S&L charters, raced to deregulate them even further. In October 1982, signing the Garn–St. Germain Act, President Reagan said with a smile, "All in all, I think we've hit the jackpot."

The gambling metaphor was inadvertently appropriate, since savings and loans—quickly snapped up by real estate developers—used their new powers to gamble away billions of dollars. S&Ls now invested heavily in commercial real estate, junk bonds, and other newfangled debt instruments, and even direct equity investments in ongoing businesses. Many investments, aided by loose accounting standards, showed profits briefly and then soured. The Texas real estate market collapsed in the mid-1980s, the junk bond market in 1990. The industry was also consumed by widespread fraud; according to the FDIC, the failure of some 50 percent of seized S&Ls was due, in part, to fraud or misconduct.

In 1986, regulators began pressing for more funds to close down insolvent S&Ls. Due to S&L industry lobbying, Congress delayed until 1987, when it allocated only $7 billion to address the problem. During 1988, regulators scrambled to keep the thrift crisis from exploding during an election year. A week before the election, campaign manager James Baker told reporters that George Bush opposed a taxpayer bailout.

One week after taking office, President Bush proclaimed the need for a swift response to the suddenly discovered S&L crisis. In August 1989 he signed into law the landmark S&L bailout bill—the Financial Institutions Reform, Recovery, and Enforcement Act (FIRREA). FIRREA authorized $50 billion for the bailout, tightened capital standards for thrifts, and reined in thrift investment standards. To manage the assets of failed S&Ls, it created the new Resolution Trust Corporation (RTC), to operate as an arm of the FDIC. At first the administration vowed that $50 billion would be enough for the rescue. Soon, however, it sought more money. In 1991, Congress authorized the borrowing of another $30 billion. In early 1992, the RTC returned for still more funds, this time seeking $25 billion. In April 1992, the House of Representatives balked at voting new money for the RTC.

COMMERICAL BANKS

Commerical banks, like S&Ls, plunged into risky investments, and many are now suffering the consequences. Banks faced the same competition for depositors as S&Ls and money market funds. To some extent banks were driven into new, riskier markets because their traditional blue-chip borrowers were finding it cheaper to raise money in the commercial paper market. Just as significantly, banks discarded decades of prudent credit practices in an effort to earn high returns. Loans to less-developed countries (LDCs) in the late 1970s cost banks hugely by the 1980s, as did energy loans. Big banks also played a central role in the hostile takeover and leveraged buyout wave, including providing "bridge loans" to help facilitate junk bond takeovers. The top one hundred banks were owed $44 billion on these "highly leveraged transaction" loans as of September 1991, and interest wasn't being paid on $5 billion worth.

Most dramatically by far, however, banks invested in commercial real estate. (The 1982 Garn–St. Germain Act, as a sort of consolation prize to banks, removed the cap on the percent of loans that could be invested in commercial real estate.) "The deregulated bankers jumped in with an ecstasy previously reserved for, well, Peru," writes journalist L. J. Davis. "With banks pouring in some $350 billion (representing 370 percent of their equity), a staggering 32 percent of all the existing office space in America was built in the 1980s." Bank portfolios of commercial real estate grew from $132 billion in 1982 to $385 billion eight years later, at a time when the population grew only 7 percent. Real estate is intensely cyclical, and the boom was followed inexorably by a crash.

The Bush administration's commercial bank regulators, like their thrift counterparts, repeatedly asserted that the situation was well in hand and that no taxpayer funds would be needed. In 1991, however, officials acknowledged that the Bank Insurance Fund was nearly broke. In December 1991, President Bush signed into law legislation that authorized the BIF to borrow up to $70 billion. This taxpayer "loan" was to be paid back by the banks through an increase in their deposit insurance premiums. However, on September 15, 1992, the FDIC board exempted three quarters of the banking industry from paying an increase in insurance premiums. Senator Donald Riegle, chair of the Senate Banking Committee, said that the FDIC decision "puts repayment of the $70 billion taxpayers loan at greater risk— and eases the insurance costs the banks should properly bear."

THE RISE OF THE "PARALLEL BANKING SYSTEM"

Competing with the regulated and insured banking system is what industry analysts Jane D'Arista and Tom Schlesinger call the "parallel banking system."

Today, at least sixty large firms act in much the same way as banks, but, rather than seeking deposits from the public, they primarily obtain funds from money-market mutual funds through the commercial paper market. By year-end 1990, for example, GE Capital, the nation's largest finance company, reported assets of $70.4 billion, more than all but six of the largest U.S.-based bank holding companies. GE Capital and General Motors Assistance Corporation have more equity capital than any bank except Citicorp. These firms invest in real estate, securities, and other instruments just like banks. But they do not have to comply with capital and reserve requirements, lending limits on loans to single borrowers, or conflict-of-interest rules, as do banks. The investments of these firms are backed by lines of credit from banks. So a failure of a major finance company could ripple through the financial system, just as the collapse of tiny Penn Square Bank eventually brought down giant Continental Illinois in 1984.

The other major trend affecting the financial system is the rise of "securitization," also abetted by government policy. Securitization is the practice of bundling together loans—say, home mortgages—and selling them as securities in a secondary market. Beginning in the mid-1970s, three government agencies have insured the secondary market for home mortgages (Ginny Mae, Fannie Mae, and Freddy Mac), one for student loans (Sallie Mae), and one for agricultural loans (Farmer Mac). By 1990, half of all newly issued securities were bundled bank loans. Securitization has enabled many new lenders to enter cheaply fields such as home mortgage lending, though it has added to the competitive pressure on thrifts and may drain funds from less standardized borrowers (e.g., small businesses).

Short-Term Measures

TO DEMONSTRATE THE SERIOUSNESS of the problem and halt runaway deregulation and consolidation, the President should declare a ninety-day freeze on the practices that are most hindering the economy in the banking realm. During that time, a more comprehensive reform program should be drafted and submitted.

1. *A moratorium on deregulation by regulatory fiat.* The Federal Reserve and other regulatory agencies have effectively repealed many safety and soundness rules by letting banks underwrite securities and insurance without adequate safeguards and public quid pro quos, and by letting S&Ls branch across state lines. Moreover, in many instances these moves have been taken despite clear congressional opposition. The new President should immediately issue an executive order halting such unilateral actions until a coherent new banking policy is instituted. He should ask the Fed, an independent entity that cannot be ordered to obey a moratorium, to comply voluntarily.

2. *A moratorium on foreclosures and calling of loans by federally controlled institutions.* Too often, when the FDIC takes over a bank or thrift (putting it into conservatorship or receivership), the officials in charge begin calling in loans to borrowers. This can result in an arbitrary and destructive constriction of credit, often in a local community that has already been hard hit by recession. A ninety-day moratorium on calling of loans and foreclosures would give borrowers some breathing space and allow the new Administration to set its own course on monetary and regulatory policy.

3. *An immediate end to the practice of dumping real estate by the RTC*. As discussed above, the RTC's asset disposition policies have helped deepen the real estate slump. The RTC should immediately stop bulk sales and other practices that undercut real estate prices, until a new system can be implemented.

4. *Assignment of capital requirements to government securities*. Capital requirements should be assigned to government securities to reflect interest rate risk. Requiring banks to hold capital reserves for government bonds will safeguard against a bond market downturn, enhance the appeal of business lending, and ease the credit crunch.

Restructuring the Financial System

GIVEN THE AMOUNT OF MONEY INVOLVED and its generalized economic impact, resolving the banking crisis—as arcane and politically painful as it is—must be a top priority of the next President. A comprehensive approach will have several elements.

RESTORING THE SOCIAL CONTRACT: INDUSTRY STRUCTURE

The massive taxpayer subsidy of deposit insurance must be reciprocated by a renewed commitment to safe lending and to funding the real, productive needs of society. A comprehensive, progressive financial restructuring plan would include the following efforts:

Put Banks and Their Competitors on a Level Playing Field. Finance companies and other nonbank banks currently have a competitive edge over banks, which must comply with safety-and-soundness laws. Moreover, the investments of these firms are backed by lines of credit from banks, which are backed by deposit insurance, so a failure of a major finance company could ripple throughout the financial system. All financial firms that directly or indirectly intermediate the public's money should be required to adhere to some minimum prudential standards.

Banking for Economic Growth. An overhaul of the banking laws should provide incentives for banks to lend to small and medium-size businesses, as these are the engines of growth in the economy. Large money-center banks, such as Citicorp and Wells Fargo, have suffered big blows in the eighties due to the crash in the real-estate market, defaults on loans to less-developed countries, and the unsuccessful financing of other speculative ventures. Regional banks, such as Banc One of Ohio and Great Western Bank of Los Angeles, have focused on consumer loans and loans to small- and medium-size businesses. These banks have been some of the most profitable banks and have contributed to job creation and the growth of local economies. Regulations and incentives should be put in place that reward this type of lending.

Creation of Community Development Banks. There are several models of community development banks that currently exist, the most famous being the South Shore Bank in Chicago's South Side. The bank targets five minority communities on Chicago's South and West sides for its development lending efforts. It has made more than $220 million in loans in those targeted communities and, through subsidiary and affiliate companies, has leveraged an additional $100 million in economic development finance. The result has been not only rising real estate values in what used to be a slum, but also a prosperous new class of black entrepreneurs.

Community development banks now operating are generally holding companies consisting of several subsidiaries, including a federal depository institution providing traditional bank services, a for-profit real estate development company, an SBA-approved small business development investment company, and one or more nonprofits that provide development services, such as business counseling or job training. In addition to the holding company model, there are several types of community lenders, self-help credit unions, and community development loan funds, many of which are owned by their depositors, insuring the reinvestment of their funds back into the local community.

A network of these community development banks should be created to lend to new, expanding, or troubled businesses in traditionally underserved areas, such as the inner cities and rural regions.

Enforcement of Fair Lending Laws. "New" 1990 Home Mortgage Disclosure Act data revealed that African Americans and Hispanics were rejected between two and four times as often as white applicants of comparable income for home loans. Enforcement of the nation's fair lending laws—the Fair Housing Act and the Equal Credit Opportunity Act—under the Reagan and Bush Administrations has been almost nonexistent. The new Administration should enforce these laws so that banks serve communities from which they take deposits.

Expanded Powers. Any restructuring of the financial system should guard against attempts to breach the prohibitions against mixing banking and commerce. Deregulation proponents argue that "firewalls" can be constructed between insured bank deposits and investment banking activities. In reality, however, such "firewalls" would prove almost impossible to enforce. In time of need, such as a market break, bankers would willingly slosh funds over the "firewalls"—consequences be damned. (That occurred at Continental Illinois during the 1987 stock market crash, when the bank raided depositor funds to bail out its commodities affiliate, an action that was retroactively approved by regulators.) Recent performance of financial regulators gives little reason to think that they are capable of monitoring the complex fund transfers that could milk dry banks and S&Ls. The only way to prevent such abuse is to sever the corporate link between these firms. To be sure, many expanded powers have been granted piecemeal by federal regulators. But as Bob Kuttner has written, "The genie was squeezed back into the bottle during the New Deal, and with good effect."

THE RESOLUTION TRUST CORPORATION (RTC)
The RTC is the fastest-growing economic agency since the New Deal. It is the largest real estate holder in the country; it held the biggest portfolio of junk bonds; its budget dwarfed that of many countries. Yet the RTC has mismanaged the S&L bailout, costing taxpayers billions of dollars more than necessary and helping to worsen the recession.

To be sure, the RTC would have a difficult mission under any circumstances. But by any definition, the bailout has been poorly executed. Accounts of mismanagement are legion. The RTC spent $100 million on a computer information system that was so flawed that the agency returned to keeping records *by hand* in the spring of 1992. Recordkeeping has been so sloppy that the GAO has been unable to audit the RTC, as required by law. In Operation Western Storm, the agency scrambled to find $7 billion it had misplaced; the accounting effort cost $24 million. Moreover, basic public purposes have been downplayed. The agency was directed to make properties available to the poor through an affordable housing program, yet few such properties have been sold; rules are so lax that one Texas executive used the affordable housing program to buy a house adjacent to his country club. The effort to recover funds from those who swindled S&Ls is anemic at best.

But most damaging to taxpayers and the overall economy has been the RTC's effort to sell off assets of failed S&Ls. Congress gave the agency a thoroughly contradictory mandate in 1989: It was to sell its assets as quickly as possible *and* at the best price. The agency has responded with a program of bulk sales and scheduled markdowns that primarily reward a small number of financial players. Asset sales have lost an average of forty cents on the dollar, according to the most complete study. This practice of dumping property cannot help but compound the regional real estate slump and thereby worsen the condition of still-open banks. Common sense suggests that the agency should sell when appropriate, but be equipped (and funded) to manage properties until the market recovers. A 1987 GAO study concluded that such patient sales are better bargains for taxpayers. At present, the RTC does not even do market analysis to project what the future value of property will be, or what impact its sales are having on local economies.

In short, the RTC should be thoroughly overhauled. First, officials should end the pretense that the agency's job is over. Second, the RTC should be formally designated a federal agency, which would subject it to open government and procedural rules from which it is currently exempt. Finally, and most important, the RTC should be reconfigured to operate as the economic development agency that it is. When appropriate, aggressive efforts should be made to link properties with public uses (i.e., nonprofit organizations, environmental preserves, etc.).

INTERSTATE BANKING

Big banks continue to lobby hard to be allowed to open branches nationwide, saying they need to be able to diversify geographically to protect against local economic downturns and to cut costs. In reality, the prohibitions against interstate banking have been greatly eroded. At present, state law controls interstate banking, and most states have allowed out-of-state banks to operate. Fifteen of the twenty-five biggest financial institutions carry on substantial interstate banking activity. Moreover, banks today can lend anywhere they want, and this has not proven to be a cure-all. (For example, the Bank of New England lost more on real estate loans in Florida than in neighboring Connecticut.)

Interstate branching, most dangerously, allows centralized banks to suction deposits out of local communities. There are three ways to avoid this consequence. The first is to allow banks to expand using only a holding company model; the local bank then retains a board of directors and is more prone to invest in the community.

The second is to strengthen the Community Reinvestment Act (CRA)— one of the success stories of American government. At no cost to the taxpayer, and at minimal cost to banks, it channels capital into neighborhoods that need it most. The CRA, passed in 1977, imposes on banks an "affirmative obligation to help meet the credit needs of the local communities in which they are chartered." Since its enactment, the CRA has been responsible for channeling at least $30 billion in loan commitments to low-income housing and small businesses, during the course of negotiations with community groups.

Untrammeled interstate branching could entirely undercut the rationale of the CRA. At present, banks are evaluated in totality, not on a branch-by-branch basis. If banks are allowed to expand by branching, citizens and regulators could be faced with the prospect of having to analyze the CRA compliance of a bank with branches in fifty states and hundreds of communities. The CRA should be applied on a branch-by-branch basis, or at least to metropolitan areas. All report data should be collected on a state-by-state basis.

The third way the Administration can ensure that credit continues to flow to local communities in the event of interstate branching is to strengthen current law that requires banks to report lending activity to small businesses and small farms. In this way, communities can monitor whether or not their local banks are draining funds from their community or reinvesting in it.

Current law provides for reporting of lending only by loan size, not by size of business. This reporting requirement shows whether small loans are being made, but it does not show whether small businesses are being served. Furthermore, reporting is not done by geographic region, and so it will not show capital flight from local communities. The new Administration should make it a priority to press for regulations that can adequately track lending to small business and small farms by geographic region.

REGULATORY REFORM

Banks and S&Ls are regulated by a jumble of agencies with overlapping jurisdictions and inadequate resources. Moreover, these agencies are dominated by the industries they regulate. To prevent a recurrence of the S&L fiasco, regulation must be made to work.

Consolidation of Regulatory Agencies. Bank regulation is a Rube Goldberg machine of overlapping jurisdictions, duplicative agencies, and mind-numbing nuances. At present, savings and loans are regulated by the Office of Thrift Supervision in the Treasury Department; deposits are insured by the Savings Association Insurance Fund of the FDIC; resolutions of failed institutions are handled by the RTC. Bank holding companies, meanwhile, are regulated by the Federal Reserve Board. National banks are regulated by the Office of the Comptroller of the Currency (OCC) in the Treasury

Department; state-chartered banks are regulated by the FDIC, which also insures all banks through the BIF.

The regulation of banks and S&Ls should be consolidated into one streamlined, adequately funded, independent agency. This would free banks from having to answer to different, and sometimes conflicting, examination procedures and requirements. Bank examiners should be encouraged in their vigilance; instead, since 1991, the Bush administration castigated officials for excessive stringency.

Citizen oversight of financial regulation. In the words of former FCC commissioner Nicholas Johnson, "The only way to keep the government upright is to lean on it from all sides." But the regulators and legislators charged with overseeing the financial industry effectively are leaned on from only one side—the bankers, thrift executives, and others who can afford lobbyists, think-tank studies, and full-page ads. Too often, policymakers are reduced to refereeing turf struggles among competing trade associations. Consumer or citizen participation in regulatory proceedings is slim to non-existent. To prevent another taxpayer-subsidized fiasco, the next President should propose (or institute by executive order) empowering consumers and taxpayers to represent themselves in the regulatory process.

A federally chartered Financial Consumers Association (FCA) would cure this representation gap. An FCA would be a voluntary, democratically run, nationwide organization established to represent and educate consumers. Consumers would be notified of their ability to join through a neutrally worded government insert in monthly deposit statements. The FCA would flexibly improve financial regulation without creating a new government bureaucracy. It is based on the successful Citizen Utility Board (CUB) model, which has saved ratepayers billions of dollars in Illinois, Wisconsin, and Oregon. There is ample precedent for the Federal Government organizing marketplace participants—from the producers' checkoff for agricultural marketing, to the hybrid, thrift-owned, but government-run Home Loan Bank system.

The Federal Communications Commission

TELECOMMUNICATIONS

NOLAN BOWIE, ANGELA J. CAMPBELL, AND ANDREW JAY SCHWARTZMAN

Summary

I T HAS LONG BEEN an article of faith among telecommunications policymakers that the marriage of computer, satellite, and fiber-optic technologies would one day transform our economy, our lives, and, quite literally, our democracy. That day is no longer a futurist's prognostication, for we are all now living amid a telecommunications transformation that is remaking the nature of work, play, and politics.

The 1992 presidential election has offered glimpses of what will soon be possible, as campaigns have reached out directly to voters through media opportunities and communications technologies that were not available until recent years.

Just as telecommunications have presented new possibilities to the campaigns this year, telecommunications policy will pose a major test for the new Administration. If the United States regains world leadership in telecommunications, this will go a long way toward rejuvenating the domestic economy. While development of an effective twenty-first century telecommunications infrastructure will not guarantee economic prosperity, it is impossible to envision a future of economic growth without one.

To put it simply, the next Administration can help guarantee affordable access to data, news, entertainment, and information. It can enable more

Nolan Bowie is Professor of Communications at Temple University and the author, most recently, of Equity and Access to Information Technology Annual Review *(Institute for Information Studies, 1990). Angela J. Campbell directs the Citizens Communications Center Project of the Institute for Public Representation at Georgetown University Law Center. Andrew Jay Schwartzman is Executive Director of the Media Access Project, where he supervises telecommunications litigation and public policy advocacy.*

Americans to participate actively in the process of self-governance. And it can foster literacy—or stifle opportunity—in the electronic vocabularies that will determine success in the marketplace of the next century.

Yet, recent administrations have lacked a coherent telecommunications policy. To the extent that such a policy exists, it has been developed and defined piecemeal to protect and further the interests of the existing broadcast, cable, and telephone industries. Continuing on this course will accelerate the division of Americans into classes of information-rich and information-poor, increasingly depriving citizens of the opportunity for meaningful participation in the process of determining their own future.

In the short term, the new Administration should halt recent changes in the FCC's ownership rules that permit further concentration of control of the media; reinstate the fairness doctrine to help ensure that citizens have access to competing viewpoints on important public issues; and strictly enforce existing regulations concerning equal employment opportunities and children's television.

Over the longer term, the critical goal is to develop the telecommunications infrastructure of the next generation under a common carrier scheme. Under this model, the owners of the interactive multichannel fiber-optic video delivery systems of the future will have no control over content, and all speakers will have nondiscriminatory access. Because this new electronic highway will be used to supplant or replace many public services, all Americans must be connected to it. Without this "universal service," we run the risk of disenfranchising millions of Americans in an "information underclass" that will impede our economic and social development.

Introduction

TELECOMMUNICATIONS POLICYMAKERS and futurists have long anticipated that the marriage of computer, satellite, and fiber-optic technologies would one day transform our economy, our culture, and our politics. But for most Americans and the representatives they elected (in the old-fashioned, nonelectronic way), 1992 was the year when they first confronted the potentially far-reaching impact of the telecommunications revolution upon the democratic process.

The 1992 presidential election offered glimpses of what will soon be possible. The 800 numbers, 900 numbers, computer bulletin boards, "infomercials," talk shows, interactive TV, videocassettes, teleconferencing, and fax machines that candidates and the mass media tested that political season have all been available in one form or another for some time now. But the potential impact of these technologies on campaign techniques is a portent of much more far-reaching developments that will soon be upon us.

The telecommunications transformation is literally remaking the way we work, play, and govern. Not long ago, telephones were merely devices that enabled two people to talk to each other by transmitting electric pulses through a copper wire. Radios were used for transmitting news and information over the air to large numbers of people, or on a very limited basis, for rudimentary two-way communications. The American Telephone and Telegraph Company was "the telephone company," and it controlled most of the nation's voice traffic, communications, and related manufacturing and research. Three television networks controlled most of what was available for Americans to watch.

But in a few short years, almost everything has changed. One-on-one conversations are increasingly carried over the air through the digital (rather than the traditional "analog") mode. Wire transmission, when used, is likely to be by fiber optics. Video and audio entertainment is frequently delivered over those wires. The amount of voice and data transmitted by wire is growing exponentially.

What has not changed are the importance of the regulatory process in shaping telecommunications policy, and the impact of the regulatory process on the American economy. It is impossible to overstate the economic impact of telecommunications, for telecommunications technology will be the backbone and nervous system of domestic and international commerce. Data, journalism, and television and motion picture programming are themselves increasingly important commodities. International competition in hardware design and manufacturing will become ever more fierce, and our ability to retain a significant share will determine the future of millions of jobs over the next decade.

Investment in domestic infrastructure can yield long-term dividends not just in the domestic economy but in world trade as well. The newly opening multibillion-dollar markets for telecommunications hardware and systems in Asia, Eastern Europe, and the former Soviet Union offer vast opportunities, especially if American systems and protocols are employed from the outset. Successful domestic deployment of these technologies can turn our nation into a telecommunications "showroom" for potential overseas customers.

Thus far, many of the most dramatic cost reductions and productivity improvements from telecommunications technology have been enjoyed by big businesses capable of benefiting from "private networks"; maximum benefits, however, will come from making these advances available to smaller businesses, government, the nonprofit sector, and individual consumers.

How we handle these access issues will also go a long way toward determining how we protect and nurture the democratic institutions and individual liberties that are our national heritage. The telecommunications decisions made by the new Administration will determine who has editorial control over program content in the next generation. By exercising authority to maximize access and opportunity, the forty-second President can ensure that America continues to democratize, industrialize, educate, and grow.

The right to speak and to receive access to information is meaningless if it is reserved only for those with deep pockets. Telecommunications can and should promote inclusion, linking each of us to each other and the world, enabling us to share common cultures and differing traditions. What may be perceived as efficient and cost-effective in the short run could well prove to be disastrous over time. If access to "free" television and low-cost universal television service is not assured, the cost will be measured in ignorance, illiteracy, innumeracy, and divisiveness. If the rate of residential telephone installations continues to erode, or even remains static, there will be millions more Americans left unable to speak to friends, family, and employers by this medium.

Another dimension that has been largely ignored in the rush to install a new technological infrastructure is the threat to individual privacy. Clearly, there can be no "electronic democracy" if there is no secret ballot, and there can be no civilian control if there is military and police access to private communications. The threat posed by corporate access to and misuse of personal information is no less dangerous. Every commercial transaction, no matter how trivial, can be recorded and aggregated with other data to develop excruciatingly intimate "profiles" of every citizen's life, beliefs, and actions. Voluntary self-restraint by the Federal Government and the private sector is not enough; affirmative protections must be built into the system and strictly enforced.

Unlike many of the challenges that the new Administration will face, telecommunications is one policy area in which the Federal Government has the power to help Americans better control their destiny without extensive federal expenditures. Washington can and should help shape the future by encouraging the development of mass media and common carrier services that promote democracy, literacy, and growth.

Recent Legacy: Regulation Through Deregulation

INTERSTATE WIRE AND RADIO COMMUNICATIONS are governed under a New Deal law, the Communications Act of 1934. In the absence of a consensus on how to update it, Congress has proven willing to debate, but unwilling to adopt, major amendments. This inertia may have been a blessing, judging from the one major exception. The disastrously anticonsumer 1984 law that largely deregulated cable TV was predicated on the theory that competing pay-TV services would emerge. But the law permitted cable to use its monopoly power to stifle new entrants. As a consequence, the cost of basic cable service has increased at three times the rate of inflation, and consumers have been forced to rent decoders and other equipment at exorbitant rates, while local government and other service channels have often been diverted to home shopping and similar revenue-generating purposes. The newly enacted 1992 legislation reregulating cable may prove to be too little, too late.

Congressional inaction has permitted the Federal Communications Commission (FCC) and the federal courts each to play an increasingly influential role in shaping telecommunications policy over the past two decades.

Since 1981, the FCC has largely abrogated its statutory responsibility to shape the development of telecommunications. Under the "unregulation" doctrine of Reagan-era FCC chairman Mark Fowler, the commission placed unyielding reliance on the marketplace to discipline anticompetitive urges of monopolies and oligopolies, eliminating in the process many of the FCC's media ownership rules. The commission began to replace traditional telephone rate regulations with "caps" and other devices designed to remove oversight over phone company actions.

Under the Bush administration, policy has been driven less by ideological purity than by more traditional Republican sympathies for big business. The FCC has shown a greater willingness to pick favorites among companies and industries (e.g., giving advantages to networks over smaller TV stations and to AT&T over smaller long-distance companies). Similarly, the FCC has paved the way for large broadcasters to acquire many more stations while leaving smaller, newer competitors out in the cold. This, combined with the continuing reluctance of the Justice Department and the Federal Trade Commission to intervene to stop anticompetitive practices or to block even the largest mergers, has resulted in a dramatic diminution of diversity in mass media ownership and in an ongoing consolidation in common carrier and other telecommunications services.

President Bush's FCC chairman Alfred Sikes has placed particular emphasis on paving the way for new technologies such as PCS, a modern-day walkie-talkie service. But his approach has tended to give an upper hand in these innovative services to telecommunications giants while often shutting out entrepreneurs, especially minorities.

The judiciary has been especially influential in the area of telephony. Indeed, for nearly a decade it has often been said that Judge Harold H. Greene of the U.S. District Court for the District of Columbia is the single most powerful regulator in the Federal Government because of his day-to-day administration of the 1982 AT&T consent decree. Over time, Judge Greene (a Carter appointee) has lifted a number of restraints on AT&T and the seven "Baby Bells" while resisting the Baby Bells' demands for major modifications of provisions that prohibit them from manufacturing equipment and providing "information services." But in decisions over the past several years, Reagan appointees on the federal appeals bench (supported by the Reagan and Bush administrations) have reversed many of Judge Greene's decisions, thus setting the stage for a sea change in the scope and freedom of local phone companies' operations.

The public has been largely shut out of the communications policy process. Although the Communications Act of 1934 mandates that all actions implementing it be based on determinations that they are in "the public interest," the FCC has viewed the public as nothing more than customers. It has let those who sell services to the public decide what is best for them. The public's right to protest changes in TV and radio station licensees based on programming concerns has been extinguished, along with the all-important fairness doctrine in broadcasting. The substitution of "price caps" for rate regulation, use of lotteries rather than qualitative judgments to award licenses, and abolition of disclosure and reporting requirements have not only made it impossible for the FCC to oversee telephone and other voice services but also have rendered it impossible for citizen groups to monitor the practices of these companies.

Public participation in the regulatory process has been further hampered by the federal appeals courts. Many FCC actions have been rendered essentially unreviewable by procedural decisions of the U.S. Court of Appeals for the District of Columbia, which has jurisdiction over the majority of these cases. Even when the substance of a ruling can be brought to the court, it has upheld FCC policies that remove the public from meaningful participation in the process.

Exclusive reliance on marketplace forces has not worked for the public. Local programming addressing the needs of demographically unattractive segments of the population—those too young, too old, or too poor to be of interest to advertisers—has largely disappeared in many markets. Service to children, who cannot express their preferences in a market-driven economy, has deteriorated so badly that Congress enacted the Children's Television Act of 1990 to restrict excessive commercialization. Local telephone companies have concentrated on the introduction of new and profitable business-oriented "enhanced" services such as voice mail, while shifting costs to residential service.

Mass Media Initiatives

THE IMPACT OF UNFETTERED "COMPETITION" in a highly concentrated media marketplace has been especially apparent in the mass media, where we have witnessed a diminution in diversity and access. Despite the explosion in the number of media outlets, less time is being devoted to informing the public about important local public issues. The multiplicity of channels has been accompanied by a concentration of ownership in a small number of large corporations. Efforts to increase minority ownership have not been very successful.

SHORT-TERM INITIATIVES
The short-term initiatives we recommend focus largely on proceedings already under way at the FCC and are designed to recommit our country to the principles of fairness and diversity.

• *Cable legislation*. In its final moments, the 102d Congress overrode President Bush's veto of the Cable Television Consumer Protection and Competition Act of 1992 (the Cable Act). Passage of the new law makes it a top priority to appoint a new FCC chair and fill the one or two vacancies that will exist as of inauguration day. Under the Cable Act, customer service, price regulation, and other implementing rules must be adopted by April 1993. Moreover, the new law gives very broad discretion to the FCC. If the FCC so chooses, it can use those new powers to roll back excessive price increases of recent years and to establish strong standards for addressing billing and service problems. Most lobbying against the Cable Act centered on cable's claim that the law's requirement that cable operators pay broadcasters for consent to retransmit their signal will force up prices. However, the most important provision of the Cable Act is actually its "program access" provision. If properly implemented, this will have a much greater impact over the next decade by breaking up cable's monopoly on programming. This could well permit development of cheaper competing technologies such as "wireless cable" and satellite-to-home "DBS" services.

• *Retain the TV ownership rules*. Present rules limit a single entity to owning a single television station within a local market and twelve stations (fourteen if minority-controlled) nationwide. Such rules foster diversity of viewpoints by limiting the number of channels that can be controlled by a single entity. Ownership limits likewise increase opportunities for new entrants, such as minorities, who at present own only 2.7 percent of broadcast stations. Ownership rules also foster competition in programming and in advertising rates.

• *Improve the comparative broadcast hearings process.* At present, new broadcast licenses are awarded to the applicant judged most likely to serve the public interest best, after a hearing in which competing applicants are compared on the basis of certain criteria. The FCC has initiated a proceeding (Docket No. 92-52) to reexamine the criteria for awarding new broadcast licenses.

In this proceeding, the FCC should reaffirm and increase the preference for minority applicants, and it should reinstitute the preference for female applicants. Minority and female ownership of broadcast stations lags far behind the presence of minorities and women in our society, so increasing minority and female ownership will increase the diversity of viewpoints.

The FCC should also impose a ban on trafficking in broadcast licenses. Imposing an antitrafficking rule would ensure that the applicant selected as the one who would best serve the public interest would actually operate the station. An antitrafficking rule, which would require the applicant to operate the station for three years, would also deter the filing of sham applications, thus speeding up the licensing process.

• *Enforce equal employment opportunity.* The FCC currently requires each broadcaster to file annual Equal Employment Opportunity (EEO) reports and to report on affirmative action plans when the license comes up for renewal. The FCC should take a closer look at these filings, especially in light of recent reports that the percentages of minorities and women employed in the broadcast industry are declining.[1] Despite its stated intent to use a contracting "zone of reasonableness" in analyzing a station's employment profile, the FCC has never required stations to employ minorities or women at more than 50 percent of their presence in the work force. By moving the benchmark toward full parity, the FCC could send a signal that it really cares about EEO. The FCC should also examine the percentages of minorities and women employed in decisionmaking positions.

• *Require fair coverage of controversial issues.* The fairness doctrine is the term used to refer to the long-standing requirement that broadcast stations both cover controversial issues of public importance and present both sides of such issues. Despite the fact that many people believe the Communications Act of 1934 mandates fairness, the FCC "repealed" the fairness doctrine in 1987. In a recent case, the FCC extended the repeal to ballot issues. The application of the fairness doctrine to ballot issues has been particularly important because often in ballot issues one side has a lot more money to spend on advertising than the other. Unless broadcasters have an obligation to air both sides of a ballot issue, the public will be aware of only the well-funded view and will not be able to make an informed decision at the polls.

The fairness doctrine should be restored by either legislation or FCC action. The fairness doctrine enjoys strong bipartisan support in Congress, as seen by the passage of legislation that would have restored the fairness doctrine but that was vetoed by President Reagan.

• *Improve the quantity and quality of children's programming.* The FCC should take a close look at license renewal applications to determine whether television stations are complying with the 1990 Children's Television Act, which requires every station to air some programming designed specifically to educate and inform children.

The FCC should empower citizens to help broadcasters identify and address children's educational and informational needs by instituting a public education program to make citizens aware of broadcasters' legal obligations and what they can do if broadcasters do not comply. The FCC should issue a citizen's guide and require each station to retain a copy in its public inspection file.

The FCC should also limit excessive commercialization on children's television. Rules adopted in 1991 by the FCC failed to end the practice of airing children's programming based on toys or advertising characters. Such programs are really little more than advertisements. The FCC could prohibit such programs simply by amending its definition of "program-length commercials."

LONG-TERM INITIATIVES

The new Administration's long-term goal should be to shape the communications infrastructure to foster economic growth and affordable access for all to the telecommunications opportunities of the future. Attaining this goal will not be easy given the many different types of media, the differing regulatory schemes, and the continuing development of new technology. Several past attempts to "rewrite" the Communications Act of 1934 have failed. Yet, it is clear that this act requires substantial revision to take into account the tremendous changes that have taken place since 1934.

New legislation should ensure that the public obtains maximum benefits from the deployment of new technologies such as fiber-optic networks and high-definition television. The huge capital requirements for such systems will make it difficult to rely on ownership diversity alone.

Common carrier regulation is the best way to ensure access for those who do not have ownership in the relevant medium, particularly when that medium has a monopoly or near monopoly, as in the case of cable and telephone companies today. Common carrier regulation requires access on a nondiscriminatory basis at just and reasonable rates. If telephone companies are permitted to offer cable television and other broadband services, they should do so only on a common carrier basis with strict safeguards to prevent discrimination and to protect ratepayers from cross-subsidies.

New legislation should recognize that certain desirable services (such as public affairs programs and children's programs) will not be provided in sufficient quantities if left solely to market forces. Market forces are inherently more responsive to those with money to spend. Certain segments of our society (such as disabled persons and persons with low incomes) will not receive adequate services if we rely on market forces alone. Thus the legislation should set up a fund to provide these services directly.

The fund could be provided by the spectrum or other fees imposed on industry or by tax dollars. If tax dollars are used, care must be taken to limit the danger of abuse of government power to restrict free speech created by the U.S. Supreme Court's 1991 decision in *Rust* v. *Sullivan* (the abortion "gag" rule case). This potentially far-reaching decision may encourage some legislators and regulators to impose conditions on speech where there is public funding. The new Administration must disavow such intentions.

Common Carrier Initiatives

SINCE THE UNITED STATES has lacked a coherent long-term telecommunications policy, the next Administration will have an opportunity to develop a new information and telecommunications order based on democratic participation and First Amendment principles.

A new telecommunications policy must come to grips with the fact that many people have been left outside the communications network. For instance, at this late date, 7 percent of Americans do not have telephones and 40 percent do not subscribe to cable television.

Moreover, development of a new telecommunications infrastructure poses increased opportunity for private restrictions on speech. A single fiber-optic network into the home and office can be a vehicle for transmitting an essentially unlimited variety of issues and ideas. However, if the owner of the network can prevent access to the network for economic or political reasons, the constitutional ideal of unlimited debate will be stymied.

The threat to privacy is also exacerbated by the new technologies. For example, the widespread uneasiness over the introduction of "caller ID" services by many local telephone companies gives just a hint of the intrusiveness that will be possible in the near future. Existing statutory mechanisms are woefully inadequate to address the issues raised by new capabilities to compile, retrieve, disclose, and manipulate personal information without the subject's knowledge.

SHORT-TERM INITIATIVES

• Strengthen current programs (such as telephone lifeline) to advance access for low-income households, rural areas, and individuals with special needs.

• Carefully review the impact of price cap regulation of telephone rates to determine whether consumers would be better off under traditional rate-of-return regulation.

• Implement the Telephone Consumer Protection Act of 1991. The rules proposed by the FCC in Docket No. 92-90 do not go far enough to protect consumers from "junk phone calls." The FCC should establish a national "do not call" database and regulate "live" calls as well as autodialed calls to protect citizens from unwanted telemarketing solicitations. The experience gained in this process will serve as a model for developing protections to accompany other new and more powerful technologies.

LONG-TERM INITIATIVES

Over the longer term, the critical goal is to develop the telecommunications infrastructure of the next generation. The central policy debate is over the relevant costs and benefits of accelerating the deployment of the telecommunications infrastructure to support more advanced information-age services. While the current administration is examining these issues, it has done so with very little input from the public. Just being open to the views of the public, however, may not be enough. It is difficult for members of the public to grapple with issues that require knowledge of technology as well as to envision what the future may bring.

Thus the new Administraton should make a careful and unbiased examination of what benefits are likely to be gained from an advanced telecommunications infrastructure, how much they will cost, who will bear the cost, and whether the intended beneficiaries are likely actually to receive the promised benefits. The relative merits of a centralized model should be compared with those of a decentralized model.[2]

The new Administration should also give considerable attention to mounting evidence that similar benefits could be obtained by merely upgrading the existing infrastructure, and delaying installation of the so-called broadband technologies touted by many policy advocates and the telephone companies. A recent study by the Consumer Federation of America found that a "Widespread Integrated Narrowband Network" based on use of Integrated Services Digital Networks, or ISDN (an acronym used to describe conversion of existing copper wires to multichannel use), would deliver 80 percent of the capabilities of a ubiquitous, broadband fiber-optic network at 10 percent of the cost.[3] This less capital-intensive approach has the additional benefit of concentrating job creation in high-tech industries that better suit the economy for worldwide competition.

The new Administration should strongly consider imposing a common carrier scheme on the new infrastructure. Under this model, the owners of any interactive multichannel fiber-optic video delivery systems of the future would have no control over content, and all speakers would have nondiscriminatory access, thus maximizing First Amendment principles of diversity.

Because this new electronic highway could be used to supplant or replace many public services, such as the post office and, perhaps, even the election board, all Americans must be connected to it. Without this "universal service" we run the risk of disenfranchising millions of Americans, creating an "information underclass" and thus impeding our economic and social development.

Thus the challenge for the new President will be to bring into the policy debate the perspectives, needs, and interests of all Americans, not just the interested industry groups. It must develop an overall telecommunications policy that is both consistent with the ideals of our democratic government and flexible enough to accommodate uncertainty and change.

NOTES

1. FCC Public Notice, "1991 Broadcast and Cable Employment Report" (June 24, 1992).
2. See M. Cooper, "Expanding the Information Age for the 1990s: A Pragmatic Consumer Analysis" (AARP, CFA, Jan. 11, 1990).
3. M. Cooper, "Developing the Information Age in the 1990s: A Pragmatic Consumer View" (June 8, 1992), p. 1.

SECURITIES REGULATION

HARVEY J. GOLDSCHMID

Summary

THE EXCESSES OF THE 1980S AND EARLY 1990S in the securities area have left the nation with a profound—and wholly justified—sense of concern. During these years, financial markets were manipulated, and counterproductive takeover tactics (e.g., greenmail, poison pills, lockups) and misallocated resources played havoc with efficiency and left many corporations grievously in debt. Largely unaddressed were critically important issues related to new financial products, new trading strategies and technologies, the internationalization of capital markets, the blurring of boundaries between previously diverse financial markets, the accountability of corporate managements, and the shareholder's proper role. Throughout the period, the Securities and Exchange Commission (SEC) stuck to its knitting, by and large properly regulating disclosure and insider trading but remaining inexcusably passive with respect to the regulatory implications of market change. Not since the trauma of the stock market crash of 1929 and the various crises of the early 1930s have our financial markets and corporate governance system been so urgently in need of reform.

The next President should recognize that the regulatory road the SEC elects to travel starting in 1993 will fundamentally affect the economic health of the nation. Financial markets allocate capital and influence business and consumer conduct in the most basic ways. The new Administration should take the following steps to restore the vigor and integrity of our financial markets and to generate proper incentives for corporate productivity, efficiency, and innovation:

Harvey J. Goldschmid is Dwight Professor of Law at Columbia University. He is a Reporter for the American Law Institute's Corporate Governance Project, and Chair of both the Committee on Securities Regulation and the Audit Committee of the Association of the Bar of the City of New York.

- Enact new federal merger and acquisition legislation that would (1) substantially extend the time required for hostile takeovers; (2) encourage accountability and discourage managerial "empire building" by requiring the shareholders of both the acquiring and target companies to approve all significant acquisitions; and (3) prohibit or sharply curtail counterproductive offensive and defensive takeover tactics.

- Revise SEC statutes and rules to (1) mandate additional disclosure in areas such as executive compensation; (2) reduce the unnecessary chilling of communications among shareholders; (3) provide greater room for shareholder dialogues with management and for collective action by shareholders; and (4) create a more level playing field during proxy contests by authorizing the SEC to preempt state law with respect to proxy expenses, shareholder disenfranchising provisions, and similar matters.

- Simplify the capital formation process for small businesses to encourage economic expansion and new, innovative activities.

- Because the SEC during the past twelve years has largely turned a blind eye toward calls for evaluation of new financial products, new trading strategies and technologies, the internationalization of capital markets, and other major issues, the nation needs the most thoroughgoing examination of the securities markets since the Kennedy administration's special study (under similar circumstances) in the early 1960s.

- Early in 1993, action should be taken to (1) significantly strengthen the regulatory scheme for investment advisers; (2) enact substantive insider trading legislation and extend the statute of limitations for insider trading and other securities act violations; (3) impose stricter disclosure requirements on certain debt issuers; (4) reform securities industry arbitration; and (5) provide new budgetary resources for the SEC.

History of the SEC

SECURITIES REGULATION FROM 1933 TO 1980[1]

The federal securities acts of 1933 and 1934 mandated broad disclosure about securities being sold for the first time or publicly traded, provided for the prosecution of misrepresentation, and regulated various Wall Street practices. Congress acted in response to public demand. Between September 1, 1929, and July 1, 1932, the value of stocks listed on the New York Stock Exchange shrank from nearly $90 billion to just under $16 billion. "The annals of finance," the Senate Banking Committee wrote, "present no counterpart to this enormous decline in security prices."[2] Approximately half of the $50 billion of new securities that were sold in the United States from

1920 to 1930 proved nearly or totally valueless. From 1934 through 1980, Congress enacted legislation regulating investment advisers, investment companies, tender offers, and other aspects of the nation's securities markets.

The SEC, created in 1934, is a traditional independent administrative agency. It has five commissioners (no more than three may be appointed from the same political party) and has in general been blessed by high-quality leadership and able staff. Professor Joel Seligman, who has written the definitive history of the SEC, summarized the commission's early years as follows:

> Gone are the days when new securities sales were dominated by private investment banks, such as J. P. Morgan and Company, when references to "bear raids" or stock market "pools" daily appeared in the nation's press, when the New York Stock Exchange fairly could be described as a "private club," when Senate hearings riveted the nation's attention with revelations of fraudulent Peruvian bond sales, "preferred" stockholder lists, bribed journalists who "touted" securities, or stock price manipulation. . . . The principal actor in this transformation of corporate finance has been the Securities and Exchange Commission.[3]

The SEC's performance after World War II receives mixed reviews. Indeed, in December 1960, President-elect John Kennedy was advised by James Landis, a former SEC chairman and dean of Harvard Law School, that federal regulatory agencies were in a state of disarray. The SEC suffered from "budget starvation," and Kennedy was advised that "the key to improvement" was "the selection of qualified personnel."[4] For the chairmanship of the SEC, the president nominated my late colleague William L. Cary of Columbia Law School.

Cary recognized that while the nation's securities markets had changed greatly between the New Deal and the New Frontier, the SEC had not done an in-depth study of these markets in over twenty years. In 1961, a special study of securities markets was commissioned. It "undoubtedly was the single most influential document published in the history of the SEC," concluded Professor Seligman. "It provided a foundation for most of the reforms that occurred in the securities industry during the ensuing fifteen years."[5]

Chairman Cary and his successors at the SEC reinvigorated a tired agency, and the special study and other initiatives produced a process of reform that changed securities laws and financial markets enormously for the better.[6] But as a new chairman takes office sometime after January 1993, he or she will face a situation remarkably similar to the one Cary faced in 1961.

THE UNFORTUNATE LEGACY OF RECENT YEARS

The nation's securities markets have changed more dramatically since 1980 than in any comparable twelve-year period of our history. The Bush and Reagan administrations have, however, inexcusably neglected many areas of fundamental importance. A rigid free-market, hands-off approach has characterized much of their thinking.

A review of the following areas of neglect illustrates the high cost to the nation of twelve years of SEC passivity. What is needed now is a rejection of the view that free markets will solve all problems more quickly and efficiently than any regulatory regime. Instead, it must be recognized that when it comes to financial markets and corporate governance, limited, informed, effective government intervention is a modern necessity. Such intervention played a major role from 1933 to 1980 in making the nation's securities markets the most respected and successful in the world. There will, of course, be instances where deregulatory steps to remove unnecessary impediments to the working of markets make sense, but the Bush-Reagan neglect in each of the follow areas appears to have no sound policy underpinning:

• *New financial products, trading strategies, and technologies.* Since 1980, futures products, various kinds of options, swaps and swap derivations, program trading, portfolio insurance, and index buying and arbitrage have become of great financial importance. Valid questions have been raised about, for example, whether these new products and strategies increase speculation, increase volatility, are being appropriately monitored, work unfairly from the standpoint of the small investor, or interfere unduly with long-term corporate governance goals. The SEC has largely ignored these issues.

• *The internationalization of securities markets.* By every statistical measure, the internationalization of securities markets has sharply increased during the past twelve years.[7] This internationalization is both unavoidable and economically desirable in many respects. What is troubling, however, is that the United States is losing its role as the world's preeminent capital market. To meet the challenge of internationalization, Bevis Longstreth, a recent commissioner of the SEC, recommended paring away rules that "impose unnecessary burdens on foreign issuers." He urged, instead, "a careful review of the SEC's role in a global competitive and multimarket setting, looking to balance investor protection interests with the national goal of maintaining our nation's preeminence as a capital market center."[8]

• *The growth of institutional investors.* In 1980, institutional investors (e.g., pension funds, mutual funds, banks, insurance companies) held 33.1

percent of the nation's outstanding equities. By 1990, institutional investors controlled $6.52 trillion in assets and held 53.3 percent of the outstanding equities in the United States.[9] The mutual fund industry has grown from less than $200 billion under management in 1980 to an estimated $1.5 trillion today. The number of investment advisers has grown from about 5,100 in 1981 to approximately 17,500 today.[10]

This growth of institutional investors raises two critical questions: (1) Has our regulatory scheme kept up with the growth? (2) Has the SEC, by revision of its proxy rules and other corporate governance regulations, provided these institutional investors—and other shareholders—adequate room to demand managerial accountability and corporate efficiency and to take collective action where appropriate? The short answer to these questions is no.

While these questions are discussed below, a feel for the scope of the problems created by SEC neglect is provided by Chairman Richard Breeden's recent admission that the SEC's current program to monitor investment advisers is "totally inadequate."[11] Today, most investment advisers are inspected only once every thirty years.[12]

• *The corporate governance dilemma.* The bottom line on the struggles for corporate control that dominated the 1980s is summarized by the word "waste."[13] During these years, while mergers and acquisitions accounted for about $1.4 trillion of corporate assets changing hands, counterproductive tactics by both acquiring corporations and targets resulted in gross misallocations of resources, costly inefficiencies, and the imperiling of many corporations that ended up deeply in debt.[14]

In general, corporate managements emerged from the 1980s even more insulated and entrenched than they entered the decade. Of great significance for the 1990s is the fact that while some of the financial devices of the 1980s, such as highly leveraged buyouts, are now largely in disrepute, the fundamental government attitudes that helped fuel the merger frenzy—outdated and paralyzed securities regulation, permissive attitudes toward antitrust enforcement, and misperceptions about the realities of corporate governance—remain largely unchanged.

During the 1980s, the SEC and the Council of Economic Advisers considered the takeover craze and concluded that no federal action was necessary.[15] They were "committed to states' rights and generally. . . [were] opposed to any corporate governance regulation."[16] Indeed, the SEC's "obeisance to states' rights dogma led to the rather incongruous result that the SEC opposed its own [earlier] recommendations to reform the Williams Act."[17]

As the next section indicates, what is needed in the 1990s is new federal merger and acquisition legislation that would prevent recurrence of the abuses of the 1980s, and revision of the SEC's proxy rules and other corporate governance regulations to encourage "shareholder democracy" by providing greater room for shareholder communications, dialogues with management, and collective action.

Principal Challenges and Reforms

EARLY PRIORITIES

New Federal Merger and Acquisition Legislation. Mergers and acquisitions—both friendly and hostile—may play an important role in furthering basic corporate law and industrial organization goals. They may, for example, prune "deadwood managements," create synergy and other incentives for efficient operation, provide liquidity for shareholders, encourage capital formation, and move corporate assets to those who can use them best.

Mergers and acquisitions may also have efficiency-retarding effects. They may, for example, be the product of career-protection and empire-building instincts among managers. Or they may result from perverse monetary, career, and psychological incentives for investment bankers, lawyers, and other professionals; anticompetitive market power incentives may also play a role.

The overall economic impact of takeovers remains the subject of legitimate dispute. But measuring or averaging the impact of *all* acquisition activity, even if feasible, has little utility. Public policy benefits lie in encouraging mergers likely to have "good" effects and discouraging those likely to be "bad." In this regard, a fundamental policy theme emerges from the studies of what went wrong in the 1980s. Since an acquiring company may not be trying to increase efficiency when making a bid, and since senior managers and other key players (e.g., investment bankers and lawyers) may be driven by self-advancing motivations that have nothing to do with efficiency, securities and corporate laws should be reoriented to maximize the chance that a proposed acquisition will, in fact, enhance efficiency, competitiveness, and the economic goals of corporate shareholders. This cannot be done under state law, which now largely governs mergers and acquisitions.

Under "enabling" state corporation laws, corporate managements are left free to run the business—and to reject acquisition proposals or to attempt to acquire other corporations—with very limited legal constraints. U.S. Supreme Court Justice Louis D. Brandeis, in 1933, regretted that the race among the states "was not one of diligence but of laxity."[18] William L. Cary, more bluntly, placed Delaware in the lead in "the race to the bottom."[19] Recently, Professor Lucian Bebchuk, of Harvard Law School, extensively reviewed the "race to the bottom" thesis and its modern critics and concluded:

> The important role of state law in the governance of corporate affairs makes critical to any corporation the corporate law rules of its state of incorporation. Because corporations are relatively free to select their states of incorporation, and because states benefit from having corporations incorporate within their boundaries, states are likely to compete to attract incorporations.
>
> One major source of the shortcomings of state competition is the possible divergence between the interests of managers and controlling shareholders and the interests of public shareholders. Notwithstanding market forces and the need for shareholder approval to reincorporate, there are many issues with respect to which managers may well seek, and states in turn may well provide, rules that do not maximize shareholder value but rather serve the private interests of managers and controlling shareholders. . . . Federal rules, or at least federal minimum standards, are warranted with respect to self-dealing transactions, taking of corporate opportunities, freezeout mergers, all aspects of takeover bids and proxy contests.[20]

Federal legislation should encourage accountability and discourage managerial empire-building by requiring the shareholders of both the acquiring and target corporations to approve all significant acquisitions. Under present state law, corporate managers are left free to select the method of acquisition and thus may avoid—in whole or in part—the necessity of securing affirmative shareholder votes.[21] There is no satisfactory rationale for taking from shareholders the right to participate in decisions basically affecting the direction and structure of their corporations.

Federal legislation, in brief, also should (1) substantially extend the time required for hostile takeovers (buying or selling important, complex industrial or financial businesses in days, as opposed to months, is simply mad in industrial organization terms); (2) prohibit or sharply curtail counterproductive offensive tactics (e.g., two-tier, front-loaded offers; greenmail) and defensive tactics (e.g., poison pills; lockups); and (3) clean up various technical problems (e.g., closing the "ten-day window" for share acquisitions after a purchaser has accumulated 5 percent).

Revised SEC Statutes and Rules to Encourage Shareholder Communications, Dialogues with Management, and Collective Action. In 1985, in the context of resolving issues during a classic takeover battle, the Supreme Court of Delaware set forth the traditional theory of shareholder power: "If the stockholders are displeased with the actions of their elected representatives [who were blocking a hostile takeover], the powers of corporate democracy are at their disposal to turn the board out."[22]

But the reality of modern corporate governance is quite different. As Professor Bernard Black put it in the course of an extensive review of shareholder passivity:

> In theory, the shareholders of public companies elect directors, who watch corporate officers, who manage/watch the company on the shareholders' behalf. But since Berle and Means [wrote in 1932], we have understood that this theory is a fiction. The managers—the current officers and directors—pick the directors, and the shareholders rubberstamp the managers' choices. Perhaps thrice in a thousand cases, unhappy shareholders mount a proxy fight. About one-fourth of the time, they win.[23]

Professor Black correctly concluded that the SEC's proxy rules and other commission regulations were unnecessarily hindering shareholder communications and collective action.

The growth of institutional investors has made effective shareholder action more practicable. Reform of the proxy process is of particular importance because the process can be used to effect a wide variety of changes (e.g., recommending the reversal of specific corporate policies, replacing directors, presenting alternative long-term strategies) without the massive ownership change—and other associated dislocations—inherent in a hostile takeover.

Revised SEC statutes and rules should do the following: (1) reduce the unnecessary chilling of communications among shareholders by narrowing the SEC's definition of solicitation or by widening the exemption for communications among certain shareholders; (2) clarify Sections 13(d) and 16(b) of the Securities Exchange Act to afford institutional investors greater room for shareholder communications; (3) modify Rule 14a-8 to encourage dialogue between shareholders and managers on a broad range of issues; and (4) encourage collective action by shareholders by revising federal standards,[24] and by providing the SEC with statutory and rulemaking power to preempt aspects of state law (e.g., proxy expense provisions, shareholder disenfranchising provisions, and the part of Pennsylvania's antitakeover statute that discourages proxy contests[25]). In addition, more complete disclosure should be mandated in areas such as executive compensation.[26]

Steps to Deal with Changing Financial Markets and the Blurring of Boundaries Between Previously Diverse Financial Markets. Many of our principal financial markets and the key players in them (e.g., securities firms, investment banks, commodities firms, commercial banks, and insurance companies) are inextricably linked in economic terms but are separately regulated. We have too many different financial regulators at the federal and state levels. Predictably, this has led to duplicative, inconsistent, and lax regulation. It is, for example, unwise today to regulate different kinds of bond issuers separately or to regulate the trading of stocks, options, and financial futures separately. Explanations for this regulatory crazy quilt focus on some combination of history, accident, expertise accumulated over time, political clout, and the preservation of executive, legislative, or administrative turf.

The SEC in the next Administration should play a significant role in helping to consolidate and rationalize our structure for regulating financial markets. Transfers of jurisdiction, deregulatory actions, and new regulatory steps will all be necessary. Early in the new Administration, the following steps should be taken to deal with changes in financial markets and the blurring of boundaries between previously diverse financial markets:

1. *Adopt single-source (SEC) regulation of the stock, option, and futures markets*. The SEC has jurisdictional responsibility for stocks and options. The Commoditites Future Trading Commission regulates stock index futures. According to Stephen Friedman, a former SEC commissioner, "there is no intellectually respectable argument for the existing system of separate regulators for securities and options on securities, and for financial futures and options on financial futures."[27] Similarly, economist Henry Kaufman concluded that "the current system of regulation and surveillance [of financial markets] is really archaic."[28] Single-source regulation would allow for both consistent regulatory requirements and more effective monitoring and prohibition of counterproductive practices. Although the political difficulties are real, Congress should be asked to transfer jurisdiction over "all stock products"—no matter how denominated—to the SEC. The SEC's track record and general expertise dictate this organizational solution.

2. *The SEC should be provided with broad new authority over governmental debt issuers*. The bond default by the Washington Public Power Supply System (WPPSS) in 1983 (at $2.25 billion, one of the largest bond defaults in securities history) and the recent scandal involving U.S. Treasury securities demonstrate the need for enhanced SEC powers. With respect to bonds issued by state and local governments, a 376-page report released by

the SEC in 1988 indicates why these issuers should be subject to stricter disclosure obligations—i.e., closer to those the SEC administers for corporate issuers. According to the SEC, WPPSS "avoided disclosure of negative developments." WPPSS's financial advisers "did not seek negative information from the Supply System to the degree they might have, and some information was withheld from them. They also tended to avoid causing full disclosure of negative information in their areas of expertise."[29] The SEC concluded that the bond underwriters also might have discovered disclosure inadequacies if they had conducted a more probing investigation of the offerings. In 1988, SEC chairman David Ruder indicated that the SEC's budget squeeze and the pendency of private litigation (now settled) affected the commission's decision to close its WPPSS investigation without bringing an enforcement action.

In general, more than a decade of experimentation with industry-generated disclosure guidelines for municipal bonds puts in doubt their efficacy.[30] SEC-mandated disclosure (at least for large issuers) would create uniform standards of reference for investors, rating agencies, and the financial media.

3. *The regulatory scheme for investment companies and investment advisers should be strengthened.* On May 21, 1992, the SEC's Division of Investment Management released a two-year study of the regulation of investment companies and investment advisers. Many of the study's wide-ranging recommendations appear sound (e.g., those relating to an enhanced role for independent directors of investment companies, some of the recommendations for increased competition and deregulation, and some of the recommendations to encourage new financial products). The study, which will require legislation for a number of its most important recommendations, should provide the basis for activity in these areas during the first years of the next Administration. As indicated earlier, however, an immediate priority is the significant strengthening of the inspection program for investment advisers.

Steps to Fine-Tune the Existing Regulatory Scheme. Among various other legislative or administrative changes proposed during the past twelve years, the best candidates for early action in 1993 are: (1) substantive insider trading legislation and the extension of the statute of limitations for insider trading and other securities act violations; (2) legislation providing new budgetary resources for the SEC; (3) proposals to simplify and encourage the capital formation process for small business; and (4) proposals for reforming securities industry arbitration.

• The names Boesky, Levine, Milken, Siegel, Winans, and Drexel Burnham, among others, dominated insider trading headlines during the late 1980s and early 1990s. In general, those who have admitted guilt, or been found guilty, in these scandals have committed hard-core, willful offenses and deserve harsh criminal and civil sanctions. They have seriously undermined the honesty and integrity of our securities markets; unfairly accumulated huge, unearned profits; and jeopardized the willingness of potential investors to support the nation's capital formation needs.

But a number of important legal questions related to insider trading (e.g., the definition of "insider," standing to sue, and the damage and "aiding and abetting" concepts) have not yet been definitively answered or are in dispute in the federal courts. The result has been unnecessary litigation expense and judicial burdens, potential traps for the unwary, and a danger that significant issues could be resolved the wrong way. Insider trading law, which has grown out of the very general language of Section 10(b) of the Securities Exchange Act of 1934,[31] now constitutes "a judicial oak which has grown from little more than a legislative acorn."[32] At this time, however, legislation should better define what it prohibits.

New insider trading legislation should resolve a 4–4 deadlock in the U.S. Supreme Court[33] by incorporating a "misappropriation" approach as part of its "insider" definition. Such a step would prevent a crimped, unworkable definition from developing and would broadly strengthen the SEC's enforcement hand. Legislative proposals made during the past few years demonstrate that important insider trading questions can be resolved fairly and with enough breadth to preserve judicial flexibility in the future. Similarly, to prevent forum shopping, unnecessary litigation expense, and judicial burdens, a uniform federal statute of limitations period for violations of Section 10(b) is desirable; a 10(b) action should be available to plaintiffs for at least five years.

• In 1988, the SEC's chairman, David Ruder, acknowledged that the commission lacked the funds to carry out its responsibilities. "We are a peanut agency" doing a large job, he testified; "we have reached limits of efficiency with current resources [then about $135 million]."[34] In 1992, Chairman Richard Breeden asked Congress for a budget of $249.8 million for fiscal year 1993 (up $24 million from fiscal year 1992) but had to concede that the investment adviser inspection program was "totally inadequate" and that only twenty-two full-time staff positions—an increase of less than 1 percent—would be added at the SEC.[35]

There can be no doubt about the reality of the budget squeeze at the SEC. When inflation is taken into account, the SEC's budget has been relatively flat from 1980 through 1992. During this period, however, there have been dramatic increases in the volume of trading on the New York Stock Exchange and other exchanges, in the assets of investment companies, in the number of investment advisers, and in the number of filings with the SEC. Moreover, securities markets have grown increasingly more complex and have changed dramatically during the past twelve years, and major areas of change have been neglected by the commission.

The irony is that even if the SEC's budget were increased substantially, there would be no cost to the U.S. Treasury in terms of general tax revenues. The SEC estimates that it will collect about $311 million in fees in fiscal 1992, equivalent to 138 percent of its budget, and $340 million in fees in fiscal 1993, equivalent to 136 percent of its proposed budget.[36] The SEC's efforts are, of course, supplemented by state securities regulators and private plaintiffs, and both have served the nation well during a difficult period. The stakes, however, are too high to continue to underfund the SEC drastically. In the new Administration, the SEC must be given a budget commensurate with its critical responsibilities.

• Proposals have been made to simplify reporting requirements for small public corporations and to encourage mutual funds and other investors to put capital into emerging businesses. In general, the new Administration should support such proposals in order to encourage economic expansion and new, innovative activities.

• During the past twelve years, arbitration has become the almost exclusive means of resolving disputes between investors and the securities industry. For many claimants, arbitration offers a relatively fast, efficient, and inexpensive means of resolving disputes. For an arbitration process to be successful, however, it must be procedurally fair and impartial. In May 1992, the General Accounting Office (GAO) issued a report that "showed that [securities industry-sponsored] arbitration forums lacked internal controls to provide a reasonable level of assurance regarding either the independence of the arbitrators or their competence in arbitrating disputes."[37] Reform recommendations made by the GAO and others, to help ensure procedural fairness and impartiality, should provide the new Administration with the basis for action in early 1993.

Long-Term Priorities

SINCE 1980, a large number of important financial products, trading strategies, and technologies have been developed, but we do not now have a theoretical or empirical basis for making definitive judgments on most of the

products, trading strategies, and technologies developed during the past
twelve years. The same conclusion applies to major issues raised by the
internationalization of securities markets, the growth of institutional investors, and the blurring of boundaries between previously diverse financial
markets.

Clearly, in these areas as well as in others, what is called for is the most
thorough examination of the securities markets since Chairman Cary's special
study in the early 1960s. Such a study has the potential to rival Cary's study
in influence and to set the SEC's reform agenda well into the next century.

As is obvious, the reform agenda for the SEC—in terms of both action
and study—is large, yet is commensurate with the gravity of the issues facing
our financial markets. William L. Cary was fond of quoting two aphorisms.
The first counseled patience. "Law reform is not for the short-winded," he
would say. The second urged both idealism and professional skill: "Technique
without ideals is a menace; ideals without technique are a mess."[38] The next
President should be mindful of both aphorisms as he entrusts a new chairman
of the SEC with the task of restoring vigor, decency, and fairness to the
nation's securities markets and corporate governance system.

NOTES

1. This discussion is based on chapters 1–4 and 9–11 of Joel Seligman, *The Transformation of Wall Street* (1982).

2. Ibid., p. 1.

3. Ibid., p. x.

4. Ibid., p. 291.

5. Ibid., p. 299.

6. See C. McGowan, W. Werner, and H. Goldschmid, "In Memoriam—Professor
William L. Cary," 83 *Columbia Law Review* (May 1983): 765, 767, 769.

7. See SEC, *Staff Report on Internationalization of the Securities Markets* (July 1987):
p. 1-1; I. Walter and A. Saunders, *National and Global Competitiveness of New York
City as a Financial Center* (1991).

8. Bevis Longstreth, "Global Securities Markets and the SEC" (unpublished paper,
March 1988), pp. 8, 20–21.

9. See C. Brancato and P. Gaughan, *Institutional Investors and Capital Markets: 1991
Update* (1992).

10. 24 *Securities Regulation & Law Report* (June 1992): 796.

11. 24 *Securities Regulation & Law Report* (March 1992): 225.

12. 24 *Securities Regulation & Law Report* (June 1992): 796.

13. This discussion is based on the Prologue to Robert Pitofsky and Harvey J. Goldschmid,
American Competitiveness and Recent Merger Movements: Lessons for Public Policy
(forthcoming).

14. One obvious consequence of the mountain of corporate debt created during the 1980s was a string of major bankruptcies; six of the ten largest bankruptcies in the history of the nation occurred in the late 1980s or early 1990s; ibid.

15. See Council of Economic Advisers, *Economic Report of the President* (1985), p. 196; R. Karmel, "Is It Time for a Federal Corporation Law?," 57 *Brooklyn Law Review* (Spring 1991): 55, 82.

16. Karmel, "Is It Time for a Federal Corporation Law?": 82.

17. Ibid.

18. *Liggett Co. v. Lee*, 288 U.S. 517, 559 (1933).

19. William L. Cary, "Federalism and Corporate Law: Reflections Upon Delaware," 83 *Yale Law Journal* (November 1974): 663, 665–66; see R. Nader, M. Green and J. Seligman, *Taming the Giant Corporation* (1976); W. Cary and H. Goldschmid, "Foreword to the Corporate Responsibility Symposium: Reflections on Directions," 30 *Hastings Law Journal* (May 1979): 1247, 1258–59; H. Goldschmid, "The Greening of the Board Room: Reflections on Corporate Responsibility," 10 *Columbia Journal of Law and Social Problems* (Fall 1973): 17, 28.

20. Lucian. Bebchuk, "Federalism and the Corporation: The Desirable Limits on State Competition in Corporate Law," 105 *Harvard Law Review* (May 1992): 1435, 1438, 1507–8.

21. Numerous methods, (e.g., asset acquisitions, tender offers, and triangular mergers) are available for reaching the same result as a formal merger (which requires the vote of shareholders of the acquired and acquiring firm) and require only the vote of the shareholders of the acquired corporation or no vote at all. See M. Eisenberg, *The Structure of the Corporation* (1976), pp. 215–17.

22. *Unocal Corp. v. Mesa Petroleum Co.*, 493 A.2d 946, 959 (Del. Sup. Ct. 1985).

23. Bernard Black, "Shareholder Passivity Reexamined," 89 *Michigan Law Review* (December 1990): 521.

24. For example, Section 14(a)'s various rules, including Rules 14a-4(d) and 14a-7, which would facilitate the election of a minority of directors. See R. Gilson, L. Gordon, and J. Pound, "How the Proxy Rules Discourage Constructive Engagement: Regulatory Barriers to Electing a Minority of Directors," 17 *Journal of Corporation Law* (1991): 29.

25. 15 Pa. Const. Stat. Ann., Sec 275 (Purdue 1991).

26. The SEC in mid-1991 proposed more modest revisions to the proxy rules than those recommended above. Under pressure from corporate groups, however, the SEC withdrew its proposals, promising that they would be reintroduced. On June 23, 1992, the SEC set forth revised proxy proposals that still have not been formally enacted into law by the commission. The SEC's proposals for enhanced communications, which represent a step in the right direction, "modify similar, even more ambitious ones, put forward in June 1991." Hershey, "SEC Acts on Behalf of Holders," *The New York Times* (June 24, 1992), p. D1.

27. *The New York Times* (January 14, 1988), p. A31.

28. *The New York Times* (December 17, 1987), p. A1.

29. 20 *Securities Regulation & Law Report* (September 1988): 1435–36.

30. See J. Seligman, *The SEC and the Future of Finance* (1985), pp. 281–94.

31. 48 Stat. 891, 15 U.S.C. Sec. 78j(b). Section 10(b) has been supplemented by other federal securities law provisions and by federal mail and wire fraud statutes.

32. *Blue Chip Stamps* v. *Manor Drug Stores*, 421 U.S. 723, 735 (1975).

33. See *Carpenter* v. *United States*, 484 U.S. 19 (1987).

34. 20 *Securities Regulation & Law Report* (September 1988): 1394.

35. 24 *Securities Regulation & Law Report* (March 1992): 225, 409–10; although not reflected in the SEC's proposed budget for fiscal 1993, legislation supported by the commission would add 175 additional inspectors to the investment adviser program (see p. 375).

36. 24 *Securities Regulation & Law Report* (March 1992): 375.

37. 24 *Securities Regulation & Law Report* (May 1992): 719.

38. The first aphorism is generally attributed to Chief Justice Vanderbilt of the Supreme Court of New Jersey and the second to Professor Karl Llewellyn of Columbia Law School.

EXECUTIVE MANAGEMENT

GARY D. BASS

Summary

A LTHOUGH BEST KNOWN FOR DEVELOPING and supervising the federal budget, the White House Office of Management and Budget also has significant and far-reaching additional powers that it wields over the federal agencies. For example, OMB oversees the development of virtually all government regulations; the collection, management, and dissemination of public information; and the management practices used in each agency.

Recently, OMB has subordinated good management practices to ideological control over and implementation of the president's policies. It has repeatedly put private, free market interests ahead of efforts—even congressionally mandated efforts—to clean up the environment, to protect worker health and safety, and enforce consumer protection. Because OMB operates under a veil of secrecy, it has been able to delay or circumvent legislative and judicial deadlines as well as displace agency decisionmaking authority.

The emergence of the Vice President's Council on Competitiveness, chaired by Dan Quayle, has worsened this problem, since the council now oversees OMB's regulatory review activities and cloaks all its work under executive prerogatives, making it impossible for the public and Congress to know truly the extent of its activities. Anecdotal information, however, has revealed the council as a conduit for business to impose its will on the regulatory decisions of government—further politicizing the process.

To both improve OMB's efficiency and stop the political contamination

Gary D. Bass is Executive Director of OMB Watch, a nonprofit research and advocacy organization that monitors the White House Office of Management and Budget. Dr. Bass has written extensively on federal budgetary, program management, regulatory, and information policy issues.

of the regulatory process, the next President must change the focus of the Council on Competitiveness from a regulatory wrecking crew to a serious effort to review ways to make this country economically competitive; in other words, get the council out of the regulatory review business. Regulatory reviews by OMB or others must be made to: (a) follow open government standards in order to promote improved record-keeping and greater public accountability; (b) require that recommendations to agencies be in writing, with justification; and (c) impose a maximum ninety-day regulatory review period.

Background

ORIGINALLY ENVISIONED AS A TECHNICAL budget office, OMB has become a very powerful, politically charged arm of the president. During the Ronald Reagan and George Bush administrations particularly, OMB has come to exercise more power than perhaps at any other time in its history.

Established in 1921 as a part of the Department of the Treasury, the office was called the Bureau of the Budget (BoB). BoB's primary task was to coordinate the annual preparation of the federal budget. Prior to that, agencies sent their budgets directly to Congress without any Executive Branch review.

Shortly after its creation, BoB's authority was enlarged with management functions, such as the authority to "clear proposed legislation." This process accelerated during the administration of Franklin Delano Roosevelt when, in 1939, BoB was moved to the newly created executive office of the president and given more power, ranging from fiscal policy and planning to administrative research and the review of agency information services. This concentration of powers established a precedent for the modern-day OMB as a very powerful office closely identified with the policies of the president.

After World War II, BoB's management responsibilities continued to grow. By 1970 it was involved in management reform, agency organization, personnel management, regulatory matters, grants-in-aid programs, and policies on intergovernmental relations. The extent of these powers was finally acknowledged when, on July 1, 1970, BoB became the Office of Management and Budget (OMB).

Still, OMB was not expected to do everything. For example, when OMB was created, the White House Domestic Council was also formed, with the idea that the council, as President Nixon put it, "will be primarily concerned with what we do; the Office of Management and Budget will be primarily concerned with how we do it and how well we do it." This neat division of labor quickly dissolved—partly because John Ehrlichman, the first director of the Domestic Council, was busy with operational problems, including Watergate, and the then OMB director, George Shultz, was relied on for help with policy decisions. Thus, while the council was to be the policy-maker and OMB the administrator, from the beginning OMB was deeply involved in both policy and administration. The failure to divide the labor remains a continuing dilemma today for OMB—how to justify deep involvement in both policy and administration, and how to respond to the accompanying charges of overpoliticization.

Another functional problem was the balance between OMB's budget and management activities. Although the management side appeared to have nearly equal weight on the organizational chart, it languished in practice. The real power of OMB rested with the budget examiners. Management staff simply lacked the clout to influence agency personnel, let alone the budget examiners.

Although maligned for its management failures, OMB did leap at some opportunities. The Paperwork Reduction Act of 1980 established the OMB Office of Information and Regulatory Affairs (OIRA) to coordinate the information collection activities of federal agencies, with a thrust toward reducing their cost to government, businesses, and individuals. OIRA was also given other information management responsibilities, such as developing information resources management policies, promoting greater information sharing among agencies, and overseeing planning for the use of computers and other information technology.

Within two months of the law's enactment, newly inaugurated President Reagan added to OIRA's powers with Executive Order 12291, which called for review of agency regulations according to a test of economic costs and benefits. OIRA combined this process with paperwork clearance to create an integrated review system.

This regulatory and paperwork review process has become one of the most controversial and politically charged activities in OMB's history. With it, OMB has subordinated its management improvement mandate to that of political censor—reviewing substantive agency decisions for consistency with presidential policies and priorities. Not surprisingly, OIRA's emergence as the president's "hit man" in such areas as occupational health and safety, environmental protection, and food and drugs has contributed to OMB's image as being overly politicized. Nearly all nonpartisan observers now decry the loss of OMB's "neutral competence."

OIRA will play a significant role in the next Administration for several reasons. First and foremost is that the Paperwork Reduction Act was to be reauthorized in 1989 but still has not been. The Chamber of Commerce and the National Federation of Independent Business, along with other business interests, have waged a campaign to grant OMB *greater* review authority over agency actions. In particular, they want to overturn the February 21, 1990, U.S. Supreme Court *Dole v. United Steelworkers of America* decision dealing with worker exposure to hazardous chemicals, which limits OMB's paperwork review authority. Labor unions and public interest groups, however, strongly oppose overturning the Supreme Court decision and favor greater public access to and accountability of the regulatory review process. But because President Bush promised to veto any legislation encroaching on what he has called presidential prerogative, Congress has been stalemated on reauthorization of the Paperwork Reduction Act.

Second, there has been no administrator of OIRA since 1989. The Paperwork Reduction Act requires the administrator to be confirmed by the Senate. The Senate is not prepared to confirm an administrator while the act remains unauthorized.

Finally, the emergence of the Quayle Council on Competitiveness as overseer of OMB's actions has punctuated the politics of this relatively new process—one in which big business interests outrank and outflank protection of the public. At the Quayle council's urging, for example, President Bush initiated a ninety-day regulatory moratorium during his 1992 State of the Union address; the moratorium, upon its conclusion, was extended for another four months. The moratorium also required agencies to review all existing rules and report to Quayle on how to revise regulations that "hinder growth."

Bush exempted from the moratorium all regulatory "emergencies" and initiatives dealing with "imminent danger to human health or safety." Although there was little explanation of what this meant, White House counsel C. Boyden Gray stated on the *MacNeil/Lehrer Newshour* that "exempted from this moratorium are regulations . . . which are necessary to protect against harm to the safety of workers or to the environment." Yet the very day that Secretary of Labor Lynn Martin reaffirmed that no worker health and safety rules would be affected, OMB rejected an OSHA regulation dealing with exposure to hazardous substances used in the construction, maritime, and agriculture industries.[1] According to OSHA, eight to thirteen lives are lost each year because of exposure to these toxics.

Indeed, to date the Quayle council has interfered with numerous health, safety, and, in particular, environmental regulations by secretly inserting weakening changes designed to benefit affected industries. Quayle's antipathy toward government regulation was made clear in an address to business lobbyists, where, speaking of agency regulators, he said, "[T]hey have met the enemy, and it's called the Competitiveness Council." And Quayle boasted about the council's style of operation to *Washington Post* reporters David Broder and Bob Woodward, claiming that it "leaves no fingerprints" on regulations it meddles with.

First Steps for the New President

REGULATORY REVIEW

On February 17, 1981, shortly after taking office, President Reagan issued Executive Order 12291, "Federal Regulation." Reagan's Executive Order 12291 went far beyond its predecessors by requiring that agencies not only assess the economic costs and benefits of every proposed rule but also be guided by the results of those assessments as reviewed and interpreted by OMB.

Strictly speaking, E.O. 12291 does not grant OMB control of agency regulations. The order states that its requirements shall not be "construed as displacing the agencies' responsibilities delegated by law." Yet an agency cannot issue a rule until completion of the OMB review. As a practical matter, this gives OMB veto power over agency regulations.

OMB interference in agency decisionmaking under E.O. 12291 has ranged from delaying to changing and halting regulations as diverse as pollution prevention requirements on manufacturing firms, consumer product safety requirements, safety standards in the workplace concerning asbestos and grain dust, underground storage of dangerous chemicals, and worker exposure to hazardous chemicals. OMB's actions in these cases have been documented and criticized in academic studies, congressional hearings, and court decisions.

The Reagan Administration, however, was far from satisfied with E.O. 12291. In 1984, Douglas Ginsburg, then head of OIRA, said: "Agencies have been working on proposed regulations long before they come to notice and comment. Then we get ourselves in a confrontation with the agency over the end product."

The solution was found in Executive Order 12498, which established a "regulatory planning process." The order had three significant elements:
- It increased the scope of OMB review of agency rulemaking to include "prerulemaking" activities. Prerulemaking includes *any* activity that *may* lead to regulatory action at some future date.
- Unlike E.O. 12291, which halts rulemaking only until OMB finishes its review, E.O. 12498 prohibits an agency from doing *any* work unless OMB gives the go-ahead.

- The standard of review is not a single objective, such as cost/benefit analysis, but rather a broader concern about "consistency with administration policies and priorities"—in essence, a political litmus test.

While a few cases of E.O. 12498 review have received public attention, most have not. It is nearly impossible to determine OMB's role, because the entire process is cloaked in secrecy. The only product available to the public is a description of what has been approved by OMB; those proposals disapproved never appear.

In the last year of the Reagan administration, the president issued three executive orders that increase OMB's control of agency regulations. These orders, "The Family" (E.O. 12606), "Federalism" (E.O. 12612), and the so-called "Takings" (E.O. 12630), add substantive criteria to the generic themes of the regulatory review orders.[2]

The combination of regulatory review with the paperwork clearance process created by the Paperwork Reduction Act of 1980 gave an additional dimension to OMB review of agency decisions. Under the Act (discussed in the following section), OMB reviews information collection activities, many of which lead to or are required by regulations. Consequently, OMB rejection of agency "paperwork" can have a significant impact on agency regulatory activities.

The paperwork process is far more open than the regulatory review process, and provides substantial documentation of OMB interference in agency rulemaking through paperwork review. Examples range from the development of reporting standards under the Pollution Prevention Act to prerulemaking studies of the health risks of personal cosmetics. Probably the best-known example was OMB's interference with OSHA's worker right-to-know regulation, which was held up and altered despite repeated court orders. The Supreme Court ruled in this case that OMB had misused its authority under the Act and that OMB should not be reviewing third-party notifications (e.g., information not collected by the government even though it may be required by the government, such as labeling notices) under the Act. (The Court did not go as far as to say that OMB did not have the authority to review third-party notifications under its other powers, such as regulatory review executive orders.)

The Reagan-Bush regulatory program has been a flagrant misuse of executive power. It has gone beyond the constitutional mandate that the president "take care that the laws be faithfully executed," by subordinating statutory mandates and agency discretion to the political priorities of the president. And it undercuts the Administrative Procedure Act, especially its requirement for public participation in agency decisionmaking, for by the time the public is informed, the most significant decisions have already been made—with the Quayle council's and OMB's unrecorded pressure.

To address the systemic problem, one must return to basic principles: Substantive decisionmaking should rest with those who possess substantive expertise and authority. This can only be the agencies, which exercise authority delegated to them by Congress. The issue, therefore, is not simply one of centralized regulatory review, but centralized review that interferes with or controls substantive agency decisionmaking. Review to eliminate duplication or unnecessarily burdensome agency activities is not synonymous with review for consistency with presidential policies and priorities. Unfortunately, at OMB, the search for effective *management* has been subverted by the desire for unilateral political *control*.

To reorient OMB regulatory review, the new President should take the following steps:

1. *Change the focus of the Council on Competitiveness and OMB.* The Bush administration has argued that the regulatory moratorium and the work of the council is a key element in revitalizing the economy. This notion is absurd. Even conservative pundits have found it hard to believe that the regulatory moratorium will boost the economy, especially after living through the S&L debacle. In practice, the council's form of "competitiveness" is nothing more than a euphemism that cloaks micromanagement of a dizzying array of scientific and technical matters better left to agency experts.

It is appropriate for the White House genuinely to coordinate the regulatory policies of government agencies. After all, these agencies are led by presidential appointees, and presumably support the administration's general philosophy. The problem does remain that too many regulatory agencies act without coordination, in a duplicative or even contradictory manner.

Rather than dismiss the Council on Competitiveness, the new President should continue to make its work a high priority, emphasizing the importance of making America competitive. The council's agenda, however, should shift from promoting deregulation to a coordinated initiative on what it means to invest in America to make it economically competitive in the world today.

2. *Rescind the regulatory review executive orders,* especially E.O. 12291 and E.O. 12498.[3] This should be accompanied by implementation of a significantly revised regulatory review process. All regulatory reviews conducted by entities outside the regulatory agency should be conducted in the sunshine so the public knows what is being reviewed and has an opportunity to participate, consistent with the Administrative Procedure Act and the Freedom of Information Act.

Records of all communications, written and oral, with OMB and other reviewing entities concerning a regulatory proposal should be placed in a public record. A ninety-day time limit should be established for review of regulations. And most important, any comments by reviewing entities must be explained in writing and be placed in the public record. Comments from reviewing entities should not, however, compel agencies to refrain from or to take any specific action.

The new Administration can make these changes unilaterally and immediately. It should also work with Congress to codify these changes and pass added legislation that may be necessary.

MANAGEMENT OF INFORMATION RESOURCES

One of the last acts of President Carter was to sign into law the Paperwork Reduction Act of 1980, which was partly designed to correct the failings of the Federal Reports Act of 1942. Under the 1980 act, OMB was given renewed power over government paperwork and other information activities.

The act eliminated the exemptions that had hobbled the 1942 act, to ensure OMB review of virtually all federal information collection activities (including surveys, questionnaires, and record-keeping requirements) that affect ten or more people. It also mandated that OMB generally improve management of federal agency information activities through the concept of "information resources management" (IRM).

The IRM concept was undermined by Reagan's OMB, which viewed the Paperwork Reduction Act almost exclusively as a way to assist the administration's agenda of deregulation and reduction of Federal Government operations. OMB used the Act's paperwork clearance process as an adjunct to its regulatory review powers and virtually ignored the rest of the act. Federal programs suffered accordingly—from delays in releasing the new IRS W-4 tax form to second-guessing the formulation of the decennial census, and from weakening health research on worker exposure to dioxin and video display terminals to curtailing evaluation of housing programs.

OMB also thwarted the public's right to know in several ways. In 1981, OMB mandated wholesale cutbacks in agency publications. By early 1984, OMB claimed to have eliminated a quarter of all federal publications and reduced government spending on nearly another quarter. While costs were cut, the public also lost. Eliminated publications ranged from educational pamphlets, such as *Infant Care* and *Your Housing Rights,* to comprehensive reports, such as the annual *Geographic Distribution of Federal Funds,* which lists the distribution of federal program dollars by congressional district.[4]

When OMB finally issued its directive, Circular A-130, for the management of information resources in December 1985, it restricted information dissemination even further. It stated that unless specifically required by law, federal agencies should not disseminate information that "would otherwise be provided by other government or private sector organizations." OMB added that agencies should place "maximum feasible reliance on the private sector" in disseminating information to the public. This criterion is unprecedented in its subordination of public service information planning to the marketing whims of the private sector.

The free flow of information is the lifeblood of our democratic society— and the 1990s offer new opportunities to improve the flow of information from government to citizenry and the reverse. The new President will have an opportunity to establish federal policy on public access through promoting legislation that calls for affirmative responsibilities to disseminate information in electronic and other means, as well as by shaping the cultural climate within the bureaucracy.

More specifically, the new President should immediately:

• Issue a final Circular A-130 that articulates the government's responsibility to disseminate government information, including in electronic formats, in a timely, equal, and equitable manner. It is essential that federal policy ensure that those without adequate resources are not restricted from access to information.

• Encourage agencies to develop directories of information resources and make such information publicly available.

• Initiate a public/private sector task force to develop standards for collecting, handling, and storing electronic information, as well as more fully articulating public access needs.

Over the longer term, the President should:

• Work with Congress to advance a national information policy that encompasses the electronic information age.

• Implement a Federal Information Locator System that provides a publicly accessible "electronic yellow pages" of government's information and regulatory holdings. FILS should be able to expand in a way that permits the public access to various government databases and that allows the public to do business (e.g., order publications, complete forms).[5]

GRANTS MANAGEMENT AND INTERGOVERNMENTAL RELATIONS

State and local governments, working hand in hand with the private nonprofit, voluntary sector, have formed an integral partnership with the Federal Government in delivery of services to the public. From the delivery of day care to services for the aged; from job training to community development; from community services for low-income people to services for the disabled; from preschool programs to adult education; from general health care to mental health services, the Federal Government has traditionally depended on the nonprofit sector and state and local governments to help get the job done.

Despite the important connections and the need for continued partnerships, the relationship between these entities and the Federal Government has deteriorated, especially for the private nonprofit sector. At the heart of the problem are OMB's policies affecting intergovernmental activities and its grants management policies, which affect every federal agency and ultimately nonprofits.

As recommended in the 1981 transition report of the Heritage Foundation, in January 1983 OMB proposed to revise Circular A-122, *Cost Principles for Nonprofit Organizations*, to restrict greatly the role of nonprofits in public policy debates.

After fifteen months of controversy, more than 140,000 public comments, and several redrafts of its proposal, OMB issued a final rule that was greatly scaled back from the original.[6] Even though the final rule was not nearly as onerous as the original proposal, it has had a lasting chilling impact on the nonprofit sector. Even now, many nonprofits continue to fear that commenting on regulatory proposals, attending public hearings, or being involved in policy debates may cause them to lose their federal funds or pay heavy penalties.[7]

In 1988, OMB again demonstrated its antipathy toward the nonprofit sector with proposed nonprocurement (e.g., grants and loans) suspension and debarment rules that established a national computer blacklist—without adequate due process—of people and organizations deemed "irresponsible" or "seriously improper" and that would be barred from federal subsidies. After much controversy, OMB issued final rules that make the nonprocurement rules comparable to those for contractors, showing its lack of understanding about the nonprofit world.

There is great irony in OMB's attack on the nonprofit sector. OMB's stated goal is to stop the misuse of federal funds. However, there is neither evidence of significant violations of federal grant rules, nor of significant sums wasted out of the small portion of direct federal grants for nonprofits. On the other hand, federal procurement, which involves a much larger pool of federal funds, appears to be subject to considerable abuse—witness defense contracts. Nevertheless, OMB has never vigorously pursued procurement reform.

For the past three years, OMB has proposed massive cuts in postal subsidies that nonprofits receive when mailing for charitable purposes. Like the message of Circular A-122, the proposed cuts were targeted to mailings containing "political advocacy." OMB did not define political advocacy, leaving unclear whether there would be exemptions for nonpartisan analysis, discussions of broad social problems, or recommendations for policy changes.

Even if the information was not considered "political advocacy," OMB proposed that only schools could qualify for third-class nonprofit postal rates. Thus all other public charities would no longer receive postal subsidy.

The attack on the nonprofit community has seemed to come full circle with the May 24, 1991, U.S. Supreme Court *Rust* v. *Sullivan* decision to uphold Reagan-era regulations prohibiting recipients of Title X family planning funds from counseling patients about abortion. While the case was widely perceived as an abortion case, the fundamental issue is really freedom of speech. If it is constitutional to limit free speech about family planning options, why not limit the free speech of scientists conducting fetal tissue research or freedom of expression of artists receiving federal grants?

The *Rust* decision also renews the 1981 Circular A-122 "taint" principle all over again. The HHS-proposed regulation requires that "programs be organized so that they are physically and financially separate from other activities which are prohibited. . . ." HHS goes on to say that "while accounting separation is necessary, it is not sufficient. There must also be a visible separation between the Title X program and other activities which are prohibited from the Title X program."

The new President must take decisive action that alters the currently unhealthy relationship between the nonprofit, charitable community and the Federal Government. The President must immediately put an end to the ambiguity nonprofits face about exercising their right to advocate by issuing a governmentwide bulletin indicating a repudiation of the "taint" principles advocated by OMB and others over the past eleven years.

In addition, the President should appoint an advisory board, comprised of leaders from the nonprofit sector and government (federal, state, and local), to review policies and procedures affecting the nonprofit, charitable community and to recommend changes that will strengthen the partnership between government and nonprofits. Since the "Defund the left!" political slogan has become viewed as government principle, the new President's actions will be keenly watched by nonprofits as a guide to whether the relationship with government will change for the better.

NOTES

1. Secretary Martin's March 10, 1992, testimony was before the Senate Labor and Human Resources Committee. See letter of March 10, 1992, from James B. MacRae, Jr., acting OIRA administrator, to Nancy Risque-Rohrbach, assistant secretary for policy, Department of Labor. OMB claimed the rule would lead to wage cuts (because employers would have to spend more on complying with government regulations), and that since rich people are generally healthier than poor people, such a regulation might actually hurt more than help workers.

2. The Takings Executive Order invites property owners burdened by federal regulations to sue the government. But that's not all. It uses the prospects of those suits and their potential monetary awards as an excuse to reduce federal regulatory activity. Vice President Dan Quayle has vowed to place the order in statute.

3. The new President should also rescind three related executive orders that are largely implemented through regulatory review: "The Family" (E.O. 12606), "Federalism" (E.O. 12612), and the so-called "Takings" (E.O. 12630).

4. When Congress subsequently learned of the demise of this report, it voted to reinstate it by having the Census Bureau publish an annual report. Most other lost publications did not have constituencies with comparable power.

5. See Gary D. Bass and David Plocher, "Finding Government Information: The Federal Information Locator System (FILS)," *Government Information Quarterly*, 8 (1): 11. Also see Charles R. McClure, Ann Bishop, Philip Doty, and Pierrette Bergeron, "OMB and the Development of a Government-Wide Information Inventory/Locator System," *Government Information Quarterly*, 8 (1): 33.

6. The initial proposal, characterized as a "gag rule," would have: (1) redefined lobbying in such broad terms as to include nearly any type of public policy initiative, including commenting on proposed regulations at any level of government, and (2) disallowed federal payment for any activity covered by the new definition and any activity associated with it. Further, the disallowed activity and associated costs would then be "tainted" so that no portion of the costs, even when not involving the expanded definition of lobbying, could be billed to the Federal Government.

7. In 1986 the Internal Revenue Service proposed regulations implementing nonprofit lobbying provisions from the Tax Reform Act of 1976. The proposal was very similar to the OMB Circular A-122 proposed rule, adding to the confusion and nervousness of nonprofits. Thus between 1981 and 1990 the Federal Government waged a campaign that has been interpreted by many nonprofits as an attack on their advocacy voice.

PART VI

ENVIRONMENTAL POLICY

OVERVIEW: ENVIRONMENTAL POLICY

THOMAS B. STOEL, JR.

The Environmental Challenge

NOW THAT THE THREAT OF NUCLEAR WAR has receded, protection of the environment presents the single greatest challenge to the future of our country and the world. We face environmental problems that are unprecedented in scope. If we fail to solve them, the future for the United States and the rest of the world will be grim. And we cannot hope to solve them unless the next President of the United States provides more leadership than we have seen during the past twelve years.

The world's human population, now more than 5 billion, is growing by 1 billion people per decade; every ten years we are adding to the earth three times the population of North America. Throughout the world, economic activities are increasing to meet the needs of these additional people and to satisfy the hopes of all people for a better life. World economic output has tripled since 1950, and is estimated to triple again in the next fifty years— a ninefold increase in less than a century.

Life on earth depends on the complex web of water, air, land, and living things that provide us with clean air, fresh water, food, and other essential products and services. Because of rapid economic and population growth, human activities now are altering the conditions of this biosphere on a global scale and reducing its capacity to sustain life. The discovery that we are depleting the stratospheric ozone layer, through emissions of artificial chem-

Thomas B. Stoel, Jr., is an environmental attorney and consultant in Washington, D.C. He formerly was Director of the International Program at the Natural Resources Defense Council and President of the Global Tomorrow Coalition.

icals that only began to be produced in the 1950s, shows how quickly and fundamentally we can affect basic elements of the biosphere.

Similarly, scientists now are warning that emissions of greenhouse gases due to human activities will increase the temperature of the entire atmosphere significantly. One prominent scientist has said that we are playing Russian roulette with the climate.

The oceans also are threatened by human activities. We are depleting fish stocks on which humanity depends for much of its protein. Global warming may have profound effects on the oceans. Some fear that changes in the salinity of the North Atlantic Ocean due to melting of ice induced by global warming could cause the entire Gulf Stream to "shut off," as it apparently has in the past. This would be catastrophic, since the Gulf Stream carries twenty times more water than all the earth's rivers and contributes 30 percent as much heat as the sun to the North Atlantic region.

Since the beginning of this century, we have reduced substantially the earth's total amount of arable land through erosion and salinization, and have destroyed about half of the world's tropical forests. Due in large part to this forest loss, the earth's stock of animal and plant species—a priceless genetic heritage that was formed over millions of years and can never be replicated—is beginning to decline rapidly.

These and other human impacts on the biosphere are still accelerating. Effects that forty years ago were foreseen by only a few visionaries, such as widespread deforestation and desertification, are now apparent to any informed person. Effects that were unknown twenty years ago, such as depletion of the stratospheric ozone layer, now are subjects of intense international concern.

In addition to this global challenge, we face severe environmental problems within our own borders. Air pollution—urban smog, acid rain, and airborne toxic pollutants—remains a serious threat. We are overusing and polluting our groundwater. Because our nation is one of the greatest wasters of energy, we needlessly emit huge quantities of greenhouse gases and pollutants that are harmful to human health and natural systems. Human health also is threatened by improper disposal of hazardous wastes and by pesticides and other toxic substances.

Our federal lands are badly managed. Overgrazing is doing further harm to already damaged western rangelands—this is our contribution to the global phenomenon of desertification. Our national parks, the "crown jewels" of our federal lands, are being degraded by forces beyond their borders, such as acid rain and depletion of water supplies. The ancient forests of the Pacific Northwest are threatened by logging even as we urge poor countries to conserve the forests of the tropics.

The Past Twelve Years: A Legacy of Neglect

THE EXECUTIVE BRANCH LARGELY ABDICATED its environmental responsibilities during the twelve years between 1980 and 1992. Within days after his inauguration, President Reagan repealed U.S. controls over international trade in toxic substances. The United States, the first country to ban ozone-depleting chemicals, began to assert that the problem of ozone depletion did not exist. The Reagan administration tried to weaken important global institutions, such as the U.N. Environment Program. It refused to ratify the Law of the Sea Treaty—the product of years of negotiation in which a U.S. team led by Republican Elliot Richardson played a leading part. In 1984, a U.S. delegation led by Reagan administration ideologues tried to prevent the U.N. Population Conference in Mexico City from acting effectively to slow world population growth.

The Reagan record concerning the domestic environment was even worse. Under James Watt, the Interior Department actively promoted unsustainable exploitation of our federal lands. The Environmental Protection Agency under Ann Gorsuch Burford undermined, through lack of enforcement, the system of laws and regulations that protect human health from dangerous pollutants. The Energy Department's overriding concern was to maximize energy production regardless of harmful impact on the environment.

The Bush administration's record was little if any better. As described in the chapter by Sharon Camp, the Bush administration continued to deny funding to the U.N. Fund for Population Activities and the International Planned Parenthood Federation, thus hampering international support for family planning. Instead of leading the world toward cost-effective actions to minimize global warming, the Bush administration in May 1992 refused to sign a carefully negotiated U.N. treaty on climate change until it was stripped of provisions requiring industrialized nations to achieve specific reductions in their emissions of greenhouse gases. This threat was effective in part because the United States is the world's largest emitter of greenhouse gases. A month later, President Bush refused to sign a pathbreaking international agreement aimed at conserving the earth's biological diversity. That treaty was signed by more than 150 countries, including all the other major industrial nations.

On the domestic side, the White House Council on Competitiveness acted behind the scenes to prevent effective implementation of the 1990 amendments to the Clean Air Act and attempted to open half of all U.S. wetlands to development. In these and other areas, the Competitiveness Council, with approval from President Bush, sabotaged environmental regulatory decisions based on *ex parte* arguments by industrial and commercial interests. Secretary of the Interior Manuel Lujan, a throwback to the time of James Watt, proposed to allow loggers to destroy the ancient forest ecosystem of the Pacific Northwest (including habitats of rare species such as the spotted owl), tried to permit oil drilling in the fragile Arctic National Wildlife Refuge, and sought to continue federal subsidies that promote overgrazing of rangelands and overuse of scarce western water.

What the Next President Should Do

TO MEET THE ENVIRONMENTAL CHALLENGE and reverse this legacy of neglect, we must make fundamental changes in our foreign and domestic environmental policies—changes that can occur and continue only if the forty-second President furnishes inspiration and guidance.

EARLY ACTIONS

If environmental protection is to be a priority for the next Administration, the President must take key actions in its first hundred days.

To signal his strong interest in environmental protection, the President should, within a few days after taking office, issue executive orders putting into effect reforms recommended in these chapters, not only to undo bad policies as soon as possible but also to signal his strong concern about environmental protection.

Early in 1993 the President also should:

• *Deliver a major environmental message to the Congress and the nation* that lays out his domestic environmental program and the elements of his environmental foreign policy. This environmental message will achieve purposes beyond the programmatic initiatives it announces. The process of preparing it will compel key figures in the new Administration to focus early on environmental policies at a time when environmental issues might otherwise be pushed aside, a point discussed in the chapter by past Environmental Protection Agency official William Drayton. The message also will ensure that Congress addresses the President's environmental proposals early in the 103d Congress; will help to mobilize a citizen constituency for the President's proposals; and will notify foreign leaders that this President will make the environment a cornerstone of his foreign policy.

• *Carefully organize and staff the Executive Branch to meet the environmental challenge.* The President should name a person of stature and great ability to be the administrator of the Environmental Protection Agency. The administrator should be a member of his cabinet, and the EPA upgraded to a cabinet department.

The President should act early to establish high-level interagency groups to ensure governmentwide action on key issues—such as global warming, sustainable development in developing countries, and population stabilization—that cut across agency lines. In particular, he should abolish the White House Competitiveness Council and establish a White House Council on the Environment and the Economy, chaired by the Vice President and charged with ensuring that environmental and economic policies (both domestic and international) are mutually reinforcing and that relevant decisions are based on the best environmental and economic evidence.

• *Establish a fair and open decisionmaking process.* The back-room decisions of the past twelve years can no longer be tolerated. A fair and open process is especially important in the environmental arena. Governmental actions to protect the environment often benefit large numbers of people while initially imposing economic costs on a much smaller number of individuals or businesses. In this situation, it usually is easier for the economic interests that oppose environmental protection to lobby quietly for their position than it is for the millions of citizens who would benefit from greater protection. If decisions are to be fair and reflect the real costs and benefits, it is essential that the decisionmaking process be accessible to everyone, including individuals and national and local citizen groups.

To correct abuses, the next President should announce that whenever he or his staff decides to review a proposed environmental regulation or other action, all interested parties will have the right to participate and to see the proposals that have been made by others.

At all levels of federal decisionmaking, the new Administration should make special efforts to ensure that citizens who are often excluded—such as poor people and members of minority groups—can participate effectively in environmental decisions that affect them. Federal agencies should be required to establish procedures that facilitate this kind of participation, including public hearings in affected localities and, when necessary, federal grants for travel, technical assistance, and other essential expenses.

• *Act on key global issues.* Many important issues involving protection of the global environment are covered in the following chapters. In addition, the next Administration should move to remedy government neglect in three main areas:

1. *Global warming of the atmosphere.* The new Administration should make the United States a leader in this field by reducing our own greenhouse gas emissions, in ways discussed in the chapter on energy policy. In addition, we should provide assistance to developing nations to help them reduce their emissions, as recommended by Gus Speth in his discussion of North–South

relations on development. We should reverse our current position and urge rapid amendment of the recently negotiated climate change treaty to include goals and timetables for achieving specified reductions in greenhouse gas emissions.

2. *Loss of the earth's biological diversity*, due mainly to destruction of tropical forests and other habitats in developing nations. The United States must put its own house in order by acting to preserve our own endangered species and ecosystems, as well as pushing for concerted global action focused directly on habitat protection—subjects discussed by Albert Appleton and Gus Speth in this book. The United States should sign the U.N. Convention on Biological Diversity and then work to correct a major flaw in the convention: its failure to identify on a global basis those habitat areas that most need protection in view of their biological richness and the threats to their integrity. Without guidance of this kind, there can be no assurance that the resources deployed under the convention will be used to maximum effect.

3. *Protection of the oceans*. Here the first task for the new Administration should be to rectify another error of the Reagan-Bush years: the failure of the United States to ratify the 1982 U.N. Convention on the Law of the Sea. International cooperation under this pathbreaking convention is badly needed to protect the marine environment.

• *Propose a fully adequate environmental budget for fiscal year 1994.* It is essential that the budget proposed in February or March 1993—a budget that will govern federal expenditures until October 1994—include the resources required to meet pressing environmental needs.

The chapter by William Drayton, for example, details the urgent need for a larger EPA budget. To offset increased environmental expenditures, the next Administration should work with Congress to curtail environmentally destructive, economically wasteful subsidies for irrigating surplus crops, pork-barrel water projects, below-cost timber sales from national forests, and the like. Additional revenues can be generated by imposing fees on environmentally harmful activities, including emissions of carbon dioxide that contribute to the greenhouse effect, and on those who use federal resources.

LONGER-TERM ACTIONS
The next Administration's main longer-term concern in the environmental arena should be to implement fully the initiatives of its first hundred days. In addition to the actions proposed in the following chapters, there are two important cross-cutting needs: to build a political consensus in support of

the Administration's environmental agenda, and to establish a new framework for environmental policy.

• *The new Administration's environmental agenda cannot be enacted or sustained without actions to ensure a political consensus.* In addition to delivering an early environmental message (and making this message an annual event), the President should convene in 1994 a White House Conference on a Sustainable Future, resuming a tradition begun by Theodore Roosevelt, who in 1908 hosted the highly influential Governors' Conference on Natural Resources. The participants in this White House Conference should include governors, mayors, members of Congress, scientists, educators, environmentalists, and representatives of business, labor, religious, women's, minority, and other interests. The purpose should be to promote wide understanding of the environmental problems we face and to build broad support for actions to ensure a sound environment *and* a sound economy. The conference could be linked to processes in individual states and cities aimed at ensuring sustainability at those levels.

• *The new Administration's environmental initiatives will be short-lived if the nation continues to be plagued by the notion that we must choose between American jobs and a clean environment.* The alleged conflict between economic growth and environmental protection is probably the biggest obstacle to U.S. environmental progress. Because of our influence in the world, it also may be the largest barrier to global environmental protection.

Yet from the viewpoint of most U.S. citizens, there is no fundamental conflict between economic and environmental objectives—they are complementary parts of a larger effort to improve the quality of life. Part of the problem is that we are using false measures of economic progress. Something must be wrong when one of our major measures of economic improvement—maximizing the Gross National Product—tells us that pollution is a benefit because the cost of cleaning up pollution adds to the GNP. The new Administration should devise and use better measures.

Another part of the problem is that the Federal Government is contributing financially to environmental destruction. Federal subsidies such as those for logging in national forests, grazing on western public lands, and overuse of scarce water harm the environment, the federal budget, and our economy. The new President should seek to eliminate these subsidies while working with affected industries and regions to ease the transition to economic activities that pay their own way and are environmentally sound.

Finally, the Administration should work with the business community to take advantage of the opportunities presented by the worldwide need for environmental protection. Many believe that in the next few decades the market for "environment-friendly" goods and services will be the largest market in history. Japanese and European firms are gearing up to meet that demand. The United States is currently a leader in that market and can be even stronger in the future. However, for our businesses to succeed in this field, U.S. environmental standards must remain high. If goods made for the U.S. market are not required to be at the environmental cutting edge, our companies will lose out in the larger global marketplace.

• *The next Administration's environmental policies should be based on four fundamental principles*:

1. *Follow a long-term, comprehensive approach in managing natural resources.* As illustrated by the severe overgrazing of federal lands in the West, federal management of natural resources too often has been short-term and piecemeal, usually in response to the narrow interests of influential "client groups." As a result, we are left with a natural resource base that is degraded and vulnerable to further destruction.

It is essential that the new Administration abandon these shortsighted policies and follow a "stewardship" approach aimed at ensuring long-run sustainability. National parks and other unique ecosystems should be managed *as* ecosystems, under management systems that ensure the ecological integrity of these areas and take into account threats from outside their borders, such as threats to water supplies. Funds for resource management must be made available on a steady, long-term basis. Much of this can be accomplished through executive orders or changes in regulations, but some new legislation will be needed (e.g., the antiquated Mining Law of 1872 should be replaced by an environmentally sensitive statute).

2. *Achieve environmental goals at least cost.* In the early 1970s the United States began a crash effort to reduce air and water pollution. We relied mainly on detailed governmental regulations enforced by strong penalties. Typically, polluters were allowed to emit specific amounts of pollution based on estimates of technological feasibility and were subject to fines or even imprisonment if they exceeded these limits.

We have come to see that this "command and control" approach has severe drawbacks:

A. By telling all polluters in an industry that they must meet the same goals, it does not allow society to benefit from the fact that some polluters can eliminate a given amount of pollution more cheaply than others.

B. By focusing on short-run, "end of the pipe" methods of cleaning up pollution, it does little to encourage changes in industrial processes or other techniques that can prevent pollution entirely.

C. By imposing penalties so severe that they rarely are enforced, it encourages polluters to ignore legal requirements in the belief that they will get off with a small fine or no penalty at all.

D. By allowing polluters to emit certain amounts of pollution without any penalty, it provides no incentive to continue reducing pollution after the legal limit has been reached.

The EPA is already moving away from this approach. The new Administration should accelerate this process by:

A. Encouraging fundamental changes in production and consumption that prevent pollution from occurring at all. For example, the use of energy-conserving light bulbs can avoid the necessity of building environmentally harmful power plants.

B. Allowing pollution permits to be traded so that pollution control is undertaken by those who can reduce emissions at the least cost.

C. Using fees and charges as a way of discouraging environmentally harmful activities. For example, to discourage activities that contribute to global warming, a carbon dioxide fee should be included in the cost of gasoline and other fuels that contain carbon. The resulting revenues could be used to reduce the federal deficit, to fund environmental protection activities, or to replace other taxes, such as those on incomes or payrolls.

D. Requiring polluters to pay when they emit even small amounts of pollution, thus providing an incentive to reduce pollution to the lowest feasible level and generating revenues that can pay for governmental costs of pollution control.

E. Compelling polluters and others to pay the full cost of activities that might cause environmental damage, including not only the cost of any environmental harm but also the cost to the government of controlling or preventing harm.

F. Whenever possible, setting clear environmental goals and leaving it to businesses to decide how to meet them.

3. *Base environmental decisions on the best evidence of costs and benefits.* Some in industry and the Bush Administration argue that environmental regulation is warranted only when there is scientific certainty that serious harm will occur in the absence of regulation. This attitude ignores the risk we run when we do *not* act to protect the environment. It led, for example, to delays in controlling ozone-depleting chemicals, thereby subjecting the world to higher levels of harmful ultraviolet radiation, and it prevented actions to combat global warming.

On the other side, some environmentalists argue that environmental decisions should not include any weighing of costs and benefits—if something is good for the environment, it should be done regardless of cost. But in the real world, decisionmakers inevitably will take economic costs into account. If there is no established process for doing so, the costs may be exaggerated because the only evidence comes from affected industries. And failure to analyze the benefits of regulation may cause decisionmakers to ignore major environmental problems or to spend large amounts to eliminate minuscule risks. Of course, the benefits taken into account must include not only those that can be expressed in dollars but also in less tangible benefits, such as conservation of animal and plant species whose value is not yet known or preservation of especially beautiful natural areas, unsullied views, and other joys to the spirit.

The new Administration should base its environmental decisions on the best evidence of costs and benefits. To ensure that decisionmakers have the best evidence, the Administration should strengthen the mechanisms by which the National Academy of Sciences and other expert bodies can make objective assessments of costs and benefits in specific situations. It should make special efforts to ensure that it has objective estimates of the *economic* impacts of proposed actions to protect the environment, so it will not have to rely solely on estimates by affected industries.

4. *Empower citizens.* One environmental success story of the 1980s was the requirement that businesses publicly report the amounts of toxic substances released from specific facilities. The resulting public concern caused many polluters to find ways to reduce their emissions. Another success story involved the "citizen suit" provisions of the Clean Water Act, under which citizens and citizen groups won many lawsuits against companies that violated pollution regulations.

Building on these experiences, the next Administration should further empower citizens by supporting legislation that would require more public reporting by companies on their use and production of toxic substances. It should also seek to broaden the right of citizens to sue polluters that violate federal laws and federal agencies that fail to enforce those laws.

All these short- and long-term steps are needed to meet our grave environmental challenges. U.S. leadership, beginning after World War II and continuing for more than forty years, brought the Cold War to a successful conclusion. The next President should launch—in the first hours of his Administration—an equally strong and determined effort to meet the new global threat.

ENVIRONMENTAL PROTECTION[1]

WILLIAM DRAYTON

Summary

I N THE 1970S THE SECOND GREAT WAVE of public health legislation in U.S. history promised protection from the tens of thousands of man-made substances pouring into the environment. Since then science has corroborated the problem, and new laws have compounded the government's load.

There is also mounting evidence of significant damage to the world's ecosystems, including the climate and oceans. We have also learned that the most important environmental interventions are not atop smokestacks but far earlier in economic, energy, research, and tax decisionmaking.

For the past twelve years, however, the Federal Government made it impossible to implement the new laws to control toxics. It ghettoized the field and deeply damaged its institutions.

The new Administration will want to provide the promised protections and undo the damage. It will have to innovate and manage skillfully at each step of the process:

• *Research*. Strategically managed research on indoor pollution, the synergistic effects of multiple substances on health, waste disposal alternatives, and many other critical unknowns would save both lives and billions of dollars. We need boldly focused researchers backed by new approaches and resources greater than the current levels of slightly more than 0.5 percent of

William Drayton, a former Assistant Administrator of the Environmental Protection Agency (1977–81) and MacArthur Fellow, was a McKinsey & Co. consultant for nine years and is currently President of Ashoka: Innovators for the Public, and Chair of Environmental Safety and of Appropriate Technology International.

government environmental expenditures and some 0.0006 percent of society's overall cleanup budget.

• *Screening*. Tens of thousands of chemicals in commerce and pesticides in the food chain will remain untested regardless of the laws until economic, reliable, short tests for the full array of health risks (not just cancer) are devised. The new Administration should create a national challenge competition to fill this critical missing link.

• *Standards*. Illustrating the need for clearer standards is the regulatory backlog concerning major cross-border risks, including climate change; the importance of ending long logjams in key areas, including pesticides and toxic substances; and the growing recognition that very serious problems remain in "conventional" areas such as drinking water and particulate air pollution. Once the Administration frees research, makes broad chemical screening possible, and installs effective monitoring systems for toxins, the pace and intelligence of standard-setting (and follow-on field compliance work) should accelerate sharply.

• *Compliance*. Restoring voluntary compliance will require regaining the confidence of millions of decisionmakers roughly simultaneously. Presidential leadership, attention-riveting process change, and credible follow-through will all be necessary.

• *Infrastructure*. Public investment in water and sewer systems lags behind needs hopelessly and must be reformed to encourage innovation, modular production with much enhanced reliability, far lower unit costs, and export sales. Private environmental investment is far larger. Its demand should undergird a major export industry but doesn't. Intelligent incentives are needed here as well.

• *Work load*. In the first several years of the 1980s, EPA's work load doubled as all the new statutes enacted to protect the public against man-made toxins reached the stage requiring field implementation. The impact on the states was even greater. Since then Congress has added further requirements, and the decline in voluntary compliance has sharply increased both the number of cases and the amount of staff time required per case. The Reagan administration, nonetheless, tried to cut EPA's budget by two thirds. Tremendous rebuilding is necessary. Added resources and many new, smarter ways of approaching the work will both be essential. For example, emulating relatively successful securities and financial regulation, we should create certified environmental auditors, paid for by business but strongly accountable to the public, to evaluate and certify that regulatees are performing in a generally safe manner.

America led this century's historic movement toward a safe environment and a sustainable relationship with nature. A decade of consumption of all forms of capital has, however, not spared the environment. Bold, strategic management and leadership are essential now if America is to catch up to the historic need.

A Greek Tragedy

IN 1981 TWO HISTORIC EVENTS COLLIDED: the second great wave of public health law in U.S. history, and the Reagan administration. The effects of this encounter have unfolded over the ensuing dozen years with the fatefulness of a classical Greek tragedy.

PROLOGUE

At the beginning of the 1970s America set out to control the few relatively easily observed pollutants then recognized as problems. By 1980, environmental regulation had reduced many of these pollutants significantly. For example, clean water regulation had cut biological oxygen demand by 71 percent, phosphate demand by 74 percent, and heavy-metals demand by 78 percent.

However, within a few years of the EPA's birth, science was demonstrating that hundreds of other substances man had let loose were dangerous (albeit often invisible). The public demanded action. Large bipartisan majorities in Congress and presidents of both parties joined to launch the second public health revolution in American history. Just as an earlier generation insisted on the "sanitary revolution" once it understood that biological contaminants were responsible for cholera and other epidemics, in the 1970s America promised itself to control man-made contaminants.

Over 1976–80, the country enacted a dozen major statutes promising protection. Tens of thousands of suspect substances were to be screened for safety and regulated when necessary. Drinking water, food, the air, where we work and live, the products and materials we use, and our lands were to be made safe again.

Moreover, our rivers and streams were to become "fishable and swimmable." The smog obscuring national park vistas was to disappear. We promised to protect all life, and the quality of life.

By 1981 it was time to deliver on all these promises. The preparatory research and regulations were done. They had to be turned into real safeguards changing behavior in hundreds of thousands of firms and communities. Government data showed that doing so would double EPA's ongoing work load by 1983–84.

UNDOING

But in January 1981, the Reagan administration came to office with a very different agenda—to *remove* the regulatory restraints, most especially EPA's, that it perceived to be limiting personal freedom and economic growth.

Recognizing the likely failure and huge political cost of trying to repeal major environmental laws, the administration set out instead to neuter their institutions. First it sought to cut EPA's (inflation-adjusted) budget by more than 60 percent. Requiring any organization suddenly to do twice the job with half the budget ensures damage.

The administration's personnel policies were even more radical. EPA's work is enormously technical and depends on complex patterns of specialization and interaction developed over years of institution-building. (Three quarters of the agency's senior civil servants in 1980 were scientists and engineers.) The administration, blocked only at the last moment, planned a series of "reorganizations" and firings that, using its own figures, would have meant that by June 1982 only three hundred of the fifty-four hundred headquarters and research staffers would still have been at their desks.

This fateful collision of an administration committed to radical "regulatory relief" with the country's historic wave of environmental decisions caused profound damage, damage that defined and limited the prospects for the following ten years:

- By the mid-1980s the typical EPA protective program lost 20 to 40 percent of its purchasing power—far less than the administration planned but still devastating. The water program, for exmple, is smaller now than in the 1970s but nonetheless must manage three times the number of regulatees (not including millions of "nonpoint"—e.g., agricultural runoff—sources) and twenty times the number of pollutants. EPA has also lost critical experts, monitoring coverage, and long-term databases. The states cannot fill the breach: Their job has grown faster than EPA's, and they, too, have lost capacity.

- Business confidence that competitors were being made to comply with environmental laws was compromised, and with it the voluntary compliance so essential to effective regulation. Consequently, by 1984 business *cut* abatement investments 38 percent—just as the new laws should have made them jump. By late 1983 the General Accounting Office reported 78 percent *non*compliance with one of the highest-priority hazardous waste requirements and 82 percent *non*compliance (largely continuous and gross) with the Clean Water Act. This lost confidence multiplied the regulators' work load many times: Going from 98 to 96 percent compliance doubles the number of firms requiring enforcement action. Consider what 80 percent *non*compliance—even 10 to 20 percent—means.

• Repeated government studies find EPA able to undertake only token portions of its statutory responsibilities. For example, of the 66,000 existing chemicals in commerce that EPA was supposed to review for safety over the 1980s, it incompletely screened less than 1 percent.

• Scandals damaged the agency's reputation for professionalism—essential for a quasi-judicial organization. Most of the administration's early presidential appointees, including Administrator Gorsuch, were forced out under clouds. The assistant administrator responsible for the Superfund program went to jail.

The administration's early shock policies largely succeeded; but, once made visible, they triggered public alarm. To "anesthetize" the issue it appointed new moderate leadership. William Ruckelshaus, Lee Thomas, and William Reilly restored professional standards—and political calm. Their decency and professionalism preserved much of an excellent institution. Consequently, rebuilding remains possible.

Still, EPA's recent administrators have operated within narrow constraints. Bill Reilly's public humiliation by the White House at the June 1992 world environmental summit in Brazil was only a particularly visible demonstration of how little room for initiative EPA has had since 1981. All three post-Gorsuch administrators tellingly had to defend budgets that make it impossible for their agency to do its job.[2]

Hunkered down defensively, ghettoized within the administration, leading a siege-insecure staff, and confronting key constituencies and a Congress with little trust in their administrations, they could move the field only modestly.

Renaissance

THE NEXT ADMINISTRATION MUST CATCH UP with fast-moving, historic changes too long denied:

• Several key statutes to control toxins don't work, and none is being implemented well.
• Evidence of significant damage to major ecosystems (from climate to oceans) is mounting.
• The most important environmental interventions are not atop smokestacks, but in structural economics; tax, energy, research policy; and other underattended areas. New approaches and new collaborations, globally and at home, are necessary.

To succeed, the next Administration will have to rebuild capacity, esprit, and credibility; pull down the ghetto walls; and experiment widely.

• *Rebuilding*: The first prerequisite for success is to rebuild the country's environmental team. They have extraordinarily complex and rapidly changing responsibilities. They need equivalent authority; respect; and some combination of new resources, methods, and incentives. They need a non-bureaucratic, decentralized-yet-integrated organizational framework that encourages initiative *and* collaboration. Scapegoating must stop.

Among the environmental agencies, the risk of EPA's seizing up is greatest. It urgently needs a coherent team of appointees who are sensitive, skilled managers, not just political and policywise individuals.

• *Thinking again*. These managers' first challenge will be to free their environmental staffers from their mental bunkers—to release the energy, creativity, and confidence they need to conjure up intelligent solutions to this field's constantly emerging problems in time—that is, to think ahead of the curve. A few examples:

1. We are ignoring major areas of risk—for example, indoor pollution. Because pollutants are trapped inside, concentrations there are typically far higher than outside. People (especially the frail and vulnerable) spend much of their lives indoors. Yet the White House over the 1980s has fought to eliminate even research regarding indoor pollution, lest it trigger new regulations. Indoor pollution of all sorts deserves priority attention. Some conventional areas—for example, particulates and drinking water—also pose levels of risk warranting priority review.

2. Knowing the levels of particular pollutants accurately in the air, water, inside structures, and on land is fundamental for research, policy, standard-setting, and compliance. EPA built national monitoring networks for the traditional pollutants it went after in 1970, but so far it has not contrived even effective monitoring tools for the newer toxic pollutants.

3. The synergistic and cumulative impact of pollutants is significantly different from and often more serious than the sum of the impacts of the individual substances. Yet the field's approach at each level (research, legislation, standards, field implementation) deals with one pollutant in one medium almost in isolation. This is an area that requires not only scientific research but also dramatic organizational creativity and experimentation.

4. There are whole programs that need fundamental reexamination. For example, why has the toxic substances program accomplished so very much less than the air program dollar for dollar? What changes are needed, and how might they be made to fly politically?

5. America's environment will be affected more and more by international decisions—for example, by China's new coal-fired power plants. What concrete policies, what bargains might we propose to the world to deal with such cross-border questions?

When EPA's people once again take the initiative and engage such challenges with excitement and pleasure, then these issues will be well on the way to resolution.

Firing this energy will take serious investment and leadership. For example, in the research area, an early Reagan target, it will take three to five years' determined work to rebuild the lost capacity, public and private—the closed laboratories, the senior researchers who have refocused their careers elsewhere, and the wide gaps in the ranks of graduate students and junior researchers.

The New Administration

BY INAUGURATION DAY

The new Administration must break with the past in two key areas before Inauguration Day. First, it must replace the outgoing administration's budget or live with the past's priorities for most of its first two years. This is a problem affecting all agencies, but the risks for EPA are especially great.

Those OMB staff who carried out the cuts are unlikely to propose significant change. Usually EPA gets its senior presidential appointees late, long after State and Defense. Consequently there may be no appointees of the new Administration at the agency until well after the budget has gone to Congress. Even if there are, they may not be familiar with EPA's complex budget and management needs. If so, it will be very difficult for the Administration-elect to turn the agency around.

Even with quick, significant budget relief beginning in October 1993, it will be well into the new Administration before the Agency can begin to rebuild. It is urgent that the transition staff devote a good deal of its time to ensuring that the President-elect, his White House staff, and eventually his EPA appointees have and focus quickly on an honest, nonincremental set of budget options.

The Administration-elect's environmental staffers should also begin immediately to contribute collegially to solving immediate policy issues—for example, how to develop trade policies that won't leave the President (and the environment) caught in a no-win crossfire.

Second, the President-elect must think through how he wants to manage his line agencies. Does he want to lead through his line appointees? Or will he rely chiefly on large White House and OMB staffs, who in turn will try to keep the departments in line through a series of controls? Given the painful history, this is an especially sensitive choice for EPA and several of the other regulatory agencies.

Almost all recent presidents have started off saying that they planned to follow the first model but have in fact fallen 70 to 90 percent into the second path. This pattern is largely set in the months right after the election. The President needs immediate help on his budget, and OMB is ready. He needs other immediate staffing help, and the senior political and personal advisers who ran his campaign are the obvious, tried people to whom he will turn. Their skills, stature, and role make them gravitate to White House jobs.

By contrast, most of the President's cabinet appointees are not yet in place, let alone in effective control; and their deputies and assistants have not yet gone to, let alone emerged from, the by then clogged FBI clearance process. So lacking a clear alternate vision of how he should lead and manage, the President by Inauguration Day will probably have created a large White House staff and have begun to operate through it and OMB. This structure makes it likely that many of the past decades' all-too-familiar repeat failings of the presidency will recur.

The problem of executive office/line department relationships is probably more troubled in the regulatory field and for EPA specifically than it is in most other parts of the government. The agency perceives itself, properly, as a quasi-judicial agency responsible for setting difficult regulatory balances defined by statutory criteria. Strong interventions by often junior executive office staffers responding to requests from regulated parties often have seemed improper, especially during administrations intent on rolling back regulations.

The new Administration needs a new approach if it is not to sink into this historical pattern of distrust, now etched in the behavior of the several bureaucracies and constituencies involved. If it shifts more authority to line appointees, making such a break will flow naturally. Even if the new President opts generally to work heavily through staff, he would be wise to insist on a redefinition of the particularly troubled executive office/EPA relationship.

This redesign should accomplish two key objectives. First, it should return true responsibility for balanced regulatory decisionmaking to the EPA administrator. Letting the White House escape the role of semiofficial court of last resort will allow it to shed a politically dangerous operating responsibility as well as put the burden for sensible decisions clearly with the one person and institution designed for the job.

Second, the President should find an effective way to lead the administrator and his other key regulators. He should give them—collectively and individually—clear objectives, challenge them to perform, and hold them accountable. Regulation is so important a functional crosscut of his Administration that it warrants this leadership investment. The common pattern of the President never seeing his regulators once appointed and leaving them to the small-scale agendas of junior OMB staffers is an invitation to drift and disappointment.[3]

The executive office staffs will gain, not lose, impact once their role changes to facilitating line agency relations with the President, serving as trustworthy managers of crosscutting decision processes, and focusing on presidential-scale issues.

THE PRESIDENT'S AGENDA

Serving the President's core agenda should be central to the environmental agenda. The President-elect will probably have the opportunity to lead the country and world to a very few historic decisions. How well he understands the historic moment and how effectively he can focus his government's and his public's energies on these opportunities more than anything else will define his contribution.

Protecting the public from toxins or the planet from us are among the ideas he may want to consider. However, even assuming he does not, it is critical that he and his senior environmental managers from the start of the Administration lead the environment out of its distant ghetto. For, as society's growth increasingly presses against both the limits of the planet's life support systems and also of the human body's defenses, environmental considerations have become essential ingredients in broader decisionmaking. How can one intelligently consider economic or energy strategy, domestically or internationally, without considering the environment?

Creating millions of good new jobs through structural reform will probably be a central presidential goal. His environmental managers should ensure that he considers the powerful option of shifting relative factor prices in the economy in favor of labor at the expense of natural resources. This could be done without distortion or bureaucracy by removing payroll taxes on labor (over 30 percent) and substituting equal revenue taxes on natural resources. Not only would employment rise and dependency payments and many social ills fall, but also the economy would jump to conserve resources and accelerate its transition to cleaner industries.

Another example: The President probably will want to make a mark in bringing the world together. As Jean Monnet demonstrated in launching

Europe's union, the key is building momentum by seizing specific, feasible collaborations. The environment offers him many of the best opportunities.

Strategy is not enough. The President's environmental team must also be able to help with the design, implementation, and underlying politics of the options he chooses. Coming out of the ghetto requires developing new organizational competencies and attitudes as well as a patient welcome from the President. It will also require the President's environmental managers to work intensively with their field's constituencies.

These two quick examples illustrate the importance of drawing the environment into the Administration's center. Making EPA a cabinet department is less important but would usefully symbolize the change.

REFITTING REGULATION

For over a decade America has had statutes and regulations on the books promising to make our air, water, food, land, etc., safe and spelling out how the job should be done. Policy improvements are needed, but what's missing is implementation.

We've cut research; we've screened only a few chemicals, and then for only a few of the possible risks; standard-setting lags proportionately; and voluntary compliance has crumbled dangerously. Let's look at how to make each of these components work.

Research. Environmental science suffered heavily in the 1980s. Radical cuts at the beginning of the decade did deep institutional damage. Failure to invest in information, facilities, or people despite rapidly rising and new sorts of needs since 1981 deepened the damage and left a massive backlog. (EPA's budget still provides 11 percent fewer real resources for research in 1992 than it did in 1980.) This failure also leaves us both exposed to health and ecological risks we could have avoided and spending billions of dollars in wasteful ignorance.

Rebuilding a strong national research capacity requires: (1) investing seriously; (2) installing research management that will generate a bold, strategic focus and engaged creativity in the laboratories; and (3) experimenting with new institutional arrangements.

The cuts and intellectual timidity of the past decade have been extraordinarily wasteful. Not providing guarantees and other incentives for fundamental research in hazardous waste abatement techniques when it is clear the industry doesn't have sufficient market certainty to do so locks the country into ineffective remedies and billions of dollars in avoidably expensive investments. Not defining and regularly updating what disposal techniques do and don't make sense for each major waste stream leaves ill-trained local junior engineers substituting their "best engineering judgment." And it forces legislators to act blindfolded without being able to weigh the alternatives. Not researching how to prevent pollution through increased reuse, recycling, and materials substitution leaves us dependent on expensive, often unreliable end-of-pipe treatment and disposal.

No private company could survive, especially one operating in a new scientific field such as the environment, with the government's current lack of research investment and weak strategic sense. Environmental research is now only slightly more than 0.5 percent of government environmental expenditures and some 0.0006 percent of society's overall cleanup expenditure.[4]

EPA and the rest of society need to invest far more talent and resources in mapping our environmental frontiers and devising intelligent approaches. To be effective in dealing with the long series of challenges the field poses, the country needs to develop flexible, open mechanisms that will bring to bear whatever combination of people and institutions work best. Environmental research needs to be far more closely tied to policy analysis,[5] and both should have much stronger international ties. Most important, the fortified walls of bureaucratic and disciplinary division need to be shattered.

Applying such simple tools as performance centers (called "profit centers" in business) and open bidding for services among them, ideas that animated well-run corporations several generations ago can bring a quantum leap in the quality and cost-effectiveness of research. If OSHA needs good health effects research on certain types of workplace exposure, it should be easy for it to purchase that research at least from any part of the government (e.g., EPA or DOE), and, ideally, from anyone outside as well. If an EPA lab can do a better job than OSHA's captive lab, giving OSHA marketlike freedom to use EPA scientists will strengthen good, responsive science where it exists and send a clear, unambiguous signal to ineffective, previously monopoly suppliers. The government could further encourage its scientists and workers to be imaginative and entrepreneurial by providing many alternative places outside their formal chain of command from which they can seek venture support for new ideas. Such changes would empower good workers and good units. They would also enable and encourage workers to collaborate across the parochialism that now so keeps government bureaus, divisions, and departments apart.

Providing incentives for the broader society to seek new environmental approaches is, for many problems, even more important. Giving tens of thousands of plant engineers the motivation to find new, cleaner production processes is, for example, probably the only way to accelerate significantly the snail's pace of control technology innovation.

Screening. One such research omission leaves the government able to screen only a tiny portion of the suspect substances it should by law be evaluating—and then only for a small portion of the potential risks.

There are more than seventy-six thousand chemicals now in use, and several thousand new substances are created each year. The Toxic Substances Control Act, the pesticides law, the Safe Drinking Water law, and other statutes require the government to screen all these substances (and more) for possible risk and to impose safeguards where necessary. These laws can be effective only to the degree that such screening is possible.

A few statistics tell the story. Over the 1980s the government was *un*able to complete action on 99 percent of these chemicals. In 1984 the National Academy of Sciences reported that we do not have adequate information to conduct health hazard assessments on more than 90 percent of such chemicals and pesticides. That is still so.

Moreover, when the government says it has screened a substance, the screen is almost always incomplete. It can spot acute, immediately visible effects. It has a reasonably reliable screen for cancer. However, from that point on it must rely heavily on animal tests—that is, on epidemiology by analogue—an analogue that is imperfect and that largely precludes observing many types of effect. How can one, for example, reliably spot and measure other than acute psychological change in a rat?

Until science can produce a set of economic, simple, quick tests for a full range of health risks, not just cancer, the environmental statutes that depend on chemical screening will remain in very large degree empty promises.

EPA should launch a national-challenge, five-year competitive research program to develop such a battery of short tests. The agency should go to twenty to twenty-five top research teams wherever they are around the country; explain the country's critical need; give each team two to five of the one hundred high-volume, most suspect chemicals in use; and ask them (1) to do as comprehensive a risk analysis of each chemical as they can and, in the process, (2) to develop practical, easily used short tests for whatever health effects they can.[6]

Standards. Despite these failures, we have learned enough to have created an extensive set of basic safeguards against unduly risky exposure to both biological contaminants and a great many suspect new, man-made substances.

There is, of course, a great deal more to do. How will the country keep automobile emissions from beginning to increase again in a few years? How can we help the FDA for the first time truly to ensure that food imports meet U.S. pesticide contamination standards? How can we best cut the emissions responsible for global warming and other atmospheric changes? The need to manage human behavior environmentally will always create new regulatory needs.

Compliance. In the 1970s almost everyone complied voluntarily with most of these laws. Of fourteen thousand registered sources of air pollution in Connecticut during five years in the middle of the decade, for example, only three hundred required administrative orders, and of these, only twenty to thirty became enforcement problems. Regulation cannot succeed without this sort of voluntary compliance.

As noted, environmental regulation forfeited much of business's voluntary compliance in the 1980s. *Non*compliance became common in many areas. Restoring voluntary compliance is essential for the new Administration. The best research and the best standards at the end of the day mean little unless they change behavior.

To succeed, the next Administration will have to regain both the attention and the confidence of hundreds of thousands of decisionmakers roughly simultaneously. After all, the collapse took place—even in the face of the very substantial pressures exerted by the expanding new rules of liability— largely because businesses correctly concluded that they could no longer assume that the government would ensure that their competitors were shouldering equal costs. Success will probably require a combination of a visible presidential intervention; a change in the regulatory process that simultaneously forces itself on everyone's attention; and visibly adequate enforcement staff to make a skeptical audience believe.

There is only one other area where regulation must cover almost all of society: tax, securities, and financial regulation. It has worked effectively for fifty years without generating the chronic pattern of political backlash that has been so harmful to environmental management. Its success is certainly not because it is less intrusive or imposes smaller costs.

Environmental regulation needs to learn from its more successful financial cousin. Probably the most important single lesson is the value of creating a profession working at the interface between government and those subject to regulation. The environmental field could similarly develop certified public environmental auditors who would, rather like CPAs: (1) evaluate the procedures and safeguards of firms handling hazardous materials and certify in their annual reports whether they are doing so in a generally accepted safe manner; and (2) collect, lab-test, certify, and report ambient and workplace conditions. They would be engaged and paid by business, held legally liable to the public, and supervised by the government.

A new profession of environmental auditors would do the vast volume of routine inspecting and evaluating that the government is not now doing and never will be able to do. Even more valuable, such auditors would develop and constantly evolve methodologies that fit the infinitely varied circumstances of particular industries, companies, processes, ambient conditions, and laws. They would occupy the middle ground, and they would have the strongest possible interest in defending it. They would also act as much-needed interpreters between government and business.

Government is already moving in this direction. California has established a registry of state-certified environmental auditors—to the applause of small business, which is unable to afford the in-house auditors the larger firms have hired or to evaluate the competency of available consultants in this new, highly technical field. A number of other states have started to require auditors for special purposes, ranging from radon inspections to certifications that a property is environmentally safe at transfer. Most large companies that deal with dangerous substances have set up their own environmental auditors, and their work has created the sophisticated techniques that make the broad application of the idea now possible. The growing use of the idea in such diverse circumstances is a reflection both of its now proven utility and also of a growing awareness that the old approaches are no longer able to do the job.

Expanding the use of environmental auditors is only one example of how the environmental field will have to experiment with new tools to get the massive job of the 1990s done. A few other examples will give a sense of the range of approaches needed.

EPA runs two of the country's largest capital public works programs. The wastewater treatment construction grants program needs to encourage innovation, ranging from novel treatment approaches to the introduction of assembly-line modular treatment units that will be both cheaper and far more reliable than the traditional plant that is custom-designed for each small town. The Superfund must create new incentives that will induce, not inhibit, quick cleanups. Both need stronger means of ensuring contractor performance and project financial integrity.

The program charged with controlling automotive and truck emissions has traditionally focused its attention on premanufacture prototypes and the subsequent manufacturing stage. As more states and cities are running mature periodic inspection and maintenance programs, they are building a model-specific database regarding actual performance. This information opens the door to regulation based on performance, not prototypes.

Stabilizing the Political Foundations

BUILDING A SOLID, SUSTAINABLE POLITICAL BASE for environmental regulation is one of the new Administration's most critical tasks. Without such a foundation we will never make our environment reasonably safe, let alone escape the terribly destructive policy swings of the past years.

There are three broad strategies essential to building such a foundation.

First, EPA must build up such a solid reputation for quasi-judicial probity and professional competency that it informally becomes "good government" to give it respectful autonomy. The Internal Revenue Service and the Securities and Exchange Commission earlier won such standing. The political insensitivity and costly overinvolvement of some executive office staffers in what should be quasi-judicial decisions, especially recently, have hurt. Restructuring these relationships and restoring the agency's capacity and morale are important. However, these changes must be complemented by a relentless management commitment (1) to reinforce everything that is professional and truth-telling in the agency's culture and (2) to ensure the staff's commitment to the idea that they are servants to all the people, not to any one group or perspective. Once this truly and deeply is the agency's culture, the staff will know it, and they will convey it to the agency's public in a thousand ways.

Second, EPA should try to build the sort of professional intermediation that the introduction of certified public environmental auditors promises. One suspects that future reactions will be much less likely and less severe if such a profession has a chance to become a heat shield between the parties and as its members become established in city after city and town after town across the country.

Finally, and quite critically, the next Administration's environmental leadership must actively reach out to build new constituency alliances. Environmental regulation annoys a great many powerful people, which has meant more years of destructive reaction than of advance since Earth Day. Victims; international allies; and, especially, those with religious faith who have an awakening sense of trusteeship for God's creation[7] could all be important new allies. Building such alliances will require considerable and sustained effort. The pressures of immediate events will seem more urgent.

But everything else will be built on quicksand until the field's base of active support is very significantly broadened.

NOTES

1. This chapter is much briefer than the memorandum sent the campaigns. For copies of the original, write the author at 1200 North Nash Street, Arlington, VA 22209.

2. The budget situation became so absurd that a coalition of major chemical company presidents responded to a briefing on the budget cuts in EPA's research by testifying before the House Appropriations Committee in favor of sharp, immediate, and continuing increases.

3. The U.S. Regulatory Council, created in the late 1970s, was one organizational experiment that served this purpose. Never loved by OMB, it was dubbed "proregulation" and disbanded as quickly as possible in the first months of the Reagan administration.

4. See "Future Risk. Research Strategies for the 1990s," U.S. Environmental Protection Agency, Science Advisory Board (SAB-EC-88-040) (September, 1988).

5. The Carnegie Commission on Science, Technology, and Government's Task Force on the Organization of Federal Environmental Research and Development Programs will very probably recommend that policy analysis be funded at no less than 5 percent of the amount budgeted for research. Draft Report of June 17, 1992, p. 62.

6. The costs of this special program could properly be assessed against the affected industries under the Toxic Substances Control Act and Superfund laws.

7. See Senator Al Gore's *Earth in the Balance* (Boston: Houghton Mifflin, 1992), chap. 13, "Environmentalism of the Spirit," for a thoughtful reflection on why Western religion is only now engaging with this concern.

ENERGY POLICY

L. HUNTER LOVINS, AMORY B. LOVINS, AND H. RICHARD HEEDE

Summary

THE CONCEPTUAL ANSWER TO THE ENERGY CHALLENGE is clear: Focus our national energy strategy on *best buys first*. Previous national energy policies have subsidized uneconomic and environmentally damaging fossil and nuclear supply boondoggles. The newest national energy strategy is no exception.

In contrast, a best-buys approach, featuring more efficient use of energy and the wider harnessing of cost-effective renewable resources—sources that don't run out, such as solar energy, wind, flowing water, and biomass—can together provide affordable and sustainable energy supplies that can outcompete and outpace both fossil and nuclear fuels. Today the United States can cost-effectively save over half of all the electricity, oil, and gas we use, trimming about $200 billion off our total energy bill while dramatically reducing environmental impacts. Achieving these technical potentials would take several decades, but it is worth doing.

The next Administration's Department of Energy should take economics seriously, objectively cataloging energy alternatives and systematically eliminating market-busting subsidies and numerous institutional barriers. Specifically, the DOE, Congress, and the Treasury should eliminate taxpayer-funded subsidies that artificially lower energy prices and cause consumers to waste energy and undervalue savings. Environmental and societal costs

L. Hunter Lovins cofounded and is President of the Rocky Mountain Institute. Amory B. Lovins—RMI's cofounder and Director of Research—previously served on the Department of Energy's senior advisory board and published, mainly in collaboration with Hunter, a dozen books and several hundred papers on energy policy. H. Richard Heede is Director of the RMI's Energy Program.

of energy extraction, transportation, and use should be accounted for by assessing and gradually phasing in energy surcharges reflecting such costs. These revenues should be used for environmental restoration or compensation to offset the regressive hardship on the low-income, fund energy education and local implementation, and reduce income taxes. The DOE should promote efficiency standards on electricity-consuming equipment and feebates for automobiles, better labeling and other education; support progressive state utility policies; and implement least-cost procurement practices.

Pursuing such an energy policy could displace all the oil imported from the Persian Gulf, thereby improving American security. Saving energy could abate global warming, acid rain, and urban smog, and solve many other environmental challenges. Unlike coal, oil, and nuclear power, efficiency and renewables do not require draconian government mandates. They produce no "national sacrifice" areas, they generate more jobs, and they lend themselves to delivery by small businesses and to decisionmaking by local authorities. They are cheaper, more environmentally benign, and inherently more democratic.

So why are they officially ignored?

Introduction

WHEN POGO SAID, "We are confronted by insurmountable opportunities," he could have meant U.S. energy policy. So-called national energy strategies have only been wish lists for energy industries eager to bail out their favorite technologies. In contrast, a policy encouraging more efficient use of energy and the wider harnessing of cost-effective renewable resources can provide abundant affordable and sustainable energy supplies.

Energy *efficiency* does not mean curtailment. It means using smarter technology and flexible, market-driven implementation to do the same or better job as before while using less energy. It means improving the American standard of living and saving money at the same time.

In fact, the transition to a sustainable, efficiency-oriented energy system is under way, even without a coherent national policy. Since 1980 the United States has gotten more than four and a half times as much new energy from savings as from all net expansions of energy supplies put together. The United States could still cost-effectively save over half of the remaining electricity, oil, and gas used. Fully achieving this would take decades, but already the energy efficiency measures the United States has implemented are saving upward of $130 billion a year, compared to what we would be spending if we used energy as wastefully as we did in 1973. If America were as energy-efficient as some of our West European and Japanese competitors, we would save an additional $210 billion a year.

Energy Misconceptions

A PERSISTENT PERCEPTION OF ENERGY SHORTAGE has underpinned official energy policy. That belief is wrong. The world has ample supplies of both fossil and renewable energy of many different types. Proven oil and natural gas reserves are expanding rapidly and will continue to grow over the next decade. Obviously, finite sources of raw materials cannot forever be gobbled by an exponentially growing population, but declarations of energy shortages are premature. We are not going to run out of oil any time soon.

The use of oil and other carbon fuels from any source will likely be checked, however, not by available supply but rather by such environmental constraints as CO_2 emissions, habitat preservation, compliance with federal clean air standards, and such national security concerns as dependence on unstable or hostile regimes or an unfavorable balance of payments.

Supply-oriented government programs rest on another misconception and create more distortions in the U.S. energy picture. U.S. energy needs are overwhelmingly for heat and liquid fuels (58 percent and 34 percent, respectively). Only 8 percent of our energy must be in the form of electricity. Yet most federal attention and two thirds of federal subsidy have been directed to the production of more electricity in large, centralized power plants.

More fundamentally, almost no one wants raw energy. Barrels of black goo, lumps of coal, and kilowatt-hours of electricity are valuable only as they are used to perform such work as delivering hot showers, shaft power, and personal mobility. Yet there are many ways to obtain these services. For example, mobility and access can be delivered by inefficient brontomobiles, by 100-mile-per-gallon, four-passenger cars (already demonstrated), by mass transit options, or by sensible land use so people are already where they want to be. Honest policymaking would compare all ways to deliver energy services to the country and choose the cheapest options first, or at least allow the market to make that choice without distortion. Had our government undertaken such an end-use, least-cost analysis, it would realize that most of the energy options it promoted and subsidized for decades are uneconomic.

A Short History

FEW GAVE ENERGY POLICY MUCH THOUGHT until 1973. Energy was left to utilities' and fuel companies' engineers and accountants until the Arab oil embargo. The ensuing energy crisis hit America like an invasion and brought two decades of dramatic change.

The spot shortages of gasoline caused by the government's reaction to the embargo gave rise to America's first official energy policy: We're running out, let's get more. President Nixon, having the dubious fortune to be in office when the embargo hit, responded with Project Independence, a proposal for a rapid expansion of coal-fired electricity, oil and gas drilling, and nuclear fission. Complex regulations and expensive subsidies were prescribed to hold energy prices below market levels so as not to "constrain economic growth."

President Ford's 1975 State of the Union message called for a scaled-down version of Nixon's efforts that, still, by the year 2000 was to build 450 to 800 new nuclear reactors, 500 to 800 new coal-fired plants, and was to continue rapid electrification and oil displacement. The cost from 1976 to 1985 would have been over $1 trillion, or three fourths of all available domestic investment in the whole economy. The grandiose schemes collapsed of their own weight, but in the meantime diverted attention from cheaper energy options.

In 1977 President Carter announced his national energy program. Describing energy as *the* factor that makes a market possible, and the basis of American foreign policy, Carter called for the moral equivalent of war (MEOW). He appeared on national TV wearing a sweater and sought to elicit the sacrifices appropriate to a time of war: "carless Sundays," thermostats set to government-ordered levels, and other curtailments. He proposed the Energy Mobilization Board, modeled on the War Production Board of World War II, to override local citizen opposition to "necessary supply projects," and the Energy Security Corporation to ensure funding if the market wouldn't. The former was not enacted; the latter, reincarnated as the Synthetic Fuels Corporation, spent billions of dollars and produced almost nothing.

On the positive side, Carter created the beginnings of real competition in electric generation (by 1990 utilities were building the minority of new capacity, private entrepreneurs the majority); greatly expanded R&D in efficiency and renewables with enormous payoffs in the 1980s; and began dismantling of the nutty price controls that created first a shortage and then a glut of gasoline.

A few officials in Carter's newly created cabinet-level Department of Energy understood that if the American people had information and opportunity, they could solve the energy problem themselves. The DOE's Office of Consumer Affairs published *The Energy Consumer*. This excellent periodical gave citizens information on cost-effective energy supply and efficiency technologies, examples of what community groups were doing to become more energy self-reliant, and lists of energy organizations and state and local offices supplying reliable information.

Such publications, coupled with technical advances and an even sharper 1979 oil price shock, helped to guide an energy revolution. From 1979 to 1986, energy efficiency delivered over four times as much new energy as did all forms of supply expansion. Renewable sources came to supply at least a tenth of the nation's total energy and the fastest-growing part.

President Reagan rode into office promising to eliminate the DOE. (He found that he couldn't, since most of what it does is build the nation's nuclear bombs.) He also sought to gut car and appliance efficiency standards and nuclear licensing procedures. He cut federal R&D for efficiency by 70 percent, and renewables by almost 90 percent. President Reagan, like administrations before and after, sought to focus federal assistance on favorite supply options, with minimal economic rationale.

By 1984, the last year for which the numbers have been studied, American taxpayers spent almost $50 billion *per year* on direct federal energy subsidies, mostly in tax preferences. A total of 92 percent of this went to conventional fuels. Oil and gas received $20.7 billion, nuclear power over $12 billion. Energy savings received less than $1 billion, and returned 185 times as much in savings per federal dollar invested than a dollar invested in nuclear power.

In 1986 the Reagan administration rolled back efficiency standards for light vehicles from 27.5 miles per gallon to 26 miles per gallon (mpg), contributing to a doubling of oil imports from the Persian Gulf and wasting more oil than the Reagan and Bush administrations hoped to find under the Arctic National Wildlife Refuge. The rollback also contributed to Japan's growing share of the U.S. car market.

The Reagan and Bush administrations also spent tens of billions of dollars safeguarding the flow of Mideast oil, gave eleven Kuwaiti oil tankers American flags and an escort service, and fought Iraq, in large part to maintain access to "vital" Persian Gulf oil. Adding the costs of U.S. forces in or committed to the Persian Gulf—estimated at $40 billion per year—to oil's commodity price, each imported barrel costs about $80, even in peacetime.

At the end of the Gulf War, the Bush administration proposed a national energy strategy (NES) that by its own projection would *increase* dependence on Mideast oil; increase the U.S. emission of carbon dioxide—the main threat to the earth's climate—by 25 percent over the next twenty five years; and hike the U.S. annual trade deficit in oil to $100 billion by the year 2000.

Bush's NES would further subsidize nuclear fission and alternative liquid fuels, sacrificing the national interest in energy security and environmental stability to retreaded boondoggles and corporate welfare programs.

Opportunities for Energy Efficiency

THE NEXT ADMINISTRATION MUST DO MUCH BETTER. Vast opportunities to meet U.S. energy needs with maximum benefit to the economy and the environment lie mainly in three areas: electricity, oil and gas, and renewable energy.

ELECTRIC EFFICIENCY

Electricity costs Americans $180 billion and the world over $500 billion per year. Expanding its supply has lately consumed as much U.S. capital (directly and in federal subsidies) as all investment in durable-goods manufacturing; ever wonder why we have a rust belt? Electrification consumes one fourth of global development capital, and by official projections will consume all of developing countries' growth, leaving little capital to buy things that were to *use* electricity. Already, interlinked shortages of power and capital are hobbling many countries' progress. And power plants consume a third of the world's fuel, releasing a third of the resulting carbon and nitrogen oxides and two thirds of the sulfur oxides.

Electricity-saving technologies aren't glamorous. Motor controls, more efficient refrigerators, and modernized light bulbs seem insignificant compared to a shiny new nuclear plant. However, the thousand or so best electricity-saving innovations now on the market, if fully used throughout the United States, would displace over *half* of all the electricity the country now uses. The average cost of implementing these savings is a couple of cents per kilowatt-hour (kwh). A kwh generated by an existing power plant costs upward of five cents. A new nuclear plant can cost as much as twenty cents per kwh.

Lighting uses roughly 20 percent of U.S. electricity. Just the lighting improvements now commercially available can, if fully used, cost-effectively save enough electricity to displace 120 Chernobyl-size power plants. A compact fluorescent lamp uses 18 watts to deliver the same illumination as a 75-watt incandescent bulb and lasts about a dozen times as long (saving enough installation labor and replacement bulbs to more than pay for the lamp). Over the bulb's lifetime, the electricity saving displaces 662 pounds of coal (if your utility runs coal plants) or 53 gallons of oil. Roughly 1,600 pounds of carbon dioxide and 18 pounds of sulfur dioxide don't get released into the air, helping to abate global warming and acid rain. The bulb more than pays for itself and pays environmental dividends as well. A utility can give away the lamp more cheaply than it can fuel its existing power plants. Southern California Edison Company, for example, has already *given away* more than 1 million such lamps.

FUEL SAVINGS

From 1973 to 1986, the United States cut the energy intensity of the economy by a fourth, its oil and gas intensity by a third, and OPEC's market share by half. Oil imports fell from 46 percent of consumption in 1977 to 28 percent five years later. By 1985, Persian Gulf oil imports were only one tenth their 1979 peak. By 1986, U.S. energy savings, chiefly in oil and gas, had become a national energy source two fifths larger than the entire domestic oil industry.

Transportation, burning nearly two thirds of U.S. oil, is the key to cutting oil dependence. The U.S. household vehicle fleet now averages 19 mpg. Improving that to an average of 22 mpg could displace all oil the U.S. imported from Iraq and Kuwait before the hostilities of July 1990. Increasing the vehicle fleet average by another 10 mpg would displace all oil we import from the Persian Gulf. We almost did it anyway. From 1977 to 1986, the rise in U.S. oil productivity averaged 5 percent per year, four fifths faster than needed to keep up with both economic growth and the decline in domestic oil extraction. Had the United States just maintained that pace, it would have needed no Persian Gulf oil from then on.

A dozen automakers worldwide have demonstrated comfortable, fast cars two to four times as efficient as today's new U.S. models, with improved safety and competitive manufacturing cost. Raising light vehicles' efficiency 50 percent by the year 2005 would save 2 million barrels of oil per day, more oil than we import from the Persian Gulf. But we can do even better. Advances in aerodynamics, new materials, ultralightweight construction, new engine and energy-storage technologies, microelectronics, and computer-aided design and manufacturing can yield a 150-mpg safe, peppy, comfortable, and affordable station wagon. Further gains in both safety and economy can come from carbon-fiber composites and crushable metal foam.

Large oil savings are also available in heavy transport. Boeing's new 777 jetliner, for instance, is twice as fuel-efficient per seat-mile as the 727. Savings are also large in nontransportation uses. For example, energy lost through U.S. windows totals twice the output of the Trans-Alaska Pipeline. Super-windows can dramatically reduce that loss in both heating and cooling climates in the United States and around the globe. Overall, the United States could save much of its oil more cheaply than drilling for more. In the longer term, biofuels from farm and forestry wastes, and efficient land use (building communities around people, not cars) can eliminate oil use.

RENEWABLE ENERGY

From 1979 to 1986 there was more net increase in U.S. energy supplies from solar energy, wind, water, and wood than from oil, gas, coal, and uranium. Many renewable energy sources are already cheaper than today's fossil fuels: passive solar space and water heating, much solar process heat for industry, some biofuels, small hydropower wind machines in good sites, and at least two kinds of solar-thermal-electric generation. Wind power has recently fallen below the cost of new coal plants, even ignoring coal's greater subsidies and pollution.

A study by five national laboratories recently concluded that increasing R&D budgets by the cost of building one nuclear power plant ($160 million a year for twenty years) could, by the year 2030, enable renewable energy to provide about half the total energy and all the electricity used in the United States in 1989, including the equivalent of 9 million barrels of oil per day, directly replacing oil and natural gas.

Nuclear power, in contrast, cannot compete with either efficiency or renewables. It cost the United States about $200 billion in public and private investment—by one government estimate over $1 *trillion* if all the taxpayer-provided R&D is included. That is more than the Vietnam War and the space program combined, to deliver to the United States just over half as much energy as *wood.* Because devices now on the market can save more electricity than all U.S. nuclear plants generate, at roughly 15 percent of the cost of just running the plants, or 5 percent of the cost of building and running them, it's cheaper to write off a new nuclear plant and provide customers with efficiency. Yet nuclear power remains the current centerpiece of federal energy policy.

The Department of Energy as Advocate

FEDERAL ENERGY AGENCIES have consistently been advocates for conventional supply technologies. The history of the agencies shows why. The Department of Energy, in particular, grew out of the original Atomic

Energy Commission and inherited many of its staff and policies. The DOE has always had a nuclear bias reflected in its research priorities, and a fondness for large electrification projects. Even the department's minor efforts to promote renewables have focused on large central station photovoltaic (solar cell) "farms" or solar "power towers" and megawatt-scale wind machines too big to work reliably.

The DOE encouraged and paid for energy supply and sought to make its favorite technologies look cheaper through subsidies and price regulation. It forecast what it believed energy demand would be, and encouraged utilities and other energy companies to build supply capacity to meet that demand as though it were fate and not choice. To date, the DOE has never published an honest comparison of the costs and productivity of various energy options, or sought to foster full and fair competition among different energy technologies.

The DOE's irresponsibility runs from physical destruction of citizen information publications printed at taxpayers' expense during the Carter administration and pulped under Reagan—even the Los Alamos National Laboratory's solar library was burned—to efforts to dictate a political solution to the nuclear waste problem, to a landscape littered with the wreckage of such grandiose supply schemes as the Clinch River Breeder Reactor, synfuels, ocean thermal energy conversion, nuclear fusion, and solar power satellites. Billions of dollars are being spent on "clean coal" (it isn't) technology. Until 1990, the Energy Information Administration statistics didn't even include half of the renewable output. The DOE sought to suppress the only honest attempt to quantify the contribution that renewables could make to the United States, written by the government's own Solar Energy Research Institute. Only smuggling a copy to Congressman Richard Ottinger (D., New York) so he could release it in the *Congressional Record* enabled the excellent book *A New Prosperity* to contribute to public debate.

Now federal leadership in energy efficiency is provided not by the DOE but by the Environmental Protection Agency. The EPA's Green Lights and Golden Carrot programs are excellent examples of highly cost-effective (yet underfunded) government support of industry efforts to implement energy-saving programs for both private and national benefit.

The DOE, as now constituted, is unlikely ever to be an effective force for promoting a rational energy policy, because its primary mission is the production and civilian oversight of nuclear bombs. At least $12 billion of $17 billion of the 1993 estimated budget and at least that much of its managerial attention will go for bombs, most aimed at a country that no longer exists and that wants to dismantle its own nuclear weapons as quickly as possible. This fixation diverts money and other resources to nonproductive and polluting activities: Virtually all of the DOE weapons facilities are badly managed, strew radioactive materials about the countryside and into the groundwater, and are facing a $100 billion cleanup bill. Worse, the secretary of energy must be a person acceptable to the military and the bomb builders. This virtually ensures the appointment of a person inimical to "softer" technologies and market economics. While many of the DOE's Civil Service employees are honest and conscientious, they are politically constrained in what options they can put forward.

The department itself is inhospitable to citizens. The bomb-related work is, understandably, highly classified. Access to such information limits the ability of staffers to interact with the public and tends to develop a mind-set of secrecy. Physically, the high level of military-style security inhibits citizen access to the DOE.

What's a Government to Do?

"THE PROPER ROLE OF A GOVERNMENT IS TO STEER, not row," says one of the DOE's finest analysts, H. Richard Holt. Yet government has so far sought not to set guidelines for a market-based energy strategy but to build and pay for devices it believes should be in place, whether or not they are cost-effective.

In an ordinary world, energy would hardly merit a cabinet-level department. Like other commodities, it should be allocated by the ordinary workings of market mechanisms. But this ignores several realities. First, there isn't a real marketplace in energy. Numerous subsidies and institutional barriers inhibit market performance. Perhaps most important, would-be market participants lack information about their energy options, and fair access to capital. Both of these are, in market theory, prerequisites to the functioning of a free market.

Government's first role in energy policy should be to move the nation in the direction of a true market in energy services. Specifically, the DOE should honestly catalog all barriers to market performance, from lack of information to obsolete and bothersome regulations. Once the factors that inhibit the market are understood, federal agencies should move systematically to clear these barriers.

The most urgent need is for accurate information. Citizens, industrialists, utility managers, local businesses, and government officials all need accurate analysis of their options. Under the Carter administration, the DOE began to serve as an honest broker of information. The succeeding administrations, however, have given every appearance of the baldest hypocrisy by mouthing the free-market ideology while seeing to it that only favored technologies could play in their "market." The Reagan administration slashed by 70 percent the print run of the government's *Gas Mileage Guide* so that two thirds of new-car buyers couldn't get one.

The DOE should recognize when it would better serve by empowering others. Energy is inherently a local issue. The Federal Government acts most efficiently when it empowers individual citizens, corporations, and local agencies. Most of the real action in energy policy is at the state and local levels in regional collaborative efforts among regulators, citizen groups, legislatures, and energy producers. An effective national government would lead by encouraging such efforts—and getting out of the way.

Many observers, including Japan, realize that the modern market is a partnership among citizens, businesses, and the government. As it sets rules for the market, the government should use common sense, encouraging analysis of and equitable support for least-cost technologies. *Best buys first* should underlie national policy. Taking economics seriously must also include externalities—the "larcenous" costs otherwise imposed on people in other times and places rather than paid for by today's consumers.

Government policy should favor, or at least not disfavor, democratic technologies—those that are relatively accountable and understandable to ordinary people. Such energy options as nuclear power require a technological priesthood to administer them and dictate to citizens how these inherently dangerous facilities will be treated. The history of nuclear power overflows with secrecy, police-state behavior, government duplicity, and the abrogation of civil liberties. Precisely the need to shield nuclear power from the market and political accountability it could not withstand led to its squandering the most resources and suffering the biggest collapse of any enterprise in industrial history. Systems that lack feedback are, by definition, lacking in intelligence. We need fewer of them, not more.

Practical Actions for a New Government

THE FIRST TASK SHOULD BE TO ANNOUNCE that it will henceforth be the policy of the nation to pursue least-cost energy services at every conceivable opportunity from Main Street to Pennsylvania Avenue.

Most of the real action in federal energy policy is not in the Oval Office but in various agencies and in Congress. The list of priorities that follows focuses on direct Executive Branch actions and also includes those in which the President's role is an indirect one, a matter of setting the context, tone, and pace, and exhorting others to act.

SUBSIDIES

America should desubsidize, not resubsidize, the energy sector. Government could still lend support to promising new technologies. The nation's wind-power industry, which can now deliver electricity at five cents per kilowatt-hour in California and appears very promising in the Midwest, owes its success—indeed, its existence—to limited and short-term tax credits. But it is contrary to free market principles to continue the multibillion-dollar subsidies to mature industries.

The President should:

• Request that the Office of Science and Technology Policy (or other suitable executive or congressional agency, or the NAS) define, quantify, and assess federal energy subsidies biannually. Policy recommendations should focus on eliminating tax preferences and biases in agency budgets.

• Encourage Congress to phase out the most expensive, market-busting subsidies and preferences systematically and rationally. The Tax Reform Act of 1986 eliminated many egregious tax preferences, but several remain. Furthermore, no attempt has been made to redress biases in the energy-related R&D budgets of numerous federal agencies (most notably the DOE) or with respect to federal loans and loan guarantees.

• Order the DOE to focus its R&D efforts on least-cost opportunities over the near term rather than, as now, pursuing high-cost or long-term supply technologies. The President, or Congress, should write similar leg-islation for tax expenditures, on- and off-budget loans and loan guarantees, and energy-related R&D programs at other federal agencies.

COUNT EXTERNALITIES

The environmental and health costs of energy extraction, conversion, trans-portation, and use are not included in energy prices. It is a complex but necessary task to monetize environmental and societal costs accurately. En-ergy surcharges should be gradually phased in, properly reflect the external costs of each energy source, and not be used simply to raise revenues or force conservation. How to spend the revenues is equally important. Since such surcharges are regressive, revenues should be used to offset the greater hardship on low-income families. The costs of environmental restoration, amelioration, or compensation should be drawn from this fund. Other prior-ities include adequately funding federal R&D and state and local imple-mentation of additional cost-effective, energy-saving opportunities and alternatives to depletable fuels. International sustainable development programs could be funded. Finally, revenues could reduce the federal budget deficit or lower income taxes.

The President should:

• Request that the National Academy of Sciences quantify societal and environmental costs of energy consumption (using a discount rate the President's grandchildren would appreciate) and recommend appropriate and phased-in surcharges for each fuel at convenient taxation points in the system.

• Establish an Advisory Committee on Resource Economics and Externalities.

• Direct his staff to assess the possibility of creating an international market in pollution avoidance.

FUEL ECONOMY STANDARDS, FEEBATES, AND TRANSPORTATION POLICIES

Automobile fuel economy (CAFE) standards have helped improve U.S. average new-car fuel economy from 18.7 mpg in 1978 to 28.5 mpg in 1988, saving billions of dollars in imported oil every year. Strengthening CAFE remains one of the most effective, energy policy tools. Saving oil is still principally a matter of vehicle efficiency, though large savings are available in residential, industrial, and nonfuel uses. Detroit complains about political meddling, but improved minimum standards are very much in the national interest, and without them the country will repeatedly be forced into international conflict and draining domestic oil resources.

A more popular alternative, a feebate system, is a market-oriented, revenue-neutral approach that would charge a higher registration fee for inefficient cars and light trucks and lower the registration fee to purchasers of more efficient vehicles. Rebates can even be based on the difference in efficiency between the new car you buy and the old one you swap—thus getting old, dirty, inefficient cars off the road much sooner while enabling low-income people to trade up to cars they can afford to run.

The President should:

• Call for a national vehicle feebate system designed to augment tougher economy standards—coupled with higher gas-guzzler taxes and significant rebates on the most efficient vehicles.

• Propose increased R&D funding on energy-saving transportation technology and policy innovation. He should also encourage interagency coordination (among the DOE, the DOT, NASA, the EPA, etc.) and technology transfer to the private sector.

• Strengthen and improve existing fuel economy standards for auto-mobiles and light trucks. Standards for heavy trucks, buses, and other vehicles should be implemented.

• Eliminate tax code preferences that encourage auto use—such as corporate credits for parking construction—and that inhibit use of mass transit systems.

BUILDING, EQUIPMENT, AND APPLIANCE STANDARDS AND INITIATIVES

Federal standard-setting is an important policy goal. Stricter standards on the efficiency of buildings, lighting, motors, heating and air-conditioning systems, and myriad other appliances and equipment are all in the national interest. The DOE's approach to standard-setting is now shifting from a payback period of two to three years to a more comprehensive look at proposals that are economically justified based on life-cycle costing—as the law requires. Building energy codes are often antiquated and do not reflect opportunities for the occupant or homeowner to save energy over the life of the building.

The President should:

• Direct the DOE to adopt a national building energy rating system, set national guidelines for energy-efficient mortgages, and periodically review the adequacy of federal and other building energy codes.

• Direct the DOE to promote industrial energy management, waste heat recovery, and efficiency by improving federal R&D and information and technology transfer.

• Encourage the DOE to broaden its research and implemention of cost-effective appliance and systems efficiency standards.

UTILITY PROGRAMS AND POLICIES

Standards merely set a floor for energy performance. Utility rebates for the purchase of superior equipment are an important complement. Sliding-scale hook-up fees for new buildings would give designers and prospective oc-cupants a financial incentive to exceed building and equipment efficiency standards. Revenue-neutral feebates charge fees to purchasers of inefficient products and use those funds to rebate purchasers of efficient electrical and fuel-consuming items, from air conditioners to aircraft. Rebates should also go directly to architects and engineers for designing efficient buildings—for which conventional design fees otherwise penalize them.

At a minimum, the Federal Government should encourage states to practice least-cost, demand-side-oriented policies. Currently the DOE's utility intervention program, mandated by Congress to promote utility regulatory reform, is being perverted into sponsoring interventions *against* reforms. The most important policy option for changing utility behavior is to allow utilities to profit from making least-cost investments, which are almost always electricity savings.

The President should:

• Require the TVA and the federal power marketing authorities to implement least-cost plans.

• Direct the Federal Energy Regulatory Commission to require least-cost plans for bulk power providers, interstate transmission, and regulated utilities. Regional planning structures, based on the successful Northwest Power Planning Council format, should be established in regions lacking this mechanism.

• Encourage state legislatures and regulators to decouple utility profits from power sales, and promote the establishment of progressive integrated resource planning.

• Direct the DOE to monitor and distribute information on least-cost planning successes (and cost-effective technical innovations) in other countries.

• Request the DOE to cooperate with the State Department and other agencies in improving information, training, and technology transfer to energy ministries, planners, financiers, and regulators in, particularly, developing and newly industrialized countries.

• Encourage the World Bank and regional lending banks to improve their least-cost planning and investment portfolio, develop more sound investment and pricing policies in recipient countries, and assist in developing market-oriented policies.

FEDERAL ENERGY MANAGEMENT AND R&D

Federal R&D should be allocated on a rational basis: Those options that can supply or save energy at the least cost should get priority funding. Materials and equipment (including buildings) in government procurement should be costed on a whole-system, life-cycle basis in fact, not just in theory. Government procurement of cost-effective efficiency and renewable energy sources should be mandated to enable the private sector to cut costs of new technologies further. It would save federal dollars and act as a powerful example for the nation.

The Federal Government is the largest single property owner in the nation, and pays $3.6 billion to light, heat, and cool federally owned buildings each year. The Office of Technology Assessment estimates that at least $900 million worth of savings is feasible and economically attractive. Numerous cost-effective measures can be used to trim the $4 billion Washington spends in energy subsidies to low-income households.

The President should draft legislation that will:

• Reward federal agencies and energy managers' cost reduction successes. Savings should be shared by the individual agencies, be invested in additional efficiency opportunities, and returned to the Treasury.

• Revise federal procurement guidelines, improve information on energy-consuming equipment, and incorporate life-cycle costing criteria.

• Increase investment in cost-effective efficiency improvements in federal domestic buildings and facilities.

• Improve the effectiveness and funding for low-income weatherization and state, institutional, and Energy Extension Service energy efficiency programs.

Confronting the "Insurmountable Opportunities"—Conclusion

CUTTING ENERGY WASTE REDUCES ENVIRONMENTAL IMPACT, improves security by lowering oil imports from politically unstable regions, puts more money in consumers' pockets, and need not compromise our standard of living. Improving energy productivity reduces the trade and federal budget deficits, eases interest rates by virtue of lowered federal borrowing, and preserves vital resources for international development and future generations.

The potential to save electricity and oil will not be fully realized until programs are planned, designed, financed, built, commissioned, and maintained with the same level of professionalism and commitment given to our energy supply. The nation has a reserve of wasted energy we can tap with existing technology. The size of this resource is roughly known; what is needed are good implementation techniques to convert this reserve into actual production, and an Administration in Washington with the intelligence to confront its opportunities.

NATURAL RESOURCE USE

ALBERT F. APPLETON

Summary

THE RESOURCES THAT COMPRISE THE AMERICAN LAND—its forests, farms, rivers, lakes and aquifers, wetlands, shorelines, minerals, grasslands, wilderness areas, wildlife, scenic vistas, parks, historic sites, suburbs, and cities—are the raw material of America's economy and culture. Managed as national capital, they will generate wealth for America. Abused, they will drain away wealth to serve narrow self-interests.

The Interior Department holds a central but not exclusive place among a knot of federal departments that together are responsible for natural resource policy. Interior has the national park system; the National Wildlife Refuge system; the vast holdings of the Bureau of Land Management in the American West; the water responsibilities of the Bureau of Reclamation; and the Bureau of Indian Affairs, with its shifting and uneasy role in Indian reservations and Native American affairs. But the Department of Agriculture sets farm and forest policy; the Army Corp of Engineers controls wetlands, stream corridors, and a significant portion of the nation's dam and reservoir building; and the Department of Commerce runs coastal zone management and marine fisheries. The Departments of Transportation, Energy, and Housing and Urban Development are also major, if more indirect, players in shaping natural resources, particularly in land-use aspects.

Virtually every aspect of natural resource administration is now subject to bitter and relentless controversy as new environmental values and constituencies challenge embedded patterns of federal policy. It will be imperative for a the new Administration to recognize that these controversies will

Albert F. Appleton is Commissioner of the New York City Department of Environmental Protection. He has served as a volunteer officer, as director of many conservation organizations, and as an adjunct faculty member at St. John's University and the New School, teaching Environmental Studies and Public Administration.

be much harder to resolve than deciding on the scope of new environmental regulation. Strategies must be evolved that recognize the difficulties and minimize the burdens of changing natural resource policy in the United States into an environmentally responsible, economically defensible, and socially successful tool for future prosperity.

Natural resource agencies most often govern by setting the terms under which the Federal Government grants access to its lands, waters, and minerals; by making direct federal investment to influence the private use of natural resources; and through direct federal service delivery such as road and dam building, under the National Park Service, or the soil conservation service programs. For example, the Interior Department has only one really critical regulatory program, under the Endangered Species Act. Instead, Interior allocates to various private users a major portion of the nation's capital, its lands and waters, through management of its four great resource systems: the national parks, the National Wildlife Refuge System, the immense holdings of the Bureau of Land Management, and the Bureau of Reclamation's water programs.

Negatively, this means that much of the interest balancing that takes place in regulatory design, and much of the structure for public participation and ratification of that interest balancing, is a pro forma exercise carried out under the careful eyes of the dominant interest group. Positively, it gives the new Administration the opportunity in the natural resource area to be much more entrepreneurial in implementing solutions that will provide concrete, immediate progress.

Briefly put, the new Administration needs to move federal natural resource policy from its traditional extractive base to a new strategy that recognizes that the economic value of environmental protection is grounded in free market management principles and that uses sound science to set its management standards. Federal programs that provide below-market access to public resources, whether it be grazing rights, timber, water, park concessions, or mining leases, should, over a reasonable period of time to protect community economic investments, be shifted to management based on true costs and preservation of environmental assets.

Federal Policies Challenged

THE TRADITIONAL FEDERAL POLICY of promoting extractive use of natural resources, particularly in underdeveloped areas of the country, has never gone unchallenged.

Since the first decade of this century, advocates of wise stewardship, or conservation, the forerunners of today's environmentalists, have challenged the extractive bias of federal management of natural resources. They have first argued that many resources have such an intrinsic value as nature, as beauty, as part of a unique American landscape heritage, that their unspoiled preservation overrides any gains from economically exploiting them. These advocates have spawned the national parks system, the wilderness movement, the wild and scenic rivers program, and other systems of land set-asides.

Even where natural resource exploitation was conceded to be appropriate, the Federal Government was then attacked for permitting greedy, politically powerful special interests to avoid obvious responsibilities so that these interests could maximize their profits. Institutions such as the National Wildlife Refuge system (preserve enough ducks for good hunting) and the Soil Conservation Service reflect the demand for responsible resource management, as do the present bitter debates over such topics as forest clear-cutting, strip mine restoration, beach management and coastal erosion, and dolphin and turtle kills by various fisheries.

Though critics have had a profound influence on softening and balancing the extractive character of federal natural resource policy, they have never fundamentally altered it. And when they came closest, in the 1970s, they provoked the Watt policies of the early Reagan years, a counterrevolution that has been essentially continued, albeit in a kinder, gentler way, under Watt's successors at Interior and elsewhere. In a macro sense this was inevitable, for those who have been the traditional beneficiaries of federal natural resource policy have too many vital interests (both legitimate and not) to surrender, without an all-out fight, their historical control over the disposition of federal resources.

At the same time, the Watt counterrevolution has only delayed but not fundamentally resolved the basic disputes that now rage over the natural resource landscape. Natural-resource-based rural economies are everywhere in decline in the United States, substantially narrowing what their participants regard as their room for maneuver. Meanwhile, the scope and demands of the environmental crisis are steadily accelerating. The result is an acrimonious and bitter stalemate. Today the users of American natural resources and their ever more insistent challengers are poised like German fencers who begin a duel with arm's-length rapiers poised exactly at each other's face, with almost no room to engage in anything but a perpetual, slashing duel.

The list of issues on which there is increasing polarization is now virtually the entire menu of federal natural resource concerns: forest management and clear-cutting, endangered species, off-road vehicles, rancher grazing rights, mining access to federal lands and strip mine restoration, wetlands preservation, coastal development and federal flood insurance, river damming, urban versus agricultural water use, airplane tours versus silence over national parks airspace, Everglades restoration versus traditional water use, oil drilling in the Arctic Wildlife Refuge, and on and on.

The new Administration cannot tiptoe from issue to issue on this menu with any hope of success. It must have a workable perspective on the two core problems: how to value natural resources, and how the Federal Government should manage the transition from its traditional policy of promoting natural resources in now obsolete ways (e.g., through below-market charges and fees; by providing other services, such as road building for timber companies, essentially gratis; and by ignoring environmental needs or underenforcing environmental standards). Without a clearly enunciated and publicly supported approach to these questions, the Administration will lose a historic opportunity to use natural resource policy as a coherent tool of national reinvestment and instead be buried in acrimonious lose-lose political controversy.

The new Administration must also address several other generally unrecognized aspects of federal natural resource policy:

• First, both sides are raising the stakes very rapidly. Traditional environmental battles started from a straightforward, use-it/don't-use-it choice. Battles were discrete, often virulent and emotional, but they ended in a resolution: Either land was developed, or it wasn't. But over the past decade, the growing recognition of environmental crisis has expanded the scope of environmental concern to where it is virtually identical with that of all organized social and economic activity. Endangered species don't live in a few convenient, out-of-the-way places that can be safely set aside. When it comes to resource use, every decision now has basic environmental implications.

As this principle has been asserted, and partially in response to it, the other side has also been raising the stakes. Real-estate developers have realized that environmental amenity sells the same house for 30 percent more, and they are making a beeline for unspoiled vistas and proximity to water. More traditional extractive interests are now scavenging the last remnants of old-growth forest, ungrazed areas, offshore oil and mineral sources, etc. Places in the National Wildlife Refuge system face continuing demands to be opened for "compatible" commercial exploitation. Even areas that traditionally would have been utterly sacrosanct environmentally—for instance, the Arctic Wildlife Refuge—are no longer safe. In short, there is no point of calm that the new Administration can hope to retreat to. An active policy is imperative.

- Second, there is a special controversy about areas immediately adjacent to federal reserves. Whether it is a matter of real estate ads extolling property with protected views, concessionaires who want to harvest the traffic attracted to national parks, or environmentalists who have discovered that most wildlife migrate outside federal boundaries and are often shot in the process, those areas adjoining federal lands—particularly national parks and refuges—are now particularly virulent environmental battlegrounds.

- Third, there has been a growing challenge to the Interior Department and other agencies from urban and suburban advocates who see federal policy contributing to urban sprawl and ignoring the claims of urban and suburban areas to more open space.

- Fourth, there is a parallel concern about a federal antirural bias. Many rural interests are perceived to be the principal beneficiaries of federal resource programs, but if judged by the larger criteria of whether they are protecting and enhancing the economic viability of rural communities, the answer has to be a resounding no. Since 1950, rural populations have plummeted as much as four fifths in places. No policy that records such a result among those it is supposed to benefit can be called a success.

The current controversy over the spotted owl and old-growth Northwest forests illustrates the point. Industry claims that logging jobs are being lost because old-growth timber is being set aside to preserve spotted owl habitats. At some level fewer logs in the short term do mean fewer jobs. But the principal beneficiaries of cutting irreplaceable environmental resources are not the loggers at the margin of employment or unemployment, but the sawmill operators and log exporters who are taking advantage of a bloated amount of below-cost federal timber to amortize rapidly their current fixed investments in the Northwest. By failing to hold the old-growth and other timber cuts on federal land to sustainable levels, current federal policy may be providing a short-term employment stimulus but at the expense of ensuring that in the middle and the long term local timber business will collapse for lack of product.

- This harsh reality highlights the fifth and final concern for future federal natural resource policies. Traditionally, the media and others have viewed resource battles as two-sided: save-it environmentalists versus use-it business interests. But there is a third side in these debates that is becoming increasingly apparent—the local communities that have relied on the revenues from the extractive use of the federal natural resources. For obvious reasons, these communities have tended to ally with traditional business users. Environmentalists and others have begun to propose more sustainable alternatives designed to maintain local economic viability, but so far without much success. The reason has been the lack of a viable strategy for rural-based natural resource economic activity that achieves environmental and social goals. The core of the proposals that have been made so far—generally some form of a tourist- or recreation-based economy—has not proven to be particularly attractive to local residents. Tourism is a hit-or-miss business from the local perspective, it does not use traditional skills, and communities often fear it will bring in undesirable elements. Moreover, when aggressively pursued, it tends to take the form of subsidizing the growth of vacation homes and leisure resorts, which bring with them their own environmental problems.

Nevertheless, a federal natural resource policy, whatever its environmental merits, that does not address the economic needs of communities that have grown up in dependence on traditional federal resource policy use is going to generate a major backlash. The challenge the new Administration faces is to find ways to defuse this backlash by addressing legitimate concerns without compromising long-term environmental and economic goals.

New Initiatives

SPEND THE LAND AND WATER CONSERVATION FUND

Reforming natural resources policy could start with the Land and Water Conservation Fund. The fund receives about $1 billion dollars a year in revenues that are dedicated to various programs of federal land purchase and support of state and local open-space initiatives. Under President Reagan virtually none of it was spent. Under President Bush the amount has edged up to about $300 million annually. The result has been to leave the fund with a paper surplus well in excess of $5 billion dollars.

The reentry of the Federal Government into land acquisition would have an immediate twofold benefit for the new Administration. First, there is a large backlog of areas that should be owned by the public, whose purchase would send an immediate signal of the Administration's intent to take the environment and open space seriously. A particular target should be coastal areas, where expanded public access and facilities would be not only good environmental policy but also a public opinion home run.

Second, there are many natural resource conflicts to which the best solution is to buy out the private developer. The wetlands debate would be far less acrimonious if the Federal Government were actively purchasing wetlands or wetland easements. The Land and Water Conservation Fund's resources are a major tool the new Administration can use as part of a flexible, entrepreneurial approach to forging new natural resource programs and defusing natural resource conflicts.

The new Administration should seek to restore the full expenditure of the Land and Water Conservation Fund and, over its first term, to spend down the current surplus. This would create a program of roughly $2.5 billion a year for the first four years. Of that, roughly half should be funneled to state and local governments, to be targeted on three systems—ocean, river, and lake access; urban and suburban park facilities; and wetlands protection—thereby creating broad national support for this investment program while rationally dividing the administrative burdens.

Obstacles can be expected to achieving this expenditure level. There are spotted pockets of vociferous opposition to further public land acquisition (i.e., coastal land developers). The next President should use his "bully pulpit" to mobilize widespread support for land preservation to ensure investments can be made successfully and promptly. Another obvious obstacle is budgetary. Though the Land and Water Conservation Fund is a dedicated fund, under the current rules of federal budgeting, underspending the fund's revenue lowers the federal deficit, while spending down the fund's accumulated surplus increases it. This deficit politics box has proved to be a major impediment to effective use of a number of other dedicated funds as well, most notably the Airport Fund. The new Administration will need to formulate a policy and a strategy that resolve these concerns in a way that allows it to tap into these available resources.

RESTORE NATIONAL PARKS

Another early initiative of the next Administration should be to focus on the most popular federal bureaucracy, the National Park Service, and the most popular federal service, our national parks. National park facilities and the National Park Service have been on a slow but steady downward slide over the past decade. A relatively modest level of investment would produce major gains in National Park Service performance and public enjoyment of the national parks, to virtually universal satisfaction. Budget concerns will again be a limiting reality, but they must be traded off here against a program that would probably produce more favorable public satisfaction per dollar than nearly any other federal program.

PROMOTE A FREE-MARKET WATER SUPPLY SYSTEM

An economically rational, environmentally responsible land use program would help shift water supplies from agricultural uses to growing urban needs. Recent western droughts have highlighted this problem and dramatically sharpened the urban-agricultural water-use conflict. Agriculture uses as much as 85 percent of federal water, despite having as little as 4 percent of the total population of areas in which water is available. Real-locating these numbers would eliminate most urban water problems, provide more water than highly controversial dam projects, and would also promote sounder agriculture by giving farmers an incentive to switch to modern, water-efficient irrigation practices.

The new Administration should not only actively promote the emerging free market in western water rights but also strive to make that market compatible with three concerns:

1. To ensure that critical agricultural interests are not harmed, sales to urban water users would ideally come from water that is currently used to irrigate crops for which there are ample production opportunities elsewhere. For example, the use of irrigated water to support a dairy industry in California makes little sense when there is abundant dairy production available in the well-watered Northeast and Midwest.

2. To ensure that a water market does not become an easy way for urban markets to engage in profligate use, water conservation standards should govern urban water purchases, including such measures as installation of low-flow fixtures and elimination of declining block rates that promote excessive water use.

3. Water rights to federally funded water sources should not be resold in ways that provide windfall profits at federal expense.

ANTICIPATE STEPS FOR PROTECTING BOTH SPECIES AND LEGITIMATE INTERESTS

The real story of the spotted owl controversy is that it was totally unnecessary. It was the product of years of ignoring obvious planning realities until everyone's room for maneuver was eliminated. The new Administration's first response should be to send a clear signal that it will avoid elsewhere that kind of irresponsible policy drift and what it meant for the Northwest.

Endangered-species programs are grotesquely underfunded. Here, as in the National Park Service, a relatively modest amount of money would produce enormous returns. Those involved in Endangered Species protection need to develop plans and programs for the future that protect endangered species while steering away, wherever possible, from legitimate economic interests. This should not be difficult. Community impacts like those in the Northwest are rare events and should not be confused with the exaggerated claims of financial hardship that particular individuals or interests often put forward and that rightfully weigh little against the historic goal of preserving the planet's natural heritage.

The next Administration can take two other steps in this area that would bring it quick and major environmental prestige. First, the United States should be a far more aggressive international participant in protecting the world's wildlife base against those who illegally trade in endangered flora and fauna.

In addition, it should think not only about endangered species but also about endangered American habitats. It should be a leader in promoting the preservation of viable examples of all significant American habitats, a goal to which a revived Land and Water Conservation Fund should contribute.

ESTABLISH A SCIENTIFIC WETLANDS POLICY

The new Administration should quickly formulate a successful wetlands policy. The Bush administration attempted to resolve this problem by defining out of existence what are, in biological and hydrological terms, areas that are indisputably wetlands. This distortion of both science and common sense can only produce bad policy and endless conflict, for it undercuts what is the basis of any responsible democratic government, its credibility and legitimacy. The next President must reject such an approach out of hand and start with a firm commitment to characterize the wetlands' natural resources solely on the basis of genuine science.

Decisions about using the country's wetlands should be based on whether there is a competing use that is publicly more valuable than what a particular wetland contributes environmentally. This does not mean a determination of the relative value of various wetlands. Though not without some basis and merit in particular instances, making relative distinctions among wetlands based on generalized categories of current conditions has a great potential for abuse. Even badly degraded wetlands often have an important value as part of an overall hydrological system. Moreover, nature tends to restore wetlands over time and, in terms of engineered wetland restoration, the record is clear that restoring wetlands in areas that once were wetlands works a lot better than just picking some site and trying to build a wetland on it. The reason is the same in both instances. Wetlands are a child of hydrology, and hydrology tends to re-create itself.

In short, wetlands generally have a significant value. They protect water quality, stop erosion, uptake water-polluting nutrients, serve as habitat for fish and waterfowl, provide flood protection, and are fundamental to the functioning of estuarine and river systems. New York City's innovative Bluebelt program to preserve freshwater wetland corridors for stormwater management is saving the city a net of at least $30 million dollars in storm sewer construction while adding additional value to surrounding neighborhoods by preserving open-space amenities. This use of wetlands as a component of infrastructure is a rapidly growing innovation in urban and suburban design.

The main way to approach wetland trade-offs should not be the current status of the wetland. The key issue should be the value to the public of development and any alternative ways of obtaining such value through using nonwetland sites. From a private developer's perspective, these are perfectly legitimate concerns. But from the perspective of public welfare, rarely will they outweigh the value of wetlands as a public resource.

Much different and more difficult is a policy for agricultural wetlands. Unlike new residential, commercial, or industrial development, which can readily be sited elsewhere, a farm cannot pick up and move; it is where it is. This makes the equities far different and calls for a far more flexible approach in dealing with agricultural wetlands. That approach, however, should not, except as a last resort, involve wetland filling. Instead, by using Land and Water Conservation Fund monies, by beefing up current agricultural programs for wetland protection, and by creative farm planning, the new Administration could develop a program in which wetland preservation for farmers was made more profitable than wetland destruction for agricultural purposes.

By removing the wetlands debate from its current realm of pseudoscience and refocusing it on the real issues—what uses of wetland areas are valuable enough to warrant a wetland sacrifice and how to deal with the special problems of agricultural wetlands—a new Administration will clear the air, send a decisive signal about its commitment to good science, and affirm the fact that, in an environmentally stressed world, what's left of the American wetland heritage is too valuable to lose.

Long-Term Policy Changes

FOR THE LONG TERM, one task is paramount: The new Administration must safely steer through the dozens of natural resource choices that face it. *Federal natural resource policy needs to be moved from its traditional extractive base to a new cost base that recognizes economic values, is grounded in free market principles, and uses sound science to determine its management needs. Federal programs that provide below-market access to public resources, whether it be grazing rights, timber, water, park concessions, or mining leases, should, over a reasonable period of time, be shifted to management based on true costs and preservation of environmental assets.*

At the same time, that valuation process must also recognize the economic and social values of the communities that have been created by the current patterns of federal resource use. Existing and historic users of federal resources who have made business and community investments on the basis of access to them under current policies have a legitimate claim to have their interests included in any new natural resource policy. The economic and public value of the environment cannot be recognized without also recognizing the economic and social value of the current communities that benefit from federal resources, however much standards and values for the use of national resources have changed.

This means that a long-term commitment to protect America's natural resources by incorporating environmental values and their costs into their use must break new and creative ground. This will require that two new features become standard operating procedures for federal natural resource bureaucracies:

• *Use collaborative approaches to reforms.* First, the process of developing and implementing natural resource policy must be one that, to the greatest extent possible, uses collaborative involvement of all competing interests to find innovative ways to design environmental reforms in ways that protect, not attack, existing rural economies and traditional natural resource users. A delicate balance is required so that, under the guise of fairness, large and well-protected economic interests do not get bought out at windfall profits or that long-term environmental and economic objectives are not compromised.

• *Invest for transitions.* Second, a key element in developing new natural resource strategies in which current users are partners with both the government and the new environmental interests will have to be transition investments, either direct to the user or indirect to the local community. Ideally, these should be funded as a sharing of the new public value from the recaptured resource. Such an investment program would properly balance environmental and economic realities with traditional history and expectations about natural resource policy.

There are models for doing so. The Canadian Government, in its recent plan to preserve the Atlantic salmon, spent $45 million buying out existing fishing rights, essentially making the local fishermen whole. Proposals for new environmental protections in the New York City watershed have evolved into a collaborative program using cost sharing to fund certain key elements, as in agricultural pollution control systems that will be integrated into the particular economic strategy of the participating farms. Pollution trading proposals, as recently proposed for the Everglades cleanup, might well be able to be applied here. Such programs are compatible with the strongest possible environmental objectives. But they recognize that the emphasis must be on attaining the goal of environmental improvement, not on the process of environmental regulation—that environmental policy cannot be made in a political or historical vacuum, that most of the public is willing to accept its environmental responsibilities but does not wish to be singled out unfairly to pay the price of environmental reform, and increasingly demands a direct voice in how those reforms are carried out.

Managing this strategic shift is key. The short-term measures recommended above are designed to set the stage for such a program and then support it.

While everyone praises flexible policies, too often government ignores their essential prerequisite. Life is a matter of logistics and never more so than when one seeks to be flexible and participatory. Such an approach means an investment in staff, integrating public participation into the structure of federal resource agencies, and disciplining all parties to avoid not undercutting the collaborative process politically. It also means much more significant attention to planning and advanced problem identification. Most, though not all, natural resource conflicts can yield to good-faith mutual effort, if all sides respect each other's legitimate goals and if the problem is addressed before it reaches the crisis stage. It is a truism that government always talks about doing this but never does. That might be the most significant ground of all for the new Administration to break. As the spotted owl controversy has shown, it would be well served to do so.

Land Use and Transportation Planning

SUSTAINABLE GROWTH

PETER CALTHORPE AND HENRY RICHMOND

Summary

U NRESTRAINED URBAN SPRAWL is generating profound environmental stress, intractable traffic congestion, a dearth of affordable housing, loss of irreplaceable open space, disinvestment
in our inner cities, and life-styles that burden working families and isolate
elderly and singles. Instead, America needs to abandon obsolete land planning strategies and return to the values and patterns of our traditional
towns—diversity, community, frugality, and human scale. We must move
from cul-de-sac subdivisions to Elm Street neighborhoods, from drive-
through commercial strips to Main Street communities, from segregated
sprawl to places more like traditional American towns. We must reinvest in
an America that ensures a new and accessible American Dream for all, not
just the fortunate few.

Rather than subsidize sprawl, our investment must encourage land use
policies oriented toward affordable neighborhoods where transit, walking,
and biking as well as driving are supported. We must create communities
where homes are near transit, parks, schools, and services; where neighborhoods are safe and walkable for kids and the elderly; and where diverse
housing opportunities coexist with commercial, civic, and employment uses.

Our investments in transit must be supported by land use patterns that
put riders and jobs within an easy walk of each station. Our investments in
affordable housing should place families in neighborhoods where they can
save dollars by using their auto less. Our investments in highways must
eschew sprawl, inner-city disinvestment, and random job decentralization.

*Peter Calthorpe is President of Calthorpe Associates in San Francisco, Cal-
ifornia. He is coauthor of* Sustainable Communities. *Henry Richmond is the
Executive Director of 1000 Friends of Oregon and founder of the National
Growth Management Leadership Project.*

Our investments in inner cities and urban businesses must be linked through transit to the larger region, not isolated by increased gridlock.

A new federal initiative should require local and state integrated land use plans *before* granting federal funds for transit, highways, affordable housing, or open space. Such regional planning would be supported by and supportive of diverse, affordable, and livable communities and provide a sound foundation for rebuilding America.

Introduction

OUR LAND USE PATTERNS ARE THE physical foundation of our society and, like our society, they are becoming more and more fractured. They increasingly isolate people and activities in an inefficient network of congestion and pollution rather than joining them in diverse and human-scaled communities. Our faith in government and the sense of common purpose essential to any vital democracy are eroding in suburbs designed more for cars than people, more for market segments than communities. Local zoning laws and development patterns designed to separate and segregate us make it difficult for Americans to work together on the social issues facing the country.

Suburban sprawl increases pollution, saps inner-city development, and generates enormous costs that are ultimately borne by taxpayers, consumers, or businesses. America is using obsolete land planning strategies that fail to account for changing household makeup,[1] a transformed workplace and work force, shrinking average family wealth, and environmental concerns. We are still building World War II suburbs as if families were large and had only one breadwinner, the jobs were all downtown, land and energy were endless, and another lane on the freeway would end traffic congestion.

The alternative, transit-oriented developments (TODs), is simple and timely. TODs cluster housing, parks, and schools within walking distance of shops, civic services, jobs, and transit. A TOD planning strategy preserves open space, supports transit, and reduces auto traffic. It creates regional order in our balkanized metropolises, balancing inner-city development with suburban investment. The increments of growth are small but will accommodate regional growth with minimal environmental impact: less land consumed, less traffic generated, less pollution produced. Mixed-use, walkable TODs will ultimately be more affordable for working families, business, and government, and are environmentally sound. But implementing this strategy will require overhauling the regulatory priorities and federal programs that shape our cities. It will also require political commitment to the investment needed to realize the transformation of our communities.

Integrated Regional Planning

TO BE SOLVED EFFECTIVELY, THE PROBLEMS of open-space preservation, affordable housing, highway congestion, air quality, and infrastructure must be seen as an integrated system, not disparate problems. Sprawl and its low-density, segregated uses, combined with chronic highway congestion, deteriorating air quality, and lack of affordable entry-level housing, have been indirectly subsidized since World War II by our federal highway program, VA loans, tax policies, mortgage insurance, and other federal and state programs. Worse, policymakers have persisted in unsuccessfully treating only the symptoms of sprawl rather than addressing the development patterns that are the root cause of the problem. We control air pollution with tailpipe emissions, fuel consumption with more efficient engines, and congestion with more freeways rather than creating cities and towns in which people are less auto-dependent.

Public investment in roads, transit, housing, civic facilities, and open space must be tied to more efficient and sustainable patterns of community development. But more sustainable and efficient patterns of community development cannot be realized by ad hoc, localized antidevelopment growth control measures. Development is not the problem. Rather, development in the right place, time, and form is the key to sustainable communities.

The land planning principles of TODs have been developed in several major regions across the United States. These principles involve clustering mixed uses within walking distance of transit service. Studies show that people in households in similar mixed-use neighborhoods developed prior to World War II typically travel half the auto miles per year that people in modern suburban households drive. In the past twenty years, while the population increased by 40 percent, the vehicle miles traveled per capita have increased by 100 percent. The highway congestion and air quality implications are plain. The structures of our communities, however, offer us few viable alternatives.

The Problem of Growth in Our Metropolitan Regions

POST-WORLD WAR II PATTERNS OF URBAN and suburban development in America are undermining long-standing national goals of economic strength, equal opportunity, and environmental quality. Development patterns thus are a major national problem. The absence of competently administered, binding state and regional policies that determine the location and fundamental quality of development results in development patterns that do not adequately consider the environmental and economic implications of piecemeal growth. The problem is twofold: First, local land use control is balkanized and unable to balance the regional issues of jobs/housing distribution, regional transit, air quality, traffic, and open space; and second, current land use policies respond to outdated conditions with outdated strategies. In response to sprawl, building moratoriums and downzoning are becoming common. The result is a policy gridlock in which development is endlessly delayed, adding cost but not quality to growth.

Consequently, development decisions consider only the local cost impacts, municipal or private. The low land price paid by the developer of the suburban shopping mall or the office tower at the freeway intersection may allow lower-than-downtown rents, which accelerates inner-city disinvestment while generating proportionally more traffic congestion and air pollution. Use of these suburban facilities generates costs not totally borne by facility users. For example, free suburban parking lots discreetly subsidize auto use without truly covering the long-term cost of the agricultural land and open space displaced. Taxpayers and industry often pay for the air pollution and congestion indirectly, in health costs and time.

Moreover, inner-city residents have been left behind by job flight, white flight, and dollar flight. Results? High unemployment. Low income. Substandard housing. A flattened tax base. Poor schools. Drugs. Teens with fatherless babies. Violence. Consequences, in part, of land development policies that respond to artificially attractive financial opportunities in the suburbs. Subsidies in the form of public highway investments and tax policy and an "anything goes" regulatory context have allowed the true cost of development to be delayed into the future.

The inner city is a trap. The high cost of housing in large-lot, apartment-short suburbia is a barrier to urban Americans and, ironically, a barrier to the children of suburbanites, who, like many inner-city citizens, cannot afford the current cost of the suburban dream. The inadequacy of public bus or rail transportation to suburbia reduces access for the working poor to decentralized job centers that are home to suburban-based service jobs, the fast-growing part of the American economy. With up to 50 percent of urban disposable income going to pay for housing, owning a car necessary to get to a suburban job is prohibitive for many.

Affordable housing and the costs of transportation are closely linked. The average American household spends more than 20 percent of its annual budget on automobiles and transportation. But the household economic implications of land use decisions are not always obvious. Reductions in auto ownership, use, insurance, and time can free critical dollars for home purchase or rent. Walkable, transit-oriented communities can render investments in transit facilities more effective while giving homebuyers the opportunity to save auto expenses.

Household budgets and tax payments are not the only economic measures of the cost of sprawl. Business is affected as well. American employers—public and private—face compensation demands that reflect high transportation and housing costs. Worker productivity declines with congestion and long commutes. Raw material and product movement is costly and uncertain. When auto exhaust "uses up" the air shed, building new manufacturing facilities in Mexico or Korea looks good. And uncertain land use decisions delay and increase the cost of commercial development, causing investors to look elsewhere.

The harms resulting from disinvestment in the inner city and high-cost, low-density development in the suburbs cannot be quickly remedied, and the Federal Government cannot alleviate them directly. The constitutionally based power to legislate land use policy lies with the states. But much of the critical infrastructure investment comes from the Federal Government, and with it the power to set a new direction.

Without investment dollars, adoption of socially responsible land use policy would accomplish little. The social goals of such an investment strategy cannot be achieved without careful decisions about the places and patterns of development those investments are intended to sustain. Congress should invest in American cities only if Congress also requires state and local land use plans that will assure efficient expenditures to advance national goals.

Treating Root Causes, Not Symptoms

WITHOUT AN INVESTMENT-BASED LAND USE POLICY reform strategy, Congress and state legislatures will continue to treat merely the symptoms of socially harmful development patterns instead of their cause. For example, fuel consumption is largely a result of sprawl patterns that compel use of a car. Congress has attempted to cut fuel consumption not by reducing sprawl but by increasing the fuel efficiency of cars. The new car fleet went from 13 mpg in 1973 to 29 mpg in 1989. Yet even this impressive doubling of fuel efficiency was outstripped by the continuing explosion of sprawl-driven auto use: The U.S. transportation sector burned 19 percent more fuel in 1989 than in 1973.[2]

Air pollution is another symptom of sprawl that cannot be cured without treating the disease itself. The 1990 amendments to the Clean Air Act are predicted to cut carbon monoxide, nitrous oxide, and hydrocarbons in the air by 10 percent by the year 2000. However, notwithstanding the tightened tailpipe emission standards, sprawl-induced increases are projected to make these same pollutants 30 percent worse in 2010 than they were in 1989.

Highway congestion also results from the trips generated by sprawl. Yet the usual response—adding new freeways and beltways at the urban fringe—does not reduce trips, and often increases trips by inducing more sprawl. Moreover, the money available to deficit-strapped federal and state legislatures is inadequate to build freeways fast enough to keep up with traffic growth, even assuming freeways had no other problems.

Joblessness, homelessness, and immobility of the urban poor are in part a result of *underdevelopment*. Unaccompanied by improvements to urban economies, welfare payments and food stamps are ultimately ineffective cosmetics. Similarly, job training programs without jobs are a mirage. These critical social problems cannot be adequately addressed until we deal with one of the root causes—a land use policy that allows too much counterproductive development to leak into the metropolitan fringe.

Integrated Investments and Political Consensus

STUDIES BY FORMER FEDERAL RESERVE ECONOMIST David Aschauer and others conclude that increased public investment heightens economic productivity, increases business revenues, and improves return on private capital. Moreover, targeted integrated infrastructure investments—instead of random building of bridges, lighting, and treatment plants—can address specific social goals as well as boost the economy. Targeted, integrated investments also can help build the public consensus needed to breathe political life into ideas, uniting environmentalists and social justice activists and no-growth advocates and developers.

Environmentalists increasingly recognize that America must selectively build its way out of the nation's problem of low-density suburbia to overcome the harms of sprawl. This means building housing and jobs in concert with rail or bus service investments. Without housing close to transit, minimum ridership is impossible. Thus, housing linked to transportation is a central part of any environmentalist's metropolitan conservation strategy.

Urban residents can support regional transportation systems as part of a strategy to encourage housing and commercial development. Inner-city investment is bolstered by conservation when joined with proposals for regional transportation and open-space systems. By linking the two objectives and by transcending the urban/suburban boundary, both environmentalists and social justice activists can create broader coalitions for change.

The private sector also can become an ally in this strategy. The development community needs financing for adequate infrastructure and certainty regarding land use policy. Regional plans providing this certainty would be a boon to the industry. More compact, infrastructure-efficient development patterns would reduce costs further. But ultimately the development community must respond to the marketplace, what the homebuyer or business seeks. Mixed-use, walkable, and transit-served developments are gaining broad acceptance in a market wise to the shortcomings of standard office parks, subdivisions, and shopping malls. The TOD strategy can help developers join with environmentalists to create "corrective development."

Land Conservation Supports Urban Investment

WHILE IT IS CLEAR THAT ONE path to urban revitalization and metropolitan environmental quality is "corrective development," sprawl containment and rural land conservation are also essential. Land use decisionmaking must address the *open space* side of the equation, too. The current situation in Washington, District of Columbia, exemplifies the economic stake urban America has in open space conservation.

It is estimated that 210 million square feet of new commercial/residential development are needed to retire the existing bonded indebtedness of District of Columbia area local governments, including the local share of the $10 billion METRO system. One hundred sixty-five million square feet of the 210 million square feet are available within a walkable 440 yards of existing METRO rural stations. As a result of rural sprawl and the failure to develop space within the city, tax revenues are lost and the D.C. government is spending $200 million per year in general funds to subsidize METRO. This is money that could be spent for other urban problems, such as housing, crime, and AIDs. The regional "leakage" is $700 million. Hence, the District of Columbia won't get the development investment its citizens need unless the countryside is saved by channeling development demand back to the city and organizing it around transit. Likewise, unless the region has a city that works, accommodating development efficiently and humanely, environmental efforts to prevent sprawl will fail.

The urban poor have a critical stake in the "property rights" debate. If local government lacks the authority to adopt local legislation to direct development to accomplish critical metropolitanwide investment goals, urban America will suffer. The capacity to direct and order environmental and economic growth depends on empowering the public sector at the regional level and setting policies that integrate federal, state, and local investments.

The Transition-Oriented Development Strategy

THE TOD LAND USE STRATEGY ADOPTED, analyzed, and tested in various forms in San Diego; Portland, Oregon; Montgomery County, Maryland; and Sacramento maps out the new integrated approach to land use. Federal policy should build on these pilot programs, which demonstrate the economic, environmental, and political feasibility of these concepts. It must help state and local governments create regional planning agencies that comprehensively address problems that transcend the balkanized jurisdictions that make up our metropolitan areas.

The TOD concept is simple: Moderate and high-density housing, along with complementing public uses, jobs, retail stores, and services, is concentrated in mixed-use developments at strategic points along an expanding regional transit system. The TOD provides an alternative to standard development by emphasizing a pedestrian-oriented environment and reinforcing the use of public transportation.

Although focused on reinforcing transit, the mixed-use and walkable neighborhoods would equally support car pools, bus, trolley, biking, walking, and more efficient auto use. A *"walkable" environment is perhaps the key aspect of TODs*. The alternatives to drive-alone auto use depend on creating comfortable pedestrian environments at the origin and destination of each trip. Placing local retail stores, parks, day care, civic services, and the transit stop at the center of each TOD reinforces the opportunity to walk or bike for many errands, as well as combine a trip to transit with other stops. Tree-lined streets and building entries that connect transit stops with local destinations also help to make the neighborhood "pedestrian-friendly." It has been shown that a higher percent of people are likely to use transit if they can walk to the station, rather than get in their cars to drive to a "park and ride" lot. Initial samplings have found that people living or working within three to five blocks of high-frequency bus or trolley service use the transit system more than any other group.

From a traffic-engineering standpoint, walkable places can affect the average household percentage of trips taken on foot, or by bike, bus, trolley, car pool, or auto. For example, in European communities, auto use generally constitutes 30 to 48 percent of all trips; transit trips comprise only 5 to 20 percent of trips; and pedestrian trips equal 30 to 50 percent of total trips. In comparison, U.S. auto use accounts for 82 percent of all trips, walking constitutes 11 percent, and public transit comprises only 3 percent. If we increased walking trips to a modest 20 percent (half that of Europe), we could potentially double transit ridership. To achieve these goals, we must provide amenities for pedestrians consistent with American life-styles.

Through regional planning efforts, TODs offer an opportunity to promote efficient development patterns. Three types of settings have been identified that broadly characterize the physical pattern of development throughout the typical city: redevelopable sites, infill sites, and new growth areas. These three areas represent the range of conditions where TODs could be located: in existing developed areas that have the potential to be "revitalized" with a mix of transit-supportable uses; in small to moderate-sized undeveloped parcels within the urbanized portions of the city that could be "infilled" with new uses; and in areas typically on the fringe that are scheduled for urban expansion. In each of these settings, TOD plans must respond to sensitive environmental resources and to the context and character of existing adjacent neighborhoods. The overall distribution of development rights across these three areas must be balanced and analyzed from a regional perspective to enhance the quality of life in each zone.

Federal Initiatives for Sustainable Communities

THERE IS A RANGE OF POLICIES and programs the Federal Government can implement to encourage and foster the kind of sustainable development our cities and metropolitan regions need:

1. *Tie federal highway and transit funds to a requirement for regional land use policies and plans that create more pedestrian and transit-oriented developments (TODs).* In reauthorizing the federal transportation program (ISTEA) in 1991, Congress required state transportation improvement plans to conform to state implementation plans to achieve federal air pollution requirements. In many cases suburban freeway or beltway projects funded in large part with federal gasoline tax dollars will increase traffic and cause federal air pollution laws to be violated. The "conformity" requirements of ISTEA would require federal funding for such a freeway to be disapproved. The effect of this new policy will be to require states and localities to try alternatives to building freeways to meet the mobility and access needs of local businesses and citizens.

The U.S. Department of Transportation should insist that localities use land use policy as a dynamic variable in environmental impact and transportation planning, instead of treating existing zone maps as a static "given." The latter approach simply compels new freeways to handle sprawl-generated traffic. Transit funds should not be given without analysis, plans, and demonstrated local commitment to use land use policy to discourage sprawl. Federal highway and transit funds should be denied to jurisdictions that do not adopt transit-oriented development land use policies.

2. *Require "mode split" and VMT performance standards for all local general and comprehensive plans.* In a modern suburb, the average household travels approximately thirty thousand miles per year. However, those in the average household in a city travel only eight thousand miles per year and, in older mixed-use neighborhoods, an average of fifteen thousand miles per year. This is a broad range influenced by many factors, including land use, household size and income, proximity of major employment centers, and convenience of transit. A more balanced "mode split" and reduced VMT (vehicle miles traveled) can be achieved by many programs on state and local levels. Performance standards should be developed on the federal level to set goals and to encourage measures to achieve the standards. In 1991 Congress began considering legislation that would reward states for encouraging more balanced mode split strategies and reduced VMT. Under the proposed legislation, states in which VMT per person increased 10 percent would receive a 10 percent cut in highway funds, which would then be used to reward states with a declining VMT. An alternative to this legislation may be to set federal standards and goals and make highway and urban mass transit authority money contingent on reasonable compliance.

3. *Develop banking policies that would provide homebuyers with credits for reduced auto ownership and/or usage.* Fannie Mae regulations can be reworked to credit households with reduced auto ownership and VMT with more financial capacity for mortgage payments. On average, a household will spend up to $6,000 per car per year or about 25 cents per mile on insurance, maintenance, payments, and parking. Savings in this area should be available for home purchase. It can be shown statistically that in certain Zip code areas, because of existing land use patterns (density, transit service, and proximity to employment), households have lower VMT. Mortgagors in these designated areas should be eligible for a lower-rate "walking home" mortgage. New growth areas would qualify for the program if the land use pattern met stipulated standards and transit service was provided. This policy would be particularly effective in encouraging new development in TOD-like patterns because private sector builders would have the incentive of increased purchasing capacity in the market.

4. *Tie affordable housing tax credits and subsidies to requirements that projects take place in mixed-use, walkable, and transit-served communities.* HUD secretary Jack Kemp proposed amending the Affordable Housing Act of 1992 so localities would have to remove land use barriers to affordable housing to be eligible for federal housing grants. Among those barriers are excessive amounts of high-cost, large-lot, single-family zoning; shortages of

multifamily, duplex, and other higher-density zoning; and excessively long time periods for project approval. Kemp's proposal was the most important explicit federal recognition since the Jackson-Udall bill of the early 1970s (1) of how long-standing national policy and financial commitments are being thwarted by local land use policy, and (2) that the Federal Government should use whatever carrots and sticks are available to correct the situation. Even though amendments were offered to clarify that Kemp's local "barrier reduction strategies" were not aimed at local rent control programs, local government lobbyists killed this important proposal.

Housing built in connection with transit (and also immediately connected to retail stores, employment, day care, public offices, and recreational activities) reduces VMT, reduces household expense for transportation, and creates pedestrian street activity that inhibits crime. Beyond reducing obstacles to affordable housing, new policy should emphasize those areas with TOD land use policies.

5. *Develop policies and programs to support urban infill and mixed-use intensification at transit stations through redevelopment agency, block grant, and CDC entities.* Redevelopment agencies have the experience, the tools, and the structure to realize much of the TOD land use goals in inner-city and infill locations. Their tax structure and power of eminent domain can provide the funds and the land assembly tool to make integrated mixed-use infill at transit stations a reality. Their legislative mandate must include reinforcing a region's expanding transit system in its often troubled inner-city locations. Block grant money and local Community Development Corporations should be integrated into this effort. In all possible cases, HUD housing programs should also be focused on these transit/redevelopment areas.

6. *Develop federal open-space investment criteria that credit a jurisdiction for compact land use planning and urban limit lines.* States and localities exercising their legislative authority to protect open space for economically productive and aesthetic purposes and to channel local development demand to urban areas should receive first priority for federal open-space acquisition dollars. States not exercising legislative authority to protect open space should receive bottom priority. Congress can create competition for its land conservation dollars.

7. *Create a federal demonstration project to build model TODs in redevelopment, infill, and new growth sites.* Much like the HUD and DOE energy-efficient buildings demonstration project of the late 1970s, a new program should be developed to support the development of model TOD

communities across the country. The concept should be tested and modified in a range of cities representing the diversity of physical, political, and economic conditions throughout the country. In each city, three projects should be supported: inner-city redevelopment, infill, and a new development area. The sites must be coordinated with local and federal transit, infrastructure, and housing programs. Such a demonstration project would have multiple goals: demonstrating how the concepts can be modified to fit local conditions, testing the market viability of the real estate products, and providing the regions with planning tools to replicate the demonstration.

NOTES

1. Of the approximately 17 million new households formed in the 1980s, 51 percent were occupied by single people and unrelated individuals, 22 percent by single-parent families, and only 27 percent by married couples with or without children. Of those with children, the family now typically has two workers. People over sixty-five years make up 23 percent of total new households.

2. The typical suburban home now generates twelve auto trips per day. The increasingly lower-density development patterns that generate those trips have pushed up vehicle miles traveled (VMT) three times faster than human population for four decades. That is why the oil spilled by the *Exxon Valdez* is a land use policy issue. And why foreign policy is, too. Our nation's sprawl-generated transportation "system" burns up 69 percent of the nation's oil, half of which is now imported.

Agency for International Development,
Department of Health and Human Services

POPULATION AND FAMILY PLANNING

SHARON L. CAMP

Summary

W
HAT THE UNITED STATES DOES in the very near term will substantially affect whether world population stabilizes at slightly less than double the current 5.4 billion or eventually triples. The two scenarios have important implications for broad U.S. national interests, including efforts to protect the global environment, alleviate world poverty, and promote peaceful democratic change. The future U.S. response to this challenge at home and abroad is crucial.

Some twenty-five very large countries account for 80 percent of world population growth. Nearly all twenty-five now have national policies to slow population growth, except the United States, which adds 2 million people a year to the world population, exclusive of legal and illegal immigration. Because of high U.S. consumption levels, U.S. population growth has a substantial impact on the global environment. Largely because of inadequate birth control choices, half of all pregnancies in the United States are unintended.

The administration of President Reagan sacrificed long-standing U.S. leadership on world population issues to domestic abortion politics. Since 1980, funding for the domestic family planning program has declined by two thirds, and U.S. foreign aid for family planning is below levels provided in the early 1970s, in inflation-adjusted dollars. New abortion-related restrictions have undermined the integrity of both programs.

In its first hundred days the new Administration should:

Sharon L. Camp is Senior Vice President of the Population Crisis Committee. She has authored many publications, including Population Pressure, Poverty, and the Environment *(Population Crisis Committee, 1990).*

- Seek a fiscal year 1993 appropriation of $320 million for Title X domestic family planning programs and an appropriation of $200 million for contraceptive and related research at the National Institutes of Health.
- Seek a fiscal year 1993 appropriation of $650 million for international population assistance, including a contribution of $90 million to restore U.S. participation in the U.N. Population Fund.
- Abolish the "gag rule" and seek congressional support for federal funding of abortions for medically indigent women under the Medicaid program.
- Work with Congress to pass a Freedom of Choice Act.
- Press for timely FDA consideration of the French "mini-abortion" pill.
- Abolish the international abortion "gag rule" (the Mexico City policy).

Over four years the next Administration should:

- Appoint a new blue-ribbon commission on "population growth and the American future" to initiate a national discussion on international population issues and alternative paths to early U.S. population stabilization.
- Increase foreign aid programs aimed at poverty alleviation, environmental protection, and human resources development, including specific new initiatives in women's health and development, through reductions in military assistance.

Introduction

THE 1990S REPRESENT the most critical decade in the history of human population growth. What the world community does or fails to do in this decade, including the role played by the U.S. Government, will largely determine whether the world's population can be stabilized in the first half of the next century at somewhat less than double its current size of 5.4 billion, or whether it will eventually grow to at least triple its current size. For many countries in Africa and the Middle East, this latter scenario actually implies a sixfold increase in population. Many of these countries are not now meeting the basic needs of their current populations and almost certainly cannot achieve environmentally sustainable economic development with the levels of population growth projected.

Because of the momentum of population growth, time is of the essence. For each decade of delay in reaching a two-child family average globally, the eventual world population will be about 1 billion people larger, and stabilization will take considerably longer. For example, if by the end of this decade about three quarters of the world's couples, on average, regularly practiced some method of fertility control, the world could expect to reach a two-child family average between about the years 2010 and 2015. This would result in approximate population stabilization before the middle of the next century at about 9 billion people. But if a two-child family average were not reached until about the year 2060—the likely result of current levels of effort—world population would not stabilize until it reached 15 billion or 16 billion people.

The implications of these two different population scenarios for U.S.-supported efforts to alleviate world poverty, protect the global environment, and promote peaceful democratic change are extremely serious. Despite recent declines in birth rates, virtually all of the developing countries in whose future the United States has some important interest still face future population pressures sufficiently serious to jeopardize their long-term economic and political development.

Population growth has helped hold down gains in per capita income in a number of African, Asian, and Latin American countries that would otherwise be—and during the 1970s were—increasingly important U.S. trading partners. Differences in fertility around the world have also aggravated the gap between rich and poor both within and among countries. Future world prosperity and security are closely tied to prospects for equitable economic progress in the developing regions, and those prospects are undermined by continued rapid population growth.

Environmental Impact

OVER THE NEXT ONE TO TWO DECADES, population growth worldwide, especially when combined with widespread poverty, will also contribute to a number of international environmental problems. Although high levels of consumption in the world's wealthy countries account for many of the most serious global environmental problems, world population growth nonetheless multiplies and accelerates the stress on renewable natural resources such as clean air, arable land, fresh water, fisheries, and forests.

In many parts of the developing world, where populations have doubled over the past twenty to thirty years, families living on the edge of subsistence can now meet their needs only by overexploiting natural resources and causing possibly irreversible environmental damage. In some rural communities in Africa, soil productivity has declined and local farming now meets less than half of local food needs. Trees are being cut down for firewood four times faster than sustainable levels, creating a fuelwood crisis that adds substantially to the burden of women's daily lives and that may disrupt hydrological cycles sufficiently to make local climates drier, contributing to cycles of severe drought.

Some of these trends, as in the case of deforestation, can also have important consequences for the global environment. The loss of tropical forests is a major threat to the survival of a diverse range of plant and animal species and an important contributing factor in global climate change through its effects both on "carbon sinks" and on future carbon dioxide emissions. Among the nine countries accounting for some 80 percent of remaining tropical forests, population doubling times range from just twenty-three years for Zaire to thirty-eight years for Colombia.

Moreover, even with small improvements in living standards, large and growing developing countries such as China and India could cancel out future conservation or pollution control measures in the industrialized countries of the North. If current trends continue, U.N. experts estimate that developing countries could account for half of all greenhouse gas emissions and 60 percent of all new waste by the year 2025. Unfortunately, few developing countries now have the financial resources to fund pollution controls, reforestation, new energy technology, and other environmental initiatives. While industrialized countries can and should help support such initiatives, even very substantial additional amounts of foreign aid could be overwhelmed if developing-country populations quadruple over the next fifty years.

The most serious consequences for the global environment may stem from continued population growth in the United States, with the world's third-largest population. Excluding immigration, the U.S. population of 252.8 million grew in 1991 by 0.8 percent, adding some 2.024 million people to the world's numbers. (The populations of Japan and most European countries are at or near stabilization.) Because U.S. per capita energy consumption is among the highest in the world, the 2 million additional Americans will contribute some 42 million additional tons of greenhouse gases annually to the world's atmosphere, significantly increasing prospects for global warming. For comparison, India added 18 million people to the world's population in 1991—more than in all of sub-Saharan Africa combined. But with very low levels of per capita energy consumption, India's annual population growth adds a smaller amount—27 million tons—of greenhouse gases to the atmosphere than does that of the United States. From a global environmental perspective, both the United States and India have serious population problems.

Worldwide Success of Organized Family Planning Efforts

FORTUNATELY, AFTER SOME TWENTY-FIVE YEARS of experience, we now know how to slow rates of population growth humanely, quickly, and cost-effectively. Although it is now recognized that many factors can indirectly influence family size—most particularly the role and status of women in the society and the availability of economic opportunities for the poor—good-quality subsidized family planning programs by themselves can produce very rapid changes in reproductive behavior. This is because they give low-income women the same reproductive choices that have been available to wealthier women since the 1960s revolution in birth control technology. In most parts of the world young women today say they want only two or three children. This is true even in very poor countries such as Bangladesh, where the status of women is very low. Over the past twenty-five years, almost thirty countries have reduced average family size by 50 percent or more.

In synergistic combination with other social and economic initiatives, organized family planning programs can bring about a demographic transition from high to low birth rates in less than a single generation. This has now occurred in considerable areas of Asia and Latin America over the past twenty-five years, and a similar transition has recently begun in parts of Africa. Worldwide an average of 75 percent of women in most countries outside Africa say they want help to have smaller families. That is the good news. The bad news is that many are still not getting it, thanks in part to political controversies in the United States.

Family Planning in the United States

THE CONSTRAINTS ON FUNDING for family planning and increasing restrictions on safe abortion have slowed declines in U.S. fertility during the 1980s and 1990s. Between 1988 and 1991, U.S. average family size actually rose by 16 percent. Recent surveys indicate that over half of all pregnancies in the United States are unintended—either ill-timed or unwanted. Of the approximately 3 million unintended pregnancies, about 1.5 million end in abortion. U.S. adolescent pregnancy and abortion rates are twice as high as those of most West European countries, where contraceptives are generally less expensive, where sex education provides explicit information about preventing pregnancy, and where young adults have relatively unrestricted access to most birth control methods, including safe abortion.

The 1992 average number of children of 2.0 for the United States is substantially higher than that for most industrialized countries. The comparable rate for Western Europe is 1.6 children. If the majority of unintended pregnancies in the United States could be avoided through better education and wider availability of contraception, U.S. family size would probably drop to that of Western Europe. Since America's baby boom generation from the 1950s will soon move out of the reproductive years, this lower fertility rate would lead fairly quickly to U.S. population stabilization (excluding net immigration).

However, with the current fertility rate of 2.0 children and net legal and illegal immigration of perhaps 1 million people a year, the U.S. population could almost double over the next century. For states such as California, New York, Texas, and Florida, which together absorb some two thirds of new immigrants, the social and environmental stresses of population growth rates rivaling those in the Third World are already apparent.

The Reagan Legacy

SOME OF THE MOST IMPORTANT POLITICAL OBSTACLES to worldwide family planning availability have occurred in Washington, D.C., where anti-abortion pressure groups opposed to artificial contraception and organized family planning efforts have been able to dictate new U.S. government policies on domestic and international programs. In contrast to these regressive trends in the United States, most developing-country leaders understand firsthand the problems associated with rapid population growth. Consequently, over 120 governments now subsidize family planning services. Conservative religious opposition to family planning has, however, increased, fueled in part by the anti-choice Reagan administration.

In his first year in office, President Reagan proposed to eliminate the $160 million domestic Title X family planning program by rolling it into a health block grant to the states and then substantially reducing federal health funds available through that mechanism. And his Office of Management and Budget also proposed eliminating the entire $235 million budget for U.S. population assistance internationally. Both these proposals, made in one form or another in most subsequent years of the Reagan and Bush administrations, failed in part as a result of strong congressional and public support for family planning.

But other efforts succeeded, specifically those that (1) crippled family planning programs with additional restrictions; (2) diverted federal funding to "pro-family" groups opposing all forms of contraception; and (3) defunded family planning organizations specifically targeted by the anti-abortion lobby.

This lobbying effort was singularly successful on the international front.

In 1984, at the U.N. International Conference on Population held in Mexico City, a U.S. delegation controlled by anti-abortion and antipopulation activists announced that the U.S. Government no longer considered population growth a serious world problem and that it found abortion so abhorrent that organizations that provided abortion information or services, even with their own funds, would henceforth become ineligible for any kind of U.S. family planning assistance.

The so-called Mexico City policy led almost immediately to U.S. withdrawal, after seventeen years of support, from the International Planned Parenthood Federation (IPPF), based in London and representing voluntary family planning associations in 125 countries. Next to the Red Cross, the IPPF is the world's largest nongovernmental charitable organization.

Congress has attempted but failed several times to overturn the policy. In both Houses of Congress a clear majority favors reversal of the policy, but the 102d Congress lacked sufficient votes to override a presidential veto.

Planned Parenthood was clearly the major target of parallel Reagan-era changes in Title X domestic family planning regulations, which followed within a year the announcement of the Mexico City policy. Widely known as the "gag rule," these regulations deny Title X domestic family planning monies to any family planning program that provides abortion services, counseling, or referral. The Reagan Title X regulations, subsequently supported by President Bush, were upheld by the U.S. Supreme Court in 1991, in *Rust* v. *Sullivan*.

In 1986, the U.S. Government also withdrew its $38 million in support to the U.N. Population Fund, which supports programs in about 140 countries and territories, including a number that receive no U.S. foreign assistance. The fund does not provide support for abortion services or counseling. It does, however, support family planning projects in countries that include abortion as part of reproductive health care, among them the often controversial program in the People's Republic of China. In 1986, the Reagan administration reacted to mounting controversy over China's population program by withholding U.S. contributions to the U.N. Population Fund.

An equally serious legacy of Reagan-era attacks on family planning has been the loss of overall financial support for programs, when adjusted for inflation. In fiscal year 1981, domestic Title X family planning programs were funded at $160 million. The Alan Guttmacher Institute estimates that the purchasing power of Title X funding dropped by roughly two thirds in the decade of the 1980s, just as large numbers of low-income women and young adults were increasingly turning to family planning clinics as their primary health care providers.

In response to rising costs and shrinking public funds, family planning programs have had to raise more money from client fees, and in some cases have shifted the focus of services to middle-income women who can pay. This latter trend has increased the number of low-income women and men, especially young adults and those in minority communities, who are now underserved. Although many state and local governments have attempted to make up the shortfall in federal family planning funds, total public spending has declined in real dollars by about one third since the early 1980s.

International family planning assistance followed a similar pattern, beginning with sharp cuts by President Reagan to President Carter's last foreign aid budget request for fiscal year 1982. President Carter asked Congress nearly to double international population assistance as part of initiatives growing out of the Global 2000 Report. Instead, President Reagan and President Bush routinely asked for less in population assistance than Congress appropriated in the prior year.

The U.S. Government's retreat from the leadership of world population efforts during the 1980s may bear at least part of the blame for the slower progress made during the past decade, as compared with the 1970s. Official U.S. ambivalence about population problems and its preoccupation with abortion helped delay a global commitment to early population stabilization and derailed progress in many countries on reproductive rights for women.

Challenge for the Critical Decade of the 1990s

GIVEN THE IMPORTANCE OF WORLD POPULATION stabilization to broad U.S. national interests, the new President and Administration should seek to close—both at home and abroad—the substantial gap between the growing demand for family planning and the still-inadequate availability of affordable services. In the longer term, U.S. policy should seek, through humane and voluntary means, to achieve early world population stabilization. During this critical decade, the United States should take all steps necessary to ensure a rise in worldwide expenditures on family planning adequate to achieve universal availability of a wide choice of safe and effective birth control technologies by the year 2000, including, where culturally acceptable, safe abortion.

Fortunately, there is still time to recoup international and domestic family planning efforts. Despite the political difficulties, population programs are some of the few successful initiatives to have survived a general deterioration recently in the quality of U.S. foreign aid programs.

The American people strongly support both domestic and international family planning programs—a fact that is probably reflected in the strong support Congress has always given the programs. According to recent polls, virtually all Americans worry about world population growth, believing by wide margins that it will aggravate world poverty and environmental degradation. At a time when public support for many types of foreign aid (especially military aid) is exceedingly low, a majority of Americans want to see some of their tax money used to support family planning programs overseas. The next President will have broad public support for new family planning initiatives.

Short-Term Initiatives

DEPARTMENT OF HEALTH AND HUMAN SERVICES

The following initiatives of the next President would immediately help restore integrity to domestic family planning and reproductive health programs and would, over time, help ensure that all American women and men in the future bear children by choice, not by chance. Universal availability of a wide choice of safe and effective contraceptives and safe methods of pregnancy termination—regardless of the age, income, or marital status of the client—would almost certainly result in an average family size for Americans of slightly below replacement-level fertility. This would allow early U.S. population stabilization, provided some limits were placed on immigration.

• *The next President should seek a fiscal year 1993 appropriation of $320 million for Title X domestic family planning programs*, essentially double the fiscal year 1992 appropriation of $155 million.

• *The next President should abolish the "gag rule" restrictions on the Title X domestic family planning program* that prohibit federal grant recipients from counseling or referring for abortion or from providing medically necessary abortion services. The President should immediately urge Congress to remove restrictions on federal funding for early and for all medically necessary abortions. The President should appoint a commissioner for the Food and Drug Administration who is committed to a fair, impartial, and timely review of the French "mini-abortion" pill, RU-486, and similar products that might make early pregnancy termination safer and less costly.

• *The next President should seek a fiscal year 1993 appropriation of $200 million for the Center for Population Research at the National Institute for Child Health and Human Development,* including $20 million for the three new contraceptive research and development centers recently authorized by Congress. Abortion-related restrictions on biomedical research that have prevented federal support for safe and effective new contraceptives that might work postcoitally should be immediately abolished. To ensure that new birth control technologies approved for use in the United States are widely available, the President should ask the Secretary of Health and

Human Services to establish at the Centers for Disease Control a task force
to monitor the availability and safe use of new methods, such as the contraceptive implant Norplant, and to report any abuse of informed consent
involving any method of birth control.

AGENCY FOR INTERNATIONAL DEVELOPMENT

The following actions of the next President would immediately return the
United States to the leadership ranks of world population efforts and would
over time substantially increase prospects for early world population stabilization at somewhat less than double current levels:

• *A growing number of informed observers believe that the Agency for
International Development, as presently constituted, is not capable of restoring integrity to U.S. population assistance programs*, much less of taking
the other initiatives in reproductive health care, women's development, the
environment, and other sectors that would help to put the world on the road
to population stabilization and sustainable development. Many international
development experts believe that the agency—essentially leaderless since
1987, bogged down by massive red tape and too many competing priorities,
and increasingly dominated by ideological appointees with no real experience
in Third World development—is not salvageable. At the very least, what's
needed is dynamic new leadership and a major organizational overhaul. To
that end the next President should appoint early on, as administrator of the
Agency for International Development, someone of sufficient national stature
and international experience to define and articulate the broad American
interest in environmentally sustainable global development.

The next President should give strong consideration to transferring to
the Department of State those foreign aid programs tied to U.S. security
and related foreign policy objectives (including balance of payments support,
democracy initiatives, and economic policy reform efforts such as structural
readjustment) and creating an independent, privately administered agency
to manage U.S. international cooperation in long-term development efforts
such as population stabilization, environmental protection, family health,
food security, and education. A new vision for U.S. foreign aid programs in
the post–Cold War world is clearly needed—one that Americans can more
readily support than the generally unpopular foreign aid programs of the
past decade. The reform and reorganization of the foreign aid program should
reflect a new vision of U.S. interests and be actively sold as such to Congress
and the American people.

• *The next President should increase total U.S. population assistance
levels for fiscal year 1993 to $650 million.* He should also signal other donor
countries of long-term U.S. support by publicly committing the U.S. Gov-

ernment to provide, in fiscal years 1994 through 2000, incremental increases in funding levels sufficient to reach a level of $1.2 billion (in 1990 dollars) by the end of the decade. This figure represents an appropriate 10 percent U.S. share of the expenditures needed to pay for family planning services and related programs in the year 2000 for three quarters of the developing world's reproductive-age couples.

• *The new President should provide a contribution of at least $90 million (or 15 percent of whatever funds Congress appropriates for U.S. population assistance) to the U.N. Population Fund for fiscal year 1993.* In this and other ways, he can signal the return of the United States to full participation in multilateral cooperation on family planning. In many cases, family planning assistance from multilateral agencies is much more acceptable than direct U.S. bilateral assistance. No congressional action is required to refund the U.N. Population Fund. The new President should instruct the U.S. executive directors to the World Bank and the regional development banks to press these development lending agencies to increase lending for population programs.

• *He should immediately abandon Reagan-era restrictions on U.S. population assistance that prohibit aid to or through any foreign organization that provides information about abortion.* This international "gag rule," known as the Mexico City policy, denies U.S. support to the London-based International Planned Parenthood Federation, with grass-roots affiliates in 125 countries, and to the highly experienced Planned Parenthood Federation of America and others. The policy has had a chilling effect on international commitments to population stabilization and women's reproductive health care by signaling other governments that the powerful U.S. Government is much more concerned about stopping abortion than about stopping population growth or saving women's lives. No congressional action is required to abolish the Mexico City policy.

Long-Term Priorities

DEPARTMENT OF HEALTH AND HUMAN SERVICES

To estimate more precisely the level of support and specific programs needed to ensure universal reproductive choice and responsible parenthood in the United States, the next President should ask the Secretary of Health and Human Services, in collaboration with other appropriate departments and state governments, to:

• make an early assessment of unmet needs for reproductive health care (including safe abortion) in the United States and develop a plan for meeting them within the President's first term;

• promote the further development and widespread adoption by local

school systems of model sex education and family life education curricula, incorporating communications research on responsible parenthood themes;

- use existing authorities under the Adolescent Family Life Act to launch
an enlarged program to reach very poor adolescent women with a
broad complex of services designed, among other things, to improve
basic health and nutrition, ensure high school graduation, delay childbearing until the early twenties, and launch more young women into
long-term productive careers.

AGENCY FOR INTERNATIONAL DEVELOPMENT (OR ITS SUCCESSOR)

The President should ask his foreign aid appointees to assess systematically
the quality of family planning services around the world. Real success in
family planning depends not just on how many people use contraceptives
but also on how well and how consistently they use them over time. Most
important is the question of whether clients are making free and informed
choices among a variety of birth control methods and whether they understand how to use the methods safely and effectively.

In addition to the funds made available for population and family planning efforts, the next President should seek to increase substantially foreign
aid funding for worldwide programs to reduce all major reproductive health
risks. The President should announce that the U.S. Government will support
international cooperation in new initiatives to reduce maternal and child
mortality rates by at least 50 percent by the end of this decade, through
expansion of existing child survival and safe motherhood programs.

OFFICE OF THE PRESIDENT

The next President should appoint a blue-ribbon presidential commission
on "population growth and the American future," similar to the 1972 commission. The new commission should, in the context of a post–Cold War
world, examine the rationale for U.S. participation in efforts to stabilize
world population. The commission should also examine various scenarios for
early U.S. population stabilization and their implications for the environment
and the future quality of American life. The commission should seek also
to develop a coherent rationale for future U.S. immigration law and policy
that is equally consistent with the desirability of U.S. population stabilization
as an environmental priority on the one hand, and with American history,
humanitarian values, and traditions of individual freedom on the other hand.

Agency for International Development,
Department of State,
and Others

MEETING THE NORTH–SOUTH CHALLENGE: DEVELOPMENT AND ENVIRONMENT

JAMES GUSTAVE SPETH[1]

Summary

THE U.S. STAKE IN THE FUTURE OF THE DEVELOPING world, already large, will grow dramatically in the future. The more than 130 developing nations of the South account for four fifths of the world's consumers and one sixth of the economic output, and much of the economic expansion will occur in these regions. Most of the flash points for military violence are there, as are the principal challenges of democracy and human rights. The gravest problems of hunger, disease, and poverty are there. The most serious deteriorations of natural resources and local environments are in these countries, and there is no prospect of meeting threats such as global climate change, biodiversity loss, and overpopulation without their cooperation.

Yet, U.S. policy toward developing countries is in disarray. U.S. programs are dominated by our own military security concerns and a shifting array of immediate political interests; burdened by conflicting objectives; and inadequate in relation to the needs of the developing world, our own long-term interests, and our ability to contribute.

The time has come to reinvent U.S. policy toward the developing world.

James Gustave Speth is President of the World Resources Institute. He formerly chaired President Carter's Council on Environmental Quality.

Early in 1993, the new Administration and Congress should turn to the task of forging a new U.S. program aimed at cooperating with developing countries to achieve broad-based and environmentally sustainable growth. This program should be responsive to the gravity of the environmental, poverty, and population challenges these countries face. It should be viewed as a long-term investment that can yield large benefits for our country: more prosperous trading partners; greater prospects for democracy and stability; a lessening of international tensions; a safer global environment; and enhanced international cooperation on U.S. objectives, ranging from halting nuclear weapons proliferation and slowing the buildup of conventional arms to controlling illegal immigration and drug trafficking.

This new U.S. program must expand U.S. development assistance significantly but also recognize the limits of traditional "foreign aid" approaches. A responsive program must integrate U.S. policy across a wide front: public and private development financing, technology cooperation, debt reduction, mutually advantageous trade reforms, and setting the right example here at home.

Two major steps are needed. First, the next President and Congress should cooperate in creating a new high-level council located and chaired within the executive office of the President to develop governmentwide, integrated U.S. policies relating to developing countries.

Second, the President and Congress should collaborate in the total rewriting of the Foreign Assistance Act. Recognizing the need for new directions and a fresh start in development assistance, the Agency for International Development (AID) should be replaced by a new agency—the Sustainable Development Cooperation Agency (SDCA). The SDCA should be organized into three primary units: a core agency, the Sustainable Development Foundation (SDF), and the Institute for Scientific and Technical Cooperation (ISTC). The SDF would provide grants on a competitive basis for education, training, and capacity-building for sustainable development. The ISTC would work to strengthen developing-country capacity to design, adapt, and utilize the latest technology and to link U.S. private sector capabilities to needs of developing countries.

Lessons of Rio

WITH THE SUDDEN COLLAPSE OF THE COLD WAR, American foreign policy was severed from its traditional moorings and set adrift. Neither the Bush administration nor Congress has responded adequately to the need to articulate a new set of principles and objectives to guide U.S. foreign policy in the post–Cold War era.

Meanwhile, whether America is ready or not, events are pressing forward, driven by powerful currents of change. One such event was the Earth Summit held in June 1992 in Rio de Janeiro, where several important dimensions of the emerging post–Cold War order came into focus.

First, the Rio conference concentrated on environmental security and on the need to close the widening gap between the haves and the have-nots through accelerated, broad-based development in the poorer countries. The greatest accomplishment of the Earth Summit may lie not in the concrete commitments made by governments (they were mostly modest steps, not giant ones) but in the likelihood that the conference has shaped the international agenda for years to come, elevating the issues of environment and equity, linking them inseparably, and dramatizing how powerfully they inject North–South relations into international affairs.

Second, Rio indicates that, with the end of the Cold War, the goal of diplomacy is shifting from conflict management to common endeavor. Earth Summit diplomacy had little to do with superpower conflict; instead, it focused on building a new system of shared international responsibilities through inclusive multilateral agreements. By its close, 154 countries had signed the climate protection convention; 156 had signed the biodiversity protection convention; and 178 had agreed to Agenda 21, an impressively detailed manual that translates the vague concept of sustainable development into actionable policies and programs.

Third, Rio signaled the rise of an increasingly powerful group in international diplomacy: nongovernmental organizations (NGOs). The Earth Summit brought together an international community of scientists, policy experts, business groups, and activists representing a wide array of interests. Although far from cohesive themselves, NGOs worked together surprisingly well throughout the Earth Summit process, lobbying and educating delegates, helping draft agreements, and communicating with the nine thousand journalists who covered Rio.

Finally, the Earth Summit suggests that the new axis of world affairs is not East–West but North–South. Summit negotiators from Europe and Japan seemed to understand the rise of North–South issues in the post–Cold War world. In the end, the North–South standoff that many anticipated and feared at Rio was largely averted because, though it sounds too good to be true, most governments appreciated that the challenges of the global environment and international development can be met only through North–South partnership and cooperation. In its editorial "Limping Home from Rio," *The Washington Post* correctly noted that if the industrial countries want meaningful environmental cooperation from the rest of the world, they are going to have to propose a North–South compact. "If they want the [poorer countries] not to struggle laboriously through the slash-and-burn, coal-and-sulfur stages of development, the rich are going to have to provide them with the resources to bypass it. That means money and technology." In fact, such a compact began to take shape during the Earth Summit. North–South technology cooperation and financing Agenda 21 in developing countries were among the most difficult issues at Rio, but a foundation was laid for addressing them, including new financial commitments from Japan and European countries.

If the U.S. ship of state has been adrift since the Cold War ended, it hit the shoals at Rio. On issue after issue, the United States was odd man out. The roots of the U.S. differences with Europe, Japan, and the developing countries at Rio are not difficult to identify. The Bush administration feared that a tougher climate protection agreement would require a serious national energy policy and that that would cost America jobs. Many in the administration see a fundamental conflict between environmental and economic performance. They also seem to doubt the seriousness of the global warming threat. The Europeans and the Japanese, on the other hand, are seeing economic advantage, not loss, in environmental performance and energy efficiency, and they are farther along in recognizing the implications of widespread climate change.

These are fundamental differences in perception with our OECD partners, but even more significant at Rio was the U.S. failure to perceive our own long-term interests in the success of the developing countries of Latin America, Asia, and Africa. The administration's go-it-alone policies sparked repeated North–South confrontations. On issues such as financing Agenda 21 and signing the biodiversity convention, U.S. policy at Rio would likely have been different had there been greater recognition of our national stake in forging a North–South compact for environment and development.

The United States must reorient its policies or face political obsolescence. Three major changes stand out: the need for new energy and environmental policies that can put the U.S. economy on an environmentally sustainable footing; the need to strengthen international institutions for environmental governance, including an active commitment to the success of a family of treaties addressing ozone layer protection, climate, biodiversity, forests, desertification, hazardous waste, and other issues; and—the primary subject of this chapter—the need for a completely revamped and revitalized program of U.S. cooperation with and assistance to the developing countries.

That the United States' vision regarding the developing world failed at Rio should surprise no one who has watched the deterioration of the U.S. development assistance effort and its political support. The easy defeat of the foreign aid authorization bill in the House of Representatives in 1991 led to a spate of stories in the national press on "foreign aid's eroding consensus" and the growing public support for a "smaller U.S. role abroad." "Foreign aid" and "Third World development" have acquired negative connotations with many voters and politicians, reminding them of giveaways, corrupt leaders, and threats to U.S jobs.

Disturbing as this state of affairs is, it has its positive side. In truth, U.S. policy toward developing countries has been in disarray for years. Numerous reviews and reports have concluded that U.S. programs are dominated by our own military security concerns and burdened by multiple, conflicting objectives, and they are inadequate in relation to the needs of the developing world, our own long-term interests, and our ability to contribute. Although the dollar amount of our development assistance is only a partial measure of the U.S. effort, U.S. assistance as a percentage of GNP now ranks next to last among the eighteen OECD donor countries, ahead only of Ireland. Thus, ending the Cold War has not so much created a problem as revealed one, and in so doing has opened the door to the possibility of positive change.

It is time to reinvent U.S. policy toward the developing world. With the Cold War at last over and democracy emerging around the globe, America should commit itself to a new era of concerted international action against world poverty and environmental deterioration. To carry this mission forward, the new Administration and the new Congress should turn now to the task of forging a new U.S. program aimed at cooperating with developing countries to achieve broad-based and environmentally sustainable growth.

Crisis in the South

THE SOUTH IS IN THE MIDST OF CRISIS. In the developing countries, an estimated 13 million to 18 million people, mostly children, die from hunger and poverty-related causes each year. That's the same human toll as 100 fully loaded 747 jets crashing every day. More than 1 billion people— 20 percent of the global population—live in households too poor to obtain the food needed for normal work, and 500 million people live in households too poor to obtain the food needed for minimal activity. Only 10 to 15 percent of hunger stems from emergencies; most hunger—85 to 90 percent—is born of poverty. Moreover, the United Nations projects that the number of people in "absolute poverty" by the year 2025 will have increased from 1.2 billion today to 1.5 billion.

While the South is slowly gaining on the North in some respects (e.g., in life expectancy and adult literacy), it is falling farther behind in others.

In the 1980s, per capita income in the developing world grew at 1.5 percent annually. In the industrial countries, the rate was 2.4 percent. Today the average per capita income in the developing countries of the South is only about 6 percent of that in the industrial North.

By 1990, external debts of the developing countries had increased from just more than $50 billion in 1970 to $1.3 trillion. In part because of service on that debt, the $40 billion transferred yearly from industrial to developing countries in the early 1980s had by the late 1980s reversed to a $20 billion to $30 billion transfer from poor to rich.

Environmentally, the developing countries today face mounting public health problems and depleting resources. Industrialization and urbanization have led to some of the most serious pollution and sanitation problems ever seen. Other environmental challenges stem not from growing affluence but from growing poverty. As a result of high population growth rates and the absence of other economic alternatives, swelling numbers of poor and landless people are putting unprecedented pressure on natural resources as they struggle to survive. Governmental policies that favor urban areas, the middle classes, and large landowners compound the situation. The poor and the environment are often caught in a downward spiral: The poor are forced to deplete resources in order to live, and that impoverishment of the environment further impoverishes the people.

The global rate of tropical deforestation jumped by more than 50 percent between the late 1970s and the late 1980s. With the rate of forest loss reaching an acre and a half per second, an area of tropical forest about the size of the state of Washington is now lost every year. As those forests are degraded, an important economic resource is lost. Moreover, tropical forests are the planet's greatest storehouse of biological diversity, and hundreds of thousands of species will become extinct by the year 2000 if current destruction continues.

Agricultural trends are also disturbing. Today, the average person among the 4 billion in the developing countries consumes about 2,500 calories of food each day. The average person consumes 3,400 calories per day in Western Europe and more than 3,600 in North America. If the world's people are to have a nutritionally adequate diet, world food output must triple over the next half century. It will be difficult enough to meet those needs under favorable circumstances, and conditions may be far from favorable. According to recent estimates by the world's leading soil scientists, an area of about 1.2 billion hectares—about the size of India and China combined—has experienced moderate to extreme soil deterioration since World War II as a result of human activities.

Another concern is the use of fossil fuels, which provide about 95 percent of the world's commercial energy. Burning large amounts of coal, oil, and natural gas already causes serious local pollution and acid rain over large regions, but many scientists believe that it is also changing the planet's climate as carbon dioxide (CO_2) and other greenhouse gases are pumped into the atmosphere. In the most thorough and widely accepted investigation to date, scientists of the Intergovernmental Panel on Climate Change concluded that it would take a 60 percent reduction in CO_2 emissions to stabilize atmospheric CO_2 at current levels. Thus, even accepting a fair amount of human-induced climate change and allowing for some improvement through slowing or halting deforestation, protecting the Earth's climate may well require that fossil fuel use be cut by more than half during the same fifty-year period in which the world economy is expected to expand severalfold and the developing world will be rapidly industrializing. Today, developing countries consume about 25 percent of world energy; but by the year 2020 that portion is projected to climb to 40 percent.

All of these challenges will be heightened over the next half century as world population roughly doubles. In that population wave, nine of every ten births will be in the already stressed developing world. Also, if economic growth continues at 3 percent annually until the year 2050, world economic activity will have expanded fivefold. Such phenomenal growth in world population and economic activity could dramatically increase stresses on both natural and social systems, with the most severe effects in the developing regions.

U.S. Interests

THE CASE FOR A NEW U.S. COMMITMENT to work with developing countries is firmly grounded in America's own long-term interests—economic, environmental, and political—as well as in humanitarian concerns.

The U.S. economic interest in the developing world has intensified with the emergence of a single global marketplace. The developing world holds vast potential markets for the United States. More than one third of its exports now go to developing countries, and almost 60 percent of Latin America's imports come from the United States. In 1990, U.S. exports to developing countries totaled more than $128 billion, a total that includes more than half of U.S. agricultural exports. Millions of U.S. jobs already depend on the economic health of the developing world, and the failure of heavily indebted countries to grow in the 1980s cost the United States an estimated 1.7 million jobs. But if the poorer countries grow again at rates common in the 1970s, U.S. exports could jump by as much as $30 billion a year within three years, creating another 600,000 U.S. jobs.

There are other economic reasons for the United States to promote development and stability abroad. One quarter of all U.S. private investment overseas is in the countries of the South. The developing world currently owes over $110 billion to the U.S. Government and to U.S. commercial banks. Half of the oil consumed in the United States is imported, and half of that comes from developing countries outside the Persian Gulf. And current efforts to negotiate for freer trade both regionally, with Latin America, and globally, through the Uruguay Round of the General Agreement on Tariffs and Trade (GATT), will deepen economic interdependence and U.S. integration with the world economy.

America's political and security interests also depend on the friendship and progress of nations in Asia, Latin America, and Africa. The United States seeks cooperation on a wide range of objectives: from halting nuclear weapons proliferation and slowing conventional arms buildups to controlling illegal immigration and drug trafficking, fighting the global spread of AIDS and other infectious diseases, combating international terrorism, and participating in regional security arrangements and peace settlements. In each of those transnational areas, the United States will find more cooperative partners in countries where it is supporting sustainable development.

America's fundamental interests in peace and human rights are also at stake. If the legions of the poor swell, if pressures on resources mount and growth proves unsustainable, if population growth continues to outpace the creation of new jobs, if social and ethnic tensions increase, the effects could be felt in many spheres—from the collapse of governments, to the adoption of authoritarian measures, to waves of ecological refugees, to civil unrest and regional conflict.

With the demise of communism, the popular view holds that U.S. development initiatives are now much less of a security imperative. The opposite is probably closer to the truth. While direct security threats to the United States have diminished, outbreaks of armed conflict in the developing world now threaten global peace and order. One hundred twenty-five wars have been fought in the developing world since World War II. While some were linked to superpower activity, most were rooted in national and regional tensions. The frequency of such conflicts could increase with the decline of superpower presence and the heightened scarcity of resources and other pressures resulting from the failure of sustainable, broad-based development.

Lastly, solving global environmental problems will require the full participation of the developing countries. Put simply, the United States needs the cooperation of the developing world to protect its own environment.

Consider global warming. Leaders of the developing world expect the North to take the first and strongest actions on global warming because, as they correctly point out, the industrial countries are largely responsible for the problem and have the most resources to solve it. But even here the problem is fundamentally intractable without the cooperation of the developing countries. Developing countries already account for 40 to 45 percent of annual greenhouse gas emissions, and their share will grow as they continue to industrialize. International cooperation aimed at helping the developing world leapfrog the energy and industrial patterns of the North is the only attractive course.

Another major U.S. and world interest—meeting the threat of runaway population growth—also requires leadership in the developing world, but success will hinge on whether the industrial countries are farsighted enough to provide financial and political support, as Sharon L. Camp discusses at length in her chapter in this book.

Developing-country cooperation with the United States across this spectrum of economic, political, and environmental issues will be enhanced where there is widely shared economic progress and a conviction that the United States is genuinely committed to helping the country realize its own aspirations. On the other hand, the persistence of large North–South disparities, and industrial country failure to respond to developing country needs, could make cooperation difficult on many issues of concern to the United States.

A New U.S. Program

EARLY IN 1993, the new Administration and the Congress should turn to the task of forging a new U.S. program aimed at cooperating with and assisting developing countries in achieving broad-based and environmentally sustainable growth.

Only the President can bring home to the American people the far-reaching transformations that are occurring in the post–Cold War world; the importance of North–South relations; and the need for a major, new integrated program of U.S. cooperation with the developing countries. Given the public's negative views of "foreign aid," if ever there were a compelling case for presidential leadership, this is it.

As a priority of the 1993–94 Congress, the next President and Congress should collaborate in the total rewriting of the Foreign Assistance Act. The following are key elements of a new U.S. program responsive to the environmental and economic needs of the developing world in the 1990s as well as to our own long-term interests.

1. The prime objective must be to promote sustainable development—
that is, economic and social progress that both alleviates poverty and protects
the environment for future generations. The new U.S. program must be a
development program, but one that moves beyond the outmoded concept
of the environment as another cost burdening the economy. Many Third
World development projects have simply not worked because they were not
environmentally sound and therefore were not sustainable.

Thus the new U.S. program should stress goals such as these:

- effective family planning and programs to improve maternal and child
  health care and to raise the status of women, with slowed population
  growth as one consequence;
- sustainable agriculture and fisheries, with the aim of meeting food and
  other agricultural needs while enhancing the natural resource base;
- sustainable energy production, with the goal of providing energy services for rapidly growing economies while reducing urban pollution
  and helping prevent global warming;
- sustainable forestry, with the goal of providing forest resources for
  community and national development while conserving biodiversity;
- effective pollution control and environmental protection programs,
  with the objective of protecting air and water and guarding public
  health.

In those and other areas, the U.S. program should focus on the needs
of the poor and promote what has come to be called "primary environmental
care." Primary environmental care combines three elements: meeting basic
human needs, protecting the local environment for future production, and
empowering local groups and communities. Projects based on those tenets
tend to be small in scale; to use locally developed technology; and to involve
local people in project design and implementation, especially women in their
role as resource managers.

2. The traditional development assistance programs, such as those carried out by the AID and other bilateral aid agencies, will not be sufficient
to support sustainable development fully or to ensure cooperation on global
environmental challenges. A successful program must extend to other critical
areas affecting the prospects of developing countries, including access to
capital and technology on favorable terms, reductions of external debt, and
mutually advantageous trade reforms.

3. The bilateral foreign assistance portion of the new U.S. program
should concentrate heavily on up-front needs—on building the human and
institutional capacities needed for sustainable development. That is pioneer-

ing work. The United States should stress education and training, increased capabilities for local governments and NGOs, national planning and policy development, technical and scientific cooperation, information and monitoring services, private sector partnerships, and demonstration projects in areas such as sustainable agriculture and sustainable energy.

This capacity-building effort should shape the international activities of many federal agencies, such as the Environmental Protection Agency and the Department of the Interior. It should also stress international cooperation in science and technology and seek to link the U.S. private sector's strengths in these areas to developing countries' opportunities and needs.

4. The United States should sharply increase its overall financial support for development assistance, perhaps doubling it. While obviously politically unpopular now, such a step would bring its contribution as a percentage of the GNP into the same league as Canada's, France's, and Germany's. The 1989 report of the Schmidt Commission, *Facing One World*, called on the OECD countries to double their development assistance, and the Earth Summit's Agenda 21 seeks a similar increase.

The Schmidt Commission also urged donor countries to give special consideration to countries that emphasize poverty-reduction programs, spend less than 2 percent of their GNP on the military, take steps toward efficient family planning policies, or implement policies aimed at environmental preservation. The United States should follow Japan's recent example and adopt that approach.

As long as U.S. bilateral foreign aid remains tied to national security considerations, it will remain strongly influenced by factors other than the honesty, commitment, need, and performance of recipients. It is time to restore the integrity of development assistance. The new U.S. program should offer assistance only when recipients demonstrate a political commitment to performance. Assistance should also be provided in a more "responsive" manner, with recipients taking more responsibility for identifying and justifying the projects they desire.

As political leaders move to overhaul development assistance, they should dispel an illusion: Public opinion polls indicate that many in the general public believe that "foreign aid" constitutes 15 percent or more of the federal budget. In fact, economic assistance of all types—including bilateral and multilateral development aid, Food for Peace, and other categories—totals considerably less than 1 percent of the federal budget. With the opportunity now before the country to reduce its military commitments, the funds should be available to invest in a stronger America at home and abroad.

5. Efforts to promote wise investments will be undermined unless coupled with internal policy reforms in many areas. To cite one example, studies in numerous countries (including the United States) have shown that substantial direct and indirect subsidies resulting from government policy encourage deforestation and the waste of water, energy, pesticides, and other resources. Economies rich and poor need signals, including prices and national accounting systems, that reflect the true long-term costs of production.

6. Wherever possible the new U.S. program should promote multilateral approaches. The United States should seek to strengthen the capabilities of the agencies of the U.N. system (such as the U.N. Environment Program and the U.N. Development Program), the World Bank, and regional development banks. The United States should also join its European allies in supporting the new Global Environment Facility sponsored by the U.N. agencies and the World Bank.

The recent emergence of what promises to be a growing family of international conventions on the environment adds a special dimension to multilateral assistance. Several of the conventions—such as the ones on climate and biodiversity—establish funds through which industrial countries assist developing countries to meet the additional costs of complying with international agreements. The Global Environment Facility has been asked to administer the funds. Eventually, the sums involved promise to be quite large.

Given that U.S. policy toward developing countries needs a fresh start and that more than marginal changes are required, U.S. institutional arrangements should be reworked along the following lines:

• The next President and Congress should cooperate in creating a new high-level council located and chaired within the executive office of the President to develop governmentwide, integrated U.S. policies relating to developing countries and to ensure a concerted interagency effort to carry out these policies. Such an entity could be part of the new Global Policy Council recently proposed by Rick Inderfurth to replace the National Security Council. It would develop appropriate bilateral and multilateral initiatives in debt reduction, trade relations, the integration of trade and environment, technology cooperation, promotion of U.S. private sector investment in developing countries, and multilateral development bank policy. It would also develop Administration initiatives in areas such as protecting world forest resources.

• AID should be replaced by a new agency—the Sustainable Development Cooperation Agency (SDCA). Although subject to the foreign policy guidance of the Secretary of State, the SDCA would be independent of the Department of State. The United States has long-term interests in Third World development that are different from the State Department's interest in day-to-day—and often changing—political, economic, and security relations. Many of AID's problems today stem from an attempt to impose short-term political objectives on a long-term development program.

The SDCA's administrator would be charged with primary responsibility for establishing overall development assistance policy and coordinating interagency implementation of U.S. international development policies. The administrator would report to the President and would serve as principal adviser to him on international development. The administrator would chair a high-level interagency body, the Sustainable Development Coordinating Committee, charged with coordinating the work of the many federal agencies carrying out these related international activities. The SDCA must come to be seen as a major and influential agency with strong leadership, not as a backwater passed over when important tasks are assigned. These goals can be furthered through appropriate statutory responsibilities and by appointing an administrator of cabinet-level stature with presidential backing and access.

• The SDCA should be organized into three primary units. The core agency would have responsibility for the majority of SDCA funds. It would operate through a policy center and regional bureaus. The policy center would bring together outstanding talent on development issues, recognizing the importance of ideas, analysis, and expertise in coordinating Washington agencies, influencing multilateral bodies, providing guidance to the regional bureaus and other SDCA entities, and developing policy dialogue and bilateral programs with developing countries. The core agency would support the administrator in carrying out statutory and special assignments, administer disaster assistance, respond to special situations (such as support for the nations of the former Soviet Union), provide technical and scientific backing for the SDCA's activities, and administer a greatly reduced Economic Support Fund program.

The SDCA's second component, the Sustainable Development Foundation (SDF) would provide major new financial resources for education, training, and capacity-building for sustainable development; for technical assistance, strategic planning, and institutional strengthening; and for grassroots initiatives and primary environmental-care projects. With units focused on each of the three major developing-country regions, it would operate on the foundation model, making grants to governmental and nongovernmental groups on a competitive basis in response to promising proposals. The SDF would both use and build talent in the NGO community, including private voluntary organizations in both the United States and developing countries. It would rely heavily on these groups as intermediate organizations for planning and carrying out sustainable development programs and implementing primary environmental-care approaches. It is envisioned that, after a phase-in period, the SDF would disburse $1 billion to $2 billion annually. Its head would be a presidential appointee reporting to the SDCA administrator.

The SDCA's Institute for Scientific and Technical Cooperation, the agency's third component, would work to strengthen developing countries' capacity to design, adapt, and utilize the latest technology and to carry out applied research for development needs; support joint scientific research and technology development of great importance to developing countries; and forge long-term linkages between the U.S. private sector and developing country enterprises.

NOTE

1. The author has benefited greatly from three reports in which he collaborated—"New Challenges, New Opportunities" (1988) by Ralph H. Smuckler and Robert J. Berg; "Partnership for Sustainable Development" (1991) by an Environment and Energy Study Institute task force chaired by the author; and "Compact for a New World" (1991), the report of the New World Dialogue convened by the WRI. He also benefited from the Overseas Development Council's "Challenges and Priorities in the 1990s" (1992); and from his WRI colleagues and their research.

PART VII

OTHER RECOMMENDATIONS

PERSONNEL PROCESS FOR A PRESIDENTIAL TRANSITION

ARNIE MILLER

Summary

T
O MOVE HIS POLICY AGENDA during the first hundred days, the President-elect will need five to six hundred key people in place shortly after his inauguration.

He must start early, establishing transition teams for each of his major policy objectives. The transition teams should identify all of the key jobs within the government necessary to achieve each major objective—jobs that must include both presidential appointments as well as career and noncareer senior executive service positions. Media expectations must be shaped so that the Administration is evaluated on the filling of key jobs rather than all jobs and so that quality rather than speed is paramount.

The transition teams should establish one- and two-year management and policy objectives for each of these key positions and then develop diverse pools of three to five candidates for each key job. Recruiters must reach out quickly and broadly to state and local governments, universities, advocacy groups, the business community, and elsewhere to identify first-rate candidates in addition to the thousands who will apply. To ensure that substantial numbers of women and people of color are appointed, advocacy groups especially should be invited to assist with outreach and identification of candidates beyond merely a Beltway–old-boy network.

The transition team and the Presidential Personnel Office (PPO) must

Arnie Miller served as the Director of the Presidential Personnel Office in the Carter administration. He is President of Isaacson, Miller, Inc., an executive recruiting firm in Boston. He specializes in recruitment of senior executives for state and local governments and nonprofit organizations.

also test for loyalty. While participation in the campaign is, of course, relevant, agreement with policies and examples from previous work are more reliable indicators of a capacity for loyalty.

The process of selecting candidates for major cabinet and subcabinet positions should serve as the first step in team-building across agency lines. Candidates for subcabinet posts should be screened by teams of people with whom they will work. Screening committees should include people from the same policy cluster and from a number of agencies as well as policy people from the new White House and OMB. Each committee should be staffed by a recruiter or personnel specialist from the transition staff or the PPO. And departmental distinctions must be downplayed. The President's agenda must replace territorial integrity or bureaucratic turf as the overriding concern.

The President, Vice President, and other senior people must work hard to foster a sense of belonging and loyalty to the Administration. An orientation program for the new appointees can help them understand overall themes as well as learn about how to do their jobs. A separate confirmation unit should be established at the White House to assist nominees with conflicts of interest and disclosure questions and to prepare them for confirmation hearings.

Efforts at team-building will be helpful but are not enough. A new way of thinking about government is needed—an American *perestroika*. Systems for budgeting and accounting; evaluating performance; hiring, firing, and promotion of personnel; and procuring of goods and services must all be revamped so that competent and committed people, pursuing progressive policies, are not bogged down in the swamp of bureaucratic process.

Organize Transition Teams Around Policies Quickly

THE NEW PRESIDENT CAN'T DO IT ALONE. He didn't win on his own, and he certainly can't govern on his own. Rather, he will need several large teams of people to help him carry out his agenda. He won't need all of his allowed thirty-five hundred presidential and political appointees in order to succeed, but he'll certainly need the help of five to six hundred key people shortly after his inauguration.

While the rest of this book deals with policy, this chapter focuses on the personnel process. It concentrates on the several hundred subcabinet appointments that must be made quickly, in addition to the fifteen to twenty department and agency heads whom the President must select.

One of the most important things to do is to start early, which means immediately after the convention. January 20 comes very quickly, and a lot must happen in the seventy-eight days between the election and the inauguration.

The first step is quietly to create skeletal transition teams during the campaign. In the past, most of the members of transition teams have been people angling for jobs in a new administration, augmented by people from the campaign after the election. Often this "augmentation" is accompanied by a struggle. In 1976, campaign manager Hamilton Jordan nudged transition director Jack Watson out of the way and, with Carter's blessing, set himself up to manage the appointment process. In 1980–81, Pendelton James was hit with a broadside from Lynn Nofziger, who accurately complained that tried-and-true Reaganites were being ignored and the government was filling up with corporate Republicans. The lesson is clear: Transition teams can't ignore people from the campaign. They must be structured from the beginning to prepare for the absorption of the victorious, battle-tested campaign staff. Ideally, campaign and transition staff will interact if not overlap before the election.

The transition team should organize itself around the President-elect's major policy objectives. Each cluster of the transition team should then translate these major policy objectives into specific steps that will have to be taken at the start of the new Administration. Next, they should identify all the positions required to achieve these objectives. The result of this effort should be clusters of positions—teams organized around each major objective.

For example, if the President has announced the goal of creating hundreds of thousands of new jobs in America by a certain date, he will need the help of people from all across government who have a hand on the rudder of job creation—from the Defense Department to the Departments of Labor, Housing, Agriculture, Health and Human Services, Commerce, and the Treasury; the Council of Economic Advisers; the Domestic Policy Staff; and the Office of Management and Budget. Similarly, an effort to reduce the deficit will require the collaboration of people at the Federal Reserve Board, the OMB, the Council of Economic Advisers, the Domestic Policy Staff, the Department of Defense, the Treasury, and the budget, procurement, and congressional liaison shops in each of the major departments and agencies. The positions identified must include not just the assistant secretaries and above who are presidential appointees, but also the deputy assistant secretaries, and those career and noncareer senior executive service, Schedule C, and Schedule A positions who will be key to the formulation and execution of new policies. According to Carl Brauer in his

1986 book *Presidential Transitions*, the Reagan transition team identified "eighty-seven appointive positions in the economic policy area" alone.[1]

Before the election, these key positions must be assembled from a variety of sources: former appointees; congressional committee staffs; the *Government Manual;* the *Plum Book*, published by the House Post Office and Civil Service Committee; and key interest groups. After the election, if a new Administration takes office, it should quickly receive the lists of incumbent appointees from the outgoing president.

While that suggestion may appear obvious, it rarely occurs. Prior to 1980, new presidents inherited empty file cabinets in the Personnel Office. Jimmy Carter was the first president to transfer a complete database of all political appointees to his successor. Ronald Reagan and George Bush, predictably, similarly collaborated. The Carter precedent should govern all future transitions.

Assuming such cooperation, the new Administration should concentrate first on filling the key positions. Everyone involved in the personnel process— transition staff, and later PPO staff; department and agency heads and staff; the Counsel to the President; the Special Inquiries Unit (SPIU) of the FBI, which conducts full field investigations; the IRS; and the congressional liaison people working on confirmations—must all know which appointments are to be made first. Without such an agreed-on priority, key positions simply won't get filled and the new President will hit the ground crawling.

Shortly after the election, the press will develop scorecards to measure progress in filling appointments. Expectations among the press must be shaped so that the new Administration is evaluated on filling key jobs rather than all jobs and so that quality rather than speed is paramount. The republic will survive if most of the thirty-five hundred presidential and political appointments aren't filled before, say, June of the first year. But the President won't be able to move his agenda in the first hundred days if five to six hundred key people are not in place.

Establish Objectives for Each Key Job

BASED ON THE NOMINEE'S GOVERNMENT RECORD and campaign speeches, the transition team should establish one- and two-year management and policy objectives for each of those key positions. These objectives ultimately must be approved by the President, his key advisers, and the relevant cabinet members. But the process must begin during the campaign, well before many of the key people can devote very much attention to it. Starting early is necessary so that, upon appointment at about around the turn of the year, an assistant secretary would know roughly what budget changes must be made, regulations revised, legislation changed, funding formulas altered, and procurements slowed down or speeded up. All major appointees must know specifically what is expected of them and how they fit into the overall effort to fulfill the President's policy objectives.

Before they are selected, candidates for each job should be specifically evaluated according to their ability to achieve those objectives. Do they understand and agree with the President's policy objectives, and do they have the requisite experience, talent, integrity, and capacity for loyalty to accomplish them? As more is learned and new people are added to the administration, these objectives may become changed or refined. But they must conform to what the President wants. And they must be specific to each President. It is not enough to define a position by listing the duties and responsibilities from standard personnel job descriptions. The role and importance of many assistant secretaries and what is expected of them in one administration will be totally different in the next.

Develop Pools of Three to Five Candidates for Each Key Job

AFTER OBJECTIVES ARE ESTABLISHED, excellent candidates must be found. Especially if the White House changes parties, transition and PPO recruiters will have no trouble finding candidates, who will appear from every conceivable source: the Hill, the campaign, interest groups, cabinet members, governors, mayors, and other White House staff will have recommendations, and many people will recommend themselves. And then there are the President and the Vice President. They will undoubtedly have ideas, too. Their recommendations must be subjected to the same scrutiny as those of others. Transition and PPO staff owe it to the President to provide him with their best judgments about all candidates. Of course, the President should have people he knows and trusts, but he must also have honest advice. Too often at the beginning of an administration, as people are establishing relationships and feeling their way, they are reluctant to take on the boss.[2]

Thus the challenge for the transition team, the PPO, and the departmental recruiters will be to reach out beyond this group of candidates to a broader network of excellent people who may not be thinking about or campaigning for a presidential appointment. This is not to imply that someone is not appropriate because he or she has applied for a position. It does mean, however, that harried recruiters, under great pressure to fill positions, must rigorously hold to their standards and resist the temptation to choose from among an existing group of familiar candidates if none is appropriate. They must then reach out to successful public servants in state and local government, universities, advocacy groups, the business community, and elsewhere to identify first-rate people.

A very substantial pool of candidates will come from the campaign. Our system of primaries requires every presidential candidate to build a personal organization, state by state. People who have helped in the primaries or in the general election will now want to help govern. Thousands will come to Washington or will write or call. Many will organize campaigns for themselves. A goodly number of first-rate people will assume major roles in the White House and in various departments and agencies. Many others will be appropriate for Schedule C or other appointments that do not require nomination by the President or confirmation by the Senate. Yet there will never be enough jobs to satisfy the demand. If people are not hired, they must know that they have been considered fully and fairly.

A system must be developed for interviewing, counseling, rating, and referring campaign staff and volunteers to appropriate contacts in each department and agency of government. Every person who has helped should be treated with respect and appreciation. As many supporters as possible and certainly every key supporter must be interviewed and counseled as to how their skills and experience match the needs of the Administration. Expectations will be extremely high and must be managed with care and honesty. People must know that there are relatively few full-time political appointments available. Part-time appointments to advisory committees, invitations to White House functions and briefings, and other opportunities to serve must be made available where appropriate.

The transition effort needs to develop pools of three to five excellent people for each position because some people will decline to serve, or be unable to clear conflict-of-interest or background investigations, and backups will be needed. Additionally, department and agency heads should be offered some choice in putting together compatible and diverse teams.

Diversity

TO ENSURE THAT SUBSTANTIAL numbers of women and people of color are appointed throughout the Administration, advocacy groups that are supportive of the Administration and represent women and/or minorities should be brought in early to assist with outreach and the identification of candidates. Such organizations should be informed, in detail, of the specific requirements for particular positions and encouraged to identify prospective candidates who meet these requirements. It may take longer to identify minorities because, by definition, there are fewer experienced people from whom to recruit.

But "we couldn't find any" is no longer a legitimate excuse. Nor is it acceptable to have "diverse pools" of candidates considered for each position but none selected. If the President wants substantial numbers of women and members of minorities serving in his government, then the transition team and the PPO must be enforcers and enablers of this policy. To be effective, they must have the power to turn down recommendations from cabinet members. More importantly, they must become a resource for candidates and networks to be tapped for candidates. It goes without saying that these offices themselves must have diverse staffs.

Loyalty

IN ADDITION TO COMPETENCE AND DIVERSITY, the transition team and the PPO must also test for loyalty. The President must have people whose work history clearly demonstrates a capacity for loyalty, which means thinking about and protecting the President's political and policy interests before one's own or those of an agency or agency head. Operationally, it can mean carrying out policies with which one doesn't agree. The problem, however, is always, Who gets to define the President's political interests? Is it the cabinet member, or the President's staff?

In the last analysis, this responsibility belongs with the White House staff. However, too often White House staffers confuse their personal predilections with the President's political interests. Strong cabinet members will be able to keep that in check, and a respected chief of staff should be empowered to arbitrate when necessary. Ultimately, a climate of mutual respect and collaboration (discussed below) must be fostered. This collegiality will go a long way toward minimizing tensions between the cabinet and the White House staff.

Particularly at the start of an administration, loyalty is typically measured by early participation in the campaign. Others who came later, or not at all, must prove themselves. While these distinctions are important, they are clearly insufficient. Many a president has been badly hurt by "early supporters" who were looking out for themselves. Alternatively, presidents have been served loyally and well by more recent supporters. Recall that President-elect Ronald Reagan chose a primary opponent's campaign manager, James Baker, to be his first chief of staff. Baker, in turn, brought many people into the White House who had not worked in the Reagan campaign.

As Carl Brauer points out, "Reagan self-confidently and wisely assumed their loyalty and Reagan got off to a much more effective start."[3]

The point is not that the President will be well served only by people who know how to salute and follow orders. Rather, the President must surround himself with people who will argue vigorously for a point of view but will know when to stop after decisions have been made and a plan must be executed.

To test for loyalty, recruiters must probe for a number of indicators: Agreement on policies is a good start, but history is better. Candidates for jobs should be encouraged to tell stories about policies they didn't agree with that they nevertheless carried out or specific instances when they subordinated their own interests to those of their superiors. These stories will be revealing. Recruiters must use them to develop an understanding of what it takes to win and hold a person's loyalty.

Selecting Appointees Should Be a Team Effort

CANDIDATES FOR SUBCABINET POSITIONS should be screened and pools developed by teams of people with whom they will work. Screening committees should include people from the same policy cluster—department and agency personnel (some from different departments) and policy people from the EOP and the OMB, as well as White House political people. Each committee should be staffed by a personnel specialist or recruiter from the transition staff and later the PPO. These specialists should drive the process along and ensure that all appropriate bases are touched as decisions get made.

The process of selecting members of the Administration should serve as the first step in team-building across agency lines. But all teams have leaders, and the President must retain for himself the responsibility to select his key appointees. This can't be delegated to the cabinet. On the other hand, department and agency heads, if they are to become active team members, can't be ignored or repeatedly overruled. When disagreements develop among staff and agency heads, the chief of staff or the Vice President should be called in to help work them out. In the end, if necessary, the President must decide.

While obviously the President can't interview all of his subcabinet appointees, he should interview all deputy secretaries and undersecretaries. He may also want to interview some key assistant secretaries. While he can't interview each assistant secretary, he should at least meet them all.

Once the Administration takes power, departmental distinctions must be downplayed. People must join together across agency lines to seek solutions to problems collectively. The mission—the President's agenda—must replace territorial integrity or bureaucratic turf as the overriding concern. People must be encouraged to collaborate and focus on the mess confronting the country rather than the interests of their particular department or agency. They must see themselves as members of an Administration rather than as employees of a particular department.

The President, the Vice President, and senior people throughout the Federal Government will have to work hard to foster a sense of belonging and loyalty to the Administration. They must start by modeling their own behavior. The style of the leaders will greatly influence the style adopted by people throughout the Administration. If White House staff are allowed to bicker and intramural politics get out of hand, the cancer will spread throughout the departments and agencies. People who are busy and feel involved don't have time for intramural politics. People who feel uninvolved grow alienated and start to leak stories or look for other ways to assert their importance.

An Orientation Program

A GOOD WAY TO START is with an orientation program for all new key appointees. This has been recommended, for many years, by observers of the presidential personnel process such as Professor Calvin Mackenzie of Bowdoin College and the Council on Excellence in Government.[4] An effective orientation program should begin building a sense of belonging and loyalty to the Administration by addressing policy, process, and politics.

Appointees should meet with the President, the Vice President, and senior White House staff. They should come away understanding the President's overall themes and their particular role in the achievement of policy outcomes. The orientation program ought to become not a place for the development of policy, but a place where themes are articulated and internalized. Appointees must also learn how to do their jobs. They will need to become familiar with the budget process and regulations governing personnel, procurement, and ethics. They should be trained regarding media, congressional, and interest group relations, and they should be provided with in-depth assessments of the political strengths and vulnerabilities of the Administration and enlisted in efforts to enhance the President's political strength.

Orientation programs, however, are only the beginning. A system of rewards must be developed that encourages collaboration and the sharing of innovative ideas. (Currently most incentives reward only bigger budgets and bigger staffs.) Appointees should be invited to the White House for briefings and discussions of policy and politics. But also the President, the Vice President, and senior staff should actually go out to the agencies to talk about issues. Appointees should be invited to dinners, movies, and other social events at the White House or elsewhere in Washington. They should have their pictures taken with the President and the Vice President. As Professor Calvin Mackenzie recommends, "Make them feel that they are special and important."[5] They are.

Getting Nominees Confirmed

ONCE PEOPLE ARE SELECTED, a great deal must take place before they are nominated and confirmed. Financial-disclosure and conflict-of-interest forms must be completed. Full field investigations must be conducted by the Special Inquiries Unit of the FBI. Tax checks are completed by the IRS. Other agencies may also be involved in granting appropriate security clearances. Many Senate committees have their own questionnaires to be completed.

For years the FBI has resisted tailoring its procedures for full field investigations to the requirements of particular positions. The bureau conducts the same number of interviews in the field for appointees to the National Advisory Commission on Library and Information Science as it does for the assistant secretary of the Treasury for tax policy, since both are presidential appointments that require Senate confirmation. The FBI's obstinance has often resulted in unnecessary delays in getting names to the Senate. The leadership of the transition team and the staff directors of the relevant Senate committees should meet with the director of the FBI to rationalize this process.

To prepare for press inquiries and confirmation hearings, nominees must internalize the President's values, approaches, and policies. Key senators and committee staff members must be visited. In some instances, it may also be necessary to visit with key members of the House and leaders of relevant interest groups. In all instances, notification and/or political clearance from these essential people must be accomplished before nominations are announced. Those to be cleared with include the leaders of the relevant House and Senate subcommittees, and the political campaign director and senators from the appointee's home state. To avoid sowing a harvest of ill will, the PPO and congressional liaison staff should also notify unsuccessful candidates and important political supporters of unsuccessful candidates.

A separate confirmation unit should be established in the White House with members of the PPO, the counsel's office, and the Office of Congressional Liaison to assist nominees with conflict-of-interest and disclosure questions and prepare them for confirmation hearings. From the moment they are selected, appointees should feel well supported by the confirmation unit and already a part of an Administration they will be proud to serve.

While these efforts at team-building and changing the culture of the Federal Government will be helpful, they will clearly not be enough to make government work effectively. As David Osborne and Ted Gaebler put it in their important new book *Reinventing Government*, "a new paradigm—a new way of thinking about government is needed"[6] They call for an American *perestroika*. Systems for budgeting and accounting; evaluating performance; hiring, firing, and promotion of personnel; and procurement of goods and services—some of these systems designed over a hundred years ago—must all be revamped to free the President and his appointees to address the nation's problems. "Hierarchical centralized bureaucracies designed in the 1930s or 1940s simply do not function well in the rapidly changing, information-rich, knowledge-intensive society and economy of the 1990s,"[7] conclude Osborne and Gaebler. "If leaders tell their employees to focus on their mission, but the budget and personnel systems tell them to follow the rules, . . . the employees will listen to the systems. The leaders' mission will vanish like a mirage."[8]

Much more work needs to be done to redefine the purposes of government, as well as the ways in which it is organized and operates to achieve those purposes. For example, our society must rethink how we can foster greater independence among our people. We should then consider what we expect government to do, what citizens should do for themselves, and what responsibilities should be assumed by other organizations or institutions in the society. Americans must redefine what we mean by national security to include economic and environmental security. Other chapters in this volume address these and other questions. However, even if the President-elect quickly chooses competent and committed people and then motivates them to advance his agenda, policy will be lost in the swamp of a bogged-down process if fundamental changes are not made in the ways our government operates.

NOTES

1. Carl Brauer, *Presidential Transitions* (New York: Oxford University Press, 1986), p. 233.
2. For a further discussion of this, see ibid., chap. 2 and 4.
3. Ibid., p. 223.
4. See, in particular, the work of Calvin Mackenzie, Director of the Presidential Appointee Project of the National Academy of Public Administration. Several of his recommendations are included in Calvin Mackenzie, *The Presidential Appointees Handbook* (National Academy of Public Administration, undated). Many of his recommendations have been adopted.
5. Calvin Mackenzie, unpublished memo to the President-elect, 1988.
6. David Osborne and Ted Gaebler, *Reinventing Government* (Reading, Mass.: Addison-Wesley, 1992).
7. Ibid., chap. 9.
8. Ibid., p. 117.

RACE AND CLASS

HENRY LOUIS GATES, JR.

EVERYONE KNOWS THERE ARE TWO NATIONS in this country, white and black, right? That's what the Kerner Commission Report said in 1968, and that's what the title of Andrew Hacker's best-selling sequel to that report says today. And for good reason. Track the statistics for public health, educational attainment, and income, and they all seem to point to the same thing—that African Americans are the ultimate unassimilables of the American mix, the pebble in the ethnic soup.

This has become our role, as well, in American political discourse: the ultimate special interest group; the people politicians speak to about drugs and riots; the resentful charity case. Yet the way African Americans are spoken about and pandered to in our quadrennial political parade no longer reflects the reality of the lives African Americans lead.

Peer a little closer, and the familiar image splits in two. Even as the ranks of the underclass expand, a second nation-within-a-nation has formed. The fact is, Afro America's affluent elite is larger than it has ever been—a legacy of the post–civil rights era and just the kinds of corporate and governmental programs of intervention that have fallen into such disfavor of late.

Now, most of the black community's leaders, self-appointed or otherwise, are loath to acknowledge the existence of this class. And that's because they take it as part of their role to publicize the dire condition afflicting so much of black America, as do those white politicians who seek and receive support from black America. Why distract from the real problem? But here's the rub. Opponents of these post–civil rights era programs are consequently in

---

Henry Louis Gates, Jr., is W. E. B. Du Bois Professor of the Humanities, Chairman of the Department of Afro-American Studies, and Director of the W. E. B. Du Bois Institute at Harvard University. He is a MacArthur Prize Fellow. His books include Figures in Black; The Signifying Monkey, *for which he received a 1989 American Book Award; and* Loose Canons: Notes on the Culture Wars.

a position to declare, flatly, that all such remedies have failed—while the voices of those programs' defenders are often faint and contradictory. How to explain the complicated truth: that for black America, these are the worst of times. . . and the best of times? That is the challenge the next President will face.

For there are two nations in this country—both black. Today, many black Americans enjoy a measure of economic security beyond any we have known in the history of black America; and yet their very existence seems an affront to the swelling ranks of the poor. Nor have black intellectuals ever quite made peace with the concept of the black bourgeoisie, a group that is typically seen as devoid of any cultural authenticity, doomed to mimicry and pallid assimilation. Indeed, nothing is more characteristic of the black bourgeoisie than the sense of shame and denial that the identity inspires. You may well ask, What did we do to be so black and blue?

But it's unfortunate that the denial of our measure of success, however limited, is seen as necessary to keep attention on our failures. For if we confronted the ambiguous legacy of the civil rights era with greater candor, we'd also have to get beyond the old either/ors of social explanation. Too many people on the right are still inclined to explain poverty as the result of bad behavior, bad values, bad morals—and nothing more. "They understand loss of values as simply choices made by individuals," the philosopher and theologian Cornel West astutely notes, "as if they are not shaped by the larger structural institutional realities of cultural consumption." In the meantime, too many apologists on the left are still inclined to explain poverty as determined solely by brute structural inequity, denying the importance of the choices we make and condescendingly treating us as helpless rag dolls tossed around by economic fate.

The dramatic growth of the black middle class gives the lie to both extremes. On the one hand, it shows that affirmative intervention, on the part of government and the private sector, does make a difference: It can change lives, transform families. On the other hand, personal responsibility is where the buck stops. One of the many vicious circles of the underclass— to use a controversial but useful term—is that poverty and hopelessness breed the kind of values that perpetuate those very conditions.

The left doesn't like to talk about culture: Why give their opponents more fodder for their benighted views? The right doesn't like to talk about racial economics: They figure the liberals are doing enough mollycoddling as it is. As a result, the main participants in the great race-and-poverty debate are more interested in scoring points off each other than they are in analytical rigor.

And what allows the game to continue is the stereotype that both sides share of a homogeneous black America still innocent of class stratification. Since many of the most prosperous of the black middle class are afflicted by the guilt of the survivor, they're not inclined to disabuse anyone of this conception. The black advertising exec may live in White Plains, but he's buried his heart in Harlem.

The truth is that black Americans have always been uncomfortable with the fact of black America's divisions, and none more so than the members of the elite themselves. Here's W. E. B. Du Bois, black America's greatest intellectual, writing in 1903:

> Can the masses of Negro people be in any possible way more quickly raised than by the effort and example of this aristocracy of talent and character? Was there ever a nation on God's fair earth civilized from the bottom upward? Never; it is, ever was and ever will be from the top downward that culture filters. The Talented Tenth rises and pulls all that are worth the saving up to their vantage ground. This is the history of human progress; and the two heroic mistakes which have hindered that progress were the thinking first that no more could ever rise save the few already risen; or second, that it would better the unrisen to pull the risen down.

Today, we may cringe at Du Bois's blatant vanguardism, but we must admire his courage in articulating what remains a taboo subject. It's too painful to admit that there is a Talented Tenth and that they may have a special role to play in the destiny of their people.

So many things have changed since then, of course. That was a colored world then, back in 1903, when W. E. B. Du Bois wrote his famous essay "The Talented Tenth." It was a world that in some sense has shaped and nurtured many of us, a world in which both our purpose and our enemies were clear. We were to get just as much education as we possibly could, to still the enemies of racism, segregation, discrimination. If we heard it once, we heard it a thousand times: Get as much education as you can, boy; nobody can take your education away from you. It was a world in which we strove to comport ourselves with dignity and grace, strove to "know and test the cabalistic letters" (as Du Bois put it) of the white elite, acknowledging and honoring those of us who had achieved—it was a world in which all these things were central to being a colored person in America.

We, too, were a people of the Book. When Du Bois was the editor of the *Crisis* magazine, he published the portraits of black college graduates, lawyers and doctors, on its cover and in its pages. Being an athlete or an entertainer was fine and good, for Du Bois; but these were solitary professions whose import was, if not ephemeral, then still not central to the collective life of the race. Playing baseball or knocking out boxers had its place . . . but these were not *serious* occupations for Du Bois and other great race leaders. Law and medicine, education and scholarship—these were the pinnacles of achievement, these the province of the Talented Tenth.

I don't claim that we ever lived up to this idealized image. But at least these were the images, the ideals, that were presented to us. Once upon a time, so we could imagine, our communal values and aspirations were intact. Only racism and segregation stood between our people and the fullness of American citizenship. If only we could secure our legal rights, the argument went, if only we could use the courts to strike down segregation; if only *de jure* segregation could be banished from the land once and for all—then all else would follow, as day upon night. The world was simple then; our enemy was an easy target.

And then the obvious obstacles tumbled and fell. *De jure* segregation was killed in the American judicial system. *Brown* v. *Board of Education* is such a great triumph of decades of legal scholarship, under the leadership of such stellar jurists as Charles Hamilton Houston, Thurgood Marshall, and Constance Baker Motley—the list is long and noble—that its anniversary still has resonance in black America. So much went into the preparation of that brief before the Court—a rare collaboration between our legal practitioners and our scholars, between politicians and political activists, between whites and blacks, Jews and Gentiles, working together in an interracial compact that few of us can even *remember*, let alone imagine happening again. There can be little doubt that the period between 1954 and the passage of the Voting Rights Act of 1965 was the decade when the Negro felt more optimism than would be justified in any other single decade in our century.

To be sure, the three years between 1965 and 1968 were bloody and turbulent ones—we could think of these years as framed by the assassinations of Malcolm X and Martin Luther King, Jr., or by the riots in Watts in 1965 and the riots just about everywhere in 1968, especially those surrounding the Democratic National Convention in Chicago. And yet despite all this, the grandchildren of the Talented Tenth—those of us who had been trained to succeed, geared to prosper, adequately prepared by family and teachers to "cross over" into the white world once the walls of segregation came tumbling down—plunged headlong and joyously into the abyss of integration.

How have we fared since 1965? In so many ways, as I insist, our progress is astonishing, something we may need to be reminded of even in the wake of the Rodney King riots, and the stark statistics that measure the gap within our community between the haves and the have-nots. The "black" community, as we knew it before 1965, simply does not exist any longer. And we do great harm to the truth when we pretend that the woes confronting the black underclass are identical to those confronting the black middle class. For a new crop of black youth, whose only experience has been of our affluent suburbs, Mattie Rich's grim film of life in the projects, *Straight out of Brooklyn*, would have to be retitled *Straight out of Brookline*. And who would ever have thought that any of us growing up would have considered enrolling our kids in "Jack and Jill"—not to advance them socially (as many of our parents hoped), but so that they would be with other black kids and learn about their ethnic heritage?

This is where we are in 1992, we members of the black upper middle class, the heirs of the Talented Tenth, isolated from the black underclass and yet still humiliatingly vulnerable to racism, in the form of random police harassment; individual racial insults from waitresses and waiters, attendants in stores, and taxi drivers unwilling to pick us up; systematic discrimination by banks and bank loan officers; wage discrimination in the workplace; and the well-known "glass ceiling" in the corporate world. The questions that greeted our arrival at white colleges in the late sixties and seventies—"Do you play basketball, football, or baseball?" (translated: "Which sport got *you* to Yale?")—have been supplanted by more subtle forms of questioning about our right and ability to *hold* the positions for which we have worked so diligently. Far too often, white colleagues at school, in our new, mostly white neighborhoods and in the workplace see blackness as a sign of inferiority, our meal ticket into the middle class as an affirmative action quota. If it is true that petty American apartheid—the sort of legal segregation that existed before 1965—has largely disappeared, it is equally true that the most pernicious form of racism—the stereotyping of an individual by the color of his or her skin—still pervades white America. And caught in this no-man's-land of alienation and fragmentation is the black middle class.

What do we do about this? What do we not do? First of all, it's time for the black middle class to stop feeling guilty about our own success while our fellow blacks languish in the inner city of despair. Black prosperity does not derive from black poverty: Those who succeed are those whose community, whose families, *prepared* them to be successful. As Stanley Crouch and others remind us, the familiar exhortation in those days was to "get all the education that you can"—and we did. When I left home for Yale, virtually my whole hometown celebrated that fact. "The community," as we put it, however sentimentally, wished us to succeed. Talking black, walking black, wearing kente cloth, listening to black music, and filling our walls with black art—as desirable as these things can be in and of themselves—are not essential to "being black." You can love Mozart, Manet, and ice hockey, and still be as black as the ace of spades.

Second, we don't have to fail in order to be black. As crazy as this sounds, recent surveys of young black kids reveal a distressing pattern. Far too many say that succeeding is "white," education is "white," aspiring and dreaming are "white," believing that you can make it is "white." Had any of us said this sort of thing when we were growing up, our families and friends would have checked us into a mental institution. We need *more success* individually and collectively, not less.

Third, we don't have to pretend any longer that 35 million people can ever possibly be members of the same social class. After all, the entire population of Canada is 26 million. Canadians are not all members of one economic class. Nor do they speak with one single voice of one single leader. As every black person knows on some level, we have never been members of a single social or economic class, and never will be. The best we can strive for is that the class differentiation within the black community ceases to be so lopsided in favor of underprivilege. Even without racism and the legacy of racism, we will still have rich and poor in the black community.

Fourth, we don't have to demand a lockstep rhetoric from the President and other political leaders that pits the black vote against the middle class and poses an irreconcilable division between personal responsibility and progressive social policy. For the fact is that millions of black voters identify themselves as middle-class, and much in the way of progressive social policy needs to be designed to foster and promote the ability of poor people, whether black or otherwise, to take personal responsibility. As the black community evolves a new maturity in recognizing our own diversity, our myriad social and economic circumstances, so, too, must a more mature discourse about African Americans and our political interests develop during the next Administration.

How do we "fight the power" in a post–civil rights world in which white racists are no longer the easy targets that Bull Connor and George Wallace used to be, a world in which the rhetoric of the civil rights era sounds tired and empty? (If George Bush, the congressional leadership, or anyone else had turned up at the spring 1992 March on Washington on behalf of the cities, and handed over a check for $500 billion to heal the ills of the inner cities, I wonder if anyone there would have known what to do with it.)

The time has come for honesty within the black community. The causes of poverty within the black community are *both* structural and behavioral, as scholars as diverse as philosopher Cornel West at Princeton and sociologist William Julius Wilson at Chicago have insisted and as most polemicists still shy away from acknowledging. A generation of well-meaning social scientists have made the notion of "the culture of poverty" taboo, correctly observing that the concept, as originally introduced, ignored the economic and structural dimensions of the problem. But having acknowledged those dimensions, it's time to concede that, yes, there is a culture of poverty. How can there not be? How can you think that culture matters and deny its relation to economic success? In general, a household composed of a sixteen-year-old mother, a thirty-two-year-old grandmother, and a forty-eight-year-old great-grandmother is not a site for hope and optimism. It's also true that not everyone in any society wants to work, that not all people are equally motivated.

There—was that so hard to say?

Our task, it seems to me, is to lobby for those social programs that have been demonstrated to make a difference for those sufficiently motivated to seize these expanded opportunities. More importantly, however, we have to demand a structural change in this country, the equivalent of a Marshall Plan for the cities. We have to take people off welfare and train them for occupations relevant to a twenty-first-century economy. And while I'm sympathetic to such incentives as tax breaks to generate new investment in the inner cities, youth apprenticeships with corporations, expanded tax credits for earned income, and tenant ownership of inner-city property, I believe that we will have to face the reality that our inner cities are simply not going to become oases of economic prosperity and corporate investment, and we should probably think about moving black inner-city workers to the jobs rather than to hold our breath waiting for new factories to resettle in the inner cities.

It is only by confronting the twin realities of the legacy of racism, on the one hand, and our failure to take the initiative and break the cycle of poverty, on the other, that the remnants of the Talented Tenth will be able to assume a role of leadership within the black community. To continue to repeat the same old stale formulas—to blame, in exactly the same ways, "the man" for oppressing us all, to scapegoat Koreans, Jews, or even Haitians for seizing local entrepreneurial opportunities that have, for whatever reasons, eluded us—is to fail to accept moral leadership. To fail to demand that members of the black community accept individual responsibility for their behavior—whether that behavior assumes the form of gang violence, unprotected sexual activity, you name it—is another way of selling out a beleaguered community. It's to surrender to the temptation to act as ethnic cheerleaders "selling woof tickets" from the suburbs instead of speaking the hard truths that may be unpopular with our fellows. Being a leader does not mean being loved; it may mean risking estrangement and alienation from the community you care most about. But Du Bois—who was himself such a leader—dared to speak an uncomfortable truth when he addressed the responsibilities of the black elite. For them, the challenge awaits of healing the rift within black America, and the larger nation as well.

And for the next President, the challenge will be to create an Administration and an atmosphere in which the interests and needs of both black Americas can be aired and advanced, just as the deep divide that separates the poor from the middle class—and the cities from the suburbs—can be bridged. We need leadership that heals, not with naive nostrums but with a sophisticated maturity that recognizes the differing social and economic conditions of Americans, black and white. Breaking through the barriers that have frozen the political discourse of race into a place we passed by a generation ago will be necessary if we are to deal with hard issues honestly. A President who spoke to both Harlem and Howard would be a good place to start.

DEMOCRATICALLY FINANCED ELECTIONS

ELLEN S. MILLER AND PHILIP M. STERN

Summary

T HERE IS A CRISIS TODAY in American politics—a crisis of confidence in our elected officials, a loss of faith in our democratic
government, and an increasing frustration at the irrelevance of individual voters in our political process. This is a crisis so fundamental that
it threatens to shake the very roots of our political democracy. It is a crisis
that has so turned off voters that more often stay home than go to the polls.
Public approval of Congress has plunged to 16 percent—its lowest level ever
recorded.

It is a crisis caused, in major part, by the unholy alliance of private
money and public elections. The heart of the debate over money and politics
concerns the very survival of our democratic process.

Reform has eluded the reformers for decades. In part this is because
campaign finance reform has generally been looked at from the perspective
of ways in which we can make the situation marginally better, and these
piecemeal reforms have met resistance from members of Congress and the
public alike. But if real reform is to be achieved, it must be looked at from
the perspective of creating a political system that would be truly fair and
equitable. Reforms must eliminate access to wealth as a determinant of a

*Ellen S. Miller is the Executive Director of the Center for Responsive Politics.
Prior to coming to the Center in 1983 she held several senior staff positions
on Capitol Hill and in the public interest community. Philip M. Stern, the
author of (Still) The Best Congress Money Can Buy (1992), was a pioneer
in exposing the role of money in politics. The author of numerous books, a
former congressional aide, research director for the Democratic Party, Co-
Chair of Citizens Against PACs, and philanthropist, Phil Stern passed away
on June 1, 1992.*

citizen's influence within the political process; increase an officeholder's accountability to ordinary voters; end the inherent conflict of interest caused by the private financing of public servants; halt and reverse the escalating cost of elections; create a more level playing field between incumbents and challengers; and free members from nonstop fundraising. To put it simply, real reform would eliminate private money from congressional campaigns (and eventually from presidential elections as well) and substitute instead a system of democratically financed elections.

This approach would include a system of total public financing for primary and general campaigns, discount postal rates, free or low-cost media time, and money to match the expenditures of candidates who still choose to run with private money. Soft money would be strictly prohibited, and a wholly restructured campaign finance regulatory agency would be in charge of administration and enforcement. Such comprehensive reform would address the full extent of the problem and would be more palatable to a cynical public that doubts the efficacy of incremental change. Importantly it would avoid past pitfalls, which have resulted from partial reforms that allow money to migrate to new uses.

Neither Congress nor the President should be looked to as the engine of reform; the impetus for democratic change in the past has always come from the people, particularly those most disenfranchised. It will be in this way as well that we restore equality and fairness in our elections.

Background

MORE THAN THREE QUARTERS of the American people believe that elected officials care more about special interests than they care about them. They believe that this government no longer represents their interests. They are angry about the hostile takeover of the electoral process by a moneyed elite. They are angry that lawmakers are unable to confront our most serious problems, all at a time when the inventory of our ills seems almost infinite. And the ultimate anger comes from a deep-seated resentment that America's democracy has become one in which you have to "pay to play," leaving them on the sidelines.

Money has become the medium of political participation in America today. A wealthy elite with precise economic and legislative agendas has taken hold of our elections and today holds sway over public policy. A fundamental inequality threatens to overwhelm the practice of our political democracy. Today, a political system driven by money disenfranchises all but an elite phalanx of campaign contributors, a system that forces politicians who want to change society to become dependent on the very same economic and social forces that often want to hold change back. It is a system in which public policy is determined more and more by campaign dollars and those who supply them. It is a system that directly challenges our idea of "one citizen, one vote."

Private money now controls the outcome of our public elections. Because we have money-based politics, we have money-biased policies. Wealth and the state are joined, and the majority of citizens are denied equal opportunity to shape the decisions that affect their lives. Private money's dominance in politics has fractured our democracy, creating a political process in which vested interests predominate and the public interest is forgotten. The people of this country have been shut out of the conversation of democracy. It's the individuals and interest groups with money—the cash constituents—who invest in officeholders and use their money to gain access to elected officials who wield power in politics today. The ordinary voters with ballots to give rather than dollars are powerless, and they know it. Private money undermines our political democracy in three fundamental ways: First, it determines, in nearly every race, who competes and who wins the election; second, it skews our national priorities and the outcome of legislation decisions; and third, it makes Congress less representative and less responsive.

First, it biases the outcome of elections. Money establishes a credibility threshold in campaigns. If you don't have it, then you are not judged to be a viable candidate. In district after district throughout the country in 1990, credible opponents were unable to raise the money it took to wage a competitive campaign. Fewer and fewer congressional challengers can raise sufficient sums of money to oppose incumbents. While spending by incumbents continues to rise with each election, the spending by challengers has slowly but steadily declined. In 1990 the average gap in spending was $308,000; in 1974 the average gap was only $17,000. Few House incumbents faced serious challenges in the 1990 elections—at least financially. In 250 of the nation's 435 congressional districts, the winning candidate outspent the loser by a factor of ten to one or greater. In nearly all these cases the winner was an incumbent seeking reelection. This towering financial advantage of incumbents has insulated them from voter anger. Contribution patterns reinforce the incumbent fundraising advantage. A total of 80 percent went of all PAC money to incumbents in 1990; only 10 percent went to challengers and 10 percent to candidates for open seats.

Success at the polls has become a situation in which the outcome is usually determined by how much "interested money" you can raise. It is not always true that you always have to raise the most money to win a race. But it is always true that if you don't raise substantial money (at least half as much as the incumbent), you will lose.

Second, private money in our elections has a direct influence on the outcome of public policy. Not only does the money often make the electorate largely superfluous on election day, it also directly and subtly corrupts the legislative process. You can see how the money works when you begin to follow it. It thwarts legislative initiatives, makes compromise difficult, determines bills and amendments introduced and not introduced, and affects the substance once they are presented for consideration. The money chase affects the choice of committee assignments and sets overall legislative priorities. It affects directly how a legislator spends his or her time in Congress.

For most members of Congress, it is possible to link their major campaign contributors to the legislative committee on which they sit. In 1990, the finance, insurance, and real estate interests gave their biggest share of money to members of the Senate Finance, House Ways and Means, and House Banking committees. For members on those committees, this generosity was the largest source of funds for their reelection campaigns. Within the finance industry, far and away the biggest donors were individuals and PACs affiliated with the insurance industry, who gave altogether $10.8 million; $1.7 million went to members of the House Ways and Means Committee. Much of that money was focused on incumbent members of the tax-writing committee, who received an average of nearly $48,000 per member.

Industry giving patterns are easily identified: The top seven recipients of money from agribusiness sit on the House Agriculture Committee. Contributions from the agriculture industry to Agriculture Committee members totaled $3.1 million. All but one member of the top ten House and Senate recipients of campaign money from the military industry sit on congressional committees dealing with military spending. Total defense giving was $7.9 million. Senator Bennett Johnston and Representative Phil Sharp, who head the congressional committees that shape energy policy, were the top recipients of money from the energy and natural resources PACs. Altogether individuals and PACs with energy interests gave $2.4 million to Senate Energy Committee members and $1.9 million to House Energy Committee and Commerce Committee members. Health care interests gave over $16 million, with the largest share of their funds going to members of the House committees responsible for health care legislation. Commerical banks were far and away the largest contributors to members of the House Banking Committee.

In short, we would never allow competing litigants to pay jurors or judges. Similarly, self-interested private money has no place in our public legislature and elections.

Third, due to private money in our elections, Congress no longer reflects the public at large. Members of minorities and women have little chance of being elected because they can't raise the money and don't have it or don't want to become beholden to the interests that can provide it. Because candidates are required to raise or have large amounts of money to wage competitive campaigns, today's money and politics system discriminates against people who are not wealthy, preventing them from participating— either as candidates or as voters. This is particularly true for lower-income and poor people, and for certain racial minorities—African Americans and Hispanics, for example—because they are statistically poorer than the population at large.

While most attention is paid to the power and influence of PAC contributions, the role played by individual givers receives insufficient attention. Individual contributors who gave $200 or more accounted for more than $101 million in contributions to winning members of the House and Senate in the 1990 elections. Until recently, little has been known about the details of that money—where it came from, who were the top contributors, and what were the patterns by which it was dispensed. Research by the Center for Responsive Politics has shown that many of the same industries and interest groups that have come to dominate the PAC world also give heavily through individual contributions. For example, interests representing the financial industry were the biggest contributors overall, accounting for some $43 million, with 38 percent of this money coming from individuals. Individual contributors from the securities and investment sector represented 65 percent ($3.8 million) of the total money ($5.9 million). Similarly, 59 percent ($5.9 million) of the real estate money was given by individuals, not PACs.

Another illustration: Legal-industry PACs, led by the Association of Trial Lawyers of America, gave $4.3 million in contributions in 1990. In fact, lawyers and lobbyists were responsible for a total of $18.6 million in contributions in the 1990 election cycle—more than any other business sector except finance. A total of 75 percent of this money came through individual contributions.

In the past we have known that business PACs outspent labor PACs by a factor of 3 to 1. Now that we have been able to classify individual givers, we know the ratio is conservatively 4.5 to 1 (business givers, $180 million; labor givers, almost exclusively PAC contributions, $40 million). Labor was one group that was scarcely in evidence among individual contributions. But for companies as diverse as Goldman Sachs, Time Warner, Solomon Brothers, the Walt Disney Company, Cassidy and Associates, the law firms of Skadden Arps, Williams & Jensen, and Camp, Barsh, Bates & Tate (to name just a few), accumulated contributions from individuals were larger than the corporations' PAC contributions.

If we want to know why we don't have a system of universal health care, we should look at the impact of the $16 million given by health care interests to legislators in 1990. Why do the real estate, finance, and insurance interests dump $43 million into congressional campaigns? Why do communities of color struggle against the placing of toxic waste dumps on their doorsteps? What is the impact of the almost $16 million that energy interests gave to winners of congressional races? How influential are lobbyists in making public policy? Ponder for a moment the $18.6 million they gave in campaign contributions in 1990. Why does labor struggle in a probusiness climate?

The Solution

THE DISTORTION OF THE POLITICAL SYSTEM brought on by private money is a systemic problem, not easily remedied. What is critically important in outlining a solution is understanding that the problem of money in politics extends well beyond special-interest PAC contributions to the entire spectrum of private-money contributions. The next President must cut this Gordian knot by endorsing—and lobbying for—radical campaign finance reform.

The Working Group on Electoral Democracy, a group of grass-roots organizers, activists, and political researchers, has drafted a model bill to provide for democratically financed elections, prohibiting virtually all private campaign contributions to primary and general elections and providing qualified candidates with total public financing, a credit line of government money from which all candidates would have to pay all campaign expenditures. This model challenges the basic assumption that public elections ought to be privately financed.

This system would provide a system of near total public financing for primary and general congressional campaigns; the concept could be adopted for use in presidential races and in state elections. Under the provisions of this model, candidates who opted into the system would get discount postal rates, free or low-cost media time, and money to match the expenditures of those candidates who ran with private money. Under this proposal soft-money abuses would end and a wholly restructured campaign finance regulatory agency would be in charge of administration and enforcement.

QUALIFICATIONS
Eligibility for total public financing would be based on the demonstrated ability to raise a relatively high number of low-dollar ($5 to $10) qualifying

contributions from in-district sources. Though the exact number of qualifying contributions is subject to debate, the goal would be to provide a number (say, one thousand) that would not be easy but not impossible for challengers to achieve.

Prospective candidates would be allowed to raise seed money to get their campaign efforts off the ground. They could raise a limited amount of this money (a $100 limitation on individual and organization contributions) before the time-specific preprimary qualifying period. This (and the $5 and $10 qualifying contributions) would be the only private money allowed. The seed money could be spent only for start-up costs. Citizens who gave the money would feel that their contribution counted for something, because it would enable the candidates of their choice to qualify for the total public financing. Using privately raised money for media advertisements or direct mail campaigns, for example, would be prohibited.

TOTAL CAMPAIGN FUNDING

Candidates who raised the required number of qualifying contributions would then qualify for a fixed amount of public financing for the primary campaign. But it would be the political party rather than the individual candidate that established eligibility for funds in the general election. Candidates or parties that received more than 20 percent of the vote in the previous general election would automatically qualify for the public stipend in the next general election, while candidates of parties that received 5 to 20 percent would receive a proportional amount. Independent candidates would also have a mechanism for qualifying for public money, and new or third parties without a track record but with growing popular support would not be shut out of the system. Their candidates could qualify in the primary by getting the same number of low-dollar qualifying contributions as the candidates of major parties. Their candidates could further qualify for public financing in the general election by getting a qualifying percentage of the total primary vote of all the candidates of all the contesting political parties. The primary election would thus serve a dual function. It would determine a party's candidate in intraparty competition and provide a fast-track qualifying test for candidates from new or third parties.

IMPROVING THE QUALITY OF DEBATE

A key component of this system would be provisions to get political information out to the public. Candidates who proved their eligibility would be eligible to send mail to voters at low-cost bulk rates as a means of offsetting the franking privilege that benefits incumbents. Candidates would be able to buy time on the broadcast media at low discount rates. Importantly, this proposal includes a free media provision in which broadcasters would be required to set aside some prime time for qualified candidates in extended-format programs. In both cases, candidates would have to abide by format restrictions (e.g., candidates might have to appear in person in their ads for at least 50 percent of the time). Participation in debates would also be required as a condition of receiving total public financing.

THE FEDERAL ELECTION COMMISSION

The Federal Election Commission (FEC) would be radically restructured to ensure fair and tough enforcement of the campaign finance laws. For a start, the commission should be made up of only five members, with no more than three from the same political party, each serving only one five-year (staggered) term. The chairman would be appointed by the President. Ex-officio members would be eliminated. The appointment process would be substantially changed, with the President nominating commissioners from a list of names provided by a nonpartisan panel and with no appointee having served as an official for any organization or committee required to file with the commission in the previous two years. The commission would be given authority to conduct random audits and to seek injunctions against violators after a finding of "clear and convincing evidence" that a substantial violation had occurred, and the standard for opening investigations into possible illegal campaign activities would be eased.

ADMINISTRATION

This system of democratically financed elections would be surprisingly easy to enforce. Eligible candidates who agreed not to accept or spend private money would receive not money but credit from a federal account regulated by the Federal Election Commission. The credit line would be large enough for challengers to compete effectively against incumbents (who have the inherent advantage of name recognition and an existing campaign organization). Candidates and their staff would be issued special FEC "expense cards" with which they would make campaign purchases and pay their bills. This proposal would actually result in lower bookkeeping costs than, say, the current presidential-election system.

THE ROLE OF PARTIES

This system of democratically financed elections is biased toward strong and cohesive political parties. As private associations, parties can, of course, raise private money, but there would be a limit of $100 on the amount an individual or an organization could give to a party. Money could be spent for issue development, leadership training, and other ongoing non-electoral-season organizing work, but parties would not be able to contribute directly to individual candidates. Yet, it is essential that parties have some hold over their candidates. So national and state political parties would be able to fund grass-roots, volunteer activities such as door-to-door canvassing efforts, leaflet distribution, and get-out-the-vote drives. The crucial point, however, is that party money could not be used to buy media ads and underwrite other campaign costs. This prohibition would be reinforced by a clause strictly prohibiting the use of soft or non-federally-regulated money in political campaigns.

INDEPENDENT EXPENDITURES

Independent expenditures—money spent by private citizens or independent political groups on behalf of a candidate without the candidate's knowledge— might be the one potential serious problem. Unable to contribute to the candidates of their choice, groups such as the American Medical Association and the NRA (as well as progressive groups for peace, environmental protection, and the rights of labor) might organize parallel campaigns independent of their favored candidate. The protection against this would be the requirement that individuals and organizations planning independent expenditures would have to notify the FEC in advance and indicate which candidate their expenditure was intended to help or defeat. This disclosure would free an equivalent amount of public money (actually credit) to the candidates who were the designated targets. Because independent expenditures on behalf of one candidate would provide opposition candidates with additional financial resources, the practice would be discouraged.

COST

The cost of democratically financed elections would be approximately $5 per taxpayer, with the money appropriated out of general revenues. Compared with the billions of dollars that vested interests take from the Treasury in the form of corporate bailouts, tax breaks, subsidies, and regulatory favors—estimated at $50 billion a year by the Democracy Project—$500 million a year is a small price to pay for fair democratic elections. Compare, for example, the $2.5 billion cost of bailing out Charles Keating's Lincoln savings and loan association, whose losses were greatly worsened by campaign finance–related corruption.

This model reform embodies two overarching goals. The first is to lessen the role and influence of interested money given by people and groups who hope to benefit financially from their contributions. The second principle—a corollary of the first—is the need to liberate House and Senate candidates from their obligations to special-interest contributors, enabling them to pay for their campaigns with funds for which they feel no special obligation. America needs a system where campaigns are paid for by "disinterested money" and where candidates can enter office with no strings attached. In a democracy, the quintessence of disinterested money is money that comes from all citizens equally, through their government.

This system has many advantages. It is simple. It draws a clear distinction between what is legal (public financing) and what is not legal (private contributions, whether by individual citizens or by PACs). The very simplicity and clarity of the model will minimize the flow of special-interest money into the congressional system.

Otherwise reform-minded individuals who feel empowered by their ability to give money to political candidates may object to this approach because it denies them their right to spend money on behalf of the candidates they support. Such a view is both narrow-minded and shortsighted because as long as money remains the driving force in American politics, all politicians will be under the thumb of donors, and programs big donors don't like will get shortchanged by elected officials. And rather than raising money, labor and progressive organizations will be able to focus on the electoral activities they do best: canvassing (and raising small contributions) so that candidates they support can qualify for public money; campaigning for candidates among their members; and voter education, issue development, and movement building nationwide and at the grass roots.

Existing reform proposals tinker with the mechanics of election financing without dealing with their most basic and easily identifiable flaw—the corrupting influence that private money has over the political system. Most recent reform proposals provide for partial public financing. These proposals are predicated on the premise that some public financing is better than the existing system.

But partial public financing plans that require candidates to raise a significant portion of their campaign funds from private sources leave untouched (or only marginally improve) all the major deficiencies in the existing system. They fail to rein in the cost of campaigns because they set unrealistically high ceilings on campaign expenditures, not addressing the problem of candidates' appetite for more and more money; fail to liberate candidates from their dependence on special-interest campaign contributions; fail to diminish the pervasive corruption of Congress because of the continuing conflicts of interest; fail to arrest significantly the "arms race" that now accounts for spiraling campaign expenditures; and fail to open up candidacy to all citizens, regardless of their own wealth or their access to wealthy contributors.

How We Get from Here to There

THE CRISIS OF CONFIDENCE in our political system offers an opportunity for advocates of new ideas. The barriers to true democratic participation in our political process are serious, long-standing, and deeply ingrained. To the extent that our system of political democracy "works," in most instances and over the long haul it works only for a very small percentage of the citizenry: people of wealth or those who represent powerful moneyed interests—that is, those who can "afford" access to and influence over public policy decisionmakers. It is a truism of history, including America's history, that elites rarely if ever give up their power and privilege of their own accord. The British did not do so, nor did slaveowners, nor industrial tycoons, nor white supremacists. Similarly, elected officials are seldom inclined to initiate or support reforms that threaten their own incumbency as well as the interests of their financial benefactors. This is why election reform legislation in Congress has been so slow and tepid, and why, without a powerful citizens' reform movement that in itself threatens incumbency, no real reform will take place and short-term lobbying efforts will continue to fail.

The task of remaking our political system depends on four basic components. First, we must transcend our current way of thinking about what is possible; second, we must have a vision of what systemic change might look like; third, we must understand that the power to create this great change lies with the citizens of this country and that only a broad-based, grass-roots movement will be capable of creating and sustaining the necessary challenge to the status quo; and fourth, we must understand that it requires a long-term commitment and a lot of patience to build what is in essence a "prodemocracy" movement, a building-block process of slowly getting people and organizations into place to make an educated, focused demand for structural reform. Comprehensive, bold reform is going to happen only when people outside of Washington begin to demand it.

Although it may be idealistic to think that deeply ingrained political practices and long-standing power relationships can be fundamentally altered, as would be the case in a system of democratically financed elections, the history of democracy in the United States offers encouragement. Justice Brandeis once remarked that everything worth doing was at one time thought to be impossible. Our system of political democracy began as a revolutionary eighteenth-century experiment, but it has unfolded since then as an evolutionary series of major democratic reforms. It is worth remembering that a generation after the American Revolution, full and equal political opportunity was still reserved for white, male property owners—a small fraction of the adult population. As time passed, however, each restriction came to be considered unjust and undemocratic, and after years of struggle by long-enduring citizen movements, each restriction was eventually eliminated.

Thomas Paine wrote two hundred years ago, "A long habit of not thinking a thing wrong, gives it a superficial appearance of being right, and raises at first a formidable outcry in defense of custom." We can no longer ignore what is wrong with our politics today. Our sights must be set high.

About the Contributors

Robert Adler is Associate Professor of Legal Studies in the School of Business at the University of North Carolina and the publisher of Consumers Union's *Consumer Reports*. He formerly served as Counsel to the Subcommittee on Health and the Environment on the Energy and Commerce Committee in the House of Representatives.

Albert F. Appleton is Commissioner of the New York City Department of Environmental Protection. He previously served as Assistant Attorney General in the New York State Medicaid Fraud Control Unit.

Sue Armsby is a member of the public policy department of People for the American Way Action Fund.

John Atlas, a public interest lawyer, is founder and President of the National Housing Institute, editor of the housing magazine *Shelterforce*, and founder and vice-chair of New Jersey Citizen Action.

Mary Jo Bane is Commissioner of the New York State Department of Social Services. She was previously Director of the Malcolm Wiener Center for Social Policy at the Kennedy School of Government at Harvard University, and is the author of many books and articles on poverty, welfare, and social and public policy.

Michael Barr, a recent graduate of the Yale Law School, has written articles for *The New York Times*, *The Yale Law and Policy Review*, and *The Houston Journal of International Law*.

Gary D. Bass is Executive Director of OMB Watch, a nonprofit research and advocacy organization that monitors the White House Office of Management and Budget. Dr. Bass has written extensively on federal budgetary, program management, regulatory, and information policy issues.

Samuel R. Berger, the former Deputy Director of the State Department Policy Planning Staff (1977-81), has been engaged in international trade law at Hogan & Hartson in Washington, D.C. He is the author of *Dollar Harvest* (Heath Lexington Books, 1971) and has written editorial articles on international issues for *The New York Times* and other publications. He is Foreign Policy Director of the Clinton/Gore transition team.

Nolan Bowie is Professor of Communication at Temple University and the author, most recently, of *Equity and Access to Information Technology Annual Review* (Institute for Information Studies, 1990).

Lee P. Brown, the former Commissioner of the New York City Police Department, has authored many articles and papers on police management, community relations, crime, and the criminal justice system, and is coauthor of the book *The Police and Society: An Environment for Collaboration and Confrontation*.

Holly Burkhalter is the Washington Director of Human Rights Watch. She is the coauthor of *With Friends Like These* (Pantheon, 1985) and contributor to *The Human Rights Leader* (American Library, 1989).

Peter Calthorpe formed Calthorpe Associates in 1983 and lectures extensively throughout the world on city and regional planning issues. He has authored many articles and coauthored a Sierra Club book, *Sustainable Communities*.

Sharon L. Camp is Senior Vice President of the Population Crisis Committee. She has authored several publications, including *Population Pressure, Poverty and the Environment* (Population Crisis Committee, 1990).

Angela J. Campbell directs the Citizens Communications Center Project of the Institute for Public Representation at the Georgetown University Law Center. She recently published an article analyzing the First Amendment aspects of video dialtone in the *North Carolina Law Review*.

Lawrence Chimerine is a Fellow at the Economic Strategy Institute, Senior Economic Advisor to DRI/McGraw-Hill, and President of Radnor Consulting Services. He has published extensively, including *Business Opportunities and Practices in the Far East* (Dow Jones-Irwin).

Joan B. Claybrook is President of Public Citizen. She served as Administrator of the National Highway Traffic Safety Administration of the U.S. Department of Transportation under President Carter. Her publications include *Freedom From Harm: The Civilizing Influence of Health, Safety and Environmental Regulations*.

Jonathan W. Cuneo is counsel for the Committee to Support Antitrust Laws (COSAL) and the National Association of Securities and Commercial Law Attorneys (NASCAT). He formerly served as counsel with the Federal Trade Commission.

Kristin Dawkins is a Senior Fellow at the Institute for Agriculture and Trade Policy. She is the author of *Balancing: Policies for Just and Sustainable Trade* (IATP, 1992) and *Environmental Impacts and Possibilities of the GATT* (IATP, 1991).

Clarence M. Ditlow is Executive Director of the Center for Auto Safety and author of numerous publications on consumers, auto safety, air pollution, and transportation, including *The Lemon Book* and *The Safe Road to Fuel Economy*.

William Drayton, a former Assistant Administrator of the Environmental Protection Agency (1977-81) and MacArthur Fellow, is currently President of ASHOKA: Innovator for the Public and Chair of Environmental Safety and of Appropriate Technology.

Peter Dreier is Director of Housing at the Boston Redevelopment Authority and housing policy advisor to Boston Mayor Ray Flynn. He drafted the Community Housing Partnership Act, legislation which became part of the National Affordable Housing Act enacted by Congress in 1990, and has written widely on urban politics and housing policy.

Marian Wright Edelman is president and founder of the Childrens Defense Fund. In 1985 she became a MacArthur Foundation Prize Fellow.

Mathea Falco is Visiting Fellow at New York Hospital-Cornell Medical Center in New York City and served as Assistant Secretary of State for

International Narcotic Matters for the State Department from 1977-81. She has authored many books and articles, including *The Making of a Drug-Free America: Programs That Work* (Random House, 1992).

Jeff Faux is President of the Economic Policy Institute in Washington, D.C. He is the coauthor of *Rebuilding America* (Pantheon) and author of *New Hope of the Inner City* (Twentieth Century Fund).

Eleanor M. Fox is Professor of Law at New York University School of Law. She was appointed by President Carter to the National Commission for the Review of Antitrust Law and Procedures. She is the author of several books and articles, including a four-volume treatise, *Corporate Acquisitions and Mergers*, coauthored with Byron E. Fox (Matthew Bender).

James K. Galbraith is Professor at the Lyndon B. Johnson School of Public Affairs at the University of Texas at Austin. He was formerly Executive Director of the Congressional Joint Economic Committee. He is the author of *Balancing Acts: Technology, Finance and the American Future* (Basic Books, 1989) and coauthor with Robert L. Heilbroner of a textbook, *The Economic Problem*.

Mark Garrison is founding Director of the Center for Foreign Policy Development at Brown University. He served as Deputy Ambassador in Moscow from 1978-80 and Director of the Office of Soviet Union Affairs in the State Department from 1974-78. He is coeditor of *Shared Destiny: Fifty Years of Soviet-American Relations*.

Henry Louis Gates, Jr. is coeditor of *Transition*, a quarterly review, and the author most recently of *Loose Canons: Notes on the Culture Wars* (Oxford, 1992).

Pamela Gilbert is the Acting Director of Public Citizens Congress Watch.

Stephen Gillers is Professor of Law at New York University School of Law. He has authored many articles and books, including his most recent *Regulation of Lawyers: Problems of Law and Ethics* (Little, Brown and Co., 2d ed., 1992).

Mark Gitenstein, former Chief Counsel of the Senate Judiciary Committee, is a Partner at Mayer, Brown & Platt in Washington, D.C.

Harvey J. Goldschmid is Dwight Professor of Law at Columbia University. He is Chair of the Securities Regulation Committee and of the audit committee of the Bar of the City of New York. Professor Goldschmid has written widely in the securities and antitrust fields.

Susannah Goodman is the banking policy analyst at Public Citizen's Congress Watch.

Peter Gray is a senior science and policy writer for the Nuclear Weapons Production Project at Friends of the Earth in Washington, D.C. In addition to writing articles for *The Washington Monthly* and *Arms Control Today*, Gray was the editor of *Facing Reality: The Future of the U.S. Nuclear Weapons Complex* (1992).

Mark Green is the New York City Commissioner of Consumer Affairs. He was the 1986 Democratic U.S. Senate nominee for New York, and is author or editor of fifteen books, including *Who Runs Congress?* (4th ed., Dell, 1984) and *America's Transition: Blueprints for the 1990s* (UPA, 1989).

Robert Greenstein is Executive Director of the Center on Budget and Policy Priorities. He served as Administrator of the Food and Nutrition Service of the U.S. Dept. of Agriculture (1979-80). He has written articles for *The New York Times* and *The Washington Post* and contributed to a number of books, including the 1991 Brookings Institute volume *The Urban Underclass*.

Agnes Gund is President of the Museum of Modern Art in New York City and the Founder and Trustee of The Studio in a School Association.

Penda D. Hair is Director of the Fair Housing Program at the NAACP Legal Defense Fund. She was formerly a Law Clerk for Justice Blackmun of the U.S. Supreme Court.

Richard Heede is acting Director of the Mountain Institute's Energy Program. He has conducted research on and developed policy proposals for strategic materials concerns for the Institutes Global Security Program.

Jan Kalicki is senior vice president at Lehman Brothers. He has served as a member of the policy planning staff under Secretaries of State Kissinger and Vance and as a chief foreign policy adviser to Senator Edward M. Kennedy.

Elaine Ciulla Kamarck is a Senior Fellow at the Progressive Policy Institute and a regular columnist for *Newsday* and *The Los Angeles Times*. She is the author of *The Politics of Evasion*, with William Galston, and of numerous articles on American politics.

Ronald A. Klain is Chief Counsel of the U.S. Senate Judiciary Committee. He has also served as a member of the President's Commission on the Federal Appointments Process.

Michael Klare is the Five College Associate Professor of Peace and World Security Studies at Hampshire College, *The Nation's* Defense Correspondent and the author of several books, including *World Security: Trends and Challenges at Century's End* (St. Martins, 1991).

Robert Kuttner is coeditor of *The American Prospect*, columnist for *Business Week*, and the author of four books on political economy, including *The End of Laissez-Faire* (1991).

Nick Littlefield is Staff Director and Chief Counsel of the U.S. Senate Committee on Labor and Human Resources.

Amory B. Lovins founded the Rocky Mountain Institute. He previously served on the Department of Energy's senior advisory board, briefed eight heads of state, and published, mainly in collaboration with Hunter Lovins, a dozen books and several hundred papers on energy policy.

L. Hunter Lovins is the Rocky Mountain Institute's President and Executive Director. She cofounded and was Assistant Director of the California Conservation Project "Tree People" and has coauthored six books and written many papers.

Mimi Mager, a former VISTA official in the Carter Administration and Executive Director of Friends of VISTA, is currently Director of Congressional Relations with the Office of the Mayor of the District of Columbia.

Michael Mandler is an assistant professor at Harvard University. He writes mainly on policy issues and microeconomic theory.

John Tepper Marlin is Project Director of the Council on Economic Priorities and served as a Federal Government Economist in Washington, D.C. He has authored several studies, including *Building a Peace Economy* (Westview Press, 1992).

Theodore Marmor is Professor in the School of Organization and Management at Yale University and has written over a hundred articles on the politics and economics of the modern welfare state and on comparative health policy, including *The Politics of Medicare*. He was on President Carter's Commission on the Agenda for the 1980s.

Robert S. McIntyre directs Citizens for Tax Justice in Washington, D.C., and is the co-author of *Inequity & Decline: How the Reagan Tax Policies are Affecting the American Taxpayer and the Economy* (1983). His articles regularly appear in *The New York Times*, *The Washington Post*, and *The New Republic*.

Walter Russell Mead is Senior Fellow for International Economics at the World Policy Institute and a contributing editor at *Harpers* and at *The Los Angeles Times*. He is currently working on book projects for Alfred A. Knopf and the Twentieth Century Fund.

Arnie Miller is founder of Isaacson Miller. He was the White House Director of Personnel under President Carter (1978-81).

Ellen S. Miller is Executive Director of the Center for Responsive Politics. She has authored many publications, including *Open Secrets: The Dollar Power of PACs in Congress* and *The Price of Admission: Campaign Spending in the 1990 Congressional Elections*.

Ralph Nader, the well-known consumer advocate, has started dozens of ongoing organizations advocating consumer and environmental interests.

Aryeh Neier is the Executive Director of Human Rights Watch and previously was the National Executive Director of the American Civil Liberties Union (1970-78). He has authored many books and articles, including *Only Judgment* (Wesleyan University Press, 1988).

Janne E. Nolan is a Senior Fellow at the Brookings Institution and the author of *Trappings of Power: Ballistic Missiles in the Third World* (Brookings, 1991).

Robert Pitofsky is Professor of Law at Georgetown University and formerly served as Director of the Bureau of Consumer Protection, Federal Trade Commission. He has authored many books and articles, including *Cases and Materials on Trade Regulation*.

David Pittle is Technical Director for Consumers Union and served as Commissioner on the U.S. Consumer Product Safety Commission in Washington, D.C. He has authored numerous articles in professional publications.

Henry Richmond is the Executive Director of 1000 Friends of Oregon and founder of the National Growth Management Leadership Project.

Mark Ritchie is President of the Institute for Agriculture and Trade Policy. He has published numerous books, including *Trading Away Our Environment: GATT and Global Harmonization* (IATP, 1990).

Estelle H. Rogers, a lawyer and public policy consultant in Washington, D.C., coordinated all of the pro-choice friend of the court briefs in the Supreme Courts 1989-90 and 1990-91 terms.

Enid C. B. Schoettle is Director of the Project on International Organizations and Law and Senior Fellow at the Council on Foreign Relations. She has published, among other works, *Postures for Non-Proliferation: Long-Term Arms Limitation and Security Requirements for Minimizing the Proliferation of Nuclear Weapons* (1979).

William B. Schultz is Counsel to the House Subcommittee on Health and the Environment where he is responsible for legislation affecting products regulated by the Food and Drug Administration. He is also an Adjunct Professor at Georgetown University and previously served at the Public Citizen Litigation Group.

Andrew Jay Schwartzman is Executive Director of Media Access Project where he supervises telecommunications litigation and public policy advocacy. His articles have appeared in many trade and legal publications, including *The American Bar Journal*.

Margaret Seminario directs the Occupational Safety and Health activities of the AFL-CIO. She is a member of the National Advisory Committee on

Occupational Safety and Health and of the Federal Advisory Council on Occupational Safety and Health.

Robert J. Shapiro is Vice President of the Progressive Policy Institute where he directs economic studies. He served as Deputy National Issues Director and economic adviser for the Dukakis-Bentsen campaign and was also Associate Editor at *U.S. News & World Report*. He was a senior economic advisor to the Clinton presidential campaign.

David E. Shaw is the managing partner of D. E. Shaw & Co., a group of financial companies based in New York, and the chairman of the National Economic Council. Earlier, Dr. Shaw served on the faculty of the Computer Science Department at Columbia University, and as a vice president at Morgan Stanley & Co.

Lee Smith is the Executive Director of Governor Cuomo's Commission on Competitiveness and Director of Economic Policy and Research for the NYS Department of Economic Development. He is editor of the Cuomo Commission report *America's Agenda: Rebuilding Economic Strength* (M. E. Sharpe, 1992).

James Gustave Speth cofounded and is President of the World Resources Institute. He formerly chaired President Carter's Council on Environmental Quality.

John D. Steinbruner has been Director of Foreign Policy Studies at the Brookings Institution since 1978. He has authored and edited a number of books and monographs, including *Decisions for Defense: Prospects for a New Order* (Brookings, 1991) and *Restructuring American Foreign Policy* (Brookings, 1989).

Philip M. Stern, the author of *Still The Best Congress Money Can Buy*, was a pioneer in exposing the role of money in politics. The author of numerous books, a former congressional aide, research Director for the Democratic Party, Co-Chair of Citizens Against PACs, and philanthropist, he passed away June 1, 1992.

Thomas B. Stoel, Jr., an environmental attorney and consultant, is the former Director of the International Program of the Natural Resources Defense Council and President of the Global Tomorrow Coalition. In 1987-88, he chaired Project Blueprint, a environmental transition agenda for the next president.

Bruce Stokes is the international economics correspondent for *The National Journal*. A member of the Council on Foreign Relations, he is the coauthor of the forthcoming book *The European Challenge* (Council on Foreign Relations, 1992).

Olivier Sultan is a Yale Law School student who previously was the executive assistant to the Consumer Affairs Commissioner of New York City. He was the Director of Research at Democracy Project.

Melanne Verveer is Executive Vice President and Public Policy Director of People for the American Way. She directs the lobbying effort through the Action Fund and represents the organizations members before Congress and the executive branch.

David C. Vladeck is an Attorney at Public Citizen Litigation Group and Adjunct Professor of Law at Georgetown University. He has written monographs in various publications, including *Litigation Under the Freedom of Information Act* (ACLU, 1978-92).

About the Editors

Mark Green is the Commissioner of Consumer Affairs in New York City. Founder and President of the Democracy Project (1981-89) and Democratic nominee for the U.S. Senate from New York in 1986, he is the author or editor of fifteen books on government, business, and law, including *Who Runs Congress?* (4th ed., Dell, 1984), *The Challenge of Hidden Profits* (1985), *Reagan's Reign of Error* (1987), and *America's Transition: Blueprints for the Nineties* (1989).

Wade Greene is a writer and a philanthropic adviser on environment and national security issues. He is a former editor of *Newsweek*, *The New York Times Magazine*, and *Saturday Review*.

John Siegal practices communications and commercial law in New York City. He formerly served as campaign issues director, chief speechwriter, and a criminal justice counsel to Mayor David N. Dinkins.

Olivier Sultan is a Yale Law School student who previously was the executive assistant to the Consumer Affairs Commissioner of New York City.

Michael Waldman, the executive director of Public Citizen's Congress Watch (1989–92), is currently a deputy director of Communications for the Clinton–Gore Transition.